Human Rights and Civil Liberties

Visit the *Human Rights and Civil Liberties*,
third edition, **mylawchamber** site at
www.mylawchamber.co.uk/fosterhumanrights
to access valuable learning material.

FOR STUDENTS
Companion website support

- Use the questions in the book alongside answer guidance on the website
  to test yourself on each topic throughout the course.
- Use the updates to major changes in the law to make sure you know the
  latest developments.
- Use the live weblinks to help you read more widely around the subject.
- Use the further case studies to help you think through contentious issues
  in detail.

FOR LECTURERS
Teaching support materials

- Use the Case Studies to set reading for seminars.

PEARSON

We work with leading authors to develop the strongest educational materials in law, bringing cutting-edge thinking and best learning practice to a global market.

Under a range of well-known imprints, including Longman, we craft high quality print and electronic publications which help readers to understand and apply their content, whether studying or at work.

To find out more about the complete range of our publishing, please visit us on the World Wide Web at: **www.pearsoned.co.uk**

Human Rights and Civil Liberties

Third Edition

Steve Foster

Coventry University

Longman
is an imprint of

Harlow, England • London • New York • Boston • San Francisco • Toronto
Sydney • Tokyo • Singapore • Hong Kong • Seoul • Taipei • New Delhi
Cape Town • Madrid • Mexico City • Amsterdam • Munich • Paris • Milan

Pearson Education Limited
Edinburgh Gate
Harlow
Essex CM20 2JE
England

and Associated Companies throughout the world

Visit us on the World Wide Web at:
www.pearsoned.co.uk

First published 2003
Third edition published 2011

ISBN: 978-1-4082-5931-3

British Library Cataloguing-in-Publication Data
A catalogue record for this book is available from the British Library

Library of Congress Cataloging-in-Publication Data
A catalog record for this book is available from the Library of Congress

ARP impression 98

Typeset in 9/12.5pt ITC Giovanni by 35
Printed in Great Britain by Ashford Colour Press Ltd

The publisher's policy is to use paper manufactured from sustainable forests.

Brief contents

Contents

Visit the *Human Rights and Civil Liberties*,
third edition, **mylawchamber** site at
www.mylawchamber.co.uk/fosterhumanrights to
access valuable learning material.

FOR STUDENTS
Visit the *Human Rights and Civil Liberties*, third edition, **mylawchamber** site at
www.mylawchamber.co.uk/fosterhumanrights to access:
- **Companion website support:** Use the questions in the book alongside answer
  guidance on the website to test yourself on each topic throughout the course.
  The site also includes updates to major changes in the law to make sure you
  are ahead of the game, weblinks to help you read more widely around the
  subject, and further case studies to help you think through contentious issues
  in detail.

Preface

As with the last revision of this text, since the publication of the second edition in 2008 there has been a tremendous amount of case and legislative changes in the field of human rights and civil liberties. This has made the updating of the text both frustrating and exciting, as I am sure it does the studying of this area of law. At the time of writing there is great public, legal and political debate on matters such as the introduction of a bill of rights for the United Kingdom, religious rights and the law relating to human rights as they affect the fight against terrorism, and these discussions are included in the text and the book's update. In addition, the text has incorporated a variety of developments in areas such as privacy and free speech, freedom of assembly and the interpretation and application of the Human Rights Act 1998. Barely a week has gone by without the law of human rights being affected by a groundbreaking judicial decision or legislative change and proposal, and the author has attempted to include these developments in both the main text of the chapters and relevant footnotes. Needless to say, it is essential that students remain up to date in this dynamic field, and the book's website (below) will assist in this respect.

Since the publication of the second edition I have received constructive advice and criticism of the book's coverage from students, colleagues and independent referees, and as a result a number of changes have been made to the text. First, this edition contains a new chapter on terrorism and human rights, which provides the opportunity to revisit a number of issues explored in previous chapters on aspects such as liberty of the person, the right to a fair trial and the prohibition of torture and to place those topics in the context of the fight against terrorism. The chapter also provides an overview on the domestic law relating to the proscription and regulation of terrorist groups. This has increased the size of the text somewhat, but the author has tried to retain the succinct and user-friendly style of the first and second editions whilst providing greater substance. Secondly, the author has removed the specific chapter on prisoners' rights, but has placed much of the information contained in that chapter in other chapters so as to deal with matters such as the right to life and those in detention, inhuman and degrading treatment and prison conditions, and the right of prisoners to private and family life. Thirdly, each chapter begins by highlighting a high-profile case, or number of cases, to introduce the reader to the area and its underlying issues.

As with the second edition, the case studies, which in the first edition were located at the end of the text, have been incorporated in each respective chapter, and in some cases there is more than one case study in each chapter. Further case studies are available on the website (below). We have also retained the additional reading lists at the end of each chapter, an introduction feature at the start of each chapter together with a list of bullet points, to enable the reader to get an overall picture of the content and aims of each chapter, and a number of self-assessment questions, posed at appropriate points in the text, which allow the reader to reflect on the legal and moral issues already discussed. I would be delighted to receive your feedback on these matters and indeed any other aspect of the text: aa5961@coventry.ac.uk.

The main aim of this text continues to be the provision of a clear, coherent and up-to-date account of the law of human rights and civil liberties for use (mainly) on undergraduate law programmes. Because of recent developments, the text concentrates on the position of civil liberties and human rights protection in light of the Human Rights Act 1998 and the standards of human rights' protection laid down, principally, by the European Convention on Human Rights and its case law. The reader will be introduced to the meaning and scope of human rights and civil liberties, the reasons for their recognition and enforcement, the machinery available for redress and, equally importantly, the reasons why they need to be restricted, including the limitations of those restrictions. These themes will form the basis of the first part of the text, and specific areas of civil liberties, covered in Part Two of the text, will be studied in the context of those themes and principles. By adopting this approach, the student will, hopefully, appreciate the dilemma of civil liberties and their legal protection, and become aware of the techniques used in national and international law in the balancing of such liberties with other rights and interests.

Although there are several excellent texts in this area, this text attempts to provide a different angle on the study of civil liberties law, avoiding, where possible, a black letter approach and allowing the reader to place the study of the subject in the context of the passing and implementation of the Human Rights Act 1998 and the principles and case law of the European Convention. Because the direction of civil liberties has been so influenced by the Convention and the 1998 Act, the book will place specific weight on the European Convention and its principles and case law, which will pervade the whole text and all arguments relating to the protection of human rights and civil liberties. In particular, the text attempts to address the dilemma of protecting human rights and civil liberties when they come into conflict with other individual or group interests. In this respect the various case studies allow the reader to reflect on the principles and machinery necessary to resolve such issues and to apply those principles to a specific situation.

Part One of the text deals with the enforcement of human rights and civil liberties, covering the definition and enforcement of civil liberties, the protection of civil liberties in both domestic and international law, and, in particular, the protection under the European Convention and in our domestic law. Particular attention is paid to the machinery and principles of the European Convention and how these will inform the protection of human rights in the post-Human Rights era. Part Two will then cover the protection of specific areas of civil liberties, such as freedom of expression, the right to demonstrate and privacy. Because the text has taken this approach, it has been necessary to omit certain specific areas such as police powers and civil liberty, although aspects of these areas are covered in the relevant sections on the Human Rights Act, the European Convention on Human Rights, liberty of the person and the right to privacy. The text now contains a specific chapter on terrorism and human rights, although this area is also reflected in the chapters on rights theory, the Human Rights Act, liberty of the person, the right to a fair trial and freedom of association. In addition, a number of case studies are dedicated to this area, in both the specific and other chapters.

As expected, since the final draft there have been a variety of case and statutory developments, which are briefly referred to below; further details and future developments will be made available on the book's companion website: **www.mylawchamber.co.uk/fosterhumanrights**.

For chapter 2 on the European Convention on Human Rights, in 2011 the Coalition government announced that they would introduce amendments to domestic law, allowing some prisoners the right to vote – those sentenced to one year or less. This followed an ultimatum from the Council of Europe to comply with *Hirst* (see page 93 of the text) and a 'pilot' judgment of the European Court in *MT and Greens v United Kingdom* (*The Times*, 23 November 2010), which gave the government six months to comply with *Hirst*. A free vote was held in parliament in February 2011 to consider the proposals. With respect to s.2 of the Human Rights Act 1998 and the doctrine of precedent, in *Manchester City Council v Pinnock* ([2010] UKSC 45) the Supreme Court held that following *Kay v United Kingdom* (pages 128–9 of the text), Article 8 required that a court had to assess the proportionality of an order of possession under the Housing Act before making such an order. The Supreme Court held that it would be wrong not to follow a clear and consistent line of authority from the ECHR where such decisions were not inconsistent with some fundamental substantive procedural rule of UK law.

Under Article 2 (see chapter 4), with respect to the state's positive duty to protect life, note that an application is now before the European Court with respect to the shooting of Jean Charles de Menezes in Stockwell station in 2005: *Armani de Silva v UK* (Application No 5878/08). It is alleged that the shooting constituted a breach of Articles 2, 3 and 13 of the European Convention on Human Rights. With respect to freedom from torture, etc. (see chapter 5), in *R v Qazi* ([2010] EWCA Civ 2579) the Court of Appeal provided guidance on when it would be a violation of Article 3 for a court to impose a custodial sentence on a prisoner with a serious medical condition. It was held that a custodial sentence was not necessarily in breach of Article 3 and that the sentencing court would order release if that was the only way to comply with Article 3. The European Court will announce its judgment in *Othman v United Kingdom* (Application No 8139/09), with respect to the deportation of the applicant, a terrorist suspect, to Jordan and the compatibility of such with Article 3. In *Al Hassan-Daniel v Revenue and Customs Commissioner* ([2010] EWCA Civ 1443) the Court of Appeal held that the illegal conduct of an individual (in this case drug smuggling) did not bar a claim under Article 3 of the Convention; the principle of *ex turpi causa* did not apply in such a context. In *R (Mousa) v Defence Secretary* ([2010] EWHC 3304 (Admin)), it was held that the failure to order a public inquiry into allegations of physical abuse of detainees by the armed forces in Iraq was not unlawful as two adequate and independent inquiries had already been established to investigate allegations of mistreatment.

With respect to liberty of the person and control orders (chapters 6 and 14), in *N and E v Home Secretary* ([2010] EWCA Civ 869), the Court of Appeal confirmed that a legally flawed non-derogating control order was void *ab initio* and would be quashed with retrospective effect. Under Article 6 (see chapter 7), the meaning of 'civil rights' was considered in *R (King) v Secretary of State for Justice* ([2010] EWHC 2522 (Admin)), where it was held that disciplinary proceedings against a young offender determined his civil rights of association and private family life, even though it was not a criminal charge (as the penalty was only cellular confinement). In that case it was also held that disciplinary proceedings conducted by a prison governor against a young offender did not constitute an 'independent court' but that the availability of judicial review met the requirements of impartiality under Article 6. In *Cadder v HM Advocate* ([2010] UKSC 43) it was held that a detainee was entitled to have access to a lawyer from the time of his first interview unless there were compelling reasons on the facts that made the presence of a lawyer impracticable. The Scottish Parliament immediately passed the Criminal Procedure (Legal Assistance, Detention and Appeal) (Scotland) Act 2010.

With respect to Article 8 (see chapter 11), in *ZH v Home Secretary* ([2011] UKSC 4), the Supreme Court held that the child's best interests was the primary consideration in deciding whether the removal of his mother to another country was proportionate under Article 8.

Also, in *QJ (Algeria)* v *Home Secretary* ([2010] EWCA Civ 1478) it was held that the statutory regimes of deportation and extradition were wholly separate and served different purposes, and thus deportations might justify a much greater degree of interference with family life than would be proportionate in the case of extraditions. In *A, B and C* v *Ireland* (*The Times*, 16 December 2010) the European Court found a violation of Article 8 in respect of the third applicant when there was no effective procedure for her to confirm whether she was entitled to an abortion under Irish national law (risk to life). The other two applications were dismissed as the Court found that the general prohibition on abortion in Irish law was necessary and within the state's margin of appreciation.

With respect to free speech, in *Naik* v *Secretary of State for the Home Department* ([2010] EWHC 2825) it was held that there had been no violation of Article 10 when a leading Muslim speaker had been excluded from the UK by the Home Secretary. The claimant had no legitimate expectation of continuing to visit the UK and the interference with his right of free speech had been lawful and proportionate given the risk of his speeches having a likely effect of instigating terrorist attacks (see *ex parte Farrakhan*, on page 747 of the text). The restrictions were proportionate as they only prevented him from addressing crowds at public events in the UK and did not prevent him disseminating his views from outside the territory. In *Sanoma Uitgevers BV* v *Netherlands* (*The Times*, 14 September 2010) the Grand Chamber overruled the European Court (see page 420 of the text) and held that there was a violation of Article 10 when a magazine was forced to hand over a CD-ROM of a street race, having promised the participants that they would not be identified. The relevant law was insufficiently clear and lacking in adequate safeguards to be 'prescribed by law'. In the law of defamation, in *McLaughlin and Others* v *Lambeth LBC* ([2010] EWHC) it was held that the rule in *Derbyshire CC* v *Times Newspaper* (see page 439 of the text) did not preclude individual officers of a local authority body from bringing an action in defamation provided they were identified and could prove that the accusations were defamatory of them. In *Spiller* v *Joseph* ([2010] UKSC 53) the Supreme Court held that the requirement in the defence of fair comment that the statement refer to facts, should now be 'whether the comment explicitly or implicitly indicates, at least in general terms, the facts on which it was based'. With respect to press freedom and privacy, following *Mosley* v *News Group Newspapers* (on pages 626–7 of the text) Mosley has petitioned the European Court claiming the right to be informed of intended publication so that claimants can apply for interim injunctions. Meanwhile, in *MGN* v *United Kingdom* (*The Times*, 18 January 2011) the European Court found no violation of Article 10 in respect of the complaint that the decision in *Campbell* v *MGN* (see pages 621–2 of the text) was in breach of press freedom. The European Court found that the House of Lords decision struck a fair balance between press freedom and privacy, and that there was no public interest in the publication of photographs and the story of Ms Campbell attending a drugs clinic. However, it held that the award of £1 million costs against MGN including liability to pay the success fees of her lawyers was excessive and therefore a breach of Article 10 in that respect. The issue of 'super injunctions' and anonymity orders have been considered in a number of cases: *DFT* v *TFD* [2010] EWHC 2335; *AMM* v *HXW* [2010] EWHC 2457; and *Gray* v *UVW* [2010] EWHC 2367 (QB), which will be detailed in the online supplement. In *JIH* v *Newsgroup Newspapers* ([2011] EWCA Civ 42) the Court of Appeal stated that, generally, on an application for anonymity in proceedings concerning the publication of a newspaper story about an individual's private life, the media and public interests would be better served by an order granting anonymity, but allowing limited details of the case into the public domain, as opposed to publishing the claimant's name with little else.

With respect to discrimination (see chapter 13), in *JM* v *United Kingdom* (*The Times*, 29 September 2010) it was held that there had been a violation of Article 1 of the first protocol and Article 14 with respect to the rules on child maintenance and same-sex couples prior to the passing of the Civil Partnership Act 2004.

I would like to thank everyone at Pearson Education Limited for their assistance in the writing and presentation of this text, in particular my thanks go to Owen Knight (Acquisitions Editor) and David Hemsley who have overseen this edition and have been of great assistance and support. This edition of the book is dedicated to my children, Tom, Ben and Ella, and to my late mother and father.

Steve Foster
Coventry University
April 2011

Guided tour

Chapter introductions outline the key themes that are to be covered and help you organise your learning.

Real-life cases and stories within the introductions place the material that is to come in the chapter into context, and show the many arenas in which human rights issues play out.

Clear headings and sub-headings keep you firmly focused and constantly aware of the progression and structure of each chapter.

Questions feature throughout chapters and offer you a chance to reflect on what you've read, test how thoroughly you've understood the topics discussed, and also to apply your knowledge of the law.

Case studies highlight and discuss the facts and key legal principles of important cases, helping to contextualise the theory you've been learning. Questions at the end of each case study aid critical examination of the principles involved.

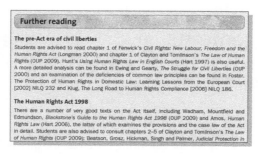

Further reading sections at the end of each chapter. These point you to a wealth of further text and journal resources which can be used as a starting point for essay research, or just help deepen your understanding of a given area.

Your complete learning package

Visit **www.mylawchamber.co.uk/fosterhumanrights**
to access a wealth of resources to support your studies:

- Weblinks to help you read more widely around the subject and really impress your lecturers
- Answer plans to questions in the book to compare with your own responses
- Additional case studies to help you get to grips with case law
- Legal updates to help you stay up to date with the law and impress examiners.

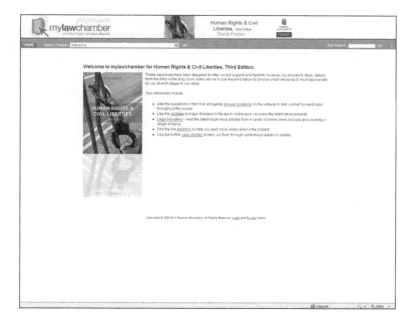

Acknowledgements

The publisher would like to thank the following reviewers for their valuable comments on the book:

Philip DH Jones (LLB, LLM, Solicitor), Senior Lecturer, Law Department, University of the West of England

Nicola Aries, Principal Lecturer, Kingston University

David Mead, Senior Lecturer, Norwich Law School, University of East Anglia

Table of cases

Table of legislation

Table of statutory instruments

Table of EU and other European legislation

Directives

Directive 73/148/EEC (Freedom of Movement)
28
   Arts 1, 2 *28*
Directive 76/207/EEC (Equal Treatment) *27,
728*
Directive 83/189 *390*
Directive 95/46/EC (Data Protection) *633*
   Art 14 *596n*
Directive 2000/78/EC (Employment Equality
   Work Directive) *729*

Treaties and conventions

Community Charter of Fundamental Social
   Rights for Workers *29*
Council of Europe Recommendation No 799,
   25 January 1977 *76n*
Council of Europe Recommendation No 1418,
   25 June 1999 *196*
EC Treaty 1991
   Art 28 *6, 7, 8, 335, 393*
   Art 29 *560*
   Art 30 *393, 560*
   Art 34 *28*
   Art 36 *28*
   Art 49 *6, 7, 8, 27n, 338*
   Art 141 *27n, 728, 735n*
   Art 234 *7*
EEC Treaty 1957 (Treaty of Rome) *6*
   Art 34 *560*
   Art 36 *560*
   Art 119 *27n, 728*
European Convention for the Prevention of
   Torture and Inhuman or Degrading
   Treatment or Punishment 1987 *21,
   224n*
European Convention for the Protection of
   Individuals with regard to the
   Automatic Protection of Data 1980
   27n

European Convention on the Protection of
   Human Rights and Fundamental
   Freedoms 1950 *passim*
Art 1 *25, 46, 50n, 66, 87, 120, 121, 188,
   189, 208, 219, 707*
Arts 2–18 *78*
Arts 2–12 *126*
Art 2 *xxi, 13, 18n, 50n, 51, 58, 61, 74, 79,
   80, 94, 104n, 106n, 121, 122–4, 126,
   131n, 150, 160, 168, 185–222, 227,
   230, 238n, 239, 246, 258, 270, 317,
   427, 468, 580, 581, 604, 639, 673,
   740, 744, 759–61*
Art 2(1) *216*
Art 2(2) *80, 187, 220, 759, 760*
Art 3 *xxi, 11, 31–3, 38–9, 43, 49, 50n, 55,
   74, 78, 79, 80, 81, 82n, 83n, 94, 95n,
   104n, 115, 122, 131n, 134, 140, 150,
   158, 186, 188, 189, 196, 197, 199,
   200, 201n, 203, 206n, 207, 208,
   215–20, 223–66, 270, 302, 312, 573,
   578, 594, 637–9, 707, 712, 724, 729,
   740, 744, 759, 761–3, 768–70, 775n,
   776, 778*
Art 4 *81–83*
Art 4(1) *74, 79, 81, 744*
Art 4(3) *81, 82*
Art 5 *13, 27, 38, 49, 61, 63, 64, 81, 83,
   121n, 123n, 136, 140, 142, 147,
   148, 150, 164, 173–5, 187n, 196,
   229n, 259, 262, 268–302, 305, 311n,
   335, 510n, 511, 545, 554–7, 559,
   561, 562, 572, 583, 641, 649, 717,
   740, 741, 744–6, 757, 759, 765–8,
   770–2*
Art 5(1) *40, 173, 274, 275, 277, 279, 280,
   283n, 289, 294, 298, 299, 302, 745,
   767–70*
Art 5(1)(a)–(f) *83, 274*
Art 5(1)(a) *40*
Art 5(1)(b) *276, 287, 556n, 559*

Table of overseas and international legislation

Part One

The enforcement of human rights and civil liberties

1 Human rights and civil liberties: definition, classification and protection

Introduction

In *R (G)* v *Nottinghamshire Healthcare NHS Trust* [2009] EWCA Civ 795, it was held that a ban on smoking in mental health units did not engage the inmates' right to private life under Article 8 of the European Convention on Human Rights, and in any case the ban was necessary to protect the health of patients. Similarly, in *R (Howitt)* v *Preston Magistrate's Court* (19 March 2009) it was held that the Health Act 2006, which made it an offence for pub landlords to allow smoking on their premises, was not incompatible with any article of the European Convention.

In *Friend* v *UK*; *Countryside Alliance* v *UK* (Application Nos 16072/06 and 27809/08), the European Court of Human Rights held that the ban on hunting with hounds was not in breach of anyone's right to private life, association or peaceful assembly, and that any interference with property rights was justified on grounds of public morals.

In May 2010 the conditions of an Anti-Social Behaviour Order that a young man should not wear low-slung trousers and hooded tops were withdrawn by the Magistrate's Court because such conditions interfered with the boy's human rights.

These cases, and hundreds of others, will be explored in this text to examine whether there has been a violation of a human right and if so whether that interference can be justified. But how do the courts decide whether a human right has been engaged, and whether any interference is justified?

This chapter introduces the reader to the meaning, scope and protection of human rights and civil liberties, and the legal and moral dilemmas involved in their recognition, interpretation and limitation. In particular the chapter will examine:

- The definition of human rights and civil liberties and different theories on human rights protection.
- The classification of human rights.
- The mechanism for protecting rights and liberties, at both the national and international level (including the protection of human rights in Europe).
- The dilemma of protecting human rights and civil liberties and the balance with other rights and interests.

Included at the beginning and end of the chapter are case studies, allowing you to study human rights disputes and to reflect on the legal and other issues raised by the case.

At the end of the chapter the reader should be able to appreciate the mechanics of protecting human rights, and the incidental dilemmas, using that knowledge to study the remaining chapters of the text on national and international machinery for enforcement (chapters 2 and 3) and substantive human rights covered in the remaining chapters of the book.

What are human rights and civil liberties?

We often hear individuals or groups of individuals claim that their human rights or civil liberties have been violated – those who claim to have been ill-treated in detention, those denied welfare benefits – but what do they mean? Are they merely seeking to make their claim sound more important, or are those terms actually capable of definition?

This section of the book will attempt to explain the fundamental importance of human rights and civil liberties and to explore the main theories behind their recognition and protection. Subsequent sections will then examine the classification of such rights, the mechanisms for their protection and the dilemmas of protecting them when they come into conflict with other rights and interests. With respect to the United Kingdom, most people now relate the terms 'civil liberties' and 'human rights' to the passing of the Human Rights Act 1998 and the European Convention on Human Rights, which has been given effect to via the 1998 Act. That Act, passed to ensure that our domestic law complies with the standards laid down in the Convention with respect to the protection of fundamental rights, has raised the profile of such rights and this textbook deals essentially with the 1998 Act and the Convention and uses those terms in that context.[1]

'Human rights' and 'civil liberties' refer to those rights that for one reason or another are regarded as fundamental or basic to the individual, or group of individuals, who assert them. Thus, human rights and civil liberties are primarily *individual* rights, claimed by the individual or group of individuals as part of, and which relate to, the position of the individual within an organised state.[2] Accordingly, the collective rights of society to peace, security or freedom from crime have not traditionally been classed as human rights or civil liberties, although they will be strongly protected by society via the traditional law, and can, in many cases engage individual human rights.[3] Instead, these rights and liberties are referring to individual benefits and enjoyment, for example the right to freedom of speech. Such rights are seen as inherent to our status as human beings – violations of them being considered as an

---

[1] Accordingly this section will refer to those instruments and such rights when attempting to explain the meaning of the general terms 'human rights' and 'civil liberties'.

[2] The present definition does not cover fundamental rights such as environmental rights, which more obviously directly benefit society as a whole.

[3] For example, the failure of the state to protect property and personal safety would engage the right to property, private life, and in some cases, the right to life. The 'right' of society to peace and security, etc. can also be used to justify the limitation of individual human rights.

affront to that status – and regarded as fundamental and in need of protection from arbitrary interference. Primarily couched in negative terms, they represent a notion of individual liberty and are usually given an enhanced status in each country's constitutional arrangements, limiting the power of government to legislate or act in contravention of these liberties or freedoms.[4]

These rights, or liberties, or freedoms, are contained in both domestic and international instruments and although there may be arguments as to why one right or claim should be fundamental, these domestic and international documents display a reasonably common content. Thus the legal system of a state, and international treaties, will attempt to protect rights such as the right to life, the right to property, the right to a fair trial and freedom of expression and peaceful assembly. Similarly, basic needs – the right to food, shelter, clothing, and the right to education – will be regarded as fundamental by most societies and accommodated in the legal and constitutional system in some way. The fact that these liberties and rights are bolstered by international treaties supports the assertion that they are regarded, globally, as fundamental, and the fact that there will be great controversy over their weighting with other interests should not detract from the premise that such claims are superior to other rights or interests. Thus, for example, the right to free speech and freedom of assembly will be regarded as more important than other manifestations of individual liberty and autonomy. Consequently the right to protest should generally override the 'right' to shop in an area free from demonstrations. Although the latter interest might, in some circumstances, override our fundamental right, there is no serious argument that the right to shop has a fundamental status and is, therefore, worthy of inclusion in any domestic or international bill of rights.[5] Similarly, taking part in pursuits and pastimes will not, generally, engage one's fundamental rights.[6]

Fundamental rights, thus have a common quality: they are regarded as basic to human worth and dignity or individual liberty and are protected as such. This is illustrated in the case of *R (G) v Nottingham Healthcare NHS Trust*.[7] In this case the applicants sought to quash regulations made under the Health Act 2006, which provided a temporary and partial exemption from smoking in public places for mental health units as being incompatible with Article 8 of the European Convention. The court recognised that the right under Article 8 covered many facets such as development and autonomy, physical and moral integrity, mental stability, the integrity of identity and the protection of private sphere and space, but refused to accept that it was coextensive with the right of absolute independence so as to protect anything that a person might want to do in a private space. In the court's view, preventing a person from smoking did not generally involve such adverse effect upon the person's physical or moral integrity or other facets, above, so as to amount to an interference with the right to private or home life. Thus the court did not accept a right to smoke wherever one is living.

---

[4] For an overall account of human rights theory, see Gorman, *Rights and Reason: An Introduction to the Philosophy of Rights* (Acumen Publishing 2003). See also Harris, Human Rights and Mythical Beasts [2004] 120 LQR 428.

[5] The fundamental right to protest might, of course, interfere with business and property interests, which will be regarded as more important and might engage Article 1 of the First Protocol to the Convention.

[6] See *R (Countryside Alliance) v Attorney General and Another* [2007] 3 WLR 922; *Friend v Lord Advocate* [2008] HRLR 11, detailed in the case study, below.

[7] [2009] EWCA Civ 795. See also *R (Foster) v Secretary of State for Justice* [2010] EWHC 2224 (Admin), where the disciplining of a young prisoner by withdrawing his tobacco allowance was held not to engage the right to private life under Article 8 of the European Convention.

The court then considered whether, had it been wrong on the first issue, the regulations were a disproportionate and arbitrary interference with the applicants' Article 8 rights; the claimants' argument being that the regulation went further than necessary to achieve any legitimate aim and that it would have been proportionate to allow the continuation of the exemption where it was not feasible for patients to smoke outside. On this issue, the court felt that given the need to protect both health and the rights of others in the enclosed environment of mental health units, and the security reasons for restricting outdoor access to many patients, the measures could be regarded as necessary and proportionate.

CASE STUDY

R (Countryside Alliance) v Attorney General and Another [2007] 3 WLR 922; Friend v Lord Advocate [2008] HRLR 11; Friend v UK; Countryside Alliance v UK (Application Nos 16072/06 and 27809/08) (2010) 50 EHRR SE 6

This dispute has been chosen for our first case study for two primary reasons. First, it highlights the controversy surrounding human rights claims and the social, economic and political arguments that need to be resolved when passing and interpreting legal measures. Secondly, and more specifically, it provides us with some guidance as to what is, and what is not a human rights claim, and can thus be used in the context of our present discussions. In addition, as you will see, the dispute raised issues under both European Convention law and EU law, allowing you to see how such laws and claims are separate. The dispute, heard in both the domestic courts and the European Court of Human Rights, revolved around the passing of legislation which made it unlawful to use a live quarry (for example a fox) whilst hunting.

You will revisit some of the areas raised in the case in more detail in subsequent chapters, so do not be too concerned about the details of the issues at this stage.

The facts and decision in the domestic proceedings

In *Countryside Alliance* the appellants claimed that the Hunting Act 2004 was incompatible with the European Convention on Human Rights and inconsistent with the European Community (EC) Treaty 1957. The applicants included those involved in hunting for their occupation and livelihood, and landowners who either permitted the pursuit on their land or managed their land for that purpose. A second set of appellants included dog breeders who had formerly sold their dogs in the United Kingdom, and UK providers of livery services, all of whom were, they claimed, affected by the ban. The first set of appellants claimed that the ban infringed Article 8 of the Convention – guaranteeing the right to private life and the home – because it adversely affected their private life, their cultural lifestyle and the use of their home; all resulting in the loss of their livelihood. They also argued that the ban interfered with their right of association and assembly under Article 11 of the Convention; their property rights under Article 1 of the first protocol to the Convention; and that they were subjected to adverse treatment with respect to the enjoyment of the above rights on the basis of their 'other status' within Article 14.

The second set of appellants argued that the Act was inconsistent with both Articles 28 and 49 of the EC Treaty. Article 28 prohibits national non-fiscal measures which prevent the free movement of goods and Article 49 prevents Member States employing rules which restrict the provision of services by EU nationals. The appellants requested that the preliminary reference procedure, under Article 234 EC Treaty, be invoked and the Court of Justice (ECJ) asked to rule on whether national measures prohibiting the economic activity of hunting breached Articles 28 and 49 where it diminished the market for products and thus reduced cross-border trade and prevented providers of hunting-related services from providing those services.

The decision of the House of Lords

With respect to Article 8 of the ECHR, the House of Lords held that fox hunting was a very public activity, lacking the personal and private aspects inherent in Article 8. Thus, the appellants' claims – based on autonomy, cultural lifestyle, the use of the home, and loss of livelihood – all failed to engage Article 8. Although the term 'home' should not be too strictly defined, it could not cover land over which the owner permitted a sport to be conducted. Equally, the activities of the hunting fraternity did not show the characteristics of a distinctive group with a traditional culture and lifestyle that was sufficiently fundamental to form part of its identity. Dissenting on this specific point, Lord Rodger of Earlsferry was prepared to accept that taking part in the hunt was sufficiently integral to their identity to engage the right to private life under Article 8, although felt that the public spectacle of the event took it outside the article for that reason. Their Lordships also rejected the claim that the ban impacted on and interfered with the right of association and assembly as guaranteed by Article 11 of the Convention. Their position was no different from that of other people who wished to assemble in a public place for sporting or recreational purposes, and fell well short of the kind of assembly whose protection was fundamental to the proper functioning of a modern democratic society.

Their Lordships then held that if the above rights had been engaged, any interference was both in accordance with the law (the clear provisions of the Hunting Act 2004) and necessary in a democratic society for the 'protection of morals'. Although many people did not consider that there was a pressing social need for the hunting ban, nevertheless a majority of the country's democratically elected representatives (parliament) did, and had decided otherwise. The democratic process was likely to be subverted if, on a question of moral and political judgment, opponents of the Act could achieve through the courts what they could not achieve through parliament.

Their Lordships did, however, find that the appellants' property rights had been clearly engaged under Article 1 of the First Protocol to the Convention – because the legislation restricted the use to which certain property could be put. However, that interference was justifiable and respected the recent and closely considered judgment of parliament on this matter. Finally, the House of Lords rejected the claim that the ban engaged the appellant's rights under Article 14 of the Convention – to enjoy their Convention rights free from unjustifiable discrimination. Even if the appellants had been the subject of any adverse treatment compared to those who did not hunt, such treatment was not on the grounds of 'other status' within Article 14 because the treatment could not be linked to any personal characteristic of any of the appellants or anything that could be meaningfully described as status.

With respect to the claims under EU law, Articles 28 and 49, the House of Lords held that the measures under the Hunting Act 2004 were not caught by these provision, but even if those articles were engaged, Lord Bingham was of the opinion that the Hunting Act 2004 was justified on the grounds of '. . . social reform, not directed to the regulation of commercial activity . . .'. Citing the ECJ's acceptance of infringement of human dignity as justification for a measure preventing the exploitation of games involving simulating the killing of people in *Omega Spielhallen -und Automatenaufstellungs-GmbH* v *Oberbürgermeisterin der Bundesstadt Bonn* (36/02) [2004] ECR I – 9609, Lord Bingham felt that parliament justifiably considered that the 'real killing' of wild animals similarly infringed a fundamental value.

At the same time the House of Lords heard the appeal in *Friend* v *Lord Advocate*, where it held that the restrictions imposed by the equivalent Scottish legislation (The Protection of Wild Mammals (Scotland) Act 2002) was lawful and not incompatible with the European Convention on Human Rights.

In particular the House of Lords rejected the submission that the ban infringed Article 9 of the Convention, guaranteeing freedom of thought, conscience and religion. Hunting with hounds was a pastime mainly for pleasure and relaxation and a person's belief in his right to engage in a recreational activity, however fervent or passionate, could not be equated with beliefs of the kind that were protected by Article 9. The Act did not compel anyone to act contrary to his conscience or to refrain from holding and giving visible expression to his beliefs about the practice of hunting in the way he dressed.

Further, there had been no violation of Articles 8 or 11. Hunting with hounds did not involve issues of personal autonomy. It was conducted in public and had social aspects involving the wider community; the right to establish and develop relationships with others was only protected to a degree and could not be extended to a generalised right of respect for minority community interests. Article 11 (freedom of assembly and association) also did not extend the right of assembly for purely social purposes and the hunter's position fell well short of the kind of assembly whose protection was fundamental to the proper functioning of a democratic society.

Finally, the appellant in the present case failed to prove that Article 14 (prohibition of discrimination in the enjoyment of Convention rights) had been violated. To prove a case under Article 14 it was necessary to prove that other articles had been engaged or the case fell within the core of the values guaranteed by those articles. In the present case the activity was one that individuals were free to participate in (before the ban) but not one which had been provided previously by the state or which restricted on the core issues of the relevant Convention rights.

The decision of the European Court of Human Rights (admissibility)

In *Friend* v *United Kingdom; Countryside Alliance* v *United Kingdom*, the European Court declared as inadmissible applications alleging that the ban on hunting with hounds was in breach of the European Convention.

With respect to Article 8 it was held that not every activity a person might engage in with others was protected by the article. Article 8 will not protect interpersonal relations of such broad and indeterminate scope that there can be no conceivable direct link between the action or inaction of the state and a person's private life. Hunting, by its very nature, was essentially a public activity and the hunting community could not be regarded as an ethnic or national minority or represent a particular lifestyle which was indispensable to a person's identity. The concept of home did not include land over which the owners practised or allowed sport to be practised and there was no evidence that the applicants would indeed lose their homes as a result of the ban. Also the ban had not created serious difficulties for earning one's living.

In respect of Article 11 the Court held that the ban did not prevent or restrict the applicants' right to assemble with other huntsmen and to engage in alternatives; the ban had been designed to eliminate the hunting and killing of animals for sport in a manner causing suffering and being morally objectionable – the ban had been introduced after extensive debate by the democratically elected representatives of the State on the social and ethical issues raised by that type of hunting.

Finally, as to Article 1 of the First Protocol the Court found that it was not arbitrary or unreasonable not to compensate for the adverse consequences of the ban, given the fact that there had been extensive debate, above, and that people had continued to gather for hunts without live quarry after the Act had been passed. (The claims under Articles 9, 10 and 14 were also dismissed as manifestly ill-founded.)

Questions

1 What 'human' rights were being claimed by the parties to the domestic proceedings?
2 Is it possible to distinguish between fundamental human rights and other rights?
3 Why did the House of Lords reject all but one of the claims based on the European Convention on Human Rights?
4 Do you agree with the House of Lords with respect to its findings in 2, above? In particular, do you agree that the claims lacked the necessary ingredients to be labelled fundamental (Convention) rights?
5 What effect does such a finding have on the enforceability and status of the claims made by the hunters and landowners?
6 Why did the House of Lords reject the claim based on the landowner's property rights?
7 Do you agree that the ultimate decision upholds the democratic legitimacy of parliament's decision in this area?
8 Does the European Court of Human Right's decision vindicate the House of Lords' decision?
9 Is it possible to answer any of the above questions without reference to your personal or political views on the ban?
10 If the law was changed by a subsequent parliament so as to allow 'hunting with hounds' are there any human rights claims that could be brought to *challenge* such a law?

Why protect human rights and civil liberties?

Where does the notion of fundamental rights come from? The text will now explore some of the leading theories on human rights and civil liberties, thus providing you with some idea as to why those rights are fundamental and why they are given enhanced protection in both national and international law.

Human rights and the social contract

Many theories on fundamental rights derive from the idea of individual liberty, based on the notion of the 'social contract' as expounded by such writers as Locke and Rawls.[8] John Locke (1632–1704) was a British philosopher who greatly influenced the political ideas of the eighteenth century. Although versions of the social contract theory had existed before Locke, his version, in its more basic format, held that in being a member of the state every individual enters into a contract with the state under which the latter agrees to protect the fundamental rights of each citizen. Thus, although each citizen agrees to allow the state power to regulate and govern, and to abide by the actions and laws of that state, that agreement is made in return for the guarantee of certain fundamental rights. The citizen's promise of allegiance to the state is, therefore, conditional on the retention of these fundamental claims, which include the right to life, liberty and property. The notion of the social contract has been expanded in more recent times by John Rawls (1921–2002), an American professor at Harvard and regarded as one of the last century's most important philosophers. He imagined a hypothetical social contract, whereby each individual, not yet knowing his or her ultimate destination or choices, seeks to achieve a society that will best allow him or her to achieve those individual goals and enjoy the 'good life'. Thus, to achieve that good life the individual will require freedom of choice, including freedom of religion and expression, and freedom from arbitrary arrest and detention. Importantly, he or she will demand these rights irrespective of social standing and the choices that he/she ultimately makes, insisting on a society that is tolerant and which does not have the arbitrary power to interfere with the enjoyment of those rights. These theories form the basis of the majority of national and international human rights documents, which we will examine later in this chapter.

Of course, social contract theory is not popular with those who feel that the main purpose of the state is to protect the state as a whole, and who thus see the protection of individual liberty at the expense of the public or state interest as dangerous and divisive. This view, commonly known as **utilitarianism**, does not see individual liberty as a good in itself, and its followers are thus prepared to sacrifice individual liberty for the common good.[9] Although utilitarianism is not opposed to individual rights, and indeed sees their protection as beneficial to society as a whole, its basic principles are cited today by those fearful that increasing the rights of individuals via such documents as the European Convention on Human Rights and the Human Rights Act 1998 will be detrimental to the public good. In response, it must not be forgotten why such documents were agreed to in the first place, and why indeed the idea of the social contract was devised. Such instruments and ideals were introduced to combat the threat of despotic and arbitrary governments, who were prepared to violate individual freedoms at any cost. Thus, as the public, aware from past experience of the dangers of the exercise of individual freedom, are naturally sceptical of the notion of the social contract, so too civil libertarians draw on previous state abuse of human rights to justify their views.

---

[8] See Locke, *The Second Treatise of Government* (1698); Rawls, *A Theory of Justice* (Harvard University Press 1972).

[9] The theory is often credited to Jeremy Bentham (1748–1832) who described the notion of natural rights as 'nonsense upon stilts', and the American Declaration of Independence as 'bawling upon paper': Bowring (ed.) *Collected Works of Jeremy Bentham* (Edinburgh, William Tait 1843).

Human rights and the protection of human dignity

The next theory that we will examine is the idea that protecting human rights is essential to maintaining the dignity and integrity of the human being. Thus human rights uphold the basic dignity of the individual as a human being; every human being, because they *are* human, is said to deserve humane treatment, and they should not, therefore, be subject to torture or other ill-treatment, or to slavery and servitude, as such treatment is an affront to human dignity. Those who advocate the abolition of the death penalty, therefore, do not always do so for practical reasons such as the possibility of sentencing the wrong person to death, but do so because they feel that such an activity is inconsistent with human dignity and of civilised behaviour. Equally, restricting an individual's right of choice, whether it be to what religion they are allowed to practise, or what they choose to say or who they are allowed to marry or associate with, could be said to be an attack on human worth and dignity. More specifically, discriminating against an individual or group of individuals because of their sex, race, religion, etc. could be said to amount to a violation of human dignity and pride.[10]

This basis for protecting human rights is, of course, vulnerable to attack from those who feel that certain individuals, because of their conduct, have forsaken their right to dignity. For example, prisoners claiming that their basic rights are being denied while in prison are often reminded by politicians and members of the public that they themselves have violated their victims' rights and should consider this when staking their claim. Such critics find it difficult to accept that documents such as the European Convention on Human Rights protect individuals from attacks on their dignity and worth irrespective of what they have done or what danger they pose to society or to particular individuals. This attack on the protection of rights can be answered in a number of ways. First, the prohibition of torture and other ill-treatment does not merely protect and benefit the individual; provisions such as Article 3 of the European Convention ensure that states do not violate the standards of civilised society. There is, therefore, a public benefit in the prohibition of torture, or arbitrary censorship or discrimination. Secondly, the vast majority of people will agree that there are limits to the manner in which an individual should be treated. Arguments about whether a person should serve life in prison, or the conditions in which they will serve their sentence, are ones of *degree*; in general everyone agrees that nobody should be subjected to torture or degrading treatment, but some feel that the state should be allowed the choice to elect a particular penalty. Thirdly, past experience tells us that these choices cannot be the sole prerogative of public opinion or of the state. It is preferable, therefore, to have a rule that insists that *all* individuals are treated with a minimum amount of respect and dignity, and that the relevant thresholds be decided within the parameters of human rights principles.

Human rights and equality

The next theory that we will examine is the idea that human rights and civil liberties are a necessary product of the notion of equality. Many human rights in domestic and international treaties are based on the idea of equality and freedom from discrimination.

---

[10] For an analysis of the role of equality and dignity in the protection of human rights, see Feldman, *Civil Liberties and Human Rights in England and Wales* (OUP 2002), chapter 3. See also the Special Issue of *European Human Rights Law Review* on Human Dignity and Equality [2006] (6) EHRLR.

International treaties and domestic bills of rights insist that rights are enjoyed free from discrimination on a variety of grounds, such as sex, race, national origin and religion. Equally, specific laws will be passed to ensure that individuals and groups are not subject to unlawful discrimination, often providing the individual with a specific remedy against the perpetrator of the discrimination. In addition, discriminatory treatment might give rise to a violation of another human right, such as freedom from inhuman or degrading treatment.

More generally, the principle of equality is often put forward as the theoretical basis for human rights protection. Treaties such as the European Convention on Human Rights advocate that the rights contained in the Convention are available to all, irrespective of personal or group characteristics, or of what the person is or has done. This principle is expounded by Ronald Dworkin (1931–), an American Professor and a leading exponent of rights and equality, who believes that every state has a duty to treat all of its citizens with equal concern and respect.[11] This is a modification of the social contract theory, and ensures that every person, particularly those who espouse unpopular views and who would not otherwise benefit from the choices made for the majority of society, are allowed to enjoy these fundamental rights. Thus, the European Convention has been used consistently by groups such as prisoners, sexual minorities and those whose views and expression of their views cause offence, providing evidence that those groups are most vulnerable to human rights abuses, and that their rights require protection from the traditional law and its enforcement. The protection of such groups gives rise to enormous public controversy, which will be examined later in this chapter, and such protection is defended via the principles of dignity and equality, which are so entrenched in all human rights documents.

Human rights and the rule of law

The fourth theory that we will examine is based on the notion that human rights uphold and maintain the basic tenets of the rule of law. Most international treaties on human rights stress the fundamental importance of the protection of such rights in upholding the rule of law. The idea that people are ruled by the law and not by men has been a central feature of democratic government since the birth of civilisation and ultimately human rights and individual liberty depend upon its maintenance. The doctrine accepts that the law has essential characteristics which distinguish it from arbitrary and unfair rules and in turn the human rights movement presupposes that the legal system will reflect those characteristics and provide the basis for protecting our fundamental rights. The doctrine is an essential feature of the British Constitution and as all students of constitutional law will recall was encapsulated by A.V. Dicey in his ideas of the predominance of regular law and the absence of arbitrary power, of equality under the law, and of the notion that individual rights will be protected by the courts.[12]

In essence the rule of law insists that states and governments follow basic principles of constitutional fair play. Law should be open, clear, general, prospective and stable,[13] and

---

[11] Dworkin, *Taking Rights Seriously* (Duckworth 1977). See also McColgan, Principle of Equality and Protection from Discrimination in International Human Rights Law [2003] EHRLR 157; Singh, Equality: The Neglected Virtue [2004] EHRLR 141.

[12] A.V. Dicey, *The Law of the Constitution* (Macmillan 1959).

[13] See Raz, The Rule of Law and its Virtue (1977) 93 LQR 195.

government should not interfere with people's rights in an arbitrary fashion. The rule of law also insists on equality, in the equal application of the law to all classes, including government officials, and on due process, including the principles of a fair trial, the presumption of innocence, the prohibition of retrospective penalties and the guarantee of judicial impartiality and independence. All these aspects of the rule of law not only protect the individual from arbitrary, irrational and unreasonable interference, but also provide a public good – an impartial and independent judiciary, an accountable and restricted government and the appearance of fair play and equality.

The 'due process' rights in the European Convention on Human Rights provide the clearest examples of how human rights can assist the rule of law. The Convention – the main treaty protecting human rights to Council of Europe countries – will be examined in detail later in this chapter and in chapter 2, but for present purposes we will examine its provisions to see how they reflect and uphold the rule of law. For example, Article 5 of the Convention provides that everyone has the right to liberty and security of the person and that such a right can only be interfered with in a number of specific circumstances, including lawful arrest and detention for specified purposes, and then only 'in accordance with a procedure prescribed by law'. Article 6 then provides that everyone has the right to a fair trial, upholding the principles of the rules of natural justice, of the independence and impartiality of the judiciary and the right of equal access to justice. More specifically, Article 7, which prohibits retrospective criminal law and penalties, supports the principle that there should be no punishment without law and that laws should be prospective and foreseeable.

Apart from the due process rights, the requirements of certainty and accountability are present throughout the Convention. Article 2 of the Convention, guaranteeing the right to life, includes the duty to conduct proper investigations into unlawful killings.[14] The 'conditional rights', contained specifically in Articles 8–11 of the Convention,[15] can only be interfered with when such restrictions are prescribed by law, or in accordance with law, and this has been interpreted by the European Court to mean that the relevant restriction must not only have a legal basis, but also that it be accessible and sufficiently certain to allow an individual to foresee the likely consequence of his or her actions.[16]

Treaties such as the European Convention on Human Rights and the Human Rights Act adopt, to some extent at least, the rights theories that have been examined above, giving a special status to individual freedom and individual rights. This does not mean that these rights can be enjoyed absolutely, or that individual freedom will always win when pitted against other interests. What these theories do espouse, however, is that these rights are normally more important than anything else, and can only be overridden in exceptional circumstances and under certain prescribed conditions. Thus, in *A* v *Secretary of State for the Home Department*[17] the House of Lords stressed that even in a terrorist situation the domestic courts were not precluded from discharging their role of interpreting and applying the law, which was an essential feature of democracy and the cornerstone of the rule of law.

---

[14] See *Jordan and Others* v *United Kingdom* (2003) 37 EHRR 2.

[15] Even other articles, such as freedom from discrimination, and the right to marry and found a family, which do not employ such phrases, have been interpreted so that they can only be violated by restrictions which possess the characteristics inherent in specific phrases such as 'prescribed by law'.

[16] See *Malone* v *United Kingdom* (1984) 7 EHRR 14 and *Sunday Times* v *United Kingdom* (1979) 2 EHRR 245.

[17] [2005] 2 AC 68.

> **Questions**
> What are human rights and civil liberties and what are their essential characteristics?
> What are the principal arguments in favour of protecting human rights and civil liberties?
> Do such rights protect a good beyond the protection of the individual, and, if so, what public good do they promote?

The classification of human rights and civil liberties

> Why do some people refer to their 'human rights' and others to their 'civil liberties'?

Although the terms 'human rights' and 'civil liberties' are related – primarily because of their fundamental status – you should be aware that at times the terms are used deliberately in order to distinguish particular rights and claims. This section will examine the ways in which these terms are used in various circumstances.

Civil liberties as civil and political rights

First, the phrase 'civil liberties' is often employed to refer to rights labelled as 'civil and political rights' – those rights which regulate an individual's relationship with the state *vis à vis* their liberty and security. These rights form the main content of documents such as the European Convention on Human Rights (and the Human Rights Act 1998) and a variety of other international treaties and national bills of rights. Often referred to as 'first generation' rights, they include the right to life, freedom from torture and slavery, freedom of the person, the right to a fair trial, the right to private life, freedom of thought, conscience, religion, speech and assembly and association, the right to marry and found a family, the right to vote and the right to personal property. They are regarded as part of every person's birthright and thus should be enjoyed against, and protected by, the state. On the other hand in this context 'human rights' refer to what are called economic, social and cultural rights, or 'second generation' rights. These include the right to food, shelter and housing, the right to education and the right to employment, and are consistent with every person's basic human needs in that society, thus attracting the liability of the state to provide such needs. International and national law will often distinguish these rights and provide different machinery for the recognition and protection of such rights. Thus, from the Universal Declaration of Human Rights there was formed both the International Covenant on Civil and Political Rights (1966) and the International Covenant on Economic, Social and Cultural Rights (1966), covering respectively these different, albeit overlapping, rights.

Human rights in an umbrella sense

Secondly, the phrase 'human rights' is also used in a generic or global sense to include *all* rights or claims that are regarded as fundamental or inalienable, and thus including first, second, and indeed third generation rights, such as the right to self-determination and the right to enjoy the environment. For example, the Universal Declaration on Human Rights

(1948) contains both groups of rights, and the European Convention on Human Rights contains the phrase 'human rights' in its title, and includes the right to education,[18] which might be regarded as belonging to economic, social and cultural rights.

Human rights and civil liberties as positive and negative rights

Thirdly, the distinction between 'human rights' and 'civil liberties' may be drawn with regard to the terms 'rights' and 'liberties'. Human rights, in the form of economic and social or cultural rights, may refer to those claims that an individual has a *right to*, imposing on the state a positive obligation to provide the necessary resources so that individuals can gain such rights. Civil liberties on the other hand usually involve the individual claiming a *freedom from* interference with that claim and thus imposing a negative duty on the state not to violate that claim. Thus, in its full title the European Convention refers to human rights and *fundamental freedoms* and, to a great extent, concentrates on the individual's right to be left alone and to enjoy his fundamental liberty. However, this distinction is not watertight. The European Convention often refers to rights, such as the right to life and the right to a fair trial, and these rights are included alongside fundamental freedoms such as freedom from torture, freedom of speech, conscience and religion, and freedom of assembly. In addition, although many of the rights in the Convention can be enjoyed by non-interference from the state, many of the rights, or aspects of those rights, do depend on the state providing resources for their enjoyment, such as the right to education, the right to a fair trial and the right to vote, which will require enormous financial and other resources. Equally, the enjoyment of freedom of speech and the right to private life demands not only non-interference, but also freedom of and access to information. In addition, although many of the 'second generation' rights are absent from the European Convention, and the Human Rights Act, the failure to provide such rights may lead to a breach of Convention rights.[19]

Human rights as opposed to residual liberties

Fourthly, the terms 'rights' and 'liberties' can be used to distinguish between the legal status of a particular claim. Thus, whereas human rights are often equated with legally enforceable claims against the state and/or other individuals, civil liberties represent the residual liberty to do anything that one wants unless the law provides otherwise. Such a distinction is drawn between the traditional method of protecting civil liberties in the United Kingdom, and the system employed under the Human Rights Act 1998. Whereas before the Act a person had the residual right to enjoy their liberty, including their fundamental civil liberties, the Human Rights Act provides a system of rights, which are laid down in statutory form and which are enforceable in a court of law against those who violate them.

Notwithstanding this, a bill of rights might give a special legal status and entrenchment to either, or both, civil and political rights and social and economic rights. What is relevant is the extent to which those rights or liberties can be legally enforced, and to what extent the normal law can override them. It is in this respect that the distinction between rights, liberties

---

[18] In Article 2 of the First Protocol to the European Convention on Human Rights.

[19] For example, a failure to provide adequate welfare benefits may lead to a breach of the right to family life or, in extreme cases, may amount to inhuman or degrading treatment or punishment: see *(R) Limbuela* v *Secretary of State for the Home Department* [2005] 3 WLR 1014.

and immunities becomes central. Wesley Hohfeld (1879–1918), an American jurist, stated that whereas a person who enjoys a right can enforce such a claim legally, other people having a legal duty not to interfere with that right, a person enjoying a liberty merely does no wrong in exercising that liberty; other people have no corresponding duty to allow the claim-holder to exercise that liberty.[20] For example, it might be said that a person has the liberty to assemble, provided he does not break any other law, but that he has no such right to assemble, because others will not be in breach of the law if they interfere with that liberty. On the other hand, freedom from discrimination becomes a right if a person who is discriminated against can bring a legal action against another who violates that right. Liberties thus are legally vulnerable and inferior to rights.

As both residual liberties and legal rights are often subject to legal interference and change, the classification of claims into *immunities* becomes fundamental. An immunity is a claim enjoyed by a person that another may not interfere with. Thus, bills of rights, whether national or international, often attempt to give certain claims an enhanced status, elevating them above regular rights and protecting them from legal and other interference. This characteristic of fundamental rights is central to the protection of both human rights and civil liberties, and provided such rights and liberties are given *legal* protection in respect of this immunity, the individual will at least start from the strongest position possible.

> **Question**
> What do you understand by the terms 'human rights' and 'civil liberties'? What have those terms got in common and when is it necessary to distinguish between them?

The mechanism for protecting rights and liberties at national and international levels

> Although it is easy to talk of the need to protect human rights and to impose moral obligations on states to protect them, both national and international law will need to provide some mechanism whereby such rights can be recognised, protected and enforced; otherwise talk of rights becomes meaningless.

This section of the text will examine the methods by which human rights and civil liberties can be recognised and protected in both domestic and international law (including how human rights are protected in Europe). It will also examine the manner in which both systems can both complement and conflict with each other.

Protecting human rights and civil liberties in domestic law

Every legal system will need to decide how human rights and civil liberties will be protected, and what status to give them in relation to other rights and interests.[21] Central to this issue

---

[20] Hohfeld, *Fundamental Legal Concepts as Applied in Judicial Reasoning* (Yale University Press 1920).
[21] See Gearty, *Civil Liberties* (OUP 2007).

will be the role of the courts, and whether they will have a power to question or set aside the acts and decisions of the other organs of government.[22] It will also involve the question of whether international human rights treaties and norms will form part of domestic law and what will be the position when national and international laws come into conflict.

One method might be to identify the rights and liberties in the constitution of the state, thereby giving those rights and liberties some special constitutional standing. Thus, the protection of these fundamental rights can be stated in the constitution to be one, or the main, aim of the state. This declaration may be merely aspirational in that the constitution does not provide any mechanism for the *legal* enforcement of these rights or liberties, but more often than not the constitution will provide some way of ensuring that these claims are given some higher or entrenched legal status. This position is then usually, but not always, supported by giving the ultimate power of interpretation and enforcement to the courts, thus restricting the power of the lawmakers and the executive to interfere with these rights. The best-known example of this 'constitutional' method of protection is the constitution of the United States, under which the courts have the ultimate power to interpret both the Constitution and the Bill of Rights and are allowed to declare legislative acts unconstitutional.[23]

Another method, and the one adopted by the United Kingdom before the passing and coming into force of the Human Rights Act 1998, is to resolve human rights disputes within the regular law. In theory at least, human rights law will have no higher or different status than any other law; the law will be passed and declared in the same manner, there will be no constitutional court, and there will be no formal system of entrenching these rights and protecting them from the regular law or the institutions of the state. This approach, referred to as the 'common law' method when applied to the system adopted by the United Kingdom, is contrasted with the 'constitutional' method employed by the vast majority of other states. It should be noted, however, that although fundamental rights might not be contained in a formal document, and given a formal special status within the legal and constitutional order, that does not mean that such rights are not regarded as fundamental and given an enhanced protection by both lawmakers and the judiciary.

As we shall see, even in the absence of a formal constitutional document, fundamental rights can be recognised and protected by the courts by a process of implied constitutional interpretation that protects such rights from arbitrary and unreasonable interference. Equally, a formal system of rights protection depends heavily on the content of the bill of rights document, the number of restrictions permitted by it and the attitude of the judiciary in interpreting that document. Ultimately, therefore, the effectiveness of a system of rights protection should not be judged by the formal method adopted within that state, but by determining whether these rights, in law and practice, are given adequate protection, and whether that system results in unjustifiable restrictions on those rights.

Whatever formal system is adopted, state law will need to address two fundamental questions. First, who is to be the final arbiter on whether these rights are to be afforded protection against legislative or other interference? In other words, will the constitution give the courts the power to declare legislative and administrative acts as inconsistent with fundamental

---

[22] For a discussion on the variety of domestic methods of protection, including under the Human Rights Act 1998, see Black-Branch, Parliamentary Supremacy or Political Expediency?: The Constitutional Position of the Human Rights Act under British Law [2002] Stat LR 59. See also, Hiebert, Paliamentary Bills of Rights: An Alternative Model? (2006) MLR 7.

[23] *Marbury* v *Madison* 1 Cranch 137 (1803) and *Roe* v *Wade* 93 S Ct 705 (1973).

rights, or will it give a residual power to the legislature and/or the executive to compromise these rights in the name of social justice or other interests? Secondly, what restrictions will the constitution allow on these rights and liberties, and what procedural or substantive limits will it place on lawmakers or law enforcers if they are allowed to compromise these rights?[24]

In relation to the first question, even within a formal system the constitutional and legal order may allocate judicial power in a number of different ways. Thus, as with the American constitution, the constitution might give the courts the power to enforce the constitution, including its bill of rights, against incompatible legislative and executive acts. Accordingly, the legislative and the executive are disentitled from passing or executing inconsistent provisions. A similar method – but one which allows the legislature the ultimate power to interfere with fundamental rights – is the one adopted by the Canadian constitution. Under this system the legislature is allowed to pass legislation with a 'notwithstanding' clause, so that legislation is regarded as legitimate notwithstanding the fact that it is inconsistent with the fundamental rights contained in the Canadian Charter on Fundamental Rights.[25] This reflects the Westminster parliamentary model and the desire to maintain legal and political sovereignty.[26] Another system, and one that is adopted by New Zealand, and by the Human Rights Act 1998, is for parliament to give the judiciary the power to interpret legislation, wherever possible, in conformity with fundamental rights, but leaving the legislature the power to pass clearly inconsistent legislation that overrides such rights.[27] Thus, although the judiciary is allowed to presume that parliament intends the government to uphold human rights and to abide by human rights standards, it will not be given the mandate to strike down clear legislative provisions which parliament clearly intends to apply irrespective of the potential violation of human rights. In this way, parliamentary sovereignty is retained and the democratically elected government remains the ultimate arbiter on questions relating to the protection of human rights and civil liberties. On the other hand, in the absence of such clear legislative intent the courts are given a wide power to uphold human rights and to protect them from encroachment where such violations would offend constitutional or international standards.

With regard to the second question, all legal systems will need to provide for circumstances where it is permissible to violate, or compromise, fundamental rights. This can be done, as is evident in the European Convention, by either stating express exceptions to the scope of a particular right or by allowing interferences provided they possess the characteristics of legitimacy and reasonableness.[28] In addition, even where fundamental rights appear to be guaranteed absolutely, they can in practice be limited by judicial interpretation. For example, although the first amendment to the American Constitution provides that no law shall be passed which abridges freedom of speech, the American courts have limited the enjoyment of freedom of expression by deciding either that certain speech is not within the ambit of the article (or that certain speech is *less* worthy of protection than others), or by

---

[24] For an excellent overview of the various methods employed by domestic jurisdictions in the protection of human rights, see Alston (ed.), *Promoting Human Rights Through Bills of Rights* (OUP 1999).

[25] See Beatty, The Canadian Charter of Rights: Lessons and Laments (1997) 60 MLR 481; Ison, A Constitutional Bill of Rights – The Canadian Experience (1997) 60 MLR 499.

[26] See G. Anderson (ed.), *Rights and Democracy: Essays in UK Canadian Constitutionalism* (Blackstone Press 1999).

[27] See the New Zealand Bill of Rights Act 1990. See Taggart, Tugging on Superman's Cape [1998] PL 266.

[28] Thus, Article 2 of the European Convention protects the right to life but provides for exceptions, for example, in cases of the defence of others from unlawful violence. In addition, the Convention makes certain rights, for example freedom of expression, conditional, allowing interference with that right provided it is prescribed by law and necessary in a democratic society for the purpose of achieving a legitimate aim.

developing a number of instances and conditions where it is permissible to restrict this fundamental right.[29]

In a system where fundamental liberty is residual and conditional on non-interference by the law, there appears to be no limit to the restrictions that could be placed on the enjoyment of those rights. For example, although one might say that everyone has the residual freedom to demonstrate subject to relevant laws prohibiting such demonstrations, unless there are means to ensure that those laws are necessary and proportionate, then the very essence of the right to demonstrate will be cancelled out by such laws. However, provided democracy and the rule of law thrive, both lawmakers and the judiciary will impose limits on the power of the law to interfere with these basic rights. As with the method of enforcement, whether the more formal and entrenched system is more effective than one that relies on the goodwill of legislators, public opinion and judges cannot be answered simply by looking at the type of system adopted within that jurisdiction. Rather, one must examine the practice of that system and see whether it complies with recognised standards of legality and fairness, which are enshrined in documents such as the European Convention, and which insists that restrictions are clear and accessible, serve a legitimate aim and are necessary and proportionate.

Questions

What constitutional and legal difficulties are involved in the protection of human rights and civil liberties in domestic law?

Which system of rights protection do you feel is most desirable in resolving those difficulties?

The protection of human rights in international law

In addition to the domestic law's attempts to uphold the fundamental rights of its citizens, the protection of such rights has benefited from the movement to protect these rights in international law.[30] Such a movement gives human rights a global significance and provides a mechanism by which to use universally agreed standards to judge the legitimacy of each state's record of protecting such rights.[31]

The dilemma of protecting human rights in international law

The protection of human rights at the international level gives rise to a number of diplomatic, legal and moral dilemmas. As international law was traditionally concerned with the relationship between member states, the protection of individual human rights raises issues regarding the proper role of international law and its institutions. Most significantly, any treaty that prescribes the manner in which a signatory state treats its individual citizens impinges on that state's right to self-determination, a fundamental principle in international law. Thus, whatever enforcement mechanism a particular treaty adopts, a balance will need to be maintained between the right of each state to its individual autonomy and the protection of individual fundamental human rights.

---

[29] See Abraham, *Freedom and the Court* (OUP 1977); Tushnet, Living with a Bill of Rights, in Tompkins and Gearty, *Understanding Human Rights* (OUP 1995).

[30] For a comprehensive coverage of this topic, see Steiner and Alston, *International Human Rights in Context: Law, Politics, Morals* (OUP 2007, 3rd edn). See also Rehman, *International Human Rights Law* (Longman 2010, 2nd edn), and Moeckkli et al., *International Human Rights Law* (OUP 2010).

[31] See Lord Hoffmann, The Universality of Human Rights [2009] 125 LQR 416, where it is argued that such rights are universal in the abstract, but national in their application.

Even if a state recognises the legitimacy of international intervention and of universal rights, there will be difficulty in achieving a consensus among member states on what rights should be included in such treaties and to what extent they should be protected.[32] Although such rights are referred to as universal, inalienable and fundamental, there will often be a basic disagreement on the validity and importance of such claims, particularly from states which do not regard the protection of individual freedom and human rights as the primary objective of their society. For many societies, freedom of speech and religion or the right to equality on grounds of sex and race are regarded as inferior, or contrary, to the fundamental aims of that society. Even if there is a basic agreement in this respect that, for example, the rights to life and freedom from torture are fundamental, there will be deep disagreements as to whether such rights preclude, for example, the death penalty, corporal punishment or different treatment of women or racial or other groups.

These differences, articulated in the phrase 'cultural relativism',[33] can be accommodated in a number of ways. First, a particular state may be allowed to make a reservation when ratifying a treaty, reserving its right to carry out a practice that might otherwise be regarded as incompatible with its treaty obligations. Secondly, human rights treaties will make provision for the state to derogate from its obligations in time of war or other emergency. Thus, Article 15 of the European Convention on Human Rights, and Article 4 of the International Covenant on Civil and Political Rights, provide for the right of derogation in times of war or other public emergency. This compromise will be particularly appropriate in the case of states that do not enjoy the political, social and constitutional stability necessary to provide for the protection of fundamental rights. Thirdly, the international machinery for enforcing these fundamental rights might allow some latitude to each individual state in how they achieve the basic aims of the treaty. In relation to treaties that are enforced judicially, such as the European Convention on Human Rights, this will involve the adjudicating body, the European Court of Human Rights, allowing each member state a certain margin of appreciation, or margin of error, in how they achieve a proper balance between the protection of human rights and the power to achieve other social or individual interests.

Enforcing international human rights standards

Consequently, it is unsurprising that the methods of enforcement fall short of the full judicial method often adopted at national level. If such a method is available under the relevant treaty, as with the European Convention and the International Covenant on Civil and Political Rights, then member states will wish to either make reservations or opt out of these optional enforcement machineries. Alternatively, they will insist that the enforcement body afford to them a wide margin of discretion in attaining the universal standards. Accordingly, a more cautious and less confrontational method of enforcement is often available. For example, the United Nations Charter lacks any machinery for the enforcement of the rights it espouses and relies purely on declaring the importance of such rights and their protection by each and every member state. This method can also be bolstered by a body responsible

[32] See Feldman, Human Rights Treaties, Nation States and Conflicting Moralities (1995) 1 Contemporary Issues in Law 61. See also Steiner and Alston, *International Human Rights in Context: Law, Politics, Morals* (OUP 2007, 3rd edn), chapters 5 and 6.

[33] For discussions on this concept, see Tierney, Beyond Cultural Relativism: Re-thinking the Human Rights Debate [2004] Juridical Review 75; Walker and Poe, Does Cultural Identity Affect Countries' Respect for Human Rights? (2002) Human Rights Quarterly 237.

for the promotion of particular fundamental rights, such as the UN Economic and Social Council. In this way human rights might be enhanced by greater awareness and international support. Another, non-judicial method is the one adopted by such treaties as the International Covenants on Civil and Political and Economic, Social and Cultural Rights, involving a system of state reporting, whereby each member state makes periodic reports to an international institution, giving details of the measures adopted so as to secure fundamental rights within their jurisdiction and the success of such measures. This will give the international body the opportunity of inspecting those measures and, in certain cases, of commenting critically. A similar, but slightly more proactive, method of international enforcement is the one adopted under the European Convention on the Prevention of Torture 1987.[34] Under this Convention, the European Committee for the Prevention of Torture is charged, *inter alia*, with the duty to make visits to member states, visiting various places where individuals are detained, for the purpose of assessing whether the conditions of such detention constitute torture or inhuman or degrading treatment or punishment.[35]

All these non-judicial and non-binding methods are very different from the methods employed by domestic law and by bodies such as the European Court of Human Rights, and might be regarded as ineffective. The various methods should, however, be seen as fulfilling the aims of international recognition, respect, promotion and protection of fundamental rights and should not be dismissed solely on the grounds that they do not involve judicial enforcement of such rights.

International human rights treaties: the United Nations[36]

The United Nations Charter 1945

Although not strictly an international treaty for the protection of human rights, the preamble to the Charter states that the peoples of the United Nations reaffirm faith in fundamental human rights, in the dignity and worth of the human person, and in the equal rights of men and women. Further, Article 1 of the Charter states that one of the purposes of the United Nations is to promote and encourage respect for human rights and for fundamental freedoms for all without distinction as to race, sex, language or religion.[37] Although the Charter and its declarations are no more than aspirational, those ideals nevertheless reflect the principles of liberty and individual freedom, which form the basis of the rights theory that we have discussed earlier in this chapter.

The Universal Declaration of Human Rights 1948

Article 68 of the United Nations Charter provides that the Economic and Social Council of the United Nations shall set up commissions in economic and social fields and for the promotion of human rights. Accordingly, the Council established the Commission on Human Rights, who in turn drafted the Universal Declaration of Human Rights, which was

---

[34] The full title is the European Convention for the Prevention of Torture and Inhuman or Degrading Treatment or Punishment.

[35] For a comprehensive account of Convention and the work of the European Committee, see Morgan and Evans, *Protecting Prisoners: The Standards of the European Committee for the Prevention of Torture in Context* (OUP 1999).

[36] See Alston and Megret, *The United Nations and Human Rights: A Critical Appraisal* (OUP 2010).

[37] Under Article 62 of the Charter the United Nations Economic and Social Council can make recommendations for the purpose of promoting respect for, and observance of, human rights and fundamental freedoms for all.

adopted by the UN General Assembly in 1948.[38] This Declaration, which is not binding on member states in international law, contains a commitment to the protection of human rights and lists a full range of both civil and political and economic and social rights.[39]

Although the Declaration was only intended to be aspirational, the United Nations did establish a system whereby the UN Commission of Human Rights could consider communications that appeared to reveal a consistent pattern of gross violations of human rights and fundamental freedoms.[40] This represented a radical departure from the basic principles of international law, which stated that such law was concerned with the relationships between states and should not interfere in the domestic affairs of each state. It also led the way to the passing of two separate covenants on human rights – the International Covenant on Civil and Political Rights and the International Covenant on Economic, Social and Cultural Rights (both examined below) – with their own mechanism for enforcement. In addition, the UN Commission, and its Sub-commission, performed a variety of tasks with regard to the promotion and encouragement of human rights protection, including undertaking investigations into the position of human rights in particular countries. In 2006 the Commission was replaced by the Human Rights Council by UN Resolution 60/251. The Council will take over the functions of the Commission and it is proposed that it will have the power to undertake a universal periodic review of the fulfilment of each state's obligations and commitments.[41]

The International Covenant on Civil and Political Rights 1966

This Covenant was adopted by the UN General Assembly in 1966 and came into force in 1976.[42] It contains a list of civil and political rights similar to that of the European Convention, although there are a number of differences with regard to the ambit of such rights.[43] The Covenant also contains a number of exceptions and restrictions similar to those contained in the European Convention. For example, a power of derogation is contained in Article 4 of the Covenant, and rights such as freedom of expression, contained in Article 19, are subject to restrictions which are provided by law and necessary for the respect of the rights or reputations of others, or for the protection of national security, of public order, or of public health or morals.[44]

---

[38] See Klug, The Universal Declaration of Human Rights: 60 Years On [2009] PL 205.

[39] The Declaration also refers to a number of 'third generation' rights, such as the right to freely participate in the life of the community (Article 27), and the right to a social and international order in which the rights laid down in the Declaration can be realised (Article 29).

[40] ECOSOC Resolution 1503.

[41] The status of the Council will be reviewed in 2011 and it may at that time become a full organ of the UN.

[42] For general reading, see Joseph, Schultz and Castan, *The International Covenant on Civil and Political Rights: Cases, Materials and Commentary* (OUP 2004, 2nd edn); Alston and Steiner, *International Human Rights in Context: Law, Politics, Morals* (OUP 2007, 3rd edn), chapter 3; Rehman, *International Human Rights Law* (Longman 2010), chapter 5.

[43] For example, under Article 24 every child is guaranteed the right to protection of his or her status as a minor, and Article 10 contains specific protection for those deprived of their liberty, stating that such persons shall be treated with humanity and with respect for the inherent dignity of the human person. In addition, the equality clause under Article 26 is wider than that contained in Article 14 of the European Convention, in that it provides that all persons are equal before the law and entitled without any discrimination to the equal protection of the law.

[44] Note that the Covenant does not use the phrase 'democratic society', employed in various articles in the European Convention, when qualifying the enjoyment of its rights.

The Human Rights Committee

The Covenant is monitored by the Human Rights Committee, established under Article 28, which has three principal functions: to receive and study reports submitted by the state parties (Article 40); to receive communications to the effect that a state party is not fulfilling its obligations under the Covenant (Article 41); and to receive communications from individuals claiming to be a victim of a violation of his or her Covenant rights by a state party (Optional Protocol to the Covenant, Article 1). The state reporting system consists of self-regulation whereby each state reports to the Committee on how it has given effect to the rights recognised in the Covenant. The second process, of receiving communications from other state parties, is more dynamic and requires a declaration from the relevant state recognising the competence of the Committee to receive and consider such complaints. In such cases, however, the Committee has no power to make a binding judgment, but may use its powers to achieve a friendly settlement between the parties.

The power to receive individual communications under the Optional Protocol is similar to the enforcement mechanism employed under the European Convention on Human Rights. Communications can be received by an individual, either personally or through another individual where the victim is prevented from communicating directly and is claiming to be a victim. The Committee has the power to declare communications inadmissible, and must be satisfied that the complainant has exhausted all available domestic remedies and that the complaint is not being considered by any other international procedure. The defendant state party is provided with the opportunity to forward its views on the allegations, but if it finds against the state the Committee has no power to enforce the finding and must leave it to the state to take any remedial action.

The United Kingdom has decided not to ratify this optional protocol, and is thus bound only by the process of state reporting explained above. The initial reluctance to sign up to the Protocol might have been that the United Kingdom, as with any other state, did not want to commit itself to a binding judicial process in relation to human rights violations. However, its commitment to the enforcement mechanism of the European Convention appears to refute that reason, and a better explanation would appear to be that as the government is already a party to the European Convention's machinery there is little need to commit itself to the Covenant in a similar fashion. In addition the International Covenant's system is less predictable than that of the European Convention in the sense that its provisions are more general and its jurisprudence less well established.[45]

The International Covenant on Economic, Social and Cultural Rights 1966

This Covenant is concerned with the protection of what has been generally defined as 'second generation' rights.[46] In the preamble to the Covenant it is recognised that these rights derive from the inherent dignity of the human person and that the idea of free human beings enjoying freedom from fear and want can only be achieved if everyone enjoys his or her economic, social and cultural rights, as well as his or her civil and political rights.

---

[45] For an analysis of the compatibility of United Kingdom law with the Covenant, see Harris and Joseph, *The International Covenant on Civil and Political Rights and United Kingdom Law* (Clarendon 1995).

[46] For a full account of the Covenant and its operation, see Craven, *The International Covenant on Economic, Social and Cultural Rights* (Clarendon 1995); Baderin and McCorquodale (eds), *Economic, Social and Cultural Rights in Action* (OUP 2007). See also Steiner and Alston, *International Human Rights in Context, Law, Politics, Morals* (OUP 2007, 3rd edn), chapter 4; Rehman, *International Human Rights Law* (Longman 2010), chapter 6.

Thus, Article 1 states that all peoples have the right of self-determination and the right to pursue their economic, social and cultural development, and Article 3 that the state parties undertake to ensure the equal right of men and women to enjoy the rights laid down in the Covenant. These general statements and duties are then supplemented by more specific rights, such as the right to work, including the right to just and favourable conditions of work (Articles 6 and 7); the right to form trade unions (Article 8); the right to social security (Article 9); the right to an adequate standard of living, including adequate food, clothing and housing (Article 11); the right to enjoy physical and mental health (Article 12); the right to education (Article 13); and the right to take part in cultural life (Article 14).

These rights are phrased in a very general manner, imposing on each state the general duty to attempt to ensure the conditions whereby such rights might be realised. This reflects the nature of economic and social rights, which impose a positive obligation on the state to provide resources and which are, therefore, heavily dependent on the economic resources of each individual state. This is duly reflected in the enforcement mechanism in the Covenant, which is based on the principle of self-monitoring and regulation. Thus, under Article 16 of the Covenant, the state parties agree to submit reports on the measures that they have adopted and the progress made in achieving the observance of the rights recognised under the Covenant.[47] Despite the general lack of direct judicial enforcement, the commitment to such economic, social and cultural rights can inform domestic law and practice, and domestic and international charity work, in this area. In addition, some of these rights are related to the more enforceable civil and political rights contained in the International Covenant on Civil and Political Rights and the European Convention. For example, the lack of social security provision might constitute inhuman or degrading treatment, and the lack of education and access to a cultural life might impact on an individual's right to freedom of expression.

Questions

Why is there a need for human rights protection at the international level?

What difficulties are evident from attempting to protect human rights at this level?

What can international law realistically seek to achieve in this area?

Human rights and Europe

Human rights (civil and political and economic and social) are protected regionally in Europe via a number of organisations and treaties. This section of the text will concentrate on the treaties that are the product of the Council of Europe and the European Union. A third body, the Organisation for Security and Co-operation in Europe (OSCE), is also charged with protecting and monitoring human rights in Europe, but will not be examined in this text.[48]

The European Convention on Human Rights and Fundamental Freedoms 1950

The European Convention on Human Rights will be studied in detail in chapter 2 of this text, but for present purposes it is worth noting the central characteristics of the Convention with regard to the protection of human rights in international law. The European Convention

---

[47] These reports are submitted to the Secretary-General of the United Nations, who transmits copies to the Economic and Social Council for consideration.

[48] All three bodies' work are examined in Rehman, *International Human Rights Law* (Longman 2010), chapters 7 and 8.

on Human Rights and Fundamental Freedoms is a regional treaty, applicable to members of the Council of Europe. This feature of the Convention is significant in that the member states shared many common characteristics in terms of their constitutional and legal systems and their views on the identification and protection of human rights and fundamental freedoms. This feature is now not so distinct because of the extension of membership and ratification to and by many new members of the Council of Europe, including a number of eastern European countries. Accordingly, membership of the Council of Europe is no longer dictated entirely by western democracies, giving rise to potential conflict over the protection of human rights in Europe.

The most striking feature of the European Convention as an international treaty on human rights relates to the machinery for the enforcement of the rights and freedoms that are contained within the main text of the Convention. Although many states will be reluctant to commit themselves to a binding and legally enforceable obligation with respect to the protection of human rights, the European Convention establishes a judicial body – the European Court of Human Rights – which not only has the power to make judicial declarations on the Convention, which are then binding in international law on the relevant state party, but which also has the power to award remedies, including compensation, in the form of 'just satisfaction'. In addition, the Court has the power to receive applications from individuals claiming to be a victim of a violation at the hands of a member state.

One of the central aims of the Convention is to effect incorporation of the Convention and its principles into the domestic law of member states. Thus, Article 1 of the Convention provides that the High Contracting Parties undertake to secure to everyone within their jurisdiction the rights and freedoms set out in Section 1 of the Convention. Accordingly, Article 1 not only places a duty on each member state to ensure that the standards of the Convention are applied in domestic law, but also, albeit implicitly, calls for incorporation of the Convention into the domestic legal structure. With regard to the United Kingdom, the Human Rights Act 1998 all but incorporates European Convention rights into domestic law, and even before the Act the Convention had a very large impact on the development of human rights principles in domestic law.

The European Social Charter

The European Social Charter (ESC) is a product of the Council of Europe. Signed in 1961, it attempts to complement the European Convention on Human Rights by providing for the enjoyment of a variety of social rights by those within the jurisdiction of the member states.[49] Part One of the Charter imposes a flexible duty on the Contracting Parties to 'accept as the aim of their policy' to pursue all appropriate means to attain the conditions in which the rights laid down in Part One may be effectively realised. Part One then lists a number of rights, including the right to earn a living, the right to just conditions of work and to safe and healthy working conditions, the right to a fair remuneration, the right to freedom of association and the right to bargain collectively. There are also references to the rights of children and young persons and to maternity and welfare benefits. Part Two of the Charter then expands on these rights, stating that the Contracting States consider themselves bound by the obligations to ensure the observance of such rights.

The ECS operates by means of a reporting system whereby Contracting Parties submit reports to the Committee of Experts, a body appointed by the European Convention's

---

[49] See Harris, *The European Social Charter* (Virginia Press 1984). See also Betten and Grief, *EU Law and Human Rights* (Longman 1999), pages 42–52.

Committee of Ministers. A revised version of the Charter entered into force in 1999, establishing a system of adjudication to deal with collective complaints by employers' and trade union organisations with regard to alleged breaches of the Charter. However, although the United Kingdom has signed the Revised Charter, it has not ratified it and will not be bound by the collective complaints system even after ratification.

Human rights and the European Union

This textbook concentrates on the rights contained in the European Convention on Human Rights as enforced under the Convention machinery and domestically via the Human Rights Act 1998. However, this section provides a brief overview of the position of human rights within the European Union and how that recognition complements the position under the Convention and the 1998 Act.

A common confusion among law students, and others, relates to the distinction between the European Convention on Human Rights and European Union (EU) law. First, the European Convention on Human Rights is a product of the *Council of Europe*, a larger body than the EU (originally the European Community), whose main concern was the recognition and protection of fundamental human rights in European states. Secondly, the judicial body of the European Convention is the *European Court of Human Rights*, and not the *European Court of Justice*, which is the judicial arm of the EU. Thirdly, an essential feature of EU law is its primacy over domestic law. EU law is by the nature of treaty membership supreme and thus overrides domestic law,[50] whereas the European Convention on Human Rights is not necessarily supreme, Article 1 of the Convention merely imposing a duty on each member state to protect the rights identified in the Convention. The extent to which the Convention is binding is, as explained below, left to each member state. Fourthly, although the decisions of the European Court of Human Rights are binding on the member states in international law, imposing on that state a duty to pay compensation or to change its law, such decisions, unlike those of the European Court of Justice, do not automatically change domestic law or allow a person to rely on that decision in contradiction to the existing domestic law. Fifthly, and in respect of the United Kingdom, EU law became part of domestic law as a result of the European Communities Act 1972, which *incorporated* EU law (and its binding status) into English law, whereas the European Convention on Human Rights was *given effect* to by virtue of the Human Rights Act 1998.

Despite this, and even though European Community (Union) law is *primarily* concerned with economic rights and security, and not with the protection of those human rights that are contained in documents such as the European Convention, the European Union and its organs play a vital role, both directly and indirectly, in the protection of human rights in the domestic states.[51]

---

[50] See *Costa* v *ENEL* [1964] ECR 585. This includes the power of the domestic courts to disapply an Act of parliament that is inconsistent with EU law: *Factortame Ltd* v *Secretary of State for Transport (No 2)* [1991] 1 All ER 70.

[51] For a detailed account of human rights and the EU, see Alston (ed.), *The EU and Human Rights* (OUP 1999); Williams, *EU Human Rights Policies: A Study in Irony* (OUP 2004); Betten and MacDevitt (eds), *The Protection of Fundamental Rights in the European Union* (Kluwer International 2006). For a briefer account, see Betten and Grief, *EU Law and Human Rights* (Longman 1998). See also Craig and De Burca, *EU Law: Text, Cases and Materials* (OUP 2007, 4th edn), chapter 11; Arnull et al., *Wyatt and Dashwood's European Union Law* (Sweet & Maxwell 2006, 5th edn), chapter 8.

First, certain rights protected by the treaties of the European Union, such as freedom of movement and freedom from discrimination on the grounds of sex, belong to the class of human rights that we have identified above, and can be equated with such rights as liberty and security of the person, contained in Article 5 of the European Convention, and the prohibition of discrimination, contained in Article 14. As we shall see, these EU provisions will be interpreted and applied in conformity with certain principles of fundamental human rights, and often the case law of both the European Court of Justice and European Court of Human Rights can be used complementarily.[52] In addition, much EU law has inspired the protection of privacy and equality laws in domestic law. For example, domestic law relating to sex discrimination, in the form of the Sex Discrimination Act 1975 and the Equal Pay Act 1970, and the Data Protection Acts 1984 and 1998, were passed and have been amended so as to comply with relevant EC provisions.[53]

Secondly, although the European Convention has not been formally adopted as EU law,[54] the Convention has been allowed to inform EU law and indirect use is made of the Convention by the organs of the EU.[55] Thus, although the European Court of Justice has held that the Community did not have the power to become party to the European Convention on Human Rights,[56] Article (6)(2) (formerly F(2)) of the Treaty on the European Union states that the EU will respect fundamental rights as recognised by the European Convention. Although the ECJ initially refused to accept that it had jurisdiction to question national or European Community law that was inconsistent with fundamental human rights,[57] later cases accepted that human rights were enshrined in the general principles of Community law and that such law should be interpreted to avoid conflict with those principles.[58] For example, in *Internationale Handelsgesellschaft*[59] the ECJ observed that the protection of fundamental human rights must be ensured within the framework of the structure and objectives of the Community, and in *Nold* v *Commission of the European Communities*[60] it held that both it and the domestic courts should have regard to those fundamental rights when reviewing or interpreting domestic and EC laws.

Thirdly, both EU law and the European Convention on Human Rights have adopted principles such as certainty, legality, equality and proportionality in determining the legitimacy

---

[52] For example, in *P* v *S and Cornwall CC* [1996] ECR I-2143 the ECJ held that transsexuals were protected by the Equal Treatment Directive on the basis that the Directive protected the principle of equality, one of the fundamental principles of Community law.

[53] The sex discrimination provisions derived from such provisions as Article 119 of the Treaty of Rome (now Article 141 of the EC treaty). The data protection laws derive from the European Convention for the Protection of Individuals with regard to the Automatic Protection of Data, 17 September 1980.

[54] The draft reform Treaty expresses the unanimous intention of the European Union member states to proceed to the accession of European Convention rights. At the time of writing the European Union member states have expressed a unanimous intention to proceed to accession to the Convention (Lisbon Agreement). In July 2010 discussions took place between the Secretary General of the Council of Europe and the Vice President of the European Commission on the EU's accession to the European Convention.

[55] See Jacobs, Human Rights in the European Union: The Role of the Court of Justice (2001) 26 ELR 331.

[56] Opinion 2/94 [1996] ECR 1-1759.

[57] *Stork* v *High Authority* [1959] ECR 17 and *Geitling* v *High Authority* [1960] ECR 423.

[58] *Stauder* v *City of Ulm* [1969] ECR 2237. For a more recent example, see *Carpenter* v *Secretary of State for the Home Department*, Case C-60/00, [2002] CMCR 64, where the European Court of Justice held that the deportation of an immigration overstayer was in breach of both Article 49 EC and Article 8 of the European Convention on Human Rights.

[59] [1970] ECR 1125.

[60] [1974] ECR 491.

and reasonableness of measures that interfere with fundamental rights. These principles have been used by the ECJ in enforcing EU law, and have been used by the domestic courts to increase their powers of judicial review in areas such as natural justice and the doctrine of legitimate expectations.[61] For example, the ECJ has used the doctrine of proportionality to measure the legitimacy of acts and decisions of domestic authorities and EU institutions, including those that interfere with fundamental human rights.[62] Thus, in *Fromancais SA v FORMA*[63] it was held that the Court should ask whether the disputed measure was the least restrictive which could be adopted in the circumstances and whether the means adopted to achieve the aim correspond to the importance of the aim.

Although European Union law and the European Convention operate according to different rules of direct effect and enforceability, the two systems are often connected and in many cases an individual will bring an action making claims under both treaties.[64] In such a case the domestic courts will need to adjudicate on domestic law and practice with regard to both European Convention and EC principles. For example, in *R v Chief Constable of Sussex, ex parte International Trader's Ferry*,[65] the House of Lords had to decide the legality of the Chief Constable's decision to limit the number of police at a protest at the applicant's premises. In doing so their Lordships not only had to judge the reasonableness of the decision in line with traditional principles of judicial review, but also had to consider the impact the decision had on the fundamental right of peaceful assembly and the right of movement of goods under Article 34 of the EC Treaty.[66]

The case of *Gough, Miller and Lilly v DPP*,[67] concerning the lawfulness of banning orders placed on football spectators provides another example. A number of people had received banning orders under s.14A of the Football Spectators Act 1989 after being convicted of violent offences at football grounds. The orders prohibited the claimants from attending football matches for a period of six years and also prevented them from travelling to football matches abroad for a period of two years. It was argued that the penalties derogated from the rights of freedom of movement and freedom to leave their home country as conferred by Articles 1 and 2 of Council Directive 73/148/EEC and that they infringed Articles 6 and 8 of the European Convention on Human Rights. The Court of Appeal held that the EC Directive did not provide an absolute right to leave one's country and thus allowed a public policy exception. The orders were only imposed where there were strong grounds for concluding that the individual had a propensity for taking part in football hooliganism, and it was proportionate that those who had shown such a propensity should be subjected to a scheme that restricted their ability to indulge in such behaviour. Dealing with the claims under the European

---

[61] See *R v North and East Devon Health Authority, ex parte Coughlan* [2000] 2 WLR 622.

[62] For a useful account of the ECJ's use of the doctrine of proportionality, see Craig and De Burca, *EU Law: Text, Cases and Materials* (OUP 2007, 2nd edn), chapter 15. See also Fordham and de la Mere, Identifying the Principles of Proportionality, in Jowell and Cooper (eds), *Understanding Human Rights Principles* (Hart 2001).

[63] [1983] ECR 395.

[64] See, for example, *R (Countryside Alliance) v Attorney General and Another* [2007] 3 WLR 922, detailed in the case study at the beginning of this chapter.

[65] [1999] 2 AC 418.

[66] The House of Lords held that the decision was both reasonable and a proportionate measure on grounds of public policy under Article 36 of the EC Treaty. Contrast *Eugen Schmidberger Internationale Transporte Planzuge v Austria* [2003] 2 CMLR 34.

[67] [2002] 3 WLR 289. For an account of the case, see Deards, Human Rights for Football Hooligans? (2002) 27 ELRev 206.

Convention, the Court held that although the legislation applied a civil standard of proof, that standard was flexible and had to reflect the consequences that would follow if the case for such an order was made out. Further, the Court was satisfied that provided that a banning order was properly made, and that any interference with the individual's right to private life was justified on the grounds of the prevention of disorder, as permitted under Article 8(2), then such a ban was not in violation of the applicants' right to private life.

The Community Charter of Fundamental Social Rights for Workers

In addition to the European Social Charter, above, as part of EU law the Community Charter of Fundamental Social Rights for Workers constitutes a political declaration of intent by Heads of State of the European Community relating to the protection of various social and economic rights of workers. By virtue of the Treaty of European Union 1992, the Community and its member states became committed to a number of objectives, including the promotion of high employment, improved living and working conditions and equal pay for equal work. The United Kingdom accepted the Community Charter in 1997 and the Treaty of Amsterdam 1997 contains in its preamble an undertaking that member states confirm their attachment to fundamental rights as defined in both the European Social Charter and the Community Charter. Thus, by drawing economic and social rights into primary EU Law, there now exists a firmer basis for the protection of social and economic rights under EU law. For example, the 1997 treaty expands the jurisdiction of the ECJ to various matters relating to cooperation between member states in justice and home affairs, and the Council of Ministers may under Article 13 of the consolidated treaty take appropriate action to combat discrimination based on sex, racial or ethnic origin, religion or belief, age or sexual orientation.

The EU Charter of Fundamental Rights

The EU Charter of Fundamental Rights seeks to further the EU's recognition and protection of human rights.[68] The Charter, drawn up by a special body including representatives of the member states, of the national parliaments and of the European parliament, was published in May 2000 and contains a variety of both civil and political rights – including (in Article 1) the right to human dignity – and social and economic rights.[69] Although the United Kingdom's stance is that the Charter should remain totally aspirational, other member states believe that it should become part of EU law. If the latter approach is adopted, then the full, or at least fuller, range of human rights will become legally enforceable under the protection of supreme EU law.[70] This would represent a radical departure of rights protection in international law, which has always distinguished between civil and political, and economic and social rights with regard to enforcement mechanisms.[71]

---

[68] See Jacobs, Human Rights in the European Union: the Role of the European Court of Justice (2001) 26 ELRev 331.

[69] For an account of the Charter and its formation, see De Burca, The Drafting of the European Union Charter of Fundamental Rights [2001] 26(2) ELR 126; Fredman, A New EU Charter of Fundamental Rights [2000] PL 170. See now Peers and Ward, The EU Charter of Fundamental Rights: Politics, Law and Policy (Hart 2004); Arnull et al., Wyatt and Dashwood's European Union Law (Sweet & Maxwell 2006, 4th edn), chapter 9; Denman, The Charter of Fundamental Rights [2010] EHRLR 349.

[70] There already exists the European Social Charter, a Treaty of the Council of Europe, and the Community Charter of Fundamental Social Rights for Workers, which recognise a number of social, economic and employment rights. For an account of those treaties, see Betten and Grief, EU Law and Human Rights (Longman 1999).

[71] See Ashiagbor, Economic and Social Rights in the European Charter of Fundamental Rights [2004] EHRLR 62.

Questions

How are human rights protected under both EU law and the European Convention on Human Rights?

What advantages might there be to the United Kingdom in having obligations under the European system as well as in international law generally?

Other international and regional treaties

In addition to the UN and European treaties outlined above, there is a plethora of other international and regional treaties concerned with the recognition and protection of human rights and fundamental freedoms. Many of these treaties attempt to address a particular issue of human rights, such as the protection of refugees, women, children or prisoners.[72] Thus, in addition to the general UN Conventions, there exist UN treaties such as the Convention on the Elimination of All Forms of Discrimination 1966, which imposes an obligation on all states to make it an offence to disseminate ideas based on racial superiority or hatred; the Convention on the Elimination of All Forms of Discrimination Against Women 1967, supplementing anti-discrimination provisions contained in more general international treaties and monitored by the Committee on the Elimination of Discrimination Against Women; and the Convention Against Torture and other Cruel, Inhuman or Degrading Treatment or Punishment (1984), monitored by the Committee Against Torture.

The dilemma of protecting human rights and civil liberties

'The Human Rights Act has introduced a culture that has inhibited law enforcement . . .'

David Cameron, Conservative Party Leader, in a speech to the Centre for Policy Studies, June 2006

This section of the chapter examines the various moral and legal difficulties inherent in the recognition and protection of human rights and civil liberties in practice: in particular, of giving such rights and liberties an elevated status in domestic and international law when such rights conflict with other rights and interests. Although this textbook is not exclusively about the European Convention and the Human Rights Act 1998, the introduction of the 1998 Act has brought about many decisions which highlight the complex nature of human rights and civil liberties issues. The following passages will therefore consider how both the Convention and the Act and the case law resulting from them have tackled contentious areas, for the purpose of illustrating and, to an extent, resolving many dilemmas which are involved in human rights disputes and which give rise to so much concern.

The Human Rights Act 1998 was passed for the primary purpose of bringing the European Convention of Human Rights, and its case law, into domestic law.[73] Although one of the aims

---

[72] See Wallace and Dale-Risk, *International Human Rights: Text and Materials* (Sweet & Maxwell 2001, 2nd edn) for a comprehensive list of such treaties.

[73] See Straw and Boateng, *Bringing Rights Home: Labour's Plans to Incorporate the ECHR into UK Law: A Consultation Paper*, 1997. The background to the introduction of the Human Rights Bill, and the passing of the Act, will be examined in detail in chapter 3.

of the Act was to enhance human rights protection in domestic law, the European Convention, and most notably the cases that had been decided by the European Court of Human Rights against the United Kingdom government, became the main focus of attention. The traditional method of protecting rights and liberties in the United Kingdom was to be enhanced and, to an extent, replaced, by a system that has been responsible for highlighting a variety of laws, administrative practices and judicial decisions that were held to be incompatible with the Convention and its principles. The future of the protection of rights in domestic law is to be, and has been, fundamentally informed by the cases that have been brought before the Convention machinery, together with those decided in the post-Human Rights Act era.

Since the first decision of the European Court of Human Rights relating to an individual application was decided,[74] the United Kingdom has regularly been found to be in violation of the European Convention. The decisions have covered a variety of areas, including prisoners' rights, freedom of expression, the right to peaceful assembly, private and family life, the right to a fair trial, arrest and detention, deportation and extradition, corporal punishment and the right to life.[75] Almost all of the cases have been controversial in the sense of arousing intense political, constitutional and legal debate regarding the importance of human rights and civil liberties and the need for the state to limit such rights and liberties for some national or individual good.[76] We will now examine some of the fundamental moral and legal dilemmas that the Convention and the Act have illustrated.

Absolute rights and the European Court of Human Rights

The first issue we shall examine is the controversy surrounding cases where the European Court has found states in contravention of what are referred to as 'absolute' rights: those rights that cannot be interfered with whatever the justification. The cases below involved the interpretation of Article 3 of the Convention, which states that no one shall be subject to torture or to inhuman or degrading treatment or punishment. Although the European Court has never found the United Kingdom government in violation of the right to be free from 'torture' under Article 3, the government has on a number of occasions been found guilty of inflicting inhuman or degrading treatment or punishment. In *Ireland* v *United Kingdom*[77] the European Court held that the application of various interrogation techniques applied to individuals suspected of terrorist offences amounted to inhuman and degrading treatment. In addition, the United Kingdom has violated Article 3 in relation to decisions to deport or extradite persons to states where they faced a real risk of being subjected to ill-treatment.[78] The government was also found to have violated Article 3 when a nine-year-old boy had been beaten by his stepfather, the Court finding that he had been subjected to inhuman and degrading treatment or punishment.[79]

---

[74] *Golder* v *United Kingdom* (1975) 1 EHRR 524.

[75] See Foster, The Protection of Human Rights in Domestic Law: Learning Lessons from the European Court of Human Rights [2002] 53 NILQ 232.

[76] These cases are detailed in both chapters 2 and 3 of this text, and throughout all chapters dealing with specific rights.

[77] *Ireland* v *United Kingdom* (1978) 2 EHRR 25.

[78] See, for example, *Soering* v *United Kingdom* (1989) 11 EHRR 439 and *Chahal* v *United Kingdom* (1997) 23 EHRR 413, examined in chapter 5 of this text.

[79] *A* v *United Kingdom* (1999) 27 EHRR 611. This case raises another issue of whether states should be liable for violations of human rights committed by private individuals as well as state actors and public authorities.

Article 3 is referred to as an 'absolute' right, allowing no possible justification for any violation. Article 3 thus poses a number of dilemmas, not least of a legal nature. How do the courts determine the criteria upon which they are to decide whether treatment or punishment falls within the terms used in the Article? The Court will attempt to employ internationally accepted standards of civilised behaviour, but in doing so it will need to decide whether particular treatments or punishments carried out in different jurisdictions are acceptable. The Court will have to decide whether to reflect the different cultures of each member state, or to strive for a common standard applicable to all states, thus outlawing a practice regarded as acceptable within a particular community. The Court will then face the difficulty of applying the relevant criteria to the facts of the case, involving difficult and often clinical decisions regarding the amount of suffering that the victim has been subjected to.

In the *Ireland* case, above, the Court held that the subjection of the victims to the so-called five techniques,[80] which included subjecting the detainees to noise and depriving them of sleep and food, constituted inhuman and degrading treatment, but not torture. Thus the Court had the *legal* difficulty of defining the particular terms and of applying them to that case, finding that the treatment did not constitute a deliberate and particularly cruel form of inhuman treatment. The Court also held that the treatment of the detainees could not be justified in any circumstances, even though the authorities were employing the techniques in an attempt to protect national security by combating terrorism and gathering intelligence information for that purpose. The Convention, therefore, outlaws such practices whatever their social utility.[81] Many people would find it hard to accept that a court can legitimately place restrictions on the powers of domestic authorities to deal with the suppression and detection of crime, particularly in the case of acts of terrorism where others' rights and social stability are threatened. Indeed it might be argued by many that the 'victims' in this case were not deserving of the Convention and the Court's protection, and had forgone their rights when they took part in their criminal activities. Notwithstanding the fact that the victims in this case were suspects, rather than convicted terrorists, the Convention offers everyone protection against such treatment. This aspect of the Convention's protection was highlighted in the House of Lords' decision in *A v Home Secretary (No 2)*[82] where it was held that the Convention, and other international treaties, outlawed the admissibility of torture evidence in any legal proceedings.

Further legal and moral problems are evident in extradition and deportation cases. The Court has established that one member state can be responsible for the violations, or likely violations, of the Convention rights of individuals committed by another state, for example where one state deports an individual who is then subjected to ill-treatment in the receiving state.[83] Such cases give rise to a number of difficulties, some of a legal or jurisdictional nature; for example, whether the Convention can engage the liability of a member state in cases where the deporting or extraditing state has not committed any direct violation of Article 3 itself and it is the receiving state which commits the actual violation. This inevitably gives rise

---

[80] The techniques are detailed in the judgment. For an analysis of the judgment and of rights protection, see Waldron, *The Law* (Routledge 1990), chapter 5.

[81] For a discussion of this dilemma, see Ginbar, *Why not Torture Terrorists?: Moral, Practical and Legal Aspects of the Ticking Bomb Justification for Torture* (OUP 2009).

[82] [2005] 3 WLR 1249. The case will be examined in chapter 5 of this text.

[83] *Soering v United Kingdom*, n 78 above. The UK government's efforts to modify this principle in the context of terrorism is considered in chapter 5 of this text.

to legal and diplomatic concerns, and the British judiciary has declared incompatible detention provisions passed by the British parliament to deal with such a situation.[84] A similar jurisdictional concern is evident when individual rights are violated by other private individuals. Thus in *A v United Kingdom*[85] the European Court held that the United Kingdom government were responsible for the actions of an abusive stepfather because domestic law failed to provide adequate protection and remedies to persons who were subjected to ill-treatment within Article 3. The Convention and the Court will, thus, need to determine the possible 'horizontal' effects of the state's obligations.

The balancing of rights and liberties with other interests: necessity and proportionality

The second issue we shall consider relates to the difficulty of balancing rights and liberties with conflicting interests or other rights. As we shall see throughout this text, some human rights conflict with other fundamental rights, and in such cases the legal system must provide an answer as to how those rights will be balanced. In doing so, the system is not denigrating the value of the rights in question, but simply offering a method by which those rights can be most effectively reconciled with other rights and interests. In other cases a human right might be compromised by a claim that is not regarded as fundamental. To allow the fundamental right to be compromised in such a situation *does* at least threaten the sanctity of that right and systems must be in place to make sure that the value of those rights are not lost for unnecessary or unsubstantiated reasons.[86]

This involves placing restrictions on the validity of any provision or act that interferes with fundamental rights. One method is to elevate the fundamental right, by perhaps including it in a bill of rights, thereby giving it a superior status over other claims. By doing this, any interference with such a right is regarded as *prima facie* unlawful, and although this will not prohibit *any* interference, those who seek to restrict the fundamental right will need to justify that breach from a weak position. Initially, any interference will need to have a foundation in law. In setting these limits treaties such as the European Convention try to ensure that interference with fundamental rights is the exception rather than the norm, protecting such rights from arbitrary, unnecessary and convenient compromise.[87]

Thus, some rights are regarded as 'conditional' and can be interfered with in particular circumstances. For example, freedom of expression and the right to private life are expressly stated in the European Convention to be subject to restrictions, provided those restrictions are in accordance with the domestic law and are deemed necessary for the purpose of achieving some legitimate purpose.[88] In these cases the domestic authorities, and ultimately the European Court of Human Rights, will need to carry out a balancing exercise to determine whether the Convention right has been justifiably interfered with. This balancing exercise is beset with difficulties of a legal and moral nature, raising all manner of questions as to how

---

[84] See *A v Secretary of State for the Home Department* [2005] 2 AC 68, examined in a case study in chapters 6 and 14.

[85] See n 79 above.

[86] See Gearty, *Can Human Rights Survive?* (Cambridge University Press 2006).

[87] See Gearty, *Principles of Human Rights Adjudication* (OUP 2005). These principles and their application are discussed in detail in chapters 2 and 3 of this text.

[88] For an excellent explanation and analysis of these principles, see Gearty, *Principles of Human Rights Adjudication* (OUP 2005), chapters 4 and 7.

that exercise should be carried out, by whom, and what weight should be given to each conflicting interest.

In the case of the United Kingdom, a country which principally follows the rule of law and which respects the notion of human rights, most human rights disputes will fall into this category and the European Court has been asked on innumerable occasions to determine whether the United Kingdom has got the balance right. For example, the European Court has held that the domestic law of contempt of court was applied disproportionately to a newspaper which commented on the 'Thalidomide' disaster;[89] that the prohibition of homosexuals serving in the armed forces was a disproportionate and unnecessary restriction on the applicants' right to private life;[90] and that the arrest and detention of demonstrators who were handing out leaflets outside a conference centre was a disproportionate interference with their right to freedom of expression and liberty of the person.[91] In these cases the domestic law and practice has attempted to balance the applicants' human rights with other interests, but the European Court has nevertheless found that there has been a violation of the Convention.

It may indeed be questioned whether the European Court, or indeed any court, is an appropriate body to judge on the appropriateness and necessity of the state's laws and practices. The European Court must not only be satisfied that the domestic state has considered the problem of balancing rights with other rights and interests, and thus has made provision for such in their domestic law, but that such restrictions are both legitimate in their nature and necessary in a democratic society for the fulfilment of that aim, for example, public safety. This is a role which has, theoretically, been alien to the United Kingdom judiciary, and involves judges (as opposed to elected representatives) and, worse still, judges from other countries, making decisions on the facts of the case and in relation to the respective merits of the parties' case. In addition, these cases will pose a host of legal and moral difficulties for the judges who have to balance those rights and interests, and indeed for the drafters of the Convention:

- Will it be sufficient that the relevant legal restriction is accepted as law in that domestic state, or will that law have to conform to certain requirements that are consistent with the rule of law?
- Will the courts simply balance those rights or interests in a pragmatic, utilitarian manner, or is it permissible to give certain rights or conflicting interests a superior status, thus making it more difficult, or easier, to interfere with certain rights in particular circumstances?
- To what extent will the Court be equipped or prepared to interfere with particular decisions?[92]
- To what extent should the cultural and legal differences inherent in each state be relevant in determining those questions?

---

[89] *Sunday Times* v *United Kingdom* (1979) 2 EHRR 245. The litigation concerned the use of the thalidomide drug by pregnant women which caused their babies to be born with deformities.

[90] *Smith and Grady* v *United Kingdom* (2000) 29 EHRR 493; *Lustig-Prean and Beckett* v *United Kingdom* (2000) 29 EHRR 548.

[91] *Steel* v *United Kingdom* (1999) 28 EHRR 603.

[92] This was highlighted most dramatically in *A* v *Secretary of State for the Home Department* [2005] 2 AC 68, where the House of Lords had to decide not only whether there was an emergency threatening the life of a nation so as to justify the government's derogation from the Convention, but also whether particular measures were proportionate and non-discriminatory.

Turning to the examples given above, it is apparent that the rights claimed by the applicants are in conflict with other interests. In the *Sunday Times* case, the newspaper's right to comment on the possible negligence of the company in manufacturing a drug which caused deformities in children was in conflict with the laws of contempt, which attempt to safeguard the impartiality and independence of the judiciary – an aim which is expressly recognised as legitimate in Article 10 of the Convention. In fact, that right was also in conflict with a person's right to a fair trial, which is a right recognised by the Convention itself, not just as a reason to interfere with free speech, but as a fundamental right.

Nevertheless, the Court decided that the interference in question, albeit applied for legitimate reasons, was a disproportionate and unnecessary response. Cases such as *Steel* and *Smith and Grady* (above) are also controversial. The Convention has relegated these conflicting interests – public order and national security – to mere legitimate aims, which *might*, in exceptional cases, justify the interference with the fundamental rights laid out in the Convention articles themselves. This poses the question *why* the right to demonstrate, or the right to private sexual life, is more important or fundamental than the right to enter a building without being troubled by demonstrators, or to insist on measures which ensure that the country has an effective and confident fighting force. To reply that the right to private life and the right to assemble peacefully *are* guaranteed in the European Convention, while the other claims are not, and that fundamental rights cannot be compromised on grounds of intolerance or of convenience, will not satisfy those who believe that individual rights should not be enjoyed at the expense of other people's rights and that any right should be enjoyed in the context of majority public opinion.

Human rights and the protection of unpopular causes

The third issue we shall consider is the difficulty of protecting the rights of unpopular causes, which was touched upon earlier in this chapter. When one looks at the case law of the Convention, particularly the high-profile cases, what is revealed is that on a high number of occasions the Convention has been used by persons who can be categorised as minority groups who will not attract the sympathy and support of the public.[93] The European Court has found that young offenders who have murdered had their liberty, and their right to a fair trial, violated by ministerial discretion.[94] Similarly, prisoners who have received life sentences for manslaughter or serious sexual offences were found to have had their right to liberty violated, domestic law and practice being found to be incompatible with the Convention and its principles.[95] Individuals who pose a threat to national security and public safety, and who have allegedly committed offences in other countries, have had their deportations or extraditions challenged on the grounds that such decisions would subject them to the risk of torture or other inhuman or degrading treatment.[96] Those individuals have also had their rights to

---

[93] This discussion excludes traditional and recognised minority groups, such as children, racial and ethnic groups.

[94] *Hussain and Singh* v *United Kingdom* (1996) 22 EHRR 1; *V and T* v *United Kingdom* (1999) 30 EHRR 121.

[95] *Weeks* v *United Kingdom* (1987) 10 EHRR 293; *Thynne, Wilson and Gunnell* v *United Kingdom* (1990) 13 EHRR 666. This protection was also extended to mandatory life sentence prisoners in *Stafford* v *United Kingdom* (2002) 35 EHRR 32, and recognised by the House of Lords in *Anderson and Taylor* v *Secretary of State for the Home Department* [2002] 3 WLR 1800.

[96] See *Chahal* v *United Kingdom* and *Soering* v *United Kingdom*, n 78 above; *D* v *United Kingdom* (1997) 24 EHRR 423.

due process upheld by the British judiciary, despite strong arguments on behalf of the government that their rights should be compromised for the purpose of national security.[97] In addition, those who practise non-traditional sexual practices have had their rights recognised and respected under the Convention.[98]

Indeed in most of the cases that have been tested under the machinery of the Convention, there are relatively few cases that involve what many might refer to as 'popular' applicants. Accordingly, the European Convention is seen by some as a 'rogues' charter', there to protect those who have deliberately transgressed society's laws or morals, and who, in extreme cases, have forfeited their rights, fundamental or otherwise.[99] For many, therefore, human rights treaties should protect 'innocent' victims of unnecessary and arbitrary acts of government, and not provide those who have broken legal and moral standards and who now seek legal protection of their so-called basic human rights and civil liberties. In addition, even if the majority of society believes that everyone should retain their basic rights, in cases such as those above, many people are unwilling to relinquish the power to punish and deal with such individuals and to agree that some form of bill of rights, policed by a court of law, should set the limits of those powers.

The protection of human rights and civil liberties, therefore, gives rise to various dilemmas and difficulties. Although the protection of these rights and liberties is not unique in this respect, the dilemmas are perhaps more pronounced and controversial than in other legal areas, even those areas which impact on and are developed by social policy. The protection of human rights and civil liberties comes at enormous cost and involves what appear to be irreconcilable differences of opinion.

States of emergency, terrorism and the protection of human rights

The fourth issue relates to the difficulty of protecting individual human rights in times of war or other public emergency, such as the threat of terrorism. In such situations the need to secure public safety and national security can justify the compromising of individual liberty and other rights, and it might be argued that fundamental human rights have to come second to the protection of the state and its citizens. As the former Prime Minister, Tony Blair, famously stated in the aftermath of the London bombings in 2005, 'the rules of the game have changed'. Indeed, following an increase in terrorist attacks around the world the British government introduced new measures to provide greater powers to the police and other authorities with respect to the arrest and detention of those suspected of terrorism.[100] This dilemma will be examined in detail in chapter 14 of the text.

In such situations both international and domestic law have to decide where the balance lies between the protection of human rights and the protection of the state, and how that

---

[97] See *A v Secretary of State for the Home Department*, n 92, above; *Secretary of State for the Home Department v JJ* [2007] 3 WLR 642; *AF v Secretary of State for the Home Department* [2009] 3 WLR 74.

[98] *Dudgeon v United Kingdom* (1982) 4 EHRR 149; *Sutherland v United Kingdom*, *The Times*, 13 April 2001; *ADT v United Kingdom* (2001) 31 EHRR 33. All these cases declared restrictive legislation and its application contrary to the right of private sexual life; they are dealt with in detail in chapter 13.

[99] These arguments will be examined briefly in chapter 3 when considering recent suggestions for the reform of the Human Rights Act 1998.

[100] These measures, beginning with the Anti-Terrorism, Crime and Security Act 2001, are discussed in chapters 6, 7 and 14 of this text.

balance is achieved will, inevitably, fuel debate between politicians, judges and the public. International law allows states to 'derogate' from their normal treaty obligations in times of war or other emergencies which threaten the life of the nation,[101] and similar provisions exist in the domestic Human Rights Act.[102] Although this right to derogate will be subject to certain procedural limitations, the real dilemma is faced when the domestic lawmakers decide the extent to which the law must erode civil liberties, and the domestic judges decide the extent to which they are going to subject that decision to judicial control.

To allow the government and parliament an unqualified margin of discretion in such cases might appear to accord with democracy: fundamental issues of public safety and national security will be decided by elected and accountable politicians free from supervision by unelected judges. However, as the House of Lords have recently reminded us, the protection of individual liberty and other rights to due process are part and parcel of a civilised, democratic society, and an attack on such individual freedoms might be regarded as an affront to those collective democratic goals.[103] This does not resolve the substantive issue of whether the courts should ultimately decide the legality and reasonableness of government measures intended to combat terrorism, but at least it reminds us of the advantages of upholding human rights, from both the individual and the collective perspective. It should also defeat the argument that in times of terrorism we simply cannot afford to protect individual human rights, for such an argument ignores the fact that democratic societies cannot afford *not* to uphold them.[104]

Questions

What moral and legal dilemmas are posed by the protection of human rights and civil liberties? Can the law of human rights ever hope to rationally balance the enjoyment of human rights with other rights and social interests?

CASE STUDY

V(enables) and T(hompson) v *United Kingdom* (1999) 30 EHRR 121

This case has been chosen because it raised many of the dilemmas that have been identified in this chapter, in particular the availability of human rights to 'unpopular' individuals and the challenge of executive action. The case can also be used to examine how the courts can employ human rights principles to uphold fundamental values of liberty and fairness. The case study concentrates on the proceedings before the European Court of Human Rights, but an outline of the domestic law proceedings has been given to provide a complete picture of the legal and other issues raised by the case.

---

[101] See, for example, Article 15 of the European Convention on Human Rights, discussed in chapters 2 and 3, and Article 4 of the International Covenant on Civil and Political Rights 1966.

[102] Section 14, Human Rights Act 1998.

[103] See, in particular, Lord Hoffmann in *A* v *Home Secretary*, n 84.

[104] See Sottiaux, *Terrorism and the Limitation of Rights* (Hart 2008); Feldman, Human Rights, Terrorism and Risk: The Role of Politicians and Judges [2006] PL 364; Dickson, Law versus Terrorism: Can Law Win? [2005] EHRLR 11; Walker, Prisoners of 'War all the Time' [2005] EHRLR 50; McKeever, The Human Rights Act and Terrorism in the UK [2010] PL 110.

Once you have read the case study, and when you are studying this area in detail, you can access the full report of the case(s) to see whether the courts' views coincide with yours and to examine the courts' rationale in detail in the context of your study of that area (chapters 6 and 7).

The case arose out of the murder of two-year-old James Bulger by two young boys, Robert Venables and John Thompson, in 1993. The horrific nature of the kidnapping and the murder attracted an enormous amount of publicity and the boys' trial had taken place in an adult court accompanied by the expected level of media coverage.

The two boys were charged with and convicted of murder and were sentenced to be detained at Her Majesty's Pleasure by virtue of s.53 of the Children and Young Persons Act 1933. Acting under his powers under that legislation the Home Secretary set a tariff period (the minimum period that a prisoner should serve in prison before being considered for release) of 15 years for the boys. In setting that tariff period, the Home Secretary ignored the recommendations of both the trial judge and the Lord Chief Justice, who had proposed shorter tariff periods, and took into account public opinion, and in particular a petition which had been signed by readers of the *Sun* newspaper which had called on the Home Secretary to impose a substantial period on the boys.

The boys challenged the decision of the Home Secretary in domestic law, claiming that he had acted unlawfully in setting the tariff and had taken into account irrelevant factors in setting that period. In the House of Lords (*R* v *Secretary of State for the Home Department, ex parte Venables and Thompson* [1998] AC 407) it was held that the Home Secretary had acted unlawfully by expressly taking into account public opinion when setting the tariff period. The House of Lords also held that the Home Secretary had acted unlawfully by treating the offenders in the same way as adult offenders for the purpose of setting their tariff periods.

As a result of the decision of the European Court of Human Rights in *Hussain and Singh* v *United Kingdom* ((1996) 22 EHRR 1), those detained under the 1933 Act received the same rights as discretionary life sentence prisoners, and were released on the order of the Parole Board. Thus, s.28(4) of the Crime (Sentences) Act provided that the Parole Board had the discretion to release a young offender after the expiry of the tariff period and that such a recommendation had to be accepted by the Home Secretary. Meanwhile, Venables and Thompson brought proceedings under the European Convention on Human Rights, claiming that their trial for murder contravened their rights under Article 3 (freedom from inhuman or degrading treatment or punishment) and Article 6 (guaranteeing the right to a fair trial). In addition, they claimed that the Home Secretary's tariff period had violated their rights under Articles 3 and 6 of the Convention, and their right, under Article 5, to liberty and security of the person. The European Commission declared their applications admissible and their cases were referred to the European Court of Human Rights (*V and T* v *United Kingdom* (1999) 30 EHRR 121).

The trial proceedings

The Court first considered whether the attribution of criminal responsibility to the applicants amounted to a violation of Article 3 of the European Convention, which states that no one shall be subject to inhuman or degrading treatment or punishment. The Court held that as there was no common European standard among the member states on this issue, the domestic law, which attributed criminal responsibility to a person from the age of 10, was not so disproportionate as to amount to a violation of Article 3. The applicants also argued that their subjection to the trial proceedings constituted a violation of Article 3. In this respect the Court held that while the public nature of the proceedings exacerbated feelings of anguish, distress, guilt and fear, it was not satisfied that those features caused, to a sufficient degree, suffering beyond that which would have inevitably been engendered by any inquiry, whether carried out in public or private, or in the Crown Court or a youth court.

The applicants then argued that the subjection to an adult trial with such intense media coverage constituted a violation of their right to a fair trial and thus a violation of Article 6 of the Convention. The European Court held that it was essential that a child charged with an offence should be dealt with in a manner which took full account of his age, level of maturity and intellectual and emotional capacities, and that steps should be taken to ensure his ability to understand and participate in the proceedings. In the Court's opinion that might mean that in the case of a young child charged with a grave offence attracting high levels of media and public interest, the hearing should be held in private so as to reduce the child's feeling of intimidation.

In the present case, the Court noted that the trial had taken place over a period of three weeks, in public and in an adult court, and had generated high levels of press and public interest. Despite the measures taken to ensure that the applicants understood the surroundings and the proceedings and to shorten the hearing times, the court found that the formality and ritual of the Crown Court must at times have been incomprehensible and intimidating for a child of 11. In addition, the measure taken to raise the defendants' dock – to ensure that the boys could see what was going on – had the effect of exposing them further to the scrutiny of the press and thus increased their sense of discomfort. It was accepted that at the time of the trial the applicants were suffering from post-traumatic distress and had found it impossible to discuss the offence with their lawyers. In the Court's opinion, given the tense courtroom atmosphere and the public scrutiny it was unlikely that the applicants would have felt sufficiently uninhibited to consult freely with their lawyers and to be able to cooperate with them so as to provide the necessary information for the purpose of their defence. Accordingly the Court found that in relation to the trial proceedings there had been a violation of Article 6.

The sentences

The applicants argued that because of their ages the imposition of detention at Her Majesty's Pleasure amounted to a violation of Article 3 of the Convention. The Court held, however, that the punitive element in the tariff period did not by itself give rise to a violation and that in all the circumstances of the case, including the applicants' ages and the conditions of their detention, it could not be said that the length of their detention (at that stage six years) amounted to inhuman or degrading treatment or punishment. Further, the Court held that the European Convention did not prohibit states from subjecting a child or young person who had been convicted of a serious crime to an indeterminate sentence. Thus the Court found no breach of Article 3 in this respect.

The applicants then argued that the imposition of the tariff by the Home Secretary constituted a violation of Article 6 of the Convention. The Court held that Article 6 of the Convention covered all the proceedings, including the determination of the sentence. In deciding that the tariff-setting function of the Home Secretary amounted to the fixing of a sentence for those purposes, the Court drew a distinction between mandatory life sentence prisoners and those subject to the provisions of detention at Her Majesty's Pleasure. In the Court's opinion, the former sentences constituted punishment for life, whereas the latter were open-ended; thus in those cases once the tariff is complete the offender can only be detained if it appears necessary for the protection of the public. Accordingly, the fixing of the tariff for the applicants was a sentencing exercise and fell within Article 6. As the decision maker was the Home Secretary and not the court, and there had been no hearing or opportunity for the applicants to call psychiatric or other evidence, and the Home Secretary had retained the discretion to decide how much of the material that was before him was presented to the applicants, there had been a violation of Article 6. The Court held that this article guarantees a fair hearing by an independent and impartial tribunal and that meant a body which is independent of the executive. As the Home Secretary is clearly not independent of the executive, it followed that there had been a violation of Article 6.

Finally, the applicants had argued that their detention was contrary to Article 5 of the Convention, guaranteeing liberty and security of the person. The Court held that there had been no violation of Article 5(1) of the Convention as the applicants' detention was clearly 'a lawful detention of a person after conviction by a competent court' as required by Article 5(1)(a). The applicants' detention was clearly prescribed by law and was not arbitrary. However, the Court found that there had been a violation of Article 5(4) of the Convention, which guarantees that everyone deprived of his liberty 'shall be entitled to take proceedings by which the lawfulness of his detention shall be decided speedily by a court and his release ordered if his detention is not lawful'. Given that the Court had found the failure of the courts to set the applicants' tariffs constituted a violation of Article 6, the applicants' right under Article 5(4) had not been guaranteed by the trial court's sentence in these cases. Moreover as the domestic courts had quashed the Home Secretary's tariffs and no new tariffs had been set, the applicants had been denied the opportunity to access a tribunal for the periodic review of the continuing lawfulness of their detention. The European Court thus found a violation in this respect.

Using their powers under Article 41 of the European Convention to award 'just satisfaction', the European Court awarded legal costs of £18,000 to T and £32,000 to V. As a result of the European Court's judgment the government introduced new rules on the conduct of trials. In addition the boys' tariffs were reset by the Lord Chief Justice, LORD WOOLF CJ, in accordance with his Practice Statement (Juveniles: Murder Tariff) ([2000] 1 WLR 1655). Applying those principles the Lord Chief Justice recommended a period of seven years and eight months, which meant that the boys would not serve a sentence in an adult prison, provided the Parole Board ordered their release. That decision was challenged by James Bulger's father, but it was held that the family of a murder victim did not have legal standing to seek judicial review of any tariff set in respect of the murder (*R v Secretary of State for the Home Department and Another, ex parte Bulger* (*The Times*, 7 March 2001).

In December 2000 Thompson and Venables applied for an injunction to restrain the publication of any information relating to their identity, whereabouts and physical appearance and any other confidential information relating to time in detention and throughout the immediate and long-term future. The High Court granted the injunction, holding that in exceptional circumstances the Court had jurisdiction to extend its protection where not to do so would be likely to lead to serious physical injury, or the death of a person seeking that protection (*Venables and Thompson* v *MGN* [2001] 2 WLR 1038). Departing from the normal practice of granting injunctions, these particular injunctions applied to the whole world.

Questions

1 On what basis did the domestic courts find that the Home Secretary's powers had been misused? What principles of fairness and justice did the courts rely on and were the courts exceeding their constitutional powers in deciding that the Home Secretary had acted unlawfully?

2 In particular, why was it unlawful for the Home Secretary to set a tariff on the basis of public opinion and outrage?

3 In the European Court of Human Rights, what fundamental principles did the Court feel had been violated by the Home Secretary and during the domestic legal proceedings?

4 To what extent is it true to say that the European Court ignored the nature and extent of the applicants' crimes and the level of public opinion and outrage?

5 Why, in the context of the European Court decision and any relevant human rights principles, were the changes regarding the trial of young offenders and the setting of their tariffs necessary? Do they substitute executive discretion with excessive judicial discretion?

6 Why wasn't the father of James Bulger allowed to challenge the judicial tariff? What human rights problems would that cause?

7 As a postscript, one of the defendants, Jon Venables, was returned to prison in 2010 for breaking the terms of his license. The Justice Secretary refused to identify the nature of his conduct for fear of jeopardising any subsequent trial. What human rights were in conflict in that situation and was the Justice Secretary correct to make such a decision?

Further reading

There is a wealth of literature on human rights theory and the protection of human rights and civil liberties at both the domestic and international level. The footnotes to this chapter make constant reference to other sources, but students should also consult the references listed below.

Human rights theory

Feldman's *Civil Liberties and Human Rights in England and Wales* (OUP 2002, 2nd edn), chapter 1 provides an excellent introduction, along with comprehensive references to further reading in this area. Harvey, Talking About Human Rights [2004] EHRLR 500 and Harris, Human Rights and

Mythical Beasts [2004] 120 LQR 428, also provide enlightening reading on modern approaches to human rights theory. See also Gearty, *Civil Liberties* (OUP 2007) for an incisive and interesting overview of human rights theory and protection. With respect to the dilemmas of protecting human rights, students are also advised to consult Gearty, *Principles of Human Rights Adjudication* (OUP 2004) and Gearty, *Can Human Rights Survive?* (Cambridge University Press 2006).

Protection of human rights in domestic law

Alston, *Promoting Human Rights through Bills of Rights* (OUP 1999) provides an excellent overview of various domestic methods for protecting human rights. In addition, consult Huscroft and Rishworth, *Litigating Rights: Perspectives from Domestic and International Law* (Hart 2002) and Campbell, Goldsworthy and Stone, *Protecting Human Rights* (OUP 2003).

Further reading on the protection of human rights in the United Kingdom will be provided in chapter 3.

International human rights

For international human rights, students should consult Steiner and Alston, *International Human Rights in Context* (OUP 2007, 3rd edn), for a definitive coverage of the topic, and may consult Rehman, *International Human Rights Law* (Longman 2010, 2nd edn) or Smith, *A Textbook on International Human Rights* (OUP 2009, 4th edn) for good, more concise, accounts. For a detailed account of the ICCPR, see Joseph, Shultz and Castan, *Cases and Materials on the International Covenant on Civil and Political Rights* (OUP 2004, 2nd edn) and Conte, Davidson and Burchill, *Defining Civil and Political Rights* (Ashgate 2004).

European human rights

Alston (ed.), *The EU and Human Rights* (OUP 1999); Williams, *EU Human Rights Policies: A Study in Irony* (OUP 2004); Peers and Ward, *The EU Charter of Fundamental Rights; Politics, Law and Policy* (Hart 2004); Betten and MacDevitt *The Protection of Fundamental Human Rights in the Europe Union* (Kluwer International 2006).

Further reading on the European Convention on Human Rights will be provided in chapter 2.

Visit **www.mylawchamber.co.uk/fosterhumanrights** to access regular updates to major changes in the law, further case studies, weblinks, and suggested answers/approaches to questions in the book.

2 The European Convention on Human Rights

Introduction

In *Al-Saadoon and Mufdhi* v *United Kingdom* the European Court of Human Rights had to decide whether the handing over by the British forces to the Iraqi authorities of two suspected murderers would be in violation of the right to life, freedom from torture and the right to a fair trial. The domestic courts had already held that the European Convention was not applicable and that in any case the death penalty did not necessarily constitute inhuman treatment or was in violation of the right to life. The European Court held that the individuals were within the UK's jurisdiction and that the death penalty was in breach of Article 3 of the Convention, which prohibits torture and inhuman and degrading treatment and punishment.

The case is but one of thousands of judgments made by the European Court, but is a good example of the importance and significance of its case law. In this case the Court had to decide whether to follow the judgment of the domestic courts; it also had to decide whether the death penalty was contrary to the Convention and international law in general. There were also, clearly, diplomatic issues at stake as to whether states should be liable for rights violations committed by other states and whether such liability is compromised during times of war and by other principles of international law and relations.

This chapter will examine the workings of the European Court and how it interprets and applies the Convention and its principles and case law to disputes brought against Member States of the Convention.

This chapter attempts to explain the role and impact of the European Convention on Human Rights, both in international and domestic law. In addition to explaining its background and its method of enforcement, particular attention will be paid to the principles underlying the Convention and the jurisprudence and case law of the European Court of Human Rights.[1] Particular, although not exclusive, regard will be made to decisions of the Court and Commission involving claims made against the United Kingdom, although examples of cases against other member states will be used in order to provide a fuller picture of the Convention's case law.

---

[1] For a detailed account of those principles and their relationship with the Human Rights Act 1998 see Jowell and Cooper (eds), *Understanding Human Rights Principles* (Hart 2001).

Included in the chapter is an overall view of the Convention's substantive rights, contained in the articles and optional protocols of the Convention, most of which have been given effect to by the Human Rights Act 1998, examined in chapter 3 of this text. Many of these rights will be examined in detail in subsequent chapters, and thus this chapter provides an overall account of the rights, only providing details of the rights and relevant case law where that right is not covered elsewhere.

Thus, this chapter will cover:

- An examination of the background, purpose and scope of the European Convention on Human Rights.

- An explanation of the machinery for enforcement of the Convention, including the role and powers of the European Court of Human Rights and the application process.

- An analysis of the various human rights norms that have informed the European Court's role and which have been given effect to in domestic jurisprudence via the Human Rights Act 1998.

- An overall examination of the rights which are protected under the Convention, including a study of some of the most pertinent case law where necessary.

Background and scope of the Convention

Although the United Kingdom is a signatory to a variety of international human rights treaties, the European Convention on Human Rights[2] has had the greatest impact on the protection of human rights and civil liberties in domestic law.[3] Whenever domestic law and practice is measured against international human rights norms, this is almost invariably referring to the provisions and case law of the European Convention.[4] The European Convention has, therefore, become central to the understanding and study of human rights and civil liberties in domestic law for two central reasons. First, the massive amount of case law involving claims against the United Kingdom government[5] has highlighted the deficiencies of our method of protecting human rights and civil liberties in domestic law and has, in many cases, resulted in important changes to domestic legislation and judicial interpretation.[6] Secondly, the Convention has had a major impact on the legal system and the enforcement of human rights and civil liberties in domestic law. Even before the European Convention was given

---

[2] The full title of the Convention is the European Convention for the Protection of Human Rights and Fundamental Freedoms (1950). It will be referred to as the European Convention on Human Rights, or the European Convention, throughout the text.

[3] For a detailed account of the European Convention see Harris, O'Boyle and Warbrick, *Law of the European Convention on Human Rights* (OUP 2009, 2nd edn). See also Van Dijk and Van Hoof, *Theory and Practice of the European Convention on Human Rights* (Intersentia 2006, 4th edn); Jacobs and Ovey, *The European Convention on Human Rights* (OUP 2010, 5th edn); Janis, Kay and Bradley, *European Human Rights Law* (OUP 2007, 3rd edn). For a detailed analysis of the Convention case law, see Mowbray, *Cases and Materials on the European Convention on Human Rights* (OUP 2007, 2nd edn).

[4] Note, however, that in *A v Home Secretary (No 2)* [2005] 3 WLR 1249 the House of Lords held that the courts could and should have regard to other international human rights instruments in assessing the legality of domestic law and practice – in this case in deciding whether it was permissible to consider evidence that may have been obtained via torture.

[5] See Foster, Learning Lessons from the European Court of Human Rights [2002] NILQ 232.

[6] See Gearty (ed.), *European Civil Liberties and the European Convention on Human Rights* (Martinus Nijhoff 1997).

effect to in domestic law via the Human Rights Act 1998, the courts were guided by the Convention and its case law when determining disputes with a human rights context and although the Convention was not directly enforceable in the courts, both advocates and judges nevertheless made constant reference to it.[7]

The Council of Europe

The European Convention on Human Rights is not a product of the European Union and is not, directly at least, part of European Union law. This, as we shall see, has profound effects with regard to the status of the Convention in domestic law.[8] The European Convention, not being part of European Union law, was not incorporated via the European Communities Act 1972, but instead was an indirect source of domestic law until it was given further effect by the Human Rights Act 1998.[9] The European Convention was devised by the Council of Europe, a body similar but more extensive in composition to the European Union, which was set up after the Second World War to achieve unity among its members in matters such as the protection of fundamental human rights.[10]

The European Convention was drafted in the light of the atrocities that took place before and during the Second World War. Accordingly, in its preamble the European Convention reminds the member states (referred to as the High Contracting Parties) of the common heritage of political traditions, ideals, freedom and the rule of law shared by their governments and resolves for them to take steps for the collective enforcement of certain of the rights stated in the Universal Declaration of Human Rights 1948. The Convention was signed by the High Contracting Parties in 1950, and entered into force in 1953.[11] It was ratified by the United Kingdom in 1957, and in 1966 the government of the United Kingdom accepted both the compulsory jurisdiction of the European Court and the power of the (then) European Commission of Human Rights to receive applications from individuals and other non-state bodies claiming to be victims of violations of their Convention rights.[12] The main body of the European Convention is supplemented by additional protocols, which may be ratified by each High Contracting Party.

The Parliamentary Council of Europe has recommended the creation of the post of Public Prosecutor and that the Commissioner for Human Rights is allowed to intervene and bring cases before the European Court in cases of gross violations of human rights in cases where the European Convention is inapplicable.[13]

---

[7] See Hunt, *Using Human Rights Law in English Law* (Hart 1998). This aspect of the Convention will be addressed in chapter 3, which will assess the impact of the Convention, including its 'incorporation' via the Human Rights Act 1998, on the development of human rights and civil liberties in domestic law.

[8] See chapter 3 of the text.

[9] This, and other differences between the European Convention and EU Law, is explained in chapter 1 of this text.

[10] Although the European Convention on Human Rights dominates the work of the Council of Europe, that body is also responsible for a vast array of treaties and processes that monitor the protection of human rights in Europe. A full list of such treaties, and other EU treaties, can be found in Part Six of Brownlie and Goodwin-Gill, *Basic Documents on Human Rights* (OUP 2010, 6th edn).

[11] For an account of the negotiation and drafting of the European Convention, see Janis, Kay and Bradley, *European Human Rights: Text and Materials* (2007, 3rd edn), chapter 1; Mowbray, *Cases and Materials on the European Convention on Human Rights* (OUP 2007, 2nd edn), chapter 1.

[12] This acceptance is renewed every five years.

[13] See Leech, Human Rights 'Hotspots' and the European Court (2004) 154 NLJ 183.

> **Question**
> Why was the European Convention on Human Rights drafted and ratified? In what ways might it enhance the international protection of human rights?

Machinery for enforcing the Convention

Although the European Convention provides legal machinery for enforcing human rights, including a European Court of Human Rights possessing the power to make judicial decisions, which are then enforceable on the member states, the main purpose of the Convention is to promote the protection of human rights by each and every member state. Thus, as with other international treaties dealing with the recognition and enforcement of human rights, the European Convention seeks to ensure that a citizen's rights and freedoms are protected in domestic law by the state's authorities and systems. The Convention machinery, therefore, is subsidiary to this purpose, and is only called upon when the individual fails to get adequate redress at a domestic level.

This is reflected in the provisions of the Convention. Thus, as we shall see, individuals and others can only make a claim under the Convention machinery if they have exhausted all effective domestic remedies.[14] The Convention, therefore, expects individuals to gain a remedy at the domestic level, under laws and procedures that hopefully reflect the principles and standards laid down in the Convention. More generally, Article 1 of the Convention provides that the High Contracting Parties shall secure to everyone within their jurisdiction the rights and freedoms defined in Section 1 of the Convention. In this sense, therefore, the Convention attempts to create within each member state a culture of human rights protection that is consistent with both the ideals contained in the preamble and the specific rights laid out in Section 1. The European Court of Human Rights has referred to this provision on a number of occasions to justify its cautious approach towards the challenge of certain domestic laws and practices.[15]

The Committee of Ministers

This body comprises one representative from each High Contracting Party, usually the Foreign Secretary of each government, and was set up by the Statute of the Council of Europe in 1949. Prior to the introduction of Protocol 11 to the European Convention in 1998, the Committee had the power in certain cases to make a judicial determination on a case. Under Article 32 of the Convention, where a case was not referred to the European Court of Human Rights within three months of its transmission by the European Commission to the Committee of Ministers, the latter had the power decide, by a two-thirds majority, whether there had been a violation of the Convention.[16] After the new protocol, the Committee's

---

[14] Article 35 of the European Convention.

[15] The provision is, therefore, central to the adoption of the doctrine of the margin of appreciation, discussed below, which allows suitable deference to be shown towards the sovereignty of each member state in its efforts to protect and balance human rights in their individual jurisdictions. See, for example, the European Court's approach in *Handyside v United Kingdom* (1976) 1 EHRR 737.

[16] For a description of the composition and role of the Committee of Ministers, including its former judicial function, see Robertson and Merrills, *Human Rights in Europe: A Study of the European Convention on Human Rights* (Manchester University Press 1993), chapter 9.

main function, under Article 46, is to supervise the execution of the European Court's judgments.[17] This includes supervising the execution of any just satisfaction award made by the Court under Article 41, and, where appropriate and necessary, ensuring that domestic law is modified so as to comply with the Court's finding.[18]

The Committee's powers are augmented by Protocol No 14 to the Convention, considered later on in this chapter. Under Article 16 of that protocol if the committee faces difficulty with the implementation of any judgment it may refer the case to the Court for an interpretation of the initial judgment. Further, after it has warned a state about non-compliance, it may refer the case to the Court to decide whether the state has in fact implemented the judgment; if the Court determines that it has not, the case will be referred back to the Committee to consider what measures should be taken. This protocol came into force in April 2010.

The European Commission of Human Rights

Before the coming into operation of Protocol 11, the European Commission of Human Rights considered the admissibility of both inter-state and individual applications, was empowered to secure a friendly settlement between the parties to the complaint, and had the power to consider the merits of the application and to consider whether there had been a violation of the Convention on the facts. Finally, the Commission had the power to refer a particular case to the European Court of Human Rights. After the coming into effect of Protocol 11 of the Convention, the Commission no longer exists and the above roles are performed by the full-time European Court of Human Rights, although the former Commission's role in the jurisprudence of the Convention is still significant.[19] Decisions of the Commission will still continue to influence the case law of the Convention, and under s.2 of the Human Rights Act 1998 domestic courts are required to take such decisions into account when determining cases raising Convention arguments.

The European Court of Human Rights

Article 19 of the European Convention establishes a European Court of Human Rights to 'ensure the observance of the engagements undertaken by the High Contracting Parties in the Convention and the Protocols thereto'.[20] In addition to its main role, discussed below, the Court has, under Article 47 of the Convention, power to give an advisory opinion on legal questions concerning the interpretation of the Convention and its protocols. Such opinions, however, cannot deal with any question relating to the content and scope of the rights and freedoms in the Convention or its protocols, or with any question which the Court or Committee might have to consider in relation to any proceedings under the Convention.[21]

---

[17] The Committee also has the power under Article 47 to request an advisory opinion of the European Court of Human Rights, and will, under Article 49, have such opinions communicated to it.

[18] See Leach, The Effectiveness of the Committee of Ministers in Supervising the Enforcement of Judgments of the European Court of Human Rights [2006] PL 443.

[19] See Robertson and Merrills, op. cit., n 16, chapter 7, and Janis, Kay and Bradley, *European Human Rights Law: Text and Materials* (OUP 2007, 3rd edn), pages 24–7.

[20] See Lester, The European Court of Human Rights after 50 years [2009] EHRLR 461.

[21] The Court delivered its first advisory opinion under Article 47 of the Convention in February 2008. Asked by the Committee of Ministers to consider the compatibility of the gender balance with respect to judges it held that it was incompatible with the Convention for a list of candidates for election to be rejected on the sole ground that there was no woman on the list: *Advisory Opinion on Female Candidates of Stares for Court*, 12 February 2008.

owing the introduction of Protocol 11 it functions on a permanent basis and is the sole body responsible for deciding the admissibility and merits of both inter-state and individual application made under the Convention.[22]

Article 20 provides that the Court shall consist of a number of judges equal to that of the High Contracting Parties, although each judge sits on the Court in his or her individual capacity. The judges are elected by the Parliamentary Assembly of the Council of Europe, and under Article 21 must be of high moral character, possessing the qualifications required for appointment to high judicial office. Further, during their term of office they must not engage in any activity that is incompatible with their independence or impartiality, or with the demands of a full-time office. Under Article 23, they are appointed for a six-year period,[23] and they cannot be dismissed from office unless the other judges decide by a majority of two-thirds that he or she has ceased to fulfil the required conditions.[24]

The European Court of Human Rights comprises Committees (which consist of three judges), Chambers of seven judges,[25] and a Grand Chamber of 17 judges.[26] The Court's Committees consider the initial admissibility of applications made under the Convention,[27] and possess the power, under Article 28, to strike out cases from its list.[28] The Chambers of the Court then decide on the admissibility and merits of the application, combining the roles formerly carried out respectively by the Commission and the old European Court. The Grand Chamber of the Court then fulfils three functions: under Article 31 it has the power to determine applications which have been relinquished by a Chamber of the Court under Article 30; it acts as an appeal court by considering requests for referrals under Article 43; and it can consider requests for an advisory opinion under Article 47. The procedure of the Court is regulated by the Rules of the European Court of Human Rights, which contain over 100 rules covering matters such as the organisation and working of the Court, its Presidency and procedure, the institution of proceedings, proceedings on admissibility, hearings, judgments and advisory opinions, and matters of legal aid.

State and individual applications

Applications under the European Convention can be either brought by member states on behalf of individual victims or from individual applicants claiming to be victims of a violation of the Convention.

---

[22] For discussion on Protocol 11 and the reform of the European Court, see Mowbray, The Composition and Organization of the New European Court of Human Rights [1999] PL 219; Shermers, The Eleventh Protocol to the European Convention on Human Rights [1994] ELRev 367. For discussions on further reform, see Mowbray, Proposals for Reform of the European Court of Human Rights [2002] PL 252; O'Boyle, On Reforming the Operation of the European Court of Human Rights [2008] EHRLR 1.

[23] Under Article 2 of Protocol No 14 to the Convention it is proposed that the period is extended to nine years.

[24] Article 24 of the European Convention.

[25] Under Article 6 of Protocol No 14 to the Convention, it is proposed that the Committee of Ministers can, for a period, decrease this number to five.

[26] For a detailed discussion, see Drzemczewski, The Internal Organization of the European Court of Human Rights: The Composition of Chambers and the Grand Chamber [2000] EHRLR 233. See the proposals for one-judge committees in Protocol No 14, discussed below.

[27] See the proposal for increasing powers of the three-man committees under Protocol No 14, considered below.

[28] Under Article 29(2) a full Chamber of the Court decides on admissibility in inter-state cases.

Inter-state applications

Article 33 of the Convention provides that any High Contracting Party may refer to the Court any alleged breach of the provisions of the Convention or the protocols by another High Contracting Party. Such applications are subject to some of the admissibility criteria laid down in Article 35 in that the Court can only deal with any application after all domestic remedies have been exhausted and within a period of six months from the date on which the final decision was made. The applicant member state may bring an application in relation to individual victims other than their own nationals, although such applications will normally involve the applicant state's own citizens.[29]

Although the idea of inter-state applications is more consistent with international law, which, traditionally, was concerned with responsibilities between states, the number of state applications has been relatively few.[30] Such cases are often brought (or perhaps *not* brought) for political reasons as well as on human rights grounds. For example, in *Ireland* v *United Kingdom*[31] an application was brought by the Irish government in relation to the treatment of Irish nationals by British authorities in army barracks in Northern Ireland, claiming that such treatment constituted a violation of Articles 3 and 5 of the European Convention.[32]

Individual applications

Article 34 of the Convention provides that the Court may receive applications from any person, non-governmental organisation or group of individuals claiming to be a victim of a violation by one of the High Contracting Parties of the rights set forth in the Convention or the protocols thereto.[33] For this purpose, 'a person' includes both natural and legal persons, such as companies.[34] A non-governmental organisation or group of individuals is eligible provided it is not in any way a public body performing public duties.[35] Individual applications are made to the Court Registry which registers the complaint and, in certain cases, takes a preliminary decision on admissibility.[36] Otherwise, the case will be referred to the Court for a determination on admissibility, considered below. Such applications may only be brought against a High Contracting Party,[37] although it is possible that such a party might be 'vicariously' liable for the violations of another state, even one which is not party to the Convention.[38]

[29] Under Article 36 of the Convention, where the High Contracting Party's national is the applicant, that party has the right to submit written comments and take part in the proceedings. In addition, the President of the Court may invite any High Contracting Party not a party to the proceedings (or any person concerned who is not the applicant) to submit written comments or take part in hearings.

[30] See Robertson and Merrills, op. cit., n 16, pages 254–5.

[31] (1978) 2 EHRR 25.

[32] The case is dealt with in chapter 3, covering Article 3 of the Convention.

[33] The applicant does not have to be a national of the defendant state provided he or she was within the state's jurisdiction at the time of the alleged violation.

[34] For example, in *Sunday Times* v *United Kingdom* (1979) 2 EHRR 245, the applicants were both a natural person (the editor) and a legal person (Times Newspapers).

[35] *Ayuntamiento de M* v *Spain* (1991) 68 DR 209, where the European Commission held that a local authority could not bring an application against the national government.

[36] For a detailed account of how to bring applications under the European Convention, see Leech, *Taking a Case to the European Court of Human Rights* (OUP 2005, 2nd edn).

[37] The extra-territoriality of the Convention, and the Human Rights Act 1998, is discussed in the next chapter.

[38] Thus, in a number of cases brought under Article 3 of the Convention, the European Court has ruled that the liability of a High Contracting Party can be engaged when it has taken action, or failed to take action, which has then resulted in an individual being subjected to a violation of their Convention rights. See, for example, *Soering* v *United Kingdom* (1989) 11 EHRR 439.

Article 34 also states that the High Contracting Parties undertake not to hinder in any way the effective exercise of the right contained in that article[39] and the European Court can find a separate violation of this article. For example, in *McShane v United Kingdom*[40] the European Court held there had been a violation of Article 34 when the police had taken disciplinary action against the applicant's solicitors, alleging that the solicitor had disclosed witness statements to the applicant's representatives before the Court. In the European Court's view this action had a chilling effect on the exercise of the right of individual petition by the applicants and their representatives.[41] Further, there may be a violation of Article 34 even where on the facts the Court is not satisfied that there is a breach of any substantive Convention right.[42]

In addition, the Court has the power to adopt interim measures, pending the determination of any application, where it considers that there is an imminent risk of irreparable damage to the applicant.[43] This can be done at the request of the applicant or other persons, or at the Court's own motion.[44] This power was exercised by the European Court in *Al-Saadoon and Mufdhi v United Kingdom*,[45] where the European Court granted an interim injunction to stop the handing over of two suspected terrorists to the Iraqi authorities, pending their claim that such a measure would contravene their Convention rights. In that case the European Court subsequently held that the failure of the United Kingdom government to abide by the interim injunction violated Articles 34 and 13 of the Convention. In the Court's view, the failure by the government to inform the Court of any attempt it had made to explain the situation to the Iraqi authorities or to reach a temporary solution which would have safeguarded the applicants' rights constituted a violation of Articles 34 and 13 of the Convention.[46]

The requirement to be a victim

Applications under Article 34 may only be brought by persons claiming to be a 'victim' of a breach of the Convention. In *Klass v Federal Republic of Germany*[47] the European Court held

---

[39] This is separate from the right to an effective remedy under Article 13 of the Convention, and to any procedural right within a specific substantive article such as the right to a proper inquiry under Article 2.

[40] (2002) 35 EHRR 23.

[41] See also *Mamatkulov v Turkey* (2005) 41 EHRR 25, where the European Court found a violation of Article 34 when the government extradited the applicant in breach of an interim order made by the European Court of Human Rights, and *Cotlet v Romania* (Application No 38565/97), decision of the European Court, 3 June 2003, where a prisoner's correspondence with the Strasbourg authorities had been interfered with by prison authorities.

[42] *Cahuas v Spain* (Application No 24668/03), decision of the European Court, 10 August 2006. The applicant had been deported to Peru to face terrorist charges in defiance of the European Court's interim measure not to deport. The refusal to obey the order constituted a breach of Article 34 even though the Court held that there was an insufficient risk of a violation of Article 3.

[43] Rule 39(1) of the Rules of the European Court.

[44] In *Hussein v United Kingdom and others* (Application No 2327/04), the Court refused to grant interim measures sought by Saddam Hussein, who alleged that his handing over to the new Iraqi authorities to face trial violated the United Kingdom's obligations under the Convention not to condemn anyone to the death penalty or to inhuman or degrading treatment or punishment. It was held that Article 1 of the Convention was not engaged and the argument that the states in question had *de facto* control over his detention because they were in coalition with the USA who had arranged his trial was dismissed.

[45] (2010) 51 EHRR 9.

[46] See also the admissibility decision of the European Court in *Ahmad and others v United Kingdom* (Application Nos 24027/07, 11949/08 and 36742/08), considered in chapter 5, at page 259.

[47] (1978) 2 EHRR 214.

that the applicant must be affected by the alleged violation and that it is not possible for a person to make a claim against a law or practice *in abstracto*: in other words merely to test the legitimacy of a particular provision or practice in domestic law. The law or practice must, normally, have been applied to the applicant's detriment, although in the above case the Court accepted that an individual might be directly affected by a provision even where it has not been specifically implemented or applied against that person.[48] In addition, in the recent case of *Gafgen v Germany*,[49] the European Court held that a detainee who had been threatened with severe physical pain during interrogation was no longer a victim once the domestic courts had found the officers guilty and had excluded any resulting evidence at the trial. This, in the Court's view, was sufficient redress in a case where the applicant had been *merely threatened* with acts of violence.

The Court is also prepared to accept applications from family representatives of the actual victim, where the latter is unable to bring proceedings personally.[50] However, the Court will not accept all representative actions brought by family members. In *Fairfield* v *United Kingdom*,[51] the European Court held that the children and executors could not bring a case under Article 10 of the Convention on behalf of a person who had been convicted under s.5 of the Public Order Act 1986 for using insulting words by referring to homosexuals as immoral and had subsequently died.[52] The Court held that the applicants had not been directly affected by the conviction, and distinguished other cases where the true victim had died after bringing an application. The Court also noted that a different, more flexible test applied in cases under Article 2 of the Convention, because of the importance of that right and the fact that the true victim's life had been taken.

Admissibility

Any person or body wishing to make use of the Convention machinery has to pass through a number of technical rules relating to the eligibility of their claim. The purpose of these rules is principally two-fold. First, they ensure that the defendant member state is protected from unmeritorious or unsubstantiated allegations. Thus, Article 34 allows the Court to declare an application inadmissible if it is anonymous, or an abuse of the right of petition, or manifestly ill-founded. Secondly, they ensure that the Convention agencies only deal with cases that are appropriate to such machinery. Accordingly, Article 34 provides that an application can only be made by a person claiming to be a 'victim' and that such a person should have exhausted all effective remedies. These ensure that the sovereignty of each member state and its legal system can operate side by side with the supervision under the Convention.

---

[48] Thus, in *Klass*, the applicants could prove that a system of secret surveillance had the potential to be applied against them and were thus victims under the Convention. Also, in *Dudgeon v United Kingdom* (1982) 4 EHRR 149, it was held that the applicant was a victim of a violation of his private sexual life even though he had never been prosecuted for his homosexual activities. In the Court's judgment the mere existence of the law, accompanied with the limited threat of legal action being taken against him, made him a victim of that violation.

[49] (2009) 48 EHRR 13.

[50] Most commonly in cases where the actual victim has lost his or her life and the representatives are bringing proceedings under Article 2 of the Convention. See, for example, *McCann v United Kingdom* (1995) 21 EHRR 97, and *Keenan v United Kingdom* (2001) 33 EHRR 38, considered in chapters 4 and 5.

[51] Application No 24790/04, decision of the European Court, 8 March 2005.

[52] See *Hammond v DPP*, *The Times*, 28 January 2004, dealt with under Freedom of assembly, in chapter 10, page 529.

The admissibility criteria

Article 35 provides that the Court may only deal with the matter (whether an inter-state or individual case) after all domestic remedies have been exhausted, according to the generally recognised rules of international law, and within a period of six months from the date on which the final decision was taken.[53] In *De Becker* v *Belgium*[54] it was held that the six-month rule related to the requirement to exhaust all *effective* remedies and was justified on the basis that the High Contracting Parties should not have their past judgments constantly called into question. The rule does not apply to continuing breaches of the Convention, in other words where the legal provision in question gives rise to a permanent state of affairs for which there is no effective domestic remedy. In *De Becker*, therefore, the applicant could bring his application after six months of the domestic court's decision because the violation, the forfeiture of his civil rights, was a continuing one lasting his whole life.

Exhausting effective remedies

The applicant must make normal use of remedies likely to be effective and adequate so as to remedy the matters of which he claims.[55] This rule only applies to remedies that can be effectively exercised in practice: it does not apply to inter-state cases where the applicant state alleges a practice of widespread and linked breaches of the Convention.[56] Similarly, in individual applications the rule has been held inapplicable where it could be established that an administrative practice existed of such a nature as to make domestic proceedings futile or ineffective.[57] In such cases it is recognised that the rule of law and principles of government accountability have broken down, thus frustrating any legal or other remedy for human rights violations.

Equally, any remedy that is available under domestic law must be effective in substance in that it is capable of providing effective reparation for any violation. Thus, if domestic law is capable of addressing the specific allegation the applicant should employ such domestic remedies.[58] For example, in *Spencer* v *United Kingdom*,[59] an allegation of breach of private life by several newspapers was declared inadmissible because the applicant had not pursued a remedy in the domestic law of confidence. Equally, the applicant should in normal cases pursue any effective appeal against an initial decision, but is not required to do so when the relevant law is clear, rendering any appeals futile. In *Handyside* v *United Kingdom*,[60] the applicant was not required to appeal against his conviction for obscenity when it was clear that the initial court's finding was within domestic law and where any appeal would almost certainly fail.

---

[53] If domestic law does not provide any remedy, the six-month period runs from the relevant act or decision which it is alleged violates the applicant's Convention rights: *X* v *United Kingdom* (1976) 8 DR 212–13.

[54] (1958) Yearbook of the European Convention on Human Rights, 214.

[55] *Donnelly* v *United Kingdom* (1975) 64 DR 4. In that case the applications were declared inadmissible when several of the applicants had received adequate compensation for their ill-treatment via civil proceedings, and others had failed to bring such proceedings in domestic law. More recently, in *D* v *Ireland* (2006) 43 EHRR SE16, the Court declared inadmissible a claim that the lack of abortion facilities in Ireland constituted a violation of her Convention rights, because the applicant could have applied for an exemption under the general rule against abortion.

[56] *Ireland* v *United Kingdom* (1978) 2 EHRR 25.

[57] *Akdivar* v *Turkey* (1996) 1 BHRC 137.

[58] *Nielsen* v *Denmark* (1958–59) Yearbook of the European Convention on Human Rights 412.

[59] [1998] EHRLR 348.

[60] (1976) 1 EHRR 737.

Other admissibility criteria

In addition to the above requirements, individual applications under Article 34 are subject to further restrictions. First, Article 35(2) of the Convention provides that the Court shall not deal with an application under Article 34 that is anonymous or substantially the same as a matter that has already been examined by the Court, or has already been submitted to another procedure of international investigation or settlement and contains no new information.[61] Although individual applications must not be anonymous, the applicant is allowed to request that certain documentation remains confidential, and often the name of the applicant will not appear if the claim refers to intimate aspects of the applicant's (or his or her family's) private life.[62] With regard to similar applications, the rule only applies to proceedings brought by the particular applicant,[63] and in cases where there has been such a claim by the applicant the Court must be satisfied that there exists relevant new information, and that the applicant is not merely putting forward fresh arguments regarding the Convention and its interpretation, as opposed to supplying new facts.[64]

An application will be rejected where it asserts a right that is not contained in the Convention or its protocols. For example, in *Bertrand Russell Peace Foundation* v *United Kingdom*,[65] the European Commission rejected an application that alleged that the United Kingdom had failed to put sufficient diplomatic pressure on the Soviet Union to deliver mail sent by the applicants, the Commission observing that no such right to diplomatic protection existed under the Convention. The rule also applies where the defendant state has either lodged a derogation or reservation in respect of the right that has allegedly been violated, or where it relates to a right in a protocol that the defendant state has not ratified.[66]

An application will be regarded as an abuse of the right of application where it appears that it has been brought for purely political or personal reasons and where as a consequence there appears to be no foundation for the claim. Thus, in *M* v *United Kingdom*,[67] the European Commission declared an application inadmissible where the applicant and his wife had brought a series of applications against the government as part of a long-running dispute regarding their treatment by the English legal system. The Commission found that the disputes were substantially similar and raised no *prima facie* case. An application may also fall foul of this rule if the applicant has been guilty of conduct that compromised the propriety or confidentiality of the Convention proceedings.

---

[61] As the United Kingdom is not party to the optional Protocol to the International Covenant on Civil and Political Rights 1966, it is unlikely that applications against the United Kingdom will fail for the reason that another institution has already received the complaint. In *Council of Civil Service Unions* v *United Kingdom* (1987) 50 DR 228, the European Commission held that as the complaint had been referred to the ILO by the TUC as opposed to the applicants themselves, the application was not inadmissible for that reason.

[62] See, for example, *ADT* v *United Kingdom* (2001) 31 EHRR 33 (applicant charged with gross indecency with other men). Such a measure will also be used where the applicants are children: *A* v *United Kingdom* (1999) 27 EHRR 611.

[63] Although if such a similar application had been unsuccessful the Court might use that as justification for rejecting a claim by another applicant.

[64] *X* v *United Kingdom* (1981) 25 DR 147.

[65] 14 DR 117 (1978).

[66] The United Kingdom has only ratified Protocols 1, 6 and 13.

[67] (1987) 54 DR 214.

Claims that are manifestly ill-founded

By far the most common reason for rejection is where the application is determined to be manifestly ill-founded; where the applicant has failed to show a *prima facie* case against the respondent.[68] At this stage the Court might be of the opinion that either the Convention, on its proper construction, does not give the applicant a right as claimed, or that the violation is clearly covered by one of the exceptions in the Convention, for example that a violation of the applicant's right to free speech is clearly necessary in a democratic society.[69] This determination will involve a consideration of the merits of the application and is a means of filtering out hopeless cases. This function was formerly carried out by the European Commission of Human Rights, and gave a wide discretion to this non-judicial body to interpret the Convention and to determine its scope.[70] Since the introduction of Protocol 11, this role has been carried out by the European Court (and its Committees).

Friendly settlements and the striking out of cases

Article 38 of the Convention makes provision for the European Court of Human Rights to effect a friendly settlement between the applicant and the defendant state in relation to any claim brought under the Convention. After receiving the application and deciding on its admissibility, the Court shall place itself at the disposal of the parties with a view to securing a friendly settlement of the matter on the basis of respect for human rights. Article 40 then provides that if such a settlement is effected the case will be struck out of the Court's list. Although the procedure of friendly settlements has been criticised as providing governments with a convenient and non-binding method of settling allegations of human rights violations, it is defended on the basis that it allows the individual state to resolve the matter without resorting to the confrontational, and last resort, remedy provided by the European Court.

Such friendly settlements may or may not involve an admission of liability of a violation of the Convention on behalf of the defendant state. In some cases the member state may be prepared to accept that they have violated the individual's Convention rights, and will be prepared to settle the matter by the payment of compensation and/or a promise to amend the relevant law or practice. For example, in *Sutherland v United Kingdom*[71] a case was struck from the Court's list and a friendly settlement was achieved between the parties when the government agreed to amend the relevant legislation and to equalise the age of consent for both heterosexual and homosexual sexual relations.[72] Other friendly settlements are effected without any admission of liability, and the member state settles the matter, usually by payment of compensation to the applicant, without accepting that it had breached its obligations

---

[68] *Boyle and Rice v United Kingdom* (1988) 10 EHRR 425.

[69] If a Committee of the Court decides on admissibility, Rule 53(3) of the Rules of the European Court requires unanimity. However, where admissibility is determined by a Chamber of the European Court, a majority decision will suffice.

[70] For example, in *X v Iceland* (Application No 8941/80), the Commission declared a case inadmissible when it ruled that Article 3 of the First Protocol did not give a person the right to insist that the country's electoral system represented the undiluted principle of majority rule.

[71] *The Times*, 13 April 2001.

[72] The Sexual Offences (Amendment) Act 2000.

under the Convention. For example, in *Amekrane* v *United Kingdom*,[73] the European Commission effected a friendly settlement, in the form of £30,000 compensation paid to a relative, when it was alleged that the United Kingdom government had violated Article 3 of the Convention by sending a member of the Moroccan Armed Forces back to his country to face the death penalty after he had fled to Gibraltar after deserting from his post.

Under the proposed Protocol No 14, below, it is intended to complement the existing facility of effecting friendly settlements in order to reduce the Court's case load. Under Article 15 of this protocol, the European Court should take note of any settlement and briefly record its terms, and the Committee of Ministers will be responsible for enforcing the settlement.

Admissibility and Protocol No 14 of the European Convention on Human Rights

The popularity of the Convention and the creation of a full-time European Court of Human Rights have led to concern regarding the Court's workload and a resultant backlog of cases.[74] This has led to proposals for further reform of the Court's procedure,[75] and specifically the Council of Europe proposed new admissibility criterion, considered below.[76] On 13 May 2004, the Committee of Ministers of the Council of Europe endorsed Protocol No 14 of the Convention. This contains various proposals for the reform of the European Convention machinery to deal with the backlog of cases pending before the Court.

Under the Protocol, in cases which are clear-cut a single judge can decide on admissibility, or strike cases out, such decisions being final.[77] In addition, three-man committees can decide on admissibility and the merits provided there is well-established case law of the Court on the relevant issue.[78] Again such decisions will be final and binding and as a consequence the work of the current seven-man committees will be substantially decreased. More controversially it is proposed to amend Article 35(3) of the Convention, above, so that applications can be declared inadmissible where the applicant has not suffered a serious disadvantage, and where respect for human rights does not require the court to examine the merits of the case.[79] This proposal would both encourage the resolution of disputes at the domestic level and allow the Court to concentrate on alleged violations which have seriously impacted on individual rights, or where otherwise a serious issue as to the protection of Convention rights is raised by the application. To safeguard the right to individual redress, the provision will not apply where the case has not been duly considered by a domestic tribunal. Further, a new procedure will enable the committee of ministers to bring proceedings before the Court

---

[73] (1974) 44 CD 101.

[74] See Lester, The European Court of Human Rights after 50 Years [2009] EHRLR 461.

[75] See, for example, the recommendations made in Lord Woolf's 'Review of the Working Methods of the European Court of Human Rights' (December 2005), which is available at www.echr.coe.int. In particular, Lord Woolf recommends greater use of alternative dispute resolution, including the mediation and the effecting of friendly settlements.

[76] For a detailed discussion of the protocol, see Beernaert, Protocol 14 and the new Strasbourg Procedures [2004] EHRLR 544, and Caflish, The Reform of the European Court of Human Rights: Protocol No 14 and Beyond [2006] HRLR 403.

[77] Article 7, Protocol No 14. The judge will be assisted by appointed rapporteurs.

[78] Article 8, Protocol No 14.

[79] Article 12, Protocol No 14. See Reudin, De minimis non curat the European Court of Human Rights [2008] EHRLR 80.

where a state refuses to comply with the judgment and European Court judges will be appointed for a single, nine-year term.

Following Russia's eventual ratification, Protocol 14 came into force in April 2010. This will allow for a speedier processing of cases.

Judgments of the European Court of Human Rights and their effect

Under Article 46 of the Convention the Court is bound to give reasons for its decisions, and this duty also applies where the Court declares an application inadmissible.[80] Where the judgment of the Court does not represent, in whole or in part, the unanimous opinion of the judges, any judge is entitled to deliver a separate opinion. The decisions of the European Court are binding in international law to those states that have accepted the compulsory jurisdiction of the Court,[81] and place a duty on the state to comply with judgment, in respect of both paying any just satisfaction awarded by the Court and of making any necessary changes to domestic law and practice.

The decisions of the Court do not automatically change domestic law, unless the Convention and its case law have been fully incorporated into domestic law so as to achieve that result.[82] In the United Kingdom, although the Human Rights Act 1998 allows the courts to take the decisions of the European Court into consideration when interpreting and applying the law, the status of such decisions with regard to a change of the law remains the same, and the domestic law remains in force until amended by parliament. This situation was illustrated by the House of Lords decision in *R v Lyons and Others*,[83] where a number of individuals sought to have their convictions quashed on the basis that the original convictions appeared to be in contravention of Article 6 of the Convention. The House of Lords held that the convictions were at the time lawful under domestic law and that the decision of the European Court[84] could not have the effect of retrospectively disturbing those convictions. Any remedy provided to the individuals in that case was the result of the Court exercising its jurisdiction under the Convention, and such a judgment did not have the effect of overturning domestic law.[85] The decision of the House of Lords was confirmed by the European Court of Human Rights when it declared inadmissible a subsequent application under the Convention.[86]

It should also be noted that even in the post-Act era a finding of a violation of the Convention by the European Court will not automatically invalidate a domestic decision

---

[80] The decisions of the European Court of Human Rights are reported in the European Human Rights Law Reports, and the judgments of the Commission and the Court are available on the European Court's website: www.echr.coe.int.

[81] Article 46 of the European Convention. Under Article 44 of the Convention, a decision of a Chamber of the European Court becomes final either at the expiry of three months of the decision, where both parties declare that they will not request a reference to the Grand Chamber, or when the Grand Chamber rejects such a request.

[82] For example, after the Court's ruling in *Malone v United Kingdom* (1984) 7 EHRR 14, the government was bound to initiate legislative changes to comply with the ruling. As a consequence, parliament passed the Interception of Communications Act 1985, but until that legislation became effective, the domestic legal situation remained as before.

[83] [2002] 3 WLR 1562.

[84] *Saunders v United Kingdom* (1996) 26 EHRR 313.

[85] If the trial had taken place after the coming into operation of the 1998 Act then the defendants could have used Article 6 to challenge the charges and any subsequent convictions.

[86] *Lyons v United Kingdom* (Application No 15227/03), decision of the European Court, 8 July 2007.

relating to the same proceedings. Thus, in *Dowsett v Criminal Cases Review Commission*[87] it was held that the Commission was entitled to refuse to refer the claimant's case for appeal despite the fact that the European Court had ruled that his Article 6 rights had been infringed in his original trial.[88] The High Court pointed out that a finding of a violation of Article 6 did not necessarily render a conviction unsafe and in breach of Article 6 and that in this case the breach had probably not made any difference to the outcome of the trial. Similarly, in *Eastaway v Secretary of State for Trade and Industry*[89] it was held that a finding by the European Court that there had been an unreasonable delay in the claimant's disqualification proceedings did not entitle him to have those proceedings invalidated. The European Court had simply found that there had been an unreasonable delay and not that a fair trial was impossible in such circumstances.

Article 43 of the Convention states that a party to the case may in exceptional circumstances, request that the case be referred to the Grand Chamber, provided that is done within three months from the date of the judgment. In such a case a panel of five judges of the Grand Chamber will consider whether the case raises a serious question affecting the interpretation or application of the Convention or its protocols, or a serious issue of general importance. If the case is referred to the Grand Chamber, then it will make a judgment on the case, which by virtue of Article 44 will become final and binding.

Just satisfaction

Under Article 41 of the European Convention, where the Court finds a violation of the Convention and the internal law of the relevant High Contracting Party allows only partial reparation to be made, it is empowered to award just satisfaction to the injured party.[90] The general aim of such awards is to place the victim into the position had the violation not occurred, compensating him or her for any financial or other loss resulting from the violation. The phrase 'just satisfaction' is employed in s.8 of the Human Rights Act 1998 and after the coming into force of the Act the domestic courts must ensure that the remedies awarded by the domestic courts reflect the principles in Article 41 of the Convention, including its relevant case law.[91]

The Court's awards come under three headings. First, pecuniary damage compensates the applicant for any direct financial loss caused by the breach itself, including loss of property and depreciation of value of property,[92] or sums incurred as fines or compensation that have subsequently been declared unlawful under the Convention.[93] Secondly, the court may award damages for non-pecuniary damage where the applicant has suffered because of the nature of the violation. This heading is particularly relevant when the applicant has suffered loss of

---

[87] [2007] EWHC 1923 (Admin).

[88] *Dowsett v United Kingdom* (2004) 38 EHRR 41.

[89] [2007] EWCA CIV 425, referring to *Eastaway v United Kingdom*; (2005) 40 EHRR 17.

[90] See Mowbray, *Cases and Materials on the European Convention on Human Rights* (OUP 2007), chapter 19; Mowbray, The European Court of Human Rights Approach to Just Satisfaction [1997] PL 647.

[91] Under s.8(4) of the Act, in determining whether to award damages, and what amount should be awarded, the Court must take into account the principles applied by the European Court of Human Rights in relation to the award of compensation under Article 41.

[92] *Hentrich v France* (1994) 18 EHRR 440 and *Lopez Ostra v Spain* (1994) 20 EHRR 277.

[93] *Jersild v Denmark* (1994) 19 EHRR 1, where the European Court reimbursed a fine imposed on the applicants under domestic law for aiding and abetting racist remarks.

liberty,[94] or where he or she has suffered physical and/or mental distress from a violation of the European Convention.[95] For example, in *Smith and Grady* v *United Kingdom*,[96] the European Court awarded non-pecuniary loss for what it saw as clear and especially grave interferences with the applicants' private lives when the applicants had been interrogated regarding their sexual orientation and subsequently dismissed from the armed forces. Thirdly, the Court can compensate for legal costs and expenses 'actually, necessarily and reasonably incurred by the applicant'.[97]

In appropriate cases the Court has the power to award no compensation other than costs and expenses. Thus, in *McCann* v *United Kingdom*[98] the European Court dismissed a claim for non-pecuniary loss after finding that a number of persons had been killed by state officials in violation of Article 2 of the Convention. In the Court's view, the fact that the victims were terrorist suspects made it inappropriate to award just satisfaction under this heading. The Court may also refuse to grant compensation where it is of the opinion that there has simply been a technical breach of the Convention or otherwise where a finding of a violation is a sufficient remedy in itself. Thus in *Kingsley* v *United Kingdom*[99] it was held that the European Court's earlier finding of a violation of Article 6 of the Convention was sufficient satisfaction for non-pecuniary damage under Article 41.[100] The European Court's Grand Chamber was of the opinion that the domestic decision was well-founded and that it had reached a decision that a properly constituted body would have reached. Further, there was no evidence that the applicant had not been provided with a fair hearing in those, and the judicial review proceedings.[101]

Questions

What is so novel and effective about the machinery of enforcement under the Convention? When does the Convention machinery come into play and how does it co-exist with the domestic law of each state?

The role of the European Court of Human Rights

The principal role of the European Court is to interpret and apply the European Convention. This involves the Court deciding whether there has been a violation of one of the substantive rights in the Convention and, in many cases, whether any and sufficient justification existed for any violation of that right. The Court will need to interpret the rights contained in the Convention so as to determine their true scope and in doing so it will attempt to determine

---

[94] *Yagci and Sargin* v *Turkey* (1995) 20 EHRR 505, where the unlawful detention had been aggravated by mistreatment by the authorities. The Court is more reluctant to award just satisfaction in cases where it is uncertain whether the applicant would have been detained in the absence of a violation of the Convention.

[95] In *Ribitsch* v *Austria* (1995) 21 EHRR 573, the European Court suggested that relatively high sums should be awarded in such cases so as to encourage applicants to bring court proceedings.

[96] (2000) 29 EHRR 493. See also *Lustig-Prean and Beckett* v *United Kingdom* (2000) 29 EHRR 548.

[97] The criteria are set down by the European Court in *McCann* v *United Kingdom* (1995) 21 EHRR 97. Since 1996 the Court awards default interest for delayed settlement of just satisfaction awards.

[98] (1995) 21 EHRR 97.

[99] (2002) 35 EHRR 10.

[100] (2001) 33 EHRR 13.

[101] The Court did, however, grant costs for legal expenses incurred in both the domestic proceedings and the proceedings before the European Court of Human Rights.

the intention of the drafters of the Convention not just from the words used in the Convention, but in the light of certain democratic and fundamental principles. The Court will also be conscious of the need to reflect recent philosophy on the protection of human rights and will thus interpret and apply it as a living instrument.[102]

The European Court is not an appeal court from the domestic courts of the member states on questions of law and fact. Indeed, by the time a case reaches a full hearing of the European Court it is assumed in the vast majority of cases that the domestic courts or other authorities have interpreted and applied the domestic law correctly.[103] This is backed up by the fact that all applicants have to show that they have exhausted all effective remedies at the admissibility stage. Rather, the role of the Court is supervisory – to see whether the domestic law and its application in a particular case were consistent with the rights laid down in the Convention. For example, if an applicant had been prosecuted under the Obscene Publications Act 1959 for publishing an obscene article – the domestic court having decided that the article tended to deprave and corrupt – it would not be the European Court's task to decide whether that article did, in fact, come within that legal definition. Instead, the Court's role would be to determine whether the prosecution of that article under existing domestic law was compatible with the principles of free speech and the doctrines of legality, necessity and proportionality that are contained in the Convention. Thus the European Court might take issue with the law itself, or an illiberal interpretation of that restrictive law,[104] but it would not, generally, be concerned with whether the domestic courts interpreted the law correctly.

The role of the European Court of Human Rights can, therefore, at least to a certain extent, be equated with the traditional function of judicial review in domestic law. The Court's function is to see whether the domestic law and its application fit within certain guidelines which are laid down by the Convention, rather than to decide the case afresh. Of course, the European Court's role is wider than that of the court in a traditional judicial review case. The Court may consider not just the legality of the law or its application, but also its compatibility with human rights, and the Convention itself, by referring to concepts such as 'necessary in a democratic society', allowing the Court to judge the merits of a particular law and its application by the domestic authorities. However, as democracy and the acceptance of the limited role of the judiciary place restrictions on the courts' jurisdiction in domestic law, so too the margin of appreciation and the general acceptance of self-determination place similar restrictions on the European Court, ensuring that it does not interfere too lightly with the decisions of democratically elected lawmakers and the decisions of the domestic courts.

Principles of human rights' adjudication

Human rights norms

The Court and Commission have developed a number of principles that have assisted them in determining the scope of the Convention rights and the legality of any interference. In the

---

[102] See Cali, The Purposes of the European Human Rights System: One or Many? [2008] EHRLR 299, where the author explores the roles of the Court in upholding human rights.

[103] An example of a case where the Court was of the opinion that the domestic law had *not* been applied correctly was the case of *Steel* v *United Kingdom* (1999) 28 EHRR 603, considered in chapter 10.

[104] As in cases such as *Sunday Times* v *United Kingdom* (1979) 2 EHRR 245; *Goodwin* v *United Kingdom* (1996) 22 EHRR 123.

preamble to the Convention the High Contracting Parties refer to their common heritage of political traditions, ideals, freedom and the rule of law and thus reaffirm their belief in those fundamental freedoms which are the foundations of justice or peace. The Convention is, accordingly, drafted and interpreted and applied in the light of these democratic and liberal principles.[105] In addition, the Court has noted that the Convention, being a living instrument, will be interpreted in the light of present-day conditions, reflecting the Court's and the member states' growing commitment to the protection of fundamental human rights.[106]

The rule of law, including the requirement of government accountability, clear and prospective laws and of procedural fairness, is at the heart of articles guaranteeing the right to liberty and security of the person and the right to a fair trial. Such articles also promote concepts such as access to the courts and the presumption of innocence, and have provided the basis of many challenges to arbitrary detention imposed by executive government rather than impartial judicial officers.[107] Such principles have also helped the European Court and Commission to determine the legality and reasonableness of certain restrictions, which under the terms of the Convention can only be justified if they are 'prescribed by law' and 'necessary in a democratic society'.

The Court and Commission have also relied heavily on the basic principles of democracy in interpreting and applying those articles guaranteeing rights such as freedom of expression, freedom of association and peaceful assembly. The Court has stressed the need for every society to possess a free press and to encourage free speech and freedom of peaceful assembly, including the reasonable but trenchant criticism of those in power.[108] Further, the European Court has referred to freedom of expression as one of the essential foundations of a democratic society, being one of the basic conditions for its progress and for the development of every man. Accordingly, pluralism, tolerance and broadmindedness demand that Article 10 is applicable not only to information and ideas that are favourably received, but also to those that offend and shock the state or any sector of the population.[109]

The Convention is also interpreted in the light of principles of equality and the protection of minorities. As a consequence, groups such as prisoners, asylum seekers and sexual minorities have enjoyed the protection of the Convention.[110] In these cases, the Court and Commission have insisted that such groups are not automatically excluded from the enjoyment of Convention rights,[111] and that in cases involving private sexual life, it would be contrary to principle to allow the majority an unqualified right to impose its standards of private sexual morality on the whole of society.[112]

---

[105] For a thorough discussion, see Merrills, *The Development of International Law by the European Court of Human Rights* (Manchester University Press 1993), particularly chapter 6. See also Greer, *The European Convention on Human Rights: Achievements, Problems and Prospects* (Cambridge University Press 2006), chapters 4 and 5.

[106] *Selmouni* v *France* (1999) 29 EHRR 403.

[107] See, for example, *Thynne, Wilson and Gunnell* v *United Kingdom* (1990) 13 EHRR 666; *V and T* v *United Kingdom* (1999) 30 EHRR 121. See also *Stafford* v *United Kingdom* (2002) 35 EHRR 32.

[108] See, for example, *Lingens* v *Austria* (1986) 8 EHRR 407.

[109] *Handyside* v *United Kingdom* (1976) 1 EHRR 737.

[110] See Livingstone and Harvey, Protecting the Marginalised: The Role of the European Convention on Human Rights [2000] 51 NILQ 445; Wheatley, Minorities under the ECHR and the Construction of a 'Democratic Society' [2007] PL 770.

[111] See *Golder* v *United Kingdom* (1975) 1 EHRR 524.

[112] *Dudgeon* v *United Kingdom* (1982) 4 EHRR 149 and *Goodwin* v *United Kingdom* (2002) 35 EHRR 18.

Permissible interferences with Convention rights

Many of the rights contained in the Convention are conditional and may be interfered with in particular circumstances. For example, freedom of expression is not intended to be absolute and there will be many cases where it will be regarded as lawful and necessary to infringe that right. However, these permitted infringements must possess certain characteristics if they are to be acceptable within the Convention and its case law. The conditional rights, contained in Articles 8–11 of the Convention, contain a particular mechanism for testing the legality of any restriction or interference: any such interference must be prescribed by, or in accordance with, the law, and be necessary in a democratic society for the protection of one of a number of legitimate aims which are recognised and listed in the Article itself. These conditions are intended to ensure that any interference with fundamental rights meets generally recognised standards of legality or fairness and allows us to distinguish between permissible and arbitrary interferences with fundamental human rights.

Prescribed by law/in accordance with law

Under the European Convention member states will need to show that any interference with a Convention right was, at the very least, justified by reference to some provision of domestic law. For example, Article 2 of the Convention allows the right to life to be taken intentionally by the sentence of a court, but only for a crime for which the penalty is *prescribed by law*. Freedom from arbitrary interference with Convention rights is also protected by Article 5 of the Convention, which allows interference with a person's liberty and security of the person only in accordance with a procedure *prescribed by law*. Such a phrase, and the phrase 'lawful arrest or detention' employed in that same Article, means not only that the law must have a legitimate source, but also that it complies with the fundamental ideals of the rule of law in that it is sufficiently fair, impartial and clear.[113] Again, the conditional rights contained in Articles 8 to 11 of the Convention insist that any interference with those rights are 'prescribed by law' or 'in accordance with the law', safeguarding human rights from arbitrary and unlawful interferences and ensuring that domestic law is consistent with ideas of procedural and substantive fairness.

The phrase 'in accordance with the law' was considered by the European Court of Human Rights in *Malone v United Kingdom*,[114] a case involving the tapping of the applicant's telephone on the authority of government circulars. According to the Court, for a measure to be prescribed by law it had to display the following characteristics: first, it must have a legal basis, in other words the law must be identified and established; secondly, the rule must be accessible – those affected by it must be able to find out what the law says; and thirdly, the rule must be formulated with sufficient certainty to enable people to understand it and to regulate their conduct by it.[115] Similarly, for any interference to be 'prescribed by law', the law has to meet the above standards and safeguards, and in *Silver v United Kingdom*[116] it was held that the same criteria should be applied to the phrases used in Article 8 and Articles 9, 10 and 11 of the Convention, both phrases to be interpreted and applied in an identical manner.

---

[113] See, for example, *Winterwerp v Netherlands* (1979) 2 EHRR 387; *Steel v United Kingdom* (1998) 28 EHRR 603.
[114] (1984) 7 EHRR 14.
[115] The European Court concluded in that case that the rules relating to telephone tapping, being included in secret administrative guidance, were not in accordance with law as required by Article 8(2) of the Convention.
[116] (1983) 5 EHRR 347.

Any provisions that interfere with Convention rights must be subject to sufficient control. Thus, in *Malone* the European Court held that there must be a measure of legal protection against arbitrary interference by public authorities with the rights in Article 8 of the Convention, especially where a power of the executive is exercised in secret where the risks of arbitrariness are evident.[117] Provisions must exist which are sufficiently independent of those who administer them and which accordingly regulate such persons, although such provisions do not have to be in the form of primary or secondary legislation.[118] For example, in *Sunday Times* v *United Kingdom*,[119] it was held that provided the law was sufficiently accessible and clear, it was not fatal that the provisions came from the common law. The key, therefore, is whether the law imposes a sufficient element of control over the relevant decision maker so as to avoid the exercise of unfettered and arbitrary action.

The requirement of accessibility

The second requirement, that the rule has to be accessible, insists that a person who is likely to be affected by the rule should have access to it. If, as in *Malone* v *United Kingdom*,[120] the rules and their scope are only available to the government or those responsible for administering the rule, such provisions will not be regarded as in accordance with law.[121] A breach of this requirement was evident in the case of *Silver* v *United Kingdom*,[122] a case involving the regulation of prisoners' correspondence via administrative guidance produced by the Secretary of State for the Prison Service. In that case the European Court held that most of the restrictions on prisoners' correspondence could be gleaned from the content of the formal law (the Prison Act 1952 and the Prison Rules 1964). However, those restrictions contained only in non-legal and non-published Standing Orders, and which did not sufficiently refer to the formal law, were not in accordance with law within Article 8(2).

The requirement of certainty

Whereas the first requirement is primarily concerned with regulating the arbitrary activities of administrators and other decision makers, the third requirement looks at the provision from the perspective of those who are to be governed by it. Law should be sufficiently clear to allow individuals to govern their future behaviour. Thus, in *Sunday Times* v *United Kingdom*,[123] it was held that a law had to be formulated with sufficient precision to enable the citizen to regulate his or her conduct: that person must be able – if need be with appropriate advice – to foresee, to a degree that is reasonable in the circumstances, the consequences which a given action may entail. Those consequences need not, however, be foreseeable with absolute certainty. While the Court noted that certainty is desirable, it also accepted that excessive rigidity

---

[117] In that case, the Court held that it could not be said what elements of the power to intercept communications were incorporated in legal rules and what elements remained within the discretion of the executive.

[118] *Barthold* v *Germany* (1985) 7 EHRR 383. In *Silver* v *United Kingdom*, n 116 above, the Court held that provided any limits of relevant discretion were referable to primary or secondary legislation then the fact that an administrator relied on non-legal guidance was not in violation of Article 8.

[119] (1979) 2 EHRR 245.

[120] (1984) 7 EHRR 14.

[121] See also the subsequent decisions of the European Court in *Halford* v *United Kingdom* (1997) 24 EHRR 523, *Khan* v *United Kingdom* (2001) 31 EHRR 45, *Copland* v *United Kingdom* (2007) 45 EHRR 37, and, most recently, *Liberty* v *United Kingdom* (2009) 48 EHRR 1.

[122] (1983) 5 EHRR 347.

[123] (1979) 2 EHRR 245.

should be avoided and that laws are inevitably couched in terms which, to some extent, are vague and whose interpretation and application are questions of practice. Similarly, although the law itself may be vague, its meaning and scope may become apparent after it has been construed and applied by the courts. Thus, in the *Sunday Times* case, although the law of contempt of court was inevitably uncertain and dependent on interpretation, a person could, by examining its application via the case law, predict with a sufficient degree of certainty whether the publication of an article would be caught by the law.[124]

If a rule is couched in terms which are so vague that its meaning and extent cannot be reasonably predicted, then the rule will not be regarded as law as required by the Convention and the interference will be unlawful irrespective of its necessity. Therefore, in *Hashman and Harrap v United Kingdom*,[125] the European Court held that the power of the domestic courts to order a person to desist in conduct that was *contra bones mores* (conduct which is seen as wrong in the eyes of the majority of contemporary citizens), was too vague to be prescribed by law for the purposes of Article 10(2), as it failed to give sufficient guidance to the applicants as to what conduct they were not allowed to partake in. In contrast, in *Steel v United Kingdom*[126] the European Court held that the concept of breach of the peace, as defined and restricted by the domestic courts, was sufficiently prescribed by law to satisfy both Articles 10 and 5 of the Convention.

Legitimate aims

As with most developed bills of rights, the European Convention recognises that the rights laid down in the Convention and its protocols may be interfered with for legitimate reasons. Specifically, in Articles 8–11, the Convention lists a number of legitimate aims, allowing the claimed right to be interfered with provided it was prescribed by or in accordance with the law and necessary in a democratic society to do so. For example, Article 10, guaranteeing the right to freedom of speech and expression, allows interferences on the grounds of national security, territorial integrity, public safety, the prevention of disorder or crime, the protection of health or morals, the protection of the reputation and or rights of others, the prevention of the disclosure of information received in confidence and the maintenance of the authority and impartiality of the judiciary.[127] Any interference with the above Convention rights has to accord to such a legitimate aim and the member state must show that the relevant legal provision pursued one of the aims laid down in the Convention, and was genuinely applied to the applicant in a particular case. Thus a legitimate aim cannot be used as a pretext for a measure taken for another, improper, purpose.[128] Thus, in *Kunstler v Austria*,[129] it was held

---

[124] Contrast *Kruslin v France* (1990) 12 EHRR 547, where the European Court found that the French law on wire-tapping, both written and unwritten, did not indicate with reasonable certainty the scope and manner of exercise of the relevant discretion conferred on public authorities and was, therefore, not in accordance with law.

[125] (1999) 30 EHRR 241.

[126] (1998) 28 EHRR 603.

[127] Article 8, guaranteeing the right to private and family life, contains similar legitimate aims, but includes the economic well-being of the country, and Articles 9 and 11, guaranteeing, respectively, freedom of thought, conscience and religion, and freedom of association and peaceful assembly, contain a limited number of the above aims. Article 11 also states that the Article shall not prevent the imposition of lawful restrictions on the exercise of these rights by members of the armed forces, of the police or of the administration of the state.

[128] Note Article 18 of the Convention, which states that the restrictions under the Convention shall not be applied for any purpose other than those for which they have been prescribed.

[129] (2008) 47 EHRR 5.

that the government could not rely on public morals as a reason for banning the exhibition of a painting when the legislation in question safeguarded individual ownership and honour rights, and was not intended to uphold public morality as such. However, a measure may pursue a legitimate aim despite its being flawed or unequal in its application. Thus, in *Choudhury* v *United Kingdom*[130] the European Commission held that the English law of blasphemy pursued the legitimate aim of the protection of the rights of others, even though the law applied only to Christianity.

In addition to the wording of those 'conditional' rights, the Convention allows other interferences by laying down exceptions or qualifications to a specific Convention right. For example, Article 5 of the Convention permits interference with liberty and security of the person in a number of circumstances, such as a person's lawful detention after conviction by a competent court, provided it is in accordance with a procedure prescribed by law. Again in Article 6 of the Convention, although everyone has the right to have their judgment pronounced in public, the press and the public can be excluded for a number of legitimate reasons, such as in the interests of morals or of juveniles.

Necessary in a democratic society

Articles 8–11 of the Convention require that all restrictions are necessary in a democratic society for achieving one of the legitimate aims listed in the article. Thus, it is not sufficient that the member state interfered with the applicant's rights for a legitimate purpose. The Court must also be satisfied that the restriction was necessary in the circumstances. This involves the Court making a qualitative decision regarding the merits of the relevant domestic legal provision and its application. Thus, although it may be beyond doubt that the prosecution of a person under the Obscene Publications Act was for a legitimate purpose – the protection of health and morals – the Court will enquire further into the necessity and reasonableness of enforcing that law on the applicant, given that such a prosecution has interfered with the applicant's fundamental rights. In this respect, although the Court's supervisory jurisdiction is limited, its role is more extensive than the one traditionally exercised in judicial review by the domestic courts. The doctrine of proportionality is at the heart of the Court's investigation into the reasonableness of the restriction, and although the Court offers a margin of appreciation to the member state and its institutions (see below), the Court's main role is to ensure that the rights laid down in the Convention are not interfered with unnecessarily.

Interpreting the phrase 'necessary in a democratic society'

The Court must define the term 'necessary in a democratic society', the definition of the word 'necessary' determining the extent of the Court's power to interfere with a legislative provision or a court decision which allegedly restricts the applicant's rights. In addition, if the Court is to be able to assess the necessity or reasonableness of any restriction it needs to define the concept of a 'democratic society' and to decide what characteristics such a society should possess and practise. In assessing whether a restriction is necessary in democratic society, the Court has stated that it must ask the following questions: is there a pressing social need for some restriction of the Convention? If so, does the particular restriction correspond to that need? If so, is it a proportionate response to that need? In any event, are the reasons

---

[130] (1991) 12 HRLJ 172.

advanced by the authorities relevant and sufficient?[131] The Court has stressed that in deciding whether a restriction is necessary it is not faced with a choice between two conflicting principles, but with a principle of, for example, freedom of expression subject to a number of exceptions, which must be narrowly interpreted.[132] Thus, although the Court may give a margin of appreciation to the member state, its prime role is to safeguard the fundamental rights in the Convention from unnecessary interference.

In *Handyside v United Kingdom*[133] the European Court ruled that the word 'necessary' did not mean 'absolutely necessary' or 'indispensable', but neither did it have the flexibility of terms such as 'useful' or 'convenient': instead the term meant that there must be a 'pressing social need' for the interference. Thus, although the Court rejects the idea that a member state would need to show that society or the legal system could not possibly do without the legal restriction, it is not prepared to accept a restriction merely because its existence and use in practice provides a useful tool in achieving a social good, particularly where there is little evidence that such a good is being achieved. Accordingly, the Court insists that there is strong objective justification for the law and its application. For example, although it might be useful or convenient to have a law that prohibits the publication of material likely to cause offence or annoyance to the majority of society, it would not for that reason alone be 'necessary' to have such a law. The existence of that law may well appease the majority of society, and provide a useful way to prohibit or sanction conduct which the majority of people regard as annoying or distasteful, but there would have to be evidence of a greater harm before one could accept that it is legitimate to restrict free speech. In such a case the Convention insists that the member state can point to a real social harm, that the legal restriction exists to preserve a legitimate aim – such as public morals or the rights of others – and that the employment of that law is, and was, *necessary* to achieve that aim.[134]

The doctrine of proportionality

This doctrine insists that a fair balance is achieved between the realisation of a social goal, such as the protection of morals or the preservation of public order, and the protection of the fundamental rights contained in the Convention. Restrictions should be strictly proportionate to the legitimate aim being pursued and the authorities must show that the restriction in question does not go beyond what is strictly required to achieve that purpose.[135] The extent to which the Court is prepared to conduct such an inquiry may well depend on other factors such as the importance of the right that has been interfered with and the nature of the legitimate aim: the more important the right that is interfered with, and the greater that interference in the particular case, the more evidence the Court will require as justification. The Court will, therefore, have regard to factors such as the fundamental character of the right in

---

[131] *Barthold v Germany* (1985) 7 EHRR 383.
[132] *Sunday Times v United Kingdom* (1979) 2 EHRR 245.
[133] (1976) 1 EHRR 737.
[134] For example, in *Dudgeon v United Kingdom* (1982) 4 EHRR 149, the European Court noted that, as opposed to the time when the legislation prohibiting homosexual conduct was passed, there was evidence of a greater understanding and tolerance of such conduct. Accordingly, the blanket prohibition of such conduct, irrespective of the age of the participants, did not correspond to a pressing social need.
[135] *Barthold v Germany* (1985) 7 EHRR 383.

question, the extent to which the right was violated, the urgency of the pressing social need, and the sanction imposed on the right user, including whether there was a less restrictive alternative available to the domestic authorities.

The European Court has adopted a variety of approaches in determining the necessity of restrictions, including whether the member state has advanced relevant and sufficient reasons for the interference. This seemingly liberal approach might be applied in a case where the Court feels that there is little evidence of a common European approach to the matter (such as in cases concerning public morality), and where the Court thus wishes to give the state a wide margin of appreciation. Conversely, where the Court is intent on thorough scrutiny, and where there is evidence of a common European standard, it might ask whether the domestic authorities had available to them a less restrictive alternative than the one applied to the applicant. This test can be employed to attack excessive penalties or sanctions, imposed by domestic law on those who have exercised their Convention rights.[136] The Court and Commission have also asked whether the restriction destroys the very essence of the Convention right in question. For example, in *Hamer* v *United Kingdom*,[137] the European Commission of Human Rights held that the prohibition on prisoners marrying while in prison destroyed the very essence of the right to marry contained in Article 12 of the Convention.

Questions

What essential human rights principles underlie the Convention and its enforcement machinery? In particular, how has the European Court of Human Rights defined and applied the terms 'prescribed by/in accordance with law' and 'necessary in a democratic society'?

The margin of appreciation

As we have seen, in many of its Articles the European Convention provides that Convention rights may be interfered with in certain circumstances and on certain conditions. Although the European Court has denied that this involves a true balancing exercise, it is prepared to accept that in certain cases it would be wrong for it to interfere with the laws and decisions of a member state when those laws or decisions have a proper legal basis, fulfil a legitimate aim, and where the domestic authorities have made a genuine and reasonable effort to balance the Convention right with those other rights or interests. Although many commentators have criticised this concept,[138] there may be a number of reasons to justify it.

First, the Court has recognised that its role under the Convention is subsidiary to the system of rights protection adopted and carried out by each member state. Article 1 of the Convention provides that it is the obligation of the High Contracting Parties to secure to everyone within their jurisdiction the rights and freedoms in the Convention and accordingly the Court has stressed that the main purpose of the Convention is to ensure that the rights laid down in the Convention are protected at the domestic level, and that the role of the European Court in pronouncing on possible violations of the Convention is secondary

---

[136] See for example *Tolstoy Miloslavsky* v *United Kingdom* (1995) 20 EHRR 442, and *Goodwin* v *United Kingdom* (1996) 22 EHRR 123, considered in chapter 9.

[137] (1979) 24 DR 5.

[138] See, in particular, Jones, The Devaluation of Human Rights [1995] PL 430. See also Lavender, The Problem of the Margin of Appreciation [1997] EHRLR 380.

to that role.[139] Secondly, natural judicial reticence might dictate that the Court would be unwilling to interfere in certain aspects of supervision relating to the law and decision making. The Court might be comfortable with deciding whether a domestic legal regulation has the necessary qualities so as to be 'prescribed by law' or in 'accordance with the law'. In such a case the judge merely has to apply an established legal principle and decide whether that regulation meets the required standards. Similarly, in deciding whether a law achieves a legitimate aim the Court is merely deciding whether the reason for the law and its enforcement falls within a list of purposes that the Convention itself has decided are legitimate. On the other hand, deciding whether a restriction, albeit lawful and relevant, is necessary and proportionate requires the Court to make a judgment on the merits of the law and its operation, and whether the law has achieved a proper balance between the protection of these fundamental rights and the realisation of these other legitimate interests. Thirdly, it might be difficult to decide whether a particular law and its application are in conformity with the standards laid down in the Convention. This will be the case where it is difficult to obtain the necessary evidence to decide whether there is a pressing social need for the existence or operation of the law, or where, given the nature of the law and its legitimate aim, it is difficult to establish any form of common European standard by which the necessity of a particular law or practice could be measured.

The doctrine was first used in the context of Article 15 of the Convention (see below, page 73), which allows member states to derogate from the Convention in times of war or other emergency. In doing so, the state is only allowed to derogate to the extent strictly required by the exigencies of the situation, and the European Court made it clear that in deciding what measures to adopt, including whether there was a state of emergency, the state, being best placed to determine the facts surrounding the derogation, would be given 'a margin of error'. This margin of error – or margin of appreciation as it is referred to in this context – has been employed by the European Court and Commission in determining whether a restriction on a Convention right is necessary in a democratic society. Thus, in *Handyside v United Kingdom*,[140] the European Court stressed that the machinery of the Convention is subsidiary to the national systems safeguarding human rights, and that consequently provisions such as Article 10(2) of the Convention leave to each state a margin of appreciation, given both to the domestic legislature and to the bodies called upon to interpret and apply the laws. This margin of appreciation, according to the Court, goes hand in hand with its powers to give the final meaning on whether a restriction is compatible with the Convention right in question.

The margin of appreciation in practice

Although the case law of the European Court on the margin of appreciation is often difficult to predict, there do appear to be some guiding principles determining the extent of discretion which the Court will allow each member state.[141] These guidelines – the status and importance of the right in question, whether the restriction infringes the enjoyment of entirely private

---

[139] See *Handyside v United Kingdom* (1976) 1 EHRR 737, below, pages 69–73. See also Lewis, The European Ceiling on Human Rights [2007] PL720.

[140] (1976) 1 EHRR 737.

[141] For a discussion and analysis of this case law see Kavanaugh, Policing the Margins: Rights Protection and the European Court of Human Rights [2006] EHRLR 422.

rights, and whether there is a discernible common European standard that the Court is able to apply – are apparent in the case law of the Convention and help us to reconcile what at first sight appears to be random application of a convenient doctrine.

The Convention organs have always afforded a wide margin of appreciation in cases where a matter of public morality is at issue. Thus, in *Handyside*, the European Court, noting that it was not possible to find a uniform conception of morals within the Council of Europe, held that states, by reason of their direct and continuous contact with the vital forces of their countries, were in a better position than the international judge to give an opinion on the exact content of the requirements of morals, as well as to the necessity of any restriction or penalty intended to meet those requirements. Thus, in that case the European Court upheld the prosecution of the applicant for obscenity for distributing a publication that was freely available in most other parts of Europe, holding that the prosecution was both necessary and proportionate. The case shows the reluctance of the Court to interfere in the area of public morality when the domestic decision is at least sustainable on legitimate grounds.[142] It also displays a propensity on behalf of the Court to defer to the member state on social issues, which it feels are better determined by the domestic authorities.[143]

The Court has given a very much narrower margin of appreciation where the restriction in question impinges on the enjoyment of the individual's right to *private* life, as opposed to the control of information disseminated to the public. This approach seeks to protect minorities from the will of the majority and in such cases the Court requires strong evidence in order to justify a violation of the applicant's Convention rights. For example, in *Dudgeon* v *United Kingdom*[144] the European Court held that as the prohibition on homosexual acts concerned a most intimate aspect of private life, accordingly there had to exist particularly serious reasons before interference on the part of public authorities could be legitimate under Article 8(2) of the Convention. The Court needed to be satisfied not only that the overriding majority of society would object, on bona fide and moral grounds, to a change in the law, but also that such a change would seriously injure the moral standards of the community. Similarly in *Smith and Grady* v *United Kingdom*,[145] it held that a restriction placed on homosexuals from remaining in the armed forces was not necessary for the purpose of achieving national security and public order. The negative attitudes of heterosexuals towards homosexuals could not, of themselves, justify the interferences in question. The European Court is, however, prepared to allow some margin to member states in the control of private life.[146]

---

[142] See Nowlin, The Protection of Morals under the European Convention for the Protection of Human Rights and Fundamental Freedoms (2002) *Human Rights Quarterly* 264.

[143] See also *Müller* v *Switzerland* (1988) 13 EHRR 212; *Marlow* v *United Kingdom*, decision of the European Court, 5 December 2000 (Application No 42015/98). A similarly wide margin of appreciation has been applied in the area of blasphemy and free speech: see *Otto-Preminger Institute* v *Austria* (1994) 19 EHRR 34; *Wingrove* v *United Kingdom* (1996) 24 EHRR 1. Note the margin will be narrower if the indecent material amounts to political satire: *Kunstler* v *Austria* (2008) 47 EHRR 5.

[144] (1982) 4 EHRR 149. See also *Modinos* v *Cyprus* (1993) 16 EHRR 485.

[145] (2000) 29 EHRR 493.

[146] See, for example, the case of *Laskey, Jaggard and Brown* v *United Kingdom* (1997) 24 EHRR 39 on the liability of individuals for taking part in consensual sado-masochistic sexual acts. See also *KA and AD* v *Belgium* (Application No 45558/99), decision of the European Court of Human Rights, 17 February 2005. Contrast *ADT* v *United Kingdom* (2001) 31 EHRR 33, where the European Court held that the conviction of the applicants for gross indecency for taking part in group homosexual activity was disproportionate and thus contrary to Articles 8 and 14 of the Convention.

The Court's margin of appreciation is, of course, subject to change if it is satisfied that there has, since its earlier case law, been a change of attitude in European society with respect to a particular issue, or if the Court believes that the balance between rights and the interests of the state need redressing. For example, the European Court now applies a relatively narrow margin of appreciation in relation to the treatment of transsexuals,[147] whereas previously it had taken a hands-off approach.[148] Further, even in cases where it would normally allow a wide margin of appreciation, it has not allowed the member state a complete discretion when domestic law interferes with the essence of a Convention right, particularly where the state has not considered the appropriate balance between rights and the respective legitimate aim.[149]

The Court has been prepared to take a robust supervisory approach, and thus to give only a narrow margin of error to the member state, in the area of press freedom. The Court regards the concept of free speech and press freedom as fundamental to the operation of any democratic state and is prepared to apply the doctrine of proportionality to its fullest extent. In *Sunday Times* v *United Kingdom*,[150] the Court accepted that the laws protecting the administration of justice from unreasonable interference, unlike domestic laws of obscenity and indecency which would inevitably vary from state to state, displayed a much more common approach, allowing the Court to more easily judge the necessity of any particular interference. In such a case a more extensive European supervision corresponds to a less discretionary power of appreciation. It was also clear from that case that the Court regarded the duty of the press to inform the public on matters of great public interest as essential to the operation of any democratic society. Thus, in that case the Court was prepared to submit the law and the measure in question to the utmost scrutiny in a desire to ensure that the press was free from all but the most necessary restrictions.

Questions

What role does the 'margin of appreciation' play in the jurisprudence of the Convention? Do you agree that it is a necessary aspect of the European Court's role in resolving human rights disputes?

CASE STUDY

Handyside v *United Kingdom* (1976) 1 EHRR 737

This case concerned the compatibility with Article 10 of the European Convention on Human Rights of the applicant's prosecution and conviction under the Obscene Publications Act 1959. The European Court of Human Rights had to decide whether the action taken against the applicant constituted a justifiable interference with his freedom ➡

---

[147] See *Goodwin* v *United Kingdom* (2002) 35 EHRR 18.

[148] *Rees* v *United Kingdom* (1986) 9 EHRR 56; *Cossey* v *United Kingdom* (1990) 13 EHRR 622; *X, Y and Z* v *United Kingdom* (1997) 24 EHRR 143; *Sheffield and Horsham* v *United Kingdom* (1998) 27 EHRR 163.

[149] See, for example, the Grand Chamber's decision in *Hirst* v *United Kingdom (No 2)* (2006) 42 EHRR 41, where the European Court held that the failure of parliament to address the question of the extent to which prisoners should forgo their right to vote fell outside the state's margin of appreciation.

[150] (1979) 2 EHRR 245.

of expression (and his right to peaceful enjoyment of possessions under Article 1 of the First Protocol), and in particular whether it was necessary in a democratic society. The case is a good example of the process of adjudication employed by the Court in the case of conditional rights. It is also instructive with regard to the role of the international court when reviewing the compatibility of domestic law and its application. The case illustrates the role of the 'margin of appreciation' in such a process and the Court's attempt to balance that concept with its role of ensuring that the fundamental rights laid down in the Convention are upheld by member states.

You can return to this case study when you acquire a more detailed knowledge of freedom of expression, covered in chapter 8, in particular when you study the domestic law relating to obscenity and indecency in that chapter.

The applicant owned the British publishing rights in the *Little Red Schoolbook*, a Danish publication that had been translated into several languages and sold in different countries. It was intended as a reference book on sexual matters and contained chapters on topics such as abortion, homosexuality, sexual intercourse and masturbation. Several hundred review copies were distributed and the book was advertised for sale at 30 pence. After several thousand copies had been sold in the United Kingdom, a number of complaints were received and the Metropolitan Police obtained a warrant to search the applicant's premises. A number of copies were seized during the search and the applicant was subsequently charged under s.1 of the Obscene Publications Act 1959 with having in his possession for gain several hundred copies of an obscene publication. He was fined £50 by the magistrates' court, and after his appeal to the Inner London Quarter Sessions was unsuccessful the remainder of the books were destroyed. Subsequent, unsuccessful, prosecutions were brought in Scotland, but no proceedings were brought in Northern Ireland, the Isle of Man or the Channel Islands, and the book circulated freely in most European countries. A revised edition of the book was allowed to circulate freely.

The applicant registered a complaint under the European Convention, claiming that the seizure and destruction of the books was contrary to his right of freedom of expression under Article 10, and of his right to peaceful enjoyment of possessions under Article 1 of the First Protocol. The European Commission declared the application admissible, deciding that the applicant had not failed to exhaust all effective domestic remedies by not appealing to a higher court against the decision of the Quarter Sessions. However, the Commission found no violation on the facts and referred the case to the European Court of Human Rights. The Court found that the applicant's criminal conviction and the seizure and destruction of the books was undoubtedly an interference with his Convention right to freedom of expression, thus constituting a violation unless falling within one of the exceptions provided by Article 10(2). It was also accepted by the Court, and by the applicant, that the interference was prescribed by law in that it had a legal basis in the Obscene Publications Acts 1959/1964 and that the Act had been correctly applied in the present case. The Court thus had to decide whether the interference was necessary in a democratic society for the purpose of achieving the legitimate aim of the protection of morals.

The Court found that the Act had the legitimate aim of the protection of morals in a democratic society. (The Court later rejected a claim that the book had been penalised purely for its anti-authoritarian views and that accordingly the restriction was not imposed for a legitimate purpose.) Accordingly, the question for the Court was whether the restriction was necessary in a democratic society for that legitimate purpose. In this respect the Court attempted to lay down the rules on determining whether an actual restriction or penalty was necessary in a democratic society. The majority of the European Commission of Human Rights was of the opinion that the Court need only ensure that the English Courts acted reasonably, in good faith and within the limits of the margin of appreciation left to the states, while the minority saw the Court's task as reviewing the publication directly in the light of the Convention and nothing but the Convention. The Court stressed that the machinery of protection established by the Convention was subsidiary to the national legal systems safeguarding human rights in that the Convention leaves to each contracting state, in the first place, the task of securing the rights and freedoms it enshrines. Thus, the Convention machinery only becomes involved through contentious proceedings and after all domestic remedies have been exhausted.

This, in the Court's opinion, applied notably to Article 10(2) of the Convention. In particular, it is not possible to find in the domestic law of the various states a uniform conception of morals; the view taken by their respective laws of the requirements of morals varies from time to time and from place to place, especially in our era that is characterised by a rapid and far-reaching evolution of opinions on the subject.

> By reason of their direct and continuous contact with the vital forces of their countries, state authorities are in principle in a better position than the international judge to give an opinion on the exact content of these requirements as well as the 'necessity' of a 'restriction' or 'penalty' intended to meet them. (para 48)

The Court then considered the meaning of the word 'necessary' in the context of Article 10(2). In the Court's view, while the word was not synonymous with 'indispensable', neither did it have the flexibility of such expressions as 'admissible', 'ordinary', 'useful', 'reasonable' or 'desirable'. Nevertheless, it is for the national authorities to make the initial assessment of the reality of the pressing social need implied by the notion of 'necessity' in this context. Consequently, Article 10(2) leaves to the contracting states a margin of appreciation, this margin being given both to the domestic legislator and to the bodies, judicial amongst others, that are called upon to interpret and apply the laws in force. Nevertheless, the Court noted that Article 10(2) does not give the state an unlimited power of appreciation. The Court is empowered to give the final ruling on whether a 'restriction' or 'penalty' is reconcilable with freedom of expression. Thus, the domestic margin of appreciation goes hand in hand with European supervision, such supervision concerning both the aim of the measure challenged and its necessity, and covering not only the basic legislation but also the decision applying it, even one given by an independent court.

The Court then turned its attention to the principles of a democratic society. In its view the Court was obliged to pay respect to the principles of such a society and noted that freedom of expression constituted one of the essential foundations of such a society, one of the basic conditions for its progress and for the development of every man. Subject to paragraph 2 of Article 10, it is applicable not only to information or ideas that are favourably received or regarded as inoffensive or as a matter of indifference, but also to those that offend, shock or disturb the state or any sector of the population. Such are the demands of pluralism, tolerance and broadmindedness without which there is no democratic 'society'. This, in the Court's view, means that every formality, condition, restriction or penalty imposed must be proportionate to the legitimate aim pursued. On the other hand, the Court noted that a person who exercises his freedom of expression undertakes 'duties and responsibilities', the scope of which depends on his situation and the technical means he uses. The Court must take this into account when deciding whether the 'restrictions' or 'penalties' were conducive to the 'protection of morals' which made them 'necessary' in a 'democratic society', and it is in no way the Court's task to take the place of the domestic courts, but rather to review under Article 10 the decisions they delivered in the exercise of their power of appreciation. The Court must decide whether the reasons given by the national authorities to justify the actual measures of 'interference' they take are relevant and sufficient under Article 10(2).

Having established the guidelines of its inquiry, the Court then considered the decision of the domestic court with regard to the publication. In this respect, the Court attached particular significance to the readership of the book, a factor that drew attention from the domestic court. The book was aimed at children and adolescents aged from 12 to 18. It was also direct, factual and reduced to essentials in style, making it easily within the comprehension of even the youngest of such readers. Although the book contained correct and useful factual information, it also included (particularly in the chapter on sex and in the passage 'Be yourself' in the chapter on pupils) sentences or paragraphs that young people at a critical stage of their development could have interpreted as an encouragement to indulge in precocious activities harmful to them or even to commit certain criminal offences. In these circumstances, despite the variety and constant evolution in the United Kingdom of views and ethics and education, the domestic judges were entitled, in the exercise of their discretion, to think at the relevant time that the publication would have pernicious effects on the morals of many of the children and adolescents who would read it.

Finally, the Court considered the measures in dispute. The applicant had argued that the failure to take legal action in other parts of the United Kingdom, that the book appeared and circulated freely in the majority of the member states of the Council of Europe, and that, even in Scotland and Wales, thousands of copies circulated without impediment despite the domestic court's ruling in 1971, showed that the judgment was not a response to a real necessity, even bearing in mind the national authorities' margin of appreciation. The Court, however, rejected those arguments. In particular, with regard to the practice of other states, it accepted that the contracting states had each fashioned their approach in the light of the situation obtaining in their respective territories, each having regard to the different views prevailing there about the demands of the protection of morals in a democratic society. The fact that most of them decided to allow the work to be distributed did not mean the contrary decision of the Quarter Sessions was in breach of Article 10. The Court also accepted that the failure to take proceedings in other parts of the United Kingdom did not call into question the necessity of the proceedings in England, and that the subsequent failure to prosecute the book was explainable on the grounds that by that time the book had been revised, in order to omit some of the more objectionable passages.

Questions

1 Why, given that the applicant had not appealed to the House of Lords, did the European Commission and Court of Human Rights accept that he had exhausted all effective domestic remedies?

2 What aspect of freedom of expression had been interfered with in this case? Is there any evidence from the judgment to suggest that the Court regarded this type of speech as less important than other expression, such as political speech?

3 Do you think that the protection of morals can be, and was in this case, a legitimate reason for restricting freedom of expression?

4 How did the European Court define the term 'necessary' when deciding whether the restriction was 'necessary in a democratic society'?

5 What did the Court identify as the necessary ingredients of a democratic society?

6 Why, in the Court's opinion, is it necessary to give the respondent state a margin of appreciation, and what sort of margin is available in cases of this type?

7 Do you think that the Court achieved a correct balance between protecting fundamental rights and preserving the state's right to protect public morals?

8 The case was decided in 1976. Having regard to changing moral values, the changing role of the European Court of Human Rights, and its subsequent case law, do you think that the case would be decided differently today?

Further restrictions on Convention rights

This section of the text examines those articles of the European Convention which allow further restrictions to be placed on the enjoyment of a person's Convention rights, including the powers of derogation (Article 15) and reservation (Article 57) and the restriction of the rights of aliens (Article 16) and those whose claims threaten the rights of others (Article 17).

Article 15 – Derogations in times of war or other public emergency

> In times of war or other public emergency threatening the life of the nation any High Contracting Party may take measures derogating from its obligations under this Convention to the extent strictly required by the exigencies of the situation, provided that such measures are not inconsistent with its other obligations under international law.

Article 15 of the Convention recognises that different considerations may apply to the safeguarding of human rights in times of war or other situations of emergency. It thus allows a member state to 'derogate' from its strict Convention obligations by, for example, passing provisions or taking action in order to deal with that emergency situation without breaching its obligations under the Convention. During such times there is often an increased threat to national security or territorial integrity, or to public safety, and in such situations it is common for a state to grant state authorities greater powers to arrest and detain individuals, to restrict free speech which might otherwise endanger national security or the successful prosecution of the war effort, to seize property or, more positively, to force individuals to comply with civic duties such as military conscription. All these measures will have an impact, or an increased impact, on the enjoyment of individual rights and liberties, and thus the obligations of the state under such treaties as the European Convention.[151]

Article 15 qualifies the right of derogation in several respects and any measures will need to be passed or carried out for a legitimate, and objectively justified, purpose and will also need to be reasonable and proportionate. First, a High Contracting Party can only take such measures as are strictly required by the exigencies of the situation. Not only does the Convention retain control over the member state during these times, deciding what measures are necessary, but by using the phrase *strictly* required, it also indicates that the measures must correspond to a very pressing social need and meet a strict test of proportionality. Thus, although the member state will be afforded quite a wide margin of error in such situations, Article 15 gives the Convention organs the right to monitor the emergency situation and to provide some objective review of the emergency and the measures necessary to deal with such. Secondly, the measures taken by the member state must not be inconsistent with its other obligations under international law. This provision strengthens the supervisory role of the Convention and makes it clear that any derogation must comply with other internationally accepted standards applying to war or other emergency situations.

Thirdly, Article 15 provides that no derogation is allowed in respect of certain Convention rights. Thus, no derogation is possible in relation to Article 2 (the right to life), (excluding deaths resulting from lawful acts of war), Article 3 (prohibition of torture, etc.), Article 4(1) (prohibition of slavery or servitude) or to Article 7 (prohibition of retrospective criminal law). This reflects the view that there are certain rights which should never be transgressed, whatever the circumstances or possible justification, and accordingly certain things which should never be carried out in the defence of the state and of social justice. Finally, Article 15 lays down a procedure that must be followed by a member state if it wishes to take advantage of its powers of derogation. Any High Contracting Party using the right of derogation must keep the Secretary-General of the Council of Europe informed of the measures which it has taken, along with the reasons thereof (the state must also inform the Secretary-General when such measures have ceased to operate and that the provisions of the Convention are being fully executed).

Both the European Court and Commission of Human Rights have considered Article 15 in a number of cases. In the early case of *Lawless v Ireland (No 3)*,[152] although the Court found that the detention of the applicant without trial for a period of five months was in violation of Article 5(3) of the Convention, it held that the Irish government was entitled to derogate from its obligations by virtue of the existence of a public emergency. The Court stressed that the measures governments can take when derogating are strictly limited to what is required by the exigencies of the situation and must not be in conflict with other international law obligations. However, the Court was satisfied that those strict limitations were met in the present case. The Court held that the respondent government should be afforded a certain margin of error or appreciation in deciding what measures were required by the situation,

---

[151] For a detailed analysis on Article 15 and terrorism law, see Warbrick, The Principles of the European Convention on Human Rights and the Response of States to Terrorism [2002] EHRLR 287. See also Allain, Derogation from the European Convention of Human Rights in the Light of 'Other Obligations in International Law' [2005] EHRLR 490; Walker, Prisoners of 'War all the Time' [2005] EHRLR 50.

[152] (1961) 1 EHRR 15.

and it was not the Court's function to substitute for the government's assessment any other assessment of what might be the most prudent or most expedient policy to combat terrorism.[153] Moreover, the Court must arrive at its decision in the light of the conditions that existed at the time that the original decision was taken, rather than reviewing the matter retrospectively.

The legality of derogation measures was considered in the case of *Brannigan and McBride v United Kingdom*,[154] concerning the United Kingdom's derogation in relation to Article 5 following the European Court's decision in *Brogan v United Kingdom*.[155] In *Brogan* the European Court held that the detention provisions contained in the Prevention of Terrorism Act 1978 were in contravention of Article 5(3) of the Convention, which guarantees the right of detained persons to be brought promptly before a judge or other officer. The government then lodged a derogation in respect of Article 5(3), claiming that the emergency position in Northern Ireland justified such derogation. This derogation was challenged in *Brannigan and McBride*, but the European Court held that it was justified, even though the derogation had not been lodged before the Court's decision in *Brogan*. The Court accepted the government's contention that there was an emergency situation, and held that the derogation was not invalid merely because the government had decided to keep open the possibility of finding a means in the future of ensuring greater conformity with Convention obligations. The Court was also satisfied that there were effective safeguards such as the availability of *habeas corpus* to safeguard against arbitrary action. The derogation was withdrawn by the United Kingdom government in 2001 when the Terrorism Act 2000 was passed,[156] but another derogation was lodged by the government in respect of Article 5(1)(f) of the Convention and the deportation of terrorist suspects.[157]

Article 57 – The power to make reservations

In addition to the right of derogation under Article 15, Article 57 of the Convention allows a state to make reservations to particular provisions of the Convention when it is ratifying the Convention. This reservation must be in relation to laws which exist at the time of ratification of the Convention and which are not at that time in conformity with the particular provision. Article 57 does not allow reservations of a general character, and any reservation shall contain a brief statement of the law concerned. The right to make reservations under an international treaty is quite common and accommodates the position where the enforcement of some rights, or their enforcement to a particular degree, would be in conflict with that state's cultural or social values. Although the Convention contains no formal control mechanism

---

[153] In *A v Secretary of State for the Home Department* [2005] 2 AC 68, the majority of the House of Lords appeared to draw a distinction between the question of whether there was a public emergency (primarily a political question for politicians to decide) and whether the measures were proportionate (primarily a legal question for the courts to determine). The case is discussed fully in chapters 6, 7 and 14 of this text.

[154] (1993) 17 EHRR 539.

[155] (1989) 11 EHRR 117.

[156] This was achieved by the Human Rights Act (Amendment) Order (2001) SI 2001/1216.

[157] The Human Rights Act (Designated Derogation) Order (2001) SI 2001/3644. This derogation was placed to accommodate provisions of the Anti-Terrorism, Crime and Security Act 2001 and was successfully challenged in *A v Secretary of State for the Home Department*, n 153, above, and in *A v United Kingdom* (2009) 49 EHRR 29. The case is explored in chapters 3, 6 and 14 of this text.

of this power of reservation, because reservations are made at the time of ratification, the Council of Europe will have the ultimate say on whether a state is allowed to ratify and thus unreasonable reservations can be controlled at that stage.

The United Kingdom made a reservation with regard to Article 2 of the First Protocol to the Convention, which states that no person shall be denied the right to education and which imposes a duty on each state to respect the rights of parents to ensure education and teaching in conformity with their own religious and philosophical convictions. When ratifying the Convention the United Kingdom government made a reservation in respect of this Article which states that the duty to ensure teaching in conformity with religious and philosophical convictions is accepted only so far as it is compatible with the provision of efficient instruction and training and the avoidance of unreasonable public expenditure.[158]

Article 16 – Restrictions on the political activity of aliens

Nothing in Articles 10, 11 and 14 shall be regarded as preventing the High Contracting Parties from imposing restrictions on the political activity of aliens.

Article 16 of the Convention seeks to restrict the rights of political aliens to enjoy their rights of freedom of expression, freedom of association and peaceful assembly. It seeks to justify, on grounds of national security and territorial integrity, a lesser protection of those rights in relation to an alien's political activities. The article also allows restrictions to be placed on the right of freedom from discrimination in the enjoyment of their Convention rights under Article 14. However, this only applies in relation to the political activity of such persons, leaving unaffected their other Convention rights, such as the right to life, freedom from torture, liberty and security of the person and the right to a fair trial where this does not involve the political activity of such persons.

The provision has been interpreted quite restrictively,[159] and the Council of Europe has called for its abolition.[160] Further, at the domestic level, in *R* v *Secretary of State for the Home Department, ex parte Farrakhan*,[161] the Court of Appeal held that Article 16 was not engaged where a person was refused entry into the country in order to prevent him from exercising his right to free speech, and the government would need to rely on the restrictions in Article 10(2) of the Convention. In the Court's view, Article 16 only applies where entry is refused, or the person is expelled, for reasons wholly independent of the exercise by the alien of Convention rights, even where the consequence is that such rights will be curtailed. In any case, it exists independently of the member state's right to take such action to protect itself and its citizens on grounds such as national security. Thus, the Court may widen the margin of appreciation given to states when dealing with matters such as the deportation of persons on the grounds of public good, provided such person's basic rights are not violated.[162]

---

[158] This reservation is contained in Schedule 3 of the Human Rights Act 1998.
[159] *Piermont* v *France* (1995) 20 EHRR 301.
[160] Recommendation No 799, 25 January 1977.
[161] [2002] 3 WLR 481.
[162] See, for example, *Chahal* v *United Kingdom* (1997) 23 EHRR 413.

Article 17 – Prohibition on the abuse of rights

Nothing in this Convention shall be interpreted as implying for any state, group or person any right to engage in any activity or perform any act aimed at the destruction of any of the rights and freedoms set forth herein or at their limitation to a greater extent than is provided for in the Convention.

Although many Convention breaches can be justified provided they meet the requirements of legality and necessity laid out in the Convention and the relevant case law, Article 17 goes further in excluding the enjoyment of Convention rights by those whose activities destroy the Convention rights and freedoms of others. In most cases the breach of the applicant's right can be justified within the other provisions of the Convention, such as Article 10(2). Article 17, therefore, operates to disqualify the applicant from even relying on the Convention right, allowing the Court to dispense with the case on the grounds that the claim is inconsistent with the terms of the Convention.

The provision is aimed particularly at extremist groups, whose primary agenda is the destruction or denial of the human rights and fundamental freedoms of others. For example, groups with a racist agenda, who take action for the sole purpose of undermining and destroying the rights of others, will fall outside the Convention's protection as that body's activities are considered to be inconsistent with the spirit of the Convention. In *Glimerveen and Hagenbeek v Netherlands*[163] the European Commission applied Article 17 in a case where the applicants had been prosecuted for the possession of leaflets likely to cause racial hatred, and had further been excluded from local elections. Hence, the applicants' claims that those measures violated their right to free speech and the state's duty to hold free elections were declared inadmissible.

Article 17 is, however, subject to limitations. It only applies to activities that threaten the enjoyment of others' Convention rights. Thus, the article does not apply to take away rights that do not impinge on others' rights, such as the right to a fair trial or liberty and security of the person.[164] In addition, any measures taken under Article 17 must be proportionate to the threat to the rights of others.[165] In the light of these restrictions, most cases will be decided on the basis of whether the restriction was in accordance with the justifiable restrictions laid down in provisions such as Articles 8–11.[166] Otherwise, Article 17 might be used to disqualify certain actions or bodies by reference only to the unacceptability of that body's political or other ideals, thus sidestepping questions regarding the legitimacy and reasonableness of the particular measure. Article 17 will, thus, be reserved for those rare cases where the person or group has resorted to acts of violence or clear racial hatred. This approach is supported by Article 18 of the Convention, which provides that the restrictions permitted under this Convention to the said rights and freedoms shall not be applied for any purpose other than those for which they have been prescribed. This provision stops the imposition of restrictions on the enjoyment of Convention rights when such restrictions cannot be justified either

---

[163] (1979) 18 DR 187.

[164] *Lawless v Ireland* (1960) 1 EHRR 1.

[165] *Lehideux and Irsoni v France* (2000) 30 EHRR 665, decision of the European Court, 23 September 1998. In this case the court held that the expression of ideas did not constitute an 'activity' within the meaning of Article 17.

[166] See, for example, *United Communist Party of Turkey v Turkey* (1998) 26 EHRR 121.

under provisions such as Article 10(2) or in cases where the exclusion of the right is justified under provisions such as Articles 15–17.

Nevertheless, Article 17 was used in conjunction with Article 10(2) of the Convention to restrict racially offensive speech in the case of *Norwood* v *United Kingdom*.[167] In this case the applicant had been convicted of a racially aggravated public order offence when he had displayed a banner proclaiming 'Islam out of Britain'.[168] The European Court declared his application inadmissible because the expression fell within Article 17. In the Court's view a general and vehement attack against a religious group was incompatible with the values of the Convention. The decision could be criticised on the basis that it allows the Court to sidestep the requirements of legality and necessity in Article 10(2) and that it instead prohibits speech of a particular nature. However, provided the Court examines Article 17 claims in the light of those requirements, Article 17 can be justified in prohibiting pure hate speech that is damaging to both individual rights and democratic values.[169]

Questions

What purpose is served in allowing a state to derogate from its obligations or to make reservations under the Convention? Are those powers destructive of the values of the Convention? What purpose does Article 17 of the Convention serve with respect to upholding the values of the Convention?

The Convention rights

The substantive rights guaranteed under the European Convention are contained in Section 1 of the Convention, Articles 2–18. This section of the Convention also guarantees an effective remedy in relation to enforcement of those rights and provides the right to enjoy those rights free from discrimination. These rights are also supplemented by subsequent protocols, which contain additional rights such as the right to education and the enjoyment of property. This part of the Convention also permits restrictions on the enjoyment of Convention rights in certain circumstances, such as war or other public emergency (Article 15), and Article 17 provides that the rights under the Convention cannot be used for the destruction of other people's rights under the Convention (see above).

Absolute and conditional rights

Some of the rights under the European Convention and its protocols are referred to as absolute rights, whereas others are referred to as conditional. This distinction is based on two factors. First, certain rights under the Convention are regarded as so fundamental that they are not capable of being derogated from, even in situations of war or other public emergency, as provided in Article 15. For example, Article 3, prohibiting torture and other forms of

---

[167] (2005) 40 EHRRR SE 11.

[168] *Norwood* v *DPP*, *The Times*, 30 July 2003.

[169] See Geddis, Free Speech Martyrs or Unreasonable Threats to Social Peace: 'Insulting' Expression and Section 5 of the Public Order Act 1986 [2003] PL 853.

ill-treatment, cannot be violated by a member state under any circumstances. Similarly the rights contained under Article 2 – the right to life (although Article 15 makes an exception for deaths resulting from lawful acts of war), Article 4(1) – freedom from slavery, and Article 7 – prohibition of retrospective criminal law, are similarly excluded from Article 15, thus attaining an absolute status under the Convention.[170]

Secondly, and more generally, the Convention makes the distinction between absolute and conditional rights in relation to whether that right can be interfered with in normal circumstances. In this sense some of the Convention rights, including the right not to be subject to torture or other ill-treatment, are regarded as absolute, while rights such as freedom of speech and the right to private life are expressly subject to restrictions, allowing the state to interfere with those rights within certain limits. Thus, in the case of Article 3, once it has been established that a violation has taken place, there can be no justification for that violation. In comparison, once it is established that a person's freedom of expression has been violated under Article 10, a member state may justify that violation by proving that the restriction was prescribed by law and was necessary for the purpose of achieving a legitimate aim, such as public morality. Freedom of expression is, therefore, a *conditional* right: it is not to be enjoyed absolutely in every situation and has to be balanced against other interests.

This distinction between absolute and conditional rights determines the role of the European Court of Human Rights, which is primarily to interpret and apply the terms of the Convention. In the case of an absolute right, such as freedom from torture under Article 3, the Court's role is to interpret the term 'torture' and then to decide whether the particular case before it reveals a violation of that term. Once that function is performed there is no further inquiry into possible justifications for that act, the right is absolute and the Court's finding determines the case.[171] In the case of conditional rights, however, the Court must first determine whether there has been a violation of that right on the facts. This will involve the Court in determining the meaning and scope of particular terms in the relevant article, such as 'private life' or 'expression'. The Court must then determine whether there has been a violation of that right on the facts, for example whether the applicant's freedom of speech was interfered with in that case. Once the Court determines that there has been a *prima facie* violation, it must then consider whether that violation can be justified within the exceptions allowed under the Convention: whether the interference was prescribed by law, whether it pursued one of the legitimate aims laid down in the Convention, and whether the interference was necessary in a democratic society. Thus, the Court seeks to perform some sort of balancing act between that right and other rights or interests with which the Convention right appears to conflict.[172]

There are also rights which appear to be absolute but which have been interpreted either to include implied exceptions or to be subject to legitimate and necessary restrictions. For example, Article 14, which provides that no one shall be subject to discrimination in the

---

[170] That is absolute in the sense of the right being non-derogable. Both Articles 2 and 7 contain express limitations making the right not absolute in every sense.

[171] It is, however, argued that the European Court employs the principles of necessity and proportionality in the *interpretation* of the terms employed in Article 3. See Palmer, A Wrong Turning: Article 3 ECHR and Proportionality [2006] CLJ 438.

[172] In such a case the Court is concerned not with a choice between two conflicting principles, but with a principle of freedom of expression subject to a number of exceptions which must be narrowly construed: *Sunday Times v United Kingdom* (1979) 2 EHRR 245.

enjoyment of their Convention rights, has been interpreted to allow rules or practices of discrimination that have a reasonable and objective justification, and which are legitimate and proportionate according to the tests applied to interferences with conditional rights such as freedom of expression.[173] Similarly, some Convention rights appear to allow a member state an unlimited discretion to exclude persons from the enjoyment of their Convention rights, yet the European Court has insisted that they must only be applied to a degree that does not destroy the essence of that right, and in accordance with principles of proportionality. For example, although the right to marry in Article 12 is stated to be dependent on national laws governing the exercise of that right, any limitations must not destroy the essence of the right to marry.[174]

Article 2 – The right to life[175]

> Everyone's right to life should be protected by law. No one shall be deprived of his life intentionally save in the execution of a sentence of a court following his conviction of a crime for which the penalty is provided by law.

Article 2 of the Convention protects the most fundamental of human rights, the right to life.[176] The right cannot be derogated from even in times of war and other public emergency, except in respect of deaths resulting from lawful acts of war, but under Article 2(2) the taking of a person's life can be justified when it results from the use of force, which is no more than absolutely necessary, in order, for example, to effect a lawful arrest. Article 2 applies to deliberate and disproportionate acts committed by state officials,[177] the acts of private individuals, which the state authorities should have prevented,[178] and the deliberate acts of the victim.[179] It also imposes a duty on every member state to carry out a proper investigation into any deaths that have occurred within its jurisdiction.[180]

The death penalty is expressly provided for in the first sentence of Article 2, although optional Protocol No 6 of the European Convention provides that the death penalty shall be abolished and that no one shall be condemned to such penalty or executed, and Protocol No 13, abolishes the death penalty in all circumstances. Both protocols have been ratified by the United Kingdom. In addition, it is has now been held that the death penalty is contrary to Article 3 of the Convention, prohibiting inhuman treatment.[181]

---

[173] *Geillustreerde Pers NV* v *Netherlands* (1977) DR 8. See Livingstone, Article 14 and the Prevention of Discrimination in the ECHR [1997] EHRLR 25.

[174] See, for example, *Hamer* v *United Kingdom* (1979) 24 DR 5 – a prohibition on convicted prisoners marrying while in prison was contrary to the right to marry under Article 12. See also *B and L* v *United Kingdom* (2006) 42 EHRR 11, dealt with in chapter 12.

[175] This right is examined in detail in chapter 4 of this text.

[176] In *Pretty* v *United Kingdom* (2002) 35 EHRR 1, it was held that the right to life under Article 2 did not guarantee the right to die, and in *Vo* v *France* (2005) 40 EHRR 12 it was held that Article 2 did not guarantee the right to life of the unborn child.

[177] *McCann* v *United Kingdom* (1995) 21 EHRR 97.

[178] *Osman* v *United Kingdom* (2000) 29 EHRR 245.

[179] *Keenan* v *United Kingdom* (2001) 33 EHRR 38.

[180] *Jordan and Others* v *United Kingdom* (2003) 37 EHRR 2.

[181] *Al-Saadoon and Mufdhi* v *United Kingdom* (2010) 51 EHRR 9, re-considering the previous judgment in *Ocalan* v *Turkey* (2005) 45 EHRR 1. The case will be dealt with in detail in chapters 4, 5 and 14 of the text.

Article 3 – Freedom from torture and inhuman and degrading treatment and punishment[182]

No one shall be subject to torture or to inhuman or degrading treatment or punishment.

This right is absolute in the sense that it admits of no exceptions or reservations once the Court is satisfied that the minimum level of severity to find a violation has been reached on the facts. The role of the European Court is simply to define the terms 'torture' and 'inhuman and degrading treatment or punishment' to see what type and level of treatment is capable of falling within their scope and then decide whether a violation has taken place.[183]

Article 3 imposes on each member state a positive obligation to ensure that a person does not suffer ill-treatment at the hands of others, including private individuals,[184] and state officers who are responsible for the care of individual persons, such as social workers.[185] A member state can also be responsible for the violations committed by another state, if they deport or extradite individuals when there is a sufficient risk of harm.[186]

Article 4 – Prohibition of slavery and forced labour

No one shall be held in slavery or servitude. No one shall be required to perform forced or compulsory labour.

Article 4(1) prohibits slavery and servitude in absolute terms and no derogation is allowed of this aspect of Article 4, even in times of war or other public emergency. Slavery and servitude refers to the civil status of a person and denotes total ownership at the hands of the state, whereas forced and compulsory labour is concerned with (usually temporary) work done under threat of some form of penalty. In this respect it has been held that the work in question must be done against the will of the person and that the work to be performed is unjust or oppressive or involves avoidable hardship.[187] This aspect of Article 4 can be derogated from under Article 15 and is also subject to a number of exceptions listed in Article 4(3), which can apply in peacetime. For example, the phrase 'forced or compulsory labour' is stated not to include work required to be done in the ordinary course of detention imposed according to the provisions of Article 5 of the Convention or during conditional release from such detention. Thus, work done in the ordinary course of a prison sentence would not normally amount to a violation of Article 4, and it has been held that such work must be aimed at the rehabilitation of the prisoner.[188] Also, such work must not contravene Article 3 of the Convention.

Article 4(3) also excludes any service of a military character, or in the case of conscientious objectors in countries where they are recognised, service exacted instead of such military service. Thus there is no right to conscientious objection, and in *Johansen v Norway*[189] the

---

[182] Examined in detail in chapter 5 and, with respect to prisoners' rights, in chapter 8.

[183] The terms employed in Article 3 were explored in *Ireland v United Kingdom* (1978) 2 EHRR 25.

[184] *A v United Kingdom* (1999) 27 EHRR 611.

[185] *Z v United Kingdom* (2002) 34 EHRR 3.

[186] *Soering v United Kingdom* (1989) 11 EHRR 439.

[187] In *X v FRG* (1974) 46 CD 22, the Commission held that a lawyer could not complain of having to act as unpaid or poorly paid defence counsel as he had entered the legal profession knowing that he might have such an obligation.

[188] *De Wilde, Ooms and Versyp v Belgium* (1971) 1 EHRR 373.

[189] (1985) 44 DR 155.

European Commission not only upheld the validity of compulsory military service but also held that the exception would, by implication, preclude any claim under Article 9 of the Convention.[190] The state is also provided with discretion whether to recognise conscientious objectors and, at its discretion, to provide alternative compulsory service in lieu of that of a military nature.

Most of the case law has emanated from the other exceptions listed in Article 4(3): service exacted in the case of an emergency or calamity threatening the life or well-being of the community,[191] and any work or service which forms part of normal civic obligations. With regard to the latter exception, the Court and Commission have offered a wide margin of appreciation to each state and have required strong evidence of unjust and arbitrary work conditions. For example, in *Van der Mussele v Belgium*[192] it was held that there was no violation of Article 4 when a lawyer was ordered to provide *pro bono* services to some of his clients. Although the Court recognised that the fact that he was aware of such an obligation was not conclusive, it also noted that the obligation involved a relatively short period of time and facilitated an individual's right to a fair trial as guaranteed by Article 6 of the Convention.

The meaning and application of Article 4 in the context of 'domestic slavery' was considered recently by the European Court in *Siliadin v France*.[193] The applicant, a young Togolese national, had been brought to France by D and had been used as an unpaid help for four years, first by D and her husband and then by another couple (B) who were friends of D. The applicant became a 'maid of all work' to the couple, who made her work every day, only giving her special permission to go to mass on certain Sundays. She slept in the children's bedroom on a mattress on the floor and wore old clothes. During this time she was never paid, although she did receive one or two 500-franc notes from Mrs B's mother. Criminal proceedings were brought against Mr and Mrs B, but they were acquitted on appeal. The Versailles Court of Appeal considered the case with respect to civil liability and found them guilty of making a vulnerable and dependent person work unpaid for them, but considered that her working and living conditions were not incompatible with human dignity. It ordered them to pay the applicant the equivalent of €15,245 in damages.

The applicant claimed a violation of Article 4 and the European Court held that her treatment did not amount to 'slavery' under Article 4 because although she had lost her autonomy there was insufficient evidence that her 'employers' had exercised a genuine right of ownership over her. However, the Court found that she had been held in servitude as she was as an unofficial immigrant and thus vulnerable and isolated and entirely dependent on her employers for all assistance. The Court also held that the failure of domestic law to create a specific criminal offence against slavery and the failure to secure a criminal conviction against her abusers for wrongfully using the services of a dependent person, meant that the state were in violation of their positive duty to ensure that individuals were not subject to treatment in violation of Article 4.

---

[190] See Gilbert, The Slow Development of the Right to Conscientious Objection to Military Service under the European Convention on Human Rights [2001] EHRLR 554. An individual might, in extreme cases, have a claim under Articles 3 or 8 of the Convention, or under Article 14.

[191] This phrase has been held to include a requirement to serve in the fire brigade or to pay a financial contribution in lieu of such service: *Schmidt v Germany* (1994) 18 EHRR 513. On the facts the Court held that there had been a violation of Article 14 of the Convention because the requirement applied only to men.

[192] (1983) 6 EHRR 163.

[193] (2006) 43 EHRR 15. See Cullen, Positive Obligations under Article 4 ECHR (2006) HRLR 585.

The case illustrates the possible liability of the state for modern practices of slavery and servitude, in that although the state might not specifically sanction such practices, its liability under Article 4 may be engaged if it either knowingly condones such practices, or fails to pass or enforce appropriate laws that provide appropriate safeguards or remedies to the individual victim.[194] It is interesting to note, therefore, that s.71 of the Coroners and Justice Act 2009, which came into effect on 6 April 2010, creates a new offence of holding someone in slavery or servitude, or requiring them to perform forced or compulsory labour.[195]

Article 5 – Liberty and security of the person[196]

Everyone has the right to liberty and security of the person.

Article 5 protects a person's liberty rather than the general right of freedom of movement, which is guaranteed by Article 2 of the Fourth Protocol.[197]

The basic right to liberty and security of the person is subject to a number of exceptions contained in Article 5(1)(a)–(f), although any interference must be 'in accordance with a procedure prescribed by law' and must safeguard against arbitrary arrest and detention. In addition, Article 5 provides that everyone who is arrested shall be informed properly, in a language which he understands, of the reasons for his arrest and of any charge against him; that everyone arrested or detained shall be brought promptly before a judge; that everyone deprived of their liberty by arrest or detention can take proceedings by which the lawfulness of their detention shall be decided speedily by a court; and that the victim of an arrest or detention in contravention of Article 5 shall have an enforceable right to compensation.

Article 6 – The right to a fair and public hearing[198]

In the determination of his civil rights and obligations or of any criminal charge against him, everyone is entitled to a fair and public hearing within a reasonable time by an independent and impartial tribunal established by law.

Article 6 guarantees the right to a hearing before an impartial and unbiased court or tribunal, the right of a person to be informed of any accusation made against them, and the right to present one's case, including the right to be presumed innocent of any criminal offence, the right to legal advice and the right to examine witnesses. It applies to all proceedings where either the applicant is facing a criminal charge, or where his or her 'civil rights and obligations' are subject to determination.

---

[194] Contrast *Tremblay v France* (Application No 37194/02), decision of the European Court, 11 September 2007, where it was held that there was no evidence to suggest that the state's insistence that the applicant pay family allowance contributions had forced her into a life of prostitution in breach of Articles 3 and 4 of the Convention.

[195] In addition, Parliament has passed the Anti-Slavery Day Act 2010, which introduces a national day to raise awareness of the need to eradicate all forms of slavery and human trafficking.

[196] See chapter 6 for a detailed analysis of the article.

[197] *Guzzardi v Italy* (1980) 3 EHRR 333. See also the House of Lords' decision in *Secretary of State for the Home Department v JJ* [2007] 3 WLR 642, and *Gillan v United Kingdom* (2010) 50 EHRR 45, both discussed in chapter 6.

[198] See chapter 7 of this text for a detailed examination of Articles 6 and 7.

The European Court has held that the right of access to the courts is implicit in the article,[199] and in *Airey v Ireland*[200] it held that the right of access may involve the provision by the state of positive facilities to allow effective access to legal redress. Article 6 also guarantees by implication the right to a fair sentence.[201]

In addition to the general right to a fair trial, contained in Article 6(1), Article 6(2) states that everyone charged with a criminal offence shall be presumed innocent until proved guilty according to law. There are further guarantees to be informed promptly, in a language which one understands and in detail, of the nature and cause of the accusation; to have adequate time and facilities for the preparation of one's defence; to defend oneself in person or through legal assistance (including the right to free representation when the interests of justice so require); and to examine, or have examined, witnesses and to obtain the attendance and examination of witnesses.

Article 7 – Prohibition of retrospective criminal law[202]

No one shall be held guilty of any criminal offence on account of any act or omission which did not constitute a criminal offence under national or international law at the time when it was committed. Nor shall a heavier penalty be imposed than the one that was applicable at the time that the criminal offence was committed.

Article 7 of the Convention upholds the basic principle of the rule of law that laws should be prospective rather than retrospective, and lays down two basic principles: that no one shall be guilty of an offence for an act which at the time of its commission was not an offence in domestic or international law; and that no one should be subjected to a heavier penalty than the one which existed at the time of the offence.

Article 7(2) states that the trial and punishment of a person for an act which at the time it was committed was criminal according to the general principles of law recognised by civilised nations will not be in violation of Article 7.

Article 8 – Right to private and family life[203]

Everyone has the right to respect for his private and family life, his home and his correspondence.

Article 8 includes the right to be free from unlawful and unreasonable interferences with the right to private and family life and the state may be responsible for providing the resources necessary for the enjoyment of these rights.[204] The European Court has also accepted that the state must ensure that an individual's Article 8 rights are not interfered with by private individuals.[205]

The Article covers a variety of private and family interests, including the right to respect for one's physical integrity, the right to one's own space, and the right to communicate private

[199] *Golder v United Kingdom* (1975) 1 EHRR 524.
[200] (1979) 2 EHRR 305.
[201] *V and T v United Kingdom* (1999) 30 EHRR 121.
[202] Covered in chapter 7 of this text, alongside the right to a fair trial under Article 6.
[203] The right to private and family life is examined in detail under chapter 11 of this text.
[204] *Marckx v Belgium* (1979) 2 EHRR 330.
[205] See *X and Y v Netherlands* (1985) 8 EHRR 235.

information with others. In addition it has been used to allow individuals to have access to personal information.[206] The right to private and family life also includes the right to a private sexual life, including the right to choose and practise one's sexual identity, and to forge relationships with others and to enjoy the benefits of family and home life. Article 8 is a conditional right and interferences with the exercise of the right by a public authority are permitted under Article 8(2) provided they are in accordance with law and necessary in a democratic society in pursuance of a number of listed legitimate aims.

Article 9 – Freedom of thought, conscience and religion[207]

> Everyone has the right to freedom of thought, conscience and religion; this right includes freedom to change his religion or belief and freedom, either alone or in community with others and in public or private, to manifest his religion or belief, in worship, teaching, practice and observance.

Article 9 supplements the rights to freedom of expression and association and protects an individual from persecution on grounds of his or her thoughts, beliefs or religion. Article 9 is not limited to religious beliefs or convictions,[208] but does not apply to every opinion and conviction of the individual.[209] The article also guarantees the right to manifest one's religion or beliefs, but this right is subject to limitations that are prescribed by law and necessary in a democratic society in the interests of public safety, for the protection of public order, health or morals, or for the protection of the rights and freedoms of others.[210]

Article 9 also imposes a positive obligation on the state to allow individuals the right to manifest and enjoy their beliefs peacefully and without undue interference.[211]

Article 10 – Freedom of expression[212]

> Everyone has the right to freedom of expression. This right shall include freedom to hold opinions and to receive and impart information and ideas without interference by public authority and regardless of frontiers.

Article 10 is concerned primarily with the right of the individual to be free from restrictions on their freedom of expression rather than the general right of freedom of information.[213] The European Court has stated that freedom of expression constitutes one of the essential foundations of a democratic society, and that Article 10 is applicable not only to information or ideas that are favourably received, but also to those that shock, offend or disturb.[214] However, it has placed special significance on public interest speech[215] and press freedom.[216]

---

[206] *Gaskin* v *United Kingdom* (1989) 12 EHRR 36.
[207] Covered in chapter 12 of this text.
[208] *Arrowsmith* v *United Kingdom* (1978) 3 EHRR 218.
[209] *Pretty* v *United Kingdom* (2002) 35 EHRR 1.
[210] *Sahin* v *Turkey* (2007) 44 EHRR 5.
[211] *Dubowska and Skup* v *Poland* (1997) 24 EHRR CD 75.
[212] Article 10 is examined in general under chapter 8 of this text and specifically in chapter 9, dealing with freedom of expression and press freedom.
[213] *Leander* v *Sweden* (1987) 9 EHRR 433.
[214] *Handyside* v *United Kingdom* (1976) 1 EHRR 737.
[215] *Sunday Times* v *United Kingdom* (1979) 2 EHRR 245.
[216] *Jersild* v *Denmark* (1994) 19 EHRR 1 and *Lingens* v *Austria* (1986) 8 EHRR 407.

Article 10 is a conditional right and paragraph 2 of Article 10 states that the exercise of the rights contained in paragraph 1 carry with it duties and responsibilities and are therefore subject to formalities, conditions, restrictions and penalties that are 'prescribed by law' and 'necessary in a democratic society' for the furtherance of a legitimate aim.

Article 11 – Freedom of assembly and association[217]

> Everyone has the right to freedom of peaceful assembly and to freedom of association with others, including the right to form and to join trade unions for the protection of his interests.

Article 11 protects two basic rights: freedom of association with others, including the right to join a trade union, and the right to peaceful assembly.

The right of association with others includes the right to form trade unions,[218] including the right to non-association.[219] However, the Court has confirmed that the inclusion of trade unions in Article 11 did not exclude political parties.[220] Article 11 also protects the right to peaceful assembly, which imposes a positive duty on every member state to ensure that everyone can enjoy the right of peaceful demonstration.[221]

Article 11 is a conditional right and restrictions may be placed on the exercise of those rights provided they are prescribed by law and necessary in a democratic society in the interests of national security or public safety, for the prevention of disorder or crime, for the protection of health or morals or for the protection of the rights and freedoms of others.

Article 12 – The right to marry

> Men and women of marriageable age have the right to marry and found a family, according to the national laws governing the exercise of that right.

Article 12 complements Article 8 of the Convention, guaranteeing the right to family and private life, by providing a right to marry and to found a family. The European Court has held that Article 12 does not guarantee the right to divorce;[222] although in *F v Switzerland*[223] it held that if national law *did* allow divorce, it must not place unreasonable restrictions on a person's right to remarry. Although traditionally the European Court and Commission had held that the right to marry applied only to persons of the opposite sex,[224] that position has been altered by more recent case law.[225]

Article 12 is a conditional right, although the European Court and Commission have interpreted Article 12 to mean that any restriction on the right to marry must not destroy the very essence of the right contained in the article.[226]

---

[217] Covered in chapter 10 of this text.
[218] *Swedish Engine Drivers' Union* v *Sweden* (1976) 1 EHRR 617. It also confers the right of that association to regulate its membership: *ASLEF* v *United Kingdom* (2007) 45 EHRR 34.
[219] *Young, James and Webster* v *United Kingdom* (1982) 4 EHRR 38.
[220] *United Communist Party of Turkey* v *Turkey* (1998) 26 EHRR 121.
[221] *Platform Ärzte für das Leben* v *Austria* (1991) 13 EHRR 204.
[222] *Johnston* v *Ireland* (1986) 9 EHRR 203.
[223] (1987) 10 EHRR 411.
[224] *Rees* v *United Kingdom* (1986) 9 EHRR 56.
[225] *Goodwin* v *United Kingdom* (2002) 35 EHRR 18.
[226] See *B and L* v *United Kingdom* (2006) 42 EHRR 11 and *F v Switzerland* (1987) 10 EHRR 411.

Article 13 – The right to an effective remedy

Everyone whose rights and freedoms as set forth in this Convention are violated shall have an effective remedy before a national authority notwithstanding that the violation has been committed by persons acting in an official capacity.

Article 13 complements Article 1, which places a duty on member states to secure the rights and freedoms laid down in the Convention, and thus insists that a person should enjoy such rights at domestic level.

Article 13 does not impose an obligation on the state to incorporate the Convention into domestic law provided an individual can enjoy the essence of those rights in domestic law.[227] Thus, there will be a violation of Article 13 if domestic law fails to recognise a particular Convention right,[228] and where a person's Convention rights have been violated they are entitled to receive compensation in appropriate cases.[229] A person should also be able to argue his or her case in accordance with Convention principles, including the right to argue that any interference was unnecessary or disproportionate.[230]

Article 14 – Prohibition of discrimination[231]

The enjoyment of the rights and freedoms set forth in this Convention shall be secured without discrimination on any ground such as sex, race, colour, language, religion, political or other opinion, national or social origin, association with a national minority, property, birth or other status.

Article 14 seeks to ensure that everyone enjoys the rights and freedoms laid down in the Convention and its protocols, irrespective of their sex, race or colour, etc. It does not provide a 'free-standing' right not to be discriminated against, and any complaint of discriminatory treatment under this article must be related to the alleged violation of another Convention right.[232] However, the Court may find a violation of a Convention right when that alleged violation is considered together with a violation of Article 14.[233] In addition, the optional Protocol No 12, not ratified by the United Kingdom, imposes a general prohibition on discrimination, thus establishing a general right of freedom from discrimination.

Article 14 is not an absolute right and in the *'Belgian Linguistic' case*[234] the European Court held that the principle of equality in Article 14 is only violated if the difference in treatment has no objective or reasonable justification.

---

[227] *Silver* v *United Kingdom* (1983) 5 EHRR 347. See Lewis, The European Ceiling on Human Rights [2007] PL 720.

[228] *Malone* v *United Kingdom* (1984) 7 EHRR 14.

[229] *Z* v *United Kingdom* (2002) 34 EHRR 3.

[230] *Smith and Grady* v *United Kingdom* (2000) 29 EHRR 493.

[231] Article 14 of the Convention is examined in chapter 13 on freedom from discrimination (pages 708–17).

[232] *Choudhury* v *United Kingdom* (1991) 12 HRLJ 172.

[233] *Abdulaziz Cabales and Balkandali* v *United Kingdom* (1985) 7 EHRR 471.

[234] (1968) 1 EHRR 252.

Additional protocols to the Convention

Article 1 of the First Protocol – Protection of property

> Every natural or legal person is entitled to the peaceful enjoyment of his possessions.

This article guarantees the right to peaceful enjoyment of possessions, which includes all property rights,[235] and states that no one shall be deprived of their possessions except in the public interest and subject to the conditions provided for by law and by the general principles of international law. The article states further that the right does not in any way impair the right of a state to enforce such laws as it deems necessary to control the use of property in accordance with the general interest or to secure the payment of taxes or other contributions or penalties.[236] The article is thus divided into three rules: the principle of peaceful enjoyment of property; the deprivation of possessions; and the right of states to control the use of property in the public interest. The article can also be used in conjunction with other Convention rights, such as the right to private and family life. Thus in *Gillow* v *United Kingdom*,[237] it was held that the law of Guernsey prohibiting the applicants from residing in their own house because they failed to satisfy residence criteria was a disproportionate interference with their right to private and family life.

The Article leaves a wide discretion to each member state to deprive a person of his right to his possessions, and to regulate the ownership and use of personal and real property, including the right to raise taxes. The Court has held that the state will be afforded a wide margin of appreciation in deciding what measures are necessary in the control of a person's possessions, particularly in the area of planning control.[238] This wide area of discretion in balancing the public and individual interests was evident in *James* v *United Kingdom*,[239] where it was held that the Leasehold Reform Act 1967, which forced landlords to sell the freehold of their properties or to extend current leases, was justified as being in the public interest. The Court found that the legislation had a legitimate aim and that the scheme itself, including the provision for compensation payable to the landlords, was within the wide margin of appreciation available to the state. The Court stressed that it would not interfere unless the judgment of the national parliament was manifestly without reasonable foundation in the enactment of the statute. Similarly, in *National and Provincial Building Society* v *United Kingdom*[240] it was held that retrospective legislation passed to validate tax regulations, allowing income tax to be collected in respect of the applicant's building society accounts, was not in violation of Article 1. There was an obvious and compelling public interest to ensure that private entities did not enjoy the benefit of a windfall created by a changeover to a new tax regime, and the applicants were aware of parliament's intention to legislate in this area.

---

[235] In *Nerva and Others* v *United Kingdom* (2003) 36 EHRR 4, it was held that waiters' tips came within the term 'possessions'.

[236] For an analysis of the case law under Article 1 of the First Protocol, see Mowbray, *Cases and Materials on the European Convention on Human Rights* (OUP 2007), chapter 16.

[237] (1987) 13 EHRR 593. Article 1 of the First Protocol could not be relied upon because Guernsey was not bound by that protocol.

[238] *Allan Jacobsson* v *Sweden* (1989) 12 EHRR 56.

[239] (1986) 6 EHRR 123.

[240] (1997) 25 EHRR 127.

However, the exercise of such powers must accord, at least to a reasonable degree, with the principles of legality and proportionality. For example, in *Sporrong and Lonnroth v Sweden*[241] it was held that the right to peaceful enjoyment of possessions requires the Court to strike a fair balance between the interests of the community in general and the protection of the individual's fundamental rights. In that case it was held that the expropriation of the applicants' property was in violation of Article 1 as the relevant expropriation laws were inflexible and did not take into account the fact that the applicants' permits to use the land had been in force for extremely long periods of time. Further, there should have been some provision for review of the permits at reasonable intervals.[242]

Further, if an individual's property rights are subject to interference under domestic law, that law should provide sufficient procedural safeguards against potential unfairness.[243] This issue has been the subject of recent litigation regarding the domestic laws of adverse possession and in *Pye (Oxford) Ltd v United Kingdom*[244] the European Court held that there had been a violation of Article 1 when landowners had lost possession of their land under the domestic rules on adverse possession, allowing a non-owner's rights to usurp those of the true owner after a period of undisputed possession.[245] In the Court's view the laws provided inadequate protection to the true owners, particularly as there was no statutory right for them to be notified of the possessor's intention to claim those rights.[246] However, on appeal that decision was overturned, the Grand Chamber concluding that the law did, in fact, provide sufficient protection to the original owner.[247] The Grand Chamber held that a rule preventing the owner from recovering possession of land could not be said to be manifestly without reasonable foundation. Further, the rules, including the limitation period, had been in force for many years and the owners were aware of them. The fact that no compensation was payable was understandable given the purpose of limitation periods and the law had struck a proper balance between the interests, particularly as the owners could take steps to stop the limitation period from running.

Article 2 – The right to education

No person shall be denied the right to education. In the exercise of any functions which it assumes in relation to education and to teaching, the State shall respect the right of parents to ensure such education and teaching in conformity with their own religious and philosophical convictions.

---

[241] (1982) 5 EHRR 35.

[242] See also *Edwards v Malta*, (Application No 17647/04), where the Court found a violation of Article 1 when the applicant's house and adjoining land had been requisitioned by the government 30 years ago to provide homes for the homeless and he had received the sum of €67 per year in compensation for the loss of his house. The Court concluded that the government had imposed an excessive burden on him to provide accommodation to another family and thus had not achieved a proper balance between the interests of the community and the applicant's right to profit from his property rights.

[243] In *Stretch v United Kingdom* (2004) 38 EHRR 12, the European Court found a violation of Article 1 when the applicant had been denied the option of a further term of 21 years under an existing lease. The refusal, by the local council, disrupted his legitimate expectation and thus was a disproportionate interference with his property rights.

[244] (2006) 43 EHRR 3.

[245] *JA Pye (Oxford) v Graham* [2003] 1 AC 419.

[246] The Land Registration Act 2002 rectified this discrepancy but did not provide protection to the applicants at the time of their dispute.

[247] (2008) 46 EHRR 45.

Under this Article everyone has the right to education, which has been interpreted to mean that individuals have the right to avail themselves of the means of instruction that are provided by the state at any given time.[248] Consequently, Article 2 simply imposes an obligation to regulate its educational system in such a way that it gives access to education without discrimination. For example, in *A v Essex County* Council,[249] the Supreme Court held that the article does not impose on the state a positive obligation to provide education that catered for the special needs of a small, but significant, portion of society which could not benefit from mainstream education. The question in such cases is whether the person has been denied the very essence of the right to education and in the present case a delay of 18 months in finding a suitable school for an autistic child after he had left a special needs school because of his behaviour did not constitute a breach of Article 2.

Further, in *X v United Kingdom*,[250] it was held that the state had the right to regulate scarce resources by restricting access to certain courses to the most able students. With respect to the United Kingdom, the government made a reservation in relation to this article, and the reservation is contained in Part II of Schedule 3 of the Human Rights Act 1998 by virtue of s.17 of the Act, which allows for such reservations. The reservation is in respect of the second sentence of the protocol – guaranteeing parents the right to have their children taught in conformity with their religious and philosophical convictions – and states that its obligations are restricted to the provision of efficient instruction and training and the avoidance of unreasonable public expenditure.

In addition, under Article 2 parents are given the limited right to insist that their children are taught in conformity with their religious and philosophical convictions, thus complementing the rights to private and family life under Article 8 and the right to manifest one's religion under Article 9.[251] The Article imposes a positive obligation to provide necessary educational resources, although the Court has decided that there is no obligation to establish or fund any particular type of educational institution.[252] The right of parents to have their children taught in conformity with their philosophical convictions was raised in *Campbell and Cosans v United Kingdom*.[253] Here it was held that the imposition of corporal punishment in a school attended by the applicant's children constituted a violation of Article 2 of the First Protocol in that it interfered with the parents' convictions on discipline, which the Court accepted as falling within the phrase 'philosophical convictions'.[254] In the Court's view the duty to respect parental convictions could not be overridden by the alleged necessity of striking a balance between the conflicting views involved and although the right to education guaranteed by Article 2 by its very nature calls for regulation by the state, such regulation

---

[248] *Belgian Linguistic case* (1968) 1 EHRR 252.

[249] [2010] 3 WLR 509.

[250] (1980) 23 DR 228.

[251] For example, in *R (Begum)* v *Governors of Denbigh High School* [2006] 2 WLR 719, it was alleged that the exclusion of the applicant for refusing to adhere to the school's dress code was in violation of both Article 9 and Article 2 of the First Protocol. Both claims failed and the case is discussed in chapter 12 of this text.

[252] *Belgian Linguistic case*, n 248, above.

[253] (1982) 4 EHRR 243.

[254] As a consequence of the Court's ruling the Education (No 2) Act 1986 was passed, prohibiting corporal punishment in state schools. The domestic courts have ruled that parents do not have the right under this Article to insist that their children *are* subject to reasonable physical punishment at school; see *R (Williamson)* v *Secretary of State for Education* [2003] 1 All ER 385.

should never injure the substance of the right or conflict with other rights in the Convention and its protocols.[255]

On the other hand, the right to education, including parental choice, might have to bow to wider issues of public interest and the rights of others. Thus, in *Sahin v Turkey*[256] it was held by the Grand Chamber that although the exclusion of the applicant from University for wearing religious dress did engage the right to education (disagreeing with the European Court's decision on this point), the rules did not destroy the very essence of the applicant's rights under that article, the rule balancing the rights of religious observance with the protection of secularism. Similarly, in *R (Begum) v Denbigh High School Governors*[257] it was held that a schoolchild who had been refused entry to school because of her unwillingness to comply with a dress code had not been denied the right to education under Article 2 of the First Protocol. The disruption to her schooling had been caused by her unwillingness to comply with a rule that the school was entitled to adhere to, and by her failure to secure prompt admission to another school where her religious convictions could be accommodated.

Article 3 – The right to free elections

> The High Contracting Parties undertake to hold free elections at reasonable intervals by secret ballot, under conditions which will ensure the free expression of the people in the choice of the legislature.

This Article imposes both a positive obligation on each member state to hold free elections, and a negative duty not to restrict such.[258] The article thus promotes democracy and complements other democratic rights such as freedom of speech and freedom of assembly.[259] Although the Article principally protects the collective right to free elections, the European Court has held that the article also bestows in general an individual right to vote. Thus, in *Mathieu-Mohin and Clerfayt v Belgium*[260] it was held that the article implied both the right to vote and the right to stand for election to the legislature.[261] In that case the applicants were French-speaking Belgian parliamentarians who lived in a Flemish district of Brussels and who under the devolved linguistic constitutional arrangements in Belgium were unable to participate in the decision making of the Flemish Council. The European Court held that the claim fell within the scope of the Article but found that the restrictions fell within the wide margin of appreciation afforded to each state.

In *Mathieu-Mohin* it was accepted that the right to vote and stand for election was subject to implied limitations and that the domestic authorities could impose restrictions provided they were legitimate and proportionate and that the very essence of the duty to ensure free

---

[255] See also *Folgero v Norway* (2008) 46 EHRR 47, discussed in chapter 11 of this text.

[256] (2007) 44 EHRR 5.

[257] [2007] 1 AC 100.

[258] The article does not impose an obligation on the state to adopt a particular type of electoral system, provided the adopted system complies with the essence of the article; see *Liberal Party v United Kingdom* (1980) 21 DR 211.

[259] See, for example, the case of *Bowman v United Kingdom* (1998) 26 EHRR 1.

[260] (1987) 10 EHRR 1.

[261] In *Ahmed v United Kingdom* [1999] IRLR 188, the European Court did not address the question of whether local elections came within the scope of the article. In that case the Court found no violation of Article 10 when local government officials were prohibited from standing for election. See also *Gitonas v Greece* (1997) 26 EHRR 691, where the Court upheld the three-year prohibition on former public servants standing for election to the Greek parliament.

elections is not undermined. Accordingly, the Court and Commission have given a wide margin of appreciation in this area, reflecting the variety of state practices within the Council of Europe.[262] For example, in *Py* v *France*,[263] it was held that there had been no violation when the applicant had been denied the right to participate in referendums and elections in New Caledonia because he failed to comply with a 10-year residency requirement. In the Court's view the 'local requirements' applying to New Caledonia warranted such restrictions.

A similar margin can be granted with respect to the right to sit in parliament. Thus in *Yumak and Sadak* v *Turkey*,[264] the Grand Chamber held that a requirement that a party may not obtain seats in parliament unless they obtained 10 per cent of the vote in elections was within the state's margin of appreciation and thus not in violation of Article 3 of the first protocol. The requirement ensured non-fragmentation in parliament and was consistent with that state's party system. In the Grand Chamber's view, provided that elections were held freely and at regular intervals there was no obligation to ensure specific systems such as proportionality. In the circumstances the very essence of the right of free elections had not been interfered with as the parties still operated and the threshold had been subject to constitutional review.

In *Matthews* v *United Kingdom*[265] the European Court held that Article 3 of the First Protocol applied to give the individual the right to vote in non-national elections. In this case a British citizen residing in Gibraltar was excluded from voting in the elections to the European parliament because Gibraltar was not included in the franchise for such elections. The Court held that although the European Union could not be challenged, each member state was responsible for ensuring that Convention rights were guaranteed within their jurisdiction.[266] Further, although the Convention did not envisage the role and place of the European parliament, the Convention was a living instrument and the Court was not precluded from determining that the European parliament fell within the definition of 'legislature'. Accordingly, as the applicant had been denied any opportunity to express her opinion in the choice of that legislature, there had been a violation. In addition, any lawful and rational restriction should not be executed in a manner which interferes with the effective enjoyment of the right to vote.[267]

Article 3 and prisoner disenfranchisement

A margin of appreciation will also be offered with respect to the disenfranchisement of prisoners. For example in *H* v *Netherlands*,[268] the European Commission upheld a domestic law that disenfranchised any prisoner sentenced to prison for more than one year for a period exceeding the length of his sentence by three years. The restriction was not in violation of the Convention and the legislator of each individual state is competent to determine the conditions under which the right to vote is to be exercised.

---

[262] See Mowbray, The Role of the European Court of Human Rights in the Promotion of Democracy [1999] PL 703.

[263] (2006) 42 EHRR 46.

[264] (2009) 48 EHRR 4.

[265] (1998) 28 EHRR 361.

[266] As it is a British territory, the Convention and its protocols extend to Gibraltar.

[267] In *Santora* v *Italy*, decision of the European Court, 2 July 2004, it was held that although disenfranchising the applicant following his conviction for a criminal offence was a lawful and proportionate measure, as the penalty had been unreasonably delayed, causing the applicant to be ineligible for voting at the time of parliamentary elections, there had been a violation of Article 3 on the facts.

[268] (1974) 33 DR 242.

Presently, convicted prisoners in England and Wales are not entitled to vote in either general or local elections by virtue of s.3 of the Representation of the People Act 1983, which specifically disenfranchises convicted prisoners. This provision was challenged under the Human Rights Act, but in *R v Secretary of State for the Home Department, ex parte Pearson and Martinez; Hirst v Attorney-General,*[269] the High Court refused to make a declaration of incompatibility, finding that domestic law was within the wide margin of appreciation given to member states.[270] In the Court's opinion, disenfranchisement of convicted prisoners was based on legitimate grounds – relating to elements of both punishment and electoral law – and was not disproportionate to those aims. The Court further held that there were legitimate grounds for disenfranchising life sentence prisoners after they had served their tariff period, because in such cases the prisoner was of sufficient risk to the public to justify his or her further detention.[271]

Following that decision the prisoner petitioned the European Court of Human Rights, and in *Hirst v UK (No 2),*[272] the Court found that domestic law and practice was in violation of Article 3. The Court was prepared to find that the ban served a legitimate aim as either preventing crime and facilitating punishment or enhancing civil responsibility and respect for the rule of law. However, in the Court's view the blanket ban applied to all convicted prisoners was disproportionate and beyond the state's margin of appreciation in this area.[273] In particular the Court noted that the domestic legislature had never sought to weigh the competing interests or to assess the proportionality of the ban as it affected convicted prisoners. The decision was confirmed by the Grand Chamber of the European Court of Human Rights,[274] where it was stressed that the right to vote was not a privilege and could only be taken away on legitimate grounds.

Despite the ruling the Grand Chamber left the United Kingdom government to decide on the choice of means for securing the rights guaranteed by Article 3. In December 2006 a consultation document was published by the Department of Constitutional Affairs, setting out the principles of prisoner enfranchisement and the options available to the United Kingdom following the judgment of the Grand Chamber.[275] This was followed by the Ministry of Justice's second-stage consultation document, outlining the government's initial proposals for prisoner enfranchisement.[276] The government suggested a number of options of enfranchisement, but favoured the idea that prisoners sentenced to less than one years' imprisonment would be automatically entitled to vote (subject to certain exceptions based on the type of

---

[269] *The Times*, 17 April 2001.

[270] See *H v Netherlands* (1974) 33 DR 242 and *X v Netherlands* (1974) 1 DR 87.

[271] For a detailed analysis of that case and the subject of prisoner disenfranchisement, see Lardy, Prisoner Disenfranchisement: Constitutional Rights and Wrongs [2002] PL 524.

[272] (2004) 38 EHRR 40. See Foster, Case Analysis on *Hirst v United Kingdom (No 2)* [2004] EHRLR 436.

[273] The Court reached a similar decision in *Kiss v Hungary* (Application No 38832/06), decision of the European Court, 20 May 2010, with respect to the total disenfranchisement of the mentally ill.

[274] (2006) 42 EHRR 41. See Easton, Electing the Electorate: The Problem of Prisoner Disenfranchisement (2006) 69 MLR 443; Lewis, Difficult and Slippery Terrain: Hansard, Human Rights and *Hirst v UK* [2006] PL 209.

[275] *Voting Rights of Convicted Prisoners Detained Within the United Kingdom – the UK Government's Response to the Grand Chamber of the European Court of Human Right's Judgment* in Hirst v The United Kingdom. Consultation Paper CP 39/06, 14 December 2009.

[276] Voting Rights of Convicted Prisoners within the United Kingdom, Consultation Paper CP6/09, 8 April 2009. See Foster, Reluctantly Restoring Rights [2009] (3) HRLR 489. On 8 December 2009 the Committee of Ministers of the Council of Europe adopted an interim resolution urging the United Kingdom to adopt the necessary measures in order to comply with the judgment.

offence for which the prisoner had been convicted). Thus, those sentenced to a term of one year or more would not be entitled to vote.[277]

In the meantime, a test case was brought to challenge the present ban on prisoners' voting rights, but in *R (Chester)* v *Secretary of State for Justice*,[278] the Administrative Court refused to grant a declaration of incompatibility with respect to the Representation of the People Act 1983 and the government's decision not to allow post-tariff life sentence prisoners the right to vote. The court would not consider granting a declaration until the statutory provision was in place, otherwise the parliamentary process would be interfered with.[279] Therefore, by May 2010, the time of the General Election, no law had been passed to address the judgment in *Hirst*, leaving the government vulnerable to claims brought by prisoners under the Human Rights Act.

A further issue arose following the judgment of the European Court of Human Rights in *Frodl* v *Austria*.[280] In that case the Court held that there had been a violation of Article 3 of the First Protocol when a prisoner had been disenfranchised after committing an offence with intent that carried a sentence of more than one year. Although the Court accepted that the ban was less restrictive than the one considered in *Hirst*, it found that the lack of judicial input into the decision to disenfranchise the particular prisoner constituted a violation of Article 3. This suggests that any legislative measure passed in England and Wales would need to include this impartial judicial safeguard, although the judgment in *Hirst* indicated that such a safeguard was merely desirable rather than compulsory. More recent developments are referred to in the preface.

Protocol No 6 – Rights relating to the abolition of the death penalty[281]

The death penalty shall be abolished. No one shall be condemned to such penalty or executed.

Although Article 2 of the Convention provides an exception to the right to life by permitting executions by a sentence of a court following conviction of a crime for which the death penalty is provided by law,[282] the European Court has recently decided that the death penalty is contrary to Article 3 of the Convention (prohibiting inhuman and degrading punishment), effectively negating the death penalty exception contained in Article 2.[283]

Further, Protocol No 6 represents the growing international movement to prohibit the death penalty and provides that no one shall be condemned to such penalty or be executed.

---

[277] The government did not intend to enfranchise post-tariff or indeterminate prisoners, believing that such a move is not required by the judgment in *Hirst* and that the continued dangerousness of such offenders makes it inappropriate to extend the franchise. However, such a view appears inconsistent with the finding of the European Court, which noted that an anomaly arose in the case of post-tariff life sentence prisoners, and that it was difficult to justify a link between the government's rationale and the loss of the vote in such cases.

[278] [2010] EWHC 63 (Admin); upheld by the Court of Appeal: *The Times*, 17 January 2011.

[279] A declaration had been made by the Scottish courts in *Smith* v *Scott* [2007] CSIH 9.

[280] (Application No 20201/04), decision of the European Court, 8 April 2010.

[281] This protocol is examined in chapter 4 of this text, alongside an examination of the right to life and the legality of the death penalty.

[282] Similarly, Article 6 of the International Covenant on Civil and Political Rights permits the death penalty, provided it is for the most serious crimes and in accordance with the law in force at the time of the commission of the crime.

[283] *Al-Saadoon and Mufdhi* v *United Kingdom* (2010) 50 EHRR 9. The case will be examined in detail in chapters 4 and 5 of this text.

This Protocol, and an Optional Protocol to the International Covenant on Civil and Political Rights,[284] calls for the complete abolition of the death penalty during peacetime.[285] In addition, Protocol No 13 provides for the complete abolition of the death penalty in all circumstances, including times of war or emergency.[286] The United Kingdom has ratified both these Protocols, thus outlawing the remaining provision allowing the death penalty in domestic law (in relation to treason) and committing the government to not reintroducing the death penalty.

Other Convention protocols

In addition to Protocol No 12 on freedom from discrimination, referred to at page 87 above, there are a number of other protocols which grant particular rights, but which have not been ratified by the United Kingdom government. For example, Article 1 of Protocol No 4 provides that no one shall be deprived of his liberty merely on the ground of inability to fulfil a contractual obligation. Article 2 of the same protocol guarantees freedom of movement, providing that everyone lawfully within the territory of the state shall, within that territory, have the right to liberty of movement and freedom to choose his residence and stating that everyone shall be free to leave any country, including their own.[287] Article 3 then provides that no one shall be expelled from the territory of the state of which he is a national and that no one shall be deprived of the right to enter the territory of the state of which he is a national. Finally, Article 4 prohibits the collective expulsions of aliens.

Protocol 7 also contains a number of additional guarantees. This includes the right of an alien lawfully resident in the territory of a state not to be expelled except in pursuance of a decision reached in accordance with law (Article 1). That article also provides the right of such a person to submit reasons against his expulsion, to have his case reviewed and to be represented for these purposes, although such rights may be lost when such expulsion is in the interests of public order or is grounded on reasons of national security. Article 2 provides for the right of those convicted of a criminal offence to have his conviction reviewed by a higher tribunal, the exercise of such right being governed by law. Article 3 provides for the right to compensation for those who have been wrongfully convicted, or pardoned on the ground that there had been a miscarriage of justice, and who have suffered punishment as a result of such conviction. Article 4 states that no one shall be liable to be tried or punished

---

[284] The Second Protocol to the International Covenant on Civil and Political Rights, aiming at the Abolition of the Death Penalty (1990).

[285] For those states that have not ratified Protocol No 13, Article 2 of the Sixth Protocol allows a state to make provision in its law for the death penalty in respect of acts committed in times of war or imminent threat of war. Other than that exception, Article 3 of the Protocol states that no derogation under Article 15 of the Convention is allowed, and Article 4 of the Protocol prohibits any such reservations of the Protocol under Article 57 of the Convention.

[286] In *Ocalan* v *Turkey* (2005) 41 EHRR 45, the Grand Chamber of the European Court held that until every state ratifies Protocol No 13 it would not be appropriate to declare that the death penalty was contrary to Article 3 of the Convention, prohibiting inhuman treatment and punishment. See now *Al-Saadoon and Mufdhi* v *United Kingdom*, n 283 above. See chapter 4 for a fuller discussion on this issue.

[287] The article provides that no restriction shall be placed on the exercise of those rights other than such as are in accordance with law and are necessary in a democratic society for pursuing a number of specified legitimate aims. In addition the right to liberty of movement is said to be subject to restrictions imposed in accordance with law and justified by the public interest in a democratic society.

again in criminal proceedings for an offence for which he has already been acquitted or convicted in accordance with the law of the state. Finally, Article 5 provides that spouses shall enjoy equality of rights and responsibilities of a private law character between them, and in their relations with their children, as to marriage, during marriage and in the event of dissolution, although it is further provided that the state may take such measures as are necessary in the interests of the children.

Questions

What type and range of rights are contained within the Convention and its protocols?

Do you feel that the Convention should adopt a broader range of human rights?

Further reading

There are a number of excellent texts on the European Convention, its machinery for enforcement and its case law. For a definitive and up-to-date overview consult Harris, Warbrick, Bates and O'Boyle, *Law of the European Convention on Human Rights* (OUP 2009, 2nd edn); van Dijk and van Hoof (eds), *Theory and Practice of the European Convention on Human Rights* (Intersentia 2006, 4th edn); Clayton and Tomlinson, *The Law of Human Rights* (OUP 2009, 2nd edn). Students can also read Ovey and White, *Jacobs and White: The European Convention on Human Rights* (OUP 2010, 5th edn); Janis, Kay and Bradley, *European Human Rights Law* (OUP 2007, 3rd edn). There is also Amos, *Human Rights Law* (Hart 2006), which examines the Convention rights and case law (of both the European Court and the domestic courts under the HRA) and principles in detail.

Mowbray's *Cases and Materials on the European Convention* (OUP 2007) is an excellent text on the case law of the European Court, and Blackburn and Polakiewicz (eds), *Fundamental Rights in Europe: The ECHR and its Member States 1950–2000* (OUP 2001) provides an interesting analysis on the effect of the Convention on the domestic law of member states. With respect to the human rights norms of the Convention, students should read Gearty's excellent text, *Principles of Human Rights Adjudication* (OUP 2005). See also Greer, *The European Convention on Human Rights: Achievements, Problems and Prospects* (Cambridge University Press 2006); Lestas, *A Theory of the Interpretation of the European Convention on Human Rights* (OUP 2007); and Bates, *The Evolution of the European Convention on Human Rights* (OUP 2010) for detailed analysis of the Convention and its history and operation.

Students can access the European Court of Human Right's website, **www.echr.coe.int/echr**, for case law, press releases and other information on the work of the Court.

Visit **www.mylawchamber.co.uk/fosterhumanrights** to access regular updates to major changes in the law, further case studies, weblinks, and suggested answers/approaches to questions in the book.

mylawchamber
unrivalled support for legal education

3 Enforcing human rights and civil liberties in domestic law

Introduction

In *A v Secretary of State for the Home Department* (2004), the House of Lords had to decide whether the detention without trial of foreign terrorist suspects was compatible with the rights of liberty of the person and freedom from discrimination. In doing so their Lordships had to have regard to common law principles of fairness and justice, but in particular they needed to assess whether the legislation in question was compatible with articles of the European Convention, which in October 2000 had been given further effect in domestic law via the Human Rights Act 1998.

This new review power of the courts, given to them by parliament, raised a number of controversial and fundamental constitutional and legal issues: could the courts adopt Convention principles over existing common law principles? Were the common law rules and values applicable at all? Would these Convention principles provide the courts with excessive and undemocratic powers of review? Can the courts now strike down Acts of Parliament? Would the independence of the judiciary and the autonomy of elected government ministers be compromised by these powers?

This chapter examines how human rights and civil liberties have been and are protected in the United Kingdom and what effect the passing of the Human Rights Act 1998 has had on rights protection and the above constitutional issues.

This chapter examines how human rights and civil liberties are protected in domestic law. It begins with an account of the law before the Human Rights Act 1998, examining the traditional common law method of protection. This is necessary for a number of reasons. First, in assessing the effect of the Act on the protection of civil liberties it will be necessary to see to what extent domestic law possessed a human rights jurisprudence before the Act and how effectively such rights were protected under that system. Secondly, as the main purpose of the 1998 Act is to allow European Convention law to be used in the domestic courts, an examination of how the Convention was used before the Act came into operation will be helpful in allowing us to assess the need for the Convention and its case law. Thirdly, and perhaps most importantly, as the Convention and the Act do not replace the traditional method, a study of that method is needed to understand the effect of the new regime on the British system of the protection of rights.

The chapter then examines the central provisions of and the accompanying case law under the Human Rights Act 1998, examining the effectiveness of the Act in enhancing the domestic protection of human rights and civil liberties.

Thus, this chapter will cover:

● An examination of the traditional common law method of protecting civil liberties in the United Kingdom.

● An analysis of the effectiveness of that system, its drawbacks and its relationship with the new method under the Human Rights Act 1998.

● An examination of the reasons for passing the Human Rights Act 1998 and of its central provisions.

● An analysis of the relevant case law under the Human Rights Act 1998 and a critical evaluation of its effectiveness.

The common law protection of civil liberties

As we saw in chapter 1, in most developed countries there is special provision made for the citizen's basic or fundamental rights. These rights are contained in a special constitutional document, a bill of rights, and thus an elevated status is given to such rights. The extent of their protection will be determined by the nature of the legal system and the content of the bill of rights itself. In some cases, therefore, the bill of rights will allow the citizen to enforce those rights in a court of law and the courts will be given the power to overrule statutory provisions or executive actions which conflict with them. In other cases, however, the document will not provide a method of legal enforcement and the enjoyment of those rights will be dependent on the limitations imposed by the ordinary law. In all these cases, however, these rights are contained in a document that has a special sanctity, and the legal system has thought it appropriate to lay them down in that document.

In comparison, in the absence of a bill of rights, or indeed any entrenched constitutional rights, the British system was (and to some extent still is) based on the idea of residual rights. One was allowed to do whatever one wished unless the law prohibited that action. Thus, rather than relying on any positive rights laid down in a constitutional document, the citizen enjoyed his or her rights by implication. The basic flaw in this system is that human rights and civil liberties have no status over and above other rights and interests. The principle of residual liberty, therefore, applies to the right to do anything, whether related to the enjoyment of human rights or not. Indeed, the principle accommodates the residual right to interfere with other people's basic and fundamental rights, provided that does not involve transgressing a particular law or legal right.

This was amply illustrated in the case of *Malone* v *Metropolitan Police Commissioner (No 2)*,[1] where the domestic courts were unable to provide a remedy to an individual who had had his telephone tapped by the police authorities. In this case the plaintiff's claim failed because he was unable to point to any breach of the civil law by the police action. The law of trespass did not apply to the case as it was not the plaintiff's telephone line that had been tampered

---

[1] [1979] Ch 344.

with, and the law of confidentiality did not extend to give a person the right to private confidential telephone calls. The practice had, of course, interfered with his right of privacy, but as the
law did not protect the right to privacy *per se*, and the European Convention on Human Rights
could not be directly enforced in the domestic courts, the plaintiff was left without a remedy.[2]

Thus, had domestic law contained a bill of rights, in such a case the relevant authorities
would, at the very least, be required to provide a legal justification for their actions. A bill of
rights would recognise every individual's right to private life and would thus require legal
justification for any interference with such. In addition, given the fundamental nature of
the right to private life, any interference would need to be justified in accordance with the
principles of necessity and proportionality which govern the restriction of human rights and
civil liberties in both domestic bills of rights and international treaties such as the European
Convention on Human Rights. That case, therefore, highlights the deficiency of Dicey's theory
of the rule of law and the protection of human rights, considered below.[3] The actions of the
police could not be sanctioned because they broke no law, and to apply a sanction in
such a case would be in violation of the idea that no one shall be punished for an action that
did not constitute an offence at law. But Dicey's theory, particularly his dismissal of the notion
of public law, fails to take into account that there is a fundamental difference between public
and private bodies and that such a difference should be reflected in the law. A private citizen
could not get the relevant permission to tap a person's telephone, and would not, in general,
get access to personal information. In cases such as *Malone*, therefore, the court's refusal or
constitutional inability to develop the law so as to protect the individual from arbitrary interference highlights the drawbacks of a system based on traditional common law principles.

The citizen's seemingly precarious position under the traditional method was, however,
bolstered by other factors, which in practice ensured that there was some safeguard against
arbitrary and unreasonable interferences with human rights. Despite the court's reluctance to
recognise certain rights, and their constitutional inability to override the express will of parliament, there is said to be a tradition of human rights protection in domestic law. Neither is
this traditional approach entirely dependent on the goodwill of parliament and the hope that
principles of democracy and constitutionalism will always be upheld by those in power.
Adherence to the rule of law, principles of natural justice and fairness, and respect for human
rights are capable of *legal* enforcement as well, albeit by a constitutionally restricted judiciary.

The rule of law and *Entick* v *Carrington*

Acceptance of the rule of law – that government acts by and within the law – meant that any
interference with the rights of individuals had to be justified by law. In *Entick* v *Carrington*[4]
the courts had accepted that any interference with the property rights of an individual had to
be justified by the law and that everyone, including officers of the state, had to show legal
authority for their actions. In that case the plaintiff's property had been seized on the authority of a general warrant issued by the defendant, the secretary of state, on the grounds that

---

[2] In *Wainwright* v *Home Office* [2004] 2 AC 406, the House of Lords confirmed that there was no common law
of privacy and the claimants had to seek a remedy before the European Court of Human Rights: *Wainwright* v
United Kingdom (2007) 44 EHRR 40.

[3] A.V. Dicey, *Introduction to the Study of the Law and the Constitution* (Macmillan 1965, 10th edn).

[4] (1765) 19 St Tr 1029.

the plaintiff had been guilty of writing seditious papers. The plaintiff had brought an action against the defendant who attempted to defend his actions on the basis that such warrants were necessary for the protection of the state and had, in any case, been issued previously without objection or challenge. In rejecting the defences, LORD CAMDEN CJ insisted that any interference with the plaintiff's property rights had to have a legal basis; if it is law it will be found in our books. Lord Camden rejected the defence of state necessity, stating that the law accepted no such concept.

The decision in *Entick* is often given as an example of how the rights of the citizen can be protected by the common law in the absence of a bill of rights and any formal constitutional guarantees. The courts not only ensure that government is armed with proper and legitimate legal authority before interfering with the rights of the citizen, but also insist that law possesses characteristics that are consistent with fairness and due process and which are inconsistent with arbitrary and discretionary action. Thus, LORD CAMDEN CJ rejects the plea that such general warrants are similar to other, legally recognised, warrants such as those for the search of stolen goods, and thus should be accepted by the courts. The courts' rejection of such general and discretionary warrants is an example of the courts safeguarding the individual from arbitrary and unreasonable law and practice, and is the basis of the multitude of cases where the courts have either interpreted statutes or developed the common law to ensure that the citizen is not subject to unnecessary interference with their basic liberties.[5] In the post-Human Rights Act era such purported powers would not be regarded as 'prescribed by law' as required by the terms of the European Convention, and would be declared in breach of the relevant Convention right.[6]

The limitations of the rule of law

Before the Human Rights Act 1998 the principles employed in the above cases could only be applied if the courts recognised the right that had been interfered with. In *Entick*, the citizen's rights over property had always been recognised by the common law of trespass and thus the government had to show legal authority when interfering with that legal right, but in cases such as *Malone*, the claim would fail if the applicant could not point to a recognised legal right, even if the right which had been interfered with was a fundamental right contained in the majority of national and international human rights instruments.[7]

Cases such as *Malone* would have been dealt with differently had the European Convention, or a common law of privacy, been available to the applicants. In such a case the courts would have accepted that there had been a *prima facie* violation of that right and would

---

[5] See also *Webb and Porter* v *Chief Constable of Merseyside Police* [2000] 1 All ER 209, where the Court of Appeal held that in the absence of express statutory authority, it was not lawful for a public authority to expropriate money from an individual.

[6] However, in *R (Rottman)* v *Commissioner of Police of the Metropolis and Another* [2002] 2 All ER 865, a majority of their Lordships overruled the decision of the Divisional Court which held that there existed no common law provision additional to s.18 of the Police and Criminal Evidence Act 1986 by which police might enter and search premises without a warrant subsequent to an arrest under the Extradition Act 1989.

[7] See also *R* v *Secretary of State for Health, ex parte C, The Times*, 18 January 1999, where the applicant failed in his claim that the storing and swapping of personal data by health authorities was a violation of his right of privacy. The use of the information had, at most, deprived the applicant of his opportunity of gaining an interview for a post, a right not recognised as such in domestic law. See Zar, The Courts' Approach in Judicial Review to the Disclosure of Information between Public Authorities (2001) 6(3) Judicial Review 161.

have been forced to declare such interference unlawful on the grounds that the violation lacked the necessary legality to consider its possible justification. Additionally, in those cases where the authority did have some legal excuse, the courts in the post-Human Rights Act era will insist that the act was necessary and proportionate.

The court's recognition of fundamental rights

The case of *Entick* v *Carrington* is not merely an illustration of the court's insistence that legal justification is required if a person's rights are to be interfered with. In addition to insisting that public authorities, like everyone else, show legal justification for their actions, cases such as *Entick* illustrate the court's desire to protect the individual from arbitrary interference by public bodies. Thus in that case LORD CAMDEN CJ not only rejects the government's defence of state necessity, but also rejects the general notion of general warrants, refusing to equate them with the variety of other warrants that had been accepted in law. The case of *Entick*, therefore, is an early example of the court's desire to ensure that interferences with others' rights are not only legal but also reasonable and acceptable; that they comply with minimum standards of fairness. These principles of substantive justice were, and continue to be, used by the courts in their inherent common law power of judicial review.

On a broader level, the case of *Entick* is important because it illustrates that in the absence of a formal bill of rights proclaiming the human rights and civil liberties of its citizens, the courts are capable of recognising fundamental rights, and protecting them from illegal and unnecessary interference. Although Dicey's view that the common law method was indeed superior to the one employed in written constitutions has been subject to intense scrutiny and criticism, cases such as *Entick* illustrate that the law can recognise fundamental rights, and the principles relating to their restriction, without the formal mechanism provided by a bill of rights.[8]

Thus, in the absence of an enforceable bill of rights charging the courts with the duty to uphold fundamental rights, and allowing them to strike down acts or decisions which are incompatible with those rights, the courts, at least in theory, could regard themselves as the guardians of those rights and protect them in the same way as the written bill of rights attempts to do.[9] As we know, this role is limited by the doctrine of parliamentary sovereignty and the consequent limited role of the judiciary in our constitution. Nevertheless the common law is capable of recognising these rights and applying the principles of human rights protection in both the interpretation of statutes and the development of the common law.

These common law principles are still potent in the Human Rights Act era, and in certain cases the domestic courts prefer to rely on constitutional rights to control excessive interference with basic liberty. For example, in *A* v *Secretary of State for the Home Department (No 2)*[10] the House of Lords ruled out evidence that may have been obtained via torture by relying on both international and common law prohibition. In coming to that decision, their Lordships referred to the common law rejection of such practices and both European and United Nations treaties and instruments on torture, and stated that although it was within the power of parliament to allow such evidence to be admitted, there was no evidence to suggest that

---

[8] See Allan, Constitutional Rights and the Common Law (1991) 11 OJLS 453; Laws, Is the High Court the Guardian of Fundamental Constitutional Rights? [1993] PL 67; Lester, The Judges as Lawmakers [1993] PL 269.
[9] See Hunt, *Using Human Rights in the English Courts* (Hart 1997).
[10] [2006] 2 AC 221.

the Anti-Terrorism, Crime and Security Act 2001 intended to override the common law and international position.

Another example is provided by the Supreme Court's recent ruling in *HM Treasury* v *Mohammed Jabar Ahmed and others*,[11] where the Supreme Court considered the legality of the Terrorism Order 2006, which allowed for freezing orders to be placed on the funds of those who were reasonably suspected of committing acts of or facilitating terrorism. Using traditional principles of interpretation and legality it held that the Order was *ultra vires* s.1 of the United Nations Act 1946, which had been passed to give effect to a UN resolution intended to suppress terrorism. The Supreme Court held that if the rule of law meant anything, what amounted to decisions that were necessary and expedient within s.1 could not be left to the uncontrolled judgement of the executive. By introducing a test based on reasonable suspicion the Treasury had exceeded its powers of implementing the 1946 Act, and was a clear example of an attempt to adversely affect the basic rights of the citizen without the clear authority of parliament. The absence of any indication that parliament intended to impose restrictions on the freedom of individuals when debating the Act meant that it was impossible to say that it confronted the matter and was prepared to accept the political cost when the measure was enacted.[12] However, the limitations of this method of protection were exposed by the passing of the Terrorist Asset-Freezing (Temporary Provisions) Act 2010, which specifies that the order of 2006 was validly made under the 1946 Act. Any judicial challenge to the new Act would have to be made under the Human Rights Act, alleging a breach of rights under the European Convention.

The interpretation of statutes

As seen below, the courts, via the application of certain constitutional fundamentals, were able to interpret legislation or develop the common law in line with the principles of individual liberty and thus uphold the citizen's basic human rights. Thus, in addition to the possibility of interpreting ambiguous statutory provisions in the light of the European Convention and other treaties, the courts could also assume that parliament did not intend to interfere with fundamental human rights unless it had included express provisions to that effect: general words used in a statute were not considered sufficient to interfere with the basic rights of the individual.

This method was particularly prevalent in relation to the citizen's right of access to the courts. Thus, in *Chester* v *Bateson*[13] it was held that a regulation passed under emergency powers legislation, which prohibited landlords from evicting their tenants without the permission of the minister, was *ultra vires*; however wide the powers of the minister under that statute, parliament did not intend to deny the citizen his fundamental right of access to the courts.[14]

However, although the courts were able to use what they regarded as fundamental constitutional rights to shape and limit the law, their role as guardians of fundamental rights was always limited by the doctrine of sovereignty of parliament. Although the courts could

---

[11] [2010] 2 AC 534.

[12] The Court noted further that the Al-Qaida order which allowed designation of a person by a Sanctions Committee without judicial review denied any effective remedy and thus was also *ultra vires*.

[13] [1920] KB 829.

[14] See also *R* v *Lord Chancellor, ex parte Witham* [1998] QB 575, where it was held that a regulation which insisted that a person who wished to bring a claim in defamation had to deposit a sum of money with the court was *ultra vires* because it constituted an unreasonable interference with the citizen's right of access to the courts. See further *Haig* v *Aitken* [2000] 3 All ER 80; *Raymond* v *Honey* [1980] AC 1.

resolve ambiguities in favour of the citizen's fundamental rights, and presume that the general words of a statute were not intended to deprive an individual of such rights, they were, and to an extent still are, powerless in the face of unambiguous statutory wording clearly intended to interfere with such rights.[15] Thus, in *R v Inland Revenue Commissioner ex parte Rossminster*,[16] the House of Lords held that the power of tax officials under s.20C of the Taxes Management Act 1970 to search for and take away documents that they reasonably believed to be evidence of an offence involving fraud in connection with tax did not require the warrant to specify the particular tax offence for which the person was suspected. In the Court of Appeal, LORD DENNING MR had implied this requirement into the statutory provision so as to ensure that the Commissioner's powers were limited and accountable, but the House of Lords overruled the Court of Appeal and reminded the courts that although the statute in question allowed breathtaking inroads into a person's privacy, it was not the role of the courts to strike down or reinterpret clear legislation passed by parliament.[17]

Fundamental rights and the development of the common law

The above principles have also been used in the court's role of developing the common law. Many areas of the common law, although not specifically concerned with the protection of human rights, affect such rights. For example, the laws of defamation, confidentiality and contempt of court exist to protect the rights of others, to safeguard aspects of their privacy and their right to a fair trial as well as the protection of other individual and public interests. Their existence and enforcement, however, also impact on other fundamental rights, most notably freedom of expression.

There are numerous examples of the courts developing the common law in a manner sympathetic to human rights. For example, in the law of defamation, the House of Lords have made a number of landmark decisions which have upheld the principles of press freedom. In *Derbyshire County Council v Times Newspapers*[18] the House of Lords held that it was not possible for a democratically elected body to sue collectively in the law of defamation. This decision was clearly not made on purely technical and legal grounds, but on the basis that such actions would be contrary to principles of democracy and free speech.[19] A desire to protect free speech from unnecessary interference was also at the heart of the House of Lords' decision in *Attorney-General v Guardian Newspapers (No 2)*,[20] heralded as a great victory for press freedom and the public's right to know.[21]

---

[15] Despite s.2 and s.3 of the Human Rights Act 1998, the concept of parliamentary sovereignty has been maintained. Thus, the courts must uphold statutory provisions that interfere with Convention rights when no other interpretation is possible, and the courts' power will then be restricted to issuing declarations of incompatibility, which will not disapply those provisions.

[16] [1980] AC 852.

[17] However, in *R (on the application of Morgan Grenfell and Co Ltd) v Special Commissioner* [2002] 2 WLR 1299, the House of Lords, in applying a constitutional interpretation to s.20 of the Taxes Management Act 1970, held that in exercising their statutory powers to search a person's premises the Commissioners were precluded from seizing legally privileged correspondence.

[18] [1993] AC 534.

[19] This, and other cases in this area, are discussed in detail in chapters 8 and 9.

[20] [1990] 1 AC 109.

[21] See also *Jones and Lloyd v DPP* [1999] 2 All ER 257, where a majority of the House of Lords held that a peaceful and non-obstructive demonstration on the highway did not necessarily constitute a trespass. See chapter 10 on freedom of assembly.

Judicial review and fundamental rights

The courts have an inherent common law power to control inferior courts and other public bodies to ensure that such bodies act within the law and act consistently with a variety of principles of good administration.[22] Even before the Human Rights Act 1998, the courts were able to take into account the human rights context of the judicial review application. In particular, the courts might justify their reviewing of a decision on the grounds that it interfered with human rights. For example, although the courts might generally refuse to interfere with particular types of decision making, the human rights context of the case could justify their reviewing powers. A good example of this is the case of *ex parte Javed and Another*.[23] In that case the Court of Appeal held that a court was entitled to review subordinate legislation that had been debated in and approved by affirmative resolution of both Houses of Parliament. This decision challenged the previous House of Lords' judgment in *Nottinghamshire County Council v Secretary of State for the Environment*,[24] where their Lordships had refused to interfere with a Ministerial Order relating to local authority expenditure which had been approved by parliament. In the *Javed* case LORD PHILLIPS MR held that the court was entitled to review the legality of an asylum regulation,[25] which had designated Pakistan as a country in which there was in general no serious risk of persecution, even though the regulation had been debated in and approved by parliament. Further, it was held that the court was entitled to assess for itself the facts presented to parliament as supporting the legality of the subordinate legislation. LORD PHILLIPS MR made it clear that the court's jurisdiction in this respect depended critically on the nature and purpose of the enabling legislation and in this case declared the subordinate legislation unlawful on the ground that the evidence relating to the treatment of women and a religious minority in Pakistan did not support the Secretary of State's conclusion as to the risk of persecution.

Although the decision was made after the coming into operation of the Human Rights Act,[26] the case was decided on traditional principles of judicial review and shows that the courts could adopt a flexible approach depending on the human rights context of the case. Such an approach will, of course, continue to be applied in the post-Human Rights Act era where as we will see the level and intensity of review is dependent on the right in question and the reasons for restriction. Thus, judicial review will continue to be developed in the light of these principles, enhanced by the availability of the principles and case law of the European Convention.[27]

Human rights could, therefore, shape the courts' review of decision making in a number of respects, and in relation to all of the established grounds of review. First, in relation to the ground of illegality, the courts could often use the principles of statutory interpretation, including the principle of legality, in deciding that the action or decision was beyond the

---

[22] For a general account of this area see Craig, *Administrative Law* (Sweet & Maxwell 2008, 6th edn).

[23] *R v Secretary of State for the Home Department, ex parte Javed and Another; R v Same, ex parte Zulfiqar Ali; R v Same, ex parte Abid Ali* [2002] QB 129.

[24] [1986] AC 240.

[25] Asylum (Designated Countries of Destination and Designated Safe Third Countries) Order 1996 (SI 1996 No 2671).

[26] Thus, had the Court of Appeal entertained a challenge to the legislation after the Human Rights Act took force it would have had the power to declare the subordinate legislation incompatible with Articles 2 and 3 of the European Convention.

[27] See Hickman, *Public Law after the Human Rights Act* (Hart 2010).

powers granted by parliament. Thus, the courts would assume that parliament did not intend to interfere with basic human rights and thus would refuse to interpret the relevant statutory provision in a manner that would give the public authority a power to violate such rights. For example, in *R v Secretary of State for the Home Department, ex parte Leech*,[28] the Court of Appeal held that despite the wide wording of s.47 of the Prison Act 1952, the Home Secretary did not have the power to impose restrictions on the prisoner's correspondence with his legal advisers unless there existed a pressing need to do so on grounds of prison security.[29]

Secondly, in relation to the doctrine of *Wednesbury* Unreasonableness,[30] although the courts rejected the use of proportionality in judicial review, they established the principle that when assessing the rationality of an act or decision they were entitled to take the view that the greater the interference with human rights the greater the justification they would require from the body in question. This principle was applied in a number of pre-Human Rights Act cases in an effort to intensify the court's scrutiny of executive decisions that conflicted with the applicant's fundamental human rights. For example in *R v Ministry of Defence, ex parte Smith*,[31] the Court of Appeal, although rejecting the direct application of Article 8 of the European Convention in challenging the government's ban on homosexuals serving in the armed forces, insisted that the ministry provide cogent evidence to justify the ban. However, despite the application of this principle, the Court of Appeal refused to strike down the policy as irrational.[32]

However, the application of the principle found success in a later case, decided by the High Court and affirmed in the Court of Appeal. In *R v Lord Saville of Newdigate, ex parte A and Others*,[33] it was held that the chairman of the Bloody Sunday inquiry had acted irrationally when he had decided that in the interests of openness and justice the tribunal should waive the anonymity, given by the first inquiry, to the soldiers involved in the inquiry. The Court of Appeal held that a decision maker was not allowed to make a decision which risked interfering with a soldier's fundamental right to life in the absence of compelling justification. Accordingly, where such rights were threatened, the range of options open to a reasonable decision maker would be curtailed and the court would anxiously scrutinise the strength of the countervailing circumstances and the degree of interference with the human right involved. The more substantial the interference, the more the court would require by the way of justification before it was satisfied that the decision was reasonable. Applying that formulation to the present facts, the Court of Appeal held that the tribunal had failed to attach sufficient significance to the risk posed to the safety of the soldiers and their families and also

---

[28] [1994] QB 198.

[29] See also *Broadmoor Hospital Authority* v *R* [2000] 2 All ER 727 – refusing an injunction that would interfere with the fundamental right of the inmate to free speech. Contrast the post-Human Rights Act case of *S* v *Airedale National Health Service Trust, The Times*, 5 September 2002, where it was held that there was a pressing reason for implying into the Mental Health Act 1983 a power to seclude patients who were lawfully detained under that legislation.

[30] *Associated Provincial Picture House* v *Wednesbury Corporation* [1948] 1 KB 223.

[31] [1996] 1 All ER 257. See also *Bugdaycay* v *Secretary of State for the Home Department* [1987] 1 All ER 720.

[32] See, in addition, *R* v *Secretary of State for the Home Department, ex parte Brind* [1991] 1 AC 696. An application under the European Convention was declared inadmissible; *Brind* v *United Kingdom* (1994) 18 CD 76. See also *R* v *Secretary of State for the Home Department, ex parte Launder* [1997] 3 All ER 971, where the House of Lords accepted that decisions involving fundamental human rights called for the most anxious scrutiny by the courts; the applicant's claim under the European Convention was declared inadmissible: *Launder* v *United Kingdom* [1998] EHRLR 337.

[33] *The Times*, 22 June 1999, affirmed in the Court of Appeal [1999] 4 All ER 860.

might not have attached sufficient weight to the assurance given by the former tribunal, the significance of which had increased over time. Furthermore, it seemed that the present tribunal was not sufficiently aware that the denial of anonymity would affect the soldiers' perception of the inquiry's fairness. The Court thus concluded that the tribunal had acted irrationally, noting that anonymity would have a limited effect on the openness of the inquiry and that a particular soldier could still be named if there were good reason.[34]

The decision in *ex parte A* provides a reasonably clear example of the application of the doctrine of proportionality in the pre-Human Rights Act era, and the language of the Court of Appeal in that case indicates that the courts would be prepared in certain cases not only to closely scrutinise the decision-making process of the original decision maker, but also to judge the objective reasonableness of the ultimate decision.[35]

Finally, in relation to the ground of procedural impropriety it is evident that many of the principles of procedural fairness, including the right to a fair hearing, are founded on the right to a fair trial which is contained in most constitutional bills of rights and which is covered by Article 6 of the European Convention. These principles could be used by the courts to insist that the applicant receive a fair and unbiased hearing,[36] and, when their human rights are at risk, to insist on a stricter application of these rules.[37]

Protection of human rights via statute

The traditional common law approach has often been supplemented by parliamentary intervention, providing the citizen with concrete rights in the form of statutory provisions. For example, instead of a general equality clause protecting individuals from discrimination, a number of statutes provide a framework against discrimination on specific grounds such as sex and marital status,[38] race,[39] trade union and non-trade union membership,[40] disability,[41] and age.[42] These statutes had been passed to deal with specific aspects of discrimination as and when parliament envisaged a sufficient need for protection or where the United Kingdom's international obligations brought pressure to bear.[43] The absence of a general equality clause,

---

[34] See also the subsequent decision in *R (A and Others) v Lord Saville of Newdigate* [2002] 1 WLR 1249, where it was held that the refusal to let the soldiers give oral evidence at the inquiry so as to protect their identities was unlawful as it exposed the soldiers to a real risk of death in violation of Article 2.

[35] Subsequently a number of decisions before the coming into operation of the Human Rights Act 1998 considered the appropriate level of judicial supervision in cases where an individual's fundamental human rights had been interfered with, thus giving guidance to the courts on their role in the post-Human Rights Act era. See, for example, *R v Secretary of State for the Home Department, ex parte Mahmood* [2001] 1 WLR 840, and *R v Secretary of State for the Home Department, ex parte Isiko, The Times*, 20 February 2001. However, the approaches taken in those cases were subsequently modified by Lord Steyn in *R (Daly) v Secretary of State for the Home Department* [2001] 2 AC 532.

[36] *Ridge v Baldwin* [1964] AC 40; *R v Gough* [1993] AC 646.

[37] For example, in *R v DPP, ex parte Manning* [2000] 3 WLR 463, it was held that although there was no general duty on the DPP to give reasons for a failure to prosecute, given that the case involved a death in custody for which the state might be responsible under Article 2 of the European Convention, the DPP should have given reasons.

[38] The Sex Discrimination Act 1975 as amended by the Sex Discrimination Act 1986.

[39] The Race Relations Act 1976 and the Race Relations (Amendment) Act 2000.

[40] The Employment Rights Act 1996 and the Employment Relations Act 1999.

[41] The Disability Discrimination Act 1995 and the Special Educational Needs and Disability Act 2001.

[42] Employment Equality (Age) Regulations 2006.

[43] For an excellent coverage of the topic of discrimination, see McColgan, *Discrimination Law: Text, Cases and Materials* (Hart 2005, 2nd edn).

however, had left certain areas of discrimination unprotected. For example, until recently it was not unlawful to discriminate against an individual on grounds of their sexual orientation or religion, although certain acts of such discrimination amounted to sex or race discrimination.[44] In addition, transsexuals had been unable to obtain protection against various forms of discrimination, there being little recognition of their status in domestic law[45] – a situation which until recently had been upheld by the European Court of Human Rights.[46]

Apart from the area of discrimination, there are also an ever-increasing number of statutes that seek to supplement the common law protection of various human rights, such as freedom of expression and assembly,[47] freedom of information,[48] and privacy.[49] In addition to statutes passed specifically to recognise and protect fundamental rights, there are a number of other statutory provisions that attempt to restrict the scope of various laws in an effort to ensure that fundamental human rights are not excessively interfered with. For example, the Obscene Publications Act 1959 includes, in s.4, a public interest defence to a charge of publishing an obscene article, and the Police and Criminal Evidence Act 1984 contains numerous safeguards against the arbitrary use of various police powers.

More usually, however, statutes have been used to limit human rights, providing a legal and, to some extent, uncontrolled mechanism to take away or reduce the liberty of the individual. For example, the Public Order Act 1986 contains a variety of restrictions on the residual right of freedom of assembly and association, and the Criminal Justice and Public Order Act 1994, via s.34, made serious inroads into the ancient right of silence. Such statutes are now, of course, subject to the boundaries laid down in the Human Rights Act 1998, but given the retention of parliamentary sovereignty, legislation continues to pose a threat to the enjoyment of human rights and civil liberties. Indeed, it has been noted that in the post-Human Rights Act era there is a growing number of legislative provisions, such as the Terrorism Act 2000 and the Regulation of Investigatory Powers Act 2000, which were passed in order to comply with the 1998 Act's requirement of legitimacy, but which contain draconian powers.[50]

The effect of the European Convention on Human Rights and other human rights instruments before the 1998 Act

Even before the passing and coming into operation of the Human Rights Act 1998, the European Convention of Human Rights and the case law of the European Court and

---

[44] See *Mandla and Another* v *Lee* [1983] 2 AC 548; *Smith* v *Gardner Merchant* [1998] IRLR 510. Discrimination in employment on such grounds is now protected under, respectively, the Employment Equality (Religion and Belief) Regulations 2003 and the Equality Act (Sexual Orientation) Regulations 2007, 2007/1263. See also the Civil Partnership Act 2004 on equality for same-sex partners.

[45] Following the decision of the European Court of Justice in *P* v *S and Cornwall County Council* [1996] ECR 1-2143, the Sex Discrimination (Gender Reassignment) Regulations 1999 were passed, altering s.2 of the Sex Discrimination Act 1975 to include protection against such discrimination in employment.

[46] See now *Goodwin* v *United Kingdom* (2002) 35 EHRR 18, and the Gender Recognition Act 2004.

[47] See, for example, The Public Interest Disclosure Act 1998, and The Public Meetings Act 1908.

[48] Freedom of Information Act 2000.

[49] The Data Protection Acts 1984 and 1998.

[50] This is the constant theme of Helen Fenwick's text, *Civil Rights: New Labour, Freedom and the Human Rights Act* (Longman 2000). These provisions, including the Terrorism Act 2006 and the Prevention of Terrorism Act 2005, are considered in chapters on liberty of the person, the right to a fair trial, freedom of expression and freedom of association, and human rights and terrorism.

Commission of Human Rights had a major impact on the development and protection of human rights in the United Kingdom. In the first place, since 1966 individuals had enjoyed the right of petition under the European Convention. This resulted in countless applications brought by individuals who claimed that their Convention rights had been violated by domestic law or practice. The success of large numbers of these applications was, thus, providing some form of redress to those individuals whose Convention rights had been interfered with and in this sense the European Convention had a tremendous impact on the protection of individuals' fundamental rights.

Secondly, and often as a consequence of the above applications, domestic law was altered or introduced to comply with the standards laid down in the Convention. As a result of many of these applications, and particularly as a result of many decisions of the European Court of Human Rights, domestic law and practice was changed. For example, following the European Court's decision in *Sunday Times* v *United Kingdom*,[51] parliament passed the Contempt of Court Act 1981 which attempted to bring the law of contempt of court into line with the principles of free speech and freedom of the press.[52] Again, following the decision of the European Court in *Malone* v *United Kingdom*,[53] parliament passed the Interception of Communications Act 1985 to put the system of authorised telephone tapping on a statutory footing.[54] Thirdly, the Convention and its case law had an effect in the domestic courts in resolving disputes with a human rights context. Although the courts remained adamant that the Convention, not being part of domestic law, could not be used directly in court proceedings, the Convention could be used indirectly in a number of respects.

As seen above, the Convention could be used in the interpretation of statutes where that statutory provision was ambiguous: in other words the provision was capable of producing two plausible interpretations, one of which would be compatible with the rights laid down in the Convention. Thus, in *Waddington* v *Miah*[55] the House of Lords interpreted s.34 of the Immigration Act 1971 so as to avoid the conclusion that the provision was intended to impose retrospective criminal liability, which would have been in contravention of Article 7 of the European Convention. The Convention could also be used by the courts in their role of developing and applying the common law. Thus, in *R* v *Chief Metropolitan Stipendiary Magistrates, ex parte Choudhury*[56] the Court of Appeal allowed arguments based on Article 10 of the European Convention in deciding whether the domestic law of blasphemy applied to religious beliefs other than Christianity. In addition, decisions of the European Court also informed judicial decision making, resulting in the courts giving an added weight to human rights issues when interpreting statutes or developing the common law. For example, following the decision of the European Court of Human Rights in *Goodwin* v *United Kingdom*,[57] the domestic courts began to interpret s.10 of the Contempt of Court Act 1981 in the light of the principles of freedom of expression and, in particular, the case law of the European Court.[58]

---

[51] (1979) 2 EHRR 245.

[52] In particular, by changing the test of unintentional contempt in s.2 of the Act and by introducing a public interest defence in s.5 of the Act – see chapter 9.

[53] (1984) 7 EHRR 14.

[54] See also the decision of the European Commission of Human Rights in *Hamer* v *United Kingdom* (1979) 24 DR 5, which led to the Marriage Act 1983.

[55] [1974] 1 WLR 683.

[56] [1991] 1 QB 429.

[57] (1996) 22 EHRR 123.

[58] *Camelot Group Ltd* v *Centaur Communications* [1999] QB 124.

Many decisions, however, were based on fundamental rights generally, rather than the European Convention specifically. The courts had accepted that there had been established within the common law certain constitutional rights which possessed the same status as those rights contained in the Convention, and which thus demanded the same respect and level of protection from the courts. Thus, in *Derbyshire County Council v Times Newspapers*,[59] although the Court of Appeal had relied on Article 10 of the Convention in reaching the conclusion that it was not possible for a democratically elected local authority to sue jointly in the law of defamation, the House of Lords decided the issue without reference to the Convention. In their Lordships' opinion, such a decision could be reached by applying the common law principles relating to freedom of expression and the freedom of the press. Again in *Attorney-General v Guardian Newspapers (No 2)*,[60] although the House of Lords referred to Article 10 of the Convention and the relevant case law of the European Court of Human Rights, their Lordships were able to reach their conclusions based on the common law, which they regarded as almost identical to the principles laid down in the European Convention.

Aside from the above possibilities, the courts refused to allow the Convention to have a direct effect on the resolution of domestic disputes. Thus it was not possible for the courts to use the Convention to provide a remedy where none existed in domestic law. Accordingly, in *Malone v Metropolitan Police Commissioner (No 2)*,[61] MEGARRY VC refused to allow the plaintiff to succeed on the grounds that the telephone tapping constituted a violation of Article 8 of the Convention: the Convention was not part of domestic law and the domestic law did not otherwise recognise the right to private life in cases such as this. Similarly, in *R v Ministry of Defence, ex parte Smith*,[62] the Court of Appeal refused to allow the applicants to rely on Article 8 of the Convention to question the legality and reasonableness of the prohibition of homosexuals in the armed forces.

Similarly, the Convention could not be used to enhance the prospects of a claim in domestic law by allowing the principles of the Convention, and the case law of the European Court of Human Rights, to be used to support that claim. In *R v Secretary of State for the Home Department, ex parte Brind*[63] the House of Lords stated that the Convention could not be used to challenge the legality or reasonableness of an administrative decision which allegedly interfered with the applicants' freedom of expression. In their Lordships' opinion, Article 10 was not relevant in deciding the issue of whether the Home Secretary had acted lawfully in imposing the broadcasting ban, and the case had to be decided on traditional principles of judicial review. Equally importantly, their Lordships held that the applicants could not rely on the doctrine of proportionality to challenge the Home Secretary's decision. The decision showed that the courts were prepared to give added weight to the human rights argument, but that they wished to do so without reference to the Convention principles of legitimacy and necessity.

Questions

How were human rights and civil liberties recognised in the period before the Human Rights Act 1998 was passed?

What were the advantages of that system and why did it survive so long?

---

[59] [1993] AC 534.
[60] [1990] 1 AC 109.
[61] [1979] Ch 344.
[62] [1996] 1 All ER 257.
[63] [1991] 1 AC 696.

The limitations and disadvantages of the traditional method

Although it would be wrong to state that domestic law did not possess any human rights law before the Human Rights Act, the traditional method possessed a number of disadvantages, which made the full protection of human rights and civil liberties difficult to achieve.[64] These difficulties were reflected by the number and types of cases brought against the United Kingdom under the European Convention of Human Rights and culminated in the passing of the Human Rights Act 1998.[65]

Some rights not protected

Although the courts and parliament had developed and created a number of constitutional rights, certain rights and liberties were left largely unprotected. Thus, although the common law and statute recognised the rights of property and freedom of the person, which are covered in various articles of the European Convention, neither legislation nor the common law recognised a direct right to privacy or private life.[66] As seen above, the courts had held, reluctantly, that domestic law did not recognise the right to private life as such, and unless the victim could fit his or her case into associated legal grounds, such as trespass or confidentiality, then domestic law did not provide a remedy. This situation resulted in a number of successful claims being brought under the European Convention in relation to actions that were clearly in violation of Article 8 of the Convention.[67] The absence of a law of privacy and private life was perhaps the most glaring lacuna in the common law method, and the passing of the Human Rights Act 1998 has seen the courts rectifying the situation.[68]

In addition, a number of legal provisions and practices in effect deprived individuals of a remedy for breach of their human rights. One example was the way in which legislation and the judiciary treated certain groups, such as prisoners.[69] This situation was remedied by a change in judicial attitude, which was largely prompted by decisions of the European Court of Human Rights.[70] Other examples were where domestic law and procedure prohibited or limited individuals from bringing legal actions, usually in an effort to protect public authorities or the wider public interest. Such measures are by no means peculiar to the United Kingdom, and are not outlawed by the European Convention on Human Rights, although many of the domestic provisions have been held to constitute an unjustified violation of human rights. Thus, in *Osman* v *United Kingdom*[71] the European Court held that the blanket

---

[64] See Klug, Starmer and Weir, *The Three Pillars of Liberty: Political Rights and Freedoms in the United Kingdom* (Routledge 1996). See also Lester, Fundamental Rights: The UK Isolated? [1984] PL 46; Gordon and Wilmott-Smith, *Human Rights in the UK* (OUP 1997).

[65] See Foster, The Protection of Human Rights in Domestic Law; Learning Lessons from the European Court of Human Rights [2002] NILQ 232; Klug, The Long Road to Human Rights Compliance [2006] NILQ 186.

[66] *Malone* v *Metropolitan Police Commissioner* (*No 2*) [1979] Ch 344, confirmed in *Wainwright* v *Home Office* [2004] 2 AC 406.

[67] See, for example, *Malone* v *United Kingdom* (1984) 7 EHRR 14; *Halford* v *United Kingdom* (1997) 24 EHRR 523; and *Khan* v *United Kingdom* (2001) 31 EHRR 45.

[68] See chapter 11.

[69] For the development of prisoners' rights in domestic law see the last edition of this book: Foster, *Human Rights and Civil Liberties* (Pearson 2008, 2nd edn), chapter 8.

[70] Most notably, *Golder* v *United Kingdom* (1975) 1 EHRR 524; *Silver* v *United Kingdom* (1985) 3 EHRR 347.

[71] (2000) 29 EHRR 245.

immunity enjoyed by the police force against actions in negligence constituted a violation of the right to a fair trial under Article 6 of the Convention.[72]

Parliamentary sovereignty and the limited role of the judiciary

Although the courts gave themselves a wide power to interpret legislation in line with human rights norms, the courts did not have (and still have not) the power to disregard statutory provisions simply because they interfere with fundamental human rights. Thus, the doctrine of parliamentary sovereignty has always limited the constitutional role of the courts. For example, as was seen in the case of *R v IRC, ex parte Rossminster*,[73] the House of Lords refused to challenge legislation on the grounds that it interfered unduly with a person's fundamental right to property and privacy. Further, other than the courts' power to interpret statutes and the common law during litigation, there existed no procedure to challenge the legality and compatibility of legislative provisions. Thus, a number of legislative provisions were alleged to be in contravention of the European Convention and other human rights treaties, and the courts were powerless to challenge such provisions. This situation has led to a number of defeats for the United Kingdom government before the European Court of Human Rights. For example, in *Sutherland v United Kingdom*[74] the European Commission of Human Rights held that a law which distinguished between homosexuals and heterosexuals with regard to the age of consent was contrary to Articles 8 and 14 of the European Convention.

Inadequate weight given to the human rights issue

Although both parliament and the courts attempted to provide for the protection of human rights and civil liberties, and tried to ensure that any interference with such rights and liberties was justified as the minimum necessary in the circumstances, on countless occasions the United Kingdom was held to have failed to achieve the correct balance between the protection of fundamental human rights and the securing of other social or individual goals. Thus, in the area of free speech, the European Court of Human Rights has found a large number of domestic provisions and judicial decisions to be out of line with the jurisprudence of the Convention. For example, in *Sunday Times v United Kingdom*[75] the European Court held that the domestic law of contempt, and its application by the House of Lords, constituted a disproportionate interference with press freedom and the public's right to know, and there have been other examples where the law and its enforcement failed to achieve the necessary balance.[76]

---

[72] See also the recent decisions in *Z v United Kingdom* (2002) 34 EHRR 3; *TP and KM v United Kingdom* (2002) 34 EHRR 2; *E and Others v United Kingdom* (2003) 36 EHRR 31, where it was held that the inability of the applicants to bring actions in domestic law for breach of their Convention rights was a violation of Article 13 of the Convention.

[73] [1980] AC 852.

[74] *The Times*, 13 April 2001. The case resulted in a friendly settlement when the government agreed to pass legislation equalising the ages of consent: The Sexual Offences (Amendment) Act 2000.

[75] (1979) 2 EHRR 245.

[76] See, for example, *Observer and Guardian v United Kingdom* (1991) 14 EHRR 153; *Tolstoy Miloslavsky v United Kingdom* (1995) 20 EHRR 442; *Bowman v United Kingdom* (1998) 25 EHRR 1; *Goodwin v United Kingdom* (1996) 22 EHRR 123, with regard to freedom of speech. See also *Gaskin v United Kingdom* (1989) 12 EHRR 36 (right to access to private information); *McLeod v United Kingdom* (1999) 27 EHRR 493 (right to private and home life).

There may have been two principal reasons for this shortfall. First, although the domestic authorities may officially or ostensibly recognise the importance of the human right in question, it is clear that they did not give it the importance that is required by treaties such as the European Convention. Thus, there was a tendency on behalf of the domestic authorities to treat, for example, freedom of speech, on the same level as someone's commercial interests.[77] Secondly, domestic law lacked a doctrine of proportionality to ensure that in practice rights and liberties were not interfered with unduly or disproportionately. Although the courts often insisted that the common law doctrine of reasonableness was akin to the test of necessity and proportionality applied under the Convention, decisions of the European Court proved that that was not the case.[78]

Inconsistent legislative and judicial approach

As domestic law had no formal bill of rights and no formal system of protecting human rights and civil liberties, and instead relied on the goodwill of parliament and the intervention of the courts, it was inevitable that protection of human rights would be, at best, patchy and inconsistent. With regard to legislative protection, therefore, although parliament passed a number of provisions protecting individuals from discrimination, there was an absence of a general equality clause containing the right to be free from discrimination. Thus, although a person was protected from discrimination on grounds of sex, marital status, race and disability, the law failed, and to a great extent still does fail, to protect against discrimination on grounds such as sexual orientation, political affiliation and religion.

In relation to judicial protection, although the courts were able to recognise and develop certain 'constitutional rights', such as access to the courts, freedom of expression and the right to demonstrate, there was often great uncertainty among the judiciary as to the legitimacy of these rights and their status when pitted against other rights and interests. For example, in *Harman* v *Home Office*[79] Lords Scarman and Roskill were in disagreement as to whether a case involving the gagging of the press was about press freedom and free speech, or simply about the formal law of contempt of court. Thus, certain judges were uncomfortable with the idea of recognising 'constitutional' rights and preferred to make decisions on the basis of strict legal rules rather than on general human rights norms. This uncertainty was evident in a number of cases. For example, in *DPP* v *Jones and Lloyd*[80] the House of Lords were divided on the question of whether an individual had the right to use a public highway for the purpose of peaceful demonstration. Although the majority felt that the absence of such a right in domestic law would mean that a person would be denied his or her right of peaceful assembly, thus finding that there was such a right, the minority preferred to apply pure legal principles and formal precedent in finding that no such right existed. Similarly, in many of the prisoners' rights cases, some judges preferred to challenge administrative practices on the traditional

---

[77] See, for example, the decision of the Court of Appeal in *Camelot Group Ltd* v *Centaur Communications* [1999] QB 124, and various decisions on contempt of court and confidentiality dealt with in chapters 8 and 9.

[78] See, in particular, *Sunday Times* v *United Kingdom* (1979) 2 EHRR 245; *Smith and Grady* v *United Kingdom* (2000) 29 EHRR 493.

[79] [1983] AC 280.

[80] [1999] 2 All ER 257.

principle of *ultra vires*, rather than accept that prisoners had fundamental rights, which could only be interfered with in exceptional circumstances.[81]

Limited protection for the rights of minorities

Not surprisingly, in the absence of a formal bill of rights guaranteeing fundamental rights for each and every citizen, and within a constitution dominated by parliamentary sovereignty, the human rights and civil liberties of minorities were very precarious. In a human rights system which relied on the goodwill of parliament and the ingenuity of the courts in controlling executive power, it was not surprising that the rights of minorities were consistently overlooked and abused. Thus with regard to prisoners, both parliament and the courts continued to deny such persons their basic rights and a number of decisions of the European Court of Human Rights were required to provide prisoners with their rights of access to the courts,[82] private and family life[83] and correspondence,[84] and liberty and security of the person.[85] This was also evident in relation to deportees and asylum seekers, where a number of decisions of the European Court of Human Rights have found the United Kingdom in violation of the Convention with regard to the treatment of such persons.[86]

The lack of a formal bill of rights led to a number of violations of the rights of children. In *Tyrer v United Kingdom*[87] the European Court held that the administration of corporal punishment on a 15-year-old boy constituted degrading treatment and punishment within Article 3 of the Convention, despite the pleas of the government that such punishment was a necessary and reasonable method of punishing young offenders.[88] Further, in *A v United Kingdom*[89] the European Court held that there had been a violation of Article 3 when a young boy had been beaten by his stepfather, who was then acquitted of assault by relying on the defence of reasonable parental chastisement. This failure of the legal system to accommodate the rights of children was also evident in the European Court's ruling in *V and T v United Kingdom*,[90] where it was held that the subjection of two 11-year-old boys to a highly publicised adult trial was in violation of their right to a fair trial under Article 6 of the Convention. The discriminatory treatment of sexual minorities provides another example of the traditional common law method and its failure to provide human rights for all. Although the domestic

---

[81] See KENNEDY LJ in the Court of Appeal in *R v Secretary of State for the Home Department, ex parte O'Brien and Simms* [1998] 2 All ER 491, at 501 on the question of whether the authorities could interfere with a prisoner's right of free speech.

[82] *Golder v United Kingdom* (1975) 1 EHRR 524; *Silver v United Kingdom* (1983) 5 EHRR 347.

[83] *Hamer v United Kingdom* (1979) 24 DR 5.

[84] *Golder v United Kingdom* (1975) 1 EHRR 524; *Silver v United Kingdom* (1983) 5 EHRR 347; *Campbell v United Kingdom* (1992) 15 EHRR 137.

[85] *Weeks v United Kingdom* (1987) 10 EHRR 293; *Thynne, Wilson and Gunnell v United Kingdom* (1990) 13 EHRR 666; *Hussain and Singh v United Kingdom* (1996) 22 EHRR 1; *V and T v United Kingdom* (1999) 30 EHRR 121; *Stafford v United Kingdom* (2002) 35 EHRR 32.

[86] See, for example, the decisions in *Soering v United Kingdom* (1989) 11 EHRR 439; *Chahal v United Kingdom* (1997) 23 EHRR 413; and *D v United Kingdom* (1997) 24 EHRR 423, discussed in chapter 5.

[87] (1978) 2 EHRR 1.

[88] The dissenting judge, Judge Fitzmaurice (the British judge) felt that the treatment was acceptable, given the age of the victim.

[89] (1999) 27 EHRR 611.

[90] (2000) 30 EHRR 121.

position had often been upheld by the European Court of Human Rights,[91] a number of cases successfully challenged the discriminatory attitude of the domestic legal system, which imposed arbitrary and disproportionate interferences on the private lives of sexual minorities.[92]

CASE STUDY

R v Ministry of Defence, ex parte Smith [1996] QB 517

This case involved the challenge by a number of armed forces personnel to the legality and reasonableness of the Ministry of Defence's blanket policy on the employment of homosexuals in the armed forces. The case has been chosen as a good illustration of how the courts dealt with cases with a human rights context in the pre-Human Rights Act era and provides an interesting comparison of the approaches adopted by the domestic courts and the European Court of Human Rights.

The applicants, three homosexuals and one lesbian, all serving in the armed forces and with exemplary service records, had been dismissed from their posts in pursuance of the Ministry of Defence's policy which prohibited homosexual men and women from serving in the armed forces and which required the automatic discharge of anyone discovered to be of homosexual orientation. The justification for the policy was that the presence of homosexuals in the armed forces was a threat to the effectiveness of the armed forces and the morale of its personnel and the Ministry had conducted a research of the attitude of personnel who had expressed a strong agreement with the policy and its continuation. A committee of both Houses of Parliament had approved of the continuation of the policy. The applicants sought judicial review of that policy and its application, claiming that it constituted an interference with their right to private life under Article 8 of the European Convention, that it was contrary to Council Directive (EEC) 76/207 relating to equal treatment for men and women in employment, and that the policy and its enforcement was irrational under the *Wednesbury* principles, in that it was unreasonable in the light of changing moral standards and the changing treatment of homosexuals in the armed forces in both the United Kingdom and around the world. The High Court rejected the applications (*R v Ministry of Defence, ex parte Smith* [1995] 4 All ER 427) and the applicants appealed to the Court of Appeal.

In the Court of Appeal it was held that as the European Convention on Human Rights had not been incorporated into domestic law, the applicants could not rely directly on Article 8 of the European Convention. Also, with respect to the argument based on

---

[91] For example, in the case of *Laskey, Jaggard and Brown* v *United Kingdom* (1997) 24 EHRR 39, involving the prosecution of sado-masochistic activities. See also the cases brought unsuccessfully by transsexuals, claiming that their rights under the Convention had been violated by discriminatory domestic laws and practices: *Rees* v *United Kingdom* (1986) 9 EHRR 56; *Cossey* v *United Kingdom* (1990) 13 EHRR 622; *X, Y and Z* v *United Kingdom* (1997) 24 EHRR 143; *Sheffield and Horsham* v *United Kingdom* (1998) 27 EHRR 163. See now *Goodwin* v *United Kingdom* (2002) 35 EHRR 18, which overrules the previous transsexual cases.

[92] See *Dudgeon* v *United Kingdom* (1982) 4 EHRR 149; *Sutherland* v *United Kingdom, The Times,* 13 April 2001; and *ADT* v *United Kingdom* (2001) 30 EHRR 611.

European Community law, the Court of Appeal held that that provision only applied to discrimination based on gender and did not extend to discrimination on grounds of sexual orientation. Thus, the applicants' case relied exclusively on the argument that the policy and its enforcement was irrational under traditional *Wednesbury* principles.

The Court of Appeal held that it could only interfere with a decision on the grounds of unreasonableness when the decision was beyond the range of responses open to a reasonable decision maker. However, in judging whether the decision maker had exceeded that margin of appreciation, the human rights context involved required that the more substantial the interference with human rights, the more the court would require by way of justification before it was satisfied that the decision was reasonable. Thus, although the test of irrationality did not alter to one of proportionality because of the human rights context, the test itself was sufficiently flexible to cover all situations and to require greater justification from the decision maker in a case where the fundamental rights of the applicant had been interfered with.

Applying that test to the facts, the Court of Appeal held that it could not be said that the policy at the time of its enforcement was irrational. The policy had been presented to and approved by both Houses of Parliament. In addition, the abandonment of the prohibition in other countries was, in the Court's judgment, too recent to support a finding of irrationality. The Court also made it clear that the decision could not be impugned on the sole ground that the decision maker had failed to take the European Convention into account, thus confirming the domestic courts' stance in this area: *R v Secretary of State for the Home Department, ex parte Brind* [1991] 1 AC 696.

The service men and women made applications under the European Convention, claiming that the investigations into their sexuality and their subsequent dismissals were in violation of Articles 3 and 8 of the Convention: *Smith and Grady v United Kingdom* (2000) 29 EHRR 493 and *Lustig-Prean and Beckett v United Kingdom* (2000) 29 EHRR 548. They also contended that there had been a violation of Article 13, which guarantees an effective remedy for breach of an individual's Convention rights, and of Article 14, which safeguards against discrimination in relation to the enjoyment of one's Convention rights.

The European Court of Human Rights held that there had been a violation of Article 8 in both cases. In the Court's view the investigations and interviews that the applicants were subjected to, and their subsequent dismissals, constituted especially grave interference with the applicants' private lives. Although the Court accepted that the investigations and dismissals pursued the purposes of national security and public order under Article 8(2) of the Convention, the Court felt that the report which sought to justify the continuation of the ban was based solely on the negative attitudes of heterosexual personnel to those of homosexual orientation, which could not justify the interferences in question. (Although the Court accepted that a change of policy would cause certain difficulties, such problems could be addressed by a strict code of conduct and by means of disciplinary rules.) However, the Court held that there had been no violation of Article 3 of the Convention. Although the Court was satisfied that the policy and its application were distressing and humiliating for the applicants, it did not feel that the treatment reached the minimum level of severity which could bring it within the scope of Article 3.

The Court also held in *Smith and Grady* that there had been a violation of Article 13 of the Convention, which guarantees the right to an effective remedy in domestic law for violations of an individual's Convention rights. In the Court's opinion, the threshold at which the domestic courts could find the Ministry's policy irrational had been placed so high that it effectively excluded any consideration by the domestic courts of the question of whether the interference with the applicants' private lives had answered a pressing social need or was proportionate to the aims pursued by the government.

As a result of that judgment the policy towards homosexuals in the armed forces was changed and the old policy of automatic dismissal was replaced by a conduct-based policy, which covers behavioural standards of all personnel, whether homosexual or heterosexual. The European Court of Justice had held that sexual orientation discrimination is not covered by EC law (*Grant v South West Trains Ltd* [1998] IRLR 206), and a decision of the Scottish Employment Appeal Tribunal that held that the word 'sex' in the Sex Discrimination Act 1975 should, in the light of the decision of the European Court of Human Rights in *Smith and Grady*, be interpreted to cover discrimination against a person on the grounds of their sexual orientation (*Macdonald v Ministry of Defence* [2001] IRLR 431) was overturned on appeal by the House of Lords [2004] 1 All ER 339.

Questions
1 To what extent could, and did, the domestic courts take into account the human rights context of the application?
2 Having rejected challenges on the basis of the European Convention on Human Rights and EC law, what human rights did the domestic courts identify had been interfered with in this particular case?
3 Why did the domestic courts uphold the armed forces' policy?
4 What conclusions can be drawn from the decision of the domestic courts regarding their power to interfere with administrative discretion and to uphold human rights?
5 How were the arguments presented to the European Court of Human Rights different from those presented to the domestic courts?
6 Why did the European Court come to the conclusion that there had been a violation of Articles 8, 13 and 14 of the Convention? What margin of appreciation did the Court appear to give to the government in this case?
7 Do you feel that it was legitimate for the European Court of Human Rights to decide that the policy was in violation of the Convention?
8 How do you think the domestic courts would have decided the case had the Human Rights Act 1998 been in force at the time?

Proposals for reform of the traditional method

This section of the chapter will deal with the varied proposals for reform of the traditional method, including the introduction of the Human Rights Bill. As the Act has now been with us for over ten years, and domestic human rights law is largely being driven by its provisions and the case law of the European Convention, the account will be brief, highlighting the main reasons for reform together with the fears shared by many regarding any new powers of the courts.[93]

Proposals for reform before 1997

Before the enactment of the Human Rights Act 1998, much academic and political discussion took place regarding the reform of the traditional method of rights protection.[94] Until the Human Rights Bill, however, proposals for reform had been rejected on the related grounds that the existing mechanism was satisfactory and that a constitutional method of rights protection would detract from the principles of parliamentary sovereignty and responsible government, and give too much power to unelected judges.[95] These aspects of rights protection have been explored in chapter 1 of this text and we have also looked at the deficiencies of the traditional method of rights protection, but it may be useful to summarise the advantages and disadvantages of the formal method before looking at the passing of the Human Rights Act 1998.

The 'pros' and 'cons' of a bill of rights

The arguments in favour and against a bill of rights for the United Kingdom, or rather incorporation of the European Convention into domestic law, were summarised in 1978 by the House of Lords Select Committee on a Bill of Rights.[96]

In favour of a bill of rights, the Committee first pointed out that the incorporation of the Convention would provide the individual with a positive and public declaration of guaranteed rights with which to challenge the power of public authorities, as opposed to relying on residual liberties. Secondly, the Committee noted that domestic law often left an individual with no remedy for breach of his or her Convention rights. Thus, as we have seen, certain rights, such as a clear and complete right to privacy, were absent from the system of rights' protection, and although the regular law might make some provision for such interests, certain claims will fail because they are not covered by the formal legal rules regulating that area. Related to this point, there may be disadvantages in attempting to balance human rights claims with other competing interests within formal legal rules.[97] In the Committee's opinion, therefore, incorporation of the Convention would complement existing human rights legislation and freshen up the common law system.

---

[93] For a detailed discussion of this area, see Bailey, Harris and Jones, *Civil Liberties: Cases and Materials* (Butterworths 1995, 4th edn), chapter 1. See also Dworkin, *A Bill of Rights for Britain* (Chatto and Windus 1990); Sir Leslie Scarman, *English Law – The New Dimension* (Sweet & Maxwell 1974); Zander, *A Bill of Rights?* (Sweet & Maxwell 1996, 4th edn). See also The Institute of Public Policy Research, *The Constitution of the United Kingdom* (IPPR 1991); Liberty, *A People's Charter: Liberty's Bill of Rights* (Liberty 1991); Klug and Wadham, The Democratic Entrenchment of a Bill of Rights: Liberty's Proposals [1993] PL 579; Cooper and Marshall-Williams, *Legislating for Human Rights: The Parliamentary Debates on the Human Rights Bill* (Hart 2000).

[94] For a thorough coverage of the bill of rights debate, see Blackburn (ed.) *Towards a Constitutional Bill of Rights for the United Kingdom* (OUP 1999) and Clayton and Tomlinson, *The Law of Human Rights* (OUP 2000), chapter 1.

[95] In 1975, Alan Leith introduced the Bill of Rights Bill into the House of Commons and in 1976 Lord Wade introduced a bill to incorporate the European Convention into domestic law in the House of Lords.

[96] *Report of the Select Committee of the House of Lords on a Bill of Rights* (HL Paper No 176), paras 30–34.

[97] See, for example, the cases of *Kaye v Robertson* [1991] FSR 62 and *R v Ministry of Defence, ex parte Smith* [1996] 1 All ER 257.

Thirdly, the incorporation of the Convention would have constitutional and diplomatic advantages. For example, the Committee saw that membership of the European Community made it important that the domestic legal and constitutional system developed as part of the community rather than in isolation. In addition, a bill of rights would assist the establishment of devolved assemblies for England and Wales. The Committee noted that a bill of rights would provide a framework of human rights guaranteed throughout the United Kingdom and that the incorporation of the Convention into domestic law would have a greater practical effect on legislators, administrators, the executive and the judiciary. The Committee saw no reason to suppose that the English courts were not as capable of adjudicating on human rights as the European Commission and Court of Human Rights.

The Select Committee's summary of the arguments against a bill of rights related to the increased power of the judiciary, the potential confusion caused by the application of human rights principles, and the argument that the existing system already largely and adequately protected the individual's human rights. In particular, the Committee noted the argument that incorporation of the Convention would hand over to the judiciary wide and important areas of legislative policy, such as freedom of expression and privacy. This argument incorporates equal concern that these matters would be taken away from a democratically elected parliament and be placed in the hands of judges who many argued were both unaccountable and unrepresentative.[98] The Committee also noted the concern that under a Bill of Rights the courts would have the power to define and apply wide and general human rights principles, thus threatening the certainty of the common law and creating uncertainty through extended litigation. This is an argument against both the nature of a bill of rights and its enforcement through judges. Thus, many argue that rights are more effectively and consistently protected through clear legal principles, such as trespass and *habeas corpus*, rather than a wide declaration of the right to liberty and security of the person, which would then require interpretation, restriction and application by the courts.

The argument regarding the existing satisfaction with the state of human rights protection in domestic law was based on successive governments' belief that the existing situation complied with the philosophy of the European Convention on Human Rights and that incorporation of the Convention into domestic law would only act to address a very small number of areas, such as the law of privacy and the legal liability of prisons. The general acceptance of this argument led the Committee to conclude that there was insufficiently compelling evidence to enact a bill of rights – although the majority of the Committee did recommend that there should be a bill of rights – and subsequent proposals failed principally on that argument.[99]

The Human Rights Bill

In 1996 the Labour Party set out proposals for the incorporation of the European Convention into domestic law,[100] making the proposal part of its election manifesto in 1997. Once

---

[98] See Griffiths, *The Politics of the Judiciary* (Fontana 1997, 5th edn). See also Griffiths, The Brave New World of John Laws (2000) 63 MLR 159.

[99] For, example, a Human Rights Bill was introduced to the House of Commons in 1985, and by Lord Lester in both 1995 and 1996.

[100] Straw and Boateng, *Rights Brought Home: Labour's Plans to Incorporate the European Convention on Human Rights into UK Law* (Labour Party 1996). See [1997] EHRLR 71.

elected, the Labour government published a White Paper,[101] and then introduced its Human Rights Bill 1997 to the House of Lords. The Act was passed on 9 November 1998 after intensive parliamentary debate regarding its scope and constitutional and legal effects.[102]

Although the Labour government was adamant regarding its proposals for constitutional reform, including the 'incorporation' of the Convention into domestic law, the content of the Human Rights Bill and the subsequent debates reflected the traditional concerns about the introduction of a formal method of human rights protection in the United Kingdom. Thus, although there was general agreement that there had to be a change in the arrangements made for the protection of human rights in domestic law, the legislation was equally driven by fears of an increase in judicial power and an interference with parliamentary sovereignty. Any proposals, therefore, had to ensure not only that human rights protection be enhanced – and in particular that the record of the United Kingdom under the European Convention be improved – but that the principles of parliamentary sovereignty and strong accountable government be preserved as far as possible. To that extent the Human Rights Bill rejected the possibility of a full-blown bill of rights, bestowing powers on the courts to set aside legislation. Instead the Human Rights Bill built on the existing principles of the traditional system, merely giving further effect to the principles and case law of the European Convention.

The scope and limitations of the Bill were summarised by the then Lord Chancellor, Lord Irvine, during the parliamentary debates:

> The design of the Bill is to give the court as much space as possible to protect human rights, short of a power to set aside or ignore Acts of Parliament. In very rare cases where the higher courts will find it impossible to read and give effect to any statute in a way which is compatible with Convention rights, they will make a declaration of incompatibility. Then it will be for Parliament to decide whether there should be remedial legislation. Parliament may, not must, and generally will, legislate . . . But the remedial action will not retrospectively make unlawful an act which is a lawful act – lawful since sanctioned by the statute. This is the logic of the bill. It maximises the protection of human rights without trespassing on parliamentary sovereignty.[103]

The provisions of the Act, and the relevant case law, will be discussed below, but for present purposes the Act was never intended to radically overhaul the United Kingdom's constitutional arrangements, or to substantially shift constitutional power from parliament to the courts.[104]

Question

What were the deficiencies of the common law system and why were reform and the passing of the Human Rights Act 1998 thought necessary?

---

[101] Home Office, *Rights Brought Home: The Human Rights Bill*, Cm 3782.

[102] For an extensive coverage of the parliamentary debates, see Cooper and Marshall-Williams (eds), *Legislating for Human Rights: The Parliamentary Debates on the Human Rights Bill* (Hart 2000).

[103] *Hansard* HL col 1228 (3 Nov 1997).

[104] See Feldman, The Human Rights Act 1998 and Constitutional Principles (1999) 19 LS 165; Gearty, Reconciling Parliamentary Democracy and Human Rights (2002) 118 LQR 248; Ewing, The Human Rights Act and Parliamentary Democracy (1999) 62 MLR 79; Lord Irvine, The Impact of the Human Rights Act: Parliament, the Courts and the Executive [2003] PL 308; O'Cinneide, Democracy, Rights and the Constitution – New Directions in the Human Rights Act Era (2004) CLP 175.

The Human Rights Act 1998

Introduction

The Human Rights Act 1998 was passed on 9 October 1998 and its main provisions came into effect on 2 October 2000.[105] Strictly speaking, the Act does not *incorporate* the European Convention into domestic law. First, the Act does not refer to all of the Convention, but only the majority of rights and limitations contained in Part One of the Convention. Secondly, the Convention and its case law does not automatically become part of the domestic law, but is instead given limited effect by the courts within the ambit of its provisions. Accordingly, on the face of it at least, the Act's obligations only apply against public authorities. Thirdly, unlike the European Communities Act 1972, the Human Rights Act does not give the Convention any enhanced or supreme status. The Act preserves the doctrine of parliamentary sovereignty and, in cases of direct and inescapable conflict between domestic law and Convention rights, dictates that domestic law will prevail. Rather, the Act allows the courts to give *further* effect to the Convention, bestowing on them the *direct* right to take Convention rights and case law into account when interpreting and developing the law, and enabling individuals to rely *directly* on Convention rights in the domestic courts.[106]

Territorial scope of the Act

As we have seen in chapter 2, the European Convention can in certain circumstances impose an obligation on member states with respect to violations occurring in another state, even where that state is not a party to the Convention.[107] More generally, member states owe an obligation, under Article 1, to protect the rights of those 'within its jurisdiction'.[108] With respect to liability under the Human Rights Act 1998, this gives rise to questions of liability where the violation takes place outside the United Kingdom, particularly as Article 1 of the Convention is not specifically given effect to under the Act.[109]

The domestic courts have accepted that the Human Rights Act's territorial ambit is in any case co-extensive with Article 1, so that the failure to 'incorporate' Article 1 is not fatal in this respect. However, the victim must be clearly within the jurisdiction of the British

---

[105] For a comprehensive analysis of the Act, see Grosz, Beatson and Duffy, *Human Rights: The Human Rights Act 1998 and the European Convention* (Sweet & Maxwell 2000); Clayton and Tomlinson, *The Law of Human Rights* (OUP 2008, 2nd edn). For a briefer coverage, see Wadham and Mountfield, *Blackstone's Guide to the Human Rights Act 1998* (OUP 2009, 5th edn).

[106] For an overview of the first years of the Act, see Klug and Starmer, Standing Back From the Human Rights Act: How Effective is it 5 Years on? [2005] PL 716; Jowell and Cooper (eds), *Delivering Rights: How the Human Rights Act is Working* (Hart 2003); Lester, The Human Rights Act 1998 – Five Years On [2004] EHRLR 258; Masterman, Taking the Strasbourg Jurisprudence into Account: Developing a Municipal Law of Human Rights' under the Human Rights Act [2005] ICLQ 907; Steyn, 2000–2005: Laying the Foundations of Human Rights Law in the United Kingdom [2005] 4 EHRLR 349; Ewing, The Futility of the Human Rights Act [2004] PL 829; Bonner, Fenwick and Harris-Short, Judicial Approaches to the Human Rights Act [2003] ICLQ 350; Dickson, Safe in their Hands? Britain's Law Lords and Human Rights (2006) LS 329.

[107] *Soering* v *United Kingdom* (1989) 11 EHRR 439.

[108] *Bankovic* v *Belgium* (2001) 11 BHRC 435.

[109] Articles 1 and 13 are excluded from s.1, and Schedule 1, of the 1998 Act.

authorities.[110] Thus, in *R (Al-Skeini and Others) v Secretary of State for the Defence*[111] it was held that the death of an Iraqi civilian in the custody of British forces in Iraq might engage the Human Rights Act 1998, as the civilian's custody in the hands of British soldiers placed him within the United Kingdom's jurisdiction as required by Article 1 of the Convention, thus imposing a duty to hold a proper investigation into that death as required by Article 2 of the European Convention.[112] Their Lordships held that s.6 and s.7 of the Act should be interpreted so as to apply not only where a public authority acted within the UK but also when it acted outside that jurisdiction for the purposes of Article 1 of the Convention. The purpose of the Act was to provide remedies in domestic law to those whose rights had been violated by a UK public authority and making such remedies available for acts done on another territory.

As a consequence s.6 needed to be interpreted as applying wherever the UK had jurisdiction within Article 1. Thus, in *R (Smith) v Oxfordshire Assistant Deputy Coroner*[113] it was argued that a soldier who had died from hyperthermia whilst carrying out duties in Iraq was subject to the jurisdiction of the Human Rights Act 1998. The Court of Appeal held that members of the armed forces were subject to UK jurisdiction wherever they were without territorial limit and that the soldier was protected by the Convention and the HRA whether he was at a base or not.

However, when the case was heard on appeal by the Supreme Court,[114] it was held that unless British troops on active service were on a United Kingdom military base they were not within the jurisdiction of the United Kingdom for the purposes of Article 1 of the Convention and the Human Rights Act 1998. The Supreme Court stressed that Convention law had established that it would only be in exceptional circumstances that Article 1 would extend beyond territorial boundaries; for example, where the state had taken effective control of another state's territory. The present case did not fall within any of those exceptions. There was no basis for the proposition that the jurisdiction which states had over their armed forces abroad both in national and international law meant that they were within their jurisdiction for the purposes of Article 1.

Further, in *Al-Skeini*, above, the House of Lords stressed that Article 1 did not apply to extend a broad, worldwide extra-territorial jurisdiction arising from the exercise of authority by state party agents anywhere in the world. Hence, the shooting of civilians during the hostilities did not engage Article 1. The British forces were not in effective control of that territory despite it being an occupying force.[115] This rejection of a more general jurisdictional liability needs to be examined in the light of the European Court of Human Right's recent decision

---

[110] In *R (Quark Fishing) v Secretary of State for Foreign and Commonwealth Affairs* [2006] 1 AC 529, the House of Lords held that the Act did not extend to the South Sandwich Islands so as to engage the government's liability to a fisherman who had been refused a licence by the Secretary of State, as that act had been done on behalf of the territory not the UK government.

[111] [2007] 3 WLR 33.

[112] See also *R (B and others) v Secretary of State for the Foreign and Commonwealth Office* [2005] 2 WLR 628, where the Court of Appeal held that it was possible to engage the liability of UK diplomatic personnel under the Human Rights Act for decisions made in the Australian Embassy.

[113] [2010] 3 WLR 223.

[114] [2010] 3 WLR 223.

[115] Note, in *R (Al-Jedda) v Secretary of State for the Defence* [2007] 2 WLR 31, it was held that the detention of an Iraqi/British citizen in Iraq for reasons of security, under UN Resolution 1546, was lawful despite being in violation of Article 5 of the European Convention. Such a power existed provided that the rights were not infringed to any greater extent than was inherent in such detention.

in *Al-Saadoon and Mufdhi v United Kingdom*,[116] where the European Court, disagreeing with the national courts,[117] held that the UK authorities had exclusive control – through the exercise of military force and by law – over the detention facilities which held the applicants. Thus, the applicants had been in the UK's jurisdiction at the time of transfer of the prisoner to the Iraqi authorities so as to face trial.[118] Indeed, at the time of writing the Grand Chamber of the European Court is preparing to hear applications brought under Articles 2 and 3 by the victims, who are questioning the British courts' ruling on the question of jurisdiction.[119]

Further difficulties have arisen with respect to whether the government authorities have any duty to intervene in relation to the treatment of British nationals or residents at the hands of other countries. In such a case the victim is not within the jurisdiction of the Act, but in *R (Abassi) v Secretary of State for Foreign and Commonwealth Affairs*[120] it was recognised that the courts *might* interfere with a decision relating to foreign policy which impinged on an individual's human rights. However, such a review would be very limited and the authorities would be under a bare duty to show that they had given due consideration to the individual's claim. This approach was followed in *R (Al Rawi and Others) v Foreign Secretary and Others*,[121] where it was held that the Secretary of State's refusal to make a formal request to the United States for the return of non-British persons detained at Guantanamo Bay was in violation neither of the European Convention nor of general principles of administrative law.[122]

Retrospective effect of the Act

The provisions of the Act generally only apply to acts or decisions of public authorities taking place after the coming into operation of the Act, on 2 October 2000. This is because the Convention is not intended to have an overriding effect apart from it being given further effect by the passing of the Act. This contrasts with the position of EU law, where the relevant EU legislation can provide individual rights irrespective of whether they have been specifically implemented by domestic legislation. For example, in *Timbrell v Secretary of State for Work and Pensions*,[123] the Court of Appeal held that a male to female transsexual could rely on an EEC directive to claim a female pension despite the fact that the Gender Recognition Act 2004 had not been passed at the time of the discrimination. The directive was precise and unequivocal and obliged the secretary of state to provide protection in domestic law.

---

[116] (2010) 51 EHRR 9.

[117] See *R (Al-Saadoon and Mufdhi) v Secretary of State for Defence* [2009] EWCA Civ 7.

[118] As a result the applicants were protected by Articles 2 and 3 of the European Convention on Human Rights. The case is detailed in chapter 4 of this text at page 218–19.

[119] *Al-Skeini v United Kingdom* (Application No 55721/07); *Al-Jedda v United Kingdom* (Application No 27021/08).

[120] *The Times*, 8 November 2002. See Wilde, Casting Light on the 'Legal Black Hole': Some Political Issues at Stake [2006] EHRLR 553.

[121] [2007] 2 WLR 1219.

[122] See also *R (Gentle) v Prime Minister* [2008] 1 AC 1356, where the House of Lords held that Article 2 did not impose an obligation on member states to take reasonable steps to ensure that their armed forces were not sent on military operations that were unlawful under international law. The House of Lords held that other than Article 2 of the Convention, the issue of whether the government had complied with international law was non-justiciable. See Gordon, Global Reach (2007) 157 NLJ 237.

[123] [2010] CMLR 42.

Although initially the courts did not insist that the cause of an action occurred before the Act's implementation, subsequent case law confirms that this is indeed the case. In *Matthews v Ministry of Defence*[124] it was assumed that the claimant could rely on the Human Rights Act to challenge s.10 of the Crown Proceedings Act 1947 (which gave the Crown immunity in tort for certain actions causing injury to members of the armed forces) even though the relevant incident, an alleged act of negligence, occurred well before the Act came into force. However, in *Wilson v First County Trust Ltd (No 2)*,[125] the House of Lords overruled the decision of the Court of Appeal in that case,[126] which had allowed the claimant to rely on Article 6 of the Convention in challenging a provision under the Consumer Credit Act 1974, despite the fact that the relevant regulated agreement was entered into before the 1998 Act came into force. Further, in *Wainwright v Home Secretary*[127] the House of Lords confirmed that the 1998 Act and Convention principles could not apply to challenge searches conducted by prison officials before the Act's enforcement, and that it was not necessary to retrospectively develop a common law of privacy to remedy this gap. In such cases, therefore, the claimants would need to seek a remedy in Strasbourg.[128]

However, some judicial efforts have been made to allow the courts to use their interpretive powers under s.3 of the Human Rights Act to construe statutes in line with the Convention, even in respect of alleged violations taking place before the Act came into force. Thus, in *R (Hurst) v HM Coroner for Northern District London*,[129] the Court of Appeal held that s.3 applied the court's new interpretative power to legislation whenever enacted. Thus, a court could, in appropriate circumstances, give a Convention-compliant interpretation to any legislation even though the dispute in the case related to an act committed before the Act came into effect. In this case public policy dictated that Article 2 of the Convention, imposing a duty on the state to protect life and to conduct effective investigations into deaths, should inform the duty of a coroner under the Coroners Act 1988.[130] However, on appeal the House of Lords held that the Court of Appeal had erred in its decision.[131] In their Lordships' view the Convention rights under Article 2 only applied domestically to deaths occurring after the coming into force of the 1998 Act, and as the right to an effective investigation was an ancillary aspect of that right that too only arose in respect of deaths occurring after 2 October 2000.[132] The House of Lords also held that it was not necessary to interpret the Coroners Act 1988 in line with Article 2 of the Convention by applying the common law presumption that

---

[124] [2003] 1 AC 1163. The case failed on its facts as there was held to be no violation of Article 6.

[125] [2003] 3 WLR 568.

[126] [2001] 3 WLR 42.

[127] [2004] 2 AC 406.

[128] In *Wainwright*, for example, the claimants took a case to the European Court of Human Rights, who found that there had been a breach of Articles 8 and 13 of the Convention: *Wainwright v United Kingdom* (2007) 44 EHRR 40.

[129] [2005] 1 WLR 3892.

[130] See also *Cumming and Others v Chief Constable of Northumbria Police*, *The Times*, 2 January 2004, where the Court of Appeal held that in assessing whether the police had reasonable grounds to arrest a person a court had to take into account Article 5 of the European Convention, even though the arrest took place before the coming into operation of the Human Rights Act 1998.

[131] [2007] 2 WLR 726.

[132] The House of Lords thus upheld its previous ruling in *Re McKerr* [2004] 1 WLR 807, to the effect that Article 2 did not apply directly to deaths occurring before 2 October 2000. For further discussion, see chapter 4 of this text.

parliament did not intend to legislate in violation of its international law obligations. In this case there was no ambiguity in the 1988 Act, and, even if there was, it was not appropriate to hold that it was parliament's intention that coroners be given wider investigative powers in line with Article 2 of the Convention in all cases.

Despite the decision of the House of Lords in *Hurst*, above, the courts are still able to apply common law principles of fundamental rights, either to cases which do not come within the ambit of the 1998 Act, or in order to supplement enforceable Convention claims. Thus, in *R (Anufrijeva) v Secretary of State for the Home Department*,[133] the House of Lords held that the constitutional principle requiring the rule of law to be observed also required a state to accord to individuals the right to know of a decision before their rights could be adversely affected. Parliament had not expressly or impliedly legislated to displace the applicable constitutional principle.

Retrospectivity and appeals

Section 22(4) of the Act provides that s.7(1)(b) applies to proceedings brought by or at the instigation of a public authority whenever the act in question takes place, but otherwise s.7(1) does not apply to an act taking place before the coming into force of that section.

Section 7(1)(b) provides that a victim can rely on a Convention right 'in any legal proceedings', thus raising the question of whether such a matter could be raised in an appeal held after the Act came into force, but in connection with initial proceedings determined before the Act's operation. In the important pre-Human Rights cases of *R v DPP, ex parte Kebilene*[134] the Divisional Court had held that the Human Rights Act applied to a pre-Act prosecution because by the time the case reached appeal the Act would be in force and the defendant could rely on the Act to quash the original conviction. Again, in *R v Benjafield*[135] the Court of Appeal held that as the prosecution of a person was within the words 'proceedings brought by or at the instigation of a public authority' under s.22(4), any appeal against conviction was part of the proceedings within s.7(1)(b). Therefore the Act's provisions could apply to challenge the ordering of confiscation orders made before the Act and upheld by the court of first instance.[136]

The decisions in *R v Lambert* and *R v Yash Pal Kansal*

However, in *R v Lambert, Ali and Jordan*,[137] the House of Lords held that the Act does not have such retrospective effect. In that case the defendants had appealed against conviction for possession of cocaine with intent to supply under s.5 of the Misuse of Drugs Act, claiming that the Act was contrary to the presumption of innocence contained in Article 6 of the European Convention. The House of Lords held that s.22(4) only applied to give retrospective effect to

---

[133] [2003] 3 All ER 827.

[134] *The Times*, 31 March 1999. On appeal the House of Lords held that the decision of the DPP to prosecute was not amenable to judicial review: [1999] 4 All ER 801.

[135] [2001] 1 WLR 75.

[136] The Court of Appeal held that confiscation orders did not constitute a criminal charge under Article 6 of the Convention and thus there was no violation of any Convention rights. This decision was upheld by the House of Lords: *R v Benjafield* [2002] 1 All ER 185.

[137] [2001] 3 WLR 206.

the Act where proceedings were brought by a public authority. An unsuccessful appeal, brought by the defendant, was not to be treated as proceedings brought by or at the instigation of a public authority, and parliament had thus not intended Convention rights to be applicable to appeals which related to convictions before the 1998 Act came into force. Thus, although the Act appeared to allow Convention rights to be raised in relation to initial prosecutions brought before the Act came into force, the decision in *Lambert* closed off the possibility of pre-Act convictions being appealed on Convention grounds.[138]

The decision in *Lambert* was considered by the House of Lords in the case of *R v Yash Pal Kansal*,[139] where it was held that the majority decision in *Lambert*, that s.22(4) of the Human Rights Act 1998 could not be applied to appeals brought by defendants against convictions, could not be supported. However, their Lordships refused to depart from that decision, stating that although the case was wrongly decided, the present case was not one in which it was appropriate for the House to depart from it. Their Lordships also held that in any case, given the state of the law at the relevant time, both the trial judge and the prosecutors (as public authorities) had no choice but to act as they did.[140]

The effect of the decision in *Lambert* was illustrated in the case of *R v Lyons and Others*,[141] where the House of Lords were asked to quash the appellants' convictions on the grounds that there had been a violation of Article 6 of the European Convention. The European Court had already decided that there had been a violation of Article 6 when incriminatory statements made by the applicants in the course of investigations had been used in the criminal trial.[142] Nevertheless, it was held that the decision of the European Court could not disturb a conviction before the Human Rights Act had come into force. The decision was binding in international law and did not require the domestic courts to quash a conviction that at the relevant time was quite clearly lawful in domestic law.[143]

However, a domestic court might apply Convention case law to a pre-Act trial when the judge could have taken into account Convention law at the original trial. Thus, in *R v Beckles*,[144] the Court of Appeal allowed an appeal against conviction because it was concerned that the jury might have drawn adverse inferences against the defendant's right to silence. In coming to this conclusion the Court of Appeal referred to the European Court's decision in *Beckles v United Kingdom*[145] for the purpose of attacking the jury's decision in the original trial. Although this case appears to run counter to *R v Lyons*, above, the Court of Appeal is saying that the jury *could* and should have complied with Article 6 and the common law at the time of the trial. In *Lyons*, on the other hand, the Court had no choice but to follow incompatible domestic law at the trial.

---

[138] The courts have also held that s.22(4) does not apply to a case where pre-October 2000 proceedings were brought by an individual via judicial review. Again, this is because judicial review proceedings are not brought by a public authority so as to invoke s.22(4). See *R v Haringey London BC, ex parte Ben-Abdelaziz and Another* [2001] 1 WLR 1485, and, more recently, *R (Hurst) v HM Coroner for Northern District* [2007] 2 WLR 726.

[139] [2001] 3 WLR 1562. For a critical account of the decisions in *Lambert* and *Kansal*, see Beyeveld, Kirkham and Townend, Which Presumption? A Critique of the House of Lords' Reasoning on Retrospectivity and the Human Rights Act [2002] LS 185.

[140] It had been argued that the prosecution and conviction were in violation of Article 6 of the European Convention because the prosecution had relied on evidence that had been obtained in violation of the principle against self-incrimination: see *Saunders v United Kingdom* (1996) 23 EHRR 313.

[141] [2002] 3 WLR 1562.

[142] *Saunders v United Kingdom* (1996) 23 EHRR 313.

[143] See also *R (on the application of Hooper and Others) v Secretary of State for Work and Pensions* [2005] 1 WLR 1681.

[144] [2005] 1 WLR 2829.

[145] (2003) 36 EHRR 13.

Of course, in such a case the victim may bring an action under the European Convention machinery if no remedy is available in domestic law; for example, following the decision in *R v Kansal*, the applicant lodged such a complaint, claiming a violation of Article 6 of the Convention. In *Kansal v United Kingdom*[146] the European Court found, following the reasoning in its previous decision in *Saunders*, that the applicant had been denied a fair hearing under Article 6 of the Convention when his answers to questions made under compulsion by virtue of the Insolvency Act had been used at his criminal trial.[147]

Question
What difficulties are posed by the Human Rights Act 1998 having a limited retrospective effect?

The rights guaranteed under the Act

Section 1(1) of the Human Rights Act 1998 states that the Convention rights referred to throughout the Act are those contained in Articles 2 to 12 and 14 of the main Convention, Articles 1 to 3 of the First Protocol and Articles 1 and 2 of the Sixth Protocol. These rights are then stated to be read with Articles 16 to 18 of the Convention, and further that they are to be subject to any designated derogation or reservation made under s.14 and s.15 of the Act.

Although the Act deliberately omits Article 1 of the European Convention, which states that it is the responsibility of each member state to ensure that the rights laid down in Part One of the Convention are guaranteed to everyone within the state's jurisdiction, the House of Lords has held that that article can be employed to extend the liability of public authorities under the Act to acts outside the jurisdiction of the United Kingdom.[148] The Act also omits Article 13 of the Convention, which guarantees to every person an effective remedy for breach of his or her Convention rights. The reasons for these omissions are that the passing of the Act is seen in itself as an adequate measure to ensure that everyone enjoys their Convention rights. Their exclusion is also consistent with the Act's exclusion of certain actions, such as those clearly allowed by primary legislation, and the exclusion of certain bodies, such as parliament, from the ambit of its protection.

Use of Convention case law by the domestic courts

Before the Act came into operation, the courts refused to allow the Convention to be used directly in legal disputes,[149] and were reluctant to refer to the case law of the Convention in resolving disputes regarding the legality and reasonableness of actions that interfered with basic human rights.[150] Section 2 of the Act not only allows domestic courts to give effect to

---

[146] (2004) 39 EHRR 31.

[147] The complaint under Article 13 (failure to provide an effective remedy) had been declared inadmissible at the admissibility stage of the proceedings and was not considered again by the full Court.

[148] *R (Al-Skeini and Others) v Secretary of State for Defence* [2007] 3 WLR 33.

[149] See, for example, *Malone v Metropolitan Police Commissioner (No 2)* [1979] Ch 344; *R v Ministry of Defence, ex parte Smith* [1996] 1 All ER 257; *R v Secretary of State for the Home Department, ex parte Brind* [1991] 1 AC 696.

[150] See, for example, *R v Staines and Morrissey, The Times*, 1 May 1997.

the substantive Convention rights, but also requires them to consider the relevant case law of the Convention when determining disputes that raise such rights and their application. It provides that when a court or tribunal is determining a question involving any Convention right, it must take into account any judgment, decision, declaratory or advisory opinion of the European Court of Human Rights, any opinion of the European Commission given in a report, any decision of the European Commission, and any decision of the Committee of Ministers whenever made or given, so far as, in the opinion of the court and tribunal, it is relevant to the proceedings in which that question has arisen.

While the section states that the courts must take into account the decisions of the European (Court), the provision does not insist that they *apply* such decisions. Of course, if the courts fail to apply case law of the Convention that is favourable to the claimant's case, that claimant will be required to take his or her case to Strasbourg. As the main aim of the 1998 Act is to avoid that scenario, the domestic courts are unlikely to refuse to apply such case law when deciding cases under the Human Rights Act. However, another possibility is that the courts will ignore the Strasbourg case law where they want to give a more generous interpretation to the Convention rights. Thus, it is suggested that the courts, unrestricted by the doctrine of the margin of appreciation, might ignore the decisions of the Court or Commission where the latter have taken an unduly restrictive approach.

There have been some indications that the domestic courts will be reluctant to disturb the status quo, and will follow the Strasbourg case law instead of developing a human rights' jurisprudence independent of and superior to that of the Convention.[151] Thus, in *R v Secretary of State for the Home Department, ex parte Taylor and Anderson*[152] the Court of Appeal suggested that it would be improper for the domestic courts to decide a case in a way that was contrary to the application currently being applied by the European Court of Human Rights. In that case the Court of Appeal held that the power of the Home Secretary to set tariffs for mandatory life sentence prisoners had clearly been accepted by both the domestic legislature and the European Court of Human Rights, and that in such a case it would not be proper to act in a manner which was inconsistent with the European Court's approach to that matter.[153] The case should not be read as a warning to the courts not to expand the Strasbourg jurisprudence, and presumably the domestic courts will be less reluctant to depart from the existing case law if such decisions are dated or inconsistent with developments within the Council of Europe.[154] This was apparent in the recent case of *Re P and others*,[155] where the House of Lords

---

[151] See, for example, the decisions in *R v Secretary of State for the Home Department, ex parte Pearson and Martinez, The Times*, 17 April 2001 (prisoner's right to vote), and the decision of the Court of Appeal in *Bellinger v Bellinger* [2002] 1 All ER 311 (recognition of transsexual marriage). Both decisions were subsequently found to be in violation of Convention rights.

[152] [2002] 2 WLR 1143. See Masterman, Section 2(1) of the Human Rights Act 1998: Binding Domestic Courts to Strasbourg? [2004] PL 725, and Masterman, Aspiration or Foundation? The Status of the Strasbourg Jurisprudence and the 'Convention Rights' in Domestic Law, in Fenwick, Phillipson and Masterman (eds) *Judicial Reasoning under the UK Human Rights Act* (Cambridge University Press 2007), chapter 3.

[153] At the time of the Court of Appeal decision, the European Court was waiting to hear a similar complaint under the European Convention machinery. In *Stafford v United Kingdom* (2002) 35 EHRR 32 the European Court suggested that the Home Secretary's powers were in violation of Article 6 and the House of Lords subsequently declared such powers incompatible with Article 6 under s.4 of the Human Rights Act 1998; [2002] 3 WLR 1800.

[154] See Lewis, The European Ceiling on Human Rights [2007] PL 720; Wright, Interpreting Section 2 of the Human Rights Act 1998: Towards an Indigenous Jurisprudence of Human Rights [2009] PL 595.

[155] [2009] 1 AC 173.

declared a rule exempting unmarried couples from adopting as incompatible with Articles 8 and 14 of the Convention. Their Lordships noted that a recent European Court judgment appeared to override its previous decision on this matter and thus pointed to the conclusion that such discrimination would be unlawful.[156] In any case, their Lordships stated that where the European Court had not laid down a definitive interpretation of the legal position the domestic courts were not bound to follow those decisions – the rights in the Human Rights Act were domestic and not international human rights and the domestic courts could give their own interpretation to them and to apply the division between the decision-making powers of the courts and parliament in a way that appeared appropriate for the United Kingdom. Thus the domestic court was free to give what it considered to be a principled and rational interpretation of the concept of discrimination on the grounds of marital status. So too, the domestic courts have stressed that general principles laid down by the European Court of Human Rights with respect to Convention articles should not necessarily disturb specific rules of domestic private law, such as public authority immunity in tort.[157]

Equally, there may also be cases where the domestic courts feel that it is more appropriate to apply specific domestic precedent to a dispute, rather than relying on general principles that have been laid down by the European Court of Human Rights.[158] In *Price v Leeds County Council*[159] it was held by the Court of Appeal that when faced with a House of Lords' decision that was inconsistent with a decision of the European Court of Human Rights,[160] it should follow the decision of the House of Lords and refer the case to appeal. The House of Lords' decision was on a particular statutory scheme, and it would subvert legal certainty if the decision of the European Court was followed. When the case was appealed,[161] the House of Lords stressed that the European Court accorded a generous margin of appreciation to the national authorities, attaching much importance to the facts of the case. Accordingly, it was for the courts to decide how in the first instance the principles expounded in Strasbourg should be applied in the special context of national legislation, practice and social and other considerations.[162] In such cases, therefore, the domestic law and domestic precedent should be followed unless there was a strongly arguable case that the law and cases were incompatible with the European Convention.[163]

---

[156] The case of *EB v France* (2008) 47 EHRR 21 appeared to override the decision in *Frette v France* (2004) 38 EHRR 21. The cases are detailed in chapters 11 and 13 of this text.

[157] See, for example, *Lawrence v Pembrokeshire County Council* [2007] 1 WLR 2991, where the Court of Appeal held that the rule laid down in *JD v East Berkshire Community Health NHS Trust* [2005] 2 AC 373, to the effect that investigators into child abuse did not owe a duty of care to the parents suspected of such abuse, was not disturbed by Article 8 of the Convention. See also *Smith v Chief Constable of Sussex* [2008] UKHL 58, which upheld such immunity in respect of the police.

[158] See Lord Phillips' views in 'We will not accept your words as law, Supreme Court tells Europe', *Daily Telegraph*, 30 July 2010.

[159] [2005] 1 WLR 1825.

[160] *Connors v United Kingdom* (2005) 40 EHRR 9 on the rights of gypsies to private and home life under Article 8.

[161] *Kay v Lambeth London Borough Council; Price v Leeds City Council* [2006] 2 WLR 570.

[162] See also *Murray v Express Newspapers, The Times*, 4 October 2007; [2007] EMLR 22 (QB), where the High Court held that the courts should follow domestic precedent in the case of any conflict between the European and domestic case law on privacy and press freedom.

[163] That decision was followed in *Doherty v Birmingham City Council* [2009] 1 AC 367, where it was held that the Mobile Homes Act 1983 clearly gave the local authority the power to evict travellers from its site, despite the ruling of the European Court in *McCann v United Kingdom* (2008) 47 EHRR 40. Until the European Court developed principles of general application in English law, the House of Lords must apply the clear provisions of the Act and domestic case law.

The danger of this approach is that the domestic decision might not adequately facilitate the principles of the Convention and that this may be exposed by subsequent appeal to the Strasbourg Court. Thus, in *Kay* v *United Kingdom*[164] the European Court held that there had been a violation of Article 8 of the Convention when the applicants (the unsuccessful claimants in the domestic proceedings, above) were unable to challenge a dispossession order on grounds of proportionality and were limited, by precedent, to challenges on grounds of legality and rationality.

However, the mere fact that the United Kingdom has lost a case before the European Court on this legal matter will not necessarily mean that the domestic courts will subsequently alter its interpretation or application of the law. For example, in *R* v *Horncastle*[165] the Supreme Court, in confirming that the statutory regime on the admissibility of evidence was not incompatible with Article 6 or the case law of the European Court of Human Rights, stressed that the judgment in *Al-Khawaja* v *United Kingdom*[166] on hearsay evidence was not determinative of the case. Although s.2 of the Human Rights Act normally resulted in the national courts applying principles clearly established by the European Court of Human Rights, there would be rare occasions, such as the instant case, when the Supreme Court would have concerns as to whether such a decision sufficiently appreciated particular aspects of the domestic process. In such a case the Supreme Court could decline to follow that decision, giving reasons for adopting that course. It is worthy of note, however, that at the time of the Supreme Court's judgment the government were appealing the decision in *Al-Khawaja* to the Grand Chamber of the European Court; in such a case the domestic courts may be reluctant to relinquish their previous interpretations of domestic law until they have total clarification on the matter from Strasbourg.

This flexibility will, however, be lost where the domestic courts are satisfied that the European decision in question has general application and is clearly intended to cover the present case. In such a scenario the domestic courts (usually the House of Lords (now the Supreme Court)) will follow the European ruling in preference to the domestic decision. For example, in *R (Purdy)* v *DPP*, although the Court of Appeal recognised that it would only be in very exceptional circumstances that it would override what would otherwise be the binding precedent of the House of Lords,[167] on appeal the House of Lords followed the European Court's decision in *Pretty* v *United Kingdom*[168] in preference to the House of Lords in *Pretty* v *DPP*[169] on the question of whether the right to die engaged Article 8 of the European Convention. This was because the European Court's ruling clearly conflicted with the House of Lords' decision on a question of the interpretation of a Convention right rather than its application to specific domestic legislation.[170] Similarly, in *AF* v *Secretary of State for the Home Department*,[171] the House of Lords held that the decision of the European Court in *A* v *United Kingdom*[172] had to be followed in preference to the decision of their Lordships in *Re MB*[173] where there was any conflict between the two decisions with respect to the use of closed evidence in control order cases.[174]

---

[164] *The Times*, 18 October 2010.
[165] [2010] 2 AC 373.
[166] (2009) 49 EHRR 1.
[167] [2010] 1 AC 345.
[168] (2002) 35 EHRR 1.
[169] [2002] 1 All ER 1.
[170] The litigation in *Pretty* is detailed in a case study in chapter 4 of this text.
[171] [2010] 2 AC 269.
[172] (2009) 49 EHRR 29.
[173] [2006] 3 WLR 839.
[174] This area and litigation will be detailed in both chapters 6 and 14 of the text.

The case law in this delicate area is, thus, difficult to predict, but the High Court has recently indicated that the issue of precedent should be determined by the Supreme Court rather than by allowing the lower courts to depart from previous decisions of the House of Lords or the Supreme Court. In *R (GC) v Commissioner of the Police of the Metropolis*,[175] the court had to decide whether to follow a House of Lords' decision which justified the retention of DNA samples,[176] or to follow the European Court's subsequent ruling, that such retention was inconsistent with Article 8 of the European Convention.[177] It was held that legal certainty demanded that the court followed the decision of the House of Lords rather than the Strasbourg court, despite the fact that the claimants in both those cases were the same. However, the court also held that it was appropriate to grant the present claimants a direct right of appeal to the Supreme Court to determine the issue of precedent. The present policy, therefore, is to follow domestic case law until the Supreme Court has the opportunity to decide which decision it is appropriate to follow, taking into account both the margin of appreciation and the need to secure compliance with clear rulings of the European Court.

Section 2 and the doctrine of proportionality

In particular, s.2 of the Act allows the courts to incorporate the doctrines of legality and reasonableness employed by the European Convention machinery in adjudicating on allegations of violation of Convention rights.[178] Thus, courts may now consider whether interferences with human rights are 'prescribed by law', whether they serve a legitimate aim, and whether they are 'necessary in a democratic society'. In particular, the courts will have access to the doctrine of proportionality, a doctrine that lies at the heart of the European Court's jurisprudence, and one that had been firmly rejected by the domestic courts in the pre-Human Rights Act era.[179] The power to use proportionality can be used both to assess the necessity of administrative action that is permitted under legislation, and to decide whether such legislation allows such interference. For example, in *S v Airedale National Health Service Trust*,[180] it was held that a power of seclusion in relation to lawfully detained mental patients should not be implied into the Mental Health Act 1983 unless there was a self-evident and pressing need for the power. On the facts, the court concluded that there was such a power and although such a power was subject to anxious scrutiny, it had been exercised reasonably.

A stricter standard of review?

Early case law suggests that the courts will be prepared to take a much more interventionist approach when considering the compatibility of administrative action with Convention rights, and both the Court of Appeal and the House of Lords have given guidance in relation

---

[175] [2010] HRLR 34.

[176] *R (S) v Chief Constable of South Yorkshire* [2004] 1 WLR 2196.

[177] *S and Marper v United Kingdom* (2009) 48 EHRR 50.

[178] See Supperstone and Coppel, Judicial Review after the Human Rights Act [1999] EHRLR 301.

[179] See Elliot, The Human Rights Act 1998 and the Standard of Substantive Review [2001] CLJ 301; Clayton, Developing Principles for Human Rights [2002] EHRLR 175; Leigh, Taking Rights Proportionately: Judicial Review, the Human Rights Act and Strasbourg [2002] PL 265; Hickman, The Substance and structure of proportionality [2008] PL 694; Baker, *Proportionality under the UK Human Rights Act* (Hart 2010).

[180] *The Times*, 5 September 2002. The House of Lords confirmed that these powers had been used legally and proportionately: [2006] 2 AC 148.

to the appropriate standard of review. In *R v Secretary of State for the Home Department, ex parte Mahmood*,[181] LORD PHILLIPS OF WORTH MATRAVERS MR stated that when anxiously scrutinising an executive decision that interferes with human rights, the court will ask the question, applying an objective test, whether the decision maker could reasonably have concluded that the interference was necessary to achieve one or more of the legitimate aims recognised by the Convention. Also, in asking the question whether the decision was necessary, the court should take account of the Strasbourg jurisprudence, pursuant to its duty under s.2 of the Act. His Lordship held that in reviewing such a decision the court would require the decision maker to demonstrate either that his proposed action did not in truth interfere with the right, or if it did, that considerations existed which might reasonably be accepted as amounting to a substantial objective justification for the interference.[182]

That dictum was clarified by the House of Lords in *R v Secretary of State for the Home Department, ex parte Daly*.[183] In that case Lord Steyn observed that Lord Phillips's statement was couched in the language of the traditional *Wednesbury* grounds of review. His Lordship held that there was a material difference between the *Wednesbury* grounds of review and the approach of proportionality applicable in respect of review where Convention rights were at stake. Although his Lordship conceded that most cases would be decided the same way whatever approach was adopted, the intensity of the review was somewhat greater under the proportionality test for a number of reasons. First, the doctrine of proportionality might require the reviewing court to assess the balance that the decision maker had struck, not merely whether it was within the range of rational or reasonable decisions open to him or her.[184] Secondly, the proportionality test might go further than the traditional grounds of review in as much as it might require attention to be directed to the relevant weight accorded to the interests and considerations. In this respect his Lordship approved of the dictum of Lord Clyde in *de Freitas v Permanent Secretary of Ministry of Agriculture, Fisheries, Land and Housing*,[185] that in determining whether a limitation is arbitrary or excessive the court should ask whether (i) the legislative objective is sufficiently important to justify limiting a fundamental right; (ii) the measures designed to meet that objective are rationally connected to it; and (iii) the means used to impair the right or freedom are no more than is necessary to meet that objective. Thirdly, even the heightened scrutiny test laid down in cases such as *Smith*[186] was not necessarily appropriate to the protection of human rights. The proper intensity of review required that the limitation of the right had to be necessary in a democratic society, in the sense of meeting a pressing social need, and that it really was proportionate to the legitimate aim being pursued. His Lordship also noted that the differences between the traditional grounds of review and the doctrine of proportionality might sometimes yield

---

[181] [2001] 1 WLR 840.

[182] For an analysis of this case and the doctrine of proportionality, see Hare, Regaining a Sense of Proportion: The Human Rights Act and the Proportionality Principle [2001] EHRLR 504.

[183] [2001] 2 WLR 1622. See also *R v Secretary of State for the Home Department, ex parte Samaroo, The Times*, 18 September 2001.

[184] See, for example, the Court of Appeal decision in *R (Wilkinson) v Broadmoor Special Hospital Authority and Others* [2002] 1 WLR 419, where it was held that the Court had to reach its own view as to whether the forcible administration of medical treatment would be contrary to Articles 2, 3 and 8 of the European Convention.

[185] [1999] 1 AC 69.

[186] *R v Ministry of Defence, ex parte Smith* [1996] 1 All ER 257.

different results, and therefore it was important that cases involving Convention rights had to be analysed in the correct way.[187]

Further, it has been accepted that the ultimate decision on the proportionality of any measure has to be addressed and decided by the courts, and not by the executive.[188] In *Huang v Home Secretary*[189] the House of Lords held that special immigration tribunals hearing appeals against decisions relating to the right to enter or remain are not performing a secondary review of the decision on the grounds of illegality or irrationality, but have to decide whether the decision in question was lawful and compatible with the European Convention. Moreover, the tribunal did not have to apply a test of exceptionality to challenge the decision. The giving of weight to the original decision was not an act of judicial deference; rather it was the performance of the ordinary judicial task of weighing up competing interests and according appropriate weight to the judgment of a person with responsibility and access to special sources of knowledge. Their Lordships also held that it was not sufficient for a judicial body to simply apply the proportionality test laid down in *de Freitas*;[190] it must also strike a fair balance between individual and community rights.

Proportionality and judicial deference

Despite accepting that the standard of review is intensified under the 1998 Act, in *Daly* Lord Steyn stated that he did not believe that there had been a shift to merits review: in his view the respective roles of judges and administrators were fundamentally distinct and would remain so. It is quite clear, therefore, that there is ample room for judicial deference even in matters affecting fundamental human rights.[191]

First, there may be cases where the courts accept that even where an executive decision impacts on the enjoyment of human rights, there may be two perfectly acceptable outcomes to that determination, particularly where the right in question is qualified and the courts' role is to adjudicate on the balance between such rights and other interests. In *Edore* v *Secretary of State for the Home Department*[192] the Court of Appeal held that given the margin of discretion available to decision makers, there was often room for two possible proportionate outcomes in a particular situation. Within that margin, a decision maker may, in some circumstances, fairly reach one of two opposite conclusions. However, the Court noted that both decisions would have to strike a fair balance between the competing claims and be proportionate on its facts.[193] Further, in *R (Wilson)* v *Wychavon DC*,[194] the Court of Appeal held that the least

---

[187] The traditional principles of review might be appropriate in certain contexts. For example, in *R (Khail)* v *Home Secretary* [2006] EWHC 2139 (Admin) it was held that a pre-Act case which stated that a decision of the Home Secretary as to asylum claims was only reviewable on *Wednesbury* grounds was still good law.

[188] See Amos, Separating Human Rights Adjudication from Judicial Review [2007] EHRLR 679.

[189] [2007] 2 AC 167.

[190] Note 185, above.

[191] On the question of the appropriate standard of review and deference, contrast Ewing, The Continuing Futility of the Human Rights Act [2008] PL 668, with Kavanagh, Judging the Judges under the Human Rights Act [2009] PL 287.

[192] *The Times*, 7 July 2003; see Keene, Principles of Deference under the Human Rights Act, in Fenwick, Phillipson and Masterman (eds), *Judicial Reasoning under the UK Human Rights Act* (Cambridge University Press 2007), chapter 8.

[193] In this case, the deportation of a woman who had lived in the country for over 10 years, and who had had two children by a man who kept in regular contact with her and the children, was held not to be proportionate and was thus not a decision open to the Secretary of State.

[194] [2007] 2 WLR 798.

restrictive approach of measuring proportionality did not have to be applied in every case and that there may be cases where there is a less restrictive approach which could have been adopted, yet still the measure is necessary and proportionate.[195]

Secondly, it is quite clear that as with the pre-Act position the intensity of the review will depend on all the circumstances, including the importance of the right in question, the level of violation and, equally importantly, the type of decision that is being challenged (including the expertise and status of the original decision maker).[196] In some cases therefore, the courts will apply standards of review that barely depart from traditional *Wednesbury* grounds.[197] For example, in *R (British American Tobacco and others) v Secretary of State for Health*,[198] in considering the proportionality of regulations banning the advertising of tobacco products and their compatibility with Article 10 of the European Convention the High Court stressed that there were areas in which the courts had to be particularly wary of imposing its own value judgments upon a legislative scheme. In the present case, therefore, although the protection of commercial speech was important, the proportionality of the regulations had to be judged in the context that the protection of health was a far-reaching social policy and that the need to restrict tobacco advertising was not challenged. On the facts, the court found that the measures were rationally connected and were proportionate to promoting health by restricting advertising at the point of sale. Similarly, in *R (Countryside Alliance) v Attorney-General*,[199] the House of Lords held that the Hunting Act 2004 was not incompatible with any Convention rights as it imposed a justified and proportionate interference, within parliament's area of discretion. In coming to that conclusion their Lordships noted that a majority of the country's democratically elected representatives had decided that there was a pressing social need for the hunting ban and that the democratic process was likely be subverted if, on a question of moral and political judgment, opponents of the Act achieved through the courts what they could not achieve in parliament.

Deference will also be shown where parliament has deliberately bestowed discretion on a specific executive body. Thus, in *Belfast City Council v Miss Behavin' Ltd (Northern Ireland)*,[200] the House of Lords held that in some situations it would be fair for the courts to conclude that the relevant legislation had struck a fair balance between individual rights and the general interests of the community, in which case there would be no room for the court to strike such a balance in an individual case. Their Lordships went on to state that if there had been no indication that the balance had been struck by the decision maker then the court would have no alternative but to strike the balance itself, giving due weight to the judgments of those who were in much closer touch with the people and the places involved than the court could ever

---

[195] In that case the different treatment accorded to caravans and buildings with respect to the power to issue stop notices to compel the following of planning law was justified under Article 14 and proportionate. The court noted that a wide area of judgment would be given with respect to measures intended to achieve social and economic benefits.

[196] See Rivers, Proportionality and Variable Intensity of Review [2006] CLJ 174.

[197] Generally the courts will be more comfortable with striking down acts that are clearly irrational in addition to being disproportionate. Thus, in *R (Baiai and Others) v Home Secretary and Another* [2006] EWHC 823 (Admin) it was held that the Home Secretary's regime of limiting the right to marry for those who were subject to immigration control was disproportionate and thus in violation of Articles 12 and 14 of the Convention. The court held that the policy adopted an illogical criterion and neglected to consider the length of the relationship. Moreover it was discriminatory and thus contrary to Article 14.

[198] *The Times*, 11 November 2004.

[199] [2007] 3 WLR 922.

[200] [2008] HRLR 11.

be. A similar discretion may be given to authorities such as the police, even though their judgment may impact on human rights. Thus, in *Re E (A Child)*,[201] in deciding that the police authorities had not breached Article 3 of the Convention in attempting to protect parents and children from violence when walking to and from school, the House of Lords held that although the Court of Appeal had erred in applying the *ex parte Smith* test rather than the heightened test of proportionality, the police were not required to drive back the protestors by force and make numerous arrests irrespective of potential widespread disorder, loss of life and destruction of property. The police were uniquely placed to make a judgment by reason of their experience and intelligence and the courts' review powers were circumscribed accordingly.

Proportionality and the decision-making process

Although both the European Court of Human Rights and the domestic courts, can, and indeed must, approach cases by considering the legality, proportionality and necessity of the challenged action, it has been made clear that an executive decision should not be impugned on the sole ground that the decision maker failed to take into account a Convention right, or has failed to ask itself whether its decision was compatible with the European Convention. Thus, in *R (Begum) v Denbigh High School*[202] the House of Lords held that the Court of Appeal had erred when they had struck down a school's decision to impose its uniform policy on the applicant without considering whether such a decision was a necessary interference with the child's right to religion under Article 9 of the European Convention, and without providing a convincing reason on that basis.[203] In their Lordships' view a court had to consider the necessity and proportionality of the final decision and must not judge the compatibility of the decision-making process with the Convention.

This principle was followed in the House of Lord's decision in *Belfast City Council v Miss Behavin' Ltd (Northern Ireland)*.[204] In this case the Northern Ireland Court of Appeal had held that the decision of a local council to refuse the applicant a licence for a sex shop was unlawful because they had not specifically taken into account the applicant's Convention rights, including freedom of expression. The House of Lords held that the reviewing court was concerned with whether the company's Convention rights had been infringed, and not whether the local authority had properly taken such rights into account. In other words, what was important was the practical outcome of the decision and not the quality of the decision-making process itself. On the facts, although the company's Convention rights had been engaged, they had been engaged only at a low level, and there was thus no basis for concluding that the local authority had violated those rights. Again, in *Secretary of State for the Home Department v Nasseri*,[205] the House of Lords held that there was no obligation under Article 3 to conduct an adequate investigation into the risk of torture or death; the correct approach was to see if there had been a violation of Article 3 on the merits, not to adjudicate on the decision-making process.[206]

---

[201] [2009] 1 AC 536.

[202] [2007] 1 AC 100.

[203] [2005] 1 WLR 3273.

[204] Note 200, above.

[205] [2010] 1 AC 1.

[206] See also *MT and Others v Secretary of State for the Home Department*, [2008] 2 WLR 159, where the Court of Appeal held that although a body in deciding whether a deportation would violate an individual's rights under Article 3 had to be rigorous, that decision would not be invalid simply because the body decided it in the individual's absence.

Further, more recently in *Re S-H (Children)*,[207] the Court of Appeal held that a judge in care proceedings who was balancing the rights of the child with other interests did not have to make specific reference to the doctrine of proportionality.

This approach contrasts with the traditional purpose of judicial review, which was concerned not with the merits of the decision itself, but rather with the decision-making process, and whether the authority had provided satisfactory reasons. It is submitted that although the ultimate question should be whether a person's Convention rights have been violated unnecessarily, the fact that the decision maker had not addressed those rights or given sufficient importance to the affected party's Convention rights when making that decision, should be relevant in judging the proportionality of the final decision. This, it is submitted, accords with the idea that public authorities should openly welcome and practise Convention principles, provided, of course, they are not held to account for technical breaches of those principles.

Proportionality and detention without trial

Despite the scope for acceptable judicial deference, the courts have made it clear that when fundamental human rights are at issue they will not show the executive, or parliament, undue deference simply because the decision or act involved high levels of sensitive policy.[208] In *A and Others v Secretary of State for the Home Department*[209] the House of Lords ruled that the detention of foreign nationals suspected of terrorism under s.21 of the Anti-Terrorism, Crime and Security Act 2001 was a disproportionate response to the threat of terrorism. In that case Lord Bingham held that where the conduct of government was threatened by serious terrorism, difficult choices had to be made and that while any decision of a representative democratic body commanded respect, the degree of respect would be conditioned by the nature of the decision made. In his view the traditional *Wednesbury* approach was no longer appropriate and the domestic courts themselves had to form a judgment whether a Convention right was breached, the intensity of the review being greater under proportionality. In Lord Bingham's view, even in terrorist situations, judicial control of the executive's interference with individual liberty was essential and the courts were not precluded by any doctrine of deference from scrutinising such issues.[210]

Further, Lord Bingham justified such an approach despite the allegation that the courts' interference in such cases might be undemocratic. In his Lordship's view, given the content of s.6 of the Human Rights Act and the courts' expressly conferred role under s.2 and s.3 of the Act to consider the case law of the European Court and to interpret legislation compatibly with Convention rights, powers specifically granted by parliament itself, the courts were operating under a wholly democratic mandate.

---

[207] [2010] EWCA Civ 1184.

[208] In *Machado v Home Secretary* [2005] 2 CMLR 43, the Court of Appeal held that an administrative decision that involved issues of public policy as well as human rights issues required a more intensive review than the test of whether the decision maker's response was within the range of reasonable responses open to it.

[209] [2005] 2 AC 68.

[210] Nevertheless, the majority of the House of Lords (Lord Hoffmann dissenting) did respect the Home Secretary's decision that there existed an emergency threatening the life of the nation, recognising that that decision at least was essentially political. For a commentary on this case and the role of the courts, see Feldman, Human Rights, Terrorism and Risk: The Roles of Politicians and Judges [2006] PL 364.

Proportionality, the 'Bloody Sunday' inquiry and the right to life

An application of this new intense level of review was seen in the case of *R (A and Others) v Lord Saville of Newdigate*.[211] The chairman of the 'Bloody Sunday' inquiry had refused requests from a number of soldiers to give their evidence at a venue other than Londonderry. The tribunal felt that the objective of restoring public confidence would be seriously diminished if a major part of the inquiry were held at a place far from where the incidents took place and concluded that there was no real and immediate risk to the soldiers' lives. Allowing the soldiers' application for judicial review of that decision, the Divisional Court held that in determining whether a decision might contravene fundamental human rights, the decision maker had to consider whether interference with the rights was a serious or real possibility. In such a case it was then for the decision maker to find compelling justification for interference, not for the potential victims to provide compelling justification for deciding otherwise. The tribunal should have asked whether it, as a public authority, would be in breach of its obligation not to make a decision exposing anyone to the real possibility of a risk to life in the future.[212] Applying that test, the court felt that the tribunal had used public confidence as the determinative factor and that accordingly its decision was erroneous.[213]

Proportionality and the detention of asylum seekers

A similarly 'hands off' approach was taken in *R v Secretary of State for the Home Department, ex parte Saadi and Others*.[214] In this case it was claimed that the temporary detention of asylum seekers at a reception centre pending the determination of their claims for asylum was in breach of the European Convention. The policy allowed a person to be detained for approximately seven days while their claims were examined and the applicants alleged that this was in contravention of their right to liberty and security of the person under Article 5 of the Convention. In the High Court COLLINS J held that the detentions were unlawful and in any case disproportionate.[215] However, on appeal to the Court of Appeal it was held that the Secretary of State had not acted unlawfully or disproportionately. Disagreeing with COLLINS J at first instance, the Court of Appeal accepted that the detention of the applicants was *prima facie* lawful under the Convention and that it was in relation to the duration of the detention that the question of proportionality arose. In the Court's view the test of proportionality involved the question of whether the process of considering an asylum application, or arranging a deportation, had gone on too long to justify the detention, having regard to the conditions in which the person was detained and any special circumstances affecting him. The Court of Appeal thus felt that no disproportionality was evident in the present case. On appeal to the House of Lords it was held that, subject to proportionality, Article 5 of the Convention did not require that detention with a view to deportation or extradition had to

---

[211] *The Times*, 21 November 2001.

[212] The court applied the test laid down in *R v Governor of Pentonville Prison, ex parte Fernandez* [1971] 1 WLR 987. It was also held that the tribunal had erred by applying the test laid down in *Osman v United Kingdom* (2000) 29 EHRR 245, of whether there was a real risk and immediate risk to life. Such a test only applied in assessing whether a state was liable for breach of its positive obligations to intervene so as to protect life.

[213] This decision was upheld by the Court of Appeal, which held that by applying the test of whether there was an unacceptable risk of attack on the soldiers by Republican dissidents, there existed a compelling reason why the soldiers' evidence should be taken in another venue: [2002] 1 WLR 1249.

[214] [2002] 1 WLR 356.

[215] *The Daily Telegraph*, 11 September 2001.

be necessary in order to be justified and that neither the methods of selection of these cases as being suitable for speedy determination, nor the manner in which they had been detained, were arbitrary or disproportionate.[216]

Proportionality, sex offenders' registration and the right to private life

Under proportionality, the judicial review of measures that interfere with human rights requires a strict assessment of the necessity of those measures in achieving any legitimate purpose and often allows the courts to ask whether less restrictive measures could be employed; or whether the measure could be tempered by procedural or other safeguards. In *R (JF) v Secretary of State for Home Department*,[217] the Supreme Court considered whether s.82 of the Sexual Offences Act 2003, which subjected sex offenders to indefinite notification requirements (notifying that a person was on the Sexual Offences Register) without any sub-sequent review, was disproportionate and thus incompatible with Article 8 of the Convention. Finding that the provision was incompatible with the right to private life, the Supreme Court noted that proportionality required a consideration of the extent of the interference with Article 8, the value of the notification requirements in achieving any legitimate aim, and the extent to which that value would be eroded if the procedure was made subject to subsequent review. Although the Court accepted that the requirements were important in helping the responsible authorities keep track of those whom they were supervising, the critical issue related to those offenders who could demonstrate that they no longer posed any significant risk of committing further sexual offences. Although it could never be certain that a person was no longer a risk, that uncertainty did not justify as proportionate the imposition of the requirements for life without review. It was also noted that other jurisdictions operated systems which had provision for review, and that it must be possible in certain cases for a tribunal to asses that there was no longer such a risk.

Questions

To what extent are the domestic courts bound by the case law of the European Court and Commission of Human Rights?

How does the doctrine of proportionality differ from traditional grounds of review, and to what extent has the doctrine changed the constitutional role of the domestic courts with respect to human rights cases?

Interpreting statutory provisions in the light of the Convention

Section 3 of the Act provides that so far as is possible, primary and subordinate legislation must be read and given effect in a way that is compatible with Convention rights. This will allow the courts to adopt a different interpretation to statutory provisions than applied by

---

[216] [2002] 1 WLR 3131. In *Saadi v United Kingdom* [2007] 44 EHRR 50, it was held that the detentions were not arbitrary. An appeal to the Grand Chamber of the European Court was unsuccessful: *The Times*, 4 February 2008.

[217] [2010] 1 WLR 76.

the courts before the Human Rights Act and thus in this sense the Act disrupts the doctrine of judicial precedent, allowing a court to disregard the previous decision of a higher court.[218]

Generally, s.3 does not apply retrospectively to cover the application of the statute to a situation before the Act came into operation. Thus in *Pearce* v *Governing Body of Mayfield School*[219] the House of Lords held that s.3 of the 1998 Act did not allow the courts to adopt a different interpretation to the word 'sex' used in the Sex Discrimination Act 1975 that had been applied by the courts before October 2000 in relation to an act of discrimination committed before that date. Neither could s.3 operate in relation to an appeal heard against that decision after October 2000.[220] This was confirmed by the House of Lords in *Wilson* v *Secretary of State for Trade and Industry*,[221] where it was held that the courts could only make a declaration of incompatibility under s.4 where s.3 could be used as an interpretative tool, and that parliament could not have intended that s.3 could be used to alter the parties' activities and obligations affected before the Human Rights Act came into operation. Although in *R (Hurst)* v *HM Coroner for Northern District London*[222] the Court of Appeal stated that the rule in *Wilson* (above) was not exclusive or absolute and that in certain cases it would not cause unfairness for the courts to use their s.3 powers to interpret legislation that had impacted on Convention rights where the act in question took place before the 1998 Act came into force, that decision was overturned on appeal to the House of Lords, and the traditional position was reinforced.[223]

It should also be noted that the interpretative power under s.3 can be used with respect to statutes that govern private law. Thus, although s.6 of the 1998 Act places a duty on public authorities not to breach Convention rights, and the remedies available to the courts relate to redressing such violations, a court may still use its powers under s.3 (and s.4) to interpret legislation in line with the Convention where the Act in question governs purely private relations. Thus in *Bellinger* v *Bellinger*[224] the House of Lords interpreted, and declared incompatible, statutory provisions governing the validity of marriages and the enjoyment of the Convention rights to private and family life and the right to marry.

Although s.3 gives a statutory power to the courts to interpret legislation in the light of Convention rights, the doctrine of parliamentary sovereignty is preserved by the Act, which provides that although s.3 applies to primary legislation and subordinate legislation whenever enacted, it does not affect the validity, continuing operation or enforcement of any incompatible primary legislation, or the validity, continuing operation or enforcement of any incompatible subordinate legislation if primary legislation *prevents removal* of the incompatibility.[225] Thus, if the courts, by using their interpretation powers under s.3, are unable to interpret primary legislation in conformity with Convention rights, the primary legislation continues in force and the courts have no power to strike the Act down. Similarly, although the courts have the power to disapply secondary legislation that is incompatible with Convention rights, they do not have such a power where the primary legislation clearly

---

[218] Note, however, that the courts might find it more appropriate to follow more specific domestic precedent in certain cases; see *Price* v *Leeds City Council* [2006] 2 AC 465, discussed at page 128, above.

[219] [2004] 1 All ER 339; heard with the appeal in *Macdonald* v *Advocate General for Scotland*.

[220] Applying the principle in *R* v *Lambert, Ali and Jordan* [2001] 3 WLR 206.

[221] [2004] 1 AC 816.

[222] [2005] 1 WLR 3892.

[223] [2007] 2 WLR 726.

[224] [2003] 2 AC 467.

[225] Section 3(2) Human Rights Act 1998.

allows such legislation to be made. In such a case, the courts may use their powers under s.4 of the Act (see below) and declare the relevant legislation incompatible, leaving such measures in force. Accordingly, whether parliamentary sovereignty will be truly compromised by the courts under the Act will depend on the extent to which the courts use their interpretation powers under s.3 of the Act, and how they interpret the words 'so far as is possible'.[226]

Section 3 of the Act gives legality to the practice of interpreting legislation in conformity with human rights, furthering the courts' powers in this respect by allowing them to adopt a Convention interpretation 'so far as is possible'. Before the Act came into operation the courts were only empowered to interpret legislation in the light of the European Convention when the provision in question was ambiguous. For example, in *Waddington* v *Miah*,[227] the words of s.34 of the Immigration Act 1971 were capable of meaning two things: that a person could be guilty of an offence under the Act even if he was eligible to enter the country at the time, but had subsequently had that eligibility removed, or that the offence only applied to someone who had entered the country illegally, but who had previously entered the country legally on an earlier and separate visit. By choosing the latter of these possibilities, the House of Lords avoided a situation where the Act was imposing criminal liability in respect of an act that at the time was not unlawful. The alternative interpretation would have been in violation of Article 7 of the European Convention, which prohibits retrospective criminal law.

Section 3 of the 1998 Act extends the court's powers in at least two respects. First, the court does not have to find a true ambiguity in the statute, provided the Convention interpretation is possible. Secondly, because the courts are also empowered to take into account the case law of the Convention, it may also construe general discretionary powers granted by legislation in the light of the Convention and its principles. Thus, the decision of the House of Lords in *R* v *Secretary of State for the Home Department, ex parte Brind*,[228] to the effect that words in a statute which are uncertain in scope, as opposed to ambiguous in their meaning, cannot be interpreted and supervised in accordance with Convention rights and case law, is no longer binding. After the implementation of the Act, the courts may decide that words such as 'the minister may pass such regulations as he sees fit' mean that such acts and decisions must be in accordance with Convention rights, and specifically must be sufficiently prescribed by law and necessary and proportionate.

Automatic life sentences

An early example of the courts' enhanced powers to interpret legislation in the light of the European Convention is evident in the case of *R* v *Offen*.[229] The case concerned the interpretation and application of s.2 of the Crime (Sentences) Act 1997, which imposed a duty on the courts to grant an automatic life sentence to defendants who have committed two serious offences, unless there were 'exceptional circumstances'. The defendant had committed two

---

[226] See Lester, The Act of the Possible – Interpreting Statutes under the Human Rights Act [1998] EHRLR 665; Pannick, Principles of Interpretation of Convention Rights under the Human Rights Act and the Discretionary Area of Judgment [1998] PL 545; Young, Judicial Sovereignty and the Human Rights Act 1998 (2002) 61 CLJ 53; Clayton, The Limits of What's 'Possible': Statutory Construction under the Human Rights Act [2002] 559. See also Kavanagh, *Constitutional Review under the UK Human Rights Act* (Cambridge 2009).

[227] [1974] 1 WLR 683.

[228] [1991] 1 AC 696.

[229] [2001] 2 All ER 154.

robberies and was sentenced to life imprisonment despite the fact that the trial judge conceded that the offences were at the lower end of the scale and had been committed using a toy gun. In interpreting that exception the Court of Appeal held that a court was entitled to decide that there existed such circumstances if an offender did not constitute a significant risk to the public. An alternative interpretation would have made the sentence arbitrary and thus in violation of Article 5 and, possibly, Article 3 of the European Convention on Human Rights. Thus, although s.2 could operate in a disproportionate manner, that effect would only be realised by a restricted interpretation of the words 'exceptional circumstances'. The problem disappeared if the words were construed so that it did not result in offenders being sentenced to life imprisonment when they did not constitute a significant risk to the public. In reaching that decision the Court of Appeal insisted that the word 'exceptional' must be given its ordinary meaning and that the court must bear in mind parliament's intention in establishing the automatic life sentence; the section was not intended to apply to someone who did not pose a future risk.

Evidence in rape proceedings/proscription offences

In *Offen* the Court of Appeal appeared to employ traditional principles of statutory interpretation. However, the courts' willingness to abandon those principles was evident in *R v A (Complainant's Sexual History)*.[230] Section 41 of the Youth Justice and Criminal Evidence Act 1999 provides that evidence of the complainant's sexual behaviour, and questions asked in cross-examination in relation to such behaviour, can only be allowed with leave of the court in express circumstances. In interpreting that provision, the House of Lords held that although the adoption of traditional principles of statutory interpretation could not solve the problem of the *prima facie* excessive inroad on the right to a fair trial, the interpretative obligation under s.3 of the Human Rights Act 1998 applied even where there was no ambiguity and placed on the court a duty to strive to find a possible interpretation compatible with Convention rights. Section 3 required the courts to subordinate the niceties of the language of s.41 and to proceed on the basis that the legislature would not, if alerted to the problem, have wished to deny the right to an accused to put forward a full and complete defence by advancing truly probative evidence. Using such powers, the House of Lords thus held that the statutory provision should be read as being subject to the implied exclusion that evidence or questioning which was required to ensure a fair trial under Article 6 should not be inadmissible.[231] The decision gives some indication of the extent of the court's power, and willingness, to interpret legislation in conformity with Convention rights, and the potential of the words 'if at all possible' employed by s.3 of the Act.[232]

A similar hands-on approach was evident in the House of Lords' decision in *Attorney-General's Reference (No 4 of 2002)*,[233] where the question was whether s.11(2) of the Terrorism

[230] [2001] 3 All ER 1.
[231] See also *Secretary of State for the Home Department v MB* [2007] 3 WLR 681, considered in chapter 7.
[232] See Klug and Starmer, Incorporation through the 'Front Door': The First Year of the Human Rights Act [2001] PL 654, pages 655–9. Contrast *R (S) v Waltham Forest Youth Court* [2004] EWHC 715, where it was held that it was not possible to add words to s.16 of the Youth Justice and Criminal Evidence Act 1999 so as to allow a young defendant to give evidence via a television link where he was afraid of his co-defendants. The Act laid down clear and specific rules regarding the protection of those giving evidence; by reading in an extra provision the court would be legislating and not interpreting.
[233] [2005] 1 AC 264.

Act 2000, which made it an offence to belong or profess to belong to a proscribed organisation, imposed an evidential rather than a legal burden on the defendant so as to make that provision compatible with Article 6 of the Convention. Section 11(2) of the Act appeared to place the burden on the defendant to prove that he had not taken part in the activities of the organisation. The majority of their Lordships held that this contravened the presumption of innocence under Article 6(2), but that it was possible to read that provision down in such a way as to avoid a legal burden. Such an interpretation was possible even though parliament had when passing the legislation intended to impose a legal burden in such cases. Although parliament had had that intention when passing the 2000 Act, having regard to its intention in passing s.3 of the Human Rights Act 1998, that provisions such as s.11 should not be incompatible with Convention rights, it was permissible to eradicate that incompatibility by employing s.3.

A more cautious approach?

Section 3 does not, however, allow the courts to read words into a statute that are clearly not there, and clearly not intended by parliament to be there. Thus, in *Poplar Housing and Regeneration Community Association Ltd v Donoghue*,[234] LORD WOOLF CJ stipulated that s.3 of the Act does not entitle the courts to legislate, adding that a court should not radically alter a statute in order to achieve compatibility. This, in his Lordship's opinion, would indicate that more than interpretation is involved. Again, in *R v Taylor (Paul Simon)*[235] the Court of Appeal refused to read a religious defence into the offence of possession of drugs under the Misuse of Drugs Act 1971 so that the provision did not apply to the intended use of such drugs for religious purposes. Such a refusal may often reflect the court's view that the statutory provision is not, as in this case, in violation of Convention rights.

The House of Lords sounded a clear warning against judicial legislation in *Re W and B*.[236] In this case the House of Lords held that the Court of Appeal[237] had acted unlawfully in introducing a system allowing courts to star essential milestones in the care plan of a child so that action had to be taken by a local authority if they were not achieved within a reasonable time. This decision, in their Lordships' view, involved an unjustified exercise of the court's powers under s.3 of the Act. Their Lordships stressed that the 1998 Act maintained the constitutional boundary between the interpretation of statutes and the passing and repeal of legislation, and that a meaning that departed substantially from a fundamental feature of an Act of parliament was likely to have crossed the boundary. In this case, a cardinal principle of the Children Act 1989 was that the courts were not empowered to intervene in the way local authorities discharged their parental responsibilities, and the starring system departed substantially from that principle. In using their powers of interpretation under s.3 of the 1998 Act to ascribe a meaning to the legislation, the courts should be able to identify clearly the particular statutory provision or provisions whose interpretation led to that result. In this case, no such provision was identified and indeed the starring system was inconsistent with the scheme of this part of the 1989 Act. Thus, the courts should not allow the principles and

---

[234] [2001] 2 WLR 1546.
[235] [2002] 1 Cr App R 37.
[236] In *Re S and Others: Re W and Others Sub Nom Re W and B (Children): W (Child) (Care Plan)* [2002] 2 WLR 720.
[237] *The Times*, 6 June 2001.

case law of the Convention to overrule the clear words and intention of domestic legislation, and must use their powers under s.4 of the Act rather than distort the clear intention of parliament.[238] Thus, in *R (Anderson and Taylor) v Secretary of State for the Home Department*[239] the House of Lords held that the Home Secretary had the clear power to impose sentences for mandatory life sentence prisoners, and that any other construction would result in the vandalising of the statutory wording, giving the section an effect quite different from that which parliament intended and going well beyond any interpretative process sanctioned by s.3.[240] Similarly, in *AS (Somalia) v Secretary of State for the Home Department*[241] it was held that it was not possible to read down the plain words of s.85 of the Nationality, Immigration and Asylum Act 2002, which precluded an officer hearing appeals against refusal of entry clearance from considering fresh evidence coming to light after the original decision. The House of Lords held that the words were unyielding and unequivocal and to read them down would cross the boundary between interpretation and amendment of the Act.[242]

The courts may, however, use their interpretation powers under s.3 of the Act to ensure that the provision in question does not allow public authorities too much discretion, thus avoiding the conclusion that the provision is incompatible with the Convention and its case law. For example, in *R v Nottingham Healthcare NHS Trust and Others, ex parte IH*[243] it was held that the Mental Health Review Tribunal's powers under s.73 of the Mental Health Act 1983 to order a conditional discharge of a patient were not in violation of Article 5 of the Convention simply because it had no power to ensure that the conditions which it imposed would be implemented within a reasonable time. The relevant provision of the Act could readily be taken to ensure that a tribunal which had ordered the conditional discharge of a patient, but deferred giving effect to that decision, could reconsider its decision should there be a change of circumstances or additional material put forward. In using s.3 of the 1998 Act to imply such powers the court was able to avoid having to make a declaration of incompatibility, thus confirming that such orders should be used as a last resort.[244] Similarly, in *R (L) v Commissioner of the Police of the Metropolis*[245] the Supreme Court held that s.115(7) of the Police Act 1997, which allowed the police to include certain personal information on an individual in an enhanced criminal record certificate, was not incompatible with Article 8, provided the words 'ought to be included' were interpreted so that the chief constable gave proper consideration to the applicant's right to private life. The police would thus have to

---

[238] Indeed, in some cases the courts will apply traditional principles of interpretation without considering the human rights context of the case. See *R (Haw) v Secretary of State for the Home Department and Another* [2006] 3 WLR 40, dealt with in chapter 10 on freedom of association and assembly.

[239] [2002] 3 WLR 1800.

[240] See Nicol, Statutory Interpretation and Human Rights after *Anderson* [2004] PL 274. See also Kavanagh, The Elusive Divide between Interpretation and Legislation under the Human Rights Act 1998 (2004) OJLS 259; Kavanagh, The Role of Parliamentary Intention in Adjudication under the HRA 1998 (2006) OJLS 153; Kavanagh, Unlocking the Human Rights Act: 'The Radical' Approach to Section 3(1) [2005] EHRLR 260.

[241] [2009] 1 WLR 1385.

[242] See also *R (Chester) v Secretary of State for Justice*, *The Times*, 17 January 2011, where the court refused to read down the Representation of the People Act 1983 so as to allow sentenced prisoners the right to vote. The court would not distort the plain meaning of the statute in order to achieve possible compatibility.

[243] [2002] 3 WLR 967.

[244] See also *R v Secretary of State for the Home Department, ex parte RA* [2003] 1 WLR 330, where it was held that the power to delay a patient's discharge under s.43 of the Mental Health Act 1983 could be interpreted to stop any unreasonable delays.

[245] [2010] 1 AC 410.

consider whether such information would interfere with the person's private life and whether such interference was justified and proportionate on the facts.

Statutory interpretation or declarations of incompatibility? *Bellinger* v *Bellinger*; *Mendoza* v *Ghaidan*

In *R* v *A*, above, the House of Lords suggested that a declaration of incompatibility should be issued as a last resort once the courts have exhausted their powers under s.3 to ensure that legislation is Convention friendly.[246] This approach is, of course, subject to maintaining a proper boundary between the courts' interpretative and legislative powers, and in certain cases it would not be appropriate for the courts to reinterpret clearly worded (and intended) legislation, even where those provisions are obviously in conflict with Convention rights and the case law of the European Court of Human Rights.[247]

For example, in *Bellinger* v *Bellinger*,[248] the House of Lords held that it was not possible to use s.3 of the 1998 Act to interpret the words 'man and woman' used in s.11 of the Matrimonial Clauses Act 1971, to include a person who had undergone gender reassignment. The provision made marriages void where, *inter alia*, the respective parties to the celebrated marriage were not respectively male and female. That, in their Lordships' view would include giving the expressions 'male' and 'female' a novel and extended meaning. In contrast, however, in *Mendoza* v *Ghaidan*[249] the House of Lords held that the Rent Act 1977 could be interpreted to give a homosexual the right to inherit his partner's tenancy. According to the majority of their Lordships it was possible to interpret the legislation so as to avoid an incompatibility with Article 14 of the European Convention without breaking any cardinal principle of the 1977 Act. Thus, it was held that the words 'living together as man and wife' in paragraph 2(2) of the Housing Act 1977 could be construed as meaning *as if they* were living together as man and wife. Lord Millett dissented on the grounds that it was for parliament to change a law that was quite clearly not intended to cover same-sex relationships.[250]

In one case, therefore, the House was prepared to give a liberal and even strained construction to the statutory words in order to ensure compatibility, whereas in the other case their Lordships declared the legislation incompatible, refusing to use s.3 to achieve another construction. The difference in approaches, and the decisions, is not explainable solely on the question of which words were susceptible to construction, both provisions could, possibly, have been interpreted in a Convention-friendly manner. However, in *Bellinger* the House of Lords was not prepared to depart from the historical policy of the Act, which was clearly meant to apply to marriages between men and women defined by purely biological factors. More significantly, perhaps, was the fact that the extent to which transsexual marriages should be recognised was not best determined by the courts and that by declaring the legislation incompatible the courts could pass the task of formulating such rules to

---

[246] For a criticism of the courts' desire to avoid making declarations see Buxton, The Future of Making Declarations of Incompatibility [2010] PL 213.

[247] For a comparative view, see Masterman, Interpretations, Declarations and Dialogues: Rights Protection under the Human Rights Act and Victorian Charter of Human Rights and Responsibilities [2009] PL 112.

[248] [2003] 2 AC 467.

[249] [2004] 2 AC 557.

[250] See also *R* v *Holding* [2006] 1 WLR 1140, where it was held that it was possible to read a proviso into specific subsections of s.75 of the Representation of the People Act 1983 that were evident in other provisions of the same section, and which thereby made those provisions Convention compatible.

parliament.[251] Thus, in *Bellinger* their Lordships' held that a declaration which conferred validity upon such a marriage would represent a major change in the law relating to gender reassignment which would have far-reaching ramifications, necessitating extensive enquiry and the widest possible consultation. The recognition of gender reassignment for the purposes of marriage was not to be dealt with in a piecemeal fashion but should form part of a coherent policy, and those issues were ill-suited for determination in the courts and were pre-eminently a matter for parliament, especially where the government had announced an intention to introduce primary legislation on the subject.[252]

Questions

How does s.3 of the Act enhance the courts' powers of interpretation with respect to cases raising Convention rights?

Do you feel that the courts have crossed the constitutional boundary and begun to legislate in this area?

Declarations of incompatibility

Although the Act does not allow the courts to strike down or disallow primary legislation that cannot be reconciled with the rights laid down in the Convention, courts are allowed, under s.4 of the Act, to declare both primary and secondary legislation incompatible with the substantive rights of the European Convention. Section 4(2) states that in any proceedings in which a court is satisfied that a provision of primary legislation is incompatible with a Convention right, it may make a declaration of incompatibility. Section 4(4) then provides the same power in respect of subordinate legislation where the court is satisfied that the provision is incompatible with a Convention right *and* that the primary legislation concerned prevents removal of the incompatibility. Thus, where the court has not been able to use its powers of interpretation under s.3 of the Act to allow the Act to be read as compatible with the Convention right, and where any subordinate legislation passed under that Act is clearly permitted within the terms of the primary legislation, it may declare such legislation as incompatible with the relevant Convention right(s).[253]

Scope of the power

Section 4 restricts the power to declare legislation incompatible to courts including the High Court and above.[254] Section 4 of the Act is supplemented by s.5, which gives the Crown the

---

[251] Parliament eventually responded to the declaration of incompatibility by passing the Gender Recognition Act 2004.

[252] See Kavanagh, Choosing between sections 3 and 4 of the Human Rights Act 1998: judicial reasoning after *Ghaidan*, in Fenwick, Phillipson and Masterman, *Judicial Reasoning under the UK Human Rights Act* (Cambridge 2007), chapter 5; Kavanagh, *Constitutional Review under the UK Human Rights Act* (Cambridge 2009), Part 1.

[253] See Feldman, Institutional roles and meanings of 'compatibility' under the Human Rights Act 1998, in Fenwick, Phillipson and Masterman, *Judicial Reasoning under the UK Human Rights Act* (Cambridge 2007), chapter 4.

[254] Section 4(5) Human Rights Act 1998. Under that provision the following courts have the power to make a declaration of incompatibility: the House of Lords (now Supreme Court), the Judicial Committee of the Privy Council, the Courts-Martial Appeal Court, the High Court of Justiciary, the High Court and the Court of Appeal. The Employment Appeal Tribunal does not have such a power: *Whittaker v P and D Watson, The Times*, 26 March 2002.

power to intervene where a court is considering making a declaration of incompatibility under the Act. Section 5 provides that in such circumstances the Crown is entitled to notice in accordance with the rules of the court. On receiving that notice, relevant officers of the Crown[255] are then given the right to be joined as party to the proceedings. Such a person may then, with leave, appeal to the House of Lords (now Supreme Court) against any declaration of incompatibility made by the lower court.[256]

It is not possible to consider arguments under s.4 regarding the compatibility of legislation with the Convention where the relevant legislation has not personally affected any particular person. In *Rusbridger and Toynbee v Attorney-General and DPP*[257] the Court of Appeal accepted that in exceptional cases it would be in the public interest to rule on the compatibility or otherwise of legislation, even before proceedings had been brought under such legislation.[258] However, on appeal the House of Lords refused to make a declaration without proof that there was any victim of the legislation.[259] In the present case there was no real risk of anyone being prosecuted under the legislation thus no real risk of any interference with free speech. In their Lordship's view, it was for the legislature and not for the courts to keep the statute book up to date.[260] Similarly, if a person has been affected by a different, and compatible, provision of legislation which in some respects is incompatible, no declaration will be granted.[261] However, in *Secretary of State for the Home Department v Nasseri*[262] the House of Lords distinguished *Rusbridger* and held that a court did have the discretion to grant a declaration under s.4 in a case where although there was no evidence of an incompatible act on the facts it would have been incompatible had that act been carried out.[263]

Further, the courts will not issue a declaration of incompatibility merely because a statute contains a gap, which if included might make the statute compatible with the Convention. Thus, in *Re W and B*[264] the House of Lords held, *obiter*, that although the absence of a particular statutory right might mean that English law is incompatible with one or more provisions of the European Convention, the absence of such a provision does not, of itself, mean that the statute is incompatible with the Convention for the purpose of s.4. In such a case, there is a statutory lacuna and not a statutory incompatibility.[265] This *obiter* seems to have been accepted in subsequent decisions, and thus the courts will not grant a declaration

---

[255] Under s.5(2) of the Act these include a minister of the Crown (or a person nominated by him), a member of the Scottish Executive, a Northern Ireland minister or a Northern Ireland department.

[256] Section 5(4) Human Rights Act 1998.

[257] [2002] EWCA Civ 397.

[258] An editor and a journalist intended to publish an article calling for the abolition of the monarchy and had sought assurances from the Attorney-General that they would not be prosecuted under the Treason Felony Act 1848.

[259] [2004] 1 AC 357.

[260] See also *R (Hirst) v Parole Board* [2002] EWHC 1592, where it was held that a declaration of incompatibility could not be issued regarding the powers of the Parole Board to order release under the Crime (Sentences) Act 1997 until the Board had made a determination under the Act.

[261] *Taylor v Lancashire County Council* [2005] 1 WLR 2668.

[262] [2009] UKHL 23.

[263] On the facts, however, a declaration was unnecessary as the Secretary had conceded that had the act taken place it would have been incompatible.

[264] [2002] 2 WLR 720.

[265] Following the decision in *Re W and B*, an application was lodged before the European Court of Human Rights, alleging a violation of Articles 6 and 8 of the Convention: *S v UK* (Application No 34407/02).

unless they are satisfied that a specific statutory provision is capable of interfering with the claimant's Convention rights.[266]

The courts may also refuse to grant a declaration if to do so would pre-empt any legislative change. Thus, in *R (Chester) v Secretary of State for Justice*[267] the Court of Appeal refused to grant a declaration of incompatibility with respect to s.3 of the Representation of the People Act 1983, which disenfranchised convicted prisoners. The government had, eventually, responded to the European Court's ruling that such exclusion was inconsistent with the right to vote, but in its consultation document it had ruled out the possibility of allowing post-tariff life sentence prisoners the right to vote. Such a prisoner sought a declaration of incompatibility, but the court refused to consider granting a declaration until the statutory provision was in place; otherwise the parliamentary process would be interfered with. As the prisoner in question was seeking a declaration before the May 2010 general election, the government's refusal to pass any measures in time for the election shows the deficiencies of s.4 in providing an effective and real remedy in challenging incompatible legislation.

In *Wilson v First County Trust (No 2)*[268] the House of Lords laid down further guidance as to the scope of the courts' powers under s.4. First, the House of Lords held that the Court of Appeal had been wrong in making a declaration of incompatibility in respect of a cause of action that arose before the Act came into operation.[269] In their Lordships' view a court could only make a declaration of incompatibility where s.3 of the Human Rights Act was available as an interpretative tool. Secondly, it held that when a court was exercising its jurisdiction under the Act in assessing the compatibility of primary legislation it was entitled to have regard to the policy objectives behind the legislation by looking at ministerial statements at the time the Bill was proceeding through parliament. In considering that material, the court was not encroaching upon parliamentary privilege or questioning proceedings in parliament. However, their Lordships also stressed that the content of parliamentary debates had no direct relevance to the issues the court was called upon to decide in compatibility matters and thus those debates were not a matter for investigation or consideration.

It must be stressed that any declaration made under s.4 does not affect the validity, continuing operation or enforcement of the provision in respect of which it is given and is not binding on the parties to the proceedings in which it is made.[270] The incompatible provision continues in force and can determine the rights of the parties involved in the dispute. Any person who is a victim of a violation of a Convention right as a consequence of that provision and its enforcement must then either pursue their remedy in Strasbourg, or wait for the government to invoke its powers to change the legislation.[271]

Since the coming into operation of the Act the courts have made a number of declarations of incompatibility with respect to primary and secondary domestic legislation, many of

---

[266] See *R (J) v Enfield Borough Council* [2002] EWHC 432 (Admin); *R (Rose) v Secretary of State for Health and Others, The Times*, 22 August 2002.

[267] *The Times*, 17 January 2011.

[268] [2004] 1 AC 816.

[269] Disagreeing with the Court of Appeal it held that the 'relevant act' was not the court's order refusing to enforce the agreement, but the time the original contract was concluded.

[270] Section 4(6) Human Rights Act 1998.

[271] Under s.10 of the Human Rights Act 1998, considered below. Such action would not, however, automatically invalidate the previous action. In *Burden v United Kingdom* (2007) 44 EHRR 51 the European Court noted that a declaration of incompatibility was not an effective remedy for a violation of Convention rights, rejecting the government's claim that someone who had benefited from such a declaration was no longer a victim.

which are referred to throughout the text with respect to particular rights such as freedom of expression and liberty of the person. The examples below are used to illustrate the different contexts in which declarations have been sought and granted and the approach of the courts in using their new power.

Judicial powers of the executive and the right to a fair trial

The first declaration of incompatibility under the Act was made by the High Court in the case of *R* v *Secretary of State for the Environment, Transport and the Regions, ex parte Barnes*.[272] The court had held that the power of the Secretary of State under the Town and Country Planning Act 1990 to recover and determine planning applications that had not been determined by the local authority, to determine appeals against refusal of planning permission instead of the inspector, and to make decisions in connection with proposed highway orders, were incompatible with Article 6(1) of the European Convention in that they denied the applicants the right to a fair trial before an independent and impartial tribunal. However, on appeal the House of Lords held that the planning laws were not incompatible with Article 6.[273] The House of Lords held that although the disputes involved were 'civil rights' within Article 6(1) of the Convention, and that the Secretary of State was not an independent and impartial tribunal, the power of the High Court in judicial review proceedings to review the legality of the decision and the procedures followed was sufficient to ensure compatibility with Article 6(1). Provided the High Court had full jurisdiction to deal with the case as the nature of the decision required, when the decision at issue was a matter of administrative policy, judicial review proceedings satisfied Article 6, even though the court would not have the full power to re-determine the merits of the decision. In coming to that decision the House of Lords relied on relevant case law of the European Court of Human Rights, where it had been found that powers of appeal and review were sufficient to ensure that the decision-making process as a whole complied with Article 6.[274] Further, the House of Lords' decision was approved by the European Court when proceedings were brought under the Convention machinery.[275]

Mental health patients and liberty of the person

Domestic mental health legislation has been the subject of several challenges under both the Convention machinery and under the Human Rights Act 1998. In *R* v *Mental Health Tribunal ex parte H*[276] the Court of Appeal found that s.72 and s.73 of the Mental Health Act 1983 were incompatible with Article 5 of the European Convention. The fact that the Act placed the burden of proof on a restricted patient to show that he was no longer suffering from a

---

[272] *R* v *Secretary of State for the Environment, Transport and the Regions, ex parte Holding and Barnes; R* v *the same, ex parte Alconbury Developments Ltd and Others; Secretary of State for the Environment, Transport and the Regions* v *Legal and General Assurance Society Ltd* [2001] 2 All ER 929.

[273] [2001] 2 WLR 1389.

[274] *Bryan* v *United Kingdom* (1995) 21 EHRR 342.

[275] *Holding and Barnes plc* v *United Kingdom* (Application No 2352/02).

[276] [2001] 3 WLR 512. Following this decision the Mental Health Act 1983 (Remedial) Order 2001 was laid before parliament revising the offending sections of the Act and requiring the tribunal to direct a person's discharge if it is not satisfied that the criteria justifying detention in hospital continue to exist.

mental disorder warranting detention, in order to satisfy the mental health review tribunal that he was entitled to discharge, was incompatible with Article 5. As the provisions were only capable of being interpreted in one way, and that interpretation meant that the authorities did not have to show that the patient was suffering from a mental disorder warranting detention, any resultant detention would be in violation of Article 5 of the Convention.[277]

Further declarations of incompatibility have been made in *R (M) v Secretary of State for Health*,[278] where the High Court held that provisions allowing a patient's nearest relative to be changed without the patient's consent was incompatible with the Convention, and in *R (MH) v Health Secretary*,[279] where the Court of Appeal held that a prolonged detention under s.2 of the Mental Health Act 1983 was incompatible with Article 5(4) of the European Convention.[280]

Detention without trial and liberty of the person

The government's effort to combat terrorism by providing additional powers of arrest and detention have come under challenge under the Human Rights Act and two of its central provisions have been declared incompatible with Article 5 of the Convention. In *A v Secretary of State for the Home Department*,[281] the House of Lords decided that the detention of foreign suspects under the Anti-Terrorism, Crime and Security Act 2001 was disproportionate and discriminatory and thus not justified under Article 15 of the Convention, which allows states to derogate from the Convention in times of war or other emergency threatening the life of the nation. The majority of their Lordships accepted that there was such an emergency, but held that a right so fundamental as freedom from arbitrary arrest could not be taken away unless in the most compelling of circumstances.[282] Further, in *JJ and Others v Home Secretary*[283] the House of Lords held that control orders imposed under s.2 of the Prevention of Terrorism Act 2005 were in breach of Article 5, and that consequently the orders, which purported to be non-derogating orders because the Home Secretary regarded them as *restrictions* on liberty rather than *deprivations* of liberty, were in fact derogating orders that the Secretary had no jurisdiction to make.

However, the courts have provided the government with some latitude in this area and in *Re MB*[284] the Court of Appeal held that the procedures in s.3 of the Prevention of Terrorism Act 2005 relating to supervision orders under that Act (passed in response to the House of Lords' decision in *A*, above) were generally compatible with Article 6. The Court of Appeal had held that the provisions could and should be read to allow the courts to review those powers beyond bare legality and to insist that there were reasonable grounds for the Secretary's belief and order,[285] and the House of Lords concluded that the use of closed materials was

---

[277] The refusal to manipulate the words of the statute in order to achieve a result compatible with the Convention can be contrasted with the decision of the House of Lords in *R v A* [2001] 2 WLR 1546, considered above.

[278] *The Times*, 25 April 2003.

[279] [2005] 1 WLR 1209.

[280] On appeal to the House of Lords, [2006] 1 AC 441, it was held that the process was capable of being operated compatibly with Article 5.

[281] [2005] 2 AC 68.

[282] For full details of the case, see case study in chapter 6 on pages 299–302 of this text.

[283] [2008] 2 WLR 642.

[284] [2007] 3 WLR 681.

[285] [2006] 3 WLR 839.

not necessarily in violation of the Convention provided there were appropriate safeguards in place.[286]

Deference to parliament: freedom of expression and national security, the right to die and the Suicide Act 1961 and prisoner disenfranchisement

Although the courts are not given the power to strike down or disapply clear primary legislation, the power to declare such legislation incompatible with the Convention will involve them assessing that legislation's legality, necessity and proportionality. It is natural in such cases that the courts might show deference to legislation passed by a democratically elected parliament, particularly where that body has contemplated the possible human rights arguments in passing such provisions.

In *R v Shayler*[287] the courts were asked to consider whether s.1 and s.4 of the Official Secrets Act 1989 were incompatible with Article 10 of the European Convention. The defendant had been charged with disclosing documents relating to security and intelligence without lawful authority under s.1(1) of the Official Secrets Act 1989, and of disclosing information obtained under warrants issued under the Interception of Communications Act 1985, under s.4(1) of the 1989 Act. The defendant claimed that unless a public interest defence could be read into the legislation the provision would be incompatible with the ideas of free speech enshrined in Article 10. In the High Court MOSES J rejected the application, holding that the Act did not contain a defence of public interest and that the absence of such a defence was not incompatible with the European Convention.[288] The imposition of criminal liability without the possibility of raising a public interest defence was necessary in a democratic society for the purpose of protecting against threats to national security.

The House of Lords dismissed the appeal,[289] confirming that the provisions of the 1989 Act did not contravene Article 10 of the European Convention. Delivering the main opinion, Lord Bingham held that on its proper construction the 1989 Act did not allow a defendant to be acquitted if he could show that it was in the public or national interest to make the disclosure in question. The relevant sections imposed no obligation to prove that the disclosure was not in the public interest and gave the defendant no opportunity to show that the disclosure was in the public interest. Noting that the Act did not impose a complete ban on disclosure of information, in that it was possible to seek authorisation, such decisions being subject to judicial review, his Lordship held that the special position of those employed in the security and intelligence services, and the special nature of their work, imposed duties and responsibilities, making it appropriate for them to seek the necessary authorisation. Accordingly, s.1 and s.4 of the 1989 Act were compatible with Article 10 of the Convention.

A similar approach was evident in the controversial case of Dianne Pretty, a woman suffering from motor neurone disease who wished her husband to take her life without incurring legal liability under the Suicide Act 1961. In *R v DPP, ex parte Pretty and Another*[290] the

---

[286] [2007] 3 WLR 681. The applicants' cases were referred back to consider whether they had, in fact, received a fair trial. The case is dealt with in detail in chapter 14 of this text.
[287] [2002] 2 WLR 754.
[288] [2001] 1 WLR 2206.
[289] [2002] 2 WLR 754.
[290] [2002] 1 AC 800.

court was asked to decide whether the DPP had the power to give an undertaking that the applicant's husband would not be prosecuted under s.2(1) of the Suicide Act if he assisted her in taking her own life, and whether the legislation was incompatible with her rights under Articles 2, 3, 8, 9 and 14 of the European Convention.

The House of Lords, upholding the decision of the Divisional Court,[291] dismissed the application, and stated that her claim was inconsistent with Article 2 and domestic common law, which provided that someone else cannot take another's life. In addition, their Lordships held that because the claims under Articles 2 and 3 of the Convention failed, the right to private and family life under Article 8 was not engaged. Alternatively, if there had been a *prima facie* breach of that article, their Lordships felt that such interference was justified for protecting the rights of others – to protect the lives of vulnerable people. Agreeing with the Divisional Court, their Lordships held that Article 14 (prohibition of discrimination) could not apply as no substantive Convention rights had been violated. The 1961 Act did not give the right to commit suicide, but merely abrogated the rule whereby it was a crime to commit such an act. In any event the Act applied to everyone and could not, therefore, be regarded as discriminatory.[292]

At times, therefore, the courts have displayed a great deal of caution when considering powers under s.4 and have usually deferred to the democratic will of parliament, especially if the case law of the Convention allows such deference. For example, in *Hirst v Attorney-General*,[293] it was held that s.3 of the Representation of the People Act 1983 was not incompatible with Article 3 of the First Protocol to the Convention merely because it disenfranchised convicted prisoners. The court took into account the wide margin of appreciation offered by the European Court and Commission in this area, and thus unless the law is clearly contrary to Convention case law, the domestic courts will be reluctant to use its powers under s.4. Hence, in *R (Anderson and Taylor) v Secretary of State for the Home Department*,[294] the House of Lords eventually followed the most recent case law of the European Court of Human Rights and declared the Home Secretary's powers to set tariffs for convicted murderers incompatible with Article 6 of the Convention. However, in the absence of clear authority from the European Court, it was not prepared to declare the mandatory life sentence incompatible with Articles 3 and 5 of the Convention.[295]

Transsexuals and the right to private and family life

The eventual recognition of transsexual rights was fought out in both the domestic and European courts. A number of decisions of the European Court had upheld domestic laws that denied transsexuals full legal and civil status.[296] This position was challenged in the domestic courts and in *Bellinger v Bellinger*[297] the Court of Appeal was asked to grant a

---

[291] *The Times*, 23 October 2001.

[292] A subsequent application to the European Court of Human Rights was unsuccessful: *Pretty v United Kingdom* (2002) 35 EHRR 1.

[293] [2002] 3 WLR 1800.

[294] [2003] 1 AC 837.

[295] *R v Lichniak and Pyrah* [2002] 3 WLR 1834.

[296] *Rees v United Kingdom* (1986) 9 EHRR 56; *Cossey v United Kingdom* (1990) 13 EHRR 622; *X, Y and Z v United Kingdom* (1997) 24 EHRR 143; *Sheffield and Horsham v United Kingdom* (1998) 27 EHRR 163. See now the decisions of the European Court in *I v United Kingdom* and *Goodwin v United Kingdom* (2002) 35 EHRR 18.

[297] *Elizabeth Ann Bellinger v Michael Jeffrey Bellinger and HM Attorney-General (Intervenor)* [2002] 2 WLR 411.

declaration that a marriage celebrated between a man and a transsexual born a male was valid and subsisting. In rejecting the application, the Court of Appeal refused to disturb the current legal position, as pronounced in *Corbett* v *Corbett*,[298] and upheld by the European Court. In the Court of Appeal's view it was for parliament to decide at which point and to what extent a change of gender should be recognised.[299] An appeal was heard in the House of Lords,[300] although in the meantime the European Court had decided to depart from its old decisions and held that the discrimination was contrary to Articles 8, 12 and 14 of the Convention.[301] Accordingly, the House of Lords declared the domestic law incompatible with the Convention, leaving parliament to pass legislation – the Gender Recognition Act 2004 – protecting such rights. The case is a good example of how the mechanism of judicial supervision adopted by the Human Rights Act attempts to blend the power of the courts to promote Convention rights with the ultimate power of parliament to determine the extent of its laws. The Court of Appeal accepted the margin of appreciation then open to democratic states to decide the extent to which they are obliged to recognise individual fundamental rights, while the House of Lords, following the latest pronouncement of the European Court of Human Rights, preferred to use its s.4 powers to declare the legislation incompatible. Thus, the question of the status of transsexuals and the extent of their rights, which was open to intense moral and medical debate, was ultimately resolved within the democratic parliamentary process.

Questions

How, if at all, does s.4 of the Act change the constitutional role of the courts and the sovereignty of parliament?

Do you feel that the domestic courts have displayed appropriate deference to parliament when using this power?

Overall effect of sections 2–4 – a hypothetical case study

Sections 2–4 of the Act provide the basis of the courts' powers to use the Convention, and the case law of the relevant Convention institutions, to ensure that domestic law is interpreted and applied in a way which is compatible with a person's Convention rights, and it may be helpful to use a hypothetical situation in order to explain the new role of the courts in cases involving alleged violations of Convention rights.

Let us assume that in 2001 parliament passed the Control of Public Order Act, s.1 of which permitted the Home Secretary to pass such regulations as he thought fit to control public order. Acting under that power, the Home Secretary passes a regulation which provides that if the Secretary of State is of the opinion that the holding of any public meeting or procession poses a serious threat to public order, he may order the prohibition of that meeting for a

---

[298] [1970] 2 All ER 33. In that case it was held that the test for the determination of sex for the purpose of marriage was to be conducted at birth on chromosomal, gonadal and genital tests.

[299] THORPE LJ, dissenting, felt that medical and social change made *Corbett* wrong in 2001 and that the family justice system should be swift to recognise the right to human dignity and freedom of choice. In his Lordship's opinion, there were not sufficiently compelling reasons to deny the legal recognition of the marriage.

[300] [2003] 2 AC 467.

[301] *Goodwin* v *United Kingdom* (2002) 35 EHRR 18.

period of up to six months. Acting under that regulation he prohibits a meeting of an animal rights group, which was to be held in the centre of London and which in the Secretary's opinion was likely to attract a violent response from counter demonstrators.

A person whose rights had been interfered with could challenge that regulation, claiming a violation of their rights under Articles 10 and 11 of the Convention.[302] Provided that person is a victim, the challenge would engage the courts' new powers under the Act. That person could claim that the regulation was *ultra vires* the parent Act, because in the absence of express words parliament never intended to interfere with an individual's basic right of free speech and demonstration.[303] If that claim failed, the person could then argue that the regulation was irrational because it interfered unreasonably with his, and others', fundamental rights, and in such a case the courts would require greater justification from the Home Secretary in order to justify the regulation.[304]

Under s.3 of the Human Rights Act the courts might interpret the Control of Public Order Act in such a way as not to allow any interference with the rights of free speech and assembly and association, and thus declare the regulation void on those grounds.[305] Alternatively, and more feasibly, the court would, despite s.3 of the Act, accept that parliament clearly intended, at least in appropriate and exceptional cases, to interfere with the fundamental rights of free speech and assembly, and move to the question of whether the particular regulation was in conformity with the Convention. In this respect, the court would use its power under s.2 of the 1998 Act to refer to relevant Convention case law, beginning with the question whether the regulation was sufficiently clear to be 'prescribed by law' as required by Articles 10 and 11. Given that the regulation gives the Home Secretary the power to decide which demonstrations are likely to pose a serious threat to public order, a court might decide that the regulation has too much potential for arbitrary use by the Home Secretary. Alternatively, the court might decide that the provision, albeit wide and discretionary on its face, is sufficiently clear and restricted provided the powers were not used in an arbitrary or unreasonable way.

The court could then examine the regulation to see whether it attempted to uphold a legitimate aim, and, more importantly, whether the regulation was necessary in a democratic society: in other words whether it was a necessary and proportionate response to the threat to public order, etc. The regulation appears to pursue the legitimate aim of preserving public order, thus making it *intra vires* the Act, and potentially valid under the Convention, and thus the main question would concern the regulation's extent. Again, the domestic court would question the reach of the regulation and, in particular, the time limit of the prohibition. Having done so, it could either regard the regulation as unnecessary and disproportionate, or interpret the power in such a way that it could only be used in a proportionate manner. Only if the court felt that the Act itself allowed arbitrary use of the provision by a minister would

[302] This challenge could be raised collaterally during the individuals' criminal trial. The mechanism of using the Act and the possible remedies available are explained later in this chapter.

[303] Using cases such as *R v Secretary of State for the Home Department, ex parte Leech* [1994] QB 198 and *R v Secretary of State for the Home Department, ex parte O'Brien and Simms* [2000] 2 AC 115.

[304] See, for example, the cases of *R v Secretary of State for the Home Department, ex parte Bugdaycay* [1987] 1 All ER 940 and *R v Ministry of Defence, ex parte Smith* [1996] 1 All ER 257.

[305] In cases before the Human Rights Act the courts might interpret the Act to allow interferences with basic rights only if there was an evident and pressing need. See, for example, *R v Secretary of State for the Home Department, ex parte Leech*, n 303, above.

it then have to consider making a declaration of incompatibility under s.4 of the Act. In doing so, the court would consider the provisions and case law of the Convention to see whether such a power was consistent with any relevant Convention rights. Unless the court felt that the Act itself or the regulation were clearly inconsistent with the Convention, it would turn its attention to the particular order made by the minister. Again, the court could refer to the case law of the Convention, and in particular to the doctrine of proportionality, to decide whether the application of this provision to the current facts represented a legitimate and necessary interference with the applicant's rights. In doing so the court would question the existence of sufficiently pressing public order problems so as to justify his intervention both under the domestic legislation, and the provisions under the European Convention.

The Act's provisions can, therefore, be used to bolster and to focus challenges to provisions or actions that interfere with the applicant's Convention rights. While such regulations or decisions will continue, in most cases, to be challenged through traditional legal actions, the Act will, to a greater extent, allow the courts to have recourse to the Convention in both the interpretation and application of public law powers. In the majority of cases a declaration of incompatibility can be avoided by a generous and liberal interpretation of the provisions, and thus only in a small number of cases will the courts need to consider whether parliament has passed legislation that is inconsistent with its obligations under the Convention.

CASE STUDY

R v A [2002] 1 AC 45

This case concerned the admissibility of evidence in rape cases and specifically the interpretation of s.41 of the Youth Justice and Criminal Evidence Act 1999. That provision imposed wide restrictions on the admission of evidence and the questioning of complainants regarding their sexual history, and was introduced to protect rape victims from unnecessary and humiliating cross-examination. The case is of interest with reference to the courts' powers of interpretation under s.3 of the Human Rights Act 1998 and raises a number of constitutional issues regarding the relationship between the courts and parliament, and how that relationship has been affected by the Act.

The defendant had been tried for rape and his defence was that sexual intercourse had taken place with the complainant's consent, or, alternatively that he believed that she had consented. A had applied to the court for leave to cross-examine the complainant regarding an alleged sexual relationship between him and the complainant during the three weeks before the alleged rape, but the judge ruled that the complainant could not be cross-examined, nor could any evidence be led, about the alleged sexual relationship. In doing so, the judge relied on s.41 of the Youth Justice and Criminal Evidence Act 1999, which provides that evidence of the complainant's sexual behaviour, and questions asked in cross-examination in relation to such behaviour, could only be allowed with leave of the court in express circumstances. Section 41(3) allowed cross-examination in the situation where the issue was one of consent, and the complainant's sexual behaviour to which the evidence related was alleged to have been similar to any such behaviour of ➡

the complainant which took place as part of the event which was the subject matter of the charge, or to any other sexual behaviour of the complainant which took place at or about the same time as that event, and the similarity could not reasonably be explained as a coincidence.

The Court of Appeal held that the evidence sought in this case was not admissible to the question of consent and asked the House of Lords to consider whether a sexual relationship between a defendant and a complainant could be relevant to the issue of consent, so as to render its exclusion under the 1999 Act a contravention of the defendant's right to a fair trial. By a majority, the House of Lords held that a prior sexual relationship between the defendant and a complainant might in some circumstances be relevant to the issue of consent. Consequently, the absence of related evidence might infringe the right to a fair trial and thus be in violation of Article 6 of the European Convention. In their Lordships' view, although merely excluding some relevant evidence would not violate Article 6, in a significant number of cases s.41 of the 1999 Act would prevent the defendant from putting forward a full defence. Accordingly, the courts should use their powers under s.3 of the Human Rights Act to interpret s.41(3)(c) of the 1999 Act so as to allow the courts to admit such evidence, whenever this was considered necessary by the judge in order to ensure a fair trial.

Lord Steyn first noted that although the legislature and the executive retained a discretionary area of judgment within which policy choices may legitimately be made, when the question arises whether parliament has adopted a scheme which makes an excessive inroad into the right to a fair trial, the court is qualified to make its own judgment and must do so. With regard to the interpretation of the 1999 Act, Lord Steyn accepted academic opinion (Lester, The Act of the Possible: Interpreting Statutes under the Human Rights Act [1998] EHRLR 665) and held that the proper approach was to ask whether the legislation conflicted with a Convention right. At that stage, the purpose of the statute will play a secondary role for it will be seldom, if ever, that parliament will have intended to legislate in breach of the Convention. It is at the second stage, when the government seeks to justify the interference with a Convention right under one of the exception clauses contained in the Convention that the legislative purpose or intent becomes relevant and it is at this stage that the principle of proportionality will be applied.

Applying his mind to the provision in question, his Lordship noted that, subject to narrow exceptions, the provision contained a blanket exclusion of potentially relevant evidence. However, the provision had to be construed in order to determine its precise exclusionary impact on alleged previous sexual experience between the complainant and the accused, and for this purpose, two processes of interpretation must be distinguished. First, ordinary methods of purposive and contextual interpretation may yield ways of minimising the *prima facie* exorbitant breadth of the section. Secondly, the interpretative obligation in s.3(1) of the 1998 Act, which provides that 'so far as is *possible* to do so, primary legislation must be read and given effect in a way which is compatible with Convention rights', may come into play.

His Lordship noted that it could not be argued that on ordinary methods of interpretation, the exceptions in the Act covered a case similar to the one before the House, where it was alleged that there was a previous sexual experience between the complainant and the accused on several occasions during a three-week period before the occasion in question.

However, although the adoption of traditional principles of statutory interpretation could not solve the problem of the *prima facie* excessive inroad on the right to a fair trial, the interpretative obligation under s.3 of the Human Rights Act 1998 applied even where there was no ambiguity and placed on the court a duty to strive to find a possible interpretation compatible with Convention rights. Section 3 required the courts to subordinate the niceties of the language of s.41 and to proceed on the basis that the legislature would not, if alerted to the problem, have wished to deny the right to an accused to put forward a full and complete defence by advancing truly probative evidence. Using such powers, his Lordship held that the statutory provision should be read as being subject to the implied exclusion that evidence or questioning which was required to ensure a fair trial under Article 6 should not be inadmissible. The result will be that sometimes logically relevant sexual experiences between the complainant and the accused may be admitted and on this basis a declaration of incompatibility can be avoided: s.41 will have achieved a major part of its objective but its excessive reach will have been attenuated in accordance with the will of parliament as reflected in s.3 of the 1998 Act.

Lord Hope on the other hand felt that parliament's response to the dilemma was a proportionate one, the section preserving the defendant's right to ask questions about and adduce evidence of other sexual behaviour by the complainant where that was clearly relevant. He held that it had not been shown that the solution adopted by the section was, in every case, disproportionate and in violation of Article 6 of the Convention. His Lordship also stated that he found it very difficult to accept that it was permissible under s.3 of the 1998 Act to read into the section a provision to the effect that evidence or questioning which was required to ensure a fair trial under Article 6 should not be treated as inadmissible. Accepting that the rule of construction in s.3 is unlike any previous rule of statutory interpretation, his Lordship stressed that it did not entitle the judges to act as legislators. Compatibility was only to be achieved as far as this was possible and plainly this is not possible if the legislation contains provisions that expressly contradict the meaning that the enactment would have to be given to make it compatible. Equally, this will be the position if the provisions do so by necessary implication, for this is also the means of identifying the plain intention of parliament.

In Lord Hope's opinion on the present case, the entire structure of s.41 of the 1999 Act contradicts the idea that it is possible to read into it a new provision which would entitle the court to give leave whenever it was of the opinion that this was required to ensure a fair trial. The whole point of the section, as was made clear during the debates in parliament, was to address the mischief that was thought to have arisen owing to the width of the discretion that had previously been given to the trial judge. The Act forbids the exercise of discretion unless the court is satisfied as to the matters that the subsections identify. Thus, it would not be possible, without contradicting the plain intention of parliament, to read in a provision enabling the court to exercise a wider discretion than that permitted by the Act.

Questions

1 What human rights were in conflict in this case? Is such a conflict best resolved by parliamentary legislation or by judicial decisions?

2 Is there a difference between interpreting a statute in the light of human rights, and legislating? If so, what is it?

3 How does the power of interpretation under s.3 of the 1998 Act differ from that which existed prior to the enactment of the 1998 Act?

4 Do you think that the House of Lords' use of their interpretative powers under s.3 of the Human Rights Act allowed the courts to legislate in this case?

5 Do you think that the courts should do all they can to avoid a conflict between domestic law and the European Convention?

6 Do you agree that a declaration of incompatibility should be avoided in all but the most exceptional case? Should the court have made a declaration in this case rather than solving the problem by the use of s.3 of the Act?

7 Has the House of Lords' approach been tempered by subsequent cases decided under the Human Rights Act 1998?

8 Does the decision in this case provide strong evidence of the potential dangers of the Human Rights Act 1998, or is it an inevitable consequence of the wording and character of the Act?

Liability of public authorities under the Act

Section 6(1) of the Act provides that it is unlawful for a public authority to act in a way that is inconsistent with a Convention right. This provision, along with s.7 of the Act, which then provides a remedy to a person who claims that a public authority has acted (or proposed to act) in a way that is unlawful under s.6, provides the main basis of the Convention's application and enforcement in domestic law. However, as we shall see, the act can also operate in a 'horizontal' fashion.

'An act' includes a failure to act but does not include a failure to introduce in, or lay before, parliament a proposal for legislation, or make any primary legislation or remedial order.[306] Consequently, no action will lie against a public authority in connection with its failure to propose or pass legislation that requires parliamentary approval and which results in a person's Convention rights being violated or ignored. Thus, in *R (Smith) v Secretary of State for the Defence*[307] it was held that the failure of the Secretary to pass secondary legislation which might have cured a discriminatory practice was not an 'act' for the purposes of section 6 of the Human Rights Act 1998.[308] Despite this provision, under the jurisprudence of the European Convention on Human Rights, a member state could be held responsible for a failure to pass such measures, each member state having a positive duty to take such measures

---

[306] Section 6(6)(a) Human Rights Act 1998.

[307] [2004] EWCA Civ 1664.

[308] However, in *R (Rose) v Secretary of State for the Home Department and Others*, *The Times*, 22 August 2002, it was held that a challenge could be made of a refusal to pass regulations that did not require the positive approval of parliament: in other words, where regulations were merely subject to a negative resolution of parliament.

as are necessary to ensure that Convention rights are enjoyed by all within the member state's jurisdiction.[309]

Section 6 of the Act again is careful to retain the doctrine of parliamentary sovereignty by providing that s.6(1) does not apply to an act of such an authority if as the result of one or more provisions of primary legislation, it could not have acted differently, or in the case of a provision of, or made under, primary legislation which cannot be read or given effect in a way which is compatible with Convention rights, the authority was acting so as to give effect to or to enforce those provisions.[310] Thus, where the court has no choice but to follow the clear and express words of the legislation and accept that the public authority had no alterative but to violate Convention rights, it is limited at most to make a declaration of incompatibility under s.4 of the Act in relation to the relevant statutory provision.

Definition of 'public authority'

Although the term 'public authority' is not defined under s.6, it is expressly provided that it includes a court or tribunal and that it does not include either House of Parliament or a person exercising functions in connection with proceedings in parliament.[311] Thus, not only is the sovereignty of Acts of parliament preserved, but so too is the system of parliamentary privilege in connection with parliamentary affairs. In addition, it has been decided that the Crown is not a public authority under s.6 of the Act so as to be responsible for the negligence of a non-Crown body.[312]

The section also states that 'public authority' includes any person whose functions are functions of a public nature,[313] and also that in relation to a particular act a person is not a public authority if the nature of the act is private.[314] This, in effect, creates two types of public authority, who are and who *may* be subject to the direct jurisdiction of the Human Rights Act. The first are 'core' public authorities, where there is no doubt that the authority in question is public – because they are clearly governmental bodies – and which thus will be liable under the Act irrespective of the nature of the function in question.[315] In these cases therefore the authority are liable for violating Convention rights whether it was exercising its public or private law functions at the relevant time. The second type are referred to as 'hybrid' authorities, who are not 'core' public authorities (above) but who might be liable where their functions are of a public nature. This would cover non-governmental bodies carrying out *public* functions, but excludes the private activities of such bodies.

---

[309] Under Article 1 of the European Convention.

[310] Section 6(2) Human Rights Act 1998. In *R v Harlow District Council, ex parte Bono* [2002] 1 WLR 2475, it was held that where primary legislation was couched in very general terms, and did not clearly require a body to breach any rights in the European Convention, then the courts did not have to uphold regulations that were in violation of that Convention right.

[311] Section 6(3) Human Rights Act 1998. By s.6(4) of the Act, parliament did not include the House of Lords in its judicial capacity.

[312] *Morgan v Ministry of Justice and the Crown* [2010] EWHC 2248 (QB).

[313] Section 6(3)(b) Human Rights Act 1998.

[314] Section 6(5) Human Rights Act 1998.

[315] Such bodies would include government ministers, local authorities, the police and prison authorities, national health service trusts and regulatory bodies such as the General Medical Council. It is unclear whether *all* the purely private acts of core public authorities, such as the control of membership, or contractual matters, would fall within s.6.

The Act appears to preserve the distinction between public and private bodies, and public and private law issues, employed in judicial review to determine the courts' jurisdiction in reviewing administrative and other acts and decisions. Thus, a remedy under the Act is only directly available against a public authority carrying out its public functions, and acts falling outside the definition in s.6 are, at least on the face of it, left unprotected.[316]

Public authorities and the case law under the Human Rights Act

The courts must, therefore, distinguish between public and private bodies and then public and private functions, and in doing so must decide what factors will be relevant in deciding such, more specifically whether the distinction will be identical to the one which determines liability in judicial review.

A number of cases have raised the question of the definition of 'public authority' within s.6 of the Act with respect to the provision of housing by various care home providers. In *Heather, Ward and Callin v Leonard Cheshire Foundation*[317] the Court of Appeal held that a housing foundation, which had closed a care home, was not a public authority and did not exercise a public law function within the meaning of s.6. The Court of Appeal held that prior to the Human Rights Act 1998 it had been clearly established that bodies such as the foundation were not susceptible to judicial review and that the Human Rights Act had not done anything to alter the status of such bodies. In the present case, despite the fact that the foundation received public funding, was state regulated, and, had it not existed, its functions would have been provided by the state, the foundation was still essentially private and carrying out private functions.[318] The Court of Appeal subsequently approved of this decision in *R (Johnson) v Havering LBC*,[319] where it was held that private sector care homes were not public authorities under s.6, and that the state did not have an obligation to ensure that care provision was met by public authorities. In any case the Court of Appeal noted that the local authority still maintained its liability under the Act to ensure that the claimants' rights under Articles 3 and 8 were not breached on transfer of such duties to that body, and remained liable for some basic care of such a person.[320] This decision was upheld by the House of Lords,[321] where it was confirmed that the mere possession of special powers conferred by parliament did not of itself mean that a body had functions of a public nature, and that equally some bodies might not have statutory powers but be amenable to review. In their Lordships' view the focus was on the functions being performed and in this case the actual provision of care

---

[316] For academic opinion on the scope of s.6 of the Act, see Bamforth, The Application of the Human Rights Act 1998 to Public Authorities and Public Bodies (1999) 58 CLJ 159; Oliver, The Human Rights Act and the Public Law/Private Law Divide [2000] EHRLR 343; McDermott, The Elusive Nature of the Public Function (2003) 66 MLR 113; Sunkin, Pushing Forward the Frontiers of Human Rights Protection: The Meaning of Public Authority under the Human Rights Act [2004] PL 643.

[317] [2002] 2 All ER 936.

[318] See the similar decision in *R (Johnson and others) v Havering LBC* [2006] EWHC 1714 (Admin). See also *RSPCA v Attorney-General and Others* [2002] 1 WLR 448, where it was held that the RSPCA was not a public authority under s.6 of the 1998 Act, the body lacking any statutory or public law role.

[319] [2007] 2 WLR 1097.

[320] The Court of Appeal confirmed that the House of Lords' decision in *Aston Cantlow*, below, had not overruled *Cheshire*. The Care of Older Incapacitated People (Human Rights) Bill 2005 sought to extend the meaning of public authorities in this respect; the Bill was dropped.

[321] [2007] 3 WLR 112.

by a private care home, as opposed to its arrangement by the local authority, was not an inherently governmental function. The care home was a private profit-making company and thus not a public authority within s.6.

Despite the above rulings, there may be cases where such providers may be regarded as a public authority within s.6. Thus, in *Poplar Housing and Regeneration Community Association Ltd v Donoghue*[322] the Court of Appeal held that the role of a housing association could, in certain circumstances, be so closely assimilated to that of a local authority that it was performing public functions for the purpose of the Act. In deciding whether the association was a public authority, the court held that it should have regard to the case law regarding public bodies and judicial review.[323] The fact that the association provided a public service, was regulated by the local authority, which would have exercised its powers had the association not existed, were *relevant, yet not decisive* factors. Although the activities of housing associations do not necessarily involve the performance of public functions, in this case the role of the association was so closely assimilated to that of the local authority that it was performing public rather than private functions.[324] Similarly, in *R (Weaver) v London and Quadrant Housing Trust*[325] it was held that a registered social landlord, regulated by the Housing Corporation and operating under the Housing Act 1996, was carrying out a public function and was a public authority for the purposes of the 1998 Act. It was noted that registered landlords were taking the place of local authorities and operated under a public law scheme. On appeal,[326] the Court of Appeal held that the termination of a tenancy by the housing trust was not of a private nature so as to exclude its liability under s.6 HRA. Taking all factors such as funding and function, the trust was a public authority and the act of termination was inextricably linked to that function.[327]

An authority has not, however, been regarded as public simply because it carries out functions which affect the public and which impact on a person's Convention rights; although these factors may become relevant if proposed legislation (see below) is passed. This is the case even though the function might normally be carried out by a public authority. Thus, in *Aston Cantlow and Wilmcote with Billesley Parochial Church Council v Wallbank*,[328] a majority of the House of Lords held that the Parochial Church Council, a statutory corporation discharging certain functions as part of the Church of England, was not a public authority within the meaning of s.6. The Court of Appeal had declared it public because it was created and

---

[322] [2001] 2 WLR 1546.

[323] For example, *R v Panel of Takeovers and Mergers, ex parte Datafin* [1987] QB 815; *R v Disciplinary Committee of the Jockey Club, ex parte Aga Khan* [1993] 1 WLR 909.

[324] On the facts, however, the court held that there had been no violation of the tenant's right to private and family life under Article 8 of the Convention. See also *R v Partnerships in Care, ex parte A* [2002] 1 WLR 2610, where it was held that the decision of a private psychiatric hospital to alter the care and treatment of a patient was an act of a public nature, making it amenable in judicial review and engaging its liability under the Human Rights Act 1998. In that case the duties of the home were underpinned by statutory provisions, in the form of the Nursing Homes and Mental Nursing Homes Regulations 1984.

[325] [2008] EWHC 1377 (Admin).

[326] *London and Quadrant Housing Trust v R (Weaver)* [2010] 1 WLR 363.

[327] See also *Hampshire County Council and Another v Beer* [2004] 1 WLR 233, where it was held that a decision of the Hampshire Farmers Markets Ltd to reject an application by a trout farmer to participate in the Farmers Markets Programme was susceptible to judicial review and s.6 of the Human Rights Act, despite it being a private company. The body owed its existence to Hampshire County Council, replaced the Council's functions, and was assisted by the Council in a variety of ways.

[328] [2003] 3 WLR 283.

empowered by the law and its notice to repair had statutory force. Further, the authority possessed powers to determine how others could act, powers that private individuals lacked.[329] However, on appeal the House of Lords found that the Church of England was essentially a religious body and did not have the character of a governmental organisation.[330] Thus, the council was not a core public authority under the Act; it was not part of government and the state had not delegated or surrendered any of its powers or duties to that body. Essentially, therefore, the body was religious in nature and engaged in self-governance and promotion of its own affairs. Neither, in their Lordships' view, were the functions in question – imposing a charge for the repair property – of a public nature.

The decision of the House of Lords in *Aston Cantlow* and *Johnson* suggests that the courts will look at both the source and nature of the body and its action in deciding liability under s.6. Thus, in *Aston Cantlow* the House of Lords placed great reliance on the body's functions, rather than insisting on any institutional link between it and government.[331] On the other hand, a body which derives its powers from public law and which has ties to governmental bodies is *more likely* to be carrying out public functions and thus be liable under the Act. For example, in *Cameron and Others v Network Rail Ltd*[332] it was held that Railtrack, a company responsible for controlling the infrastructure of the national railway, was not a public authority for the purpose of s.6 of the Act. Although the company originally had public law functions, regulations passed in 2000 divested it of those duties.[333] Therefore it was not acting as a public authority at the time of an accident which allegedly rendered it in violation of Article 2 of the Convention.

Cases such as *Johnson* raise the question of whether the domestic law's refusal to subject such bodies to the Human Rights Act might lead to a breach of the European Convention. There would not appear to be a violation of Article 6 in this respect as the rule disallowing legal action against such bodies would be classed as part of the substantive law.[334] The domestic courts have also refuted the argument that such decisions are in breach of the claimant's other Convention rights. Thus, in *Johnson*, the House of Lords questioned the contention that those who funded themselves and were housed by private organisations had less protection of their Convention rights than those who were housed by the local authority. Equally their Lordships were satisfied that the general duty of the local authority to provide accommodation provided sufficient safeguards against breaches of their Convention rights.

Nevertheless, there has been criticism with respect to the scope of the Human Rights Act and its application to bodies who, despite not being public authorities as such, perform functions which have a great impact on the public, or sectors of the public. This has resulted in legislative change and proposals for such change. Specifically, The Health and Social Care

---

[329] [2001] 3 All ER 393. See Carss-Frisk, Public Authorities: The Developing Definition [2002] EHRLR 319.

[330] The House also held that in any case there was no violation of Article 1 of the First Protocol to the Convention simply because the owners of property acquired a very expensive duty to repair.

[331] An approach which appeared to be favoured by the Joint Committee on Human Rights: *The Meaning of Public Authority under the Human Rights Act 1998* (2004). In 2007 the Joint Committee published another report on *The Meaning of Public Authority under the Human Rights Act* (28 March 2007), recommending that the 1998 Act be amended to include within the definition of public authority any body performing a function of a public nature pursuant to a contract with a public body.

[332] [2006] HRLR 31.

[333] During the debates to the Human Rights Bill, bodies such as Railtrack were regarded as bodies which would be so liable under the Act: HL Deb, vol 583, col 811 (24 November 1997).

[334] See *Z v United Kingdom* (2002) 34 EHRR 3, explained in chapter 7 of this text.

Act 2008 allows residents of private care homes to bring actions under the Human Rights Act 1998. The relevant provisions of the Act came into operation on 1 December 2008.[335]

More generally, the Human Rights Act 1998 (Meaning of Public Authorities) Bill 2009, which had its second reading in April 2010, sought to clarify which bodies constitute public authorities under the Act. Clause 1 of the Bill identifies a number of factors which must be taken into account in determining whether a function is one carried out by a public authority. These factors include: the extent to which the state has assumed responsibility for the function; the role and responsibility of the state in relation to the subject matter in question; the nature and extent of the public interest in the function in question; the nature and extent of any statutory power or duty in relation to the function in question; the extent to which the state, directly or indirectly, regulates, supervises or inspects the performance of the function in question; the extent to which the state makes payment for the function in question; whether the function involves or may involve the use of statutory coercive powers; and the extent of the risk that improper performance of the function might violate an individual's Convention right.

In addition, clause 2 provides that for the purposes of s.6(3)(b) of the 1998 Act, a function of a public nature includes a function which is required or enabled to be performed wholly or partially at public expense, irrespective of the legal status of the person who performs the function, or whether the person performs the function by reason of a contractual or other agreement or arrangement. If passed, therefore, the scope of the Human Rights Act will extend to many acts that are in essence ones performed for the benefit of the public and which as a consequence should be regulated by human rights legislation. The Bill was lost when Labour lost power.

Questions

What difficulties does s.6 pose in respect to defining a public authority and its liability under the Act?

What approaches have the courts adopted in this respect and is that approach consistent with the purpose of the Act and the obligations of the government under the Convention?

How would the position be improved if the Human Rights Act 1998 (Meaning of Public Authorities) Bill 2009 was passed?

The 'horizontal' effect of the Human Rights Act

It is clear that the Act is going to be used in private proceedings and will attach liability for violation of Convention rights committed by private persons or bodies.[336] The Act provides several possibilities of its provisions being used to redress human rights violations committed by private individuals or bodies. This is achieved principally by making the courts public authorities under s.6 of the Act. Under this section, it will be unlawful for the courts to act in a way that is incompatible with Convention rights. Thus, the courts will have responsibility

---

[335] Via the Health and Social Care Act 2008 (Commencement No 4) Order 2008 (SI 2008/2994).

[336] See Buxton, The Human Rights Act and Private Law (2000) 116 LQR 48; Hunt, The 'Horizontal Effect' of the Human Rights Act [1998] PL 423; Wade, Horizons of Horizontality (2000) 116 LQR 217; Phillipson, The Human Rights Act, 'Horizontal Effect' and the Common Law: A Bang or a Whimper? (1999) 62 MLR 824; Phillipson, Clarity Postponed: Horizontal Effect after *Campbell*, in Fenwick, Phillipson and Masterman, *Judicial Reasoning under the UK Human Rights Act* (Cambridge University Press 2007), chapter 6.

not only to carry out the functions imposed on them under the Act, such as interpreting statutory provisions wherever possible in the light of the Convention, but also to develop the law, including the private law, in a manner which is consistent with Convention rights.[337] If the courts fail to do this, they will, as a public authority, be liable under s.6 of the Human Rights Act.

This is consistent with the case law of the European Convention, which has imposed liability for Convention violations committed by non-state bodies. Under Article 1 of the Convention each High Contracting Party must secure to everyone within their jurisdiction the rights and freedoms defined in Section 1 of the Convention. As a consequence, each member state owes a duty to ensure that its legal system accommodates the principles enshrined in the European Convention, by providing protection against Convention violations and ensuring that such rights are upheld within that system.[338] This is reinforced by Article 13 of the Convention, which provides that everyone whose rights and freedoms set forth in the Convention are violated shall have an effective remedy before a national authority.

Accordingly, the courts have been prepared to develop certain aspects of domestic common law in order to accommodate Convention rights and duties.[339] For example, in *Douglas and Others* v *Hello! and Others*[340] the law of confidence was developed to ensure the guarantee of a person's right to privacy in relation to materials which had not been previously recognised by the common law. Again, in *Venables and Thompson* v *Newsgroup Newspapers Ltd*,[341] the High Court held that the common law of confidence could be expanded to accommodate a claim that the release of personal information would cause a threat to the claimants' right to life.[342] However, subsequently the House of Lords showed caution in accepting the full horizontal effect of the Act. In *Wainwright* v *Home Office*[343] it was held that the common law had not developed a separate action in privacy, and that cases such as *Douglas* had merely expanded the existing common law of confidentiality in order to accommodate privacy, and Article 8 principles. Further the House of Lords felt that it was not necessary to develop such a law in order to comply with Convention case law, a statement which appeared to be contradicted when the claimants in *Wainwright* took their case to the European Court of Human Rights.[344]

There will be similar scope for the courts to develop other areas of private law in a way that is Convention compliant. Therefore, in actions for negligence the courts will need to review various rules and cases which exclude public authorities from liability or otherwise restrict individuals from bringing private law actions. Thus, following the decision of the European Court of Human Rights in *Osman* v *United Kingdom*,[345] that the blanket immunity given to the police authorities in actions in negligence was contrary to the right to a fair trial

[337] See Wright, *Tort Law and Human Rights* (Hart 2001) for an analysis of the effect of the Act and the Convention on various aspects of the law of tort.

[338] See, for example, *Young, James and Webster* v *United Kingdom* (1982) 4 EHRR 38; *A* v *United Kingdom* (1999) 27 EHRR 611; *Osman* v *United Kingdom* (2000) 29 EHRR 245.

[339] It has also been argued that the Act allows the courts to develop Convention rights outside common law actions. See Morgan, Questioning the 'True Effect' of the Human Rights Act 1998 (2002) LS 259.

[340] [2001] 2 All ER 289.

[341] [2001] 1 All ER 908.

[342] See Hare, Vertically Challenged: Private Parties, Privacy and the Human Rights Act [2001] EHRLR 526. See also the decisions in *R* v *Wakefield MBC and Another, ex parte Robertson* [2002] 2 WLR 889; *A* v *B plc and Another* [2002] 3 WLR 542; *Campbell* v *MGN Ltd* [2004] 2 AC 457. These, and other cases, will be dealt with in chapters 9 and 11.

[343] [2004] 2 AC 406.

[344] *Wainwright* v *United Kingdom* (2007) 44 EHRR 40.

[345] (2000) 29 EHRR 245.

within Article 6 of the Convention, the courts will need to be mindful that similar immunities and procedural obstacles do not violate a claimant's Convention rights.[346]

In addition the courts will need to ensure that the substantive aspects of any relevant law are sympathetic to the rights laid down in the European Convention. In *X* v *Y*[347] the Court of Appeal attempted to clarify the application of the Human Rights Act to unfair dismissal disputes in the private sector. In this case the employee, a probation worker, had been dismissed for receiving a caution for an indecency offence committed in a public toilet with another man. He claimed unfair dismissal and asserted that the dismissal was in breach of his Convention rights under Articles 8 and 14 of the Convention and that by employing s.3 of the Human Rights Act the test of unfairness contained in the Employment Rights Act 1996 should be interpreted in the light of those rights. Although the Court of Appeal held that the tribunal was entitled to find that Articles 8 and 14 were not engaged on the facts, it held that the 1998 Act might have an effect on dismissals in the private sector in appropriate cases. In the Court's view a tribunal should not uphold a dismissal that was clearly incompatible with the Convention rights of the employee, although if there was a justifiable reason for his dismissal under the 1996 Act the tribunal should consider such rights in the context of the application of s.3 of the 1998 Act to the provisions of the 1996 Act.[348]

Questions

To what extent does the 1998 Act have a 'horizontal' effect?

Is it necessary for the Act to have such an effect in order to comply with the government's obligations under the Convention?

Remedies under the Act

The remedies available to those whose Convention rights have been violated revolve around s.6 of the Act, which makes it unlawful for public authorities to act in a way that is incompatible with a person's convention rights. Thus s.7(1) of the Act provides that a person who claims that a public authority has acted (or proposes to act) in a way which is made unlawful by s.6 may either bring proceedings against the authority under this Act in an appropriate court or tribunal,[349] or rely on the Convention right or rights concerned in any legal proceedings.[350]

---

[346] Decisions post-*Osman* have allowed substantive law impediments to bringing legal actions and in *Brooks* v *Metropolitan Police Commissioner* [2005] 1 WLR 1495 the House of Lords held that the police did not owe a duty of care to a victim or a witness when investigating a suspected crime and that such a finding was not inconsistent with Article 6 of the Convention: *Z* v *United Kingdom* (2002) 34 EHRR 3. See also *Matthews* v *Ministry of Defence* [2003] 1 AC 1163.

[347] *The Times*, 16 June 2004. See Collins, The Protection of Civil Liberties in the Workplace (2006) 69 MLR 619.

[348] Contrast *Copsey* v *WWW Devon Clays Ltd*, *The Times*, 25 August 2005, where the Court of Appeal held that Article 9 had limited application when considering whether a dismissal of an employee for refusing to work on Sundays was fair. On the facts the Court of Appeal held that Article 9 was not engaged and that the decision to dismiss had to be judged purely on the statutory provisions relating to unfair dismissal.

[349] This is defined in s.7(2) as such court or tribunal as may be determined in accordance with rules, and proceedings against an authority including a counterclaim or similar proceedings.

[350] Under s.7(6) of the Act 'legal proceedings' include proceedings brought by or at the instigation of a public authority and an appeal against the decision of a court or tribunal. See Leigh and Lustgarten, Making Rights Real: The Courts, Remedies and the Human Rights Act (1999) 58 CLJ 509.

Accordingly, a person claiming to have had his or her Convention rights violated can either bring a direct action, usually via judicial review proceedings, for breach of his or her Convention rights by virtue of s.7 of the Act, or use that right (or rights) in other proceedings collaterally as a means of challenging action taken against him, such as in the course of criminal proceedings.

Victims of a Convention violation

Section 7(1) limits the scope of the Act to those who are 'victims' of a violation of Convention rights and a person is only regarded as a victim of an unlawful act if he would be regarded as such for the purposes of Article 34 of the European Convention.[351] In this sense the domestic courts are expected to adopt the European Court's liberal approach in this area,[352] and thus anyone affected, or potentially affected, by the unlawful act would be considered a victim, as would the relatives and dependants of those directly affected. For example, in *R (Holub and Another)* v *Secretary of State for the Home Department*,[353] it was held, *obiter*, that the parents of a minor whose human rights had been breached had the standing to complain under s.7 of the 1998 Act.[354] However, the House of Lords has held that it is not possible for the courts to make a declaration of incompatibility in relation to legal provisions that do not personally affect the claimant, and where there is no risk of such provisions impacting on the individual's rights.[355]

Although the European Court does not always insist that the law has been applied against an individual before they are regarded as victims,[356] in most cases the domestic courts will refuse to rule on the relevant law *in abstracto*, and will insist that a specific decision has been made. For example, in *R (Hirst)* v *Parole Board*[357] it was held that a prisoner could not bring an application for a declaration that the Crime (Sentences) Act 1977 was incompatible with Article 5 of the European Convention until the Board had considered his case for release. In the court's view, it would not be proper for it to rule on the question of compatibility until the Board had considered the claim, because until that time it would not be apparent that the statutory power was capable of impacting on the prisoner's case. Although the court accepted that in certain cases it would be appropriate to make declarations before the relevant provisions had been enforced, in this case the court should not interfere until it was faced with a specific decision that might be in violation of the applicant's Convention rights.[358]

The Act envisages that proceedings for breach of a Convention right may be brought by judicial review proceedings and states that in such a case the applicant shall be taken to have sufficient interest in relation to the unlawful act only if he is, or would be, a victim of that

---

[351] Section 7(7) Human Rights Act 1998.

[352] See chapter 2, pages 50–1.

[353] [2001] 1 WLR 1359.

[354] In *Morgan* v *Ministry of Justice* [2010] EWHC 2248 (QB) it was held, *obiter*, that a fiancée could be regarded as a victim with respect to the suicide of a prisoner, but whether someone in a mere relationship would be a victim would depend on all the facts. The individual would need to have suffered gravely or be personally concerned to be considered a victim under the Act.

[355] *Rusbridger and Toynbee* v *Attorney-General and DPP* [2004] 1 AC 357.

[356] *Dudgeon* v *United Kingdom* (1982) 4 EHRR 149.

[357] [2002] EWHC 1992.

[358] *Rusbridger and Toynbee* v *Attorney-General and DPP* [2004] 1 AC 357.

act.[359] It will not be sufficient if the person has standing on other grounds, such as being a recognised representative group that has brought the action on behalf of the direct victim. Consequently, where in the past the courts have accepted such representative actions,[360] arguments on breach of Convention, or other human rights grounds, would need to be considered under the traditional position before the Human Rights Act came into force, with the courts unable to use their specific powers under, for example, s.2 and s.3 of the Act, but still subjecting the decision to a more intense scrutiny than would be the case had the application not raised a human rights argument.[361]

Further problems relating to public law actions are raised by s.7(5) of the Act, which imposes a time limit for the bringing of proceedings under this section,[362] and which makes this provision subject to any rule imposing a stricter time limit in relation to the procedure in question. This will give rise to problems where the victim's claim is a 'public law' issue, in that it raises the question of the validity of the decision makers' exercise of public law (usually statutory) powers, and thus requiring the case to be decided via the public law procedure of judicial review.[363] In such a case the courts must decide whether the proceedings can be brought directly under the Act, with its time limit of one year, or whether the victim must proceed via the procedure of judicial review and be bound by the stricter time limits.[364]

Power to award an appropriate remedy

Section 8(1) states that where a court finds that an act (or proposed act) of a public authority is (or would be) unlawful, it might grant such relief or remedy, or make such order, within its powers as it considers just and equitable. This includes the power to award damages, although only where the court has a power to award damages or order the payment of compensation in civil proceedings.[365] No award of damages shall be made unless, taking account of all the circumstances of the case including any other relief granted, or order made in relation to the act in question and the consequences of any decision in respect of that act, the court is satisfied that the award is necessary to afford just satisfaction to the person in whose favour it is made.[366] This suggests that courts should consider alternative, non-compensatory

---

[359] Section 7(3) Human Rights Act 1998. The claimant will need to exhaust alternative effective remedies, such as statutory appeals: see *R v Secretary of State for the Home Department, ex parte Kurdistan Workers' Party and Others* [2002] EWHC 644 (Admin), where it was held that a challenge to the lawfulness of proscription under the Terrorism Act 2000 should be heard by the Proscribed Organisations Appeal Commission before being challenged by means of judicial review.

[360] See, for example, *R v Secretary of State for the Environment, ex parte Greenpeace Ltd (No 2)* [1994] 4 All ER 352.

[361] For example, as evidenced in cases such as *R v Ministry of Defence, ex parte Smith* [1996] 1 All ER 257.

[362] The proceedings must be brought before the end of the period of one year with the date on which the act complained of took place or such longer period as the court or tribunal considers equitable having regard to all the circumstances. In *Somerville v Scottish Ministers* [2007] 1 WLR 2734, the House of Lords held that s.7(5) did not apply to a claim for damages with respect to an action of the Scottish Executive that was outside its powers because it was contrary to the applicant's Convention rights.

[363] As required by the exclusivity principle established by the House of Lords in *O'Reilly v Mackman* [1983] 2 AC 237.

[364] Under the Civil Procedure Rules 1998 an application for judicial review must normally be brought within three months of the decision against which review is sought. More generally, the courts will need to decide when it is appropriate for a victim to pursue an action under the Human Rights Act, and whether such a person might have to, or be able to, bring alternative actions.

[365] Section 8(2) Human Rights Act 1998.

[366] Section 8(3) Human Rights Act 1998.

remedies and award damages as a last resort. Also, in deciding whether to award damages, or in deciding the amount of any award, the court must take into account the principles applied by the European Court of Human Rights in relation to the award of compensation under Article 41 of the Convention.[367]

Early case law on the courts' power to award damages under s.8 suggested that they would take a liberal and generous view. In *R (Bernard and Another) v Enfield LBC*,[368] damages had been sought for failure to provide suitable accommodation to the claimant, who was severely disabled, and her husband and six children. It was found that the authority's failure to act had shown a singular lack of respect for the claimant and that that failure justified the court in awarding just satisfaction. In the court's view it was difficult to see why awards should not be comparable to tortious awards and that the awards recommended by the Local Government Ombudsman were of great assistance. Further, the award should not be minimal because that would diminish the respect for the policy underlying the Human Rights Act. In this case the claimant's problems were compounded by the conduct of the authority and the award should be at the top end of the £5000–10,000 range. Similarly, in *R (KB) v Mental Health Review Tribunal*,[369] it was held that damages for breach of human rights under the Human Rights Act should be no lower than for a comparable tort and should, as far as possible reflect the English level of damages. The court awarded damages of between £750 and £1000 to patients whose release had been delayed in breach of Article 5(4) of the Convention.[370]

However, subsequent cases have attempted to restrict the generosity of that approach. For example, in *Anufrijeva v London Borough of Southwark*,[371] the Court of Appeal stressed that damages for breach of Article 8 of the Convention were not recoverable automatically, and would only be awarded when necessary to give just satisfaction.[372] The court also confirmed that breach of a public law duty would not be sufficient on its own and there would have to be a degree of culpability together with foreseeable harm. Also, in the joint action in *R (N) v Secretary of State for the Home Department*,[373] it was held that damages under the Act would not be granted automatically for omissions or inactivity of public authorities that caused breaches of Convention rights and that the courts were to look critically at such claims. In the Court of Appeal's view the main concern was usually to bring the infringement to an end and that compensation was of secondary importance.[374]

---

[367] Section 8(4) Human Rights Act 1998. For those principles and their application, see chapter 2, pages 57–8.

[368] *The Times*, 25 November 2002.

[369] [2003] 3 WLR 385.

[370] However, it was held that damages would not be granted automatically for violation of that article, and that the courts should follow the principle of just satisfaction as practised by the European Court.

[371] [2004] 2 WLR 603.

[372] In *Boyle v Criminal Cases Review Commission* [2007] EWHC 8, it was held that even if a prisoner could prove that there had been an unreasonable delay by the Commission in referring his case to the Court of Appeal, it would not be appropriate to grant damages, it being a sufficient remedy that the prisoner bring an action in judicial review.

[373] [2004] 2 WLR 603.

[374] Further, in *Wainwright v Home Secretary* [2004] 2 AC 406, the House of Lords held, *obiter*, that it was doubtful whether damages could be claimed under the Human Rights Act 1998 for invasion of privacy by a public authority which had caused distress to a person, where that act was merely negligent. This *obiter* now needs to be viewed in the light of the decision of the European Court of Human Rights in *Wainwright v United Kingdom* (2007) 44 EHRR 40.

Section 8 applies to those violations coming within s.6 and s.7 of the Human Rights Act and, therefore, only covers breaches committed by public authorities.[375] However, as 'public authorities' include courts, victims will be able to rely on the principles and case law of the European Convention in all types of legal proceedings, including private actions taken against private individuals. Although the courts will be guilty of violating convention rights by the denial of appropriate legal protection, the Act provides that the remedy in such a case will be via judicial review or by appeal.[376] More specifically, s.9(3) of the Act states that damages may not be awarded under the Act in respect of a judicial act done in good faith. Consequently an award of damages is not generally available in relation to judicial acts that violate a person's Convention rights, although s.9(3) makes an exception in cases where there is a violation of Article 5(5) of the European Convention, which guarantees an effective remedy when a person's right to liberty and security of the person under Article 5 of the Convention has been violated.

Although a monetary award is thus expected in cases of loss of liberty, it is clear that Article 5(5), read in conjunction with s.8 of the Human Rights Act does not provide a freestanding right to compensation. In *R (Downing) v Parole Board*[377] the High Court stressed that s.8 of the Act provided a wide area of discretion to the domestic courts as to when to award damages for breach of Convention rights, allowing them to take into account a variety of factors. In the instant case, therefore, it refused to grant compensation to a prisoner whose parole hearing had been unreasonably delayed; the delay impinged on the prisoner's conditions of imprisonment (he had been ordered to be moved to open conditions) rather than his liberty, and there was no evidence of any mental suffering. Further, having regard to the seriousness of the original offence (sexual assault and murder), it would not have been an appropriate exercise of the court's discretion having regard to the public interest to award the prisoner damages.

Further guidance and caution was provided by the House of Lords in *R (Greenfield) v Home Secretary*,[378] a case concerning an admitted violation of Article 6 when prisoners had not been provided with legal assistance at a disciplinary hearing. In that case their Lordships confirmed that when domestic courts are considering awards under s.8 they should take into account the case law of the European Court, although they were not bound to follow such decisions. In particular, the courts should apply the principle applied by the European Court in cases where there has been held to be a breach of Article 6, to the effect that a finding of a violation of Article 6 is normally just satisfaction in itself,[379] and that it was not appropriate for such awards to be comparable to tortious awards.[380] Thus, in cases of structural bias, the practice of the European Court was not to make an award for physical and mental suffering and that where such an award is made for loss of procedural opportunity or anxiety and frustration,

---

[375] An example of the courts' ability to award damages to compensate for a violation of the claimant's human rights was seen in the case of *Adenivi v Newham* LBC, unreported, decision of the High Court, 16 October 2001, where £5000 damages were awarded to a disabled child whose photograph had been used by a local authority to promote an AIDS awareness campaign.

[376] Section 9(1) Human Rights Act 1998. Section 9(2) then provides that subsection (1) does not affect any rule of law which prevents a court from being the subject of a judicial review.

[377] [2008] EWHC 3198 (Admin).

[378] [2005] 1 WLR 673.

[379] See, for example, *Kingsley v United Kingdom* (2002) 35 EHRR 10, noted in chapter 2, page 58.

[380] See Gordon, HRA Damages after Greenfield: Where are We Now? [2006] Judicial Review 230; Clayton, Damage Limitation: The Courts and the Human Rights Act Damages [2005] PL 429.

the sums were modest. In the present case the conduct of the adjudication itself appeared to have been exemplary, and there was no special feature warranting an award of damages.[381]

Further, it was only where the European Court found a causal connection between the violation and the loss for which an applicant sought to be compensated was it ordinarily willing to depart from its practice of finding a violation of Article 6 to be, in itself, just satisfaction under Article 41 of the Convention. While it might be appropriate to make an award if the court feels that the applicant had been deprived of a real chance of a better outcome, in the instant case it was inappropriate to speculate whether a legal representative might have persuaded the adjudicator to take a different view.[382]

A more protectionist approach will be taken where there has been a serious violation of the victim's Convention rights, particularly where there has been a violation of the state's obligation to protect life, under Article 2 of the Convention. In *Van Colle* v *Chief Constable of Hertfordshire*[383] the court at first instance had found a violation of Articles 2 and 8 when the police authorities had taken inadequate steps to safeguard the life and private and family life of a prosecution witness (G) from attacks by suspects in a forthcoming trial. It was held that in deciding the level of damages the court should consider the character and conduct of the parties and the extent and seriousness of the breach, taking into account the negligence of the police officer, the distress suffered by the death victim and the mother, and the fact that there had been no apology from the force or the individual officer, who had faced only minor disciplinary charges. On those facts the court awarded £15,000 for G's distress suffered before his death and £35,000 for the grief and suffering of the parents caused by the breach. On appeal,[384] the Court of Appeal upheld the finding on liability, but held that the judge at first instance had erred by considering the lack of a proper apology and the fact that the officer had been found guilty of failing to perform his duties conscientiously. In the Court of Appeal's view the awards were too high; the judge should have awarded £10,000 to the deceased's estate and £15,000 to the family personally. This guidance can still be regarded as good law despite the Court of Appeal's decision being subsequently overturned by the House of Lords on the question of substantive liability.[385]

Such compensation can often reflect the seriousness of the state's initial obligation and breach of this fundamental right, despite evidence of the victim's specific financial or other loss. Thus, in *Savage* v *South Essex Partnership NHS Trust*[386] the court granted damages of £10,000 to the daughter of a woman who had committed suicide after absconding from a mental hospital as a 'symbolic acknowledgment' that the trust ought to properly compensate her for her loss. In doing so the court took into account that the victim had not brought the case for financial reasons and that no award could compensate the victim for the loss of her mother.

---

[381] See also *Re P, The Times*, 1 February 2007, where it was held that damages were not available to a mother who had not been consulted before a care plan had been abandoned. In the Court's view the breach was purely procedural and would not have materially affected the mother's position. However, it held that damages were available in appropriate cases where parents are not involved in decisions affecting family life.

[382] That approach is not appropriate in cases where a violation has possibly resulted in a deprivation of liberty. In *R (Hirst)* v *Secretary of State for the Home Department and Another, The Times*, 4 July 2005, the applicant was awarded £1500 for a failure to provide reasons for his recall to prison, which had led to a violation of Article 5(4).

[383] [2006] 3 All ER 963.

[384] [2007] 1 WLR 1821.

[385] *Van Colle* v *Chief Constable of Hertfordshire* [2009] 1 AC 225, examined in chapter 4.

[386] [2010] HRLR 24.

Questions
To what extent have s.7 and s.8 of the Act enhanced the remedies available in domestic law to victims of human rights violations?
Has the approach taken by the domestic courts in the post-Act era been consistent with the Convention and its case law?

Remedial action

The Act is careful to retain parliamentary sovereignty and to leave the ultimate power of deciding the compatibility of domestic legislation with Convention rights with the democratically elected legislature. Thus, where a court had declared a statutory provision as incompatible with the Convention, it has no power to disapply the provision and the ultimate decision of whether the provision remains as valid law rests with the lawmakers. Thus, parliament can either leave the provision on the statute books, risking an application under the European Convention by a relevant victim, or alter that provision in line with the Court's finding.

Specifically, s.10 of the Human Rights Act foresees that in the case of incompatible legislation the government may wish to change the law, and provides a mechanism whereby remedial action can be taken by a minister of the Crown to amend such legislation. Section 10 of the Act provides that where a provision of legislation has been declared incompatible under s.4 of the Act, or it appears to a minister of the Crown or Her Majesty in Council that, having regard to a finding of the European Court of Human Rights made after the coming into force of s.10 in proceedings against the United Kingdom, a provision of legislation appears incompatible with an obligation of the United Kingdom under the Convention, the minister may, if he considers that there are compelling reasons for proceeding under this section, make such amendments by order to the legislation as he considers necessary to amend the incompatibility.[387] Once made, a remedial order may be made so as to have the same effect as the legislation that it affects.[388] It is also clear that such an order can operate retrospectively, although it is stated that no person is to be guilty of an offence solely as a result of the retrospective effect of any order.[389]

A similar power is created in the case of subordinate legislation, where a minister considers it necessary to amend the primary legislation under which the subordinate legislation was made so as to allow an incompatibility between the provision and the Convention right to be removed. Again the minister must consider that there are compelling reasons for proceeding under this section, although the minister's action does not have to be in response to a declaration of incompatibility or an appropriate decision of the European Court of Human

---

[387] Section 10(2) Human Rights Act 1998.
[388] Paragraph 1(4) of Schedule 2.
[389] Paragraph 1(5) of Schedule 2. The above provision is limited to the situation where the court has made a declaration of incompatibility under s.4, or where, after the coming into operation of the Act, a decision of the European Court involving the United Kingdom appears to make the statutory provision incompatible with the Convention.

Rights. In such a case he may order such amendments to that primary legislation as he considers necessary.[390]

Such remedial orders are governed by the procedure laid down in Schedule 2 of the 1998 Act and provide for both a standard and emergency procedure. Schedule 2, paragraph 2 provides that no remedial order can be made unless a draft of the order has been approved by a resolution of each House of Parliament made after the end of the period of 60 days beginning on the day that the draft was laid. Thus, in normal circumstances the order is subject to the positive affirmation of parliament.[391] Further, under paragraph 3(1) of the Schedule no draft can be laid under paragraph 2 unless the person proposing to make the order has laid a document before parliament containing a draft of the proposed order and the required information,[392] and a period of no less than 60 days has expired. This is to allow relevant representations to be made, and paragraph 2(c) then provides that if representations[393] have been made the draft order must be accompanied by a statement containing a summary of such representations and the details of any change made to the order as a result of the representations.

In emergency cases where the order is made without being approved in draft, paragraph 4 provides that the person making the order must lay it before parliament, accompanied by the required information, after it is made. Then, if representations have been made during the period of 60 days the person making it must (after the end of that period) lay before parliament a statement containing a summary of those representations and, if any changes were made as a result of the representations, details of the changes.[394] If changes have been made, paragraph 4(3) requires the person making the statement to make a further remedial order replacing the original order and to lay a replacement order before parliament. The paragraph then provides that if, at the end of the period of 120 days after the original order was made, a resolution has not been passed by each House approving the original or replacement order, the order ceases to have effect.[395]

Statements of compatibility

Section 19(1) of the Act provides that a minister of the Crown in charge of a bill in either House must, before the Second Reading of the bill, make either a statement of compatibility

---

[390] Section 10(3) Human Rights Act 1998. Under s.10(4) the section also applies where subordinate legislation has been quashed, or declared invalid by reason of incompatibility, and the minister wishes to proceed under paragraph 2(b) of Schedule 2 of the Act. These powers are, of course, additional to the general powers of parliament to change the law, but it is expected that such changes will follow the specific constitutional safeguards laid down in the 1998 Act.

[391] Under paragraph 2(b) no such procedure has to be followed where it is declared in the order that it appears to the person making it that, because of the urgency of the matter, it is necessary to make the order without such approval.

[392] This is defined in paragraph 5 as an explanation of the incompatibility that the order seeks to remove and a statement of the reasons for proceeding under s.10 and for making an order in those terms.

[393] 'Representations' are defined under paragraph 5 as representations about a remedial order (or proposed remedial order) made to the person making (or proposing) it and including any relevant parliamentary report or resolution.

[394] Paragraph 4(2) of Schedule 2.

[395] Paragraph 4(4) of Schedule 2. This will not affect anything previously done under either order or the power to make a fresh remedial order.

to the effect that in his view the provisions of the bill are compatible with the Convention rights, or make a statement to the effect that although he is unable to make a statement of compatibility the government nevertheless wishes the House to proceed with the bill.[396]

The constitutional and legal effect of this provision is uncertain. According to traditional constitutional law, an Act of parliament cannot bind parliament as to the manner in which legislation is passed. Thus, a bill that did not contain such a declaration could not be invalidated by the courts. Also, as the courts have not been bound by the pronouncements, as opposed to the formal Acts of parliament, a declaration that a bill is Convention compliant would not bind the courts and prevent them from subsequently declaring legislation incompatible with Convention rights. The courts might, however, show deference to such declarations when determining the compatibility of such legislation with Convention rights,[397] although such declarations, and general parliamentary approval, could not prevent the courts in coming to a contrary conclusion on the legislation's compatibility with the European Convention.[398]

Thus far only one statement of incompatibility has been made by a relevant minister with respect to proposed domestic law. Section 321(2) of the Communications Act 2003 makes political advertising unlawful and may be inconsistent with the European Court's decision in *VgT Verein gegen Tierfabriken* v *Switzerland*.[399] Accordingly, the minister made a statement under s.19(1)(b) of the Human Rights Act 1998 that the government intended to proceed with the Bill despite not making a declaration of compatibility.[400] The provision was challenged by Animal Rights International, who claimed that it is contrary to Article 10. However, in *R (Animal Defenders International)* v *Secretary of State for Culture and Media and Sport*[401] it was held that the prohibition was not incompatible with Article 10. In their Lordships' views the greater immediacy and impact of radio and television advertising accounted for a need for a blanket prohibition of political advertising in those media where no such prohibition applied to other communication media. Thus, the provision was not incompatible with Article 10 or the decision of the European Court in *VgT Verein gegen Tierfabriken* v *Switzerland*.

In justifying any departure from the European Court's ruling, it was held that there was no common consensus about how to legislate for religious and political advertising and each Member State appeared best fitted to judge the checks and balances necessary to safeguard the integrity of its own democracy consistently with Article 10. Further, the full arguments about equality in freedom of speech and political advertising were not considered and employed in *VgT* and it was not to be assumed that the European Court would disagree with the House of Lords in this case: the decision in the present appeal showed no more than the possibility of a divergence of opinion of the European and domestic courts, something which was implicitly contemplated by the Human Rights Act 1998. Subsequently, in *TV Vest AS* v *Norway*,[402] the European Court held that there was violation of Article 10 when a ban on

---

[396] Under s.19(2) the statement must be in writing and be published in such matter as the minister making it considers appropriate.

[397] See *Nottinghamshire County Council* v *Secretary of State for the Environment* [1986] AC 240.

[398] See *R* v *Secretary of State for the Home Department, ex parte Javed and Another* [2002] QB 129, where it was held that subordinate legislation approved by parliament could be reviewed on the grounds of illegality and unreasonableness.

[399] (2002) 34 EHRR 4.

[400] See Lewis, Political Advertising and the Communications Act 2003 [2005] EHRLR 290.

[401] [2008] UKHL 15.

[402] (2009) 48 EHRR 51.

political advertising was applied to fine the media for broadcasting an advertisement on behalf of the Pensioner's Party, a small party who wished to use the broadcast to highlight its ideals. The ruling is not necessarily decisive of the compatibility of the domestic situation, as the decision was made on the facts, the European Court holding that the reasons for the fine in this case were unconvincing as there was little evidence of the party using the media or any financial power to gain political advantage over others.[403]

Section 13 and freedom of religion

Under s.13 of the Act if a court's determination of any question arising under the Act might affect the exercise by a religious organisation (itself or its members collectively) of the Convention right to freedom of thought, conscience and religion, it must have particular regard to the importance of that right.[404] Unlike s.12 of the Act, which attempts to give added protection to freedom of expression,[405] this section does not give any specific guidance as to what aspects of that right and its enjoyment are to be given special weight, and in that sense it adds little to the general position that interference with any Convention right must be necessary and proportionate.[406] Nevertheless, the courts will be obliged to take this right into account in developing the law in favour of the enjoyment of the rights contained in Article 9, including allowing interferences with other Convention rights, such as freedom of expression, for the purpose of protecting an individual's, or group's, Article 9 rights.[407]

Derogations and reservations

In order to accommodate a state's particular emergency circumstances or special cultural or social needs, the Convention allows member states to relieve themselves of their full responsibilities or commitments under the Convention, either by lodging a derogation to deal with a state of war or other public emergency, or by placing a reservation on its commitment to a particular Convention right.

Derogations

Article 15 of the European Convention allows a member state to 'derogate' from its obligations under the Convention in times of war or other public emergency threatening the life of the nation, and s.1(2) of the Human Rights Act allows the government to avoid giving effect to the Convention to the extent that it has lodged a derogation within the provisions of s.14 of the Act.

---

[403] It would appear, therefore, that the House of Lords' ruling may be within its discretion under s.2 of the Human Rights Act with respect to following previous European Court rulings; see pages 128–30 above.

[404] See Cumper, The Protection of Religious Rights under Section 13 of the HRA [2000] PL 254.

[405] Section 12 of the Act is considered in detail in chapter 8 of this text.

[406] See Wadham and Mountfield, *The Human Rights Act 1998* (Blackstone Press 2006, 4th edn), page 49.

[407] During the passage of the Human Rights Bill church organisations were particularly concerned that the right to employ suitable teachers in religious schools and to impose requirements for religious marriages would be threatened by actions under the 1998 Act.

The Human Rights Act 1998 (Amendment No 2) Order 2001

United Kingdom derogations existing at the time of the Act's implementation were contained in Schedule 3 of the Act. The Act thus contained the government's derogation notices of 1988 and 1989, which were made after the European Court's decision in *Brogan* v *United Kingdom*.[408] In that case the Court found that domestic provisions allowing extended detention of suspected terrorists were in violation of Article 5(3) of the Convention, which states that persons who have been arrested must be brought promptly before a court. The government's derogation under Article 15 of the Convention was challenged in *Brannigan and McBride* v *United Kingdom*,[409] but the European Court held that the derogation was justified under the terms of Article 15, even though it had only been lodged after the decision in *Brogan*. This derogation was withdrawn by an order made under the Human Rights Act[410] when the relevant statutory provisions were replaced by the Terrorism Act 2000.

Using its powers under s.14 of the Act, the Secretary of State made the Human Rights Act 1998 (Amendment No 2) Order 2001, which came into force on 20 December 2001 and which gave notice to the Council of Europe of the United Kingdom's derogation from Article 5(1) of the European Convention. The derogation was in response to the terrorist attacks in the United States of America on 11 September 2001, which the government claimed caused a state of public emergency under Article 15, and which resulted in the passing of the Anti-Terrorism, Crime and Security Act 2001.[411] This Act, *inter alia*, provided for an extended power to arrest and detain foreign nationals, whom it is intended to remove or deport from the United Kingdom, but where such removal or deportation is not for the time being possible; primarily because such a person would face treatment in violation of the Convention if returned to that particular country. The extended power applied where the Secretary of State believd that the person's presence in the United Kingdom was a risk to national security where he suspected the person of being an international terrorist, and in such a case the Secretary could issue a relevant certificate, which was subject to an appeal to the Special Immigration Appeals Commission.

The derogation order explained that the provision in question was necessary in order to release the government from its obligations under the Convention and to comply with the European Court's judgment in *Chahal* v *United Kingdom*.[412] In that case the European Court held that in order to comply with Article 5 of the Convention deportation proceedings had to be prosecuted with due diligence. In the order the government argued that this measure was strictly required by the exigencies of the situation, stressing that it was a temporary measure, which would expire after 15 months unless renewed by parliament.

These powers, contained in s.23 of the Anti-Terrorism and Security Act 2001 were challenged in the domestic courts by the detainees as incompatible with Articles 5 and 15 of the Convention. Initially the Special Immigration Appeals Commission held that although there was a state of public emergency and justification for derogating from Article 5, the provisions and their enforcement were discriminatory and thus in violation of Article 14 of the

---

[408] (1989) 11 EHRR 117.

[409] (1993) 17 EHRR 539.

[410] Human Rights Act (Amendment) Order (2001) S1 2001/1216.

[411] See Warbrick, The Principles of the European Convention on Human Rights and the Responses of States to Terrorism [2002] EHRLR 287.

[412] (1997) 23 EHRR 413.

Convention. However, in *A and Others* v *Secretary of State for the Home Department*,[413] the Court of Appeal held that the detentions were compatible with the Convention, including Article 14. In the Court's view, the powers were objectively justified during a time of public emergency and were proportionate. LORD WOOLF CJ accepted that taking action against nationals as well as non-nationals would have been more effective. Equally, if the non-nationals were detained notwithstanding the fact that they wanted to leave this country, the action would be more effective. However, on his assessment of the situation, the Home Secretary had come to the conclusion that he could achieve what was necessary by either detaining or deporting only terrorists who were aliens. This was justified on objective and relevant grounds; such persons had no right to stay in the country, only a right not to be removed. The distinction between aliens and nationals was part of international law and the need to protect them from torture meant that such detention was not in violation of Article 14.

However, on appeal the House of Lords held that the measures were incompatible with the United Kingdom's obligations under the European Convention and could not be excused within Article 15 of the European Convention.[414] Their Lordships first addressed the question of whether there existed a public emergency threatening the life of the nation so as to allow derogation, stressing that great weight should be given to the judgment of the Home Secretary and parliament because they had to exercise a pre-eminently political judgment, and the more political the question was, the more appropriate it would be for political resolution and consequently the court's role in scrutiny would be smaller.[415] Nevertheless, their Lordships found that the actual measures to deal with that emergency were disproportionate because they did not deal with the threat of terrorism from persons other than foreign nationals; permitted suspected foreign terrorists to carry on their activities in another country provided there was a safe country for them to go; and permitted the detention of non-Al-Qaeda supporters even though the threat relied on to justify the measures was from that specific source. It was also held that the measures contravened Article 14 because the appellants were treated differently because of their nationality or immigration status; such a distinction could not form the legitimate basis of depriving one group of their Convention right to liberty of the person as protected by Article 5.[416]

Following the decision of the Lords in *A*, the 2001 derogation was withdrawn and parliament passed the Prevention of Terrorism Act 2005, which introduced a system of control and supervision orders to deal with such suspects.[417] These powers were passed as non-derogating orders – the government believing them to be compatible with Articles 5 and 6 of the Convention – and were challenged as being contrary to Article 6 of the Convention. In *Re MB*[418] the House of Lords held that the procedures for reviewing the use of those powers (under s.3 of that Act) were generally compatible with Article 6. However, in *Secretary of State*

---

[413] [2003] 2 WLR 564.

[414] [2005] AC 68.

[415] Lord Hoffmann dissented on this issue, concluding that the real threat to the life of the nation, in the sense of a people living in accordance with its traditional laws and political values, came not from terrorism but from laws such as those in issue.

[416] Lord Walker dissented and found that the detention provisions were necessary and proportionate. In his Lordship's opinion the Act offered protection against abuse, and the fact that in nearly three years only 17 individuals had been certified under the provisions pointed to the conclusion that the measures and any discrimination was necessary and proportionate.

[417] These measures are examined in chapters 6 and 7 of this text.

[418] [2007] 3 WLR 681.

for the Home Department v *JJ and Others*[419] the House of Lords held that control orders imposed on the applicants under s.2 of the Prevention of Terrorism Act 2005 were in breach of Article 5 of the Convention. Consequently, the orders, which purported to be non-derogating orders because the Home Secretary regarded them as restrictions on liberty rather than deprivations of liberty, were, in fact, derogating orders that the Secretary had no jurisdiction to make.[420]

These cases suggest that the domestic courts will subject anti-terrorist measures, including derogating measures, to the strictest scrutiny. Thus the House of Lords, while showing some deference to parliament and the executive when deciding whether a state of emergency existed, showed little reluctance to pass judgment on the compatibility of specific provisions that impact on fundamental rights of liberty and due process. In this respect, therefore, the domestic courts have not been prepared to offer the wide margin of appreciation that the European Court has provided in Article 15 cases.

Questions

How have the domestic courts reacted to the government's attempts to derogate from the Act with respect to the threat of terrorism?

Is this reaction consistent with the case law of the Convention and the purpose of the Human Rights Act 1998?

Reservations

Article 57 of the European Convention on Human Rights allows each member state to make reservations with regard to its commitments under the Convention to ensure observance of the Convention rights within its jurisdiction. Acting under this power the United Kingdom has made a reservation in connection with its obligations under Article 2 of the First Protocol to the Convention, so that such obligation is compatible with the provision of efficient instruction and training, and the avoidance of unreasonable public expenditure.[421] Section 15 of the Human Rights Act 1998 recognises the power to make a designated reservation, which is referred to as the United Kingdom's reservation to Article 2 of the First Protocol and any other reservation by the United Kingdom that is designated for the purposes of the Act in an order made by the Secretary of State. Under the Act, if a designated reservation is withdrawn wholly or in part, it ceases to have effect,[422] although the Secretary of State can make a fresh designation order in respect of the article concerned.[423] Such reservations are stated to cease to have effect five years after the Act came into force, or five years after the designation order,[424] although the Secretary of State may extend that period by a further five years.[425]

---

[419] [2007] 3 WLR 642.

[420] Applying the decision of the European Court of Human Rights in *Guzzardi* v *Italy* (1981) 3 EHRR 333, their Lordships held that the orders impacted severely on liberty, were expected to last indefinitely, and prevented the individuals from pursuing the life of their choice. Contrast the decision of the House of Lords in *Secretary of State for the Home Department* v *E* [2007] 3 WLR 720. These cases are examined in chapters 6 and 14 of this text.

[421] This reservation is contained in Part 2 of Schedule 3 of the Human Rights Act 1998.

[422] Section 15(3) Human Rights Act 1998.

[423] Section 15(4) Human Rights Act 1998.

[424] Section 16(1) Human Rights Act 1998.

[425] Section 16(2) Human Rights Act 1998.

Conclusions

Although the Act does not disturb the traditional principles of the British Constitution, and in particular does not create a constitutional bill of rights as such, it can be argued that it has provided us with identifiable and concrete human rights law. This is not to suggest that before the Act there was no human rights law, but the listing of specific rights in the 1998 Act and the 'incorporation' of the human rights law and principles of the European Convention and its case law, has at least guaranteed that human rights issues and disputes are dealt with directly as such, and not incidentally through formal legal rules. Thus, although most private remedies, such as defamation, confidentiality, trespass and nuisance, still govern the parties' legal position, such laws are now subject to the principles and case law of the Convention, and when legal cases raise Convention rights they are dealt with as such. For example, in pre-Act cases such as *Malone*[426] and *Kaye* v *Robertson*[427] the courts struggled to accommodate what were clearly human rights' disputes into the relevant legal principles and remedies, whereas such laws are now clearly driven by human rights principles.[428] This is particularly so with respect to the use and control of public power, which the 1998 Act is principally concerned with. Although several pre-Act cases recognised the existence and importance of human rights in the context of judicial review,[429] public power is now clearly and consistently subject to principles of legality, necessity and proportionality. Moreover, much of the judicial deference evident in previous cases with respect to the challenge of administrative and legislative policy has now been reduced because of the courts' power (and duty) under the Act to subject such actions to an appropriately intensive review.[430] At the very least, the Human Rights Act has managed to provide for greater compliance of domestic law with our obligations under the European Convention on Human Rights, which, arguably, was the essential aim of the Act.[431]

Reforming the Human Rights Act 1998?

The Human Rights Act has come under criticism from both those who believe its provisions fail to safeguard human rights effectively and those who feel that it goes too far in protecting rights over and above other rights and interests.

Strengthening the Act

There has been a great deal of academic discussion as to the efficacy of the Human Rights Act 1998, centring on the *strengthening* of the Act's provisions and ambit and calling for the extension of rights' protection in the United Kingdom.[432] Consequently, the possibility of a bill of

---

[426] *Malone* v *MPC* [1979] Ch 344.

[427] [1991] FSR 62.

[428] See the development of confidentiality law as detailed in chapters 9 and 11 of this text.

[429] See, for example, *R* v *Home Secretary, ex parte Brind* [1991] 1 All ER 696; *R* v *Ministry of Defence, ex parte Smith* [1996] 1 All ER 257.

[430] See in particular, *A* v *Secretary of State for the Home Department* [2005] 2 AC 68 and *R* v *Secretary of State for the Home Department, ex parte Daly* [2002] 2 AC 532.

[431] For an account of the United Kingdom's record before the Strasbourg Court after the Act came into force, see Amos, The Impact of the Human Rights Act on the United Kingdom's Performance before the European Court of Human Rights [2007] EHRLR 655.

[432] See Klug and Starmer, Standing Back from the Human Rights Act: How Effective is it 5 Years On? [2005] PL 716; Lester, The Human Rights Act 1998 – Five Years On [2004] EHRLR 258; Clayton, The Human Rights Act Six Years On: Where Are We Now? [2007] EHRLR 11.

rights for the United Kingdom, including introducing a constitutionally entrenched bill of rights has re-surfaced,[433] and it is in this context that we will examine, in brief, the recommendations of the 29th report of the Joint Committee on Human Rights on whether the United Kingdom should adopt a bill of rights.[434]

Does the United Kingdom need a bill of rights?

The Committee concluded that there was considerable scope for a bill of rights to add to what is already in the Human Rights Act 1998. In particular the Committee saw it necessary to enhance the rights of vulnerable and marginalised groups such as asylum seekers and children in custody. However, it stressed that any bill of rights should not in any way weaken the existing machinery contained in the Act for the protection of Convention rights and sought an assurance from the Justice Secretary that there was nothing in the then government's plans, below, to weaken the Act.

A 'British' bill of rights

The Committee expressed some concern that the government had linked fundamental human rights with citizenship, portraying the idea that such rights only belonged to UK citizens rather than to all individual human beings within the jurisdiction of the United Kingdom. Equally, the Committee felt that the term 'British' bill of rights would not only isolate non-citizens, but would also cause dissent from UK citizens who would not consider themselves British, but as Irish or Scottish, etc. Nevertheless, the Committee recognised that a domestic bill of rights could and should provide the opportunity to reflect particular values that are fundamental to a particular nation state. It concluded, therefore, that a United Kingdom bill of rights would constitute an accurate description of a document which sought to express the state's national identity and definition.

What should be included in a United Kingdom bill of rights?

The Committee agreed that a United Kingdom bill of rights should have a preamble that sets out the purpose of having a United Kingdom bill of rights and the values that are considered fundamental in UK society; the content of which the government should research and consult on. In its Outline of a UK Bill of Rights (included in Annex 1 of its Report) the preamble reads as follows:

> This Bill of Rights and Freedoms is adopted to give lasting effect to the values which the people of the United Kingdom consider to be fundamental.

The preamble then listed the rule of law, liberty, democracy, fairness and civic duty as those values. The outline then includes an interpretative clause, requiring any body interpreting the bill to strive to achieve its purpose and to give practical effect to the fundamental values that underpin it. Specifically, the Committee recommended the classification of rights into civil and political rights, fair process rights, economic and social rights, democratic rights and the rights of particular groups, and the inclusion of a (qualified) right to trial by jury and a right to administrative justice. In addition, it recommended giving better effect to the UN

---

[433] See Klug, A Bill of Rights of Rights: Do We Need One or Do We Already Have One? [2007] PL 701.

[434] *A Bill of Rights for the UK?* Report of the Joint Committee of Human Rights, 10 August 2008. HL Paper 165-1; HC 150-1.

Conventions on the Rights of the Child and on the Rights of Persons with Disabilities. The inclusion of other rights should then be the outcome of appropriate public consultation.

Economic and social rights and 'third generation' rights

The Committee welcomed the idea of including a limited number of economic and social rights – initially the right to health, education, housing and an adequate standard of living – in the bill of rights. However, being mindful of the question of whether courts should resolve cases involving such issues as the allocation of resources, it felt that the most appropriate way to proceed was to impose an obligation on the state to achieve those rights and to report to parliament on the progress being made in that respect. The courts would then have a limited role to play in the review of the government's policies and their progress. With respect to third generation rights, the Committee recommended the inclusion in the bill of rights of the right to a healthy and sustainable environment; such a right being capable of legal expression.

The relationship between parliament, the executive and the courts

The Committee felt that a bill of rights with the power of the courts to override Acts of Parliament would be at odds with the United Kingdom's traditional constitutional structure. So too the Committee was against the idea of entrenching the bill of rights from further amendment save by special procedure. It felt that the existing arrangements for rights protection contained in the Human Rights Act were the most appropriate and democratic. Any bill of rights should, therefore, have an express statement allowing Parliament to override the provisions in the bill. However, in order to strengthen government accountability, ministers should provide full and reasoned explanations to parliament regarding the compatibility of parliamentary bills, and this should be extended to amending secondary legislation.

Although rejecting the idea of suspended orders of invalidity, the Committee recommended that following any declaration of incompatibility the government would be required to bring forward a formal response to parliament and to initiate a debate on its response. Further, the bill of rights would require the government to come back to court to account for what it has done to implement the court's judgment.[435]

Responsibilities and duties

The Committee firmly rejected the idea that a United Kingdom bill of rights be called either a bill of rights and *duties* or a bill of rights and *responsibilities*. In its view a bill of rights was not the place to impose general obligations on the individual to obey the law. Further, the enjoyment of human rights could not be made contingent on the fulfilment of responsibilities; the limitations on the enjoyment of human rights – including the respect of the rights of others – had already been built into the Convention rights.

With respect to the application of the bill to private bodies and persons, the Committee recommended that it should be able to find a way of binding such bodies and persons who perform public functions. In addition, although rejecting the idea of the bill having

---

[435] With respect to derogation in times of emergency, the Committee recommended that the government's power to derogate should be subject to parliamentary and judicial safeguards and that the requirements and limitations of such derogation should be clearly spelled out in the bill of rights. Parliamentary confirmation that a state of emergency exists would be a requirement; and parliament would also prescribe an appropriate time limit for the period of any derogation.

full horizontal effect between private individuals, the Committee proposed that indirect horizontal effect could be achieved by imposing an express duty on all courts to interpret and apply legislation and the common law in a way which is compatible with the rights and freedoms in the bill and which promotes the purpose of the bill. The courts, as with all public bodies, would also have a duty to act compatibly with the bill and to take active steps to promote its objectives.

Weakening the Act

There has been much political and public debate on whether the Act has been successful in securing a fair balance between human rights and the more general interests such as national security, public safety and the prevention of crime. Specifically, there has been concern over the European Court's stance on the protection of the rights of those suspected of terrorism, and the United Kingdom government was joined as a party in a case which sought to question the absolute nature of the prohibition of torture in cases where suspected terrorists are being deported or extradited.[436]

A possible remedy to this situation may involve the replacing of the Act with a domestic bill of rights, which would more reflect 'British values' and allow the introduction of a more appropriate bill of rights and responsibilities for the citizen. Thus, in its Green Paper on Constitutional Reform,[437] although the then government conceded that repealing the 1998 Act would prevent citizens from exercising their fundamental rights in British courts and lead to lengthy delays while individuals appealed to Strasbourg,[438] it stressed that the Act should not necessarily be regarded as the last word on the subject and that a bill of rights and duties could give people a clear idea of what we can expect both from public authorities and from each other. Specifically, it could provide recognition that human rights come with responsibilities and must be exercised in a way that respects the human rights of others.[439]

The government and other critics of the Act are hopeful that any change to the Act would be countenanced by the European Court of Human Rights by applying an appropriate margin of appreciation. However, if a change to the Act entailed a reduction of the level of enjoyment of Convention rights, that margin would not be offered: a fact that the Green Paper concedes when it states that a framework of civic responsibilities would need to avoid encroaching upon personal freedoms and civil liberties.[440] Despite the Joint Committee on Human Rights' rejection of the ideals expressed in the government's recommendations,[441] the Ministry of Justice published a Green Paper outlining some of the earlier proposals.[442] If these proposals are pursued, by whichever government, then the bill of rights for the United Kingdom debate will resurface, including the possibility of enhancing the rights protection under the Act by the introduction of a constitutionally entrenched bill of rights.[443]

---

[436] *Ramzy v The Netherlands* (Application No 25424/05), discussed in chapter 5 of this text.

[437] *The Governance of Britain 2006–2007* (CM 7170).

[438] Ibid., para 207.

[439] Ibid., paras 208–10.

[440] Ibid., para 210.

[441] See the Joint Committee on Human Rights, 29th Report on Bill of Rights for the UK, available at www.publications.parliament.uk/pa/jt/jtrights/htm, and the government's response, 19 January 2009, at www.publications.parliament.uk/pa/jt200809/jtselect/jtrights/15/15.pdf.

[442] 'Rights and Responsibilities: developing our constitutional framework', CM 7577, March 2009.

[443] See Klug, A Bill of Rights of Rights: Do We Need One or Do We Already Have One? [2007] PL 701. See also Asmal, Designing a Bill of Rights for a Diverse Society [2007] EHRLR 597.

Questions

What are the central provisions of the Human Rights Act, and what purpose do those provisions seek to achieve?

To what extent has the traditional system of protecting civil liberties survived the Act?

How, if at all, has the Act enhanced the protection of human rights and civil liberties in domestic law?

What constitutional and legal difficulties has the Act created?

Overall, do you prefer the traditional common law methods or the system under the Human Rights Act 1998?

If the Act was to be repealed or modified, what form should a new bill of rights/duties take?

Further reading

The pre-Act era of civil liberties

Students are advised to read chapter 1 of Fenwick's *Civil Rights: New Labour, Freedom and the Human Rights Act* (Longman 2000) and chapter 1 of Clayton and Tomlinson's *The Law of Human Rights* (OUP 2009). Hunt's *Using Human Rights Law in English Courts* (Hart 1997) is also useful. A more detailed analysis can be found in Ewing and Gearty, *The Struggle for Civil Liberties* (OUP 2000) and an examination of the deficiencies of common law principles can be found in Foster, The Protection of Human Rights in Domestic Law: Learning Lessons from the European Court [2002] NILQ 232 and Klug, The Long Road to Human Rights Compliance [2006] NILQ 186.

The Human Rights Act 1998

There are a number of very good texts on the Act itself, including Wadham, Mountfield and Edmundson, *Blackstone's Guide to the Human Rights Act 1998* (OUP 2009) and Amos, *Human Rights Law* (Hart 2006), the latter of which examines the provisions and the case law of the Act in detail. Students are also advised to consult chapters 2–5 of Clayton and Tomlinson's *The Law of Human Rights* (OUP 2009); Beatson, Grosz, Hickman, Singh and Palmer, *Judicial Protection in the United Kingdom* (Sweet and Maxwell 2009); Jowell and Cooper, *Understanding Human Rights Principles* (Hart 2001); and the excellent text by Gearty, *Principles of Human Rights Adjudication* (OUP 2005); all of which provide an analysis of the principles underlying the Act and an examination of the Act's interpretation and application.

The Act in practice

Students should consult Fenwick, Phillipson and Masterman (eds), *Judicial Reasoning under the UK Human Rights Act* (Cambridge University Press 2007) for expert coverage and analysis of various aspects of the Act. See also Jowell and Cooper (eds), *Delivering Rights: How the Human Rights Act is Working* (Hart 2003); Kavanagh, *Constitutional Review under the UK Human Rights Act* (Cambridge 2009); Leigh and Masterman, *Making Rights Real; Enforcing the Human Rights Act* (Hart 2007); and Baker, *Proportionality under the UK Human Rights Act* (Hart 2010).

In addition, the following articles are recommended for an expert analysis of the Act, its case law, the role of the courts in the Human Rights Act era, and the success or otherwise of the Act: Amos,

The Impact of the Human Rights Act on the United Kingdom's Performance before the European Court of Human Rights [2007] PL 655; Bonner, Fenwick and Harris-Short, Judicial Approaches to the Human Rights Act [2003] ICLQ 350; Buxton, The Future of Declarations of Incompatibility [2010] PL 213; Clayton, Judicial Deference and 'Democratic Dialogue' [2004] PL 33; Dickson, Safe in Their Hands? Britain's Law Lords and Human Rights (2006) LS 329; Edwards, Judicial Deference under the Human Rights Act (2002) 65 MLR 859; Eleftheriades, On Rights and Responsibilities [2009] PL 33; Hickman, The Substance and Structure of Proportionality [2008] PL 694; Kavanagh, Unlocking the Human Rights Act: The 'Radical' Approach to Section 3(1) [2005] EHRLR 260; Kavanagh, The Role of Parliamentary Intention in Adjudication under the HRA 1998 (2006) OJLS 153; Kavanagh, Judging the Judges under the Human Rights Act [2009] PL 287; Klug, A Bill of Rights of Rights: Do We Need One or Do We Already Have One? [2007] PL 701; Klug, Judicial Deference under the Human Rights Act 1998 [2003] EHRLR 125; Klug and Starmer, Standing Back From the Human Rights Act: How Effective is it 5 Years on? [2005] PL 716; Lester, The Human Rights Act 1998 – Five Years On [2004] EHRLR 258; Lord Irvine, The Impact of the Human Rights Act: Parliament, the Courts and the Executive [2003] PL 308; Masterman, Taking the Strasbourg Jurisprudence into Account: Developing a Municipal Law of Human Rights under the Human Rights Act [2005] ICLQ 907; Nicol, Statutory Interpretation and Human Rights after *Anderson* [2004] PL 274; Steyn, 2001–2005: Laying the Foundations of Human Rights Law in the United Kingdom [2005] 4 EHRLR 349.

Visit **www.mylawchamber.co.uk/fosterhumanrights** to access regular updates to major changes in the law, further case studies, weblinks, and suggested answers/approaches to questions in the book.

Part Two

The protection of substantive
human rights and civil liberties

4 The absolute rights: the right to life

Introduction

In *Pretty* v *United Kingdom* the European Court of Human Rights had to decide whether the right to life, as guaranteed by Article 2 of the European Convention on Human Rights, included the right to die. It decided that it did not, but that a ban on assisted suicides could engage a person's right to private and family life. Subsequently, in *R (Purdy)* v *DPP* the House of Lords held that the DPP had to provide sufficiently clear guidance as to when prosecutions would be brought against people who assisted another's suicide.

Why did the European Court decide there was no general right to die? And how can the law reconcile the individual's right to self-determination and the state's obligation to preserve life?

This chapter examines how both the European Convention and domestic law protect the fundamental right to life. The chapter will firstly examine the nature and importance of the right to life, including its absolute and fundamental status. It will then explore the scope of that right including the nature and extent of the duties that such a right imposes on the state to preserve it. Further, the chapter will examine the procedural aspect of the right to life, detailing the state's obligation to hold investigations into deaths which may have occurred in breach of the general right to life. Finally, it will look at the legitimate exceptions to the general right – where it is permissible for a state to take life – including the legality of the death penalty.

The right will be viewed initially from the perspective of Article 2 of the European Convention on Human Rights, which provides that everyone's right to life shall be protected by law. However, a study will be made of both European Convention case law and the case law (and relevant statutory provisions) in domestic law, most notably how the right has been developed under the Human Rights Act 1998.

Thus, this chapter will cover:

- An examination of the importance and nature of the right to life under the European Convention on Human Rights.
- An examination and analysis of the scope and extent of the state's obligation to protect life under the Convention and the Human Rights Act 1998.

- An examination of the state's procedural obligation under the Convention and the Act to conduct effective investigations into deaths in their jurisdiction.
- An examination of the permitted exceptions to the right to life and the circumstances in which it is lawful to take life, including the legality of the death penalty.

All sections of the chapter will be illustrated by an analysis of the relevant case law both of the European Court of Human Rights and cases decided under the Human Rights Act 1998 and a critical evaluation of their effectiveness in protecting the right to life.

The right to life and Article 2 of the European Convention

Although the right to life has always been recognised and protected in English domestic law, since the passing of the Human Rights Act 1998 the focus has largely been on Article 2 of the European Convention on Human Rights. This right is given effect to in domestic law by the 1998 Act and the courts are bound to take into account the relevant case law of the European Court of Human Rights. Our domestic law in this area will, therefore, be shaped by Article 2, its principles and Convention case law. Article 2 of the European Convention provides as follows:

> Everyone's right to life should be protected by law. No one shall be deprived of his life inten-tionally save in the execution of a sentence of a court following his conviction of a crime for which the penalty is provided by law. Deprivation of life shall not be regarded as inflicted in violation of this article when it results from the use of force which is no more than absolutely necessary:
>
> a   in defence of any person from unlawful violence
> b   in order to affect a lawful arrest or to prevent the escape of a person lawfully detained
> c   in action lawfully taken for the purpose of quelling a riot or insurrection.

Similar provisions and protection are provided by other international instruments. For example, Article 3 of the Universal Declaration of Human Rights 1948 provides simply that everyone has the right to life, liberty and security of the person. However, Article 6 of the International Covenant on Civil and Political Rights 1966 bestows a more positive duty on the state by providing not only that every human being has the inherent right to life, but also that the right shall be protected by law and that no one shall be arbitrarily deprived of his life. Nevertheless, it will be Article 2 of the European Convention that will most influence domestic law and shape the content of this chapter.

The importance of the right to life under Article 2

Article 2 of the Convention protects the most fundamental of human rights, the right to life.[1] This right must, of course, be respected if any other human rights are to be enjoyed and can thus be regarded as the most basic of civil and political rights.[2] Further, its violation by the state represents the most serious of human rights breaches, consistent with arbitrary and uncivilised government and the lack of basic respect for the sanctity of life. Thus, the

---

[1] In *Pretty v United Kingdom* (2002) 35 EHRR 1, the European Court held that the right to life under Article 2 did not guarantee the right of self-determination so as to allow a person the right to die.

[2] The UN Human Rights Committee described it as the basic precondition of the enjoyment of other rights: (1991) IHRR 15–16.

European Court has noted that Article 2 and the exceptions listed in Article 2(2) rank as the most fundamental provisions in the Convention, and enshrine one of the basic values in the democratic societies of the Council of Europe.[3]

The right is absolute in the sense that it cannot be derogated from even in times of war and other public emergency, except in respect of deaths resulting from lawful acts of war.[4] However, the Convention recognises that even the fundamental right to life may be compromised in exceptional circumstances and thus provides a number of express exceptions, above, which, although narrowly construed, provide justification for the taking of a person's life.

Scope of the right to life under Article 2

Article 2 imposes a *negative* obligation not to intentionally deprive a person of their right to life. Additionally, as the article talks of an individual possessing a right to have his life protected by law, it also imposes a *positive* obligation on the state to preserve individual life.

Article 2 thus firstly applies to deliberate acts of ill-treatment committed by the state, usually via state officials, for example on persons in detention and via unnecessary and disproportionate acts of violence by state officials in the course of public protection.[5] Further, to augment this negative duty the European Court has also made it clear that in many cases, such as where the person is in the detention of the state, the burden of proof in relation to such deaths will be on the state authorities.[6] Thus, in *Salman* v *Turkey*[7] it was stated that where a person is brought into state custody in good health and then dies, there is a particularly stringent obligation placed on it to provide a satisfactory account of that death. Accordingly, in that case it was held that there had been a violation of Article 2 when the victim had been arrested and then died on arrival at hospital. The state argued that he had died of a heart attack, but evidence of ill-treatment contradicted this and thus the state was held in violation of Article 2. Equally, in certain cases of disappearances, the Court is prepared to assume the state liable in the absence of a body.[8] More recently, in *Tais* v *France*[9] the European Court found a violation of Article 2 when the applicant had been found dead in a police cell in a pool of his own blood and excrement, allegedly having been beaten with police batons the previous evening. The Court held that the state had failed to provide a satisfactory explanation for his death and thus were liable under Article 2.[10]

Equally the state's liability under Article 2 may be engaged with respect to acts of private individuals that the state authorities should have prevented and which have threatened the victim's life.[11] In such a case the state has a positive, albeit limited, duty to safeguard the lives

---

[3] *McCann* v *United Kingdom* (1995) 21 EHRR 97, at para 147.

[4] Article 15(3) of the European Convention and Article 14(2) of the International Covenant on Civil and Political Rights 1966.

[5] *McCann* v *United Kingdom* (1995) 21 EHRR 97.

[6] See, for example, the case of *Jordan and Others* v *United Kingdom* (2003) 37 EHRR 2.

[7] (2002) 34 EHRR 17.

[8] *Timutas* v *Turkey* (2001) 33 EHRR 121. Alternatively, in the absence of evidence of a definite death the Court might find the state to be in violation of Article 5 – guaranteeing liberty and security of the person: *Kurt* v *Turkey* (1999) 27 EHRR 373.

[9] Decision of the European Court of Human Rights, 1 June 2006.

[10] In many of these cases, including the present one, the Court will probably find a violation of the duty to conduct a proper investigation into the death, see below.

[11] *Osman* v *United Kingdom* (2000) 29 EHRR 245.

of its citizens, and may be held liable if it has failed to take appropriate action with respect to a relatively real risk to life. Further, this liability may be owed with respect to the deliberate acts of the victims themselves: the state having a duty to take reasonable steps to avoid suicides, particularly where the victim is in detention or under the control of state authorities.[12] Thus, in *Kilinc v Turkey*,[13] the European Court found a violation of Article 2 when the applicant had committed suicide whilst carrying out military service. The applicant had long-standing psychiatric problems and was deemed fit for military service. The next day he shot himself in the head with a rifle. The Court found that there was inadequate guidance given to the authorities to decide whether a person was fit for service and if so which tasks they should be allocated. Accordingly, the authorities had not done everything in their power to prevent the risk of suicide and were in violation of Article 2.

Question

Why is the right to life regarded as so fundamental in modern democracies and under the European Convention on Human Rights?

Territorial liability for deaths

As Article 1 of the Convention imposes a duty on member states to secure Convention rights to everyone within their jurisdiction, the state can be liable for deaths of foreign citizens occurring in their country. As we have seen in chapter 2, the European Convention can in certain circumstances impose an obligation on member states with respect to violations occurring in another state, even where that state is not a party to the Convention.[14] That principle and the relevant case law will be explored in the next chapter, dealing with the prohibition of torture and inhuman and degrading treatment or punishment, but its application to Article 2 can be illustrated in the case of *Bader v Sweden*.[15] In this case the European Court found a violation of Articles 2 and 3 when the applicant had been denied asylum and faced the death penalty in Syria, having been found guilty of murder in his absence. The government had not received any assurance from the Syrian authorities that his case would be reopened or that he would not face the death penalty. The applicant had, thus, been subjected to a real risk that he would be executed in violation of Article 2. Further, given the unfairness of the proceedings and the anxiety surrounding such lack of due process, there was also a violation of Article 3.

Equally, liability may be engaged where the member state has sufficient control of that territory or part of the territory in which the death has taken place. Generally, member states owe an obligation, under Article 1 of the Convention, to protect the rights of those 'within its jurisdiction'. However, the European Court has been cautious in extending liability in this area. In *Bankovic v Belgium and the United Kingdom*[16] the European Court held that it would only be in very exceptional circumstances that acts performed outside the territory of the state, or otherwise taking effect beyond the territories, would constitute an exercise of jurisdiction under Article 1. In this case the European Court declared inadmissible a claim by a

---

[12] *Keenan v United Kingdom* (2001) 33 EHRR 38.
[13] Decision of the European Court, 9 June 2005.
[14] *Soering v United Kingdom* (1989) 11 EHRR 439.
[15] Decision of the European Court, 8 November 2005.
[16] (2007) 44 EHRR SE5.

relative that his daughter's death at the hands of a NATO attack in Serbia had engaged Article 2. In the Court's view extra territoriality would occur when there was a military occupation or where the government of the state concerned had consented to the occupation. Neither of those circumstances applied in the present case and thus Article 1, and Article 2, did not apply.

With respect to liability for breaches of Article 2 in domestic law under the Human Rights Act 1998, it has been accepted that the Act's territorial ambit is coextensive with Article 1, so that the failure of parliament to 'incorporate' Article 1 is not fatal. Thus, in R *(Al-Skeini and Others)* v *Secretary of State for the Defence*[17] it was held that the death of an Iraqi civilian in the custody of British forces in Iraq engaged the Human Rights Act 1998 as the civilian's custody in the hands of British soldiers placed him within the United Kingdom's jurisdiction as required by Article 1 of the Convention, thus imposing a duty to hold a proper investigation into that death as required by Article 2 of the European Convention. However, the Court of Appeal also held that Article 1 did not apply to extend a broad, worldwide extraterritorial jurisdiction arising from the exercise of authority by state agents anywhere in the world. Hence, the shooting of civilians during the hostilities did not engage Article 1. The British forces were not in effective control of that territory despite it being an occupying force.[18] At the time of writing, the Grand Chamber of the European Court is preparing to hear applications brought under Articles 2 and 3 by the victims, who are questioning the British courts' ruling on the question of jurisdiction.[19]

Article 2 and the Human Rights Act 1998

As Article 2 of the Convention has now been given effect in domestic law by virtue of the Human Rights Act 1998, the domestic courts are bound to apply Article 2 and its case law in relevant domestic proceedings. Thus, under s.6 of the Act it is unlawful for public authorities to violate Convention rights, including the right to life, and any proceedings brought against such bodies may draw on the relevant principles and cases identified in this chapter. However, for Article 2 to apply directly the victim would need to show that the defendant is a public authority. Thus, in *Cameron and Others* v *Network Rail Ltd*[20] it was held that Railtrack (the company responsible for controlling the infrastructure of the national railway) was not a public authority because although it originally had public law functions, regulations passed in 2000 divested it of those duties. Thus, it was not acting as a public authority at the time of the accident in question. Despite the limits imposed by s.6 of the 1998 Act, Article 2 can be used in private law proceedings and might inform domestic law with respect to the application of such laws and available remedies.[21]

However, it has been established that Article 2 can only be applied in the domestic courts with respect to deaths that occurred after the Human Rights Act 1998 came into force. In *Re McKerr*[22] the House of Lords held that s.6 of the Human Rights Act applied only to an

---

[17] [2006] 3 WLR 508.

[18] The decision was upheld by the House of Lords: [2007] 3 WLR 33. The fuller implication of this rule for public authorities under the Human Rights Act 1998 is discussed in chapter 3, see pages 120–2. See also the decision of the Court of Appeal in *R (Al-Saadoon and Mufhdi)* v *Secretary of State for Defence* [2009] 3 WLR 957 and the subsequent decision of the European Court in *Al-Saadoon and Mufdhi* v *United Kingdom, The Times,* 10 March 2010, discussed in detail under the death penalty and protocols 6 and 13, below.

[19] *Al-Skeini* v *United Kingdom* (Application No 55721/07); *Al-Jedda* v *United Kingdom* (Application No 27021/08).

[20] [2007] 1 WLR 163.

[21] See, for example, *Venables and Thompson* v *Newsgroup Newspapers*, discussed below at page 193.

[22] [2004] 1 WLR 807.

unlawful killing which occurred after the Act came into force, and for those purposes it was the death, rather than the refusal to hold an inquiry into it, which triggered the state's liability under Article 2, that was the relevant date for assessing jurisdiction. Their Lordships also held that it would not be appropriate to apply a so-called common law right to an effective investigation into unlawful deaths as such a right would be inconsistent with the existing statutory framework for such investigations.[23]

The ruling in *McKerr* was upheld by their Lordships in *R (Hurst) v HM Coroner for Northern District London*,[24] where it was held that the Court of Appeal in that case had erred in finding that in appropriate circumstances s.3 of the Human Rights Act empowered a domestic court to give a Convention-compliant interpretation to legislation (the Coroners Act 1988), even though the act was committed before the Act came into effect. The Court of Appeal had held that public policy dictated that Article 2 of the Convention should inform the duty of a coroner under the Coroners Act 1988.[25] However, the House of Lords held that it was not necessary to interpret the Coroners Act 1988 in line with Article 2 of the Convention by applying the common law presumption that parliament did not intend to legislate in violation of its international law obligations; there was no ambiguity in the 1988 Act, and even if there was it was not appropriate to hold that it was parliament's intention that coroners be given wider investigative powers in line with Article 2 of the Convention in all cases.

Positive duty to protect life

Article 2 does not merely impose a negative duty on the state not to interfere with a person's right to life, but also places a positive duty on the state to ensure that an individual's life is not taken unnecessarily.

Therefore, the state must take reasonable measures to safeguard a person's life, and this duty applies whether the act is one of a state official or a private individual. The duty involves having in place appropriate laws imposing criminal liability for acts which threaten the right to life and proper procedures to ensure that persons are deterred from committing such acts and are sanctioned for breaches of such laws, thus ensuring that such risks do not materialise.[26]

However, this duty is not absolute and an applicant would need to show that there was a *real risk* of a violation of Article 2, and that the authorities had failed to take the appropriate standard of care in ensuring that the right to life was adequately protected. In *Osman v United Kingdom*,[27] the applicants, Mrs Osman and her son, Ahmet, brought a claim under Article 2 concerning the unlawful killing of Mr Osman by a Mr Paget-Lewis, one of Ahmet's teachers, who had formed an attachment to Ahmet. When the teacher shot dead Mr Osman and another person, the applicants brought an action against the police in negligence. The courts held that the police were protected by legal immunity.[28] The applicants then brought an

---

[23] The applicants in this case had already brought a successful case before the European Court of Human Rights with respect to the inadequacy of the investigation: *McKerr v United Kingdom* (2003) 37 EHRR 2. See now *Brecknell v United Kingdom* (2008) 46 EHRR 42, where the Court found a breach of Article 2.

[24] [2007] 2 WLR 726.

[25] [2005] 1 3892.

[26] See Mowbray, *The Development of Positive Obligations under the European Convention by the European Court of Human Rights* (Hart 2004), chapter 2.

[27] (2000) 29 EHRR 245.

[28] *Osman v Ferguson* [1993] 4 All ER 344.

action under the European Convention, claiming a violation of Articles 2 and 6 of the Convention. The European Court noted that Article 2 enjoined the state to take appropriate steps to safeguard the lives of those within its jurisdiction and that they had to take preventive operational measures to protect an individual whose life is at risk from the criminal acts of another individual. However, the Court noted that that obligation should not impose an impossible and disproportionate burden on the authorities. In this case, although the Court pointed to a series of missed opportunities which could have neutralised the threat imposed by Paget-Lewis, the police could not be criticised for attaching greater weight to the presumption of innocence or failing to use their powers, having regard to their reasonably held view that they lacked the standard of suspicion to use such powers, or that any action taken would not produce concrete results.[29]

The decision and approach in *Osman* was adopted by the House of Lords in the domestic case of *Van Colle v Chief Constable of Hertfordshire*.[30] In this case the victim was due to give evidence at a forthcoming fraud trial. Before the trial the prospective defendant had made several threats to the victim which the latter reported to the police officer in charge of the case. The officer decided not to take any further action in response to the complaints, despite the fact that he was aware of the defendant's interference with other witnesses and one incident where there had been a fire at the property of a witness. The Court of Appeal had held that there had been a violation of Article 2 (and of Article 8 – guaranteeing the right to private and family life) as the authority had taken inadequate steps to safeguard the life (and private and family life) of a prosecution witness from attacks by suspects in a forthcoming trial.[31] In the Court of Appeal's view the murdered witness was in a special category of person worthy of protection under Article 2,[32] and there was a real and immediate risk which the police officer was aware of and had taken inadequate steps to address. Specifically, the officer was not aware of the witness protection scheme and had not responded to a number of threats and incidents which alerted him to those risks. The Court of Appeal also held that it was not necessary for the claimant to prove that the 'but for test' in causation had been satisfied; it being sufficient that there were protective measures open to the officer, and that such measures had *a real prospect* of avoiding the death. On the evidence it was more likely than not that the death would have been avoided.

However, on appeal the House of Lords overturned the decision of the Court of Appeal, finding that the test in *Osman* – that the authorities knew at the time of the existence of *a real and immediate* risk to life – was not present in this case. Their Lordships noted that the murder had been the action of a disturbed and unpredictable individual and it could not be reasonably said that the police should, from the information available to them at the time, have anticipated that the assailant constituted a risk to the claimants' life that was both real and imminent. It was also stressed that the *Osman* test was invariable and did not impose a standard that varied from case to case. Thus in the present case it could not be pleaded that the claimant belonged to a special category where a lower threshold of predictability applied, and the Court of Appeal had thus erred in finding a violation of Article 2 for that reason.

---

[29] The Court did, however, find that the applicant's right to a fair trial under Article 6 had been violated by their inability to bring civil proceedings against the police.

[30] [2009] 1 AC 225.

[31] [2006] 3 All ER 963.

[32] Contrast with the decision in *R (Bloggs) v Secretary of State for the Home Department*, considered below.

Such a ruling ensures that those suing the police cannot avoid the general legal immunity granted to such bodies in respect of tort actions,[33] and it now appears that bringing such a case under Article 2 will require the claimant to show a very strong case in order to establish liability. Thus, in *Mitchell v Glasgow City Council*[34] the House of Lords held that there had been no violation of Article 2 and the principle in *Osman* when a man had been attacked and killed by his next-door neighbour. The man had been threatened by the neighbour seven years previously and had been invited to a meeting organised by the council in order to discuss the neighbour's recent conduct. The man was not aware that the neighbour would attend the meeting and was verbally abused by him at the meeting. Shortly afterwards, the neighbour fatally attacked the man at his home and an action in negligence and under Article 2 was brought against the council by his relatives. Dismissing both claims,[35] the House of Lords noted that the only previous act of violence against the man had occurred seven years ago and that although the neighbour had lost his temper and been abusive, he had not threatened the man, nor had the neighbour been armed. Thus, there was nothing said or done by the neighbour to alert the authority to a risk that he would attack the man when he got home, let alone inflict fatal injuries on him.

Nevertheless, the domestic courts will need to carefully assess the risk posed to the victim's life and then balance that risk with the attainment of other interests, such as the protection of the rights of others, as well as more general interests such as the due administration of justice. This duty had been imposed on the relevant authorities even before the coming into force of the Human Rights Act,[36] and in *R v Lord Saville of Newdigate, ex parte A and Others*,[37] it was held that the chairman of the 'Bloody Sunday' inquiry had acted irrationally when he had decided that in the interests of openness and justice the tribunal should waive the anonymity, given by the first inquiry, to the soldiers involved in the inquiry. The Court of Appeal held that a decision maker was not allowed to make a decision which risked interfering with a soldier's fundamental right to life in the absence of compelling justification. Accordingly, where such rights were threatened, the range of options open to a reasonable decision maker would be curtailed and the court would anxiously scrutinise the strength of the countervailing circumstances and the degree of interference with the human right involved: the more substantial the interference, the more the court would require by the way of justification before it was satisfied that the decision was reasonable. Applying that formulation to the present facts, the Court of Appeal held that the tribunal had failed to attach sufficient significance to the risk posed to the safety of the soldiers and their families and also might not have attached sufficient weight to the assurance given by the former tribunal, the significance of which had increased over time. Furthermore, it seemed that the present tribunal was not sufficiently aware that the denial of anonymity would affect the soldiers' perception of the inquiry's fairness. The Court thus concluded that the tribunal had acted irrationally, noting that anonymity would have a limited effect on the openness of the inquiry and that a particular soldier could still be named if there were good reason.

---

[33] *Smith v Chief Constable of Sussex,* discussed in chapter 7 of this text.

[34] [2009] 1 AC 874.

[35] The negligence claim was dismissed on policy grounds, which will be examined in chapter 7 of this text.

[36] Contrast the ruling in *Re McKerr*, considered above, page 189.

[37] *The Times*, 22 June 1999, affirmed in the Court of Appeal [1999] 4 All ER 860.

A similar stance was taken in the post-Human Rights Act and related case of *R (A and Others) v Lord Saville of Newdigate*.[38] Here the applicants had challenged the chairman of the inquiry's refusal of requests from a number of soldiers to give their evidence at a venue other than Londonderry. The tribunal felt that the objective of restoring public confidence would be seriously diminished if a major part of the inquiry were held at a place far from where the incidents took place and concluded that there was no real and immediate risk to the soldiers' lives. Allowing the soldiers' application for judicial review of that decision, the Divisional Court held that in determining whether a decision might contravene fundamental human rights, the decision maker had to consider whether interference with the rights was a serious or real possibility. In this case the tribunal should have asked whether it, as a public authority, would be in breach of its obligation not to make a decision exposing anyone to the real possibility of a risk to life in the future. Applying that test, the Court felt that the tribunal had used public confidence as the determinative factor and that accordingly its decision was erroneous. This decision was upheld by the Court of Appeal,[39] which found that by applying the test of whether there was an unacceptable risk of attack on the soldiers by Republican dissidents, there existed a compelling reason why the soldiers' evidence should be taken in another venue.

The Court of Appeal also clarified the appropriate threshold of risk in such cases and applied the test laid down in *R v Governor of Pentonville Prison, ex parte Fernandez*,[40] to the effect that the potential victims' fears should be objectively justified. Accordingly the tribunal had erred by applying the test laid down in *Osman v United Kingdom*,[41] of whether there was a real and immediate risk to life. Such a test, in the Court of Appeal's view, only applied in assessing whether a state was liable for breach of its positive obligations to intervene so as to protect life, and imposed an inappropriately high threshold in circumstances such as the present.[42] However, in *Re Officer L*[43] the House of Lords held that in deciding to grant anonymity to a witness, a tribunal needed to be satisfied that the risk of injury or death would be *materially increased* if evidence was given without anonymity, and that only if it is satisfied on this point did the question whether that increased risk would amount to a real and immediate risk to life arise.

It is also clear that the right to life is likely to 'trump' other rights, such as freedom of expression, where there is a real risk of the applicant's life being taken. Thus, in *Venables and Thompson v Newsgroup Newspapers*[44] the court placed the right to life above the public's right to know. In this case the claimants, the young boys found guilty of the murder of a two-year-old, sought indefinite orders to restrain publicity of their identities, fearing that such disclosure would interfere with their right to life and private life. In granting the requested orders the High Court held that in the instant case it was necessary to grant indefinite injunctions restraining the media from disclosing information about the identity, appearance or

---

[38] *The Times*, 21 November 2001.

[39] [2002] 1 WLR 1249.

[40] [1971] 1 WLR 987.

[41] (2000) 29 EHRR 245.

[42] In *R (A) v HM Coroner for Inner South London*, *The Times*, 11 November 2004, the Court of Appeal held that there had to be reasonable grounds of fear of the witness's safety before an order of anonymity could be granted. The Court of Appeal upheld the High Court's decision to quash the refusal by a Coroner's Court to grant anonymity to two police officers in respect of an investigation into an unlawful death where the court found that the officers faced a real risk to their lives if anonymity was lifted. See now *Re L Officer*, below.

[43] [2007] 1 WLR 2135.

[44] [2001] 1 All ER 908.

addresses of the claimants and when they were released from detention. The claimants were uniquely notorious and were at serious risk of attacks from members of the public as well as friends and relatives of the murdered child. In such circumstances the court had to have particular regard to Article 2 of the Convention. Similarly, in *Carr* v *News Group Newspapers*[45] an injunction was granted protecting the identity of Maxine Carr, who had been the co-defendant in a high-profile murder trial. In the court's view the injunction was an effective and proportionate way of reducing the risk of physical and psychological harm towards the claimant and aiding her rehabilitation: without the injunction the task of the police and probation authorities would have been more difficult, if not impossible.

Notwithstanding the importance attached to the right to life the court must still be satisfied that there is a sufficient risk to the applicant's life and in this respect may be prepared to offer the authorities some area or margin of discretion. For example, in *R (Bloggs)* v *Secretary of State for the Home Department*[46] the Court of Appeal held that the decision of the Prison Service to remove the prisoner from a protected witness unit in prison and return him to the mainstream prison system was not in violation of his right to respect for life under Article 2. In the Court's view there had been a substantial reduction of risk to the prisoner's life once the authorities had decided not to prosecute the person who posed the threat to the prisoner. The authorities are also allowed to consider financial matters when making decisions which might affect the individual's right to life, provided that assessment is within their margin of discretion. Thus, in *Watts* v *United Kingdom*,[47] in declaring an application inadmissible, the European Court held that there had been no breach of Article 2 when a very elderly person was moved from her care home after the council had decided to close the home and relocate her. Although such moves could reduce the life expectancy of such individuals, the move had been carefully planned to minimise any risk to her life and the council were entitled to consider the alternative of retaining the home as financially unviable.

The domestic courts have also considered the *Osman* principle with respect to the authorities' liability for suicides of mental health patients. In *Savage* v *South Essex Partnership NHS Trust*[48] the House of Lords gave a preliminary ruling and held that the test in *Osman* under Article 2 applied to a health authority's obligation to prevent suicides of mental health patients, and that such an obligation involved employing competent staff and adopting a system of work which would protect patients' lives. Their Lordships also held that Article 2 imposed an 'operational' obligation on health authorities to do all that could reasonably be expected to prevent a risk patient from committing suicide. This obligation only arose if the authorities knew or ought to have known that the patient was a real and immediate suicide risk and in such circumstances Article 2 required them to do all that could reasonably be expected to prevent the patient from committing suicide, and that priority is given to saving the patient's life. It was also stressed that the *Osman* test was different from and more difficult to prove than the test in negligence and that resources could be taken into account in determining liability on the facts.

---

[45] [2005] EWHC 971. Contrast the decision of the Chancery Division in *Mills* v *Newsgroup Newspapers* [2001] EMLR 41, where although it was claimed that the claimant (Heather Mills-McCartney) was in fear of her life and security, an injunction prohibiting the *Sun* newspaper from disclosing her new address in Hove was refused because it was already well known that she was a resident in that area.

[46] [2003] 1 WLR 2724.

[47] Application No 53586/09, 4 May 2010.

[48] [2009] 1 AC 681.

In the subsequent proceedings,[49] the High Court held that the Foundation Trust had breached its positive obligations under Article 2 when the claimant's mother, who had a long history of mental illness and had absconded on previous occasions, had absconded from the hospital and committed suicide. The court noted that despite the fact that she had been previously assessed as a suicide risk and had made a significant attempt to kill herself, only one nurse was aware of her history. In addition there had been no proper risk assessment or consideration of her level of observation and her previous absconding from hospital had been dismissed as insignificant. Although there was little risk of her committing suicide within the hospital, there was a real and immediate risk of her absconding and committing harm outside. With respect to whether the authorities had done all that was reasonably expected of them, that had to be decided in the light of all the circumstances and the claimant in this case need only show that her mother had lost a substantial chance of survival as a result of the Trust's actions. In this case increased observation would have enhanced the chances of survival.[50]

The right to die?

Article 2 protects the right to life, and specifically imposes an obligation on the state to protect a person's right to life – 'everyone's right to life shall be protected by law'. As we have seen this imposes an obligation on the state not to take life unnecessarily, and also imposes a positive obligation to safeguard the individual from threats to their life.

Further, it could be argued that the right to life under Article 2 also includes the right of an individual to choose whether to live or die: in other words the individual has the right to die, and the state has an obligation to respect, that desire. This claim could be justified on the basis that Convention rights are based on liberty and individual choice and autonomy and that accordingly Article 2 respects the general right of self-determination. This was the basis of the claim in the case study, below.

CASE STUDY

Pretty v *United Kingdom* (2002) 35 EHRR 1

This case was heard by the European Court of Human Rights in April 2002 and involved consideration of a number of 'absolute' and 'conditional' Convention rights. The case raised a variety of issues regarding the interpretation of certain Convention rights and also involved the Court in determining whether any *prima facie* violation of the Convention was justified by competing public interests. The fact that the case concerned a statutory provision passed by a democratically elected legislature, and that the case had already been heard in the domestic courts and been subject to a decision of the House of Lords, also raised the issue of the European Court's ability, and willingness, to interfere with the legislative and judicial decisions of the domestic authorities.

---

[49] *Savage* v *South Essex Partnership NHS Foundation Trust* [2010] HRLR 24.

[50] Contrast *Rabone* v *Pennine Care NHS Trust* [2009] EWHC 2024 (QB), where it was held that the Trust had no obligation under Article 2 with respect to the suicide of a voluntary mental patient who had capacity to become and remain an informal patient and who committed suicide after being allowed to leave the hospital.

Dianne Pretty suffered from motor neurone disease and faced the prospect of imminent death. She was still mentally alert and wished to control the timing and manner of her dying so as to avoid the resultant suffering and indignity of her protracted death. As she was physically unable to terminate her own life, and her husband was willing to assist her, she made an application to the Director of Public Prosecutions for an undertaking that her husband would not be prosecuted under the Suicide Act 1961 for aiding and abetting her suicide. The Divisional Court rejected her claim on the basis that the DPP had no power to give such an undertaking and that in any case the court could not review his decision. On appeal to the House of Lords the decision of the Divisional Court was confirmed and their Lordships also held that there had been no violation of the applicant's Convention rights and that the Suicide Act 1961 was not incompatible with Articles 2, 3, 8, 9 or 14 of the European Convention (*R (Pretty)* v *Director of Public Prosecutions* [2002] 1 All ER 1). Dianne Pretty then lodged an application under the European Convention on Human Rights, claiming a violation of Articles 2, 3, 8, 9 and 14 of the Convention. The European Court declared the case admissible, considering that the claim raised questions of law that were sufficiently serious to be considered on their merits.

With respect to her claim under Article 2 of the Convention, the European Court noted that Article 2 enjoins the state not only to refrain from the intentional and unlawful taking of life, but also to take appropriate steps to safeguard the lives of those within its jurisdiction. Such an obligation extended to putting in place effective criminal law provisions to deter the commission of offences against the person, including, in well-defined circumstances, a positive obligation to take preventive operational measures to protect an individual whose life is at risk from the criminal acts of another individual (*Osman* v *United Kingdom* (2000) 29 EHRR 245). The Court then found that the consistent emphasis in the case law under this article had been the obligation of the state to protect life. Thus, it was not persuaded that Article 2, unlike other articles, such as Article 11, which had been interpreted to include a negative right not to join a trade union, could be interpreted as involving a negative right. Article 2 was phrased in different terms to Article 11 and was unconcerned with issues to do with the quality of living or what a person chooses to do with his or her life. Although those aspects may be reflected in other Articles of the Convention, Article 2 cannot, without a distortion of language, be interpreted as conferring the diametrically opposite right, namely a right to die; nor can it create a right to self-determination in the sense of conferring on an individual the entitlement to choose death rather than life. Accordingly, the Court found that no right to die, whether at the hands of a third person or with the assistance of a public authority, can be derived from Article 2.

In particular, the Court took into account Recommendation 1418 (1999) of the Parliamentary Assembly of the Council of Europe, which recognised, *inter alia*, that a dying person's wish to die never constitutes any legal claim to die at the hand of another person. The applicant had argued that failure to recognise a right to die under the Convention would place those countries that do permit attempted suicide in breach of the Convention. In response, it held that it was not for the Court to assess whether or not the state of law in any other country fails to protect the right to life; in any case the right to life may have to be balanced against other provisions, such as Articles 5 and 8, and such cases would need to be determined on their particular facts. In any case, even if the circumstances prevailing in another country were not found to be in violation of Article 2, that would not assist the applicant in this case in her fundamentally different claim that the United Kingdom would be in breach of its obligations under Article 2 if it did not allow assisted suicide.

Turning to her claim under Article 3 of the Convention, the Court noted that it had previously held that where treatment humiliates or debases an individual showing a lack of respect for, or diminishing, his or her human dignity, it may be characterised as degrading and thus fall within the prohibition of Article 3 (*Price v United Kingdom* (2002) 34 EHRR 53). In addition, the Court noted that suffering that flows from naturally occurring illness, physical or mental, might be covered by Article 3 where it is, or risks being, exacerbated by treatment, whether flowing from conditions of detention, expulsion or other measures, for which the authorities can be held responsible (*Keenan v United Kingdom* (2001) 33 EHRR 38 and *D v United Kingdom* (1997) 27 EHRR 423).

In the present case, it was beyond doubt that the government had not, itself, inflicted any ill-treatment on the applicant. Nor was there any complaint that the applicant was not receiving adequate care from the state medical authorities. Unlike the case of *D v United Kingdom*, where the act of deportation would have subjected the applicant to intolerable medical conditions, in the present case there was no comparable act or treatment on the part of the government. Rather the applicant claims that the refusal of the DPP to give an undertaking and the criminal law prohibition on assisted suicide shows that the state is failing to protect her from the suffering that awaits her as the illness reaches its ultimate stages. Such a claim, in the Court's view, places a new and extended construction on the concept of treatment, which, as the House of Lords found, goes beyond the ordinary meaning of the word. While the Court must take a dynamic and flexible approach to the interpretation of the Convention, Article 3 must be construed in harmony with Article 2, which is first and foremost a prohibition on the use of lethal force or other conduct which might lead to the death of a human being and which does not require a state to permit or facilitate his or her death. Although sympathetic to the applicant's claim that she faces the prospect of a distressing death, the Court held that the positive obligation claimed in this case would require that the state sanction actions intended to terminate life, an obligation that cannot be derived from Article 3. Thus, there was no positive obligation to require the government either to give an undertaking not to prosecute the applicant's husband or to provide a lawful opportunity for any other form of assisted suicide.

The applicant also argued that there had been a violation of her right to respect for private and family life, as guaranteed under Article 8 of the Convention. The Court held that although no previous case had established any right to self-determination as such within Article 8, it considered that the notion of personal autonomy was an important principle underlying the interpretation of Articles 8's guarantees. The Court noted that the ability to conduct one's life in a manner of one's choosing might also include the opportunity to pursue activities perceived to be of a physically or morally harmful or dangerous nature for the individual concerned. Thus, even where the conduct poses a danger to health, or arguably, where it is of a life-threatening nature, the case law has regarded the state's imposition of compulsory or criminal measures as impinging on the private life of the applicant within Article 8 and requiring justification in terms of

Article 8(2) (*Laskey, Jaggard and Brown* v *United Kingdom* (1997) 27 EHRR 39). The fact that death was not the intended consequence in those cases was not decisive; the refusal to accept a medical treatment might, inevitably, lead to a fatal outcome, yet the imposition of medical treatment without the consent of the patient would interfere with a person's physical integrity so as to engage the rights protected under Article 8. Noting that the very essence of the Convention is respect for human dignity and human freedom, and without negating the principle of sanctity of life protected under the Convention, the Court considered that it was under Article 8 that notions of the quality of life took on significance. Taking into account the decision of the Supreme Court of Canada in *Rodriguez* v *The Attorney-General of Canada* ([1994] 2 LRC 136), that the prohibition of a person receiving assistance in suicide deprived her of autonomy and required justification under principles of fundamental justice, the Court held that it was not prepared to exclude that the prevention of the applicant from exercising her choice to avoid what she considers will be an undignified and distressing end to her life constituted an interference with her right to respect for private life under Article 8.

The Court then considered whether that interference was necessary in a democratic society for the purpose of safeguarding life and thereby protecting the rights of others within Article 8(2). The Court recalled that the margin of appreciation was narrow as regards interferences in the intimate area of an individual's sexual life (*Dudgeon* v *United Kingdom* (1981) 4 EHRR 149), although it noted that the matter under consideration in the present case could not be regarded as of the same nature, nor did it attract the same reasoning. Although the Court did not accept that the applicant was particularly vulnerable, it found itself in agreement with both the decision of the House of Lords and the decision of the Supreme Court of Canada in *Rodriguez*, above, that states were entitled to regulate activities that are detrimental to the life and safety of other individuals. In such cases, it is primarily for the states to assess the risks to the weak and vulnerable as well as the likely incidence of abuse if the general prohibition on assisted suicides were relaxed or exceptions made.

Although the Court conceded that it was not its role to look at the law in abstract, it noted that its judgment in this case could not be framed in such a way as to prevent applications in later cases. Accordingly, it did not consider that the blanket nature of the ban on assisted suicide was disproportionate: flexibility was provided by the need of the DPP to grant permission to prosecute in each case, and evidence indicated that convictions for murder in such cases were rare. Thus, it did not appear arbitrary to the Court for the law to reflect the importance of the right to life by prohibiting assisted suicide while providing for a system of enforcement that gave due regard in each particular case to the public interest in bringing a prosecution, as well as to the fair and proper requirements of retribution and deterrence, nor, in the Court's view, was there anything disproportionate in the refusal of the DPP to give the advanced undertaking. The Court felt that strong arguments based on the rule of law could be raised against any claim by the executive to exempt individuals or classes of individuals from operation of the law, and in any event the seriousness of the act for which immunity was claimed was such that the decision could not be said to be arbitrary or unreasonable.

With respect to the applicant's argument that the law and the DPP's refusal constituted an unjustified interference with her freedom of thought and conscience under

Article 9, the Court held that although it did not question the firmness of the applicant's views concerning assisted suicide, it did not consider that all opinions or convictions constitute beliefs as protected by Article 9(1) of the Convention. The applicant's claims do not involve a form or manifestation of a religion or a belief, through worship, teaching, practice or observance within Article 9. In addition, the Court noted that it had been held previously that the term 'practice' as employed in Article 9 does not cover each act which is motivated or influenced by a religion or belief (*Arrowsmith v United Kingdom* (1978) 3 EHRR 218). Although the applicant's claim did touch upon the principle of personal autonomy, such a claim was merely a restatement of the complaint raised under Article 8. Accordingly the Court found that there had been no violation under Article 9.

Finally, the Court considered whether the applicant's treatment was in violation of Article 14 of the Convention in that she had suffered discrimination because she had been treated in the same manner as others whose situations were fundamentally different; accordingly she was prevented, because of her disability, from exercising the right enjoyed by others to end their lives without assistance. The Court accepted that discrimination under Article 14 might occur where states, without an objective and reasonable justification, fail to treat differently persons whose situations are significantly different (*Thlimmenos v Greece* (2001) 31 EHRR 15). However, the Court held that even if that principle could be applied to the present case, there was, in the Court's view, objective and reasonable justification for not distinguishing in law between those who are and those who are not physically capable of committing suicide. When considering the applicant's claims under Article 8 the Court had already found that there were sound reasons for not introducing into the law exceptions to cater for those who are deemed not to be vulnerable, and similar cogent reasons existed under Article 14 for not seeking to distinguish between those persons. The Court noted that the borderline between the two categories will often be a fine one and that the building into the law of an exemption for those judged incapable of committing suicide would seriously undermine the protection of life which the 1961 Act was intended to safeguard.

Dianne Pretty later died of her disease.

Subsequently, in *R (Purdy) v DPP* [2009] UKHL 45, the House of Lords held that such a claim did engage Article 8 rights (following the decision of the European Court in *Pretty*) and that the failure of the DPP to promulgate clear guidelines on prosecution policies was in breach of her right to private and family life. The lack of such guidelines offended the principles of foreseeability and accessibility inherent in Article 8. Since the decision in *Purdy* the DPP has issued such guidelines, indicating in what circumstances a person might be prosecuted under the Act. Further, s.59 of the Coroners and Justice Act 2009 has replaced s.2 of the Suicide Act 1961 and creates an offence of encouraging and assisting suicide, providing guidance as to the specific components of the offence.

Questions

1 Do you feel that the Court's interpretation of Article 2 as involving a positive right to life is a correct one, or one that was driven by policy, in particular the desire to avoid the issues of euthanasia?

2 With regard to its interpretation of Article 3, do you feel that the Court is correct in considering that its decision under Article 2 determines the applicant's claim under this article? Is it not possible to imply a right to die with dignity into Article 3?

3 In respect of its decision under Article 8, why did the European Court find a violation of that article and not of the other articles? Is that decision defendable?

4 Do you agree with the Court's view that a person's views on assisted suicide are not a conviction or belief under Article 9 of the Convention?

5 Why did the applicant's claim fail under Article 14? Should the article have offered the applicant a remedy irrespective of the decision on other articles of the Convention, and would the claim have succeeded under a general equality protection clause such as that contained in Protocol No 12?

6 In what respects do you feel that the decision highlights the deficiencies of the rights contained in the European Convention on Human Rights?

7 To what extent would it have been appropriate for the European Court to develop the ambit of the relevant Convention rights and to declare a general right of self-determination?

8 What does the decision tell us about the role of the European Court of Human Rights, and in particular its relationship with domestic lawmakers and judges?

9 What is the position of euthanasia *vis-à-vis* Article 2 of the Convention?

10 To what extent does the decision in *Purdy* and subsequent legislation and guidelines resolve the above issues? (Read chapter 11 of the text for details of the new legislation and sentencing guidelines.)

A duty to preserve life?

In *Pretty* (above) the European Court of Human Rights stressed that the main thrust of Article 2 was the protection and *preservation* of the individual's right to life. Thus, it was not possible to read into Article 2 a right to die, or at least an *obligation* on the state to assist an individual in the termination their life. It is clear that the individual possesses some right to self-determination, albeit under Article 8 of the Convention rather than Article 2. However, that then begs the question of whether the state has a positive duty to preserve life, and the extent of that obligation. In *Pretty* the European Court refused to rule on the legality of any euthanasia laws, but appeared to accept that such laws were not necessarily in violation of Article 2. Any such laws would need to respect the state's obligation under Article 2 to preserve life and would need to contain sufficient safeguards against any abuse, ensuring that the right to self-determination was properly respected and that any deaths were subject to appropriate control.[51]

Certainly the state owes an obligation to provide adequate and appropriate medical care so as to comply with its obligations under Articles 2 and 3 of the Convention. This obligation will not be absolute and the courts will be cautious in imposing too strict a duty or of interfering with decisions on the allocation of scarce resources. For example, in *R (Rogers) v Swindon NHS Primary Care Trust*[52] it was held that Article 2 of the Convention would only be engaged with respect to the non-provision of medical treatment which put a person's life at risk where the state had promised treatment to the general public.[53] In this case the authority had

---

[51] At the time of writing there is no plan to legislate on this matter. The Assisted Dying for the Terminally Ill Bill was considered in the 2005–2006 parliamentary session but subsequently lost.

[52] [2006] EWHC 171 (QB).

[53] Applying *Nitecki v Poland*, decision of the European Court, 21 March 2002; neither had Article 3 been violated, as the threshold of Article 3 in cases of failure to provide treatment was particularly high and in this case the threat to the applicant's health was not immediate.

refused to provide the applicant, who was suffering from breast cancer, with such treatment, on the basis that her case did not show exceptional circumstances. On appeal it was held that such a policy was irrational as it did not relate to matters of resources and thus there was no reason to distinguish between patients. However, the Court of Appeal did not consider Article 2 and thus the dicta of the High Court in that respect still stands.

The specific issue of whether, and to what extent, the state must provide adequate abortion facilities was raised by the Grand Chamber of the European Court, which considered a number of issues relating to the availability of abortion facilities in *A, B and C v Ireland*.[54] In this case the applicants, who all had to travel to the United Kingdom to get abortions, alleged that the restriction on abortion under Irish law, and the lack of clear legal guidelines regarding the circumstances in which a woman may have an abortion to save her life, violated Article 2.[55] The outcome of the case is important in the developing jurisprudence of the Court with respect to the state's positive obligations to preserve life, and is referred to in the preface to the book.

The corresponding duties to protect life and to respect individual autonomy and the right to self-determination were at issue in the case of *A Local Authority v Z and Another*.[56] In that case a local authority sought an injunction to prevent a husband taking his wife to Switzerland for an assisted suicide. Refusing that injunction, it was held that although a local authority had a duty to investigate the position of a disabled person who wished to arrange travel abroad for her to arrange assisted suicide, in this case the person was legally competent and the authority had no duty to seek an injunction to stop her from leaving the country. Although Article 2 of the Convention was engaged, in the present case that issue was overridden by principles of self-determination. Although the police could, in appropriate cases, avail themselves of the criminal law if they felt that her husband was committing an offence under s.2 of the Suicide Act 1961, the injunction sought by the authority in this case was not necessary.

A different issue arises when the individual concerned wishes to live and claims that the state authorities are not taking adequate steps to abide by that wish, for example, by failing to provide life-preserving treatment, or an assurance that such treatment will be made available. In *R (Burke) v GMC*[57] it was accepted that if a patient was competent, or was incompetent but had made an advance directive which was valid and relevant to the treatment in question, that person's decision to require the provision of artificial nutrition and hydration in their dying days was determinative of the issue. Once a patient was admitted into an NHS hospital, a duty of care arose to provide and continue to provide treatment that was in the best interests of the patient. The doctor and the hospital were under a continuing obligation that could not lawfully be discontinued unless arrangements were made for the responsibility to be taken over by someone else and medical opinion could never be determinative of what was in a patient's best interests. If the patient was incompetent and had left no binding and effective advance directive, then in the final analysis it was for the court to decide what was in his best interests. On the facts, however, the Court of Appeal held that there was nothing unlawful about the General Medical Council's guidance on this issue, and accordingly the

---

[54] Application No 25579/05.

[55] Further, it was argued that the restriction on abortion stigmatised and humiliated them and risked damaging their health in breach of Article 3, and that the criminal law on abortion was insufficiently clear and précis and thus in breach of Article 8.

[56] [2005] 1 WLR 959.

[57] [2005] 3 WLR 1132.

claimant's request for declarations to that effect should fail. A subsequent application to the European Court was unsuccessful.[58]

Intentional deprivation of life

Cases such as *Burke* raise the question of whether it is lawful for medical staff to deliberately terminate life in any circumstances and whether such a decision could ever be compatible with the state's obligations under Article 2 of the European Convention. The moral and legal dilemma facing hospital staff in such cases may be avoided by arguing either that the death was not intentional within Article 2, because the intention was to end pain or distress rather than to kill (or that it constituted an omission rather than an act), or that Article 2 contains an implied exception when death is in the best interests of the patient.[59]

Where the patient has a capacity to refuse or accept treatment then, as discussed above, the wishes of the patient must be abided by.[60] However, with respect to patients in a permanent vegetative state who are incapable of consent, the domestic courts have held that such lives may be terminated if that is in the best interests of the patient.[61] Consequently, if the preservation of life is, in the court's view, in the patient's best interests, any termination of life would be in breach of the authority's obligations under Article 2. This inevitably involves the domestic courts judging the quality of the patient's life, something that they may be reluctant to do. Nevertheless the courts have allowed the withdrawal of life-preserving treatment where it has been necessary to allow the patient to die with dignity and humanity.[62] In contrast, in *An NHS Trust* v *MB*,[63] the High Court ruled that an 18-month old baby boy who was critically ill should not be allowed to die. The Trust had argued that to keep him alive would be intolerable and cruel, but HOLMAN J ruled that withdrawing ventilation would not be in the interests of the child. His Lordship stated that when the child begins to suffer pain it may be in his best interests to withdraw that facility.

The dilemma was particularly acute in the case of *Re A*,[64] the case involving conjoined twins – Jodie and Mary. In this case the parents of two conjoined girls sought a declaration that their surgical separation would be unlawful as it would involve, inevitably, the death of one of the children. The court at first instance had held that the operation was necessary and in the best interests of the children as one child (Mary) had severe brain abnormalities and was drawing on her sister's blood supply, thus jeopardising the latter's life. The Court of Appeal held that the welfare of the children was paramount over the wishes of the parents and ruled that the operation was clearly in the best interests of Jodie as it would offer her the prospect of an independent existence as opposed to certain death if the operation was not carried out. Although the judge had erred in stating that Mary's life was of no value to her – the operation would terminate a valuable life and could thus not be beneficial – the court had to conduct a balancing exercise and consider what would be the least detrimental course

---

[58] In *Burke v United Kingdom*, 11 July 2006, the European Court dismissed the applicant's claims under Articles 2, 3, 8 and 14 of the Convention as inadmissible. In the Court's view the domestic law and its operation did not pose a significant risk that his Convention rights would be jeopardised.

[59] For an analysis of the relevant domestic case law, see Amos, *Human Rights Law* (Hart 2006), pages 178–82.

[60] See *Burke*, n 57.

[61] See *Airedale NHS Trust v Bland* [1993] AC 789; *NHS Trust v A: Mrs M* [2001] 2 WLR 942.

[62] *NHS Trust v A*, n 61 and *A NHS Trust v D* [2002] FLR 677.

[63] [2006] FLR 319.

[64] *Re A (Children) (Conjoined Twins: Surgical Separation)* [2001] 2 WLR 480.

of action. In this case the balance fell decisively in Jodie's favour and thus the operation should be carried out.[65]

Dealing with the issues under Article 2, the Court of Appeal concluded that the operation would not constitute murder as, on the facts, the doctrine of necessity would apply: the act was necessary to avoid inevitable and irreparable evil; it involved no more than was reasonably necessary for that purpose to be achieved; and there was a proportionality between the evil to be inflicted and the evil to be avoided.

The right to life and the unborn child

One issue for the European Court to determine is at what point life begins; specifically who is a 'person' for the purpose of Article 2 and its protection? This issue raises the question of whether Article 2 protects the right of the unborn child, and whether any intentional killing of the foetus would be in violation of Article 2. If the unborn child is within the scope of the article, then the Convention machinery, and the individual member states, will need to balance the rights of such a child with the family and private rights of the mother. Abortions involve the claim of the mother to self-determination and physical autonomy, respected under Article 8 of the Convention, and in some cases will engage the mother's right to life and freedom from inhuman or degrading treatment.[66] Indeed the European Court has appeared to recognise the mother's right to an abortion and the right to have access to the necessary resources and information to undergo a termination.[67]

Although this conflict could be resolved by applying principles of proportionality, the wording of Article 2 appears to preclude such a balancing exercise, because the circumstances in which life can be taken intentionally are specifically prescribed by the article and do not appear to include a termination, albeit one conducted for the benefit of another.

The European Court and Commission of Human Rights have not finally resolved this issue, but the current position is that the European Court is not prepared to rule that the unborn child is within the scope and protection of Article 2. In *Paton v United Kingdom*,[68] the European Commission considered a claim by the father of an aborted child that the operation was in breach of Article 2. Although the Commission accepted that he was a victim for the purpose of Article 2, it ruled that the term 'everyone' employed in Article 2 did not include the unborn child. The Commission did not rule definitively on whether the term 'life' covered the foetus, but did rule out the interpretation that such a life could be enjoyed absolutely: such an interpretation being inconsistent with the conflicting family and private rights of the mother.

This area has now been informed by two decisions of the Grand Chamber of the European Court. First, in *Vo v France*[69] the applicant had complained that the domestic law's refusal to classify the intentional killing of her unborn baby as homicide contravened the duty to protect life under Article 2 of the Convention. A hospital had performed an abortion on the applicant after an administrative error confused the applicant with another patient. A criminal

---

[65] The Court of Appeal did not apply the test in *Bland*, above, as the operation in this case was a deliberate act as opposed to a refusal to give treatment.

[66] See Plomer (2005) HRLR 311.

[67] *Open Door Counselling and Dublin Well Woman v Ireland* (1993) 15 EHRR 244.

[68] (1980) 3 EHRR 408.

[69] (2005) 40 EHRR 259.

prosecution for unintentional homicide of the child failed because the French courts did not regard the child as a person. The Grand Chamber considered whether an unborn child was a person under Article 2 and decided that on the proper interpretation of Article 2 an unborn child was not such a person. In the majority's view, there was no consensus at the European level on the nature and status of the embryo/foetus, and accordingly it was neither desirable nor possible to answer in the abstract the question whether the unborn child was a person for the purposes of Article 2.

Further, the Grand Chamber held that even if the unborn child was a person under Article 2, in the present case the state had fulfilled its positive obligation to protect life, as the child was not deprived of all protection under French law. That was because the child would be indirectly protected by both the mother's right to bring a civil action in damages and by the existence of the offence of intentionally causing injury to the mother. That protection, in the court's view did not require the provision of a specific criminal law offence or remedy. Three judges gave dissenting opinions, arguing that the mother and child had separate existences and that the Convention should now be interpreted in a way which confronted modern dangers to human life posed by practices of scientific research and genetic manipulation.

In the second case, in *Evans v United Kingdom*,[70] the Grand Chamber of the European Court of Human Rights held that embryos created by the applicant and her partner did not enjoy the right to life under Article 2. The Grand Chamber's approach had been adopted in domestic law: in *Evans v Amicus Healthcare Ltd*[71] the Court of Appeal held that prior to the moment of birth, the foetus did not have independent rights or interests.[72] At present, therefore, the parents will need to seek protection of their other Convention rights, and the European Court will offer each state a margin of appreciation as to the existence and content of its abortion laws.

In addition, in *A, B and C v Ireland*,[73] the Grand Chamber of the European Court have considered Article 2 (and 3) with respect to the availability of abortion facilities to women. The case did not deal with the rights of the unborn child, and thus will be discussed elsewhere in this chapter, and is referred to in the preface to the book.

Questions

What substantive duties does Article 2 impose on member states with respect to protecting the right to life?

Why doesn't the right to life include the right to die and the right to life of the unborn child?

The right to life and those in detention

Because of the status and vulnerability of prisoners, the state will owe a more specific positive duty to safeguard the lives of those in detention. Thus, liability can be engaged with respect not only to the unlawful or excessive acts of state officials, but also to the actions of fellow inmates and from acts of self-harm.[74] The state will also owe a duty of care to ensure that

---

[70] (2008) 46 EHRR 34.

[71] [2004] 3 WLR 681.

[72] Following the pre-Human Rights Act case of *Rance v Mid-Downs Health Authority* [1991] 1 QB 587.

[73] Application No 25579/05.

[74] See Foster, The Negligence of Prison Authorities and Prisoners' Rights (2005) Liverpool LR 75.

prison conditions and practices do not threaten the lives of those in custody, although in all these cases the duty will be circumscribed by issues of security and the extent of any duty of care.

Article 2 of the European Convention guarantees the right to life, and prison authorities are responsible for protecting the prisoner from threats to his life, not only from the actions of the authorities themselves, but from the actions of others, such as fellow prisoners.[75] In addition, the common law imposes a duty on prison and police authorities to safeguard a prisoner's life: a duty which is now buttressed by the duty of all public authorities to safeguard the prisoner's right to life under Article 2 of the European Convention.[76] Thus, both the common law and Article 2 of the European Convention are capable of imposing liability on public authorities when a detainee takes his life. For example, in *Kirkham v Chief Constable of Greater Manchester Police*[77] it was held that the police authorities were liable for the suicide of a prisoner when they had negligently failed to pass on information relating to the prisoner and his suicidal tendencies to the prison authorities. As with claims arising from assaults by fellow prisoners, above, the courts are more likely to find negligence where there has been a departure from the authority's own procedures, and where the prisoner is vulnerable because of his or her mental state. However, in *Reeves v Commissioner for the Police of the Metropolis*[78] it was held that such liability might arise even in the case of a person of sound mind. In *Reeves*, a person who was a known suicide risk committed suicide while in police detention. The police authorities had been negligent in leaving the flap of the detainee's cell open and as a consequence he was able to hang himself. At first instance the judge held that although the authorities owed the prisoner a duty of care, they could rely on the defences of *volenti non fit injuria* and *novus actus interveniens*. However, the Court of Appeal and the House of Lords held that the defences of consent and *novus actus* were inappropriate, although the House of Lords held that the principles of contributory negligence could apply and that it was appropriate to reduce the compensation granted to the prisoner's relatives.[79]

The authority's duty to safeguard the prisoner's life from the dangers of custody under Article 2 was clearly illustrated in *Edwards v United Kingdom*.[80] In this case it was held that there had been a clear violation of Article 2 when the applicants' son had been beaten to death by his cellmate. Given the cellmate's psychiatric history and the failure of the prison authorities to screen and deal with his dangerousness, he should not have been placed in the same cell with the applicants' son. Article 2 of the Convention can thus be used to protect an inmate's right to life not only from the acts of public officials, but also the actions of fellow inmates.

Thus, prison authorities owe a positive duty under Article 2 to ensure that they take reasonable measures to safeguard every inmate's right to life.[81] This duty was recognised in the case of *R v A Hospital Authority, ex parte RH*,[82] where it was accepted that Article 2 could apply to

---

[75] See *X v FRG* (1985) 7 EHRR 152; *Rebai v France* 88-B DR 72.

[76] In *Morgan v Ministry of Justice and the Crown* [2010] EWHC 2248 (QB), it was held that an action with respect to the alleged negligence of the local NHS primary trust, which it was alleged had led to the suicide of the claimants' fiancée, could not be taken against the Crown as the trust were not a body of the Crown.

[77] [1990] 2 QB 283.

[78] [2000] AC 283.

[79] That part of the judgment may conflict with Article 13 of the Convention, which imposes an obligation to provide an effective remedy to victims of violations of Convention rights.

[80] (2002) 35 EHRR 19.

[81] See the principles established in *Osman v United Kingdom* (1998) 29 EHRR 245.

[82] Decision of the Administrative Court, 30 October 2001.

a claim by an inmate that the prison authorities owed a duty to protect other inmates from his actions. In this case the applicant, a detainee with hepatitis C, had claimed that the failure to provide him with condoms was unlawful on the ground, *inter alia*, that it breached the authority's duty to protect the right to life of other inmates. Although the application was dismissed on the merits, the court accepted that in this case the hospital owed a *prima facie* duty under Article 2.

However, any such duty will be limited to taking reasonable steps to combat the extent of any risk. For example, in *R (Bloggs) v Secretary of State for the Home Department*[83] it was held that the decision to remove a prisoner from a protected witness unit in prison and return him to the mainstream prison system was not in violation of the prisoner's right to respect for life under Article 2 because there had been a substantial reduction of risk to the prisoner's life once the authorities had decided not to prosecute the person who posed the threat to the prisoner. Similarly, in *R (Shelley) v Home Secretary*,[84] the Court of Appeal refused prisoners permission to apply for review of the prison service's policy to provide disinfectant tablets to clean needles used by prisoners, instead of allowing a needle exchange system. The Court held that it was permissible for the service to be led by considerations of security in considering whether to provide such a service and that the policy was not unlawful simply because other agencies offered such a service.[85] Subsequently, in *Shelley v United Kingdom*[85a] the European Court of Human Rights held that the prisoner's Article 2 (and 3) rights were not engaged as he was not a drug user and was thus in no danger. It also found that, although his right to physical health and safety engaged Article 8, there was no obligation to pursue particular policies in that respect and there was no evidence that the prisoner was in any particular danger, given that they had an alternative preventive policy.

In addition, liability can be engaged under Article 2 where the prisoner takes his own life.[86] In such a case, however, the European Court has made it clear that it will need to be satisfied that the authorities have clearly broken their duty under Article 2. Thus, in *Keenan v United Kingdom*[87] it was held that there had been no violation of Article 2 when a mentally ill prisoner had committed suicide. The prisoner, who had a history of mental illness, had been placed in the prison healthcare centre. When he assaulted two officers he was placed in segregation and received an award of 28 additional days as punishment. The day after the award he was found hanged in his cell. The Court found that although there was clear evidence that the prisoner was mentally ill, he had not been diagnosed as a clear suicide risk. The prison authorities had monitored his behaviour and on the whole had made a reasonable response to his conduct, placing him in hospital care and under watch when he showed suicidal tendencies. He had been subject to daily medical supervision by the prison doctors, who had consulted psychiatrists with knowledge of his case, and had been declared fit for segregation. Accordingly, there had been no breach of Article 2.[88]

---

[83] [2003] 1 WLR 2724.

[84] [2005] EWCA Civ 1810.

[85] See Lines, Injecting Reason: Prison Syringe Exchange and Article 3 of the European Convention on Human Rights [2007] EHRLR 66.

[85a] (2008) 46 EHRR SE16.

[86] The liability for suicides of mental health patients was examined in *Savage v South Essex Partnership NHS Foundation Trust* [2009] 1 AC 681, and is considered above at page 194.

[87] (2001) 33 EHRR 38.

[88] The Court did, however, find that there had been a violation of Article 3 of the Convention, see below.

The European Court has taken a cautious approach when determining whether there had been a violation of Article 2 because of the authorities' actions or omissions,[89] and the decision in *Keenan* displays a similar reluctance. Thus, although the Court found that the lack of medical and psychiatric expertise and supervision available to the prisoner constituted a violation of Article 3 of the Convention, it was still of the opinion that it was not apparent that the authorities had failed to take any step which should reasonably have been taken so as to avoid the prisoner's death. Similarly, in *Orange v Chief Constable of West Yorkshire*[90] the Court of Appeal confirmed that a duty of care to ensure that a prisoner does not commit suicide was owed only when the authorities knew or ought to have known of a suicide risk in an individual prisoner's case.[91] Further, the authorities will be given some discretion with respect to how they treat inmates with mental or other difficulties, even where they have shown suicidal tendencies in the past. Thus, in *Trubnikov v Russia*[92] it was held that there had been no violation of Article 2 when a prisoner with a record of suicide attempts had committed suicide in his cell. The Court held that despite his history, and the fact that the authorities were partly responsible for the fact that he had access to alcohol and should have known that his state posed risks to him while he was serving a disciplinary punishment in segregation, he had not *at the time* posed an immediate risk of suicide so as to engage the liability of the state.[93]

In contrast, in *Renolde v France*[94] the Court found that a violation of Articles 2 and 3 had occurred when a prisoner who had previously self-harmed committed suicide whilst in pre-trial detention. The prisoner had attempted to commit suicide by cutting his arm two months after admission to the prison and was prescribed medication. The medical team was informed of previous psychiatric problems and the next day he was placed in a single cell under special supervision and continued to be given antipsychotic medication which he was required to take. Two days later he assaulted a guard and was ordered to serve 45 days in a punishment cell; despite appearing 'very disturbed'. Ten days later he was found hanged in his cell and it was subsequently discovered that he had not taken his medication for three days.

The Court noted that the authorities had been aware of his condition and mental illness history and that consequently the risk of self-harm was real and thus required careful monitoring. The question, therefore, was whether the authorities had done all that could reasonably be expected of them to avoid that risk. Despite the special supervision he received there was never any question of him being moved to a psychiatric unit, and given that the prisoner was at likely risk of suicide the authorities would be expected to, if not ordering his admission to a psychiatric unit, at the very least ensure that he be provided with medical treatment corresponding to the seriousness of his condition. The facts showed, however, that he was left to take his own medication without supervision, and that the fact that he had not taken the medication was likely to be the cause of his death. In addition, the fact that three days after

---

[89] *Osman v United Kingdom* (2000) 29 EHRR 245.

[90] [2001] 3 WLR 736.

[91] See also *Younger v United Kingdom* (decision of the European Court, 7 January 2003, Application No 57420/00), where the European Court held that although the authorities had departed from safety procedures, the applicant's son was not a suicide risk so as to engage the state's liability under Article 2 of the Convention.

[92] Judgment of the European Court, 6 July 2005. Noted in [2005] EHRLR 676.

[93] The Court did, however, find a violation of the procedural obligation under Article 2 because the state had failed to carry out an effective investigation into that death.

[94] (2009) 48 EHRR 42.

his first suicide attempt he had been given the maximum penalty of 45 days' detention in a punishment cell was likely to aggravate any risk of suicide; placing a prisoner suffering from severe disturbance in solitary confinement for a prolonged period would have an inevitable impact on his mental state, particularly where he had attempted suicide shortly before the final event. The decision in *Renolde* can be distinguished from *Keenan* in the sense that Renolde's mental state was more severe and thus his medical and other needs were greater. Thus, the decision in *Renolde* does not disturb the European Court's cautious stance as evidenced in cases such as *Keenan*. However, it may cast doubts on the decision of the Court in *Trubnikov v Russia*, and it is submitted that *Trubinov* may be difficult to reconcile with the Court's robust statement in *Renolde* on the duties of prison and other authorities in respect of vulnerable detainees.

The Convention also imposes a duty to provide an official investigation into the death of a person in the State's custody,[95] and in *R v Secretary of State for the Home Department, ex parte Wright*,[96] the High Court held that the prison authorities and the domestic courts should be mindful of their duties under Articles 2 and 3 of the European Convention when reviewing investigations into deaths in custody. In this case the court ordered the Secretary of State to conduct an inquiry into the death of a prisoner from an asthma attack. Applying the decision in *Keenan* it held that it was arguable that the prisoner had suffered inhuman and degrading treatment and that the authorities were liable under Articles 2 and 3 of the Convention. That decision reflects the courts' anxiety that unless such procedures are open and full then prison or other authorities may fall short of the standards under the Convention, thus engaging the authorities under the Human Rights Act, and imposing a duty on the courts to avoid such violations.[97] The duty to hold investigations for deaths in custody is considered below as part of the general procedural obligation imposed by Article 2.

Article 2 and procedural obligations

In addition to imposing a *substantive* obligation on the state to protect life and not to arbitrarily deprive individuals of their right to life, Article 2 of the Convention also imposes a *procedural* obligation on the state. This duty will normally exist independently of the issue of substantive liability on the facts and thus it will not generally be necessary to establish an arguable breach of Article 2.[98] Accordingly, Article 2 imposes a duty on every member state to carry out a proper investigation into any deaths that have occurred within its jurisdiction.[99] In *McCann v United Kingdom*[100] the European Court noted that the general prohibition of arbitrary killings by state agents would be ineffective in practice if there existed no procedure for reviewing the lawfulness of the use of lethal force by state authorities. Consequently the Court ruled that Article 2, along with Article 1 of the Convention, requires by implication

---

[95] See, for example, *Edwards v United Kingdom* (2002) 35 EHRR 19. A similar procedural duty exists under Article 3 of the Convention. Thus, in *Indelicato v Italy* (2002) 35 EHRR 40 it was held that a delay into an enquiry into the possible ill-treatment of inmates by state officials constituted a violation of Article 3.

[96] [2002] HRLR 1.

[97] See also *DPP v Manning* [2001] QB 330, where it was held that there had been a breach of the rules of natural justice when reasons were not given for a decision not to conduct an inquiry into a prisoner's death.

[98] *R (Smith) v Oxfordshire Assistant Deputy Coroner* [2008] WLR 1284.

[99] See Mowbray, Duties of Investigation under the European Convention on Human Rights (2002) ICLQ 437.

[100] (1995) 21 EHRR 97.

that there should be some form of effective official investigation when individuals have been killed as a result of the use of force by, *inter alia*, agents of the state.[101] This duty extends to deaths at the hands of private individuals and to acts of suicide,[102] and complements Article 13 of the Convention, which guarantees the right to an effective remedy in domestic law for breach of Convention rights. As a result, it is possible to find a violation of Article 2 with respect to a breach of procedure even where the Court is not satisfied that there has been a substantive breach of that article on the facts.

The requirements of the procedural obligation under Article 2 were articulated in *Jordan and Others* v *United Kingdom*,[103] where the European Court decided that there had been a violation by the failure to conduct a proper investigation into the circumstances of the deaths of persons killed in the fight against terrorism in Northern Ireland. In one of the applications, Hugh Jordan had been shot three times in the back and killed by RUC officers in November 1992. In November 1993 the DPP declared that there was insufficient evidence to prosecute the officers and in January 1995 a coroner's inquest began. The inquest was adjourned in May 1995 to allow an application for judicial review into the coroner's refusal to allow the family access to witness statements, and when the European Court heard the case in May 2001 the inquest proceedings had not been concluded. The family had also instituted civil proceedings in December 1992, alleging death by wrongful act, and those proceedings were still at the discovery stage.

The European Court held that where the events in issue lay within the knowledge of the authorities, the burden of proof would be on the state to provide a satisfactory and convincing explanation. The Court also stated that the obligation under Article 2 required there to be some form of effective official investigation when individuals had been killed as a result of the use of force. Whatever the form of investigation, the state must take the initiative and the investigation had to be carried out by persons who were independent from those implicated in the events. The investigation also had to be effective by being capable of leading to a determination of whether the force used in such circumstances was justified, and to the identification and punishment of those responsible. Specifically, the Court held that the authorities must have taken reasonable steps to secure the evidence concerning the incident, including eyewitness testimony and the necessary forensic evidence. Any deficiency in the investigation's ability to establish the cause of death would risk falling foul of this standard, and it was also an implicit requirement of Article 2 that the inquiry be conducted with promptness and reasonable expedition.[104] Applying those principles to the cases in hand, the European Court held that although it should not specify in any detail which procedures the authorities should have adopted, the available procedures adopted in all four cases had not struck the right balance between providing an effective investigation and protecting matters such as national security. In all cases the Court had identified shortcomings in transparency and effectiveness

---

[101] Ibid., at para 161.

[102] See *Keenan* v *United Kingdom*, n 87; *Edwards* v *United Kingdom* (2002) 35 EHRR 19.

[103] *Jordan and Others* v *United Kingdom*; *McKerr* v *United Kingdom*; *Kelly and Others* v *United Kingdom*; *Shanaghan* v *United Kingdom* (2002) 34 EHRR 20.

[104] In *Demir and Others* v *Turkey*, decision of the European Court of Human Rights, 13 January 2005, it was held that there had been a violation of Article 2 when a prisoner had died from head injuries when being transferred to another prison after a confrontation between prisoners and guards in the prison and it had taken more than five years to instigate criminal proceedings against the guards and those proceedings were still pending.

and in ensuring the accountability of agents of the state so as to maintain public confidence and to meet the legitimate concerns that could arise from the use of lethal force.[105]

The European Court has taken a hands-on approach in this area and has ruled on the effectiveness of domestic investigations on a number of occasions. For example, in *McShane v United Kingdom*,[106] the European Court held that an inquiry into the lawfulness of a civilian's death during a disturbance in Londonderry fell short of an effective investigation as required by Article 2. The Court found that the police officers investigating the incident were not independent of the officers implicated in the incident, the investigation lacked expediency, the inquest proceedings were not started promptly, the soldier directly implicated in the incident could not be required to attend as a witness, and the inquest procedure did not allow any verdict which could have played an effective role in securing a prosecution. Further, in *Finucane v United Kingdom*[107] the Court held that there had been a violation when the authorities had conducted an inadequate investigation into the circumstances of Patrick Finucane, a solicitor living in Northern Ireland who was shot dead by two masked men who broke into his home. In the Court's view there had been a lack of independence in the police inquiry and the inquest had not investigated the possibility of collusion with the police authorities.[108] The first two inquiries lacked publicity and the final one was conducted ten years after the event. In addition the DPP had not been required to give reasons for his decision not to prosecute those suspected, and judicial review was not available to challenge his decisions.[109]

However, the duty under Article 2 will not be violated if the investigation displays a flaw, but nevertheless is in general compliance with the procedural obligation to hold an effective investigation. Thus, in *McBride v United Kingdom*,[110] in declaring the application inadmissible the European Court held that there had not been a violation of Article 2 merely because the armed forces had retained two soldiers who had been found guilty of the murder of the applicant's son. In the circumstances the investigation had been in compliance with Article 2 and there was no separate breach simply because the soldiers had not been discharged. However, even where there is no procedural or substantive violation of Article 2 the victim is still entitled to an effective remedy under Article 13 of the Convention, and this article, as well as Article 2, demands that the representatives are allowed to participate effectively in the investigation and are given access to appropriate and relevant evidence.[111] Thus, in *Bubbins v United Kingdom*[112] the European Court held that there had been no procedural violation of Article 2 when the police officers involved in the shooting of the deceased had been granted

---

[105] See also *Edwards v United Kingdom* (2002) 35 EHRR 19, where it was held that the inquiry into the killing of a prisoner by his schizophrenic cellmate did not satisfy Article 2.

[106] (2002) 35 EHRR 23.

[107] (2003) 37 EHRR 29.

[108] See *Brecknell v United Kingdom* (2008) 46 EHRR 42, where it was held that an inquiry conducted initially by the RUC was not sufficiently independent because officers of the RUC were implicated in the deaths.

[109] This case raises the question of the compatibility of immunity with respect to decisions of the DPP: see *R (Pretty) v DPP* [2002] 1 All ER 1.

[110] (2006) 43 EHRR SE 10.

[111] In *Brecknell, McCartney, McGrath, O'Dowd and Reavey v United Kingdom*, n 108, above, it was held that it was not necessary that the families had access to police files or copies of all documents during an ongoing inquiry. Neither was it necessary for them to be consulted or informed at every step of the inquiry.

[112] (2005) 41 EHRR 24. For commentary on this case, see Martin (2006) 69 MLR 242. See also *Hacket v United Kingdom* (Application No 34698/04), where the European Court held that the procedural obligations under Article 2 had been complied with on the facts.

anonymity at the inquest. In the Court's view the inquest had managed a careful balancing of the applicant's family interests with those of the possibility of reprisals against the officers. Nevertheless, it found a violation of Article 13 because *had* the applicants taken and succeeded in a civil action they would not have been able to recover compensation for non-pecuniary loss, and accordingly it would have been unlikely that they would have received legal aid.[113]

Inquests into deaths, Article 2 of the European Convention and the Human Rights Act 1998

In the post-Human Rights Act era the domestic courts are bound to follow the jurisprudence of the European Court (and Commission) of Human Rights when adjudicating claims that public authorities have violated the victim's right to life. Thus, the courts must apply the principles discussed above in deciding whether relevant deaths have been adequately investigated and whether the authorities have carried out their respective functions in conformity with Article 2.

There has been debate as to whether a duty to carry out the procedural obligations under Article 2 is dependent on the finding, or indeed arguable existence, of a substantive breach. Thus, In *R (Smith) v Oxfordshire Assistant Deputy Coroner*[114] the Court of Appeal held that a soldier who had died from hyperthermia whilst carrying out duties in Iraq was subject to the jurisdiction of the Human Rights Act 1998 and thus could rely on the procedural obligation under Article 2 of the European Convention. It was held that the circumstances of the soldier's death gave rise to concerns whether the army had provided an adequate system to protect his life and thus the coroner should have considered in what circumstances he died. Further, it was not necessary that the coroner should find that there was an arguable case that Article 2 had been breached as the *coroner's* duty in question in this case was a procedural one. However, the Court of Appeal's decision was overturned on appeal to the Supreme Court,[115] where it was held that unless British troops on active service were on a United Kingdom military base they were not within the jurisdiction of the United Kingdom for the purposes of Article 1 of the Convention and the Human Rights Act 1998. The Supreme Court stressed that Convention law had established that it would only be in exceptional circumstances that Article 1 would extend beyond territorial boundaries; for example, where the state had taken effective control of another state's territory. The present case did not fall within any of those exceptions.

Further, in *R (Gentle) v Prime Minister and Others*,[116] the House of Lords refused to grant relatives leave to apply for judicial review of the government's refusal to hold a public inquiry into the circumstances leading to the invasion of Iraq because Article 2 did not impose an obligation on the state to take reasonable steps to satisfy itself of the legality of another country under international law. Their Lordships stressed that the procedural duty to hold an investigation into a death was parasitic on the *existence* of a substantive right that Article 2,

---

[113] In *Cameron and Others v Network Rail Ltd* [2007] 1 WLR 163, it was held that the fact that damages caused by alleged negligence were limited to funeral expenses did not mean that the state was in violation of Article 2 by failing to provide an effective remedy for unlawful deaths. It was within the state's margin of appreciation to limit the availability of financial claims to financially dependent relatives.

[114] [2008] 1 WLR 1284.

[115] [2010] 3 WLR 223.

[116] [2008] 1 AC 1356.

and in this case the procedural duty so claimed did not arise from a substantive breach of Article 2.[117]

An early Court of Appeal decision threatened to undermine the protection offered by the European Court in cases such as *Jordan* and *Edwards*. In *R (Amin) v Secretary of State for the Home Department*[118] the Court of Appeal ruled that it was not necessary for the Secretary of State to conduct a full independent and public inquiry into the death of a young Asian prisoner at the hands of his racist cellmate. In the Court of Appeal's view, in cases where it is alleged that the state had broken its duty to take reasonable care and should thus have prevented a death, a flexible approach should be taken and publicity and participation from the family was not required in every case. That decision was overturned on appeal, where the House of Lords found that the investigation in question did not fulfil the requirements of Article 2, and that a full independent public investigation had to be held to comply with the Convention. The House of Lords stated that although the European Court had not prescribed a single model of investigation to be applied in all cases, it had laid down minimum standards that had to be met irrespective of the type of investigation that was conducted. Applying the principles laid down by the European Court in *Edwards v United Kingdom*,[119] on the facts their Lordships held that there had been no inquest to discharge the state's investigative duty, that the police investigation had raised many unanswered questions and did not discharge that duty,[120] and that the Prison Service's investigation did not enjoy independence and had been conducted in private, not being published. Finally, the family had not been able to play an effective part in the inquiry; on the facts they should have had the right to be legally represented,[121] provided with the relevant material and given the opportunity to cross-examine witnesses.[122]

Despite the robust approach taken by the House of Lords in *Amin*,[123] there is room for flexibility and it is not mandatory that there is a full judicial or public inquiry in every case.[124]

---

[117] See also *R (P) v Secretary of State for Justice* [2010] 2 WLR 967, where it was held that there had been no violation of Article 2 when there had been a delay in transferring a young prisoner with a history of self-harm from an offender's institution to a psychiatric hospital. In the Court's view there was no immediate risk to life as initial medical opinion saw no need for immediate transfer. Accordingly, Article 2 was not engaged so as to impose a duty to hold an investigation.

[118] [2002] 3 WLR 505.

[119] Note 105, above.

[120] A subsequent public inquiry disclosed 186 failings contributing to the murder, identified 19 culpable individuals and made a number of recommendations to the government with respect to such investigations: *Report of the Zahid Mubarek Inquiry*, July 2006.

[121] See *R (Main) v Minister for Legal Aid* [2007] EWCA Civ 1147, where the Court of Appeal held that it was not irrational for the minister to deny funding for full legal representation to a relative of a victim of a train crash. The Court of Appeal felt such decisions involved a good deal of discretion on the part of the minister and that the inquiry would be effective without the relative being legally represented.

[122] [2005] 1 AC 653. See also *R (Davies) v HM Deputy Coroner for Birmingham* [2004] 1 WLR 2739, where the Court of Appeal ordered that a new inquest into a prisoner's death take place in order to establish whether systemic neglect had been a cause of death. The Court of Appeal noted that the law was in an unsettled state and that the present coronial system was currently an inadequate vehicle for the procedural obligations imposed by Article 2 of the European Convention.

[123] Subsequently, in *R (JL) v Secretary of State for the Home Department* [2008] 1 WLR 158, the Court of Appeal confirmed that where there had been a suicide in custody it was for the state to investigate the facts and not for the victim's family to establish an arguable case before an investigation could take place.

[124] In addition, note that s.67 and s.68 of the Counter Terrorism Act 2008 allow the Secretary of State to certify the contents of an inquest as sensitive and to appoint a special coroner for such investigations, with no jury.

For example, in *Scholes* v *Secretary of State for the Home Department*,[125] it was held that there had been no breach of Article 2 when a full public inquiry had not been established to examine the sentencing and subsequent suicide of a 16-year-old boy at a young offender institution. The Court of Appeal held that the judge had not violated Article 2 by imposing a two-year detention, because he had not been obliged to conduct an enquiry as to where and in what circumstances the boy would be detained, and had, in fact, requested that information as to his vulnerability be passed on to the authorities. The court also held that the inquest in this case had been thorough and in compliance with Article 2. In the court's view a full public inquiry was not required in every case, and although an inquest could not always look fully at policy issues, in this case the court had done that and the coroner had forwarded its findings to the Secretary. The Secretary had responded to these issues and accordingly the combination of that response and the inquiry met the demands of Article 2.[126]

In *R (JL)* v *Secretary of State for Justice*[127] the House of Lords provided some clarification regarding the level and depth of inquiry required under Article 2. In that case their Lordships held that the near-suicide of a prisoner in custody which caused a potential for serious long-term injury automatically triggered the state's obligation to hold an enhanced investigation.[128] In such a case that duty could not be discharged by holding an internal investigation. In some circumstances an internal investigation would suffice, but in others a further, enhanced, inquiry would be needed. A 'D' type inquiry, as identified by the Court of Appeal in *R (D)* v *Secretary of State for the Home Department*,[129] requiring a full public inquiry taking oral evidence in public, was not required in every case. Thus, *D* was wrong in the sense that it indicated that all investigations into near-suicides be carried out in public; the D-investigation would be rare (in cases such as *Amin*).

In *JL* their Lordships also stated that where an initial inquiry took place it should be sufficiently close to an enhanced investigation as possible and a further inquiry may be necessary even though no fault is identified; that was because an essential object is to learn lessons for the future. Although an internal inquiry was inevitable at the outset, a further inquiry should be instigated as soon as it was apparent that the prisoner had attempted suicide and was incapacitated. Such an inquiry had to be independent, initiated by the state, accommodate family participation, be prompt and expeditious and involve public scrutiny. In the subsequent full proceedings, the High Court held that there had been no violation of Article 2 when the claimant alleged that he had been insufficiently involved in the first stage of the inquiry. There was no rigid requirement as to the means by which an individual's participation into an investigation into his attempted suicide was to be achieved consistently with Article 2; and the claimant had in this case rebuffed attempts to engage with the process. Neither was there evidence of bias simply because the psychologist conducting the inquiry had extensive experience in the prison service; she had not worked in the specific institution or had any connection with the staff.[130]

---

[125] [2006] HRLR 44.

[126] So too, in *R (S)* v *Home Secretary* [2007] EWHC 51, it was held that the normal method of investigation into a death in custody was an inquest, and that it was not always incumbent to set up a public inquiry where the inquest did not touch on broad issues of government funding or policy.

[127] [2009] 1 AC 588.

[128] Contrast *R (P)* v *Secretary of State for Justice* [2010] 2 WLR 967, where the prisoner was not at immediate risk of self-harm and the secretary had acted on medical advice that he did not require hospital treatment. In such a case there was no breach of Article 2 and thus no duty to hold an investigation.

[129] [2006] 3 All ER 946.

[130] *R (JL)* v *Secretary of State for Justice* [2010] HRLR 4.

Accordingly, the courts are more concerned with whether there has been an effective investigation in the round, rather than prescribing a specific procedure for every death. For example, in *R (Takoushis)* v *HM Coroner for Inner North London and Others*,[131] it was held that there had not been a full and fair inquest into why a mentally ill person had committed suicide after leaving the emergency department of a hospital. The Court of Appeal found that the coroner had not considered all relevant evidence before concluding that there had been no evidence of negligence so as to warrant a jury sitting on the case. More generally it was held that where a person died as a result of possible medical negligence in an NHS hospital there had to be a system that provided for an effective and practical investigation into the facts, although not necessarily in the form of a state-initiated investigation, as required for deaths in custody. In the court's view the question was whether the system as a whole, including the investigation and the possibility of civil, criminal or disciplinary, actions, fulfilled the requirements of Article 2. The court also noted that there was material difference between deaths in custody and cases such as the present where the patient was receiving voluntary treatment; in the latter cases the state need not initiate the investigation process.

So too, even where there is a full and public inquiry, not every procedural flaw will result in a violation of Article 2. Thus, in *R (D)* v *Secretary of State for the Home Department*[132] it was held that although any inquiry into the death had to be held in public to be compliant with Article 2, it was not necessary that the prisoner in question had the right to cross-examine witnesses. Moreover, although the inquiry had to be held in public, Article 2 did not require that the whole process had to be in public: simply that the Chairman would make the evidence and written submissions public and take oral evidence in public.

The domestic courts have also had to address the question of whether official inquiries should determine or at least locate guilt on the part of the relevant authorities. Some inquiries, such as coroner's inquests, deliberately avoid attaching criminal or civil liability in such cases and this limitation may well impinge on the family's right under Article 2 to receive a proper and full explanation of the death. This may, *inter alia*, provide the relatives with the necessary evidence in which to bring legal proceedings and thus provide them with an effective remedy, as required by Article 13 of the Convention. In *R (Middleton)* v *Somerset Coroner*,[133] the House of Lords held that the state's procedural obligation under Article 2 required an inquest to give an expression of the jury's conclusion on the central factual issues surrounding the death. Thus, although the finding could not implicate criminal or civil liability, in deciding how a person had died the jury must indicate not only by what means the person died, but also by what means *and in what circumstances*. In this case the inquest had not indicated the jury's findings on the relevant factual matters and thus had not, initially, complied with Article 2. However, the applicants had eventually been provided with those findings and the inquest in that case had been fair in all other respects. Further, in *R (Sacker)* v *West Yorkshire Coroner*,[134] the House of Lords applied the principle in *Middleton* and held that the Coroners Act 1988 could be interpreted in order to allow the court to inquire into how the deceased had come to her death. Accordingly, as the jury had not been given the opportunity to conclude that the prisoner's death had been caused by a systemic failure – it

[131] [2006] 1 WLR 461.
[132] [2006] 3 All ER 946.
[133] [2004] 2 AC 182.
[134] [2004] 1 WLR 796.

had been found that a locum doctor was unfamiliar with the procedure for suicide-risk prisoners – their Lordships ordered a new inquest into the prisoner's death.[135] However it has been held that there is no duty on the coroner in an inquest into a death in custody to direct a jury to consider a fact which is potentially, rather than actually causative of death.[136]

This duty to inquire into all the facts surrounding the incident may also be imposed on other investigative bodies, such as the Independent Police Complaints Commission. Thus, in *R (Reynolds)* v *Independent Police Complaints Commission*[137] it was held that the Commission had the power and the duty to investigate cases of serious injuries in police custody and in carrying out its investigations it was under a duty to determine whether the conduct of the police had caused the injury. That was not possible without evaluating any evidence that indicated an alternative cause, which included any possible cause which might have occurred before police contact.

Questions

What is the extent and purpose of the state's procedural obligations under Article 2? Is domestic law compatible with these obligations?

The right to life and the death penalty

Despite a continuing international movement to outlaw the death penalty, and a recent judgment of the European Court of Human Rights to the effect that it is now considered inhuman and degrading within Article 3 of the European Convention,[138] capital punishment is not contrary to international human rights law *per se*. Thus, those states which carry out the death penalty are not necessarily in violation of their international law obligations. Article 6 of the International Covenant on Civil and Political Rights 1966 makes provision for such circumstances and paragraph 2 states that where the death penalty has not been abolished a sentence of death may be imposed only for the most serious crimes and in accordance with the law in force at the time of the offence. Further, that paragraph stresses that the penalty must not be contrary to the provisions of the present Covenant, and must be carried out pursuant to a final judgment rendered by a competent court.

As we shall see, a large number of states have agreed to abolish the death penalty and have signed optional protocols, contained in various international treaties, to that effect. For those states which have not signed those protocols the death penalty may be carried out subject to the limitations imposed on such a practice by the relevant treaty. However, Article 6(6) of the International Covenant (above) provides that nothing shall be invoked to delay or to prevent the abolition of capital punishment by any state party, thus clearly recognising that the international community is in favour of abolition.

Despite its general legality in international law, Article 6 imposes a number of restrictions on the death penalty. First, the death penalty can only be imposed after due process has been satisfied. Thus, the imposition of such a sentence without a fair trial, or specifically where the

---

[135] See also *R (Cash)* v *HM Coroner for Northamptonshire* [2007] 4 All ER 903 (Admin), where it was held that the decision of a coroner not to leave a verdict of unlawful killing to the jury was a breach of Article 2.

[136] *R (Lewis)* v *HM Coroner for the Mid and North Division of Shropshire* [2010] 1 WLR 1836.

[137] [2009] 3 All ER 237.

[138] *Al-Saadoon and Mufdhi* v *United Kingdom* (2010) 51 EHRR 9.

sentence has been passed by a body other than a competent court, would constitute a violation of the right to life and not merely a breach of the right to a fair trial. This limitation is also evident in Article 2 of the European Convention on Human Rights, which provides that no one shall be deprived of his life intentionally *save in the execution of a sentence of a court following his conviction of a crime for which the penalty is provided by law.*[139] In addition, if a court found that the death penalty was likely to be carried out without due process it might regard that process as adding to the stress and anxiety of the victim and thus in violation of the prohibition against inhuman and degrading treatment or punishment.[140]

Secondly, international law might seek to outlaw the imposition of the death penalty on particular individuals. For example, Article 6(5) of the International Covenant provides that a sentence of death shall not be imposed for crimes committed by persons below 18 years of age and shall not be carried out on pregnant women. Although the European Convention does not include those specific prohibitions, Article 3 of the Convention, prohibiting torture and inhuman and degrading treatment or punishment, would be engaged if the death penalty was imposed on vulnerable detainees. For example, in *Soering* v *United Kingdom*[141] the European Court took into account the victim's age and mental stability in declaring that exposure to the death row phenomenon was in violation of Article 3.

Thirdly, Article 6 of the International Covenant, and Article 2 of the European Convention, is subject to the other provisions of those treaties, most notably the prohibition of torture and inhuman and degrading treatment. Consequently, if the sentence or execution is in breach of such prohibition, the latter will override the death penalty exception. An international court might thus find a violation in respect of the imposition of the death penalty if it feels that the sentence itself, or the manner of or circumstances surrounding the execution, crosses the necessary threshold. In *Soering* (above), the European Court accepted that the death penalty was not in breach of Article 2, but held that a violation of Article 3 would have taken place because of the exposure of the victim to the death row phenomenon; such conditions subjecting him to an unacceptable level of stress and anxiety while he waited for the sentence and subsequent appeals. Using that principle, it could be agued that certain forms of execution, such as those carried out in public, would be contrary to international law.

Fourthly, the European Court of Human Rights has now accepted the more general argument that any death penalty sentence or execution, by its very nature, would constitute a violation of the prohibition against torture or inhuman or degrading punishment and thus be in breach of international law. Previously, in *Ocalan* v *Turkey*,[142] the European Court considered the legality of the death sentence during peacetime, stating that it could not be excluded, in the light of recent developments that had taken place in this area, that the member states had agreed through their practice to modify the second sentence of Article 2(1) in so far as it permitted capital punishment in peacetime. Accordingly, in the Court's view it could be argued that the death penalty could be regarded as inhuman and degrading treatment contrary to Article 3. However, the Court stressed that it was not necessary to reach any firm conclusion on this point in the present case as the penalty had been imposed after an

---

[139] See *Ocalan* v *Turkey* (2005) 41 EHRR 45, considered below, where the compatibility of the death penalty with Article 3 was not clarified as any sentence would have been in breach of Article 6 and thus Article 2 in any case.
[140] *Ocalan* v *Turkey*, above. See also *Bader* v *Sweden*, decision of the European Court, 8 November 2005.
[141] (1989) 11 EHRR 439, considered below, and in chapter 5 of this text, page 237.
[142] (2003) 37 EHRR 10.

unfair trial. The case was referred to the Grand Chamber of the European Court of Human Rights,[143] which held that the second sentence in Article 2 of the Convention might now have been amended by state practice and that accordingly states would now regard it as an unacceptable form of punishment in peacetime. However, as not every state had signed Protocol No 13, prohibiting the death penalty at all times, even during war time, the Court held that it would not be appropriate to conclude that the death penalty was inhuman and degrading and thus automatically in violation of Article 3. In any case, such a finding was not necessary as in this case the Court found that the death penalty was threatened after the failure to provide a fair trial and that that constituted a breach of Article 3 as the applicant had been subjected to the threat of being unlawfully executed.

However, in *Al-Saadoon and Mufdhi v United Kingdom*,[144] the European Court revisited this issue in the light of developments since the *Ocalan* judgment; in particular that all member states apart from Russia, who had announced a moratorium on the death penalty, had legally abandoned the death penalty in its domestic law, and all but three states had ratified Protocols 6 of the Convention, below. The Court noted, therefore, that the territories encompassed by the member States of the Council of Europe had become a zone free of capital punishment. Accordingly the Court held that the death penalty could now be considered as amounting to inhuman and degrading treatment, involving as it did the deliberate and premeditated destruction of a human being by the state authorities, and causing physical pain and intense psychological suffering as a result of the foreknowledge of death. This effectively overturned the decision of the Court of Appeal in *R (Al-Saadoon and Mufdhi) v Secretary of State for Defence*,[145] where it was held that it was not unlawful for British troops to hand over two Iraqis to the Iraqi authorities to face a trial and the death penalty as there was insufficient evidence that international law prohibited executions by hanging because it was in violation of the prohibition of inhuman treatment. This European Court ruling does not affect the position of the death penalty in international law, above, affecting as it does only the contracting states to the European Convention. However, it adds to the jurisprudence of the European Court on the interpretation of Convention principles and will continue to fuel the debate with respect to the compatibility of the death penalty with more general principles and norms of international human rights law.

The death penalty and Protocols 6 and 13

As mentioned above, member states can agree to ratify additional protocols in various international treaties, agreeing not to carry out the death penalty. This will reflect their domestic law's prohibition of the death penalty and will involve the state in an automatic violation of their international law obligations, irrespective of whether the death penalty constituted a violation of any other human right, such as freedom from inhuman punishment.

Protocol No 6 of the European Convention provides that the death penalty shall be abolished and that no one shall be condemned to such penalty or executed. Thus, once a member state signs Protocol No 6 then the exemption contained in Article 2 of the Convention ceases to operate. At present all member sates have signed Protocol 6 and only Russia has not ratified

---

[143] (2006) 41 EHRR 45.
[144] (2010) 51 EHRR 9.
[145] [2008] EWHC 3098.

it (although it has agreed a moratorium during peacetime). Article 2 of the Protocol allows a state to make provision in its law for the death penalty in respect of acts committed in times of war or imminent threat of war. Other than that exception, Article 3 of the Protocol states that no derogation under Article 15 of the Convention is allowed, and Article 4 of the Protocol prohibits any such reservations of the Protocol under Article 57 of the Convention.

In addition Protocol No 13 to the European Convention provides for the abolition of the death penalty in all circumstances and was signed by the United Kingdom government in May 2002.[146] The latter protocol has now been ratified by 42 member states in the Council of Europe; Armenia, Latvia and Poland have signed but not ratified; and Azerbaijan and Russia have not signed it. Protocols 6 and 13 represent a growing international movement to prohibit the death penalty and this protocol, and an optional protocol to the International Covenant on Civil and Political Rights,[147] calls for the complete abolition of the death penalty during peacetime. In addition, in 2007 the Parliamentary Assembly of the Council of Europe adopted a resolution calling for a moratorium by all states on the death penalty in their domestic law, confirming its strong opposition to the death penalty in all circumstances, so as to reinforce the protocols under the European Convention, above, and the measures taken by European states to effectively end the death penalty in their jurisdictions.[148] The Parliamentary Assembly now insists that states joining the Council of Europe agree to apply an immediate moratorium on executions so as to delete the death penalty from its national legislation, and to sign and ratify Protocol No 6.

As the United Kingdom has signed Protocols 6 and 13, any death penalty carried out in the jurisdiction of the United Kingdom would be contrary to that Protocol and thus contrary to the United Kingdom's Convention responsibilities. In addition, as evidenced by cases such as *Soering v United Kingdom*,[149] the death penalty might also give rise to liability under Articles 2 and 3 of the Convention in that the circumstances surrounding the death penalty may well constitute inhuman and degrading treatment. Ratification of Protocol No 6 and 13 thus gives rise to a specific problem for states such as the United Kingdom which might deport or extradite a person to face the death penalty in another country, which is either not a party to the Convention, or has not ratified Protocol No 6. In such a case, the United Kingdom government's decision to deport must not be arbitrary or in conflict with Article 3. In addition, following the signing of Protocol No 6 any such action would appear to be in breach of that protocol. That is because the protocol not only provides that the death penalty shall be abolished, but also that no one shall be *condemned* to such penalty or be executed.

The death penalty, Protocols 6 and 13 and the case of Al-Saadoon and Mufdhi

The issues surrounding the surrender of individuals to face the death penalty in another state were raised in the complex case of *R (Al-Saadoon and Mufdhi) v Secretary of State for Defence*,[150] where it was held that it was not unlawful for British troops to hand over two Iraqi nationals who were suspected of committing terrorist killings to the Iraqi authorities to face a criminal

---

[146] The government had already ratified, without reservation, the Second Protocol to the International Covenant on Civil and Political Rights 1966.

[147] The Second Protocol to the International Covenant on Civil and Political Rights, aiming at the Abolition of the Death Penalty (1990).

[148] Resolution 1560, 26 June 2007.

[149] (1989) 11 EHRR 439.

[150] [2009] 3 WLR 957.

trial and the death penalty. It was decided that Article 1 of the Convention was not engaged in this case as the victims were not within the authority's jurisdiction as the British troops did not have exclusive control over the relevant territory, but that in any case the government troops were obliged under international law to hand over the individuals, unless there was a real risk that the detainees' Article 3 rights were to be violated. In the domestic court's view, although the death penalty was outlawed in the United Kingdom, it was not in breach of the Convention or international law as there was insufficient evidence that international law prohibited executions by hanging because it was in violation of the prohibition of inhuman treatment.

However, in *Al-Saadoon and Mufdhi v United Kingdom*,[151] the European Court of Human Rights held that the handing over of the detainees to the Iraqi authorities constituted a violation of Articles 2, 3 and 13 of the Convention. Disagreeing with the national courts, the European Court held that the United Kingdom authorities had, through the exercise of military force and by law, exclusive control over the detention facilities which held the applicants. As the applicants were likely to face the death penalty, Articles 2 and 3 of the Convention had to be analysed to ensure that the United Kingdom was not in breach of its obligations under the Convention. On the issue of Article 3, the Court held that the death penalty could now be considered as amounting to inhuman and degrading treatment, involving as it did the deliberate and premeditated destruction of a human being by the state authorities.

The position of the death penalty and Protocols 6 and 13 (and Article 3) with respect to the United Kingdom's surrender of the prisoners was summarised by the European Court in the following way:

> ... from the date of the [UK ratification] the respondent's obligation under Article 2 of the Convention and Article 1 of Protocol No 13 dictated that it should not enter into any arrangement which involved it in detaining individuals with a view to transferring them to stand trial on capital charges or in any way subjecting individuals within its jurisdiction to a real risk of being sentenced to the death penalty and executed. Moreover ... the applicants' well-founded fear of being executed (during the period of detention) must have given rise to a significant degree of mental suffering and to subject them to such suffering constituted inhuman treatment within the meaning of Article 3 ... .[152]

The Court also rejected the government's contention that they had no choice but to respect Iraqi sovereignty and transfer the applicants. It had not been shown that the respect of their human rights would inevitably damage sovereignty because the domestic authorities had neither negotiated with the Iraqi authorities nor explored the possibility of trying the applicants in the domestic courts.[153] Accordingly the United Kingdom was in breach of Article 3 and of its obligations under Protocol 13.

Questions

Is the death penalty unlawful in international law?

What is the position of the death penalty with respect to member states of the Council of Europe and, specifically, the United Kingdom?

---

[151] (2010) 51 EHRR 9.

[152] Ibid., at para 137 of the judgment.

[153] The Court also found a violation of Article 34 (the right to petition) because of the United Kingdom's refusal to abide by the Court's indication not to transfer the applicants to the Iraqi authorities. This also led to a violation of Article 13 because of its failure to provide an effective remedy.

The exceptions under Article 2(2) – permissible use of lethal force

Unlike Article 3 of the European Convention, which prohibits torture and other forms of ill-treatment in absolute terms, Article 2 does allow life to be taken intentionally in particular and exceptional circumstances. In doing so it accepts that it may be permissible to take a person's life for the greater benefit of other individuals or the interests of the state.

Article 2(2) of the European Convention provides that the deprivation of life shall not be regarded as inflicted in contravention of Article 2 when it results from the use of force, which is no more than absolutely necessary, in the following circumstances: in defence of any person from unlawful violence; in order to effect a lawful arrest or to prevent the escape of a person lawfully detained; or in action lawfully taken for the purpose of quelling a riot or insurrection.

Use of force against unlawful violence

This exception in Article 2(2) envisages the situation where it might be necessary to use fatal force on one individual in order to protect another or other individuals from unlawful violence. For example, the state authorities might decide to employ fatal force when an individual is being held hostage and their life is in danger,[154] or where there is an imminent danger that the individual is going to use explosives which will threaten the lives or safety of the public. In such cases they are allowed to use fatal force where it is absolutely necessary to protect others from unlawful violence. For this exception to apply, however, there should exist the most exceptional circumstances and the limitations of the state's defence were carefully considered by the European Court in the case of *McCann v United Kingdom*.[155] In this case security intelligence had been gathered to the effect that three IRA terrorists were to enter Gibraltar and commit an act of terrorism, probably via a car bomb. Three people were seen near a car, and believing that the car contained a bomb and that it was to be detonated, members of the SAS shot dead the three people. The European Court held that although the SAS members had used no more force than was necessary in the circumstances, there had been a violation of the right to life through the careless planning of the operation by the security authorities. The authorities had fed misinformation to the soldiers – that there was, for certain, a bomb in the car and that it could be detonated by a single press of the button – and crucial assumptions had been made which turned out to be untrue; insufficient allowances had been made for other assumptions.

Interestingly, the Court felt the legal test of defence in the domestic law of self-defence – that the force used was reasonably justifiable – was not inconsistent with the test of absolute necessity employed in Article 2(2).[156] Although the tests look different on paper, the application of the domestic test did not reveal any inconsistency, requiring suitably strong justification for force that takes a person's life. Nevertheless, it stated that the Convention term indicated that a stricter and more compelling test of necessity must be employed than, for

---

[154] See *Andronicou* v *Cyprus* (1998) 25 EHRR 491.

[155] (1995) 21 EHRR 97.

[156] See Leverick, Is English Self-defence Law Incompatible with Article 2 of the ECHR? [2002] Crim LR 347. In *R (Bennett)* v *Inner South London Coroner* [2006] HRLR 22, the High Court confirmed that the test of self-defence was substantially the same as the necessity test under Article 2(2). Accordingly, a coroner's direction that a jury could return a verdict of lawful death if they believed the police officer's use of force was reasonably necessary in all the circumstances was both lawful and consistent with the Convention. The decision was upheld by the Court of Appeal: *The Times*, 13 August 2007.

example, when deciding whether an interference with freedom of speech is necessary in a democratic society under Article 10(2).

The decision was also controversial because in that case it was prepared to find the death unlawful despite holding that the intensity of the public inquiry into the Gibraltar affair did not fall short of the standards expected in Article 2. The case law under Article 2 appears to support the conclusion that the European Court is more likely to overrule the findings of the domestic authorities, and substitute its own opinion on the facts, where, as in the *McCann* case, the error occurs because of a failure to carry out a proper investigation into the facts, or to plan the operation with due care. On the other hand, the Court appears to be reluctant to interfere where it is alleged that unreasonable force has been used by officers at the scene. In those cases the Court might be reluctant to question the judgment of the individual officers, who having little time to reflect have to make an instant decision.[157]

The Court will also provide some deference to the authorities in respect of the planning and execution of the operation itself.[158] For example, in *Bubbins* v *United Kingdom*[159] the European Court held that there had been no violation of Article 2 when police had shot dead the applicant's brother, mistakenly believing that he was a burglar. The victim's girlfriend had called the police to her flat believing that she had seen a burglar breaking in. When the police arrived they saw a figure in the window that appeared to be pointing a gun and after attempting to communicate with the figure one police officer shot at him and killed him. It transpired that the gun was a replica. Examining the facts, the Court found that it had not been established that there had been a failure to plan and organise the operation in such a way as to minimise *to the greatest extent possible* any risk to the right of life. Although the Court stated that deprivations of life called for the most careful scrutiny, it stated that it was relevant in this case that a law enforcement operation had been carried out. Such operations were regulated by domestic law and had a system of safeguards to prevent the arbitrary use of unlawful force. In this case, therefore, the use of lethal force had not been disproportionate and did not exceed what was absolutely necessary to avert what was honestly perceived by the relevant officer to be a real and immediate risk to his life and those of his colleagues.[160]

In such cases, therefore, the Court will be reluctant to make an *ex post facto* decision on the legality of the killing. For example, in *McShane* v *United Kingdom*,[161] where the applicant alleged that the police and armed forces had used unnecessary and disproportionate force when her husband had died during a disturbance in Londonderry, the Court held that it would be inappropriate and contrary to its subsidiary role under the Convention to duplicate the role of the domestic civil courts and to attempt to establish the facts and determine the

---

[157] See the Court's decision in *McCann*, above, with respect to the liability of the soldiers. See also the European Commission's decisions in *Stewart* v *United Kingdom* (1984) 39 DR 162, where it was held that the shooting of a 13-year-old boy by armed troops in Northern Ireland during a riot was not a violation of Article 2, and the admissibility decision of the European Court in *Caraher* v *United Kingdom* (Application No 24520/94). See also *Brady* v *United Kingdom* (Application No 85752/97).

[158] See *Andronicou* v *Cyprus* (1998) 25 EHRR 491.

[159] (2005) 41 EHRR 24.

[160] For commentary on this case, see Martin, *Bubbins* v *United Kingdom*: Civil Remedies and the Right to Life (2006) 69 MLR 242. See also *Huohvanainen* v *Finland* (Application No 57389/00), where the European Court held that there had been no violation of Article 2 when the applicant's brother had been shot dead by the police; and *Ramsahai and Others* v *Netherlands* (Application No 52391/99), where the Court found no violation where a young man had been shot dead by an officer after being told to stop brandishing a gun.

[161] (2002) 35 EHRR 23.

lawfulness of the husband's death. The Court, therefore, refused to make a finding with regard to the alleged responsibility of the state for the death.[162] However, as we have seen the Court has taken a much more robust approach when questioning the adequacy of the investigation into the legality and necessity of the deaths.[163]

Questions

In what circumstances does Article 2 of the Convention permit the intentional taking of life? How absolute is the right to life under Article 2 of the Convention?

Further reading

Texts

A number of texts on the European Convention contain excellent chapters on Article 2 of the Convention and its relevant case law: Harris, Warbrick, Bates and O'Boyle, *Law of the European Convention on Human Rights* (OUP 2009, 2nd edn), chapter 2; Ovey and White, *Jacobs and White: The European Convention on Human Rights* (OUP 2010, 5th edn), chapter 4; Mowbray, *Cases and Materials on the European Convention* (OUP 2007, 2nd edn), chapter 2. The latter is an excellent reference point on the case law of the European Court in this area. See also Clayton and Tomlinson, *The Law of Human Rights* (OUP 2009), chapter 7, for an expansive coverage of both domestic and European law in this area, and Amos, *Human Rights Law* (Hart 2006), chapter 7, for a very good account of the domestic case law.

Articles

The following articles also provide interesting reading in specific aspects of the right to life: Anthony, Positive Obligations and Policing in the House of Lords [2009] EHRLR 538; Giliker, Osman and Police Immunity in the English Law of Torts (2000) 20 LS 372; Hirst, Suicide in Switzerland: complicity in England [2009] Crim LR 335; Mowbray, Duties of Investigation under the European Convention on Human Rights [2002] ICLQ 437; Leverick, Is English Self-defence Law Incompatible with Article 2 of the ECHR? [2002] Crim LR 347; Yorke, The Right to Life and Abolition of the Death Penalty in the Council of Europe [2009] ELR 205.

Visit **www.mylawchamber.co.uk/fosterhumanrights** to access regular updates to major changes in the law, further case studies, weblinks, and suggested answers/approaches to questions in the book.

---

[162] The Court did, however, find a breach of the procedural requirements of Article 2 on the facts of the case (see above).

[163] See the cases on the procedural obligations under Article 2, discussed above, pages 208–11.

The absolute rights: freedom from torture and inhuman and degrading treatment and punishment

Introduction

In March 2010, *The Daily Telegraph* reported that a prisoner is claiming that a smoking ban imposed on him for swearing at a prison officer is a violation of Article 3 of the European Convention – which prohibits inhuman and degrading treatment – and constitutes cruel and unusual punishment.

In the same month the European Court of Human Rights decided that the surrendering of two Iraqi nationals by British forces to the Iraqi courts to face the death penalty was in breach of their Convention rights because the death penalty is considered to be inhuman and degrading treatment.

Is it possible that the prisoner in the first case could succeed in claiming a breach of Article 3? Why did the European Court decide that the death penalty is inhuman and degrading, and does that mean that the death penalty is unlawful?

Although the United Kingdom does not regularly practise torture, the prohibition of torture and other forms of ill-treatment is still relevant to the examination of the UK's human rights record under both international and national law. The government has never been found guilty of torture, but has been held responsible for inhuman and degrading treatment and punishment on a number of occasions (see below). Equally, the passing of the Human Rights Act 1998 will require the government and the judiciary to examine a number of rules relating to deportation, detention, punishment and the granting or withdrawal of welfare benefits to see if they fall foul of the Convention and the 1998 Act.

This chapter examines how the European Convention on Human Rights (and other international treaties) and domestic law prohibits the use of torture and inhuman or degrading treatment or punishment and protects the individual from such treatment. The chapter will first examine the nature and importance of that right, including its absolute and fundamental status. It will then explore its scope, including the nature and extent of the duties that such a right imposes on the state to prohibit it.

The right will be viewed initially from the perspective of Article 3 of the European Convention on Human Rights, which prohibits torture and inhuman and degrading treatment punishment. A study will be made of both European Convention case law and the case law (and relevant statutory provisions) in domestic law, and most notably how the right has been developed under the Human Rights Act 1998. Specific study will be made of Article 3 and its application to areas such as extradition and deportation, corporal punishment and prison conditions.

Thus, this chapter will cover:

- An examination of the importance and nature of freedom from torture and other ill-treatment.

- An examination and analysis of the scope and extent of the state's obligation to protect individuals from such treatment.

- An examination of the definition of the terms used in Article 3 of the Convention and the mechanisms used by the courts in assessing the appropriate thresholds in order to find a violation.

- An examination of the application of Article 3 with respect to issues such as deportation and extradition, corporal punishment, prison conditions and the admissibility of torture evidence in legal proceedings.

In examining the above the chapter will analyse the relevant case law of the European Court of Human Rights and cases decided under the Human Rights Act 1998 and provide a critical evaluation of their effectiveness in prohibiting torture and other forms of ill-treatment.

Freedom from torture and inhuman and degrading treatment and punishment

Nature and scope of the right

Article 3 of the European Convention protects the individual from torture and other acts of ill-treatment and provides as follows:

> No one shall be subject to torture or to inhuman or degrading treatment or punishment.

Article 3 is, of course, binding on the British government by virtue of it ratifying the European Convention, and decisions of the European Court of Human Rights impose an obligation in international law to comply with those judgments. In addition, Article 3 is now given effect in domestic law and the courts must take Article 3 and the relevant case law into account when adjudicating on Article 3 cases. Although the Human Rights Act has only 'incorporated' European Convention rights, the House of Lords has accepted that it might be permissible to take other international provisions on this subject into account.[1]

This prohibition is contained in all general international and regional human rights treaties, and in addition there are specific treaties and mechanisms to regulate and punish such acts.[2] The Universal Declaration of Human Rights 1945 provides, in Article 5, that no one shall be subjected to torture or to cruel, inhuman or degrading treatment or punishment,

---

[1] See *A v Secretary of State for the Home Department (No 2)* [2006] 2 AC 221, dealt with below in the second case study for this chapter.

[2] See the UN Convention against Torture and other Cruel, Inhuman or Degrading Treatment or Punishment 1984, together with the Optional Protocol of 2002; and the European Convention for the Prevention of Torture and Inhuman and Degrading Treatment or Punishment 1987. See Brownlie and Goodwin-Gill, *Basic Documents on Human Rights* (OUP 2010, 6th edn).

and Article 7 of the International Covenant on Civil and Political Rights 1966 repeats that prohibition and adds that no one shall be subjected without his free consent to medical or scientific experimentation. Further, Article 10 of the International Covenant states that all persons deprived of their liberty shall be treated with humanity and with respect for the inherent dignity of the human person. Such provisions will also be found in domestic legal systems. Both US and English law prohibit cruel and unusual punishments,[3] and English law makes it an offence for a public official to commit an act of torture.[4]

The wording of those provisions indicate that torture and other forms of ill-treatment, as with slavery and servitude, violate a human's dignity and worth, offending that individual's inherent right to be treated as a human being. Such practices, therefore, are considered inconsistent with civilised behaviour and thus justify a complete prohibition, whatever individual or collective benefit may be gained from such acts.[5] Consequently acts of torture have become accepted as crimes of international law and the international prohibition on the use of torture enjoys the enhanced status of a *jus cogens* or a peremptory norm of general international law.[6] It is also clear that the prohibition of such acts has a particular relevance with respect to the treatment of prisoners, Article 10 of the International Covenant making specific reference to the right to dignity of those in detention. As a consequence there are specific treaties and rules relating to such individuals.[7]

This right to be free from torture, etc. is couched in absolute terms and admits of no exceptions or reservations, unlike other rights such as freedom of expression and liberty of the person, which can be interfered with provided there exists a legitimate aim and the 'violation' is prescribed by law and necessary and proportionate. Such is the fundamental and absolute character of Article 3 that international law does not foresee any justification for an act which is considered to breach its terms. In other words, an act of (torture) is regarded as so contrary to human dignity and the standards of a civilised democracy that no countervailing interest could ever justify its commission. Thus, in *Chahal* v *United Kingdom*[8] the European Court stated that Article 3 enshrined one of the most fundamental values of democratic society, and that even in the context of protecting that society from terrorist violence the Convention prohibits torture or inhuman or degrading treatment or punishment in absolute terms and irrespective of the victim's conduct.

However, although the right under Article 3 of the Convention is an absolute as opposed to a conditional one, the European Court will inevitably apply some principles of legitimacy and necessity in deciding whether there has been a violation of that article: in other words, whether the act in question has crossed the requisite threshold to allow the Court to pronounce a violation. For example, with respect to prison conditions, the European Court will take into account the dangerousness of the prisoner and the nature of the offence in deciding

---

[3] See the English Bill of Rights 1689, prohibiting 'cruell and unusuall punishment' and the 8th amendment to the US Constitution, prohibiting excessive bail and cruel and unusual punishments.

[4] See s.134 of the Criminal Justice Act 1988.

[5] Derogations allowed under international treaties in times of war or public emergency do not permit derogations from the prohibition of torture or slavery. See chapter 2 of this text, at pages 73–5.

[6] See *R* v *Bow Street Metropolitan Stipendary Magistrate, ex parte Pinochet Ugarte* [2000] 1 AC 147, where the House of Lords held that state officials could have no state immunity with respect to acts of torture.

[7] See, for example, the UN Body of Principles for the Protection of all Persons under any form of Detention or Imprisonment 1988; the UN Basic Principles for the Treatment of Prisoners (1990); and the European Prison Rules 1987. See Rodley, *The Treatment of Prisoners in International Law* (OUP 2009, 2nd edn).

[8] (1996) 23 EHRR 413.

whether such conditions are in violation of Article 3.[9] Thus, sustained periods of solitary confinement and withdrawal of contact with family and friends may be in breach of Article 3 if applied to all prisoners, but if the prisoner in question is a threat to state security and to others such punishment may be acceptable.[10] This is because solitary confinement is not in breach of Article 3 *per se*, unlike an act of deliberate humiliation or cruel punishment. In determining its acceptability with respect to Article 3, therefore, it appears to be justifiable for the Court to consider the purpose and utility of that measure, provided it does not justify that treatment solely on those grounds: in other words, that unlimited and cruel solitary confinement is acceptable because of its utility.[11]

The use of proportionality within Article 3 has been strongly condemned, principally on the grounds that it allows the Court to compromise the absoluteness of Article 3's prohibition by considering whether the treatment or punishment in question serves a useful social or other purpose.[12] Nevertheless, the European Court has appeared to use it as a means of distinguishing acceptable and unacceptable treatment and in *Gafgen v Germany*[13] the Court used it to justify a finding of inhuman treatment as opposed to torture. In that case the applicant had been threatened with severe physical pain during interrogation when the police were trying to locate a child abducted by the applicant. The Court held that if the threat had been carried out that would have constituted torture, but as the interrogation only lasted ten minutes *and was done as a genuine attempt to save the child's life*, the threats constituted inhuman treatment.

Article 3 and the role of the European Court of Human Rights

The role of the European Court therefore is, first, to define the terms 'torture' and 'inhuman and degrading treatment or punishment' to see what type and level of treatment is capable of falling within their scope.[14] In doing so the Court may have to determine some jurisdictional points, such as whether a breach of the article can be committed by a private individual or a state other than the state defending the proceedings. At this stage the Court may also have to consider whether particular forms of treatment fall inside or outside those terms: for example, whether a sentence of imprisonment imposed on a young person could constitute inhuman or degrading treatment,[15] or whether handcuffing of prisoners is automatically in violation of the Convention.[16]

---

[9] See *R (Bary and others) v Secretary of State for Justice* [2010] EWHC 587 (Admin), dealt with under conditions of detention later in the chapter.

[10] See the cases dealt with under prison conditions, below 244–61.

[11] See also *R (Wellington) v Secretary of State for the Home Department* [2009] 1 AC 335 and *R (Bary) v Secretary of State for the Home Department, The Times*, 14 October 2009 with respect to the compatibility of prison conditions overseas after extradition, considered in more detail below at page 260.

[12] Palmer, A Wrong Turning: Article 3 ECHR and Proportionality [2006] CLJ 438; Nowak, Challenges to the Absolute Nature of the Prohibition of Torture and Ill-Treatment [2005] Netherlands HRQ 674.

[13] (2009) 48 EHRR 13.

[14] For an overview of Article 3, see Cooper, *Cruelty: An Analysis of Article 3* (Sweet & Maxwell 2002). See also Addo, Is there a Policy Behind the Decisions and Judgments Relating to Article 3 of the European Convention on Human Rights? (1995) ELRev 178; Yutaka Aria-Yokoi, Grading Scale of Degradation: Identifying the Threshold of Degrading Treatment or Punishment under Article 3 ECHR [2003] Netherlands HRQ 385.

[15] See *V and T v United Kingdom* (1999) 30 EHRR 121. In *DG v Ireland* (2002) 35 EHRR 33, it was held that the detention in prison of a 16-year-old boy with a personality disorder did not of itself constitute inhuman or degrading treatment.

[16] See *Raninen v Finland* (1997) 26 EHRR 563.

Secondly, the Court will have to assess whether the particular applicant has been subjected to treatment in violation of the article. This will involve the Court assessing the effect of that treatment on the applicant and, by looking at all the factors involved in the case, assessing whether the necessary threshold has been met.[17] In such cases the Court must inquire into the extent of the ill-treatment, its duration and the circumstances of its use, as well as to the personal circumstances of the applicant. In certain circumstances, for example, where the alleged violation of the article relates to a future breach, the Court will also have to address purely factual questions such as the risk of the applicant being subjected to ill-treatment by another state.[18] Other factors require a more general and objective enquiry. For example, whether the administration of corporal punishment is in violation of Article 3 will depend on the Court's acceptance, or otherwise, of that treatment and that assessment will be made on the basis of whether it considers such treatment to be consistent with the standards of a civilised democratic society. Thus, the Court may regard certain treatment or punishment, such as imprisonment, as at least *prima facie* acceptable because it is adopted commonly among all member states, whereas judicial corporal punishment would be considered to be contrary to Article 3 because it is commonly accepted as unacceptable and thus inhuman.[19]

As stressed above, because of the absolute nature of the right the Court cannot justify treatment or punishment which crosses the necessary threshold because it passes tests of legitimacy and proportionality. Thus, once it has decided there has been a breach of Article 3 it cannot look at any qualifying provisions, as are contained, for example, in Article 10(2) of the Convention, in order to justify what is in effect a violation of that article. Thus, while Article 10 cases pose two essential questions: 'was there a violation of the victim's freedom of expression?', and, if so, 'was that violation legitimate and necessary?', cases under Article 3 merely pose one question: does the act in question constitute a violation of Article 3? If the answer to that question is 'yes', then no justification can be put forward on behalf of the state. However, as we shall see, arguments of utility and necessity may well play a part in deciding whether the act in question is inconsistent with the wording and spirit of the article.

> **Questions**
> What values does a provision such as Article 3 of the European Convention uphold?
> Why is the article couched in absolute terms without any qualifying provision?
> Why is this freedom apparently better protected than the right to life?

Article 3 and the state's positive obligations

The main purpose of Article 3 is to prohibit states and state actors from committing acts of (torture) on individuals in its jurisdiction. However, as with Article 2 of the Convention, Article 3 does not merely impose a negative duty on the state to refrain from such acts. Article 3 can engage a member state in a positive obligation to ensure that a person does not suffer ill-treatment at the hands of others, including private individuals. This would also involve the duty to provide adequate compensation for those who have been subject to a violation of Article 3 and in domestic law

---

[17] See McBride, Imperfect Limits to Unacceptable Treatment (2000) 25 ELRev (Human Rights Survey) 31. See also Evans, Getting to Grips With Torture (2002) ICLQ 365.
[18] See, for example, *Chahal v United Kingdom* (1997) 23 EHRR 413.
[19] *Tyrer v United Kingdom* (1978) 2 EHRR 1.

this can be achieved through the 'incorporation' of the Convention via the Human Rights Act 1998, and by the introduction of specific statutory measures to ensure adequate compensation.[20]

The above principles are illustrated in the case of *A v United Kingdom*,[21] where the United Kingdom was held liable for the ill-treatment of the applicant at the hands of his stepfather because the domestic law allowed the stepfather to rely on a defence of reasonable chastisement, providing the applicant with inadequate protection against subjection to inhuman or degrading treatment or punishment.[22] Similarly, in *MC v Bulgaria*[23] it was held that the applicant's Convention rights under Articles 3 and 8 had been violated when the state had failed to implement and apply sufficiently protective rape laws. In this case the applicant had alleged that she had been raped, but the men were acquitted because in that case there had been no signs of force or physical resistance by the applicant. The Court held that such a requirement gave too little protection to the applicant and was inconsistent with the development of the law of rape in other European countries. Again, in *R (B) v Director of Public Prosecutions*[24] it was held that the decision of the Crown Prosecution Service to discontinue a prosecution for a serious assault because the victim was not a credible witness was both irrational and in breach of the victim's Article 3 rights; the decision was humiliating and caused the victim to feel like a second-class citizen.

The state will thus be held liable where its public authorities are responsible for subjecting individuals to breaches of Article 3. For example, in *Z v United Kingdom*,[25] the failure of the social services to provide adequate protection against physical and other abuse resulted in a violation of Article 3. The applicants were four young children whose family had been referred to the social services because of concerns about them. The family was monitored for four and a half years, but during that period problems continued. Almost five years after the referral to the social services, the children were placed in emergency foster care. The applicants brought actions in negligence against the local authority, but the case was struck out when the House of Lords held that as a matter of public policy local authorities should not be held liable in respect of the exercise of their statutory duties to safeguard the welfare of children.[26] The European Court noted that the state had a duty to take such measures to provide effective protection against acts of ill-treatment, in particular of children and other vulnerable people. Although the European Court acknowledged the difficult and sensitive decisions facing social services and the important countervailing principle of respecting and preserving family life, in the present case the system had failed to protect the applicants from serious, long-term neglect and abuse. The decision in *Z* was also applied in *E and Others v United Kingdom*[27] where the European Court, found the government in violation of Articles 3 and 13 of the Convention when a local authority had failed to protect the applicants from sexual abuse perpetrated by their stepfather.

However, for the Court to find a violation of Article 3 in such circumstances there must be evidence supporting the establishment of liability on the authority's behalf. Thus, in *DP and*

---

[20] For example, The Torture (Damages) Bill 2010 proposes to lift state immunity in tort cases and would allow victims of torture to sue those responsible. This would overturn the decision in *Al-Adsani v United Kingdom* (2002) 34 EHRR 273, where the European Court upheld such immunities.

[21] (1999) 27 EHRR 611.

[22] Such a defence was withdrawn by s.58 of the Children Act 2004.

[23] (2005) 40 EHRR 20.

[24] [2009] 1 WLR 2072.

[25] (2002) 34 EHRR 3.

[26] *X and Others v Bedfordshire County Council* [1995] 2 AC 633.

[27] (2003) 36 EHRR 31.

JC v United Kingdom,[28] it was held that there was no violation of Article 3 (or of Article 8) when the applicants complained that they had been subjected to sexual abuse perpetrated by their stepfather, because it had not been shown that the local authority should have been aware of the sexual abuse inflicted by the stepfather so as to give rise to a positive obligation to protect them from that abuse.[29] In addition, even where a duty is owed under Article 3, the courts will provide the authority with an area of discretion in deciding whether they have fulfilled their substantive obligations. Thus, in *Re E (A Child)*[30] the House of Lords held that the police authorities had not broken their obligation under Article 3 in protecting parents and children from violence when walking to and from school. Although the authorities were subject to the heightened test of proportionality, the police were not required to drive back the pro-testors by force and make numerous arrests irrespective of potential widespread disorder, loss of life and destruction of property.

As we shall see later, Article 3 can also engage the state's liability for acts of ill-treatment committed by other states where the former state has subjected the individual to a real risk of a violation of his Article 3 rights. This may occur even when the receiving state is not strictly in violation of the article because the ill-treatment may have occurred because of circum-stances beyond its control. In this case, therefore, Article 3 imposes a positive obligation on the state to prevent acts of ill-treatment.[31] However, the extent of the state's positive obligation is limited to exceptional cases and the European Court is reluctant to impose onerous or unrealistic duties on the state to facilitate individual dignity.[32]

For example, in *Pretty v United Kingdom*[33] it was held that the applicant could not claim that she had been subjected to treatment in breach of Article 3 simply because state law did not allow someone to facilitate her death. In that case the Court noted that although suffering that flows from naturally occurring illness, physical or mental, might be covered by Article 3 where it is, or risks being, exacerbated by treatment, whether flowing from conditions of detention, expulsion or other measures, for which the authorities can be held responsible,[34] in the present case, it was beyond doubt that the government had not, itself, inflicted any ill-treatment on the applicant. Nor was there any complaint that the applicant was not receiving adequate care from state medical authorities. Unlike the case where the act of deportation would subject an individual to intolerable medical conditions, in the present case there was no comparable act or treatment on the part of the government. Rather the applicant claimed that the refusal of the DPP to give an undertaking and the criminal law prohibition on assisted suicide showed that the state was failing to protect her from the suffering that awaited her as the illness reached its ultimate stages. Such a claim, in the Court's view, placed

---

[28] (2003) 36 EHRR 14.

[29] In these cases, however, the Court may find a breach of another Convention right, particularly if the victim was not allowed to pursue his or her claim in the domestic courts. In *DP*, therefore, the Court did find a violation of Article 13 because the applicants did not have available to them an effective domestic procedure of inquiry for establishing the facts and shedding light on the conduct reasonably to be expected from the social services.

[30] [2009] 1 AC 536.

[31] *D v United Kingdom* (1997) 24 EHRR 423.

[32] Note the decision in *Tremblay v France* (Application No 37194/02), decision of the European Court, 11 September 2007, where the European Court rejected the applicant's claim that her obligation to pay state contributions had forced her into a life of prostitution in breach of her rights under Articles 3 and 4 of the Convention.

[33] (2002) 35 EHRR 1.

[34] See *Keenan v United Kingdom* (2001) 33 EHRR 38; *D v United Kingdom* (1997) 24 EHRR 423.

a new and extended construction on the concept of treatment, which, as the House of Lords found, goes beyond the ordinary meaning of the word. While the Court must take a dynamic and flexible approach to the interpretation of the Convention, Article 3 must be construed in harmony with Article 2, which is first and foremost a prohibition on the use of lethal force or other conduct which might lead to the death of a human being and which does not require a state to permit or facilitate his or her death. Although sympathetic to the applicant's claim that she faced the prospect of a distressing death, the Court held that the positive obligation claimed in this case would require that the state sanction actions intended to terminate life, an obligation that cannot be derived from Article 3. Thus, there was no positive obligation to require the government either to give an undertaking not to prosecute the applicant's husband or to provide a lawful opportunity for any other form of assisted suicide.

As with Article 2 of the Convention, Article 3, together with Article 13, which provides an effective remedy for Convention violations, imposes a procedural obligation on the state to conduct an effective investigation into allegations of ill-treatment that are alleged to have violated the state's duties under this article. Thus, in *Aksoy v Turkey*[35] it was held that Article 3 had implications for Article 13 of the Convention, and required the state to carry out a thorough and effective investigation into incidents of torture.[36] Further, a failure to carry out such an investigation may frustrate any subsequent effort on behalf of the victim to bring legal action and thus constitute a violation of the right to a fair trial under Article 6.[37] The European Court has also accepted that a separate violation of Article 3 may be found for failure to investigate. In *Sevtap Veznedaroglu v Turkey*[38] it was accepted that where an individual raises an arguable claim under Article 3 that he has been ill-treated at the hands of the state and by state actors, then Article 3, in combination with Article 1 of the Convention, requires an effective investigation capable of leading to the identification and punishment of those responsible. Finally, a failure to conduct such an investigation might subject anxious and distressed relatives to treatment in violation of Article 3.[39]

As with the procedural obligation under Article 2, the courts will insist on minimum standards of procedure and a proper and full inquiry in relevant cases. For example, in *R (M and Others) v Secretary of State for the Home Department*,[40] it was held that the Home Secretary should have conducted an independent investigation into a disturbance at a detention centre where the appellants alleged that they had had their Article 3 rights violated when, during the disturbance, they had, *inter alia*, been denied toilet facilities and food and water. The Court of Appeal agreed with the judge at first instance that the circumstances triggered off a duty to hold an independent investigation and that the availability of criminal and civil proceedings and the internal inquiry did not satisfy the state's duty under Article 3.[41] Further, in *Mousa and Others v Secretary of State for the Defence*,[42] it was held that criminal and civil proceedings

---

[35] (1997) 23 EHRR 533.

[36] This obligation is imposed on state authorities, rather than the courts, and in the case of judicial review the courts' duty is to investigate the substantive merits of the claim rather than conduct a purely procedural investigation: *Nasseri v Secretary of State for the Home Department* [2010] 1 AC 1.

[37] *Assenov v Bulgaria* (1999) 28 EHRR 652.

[38] (2001) 33 EHRR 1142.

[39] *Cakiki v Turkey* (2001) 31 EHRR 133.

[40] *The Times*, 20 March 2009.

[41] On the facts, however, as the incident took place some time ago the court merely declared that the secretary *should* have held such an inquiry.

[42] [2010] HRLR 33.

would never excuse the absence of a public inquiry where there had been allegations of a serious systematic failure to safeguard human rights. Nevertheless, the courts will provide the authorities with a reasonably wide area of discretion in fulfilling that procedural duty provided that overall fairness is assured. Thus, in *Morrison v Independent Police Commissioner*[43] it was held that an investigation of a complaint of ill-treatment by the same police force was not in violation of Article 3. The availability of an appeal of that investigation to the IPA, and the possibility of criminal proceedings against the relevant officers, would ensure that the investigation was sufficiently independent.

> **Question**
>
> What positive and negative obligations does Article 3 impose on the state with respect to the prohibition of torture and other ill-treatment?

Definition of torture, inhuman and degrading treatment or punishment

The terms used in Article 3 have been defined by both the European Commission and European Court of Human Rights, although in *Selmouni v France*[44] the European Court held that the terms are flexible and that the Convention is a living instrument that must be interpreted in the light of present-day conditions. The Court took the view that the increasingly high standard being required in the area of human rights required a greater firmness in assessing breaches of the fundamental values of democratic societies. Thus, certain acts which in the past were classified as inhuman and degrading treatment as opposed to torture could be classified differently in the future. Also, in *Al-Saadoon and Mufdhi v United Kingdom*[45] the European Court took into account the changing attitude of member states towards the death penalty in deciding that such a penalty was now contrary to Article 3 of the Convention. Thus, in that case it was decided that the death penalty could now be considered as amounting to inhuman and degrading treatment, involving as it did the deliberate and premeditated destruction of a human being by the state authorities, and causing physical pain and intense psychological suffering as a result of the foreknowledge of death.[46]

'Torture' and the other terms employed in Article 3 are not specifically defined by that article, but the terms have been explored and defined by the European Court and, initially, by the European Commission of Human Rights. In the *Greek* case the Commission laid down the following guidelines with respect to the definition and scope of the respective terms. First, the Commission stated that certain treatment might apply to all three definitions: accordingly, all acts of torture would also be inhuman and degrading and all inhuman treatment would be degrading. Secondly, it stated that the notion of *inhuman* treatment covers that treatment which deliberately causes unjustifiable and severe suffering, whether that suffering is mental or physical. Thirdly, the Commission noted that the term 'torture' was often used to describe inhuman treatment, which has a purpose (such as the obtaining of information and confessions, or the infliction of punishment: in other words it was generally an aggravated form

---

[43] [2009] EWHC 2589 (Admin).
[44] (1999) 29 EHRR 403.
[45] (2010) 51 EHRR 9.
[46] The case is detailed in chapter 4 of this text, at pages 218–19.

of inhuman treatment. Finally, the Commission held that treatment or punishment could be said to be *degrading* if it grossly humiliates an individual before others or drives him to act against his will or conscience.[47]

Those individual terms were explored in the inter-state case of *Ireland v United Kingdom*.[48] The alleged violation of Article 3 centred around the application of the so-called 'five techniques' which involved detained suspects being subjected to, *inter alia*, intense noise, wall-standing, and deprivation of food and sleep. The Court found that the application of the techniques to the detainees constituted both inhuman and degrading treatment within Article 3. The five techniques were applied in combination, with premeditation and, for hours at a stretch, causing if not bodily injury, at least intense physical and mental suffering and acute psychiatric disturbances, and thus constituted inhuman treatment. Further, the Court held that the techniques were degrading since they were such as to arouse in their victims feelings of fear, anguish and inferiority capable of humiliating them and possibly taking away their physical or moral resistance.

However, the European Court held that the techniques did not amount to torture, which the Court felt was treatment constituting *deliberate* inhuman treatment causing *very serious and cruel suffering*. In the *Ireland* case the European Court stressed that the distinction between 'torture' and the other terms would be a question of degree. On the facts, the Court held that the practices, although amounting to violence which was to be condemned on moral grounds and clearly amounting to inhuman and degrading treatment, did not occasion suffering of the particular intensity and cruelty implied by the word 'torture' as understood by the Court. Also it noted that it was the clear intention of the drafters of the Convention that a special stigma be attached to a finding of torture. Consequently a finding of torture as opposed to a lesser violation is not without significance: such a finding would damage the human rights record of that state,[49] and the Court would award higher awards for non-pecuniary loss when considering just satisfaction under Article 41 of the Convention. Thus, a finding of torture is reserved for aggravated and deliberate inhuman treatment or punishment, the distinction between torture and inhuman treatment or punishment lying in the intensity of the acts and, possibly, the intention of the perpetrators. Thus, in *Gafgen v Germany*[50] the Grand Chamber of the European Court had to determine whether there had been a violation of Article 3 when the applicant had been threatened with severe physical pain during interrogation, when the police were trying to locate a child abducted by the applicant.[51]

The distinction between the terms 'inhuman' and 'degrading' then appears to be based on the type of harm suffered by the victim; inhuman treatment causing physical, mental or psychiatric harm, and degrading treatment constituting an attack on a person's dignity, although the distinction could also be made on the level of the harm suffered.[52]

---

[47] (1969) 12 YB 170. Although the treatment will normally be deliberate, a court may find an act to be inhuman or degrading despite the lack of intention on behalf of the state or state actor. See, for example, *Price v United Kingdom*, discussed under conditions of detention, below.

[48] (1978) 2 EHRR 25.

[49] For example, the United Kingdom has never been found by the European Court to have committed an act of torture under Article 3.

[50] (2010) 28 BHRC 463.

[51] The Court also found that the applicant was no longer a victim as the domestic courts had found the officers guilty and had excluded any resulting evidence at the trial. This was sufficient redress in a case where the applicant had been merely threatened with acts of violence.

[52] See Janis, Kay and Bradley, *European Human Rights Law: Text and Materials* (2007 OUP, 3rd edn), pages 181–92.

The appropriate threshold

Having defined the terms in Article 3, the Court must then determine whether the facts reveal a violation of that article. This will depend on the level of harm suffered by the victim and the intention of the perpetrator, as well as the Court's views on the acceptability of such treatment. In *Askoy* v *Turkey*[53] the Court held that when the applicant had been strung up in a cell, blindfolded and had electrodes attached to his genitals, this clearly amounted to torture, and in *Selmouni* v *France*[54] the Court made a finding of torture when the applicant had, *inter alia*, been subjected to repeated physical and verbal assaults, had been urinated on by an officer, and had been threatened with a blow lamp. In deciding whether treatment is 'inhuman' the Court will not only have to distinguish such treatment from acts of torture, but also satisfy itself that there has been a sufficiently serious attack on the victim's physical, mental or psychological well-being. In *Tomasi* v *France*[55] the applicant had been hit in the stomach, slapped and kicked, had his head knocked against the wall, and been left naked in front of a window for several hours. The Court found that having regard to the number of blows and their intensity, such treatment was both inhuman and degrading.

Similarly, in deciding whether treatment or punishment is 'degrading', the Court has held that the humiliation or debasement involved must reach a particular level, such an assessment being relative and dependent on all the circumstances of the case, including the age of the victim.[56] In *Pretty* v *United Kingdom*[57] the Grand Chamber of the European Court stressed that the treatment must attain a minimum level of severity and involve either actual bodily injury or *intense* physical or mental suffering. It is clear, therefore, that not all attacks on a person's physical or mental integrity will cross the threshold required for a violation of Article 3 and in such cases the Court will be satisfied with finding a violation of another, less fundamental, Convention right.[58] This is starkly illustrated by the recent case of *Wainwright* v *United Kingdom*,[59] below.

In this case Mrs Wainwright and her son (who suffered from cerebral palsy) visited the woman's son and the boy's half-brother in prison. Because the prisoner was suspected of supplying drugs in the prison, the governor ordered that all visitors be strip-searched before visits. Mrs Wainwright was taken to a nearby room which overlooked offices and which had blinds that had not been pulled down and was told to remove her clothes apart from her underwear. She was then asked to pull down her underwear and bend forward, at which point officers inspected her genital area and her anus. Meanwhile her son was taken to another room and told to remove the clothes on his upper body, although he was concerned that his rectum was to be searched as one of the officers was wearing rubber gloves. He was asked to remove his boxer shorts and one officer lifted up his penis and pulled back the foreskin. Both applicants were distressed during the visit (Mrs Wainwright was physically sick) and subsequent

---

[53] (1996) 23 EHRR 553.

[54] (1999) 29 EHRR 403.

[55] (1992) 15 EHRR 1.

[56] *Tyrer* v *United Kingdom* (1978) 2 EHRR 1.

[57] (2002) 35 EHRR 1.

[58] For example, in *Costello-Roberts* v *United Kingdom* (1993) 19 EHRR 112, considered below, the European Court found a violation of the right to private life even though it found that corporal punishment had not violated Article 3.

[59] (2007) 44 EHRR 40. See also *L* v *Lithuania* (Application No 27527), decision of the European Court, 11 September 2007, where it was held that a transsexual's failure to register his new sexual identity had caused him understandable distress and frustration but not to such an intense degree as to warrant considering the case under Article 3 as opposed to Article 8.

examinations revealed post-traumatic stress and the worsening of existing mental disorders. After the events Mrs Wainwright decided not to visit her son in prison again.

After bringing largely unsuccessful domestic proceedings[60] the applicants brought a case under the European Convention, claiming a violation of Articles 3 and 8 of the Convention. Dealing with the claim under Article 3, the Court accepted that the search served a legitimate preventive measure in respect of the endemic drug problems within the prison, but stressed that such an invasive procedure had to be conducted with rigorous adherence to procedure and with due respect of the applicants' dignity. Applying those principles to the facts, the Court held that although the officers had failed to comply with their own procedures and had demonstrated 'sloppiness' and a lack of courtesy, there had been no verbal abuse of the applicants and, with the exception of the touching of the boy (for which he had received compensation for battery in the domestic action), no physical contact. Although the procedure had caused obvious distress to the applicants, it did not in the Court's view reach the minimum level of severity prohibited by Article 3.[61]

Thus, it is clear that not all forms of ill-treatment will be in violation of its provisions, and in deciding whether the threshold under Article 3 has been met, the Court can take into account whether the treatment complained of is part and parcel of a necessary and civilised social order. For example, although arrest, detention and imprisonment may degrade a person, they are regarded as perfectly acceptable under the Convention. Equally, in deciding whether the circumstances of such actions cross the necessary threshold, the Court can take into account factors such as the victim's age and dangerousness.[62]

> **Questions**
> How has the European Court defined the various terms employed in Article 3?
> On what basis does the Court distinguish those terms and determine whether there has been a breach of that term on the facts?
> Has the court managed to preserve the absolute character of Article 3 in the interpretation process?

Article 3 and corporal punishment

The question of judicial corporal punishment and Article 3 was considered in the case of *Tyrer v United Kingdom*.[63] In that case the applicant, a 15-year-old boy living in the Isle of Man, had been sentenced to several strokes of the birch for an assault on another boy. The Court held that it was immaterial that the punishment was an effective deterrent, or that the majority of society in the Isle of Man approved of the punishment. Describing the punishment as institutionalised violence, it held that the applicant had been subjected to an assault on precisely that which it is one of the main purposes of Article 3 to protect, namely a person's dignity and physical integrity. The European Court regarded judicial corporal punishment as incompatible

---

[60] *Wainwright* v *Secretary of State for the Home Department* [2004] 2 AC 406.

[61] The Court did, however, find that there had been a breach of Articles 8 and 13 of the Convention. The case is dealt with in detail in chapter 11 of this text.

[62] See, for example, *V and T* v *United Kingdom* (1999) 30 EHRR 121: the European Court decided that neither the subjection of two ten-year-old boys to an adult trial nor the passing of a life sentence on them was in violation of Article 3. See also *R (Wellington)* v *Secretary of State for the Home Department* [2009] 1 AC 335, where the House of Lords noted that a life sentence without remission was not necessarily in violation of Article 3.

[63] (1978) 2 EHRR 1.

with Article 3 of the Convention; although the punishment was carried out in private and under medical supervision, the overall effect of such punishment violated Article 3.

Tyrer did not, however, clarify the question of the compatibility of other forms of corporal punishment, most notably corporal punishment in schools. In this context, the European Court and Commission have adopted a case-by-case approach to determine whether, on the facts, the necessary threshold has been met. For example, in *Costello-Roberts* v *United Kingdom*[64] the European Court held that the beating of a young boy on the bottom, through his shorts with a slipper, which caused short-term bruising, was not in violation of Article 3. In the Court's view, because the physical and psychological effects were not long-lasting, the threshold had not been met in this case.[65] There have been other cases brought against the United Kingdom in this area,[66] but the case law is inconsistent, displaying a reluctance to challenge the general compatibility of the practice of corporal punishment within the Convention. In any case domestic law took the initiative and passed the Schools Standard and Framework Act 1998, which outlawed corporal punishment in all schools.

Corporal punishment also raises questions concerning the rights of parents to have their children taught, and punished, in accordance with their religious and philosophical wishes. In *Campbell and Cosans* v *United Kingdom*[67] it was claimed that the threat of corporal punishment was contrary to both Article 3 of the Convention and the right of parents, under Article 2 of the Protocol No 1, to ensure that their children are taught in compliance with their philosophical and religious convictions. The European Court held that on the facts there had been no violation of Article 3, because it was not satisfied that the pupils at the school, by reason only of the risk of being subjected to such punishment, were sufficiently humiliated or debased. However, the Court held that there had been a breach of the parents' rights under Article 2 of the first Protocol. In the Court's view, nothing suggested that corporal punishment was of such overriding importance in the education process that it would justify an interference with the parents' philosophical convictions.[68]

That decision, of course, left open the possibility that parents who *do* wish their children to be subjected to corporal punishment in the school context, but who are denied this by prohibitive national law (as they are in the United Kingdom), could claim to have had their parental rights violated. This issue arose in the post-Human Rights Act case of *R (Williamson)* v *Secretary of State for Education*,[69] where parents and teachers claimed that the Education Act 1996 violated their rights under both Article 2 of the First Protocol and Article 9, which guarantees freedom of thought, conscience and religion. In the Court of Appeal[70] it was held both applicants' claims should fail. In the Court's view, although the belief in corporal punishment was a recognisable belief under those articles, the prohibition of such punishment in schools did not deprive the parents of those beliefs as they could carry out such punishment in the home. Further, the teachers in

---

[64] (1992) 19 EHRR 112.

[65] The Court did not regard this factor as a prerequisite of a violation, but regarded it as relevant in deciding whether the threshold is met in a particular case. Contrast the decision in *Y* v *United Kingdom* (Application No 14229/88), where the administration of four hard strokes of the cane on the bare buttocks of the applicant, causing swelling, bruising and considerable pain, constituted degrading treatment and punishment; a friendly settlement was then reached with the applicant and the government.

[66] See, for example, *Warwick* v *United Kingdom* (Application No 9471/81).

[67] (1982) 4 EHRR 243.

[68] The Education (No 2) Act 1986 outlawed corporal punishment in state schools.

[69] [2005] 2 AC 246.

[70] [2003] 1 All ER 385.

this case could not claim any right over and above that possessed by the parents. The House of Lords dismissed the appeal but refused to declare the Education Act 1996 incompatible with the Convention on other grounds. In their Lordships' view, although both articles were engaged, parliament was entitled to make an exception to those rights on the basis that they interfered with the child's rights not to be subject to inhuman and degrading treatment. Accordingly, parliament was entitled to have a broad blanket rule on prohibition, and the interference with the parents' convention rights were necessary in a democratic society for the protection of the rights of others. The statutory ban pursued a legitimate aim and was intended to protect children from the pain, distress and other harmful effects that infliction of physical violence might cause. Further, the means chosen by parliament to achieve this aim were proportionate and appropriate. The parents' beliefs involved inflicting physical violence on children in an institutionalised setting, and although parliament was bound to respect the parents' beliefs, it was entitled to decide that the manifestation of those beliefs in practice was not in the best interests of children.

The controversial topic of parental chastisement was raised in *A v United Kingdom*.[71] The applicant, a nine-year-old boy, had been beaten with a garden cane by his stepfather, medical reports suggesting that he had been beaten repeatedly and severely, although in criminal proceedings for assault the defendant was acquitted on the grounds that he had used reasonable force in exercising parental chastisement. The European Court held that given the fact that the applicant had been beaten with considerable force, and on more than one occasion, the threshold within Article 3 of the Convention had been satisfied. It also concluded that domestic law and its application had failed to protect the applicant from such treatment, thus engaging the liability of the government for such action. Again, the European Court did not outlaw physical parental chastisement, and gave little guidance on what level of such punishment would be acceptable. However, some guidance is provided by national law, as s.58 of the Children Act 2004 states that the battery of a child cannot be justified on the ground that it constituted reasonable punishment in respect of the offences of wounding and causing grievous bodily harm or assault causing actual bodily harm.[72] Despite these changes, there is still pressure on the United Kingdom from the Council of Europe to implement a full ban on corporal punishment.[73]

Questions

What is the European Court's stance on physical punishment *vis à vis* Article 3?

Should the use of any form of physical punishment on children be outlawed under Article 3?

Article 3 and deportation and extradition

Deportation and extradition raises issues of liability under the Convention when there is a real risk that the applicant will have their Convention rights violated by the receiving state.[74]

---

[71] (1999) 27 EHRR 611.

[72] See Keating, Protecting or Punishing Children: Physical Punishment, Human Rights and English Law Reform (2006) LS 394.

[73] Hirsch, UK criticised over delay in bringing in ban on smacking, *Guardian*, 26 April 2010, Law 7.

[74] In *R v Special Adjudicator, ex parte Ullah* [2004] 2 AC 323, the House of Lords held that an article other than Article 3 (in this case Article 9) *could* be engaged in relation to the removal of an individual where the anticipated treatment in the receiving state would be in breach of the requirements of the Convention, but did not meet the threshold of Article 3. Similarly, in *Razgar v Home Secretary* [2004] 2 AC 368, the House of Lords held that the rights under Article 8 of the Convention could be violated when a deportation might cause an effect on his mental health, even where the treatment did not violate Article 3.

Such acts give rise to a claim that the person will face a violation of his Convention rights when he enters the receiving country.

The jurisdictional question of whether one member state can be responsible for the violations of another state was addressed and resolved in the case of *Soering v United Kingdom*.[75] Here the European Court held that a decision of a member state to extradite a person might engage the responsibility of that state under the Convention where there were substantial grounds for believing that, if extradited, such a person would be faced with a real risk of being subjected to breaches of Article 3. In *Soering*, the United States had sought the extradition of a young German national, who was wanted to stand trial for the murder of his girlfriend's parents. The government was given an assurance that the prosecutors would forward the views of the British government that he should not face the death penalty and the government agreed to his extradition. The Court held that although the death penalty itself was not in contravention of the European Convention, the circumstances making up the death penalty, and in this case the death row phenomenon, constituted such serious treatment that extradition in this case would constitute a violation of Article 3.[76]

In coming to that decision the Court in *Soering* had to consider the acceptability of the death row conditions – subjecting American law and practice to the standards of the Convention – as well as the effect that the conditions would have on the applicant. In this case, therefore, it felt that the applicant's age and mental state were relevant in determining whether the threshold had been passed and whether there had been a substantive breach. Equally, the Court will need to assess the actual risk that the victim has been subjected to. For example, in *Iorgov v Bulgaria*,[77] it was held that the applicants had not been subjected to the death row phenomenon when sentenced to death at a time when the death penalty had been suspended under domestic law. Although the applicants would have been subjected to some initial fear and anxiety, this would have passed with time and was not comparable to the death row phenomenon so as to violate Article 3.

In these cases the Court must decide whether the applicant faced a *real risk* that he would be subject to conditions or treatment in violation of his Convention rights. This involves both the factual question of whether the risk is real enough, and whether the treatment that the applicant is likely to receive would be in violation of Article 3. In *Chahal v United Kingdom*,[78] the applicant had entered the United Kingdom in 1972 and had received indefinite leave to stay. In 1984 he had visited Punjab and become involved in the cause of a Sikh homeland, and as a result had been arrested and detained for 21 days and subjected to torture by the Punjab police. On his return to the United Kingdom the applicant became a prominent member of the British Sikh community and was charged with a number of offences relating to those activities. Although his convictions were quashed by the Court of Appeal, the Home Secretary believed that he was involved in a number of acts of intimidation and terrorism and decided to deport the applicant on the grounds that his presence was not conducive to the public good. With regard to Article 3, the Court held that despite assurances given by the Indian

---

[75] (1989) 11 EHRR 439.

[76] It should be noted that the Court considered it relevant to its finding that the United Kingdom had an alternative: to extradite the applicant to Germany so as to face trial there, without the possibility of the death penalty.

[77] (2005) 70 EHRR 7. See also *GB v Bulgaria*, decision of the European Court, 11 April 2004.

[78] (1996) 23 EHRR 413. Contrast the decision in *Singh v United Kingdom* (Application No 30034/96), admissibility decision of the European Court of Human Rights, 26 September 2000, where the applicants had not established that they were at risk of ill-treatment threatening their lives if deported to India.

government to the British government that the applicant would have no reason to expect to suffer mistreatment of any kind at the hands of the Indian authorities, the evidence, including continued international allegations of ongoing abuse and the fact that the applicant's high profile would make him a target for such mistreatment, was sufficient to lead to the conclusion that his deportation, if allowed, would lead to a violation of Article 3.[79]

The fact that the receiving state has provided assurances that individuals will not be ill-treated is often a relevant and decisive fact in determining whether there is a real risk of a violation of Article 3. However, as seen in *Chahal* (above) that assurance can be rebutted on the evidence and the reviewing court may dismiss the assurances. Guidance in this area has been provided in *RB (Algeria) v Secretary of State for the Home Department* and *Othman (Jordan) v Secretary of State for the Home Department*,[80] where the House of Lords stated that there was no principle that assurances given by third countries must eliminate *all* risk of inhuman treatment before they can be relied upon. However, their Lordships stressed that such assurances should be treated with scepticism where given by a country where inhuman treatment by state agents was endemic.

Generally, the Court must be satisfied that the facts reveal a real risk of ill-treatment in violation of Article 3.[81] This will involve both the domestic authorities, and then the European Court of Human Rights, in assessing the factual evidence and claims of both parties.[82] Thus, in *Hilal v United Kingdom*[83] the European Court found a violation of Article 3 when the applicant, a Tanzanian national who had been subjected to serious ill-treatment in his home country, was refused asylum. The Court found that there was still evidence of active persecution of members of that party and that this, together with the poor human rights record of the country, and the fact that prison conditions remained harsh and life threatening, indicated that the applicant would face a serious risk of being subjected to torture or inhuman and degrading treatment.[84]

The Court is, however, often willing to show a good deal of deference to the domestic authorities in balancing the Convention rights of such applicants with the general interests of the community in upholding immigration and asylum policies. For example, in *Vilvarajah v United Kingdom*,[85] the applicants, Sri Lankan Tamils, had entered the United Kingdom and unsuccessfully claimed political asylum because of the civil war in that country. The applicants alleged that they were subjected to ill-treatment on their return and now claim that their return to Sri Lanka exposed them to a real risk of ill-treatment in violation of Article 3. The

---

[79] See also in *Bader v Sweden* (2008) 46 EHRR 13, where the European Court found a violation of Articles 2 and 3 when the applicant faced the death penalty having been found guilty of murder in his absence. The government had not received any assurance from the Syrian authorities that his case would be reopened or that he would not face the death penalty.

[80] [2010] 2 AC 110.

[81] For example, in *R (Wellington) v Secretary of State for the Home Department* [2008] 1 AC 335, it was held that extraditing the claimant to the USA to face a life sentence without remission was not in breach of Article 3 as such a sentence was not necessarily inhuman and degrading.

[82] Under the Human Rights Act 1998, although the domestic courts have to undertake a rigorous scrutiny of the evidence, it is not always necessary that the claimant be present at such an investigation: *MT and Others v Secretary of State for the Home Department,* [2008] 2 WLR 159.

[83] (2001) 33 EHRR 2.

[84] In *R (Gedara) v Home Secretary* [2006] EWHC 1690, it was held that in assessing whether a person was at sufficient risk of ill-treatment in another country it was permissible to take into account the fact that that person was a police officer and thus faced a naturally heightened risk of harm.

[85] (1991) 14 EHRR 248.

European Court held that the general unsettled situation in Sri Lanka at the time of the applicants' deportation did not establish that they were at greater risk than any other young Tamils who were returning there; the applicants had established only a possibility rather than a clear risk of ill-treatment.[86] Although the Court held that it had a duty rigorously to examine the existence of the risk in view of the absolute character of Article 3, there were no distinguishing factors in the case of the applicants so as to enable the Home Secretary to foresee that they would be ill-treated on their return.[87] More recently, in *Nnyanzi v United Kingdom*,[88] the European Court held that there had been no violation of Article 3 when the applicant asserted that her deportation back to Uganda would result in ill-treatment and persecution on grounds of her father's political beliefs. In the Court's view there was insufficient evidence that she would face treatment in breach of Article 3; although her father had been arrested for his political activities and she had been questioned and arrested briefly on one occasion, there was no evidence of ill-treatment and her lack of political activity did not subject her to any enhanced risk.

Where, on the other hand, there are such factors, the Court will take a more protectionist approach. Thus, in *NA v United Kingdom*,[89] it was held that there had been a violation of Articles 2 and 3 when the United Kingdom authorities had threatened to deport the applicant to Sri Lanka after his plea for asylum had been refused. In the Court's assessment, considering the recent increased level of violence and the breakdown in security in Sri Lanka, together with the particular circumstances of the applicant – he had been arrested as a Tamil tiger some years ago – there was a real risk of ill-treatment at the hands of the authorities who were making strenuous efforts to combat the activities of the Tamil tigers. As the authorities had failed to consider these individual factors and thus to realise the risk that the applicant faced of identification and subsequent ill-treatment, there had been a violation of the Convention. Similarly, in *N v Finland*[90] the European Court held that there had been a violation of Article 3 when the state intended to deport the applicant back to the DRC (formerly Zaire). The applicant had left the country seven years earlier and feared persecution because he had been an informant for the former president. Despite the lapse of time and improved situation in the country there was still a real risk of recrimination, bearing in mind his particular involvement with the former government.[91] Controversially, however, the domestic courts have held that the fact that an ex-criminal and police informant subject to extradition would be in danger once at liberty and released from prison was not a matter that would engage Articles 2 or 3 or the decision to deport. In such a case the person had chosen to associate with violent criminals who may, naturally, wish to exact their revenge.[92]

---

[86] In *Sultani v France* (Application No 45223/05), decision of the European Court of Human Rights, 20 September 2007, the Court concluded that the applicant, if deported, was in no greater danger than anyone else in Afghanistan, where it was accepted that there was widespread violence. Such a finding did not mean that deportation would be contrary to Article 3.

[87] Similarly, in *Launder v United Kingdom* [1998] EHRLR 337, the European Commission held that the applicant did not face a real risk of being subjected to treatment in violation of Article 3 by being returned to Hong Kong at a time when China was to take over the Crown Colony.

[88] (2008) 47 EHRR 18.

[89] (2009) 48 EHRR 15.

[90] (2006) 43 EHRR 12.

[91] See also *SH v United Kingdom* (Application No 19956/06), where the applicant had close ties with a previous human rights activist who had sought asylum in the United Kingdom.

[92] *Radziszewski v Poland* [2010] EWHC 601.

An exception to *Soering* in the context of terrorism?

In *Chahal* (above) the European Court stressed that the prohibition under Article 3 against ill-treatment is absolute and that once substantial grounds have been shown for believing that an individual would face a real risk of being subjected to a violation of Article 3, the activities of the person, however undesirable, cannot be a material consideration. Nevertheless, the Court will consider the importance of upholding extradition agreements and diplomatic relations between the states when determining the extent of the risk to the individual. Thus, in *Cahuas* v *Spain*,[93] the European Court found that there had been no violation of Article 3 when the applicant had been deported to Peru to face terrorist charges. Spain had received assurances that he would not face the death penalty or a life sentence, and Peru was party to international human rights treaties.[94]

More controversially, the European Court has been asked to consider relaxing the absolute character of Article 3 and the judgment in *Chahal* where the individual is suspected of terrorism and the deportation or extradition is said to be necessary for national security. In *A* v *Netherlands* and *Ramzy* v *The Netherlands*,[95] the applicants, who were arrested on suspicion of committing a variety of terrorist offences, complained that their removal to their home countries would expose them to a real risk of torture. The defendant states, together with four intervening states including the United Kingdom, argued that such removals do not violate Article 3 when it is strictly necessary to secure national security and is in the interests of the state's execution of their international relations. In a unanimous decision the Court reiterated the absolute prohibition of torture under Article 3 and stated that it was not possible to weigh the risk of ill-treatment against the reasons put forward for the expulsion in order to determine whether the state's responsibility was engaged under the article. Specifically, the Court stressed that the existence of domestic laws and accession to international human rights treaties by states who were not a party to the European Convention could not by itself ensure adequate protection from ill-treatment; particularly as reliable sources had reported practices which were contrary to the Convention and actively tolerated and pursued by the authorities.[96]

This decision follows the approach in the Court's earlier judgment in *Saadi* v *Italy*,[97] where it was suggested that there would be no compromise of Article 3 and the test of assessing risk in such cases. In that case it was held that there would be a violation of Article 3 if the applicant, who was suspected of international terrorism and had been found guilty of such in Tunisia in his absence, was deported by Italy to Tunisia as part of 'urgent measures to combat international terrorism'. The Court found that there was a real risk of the applicant being subjected to ill-treatment in breach of Article 3, and that the considerable difficulties facing states with respect to terrorist violence did not call into question the absolute nature of Article 3. Thus, it was not possible to weigh the risk that a person might be subjected to ill-treatment against his dangerousness to the community if he was not sent back. Further, the argument that the risk had to be established by solid evidence where the individual

---

[93] (2009) 48 EHRR 24.

[94] The Court also held that the failure to comply with the European Court's interim measure (not to deport) did not create a violation of Article 3 even though it was in breach of Article 34.

[95] Application No 25424/05.

[96] The application in *Ramzy* was struck out as the Court and his lawyers could not locate him.

[97] (2009) 49 EHRR 30.

was a threat to national security was not consistent with Article 3 and its absolute nature. The test was whether there were substantial grounds for believing that there was a real risk and in this case there was strong evidence that those found guilty of terrorist offences had been subjected to torture and that the authorities had failed to investigate relevant allegations of such.[98]

On the other hand, whether in or outside the context of terrorism, the courts have been prepared to take into consideration the policies of extradition and punishment in deciding whether on the facts the necessary threshold required for a finding of inhuman or degrading treatment has been crossed. For example, in R (Wellington) v Secretary of State for the Home Department[99] the House of Lords held that the test of what constituted inhuman and degrading treatment under Article 3 depended on whether the treatment was to take place in the United Kingdom or another jurisdiction in the receiving country. In the latter case, Article 3 only applied in an attenuated form and reliance on it would require a very strong case. The House of Lords held that a relativist approach was essential if extradition was to continue to function, and in the extradition context Article 3 was to be treated as applicable only in a way that took account of the desirability of the arrangements for extradition. Similarly, in R (Bary and Others) v Secretary for the Home Department[100] it was held that there was no violation of Article 3 when the claimants had been extradited to the United States to face charges of terrorism, because the administrative measures applicable in the United States, together with the tough prison conditions in super maximum security prisons, did not cross the necessary threshold. It was also noted that there were sufficient protective measures available to the claimants under US law to safeguard them against abuse. These cases, although decided outside the context of terrorism, would be relevant in determining the acceptability of prison and other conditions awaiting terrorist suspects in the receiving country, but do not apply where there is a real risk of torture or other forms of ill-treatment outside lawful detention.

Deportation and inadequate medical care

A novel application of the Soering principle was evident in the case of D v United Kingdom.[101] In this case D, a citizen of St Kitts in the West Indies, had entered the United Kingdom illegally and had been charged with the importation of drugs. He was sentenced to six years' imprisonment and during his sentence he contracted AIDS. On his release he was ordered by the Home Secretary to be returned to his home country of St Kitts and claimed that because of the lack of medical and other care facilities in that country, he would face intolerable conditions in violation of Article 3. It was held that the principle in Soering could be extended to cover a case such as the present where the intolerable conditions that awaited the applicant were not the fault of the receiving state. The Court concluded that given the applicant's current condition and the inadequate medical facilities in that country, his removal by the United

---

[98] In AS (Libya) v Secretary of State for the Home Department, The Times, 16 April 2008; [2008] HRLR 28, the Court of Appeal upheld the Appeals Commission's findings that the deportation of two suspected terrorists to Libya would have been in breach of Article 3. The correct test was whether there were substantial grounds for believing that they would face a risk of suffering contrary to Article 3; and that meant no more than there must be a proper evidential basis for concluding that there was such a risk.

[99] [2009] 1 AC 335.

[100] The Times, 14 October 2009.

[101] (1997) 24 EHRR 423.

Kingdom to a country where he would face the risk of dying in the most distressing circumstances amounted to the subjection of the applicant to inhuman treatment.[102]

However, in N v Secretary of State for the Home Department[103] the House of Lords held that the deportation of an asylum-seeking Ugandan citizen suffering from AIDS/HIV to Uganda was not in breach of Article 3 even though access to medical treatment and facilities was problematic. The House of Lords held that exceptional circumstances were required to apply the decision in D v United Kingdom and thus prevent removal. The test was whether the applicant's medical condition had reached such a critical state that there were compelling humanitarian grounds for not removing him to a place which lacked the medical and social services which he would need to prevent acute suffering. Article 3 could not be interpreted so as to require contracting states to admit and treat AIDS sufferers from all over the world for the rest of their lives or to oblige contracting states to give an extended right to remain to would-be immigrants who had received medical treatment while their asylum applications were being considered.[104]

The case has now been considered by the Grand Chamber of the European Court of Human Rights,[105] and agreeing with the decision in N v Secretary of State for the Home Department (above) it was confirmed that the principle in D v United Kingdom was only to be applied in very exceptional circumstances where the humanitarian grounds against removal were compelling. The fact that the applicant's circumstances, including her life expectancy, would be significantly reduced if she were to be removed was not sufficient in itself to give rise to a breach of Article 3. Article 3 did not place an obligation on the contracting state to alleviate such disparities through the provision of free and unlimited health care to all aliens without a right to stay within its jurisdiction.[106] The case was distinguished, however, in JA (Ivory Coast) v Secretary of State for Home Department,[107] where the Court of Appeal held that the rule in N did not apply to foreign nationals who had lawfully entered the country, diagnosed as HIV positive and consequently given leave to remain so that they could receive medical treatment. In such a case whether there would be a breach of the Convention was to be determined by asking whether their removal would be proportionate. The principle in D also applies to cases involving mental illness which risk suicide, and in such cases what is required is a very exceptional case where the humanitarian grounds against removal were compelling.[108]

---

[102] The Court stressed that the decision was based on the very exceptional facts of the case and that it should not be taken to mean that persons who are imprisoned in another country are entitled to remain there on their release so as to take advantage of medical or other assistance. The case was distinguished by the European Court in Bensaid v United Kingdom (2001) 33 EHRR 10, where the European Court was satisfied that the applicant, an Algerian citizen undergoing treatment for schizophrenia, would be able to avail himself of reasonable medical facilities in his home country.

[103] [2005] 2 AC 296.

[104] See Palmer, AIDS, expulsion and Article 3 of the ECHR [2005] EHRLR 533). See also ZT v Home Secretary [2005] EWCA Civ 1421.

[105] N v United Kingdom (2008) 47 EHRR 39.

[106] See, however, RS (Zimbawe) v Secretary of State for the Home Department [2008] EWCA Civ 839, where it was held that the Immigration and Asylum Appeal Tribunal could and should adopt a broader approach to the relevant 'humanitarian considerations' which pertained to the applicant and her possible return to Zimbabwe. It was relevant and necessary therefore to consider the political instability in Zimbabwe as well as health considerations in deciding whether a breach of Article 3 would have occurred.

[107] The Times, 2 February 2010.

[108] RA (Sri Lanka) v Secretary of State for the Home Department [2008] EWCA Civ 1210. See also R (Tozlukaya) v Secretary of State for the Home Department [2006] EWCA Civ 379, where the Court of Appeal held that the Home Secretary had not erred in refusing a claim for asylum simply because one of the applicants was in greater danger of committing suicide if she were deported from the United Kingdom to Germany. There were safeguards to reduce that risk during deportation, and when she arrived in Germany.

> **Questions**
>
> How has Article 3 been employed to protect those who are subject to deportation or extradition? Why is this area so controversial and do you believe that the position should be modified in the context of the fight against terrorism?

Provision of basic needs and Article 3

Although the basic human needs of food, clothing and shelter relate to economic and social rights, and are thus beyond such treaties such as the European Convention on Human Rights (and thus the remit of the Human Rights Act), a state's failure to provide those needs might engage Article 3 of the European Convention. In other words, such omissions, or the provision of inadequate resources, may constitute inhuman and degrading treatment.

This aspect of the state's obligations under Article 3 has been the subject of a good deal of litigation with respect to the refusal to provide support to asylum seekers who do not apply for such assistance within the relevant statutory requirements. In *R (Q and Others) v Secretary of State for the Home Department*[109] the Court of Appeal held that the refusal of support for asylum seekers under s.55 of the Nationality, Immigration and Asylum Act 2002 would not amount to a breach of Article 3 (or 8) simply because the claimants could prove that there was a real risk that he would be left destitute and thus subjected to inhuman or degrading treatment. In the Court of Appeal's view it was not unlawful for the Secretary to decline to provide support unless and until it was clear that charitable support had not been provided and that the individual was not capable of fending for himself. Further it would need to be shown that the applicant's circumstances would pass the degree of severity described in the case law of the European Court.[110]

In *R (Limbuela) v Secretary of State for the Home Department*,[111] the House of Lords held that as soon as an asylum seeker made it clear that there was an imminent prospect of a violation of Article 3 because the conditions that he was having to endure were on the verge of reaching the necessary degree of severity, the Secretary of State had the power under the Immigration and Asylum Act 1999, and a duty under the Human Rights Act 1998, to avoid that situation. The act of withdrawing support from a person who would otherwise become destitute was intentionally inflicted and one for which the Secretary became responsible. Their Lordships held that withdrawal of support would not necessarily violate Article 3 but it would do so once the margin was crossed between destitution and inhuman and degrading treatment. Ill-treatment had to maintain a minimum level of severity and had to have a seriously detrimental effect and deny the most basic needs of any human being. The test was whether the treatment the person was subjected to by the entire package of restrictions and deprivations could properly be described as inhuman or degrading. The threshold might be crossed if a person with no means of support was by the deliberate act of the state denied shelter, food or the most basic necessities of life. More recently, the domestic courts have confirmed that Article 3 did not prescribe a minimum standard of social support for those in need and that the state was not required to provide a home or minimum level of financial assistance to those within its care.[112]

---

[109] [2004] QB 36.

[110] See *Pretty v United Kingdom*, discussed above.

[111] [2006] 1 AC 396.

[112] *R (EW) v Secretary of State for the Home Departments* [2009] EWHC 2957 (Admin). On the facts it was not a violation of Article 3 for the UK to transfer the applicant to Italy where he claimed he would face humiliation and destitution. There was no evidence that those conditions crossed the threshold required by Article 3.

Article 3 and those in detention

Article 3 of the Convention has been used in a variety of circumstances by prisoners and other detainees. First, it has been pleaded in relation to the deportation or extradition of persons who claimed that they would be subjected to torture or other ill-treatment in detention on their return to a particular country. For example, in *Batayav* v *Secretary of State for the Home Department*,[113] the Court of Appeal took into account the European Court's judgment in *Kalashnikov* v *Russia*[114] to support the appellant's argument that he faced a real risk of being subjected to prison conditions that were in violation of Article 3 if he was returned to a Russian prison from which he had escaped.[115] Secondly, Article 3 has been used by prisoners in relation to deliberate ill-treatment meted out by prison officers or other state officials. Cases against the United Kingdom are rare in this area, but in *Ireland* v *United Kingdom*[116] the European Court held that the subjection of detainees to 'the five techniques' of interrogation in army barracks in Northern Ireland, while not constituting torture, did amount to inhuman and degrading treatment and punishment. In this respect the deliberate use of unlawful force used by a state official against a detainee will undoubtedly be regarded as a violation of Article 3.[117]

Thirdly, Article 3 can be used to challenge the compatibility of prison conditions, including medical treatment and care, with human rights standards. Initially the European Commission of Human Rights took a cautious approach in this area, reserving findings of violations for cases of deliberate ill-treatment and refusing to rule on the compatibility of prison conditions with Article 3.[118] Subsequently, however, the European Court began to take a more positive approach and have ruled certain prison conditions to be in violation of Article 3.[119] The Court has taken a particularly robust approach with respect to the standards of medical treatment afforded to vulnerable prisoners in detention. For example, in *Keenan* v *United Kingdom*,[120] the European Court held that there had been a violation of Article 3 when there had been a lack of effective monitoring and a lack of informed psychiatric input into the assessment and treatment of a prisoner who was a known suicide risk.[121] Further, in *McGlinchey* v *United Kingdom*,[122] the European Court held that there had been a violation of Article 3 of the Convention when an inmate had died in prison after receiving inadequate medical care to deal with her symptoms of withdrawal from heroin.[123]

---

[113] [2003] EWCA Civ 1489. The Court of Appeal subsequently decided that there was no such risk: [2005] EWCA Civ 366.

[114] (2003) 36 EHRR 587.

[115] Contrast *Sorokins* v *Latvia* [2010] EWHC 1962 (Admin), where the Court assumed that the Latvian government would abide by its obligations under Article 3 with respect to prison conditions.

[116] (1978) 2 EHRR 25.

[117] *Ribitsch* v *Austria* (1996) 21 EHRR 573.

[118] See Gardner and Wickremasinghe, England and Wales and the European Convention, in Dickson (ed.), *Human Rights and The European Convention* (Sweet & Maxwell 1997), chapter 3, pages 49–63. See also *Reed* v *United Kingdom* (1979) 19 DR 113.

[119] See below, at pages 248–9.

[120] (2001) 33 EHRR 38.

[121] Contrast the decision of the European Court in *Aerts* v *Belgium* (2000) 29 EHRR 50, where the European Court held that while the conditions of the applicant's detention in a psychiatric wing of a prison were unsatisfactory and not conducive to his effective treatment, there was no proof of any deterioration of the applicant's mental health.

[122] (2003) 37 EHRR 41.

[123] See also *Price* v *United Kingdom* (2002) 34 EHRR 53, where the European Court held that there had been a violation of Article 3 when a disabled female prisoner complained that she had to endure a number of physical and medical difficulties while in detention.

In judging the compatibility of conditions and care, although the Court may be sympathetic to the social and economic resources of the member state, it can still find that state in violation of Article 3 if the conditions do not meet the standards laid down in the Convention.[124] However, the Court has stressed that the conditions or treatment must go beyond the normal harshness associated with imprisonmenghe, and in this respect it has been unwilling to lay down specific standards with respect to the detention and treatment of elderly or infirm prisoners,[125] unless it is satisfied that such prisoners cannot be properly cared for while in prison.[126] Equally, the Court is prepared to consider the dangerousness of the prisoner in assessing the compatibility of prison conditions with Article 3, as well as the public interest that sentences are served in full.[127]

Article 3 and general conditions of imprisonment

Article 3 has also been used in many cases to challenge the compatibility of prison conditions with human rights standards.[128] For many years the European Commission of Human Rights took a cautious approach in this area.[129] Thus, in *Reed* v *United Kingdom*[130] the European Commission declared inadmissible the prisoner's complaint that three months in solitary confinement amounted to a breach of Article 3, even though it accepted that his cell was infested with cockroaches and that the prison was seriously dilapidated and without adequate super-vision. Similarly, in *B* v *United Kingdom*,[131] the Commission, after conducting an on-the-spot investigation of conditions at Broadmoor, held that although the conditions at the institution were unsatisfactory, they did not constitute a violation of Article 3. In that case the applicant had been detained at Broadmoor for three and a half years at a time when there was evidence of serious overcrowding and poor facilities. Although critical of some of the aspects of the prisoner's detention, the Commission accepted the evidence of the prison psychiatric staff and held that the applicant's treatment did not amount to inhuman or degrading treatment.[132] The European Court had also held that it was permissible to consider the dangerousness of the prisoner and thus issues of public and prison safety in determining whether the conditions were contrary to Article 3.[133]

---

[124] See *Poltorastskiy and Others* v *Ukraine*, decision of the European Court, 29 April 2003, where the Court took into account the Ukraine's socio-economic problems, but held that a lack of resources could not in principle justify prison conditions so poor as to constitute inhuman or degrading treatment.

[125] See, for example, *Papon* v *France* (2004) 39 EHRR 10.

[126] See *Mouisel* v *France* (2004) 38 EHRR 34, where the Court held that the failure to release a seriously ill prisoner from prison amounted to a violation of Article 3 of the Convention. The Court also found a violation in respect of his shackling while travelling to and from prison and during chemotherapy treatment.

[127] *Sanchez* v *France* (2006) 43 EHRR 54; contrast *Henaf* v *France* (2005) 40 EHRR 44.

[128] For an overview of Article 3 as it relates to prisoners and prison conditions, see Cooper, *Cruelty – An Analysis of Article 3* (Sweet & Maxwell 2003), chapters 3 and 4. See also Yokoi, Grading Scale of Degradation: Identifying the Threshold of Degrading Treatment or Punishment under Article 3 ECHR (2003) Netherlands Human Rights Quarterly 385. See also Foster, Prison Conditions, Human Rights and Article 3 ECHR [2005] PL 33. For a view from the Chief Inspector of Prisons, see Owers, Prison Inspection and the Protection of Human Rights [2004] EHRLR 107.

[129] See Gardner and Wickremasinghe, England and Wales and the European Convention, in Dickson (ed.), *Human Rights and The European Convention* (Sweet & Maxwell 1997), chapter 3, pages 49–63.

[130] (1979) 19 DR 113. His complaints regarding physical ill-treatment at the hands of prison officers was accepted by the Commission and a friendly settlement was effected.

[131] (1978) 10 DR 37.

[132] See also the cases of *Hilton* v *United Kingdom* (1981) 3 EHRR 104; *T* v *United Kingdom* (28 DR 5); *McFeeley* v *United Kingdom* (1981) 3 EHRR 161.

[133] *Krocher and Moller* v *Switzerland* (1982) 34 DR 24.

The courts must be satisfied that the applicant's treatment goes beyond the inevitable harshness associated with incarceration. For example, in *Radziszewski v Poland*[134] it was held that there was no violation of Articles 2 and 3 when a person being returned to prison would serve his sentence with undesirable persons such as rapists and paedophiles in a vulnerable prisoners unit. There was no evidence that the authorities would not place him securely in the prison to accommodate the fact that he was a police informant. In contrast, in *Rodic v Bosnia*,[135] there was a breach of Article 3 when a vulnerable prisoner found guilty of war crimes had been kept in the same cell as other prisoners and was persecuted and beaten by fellow prisoners.

The courts will also consider the dangerousness of the prisoner in assessing the compatibility of prison conditions with Article 3, as well as the public interest that sentences are served in full. Thus, in *Sanchez v France*[136] it was held that there had been no violation of Article 3 when a prisoner (Carlos 'The Jackal') had been segregated in prison for over eight years. The majority of the Court held that he had not been subject to social isolation as he had had visits from lawyers, access to television and newspapers and time outside his cell. The majority felt that the hardship of segregation had not crossed the threshold necessary for a finding of a violation under Article 3, while the minority of the Court found that the treatment was contrary to basic minimum standards of human dignity and posed threats to his future mental health. In particular the Grand Chamber noted that the prisoner was very dangerous and had shown no remorse for his crimes.[137] The domestic courts have shown a similar deference and in *R (Bary and Others) v Secretary of State for Justice*[138] there had been no violation of Articles 3 and 8 when a number of detainees awaiting deportation for suspected terrorism were transferred to a special unit where they had limited contact with other prisoners and family visits. There was sufficient evidence, albeit based on professional judgment rather than hard evidence of specific intelligence, that one of the detainees might plan or incite a terrorist attack from within prison and would inspire and radicalise young Muslim prisoners. The governor had a wide discretion to deal with that risk and it was not irrational to subject the other suspected terrorist detainees to the same regime as there was a danger that they would indoctrinate other prisoners at the request of the other detainee. Neither had there been a violation of Article 3: the new regime was not introduced as a punishment or with an intention to humiliate and there was insufficient evidence that the detainees' mental health had been affected by the regime.[139]

The courts can also consider issues of good order and discipline in deciding whether a practice amounts to a breach of Article 3. Thus, in *R v Secretary of State for the Home Department, ex parte Carroll and Al-Hasan*,[140] where two prisoners who had been required to squat for the purposes of a strip search complained of a violation of Article 3, although it was accepted that the search involved an affront to dignity, it was held that the practice was

---

[134] [2010] EWHC 601.

[135] Decision of the European Court, 27 May 2008.

[136] (2006) 43 EHRR 54.

[137] It also noted that he had some contact with lawyers and medical staff and had not been denied family visits; consequently, this mitigated the harshness of the regime.

[138] [2010] EWHC 587 (Admin).

[139] But note the admissibility decision of the European Court in *Ahmad and Others v United Kingdom* (Application Nos 24027/07, 11949/08 and 36742/08), discussed below at pages 259–61.

[140] [2002] 1 WLR 545.

proportionate to the needs of security and thus not in violation of the Convention.[141] The Court of Appeal was satisfied that the prison regulations ensured that the search was only carried out when the authorities had reasonable grounds to believe that the prisoner was concealing items in his genital or anal area.[142] Further, the Prison Rules ensured that such searches were carried out in as seemly a manner as possible.[143] So too in *R (AN) v Secretary of State for Justice*[144] it was held that there had been no violation of Article 3 when a Syrian national imprisoned for breaching a control order had been placed in a single cell to isolate him from other prisoners who the authorities feared he might convert to radicalism. The conditions were not akin to solitary confinement, were imposed for sound security reasons, and clearly fell short of the threshold under Article 3 as there was no evidence of any adverse effect on his private life.

On the other hand, arbitrary treatment and punishment is likely to be in violation of Article 3. For example, in *Yankov v Bulgaria*[145] the European Court held that there had been a violation of Article 3 when a 55-year-old prisoner had had his head shaved and been placed in solitary confinement for publishing defamatory remarks about prison wardens and other state officials. The Court held that the act of forced shaving might have the effect of diminishing a prisoner's human dignity and of arousing feelings of inferiority capable of humiliating the prisoner. The applicant's age and the fact that he appeared in public nine days after his head had been shaved were also regarded as relevant factors. So too, punishments and restraint will be in breach of Article 3 if they do not fulfil a legitimate purpose or are otherwise arbitrary. Thus, in *R (C) v Secretary of State for Justice*,[146] it was held that the Secure Training Centre Amendment Rules 2007 – allowing restraints to be used on children in detention to secure good order and discipline – were invalid and in conflict with Article 3 because the Secretary of State had failed to show the necessity to extend the power to use restraints in order to secure general good order and discipline.[147]

Despite an initial reluctance to intervene, and following the European Court judgment in *Selmouni v France*,[148] the European Court has begun to take a more positive approach and has ruled certain prison conditions to be in violation of Article 3. In that case the European Court held that the severe beating of the prisoner by police officers in his cell constituted torture within Article 3. The Court also held that some treatment, which was formerly not regarded as severe enough to constitute torture, might in the present day be regarded as such. This gave rise to an expectation that the court might lower its threshold with regard to the concepts of inhuman and degrading treatment and lead it to take a more proactive approach to matters such as poor prison conditions.

---

[141] The European Court of Human Rights has held that such searches are not in violation of Article 3 where they are necessary to ensure prison security or prevent disorder or crime and are conducted in a proper manner showing clear respect for the prisoner. See *Valasinas v Lithuania*, decision of European Court of Human Rights, 24 July 2001. Such procedures must not, however, be arbitrary: see *Frerot v France* (Application No 70204/01), decision of the European Court, 12 June 2007.

[142] Even if the searches are carried out in an appropriate way, the policy must not be discriminatory or applied in an excessive or arbitrary manner: *Frerot v France*, n 141, above.

[143] The Court of Appeal held that there was no duty to give reasons for the search to the prisoner before the procedure was carried out. Such a duty, in the Court's opinion, would be impracticable, although it recognised that in certain circumstances it would be desirable to give reasons.

[144] [2009] EWHC 1921 (Admin).

[145] (2005) 40 EHRR 36.

[146] [2009] 2 WLR 1039.

[147] The Rules were also invalid because the Secretary had failed to conduct a proper race equality impact assessment. See also *R (Pounder) v HM Coroner for Durham and Darlington* [2009] EWHC 76 (Admin).

[148] (1999) 29 EHRR 403.

There is now evidence that the European Court is willing to challenge general prison conditions within the standards of Article 3. For example, in *Peers* v *Greece*,[149] the applicant, a British national, had been arrested on drug related charges, and complained about the conditions of his incarceration as a remand prisoner in a Greek prison. He complained that he had been detained, alongside one other detainee, in a cramped cell which had little natural light and no ventilation, and which had an open toilet, which often failed to work. He also complained that he had been provided with no access to vocational courses or activities or a library. The European Court held that although there had been no evidence of a positive intention to humiliate or debase the applicant, the fact that the state authorities had taken no steps to improve the objectively unacceptable conditions of the applicant's detention denoted a lack of respect for the applicant. Taking into account the fact that, for at least two months, he had to spend a considerable part of each day practically confined to his bed in a cell with no ventilation and no window, and had to use the toilet in the presence of another inmate (and be present while the toilet was being used by his cellmate), the Court was of the opinion that the conditions gave him feelings of anguish and inferiority capable of humiliating and debasing him. The Court thus found that the conditions amounted to degrading treatment within Article 3. Similarly, in *Dougoz* v *Greece*[150] the European Court found that the detention of the applicant in an overcrowded cell with inadequate sanitation and insufficient beds where he was deprived of fresh air, daylight, hot water and exercise, constituted degrading treatment and thus a violation of Article 3. In coming to that conclusion, the Court noted that the European Committee for the Prevention of Torture had corroborated the applicant's allegations.[151] Rather than outlawing particular practices, the European Court's approach seems to be based on the cumulative effect of the conditions and the impact they have on the particular prisoner.[152]

Although the Court may be sympathetic to the social and economic resources of the member state and thus its prison conditions, it can still find that state in violation of Article 3 if the conditions do not meet the standards laid down in the Convention. Thus, in *Poltorastskiy and Others* v *Ukraine*[153] it was held that there had been a violation of Article 3 with regard to the conditions of detention suffered by a number of death row prisoners: at one point the prisoners had been locked up for 24 hours in a room with no natural light and that there had been little or no provision for activities or human contact. The Court took into account the Ukraine's socio-economic problems, but held that a lack of resources could not, in principle, justify prison conditions so poor as to constitute inhuman or degrading treatment.[154]

With the passing of the Human Rights Act domestic prisoners have begun to challenge a number of prison rules and practices on the basis that they subjected prisoners to inhuman or degrading treatment or punishment and thus constituted a violation of Article 3. Article 3 might also be used to strengthen prisoners' civil actions. For example, in *Russell, McNamee*

---

[149] Decision of the European Court, 19 April 2001.

[150] 10 BHRC 306.

[151] In the past the European Commission had treated the Committee's findings with caution, noting that its findings and recommendations were not of a judicial nature: see *Delzarus* v *United Kingdom* (Application No 17525/90).

[152] *Kalashnikov* v *Russia* (2003) 36 EHRR 33. See *Gultyayeva* v *Russia* (Application No 67413/01), where the cumulative effect of the conditions of her cell and the effect on her health of being exposed to cigarette smoke for two months was sufficient to find a breach of Article 3.

[153] Decision of the European Court, 29 April 2003.

[154] See also *Gusev* v *Russia*, 15 May 2008, where the Court stated that the member state must organise its prisons in such a way so as to secure respect for the dignity of the detainee regardless of financial or logistical difficulties.

and McCotter v *Home Office*,[155] the High Court, in granting damages in an action for assault, noted that the injuries caused to the prisoners by the assaults of the prison officers were sufficiently serious to constitute a violation of Article 3 of the Convention.[156]

In addition, there is some evidence that the domestic courts are prepared to use the European Court's jurisprudence with respect to challenges to conditions of imprisonment in the United Kingdom. This is highlighted by our next case study, which details the decision in *Napier* v *Scottish Ministers*,[157] a case in which a remand prisoner who suffered from eczema complained that his shared living space and sanitary conditions were inadequate.

CASE STUDY

Napier v *Scottish Ministers*, *The Times*, 13 May 2004

This case has been chosen to illustrate the issues that arise when the courts are requested to judge the compatibility of prison conditions with international human rights standards. The case is the most high profile of the domestic decisions in this area and caused much legal debate surrounding the court's approach as well as political controversy with respect to the question of whether the government should fund the resulting compensation claims.

The facts

A remand prisoner detained at Barlinnie Prison complained that his shared living space was inadequate in terms of light, ventilation and space. He also complained of inadequate sanitary conditions, which involved 'slopping out', and that he was confined to his cell for excessive periods, further relying on a medical report that stated that his eczema condition was unlikely to improve whilst held in such conditions. The prisoner sought an interim order transferring him to another jail pending full trial. Granting the order, the court noted that the respondents had conceded that he had established a *prima facie* case that the conditions were in violation of Article 3 of the European Convention and that the balance of convenience favoured the granting of the order. The court thus ordered that he be transferred to conditions of detention that complied with Article 3 (*The Times*, 15 November 2001).

The decision of the Outer Session

At a subsequent hearing, the Outer Session held that the subjection of the applicant to the conditions existing in that prison at that time, and in particular to the practice of 'slopping out', constituted inhuman and degrading treatment within Article 3 of the European Convention and the prisoner was awarded £2400 in compensation (*The Times*, 14 May 2004).

---

[155] *Daily Telegraph*, 13 March 2001.

[156] The court refused to grant the claimants exemplary damages in this case, stating that it was not essential for the court to award such damages in their role of ensuring that such assaults are punished. Such a decision might give rise to a complaint that the courts have failed to give the prisoners sufficient redress for the violation of their Convention rights, as required under Article 13 of the Convention.

[157] *The Times*, 13 May 2004. See Foster, Prison Conditions, Human Rights and Article 3 ECHR [2005] PL 33; Lawson and Mukherjee, Slopping out in Scotland [2004] EHRLR 645.

In deciding whether the applicant's human rights had been violated, the court did not regard it as necessary to consider the variety of other international instruments relating to conditions of detention, such as the United Nations Standard Minimum Rules and the European Prison Rules. In his Lordship's opinion, Article 3 was expressed in clear and simple terms and recourse to other instruments would not have advanced the prisoner's case.

The Outer House compared the petitioner's claim with a number of cases brought before the European Court of Human Rights (*Yankov* v *Bulgaria* (2003) 15 BHRC 592; *Kalashnikov* v *Russia* (2003) 36 EHRR 34; *Kudla* v *Poland* (2002) 35 EHRR 11; *Valasinas* v *Lithuania* 12 BHRC 266; *Peers* v *Greece* (2001) 33 EHRR 51; *Dougoz* v *Greece* (2002) 34 EHRR 61), and in its view, although the conditions in the present case were plainly not as bad as those established in the case of *Peers* v *Greece*, the complaints in that case included a number of features of the petitioner's detention conditions, and indeed the 'slopping-out' process, which was a significant element of the petitioner's claim, was absent in that case. Having taken into consideration a number of decisions of the European Court and Commission in this area, Lord Bonomy stated:

> . . . to detain a person along with another prisoner in a cramped, gloomy and stuffy cell which is inadequate for the occupation of two people, to confine them there for at least 20 hours on average per day, to deny him overnight access to a toilet throughout the week and for extended periods at the weekend and thus to expose him to both elements of the slopping out process, to provide no structured activity other than daily walking exercise for one hour and one period of recreation lasting an hour and a half in a week, and to confine him to a 'dog box' for two hours or so each time he entered or left the prison was, in Scotland in 2001, capable of attaining the minimum level of severity necessary to constitute degrading treatment and thus to infringe article 3. (at para 75)

His Lordship then considered whether the petitioner was subjected to conditions which reached that level of severity in the light of a consideration of all the circumstances of his detention, having regard to his own personal circumstances. His Lordship, therefore, accepted that a particular prisoner at a prison with those conditions might not be subject to a violation of Article 3 because he or she might not have been subjected to the harshness of those conditions, because, for example, they had not had to make use of a chamber pot, or had in fact had more time out of his cell. In respect of the complaints about 'slopping out', it was noted that although where truly disgusting events occurred only twice in the cell, and to that extent the petitioner's experience was better than that of many other prisoners, the threat that either (he or his cell mate) would be required to defecate in the cell was ever-present because of the uncertainty about whether a request to go to the toilet would be granted. The petitioner's release for 'slopping out' first thing in the morning clearly gave him no sense of relief in view of the disgusting conditions in which it took place, the pervasive stench and the pressure and chaos of the whole exercise. Taking part in the practice made the petitioner feel small and overwhelmed his efforts to maintain his hygiene routine.

His Lordship also felt that the prisoner's eczema condition was of crucial importance to the determination of the case because, first, the condition's resurgence and persistence were caused by the actual conditions of detention, secondly, the very presence of the condition was a source of acute embarrassment and a feeling of humiliation to the prisoner, causing him a degree of mental stress, and thirdly, the fact that the infected eczema was caused by the conditions of his detention, in particular by the practice of 'slopping out'. Having regard to all the factual and expert evidence, his Lordship was thus satisfied that the prisoner had been exposed to conditions of detention which, taken together, were such as to diminish his human dignity and to arouse in him feelings of anxiety, anguish, inferiority and humiliation so as to cause a violation of Article 3 of the Convention.

Questions
1 Why did the Court refuse to consider international treaties and measures other than Article 3 of the European Convention on Human Rights? Do you agree that such an approach is sensible and effective?
2 What factors did the Court take into account in deciding that Article 3 had been violated?
3 Which of those factors could be described as either personal to the particular applicant or of more general application *vis à vis* judging prison conditions?
4 Do you think that the Court regarded the practice of 'slopping out' as inconsistent with Article 3?
5 To what extent was the Court's decision consistent with the case law of the European Court of Human Rights in this area?
6 Do you feel that the domestic courts should be more, or less, robust than the European Court in this area?
7 Do you feel that the award of £2400 compensation constitutes 'just satisfaction' for such a violation?
8 To what extent have the domestic courts developed the principles in this case in judging subsequent prison conditions claims? (Answer this question once you have completed reading this section of the chapter.)

Although *Napier* was decided on its peculiar facts,[158] the decision nevertheless mirrors the more robust approach taken by the European Court in recent years, particularly where the general conditions of detention have a specifically deleterious effect on prisoners with mental or physical disabilities. More generally, however, the courts have been reluctant to find violations of Article 3. Thus, in *R (on the application of BP) v Secretary of State for the Home Department*,[159] when a 17-year-old detainee in a young offender institution with a history of self-harm and attempted suicide sought a declaration that his confinement in a segregation unit was contrary to Articles 3 and 8, it was held that the facilities afforded to him within his cell including the number of visits, the length of time which he was kept there and the penal purpose of the segregation precluded a finding that his treatment was in breach of Article 3. Similarly, in *Broom v Secretary of State for the Home Department*,[160] the court rejected a claim when a prisoner complained that he was subjected to disgusting and unhygienic conditions;

[158] See also *Ostrovar v Moldova* (2007) 44 EHRR 19, where the European Court noted that the authorities had failed in their duty to protect his asthmatic condition from the smoking of other inmates in finding that the conditions as a whole were contrary to Article 3.
[159] [2003] EWHC 1963 (Admin).
[160] [2002] EWHC 2041.

one cell had excrement around the toilet and in another the cupboards were soaked in grease from cooking utensils. He also claimed that as in-cell modesty screens were provided in all other dispersal prisons, not to have them was humiliating because there was no privacy when using the toilet, exacerbated by the fact that female staff were present on the wing. In rejecting the claim it was noted that imprisonment itself is humiliating and the circumstances of the present case were no more than the ordinary incidence of a prison regime. In the present case the degree of suffering was relatively low when set in the overall context of a prison regime and consequently the threshold of degradation that would be required for the claimant to succeed was not evident.[161]

Prisoners with physical and mental disabilities

The detention and treatment of prisoners with physical, mental or other disabilities has excited a good deal of debate with respect to the question of whether such persons should be incarcerated in prison, and the appropriate standards of their treatment in prison. In addition to concerns expressed by the European Committee for the Prevention of Torture, there have been a number of decisions of the European Court in respect to the treatment of such detainees, raising issues of the compatibility of their detention and treatment with Article 3 of the Convention.[162] The Court's approach is to look at each case on its merits, and in *Grori* v *Albania*[163] it was held that although there was no general duty to release prisoners suffering from serious illnesses, there was an obligation to ensure that a prisoner received adequate treatment or medication and that this duty was not excused on grounds of expense.[164]

There is certainly evidence that the Court will take a robust approach where vulnerable prisoners are subjected to the harsh conditions of imprisonment. For example, in *Keenan* v *United Kingdom*,[165] the European Court held that there had been a violation of Article 3 in respect of the manner in which a mentally ill prisoner had been treated while known by the authorities to be a suicide risk. In that case the Court found that the lack of effective monitoring of the prisoner's condition and the lack of informed psychiatric input into his assessment and treatment disclosed significant defects in the medical care provided to a mentally ill person known to be a suicide risk. In addition, the imposition on the prisoner of a serious disciplinary punishment, including the imposition of 28 additional days some nine days before his expected release, might well have threatened his moral and physical resistance and was not compatible with the standard of treatment required in respect of a mentally ill person. In contrast, in *Aerts* v *Begium*[166] the European Court found that there was no violation of Article 3 when a mentally ill prisoner was detained in what the Court conceded were unsatisfactory conditions that were not conducive to his effective treatment. There was no evidence of a

---

[161] See also *R (Mackenzie)* v *Home Secretary* [2006] EWHC 1746 (Admin), where it was held that there had been no violation of Article 3 when a Category A prisoner had been subjected to regular nightly checks, involving opening his cell flap and turning a light on to see that he had not escaped. This did not come anywhere near crossing the threshold required by Article 3, despite the prisoner's physical state – he was suffering from prostate cancer.

[162] See Murdoch, The Impact of the Council of Europe's 'Torture Committee' and the Evolution of Standard-setting in Relation to Places of Detention [2006] EHRLR 159.

[163] Decision of the European Court, 7 July 2009

[164] See also *Akhmetov* v *Russia* (Application No 37463/04), where the refusal to transfer the prisoner to a civilian hospital was held in breach of Article 3.

[165] (2001) 33 EHRR 38.

[166] (2000) 29 EHRR 50. See also *Kudla* v *Poland* (2002) 35 EHRR 11.

deterioration of the applicant's mental health and thus he had not been subjected to inhuman or degrading treatment.[167]

Further, in *Price* v *United Kingdom*,[168] the European Court held that there had been a violation of Article 3 when a disabled female prisoner who had been committed to prison for seven days for contempt of court complained that she had to endure a number of physical and medical difficulties while in prison. The Court held that although there had been no evidence of any positive intention to humiliate the prisoner,[169] the detention of a severely disabled person in conditions where she was dangerously cold, risked developing sores because her bed was too hard or unreachable, and was unable to go to the toilet or to keep clean without the greatest of difficulty, constituted degrading treatment within Article 3. Although limited to its particular facts, the decision in *Price* does indicate that the Court is prepared to use Article 3 to denounce the intolerable treatment of prisoners. At the very least, the case establishes that prison and other authorities are under a positive duty under Article 3 to ensure that prisoners are provided with appropriate facilities and care while in detention.[170] Similarly, in *Vincent* v *France*,[171] the Court found a violation of Article 3 in respect of the treatment of a wheelchair-bound prisoner who had been detained for four months in a prison which had inadequate facilities to deal with his disability. The Court concluded that the applicant had been totally reliant (and therefore vulnerable) on the authorities and had lost the ability to leave his cell or move about the prison independently: a wheel had to be removed from his chair every time he entered or left his cell.[172]

That protectionist approach was evident in *McGlinchey* v *United Kingdom*,[173] which concerned the treatment of a drug addict admitted to prison while suffering from withdrawal from heroin addiction.[174] In this case a female prisoner with a long history of heroin addiction and who was asthmatic, began to suffer heroin withdrawal symptoms immediately following her imprisonment, having frequent vomiting fits and losing much weight. She was seen by

---

[167] See also *Zhu* v *United Kingdom* [2001] EHRLR 231 where it was held that there had been no violation of Article 3 when a Chinese national who had been detained under the Immigration Act 1971 complained that he had been detained in his cell for 19 hours a day, with only one hour of exercise, had received physical and verbal abuse from other prisoners, had suffered significant communication and language difficulties and had suffered mental health problems which led to him attempting suicide. See also *Koniarska* v *United Kingdom* (Application No 33670/96).

[168] (2002) 34 EHRR 53; see Foster, Inhuman and Degrading Prison Conditions (2001) NLJ 1222.

[169] This is not a prerequisite for a finding under Article 3, but can often be a relevant factor. See *Iwanczuk* v *Poland* (2004) 38 EHRR 8, where the Court held that the actions of prison officers in requiring the applicant to strip naked before exercising his right to vote, followed by verbal abuse and the making of humiliating comments regarding his body, constituted a violation of Article 3.

[170] See also the Court's decision in *AB* v *The Netherlands* (2003) 37 EHRR 48, where it was held that the inadequate implementation by state authorities of judicial orders to improve prison facilities and the failure to implement urgent recommendations from the European Committee for the Prevention of Torture, meant that the applicant who had complained about such conditions during his detention had no effective remedy under Article 13 of the Convention.

[171] Decision of the European Court, 24 October 2006.

[172] See also *Riviere* v *France*, decision of the European Court, 11 July 2006, where it was held that there had been a violation of Article 3 when the applicant, a long-term prisoner with a psychiatric disorder, had been detained in normal prison conditions without proper facilities for his disorder. He should have been detained in special conditions irrespective of his offence or perceived dangerousness.

[173] (2003) 37 EHRR 41.

[174] In November 2006 the Home Office was reported to have made out-of-court settlements to six prisoners who were claiming that their forced withdrawal from drugs on imprisonment was contrary to their human rights: *The Times*, 13 November 2006, page 13.

the prison doctor the day after her admission to prison, and the doctor prescribed medication for her condition and gave instructions that her weight be continuously monitored. Later she was admitted to hospital and moved to intensive care where she was heavily sedated and kept on a life-support system until she died some days later. The Court confirmed that the state had a duty to ensure that a person was detained in conditions that were compatible with respect for human dignity, including the duty to make proper provision for the prisoner's health and well-being in the form of requisite medical assistance. The Court found that although the prisoner's condition had been regularly monitored over one period, she had been vomiting repeatedly during that period and had lost a lot of weight. Further, in another period, despite any evidence that her condition had improved, she had not been seen by a doctor for two days while continuing to vomit and lose weight. Subsequently, despite some improvement in her condition, she continued to lose weight and had become dehydrated, which had not only caused her great distress and suffering, but had posed a very serious risk to her health. In conclusion, the prison authorities had failed to comply with their duty to provide her with the requisite medical care and their treatment of her had violated the prohibition against inhuman and degrading treatment contained in Article 3.

The decisions in *Keenan*, *Price* and *McGlinchey* are particularly relevant to the treatment of mentally ill or otherwise vulnerable persons, although the Court placed great reliance on the fact that the authorities were under an obligation to protect the health and safety of persons deprived of their liberty, thus making the decision relevant to prisoners generally and indicating a willingness on the Court's part to rule on the standards of prison conditions.[175]

Elderly and infirm prisoners

The detention of elderly and infirm prisoners may give rise to claims under Article 3 and the case law thus far suggests that the courts will attempt to conduct a pragmatic and proper balance between the functions of the criminal justice system and the human rights of the prisoners. The European Court adopted a 'hands off' approach in *Papon v France*,[176] where the applicant had argued that because of his age and the state of his health his incarceration constituted a violation of Article 3. It was held that although the Court did not exclude the possibility that in certain conditions the detention of an elderly person over a lengthy period might raise an issue under Article 3, in the instant case the applicant's general state of health and his conditions of detention and treatment had not reached the level of severity required to bring it within Article 3. In coming to that conclusion the Court noted that none of the member states had an upper age limit for detention.[177] Similarly, in *Matencio v*

[175] Contrast the decision in *James Bollan, Anne Bollan and Stephanie Bollan v United Kingdom* (Application No 42117/98), where the European Commission declared an application inadmissible when a young prisoner had committed suicide while on remand after being locked in her cell to cool down. The European Court found that the detention of the applicant in those circumstances did not reach the threshold necessary to find a breach of Article 3 of the Convention. See also *Kudla v Poland* (2002) 35 EHRR 11, where the European Court was not satisfied that the suicide attempts of the applicant were related to a lack of medical and psychiatric care.
[176] (2004) 39 EHRR 10.
[177] See also the admissibility decision in *Sawonuik v United Kingdom* (Application No 63716/00), where it was held that the detention of a 79-year-old war criminal was not, *per se*, in violation of Article 3. In *V and T v United Kingdom* (1999) 30 EHRR 121 it was held that the imposition of a life sentence on two 10-year-old boys did not constitute a violation of Article 3. The Court took into account that there was no common European policy on the minimum age for imprisonment. See also *DG v Ireland* (2002) 35 EHRR 33, where it was held that the detention of a 16-year-old with a personality disorder did not, *per se*, constitute inhuman or degrading treatment.

France[178] the Court held that there had been no violation of Article 3 when a prisoner suffered a stroke in prison and claimed that his detention and conditions of detention violated the Convention. In the Court's view he was offered adequate medical assistance and thus the threshold in Article 3 had not been reached.[179]

This approach was followed by the domestic courts in *R (Spink) v Home Secretary*,[180] where it was held that the refusal of the Secretary of State to grant compassionate release to a prisoner serving a life sentence and who had been diagnosed with terminal cancer, and whose life expectancy was estimated at between three and six months, was not in breach of Article 3. The Home Secretary had refused his request because the prisoner represented a real risk of re-offending, and had not satisfied him that there were exceptional circumstances to justify release. The Court of Appeal held that it was important to bear in mind that the claimant was a serving prisoner and that it is in general in the public interest that the allotted sentence is served. Equally, the risk of re-offending was a material factor for the Secretary of State to consider. Distinguishing the present case from the decision of the European Court in *Mouisel v France*, below, it was held that there had been no recommendation to move the claimant to a hospital, and he had, despite his condition, remained reasonably fit and mobile. Further, although he had been handcuffed when in hospital, this was after a suitable assessment had been carried out with respect to the risk of him committing acts of violence.

However, the European Court is more likely to find a violation of Article 3 when such prisoners cannot be guaranteed adequate medical and other care while serving their sentence, or have been subjected to practices which are exacerbated because of their age and health. For example, in *Mouisel v France*[181] the Court held that the failure to release a seriously ill prisoner from prison amounted to a violation of Article 3 of the Convention. In that case the prisoner had contracted leukaemia and complained of the standards of his treatment before his ultimate release. The European Court noted that the prisoner was suffering from permanent asthenia and fatigue, that he was waking up in pain in the night and that there was a psychological impact of stress on his life expectancy. Further, the Court noted that the prison was scarcely equipped to deal with illness, and had failed to transfer him to another institution. Consequently, the Court found that the authorities had failed to take sufficient care of the prisoner's health to ensure that he did not suffer treatment contrary to Article 3.[182]

The Court is also prepared to interfere in cases where the prisoner has been deliberately mistreated and the prisoner's age and state of health have exacerbated that situation. Thus, in

---

[178] Application No 58749/00.

[179] See also *Gelfmann v France* (2006) 42 EHRR 4, where the European Court held that there had been no violation of Article 3 when a prisoner, who had suffered from AIDS for nearly 20 years, 10 years before his incarceration, had had his request for release on medical grounds refused. There was no general obligation to release a prisoner on health grounds or to transfer him to a civilian hospital, even if suffering from an illness that was difficult to treat, provided the prisoner is receiving adequate treatment in prison and his condition was being monitored by an outside hospital.

[180] [2005] EWCA Civ 275.

[181] (2004) 38 EHRR 34.

[182] The Court also took into account the fact that the prisoner had been handcuffed to and from chemotherapy sessions, of which the European Committee for the Prevention of Torture had been very critical. See also *Farbthus v Latvia*, 2 December 2004, where the European Court found a violation of Article 3 when an 84-year-old prisoner suffering from very poor health had been detained in prison and prison hospitals for nearly two years. The Court found that given his very poor and worsening health – he could not stand up and wash, etc. without assistance – his delayed release on medical grounds constituted a violation of Article 3.

Henaf v *France*[183] it was held that there had been a violation of Article 3 when a 75-year-old prisoner had been handcuffed on his way to hospital to undergo an operation and had been chained to the bedpost the night before the operation. Having regard to his health, age and the absence of any previous conduct suggesting that he was a security risk, the restrictions on his movement were disproportionate to any security requirements.[184]

The use of handcuffs for security purposes on prisoners receiving medical treatment also gives rise to issues under Article 3 and in *R (Graham and Allen)* v *Secretary of State for Justice*[185] the High Court had to consider the circumstances in which it was permissible for such restraints to be used. It was held that the use of handcuffs on prisoners who posed an adequately founded risk of escape was not in breach of Article 3 and that such assessment was initially for the prison authorities. In the present case it was not unlawful for the authorities to assess a 73-year-old prisoner serving a life sentence for the murder of his wife and children four years previously as posing a sufficient risk of escape and of harm to the public during his hospital treatment. Further, there were no health reasons why he should not be restrained. However, in that case it held that there had been a violation of Article 3 when a prisoner receiving treatment for Hodgkin's lymphoma while serving a sentence of three years for drug offences had been handcuffed to officers during his medical treatment and placed in hand-cuffs during subsequent visits to receive chemotherapy treatment. The court held that because the prisoner was felt to be a serious risk to the public if he escaped, the initial decision to handcuff the prisoner did not violate Article 3 (although it came perilously close to do doing so). However, when the prison authorities became aware of the full facts of his illness and of the unlikelihood of him escaping, and recommended the removal of the restraints, the subsequent use of handcuffs during further hospital treatment and out-patient visits con-stituted both degrading and inhuman treatment. Notwithstanding this ruling the courts have subsequently upheld decisions to handcuff such prisoners, provided the medical problems are not so extreme as to outweigh any risk issues.[186]

The case law of both the European and domestic courts in this area remains cautious and highly dependent on the individual facts and it is clear that exceptional circumstances need to be present to find a violation of Article 3. For example, in *Sawonuik* v *United Kingdom*,[187] the European Court held that the imprisonment of a 79-year-old war criminal was not, in the absence of other evidence of ill-treatment or exceptional hardship, in violation of Article 3, provided the prisoner was in receipt of appropriate medical care. Further, in *Zhu* v *United Kingdom*[188] the European Court held that there had been no violation of Article 3 when a Chinese national who had been detained under the Immigration Act 1971 complained that he had been detained in his cell for 19 hours a day, with only one hour of exercise, had received

---

[183] (2005) 40 EHRR 44.

[184] The Court also noted that on its visit to France in May 2000 the European Committee for the Prevention of Torture had recommended that the practice of attaching prisoners to hospital beds should be outlawed.

[185] [2007] EWHC 2490 (Admin).

[186] In *R (Faizovas)* v *Secretary of State for Justice, The Times*, 25 May 2009, the Court of Appeal held that there had been no violation of Article 3 when a Category C prisoner had been handcuffed whilst travelling to and from and attending chemotherapy treatment at a hospital. In the court's view he had been correctly assessed as a risk to the public on escape (he was serving a sentence for sexual assault), and in the absence of other factors the issue of security justified the use of restraints. The prisoner's own sense of humiliation was not sufficient to displace that assessment.

[187] Application No 63719/00, declared inadmissible on 29 May 2001.

[188] [2001] EHRLR 231.

physical and verbal abuse from other prisoners, had suffered significant communication and language difficulties and had suffered mental health problems which led him to attempt suicide. Although the Court accepted the majority of the applicant's claims, it noted that no complaints had been made about the conditions themselves, save that too much time was spent in jail, and although there was some evidence of ill-will shown towards him by other prisoners, neither this, nor his detention in a 'ligature free' cell after his suicide attempt, constituted inhuman or degrading treatment.

The provision of food and force-feeding and medical treatment

The prisoner's basic rights to nutrition can give rise to claims under Article 3. This was evident in the pre-Act case of *R* v *Secretary of State for the Home Department, ex parte Russell and Wharrie*,[189] where the court considered whether it was lawful for a governor to reduce the diet of a prisoner as a punishment. In that case the prisoners had refused to wear prison clothes and as a consequence were not allowed to go to the food servery to collect their meals. In response the governor ordered that the prisoners be provided with one meal a day in their cells. The court held that the governor was in breach of his duty under the Prison Rules to provide the prisoners with wholesome and nutritious food. Although the case was decided principally on the interpretation of Rule 24 of the Prison Rules 1999, the court paid full regard to Article 3 and the relevant case law[190] in determining the level of the governor's duties under Rule 24.

The question of force-feeding also gives rise to questions under Article 3. In *X* v *FRG*[191] the European Commission of Human Rights held that force-feeding involves a degrading element which in certain circumstances is in violation of Article 3, and in *Herczegfalvy* v *Austria*[192] the European Court held that the medical necessity for such treatment must be convincingly shown to exist. However, such practices do not appear to be in breach of Article 3 *per se*. For example, in *Naumenko* v *Ukraine*,[193] it was held that there had been no violation of Article 3 when the applicant had been subjected to therapeutic therapy. On the facts, there was insufficient evidence that the applicant had not consented to the treatment, but in any case Article 3 did not prohibit such treatment in appropriate cases and here the applicant was suffering from serious mental disorders.

The issue was considered by the domestic courts in *R* v *Collins, ex parte Brady*,[194] a case decided before the Act came into operation and one concerned with persons detained under mental health legislation. The prisoner had decided to starve himself to death and had been force-fed by the authorities when his health deteriorated. It was held that force-feeding was 'medical treatment' given to him for the mental disorder from which he was suffering as prescribed by s.63 of the Mental Health Act 1983, and thus was lawful provided there was sufficient evidence that the applicant's desire to starve himself was connected with his mental illness. The court accepted expert medical opinion that although the applicant had made a conscious decision to starve himself, his decision was a symptom of his mental illness. Accordingly the authorities were entitled to treat that illness and to force-feed the applicant.

---

[189] [2000] 1 WLR 2027.
[190] *McFeeley* v *United Kingdom* (1981) 3 EHRR 161.
[191] (1985) 7 EHRR 152.
[192] (1992) 15 EHRR 437.
[193] Decision of the European Court, 10 February 2004.
[194] [2000] Lloyd's Rep Med 355. See Foster, Force Feeding, Self-determination and the Right to Die (2000) 150 NLJ 857.

Notwithstanding the decision in *Brady*, the force-feeding, of even a mental health prisoner without very strong medical or other reasons will be contrary to Article 3 of the Convention.[195] This matter was considered in the context of compulsory treatment of mental heath detainees by the Court of Appeal in *R (Wilkinson) v Broadmoor Hospital and Others*.[196] The applicant had sought to challenge his forcible subjection to antipsychotic medication on the grounds that such treatment was contrary to Articles 2, 3, 8 and 14 of the European Convention. In ordering that the relevant medical officers attend court for the purposes of cross-examination, the Court of Appeal held that it was for the court to consider whether the applicant was capable of consenting to the treatment, and whether the treatment would constitute a violation of the applicant's right to life, private life, and the right not to be subjected to inhuman or degrading treatment.[197] Thus, following *Wilkinson*, the courts would need to be satisfied that there were extreme and urgent reasons justifying any such compulsory treatment. The Court of Appeal also opined that if the applicant *did* have the capacity to consent, it would be difficult to suppose that he should be forced to accept it; the impact on his rights to autonomy and bodily inviolability were immense and the prospective benefits of the treatment appeared speculative. Although the courts condoned such a practice in the old case of *Leigh* v *Gladstone*,[198] more recent authority suggested that force-feeding would be unlawful, provided the prisoner remained in control of his mental faculties. Thus, in *Secretary of State for the Home Department* v *Robb*[199] the Court of Appeal made a declaration that the prison authorities had no duty to interfere with a prisoner's decision to go on hunger strike and stated that despite incarceration prisoners retained the basic right of self-determination.[200]

Article 3 and sentencing

Article 3 has also been used to challenge the lawfulness of the mandatory life sentence. In *V and T v United Kingdom*[201] the European Court of Human Rights held that it was possible that a sentence of imprisonment might give rise to circumstances that would constitute a violation of Article 3 of the Convention, although, on the facts, it held that there had been no violation as there were good reasons for imposing a life sentence on young boys found guilty of murder and there was no consensus on the age at which individuals could receive such sentences.

In domestic law, in *R v Lichniak and Pyrah*,[202] the House of Lords held that a mandatory life sentence was not incompatible with Article 3. It had been argued that the automatic imposition of a life sentence, where at the time of the sentence the prisoner posed no possible risk to the public, amounted to inhuman and degrading treatment and punishment

---

[195] In *Nevmerzhitsky* v *Ukraine*, decision of the European Court, 5 April 2005, it was held that the force-feeding of the applicant when the medical necessity of such had not been established constituted torture under Article 3.

[196] [2001] 1 WLR 419.

[197] In this respect, the court held that the test applied by the court in *ex parte Brady*, that the decision of the authorities should be measured by *Wednesbury* Unreasonableness, was no longer appropriate after the implementation of the Human Rights Act.

[198] (1909) 26 TLR 139.

[199] [1995] 1 All ER 677.

[200] This position was confirmed in the case of *Re W (Adult: Refusal of Treatment)*, *The Independent*, 17 June 2002, where it was held that a prisoner with mental capacity had the right to refuse treatment to a self-inflicted condition that was potentially life-threatening. See Williams, Hunger-Strikes: A Prisoner's Right or a Wicked Folly? (2001) Howard Journal of Criminology 285.

[201] (1999) 30 EHRR 121.

[202] [2002] 3 WLR 1834.

of the prisoner. However, the House of Lords held that despite the variety of views on the desirability of the mandatory life sentence, it was clear that such a sentence was not, by its very nature, in violation of Article 3. In practice it would be rare for a prisoner to be detained for life and in all other cases once the tariff period had been served the Secretary of State had the power to, and in practice did, refer cases to the Parole Board so as to consider release. Further, in *R v Drew*[203] the House of Lords held that the power under s.109 of the Criminal Courts (Sentencing) Act 2000 to impose an automatic life sentence on a mentally ill offender rather than order detention in a mental hospital was not incompatible with Article 3. In this case the individual was a serious risk to the public and the Home Secretary had discretion to move the prisoner to a hospital in appropriate circumstances. In the present case the eight days served in prison did not cross the threshold required for a violation of Article 3. That decision was upheld by the European Court of Human Rights, which found the applicant's case inadmissible.[204] Although the Court was concerned that the applicant had been sent directly to prison against the recommendations of the sentencing judge and two psychiatrists, it found that detention for eight days on a prison medical wing without effective access to full and medical treatment did not reach the necessary threshold.

Despite the ruling in *Lichniak and Pyrah*, there still remains the question of whether the imposition of a whole life sentence would be contrary to Article 3, although the European Court has upheld very long sentences provided they are supported on strong punitive grounds. Thus, in *Leger v France*,[205] it was held that there was no violation of Article 3 when the applicant had served a sentence of 41 years for abduction and murder. Although the Court noted that a life sentence of this length necessarily entailed anxiety and uncertainty relating to prison life and after release, in the circumstances there were no aggravating circumstances to conclude that the applicant had undergone an exceptional ordeal capable of constituting treatment contrary to Article 3. The position was clarified partially by the European Court of Human Rights in *Panayi (aka Kafkaris) v Cyprus*,[206] where it was held that the imposition of an indeterminate life sentence did not violate Articles 3 (or Articles 5 and 14). Although the imposition of an irreducible life sentence would be inconsistent with Article 3 that would only be the case where there was no hope, prospect or possibility of release. In the present case although a whole life sentence was possible there were provisions for suspension and remission of the sentence. Such a sentence entailed a level of anxiety, but not one in violation of Article 3 given the possibilities of release.

The admissibility decision in *Ahmad and Others* v *United Kingdom*

A more authoritative ruling on this issue is expected from the European Court of Human Rights after its admissibility decision in the case of *Babar Ahmad and Others v United Kingdom*,[207] which concerned the United Kingdom's intended extradition to the United States of four suspected international terrorists, including the Muslim cleric Abu Hamza al-Masri. In that decision the Court declared admissible his and the other applicants' claims that if extradited they would face inhuman and degrading prison sentences and conditions and the Court made an interim order under Rule 39 of the Rules of the European Court of Human Rights,

---

[203] [2003] 1 WLR 1213.

[204] *Drew v United Kingdom* (2006) 43 EHRR SE2.

[205] Decision of the European Court, 11 April 2006. An appeal to the Grand Chamber was subsequently struck out after the applicant died: (2009) 49 EHRR 1.

[206] (2009) 49 EHRR 35.

[207] Application Nos 24027/07, 11949/08 and 36742/08, European Court of Human Rights.

suspending any extradition until the final hearing before the Court. The applicants had unsuccessfully contested their extradition in the English courts.[208] They argued that, as non-citizens of the United States suspected of membership of Al-Qaeda or accused of acts of international terrorism, they were at risk of being designated as an 'enemy combatant' and subject to trial by a military commission and sentenced to life imprisonment or death.

Specifically, they claimed that whilst in pre-trial detention in a federal prison they would be at substantial risk of 'extraordinary rendition' to a third country and of being subjected to special administrative measures – including solitary confinement and restrictions on communication with their legal representatives. Specifically, Abu Hamza, who is blind in one eye, amputated of both forearms and suffering from high blood pressure and diabetes, argued that, if extradited, he would most likely be detained in ADX Florence (below) despite his poor health. It was also alleged that, once extradited, they were at risk of extraordinary rendition and life imprisonment without parole and/or extremely long sentences in a 'supermax' prison in the United States, such as ADX Florence, where special administrative measures would be applied to them.

The European Court held that there was no reason to believe that the United States Government would breach the terms of its diplomatic assurances, and, therefore, no real risk that the applicants would either be designated as enemy combatants (with the consequences that that entailed, such as the death penalty) or subjected to extraordinary rendition. However, with respect to post-trial detention the Court considered that Mr Ahmad, Mr Aswat and Mr Ahsan were at real risk of being held at ADX Florence if convicted and that their complaints under Article 3 concerning the stringency of conditions there for what could be the rest of their lives, raised serious questions of fact and law which needed to be examined on their merits. It also declared admissible their complaint that their conditions of detention might be made even stricter by the imposition of special administrative measures in ADX Florence.[209]

The Court also declared admissible the complaints under Article 3 concerning the length of their possible sentences – Ahmad, Ahsan and Abu Hamza facing life sentences without parole and Aswat facing a maximum of 50 years' imprisonment, meaning he would be nearly 78 before becoming eligible for release. Accordingly, the Court invited the parties to submit further written observations on the following issues: whether, given the length of the sentences faced by Ahmad, Aswat and Ahsan, if convicted, the time spent at ADX Florence would amount to a breach of Article 3 (and specifically whether they would have any real prospect of entering a 'step-down programme' whereby they would move through different levels of contact until they were deemed suitable for transfer to a normal prison); whether the 8th Amendment to the United States Constitution (prohibiting cruel and unusual punishment) provided protection which is equivalent to Article 3 of the Convention; and, if convicted, whether the applicants' sentences, in fact, would be irreducible? The decision will hopefully clarify some fundamental issues on the interpretation of Article 3 of the Convention; including the compatibility of both 'supermax prison conditions' and irreducible or very lengthy prison sentences.

In the meantime, other domestic decisions have suggested that even an irreducible term could comply with human rights law. For example, in R (Wellington) v Secretary of State for the Home Department[210] the House of Lords held that the threat of an imposition (by an American

---

[208] *Mustafa Kamel Mustafa v United States and Secretary of State for the Home Department* [2008] 1 WLR 2760.

[209] With respect to Abu Hamza's complaint about ADX Florence, as he would, at most, risk spending a short period of time there and only until such time as his state of health was assessed, his complaint should be declared inadmissible.

[210] [2009] 1 AC 335.

court) of a whole life sentence in lieu of the death penalty did not automatically violate Article 3. Although the claimant was to be subjected to a blanket rule, in this case the punishment was by no means out of proportion to the gravity of the offence. Their Lordships held that a life sentence under domestic law was not irreducible,[211] and thus did not engage Article 3. However, their Lordships also held that even if the life sentence in the United States was irreducible, which it was not, that sentence was not so grossly disproportionate to the offence so as to contravene the heightened standard for contravention of Article 3 *in the context of extradition.* Although that context appeared to be decisive to their Lordships' decision, in *R v Bamber,*[212] the Court of Appeal held that a whole life sentence for conviction of the murder of five people was justified and not in violation of Article 3; as there was nothing in the Convention precluding the making of a whole life order where it represented appropriate punishment for extreme criminality.[213] There does appear to be some conflict between the domestic and European decisions on this issue, which may have to be resolved by a further appeal to the Strasbourg court.

> **Question**
> How successful has Article 3 been in protecting those in detention from violations of Article 3?

Admissibility of torture evidence and Article 3

Various legal and moral issues are raised when there is evidence that individuals have been subjected to torture or ill-treatment in breach of Article 3 or other international rules prohibiting such treatment. This aspect of the prohibition of torture will be dealt with in detail in chapter 14 of this text in the context of the discussion of human rights and terrorism. For the purpose of present discussions, parties to a legal dispute may seek to rely on, or exclude, such evidence and the courts will need to assess the admissibility of such evidence in the light of principles of the prohibition of torture, or open justice.

For example, in *A v Secretary of State for the Home Department (No 2)*[214] the House of Lords employed the prohibition of torture in international and domestic law and held that the government could not rely on evidence that may have been extracted by torture to prove the grounds on which to justify the imposition of a control order.[215] The domestic courts have also rejected attempts by the government to claim public interest immunity with respect to official documents that are needed to verify claims that individuals have been tortured.[216]

---

[211] This had been decided in *R v Bieber* [2009] 1 WLR 223, where the High Court held that a whole life term should not be construed as a sentence that was irreducible, and that any claim that such a sentence violated Article 3 should be made not at the time of the sentence's imposition but at a time when it is claimed that any further detention would be in breach of Article 3.

[212] [2009] EWCA Crim 962.

[213] Contrast *Boucherville v Mauritius* [2008] UKPC 37, where the Privy Council held that a mandatory sentence of imprisonment for life was akin to a death sentence and thus breached the constitution. The Privy Council drew the distinction between this case and *Kafkaris* and held that the lack of release possibilities made the sentence arbitrary and disproportionate as well as inhuman and degrading.

[214] [2006] 2 AC 221.

[215] See also *Yasser Al-Sirri v Home Secretary* [2009] EWCA Civ 222, where it was held that the Immigration Tribunal had erred by giving any, albeit limited, weight to evidence that it conceded might have been obtained from torture.

[216] See *R (Mohamed) v Secretary of State for Foreign Affairs* [2009] 1 WLR 2579; *R (Binyam Mohamed) v Secretary of State for Foreign and Commonwealth Affairs* [2010] 3 WLR 554; and *Aamer v Secretary of State for Foreign and Commonwealth Affairs* [2009] EWHC 3316 (Admin), discussed in chapters 7 and 14.

CASE STUDY

A v *Secretary of State for the Home Department (No 2)* [2006] 2 AC 221

This case has been chosen because it involved a conflict between the domestic and international prohibition of torture and the successful prosecution of crime and the protection of national security. Although the practice of torture is prohibited absolutely, the House of Lords was faced with the question of whether evidence obtained as a result of such a practice could be used in legal proceedings to justify the arrest and detention of suspected terrorists. The case involved consideration of both international and domestic law and the decisions of the Court of Appeal and the House of Lords provide an interesting contrast in pragmatic and human rights approaches to the question.

Background

The detention without trial of foreign suspects under domestic legislation has already been successfully challenged in the case of A v *Secretary of State for the Home Department* ([2005] 2 AC 68), where the House of Lords held that such detention was incompatible with Articles 5 and 14 of the European Convention on Human Rights. The present case concerned the question of whether evidence which may have been extracted by torture in breach of international law was admissible with respect to such detentions.

The facts

Section 21 of the Anti-Terrorism, Crime and Security Act 2001 allowed the Secretary of State to issue a detention certificate under the Act if he reasonably believed that the person's presence in the United Kingdom was a risk to national security, and suspected that the person is a terrorist. Section 25 of the Act then provided that a person may appeal against such a certificate to the Special Immigration Appeals Commission (the Commission), who may cancel the certificate if it considers that there were no reasonable grounds for the Secretary's belief or suspicion or considers that the certificate should not have been issued for some other reason.

The appellants in the present case had been detained under such certificates and appealed to the Commission, claiming that the certificates should be cancelled because the Home Secretary may have based his suspicion under s.21 on evidence that was obtained by torture inflicted on persons in other countries. On 29 October 2003 the Commission refused to cancel the certificates and the appellants appealed to the Court of Appeal, claiming that the Commission should decline to consider any evidence unless it was shown not to have come into existence as a result of a violation of Article 3 of the Convention.

The decision of the Court of Appeal

In the Court of Appeal the appellants argued that such evidence should be excluded under the common law rule excluding evidence obtained by torture, and that the use of such evidence was contrary to both Article 6 of the European Convention on Human Rights (guaranteeing the right to a fair trial) and Article 15 of the United Nations Convention against Torture and other Cruel, Inhuman or Degrading Treatment or Punishment 1985 (which specifically provides for the exclusion of such evidence). The Court of Appeal dismissed the appeals and held that given the nature and context of the Secretary's powers such evidence was not automatically excluded. Lord Justice Pill assumed that the derogation order made in respect of the detentions was lawful, and that the 2001 Act could be expected to facilitate the Secretary's duty to safeguard national security. Consequently, the circumstances prevailing in this case were very different from those in a criminal trial where the Convention provided its basic safeguards. Here, the detention was justified upon suspicion and belief and the Secretary's value judgment would be based on an assessment of information obtained from many and varied sources. In particular, Article 15 of the UN Convention was not part of domestic law and in so far as it required an analysis of sources before a reasonable belief could be formed, such a provision would be contrary to the clear intention of the 2001 Act. Thus, although the courts should interpret legislation in conformity with the government's international obligations, such an interpretation was not possible in this case and would lead to the incorporation of Article 15 into domestic law via a different route. Lord Justice Laws held that incorporation of the European Convention via the Human Rights Act 1998 did not carry on its back an acceptance that other international obligations should drive the administration of Article 6.

The Court of Appeal then stated that although the Commission had the power to determine whether there had been an abuse of process, the Act did not permit too circumscribed a view of available material when assessing the reasonableness of the Secretary's judgment. The Secretary himself would have regard to the source of the material and the circumstances in which it was obtained, and provided he was acting in good faith the courts should recognise his responsibility for national security when they assess his approach to the material available to him.

Concurring, LAWS LJ conceded that the exclusionary rule would forbid the Secretary of State from relying upon any statement obtained by torture which the state had procured or connived at. However, he was unable to see that the Secretary was prohibited from relying on evidence coming into his hands which had or might have been obtained through torture by agencies of other states over which he had no power of discretion. The issue in such a case would be resolved by the law of evidence, and the evidence would be admissible if it was relevant, the court not generally being concerned with its provenance. His Lordship did not believe that the law should impose on the Secretary a duty of solemn inquiry as to the interrogation methods used by agencies of other states; apart from the practical reality, there was no sound juridical base for such a requirement. Once it was accepted that the scope of Article 6 was determined by the context of the case, and the nature of s.21 of the 2001 Act, then the admission of evidence of third parties which was or might have been obtained in violation of Article 3 was no more offensive to Article 6 than it was to the common law.

Lord Justice Neuberger dissented from the majority and held that in determining whether a person was entitled to a fair trial under Article 6, regard should be had to other international treaty provision, particularly the UN Convention on Torture. Noting that it was important to emphasise the general aim of the UN Convention when considering the wider context, his Lordship stated that:

> If the courts of states that were party to the European Convention decided that evidence obtained under torture was admissible, then, while not expressly condoning torture, they

would effectively be indicating that the use of torture to obtain evidence was not merely impliedly condoned, but was worthwhile, because such evidence might well be taken into account in those courts.

His Lordship also highlighted the potential prejudice to the detainee and his right to a fair trial, particularly with respect to the reliability of such evidence and the inability of the detainee to cross-examine third parties. Thus, despite the existence of the emergency situation as identified in the 2001 Act, it could not be concluded that the detainees received a fair trial if evidence obtained by torture could be taken into account.

The detainees appealed against the majority decision of the Court of Appeal and the point for the House of Lords to consider was whether the Commission might receive evidence which had or might have been procured by torture inflicted, in order to obtain evidence, by officials of a foreign state, without the complicity of the British authorities.

The decision of the House of Lords

Delivering the main opinion Lord Bingham began by stressing that English common law had, from its earliest days, set its face firmly against the use of torture. In rejecting such use, whether applied to defendants or witnesses, the law accepted both the cruelty and degradation of the practice, and the inherent unreliability of any evidence procured by it. With respect to the European Convention, although his Lordship conceded that the European Court of Human Rights had been reluctant to lay down any common rules on the use of evidence, preferring to leave such rules to individual states, it nevertheless had insisted that each state must ensure that proceedings had been fair. The Court also recognised that the way in which evidence was gathered might make those proceedings unfair (relying on *Saunders* v *United Kingdom* (1996) 23 EHRR 313) and his Lordship was of the opinion that it would take a similar view where complaints of coercion and torture appear to be substantiated.

Lord Bingham then considered the impact of general public international law on the issue. He noted that the European Court had invoked a wide range of international instruments, including the UN Convention on Torture, in interpreting and applying the European Convention (*Al-Adsani* v *United Kingdom* (2002) 34 EHRR 273) and had accepted that it should consider relevant rules of international law. In that respect it was common ground that the international prohibition on the use of torture enjoyed the enhanced status of a *jus cogens* or peremptory norm of general international law recognised as one from which no derogation was allowed. This essential character of the use of torture had been recognised by the House of Lords in *R* v *Bow Street Metropolitan Stipendary Magistrate, ex parte Pinochet Ugarte* ([2000] 1 AC 147), thus clarifying international condemnation of the practice. Further, states were now obliged not only to refrain from authorising or conniving at torture, but also to suppress and discourage it and not to condone it. Specifically, Article 15 of the UN Convention required the exclusion of statements made as a result of torture as evidence in any proceedings, and, contrary to the Secretary of State's claim, that did not merely apply to criminal proceedings or where the torture took place in the jurisdiction of the state holding the proceedings. In his Lordship's view:

> It would be remarkable if national courts, exercising universal jurisdiction, could try a foreign torturer for acts of torture committed abroad but receive evidence obtained by such torture.

Lord Bingham stated that the rationale of the exclusionary rule contained in Article 15 was found not only in the unreliability of torture evidence but also its offensiveness to civilised values and its degrading effect on the administration of justice, thus damaging the integrity of the proceedings. Nor, in his Lordship's opinion, should the above principles be undermined by measures directed to counter international terrorism. All states were strongly urged by the international community to cooperate and share information to counter terrorism, but human rights and humanitarian law could not be compromised or infringed.

His Lordship then considered whether the above principles were overtaken by the context of the case and the specific statutory powers included in the 2001 Act, together with rule 44(3) of the Commission's Rules, which allowed the Commission to receive evidence that was not admissible in a court of law. Although his Lordship held that it would be within the power of the sovereign parliament, in breach of international law, to confer power on the Commission to receive third-party torture evidence, he stressed that the common law had regarded torture and its fruits with abhorrence for over 500 years:

> His Lordship was startled, even a little dismayed, at the suggestion, and the acceptance by the Court of Appeal majority, that the deeply rooted tradition and an international obligation solemnly and explicitly undertaken could be overridden by a statute and a procedural rule which made no mention of torture at all.

Thus, the principles of the common law standing alone compelled the exclusion of third-party torture evidence as unreliable, unfair, offensive to the ordinary standards of humanity and decency and incompatible with the principles which should animate a tribunal seeking to administer justice. The common law does not stand alone in this respect and effect had to be given to the European Convention, which itself took into account the universal consensus established in the UN Torture Convention. The answer to the central question in the appeal was to be found not in a government policy, which might change, but in law.

With respect to the relevant burden of proof, his Lordship stated that in the context of the statutory regime a procedure had to be devised which afforded some protection to the appellant without imposing on either party a burden which he could not ordinarily discharge. All their Lordships agreed that a conventional approach to the burden of proof was inappropriate and that it would be unrealistic to expect the detainee to prove anything as he was denied access to much of the information to be used against him. It was agreed unanimously therefore that all the detainee could reasonably be expected to do was to raise the issue and ask the Commission to consider it. The detainees would thus have to raise some plausible reason that the information may have been obtained by torture, usually that the country in question regularly practises such acts. However, their Lordships could not agree on what the Commission should do once it had received that basic evidence. In Lord Hope's opinion, which was supported by three other Lordships, the Commission should only refuse to admit the evidence if it concluded, on a balance of probabilities, that it was obtained by torture. If, on the other hand, the Commission was left in doubt as to whether the evidence was so obtained it should admit it, although it would have to bear its doubt in mind when evaluating that evidence. Conversely, Lord

Bingham, together with Lords Nichol and Hoffmann felt that once the Commission was given that plausible reason, or where it knew or suspected that the evidence might have come from such a country, it was for the Commission to initiate or direct the necessary inquiry to form a fair judgment whether the evidence had, or whether there was a real risk that it might have been obtained by torture or not. If then the Commission was unable to conclude that there was not a real risk that the evidence had been so obtained, it should refuse to admit it; otherwise it should admit it. In Lord Bingham's view, the test adopted by Lord Hope could never be satisfied in the real world and would undermine the practical efficacy of the UN Torture Convention.

Questions

1 How does the decision of the House of Lords in this case add to international law with respect to protection against torture and other ill-treatment?
2 Do you think that the prohibition of torture evidence follows inevitably from the general prohibition of torture in international law?
3 What was the basis of the Court of Appeal's decision in this case? Was its approach entirely pragmatic or can it be justified in terms of democratic human rights principles?
4 Do you think that the Court of Appeal decision in this case undermined the absolute and fundamental nature of provisions such as Article 3 of the European Convention?
5 What was the rationale of the House of Lords' decision?
6 Do you feel that the House of Lords' decision lacks pragmatism or democratic legitimacy?
7 Was the decision based on common law principles or on provisions of international law or both?
8 Do you think the House of Lords' acceptance of provisions of international treaties other than the European Convention on Human Rights is controversial and/or erroneous?

Conclusion

Despite the current concerns that human rights should not be enjoyed over and above public safety and the security of the state, the prohibition of torture and other ill-treatment has retained its absolute status and in general the courts have adopted a robust approach in this area. However, the article is continually under threat and the judiciary will be asked to entertain the idea that it should be allowed to be violated or compromised in times of emergency. For the time being, decisions such as *Saadi v Italy*,[217] where the European Court refused to modify the *Soering* principle in the context of the deportation of suspected terrorists, are vital in retaining the absoluteness of this right.

[217] (2009) 49 EHRR 30.

Further reading

Texts

A number of texts on the European Convention contain excellent chapters on Article 3 of the Convention and its relevant case law: Harris, Warbrick, Bates and O'Boyle, *Law of the European Convention on Human Rights* (OUP 2009, 2nd edn), chapter 3; Ovey and White, *Jacobs and White: The European Convention on Human Rights* (OUP 2010, 4th edn), chapter 5; Janis, Kay and Bradley, *European Human Rights Law* (OUP 2007, 3rd edn), chapter 5; Mowbray's *Cases and Materials on the European Convention* (OUP 2007, 2nd edn), chapter 3. The latter is an excellent reference point on the case law of the European Court in this area. Clayton and Tomlinson, *The Law of Human Rights* (OUP 2009, 2nd edn), chapter 8, provides comprehensive coverage of both European and various domestic law provision; Amos, *Human Rights Law* (Hart 2006), chapter 8, provides a useful account of domestic cases on Article 3 in the post-Human Rights Act era. In addition, Cooper's *Cruelty: An Analysis of Article 3* (Sweet & Maxwell 2002) provides a comprehensive coverage of the subject.

Articles

The following articles provide expert commentary analysis of the scope and case law of Article 3: Addo, Is there a Policy Behind the Decisions and Judgments Relating to Article 3 of the European Convention on Human Rights? (1995) ELRev 178; Yutaka Aria-Yokoi, Grading Scale of Degradation: Identifying the Threshold of Degrading Treatment or Punishment under Article 3 ECHR [2003] Netherlands HRQ 385; Palmer, A Wrong Turning: Article 3 ECHR and Proportionality [2006] CLJ 438; Nowak, Challenges to the Absolute Nature of the Prohibition of Torture and Ill-treatment [2005] Netherlands HRQ 674; McBride, Imperfect Limits to Unacceptable Treatment (2000) 25 ELRev (Human Rights Survey) 31; Evans, Getting to Grips With Torture (2002) ICLQ 365.

With respect to Article 3 and prison conditions, see Murdoch, The impact of the Council of Europe's 'Torture Committee' and the Evolution of Standard-setting in Relation to Places of Detention [2006] EHRLR 159; Owers, Prison Inspections and the Protection of Human Rights [2004] EHRLR 107; Foster, Prison Conditions, Human Rights and Article 3 ECHR [2005] PL 33; Foster, The Negligence of Prison Authorities and the Protection of Prisoner's Rights (2005) (26) Liverpool Law Review 75; Evans, Torture (editorial) [2006] EHRLR 101.

Visit **www.mylawchamber.co.uk/fosterhumanrights**
to access regular updates to major changes in the law,
further case studies, weblinks, and suggested
answers/approaches to questions in the book.

6 Human rights and due process: liberty of the person

Introduction

In *Austin* v *Metropolitan Police Commissioner* (2008) the House of Lords had to decide whether the police had interfered with hundreds of individuals' liberty of the person when they cordoned them off from a mass demonstration which was threatening the peace.

In *Stafford* v *United Kingdom* (2002) the European Court had to decide whether the Home Secretary had the power to refuse to release a life sentence prisoner who the Home Secretary felt was still at risk of committing non-violent criminal offences.

These cases, and many others studied in this chapter, raise issues about the nature of liberty, the justification for its interference, and the principles underlying liberty, fairness and due process.

This chapter examines how both the European Convention on Human Rights and relevant domestic law recognises and upholds the basic right to liberty of the person. The chapter will explore the basic nature and principles of individual liberty including its values and the circumstances in which it might have to be compromised. The chapter will focus on Article 5 of the European Convention on Human Rights, examining its various guarantees and exceptions together with the relevant case law of the European Court of Human Rights. The chapter will also examine how those provisions and cases have been interpreted and applied in domestic law, particularly in the post-Human Rights Act era.

The chapter will deal with the article's provisions in turn, but, as and when relevant and necessary, particular attention will be paid to controversial issues such as liberty and police powers, release and recall of prisoners and the balance between liberty of the person and national security. With respect to the latter issue, some attention will be given to the extent to which individual liberty and Article 5 can be compromised in times of emergency; although the relevant law and its compatibility with Article 5 will be examined in detail in chapter 14 of this text.

Thus, this chapter will cover:

- An examination of the importance and nature of individual liberty.
- An examination of how that right is protected under the European Convention on Human Rights.
- An examination of the extent to which that right has been upheld in domestic law, specifically in the post-Human Rights Act era.
- A specific examination of liberty of the person and police powers, release of prisoners and the balance between liberty of the person and national security.

Liberty

The term 'liberty' used in its general sense refers to basic principles of autonomy and freedom. One is free to do what one chooses and the right to individual autonomy protects us from state interference as to what we do, with whom we associate and what choices we make with respect to our lives. Most liberal democratic states will be founded on such principles, and domestic bills of rights and international treaties will reflect them in its various guarantees. More specifically, however, liberty refers to freedom of movement and freedom from detention of the person, usually by the state. Treaties and bills of rights will thus make specific provision for individual liberty, guaranteeing freedom from detention unless specific and exacting conditions are fulfilled. These provisions will, therefore, create a presumption in favour of individual liberty and against deprivation of liberty, as well as guaranteeing against the arbitrary deprivation of liberty of the person.

The rule of law lies at the heart of the above principles, guaranteeing that liberty is only interfered with in accordance with clear and prospective laws and after following the basic principles of procedural fairness. For example, any power to arrest an individual should be in accordance with formal legal powers and based on proof or reasonable suspicion that the individual has, or is about to, transgress the law;[1] any detention should be preceded by a decision of an independent judicial officer acting within the law, and such detention should be connected to that decision and not dependent on executive or other discretion. The right to liberty, therefore, is not absolute, but should continue unless specific conditions are met and safeguards of certainty, independence and objectivity are present.[2] Further, although those principles may need to be compromised somewhat in times of emergency (including the fight against terrorism) as we shall see, those basic values and rights remain despite the existence of any threats to national security and public safety.[3]

---

[1] A law should not allow deprivation of liberty couched in terms which are so vague that its meaning and extent cannot be reasonably predicted: *Hashman and Harrap* v *United Kingdom* (1999) 30 EHRR 241.

[2] For example, Article 5 allows interference with a person's liberty and security of the person only in accordance with a procedure prescribed by law, meaning not only that the law has a legitimate source, but that it complies with the fundamental ideals of the rule of law in that it is sufficiently fair, impartial and clear: *Winterwerp* v *Netherlands* (1979) 2 EHRR 387.

[3] It has been held that the principles of Article 5 of the European Convention can be overridden in times of conflict by relevant UN Security Council Resolutions, provided the rights under Article 5 are not infringed to any greater extent than is inherent in any detention pursuant to such powers: see chapter 3, n. 115.

Liberty and security of the person and Article 5 of the European Convention on Human Rights

Article 5 provides that everyone has the right to liberty and security of the person. It also lays down the requirements of any lawful interference with that basic right and guarantees the right to compensation in law when that right is violated. The remainder of the chapter will examine the content of Article 5, together with its interpretation and application by both the European Court of Human Rights and the domestic courts.[4]

Scope of the article

Although Article 5 talks of liberty *and* security of the person the article is principally concerned with guarding against deprivations of liberty and does not provide general protection to the security and safety of the person.[5] Thus the state does not owe a general obligation under this article to protect individuals from harm. However, the state will owe a limited duty to do so under both Articles 2 and 3 of the Convention, thus safeguarding the individual from foreseeable harm.[6] More specifically, Article 5 has been used to impose a strict obligation on the state to account for the disappearance of individuals. Thus, in *Kurt* v *Turkey*[7] the Court held that a state, having assumed control over an individual by taking them into detention, must account for the whereabouts of that person, adopting effective measures to safeguard against the risk of disappearance and conducting a prompt and effective investigation into any reasonable claim.

In addition, Article 5 is not engaged by a claim of the conditions under which a person is detained.[8] Again, such conditions may give rise to a claim under other articles, most notably Article 3, and it has been held that a mental patient must be detained in an appropriate institution for the detention to be lawful under Article 5(1)(e).[9] In addition, the imposition of certain conditions on patients may amount to a derivation of liberty and not merely a restriction on their movement. In *R (Home Secretary)* v *Mental Health Review Tribunal*,[10] it was held that conditions imposed on a patient discharged from hospital that would leave him supervised or escorted at all times was a deprivation of liberty under Article 5 of the Convention, even if the patient agreed to it. Similarly, in *R (G)* v *Mental Health Review Tribunal and Another*,[11] it was held that a conditional discharge under the Mental Health Act 1983 on condition that he remain at the hospital he was already staying at engaged Article 5.

---

[4] For reading on liberty of the person and Article 5 of the Convention see Harris, Warbrick, Bates and O'Boyle, *Law of the European Convention on Human Rights* (Oxford 2009, 2nd edn), chapter 5; Clayton and Tomlinson, *The Law of Human Rights* (OUP 2009, 2nd edn), chapter 10; van Dijk and van Hoof, *Theory and Practice of the European Convention on Human Rights* (Intersentia 2006); Mowbray *Cases and Materials on the European Convention* (Oxford 2007, 2nd edn), chapter 7.

[5] For a detailed discussion of the scope of Article 5, and its possible applicability to security of the person, see Powell, The Right to Security of the Person in European Court of Human Rights Jurisprudence [2007] EHRLR 649.

[6] See chapters 4 and 5 of this text.

[7] (1999) 27 EHRR 373.

[8] *Winterwerp* v *Netherlands* (1979) 2 EHRR 387. Thus, in *Davies* v *Secretary of State for Justice* [2008] EWHC 397, it was held that the movement of a prisoner from open to closed conditions did not engage Article 5 as that article was not concerned with the location and conditions of imprisonment.

[9] *Ashingdane* v *United Kingdom* (1985) 7 EHRR 258.

[10] [2004] EWHC 2194 (Admin).

[11] [2004] EWHC 2193 (Admin).

> **Questions**
> Why is liberty of the person regarded as so fundamental in democratic states and under the European Convention on Human Rights?
> What aspects of liberty and security of the person are covered by Article 5?

What is liberty?

Article 5 is concerned with the deprivation of liberty and is to be distinguished from the general right of freedom of movement, guaranteed by Article 2 of the Fourth Protocol. Thus, in *Guzzardi v Italy*,[12] the European Court stressed that the article is not concerned with mere restrictions on liberty of movement but rather with restrictions on the physical liberty of the person, although it accepted that such a distinction is often a question of degree. In that case the applicant, who was suspected of taking part in the activities of the Mafia, had been placed under special supervision on part of a designated island, being confined to a space of 2.5 square kilometres, being forced to report to the police twice daily and being subject to a curfew between 10pm and 7am. It was held that the applicant had suffered a breach of Article 5. In the Court's view, whether Article 5 is engaged requires an examination of the individual's concrete situation, taking into account the type, duration, effects and manner of implementation of the measures. On the facts, although the Court was satisfied that the applicant's position could be contrasted with classic forms of detention, where individuals are confined to a cell, it felt that in many respects the treatment equated with conditions in an open prison and thus amounted to deprivation of liberty.[13]

Once the article is engaged, the state will need to prove that there is a legitimate reason for the individual's detention and as the state often believe that the treatment does not amount to a deprivation of liberty that justification will often be lacking. For example, in *Guzzardi*, having found a *prima facie* breach of Article 5, the Court then found that his detention did not fall within the exceptions laid down by that article, the applicant being detained for preventive reasons not sufficiently tied to the commission of any specific offence. This dilemma has arisen with respect to the British government's use of control orders under the Prevention of Terrorism Act 2005. Such measures, which controlled the movement and activities of individuals suspected of terrorism but who would not be facing criminal charges and who could not be deported, purported to be non-derogating orders under the Convention and the Human Rights Act 1998 because the Home Secretary regarded them as *restrictions* on liberty and movement rather than deprivations of liberty.[14]

The orders were thus challenged under the Human Rights Act on the basis that they involved an illegitimate violation of Article 5. In the first case, *Secretary of State for the Home Department v JJ and Others*,[15] the House of Lords held that orders imposed on the applicants

---

[12] (1980) 3 EHRR 333.

[13] See also *Ammur v France* (1996) 22 EHRR 533, where it was held that the detention of asylum seekers in an airport international transit area involved a deprivation of liberty. Contrast *Nielsen v Denmark* (1988) 11 EHRR 175, where it was held that the detention, at a mother's request, of a 12-year-old boy in a hospital did not fall within Article 5. The Court held that it must be possible for a child to be admitted to hospital in the exercise of parental rights.

[14] The measures were introduced after the decision of the House of Lords in *A v Secretary of State for the Home Department* [2005] 2 AC 68, considered in chapters 3 and 14.

[15] [2007] 3 WLR 642.

were, in fact, derogating orders that the Secretary of State had no jurisdiction to make and thus were in breach of Article 5.[16] The orders in this case were imposed on a number of asylum seekers from Iraq and Iran and obliged them to remain within their residences (a one-bedroom flat) at all times apart from a period of six hours a day. All visitors had to be screened and the residences were subject to spot searches by the police, and when the individuals were allowed to leave they were restricted to confined urban areas. Applying the principles in *Guzzardi* above, it was noted that the orders impacted severely on liberty and were expected to last indefinitely. The judge at first instance had, thus, been entitled to conclude that the restrictions imposed physical restraints on those concerned and that prevented the individuals from pursuing the life of their choice.[17]

However, the courts have not declared such orders as contrary to Article 5 *per se*, insisting that whether Article 5 is engaged depends on the cumulative effect of the restrictions. Thus, in *Secretary of State for the Home Department v E*[18] the House of Lords distinguished the case of *JJ*, above, and held that Article 5 was not engaged when the individual lived in his own home with his family and was able to leave that home for 12 hours a day with no geographical restriction. Further, he had ample opportunity to engage in everyday activities and make a wide range of social contacts.[19] Further, in *Secretary of State for the Home Department v AF*[20] the House of Lords held that an order which prohibited the individual from leaving his flat for more than ten hours a day and which imposed electronic tagging and restricted him to a certain geographical area outside the flat, did not constitute a deprivation of liberty. The domestic courts have thus stressed that whether the imposition of a curfew within the control order amounts to a deprivation of liberty under Article 5 will depend on all other considerations and conditions of the order, the essential issues being whether there is a sufficient element of confinement.[21] However, the courts have also held that a control order contains no implied power to conduct a personal search, and that such an act would constitute a violation of Articles 5 and 8.[22]

More recently the Supreme Court has held that whether such orders do engage and breach the right to liberty under Article 5 might depend on whether such restrictions impinge on the right to private life contained in Article 8. Thus, in *AP v Secretary of State for the Home Department*,[23] it was held that a condition in a control order which restricted the controlee's

---

[16] In *N v Secretary of State for the Home Department* [2010] EWCA Civ 869 it was held that a control order which had been declared *ultra vires* by the courts was void *ab initio* and would be quashed with retrospective effect. Thus the controlee could not be punished for breaking such an order and the secretary was liable in damages for any wrongful deprivation of liberty.

[17] Lord Hoffmann dissented, stressing that the courts should not give an over-expansive interpretation to Article 5 and believing that the measures were simply a restriction on movement.

[18] [2007] 3 WLR 720.

[19] See also *Rideh v Secretary of State for the Home Department* [2007] EWHC 2237 (Admin), where it was held that a modification to the individual's control orders did not involve a restriction on his liberty, and that any interference with his right to private and family life was necessary and proportionate. The court did, however, recognise that, in general, the mental state of an individual could have an impact on the severity of the restrictions.

[20] [2007] 3 WLR 681.

[21] *Secretary of State for Home Department v AP* [2009] EWCA Civ 731. See also *Secretary of State for the Home Department v GG and NN* [2009] EWHC 142 (Admin), where it was held that a control order imposing a 16-hour curfew on an individual and which required him to move to another town did not amount to a derivation of liberty under Article 5.

[22] *Secretary of State for the Home Department v GG and NN* [2010] 2 WLR 731, and *BH v Secretary of State for the Home Department* [2009] EWHC 2938.

[23] *The Times*, 17 June 2010.

rights under Article 8 could tip the balance when determining whether there had been a deprivation of liberty under Article 5, even where that restriction might be regarded as a proportionate interference with private and family life.[24] In the Supreme Court's view, in cases where a control order imposed a curfew of between 14 and 18 hours a day other restrictions apart from confinement could be relevant; although in cases where the curfew was less than 16 hours a day the other conditions would have to be particularly destructive of the life of the controlee for the court to strike it down. In the present case it was relevant that the controlee lived some distance from his family – he lived in Manchester and the family in London – and that in practice the curfew thus caused the substantial isolation of the controlee.

The question of what amounts to a deprivation of liberty is also relevant with respect to the extent to which the police can restrict the movement and activities of protestors. Often the police will prohibit protestors from entering particular areas, fearing that their presence might cause a disturbance. When the protestors' presence or behaviour is likely to cause a breach of the peace then the police intervention would fall within the permitted exceptions (see below) provided they are lawful and proportionate. However, the police may argue in some cases that the measures do not engage Article 5. In *R (Laporte) v Chief Constable of Gloucestershire*[25] the police had boarded a coach taking protestors to an air base and accompanied the coach back to London. The House of Lords held that there was nothing in domestic law which justified action short of arrest when a breach of the peace was not so imminent as to justify any arrest, and that as no breach of the peace was apprehended in this case the protestors' Convention rights had been violated. That case did not fully address the question of what level of deprivation is necessary for Article 5 to be engaged, although it accepted that detaining the protestors on the coach from Gloucester to London was such a deprivation. In contrast, in *Austin v Metropolitan Police Commissioner*[26] the House of Lords held that there had been no deprivation of liberty within Article 5 when protestors were detained for several hours in one area to prevent an imminent breach of the peace, before being released. In their Lordships view whether a situation amounted to a deprivation of liberty was fact sensitive and depended on all the circumstances including why the person's movement was restricted. The case law of the Convention did not expressly address this issue but a balancing exercise was inherent in cases such as *Guzzardi*. Although the police would have to act in good faith and in proportion, the intention of the police in the present case was to maintain the cordon only so long as was reasonably necessary to achieve a controlled dispersal and thus the measures taken were proportionate.[27]

The decision in *Austin* – that a legitimate motive in restraining individuals could mean that there had in fact been no deprivation of liberty – was called into question in the recent European Court judgment in *Gillan and Quinton v United Kingdom*.[28] In that case the European Court did not rule out the possibility that the employment of stop and search

---

[24] See *BX v Secretary of State for the Home Department* [2010] EWHC 990 (Admin), where it was held to be proportionate to relocate the individual away from London to the West of England to stop him associating with extremists.

[25] [2007] 2 WLR 46.

[26] [2009] 1 AC 564; see chapter 10 for details.

[27] See Mead, Of Kettles, Cordons and Crowd Control – *Austin v Commissioner* of the Police for the Metropolis and the Meaning of 'Deprivation of Liberty' [2009] EHRLR 376; Fenwick, Marginalising Human Rights: Breach of the Peace, 'Kettling', the HRA and Public Protest [2009] PL 737.

[28] (2010) 50 EHRR 45. See Buxton, Terrorism and the European Convention [2010] Crim Law R 533.

powers entailed a deprivation of liberty, but decided the case on the basis of Article 8 of the Convention. On the domestic front, in *R (Gillan)* v *Commissioner of the Police for the Metropolis*[29] the House of Lords had held that a stop and search under the Terrorism Act 2000 did not constitute a deprivation of liberty and that such transient interferences would not usually engage Article 5; but such a finding may now have to be reviewed after the European Court's ruling.

Question

How have the courts distinguished between loss of liberty and restrictions on freedom of movement? Is that distinction logical?

The legitimate exceptions under Article 5(1)

If the applicant's case does come within Article 5, any deprivation must conform to substantive and procedural rules of national law and must protect the individual from arbitrary deprivation of his or her liberty. The basic right to liberty and security of the person is subject to a number of exceptions contained in Article 5(1)(a)–(f), although any interference with the basic right is *prima facie* unlawful. In addition, Article 5(1) specifies that any interference will be unlawful unless it is 'in accordance with a procedure prescribed by law'. Thus, Article 5 imposes the requirements of legality and accessibility, and accordingly liberty should not be interfered with arbitrarily and any deprivation must comply with procedural and substantive principles of fairness and justice.

Those principles were considered by the Grand Chamber of the European Court in *Ocalan* v *Turkey*,[30] the Court stressing the fundamental importance of complying with those standards and confirming that for a detention to be lawful, and for it to be consistent with a procedure prescribed by law, it must be in conformity with the substantive and procedural rules of national law. Further, any detention needed to be consistent with the purpose of Article 5, namely to protect individuals from arbitrariness, and that an arrest that takes place in flagrant breach of international law may also be in violation of Article 5. The applicant was suspected of being involved in acts of terrorism and a warrant had been issued for his arrest in addition to a number of wanted notices being circulated by Interpol. He was eventually arrested at Nairobi airport when the Turkish authorities intercepted the Greek ambassador's efforts to allow the applicant to leave the country. The applicant was then blindfolded and handcuffed and forcibly taken back to Turkey by the Turkish authorities, the blindfold being removed when they reached Turkish airspace.

The European Court held that, provided extradition is the result of cooperation between the relevant states and that the legal basis for the order of the fugitive's arrest is a warrant issued by the authorities of the fugitive's state of origin, even atypical extraditions are not in breach of Article 5. In the present case there had been no breach of the Kenyan government's sovereignty and his arrest and detention had, in fact, complied with orders issued by the Turkish domestic courts for the purposes of bringing him before the Turkish courts to face

---

[29] [2006] 2 AC 307.
[30] (2005) 41 EHRR 45.

charges for breach of domestic law. The decision shows that the European Court is often willing to take a pragmatic and diplomatic approach in this area, despite the existence of practices that might, technically, fall foul of the rule of law.[31]

Lawful detention after conviction

The first exception concerns the lawful detention of a person after conviction by a competent court. The use of the word 'lawful', repeated in many of the exceptions, and the requirement that the detention be after conviction by a 'competent' court, ensure that the individual is protected by the general principles of due process and the rule of law. Thus, in *HL* v *United Kingdom*,[32] it was held that there had been a violation of Article 5(1) when a person had been detained in a mental hospital as an 'informal patient'. The domestic courts had justified the detention by reference to the common law doctrine of necessity,[33] but the European Court held that such a doctrine was too uncertain and arbitrary to be prescribed by law for the purposes of Article 5. The Court also found a violation of Article 5(4) because the applicant had no effective method of challenging that detention.[34]

Similarly, any conviction must have a sufficient basis under domestic law, and the relevant court must not interpret and apply the law in an arbitrary way.[35] This will not, however, invalidate a conviction when it is subsequently discovered that the court of first instance made an error of fact or law in convicting the applicant.[36] The European Court insists that there is a sufficient connection between the finding of guilt and the subsequent detention. Thus, in *Van Droogenbroek* v *Belgium*[37] it held that there was a sufficient connection where the applicant was subjected to a ten-year period of executive supervision after completion of a two-year fixed sentence imposed by the domestic court. The European Court noted that the executive discretion was exercised within a statutory framework and by a sentence imposed by the court. This principle was applied in *Weeks* v *United Kingdom*,[38] where it had been alleged that the power to detain and recall a discretionary life sentence prisoner once the fixed element of his sentence (the tariff) had expired was contrary to Article 5(1). In the Court's view the applicant's conviction and his recall to prison some ten years later were sufficiently connected and would only be broken if the grounds of the detention or re-detention were inconsistent with the objectives of the original sentencing court. Although that principle has been applied to other prisoners,[39] there may still be a violation of Article 5 on the facts of a

---

[31] Contrast the domestic law decision in *R* v *Horseferry Road Magistrate Court, ex parte Bennett, The Times*, 1 April 1994, where the extradition and arrest had been effected by collusion and in breach of an extradition agreement.

[32] (2005) 30 EHRR 42.

[33] *R* v *Bournewood Community and Mental Health NHS Trust, ex parte L* [1999] 1 AC 458.

[34] Contrast *R (B)* v *Ashworth Hospital Authority* [2005] 2 AC 278, where the House of Lords held that the 1983 Mental Health Act authorised a mental patient to be treated for any mental disorder, and not merely the one for which the patient was detained. His treatment to deal with other personality traits was not therefore unlawful or in violation of Article 5 of the Convention.

[35] *Tsirlis and Kouloumpas* v *Greece* (1997) 25 EHRR 198.

[36] *Benham* v *United Kingdom* (1996) 22 EHRR 293.

[37] (1982) 4 EHRR 443.

[38] (1987) 10 EHRR 293.

[39] That principle has also been applied to mandatory life sentence prisoners (*Wynne* v *United Kingdom* (1994) 19 EHRR 333) and those detained at Her Majesty's Pleasure (*V and T* v *United Kingdom* (1999) 30 EHRR 121). In *Weeks*, however, the Court did find a violation of Article 5(4); see below.

particular case if the Court is not satisfied of the causal connection between the sentence and the subsequent detention.[40]

Lawful arrest or detention for non-compliance of a lawful court order

Article 5(1)(b) permits the arrest or detention of a person who has not complied with a court order when such arrest or detention is required for the fulfilment of an obligation that is prescribed by law. The detention does not always have to be sanctioned by a court of law, but the European Court will need to be satisfied that a specific legal obligation has been, or is, in danger of being breached.[41] In this respect the European Court has taken a flexible approach, affording a fairly wide area of discretion to national law, and in *Steel v United Kingdom*[42] it held that the general powers to bind over an individual in order to keep the peace were compatible with Article 5, provided there had been some threat to the peace caused by the applicant's conduct.[43]

In addition, the sentence of the court must be within the law and must not be arbitrary. In *Benham v United Kingdom*,[44] the applicant had been sent to prison for 30 days for failure to pay his poll tax. The applicant successfully appealed against the sentence on the basis that the magistrate's court had no evidence to find him guilty of culpable neglect, but under English law he was not eligible for compensation. It was held that the European Court could declare the detention unlawful if it was arbitrary or resulted in the magistrate exceeding his jurisdiction by granting the detention. Although in this case the High Court overruled the magistrate's decision, there was evidence that he had considered the relevant factors before committing the applicant to prison and thus the detention was lawful within Article 5(1)(b). Neither, in the Court's view, was the detention arbitrary, in other words, in bad faith.[45] In contrast, in *Beets and Others v United Kingdom*,[46] it was held that there had been a violation of Article 5 when poll tax defaulters were imprisoned and where the magistrates had not properly considered whether the applicants were wilful defaulters under the relevant law.

Lawful arrest or detention following arrest

Article 5(1)(c) allows for lawful arrest or detention of a person which has been effected for the purpose of bringing him or her before the competent legal authority on reasonable suspicion of their having committed an offence or when it is reasonably considered necessary to prevent their committing an offence or fleeing after having done so. Again, the Court insists that such actions are capable of being justified on legitimate and objective grounds,[47]

---

[40] In *Stafford v United Kingdom* (2002) 35 EHRR 32, the European Court held that there was an insufficient connection between imposing a mandatory life sentence for murder and the subsequent recall and detention of that prisoner on the basis of perceived fears that he would commit crimes of a non-violent nature.

[41] *Engel v Netherlands* (1976) 1 EHRR 647.

[42] (1999) 28 EHRR 603.

[43] Similarly, in *McVeigh, O'Neill and Evans v United Kingdom* (1981) 25 DR 15, a duty to submit to an examination on entering the country satisfied Article 5, even though it was not a general obligation arising under criminal or disciplinary law.

[44] (1996) 22 EHRR 293.

[45] See also *Perks and Other v United Kingdom* (2000) 30 EHRR 33.

[46] *The Times*, 10 March 2005.

[47] In particular, a detention must accord with clear and absolute domestic law that limits the period of detention. See, for example, *K-F v Germany* (1997) 26 EHRR 390, where the detention of the applicant beyond the 12-hour period allowed by domestic law was held to be in violation of Article 5.

although the facts raising a suspicion under this provision need not be the same level as those necessary to justify a conviction, or even the bringing of a charge.[48] Further, in *Moulton v Chief Constable of the West Midlands*,[49] the Court of Appeal, in dismissing a claim for malicious prosecution, held that although the threshold of reasonable suspicion for bringing a charge was higher than that for arrest, it was not necessary to comply with Article 5 that the burden of a claimant to prove malice be reduced.

The requirements of a 'lawful arrest' within paragraph (c) were laid down by the European Court in *Fox, Campbell and Hartley v United Kingdom*.[50] The applicants were arrested under s.1 of the Northern Ireland (Emergency Provisions) Act 1978, which provided that a person could be arrested on suspicion of being a terrorist and could be detained for up to 72 hours. They were detained for between 30 and 44 hours and were then released without charge. The European Court held that a reasonable suspicion as required by Article 5(1)(c) presupposes the existence of facts that would satisfy an objective observer that the person might have committed the offence. However, the Court stressed that what might be regarded as reasonable will depend on all the circumstances, and that in respect of terrorism the test differs from that involved in conventional crime, as long as the essence of reasonableness is not impaired. The government must furnish at least some information which could satisfy the Court that the arrested person was reasonably suspected of having committed the offence. In the present case, the only evidence was that they had committed offences seven years previously and consequently the Court was not satisfied that those minimum standards laid down were met.[51]

Allowance will, thus, be made of the particular circumstances, giving a wide though not unlimited discretion with regard to the investigation of terrorism. In such cases, therefore, the Convention may excuse a less objective standard of suspicion. Although terrorism laws often dispense with the requirement of *reasonable* suspicion in relevant arrest powers, the Court will still insist on some objectivity, albeit watered down by the exigencies of the situation. Thus, in *Murray v United Kingdom*,[52] it held that in view of the difficulties inherent in the investigation of terrorism in Northern Ireland the reasonableness of the suspicion could not always be judged according to the same standards that were applied in cases of conventional crime. The Court stressed that the fact that the domestic provision was couched in subjective terms, merely requiring a suspicion that was honestly and genuinely held, was not decisive but nevertheless instructive. On the facts, the Court found no violation of Article 5(1) when the applicant had been arrested because there was sufficient evidence from her past activities and association with others to justify the suspicion that she was involved in funding terrorism.

This dilemma was considered again in *O'Hara v United Kingdom*,[53] where although the European Court confirmed that the exigencies of dealing with terrorist crime could not stretch the notion of reasonableness so as to impair the safeguards of Article 5(1)(c), it was prepared to modify the normal requirements of objectivity. In this case the applicant, a well-known

---

[48] *O'Hara v United Kingdom* (2002) 34 EHRR 32.
[49] [2010] EWCA Civ 524.
[50] (1990) 13 EHRR 157.
[51] In *Brogan v United Kingdom* (1989) 11 EHRR 117, the European Court held that it was sufficient to arrest a person on suspicion of being involved in terrorism as that phrase was defined in the relevant legislation and that in that case the applicants were questioned about specific acts and allegations.
[52] (1995) 19 EHRR 193.
[53] (2002) 34 EHRR 32.

member of Sinn Fein, had been arrested on suspicion of the murder of a German national, the arrest being based on specific information provided by informants and then passed on to the police by the Special Branch that he was involved in the murder. He was informed that he was being arrested under s.12 of the Prevention of Terrorism (Temporary Provisions) Act 1984, which allowed arrest on reasonable suspicion that a person was concerned in the (commission) of acts of terrorism, and was taken to a detention centre where he was questioned for six and a half days and then released without charge. Domestic civil proceedings failed on the grounds that the courts were satisfied that there was sufficient evidence provided to the police to justify his arrest on reasonable suspicion of involvement with terrorism.[54]

The European Court held that the reasonableness of the suspicion on which an arrest must be based formed an essential safeguard against arbitrary arrest and detention and that there must exist some facts which would satisfy an objective observer that a person may have committed an offence. Nevertheless, that had to be considered in all the circumstances, particularly that terrorist crime posed particular problems as the police may have to rely on evidence which is reliable but which cannot be disclosed for fear of jeopardising others. In the present case the suspicion was based on information passed on to the police by informers who had identified the applicant as one of a number of persons involved in the murder. The arrest was, therefore, a pre-planned operation, and was based on more substantial evidence than present in the case of *Fox, Campbell and Hartley*, above, and the purpose of the detention was to confirm or dispel that suspicion. Accordingly that arrest, and the domestic courts' assessment regarding the legality of the arrest and detention came within Article 5. Dissenting, Judge Loucaides equated the present case with *Fox* on the basis that in neither case had the courts been provided with grounds to justify the reasonableness of the suspicion.

The decision in *O'Hara* thus recognises that the full rigours of objectivity often have to be compromised in such cases so as to accommodate the difficulties of providing open and fully objective evidence. This suggests that current domestic arrest powers with respect to terrorism are probably consistent with Article 5 of the Convention, provided they are executed in good faith. Under s.31 of the Terrorism Act 2000 the police have the power to arrest, without a warrant, a person whom the officer *reasonably* suspects of being a terrorist, and thus the provision requires objectivity. However, as terrorism covers not only the commission of terrorist offences, but also 'being concerned' with such, there is the danger that individuals could be detained on the basis of association with others rather than any clear connection with criminal activities.

Lawful detention of minors

Article 5(1)(d) allows for the detention of a minor by lawful order for the purpose of educational supervision or his lawful detention for the purpose of bringing him before the competent legal authority. The European Court insists that the applicant be detained in a place that has such educational facilities. Thus, in *Bouamar v Belgium*[55] it was held that although the confinement of a juvenile in a remand prison does not necessarily contravene Article 5, the state must put in place appropriate institutional facilities to meet educational objectives. That principle was applied in *DG v Ireland*,[56] where it was held that the sending to prison of a

---

[54] *O'Hara v Chief Constable of the RUC* [1997] 1 All ER 129.
[55] (1988) 11 EHRR 1.
[56] (2002) 35 EHRR 33.

16-year-old boy, who had been originally recommended to be placed in a high support therapeutic unit because of his personality disorder, was not lawful within Article 5(1)(d). The applicant had been sent to a prison when the High Court decided that there were no secure educational facilities available elsewhere. The European Court held that the court's detention order was not based on any specific proposal for his secure and supervised accommodation, but rather that he had been sent there as the least offensive of the various inappropriate options available.[57]

Lawful detention of persons for the protection of society

Article 5(1)(e) provides for the lawful detention of persons for the prevention of the spreading of infectious diseases, of persons of unsound mind, alcoholics or drug addicts or vagrants. With regard to the detention of those of unsound mind, the European Court has stated that that person must be reliably shown to be of unsound mind; the mental disorder must be of a kind or degree warranting compulsory confinement; and the validity of the continued detention depended on the persistence of that disorder.[58] These principles were considered in *Johnson v United Kingdom*,[59] where the applicant had been recommended for release from a mental hospital subject to his living in a hostel and being supervised by social workers. This was delayed as the tribunal could find no suitable accommodation, and he claimed that the failure by the authorities to ensure that there were adequate hostel facilities for the applicant to be sent to was in violation of Article 5(1). The Court held that although it was not unlawful to continue to detain a person once the mental disorder had ceased – in other words he was not entitled to immediate and unconditional release because there might be good reasons for the authorities to defer his release until it would be more appropriate – any release must not be unreasonably delayed. In the present case the tribunal had no power to ensure that a placement was found, and thus there had been a breach of Article 5. In contrast, in *Kolanis v United Kingdom*,[60] it was held that there had been no violation of Article 5(1) when the applicant had not been conditionally released from a mental hospital because of a lack of medical and psychiatric support for supervised release. There was no absolute obligation on the state to ensure such facilities and as her mental ill health was still in existence there had been no violation of Article 5(1).[61]

The detention of vagrants was considered in *De Wilde, Ooms and Versyp v Belgium (the 'Vagrancy cases')*,[62] where the European Court held that there was no definition of such in the Convention, and that the domestic authorities would enjoy a wide power to define the term in domestic law. The Court stressed that Article 5(1)(e) was supplemented by Article 5(4), which allows a person to challenge the legality of their detention. In this case, as the applicants had been detained by order of a magistrate by a summary procedure not containing the benefits of a normal criminal process, there had been a violation of Article 5(4).

---

[57] The Court also found a violation of Article 5(5) of the Convention because the detention being lawful in domestic law, there was no enforceable right to compensation for such detention.

[58] *Winterwerp v Netherlands* (1979) 2 EHRR 387. See also *X v United Kingdom* (1982) 4 EHRR 188.

[59] (1997) 27 EHRR 296.

[60] (2006) 42 EHRR 12.

[61] However, the Court found a violation of Article 5(4) because for over a year she had not been able to have her continued detention considered by a court until her final conditional discharge.

[62] (1971) 1 EHRR 373.

Lawful arrest or detention of aliens and deportees

Article 5(1)(f) provides for the lawful arrest or detention of a person to prevent him from effecting an entry into the country, including the arrest or detention of those against whom action is being taken with a view to deportation or extradition. Such arrest or detention will be unlawful under Article 5 if the state authorities are acting in bad faith or have employed illegal means to achieve its aims. For example, in *Bozano* v *France*,[63] the European Court held that there had been a violation of Article 5 when the French police officers had forcibly escorted the applicant, an Italian national, to the Swiss border and handed him over to the Swiss authorities following a refusal by a French court to order his extradition. The applicant's liberty had been compromised in order to effect a disguised extradition and to circumvent the order of the French Court, and in such circumstances, the deprivation of liberty was neither 'lawful', nor compatible with the 'right to security of the person'.

The Court must be satisfied that the detention is effected for genuine reasons and pending deportation and is thus not being used for spurious reasons.[64] Thus, in *A* v *United Kingdom*[65] the European Court held that apart from certain individuals who had been subject to detention without trial under the Anti-Terrorism, Crime and Security Act 2001, and who been detained for short periods before leaving the country, there was no evidence that the other applicants were being detained pending 'action being taken with a view of deportation', as required by Article 5(1)(f). As a consequence there had been a violation of Article 5(1), which would remain unlawful unless lawfully derogated from under Article 15 of the Convention.

Equally, for a detention to be lawful there must exist some measures to ensure that the detention has not been ordered for arbitrary reasons or that the detention is not unreasonably prolonged. Thus, domestic law must provide some possibility of that detention being reviewed by an independent authority. For example, in *Quinn* v *France*[66] the European Court held that the detention of the applicant for a period of two years while extradition proceedings were pending constituted a violation of Article 5 as the applicant's detention had been unreasonably delayed without good reason. In contrast, in *Chahal* v *United Kingdom*,[67] the European Court held that here had been no violation of Article 5(1) when the applicant had been detained pending his deportation to India. The proceedings had to be conducted with due diligence if they were to be acceptable under the Convention, and in this case his lengthy detention – a period of six years between his initial detention and the failure of the final judicial review proceedings – was not excessive, particularly as there was an immigration advisory panel to check on any potential arbitrariness of any detention.[68]

The detention of deportees in prison has excited much criticism, but in *T* v *Secretary of State for the Home Department*[69] it was held that the detention pending deportation in prison rather than in an immigration removal centre was not contrary to the individual's Convention

---

[63] (1986) 9 EHRR 297.

[64] In *HXA* v *Home Office* [2010] EWHC 1177 QB it was held that a person detained under the Immigration Act 1971 pending deportation was being unlawfully detained if the joint purpose of the detention was to investigate whether he should be extradited to the receiving country to face criminal charges.

[65] (2009) 49 EHRR 29.

[66] (1995) 21 EHRR 529.

[67] (1996) 23 EHRR 413.

[68] See also *R (Q)* v *Home Secretary* [2006] EWCA Civ 2690, where the Court of Appeal held that there had been no violation of Article 5 when the applicant had been detained for nine months pending his deportation to Algeria. The applicant had been a master of aliases and the governments had taken constant steps to verify his identity.

[69] Decision of the Administrative Court, 18 December 2007.

rights. In this case the claimant had been detained in a secure unit in prison as he was a police informer and vulnerable to attacks and threats, and complained that this was contrary to Articles 5 and 8 of the Convention. The court held that there was no rule precluding the use of such prison facilities for persons awaiting deportation and equally there was no duty on the state to provide such facilities in immigration centres. Further, in *R (WL) v Secretary of State for Home Department*,[70] the Court of Appeal held that it would not be unlawful to detain foreign national prisoners pending deportation with a rebuttable presumption in favour of detention, subject to the period of detention being reasonable. However, it stated that it would be unlawful to operate such a policy on a blanket basis.

Similarly, domestic measures allowing the detention of asylum seekers pending the determination of their asylum claims have been declared compatible with the Convention. In *R (Saadi) v Secretary of State for the Home Department*,[71] the House of Lords held that the temporary detention of asylum seekers pending a fast-track determination of their asylum claims was not in violation of Article 5. That decision was confirmed by the Grand Chamber of the European Court of Human Rights in *Saadi v United Kingdom*,[72] where it held that the detention had been ordered as a necessary and genuine part of the immigration process under Article 5(1)(f) and was neither arbitrary not excessive in length. In the Court's view the detention of lawful immigrants was capable of being compatible with paragraph (f) since a potential immigrant had not effected a lawful entry until he was granted leave to remain in the country. Although the applicant had been granted temporary admission, his detention was still to prevent him effecting an unlawful entry in the absence of formal clearance; there was no requirement that such detention was necessary to prevent him absconding. Given the administrative problems with which the United Kingdom was confronted at the time, with an escalating flow of huge numbers of asylum seekers, it was not incompatible with Article 5 to detain the applicants for seven days in suitable conditions to enable the asylum claim to be processed speedily.[73]

In contrast, in *Nadarajah v Secretary of State for the Home Department*[74] the Court of Appeal held that the detention of asylum seekers pending their removal from the country was in violation of Article 5 of the Convention where the asylum seekers had given notice to the Home Secretary of their intention to initiate judicial review proceedings. Although the Home Secretary was entitled to have a policy encouraging expedition in appealing or applying for judicial review, the Home Secretary's policy was not generally known and accessible. In this case the applicant had given clear notice of his intention to apply for judicial review and thus his deportation was not imminent. In such a case his detention was in violation of Article 5(1)(f) of the Convention and thus lacked legality.[75]

---

[70] [2010] 1 WLR 2168.

[71] [2002] 1 WLR 3131.

[72] (2008) 47 EHRR 17.

[73] Contrast *S v Secretary of State for the Home Department* [2007] EWHC 1654 (Admin), that it was unlawful to detain a mother and her children who had stayed in the country illegally because there were no grounds for believing that they would not comply with the conditions of temporary release. In that case the mother had been in the country for two years and thus there were no grounds for believing that she would abscond pending deportation.

[74] [2003] EWCA Civ 1768.

[75] See also *R (Konan) v Secretary of State for the Home Department* [2004] EWHC 22 (Admin). Further, in *ID v Home Office* [2006] 1 WLR 1003, the Court of Appeal held that immigration officers did not have immunity from an action in damages for false imprisonment when it had been established that their decisions to detain were *ultras vires*.

> **Questions**
> In what circumstances does Article 5 allow liberty to be interfered with?
> What restrictions do the Convention and the courts place on the application of those interferences?

Right to be informed of reasons for arrest and charge

Article 5(2) provides that everyone who is arrested shall be informed properly, in a language which he understands, of the reasons for his arrest and of any charge against him. For example, in *Saadi v United Kingdom*, above, it was held that there had been a breach of Article 5(2) when the immigration authorities had taken 76 hours in informing the applicants why they were being detained at an immigration centre pending the determination of their asylum claim. Nevertheless, the Court has given some latitude to the state and has held that the individual need not be supplied with full information of the reasons for arrest at the actual time of that arrest. For example, in *Fox, Campbell and Hartley v United Kingdom*[76] it was held that an interval of a few hours between the arrest and the provisions of reasons did not violate Article 5(2). Although the fact that the applicants were simply told that they were being arrested under s.11 of the Northern Ireland (Emergency Provisions) Act 1978 on suspicion of being terrorists, and that was not sufficient to comply with the requirement that a person should know why he was being detained, the fact that they were questioned in relation to specific acts and allegations satisfied Article 5(2) and complied with the requirement that people should be informed promptly. Similarly, in *Murray (Margaret) v United Kingdom*,[77] it was held that although the reasons for the applicant's arrest had not been brought to her attention at the time of her arrest, she had been sufficiently notified during her subsequent interrogation and an interval of a few hours did not fall outside the definition of promptness as required by Article 5(2). In the Court's view, it must have been apparent to the applicant that she was being questioned about her possible involvement in the collection of funds for the IRA.

Right to be brought promptly before a judge for trial or release

Article 5(3) provides that everyone arrested or detained in accordance with Article 5(1)(c) of the Convention shall be brought promptly before a judge or other officer authorised by law to exercise judicial power. That person is then entitled to trial within a reasonable time, or to release pending trial, although Article 5(3) specifically provides that release may be made conditional by guarantees to appear for trial.

This provision ensures that there are judicial or other safeguards against arbitrary arrest and detention, ensuring impartial and independent control, and for Article 5(3) to be complied with, 'the other officer' in question must be independent of the executive and the parties to the action, and there must be an absence of appearance of bias. For example, in *Assenov v Bulgaria*,[78] the European Court held that there had been a violation of Article 5 when the applicant had been arrested and placed on remand, the decision being approved by a state prosecutor. As prosecutors could subsequently have acted against the applicant in

---

[76] (1990) 13 EHRR 157.
[77] (1994) 19 EHRR 193.
[78] (1999) 28 EHRR 652.

criminal proceedings, they were not sufficiently independent or impartial for the purpose of Article 5(3).[79] Again, in *Thompson v United Kingdom*,[80] the European Court held that there had been a violation of Article 5 when the applicant had been subjected to summary detention by his commanding officer before being tried in a Magistrate's Court. The Court found that the officer could not be regarded as independent and impartial for the purposes of Article 5(3).[81]

Article 5(3) in the terrorist context

A person must be brought before the relevant judicial authority 'promptly' and the meaning of that phrase in the context of terrorist crime was considered in *Brogan v United Kingdom*.[82] In this case the applicants had been arrested by the police having been suspected of involvement in acts of terrorism. They were all detained for periods between four and a half and six days and eventually released without charge. The European Court held that the requirement that they be brought before a court 'promptly' was violated in this case, despite the circumstances of terrorism.[83] Although the Court did not specify what delay would have been reasonable, it concluded that even the shortest of the periods involved in this case was inconsistent with the notion of promptness laid down in Article 5(3). To justify so lengthy a period of detention would involve a serious weakening of this procedural guarantee to the detriment of the individual, impairing the very essence of the right. A similar breach was found in *O'Hara v United Kingdom*,[84] where the applicant, who had been arrested on suspicion of murder, had been held for six days and 13 hours before his eventual release. Applying the principles expounded in *Brogan*, the European Court held unanimously that there had been a violation of Article 5(3) of the Convention, a finding which was conceded by the British government.

Such rulings call into question the compatibility of current domestic detention powers with respect to the prevention of terrorism. As we have seen, the government have argued, largely unsuccessfully, that detentions via control orders under sections 1–3 of the Prevention of Terrorism Act 2005, do not involve deprivation of liberty and thus do not engage Article 5 of the Convention. On the other hand, sections 4–6 of the 2005 Act provide for derogating control orders. In these cases it is conceded that Article 5 is engaged and that the detention would otherwise violate Article 5(3) of the Convention as interpreted in cases such as *Brogan*. These orders will allow detention for up to six months but can only be made once a derogation order has been made. The government believes that the provisions are compatible with Article 15 of the Convention because they are made by a court after a hearing, albeit in the absence of the individual.[85]

---

[79] See also *Hood v United Kingdom* (2000) 29 EHRR 365, and *Jordan v United Kingdom* (2001) 31 EHRR 6, where it was held that the detention of a soldier by the commanding officer pending a court martial was in violation of Article 5(3) because such an officer would play a substantial role in the subsequent prosecution.

[80] (2005) 40 EHRR 11.

[81] The European Court also held that the summary proceedings conducted by the Commanding Officer lacked impartiality and were thus in violation of Article 6, the officer being central to the prosecution and at the same time the sole judge. Military discipline is discussed in more detail in the next chapter.

[82] (1989) 11 EHRR 117.

[83] In *Ocalan v Turkey*, discussed above under Article 5(1), the Grand Chamber found a violation of Article 5(3) when the applicant had been kept in police custody for a period of seven days before being brought before the judicial authorities. The Court saw no necessity for such a delay, despite the dangerousness of the applicant and his connection with acts of terrorism.

[84] (2002) 34 EHRR 32.

[85] The compatibility of control orders with Article 6 of the Convention will be discussed in the next chapter and in chapter 14.

Apart from control orders, domestic terrorism provisions allow for extended periods of detention of terrorist suspects. Initially, a person arrested under s.41 of the Terrorism Act 2000 can be detained up to 48 hours, but that period may be extended up to 28 days by a judge,[86] the government believing that the judicial involvement complies with Article 5 of the Convention.[87] Thus, while the law before 2000 allowed extended detention at the discretion of the executive (the Home Secretary), the current law requires judicial approval and review. The government believes that these judicial safeguards make the provisions compatible with Article 5 and the decision in *Brogan*, and thus no derogation is thought necessary in this respect. Indeed, in *R (I) v City of Westminster Magistrates' Court*[88] it was held that s.41 was not incompatible with Article 5 of the Convention. In the court's view, although there was no power to release on bail, there was judicial control over whether there was to be further detention – any detention had to be justified before a Magistrate and then, if an extension was granted, by a High Court judge – and thus sufficient protection for the individual for the purpose of Article 5.

Article 5(3) and pre-trial detention

Although Article 5 does not prohibit the pre-trial detention of an individual, for such detention to be permissible there must be sufficient safeguards against arbitrary or unnecessary loss of liberty. Thus, in *Caballero v United Kingdom*[89] it was held that the automatic denial of bail pending trial was in violation of Article 5(3) and that the government was also in breach of its obligation to provide compensation for arrests in violation of Article 5.[90] That formal approach can be contrasted with the House of Lords' decision in *O v Harrow Crown Court*,[91] where it was held that s.25 of the Criminal Justice and Public Order Act 1994 (which provided that in cases where the defendant had a prior conviction for sexual offences bail would only be granted if the court was satisfied that there were exceptional circumstances to justify it) was compatible with Article 5(3). In this case, therefore, the defendant's detention in custody for a period of 22 months and beyond the 182-day custody time limit, did not offend Article 5(3), particularly as the reasons for refusing bail in this case were very strong.

This appears to be consistent with the approach taken by the European Court in *McKay v United Kingdom*,[92] which stresses that the absence of a specific right of bail is not necessarily in contravention of Article 5(3) provided there are sufficient safeguards against arbitrary detention. In that case the Court stressed that Article 5(3) provided protection in both the initial period following arrest and the period pending trial, but that both rights were distinct from each other. Judicial control over the initial decision with a power to order release provided the safeguard for the first right, and under the second limb the judges were under an obligation to review the continued detention pending trial to ensure release when it was no longer necessary. There was no requirement that the two issues be dealt with by the same

---

[86] A district judge can approve an extension up to 14 days and a High Court judge up to 28 days. Any extension must not exceed 7 days at a time.

[87] Section 41(7) (and Schedule 8 of the Terrorism Act 2000), as amended by the Terrorism Act 2006. Initially the government wanted a period of 90 days and was ultimately defeated in its efforts to increase the limit to 42 days in the Counter-Terrorism Bill 2008.

[88] [2008] EWHC 2146.

[89] (2000) 30 EHRR 643.

[90] See also *SBC v United Kingdom* (2002) 34 EHRR 1.

[91] [2007] 1 AC 249.

[92] (2007) 44 EHRR 41.

judicial officer. Accordingly, in *R (I) v City of Westminster Magistrates' Court*[93] it was held that although s.41 of the Terrorism Act 2000 contained no power to release on bail, there was judicial control over whether there was to be further detention and thus sufficient protection for the individual for the purpose of Article 5. Accordingly there was no breach of that article.

With respect to the length of pre-trial detention, in *Kevin O'Dowd v United Kingdom*[94] the European Court has stressed that it must have regard to both the presumption of innocence and all the facts in assessing whether there has been a breach and whether the public interest justified a departure form the general rule in Article 5. In addition the Court should be satisfied that the domestic authorities displayed special diligence in the conduct of the proceedings, having regard to any periods of unjustified delay, the complexity of the proceedings, and any steps taken to ensure that the length of the detention was reasonable.

Right to challenge lawfulness of detention

Article 5(4) of the Convention provides that everyone deprived of their liberty by arrest or detention shall be entitled to take proceedings by which the lawfulness of their detention shall be decided speedily by a court and their release ordered if the detention is not lawful.[95] This right is fundamental to the rule of law as a safeguard against arbitrary detention by the state, allowing the individual to challenge any detention before a court of law to ensure that the detention is both within the strict law and consistent with the basic principles of due process, even if the original detention was not arbitrary, and was *prima facie* lawful under Article 5(1)(c).[96]

Central to the protection offered by this provision is the access to an independent body with judicial powers. Thus, in *Ocalan v Turkey*[97] it was held that there had been a violation of Article 5(4) despite the fact that domestic law allowed for judicial review of the original detention. The Grand Chamber noted that there had not been any instance of a successful review, and in any case the applicant in this case had been denied access to legal advice, rendering such opportunity for review worthless. Article 5(4) has also been used domestically to challenge the legality of the parole procedure for prisoners serving indeterminate sentences. In *R (Brooke) v Parole Board*[98] it was held that the Parole Board, which considers the early release of prisoners, was not sufficiently independent so as to satisfy either Article 5(4) or the common law rule against bias. In the court's view, the Board, which was identified as an executive non-departmental public body acting under the sponsorship of the newly created Ministry of Justice, lacked the objective appearance of independence from the department, particularly with respect to funding, appointment of its members and the directions it received from the ministry.

---

[93] [2008] EWHC 2146.

[94] Application No 7390/07, decision of the European Court, 21 September 2010. The Court found that there had been no violation of Article 5(3) on the facts because the applicant had contributed substantially to the delay and the authorities had overall acted with due diligence.

[95] This would include the right to attend a hearing of an appeal against refusal of bail: *Allen v United Kingdom* (2010) 51 EHRR 22.

[96] In *Al-Jedda v Ministry of Defence, The Times*, 9 September 2010, the Court of Appeal held that the detention of a suspected terrorist was lawful under the Iraqi constitution despite the decision being made not by a judge but a specially appointed tribunal who had quasi-judicial qualities.

[97] (2005) 41 EHRR 45.

[98] *The Times*, 5 February 2008.

A detention will be lawful where the European Court is satisfied that a court has ordered the original detention and that that original order is sufficiently linked to the subsequent detention. Article 5(4) does not, therefore, confer a right of appeal where the original detention is imposed by the court, and there remains a sufficient link between that sentence and the subsequent detention.[99] However, where a decision depriving a person of his liberty is taken by an administrative body, Article 5(4) obliges the state to make available to the person detained a right of recourse to a court. In such cases, at the very least a judicial body should have the power to question the evidence upon which an individual has lost his liberty. Thus, in *Chahal v United Kingdom*[100] the European Court held that the domestic courts' inability to access the information which was the basis of the government's claim of national security, coupled with the lack of procedural safeguards in the advisory panel's proceedings, meant that there had been a violation of Article 5(4).

This issue of access to evidence was raised in *A v United Kingdom*,[101] where the European Court had to consider the detention of foreign terrorist suspects on the basis of closed evidence. In that case it was alleged that the procedure before the Special Immigration Appeals Commission (SIAC) was unfair because it had regard to closed evidence that was not made available to the applicants and their lawyers. The European Court confirmed that Article 5(4) required a detained person to be given an opportunity to challenge any allegation that formed the basis of their detention and that generally that would require the disclosure of any evidence against the detainee. Whether Article 5(4) was satisfied depended on whether the allegations made against the applicants were sufficiently specific to allow them to provide the lawyers and the special advocate with information in order to refute such allegations. On the facts, although allegations against some of the applicants had been specific and related to possession of specific documents, others had been general, such as being a member of a named extremist group. Consequently, there had been a violation of Article 5(4) in respect of these applicants.[102]

In *Winterwerp v Netherlands*,[103] the Court stressed that the review must not be limited to the bare legality of the detention, and requires a review of lawfulness to be available at reasonable intervals. However, it also held in that case that to comply with Article 5(4) it is not necessary that a court-like body be able to question and overturn every aspect of the original decision. Thus, in *X v United Kingdom*[104] the European Court held that Article 5(4) does not embody a right to judicial control of such scope as to empower the court, on all aspects of the case, to substitute its own discretion for that of the decision-making authority. Notwithstanding that, in the Court's view the review should be wide enough to bear on those conditions, which according to the Convention are essential for the lawful detention of, in this case, a person of unsound mind. Thus, in that case it held that Article 5(4) required an appropriate procedure allowing a court to examine whether the patient's disorder still existed and whether the minister was entitled to think that the applicant's continued compulsory detention was necessary in the interests of public safety.[105]

---

[99] *De Wilde, Ooms and Versyp v Belgium* (1971) 1 EHRR 373.
[100] (1997) 23 EHRR 413.
[101] (2009) 49 EHRR 29.
[102] The case is detailed in a case study in chapter 14.
[103] (1979) 2 EHRR 387.
[104] (1981) 4 EHRR 188.
[105] See also the decision in *Benjamin v United Kingdom* (2003) 36 EHRR 1, in relation to the release of discretionary life sentence prisoners who are subsequently detained in a mental hospital.

There may also be a violation of this provision if the law imposes a presumption of detention. In *R v Mental Health Tribunal, ex parte H*[106] the Court of Appeal held that s.72 and s.73 of the Mental Health Act 1983, which placed the burden of proof on a restricted patient to show that he was no longer suffering from a mental disorder warranting detention in order to satisfy the mental health review tribunal that he was entitled to discharge, was incompatible with Article 5. Following this decision the offending sections of the Act were amended requiring the tribunal to direct a person's discharge if it is not satisfied that the criteria justifying detention in hospital continue to exist.[107]

Release and recall of prisoners and Article 5

As we have seen, Article 5(1)(b) ensures that an individual is only detained within the law and after due process. In addition, someone in detention should be able to review the legality of their continued detention and at the heart of this provision lies the question of the release and recall of prisoners who have served the fixed part of their sentence, but who are nonetheless detained for the purpose of safeguarding the public from risk. A number of claims have been brought by prisoners with respect to the powers of the executive to determine the release of sentenced offenders.[108] This issue is particularly prevalent where the sentence includes a public risk period, where the prisoner can be detained beyond the punitive period set by the court. This section will first examine the position of Article 5 with respect to various life sentence prisoners, and will then briefly examine other types of sentences where the safeguards of Article 5 might apply.[109]

Discretionary lifers

These are prisoners serving a life sentence imposed in the court's discretion because of the characteristics of the prisoner and the offence. Their sentence will consist of a fixed term followed by a public risk period during which they will be eligible for release from, and then recall to, prison.[110] In relation to the post-tariff periods of discretionary life sentence prisoners, the European Court held in *Weeks v United Kingdom*[111] that because the purposes of the discretionary life sentence were susceptible to change over a period of time, the prisoner was entitled to apply to a court to decide speedily whether or not his deprivation of liberty had become lawful, both when the prisoner was recalled to prison, and at regular intervals thereafter. As in such cases the Parole Board only had an advisory power, and there was a lack of access for the prisoner to the reports before it; there had been a violation of Article 5 in this case. Similarly, in *Thynne, Wilson and Gunnell v United Kingdom*,[112] the Court confirmed that the system by which the Home Secretary determined the release of such prisoners was

---

[106] [2001] 3 WLR 512.

[107] See the Mental Health Act 1983 (Remedial) Order 2001.

[108] See Padfield, *Beyond the Tariff: Human Rights and the Release of Life Sentence Prisoners* (Willan Publishing 2002).

[109] For a comprehensive coverage of this area, see Livingstone, Owen and MacDonald, *Prison Law* (OUP 2008), chapters 13 and 14.

[110] In *Waite v United Kingdom* (2003) 36 EHRR 44, the European Court of Human Rights held that the recall of a discretionary life sentence prisoner without being afforded the right to an oral hearing was incompatible with Article 5(4) of the Convention.

[111] (1987) 10 EHRR 293.

[112] (1990) 13 EHRR 666.

contrary to Article 5(4) of the Convention. In that case three discretionary life sentence prisoners convicted of serious sexual and violent offences argued successfully that the release provisions relating to them failed to provide them with the right to challenge the legality of their continued detention, and subsequently s.34 of the Criminal Justice Act 1991 took away the Home Secretary's power to determine the prisoner's tariff and vested the ultimate decision of release in the Parole Board. The Court has also held that discretionary lifers who are subsequently detained in a mental hospital, and whose release is at the ultimate discretion of the Home Secretary, were entitled to the protection of Article 5(4) and that there had been a violation of that provision because the decision was taken by the executive without adequate review by a tribunal or the courts.[113]

The European Court has also insisted that the legality and necessity of such prisoners' detention should be reviewed at regular intervals.[114] In *Oldham v United Kingdom*,[115] the Court held that what constituted a reasonable interval depended on the facts but in this case a delay of two years between the prisoner's reviews constituted a violation of the Convention. Again, in *Hirst v United Kingdom*,[116] it was held that there had been a violation of Article 5(4) of the Convention when the applicant, a discretionary life sentence prisoner who had served his tariff period, had to wait 21 months and two years between the reviews of his detention by the Discretionary Lifer Panel. Although the European Court refused to state what in general was a reasonable period, it held that because in this case the prisoner had served a considerable period of imprisonment and had developed significantly during the course of his sentence, and could not be considered as a person in respect of whom no further change of circumstances could be envisaged, the periods in question were not in conformity with Article 5(4).[117] The domestic courts have adopted a flexible approach in this area, and in *R v HM Prison Lifer Panel, ex parte MacNeil*,[118] it was held that where the prisoner had been recalled to prison and had been recommended for detention in open conditions, it was not irrational for the panel to recommend a review in under two years. That decision can be contrasted with the European Court's ruling in *Blackstock v United Kingdom*,[119] where a life sentence prisoner had applied for transfer to open conditions as a prerequisite of his post-tariff release and had to wait a further 22 months before the Lifer Panel reconsidered that request. The Court held that the authorities had failed to have due regard to the principle of expedition and also found a violation of Article 5(5) because the applicant had no possibility of obtaining compensation in domestic law at that time. Similarly, in *R v Secretary of State for the Home Department and Another, ex parte Noorkoiv and Another*,[120] the Court of Appeal held that the policy of referring lifers' cases on a quarterly basis, which meant that the case would

---

[113] *Benjamin v United Kingdom* (2003) 36 EHRR 1. See also *R (D) v Secretary of State for the Home Department* [2002] 1 WLR 1315, where it was held that the power of the Home Secretary to detain a discretionary life sentence prisoner who had since his imprisonment been transferred to mental hospital, was incompatible with the applicant's Convention rights under Article 5(4).

[114] This also now applies to post-tariff mandatory lifers; see below.

[115] (2001) 31 EHRR 34.

[116] *The Times*, 3 August 2001.

[117] See also *Hutchison and Reid v United Kingdom* (2003) 37 EHRR 9, where there had been a violation of Article 5(4) when a patient's release had been unreasonably delayed. The Court also held that the burden of proof placed on the applicant to show that he should no longer be detained was inconsistent with that article.

[118] *The Times*, 18 April 2001.

[119] (2006) 42 EHRR 2.

[120] [2002] 4 All ER 515.

be heard by the Parole Board three months after the expiry of the tariff, was in violation of Article 5(4) of the Convention. Delays could not be justified by the Board's lack of financial resources,[121] and to avoid the delay the Board should consider the prisoner's post-release risk before the expiry of the tariff period.[122]

Mandatory lifers

These are prisoners who have received a mandatory life sentence because the law provides for such a sentence for certain offences, such as murder. Again, the sentence will consist of both a fixed and public risk period. In *Wynne v United Kingdom*,[123] the European Court drew a distinction between discretionary life sentence prisoners and those serving a mandatory life sentence for murder. In the latter case, the sentence itself, being prescribed by law and passed without any judicial discretion, constituted sufficient protection against arbitrary detention. Thus no issues under Article 5(1) or (4) were raised. The decision in *Wynne* was, however, reviewed in *Stafford* v *United Kingdom*,[124] where the European Court established that there was no significant difference between the different types of life sentence. Thus, as the mandatory life sentence in effect consisted of two sentences, the latter being based on risk to the public in the light of the changing personal circumstances of the individual, decisions on the release of such prisoners needed to be made by a court-like body with the power to order release if detention was no longer necessary.

In *Stafford* the applicant had received a mandatory life sentence in 1967. In 1979 he was released on licence, but recalled for breach of his licence conditions. He was released again in 1991, but in 1994 he was convicted of fraud and received a six-year prison sentence. In 1997 the Parole Board recommended his release, but the Home Secretary, fearing that there was still a risk of him committing further, non-violent offences, refused to release him. Stafford brought an application claiming that his detention from the time of the Home Secretary's refusal to his ultimate release was unlawful. The European Court found that his detention could only be justified on the basis of his danger to the public from the risk of further violence. Thus, there was no sufficient causal connection between the possibility that he might commit other non-violent offences and the original sentence for murder in 1967. Such a detention was not within the spirit of the Convention and was in violation of Article 5(1).[125] The Court also found that there had been a breach of Article 5(4) of the Convention in that the applicant had not had the lawfulness of his detention reviewed by a court-like body with a power to order his release.[126]

Following the decisions in *Stafford v United Kingdom*, parliament passed the Criminal Justice Act 2003, which normally requires the Home Secretary to accept the Parole Board's recommendation for release of a mandatory lifer after the serving of the tariff period.

---

[121] See *R (Cawley) v Parole Board*, decision of the High Court, 29 October 2007, where it was held that a delay caused by the shortage of Parole Board members constituted a violation of Article 5(4).

[122] However, the Court of Appeal rejected the submission that prisoners sentenced to automatic life sentences under s.2 of the Crime (Sentences) Act 1997 should take precedence over other life sentence prisoners.

[123] (1994) 19 EHRR 333.

[124] (2002) 35 EHRR 32.

[125] See also *Waite v United Kingdom* (2003) 36 EHRR 54, where it was held that the applicant's redetention on the grounds that he was a danger to himself and that he was conducting a homosexual relationship with a 16-year-old boy, was in violation of Articles 5 and 8 of the Convention.

[126] See also *Wynne v United Kingdom* (2004) 38 EHRR 42; *King v United Kingdom* (2005) 41 EHRR 2.

In addition, following the House of Lords' decision in *R (Anderson)* v *Secretary of State for the Home Department, the Home Secretary*,[127] considered under Article 6, later, the 2003 Act establishes clear guidance by which the courts can fix tariffs for mandatory life sentence prisoners.[128]

Offenders detained at Her Majesty's pleasure

In relation to young offenders who are detained at Her Majesty's pleasure, the European Court held in *Hussain and Singh* v *United Kingdom*[129] that such prisoners who had served their tariff periods were entitled to the same level of protection as discretionary lifers, and thus had the right to have their release determined by someone other than the Home Secretary. Also, in *V and T* v *United Kingdom*[130] the European Court held, *inter alia*, that there had been a violation of Article 5(4) of the Convention when the tariff had been set by the Home Secretary and had not been the subject of subsequent judicial challenge or confirmation. It also held that there had been a violation of Article 5(4) because the applicants had not since the setting of their tariff had the opportunity to challenge its legality and to get it independently reviewed.

As a result of those decisions legislation was introduced to ensure that such prisoners received the same protection as discretionary life sentence prisoners, and that the minimum terms were set and reviewed fairly. Those provisions and their application will be considered later with respect to Article 6 of the Convention.

Article 5 and other sentences

Whether Article 5 (and 6) of the Convention is engaged in the release and recall of prisoners serving determinate sentences has been the subject of a great deal of judicial debate and the principal rule is that it is not engaged because the original sentence, along with judicial review of the decision on release satisfies Article 5.

Thus, it has been held that Article 5(4) is not engaged in respect of offenders' sentences under s.80 of the Powers of Criminal Courts (Sentencing) Act 2002. This provision allows a court to impose a longer than fixed sentence in order to protect the public from serious harm from the offender. In *R* v *Parole Board, ex parte Giles*,[131] the House of Lords held that a prisoner serving an extended sentence was not covered by Article 5(4) of the Convention because the original sentence met the requirements of Article 5. Thus, the prisoner had no right to an oral hearing before the Parole Board after the punitive period of his sentence had expired. The House of Lords thus equated such sentences with determinate sentences. However, *Giles* was distinguished in *R* v *Parole Board, ex parte Sim*,[132] where it was held that Article 5 of the

---

[127] [2003] 1 AC 837.

[128] In *R (Middleton)* v *Secretary of State for the Home Department* [2003] EWHC 315 (Admin), it was held that the Secretary of State could continue with his powers to decide on the release of mandatory lifers provided his decision was not arbitrary. A member state was allowed a reasonable time to consider the implementation of interim measures prior to legislative change. However, in *King* v *Secretary of State for the Home Department* [2004] HRLR 9, it was held that there had been a violation of Article 5(4) of the Convention where a mandatory lifer's release had not been considered for nearly four years.

[129] (1996) 22 EHRR 1.

[130] (1999) 30 EHRR 121.

[131] [2004] HRLR 9.

[132] [2004] 2 WLR 1170.

Convention was engaged when a prisoner who had received an extended licence under s.85 of the 2002 Act had been recalled and detained for breach of that licence. The Court of Appeal held the Article was not satisfied by the original sentence of the court.[133]

Until recent reforms there had been some confusion because the House of Lords had held that although the Convention does not guarantee early release, such powers that do exist must comply with the Convention. In *R (Clift) v Home Secretary*[134] it was held that the early release provisions contained in the Criminal Justice Act 1991 for long-term prisoners (those sentenced to 15 years or more) were incompatible with Article 5 of the Convention because they denied such prisoners the right of access to the Parole Board. In their Lordships' view the right to early release, where domestic law provided such, clearly engaged Article 5 and needed to be inspected under Article 14. Long-term prisoners were being treated differently from short-term and discretionary life sentence prisoners and the factor of risk to the public was no longer a valid one, having become since *Stafford* an indefensible analogy.

Despite this ruling, on the facts, it was held that *Clift* had not been treated differently on grounds of 'other status' within Article 14 because that phrase referred to personal characteristics and not to what the person had done in the past. In this case the length of the sentence was not a personal characteristic falling within Article 14, and thus there had been no breach in his case. However, Clift made an application under the Convention, and in *Clift v United Kingdom*[135] the European Court held that the applicant's status was one covered by Article 14 and that, unlike the situation where the difference in treatment is based purely on the gravity of the offence,[136] his treatment was different because of the length of the sentence. Although the Court recognised that the two were related, it noted that there were other factors that were relevant to the sentence including the judge's perceived risk to the public of the prisoner. Accordingly, where early release schemes applied to prisoners depending on the length of sentence there was a risk that unless they were objectively justified they may lead to arbitrary detention. The Court also held that the prisoner was in an analogous position with the other prisoners because the purpose of excluding the applicant from the early release scheme was not to punish him but to reflect the unacceptability of the risk of his release, and in that case no distinction could be drawn between long-term prisoners serving less than 15 years, long-term prisoners serving 15 years or more and life prisoners. As the methods of assessing risk were in principle the same for all prisoners, the applicant was in an analogous position with the other categories, and although the difference in treatment between those serving less than 15 years and those serving more might be capable of justification, in this case the government had failed to demonstrate how the approval of the Secretary of State for the release of the latter group addressed concerns for public security. Further, it was not justifiable to treat these prisoners less favourably than life sentence prisoners, when lifers often posed greater risks to the public on release. In any case, the anomaly was removed by subsequent legislation, which gave the sole power of release to the Parole Board in all determinative sentences; first by s.244

---

[133] It was also held that recall was only justified when there was a risk of reoffending related to offences of a similar nature to the triggering offence. In addition, it was held that s.44A of the Criminal Justice Act 1991, which allowed release if the Board was satisfied that it is no longer necessary for the protection of the public for the prisoner to be confined, should be read in such a way that the Board would reach that conclusion unless positively satisfied that the continuing detention was necessary in the public interest.

[134] [2007] 1 AC 484.

[135] *The Times*, 13 July 2010.

[136] *Gerger v Turkey* (Application No 24919/94).

of the Criminal Justice Act 2003 and subsequently by s.145 of the Coroners and Justice Act 2009.

In the domestic courts the decisions in *Clift* and *Giles* were clarified by the House of Lords in *R (Black)* v *Secretary of State for Justice*,[137] where it was confirmed that Article 5(4) was not engaged in cases involving prisoners with determinate sentences.[138] Although the Home Secretary's role in determining the release of long-term prisoners due for parole was rightly classified in *Clift* as anomalous, it was not contrary to the European Convention. The European Court case law drew a clear distinction between indeterminate sentences and fixed sentences, the latter satisfying Article 5 through the original sentence. Parole was an administrative process not covered by Article 5 and there was no requirement that the Parole Board be involved in such sentences; and the fact that they had did not engage Article 5. In *Black* the House of Lords also stated that the decision of the House of Lords in *R (Smith)* v *Parole Board*,[139] below, was peculiar to its facts because it was concerned with the recall of prisoners on licence. In *Sim* the House of Lords held that the common law duty to act fairly, although not requiring the Board to give an oral hearing in every case where a prisoner released on licence was recalled to prison, was not so constricted as to rule out the need for an oral hearing in some cases. Although the House of Lords held that Article 5(4) was satisfied provided the procedure complied with basic fairness, in the present case the prisoners should have been offered an oral hearing because the prisoners wished to challenge essential evidence that had been used as the basis for their recall.[140] This decision now has to be looked at in the light of the decision of the European Court in *Clift* and the subsequent legislative changes, above.

There has also been much judicial debate surrounding s.225 of the Criminal Justice Act 2003, which requires a court to impose a sentence for public protection where a person over the age of 18 has committed a serious or specified offence. In such a case the prisoner will serve a minimum period but may be retained in prison for an indefinite period for public protection. It is arguable that this sentence engages Article 5 and that the prisoner is thus entitled to have his detention reviewed by an independent court-like body which should release the prisoner if they are satisfied that he is no longer a risk to the public. In *R (Wells)* v *Parole Board*[141] it was held that continued detention would be unlawful under Article 5(4) if the authorities had not put into place an effective method of assessing the prisoner's danger. Thus, because the prison service had not put into place the necessary programmes to assess risk, there was no effective way in which that risk could be assessed by the Parole Board in order to judge whether continued detention was necessary.[142] However, in *Secretary of State for Justice* v *James and Walker*,[143] it was held that although the Secretary was in breach of his

---

[137] [2009] 1 AC 949.

[138] See also *R (Robinson)* v *Secretary of State for Justice* [2010] 1 WLR 2380, where it was held that provisions relating to the early release of prisoners serving determinative sentences were concerned with the administration of the sentence rather than the original sentence and were thus outside Article 6.

[139] [2005] 1 WLR 250.

[140] See also *R (Hirst)* v *Secretary of State for the Home Department and Another*, *The Times*, 4 July 2005. It was held that there had been a violation of Article 5(4) of the Convention when *a life sentence* prisoner had been recalled to prison for breach of his licence conditions and was not provided with reasons for the recall for eight days. This had delayed his giving representations to the Board and had thus delayed the Board's ultimate decision to release him, and the claimant was awarded £1500 in damages.

[141] *The Times*, 6 February 2008.

[142] The decision in *Wells* was followed in *R (James)* v *Secretary of State for Justice*, *The Times*, 6 February 2008.

[143] [2010] 1 AC 553.

public law duty to allow the Board to assess the risk of such offenders and to decide on release, it did not follow that the detention of the prisoners beyond the tariff terms was automatically unlawful. The detention would only become unlawful where it was no longer necessary to protect the public or where there had been an arbitrary delay. Their Lordships held that where a prisoner serving such a sentence was, after the tariff period had expired, unable to demonstrate his safety for release, his continued detention was not unlawful under common law. Nor was it in breach of Article 5 unless there had been a period of years without effective review. The prisoner's remedy was declaratory relief, not release, which would be in clear breach of the relevant legislation. Thus, detention beyond the tariff was justified with respect to Article 5 because the sentencing court had decided that that the prisoner would continue to be dangerous at the expiry of the tariff. Article 5(4) required no more than that the Parole Board speedily decide whether the prisoner continued to be lawfully detained and that would be the case unless and until it was satisfied as to his safety for release or unless so much time had elapsed that the causal link had been broken.

Finally, the European Court has held that decisions relating to classification and transfer of prisoners do not fall into the scope of Article 5 (or Article 6) of the Convention. For example, in *Blackstock* v *United Kingdom*,[144] the European Court declared inadmissible the claim that his categorisation decision should be made by a court-like body (Article 5 was not engaged by such a decision) and that the timing of the review should be set by a court. In addition, the High Court has held that a claim relating to the conditions of imprisonment do not engage the protection of Article 5 of the Convention.[145] However, such decisions are subject to the principles of natural justice. Thus, in *R* v *Secretary of State for the Home Department, ex parte Sunder*,[146] although Articles 5 or 6 were not engaged, the court still insisted that such prisoners be given the gist of reasons for the decision. Similarly, in *R (on the application of Williams)* v *Secretary of State for the Home Department*,[147] the Court of Appeal held that there might be circumstances in which a post-tariff discretionary life prisoner challenging his security classification was entitled to an oral hearing before the Category A Committee and to full disclosure of reports. More importantly, in *R* v *Secretary of State for the Home Department, ex parte Hirst*[148] the Court of Appeal held that a discretionary life sentence prisoner was entitled to make representations before a decision was made to move him from category C conditions to a category B prison.

Although the prisoner might not always be entitled to full reasons and disclosure, there may be circumstances where the courts order such. For example, in *R (Lord)* v *Secretary of State for the Home Department*[149] it was held that a category A prisoner was entitled to see the reports prepared by prison staff as the basis of his security classification so that he could become aware of any matter of fact or opinion relevant to his categorisation. To provide a gist of reasons that concealed that the views were not unanimous failed to comply with appropriate

---

[144] (2006) 42 EHRR 2.

[145] *R* v *Secretary of State for the Home Department, ex parte Burgess, Daily Telegraph*, 5 December 2000. See also *S* v *Airedale National Health Service Trust, The Times*, 5 September 2002, where it was held that the seclusion of a lawfully detained mental patient did not engage Article 5.

[146] [2001] EWHC 252 (Admin).

[147] [2002] 1 WLR 2264.

[148] *The Times*, 17 April 2001; [2002] HRLR 39.

[149] [2003] EWHC 2073.

standards, and, although there may be cases where the Secretary of State might justify less than full disclosure, a policy of blanket non-disclosure could never be justified.

> **Questions**
>
> How essential is Article 5 in upholding the rule of law and individual liberty?
>
> How did the recent decisions in *Wells* and *James* (above) uphold the inherent notions of justice in Article 5?

Right to compensation for breach of Article 5

Article 5(5) provides that everyone who has been the victim of an arrest or detention in contravention of Article 5 shall have an enforceable right to compensation, thus offering specific redress in the form of monetary compensation for violations of Article 5. This provision is incorporated into domestic law by the Human Rights Act 1998, and is the one exception where the act of a judicial officer may attract liability for damages.[150]

The provision is of particular relevance where the deprivation of an individual's liberty is lawful in domestic law, but subsequently found by the European Court to be in violation of Article 5 of the Convention. Thus, in *Brogan* v *United Kingdom*,[151] the European Court, having found that the applicants had not been brought promptly before a court, noted that their detention was perfectly lawful under domestic law, and thus could not give rise to an enforceable claim for compensation. Accordingly, the Court found there had been a violation of Article 5(5) in this respect, referring the question of compensation to the parties to the government in order to reach an appropriate settlement.

The issue of compensation for such unlawful detention was considered more recently by the European Court in *A* v *United Kingdom*,[152] with respect to the detention without trial of foreign terrorist suspects. Those individuals had been denied the right to compensation in the domestic courts because the detentions were strictly lawful under domestic law. In considering the applicants' claims for just satisfaction the European Court noted that it had not found a breach of Article 3 and thus could not consider compensation for mental suffering allegedly arising from the nature of the sentence and the conditions of detention. Nevertheless, as there had been breaches of Article 5(1), (4) and (5) with respect to various applicants, it could consider awarding monetary compensation if necessary; although it had the discretion to decide that judgment alone was sufficient satisfaction. Although the Court had made no award in *McCann* v *United Kingdom*,[153] because the immediate victims had intended to carry out a terrorist act, the present case was distinguishable because it had never been established that the applicants had engaged, or attempted to engage, in such acts. In this case the applicants had been detained for long periods of time which would normally require large sums in satisfaction. However, in this case the government had acted in good faith and the measures in question had been passed and applied for the genuine purpose of dealing with an emergency, which the domestic courts accepted existed. Although both courts found the

---

[150] See s.9 (3) Human Rights Act 1998.
[151] (1989) 11 EHRR 117, discussed above.
[152] (2009) 49 EHRR 29
[153] (1995) 21 EHRR 97.

measures disproportionate, a core part of those findings was based on the discriminatory effect of the provisions. Further, as the provisions had been subsequently replaced by control orders it could not be assumed that the applicants would not have been subjected to some loss of liberty even if these violations had not taken place. Accordingly, the Court awarded sums (between €2300 and €3900) which were substantially lower than those granted in other cases of unlawful detention.

The possibility that compensation would be denied because of clear legal rules is affected by the passing of the Human Rights Act, discussed below.

Compensation for loss of liberty under the Human Rights Act 1998

Article 5(4) of the Convention has been 'incorporated' into domestic law via the Human Rights Act 1998. Thus, the individual now has a specific right to compensation against public authorities where he/she has been unlawfully deprived of his/her liberty. This right can now be used alongside the courts' power, under s.8(1) of the 1998 Act, to grant just satisfaction to victims of violations of Convention rights. More specifically, s.9(3) of the Act states that although damages may not generally be awarded under the Act in respect of a judicial act done in good faith, that provision makes an exception in cases where there is a violation of Article 5(5) of the European Convention.

Section 8(1) states that where a court finds that an act (or proposed act) of a public authority is (or would be) unlawful, it might grant such relief or remedy, or make such order, within its powers as it considers just and equitable. This includes the power to award damages, provided the court has a power to order the payment of compensation in civil proceedings.[154] However, damages are not awarded as of right and no damages award shall be made unless the court is satisfied that it is necessary to afford just satisfaction to the individual.[155] Further, a court must take into account the principles applied by the European Court of Human Rights in relation to the award of compensation under Article 41 of the Convention.[156]

There is, thus, great scope under the Act for awarding damages to those who have had their Article 5 rights violated, where they either were detained unlawfully or have had their detention unduly and unreasonably delayed. For example, in *R (Hirst)* v *Secretary of State for the Home Department and Another*,[157] a discretionary life sentence prisoner was awarded £1500 for a failure to provide reasons for his recall to prison, which had led to a violation of Article 5(4).[158] Early case law on the courts' power to award damages under s.8 suggested that they would take a generous view, and in *R (KB)* v *Mental Health Review Tribunal*,[159] it was held that damages for breach of human rights under the Human Rights Act should be no lower than for a comparable tort and should, as far as possible, reflect the English level of damages. In that case, therefore, the court awarded damages of between £750 and £1000 to patients whose release had been delayed in breach of Article 5(4) of the Convention. In doing so the court took into consideration that the loss of liberty in this case had caused undeniable

---

[154] Section 8(2) Human Rights Act 1998.
[155] Section 8(3) Human Rights Act 1998.
[156] Section 8(4) Human Rights Act 1998. For those principles and their application, see chapter 2, pages 57–8 and chapter 3, pages 165–9.
[157] *The Times*, 4 July 2005.
[158] In *R (Johnson)* v *Secretary of State for the Home Department* [2007] 1 WLR 1990, it was held that prisoners serving determinative sentences were also entitled to compensation for delay in their parole proceedings.
[159] [2003] 3 WLR 385.

distress to the individuals, who were mentally vulnerable. However, the court stressed that damages would not be granted automatically for violation of that article, and that the courts should follow the principle of just satisfaction as practised by the European Court.

Consequently, as with awards under Article 41, the court will insist that there was a causal connection between the violation and any loss of liberty and consequently the domestic courts may refuse compensation for a breach of Article 5 where it is not satisfied of such a connection. For example, in *R (Richards)* v *Home Secretary*[160] it was held that although the Home Secretary had acted in breach of the Convention in refusing to accept the recommendations of the Parole Board for the claimant's release, no compensation should be granted because in the circumstances the claimant would not have been released in any case, because of finding suitable accommodation and monitoring because of his problems with alcohol. Further, in some cases the domestic court might feel that it is inappropriate and unnecessary to award compensation. In *R* v *Home Secretary, ex parte IH*[161] the House of Lords held that the violation of the claimant's rights under Article 5(4) to have the legality of their detention reviewed by a court-like body did not give rise to a claim in compensation since the violation had been publicly acknowledged by the authorities and the offending law had been changed. This, in their Lordship's view, sufficiently vindicated the individuals' rights.[162]

The incorporation of Article 5(5) of the Convention has also given rise to difficulties where the relevant act in question was lawful at the time. Because the Human Rights Act does not apply retrospectively, the courts cannot generally provide a remedy for breach of Convention rights when the act in question was clearly lawful; in such a case the court can, at most, declare the act or the provision incompatible but such a declaration does not change the legal position of the parties. In such a case the victim may need to pursue a case before the European Court of Human Rights. Thus, following the decision of the House of Lords in *A* v *Secretary of State for the Home Department*,[163] the detainees successfully brought an action for compensation for detention which was in breach of Article 5 but nonetheless lawful under domestic law at that time.[164]

However, in *R (Richards)* v *Home Secretary*,[165] it was held that that principle does not apply when the individual has been a victim of a breach of Article 5 and is seeking to enforce his right to compensation under Article 5(5). The claimant in this case had sought compensation from the Home Secretary following the ruling in *Stafford* v *United Kingdom*[166] that the detention of mandatory lifers for non-violent offences was in violation of Article 5(4). The High Court held that Article 5(5) conferred a freestanding right to compensation for unlawful detention and that the claimant's right to compensation arose once the European Court had declared that type of detention in breach of the Convention, even though part of his detention occurred before the decision in *Stafford*. Although the court recognised that the right to compensation would not be triggered until the domestic court declared it unlawful, the decision in *Stafford* was not limited to having a prospective effect. That decision also suggests that

---

[160] [2004] EWHC 93 (Admin).

[161] [2004] 2 AC 253.

[162] A subsequent application under the European Convention was declared inadmissible: *IH* v *United Kingdom* (Application No 7111/04).

[163] [2004] AC 68.

[164] *A* v *United Kingdom* (2009) 49 EHRR 29.

[165] [2004] EWHC 93 (Admin).

[166] (2002) 35 EHRR 32.

it will be no defence that the public authority had to act as it did because of clear domestic law. Thus, in this sense Article 5(4) overrides the general principle contained in s.6(2) of the 1998 Act. However, the decision in *Richards* does not extend to providing compensation for acts done before the Human Rights Act came into force. In *R (Wright) v Home Secretary*[167] the Court of Appeal confirmed that the source of the right in domestic law to compensation under Article 5(5) was the Human Rights Act and that accordingly the Home Secretary was entitled to refuse compensation to the claimant when he had been detained in prison on the orders of the Home Secretary in circumstances which were in breach of the European Court's decision in *Stafford*, but during a period before the 1998 Act's enforcement.

The Convention and freedom of movement

As we have seen the right to liberty under Article 5 does not equate with the right to freedom of movement. Nevertheless, Article 2 of Protocol No 4 guarantees freedom of movement by providing that everyone lawfully within the territory of the state shall, within that territory, have the right to liberty of movement and freedom to choose his residence and stating that everyone shall be free to leave any country, including their own. That article provides that no restriction shall be placed on the exercise of those rights other than such as are in accordance with law and are necessary in a democratic society for pursuing a number of specified legitimate aims.

Liberty of the person and derogations in times of war or other public emergency

This chapter concludes by examining how liberty of the person is affected in times of emergency such as war or where a state is facing a threat of terrorism. As we have seen, the European Court is prepared to interpret the provisions of Article 5 so as to reflect the seriousness of the criminal investigation. This means that it is prepared to apply those provisions more flexibly with respect to domestic laws intended to tackle terrorism and other very serious crime. In addition, Article 15 of the Convention, and s.14 of the Human Rights Act 1998, provides that in times of war or other public emergency threatening the life of the nation a state may take measures derogating from its Convention obligations to the extent strictly required by the exigencies of the situation. These provisions have been discussed in chapters 2 and 3 of this text, but with respect to liberty and security of the person, it is particularly common during such times for a state to grant authorities greater powers of arrest and detention. In such circumstances both the Convention machinery and the domestic courts must ensure that there is a fair balance between individual liberty and national security and public safety.[168]

Under Article 15 a state can only take such measures as are *strictly* required by the exigencies of the situation, indicating that the measures must correspond to a very pressing social need and must meet a strict test of proportionality. In addition, the measures must not be inconsistent with its other obligations under international law and internationally accepted standards applying to war or other emergency situations.

---

[167] [2006] HRLR 23.

[168] See the Council of Europe's guidelines in this area: *The Fight Against Terrorism: Council of Europe Standards* (2005). See also Warbrick, The Principles of the European Convention on Human Rights and the Response of States to Terrorism [2002] EHRLR 287.

The Convention machinery has offered a generous margin of appreciation in this area and in *Lawless v Ireland (No 3)*,[169] the European Court held that the respondent government should be afforded a certain margin of error in deciding what measures were required by the situation. Thus, it was not the Court's function to substitute for the government's assessment any other assessment of what might be the most prudent or most expedient policy to combat terrorism. In that case, therefore, although the Court found that the detention of the applicant without trial for a period of five months was in violation of Article 5(3) of the Convention, it held that the Irish government was entitled to derogate from its obligations by virtue of the existence of a public emergency. In the present case the Court was satisfied that the strict limitations imposed by Article 15 had been met. Equally, in *Brannigan and McBride v United Kingdom*,[170] the Court concluded that a derogation from Article 5, which had only been lodged once the relevant provisions had been declared unlawful by the European Court in *Brogan v United Kingdom*,[171] was nevertheless necessary and valid. The Court accepted the government's contention that there was an emergency situation, and held that the derogation was not invalid merely because the government had decided to keep open the possibility of finding a means in the future of ensuring greater conformity with Convention obligations. The Court was also satisfied that there were effective safeguards such as the availability of *habeas corpus* to safeguard against arbitrary action.

However, a much more robust approach has been taken by the domestic courts with respect to provisions intended to combat the threat of international terrorism, and in *A v Secretary of State for the Home Department*[172] (dealt with in detail in the case study, below) the House of Lords declared as incompatible the government's derogation from Article 5(1) with respect to s.23 of the Anti-Terrorism, Crime and Security Act 2001, which provided for an extended power to arrest and detain foreign nationals, whom it is intended to remove or deport from the United Kingdom, but where such removal or deportation is not for the time being possible.[173]

The decision in *A* shows that the domestic courts are not prepared to relinquish their duty to safeguard the liberty of the individual simply because the government pleads an emergency situation. This 'hands on' approach has continued with respect to the judicial review of control orders, detailed above, and the courts are prepared to judge the necessity and proportionality of such measures in line with the standards laid down in the Convention and their mandate under the Human Rights Act. The comparison in judicial deference between the European Court and the domestic courts is interesting to note, the domestic courts perhaps feeling unhampered by considerations of diplomacy, state sovereignty and the full rigours of the doctrine of the margin of appreciation.[174] The case certainly shows the courts' belief in individual liberty and the importance of upholding it, believing, as Lord Hoffmann stressed, that the real threat to the rule of law comes not from acts of terrorism but from provisions which depart from the fundamental notions of justice and the rule of law which both Article 5 and British notions of liberty encapsulate.

---

[169] (1961) 1 EHRR 15.

[170] (1993) 17 EHRR 539.

[171] (1989) 11 EHRR 117.

[172] [2005] 2 AC 68.

[173] The details of the derogation are explained in chapter 3 of this text, pages 173–5.

[174] The case is discussed and analysed in detail by Feldman, Human Rights, Terrorism and Risk: The Roles of Politicians and Judges [2006] PL 364. See also Finnis, Nationality, Alienage and Constitutional Principle [2007] LQR 123; Walker, Prisoners of 'War all the Time' [2005] EHRLR 50.

CASE STUDY

A v Secretary of State for the Home Department [2005] 2 AC 68

This case has been chosen to illustrate the difficulty of balancing fundamental human rights with pressing issues of national security. The case caused heated political, constitutional and legal debate and pitted the courts against parliamentary will and the power of executive government. It raises issues such as the place of human rights in times of emergency, the constitutional role of the courts and the application of both common law and Convention principles of fairness and equality. More specifically, it illustrates the importance placed on the notion of individual liberty and the reluctance of the courts to abandon that notion even in times of emergency.

The case is mentioned throughout the text, particularly in the chapters on the Human Rights Act 1998 (chapter 3).

Background and facts

Article 15 of the European Convention allows member states to 'derogate' from its obligations under the Convention in times of war or other public emergency threatening the life of the nation, and under s.14 of the Human Rights Act 1998 the government may lodge and continue in force any such derogation as it affects the enforcement of that Act.

Acting under s.14, and in response to the terrorist attacks on 11 September 2001, the Secretary of State made The Human Rights Act 1998 (Amendment No 2) Order 2001, which derogated from Article 5(1) of the European Convention, guaranteeing liberty of the person. This was to accommodate the Anti-Terrorism, Crime and Security Act 2001, which, *inter alia*, provided for an extended power to arrest and detain foreign nationals, who would be removed from the United Kingdom, but where such removal or deportation is not possible because such a person would face treatment in violation of the Convention if returned to that particular country. This measure and the derogation was taken to comply with the European Court's judgment in *Chahal v United Kingdom* (1997) 23 EHRR 413, where it was held that in order to comply with Article 5 of the Convention deportation proceedings had to be prosecuted with due diligence.

Under s.21 and s.23 of the Anti-Terrorism, Crime and Security Act 2001 the Secretary of State can issue a relevant certificate ordering detention where he suspects the person of being an international terrorist and where he believed that the person's presence in the United Kingdom was a risk to national security.

The provision and the derogation were challenged by a number of foreign nationals who were suspected of international terrorism, and who were detained in Belmarsh Prison. At first instance ([2002] HRLR 45), the Special Immigration Appeals Commission held that the provisions were discriminatory, but on appeal ([2003] 2 WLR 564) the Court of Appeal held that the powers were objectively justified during a time of public emergency. Although LORD WOOLF CJ accepted that taking action against nationals as well as non-nationals would have been more effective, he concluded that the Home Secretary was entitled to come to the conclusion that he could achieve what was necessary by either detaining or deporting only the terrorists who were aliens. This, in his Lordship's view, was justified on objective and relevant grounds. The detainees appealed to the House of Lords.

The decision
A majority of their Lordships held that the measures allowing indefinite detention without trial or charge were incompatible with the United Kingdom's obligations under the European Convention and could not be excused within Article 15 of the European Convention.

Was there a public emergency?
Lord Bingham first addressed the question of whether there existed a public emergency threatening the life of the nation so as to allow derogation. In his Lordship's view, shared by all other Lordships apart from Lord Hoffmann (below), great weight should be given to the judgment of the Home Secretary and parliament because they had to exercise a pre-eminently political judgment. The more political the question was, the more appropriate it would be for political resolution and the court's role in scrutiny would, therefore, be smaller. The question here was at the political end of the spectrum and the appellants had shown no ground strong enough to displace the Home Secretary's decision on this threshold issue.

However, Lord Hoffman dissented on the emergency issue. In his opinion the government had equated a situation where there was a threat of serious physical damage and loss of life with one where there was a threat to the life of the nation. In his Lordship's view that was a misunderstanding of the term employed in Article 15 of the Convention, and terrorist violence, serious as it was, did not threaten the institutions of government or the existence of the civil community. He concluded by stating that the real threat to the life of the nation, in the sense of a people living in accordance with its traditional laws and political values, came not from terrorism but from laws such as those in issue. (The judgment was given in December 2004 and on 7 July 2005 four terrorist bombs were detonated in the middle of London, causing over 50 fatalities.)

Were the measures proportionate and strictly required?
Addressing this issue, Lord Bingham stated that the relevant question was whether the legislative objective was sufficiently important to justify the limitation; whether the measures designed to meet that objective were rationally connected to it; and whether the means used were no more than necessary to accomplish that objective. His Lordship accepted that where government was threatened by terrorism difficult choices had to be made. Further, while the decision of a representative democratic body demanded respect, the degree of respect would be conditioned by the nature of the decision. The traditional approach adopted in *Associated Provincial Picture Houses Ltd* v *Wednesbury Corporation* [1948] 1 KB 223 was inadequate, and even in a terrorist situation the domestic courts were not precluded by deference from scrutinising the issues raised in this case. Although judges were not elected, the functions of the independent judge, charged with interpreting and applying the law, was a cardinal feature of the modern democratic state and a cornerstone of the rule of law. It would thus be wrong to stigmatise judicial decision making as in some way undemocratic.

On the facts, his Lordship found that the measures were disproportionate for the following reasons:

- The sections under the 2001 Act did not deal with the threat of terrorism from persons other than foreign nationals, in other words United Kingdom nationals.

- The provisions permitted suspected foreign terrorists to carry on their activities in another country provided there was a safe country for them to go; and permitted the detention of non-Al-Qaeda supporters even though the threat relied on to justify the measures was from that source.

- Further, if the threat posed by UK nationals could be addressed without infringing the right to personal liberty, it had not been shown why similar measures could not adequately address the threat posed by foreign nationals.

It was also held that the measures were unlawful under Article 14 of the European Convention (Convention rights should be enjoyed without discrimination). The provisions allowed foreign nationals to be deprived of their liberty but not UK nationals. The appellants were therefore treated differently because of their nationality or immigration status. Although some distinction might be made between those groups in an immigration context, such a distinction could not form the legitimate basis of depriving one group of their Convention right to liberty of the person as protected by Article 5.

Lord Walker, dissenting, concluded that the detention provisions were necessary and proportionate. In his Lordship's opinion when the country was faced with immediate threats from enemies who made use of secrecy, deception and surprise, the need for anti-terrorism provisions to be strictly necessary had to be interpreted in accordance with the precautionary principle recognised by the European Court in cases such as *Lawless* v *Ireland* (1961) 1 EHRR 15. In addition, the Special Commission was an independent and impartial tribunal and thus offered protection against abuse. Although detention without trial of non-national suspects was a cause of grave concern, the judgment of parliament and the Secretary of State was that those measures were necessary. This fact, the existence of the above safeguards, and the fact that in nearly three years only 17 individuals had been certified under the provisions, pointed to the conclusion that the measures and any discrimination was necessary and proportionate.

The majority of their Lordships declared the relevant sections of the 2001 Act as incompatible with Articles 5 and 14 of the European Convention and struck down the derogation order on the same basis. This did not affect the validity of the measures, which continued in force, but the decision led the government to introduce new, non-derogating, measures allowing control orders to be placed on relevant suspects. These measures were challenged in *Secretary of State for the Home Department* v *MB*, [2007] 3 WLR 681, as being in breach of the right to a fair trial and, successfully, in *Secretary of State for the Home Department* v *JJ* [2007] 3 WLR 642, as being in breach of the right to liberty of the person (see page 271, above). The individuals in *A* took their case to the European Court of Human Rights to claim compensation for their unlawful detention; see below.

Questions

1 Why were the measures under the 2001 Act introduced?
2 What effect did those provisions have on the right to liberty and security of the person and what fundamental principles did they threaten?
3 Why does Article 15 of the Convention allow derogations in times of war and other emergency?
4 Did the House of Lords accept that individual liberty should be subject to that power of derogation?
5 Why did the House of Lords place so much emphasis on the right to liberty of the person, and were the Lords correct in giving it so much emphasis?
6 What is the European Court's approach with respect to state derogations under Article 15?
7 Is the House of Lords' decision consistent with the European Court's approach?
8 How did the House of Lords distinguish between the decision to declare a state of emergency and the measures the government put into operation to deal with that emergency?
9 Do you feel that the House of Lords achieved the correct balance between individual liberty and state security and public safety?

Following the decision of the House of Lords, the individuals petitioned the European Court of Human Rights claiming violation of Articles 3, 5, 6, 13 and 14 of the Convention, and alleging that they suffered psychiatric harm from their unlawful detention and that they were not allowed to adequately challenge or seek compensation for the detention. In *A v United Kingdom*[175] the Grand Chamber of the Court held that the treatment of the detainees failed to reach the necessary severity to constitute a violation of Article 3, but that there had been a breach of Article 5(1) as the possibility of deportation proceedings making the deprivation lawful under paragraph (f) were not sufficiently imminent. The Court also held that there was no reason to disagree with the House of Lords on the lack of proportionality of the measures with respect to the legality of the derogation under Article 15. There had also been a violation of Article 5(4) because the lack of availability to the applicants and their lawyers of closed evidence meant that they were deprived of their right to effectively challenge the continued legality of that detention. A breach of Article 5(5) – the right to compensation – was conceded by the government and the Court granted just satisfaction of £2500. The case of *A v United Kingdom* will be dealt with in detail in chapter 14 of this text.

---

[175] (2009) 49 EHRR 29.

Further reading

Texts

A number of texts on the European Convention contain excellent chapters on Article 5 of the Convention and its relevant case law. See, in particular, Harris, Warbrick, Bates and O'Boyle, *Law of the European Convention on Human Rights* (OUP 2009, 2nd edn), chapter 5; Ovey and White, *Jacobs and White: The European Convention on Human Rights* (OUP 2010, 5th edn), chapter 7; Janis, Kay and Bradley, *European Human Rights Law* (OUP 2007, 3rd edn), chapter 12; van Dijk and van Hoof, *Theory and Practice of the European Convention on Human Rights* (Intersentia 2006), chapter 9.

In addition, Mowbray's *Cases and Materials on the European Convention* (OUP 2007, 2nd edn), chapters 7 and 17, details the essential case law of the European Court in this area (including derogation); Clayton and Tomlinson, *The Law of Human Rights* (OUP 2009, 2nd edn), chapter 8, provides comprehensive coverage of both European and various domestic law provision. See also Ashworth and Emmerson, *Human Rights and Criminal Justice* (Sweet & Maxwell 2007, 2nd edn), chapter 5, and Amos, *Human Rights Law* (Hart 2006), chapter 9, which provide a useful account of domestic cases on Article 5 in the post-Human Rights Act era. See also Fenwick, *Civil Liberties and Human Rights* (Routledge 2007, 4th edn), for chapters on liberty of the person (chapter 11) and anti-terrorism and human rights (chapter 14).

Articles

For a general overview of Article 5, see Powell, The Right to Security of the Person in European Court of Human Rights Jurisprudence [2007] EHRLR 649.

There has been a vast amount written on liberty of the person and terrorism and students should at least read Bates, Anti-terrorism Control Orders; Liberty and Security Still in the Balance (2009) LS 99; Ewing, The Continuing Futility of the Human Rights Act [2008] PL 668; Feldman, Human Rights, Terrorism and Risk: The Roles of Politicians and Judges [2006] PL 364. See also Finnis, Nationality, Alienage and Constitutional Principle [2007] LQR 123; Shah, From Westminster to Strasbourg: *A and Others* v *UK* (2009) (3) HRLR 473; Walker, Prisoners of 'War all the Time' [2005] EHRLR 50.

Visit **www.mylawchamber.co.uk/fosterhumanrights**
to access regular updates to major changes in the law,
further case studies, weblinks, and suggested
answers/approaches to questions in the book.

7 Human rights and due process: the right to a fair trial

Introduction

In *V and T* v *United Kingdom* (1999) the European Court of Human Rights had to decide whether subjecting two 11-year-old boys to an adult trial to face charges of murder, and sentencing the boys to a life sentence, was in breach of Article 6 of the European Convention on Human Rights, which guarantees the right to a fair trial. (See the case study at the end of chapter 1 of this text.)

In *Steel and Morris* v *United Kingdom* (2005) the Court had to decide whether defendants in protracted and complex legal proceedings were deprived of the right to a fair trial when they, unlike the claimants, were not represented by legal counsel. (See the case study in chapter 9.)

In *Ezeh and Connors* v *United Kingdom* (2004) the court had to decide whether internal prison disciplinary proceedings were 'criminal proceedings', thus attracting the right to legal representation and the right to a fair trial.

All these cases raised various issues about the fundamental right to a fair trial and due process and they will be examined in this chapter in an attempt to explain the ambit and extent of those rights and the values underlying Article 6.

This chapter examines the fundamental right to a fair trial. The chapter will focus on Article 6 of the European Convention, examining its scope and its specific provisions, together with the relevant jurisprudence of the European Court of Human Rights.[1] The chapter will also, where appropriate, draw on the relevant case law of the domestic law, especially in the post-Human Rights Act era so as to examine the compatibility of domestic law with Article 6. The chapter will analyse specific aspects of the right to a fair trial in turn: including the right of access to the courts, the right to a fair and impartial tribunal, the presumption of innocence, the right to present legal arguments, the right to legal representation and the right to call and examine witnesses.

This chapter will also cover Article 7 of the European Convention, which protects the individual against retrospective criminal law and penalties, examining the relevant case law of both the European Court and the domestic courts in this area.

---

[1] For a comprehensive account of human rights and the criminal process, see Emmerson and Asworth, *Human Rights and Criminal Justice* (Sweet & Maxwell 2007, 2nd edn). See also Clayton and Tomlinson, *The Law of Human Rights* (OUP 2009, 2nd edn), chapter 11.

Thus, this chapter will contain:

- An examination of the importance of the right to a fair trial and the scope of Article 6 of the European Convention on Human Rights.
- An examination of the various provisions and safeguards within Article 6, together with the relevant Convention case law.
- An examination of the extent to which those principles are upheld in domestic law, specifically under the Human Rights Act 1998.
- A specific examination of Article 7 of the Convention – prohibiting retrospective criminal law and penalties – together with relevant Convention and domestic case law.

The right to a fair trial

The right to a fair trial lies at the heart of any democratic society which prides itself on fairness, justice and the rule of law. In such societies, there is an expectation that natural justice will be applied in all cases where a person's liberty, goods or welfare are at stake and the fairness and legality of judicial process will be measured against those principles. For example, it is accepted that legal disputes are resolved by access to an independent and impartial court or tribunal, and that such a body will resolve that dispute in line with established legal principles, by following a procedure which will allow both sides to present their case effectively, and by providing effective and fair remedies and sanctions. More specifically, our ideas of social justice require a legal system to provide effective access to justice via effective and, in appropriate cases, free legal assistance. These principles are especially, but of course not exclusively, important in criminal trials, where the liberty of the individual may be affected and where it is essential to preserve a presumption of innocence and to guard the individual from arbitrary and retrospective criminal law and process.

These principles are reflected in all international human rights treaties. The preamble to the European Convention refers to the High Contracting Parties' common heritage of political traditions, ideals, freedom and the rule of law, reaffirming their belief in those fundamental freedoms which are the foundations of justice or peace. As we have seen in the previous chapter, the rule of law is at the heart of Article 5, guaranteeing the right to liberty and security of the person. It is also instrumental in guaranteeing the right to a fair trial, upholding principles such as access to the courts and justice, freedom from judicial bias, the equality of arms, and the presumption of innocence. Together with the principle of equality, the rule of law will also ensure that the right to a fair trial is enjoyed by all, and in this respect the European Court has insisted that groups such as prisoners are not automatically excluded from its protection.[2]

As with other Convention articles a member state may be liable for exposing an individual to a violation of Article 6 by removing that person to another jurisdiction where they will face an unfair trial. The requirements of such liability were laid down in *RB (Algeria) v Secretary of State for the Home Department; Othman (Jordan) v Secretary of State for the Home Department*,[3] where the House of Lords stated that before the deportation of an alien was capable of violating

---

[2] See *Golder v United Kingdom* (1975) 1 EHRR 524.
[3] [2010] 2 AC 110.

Article 6 there must be substantial grounds for believing that there was a real risk that there would be a fundamental breach of his right to a fair trial, and that that breach would lead to a miscarriage of justice that itself constituted a flagrant violation of his fundamental right. In that case, therefore, it was held that it would not be unlawful to deport simply because the person would have faced a trial at the hands of a court where there were concerns as to its independence and impartiality. Such a factor would not have led to a flagrant violation of Article 6. The House of Lords also held that there was no authority for the rule that in a foreign trial the use of evidence obtained by torture *necessarily* amounted to a flagrant violation of justice.

Article 6 – The right to a fair and public hearing

Article 6 of the Convention provides that in the determination of his civil rights and obligations or of any criminal charge against him, everyone is entitled to a fair and public hearing within a reasonable time by an independent and impartial tribunal established by law. The individual's right to a fair trial also confers a benefit to society in that there is a great public interest in maintaining an impartial and fair judicial process. Article 6 is thus regarded as one of the most fundamental of human rights and a violation of Article 6 will not be excused simply because it is claimed that the outcome would have been the same irrespective of whether there had been a breach. Thus, the Court of Appeal has held that in a case where the accused had been denied his Article 6 rights it would be rare for the court to speculate as to whether adherence to those rights would have made a difference.[4] However, the courts can consider whether the defendant has received a fair trial in the round despite the violation of Article 6. For example, in *Allison* v *HM Advocate*,[5] the Supreme Court held that although the Crown's failure to disclose outstanding charges relating to one of its witnesses was incompatible with the accused's right to a fair trial under Article 6, as there was no real possibility that the jury would have come to a different verdict there had been no miscarriage of justice. Alternatively, where there is little evidence that the individual's interests have been damaged the Court will declare a violation of Article 6, but may refuse to grant compensation. For example, in *Kingsley* v *United Kingdom*,[6] the European Court found that there had been a violation of Article 6 when the applicant did not receive an impartial and unbiased hearing, but refused to grant the applicant compensation under Article 41 on the basis that despite the appearance of bias there was no evidence to suggest that the applicant had not received a fair trial.[7]

Article 6 reflects the rules of natural justice, which have been applied in English domestic law to judicial proceedings and have been extended to cover most decisions that affect the rights and expectations of the individual.[8] Thus, Article 6 guarantees the right to a hearing before an impartial and unbiased court or tribunal, the right of a person to be informed of any accusation made against them, and the right to present one's case, including the right to be presumed innocent of any criminal offence, the right to legal advice and the right to examine witnesses. However, the right to a fair trial, or at least the extent to which an individual should enjoy it, often needs to be balanced against other interests, such as the

---

[4] *Hammerton* v *Hammerton, The Times*, 12 April 2007.
[5] [2010] HRLR 16.
[6] (2001) 31 EHRR 13.
[7] (2002) 35 EHRR 10.
[8] See Craig, *Administrative Law* (Sweet & Maxwell 2008, 6th edn), chapters 13 and 14.

successful prosecution of crime and the protection of others. In some cases, therefore, the European Court will refuse to find a violation even where there has been a technical breach of Article 6 if it is satisfied that the applicant has received a fair trial in the round.[9]

This raises the question of whether it is appropriate to refer to Article 6 as an absolute or conditional right. Although Article 6 does not appear to be a qualified right, in the sense that it does not contain the qualifying paragraph evident in Articles 8–11 of the Convention, in practice the individual's right to a fair trial will be balanced against the rights of others and the general public interest. Consequently, the individual will not enjoy an absolute and unfettered right to access the courts, to bring and cross-examine witnesses or to have access to relevant evidence. Appropriate and necessary restrictions can be placed on those rights, provided they do not interfere with the tenets of due process and do not deprive the applicant of a basic right to a fair trial. For example, in *Brown v Stott*,[10] the Privy Council stated that although the right to a fair trial is an absolute right that cannot be compromised, there might be exceptional cases in which the defendant's procedural rights have to give way to the greater interests of the public that justice be done. Limited qualification of the specific rights contained in Article 6 is acceptable, provided they are reasonably directed towards a clear and proper public objective and represents no greater qualification than the situation calls for. Accordingly, the national courts need to give weight to the decisions of the representative legislature and the democratic government when such bodies have constructed rules that seek to achieve such a balance.

In *Brown* the defendant claimed that s.172(2)(a) of the Road Traffic Act 1988, which compelled a person to answer the question whether he or she had been driving a car, was incompatible with the rule against self-incrimination and thus contrary to Article 6 of the Convention. The Privy Council held that the right against self-incrimination was not absolute and that a rule which compelled drivers suspected of drink driving to admit that they had been driving the vehicle struck a fair balance between the right to a fair trial and the public interest in addressing injuries on public roads. The decision shows that Article 6 can be limited in its interpretation and its application, and that provision has been declared compatible with Article 6 by the European Court of Human Rights.[11]

The scope of Article 6

Article 6 applies to all proceedings where the applicant is either facing a criminal charge, or where his or her 'civil rights and obligations' are subject to determination. Thus, if the dispute in question does not come within the scope of Article 6, an individual cannot rely on the substantive guarantees of that article; Article 6 will not be engaged irrespective of the unfairness of the proceedings.[12] The meaning of the above phrases will be examined below, but it should be remembered that the domestic rules of natural justice might apply to a case that does not strictly come within Article 6. For example, in *R (Ullah) v Secretary of State for the*

---

[9] See, for example, the exclusion of unlawful evidence cases, such as *Khan v United Kingdom* (2001) 31 EHRR 45, discussed below.

[10] [2003] 1 AC 681.

[11] *O'Halloran and Francis v United Kingdom* (2008) 46 EHRR 21, considered below.

[12] See *R (McCann) v Manchester Crown Court* [2003] 1 AC 787, dealt with below. In that case, although Article 6 did not apply, the House of Lords held that magistrates should still apply a criminal standard of proof when making an antisocial behaviour order.

Home Department,[13] the Court of Appeal held that although a decision on entry into the country did not engage Article 6, as a matter of common law the claimant was entitled to a fair trial and that the burden of proving that leave to enter was obtained by fraud was a high one.[14] Further, although a decision on a prisoner's categorisation does not engage Article 6 because it does not determine guilt or the prisoner's civil rights, such a decision affects the prisoner and his inherent liberty and the rules of natural justice will demand that the prisoner be given full reasons for such decisions.

It should also be noted that Article 6 is concerned with procedural fairness as opposed to the legality and fairness of substantive law. In general the European Court will not allow Article 6 to be employed to question the compatibility of substantive domestic law. Thus a substantive rule of domestic law that makes it difficult or impossible for an individual to bring legal proceedings will not fall foul of Article 6, and in such a case the individual would need to show a breach of another Convention right. For example, in *A v United Kingdom*,[15] it was held that the rule of privilege exempting parliamentary speech from the law of defamation did not engage Article 6 as it was a rule of substantive law and did not come within that article.[16] However, the Court has in some cases ruled that procedural obstacles placed on potential litigants do violate Article 6,[17] and this will be discussed later in the chapter, under access to the courts.

Criminal charge

Article 6 firstly only applies when the individual is facing a criminal charge that determines his liability.[18] In *Engel v Netherlands*[19] the European Court held that in determining whether a charge was criminal within Article 6, three particular questions needed to be addressed: first, whether the offence in question had been classified as criminal within the domestic legal system; secondly, the nature of the offence; and thirdly, the severity of the punishment.[20] The Court stressed that the classification of a penalty is one, but not the decisive, factor in making that distinction. In such cases the Court is more concerned with whether the charge itself, and the accompanying penalty, has the characteristics of a criminal offence. Thus, in *Engel* the Court concluded that in those cases where the penalty was light, Article 6 was not engaged, as opposed to those cases where a substantial penalty involving loss of liberty had been imposed, and which attracted the protection of the article. Thus, although states are allowed to take measures to de-formalise proceedings in relation to lesser offences, they cannot take away the individual's right to a fair trial simply by classifying the offence as regulatory. For

---

[13] *The Independent*, 16 October 2003.

[14] Applying the previous House of Lords' decision in *R v Home Secretary, ex parte Khawaja* [1984] AC 74.

[15] (2003) 36 EHRR 51.

[16] The Court also held that any interference with the applicant's private life caused by that rule was necessary in order to protect free speech in parliament.

[17] *Osman v United Kingdom* (2000) 29 EHRR 245.

[18] Thus, Article 6 does not apply to charges that do not determine criminal liability, such as the appointment of a lawyer: *X v United Kingdom* (1982) 5 EHRR 273. It does, however, cover the sentence of the court: *V and T v United Kingdom* (1999) 30 EHRR 121.

[19] (1976) 1 EHRR 647.

[20] In *Ezeh and Connors v United Kingdom*, below, it was held that the second and third factors identified in *Engel* were alternative and not cumulative factors, although a cumulative approach might be adopted in some, unclear cases.

example, in *Ozturk* v *Turkey*,[21] it was held that classifying motor offences as regulatory did not preclude the applicant's right to rely on Article 6 and to be protected from arbitrary fines.

Thus, although the Court in *Engel* accepts that the imposition of disciplinary measures is not, in general, of a criminal character, it stressed that it had the power to displace that classification if there is evidence that in reality the applicant is facing a criminal charge that should be accompanied by a judicial process. The question, therefore, is whether the charge is *truly* disciplinary or regulatory. For example, the domestic courts have held that disciplinary proceedings by school governors against a teacher did not constitute a criminal charge; although given the seriousness of the charge and the impact on his career the proceedings engaged his' civil rights' and thus entitled him to legal representation.[22] Equally, in *R (V)* v *Independent Appeal Panel for Tom Hood School*,[23] the Court of Appeal held that Article 6 was not engaged in respect of the permanent exclusion of a child from school for possession of a knife as the proceedings were regulatory and not criminal.[24]

There may also be cases where although Article 6 is engaged, the proceedings in question are civil rather than criminal in nature and thus do not attract the specific safeguards in Articles 6 or 7.[25] For example, in *R (McCann)* v *Manchester Crown Court*[26] it was held that the making of antisocial behavioural orders under s.1 of the Crime and Disorder Act 1998 were not criminal in nature and thus were not in breach of Article 6 simply because the court was allowed to take into account hearsay evidence in making the orders. In coming to that conclusion the House of Lords noted that applications for the making of such orders did not involve the Crown Prosecution Service and that the proceedings were begun by the civil process of a complaint. Further, no *mens rea* need be proved for such an order to be made and it was unnecessary to establish criminal liability; the making of such an order, therefore, was not a conviction or a condemnation that the defendant was guilty of an offence, and such an order did not result in a penalty.[27] Accordingly, as such evidence would be admissible in civil proceedings there had been no breach of Article 6 in this case.[28] Further, in *Blake* v *United Kingdom*,[29] the European Court held that the issue of proceedings for an account of profits against the applicant made by the Attorney-General after the publication of the applicant's memoirs was civil in nature and did not amount to a criminal charge. In declaring the

---

[21] (1984) 6 EHRR 409.

[22] *R (G)* v *X School Governors* [2010] 1 WLR 2218.

[23] [2010] HRLR 21.

[24] The boy also failed to show that his exclusion impacted on his civil right to continue his studies at that school, there being no civil right to be educated at a particular school.

[25] For example, in *MB* v *Secretary of State for the Home Department* [2007] 3 WLR 681, the House of Lords held that control orders made under the Prevention of Terrorism Act 2005 were not criminal or punitive in nature, but nevertheless impacted on the individual's civil rights.

[26] [2003] 1 AC 787.

[27] For a critical commentary of the case, see Bakalis, Asbos, 'Preventative Orders' and the European Court of Human Rights [2007] EHRLR 427. See also *R (R)* v *Durham Constabulary* [2005] 1 WLR 1184, where the House of Lords held that the giving of a warning to a boy of 15 about his admitted behaviour of indecent assaults was not a criminal charge under Article 6 of the Convention. The power was intended to be used for the benefit and welfare of the person warned and was not intended as a criminal punishment.

[28] Despite that finding the House of Lords held that magistrates should still apply a criminal standard of proof before making such an order; in other words they should be sure that the defendant had acted in an antisocial manner. However, in deciding whether it was necessary to protect persons from further acts of antisocial behaviour no standard of proof was required and the court merely had to exercise its judgment.

[29] (2007) 44 EHRR 29.

application inadmissible in that respect the European Court held that reference made by both the Attorney-General and the court to the applicant's guilt did not transform the proceedings into a criminal matter. Accordingly, as no criminal proceedings were pending against the applicant the Court held that a statement of the applicant's criminal guilt during a civil trial did not violate the presumption of innocence under Article 6(2).[30]

Prisoners' disciplinary proceedings and Article 6

Article 6 is particularly relevant in challenging prison disciplinary decisions. Although the prison authorities regarded such proceedings outside Article 6 – because they are disciplinary rather than criminal in nature – the European Court has applied Article 6 in appropriate cases. In *Campbell and Fell* v *United Kingdom*[31] it held that there had been a violation of Article 6 when prisoners had received awards of 570 days' loss of remission following disciplinary proceedings at which they were refused legal representation. Given the nature of the charges and the nature and severity of the penalty, the prisoners were clearly facing 'criminal charges' within Article 6 and were thus entitled to the protection offered by that article. However, the Court did not accept the opinion of the European Commission, which had decided that prison disciplinary proceedings lacked the independence and impartiality necessary for a fair trial within Article 6.

More recently, in *Ezeh and Connors* v *United Kingdom*,[32] the European Court of Human Rights held that the applicants' right to a fair trial had been violated when they had been denied legal representation when charged under Prison Rules. One of the applicants had been awarded 40 additional days, while the other applicant had been given seven days. The Court held that having regard to the nature of the charges – assaulting an officer and using threatening language – the disciplinary charges amounted to criminal charges within Article 6. Accordingly, the applicants were entitled to legal representation under Article 6(3)(c) of the Convention. The decision was upheld by the Grand Chamber of the European Court,[33] which found that as the offences were imposed after a finding of culpability and were imposed to both punish the offenders and to deter them in the future, the penalty came within Article 6. Although the Court accepted that the imposition of the additional days was lawful, it found that the prisoners were detained beyond a date at which they would normally be released. Accordingly the additional days constituted fresh deprivations of liberty imposed for punitive purposes.[34]

Until the decision in *Ezeh* the domestic courts had rejected a number of claims that prison disciplinary proceedings were within Article 6. For example, in *R (Greenfield)* v *Secretary of State for the Home Department*,[35] the Court of Appeal held that when a prisoner had been given 21 additional days as a punishment for failing a mandatory drugs test, that procedure could be properly classified as disciplinary rather than criminal, thus not amounting to a criminal charge within Article 6 of the Convention. Although there existed a similar offence to the charge brought against him, the actual charge had a disciplinary connotation regarding the

---

[30] The case is referred to below with respect to other aspects of Article 6.

[31] (1984) 7 EHRR 165.

[32] (2002) 35 EHRR 28.

[33] (2004) 39 EHRR 1.

[34] Following the decision the Prison Rules were amended to provide for an adjudicator to inquire into serious offences against discipline and to relieve governors of the power to award additional days as a punishment. See Prison (Amendment) Rules 2002 (SI 2002/2116).

[35] [2002] 1 WLR 545.

control of prisoners and the finding against him did not result in his having a criminal record. Any contrary conclusion would, in the court's opinion, result in serious difficulties for the Prison Service in maintaining a swift and efficient disciplinary system.[36] Further, in *R v Secretary of State for the Home Department, ex parte Carroll and Al-Hasan*,[37] where prisoners had been disciplined for refusing to squat when ordered to do so by a prison officer who suspected the prisoners of concealing drugs, the court held that the offences in question were disciplinary in nature. In the court's opinion, the power to award additional days did not automatically make the proceedings criminal, being founded upon the original sentence of the court, and the prisoners were not entitled to legal representation.[38]

Those decisions are now, of course, overruled by the judgment in *Ezeh and Connors v United Kingdom*, above, wherever prisoners are subjected to additional days. The European Court did not decide that every disciplinary charge constitutes a criminal charge, or that every prisoner charged with a breach of the Prison Rules is entitled to legal representation. However, although it did not clearly decide that the imposition of additional days would *always* attract the protection of Article 6, following that decision the Home Secretary introduced new rules,[39] which provide for an adjudicator to deal with serious offences against discipline and relieve governors of their power to award additional days as a punishment.[40]

Nevertheless, the protection of Article 6 is not available to all prisoners and in all circumstances. For example, in *Tangney v Governor of Elmley Prison and Another*,[41] the Court of Appeal held that the right to an independent adjudicator under the amended Prison Rules did not apply to life sentence prisoners because additional days could not be awarded to such prisoners. In this case the punishment, and the penalty of cellular confinement, did not engage Article 6 or the rules of natural justice. Although that penalty might affect his parole chances, the effect of such was not imposed by the disciplinary adjudication, and any decision of the Parole Board would be made on risk to the public rather than punishment to the prisoner. In addition, in *Matthewson v Scottish Ministers*[42] it was held that although the Parole Board could consider the prisoner's disciplinary record when considering release, its consideration of the prisoner's case in the future did not involve the determination of a criminal charge so as to attract the protection of Article 6.[43]

---

[36] The court also held that there had been no violation of Article 5 of the Convention by the imposition of additional days. Additional days formed part of the period of the sentence that had to be served before release and the jurisdictional justification for the detention always remained the original sentence. By the time the House of Lords heard the appeal the European Court had given its judgment in *Ezeh and Connors*. Therefore, the House of Lords confined the appeal to the question of just satisfaction for breach of Article 6: [2005] 1 WLR 673.

[37] [2002] 1 WLR 545.

[38] See also *Matthewson v The Scottish Ministers, The Times*, 24 October 2001; the Court of Session held that where a prisoner serving a mandatory life sentence was charged with smoking cannabis, he had not faced a criminal charge under the terms of Article 6.

[39] The Prison (Amendment) Rules 2002 (2002/2116).

[40] The rules did not quash awards made before the implementation of the Human Rights Act, and that decision was unsuccessfully challenged in *R (Rogers) v Secretary of State for the Home Department* [2002] EWHC 2078 (Admin), where it was held that the Act could not be given retrospective effect.

[41] *The Times*, 30 August 2005.

[42] *The Times*, 24 October 2001.

[43] See also *R v Secretary of State for the Home Department, ex parte Sunder* [2001] EWHC 252 (Admin), where a prisoner claimed a violation of Article 6 of the Convention when he had been classified as Category A – high escape risk because of his association with terrorist activities in India. It was held that Article 6 was irrelevant to the committee's decision because it did not determine the prisoner's civil rights. Neither, in the court's view, did the matter constitute a criminal charge as it only affected the conditions of his detention.

Further, in *Keenan* v *United Kingdom*[44] the Court held that the absence of a remedy allowing the prisoner to challenge the immediate effect of such an award was in contravention of Article 13 of the Convention guaranteeing an effective remedy for breach of Convention rights. Although the case related to the treatment of mentally ill prisoners, it would appear that if another Convention right is violated in the disciplinary process, as in *Keenan* when the disciplinary award constituted a violation of Article 3, then an immediate and effective remedy should be available to the prisoner to challenge that decision. In the Court's opinion, neither judicial review nor the internal disciplinary system provided such a remedy as the prisoner could not realistically expect such a remedy to operate before the award had been served.

Civil rights and obligations

Outside the context of a criminal charge, Article 6 can be engaged in cases where what is in dispute is the individual's civil rights or obligations.[45] The European Court gave guidance as to the meaning of that phrase in *Ringeisen* v *Austria*,[46] and was prepared to take a reasonably flexible approach, eschewing a formal distinction between private and administrative law. In the Court's view it was not necessary that both parties to the proceedings were private individuals, provided the result of the proceedings were decisive of private rights and obligations. Thus, the fact that one party was the state, and that the proceedings had been classified as 'public', was of little consequence. In the present case, therefore, although the applicant's property rights were being determined by an administrative tribunal that had applied administrative law principles, the decision would be decisive of those private property rights and consequently the case fell within Article 6.

Further, it is not fatal to the applicant's claim that the source of the action is statutory or that it engages a person's constitutional rights. For example, in *Tinnelly* v *United Kingdom*,[47] the European Court held that a right not to be discriminated against in the offering of contracts – as protected by the Fair Employment Act 1976 – was a 'civil right' within Article 6 of the Convention. In the Court's view, the statute clearly intended to provide a civil enforceable right to an individual and the fact that the fight against discrimination has a societal benefit did not detract from the right's essential private status.[48]

The European Court has, however, excluded from Article 6 disputes between civil servants and the state with respect to recruitment, termination and conditions of service. In *Pellegrin* v *France*,[49] it was held that this principle would only apply where the public servant's duties involved responsibility for protecting the general interests of the state, for example, where the applicant is a member of the armed forces. The principle was restricted further in the recent Grand Chamber decision in *Eskelinen* v *Finland*,[50] where it was held that for Article 6 to be

---

[44] (2001) 33 EHRR 38.

[45] For a detailed discussion of this phrase and the scope and application of Article 6, see Herberg, Le Seuer and Mulcahy, Determining Civil Rights and Obligations, in Jowell and Cooper (eds), *Understanding Human Rights Principles* (Hart 2001), pages 91–137.

[46] (1971) 1 EHRR 455.

[47] (1998) 27 EHRR 249.

[48] On the other hand, if the state chooses not to create a civil right of action for the individual, there will be no violation of Article 6: see *R (Kehoe)* v *Secretary of State for Work and Pensions* [2006] 1 AC 42, dealt with below under access to the courts.

[49] (2001) 31 EHRR 26.

[50] (2007) 45 EHRR 1.

excluded the state would have to show that the restriction was justified on objective grounds in the interests of the state. Thus, not only would the civil servant have to be employed in a special category of employment where a special bond of trust and loyalty existed, but it would also have to be shown that the actual dispute related to that special bond of trust. Thus, the resolution of ordinary labour disputes would not be excluded from the scope of Article 6.

Although the classification of the case and the proceedings are not conclusive, the proceedings in question must impinge and be capable of determining the applicant's private rights. Thus, in *Al-Fayed v United Kingdom*[51] it was held that the publication of a report drawn up by inspectors who had been appointed to investigate the affairs of the applicant's company did not engage Article 6 as it could not be said that the inquiry had determined the applicant's civil right to a good reputation or that its result was directly decisive of that right.[52] Again, in *R (Harrison) v Secretary of State for the Home Department*,[53] the Court of Appeal held that the right to be recognised as a British citizen was not a 'civil right' so as to engage Article 6 of the Convention. The court held that the letter from the minister, declining his claim that he was a British citizen, did not determine his civil rights, but was simply an expression of opinion as to the likely success of his claim, or, at the most, a provisional determination of that claim. Accordingly the domestic courts were entitled to refuse permission to hear his claim for judicial review of that decision. The decision must, therefore, impact on the individual's rights, as opposed to a mere expectation that the authority in question would fulfil its duty in their favour. Thus, in *Ali v Birmingham City Council*,[54] the Supreme Court held that a decision by a local housing authority under the Housing Act 1996 to discharge its duty to secure that accommodation was available for occupation by a homeless person was not a determination of civil rights under Article 6. The right in this case was not one held by the applicant but one which was dependent upon a series of evaluative judgments by the provider as to whether the statutory criteria was met.

Equally, the decision in question will not normally engage Article 6 if it is merely a provisional measure, although an exception can be made where that decision seriously impacts on the individual's rights. Thus, in *R (Wright and others) v Secretary of State for Health*,[55] the House of Lords held that Article 6 was engaged when nurses had been placed on a provisional list which would prevent them from working as a carer with vulnerable adults. As the decision drastically affected their employment prospects as care workers, Article 6 was engaged even though the determination of their civil rights was provisional. Accordingly, the secretary would need to allow the nurses to make representations before he made any decision to place someone on the list.

Article 6 and the right of access to the courts

Although Article 6 does not provide an express right of access to the courts, the European Court has held that such a right is implicit in the article's guarantee of a right to a fair trial.

---

[51] (1994) 18 EHRR 393.

[52] See also *Murungaru v Home Secretary* [2008] EWCA Civ 1015, where it was held that the withdrawal of a visa did not engage the respondent's civil property rights. Nevertheless he was held to have a viable *common law* claim under judicial review.

[53] *The Times*, 15 April 2003.

[54] [2010] 2 AC 39.

[55] [2009] 1 AC 739.

Thus, in *Golder* v *United Kingdom*,[56] the European Court held that Article 6(1) was not limited to guaranteeing the right to a fair trial in legal proceedings that are already pending, but also secured a right of access to every person wishing to commence an action in order to have his civil rights and obligations determined by the courts: it being scarcely conceivable that the rule of law could operate without access to the courts. In that case the Court found that there had been a violation of Article 6 when a prisoner, who wished to bring civil proceedings against a prison officer, had been refused permission to consult a solicitor because he had not exhausted all internal procedures before bringing the action.

In *Airey* v *Ireland*,[57] the European Court held that the right of access under Article 6(1) might, in certain cases, involve the provision by the state to the individual of positive facilities to allow effective access to legal redress. Here the European Court held that there had been a violation of Article 6 when the applicant had been unable to obtain a judicial separation from her husband because of her limited financial resources and the absence of a system of civil legal aid, making it impossible for her to find a lawyer willing to act for her. The state's obligation under Article 6 is not merely to guarantee rights that are theoretical or illusory, and in the circumstances she had no effective right of access to the courts or a specific remedy.

However, the European Court in *Golder* held that Article 6 contains implied restrictions. While the Court refused to elaborate a general theory of limitations, it accepted that there might be implied limitations in cases, for example, of minors and those of unsound mind. However, the Court has stressed that those restrictions must be imposed for legitimate reasons and must not destroy the very essence of the right to a fair trial. While not ruling on the general compatibility of such limitations on prisoners, the Court noted that in that particular case it was not justifiable for the Home Secretary to rule on the prospects of the intended proceedings.[58] More specifically, Article 6, in combination with Article 8, guarantees the right of access to a lawyer, including the right of the individual to engage in confidential correspondence with his or her legal adviser. The European Court regards the confidentiality of such privileged correspondence as fundamental and will require very strong grounds for its violation.[59] However, it will only find a violation of Article 6 where it is satisfied that the interference has affected, or was capable of affecting, the outcome of any proceedings. For example, in *Foxley* v *United Kingdom*,[60] the Court held that although there had been a violation of Article 8 when the applicant's correspondence, including his legal correspondence, was automatically redirected and opened by an official dealing with his bankruptcy, there was no evidence to suggest that the receivership proceedings had been affected.

Fair trial and legal immunities

Domestic laws that preclude or restrict a party from bringing legal proceedings against a particular body raise the question of whether they are in violation of Article 6 in denying access to the courts. Relevant time limits or other bars to legal proceedings must pursue a legitimate

---

[56] (1975) 1 EHRR 524.

[57] (1979) 2 EHRR 305.

[58] See also *Silver* v *United Kingdom* (1983) 5 EHRR 347.

[59] In *Campbell* v *United Kingdom* (1992) 15 EHRR 137, the European Court held that there had been a violation of Articles 6 and 8 of the Convention when the applicant's legal correspondence had been opened, although not read, to ensure that they were of a legal character. The risk that the correspondence was being forged in order to smuggle prohibited materials or messages into prison was so negligible that it should be discounted.

[60] (2001) 31 EHRR 25.

aim and be proportionate to that aim, although the European Court will offer a reasonable degree of latitude to the domestic law in this respect. In *Stubbings* v *United Kingdom*[61] it was held that the application of the limitation period barring the bringing of a civil action after the expiry of a six-year period was within the state's margin of appreciation. However, this approach has been modified by the domestic courts in the post-Human Rights Act era, and in *A* v *Hoare*,[62] the House of Lords held that the six-year limitation period for bringing actions needed to be applied flexibly in order to be compatible with Article 6. The House of Lords held that the provision needed to be interpreted in a way that would allow the court to consider the inhibiting effect that sexual abuse would have on the victim's preparedness to bring legal proceedings. In this case, therefore, when the case was remitted, a victim of sexual offence was allowed to bring proceedings against the attacker when the court exercised its discretion to exclude the time limit in respect of a serious sexual assault where the defendant had won £7 million on a lottery over 16 years after the initial attack.[63] On the other hand, in *Seal* v *Chief Constable of South Wales Police*,[64] the House of Lords held that both the limitation period for bringing a civil action and the requirement to obtain leave of the court to allow actions brought against mental institutions were not in violation of Article 6, such provisions pursuing a legitimate aim and not restricting the right to access to the courts in such a way as to impair the very essence of the right.

Article 6 is clearly violated when an individual is denied their pre-existing right to seek justice before the courts.[65] Thus, in *Tinnelly* v *United Kingdom*,[66] the European Court held that there had been a violation of Article 6 when the applicants were unable to proceed with a claim for discrimination when the Secretary of State had issued the company with a certificate to the effect that the decision had been made for the purpose of safeguarding national security or the protection of public safety order.[67] The European Court has also held that the application in domestic law of a blanket rule disallowing certain claims from proceeding or succeeding whatever their merits was in violation of Article 6 of the Convention. In *Osman* v *United Kingdom*,[68] the applicant had attempted to bring civil proceedings against the police for their negligence in handling the arrest of her son's teacher, who had killed the applicant's husband and wounded the applicant's son. The domestic courts held that no action could lie against the police in negligence in relation to their actions in investigating and suppressing crime.[69] The European Court held that the exclusionary rule had a legitimate aim – the prevention of crime and disorder – but held that the blanket application of the rule in this case unjustifiably deprived the applicant of her right to have the merits of her civil action tried before a court. In this case the applicant had satisfied the court regarding proximity, the case involved serious offences where the life of a child was at issue, and what was alleged was gross negligence as opposed to minor incompetence. The application of the rule in such a case thus applied a watertight and irrebuttable defence against the applicant's legal claim and thus constituted a disproportionate restriction on the applicant's rights under Article 6.

[61] (1996) 23 EHRR 213.

[62] [2008] 1 AC 135.

[63] *A* v *Hoare* [2008] EWHC. The claimant had been initially prevented from commencing proceedings at the time due to the defendant's impecuniosity whilst serving a life sentence for the assault.

[64] [2007] 1 WLR 1910.

[65] See, for example, *Golder* v *United Kingdom*, discussed above.

[66] (1998) 27 EHRR 249.

[67] See also *Devlin* v *United Kingdom* (2002) 34 EHRR 43.

[68] (2000) 29 EHRR 245.

[69] *Osman* v *Ferguson* [1993] 4 All ER 344.

However, the ruling in *Osman*, above, seems to have been restricted by subsequent case law. Thus, it is not necessarily incompatible with the Convention to safeguard the rights of government bodies or other persons by making it more difficult for them to be sued. For example, in *McElhinney* v *Ireland*,[70] it was held that the application of the principle of sovereign immunity, which was applied to deny the applicant's claim for compensation in relation to an allegation of assault by a Northern Ireland soldier, was not in violation of the right to a fair trial as guaranteed by Article 6. Thus, provided the applicant is given an opportunity to raise the appropriate legal issues in a court of law, it will not be in violation of Article 6 that the case is struck out by applying a rule which insists that a person has to prove that they have a sustainable action in law.

Furthermore, if the application of *substantive* domestic law results in the case being unsustainable then there will be no violation of Article 6. In *Z and Others* v *United Kingdom*,[71] the European Court distinguished the case of *Osman*, and held that the striking out of the applicants' claim in negligence against the local authority resulted from the application by the domestic courts of substantive law principles which the Court was not prepared to interfere with. In the present case, therefore, the applicants had not been denied access to the courts because they were able to bring their claims before the domestic courts and have the House of Lords consider whether the law of negligence should be expanded to allow actions in negligence against public authorities when they had allegedly failed to protect individuals from sexual abuse.[72] In *Z* the European Court stressed that Article 6 was concerned with unfair *procedure* rather than *substantive* law. This distinction was applied by the House of Lords in *Wilson* v *First County Trust Ltd (No 2)*,[73] where it was held that s.127(3) of the Consumer Credit Act 1974, which barred the enforcement of regulated agreements that did not comply with the Act, did not engage Article 6 because such provisions imposed a substantive legal impediment to the success of a party's action.

The European Court in *Z* did not expressly overrule its decision in *Osman*, preferring to suggest that the decision was based on a misunderstanding of the domestic law of negligence, in that it seemed to assume that the applicants had a legal claim, which was then taken away by the defence. However, the approach taken in *Z* appears to have been applied subsequently by both the European and domestic courts.[74] For example, in *Roche* v *United Kingdom*,[75] it was held that there had been no violation of Article 6 when the applicant had been denied his right to sue for medical injuries suffered while in the armed forces. In the Court's view, s.10 of the Crown Proceedings Act 1947, which barred such claims, did not take away the applicants 'civil right' to bring an action, but rather confirmed the existing law that no such right existed.[76]

---

[70] (2002) 34 EHRR 13.

[71] (2002) 34 EHRR 3. The case is examined in more detail in chapter 5, page 228.

[72] *X and Others* v *Bedfordshire County Council* [1995] 2 AC 633.

[73] [2004] 1 AC 816.

[74] See also *TP and KM* v *United Kingdom* (2002) 34 EHRR 2; *A* v *United Kingdom* (2003) 36 EHRR 51.

[75] (2006) 42 EHRR 30.

[76] However, in this case the Court found a violation of Article 8 because the applicant had been denied access to certain health and safety records that would have allowed him to assess the risk of injury from such dangers. See also *Matthews* v *Ministry of Defence* [2003] 2 WLR 435, where the House of Lords confirmed that the barring of a civil action under s.10 of the Crown Proceedings Act 1947 was not an interference with Article 6 of the Convention. The bar was part of the legal system's substantive law and not a procedural limitation on the enforcement of a legal claim.

Thus, Article 6 does not create a substantive civil right where none exists in domestic law. For example, in *R (Kehoe) v Secretary of State for Work and Pensions*,[77] the House of Lords held that there had been no violation of Article 6 when domestic legislation omitted a right to enforce the Child Support Agency's duty to ensure that former husbands paid child maintenance. The Act gave no right of enforcement to the spouse and Article 6 could not create a substantive right where there was no legal basis for such in domestic law. Baroness Hale dissented, opining that children had a right to be maintained, which then engaged Article 6, and by not enforcing that right the CSA had failed in their duties as a public authority under s.6 of the Human Rights Act 1998. A subsequent application to the European Court was dismissed where it was held that it was within the state's discretion to provide a public law remedy instead of a private law action. Thus there had not been a disproportionate interference with her right of access to the courts, or her right to an effective remedy under Article 13.[78]

It would appear therefore that the approach in *Z* is being preferred to the decision in *Osman*, and in *Brooks v Commissioner of the Police for the Metropolis*,[79] the House of Lords applied *Z* and confirmed that the principle laid down in *Hill v Chief Constable of West Yorkshire*,[80] to the effect that the police did not owe a duty of care to a victim or a witness when investigating a suspected crime, was not inconsistent with Article 6 of the Convention.[81] The decision in *Brooks* was followed in *Smith v Chief Constable of Sussex*,[82] where the House of Lords held that the principle in *Hill* – that in the absence of special circumstances the police should not be liable in negligence for harm caused by criminals – should be preserved.[83] According to their Lordships, Article 2 (the right to life) did not disturb the common law rules of negligence, but rather provided an *alternative* course of action under the Human Rights Act. A retreat from *Hill* would hinder the role of the courts in investigating crime and protecting the rights of society.[84] Similarly, in *Lawrence v Pembrokeshire County Council*,[85] it was held that there was no breach of the claimant's Convention rights when an action against the local authority for negligently placing his children on a child protection register was struck out after applying the domestic rule that investigating officers did not owe a duty of care in such circumstances.

However, although the domestic courts are allowed to construct and apply substantive principles of law which determine the success of a particular claim without violating Article 6, that principle needs to be qualified in at least two respects. First, if the relevant claim engages another Convention right, such as the right to life or the right to private and family life, then the European Court can find that the failure of the domestic courts to provide a real and effective remedy in such a case will constitute a breach of Article 13 of the Convention, which

---

[77] [2006] 1 AC 42.

[78] *Kehoe v United Kingdom* (2009) 48 EHRR 2. In the Court's view, it was not essential to decide whether her claim amounted to a 'civil right' under Article 6 as the remedy of judicial review against the CSA provided an adequate remedy for the applicant, despite it not being her preferred option.

[79] [2005] 1 WLR 1495.

[80] [1989] AC 53.

[81] The House of Lords also held that the Court of Appeal had erred in extending the common law by imposing liability on the police to the witnesses of a crime who had suffered psychiatric harm.

[82] [2009] 1 AC 225.

[83] See McIvor, Getting Defensive about Police Negligence: the Human Rights Act 1998 and the House of Lords [2010] CLJ 133.

[84] In *Smith* an action under both negligence and Article 2 failed on the facts. See also *Mitchell v Glasgow City Council* [2009] 1 AC 874.

[85] [2007] 1 WLR 2991.

guarantees an effective remedy in domestic law. A statutory or common law bar might then breach Article 13 as well as being a disproportionate interference with the substantive Convention right.[86] Thus, in *MAK and RK v United Kingdom*[87] it was held that there had been a violation of Articles 8 and 13 when parents who had been wrongfully suspected of abuse after their child's injuries had been misdiagnosed, had had their civil actions struck out. As the actions were brought in the pre-Human Rights era they had thus been deprived of an effective remedy of compensation for violation of their Convention rights.

Secondly, in the post-Human Rights Act era a victim of a Convention right other than Article 6 may bring a direct claim under a specific Convention article rather than relying on the common law action and its obstacles. Therefore, although the common law restrictions can be maintained, the victim will be provided with a remedy by relying on his other Convention rights.[88] For example, in cases such as *MAK*, above, the law would need to provide an avenue of redress outside the law of tort for those whose Convention right to private and family life had been disproportionately interfered with. In addition, within certain boundaries, the courts, as a public authority, have a duty to develop domestic law in a manner that is consistent with the Convention and its case law. Although that does not directly disturb existing rules of substantive law, there is evidence that the courts are prepared to develop private law in line with the Convention. Thus in *D v East Berkshire Community Health NHS Trust*,[89] the House of Lords held that although there were strong policy grounds for striking out most cases brought by parents alleging negligence in investigating child abuse, there were no longer such policy reasons for denying claims brought by the affected children.[90] Similarly, in *Desmond v Chief Constable of Nottinghamshire Police*[91] it was held that the rule in *Hill* did not necessarily exclude a claim against the police when they had assumed a responsibility towards a particular individual; in this case to collate and distribute evidence for an enhanced criminal record certificate responsibly.

Questions

What values and rights does Article 6 of the European Convention seek to uphold?

To what type of proceedings does Article 6 apply?

How does Article 6, and other Convention articles, regulate the immunities from legal action of certain public authorities?

A fair hearing before an impartial court or tribunal

A fundamental aspect of the right to a fair trial is that one is entitled to a hearing before an *impartial* court or tribunal: that is, a court that is independent of government and that will resolve the dispute fairly and impartially, free from personal or other bias or prejudgment.[92]

---

[86] See *Z v United Kingdom* (2002) 34 EHRR 3.

[87] (2010) 51 EHRR 14. See also *AD v United Kingdom* [2010] 51 EHRR 8.

[88] See *Smith v Chief Constable of Sussex*, n 82 above

[89] [2005] 2 All ER 443.

[90] See also *Phelps v Hillingdon LBC* [2001] 2 AC 619, where the House of Lords refused to strike out a claim for loss caused by the misdiagnosis of an educational psychologist.

[91] [2011] EWCA Civ 3. The case failed on its facts.

[92] In *R v Dunn* [2010] 2 Cr.App.R 30, it was held that there was no bias in the Court of Appeal deciding whether to refer a case for appeal to the Supreme Court.

The European Court will insist that the judge or court is free from bias and, as in English law, this means eradicating any reasonable *appearance* of bias.[93] In *Findlay* v *United Kingdom*[94] it was held that, in order to establish whether a tribunal is independent, regard must be had to the question whether the body presents an appearance of independence. In the Court's view, the tribunal must be objectively free of personal prejudice or bias and it must offer sufficient safeguards to exclude any legitimate doubt in this respect, regard being had to the manner of appointment of its officers and their term of office, and the existence of guarantees against outside pressures.

These basic tenets of fairness and impartiality should always be adhered to, even where there is a strong public interest in the arrest and prosecution of terrorist crime. In *Ocalan* v *Turkey*,[95] the Grand Chamber of the European Court held that there had been a violation of Article 6 when the applicant, who had been accused of inciting terrorism, had been tried and convicted in the State Security Court presided over by military judges. The Court held that the presence of a military judge could only have raised doubts in the applicant's mind as to the independence and impartiality of the court, particularly in the exceptional circumstances of the case when he was being accused of acting against the interests of the state.

In particular, the principles of impartiality and independence are put in doubt where a judicial decision is made by a member of government. This issue arose in *McGonnell* v *United Kingdom*,[96] where the Deputy Bailiff of Guernsey was the sole judge in relation to the applicant's planning permission application. The Deputy is a senior judge in the Royal Court (and ex-officio President of the Court of Appeal) and is also the President of the States of Election, of the States of Deliberation and of four state committees – including the legislation committee. The Court held that there had been a violation of Article 6, noting that any direct involvement in the passage of legislation or of executive rules was likely to be sufficient to cast doubt on the judicial impartiality of a person who was subsequently called on to determine a dispute relating to the wording of the legislation or rules at issue.[97] In contrast, in *Pabla Ky* v *Finland*,[98] the Court held that no violation was found when an MP sat in the applicant's case as an expert lay member of the court. Although the European Court in *McGonnell* did not preclude the possibility of judicial officers having another governmental function, the case raised specific concerns in relation to the position of the Lord Chancellor, which have now been addressed in the Constitutional Reform Act 2005.

The right to a fair trial and military discipline

Military discipline of criminal offences gives rise to concerns whether the defendant can receive a fair trial within Article 6 and in a series of cases the European Court has held that court-martial proceedings were in violation of the Convention. For example, in *Findlay* v

---

[93] For the English test, see *R* v *Gough* [1993] AC 646, as modified in the post-Human Rights era by *Director-General of Fair Trading* v *Proprietary Association of Great Britain* [2002] 1 All ER 853 and *Porter* v *Magill* [2002] 2 WLR 37.

[94] (1997) 24 EHRR 221.

[95] (2005) 41 EHRR 45.

[96] (2000) 30 EHRR 289.

[97] See also *R (Barclay and Others)* v *Secretary of State for Justice* [2009] 2 WLR 1205, where the Court of Appeal held that as the principal judicial officer of the island of Sark was linked to the executive and the legislature there was an inconsistency with Article 6 of the Convention. The claim with respect to voting rights was defeated on appeal on other grounds: *R (Barclay and Others)* v *Secretary of State for Justice* [2009] 3 WLR 1270.

[98] (2006) 42 EHRR 34.

United Kingdom,[99] the applicant had been charged with several offences and sentenced to two years' imprisonment by a court martial, and demoted from his present rank and dismissed from the army. The convening officer took the decision to charge the applicant with a variety of civilian and military offences and appointed the prosecuting officer and the members of the court martial, all of whom were inferior in rank to him and who served in his units. The President of the court was on the convening officer's staff and the Judge Advocate was appointed by the General Office of the Judge Advocate. The convening officer also acted as confirming officer, to whom the applicant unsuccessfully asked for a reduction in sentence. The European Court held there had been a violation of Article 6(1), noting the close link between the convening officer and the members of the Court and that as a non-judicial officer he had the power to ratify the decision of the judicial court and to vary the sentence.

As a result of this case,[100] parliament passed the Armed Forces Act 1996, which abolished the role of the convening officer, allocating his role to a higher authority and court administration officers. Despite those changes, the European Court has continued to find that the general structure of the court-martial system was contrary to Article 6(1) of the Convention. Thus, in *Morris v United Kingdom*[101] the Court held that although there had been put in place certain safeguards to ensure impartiality – notably the presence of a legally qualified civilian judge who since 1966 had an enhanced role – such safeguards were insufficient to exclude the risk of undue pressure being brought to bear on two relatively junior serving officers who sat on the applicant's court martial. Those officers had no legal training and remained subject to army discipline and reports, and consequently there had been a violation of Article 6. Further, the possibility of appeal to the Court Martial Appeal Court did not rectify that breach, as that body did not have the power to hear the matter afresh.[102]

Despite the ruling in *Morris*, in *R v Spear, Hastie and Boyd*,[103] the House of Lords declared the new system as compatible with Article 6 of the Convention, distinguishing *Morris* on its facts. Further, in *Cooper v United Kingdom*,[104] it was held that there had been no violation of Article 6 when the applicant had been found guilty of theft at a court martial and sentenced to 56 days' imprisonment. In the Court's view there was no ground to question the independence of the Air Force judge advocate as he was a civilian, appointed by another civilian, the Lord Chancellor. Moreover, he had been appointed to this court martial by the Judge Advocate General, another civilian. However, further concerns have been raised by both the European and domestic courts with respect to the naval disciplinary system. In *Grieves v United Kingdom*[105] it was held that the system by which the prosecuting authority could appoint a prosecutor for a court martial from a list of uniformed naval barristers was in violation of Article 6. Further, the Court noted that the post of Permanent President of Courts Martial did not exist in naval discipline, and although the Royal Naval judge advocates fulfilled the same central roles as the Air Force equivalents, they were serving naval officers

---

[99] (1997) 24 EHRR 221.
[100] See also *Coyne v United Kingdom, The Times*, 24 October 1997; *Hood v United Kingdom* (2000) 29 EHRR 365; *Cable and Others v United Kingdom* (2000) 30 EHRR 1032; *Moore and Gordon v United Kingdom* (2000) 29 EHRR 728.
[101] (2002) 34 EHRR 52.
[102] The Court also found that the role of the reviewing authority, a non-legal body that had the power to quash convictions and to replace sentences, was inconsistent with Article 6.
[103] [2002] 3 WLR 437.
[104] (2004) 39 EHRR 8.
[105] (2004) 39 EHRR 2.

and appointed by naval officers. Thus, on the facts, there had been a violation of Article 6 when the applicant had been found guilty of malicious wounding by a Naval Court Martial and as a consequence sentenced to three years' imprisonment and discharged from the service.[106] This position was confirmed in the domestic courts, and in *R v Stow*[107] it was held that a naval court martial did not possess the necessary safeguards to ensure the prosecuting authority's independence and impartiality. The Court of Appeal stressed that Article 6 insisted on the independence and impartiality not only of the decision makers, such as judges, but also of the prosecuting authority, who in the present case was subject to too much pressure from his superiors regarding the performance of his duties to be considered impartial. Accordingly there had been a violation of Article 6 and the defendant's prosecution for drunkenness and using insubordinate language was unsafe.[108]

Freedom from bias

Article 6 includes the right to an impartial hearing, free from bias and the *appearance* of bias. Thus there should be no evidence of any predisposition by the judge or court to the case in question.[109] This issue has arisen with respect to whether prison disciplinary proceedings can be compatible with Article 6 if they are carried out by the prison authorities. The position now is that once Article 6 is engaged by the relevant disciplinary proceedings – in the sense that it involves a criminal charge within that article – a breach of impartiality is obvious. Thus, in *Whitfield and Others* v *United Kingdom*,[110] it was held that there had been a violation of Article 6(1) when four young offenders had been awarded additional days in the course of prison disciplinary proceeding; the Court held that the proceedings lacked both structural independence and the objective appearance of such.

This not only requires impartiality from judges, but also members of the jury. Bias among jury members will therefore result in a breach of Article 6, although there must be sufficient evidence to support the applicant's claim. For example, in *Gregory* v *United Kingdom*,[111] the applicant, who was black and was being tried for robbery, complained that when the jury retired for their verdict they returned with a note that said 'jury showing racial overtones, one member to be excused'. The judge directed that the trial proceed, rather than discharging the jury, with a warning to the jury to put out of their minds any thought of prejudice and to decide the case on its merits and on the evidence alone. The jury eventually returned with a 10–2 verdict after the judge said that he would accept a majority verdict. It was held that the judge had done all that was required of him under Article 6 to expel any objectively justified

---

[106] See also *GW* v *United Kingdom* and *Le Petit* v *United Kingdom, The Times,* 9 July 2004, and *R v Dudley* [2005] EWCA Crim 719, where it was held that a tribunal that was presided over by a uniformed judge advocate involved a lack of impartiality and was thus contrary to Article 6.

[107] [2005] EWCA Civ 1157.

[108] Note with respect to civil proceedings, in *Crompton* v *United Kingdom* (2010) 50 EHRR 36, it was held that the Army Board was not an independent tribunal for assessing compensation payable to a member of the Territorial Army for redundancy; although domestic judicial review proceedings remedied such lack of independence.

[109] In *R v Dunn* [2010] 2 Cr.App.R 30, the Court of Appeal held that there was no such bias when the Court was asked to decide to grant leave to appeal against its decisions. The Court was simply deciding whether there was sufficiently important point of law to justify the appeal.

[110] (2005) 41 EHRR 44.

[111] (1997) 25 EHRR 577.

doubts as to the impartiality of the jury. The defence had not specifically asked for the jury to be discharged and under the rules relating to the secret deliberations of juries it was not possible to question the jury on the circumstances that justified the writing of the note. In contrast, in *Sander* v *United Kingdom*[112] it was held that a judge's decision to deal with an allegation of racial bias in a jury by means of a redirection rather than discharging the defendant was contrary to Article 6. The European Court distinguished *Gregory* on the basis that in the present case the juror had admitted to making a racist remark and that counsel for the applicant had insisted that the jury be dismissed.[113]

Despite the possibility of jury bias, and the decision in *Sander*, the House of Lords has held that the rule which declared that evidence of jury deliberations was inadmissible to question the legality of a criminal trial was not inconsistent with Article 6. In *R* v *O'Connor and Mirza*,[114] the House of Lords noted that the rule was there to protect the secrecy of jury deliberations, and that any attempt to ignore the rule to allow evidence of a wrongful conviction should be resisted by the courts. Accordingly s.8(1) of the Contempt of Court Act 1981 was not incompatible with Article 6, although the trial court was allowed to investigate allegations of bias made known to it during the trial and would not be in contempt of court in so doing. This duty thus would give the accused some protection from bias and the risk of wrongful conviction.

In addition, the independence of the jury and its function should not be compromised by the presence of prosecution personnel or police officers. In *Szypusz* v *United Kingdom*[115] it was alleged that allowing police officers to relay CCTV footage to the jurors in the jury room for two hours breached the applicant's right to a fair trial. However, the European Court found that as all parties had agreed to the procedure, and that the jury had received a special direction not to discuss the case or communicate with the officer, there had been no violation on the facts.

The right to a fair and impartial court and prisoners' disciplinary proceedings

Although it is now accepted that some prison disciplinary charges amount to criminal charges so as to engage Article 6,[116] there has been some debate with respect to the impartiality of such proceedings. The domestic courts had refused to declare such proceedings in breach of the rules of natural justice because of actual or apparent bias, holding that such appearance of bias is specifically condoned by statutory provisions that allow prison governors to hear such cases, despite their existing knowledge of the accused prisoner.[117] However, the domestic rules against bias can be breached in certain cases. In *R (Al-Hasan and Carroll)* v *Secretary of State for the Home Department*,[118] the House of Lords held that there was an appearance of bias when disciplinary proceedings were chaired by the Deputy Governor who had been present when the governor had given instructions that the prisoner be subject to a

---

[112] (2001) 31 EHRR 44.

[113] *In R v C and Others* [2005] EWCA Crim 854, the Court of Appeal held that if a judge is in sufficient doubt about the reliability of witnesses, he should stop the case and not merely invite the jury to do so.

[114] [2004] 1 AC 1118.

[115] Application No 8400/07, decision of the European Court, 21 September 2010.

[116] *Campbell and Fell v United Kingdom* (1984) 7 EHRR 165; *Ezeh and Connors v United Kingdom* (2002) 35 EHRR 28, dealt with above.

[117] See *R v Board of Visitors of Frankland Prison, ex parte Lewis* [1986] 1 WLR 130; *R v HM Prison Service, ex parte Hibbert*, unreported, decision of the High Court, 16 January 1997.

[118] [2005] 1 WLR 688.

squat search. The House of Lords accordingly quashed the disciplinary award. In their Lordships' view the Deputy Governor should have disclosed this fact and asked for the party's permission to proceed, or stood down.

The decisions in *Campbell and Fell* and *Ezeh* had not directly approached the question of whether such proceedings are incompatible with the principles of impartiality and independence contained in Article 6, but once it was accepted that Article 6 was engaged by relevant disciplinary proceedings, a breach of impartiality was obvious. Thus, in *Whitfield and Others v United Kingdom*,[119] it was held that there had been a violation of Article 6(1) when four young offenders had been awarded additional days in the course of prison disciplinary proceeding. The Court held that the proceedings lacked both structural independence and the objective appearance of such. This case confirms that *if* the disciplinary charge amounts to a criminal offence under Article 6, which it always will if additional days are imposed, then the governor will not be an impartial tribunal for the purposes of Article 6.

Following *Ezeh* disciplinary charges that constitute criminal charges are presided over by an Independent Adjudicator.[120] However, in *R (Bannatyne) v The Independent Adjudicator and the Secretary of State for the Home Department*,[121] the High Court held that the fact that prison disciplinary proceedings were generally not held in public was not contrary to Article 6 of the European Convention. In the court's view it had been accepted in *Campbell and Fell v United Kingdom* that that aspect of Article 6 was not absolute and that there were good policy reasons for not allowing a public hearing in disciplinary proceedings. The recent decision of the European Court in *Ezeh and Connors* did not establish that principle. Further, in *R (Haase) v Independent Adjudicator*[122] it was held that the presentation of the prosecution case in a disciplinary adjudication by a prison officer who may have been a witness to the alleged offence was not incompatible with Article 6 of the Convention. The court drew a distinction between the requirements in military discipline and prison discipline on grounds such as the seriousness of the offence, the need for speed and the inquisitorial nature of the proceedings.

The appearance of bias, judicial review and Article 6

The European Convention does not prohibit executive involvement in judicial decisions provided there is a sufficient opportunity for judicial review of such a decision. In *Bryan v United Kingdom*[123] it was held that whether the process of judicial review of administrative action satisfied the requirements of Article 6 depended on factors such as the subject matter of the decision appealed against, the manner in which that decision was arrived at, and the content of the dispute. Thus, the fact that judicial review does not always allow the court to consider every aspect of the original decision and its merits is not inconsistent with Article 6 when the nature of the dispute is policy-based. In contrast, in *Kingsley v United Kingdom*[124] the Court held that one essential feature of judicial review is that the reviewing court should be able to quash the impugned decision and remit the case for a new decision. The Court noted that the domestic courts were unable to remit a flawed decision of the Gaming Board to an independent tribunal, because although the court accepted that there had been an appearance

[119] (2005) 41 EHRR 44.
[120] Prison Amendment Rules 2002 (SI 2002/2016).
[121] [2004] EWHC 1921 (Admin).
[122] [2008] 1 WLR 1401.
[123] (1995) 21 EHRR 342.
[124] (2001) 33 EHRR 13.

of bias, such a decision had to stand because under domestic law no other body could make that decision.[125]

The question of the adequacy of judicial review of executive decisions was raised in *R v Secretary of State for the Environment, Transport and the Regions, ex parte Barnes*,[126] where the courts considered whether the power of the Secretary of State under the Town and Country Planning Act 1990 to recover and determine planning applications that had not been determined by the local authority, and to determine appeals against refusal of planning permission instead of the inspector were compatible with Article 6. Relying on the decision of the European Court in *Bryan*, above, the House of Lords held that although the disputes involved 'civil rights' within Article 6(1), and that the Secretary of State was not an independent and impartial tribunal, the power of the High Court in judicial review proceedings to review the legality of the decision and the procedures followed by the Secretary was sufficient to ensure compatibility with Article 6(1). Provided the High Court had full jurisdiction to deal with the case as the nature of the decision required, when the decision at issue was a matter of administrative policy, judicial review proceedings satisfied Article 6, even though the court would not have the full power to re-determine the merits of the decision.[127]

That principle has been upheld in a number of cases. For example, in *Begum v Tower Hamlets LBC*,[128] the *Alconbury* case was followed when it was held that the opportunity to appeal against housing decisions by internal review and appeal to the county court on a point of law satisfied Article 6 of the Convention. Further, in *R (Kehoe) v Secretary of State for Work and Pensions*,[129] the High Court accepted that the right of judicial review of the Child Support Agency's decisions provided adequate redress and was thus compatible with Article 6.[130] However, the court's review must provide a real and effective remedy. Thus, in *R (Wright and Others) v Secretary of State for Health*,[131] it was held that s.82 of the Care Standards Act 2000, allowing for the listing of care workers thought unsuitable to provide care, was incompatible with Article 6 because it only allowed workers to appeal nine months after the listing and judicial review of that decision was not thought to be an adequate remedy because a successful action could not lead to reinstatement of the victim.

In the post-Human Rights era, therefore, the courts must ensure that executive decisions that do not initially comply with Article 6 can be reviewed not only with respect to legality, but also on grounds of necessity and proportionality. In *Re MB*,[132] the High Court held that the procedures in s.3 of the Prevention of Terrorism Act 2005 relating to the granting and supervision of control orders were incompatible with Article 6 because they merely allowed the court to review the legality of the Secretary's decision to make a detention order, which

---

[125] However, on the hearing on just satisfaction, the European Court held that the finding of a breach of Article 6 was sufficient satisfaction and rejected the applicant's claim for compensation: *Kingsley v United Kingdom*, *The Times*, 4 June 2002.

[126] *R v Secretary of State for the Environment, Transport and the Regions, ex parte Holding and Barnes; R v the same, ex parte Alconbury Developments Ltd and Others; Secretary of State for the Environment, Transport and the Regions v Legal and General Assurance Society Ltd* [2001] 2 WLR 1389.

[127] A subsequent application under the European Convention was declared inadmissible: *Holding and Barnes plc v United Kingdom* (Application No 2352/02), 12 March 2002.

[128] [2003] 2 WLR 388.

[129] *The Times*, 21 May 2003.

[130] Subsequently, the House of Lords decided that Article 6 was not engaged because the claimant had no civil right under the statute: [2006] 1 AC 42.

[131] [2007] 1 All ER 507.

[132] *The Times*, 17 April 2006.

was in the court's view conspicuously unfair. The court concluded that the thin legality of the procedure could not disguise the fact that the controlees' rights were being determined by the executive and not by an independent court as required by Article 6. However, on appeal it was held that the procedure could and should be read to allow the courts to review those powers beyond bare legality and to insist that there were reasonable grounds for the Secretary's belief and for making the order.[133]

Questions

How has Article 6 and the case law of the European Court ensured the right to a fair and impartial hearing?

To what extent can it be said that the case law of both the European Court and the domestic courts has displayed a pragmatic approach in this area?

Article 6 and the right to a public hearing

Article 6 provides that everyone is entitled to a fair and *public* hearing. The European Court has held that the right to a public hearing is fundamental to the protection of public scrutiny, providing the means by which public confidence in the courts could be maintained and rendering the administration of justice visible.[134] However, it has also held that the right to a public hearing is subject to restrictions, this being apparent from the text of Article 6(1), which allows the press and public to be excluded (see below). Also, the Court has accepted that even in criminal trials it might be necessary to limit the open and public nature of the proceedings in order to protect, for example, the safety or privacy of witnesses or to promote the free exchange of information and opinion in the pursuit of justice.[135] The domestic courts must therefore balance the privacy rights of the claimants with the need for open justice. For example, in *Revenue and Customs Commissioners* v *Banerjee*[136] it was held that a taxpayer was not entitled to an order of anonymity with respect to her tax proceedings as the principle of public justice outweighed concerns of the claimant's personal vulnerability and her wish to avoid publicity of any kind. Taxpayers did have an expectation of privacy, but on the facts no order would have been given for a private hearing and the details of the claimant's finances were relatively routine. Generally the court accepted that there was a strong public interest in the publication of tax proceedings as they affected other taxpayers.

The article provides that judgment shall be pronounced publicly, although the press may be excluded from all or part of the trial 'in the interests of morals, public order, national security in a democratic society, where the interest of juveniles or the protection of the private life of the parties so require or to the extent strictly necessary in the opinion of the court in special circumstances where publicity would prejudice the interests of justice'. In *B and P* v *United Kingdom*[137] it was held that the denial of a public hearing and a pronouncement of

---

[133] [2006] 1 WLR 839. On further appeal to the House of Lords it was held that the procedure for accepting closed evidence could be compatible with Article 6 of the European Convention: [2007] 3 WLR 681.

[134] *Sutter* v *Switzerland* (1983) 6 EHRR 272.

[135] See, for example, *Doorson* v *Netherlands* (1996) 22 EHRR 330; *Jasper* v *United Kingdom* (2000) 30 EHRR 441; *Z* v *Finland* (1997) 25 EHRR 371; *T* v *United Kingdom* (2000) 30 EHRR 121.

[136] [2009] 3 All ER 330.

[137] (2002) 34 EHRR 19.

judgment in public in child custody proceedings did not violate the right to a fair trial as guaranteed under Article 6. The judge had discretion to allow a public hearing in such cases and had in the present case reasonably exercised that discretion in the interests of the child. Further, the judgment and its reasons were available to all affected parties.

Domestic courts will, therefore attempt to balance the conflicting interests so as to secure privacy, open justice and press freedom. Thus, in *Independent News and Media Ltd v A*,[138] the Court of Appeal held that although hearings before the Court of Protection should be held in private unless there was a good reason why they should not, in the present case the presence of selected members of the press would ensure that matters of public interest would be made available for discussion. In contrast, it was held in *R (Bannatyne) v The Independent Adjudicator and the Secretary of State for the Home Department*[139] that the fact that prison disciplinary proceedings were generally not held in public was not contrary to Article 6 of the European Convention. In the court's view it had been accepted by the European Court that that aspect of Article 6 was not absolute and that there were good policy reasons for not allowing a public hearing in disciplinary proceedings.

The preservation of national security may also provide an exception to the principle of open justice. Thus, in *R v Crown Court ex parte Times Newspapers*,[140] the Court of Appeal held that both an order by the trial judge that a terrorist trial be held *in camera* and an order that an appeal against that decision be held without a hearing and restricting public access was not incompatible with Article 6. The decision was justified because of the substantial risk to national security if the hearing was held in public, and the procedure would allow the defendant to be presented with relevant evidence while ensuring that the prosecution could be continued without diminishing the risks to national security. More recently, in *Kennedy v United Kingdom*[141] it was held that there was no violation of Article 6 when the applicant's complaints of unlawful surveillance were heard by the Investigatory Appeals Tribunal in private and he was simply informed that 'no determination had been made', meaning either that there had been no surveillance or that it was lawfully carried out. The Court held that restrictions on the right to adversarial proceedings in cases such as the present were justified by issues of national security – bearing in mind the importance of secret surveillance to the fight against terrorism and serious crime – and that it was sufficient to inform the applicant of the determination in those general terms.

The right to present legal arguments

A person should be given an opportunity of putting forward legal arguments in support of their case or defence, and the general right to a fair trial contained in Article 6(1) goes hand in hand with the more specific right of participation and legal representation contained in Article 6(3)(c), discussed below. For example, in *P, C and S v United Kingdom*[142] it was held that there had been a violation of Article 6(1) when the applicants, the mother and father of a child who was felt to be in danger from the mother, were not legally represented in neither the care order nor adoption proceedings. Although the domestic courts had to strike a

---

[138] [2010] 1 WLR 2262.
[139] [2004] EWHC 1921.
[140] [2006] 1 WLR 1361.
[141] *The Times*, 3 June 2010.
[142] (2002) 35 EHRR 31.

balance between the interests of the parents and the welfare of the children, the refusal of the courts to defer the proceedings and to allow the applicant to obtain legal representation prevented the applicants from putting forward their case in a proper and effective manner.

However, Article 6 does not guarantee an absolute right to an oral hearing. In *Eskelinen* v *Finland*,[143] the Grand Chamber of the European Court held that there had been no violation of Article 6(1) when the applicants, police officers that were seeking to claim mobility bonus payments from the state, were denied an oral hearing by the domestic courts. In this case the applicants were allowed to request such a hearing and the administrative courts had provided reasons for not granting the request – that the evidence that the applicants wanted to put forward was not instrumental to the case. Further, the applicants had been given ample opportunity to put forward their case in writing and to comment on the submissions of the parties.

The right under Article 6 might also impose a duty on the court to modify it procedures so as to allow the party to present their case. In *Polanski* v *Conde Nast Publications*,[144] the House of Lords held that there had been a violation of Article 6 when a claimant in a defamation action had been refused permission by the court to give evidence by video link and instead was ordered to give evidence in court. The claimant, the well-known film director, had wished to avoid the risk of being arrested in the United Kingdom and deported to the United States to face charges of sexual abuse. The Court of Appeal held that the courts' general policy should be to discourage litigants from escaping the normal legal process and it had been legitimate and proportionate for the court to insist that he attend court to give evidence.[145] However, on appeal the House of Lords held that despite his status as a fugitive the claimant was entitled to seek the assistance of the courts in seeking to enforce his civil rights. In the present case, his absence from the court would not prejudice the other party but a failure to give evidence by video link would gravely handicap the conduct of his case and of the proceedings.[146]

Ability to present evidence/equality of arms

Both parties to a case have the right to present their case to the court, although in *Ebanks* v *United Kingdom*[147] the European Court held that there would be no violation of Article 6 where a defendant chose not to give oral evidence on the advice of his counsel and where such evidence was not essential to guarantee a fair trial. Equally both parties should have the right to access all relevant evidence before the court and should, as far as possible, enjoy this right equally. The general right to equality of arms was upheld in *Rowe and Davis* v *United Kingdom*,[148] where the European Court found a violation of Article 6 when during the applicants' trial for murder the domestic courts had refused to order the disclosure of a document, referring to evidence given against them by a police informant, on the grounds of public interest immunity. Noting that it was a fundamental aspect of the right to a fair trial in criminal proceedings that there should be equality of arms between the prosecution and defence, the Court held that there had been insufficient opportunity for the applicants to

---

[143] (2007) 45 EHRR 1.

[144] [2005] 1 WLR 637.

[145] [2004] 1 WLR 387.

[146] The decision was upheld by the European Court of Human Rights in *Conde Naste Publications* v *United Kingdom* (Application No 29746/05).

[147] Application No 36822/06, 26 January 2010.

[148] (2000) 30 EHRR 1.

scrutinise the decision of the judge to withhold that evidence. The subsequent review of that decision by the Court of Appeal did not, in the European Court's view, remedy that unfairness as it was carried out *ex post facto*, and was possibly influenced by the finding of guilt.[149]

Accordingly, rules of domestic law that exclude a party from relying on evidence which is central to their case can be challenged as being in violation of Article 6. In *Dowsett* v *United Kingdom*,[150] the European Court held that there had been a violation of Article 6 when relying on public interest immunity the prosecution had failed to disclose the fact that the defendant's alleged accomplice in a murder trial had been offered an inducement to provide evidence against the defendant. The Court noted that the information may have been vital to the defence case and stressed that such information should have come before the trial judge to rule on its possible disclosure. Further, in *Edwards and Lewis* v *United Kingdom*,[151] it was held that there had been a violation of Article 6 when substantive evidence relating to the applicant's entrapment was withheld on grounds of public interest immunity. The applicant had been convicted of possessing a Class A drug with intent to supply following an entrapment operation by the police, but evidence of the operation and the identity of those involved had been withheld on public interest immunity grounds. The trial judge also refused an application to exclude evidence relating to the entrapment and the Court of Appeal found that the withheld evidence would not have assisted his defence and refused to order disclosure. The European Court held that the right to a fair trial precluded the use of evidence obtained by entrapment, although the right to disclosure was subject to restrictions that were necessary to safeguard another person's fundamental rights or an important public interest. In the present case the applicant had been denied access to evidence that could have related to the entrapment issue and the failure to allow disclosure was contrary to the requirements of adversarial proceedings and equality of arms.

However, exclusionary rules can be applied in appropriate cases, provided their application does not interfere with the fundamental right to a fair trial. Thus, in *Jasper and Fitt* v *United Kingdom*[152] there had been no violation of Article 6 when evidence had been excluded under the doctrine of public interest immunity. The judge had been able to look at the relevant evidence and balance the rights of both the prosecution and the defence. In particular, the defence had been able to outline its case to the judge and, where the information was not put to the jury, had been informed of the relevant information as far as possible without revealing the material that the prosecution sought to keep secret.[153] The question is, therefore, whether the original non-disclosure can be remedied by other court procedures and whether in the round the defendant has received a fair trial. Thus, in *Alami and Botmeh* v *United Kingdom*,[154] it was held that there had been no violation of Article 6 when information relating to a terrorist organisation's plot to attack the Israeli Embassy had not been put before the court at the applicants' trial. In the European Court's view the Court of Appeal was able to consider fully the impact of that evidence on the safety of their convictions, which they

---

[149] The case was ultimately referred back to the Court of Appeal and the convictions were quashed: *R* v *Rowe, Davis and Johnson, The Times*, 25 July 2000; [2000] HRLR 527.
[150] (2004) 38 EHRR 31.
[151] (2005) 40 EHRR 24.
[152] (2000) 30 EHRR 97.
[153] Contrast *Atlan* v *United Kingdom* (2002) 34 EHRR 33.
[154] (2008) 46 EHRR 31.

considered added nothing to the case presented at trial. Further, the applicants were presented with the evidence and allowed to use it in their appeal.

Recently, the domestic courts have had to consider whether they could admit evidence from military intelligence sources that passed between allies in the determination of civil actions alleging the torture of terrorist suspects. In doing so the courts have had to balance open justice with national security and have thus far taken a robust approach in the protection of due process. Thus, in *R (Binyam Mohamed)* v *Secretary of State for Foreign and Commonwealth Affairs*,[155] the Court of Appeal ordered the publication of documents passed between the UK and US authorities relating to a suspected terrorist's detention and treatment so that they could be used in legal proceedings. Rejecting the Secretary's claim of public interest immunity in respect of the information, it was noted that confidentiality as to working arrangements between allied intelligence services was not absolute, and in balancing national security with the public interest in open justice as safeguarding the rule of law those reports should be included as they did not contain any information which would pose a risk to national security but did contain information that it was in the public interest to disclose. The Court of Appeal rejected the claim that such correspondence was automatically confidential to the receiving country, and that disclosure would lead to less productive intelligence sharing. The court also noted that some of the allegations had entered the public domain because of a court action pursued by the suspect in the United States.[156]

The legality of relying on undisclosed material has been considered by both the domestic and European courts with respect to the making of control orders under s.3 of the Prevention of Terrorism Act 2005. This area will be examined in detail in chapter 14 of this text.[157] Outside this context the domestic courts have taken a robust approach to the requirements of Article 6. For example, in *Bank Mellat* v *HM Treasury*,[158] the Court of Appeal held that when the Treasury made an order against a bank under the Counter Terrorism Act 2008 it had to disclose sufficient information, not only to allow the bank to deny the allegation made against it, but to refute the essential allegations upon which the Treasury justified the making of such an order. Further, in *Al Rawi* v *Security Services*[159] it was held that the domestic courts had no power to adopt closed material procedures in an ordinary civil claim in the absence of a clear statutory power to do so, or with the consent of all parties to the litigation. Although different considerations might apply where the litigation might have a significant effect on vulnerable third parties or the wider public interest, in the present case the litigation – a civil action against the security services for complicity in the claimant's ill-treatment at a US detention facility – affected only the parties to the action. However, the courts are prepared to allow some departure from the traditional procedure in the context of terrorism, provided the essential principles of fairness are adhered to. Thus, in *Tariq* v *Home Office*[160] it was held that tribunal procedure allowing a private hearing and the exclusion of the claimant (on grounds of national security) from parts of the discrimination hearing where closed evidence was

---

[155] [2010] 3 WLR 554.

[156] See also *Aamer* v *Secretary of State for Foreign and Commonwealth Affairs* [2009] EWHC 3316 (Admin), where a court ordered the disclosure of documents that a detainee at Guantanamo Bay needed in order to prove before a US task force that his original confessions during detention were induced by torture.

[157] See chapter 14, at page 764.

[158] [2010] 3 WLR 1090.

[159] [2010] 3 WLR 1069.

[160] [2010] 1 CR 223.

being considered was not incompatible with Article 6 provided he was given sufficient evidence of the allegations to allow him to instruct his legal representative.[161]

Equality of arms and legal representation

The right of equality of arms can also be combined with the right to legal representation under Article 6(3) to ensure that one party is not unduly disadvantaged with respect to the presentation of relevant legal points. This is illustrated in the case of *Steel and Morris* v *United Kingdom*,[162] below, where it was claimed that the denial of full and free legal aid in a defamation action deprived the defendants of their right to a fair trial.

CASE STUDY

Steel and Morris v *United Kingdom* (2005) 41 EHRR 22

Substantively, this case is concerned with the conflict between free speech and the law of defamation: that is whether the law should be used to suppress or penalise speech where the subject matter of the claim constitutes ideas expressed on matters of undoubted public interest. The case will be examined in that context in chapter 9 of this text. For our present purposes the case will be examined with respect to Article 6 of the Convention and the right of litigants to present their case in court proceedings; and more specifically the right to legal representation in presenting that case. It has been chosen to illustrate the fundamental nature of the right to a fair trial and the consequences of its absence, not only to the parties to but to justice as a whole. The reader should note the relationship between the substantive issues of free speech raised under Articles 10 and the procedural issues raised under Article 6. You should revisit this case study and the questions at the end when you have read the text on the law of defamation.

The applicants, well-known peace activists, had been involved in the distribution of a six-page leaflet entitled *What's wrong with McDonald's?* The leaflet made certain allegations about the fast-food company, claiming that it was guilty of abusive and immoral farming, deforestation, the exploitation of children and their parents through aggressive advertising, and the sale of unhealthy food. McDonald's issued a writ against the applicants claiming damages in libel and at the trial (known as the 'McLibel' case and the longest libel trial in English history: *McDonald's Corporation* v *Steel and Morris*, unreported, 19 June 1997), the applicants denied responsibility for publication, and also denied that the words in the leaflet (and later placed on a website) were defamatory. The applicants also raised defences of fair comment and justification. Both applicants were denied legal aid and represented themselves at the trial, although they did receive some legal assistance through volunteer lawyers. On the other hand McDonald's were represented by lawyers experienced in defamation law. The applicants' defences were rejected

---

[161] See also *R (Roberts)* v *Parole Board* [2005] 2 AC 738, where it was held that there had been no unfairness when the Board refused to release the prisoner to open conditions on the basis of both open and closed, sensitive, material.

[162] (2005) 41 EHRR 22.

at first instance and the Court of Appeal upheld that decision (*The Independent*, 10 May 1999), although it did reduce the damages awarded by the trial judge so that £36,000 was awarded against Steel and £40,000 against Morris. McDonald's never sought to enforce those sums and the applicants were adamant that they would never pay.

The applicants petitioned the European Court of Human Rights claiming that the denial of legal aid at the trial deprived them of the right to a fair trial (guaranteed under Article 6) in that they were severely hampered with respect to the gathering of evidence and the general organisation of their case. Consequently, they claimed that there had been a violation of Article 6 of the European Convention. In addition they claimed that the trial and the damages award constituted an unnecessary and disproportionate interference with their right to freedom of expression as guaranteed by Article 10 of the Convention.

The decision of the European Court of Human Rights under Article 6

With respect to the claim under Article 6, the Court noted that it was central to the concept of a fair trial that the litigant was not denied the opportunity to present his or her case effectively before the court and was able to enjoy equality of arms with the opposing side. Whether a party was entitled to legal aid depended on the particular circumstances of the case, including the importance of what was at stake, the complexity of the relevant law and procedure and the person's capacity to represent him or herself effectively. In this case, in terms of what had been at stake, the Court noted that the financial consequences had been potentially severe. Further, with respect to the complexity of the case, it noted that the trial had lasted 313 days and that the factual case that had to be proved by the applicants was highly complex; extensive legal and procedural issues had to be resolved before the trial judge.

Against that background the Court noted that the applicants appeared to be articulate and resourceful and were successful in proving the truth of a number of allegations. They had also received some limited assistance from volunteer lawyers, including help in drafting their initial pleadings. However, for the bulk of the proceedings they had acted alone and in an action of such complexity neither the sporadic help nor the latitude granted to them by the court as litigants in person, was a substitute for competent and sustained representation by an experienced lawyer familiar with the case and the law of libel. The Court held that the denial of legal aid deprived the applicants of the opportunity to present their case effectively and contributed to an unacceptable inequality of arms with McDonald's, and that consequently there had been a violation of Article 6.

The decision of the European Court under Article 10

Turning to the claim under Article 10 of the Convention, the Court noted that the question in the present case was whether the interference with the applicants' right to free speech was necessary and proportionate, it being accepted that there was such interference and that it was prescribed by law and done in pursuance of a legitimate aim.

The Court addressed the applicants' specific claim that it was unfair for them to have to prove the truth of the allegations when they had denied publication and where they ➡

had simply distributed leaflets to the public. Rejecting those arguments the Court held that it was not in principle incompatible with Article 10 to require a defendant to prove the truth of those statements in accordance with the civil standard of proof. Nor should the fact that the claimants were a multinational company deprive it, in principle, of the right to bring proceedings or to require the defendants to prove the truth of the statements. Such companies inevitably laid themselves open to increased public scrutiny, but in addition to the public interest in free speech, there was a competing interest in protecting the commercial success and viability of companies, for the benefit of shareholders and for the wider economic good.

However, the Court added that notwithstanding the state's margin of appreciation in the operation of such laws and the relevant burden of proof, if a state does provide a remedy to such corporations, it was essential, so as to safeguard the countervailing interests in free speech and public debate, that a measure of procedural fairness and equality of arms was provided for. The more general interest in promoting the free circulation of information and ideas about the activities of powerful commercial entities and the possible chilling effect on others were also important factors to be considered in that context, bearing in mind the legitimate and important role campaign groups could play in stimulating public discussion. Consequently, the lack of procedural fairness and equality gave rise to a breach of Article 10. Further, the Court noted that under the Convention any award of damages for defamation had to bear a reasonable relationship of proportionality to the injury to reputation. In the present case, while no steps had been taken to enforce the damages award against the applicants, the fact remained that the substantial sums awarded against them had remained enforceable since the decision of the Court of Appeal in 1999, and in those circumstances the award of damages could be said to be disproportionate to the legitimate aim of protecting the corporation's reputation.

The Court thus found a violation of both Articles 6 and 10 of the Convention. It awarded the applicants compensation for the distress and anxiety caused by representing themselves in the long and complicated proceedings and also reimbursed their costs and expenses.

Questions

1 Why was this case dealt with under both Articles 6 and 10 of the Convention?
2 Identify both the substantive and procedural issues raised by the applicants' claims.
3 What specific issues were raised under Article 6 of the Convention?
4 What role does Article 6 of the Convention play in resolving substantive legal issues?
5 How did the principles and values of Article 6 combine with those in Article 10 in this case and how did they both shape the Court's judgment under Article 10?
6 How did the European Court of Human Rights' judgment and use of Article 6 accommodate the moral and practical problems of large and powerful claimants using the law of defamation to suppress free speech?
7 What did the European Court decide with respect to the question of whether the burden of proof should be on the publisher? Do you agree with that finding?
8 To what extent does the decision guarantee a right to legal representation and participation in civil disputes?

The use of unlawful evidence

The fact that the applicant's Convention rights have been violated in the obtaining of evidence will not automatically lead to a violation of Article 6. Thus in *Khan v United Kingdom*[163] it was held that although evidence used against the applicant in his criminal trial had been obtained in violation of Article 8, because it had been obtained via surveillance techniques that were not in accordance with law, the admission of that evidence did not violate the applicant's right to a fair trial within Article 6. Article 6 did not lay down any rules on the admissibility of evidence, and the domestic authorities had the initial right to regulate such matters provided the proceedings as a whole were fair.[164] Although the applicant's conviction was based solely on the use of that evidence, he had been given an opportunity to question the admissibility of the evidence and the domestic courts had carefully assessed the evidence to see whether its inclusion would cause substantive unfairness.[165] Similarly, in *PG and JH v United Kingdom*,[166] there was no violation of Article 6 when the police had tapped the applicants' telephone and then recorded their voices in police cells to confirm that the taped voices belonged to the applicants. The European Court held that Article 6 had not been breached in respect to the non-disclosure of that material because sufficient safeguards had been taken to protect the defendant's interests and there had been no unfairness in leaving the taped evidence to the jury as a thorough summing up had been provided to the jurors.

The position is different, however, where on the facts it is shown that the use of the information impinges on the applicant's right to silence and the privilege against self-incrimination. In *Allan v United Kingdom*,[167] the applicant complained of a violation of, *inter alia*, Article 6 with respect to the use at his trial of covert surveillance evidence taken while he was in his cell. The evidence comprised tape recordings of the applicant in the police station and in prison with three men, including a long-standing informer who had been placed by the police in the cell in order to obtain evidence against the applicant after he had indicated that he was not prepared to answer police questions. The informant's testimony formed the principal prosecution evidence at the trial and the applicant was convicted of murder. The European Court held that although the recordings were not unlawful because the applicant had not been coerced or entrapped into making the recorded statements and had been able to challenge the admissibility of the evidence at the trial, there had been a violation of Article 6(2). In the Court's view, the privilege against self-incrimination was not limited to cases in which the accused's will had been directly overcome by duress and also protected the freedom of a suspect to choose whether to speak or to remain silent under police questioning. This freedom could be undermined where the authorities elicited evidence from the accused by subterfuge, once they had failed to elicit that evidence through questioning, and in the present case the applicant would have been open to persuasion to take the informant into his confidence. In that sense, therefore, the evidence obtained by the informant was obtained against the applicant's will and the use of that evidence at trial violated the right to silence and privilege against self-incrimination.

---

[163] (2001) 31 EHRR 45.

[164] *Schenk v Switzerland* (1988) 13 EHRR 242; *Teixeira de Castro v Portugal* (1998) 28 EHRR 101.

[165] The Court also held that the taking of the voice samples did not infringe the applicant's right against self-incrimination.

[166] *The Times*, 19 October 2001.

[167] (2003) 36 EHRR 12.

> **Question**
> To what extent has the European Court ensured equality of arms in judicial proceedings?

The right to a fair sentence

In *V and T v United Kingdom*[168] it was confirmed that the concept of trial in Article 6 extended to giving a person the right to a fair sentence. In that case the applicants, who had been found guilty of murder and who under domestic law were detained at Her Majesty's Pleasure, had had their sentences fixed by the Home Secretary. The European Court held that the applicants had the right to have their sentences set by a fair and impartial body and that there had been a violation of that safeguard in the present case because the sentence had been set by a politician without sufficient judicial safeguards.

The ruling in *V and T* was stated to apply only to the type of prisoners in question and was not intended to apply to mandatory lifers, but in *Stafford v United Kingdom*[169] the European Court accepted that there was no effective difference between these sentences and overruling its previous decisions it held that Article 5(4) applied to decisions as to those prisoners' release. After *Stafford*, in *R (Taylor and Anderson) v Secretary of State for the Home Department*,[170] the House of Lord agreed with the European Court that the Home Secretary's role in fixing the tariff had become increasingly difficult to reconcile with the notion of the separation of powers and that tariff fixing was a sentencing exercise representing the element of punishment. Their Lordships stated that Article 6 was one of the most important rights in the Convention and the protection under that Article applied equally to the fixing of a sentence as it did to the determination of guilt. The Home Secretary should not fix the tariff of a convicted murderer, even if he did no more than confirm what the judges had recommended. Accordingly, as the Home Secretary was acting so as to give effect to s.29 of the Crime (Sentences) Act 1997 when deciding himself on the minimum period which must be served by a mandatory life sentence prisoner, the House of Lords made a declaration that s.29 was incompatible with the right under Article 6 to have a sentence imposed by an independent and impartial tribunal.

The Home Secretary's powers were amended so as to comply with the House of Lords' judgment,[171] and now all tariffs (or, as they are now known, minimum terms) are set by the courts in accordance with statutory guidelines.[172] This complies with the basic principles in Article 6, although new issues are being raised with respect to these sentences and their review. For example, with respect to the setting of minimum terms for offenders detained at Her Majesty' Pleasure, in *R (Smith) v Secretary of State for the Home Department*[173] the House of Lords held that, where an offender under 18 had been detained during her Majesty's Pleasure, the minimum term of a young offender should be subject to review by the Home

---

[168] (1999) 30 EHRR 121.

[169] (2002) 35 EHRR 32.

[170] [2002] 3 WLR 1800.

[171] See schedule 21 Criminal Justice Act 2003 and s.82A Powers of the Criminal Courts (Sentencing) Act 2000.

[172] In *R (Nejad) v Secretary of State for the Home Department, The Times*, 13 February 2004, it was held that in those remaining cases where the Home Secretary had the power to fix a sentence for discretionary life sentence prisoners, that he should always follow the judicial view unless there were good reasons to depart from such view and the Home Secretary had put forward such reasons for departing from the judicial view.

[173] [2006] 1 AC 159.

Secretary even though it had been reviewed subsequently by the Lord Chief Justice. The House of Lords held that, although Article 6 would preclude a sentence being increased, it did not preclude the reduction of that sentence. However, in *R (Dudson) v Secretary of State for the Home Department*,[174] the House of Lords held that there was no automatic right to an oral hearing where a young person's tariff was being reviewed. A fair and public hearing under Article 6 did not require an oral hearing at every stage of the proceedings. The prisoner had had a fair hearing at this trial and the overriding question was whether the issue could be dealt with properly as a matter of fair trial without hearing the applicant orally. An oral hearing would have caused considerable delay and would not have served any useful purpose, and there was no argument that an oral hearing was needed over and above the argument that it was required as part of the normal process.[175]

Equally, the imposition of arbitrary and disproportionate criminal penalties might lead to a violation of Article 6, or other Convention rights. In *International Transport Roth GmbH and Others v Secretary of State for the Home Department*,[176] lorry drivers and the owners of their vehicles had all been subjected to penalties as persons responsible for clandestine entrants to the United Kingdom by provisions made under s.32 of the Immigration and Asylum Act 1999.[177] They claimed that their arrests and the subsequent penalties were contrary to Articles 5 and 6 of the Convention, to the right of property under Article 1 of the First Protocol, and Articles 28 and 49 of the EC Treaty. The Court of Appeal held that the penalty regime in question did not adequately protect the rights of those alleged to be responsible for clandestine entrants. The scheme was unfair in that its essential approach in imposing strict liability was unfair to carriers, and although the reverse burden of proof did not in itself violate Article 6, that aspect could not be ignored. In the Court's view the scheme should properly be regarded as criminal and it was not right to impose so high a fixed penalty without the possibility of mitigation. The fixed nature of the penalties offended the right to have a penalty determined by an independent tribunal and although the inflexibility of the penalty did not deprive the carriers of a right to a fair trial under Article 6, they did impose an excessive burden on the carriers in breach of Article 1 of the First Protocol.

A fair hearing within a reasonable time

Article 6(1) provides that an individual should receive a fair trial within a reasonable time, and this includes the right to an effective remedy in domestic law when there has been an unreasonable delay.[178] This supplements the right under Article 5(3) of the Convention to be brought promptly before a judge or other officer and to have the right to trial within a reasonable time or to release pending trial. Article 6(1) goes further than that provision and applies to the length of the judicial proceedings, including appeals. It is also concerned with both criminal and civil proceedings, even where loss of liberty is not at stake. Thus, in *Mitchell v*

---

[174] [2006] 1 AC 245.

[175] In *R (Robinson) v Secretary of State for Justice* [2010] 1 WLR 2380, it was held that provisions relating to the early release of prisoners serving determinative sentences were concerned with the administration of the sentence rather than the original sentence and were thus outside Article 6.

[176] [2002] 3 WLR 344.

[177] The Carrier's Liability (Clandestine Entrants and Sale of Transporters) Regulations 2000 and The Carrier's Liability (Clandestine Entrants) (Code of Practice) Order 2000.

[178] See *McFarlane v Ireland* (Application No 3133/06), decision of the European Court, 10 September 2010.

United Kingdom,[179] it was held that there had been a violation of Article 6 when there had been an excessive delay in the applicants' domestic civil proceedings for breach of contract, which had lasted nearly nine and a half years.[180] Further, in such cases the European Court may award compensation for non-pecuniary loss even though the applicant received a fair trial in the round. For example, in *Blake v United Kingdom*,[181] the European Court awarded €5000 to the applicant for distress after it had found that there had been a violation of Article 6 when proceedings to recover profits he had gained from writing his memoirs, in breach of his duty of confidentiality, had lasted nine and a half years.

What amounts to a reasonable time depends on the circumstances of the case, taking into account factors such as the complexity of the charge or the claim, the need to investigate the facts for the benefit of the parties and third parties, and the conduct of the parties if, for example, they have been responsible for the delay.[182] For example, in *Robins v United Kingdom*[183] Article 6 was violated when there was a delay of ten months between judgment and the ordering of costs, and a further delay of 16 months before the costs were confirmed on appeal. Although the European Court is reluctant to interfere with the domestic legal system of each state, it insists that the state takes reasonable measures to ensure that the courts provide reasonably prompt remedial action, including clearing backlogs in the judicial system.[184] Thus, in *King v United Kingdom*,[185] the European Court found a violation of Article 6 when the applicant's tax penalty proceedings lasted nearly 14 years. Although the applicant had been guilty of some time-wasting the authorities had contributed significantly to the delay of the proceedings, which, on analysis, took an excessive length of time. Similarly, in *Deak v United Kingdom*,[186] it was held that there had been a violation of Article 6 when proceedings under the Hague Convention on Child Abduction challenging a child's removal from the United Kingdom lasted five and a half years. Although the UK proceedings (lasting three and a half years) did not breach the article – because they had to await the conclusion of the Romanian proceedings – the later proceedings of six years did as they involved long periods where no judicial or procedural activity was evident.[187]

The requirement of expedition is particularly important in criminal proceedings, where the applicant's liberty might be at stake. In *Mellors v United* Kingdom[188] it was held that there had been a violation of Article 6(1) with respect to the length of the applicant's criminal

---

[179] (2003) 36 EHRR 52.

[180] See also *Obasa v United Kingdom* (Application No 50034/99), decision of the European Court, 16 January 2003, where it was held that there had been a violation of Article 6(1) in respect of the length of proceedings regarding the applicant's discrimination claim – a period of over seven years from the instigation of the claim until the final decision to refuse leave to appeal to the House of Lords.

[181] (2007) 44 EHRR 29.

[182] See *Konig v Germany* (1978) 2 EHRR 170. In *Davies v United Kingdom* (2002) 35 EHRR 29, the Court found a violation of Article 6 regarding the state's proceedings against the applicant and his company, even though it accepted that some of the delay was caused by the applicant's tactics and that the proceedings were complex.

[183] (1997) 26 EHRR 527.

[184] See *Zimmermann and Steiner v Switzerland* (1983) 6 EHRR 17; *Guincho v Portugal* (1984) 7 EHRR 223.

[185] (2005) 41 EHRR 2.

[186] (2008) 47 EHRR 50.

[187] See also *Crompton v United Kingdom* (2010) 50 EHRR 36, where there was a breach of Article 6 with respect to the length of proceedings (11 years) of a redundancy payments claim and a subsequent judicial review of the claim.

[188] (2004) 38 EHRR 11.

proceedings. Although the European Court held that a delay of eight months between arrest and conviction was not unreasonable, it found a violation with respect to the appeal proceedings, which took three years to conclude.[189] In such cases the Court will be inclined to award compensation to the victim. Thus, in *Massey v United Kingdom*,[190] it awarded the applicant €4000 for non-pecuniary loss after it had found a violation of Article 6 when the criminal proceedings against the applicant for indecent assault lasted nearly five years. The Court noted that the case had not been particularly complex and stressed that in a case where there had already been some delay in bringing the matter to trial the need for processing the appeal expeditiously took on more urgency.

In cases where the defendant is charged with particularly serious offences, the European Court must ensure that there is a proper balance between ensuring expedition and granting the applicant a fair and proper trial. In *Henworth v United Kingdom*[191] the applicant's murder trial and three subsequent retrials had lasted six years. The applicant was arrested and charged with the murder of his flat-mate in June 1995 and convicted in July 1996. He successfully appealed against that decision because the judge had misdirected the jury, and in July and August 1998 a retrial took place at which he was discharged because the jury was unable to reach a verdict. A further retrial commenced in July 1999 where his legal representative unsuccessfully argued that it was an abuse of process to try him after two unsuccessful trials. During the third trial he dispensed with legal representation and represented himself, but after feeling unable to do so a fourth retrial began in September 1999, where he was convicted and sentenced to life imprisonment. In October 1999 he appealed against his conviction, arguing that the second retrial was an abuse of process as it flouted the convention in English law that if the prosecution has failed to secure a conviction on two occasions it should not then seek a further trial. This claim was dismissed by the Court of Appeal in January 2001 and appeal to the House of Lords was refused in June 2001.

The European Court held that while the gravity of the offence was a relevant factor to be taken into consideration, it noted that the proceedings were relatively straightforward considering that they concerned a murder case. The period that elapsed between his first conviction in July 1996 and the appeal judgment being given in February 1998 was unduly long and the government had not provided any explanation for this delay. However, the period of five months between the quashing of the conviction in February 1998 and his first retrial in July 1998 could not be regarded as excessive, and although there was a delay of 12 months before the second retrial, responsibility for this was in part due to the unavailability of legal representation. Equally, the short delay between the second and third retrials was not excessive. However, although the time that elapsed between his conviction and judgment being given by the Court of Appeal was not excessive, the state was obliged to proceed with particular diligence at this time because the applicant was in custody and the authorities had decided to try him for a second time. While there were no unusually long and unexplained periods of inactivity, there had been a number of delays which, taken together and in light of the

---

[189] See also *Yetkinsekerci v the United Kingdom* (Application No 71841/01), decision of the European Court, 20 October 2005, where the Court held that there was a violation of Article 6 when the applicant's criminal appeal took over three years.

[190] *The Times*, 23 November 2004; joined with *King*, above.

[191] (2005) 40 EHRR 33.

decision to retry him again after July 1998, disclosed that the proceedings did not proceed with the necessary expedition.

Article 6 and the presumption of innocence

Article 6(2) states that everyone charged with a criminal offence shall be presumed innocent until proved guilty according to law.[192] For example, in *Minelli* v *Switzerland*[193] there was a violation of Article 6(2) when the domestic courts awarded court costs against the applicant on the basis that had it not been for a limitation period barring action against him a complaint would very probably have led to his conviction because a similar claim against another person had been upheld. The domestic court had satisfied itself of the applicant's guilt without the applicant receiving the benefit of the guarantees and accordingly there had been a violation of Article 6(2).[194] The principle does not apply, however, to the imposition of every penalty. Thus, in *Phillips* v *United Kingdom*,[195] there was no violation of Article 6(2) when domestic law allowed the courts to confiscate an individual's property and to assume that all the proceeds held by a person convicted of drugs trafficking represented the proceeds of such activity. Such a presumption did not go to the individual's guilt and in any case the procedure was subject to certain judicial safeguards.[196]

Article 6(2) thus only applies to criminal proceedings, and in *R (Allen)* v *Secretary of State for Justice*[197] it was held that a person could not apply the presumption of innocence under Article 6(2) to prove that her quashed conviction had automatically led to a miscarriage of justice for the purpose of claiming compensation under the Criminal Justice Act 1988. Article 6(2) only applied to criminal proceedings and not to claims for compensation; the right to compensation was only available where the miscarriage of justice had occurred, and the claimant was thus innocent, beyond reasonable doubt. Also, in *R* v *G*[198] the House of Lords held that Article 6(2) was concerned with the *procedural* fairness of the system for the administration of justice and dealt with the burden of proof regarding the elements of the offence and any defences to it; it did not deal with the *substantive issue* of what those elements were or what defences *ought* to be available. Thus the conviction of a 15-year-old boy for rape under s.5 of the Sexual Offences Act 2003 was not incompatible with Article 6 of the Convention, despite the lack of defence of reasonable belief that the victim was over 13.

---

[192] In *Allison* v *HM Advocate* [2010] HRLR 16, the Supreme Court held that although a person was presumed to be innocent it was still a breach of an individual's right to a fair trial when the court had not been told of charges brought against a witness so as to allow the defendant to question the credibility of the witness' evidence.

[193] (1983) 5 EHRR 554.

[194] See also *Yassar Hussain* v *United Kingdom* (2006) 42 EHRR 33, where the domestic judge in refusing the applicant's costs order after acquittal (caused by the prosecution witness being absent) intimated that the applicant had been guilty as there was compelling evidence against the defendant. The European Court found that such a statement violated the applicant's right of presumed innocence under Article 6(2).

[195] *The Times*, 13 August 2001. See also *McGuiness and Heaney* v *Ireland* (2001) 33 EHRR 12.

[196] However, in *R* v *Briggs-Price* [2009] 1 AC 1026, the House of Lords held that although Article 6(2) did not apply to confiscation orders, the presumption of innocence inherent in Article 6(1) did. Consequently, a criminal standard of proof should be applied when a judge decided whether a criminal had benefited from a drugs trafficking offence.

[197] [2009] 2 All ER 1.

[198] [2009] 1 AC 92.

In particular, Article 6(2) protects an individual from self-incrimination.[199] In *Saunders* v *United Kingdom*[200] the applicant claimed that the requirement that he answer questions put to him by the Department of Trade and Industry, which then formed a significant element of the evidence in a subsequent criminal investigation, offended the principle against self-incrimination. It was held that the use by the prosecution at the applicant's trial of statements given under legal compulsion during a statutory investigation into corporate fraud infringed the applicant's right against self-incrimination. That right, like the right to silence, was a generally recognised international standard that lay at the heart of the notion of a fair trial. The right had close links with the presumption of innocence contained in Article 6(2) and was primarily concerned with respecting the will of the accused to remain silent.[201] In this case the prosecution had made use of these statements to question the applicant's honesty and integrity and it was irrelevant that the statements were not self-incriminating.[202] Again, in *Kansal* v *United Kingdom*,[203] it was held that the use at a subsequent criminal trial of answers given under compulsion to the Official Receiver under s.291 of the Insolvency Act 1986 breached the guarantees under Article 6. The Court noted that the information received from those answers played a significant part in the criminal trial against him and that consequently the applicant had been denied a fair trial.

However, the protection against self-incrimination is not absolute and both domestic and European courts have upheld provisions which compel a defendant to make statements. In *Brown* v *Stott (Procurator Fiscal)*,[204] the Privy Council held that s.172(2)(a) of the Road Traffic Act 1988, which compels a person to answer the question whether he or she had been driving a car when arrested on suspicion of committing a driving offence, was compatible with the rule against self-incrimination. The provision was necessary to fulfil a clear and proper public objective and did not sanction prolonged questioning, providing simply for the putting of a single question which could not, without other evidence, incriminate the suspect. Further, the trial judge had the right to exclude admissions where there was a suggestion of improper coercion or oppression. The compatibility of that principle was confirmed by the European Court in *O'Halloran and Francis* v *United Kingdom*,[205] where it was held that s.172 was not incompatible with the right to a fair trial. In the Court's view, although the provision allowed direct compulsion because it made it an offence to refuse to give such evidence, it was part and parcel of a legitimate national regulatory scheme to monitor the ownership of motor vehicles. Again, although the statement was then used in subsequent criminal proceedings, the defendants were able to question the propriety and reliability of that evidence and the prosecution still had to prove the offence beyond all reasonable doubt. Given the limited use

---

[199] *Funke* v *France* (1993) 16 EHRR 297. See Berger, Self-incrimination and the European Court of Human Rights: Procedural Issues in the Enforcement of the Right to Silence [2007] EHRLR 514.

[200] (1996) 23 EHRR 313.

[201] In *PG and JH* v *United Kingdom*, *The Times*, 19 October 2001, it was held that voice samples, taken covertly in the defendant's cells were akin to physical examples and thus did not constitute incriminating evidence in breach of Article 6(2).

[202] See also *IJL, GMR and AKP* v *United Kingdom* (2001) 33 EHRR 11, where Article 6(1) was violated when the applicants had been interviewed by DTI inspectors in the course of an investigation of a takeover bid and the transcripts of those interviews had been used by the prosecution in the applicants' subsequent criminal trial.

[203] (2004) 39 EHRR 41.

[204] [2001] 2 All ER 97.

[205] (2008) 46 EHRR 21.

of the statement, in the circumstances the right to remain silent and to be free from self-incrimination had not been destroyed.

Article 6 and the right to silence

Article 6 gives general recognition to the individual's right to remain silent. In *Condron* v *United Kingdom*[206] the European Court affirmed that the right to silence lay at the heart of the notion of a fair procedure and that particular caution was required before a domestic court invoked an accused's silence against him. In that case the Court held that there was a violation of Article 6 when the trial judge had given a direction to the jury that might have left them at liberty to draw an adverse inference from the applicant's silence despite the plausibility of the applicant's explanation for his silence. Similarly, in *Beckles* v *United Kingdom*,[207] there had been a violation of Article 6 when the trial judge had left the jury to draw an adverse inference after he had failed to alert the jury of all the possible explanations for the applicant remaining silent.

The right is not, however, absolute, and the question for the Court is whether the applicant received a fair trial in all the circumstances. In *Murray* v *United Kingdom*,[208] the applicant had been arrested and cautioned under the Criminal Evidence (Northern Ireland) Order 1988. He said he had nothing to say and was taken to a police station and asked to account for his presence in the house where he had been arrested, but again said nothing. His right of access to a solicitor was delayed for 48 hours and at his trial he was convicted, adverse inferences being drawn against him for failing to give evidence in court and for failing to account for his presence at the house. The European Court held that Article 6 did not prevent the applicant's silence from being taken into account in assessing the prosecution's evidence provided there are sufficient safeguards. The overall evidence against the applicant was formidable and the drawing of the inference in this case was more a matter of common sense.[209]

In such cases the Court has insisted on access to legal advice, and in *Murray* it held that as such inferences could be drawn under the Order, it was important that the accused be given the benefit of legal assistance, and the denial for 48 hours of access to his solicitor in this case violated Article 6(1) in conjunction with Article 6(3)(c) of the Convention. Further, in *Averill* v *United Kingdom*,[210] it was held that the deferral of the right of access to a lawyer for 24 hours had deprived the applicant of effective advice during his initial period of detention, particularly as the trial judge had drawn a very strong adverse inference from the applicant's silence during interrogation. Thus, the Court found a violation of Article 6(3)(c) in that case, despite holding that the right to silence had not been violated on the facts.

Article 6, the presumption of innocence and reverse burdens

Much case law has been generated in the domestic courts since the coming into force of the Human Rights Act 1998, involving claims that statutory provisions reversing the burden of

---

[206] (2001) 31 EHRR 1.
[207] (2003) 36 EHRR 13.
[208] (1996) 22 EHRR 29.
[209] See also *Adetoro* v *United Kingdom* (Application No 46834/06), where there was no violation of Article 6 as the defendant was not convicted on basis of silence, despite the trial judge giving a deficient direction to the jury on drawing adverse inferences.
[210] (2001) 31 EHRR 36.

proof are contrary to the presumption of innocence contained in Article 6(2). The courts have taken a broad approach, and have considered each provision on its merits; neither the domestic nor European Courts have declared such provisions as incompatible with Article 6 *per se*.

The compatibility of s.16 and s.16A of the Prevention of Terrorism Act 1989, which appeared to reverse the normal burden of proof when a person is charged with being in possession of articles for terrorist purposes, was considered in the pre-Human Rights Act case of *R v DPP, ex parte Kebilene*.[211] In this case, the courts considered whether the DPP should give consent to a prosecution under s.16 and s.16A of the Prevention of Terrorism Act 1989, which placed a legal burden of proof on the accused to prove that the items found in his possession were neither not in his possession nor not in his possession for a terrorist purpose. The Divisional Court held that those provisions were contrary to the presumption of innocence contained in Article 6 of the Convention in that they would allow a court to convict even when the jury entertained a reasonable doubt as to the defendant's guilt. On appeal to the House of Lords it was held that the DPP's decision to proceed with a prosecution was not subject to judicial review and thus the House of Lords did not have to deal directly with the question of whether s.16 and s.16A of the Prevention of Terrorism Act 1989 were contrary to Article 6(2). In any case, the House of Lords noted that the Convention case law does not necessarily preclude the reversal of the burden of proof, provided such does not interfere fundamentally with the defendant's right to a fair trial and the principle of the presumption of innocence.[212]

This type of provision has been considered by the domestic courts in the post-Act era, and in *Attorney-General's Reference (No 4 of 2002)*[213] the House of Lords considered the compatibility of s.11 of the Terrorism Act 2000, which makes it an offence to belong to or take part in the activities of a proscribed organisation and which provides a defence if the charged can prove that he had not taken part in such activities at any time at which it was proscribed. The question for the House of Lords was whether the provision imposed a *legal* burden on the defendant, in which case the presumption of innocence would be violated, or simply an *evidential* burden, in which case the defendant would have to adduce some evidence but the burden of proving beyond reasonable doubt that the offence had been committed would still remain with the prosecution. The House of Lords held that parliament had intended that s.11(2) impose a legal burden on the defendant and that in such a case a conviction would be a disproportionate breach of Article 6 because a person could be convicted on the basis of conduct which was not criminal at the date of commission. However, in their Lordship's view that section could be read down so as to impose an evidential burden only, in which case the provision could remain compatible with Article 6 and the Human Rights Act.[214] Similarly, in *R v Keogh*,[215] the Court of Appeal held that the reverse burden of proof in s.2 and s.3 of the Official Secrets Act 1989 of making damaging disclosure of prohibited information was incompatible with Article 6. The Court of Appeal held that the question was whether the reverse burden of proof was necessary for the effective operation of those offences. It noted that the trial would be

---

[211] [1999] 4 All ER 801.

[212] When the *Kebilene* case was returned to trial the incompatibility issue was in fact resolved by the court interpreting the provisions so as to require the prosecution to discharge the ultimate, legal, standard of proof: decision of the Crown Court, 14 February 2000.

[213] [2005] 1 AC 264.

[214] The implications of that case on the court's powers of interpretation under s.3 of the Human Rights Act 1998 are discussed in chapter 3, pages 140–1.

[215] [2007] 1 WLR 1500.

completely unbalanced if the Crown waited until a defendant had advanced his case before advancing a positive case in relation to the *mens rea* of the offences and that procedurally the trial was likely to proceed as if the burden of proof of *mens rea* lay at the outset upon the Crown. Accordingly, the 1989 Act could operate effectively without the imposition of the reverse burdens of proof. Thus, to give the sections their natural meaning would be disproportionate and unjustifiable, although those provisions could be read down so as to be compatible.

In *R v Lambert, Ali and Jordan*[216] the House of Lords considered whether s.28 of the Misuse of Drugs Act 1971 was compatible with Article 6(2) of the European Convention. The defendant appealed against his conviction for possession with intent to supply cocaine contrary to s.5 of the 1971 Act. He relied on s.28 of the Act and claimed that he did not know that the bag that he was in possession of contained cocaine, but the trial judge held that the Crown only had to prove that the defendant knew that he possessed the bag and that the defence required proof on the balance of probabilities. The House of Lords confirmed that all that had to be proved was that the defendant knew that he possessed a bag with something in it and that s.28 imposed on the defendant a legal rather than an evidential burden of proof. In that respect therefore, s.28 derogated from the presumption of innocence and was thus not justified under Article 6(2), although it was held that the Human Rights Act could not be applied retrospectively in this case.[217] Again, in *R v Benjafield and Others*,[218] the Court of Appeal held that although Article 6(2) did not apply to confiscation orders under the Drug Trafficking Act 1994, the defendant was still entitled to a fair trial under Article 6(1). In their Lordships' view the 1994 Act pursued a legitimate aim in the public interest and the procedure adopted by parliament was a fair and proportionate response to that aim. The judge had the power to avoid injustice and in a case where there was or might be a serious risk of injustice, a confiscation order should not be made.

The distinction between an evidential and legal burden is important in judging compatibility with Article 6(2) although it is not exclusive and there may be cases where it is lawful to impose a legal burden.[219] For example, in *Sheldrake v DPP*[220] the House of Lords held that s.5(2) of the Road Traffic Act 1988, which provides that it is a defence for a person charged with drink driving to prove that at the time he is alleged to have committed the offence there was no likelihood of his driving the vehicle, was not in violation of Article 6 despite imposing a legal burden of proof. In their Lordships' view, the provision pursued a legitimate aim (the prevention of death and other injury) and it was not in such circumstances objectionable to criminalise a defendant's conduct without requiring the prosecutor to prove criminal intent. The defendant would have full opportunity to show that there was no likelihood of his driving, and in the event a conviction would not rest on a presumption that the person was likely to drive, but rather that he was in charge of a car while unfit to drive. Again, in *Grayson and Barnhum v United Kingdom*,[221] the European Court held that there had been no violation of Article 6 when the burden of proof had been placed on the applicants in confiscation proceedings to

---

[216] [2001] 3 All ER 577.

[217] Contrast *L v DPP* [2002] 2 All ER 854, where it was held that it was not an infringement of Article 6 to require a person accused under s.139 of the Criminal Justice Act 1988 of possessing an offensive weapon to prove on the balance of probabilities that he had a good reason for having such an article in his possession.

[218] [2001] 1 WLR 75. The decision of the Court of Appeal that the Act's provisions could be applied retrospectively was overruled by the House of Lords in *R v Lambert, Ali and Jordan* [2001] 3 All ER 577.

[219] See Dennis, Reverse Onuses and the Presumptions of Innocence: In Search of Principle [2005] Crim LR 901.

[220] [2005] 1 AC 264; heard jointly with *Attorney-General's Reference (No 4)*, above.

[221] (2009) 48 EHRR 30.

show that they did not have any reliable assets equivalent to the calculated benefits from the offences. The Court held that it was not unreasonable to expect them to show to the prosecution what had happened to all the money which had been proved to be in their possession.[222]

Question

To what extent do the European Convention and the Human Rights Act 1998 guarantee the right to the presumption of innocence, including the right to silence and freedom from self-incrimination?

Article 6 and the individual's right of participation

An individual should be aware of the nature of the charge or other proceedings, and must be allowed to participate constructively in such proceedings.[223] Thus, in *V and T v United Kingdom*[224] Article 6 was violated when two 11-year-old boys charged with murder had been subjected to an adult-like trial under conditions that must have made it almost impossible for them to comprehend what was going on or to effectively consult with their lawyers. Subsequently, in *SC v United Kingdom*,[225] it was held that there had been a violation of Article 6(1) when a young person of 11 was tried in an adult court and sentenced to two-and-a-half year's detention for attempted robbery. The Court accepted evidence that given the boy's low intellect he was incapable of fully understanding the proceedings and their consequences; consequently the applicant was not capable of participating effectively in his trial to the extent required by Article 6. In the Court's view, where a decision was taken to deal with a young person by means of criminal trial, it was essential that he or she should be tried in a specialist tribunal which was able to give full consideration to and make proper allowance for his particular difficulties and to adapt its procedure accordingly.

In particular, the domestic judge and other authorities have an obligation, both under Article 6 and under the Human Rights Act 1998, to ensure that the proceedings are conducted in a manner that is consistent with the individual's right to a fair trial. This includes the duty to ensure that the parties have sufficient access to their lawyers and the details of the case.[226] Thus, in *Ocalan v Turkey*,[227] the Grand Chamber found a violation of Article 6 when the defendant had been denied access to the case file until a late stage in the proceedings. In contrast, in *CG v United Kingdom*,[228] although the European Court was satisfied that there was some substance to the applicant's complaint that the trial judge had frequently disrupted the giving of her evidence, it was satisfied that the interruptions did not prevent the applicant's counsel from continuing his line of defence. In any case, the disruptions were offset by the opportunity at the end of the trial for counsel to address the jury without interruption.

Specifically, Article 6(3)(a) provides that every person has the right to be informed promptly, in a language which he understands and in detail, of the nature and cause of the

---

[222] Neither did the confiscation order amount to a disproportionate interference with the right to enjoyment of possessions under Article 1 of the First Protocol.

[223] *Stanford v United Kingdom, The Times,* 8 March 1994.

[224] (1999) 30 EHRR 121.

[225] *The Times,* 29 June 2004.

[226] See *Hammerton v Hammerton, The Times,* 12 April 2007, discussed below under legal representation.

[227] (2005) 41 EHRR 45.

[228] (2002) 34 EHRR 31.

accusation made against him. In *Broziek* v *Italy*[229] the applicant, a German national, was sent information regarding his pending criminal charge that was written in Italian. The applicant explained that he needed to be informed in his mother tongue but this was ignored and he was convicted in his absence. It was held that the domestic court should have taken steps to ensure compliance with Article 6 and in the absence of such evidence found that Article 6 had been violated. In addition, Article 6(3)(b) provides the right to have adequate time and facilities for the preparation of one's defence, and the Court has held that what amounts to a reasonable time depends on the circumstances of the case, including in particular the complexity of the charge.[230] Finally, Article 6(3)(e) guarantees the right to have the free legal assistance of an interpreter if he cannot understand or speak the language used in court.[231] In *Cuscani* v *United Kingdom*[232] it was held that there had been a violation of this provision when a trial judge had allowed the proceedings to continue despite the defendant's clear lack of proficiency in English and his inability to understand the proceedings.

The right to defend oneself in person or through legal assistance and the right to free legal assistance

Article 6(3)(c) provides three separate due process rights to the individual when they are charged with a criminal offence: first, a general right to defend oneself against any criminal charge; secondly, the right to have legal representation of one's choosing if one does not wish to defend oneself;[233] and thirdly, to be given free legal assistance when one has not got sufficient means to pay for legal assistance, and the interests of justice require such provision. Thus, once Article 6 is engaged in the sense that the individual is facing a criminal charge, there is a technical breach of Article 6(3)(c) when the defendant is denied legal representation. This will inevitably render the trial unfair where the charge is serious and the defendant's liberty is at stake. Thus, in *Campbell and Fell* v *United Kingdom*,[234] it was held that there had been a violation of Article 6(3) when prisoners facing serious disciplinary charges and penalties involving the loss of liberty had not been allowed to be legally represented during the hearing.[235] Further, as we shall see, there is no automatic right to *free* legal assistance; whether the individual is entitled to such depends on their financial means and whether the interests of justice demand such assistance.

It should also be noted that this specific right exists alongside a general right to a fair trial and the right to present one's case, and thus the non-provision of legal assistance can result in a breach of Article 6(1) even where there is no criminal charge, for example in the context of civil proceedings.[236] Thus in *K* v *Authority Reporter*,[237] the Scottish Court of Session held that

---

[229] (1989) 12 EHRR 371.

[230] *Albert and le Compte* v *Belgium* (1983) 5 EHRR 533.

[231] *Luedicke, Belkacem and Koc* v *Germany* (1978) 2 EHRR 149.

[232] (2003) 36 EHRR 2.

[233] This includes a limited right to refuse a lawyer provided by the state: *Croissant* v *Germany* (1993) 16 EHRR 135.

[234] (1984) 7 EHRR 165.

[235] See also *Ezeh and Connors* v *United Kingdom* (2002) 35 EHRR 28.

[236] See *Steel and Morris* v *United Kingdom*, detailed in the case study above. However, such a finding is not automatic if the court is satisfied that the denial of representation has not resulted in injustice. See, for example, *Pine* v *Law Society* [2002] UKHRR 81 – disciplinary charges against a solicitor did not require legal assistance given the solicitor's expertise and the uncomplicated proceedings.

[237] [2009] SLT 1019.

the lack of state funded legal representation at a children's hearing available to relevant participants was incompatible with Article 6 (and 8 and 14) of the Convention, when without such representation they would be incapable of participating effectively in the proceedings.

Consequently, Article 6 guarantees the right to effective legal representation and a court might find a breach of both aspects of Article 6 where the defendant and the legal representative are not allowed to put forward their case effectively. For example, in *Ocalan v Turkey*,[238] the Grand Chamber held that there had been a violation of Article 6 when the defendant had not been assisted by his lawyers when being questioned in police custody and where the authorities had restricted the number of legal visits from his lawyers. Further, those meetings were not conducted with sufficient secrecy and the lawyers had been denied full access to the case file for an unreasonable length of time. Again, in *Hooper v United Kingdom*,[239] the European Court held that there had been a violation of Articles 6(1) and (3)(c) when the applicant and his legal representative had been denied the opportunity to address the magistrate before it had imposed a binding over order on him and the applicant had been committed to prison on the basis of that order.

Article 6(3)(c) also guarantees the right to have pre-trial legal assistance, for example during detention and interrogation, as in *Ocalan*, above. Thus, in *Brennan v United Kingdom*[240] Article 6(3) had been violated when a police officer had been present within hearing during the applicant's first consultation with his solicitor, having been arrested on suspicion of a terrorist murder. The presence of the officer infringed his right to an effective exercise of his defence rights. However, the Court also held that there had not been a violation of Article 6(3) when the applicant was denied access to his solicitor for 24 hours. The Court found that the solicitor's late arrival was not attributable to the authorities and was satisfied that the applicant had not made any incriminating admissions during this period.[241]

The right to free legal assistance

Article 6(3) specifically provides that if a person has not sufficient means to pay for legal assistance he should be given it free when the interests of justice so require.[242] In *Granger v United Kingdom*,[243] a man of limited intelligence had been charged with a particular offence and had been refused legal aid and the right to be provided with a counsel at appeal. He did have notes from his solicitor but he clearly did not understand them when he read them out in court. In particular, there was one complex ground of appeal that he could not deal with. It was held that having regard to his intelligence and the complexity of the case, he should have been given legal aid. Articles 6(1) and 6(3)(c) should be read together, and where, as in the present case, it was apparent that a fair hearing could not take place without legal advice, then both provisions would be violated. The European Court assesses the need for legal assistance on the particular facts of the case, taking into account such factors as the seriousness of the charge and the complexity of the case. In *Benham v United Kingdom*[244] Article 6 was

---

[238] (2005) 41 EHRR 45.

[239] (2005) 41 EHRR 1.

[240] (2002) 34 EHRR 18.

[241] Contrast *Magee v United Kingdom* (2001) 31 EHRR 35: a violation of Article 6 was found when the applicant had been deprived of legal assistance for over 48 hours and where the incriminating statements he made at the end of the first 24 hours became the basis for his conviction.

[242] See *Artico v Italy* (1980) 3 EHRR 1.

[243] (1990) 12 EHRR 469.

[244] (1996) 22 EHRR 293.

violated when the applicant had not been provided with legal representation when charged with culpable neglect in not paying his community charge. Given the nature of the proceedings, he was entitled to the protection of Article 6(3)(c); the law – culpable negligence to pay – was not straightforward, and the applicant's liberty was at stake.[245] So too, in *Hammerton* v *Hammerton*,[246] the Court of Appeal held that in the absence of unreasonable behaviour on the part of the litigant, a person who was liable to be sent to prison for contempt of court was entitled to legal representation under Article 6. Thus, the judge in the case had a duty to adjourn the proceedings until the issue of the individual's legal representation in a breach of court order case had been resolved.[247]

Witnesses and the right to a fair trial

Article 6(3)(d) confers on the individual the right to examine, or have examined, witnesses against him and to obtain the attendance and examination of witnesses on his behalf. This right, in combination with the general right to a fair trial under Article 6(1) provides the opportunity to confront witnesses.[248] Thus, in *Saidi* v *United Kingdom*[249] it was held that Article 6 had been violated when the applicant's conviction for drug offences was based solely on identification evidence, the applicant being given no opportunity to confront and question that evidence.[250] So too, in *R* v *Davis (Iain)*,[251] the House of Lords held that the defendant's conviction for murder had been in breach of Article 6 (and the principles of English common law) when the material witnesses remained anonymous and counsel was not allowed to ask questions which would identify them. The House of Lords held that given that he was convicted solely on their evidence and the defendant was effectively obstructed in his wish to discredit the witnesses there had been a breach of the right to cross examine witnesses and thus to a fair trial. The House of Lords referred the case back and at a subsequent hearing it was decided that the interests of justice demanded a retrial.[252] However, in response to the House of Lords' decision the Criminal Evidence (Witness Anonymity) Act 2008 was passed, which replaced the common law rules and overturned the decision in *Davis*.

Although the law can seek to protect vulnerable witnesses, it must strike an appropriate balance between the conflicting rights of the parties and such witnesses. Accordingly, a blanket or inflexible rule against the right to examine witnesses may be in breach of Article 6. For example, in *Re W (Children)*,[253] the Supreme Court held that there should be no presumption

---

[245] As there was no guarantee that the applicant would not have been sent to prison had he received legal representation, the Court would not grant compensation for a violation of Article 6. In *Edwards* v *United Kingdom* (Application No 38260/97) the Court effected a friendly settlement when the applicants had been denied legal representation in proceedings for non-payment of poll tax, which led to their detention. See also, *Townsend* v *United Kingdom, The Times,* 27 January 2005.

[246] *The Times,* 12 April 2008.

[247] Contrast *Blake* v *United Kingdom* (2007) 44 EHRR 29, where it was held that the lack of legal aid and representation was not in breach of Article 6 as the applicant had been represented in part and had divested himself of funds that could have been used for legal assistance.

[248] In appropriate cases the court should stop proceedings if it believes that adverse witnesses are unreliable: *R* v *C and Others* [2007] EWCA Crim 854.

[249] (1993) 17 EHRR 251.

[250] See also *Kostovski* v *Netherlands* (1989) 12 EHRR 434; *Doorson* v *Netherlands* (1996) 22 EHRR 330.

[251] [2008] 1 AC 1128.

[252] Subsequently the Court of Appeal ordered a retrial: *R* v *Davis (Iain)* [2008] EWCA Civ 1735.

[253] [2010] 1 WLR 701.

that a child would not be required to attend court to give evidence in family care proceedings. Such a presumption could not be reconciled with the need to strike a fair balance between the right to a fair trial and the right to private life under Article 8. A court should weigh the advantages of bringing the child to court against any damage it might do to the child's welfare.[254]

Article 6 does not guarantee to the accused an unlimited right to attendance of witnesses in court, and the necessity of witnesses, and the question of how many witnesses are allowed, is within the discretion of the domestic courts, provided the European Court is satisfied that the applicant has received a fair trial. Thus, in *Van Mechelen v Netherlands*,[255] the European Court held that there had been no violation of Article 6 when the applicants had been convicted of attempted manslaughter and robbery on the basis of anonymous witnesses provided by the prosecution. There had been ample opportunity to challenge those witnesses and the convictions did not rest solely upon the statements made by such witnesses.

The use of hearsay evidence and the case of *Al-Khawaja* v *United Kingdom*

This area often involves a conflict between the rights of the defendants and those of witnesses and the administration of justice, and the question is whether the domestic law has achieved the right balance within the area of discretion allowed by the Convention and the European Court. In the case below both the European and domestic courts have had to consider the use of hearsay evidence at criminal trials and there is clearly a difference of opinion as to how Article 6 and the general right to a fair trial impacts on the use of such evidence.

In *Al-Khawaja and Tahery* v *United Kingdom*,[256] the European Court held that there had been a violation of Article 6(1) and 6(3)(d) when witness statements from absent witnesses were read out at the applicants' trial. In one case the applicant had been charged with assault and convicted on one count when the complainant's statement, made before her death, was read out in court. In the other case the applicant was convicted on the basis of evidence provided by a sole witness who did not appear in court because of fear to his safety. In both cases the European Court held that the unfairness to the defendants in not being able to question those witnesses and their statement could not be offset by any direction of caution made to the jury by the judge.

Meanwhile, the domestic courts have maintained that provided hearsay evidence was reliable and tested and assessed as such there is no violation of Article 6(3)(d), even where a defendant is convicted solely or decisively on such evidence. Thus, in *R v Horncastle*,[257] the Supreme Court agreed that the admissibility of evidence was for the national courts and that the decision in *Al-Khaawja* did not justify the domestic courts from departing from its previous decisions in this area. The Supreme Court held that the statutory regime on the admissibility of evidence was not incompatible with Article 6 or the case law of the European Court of Human Rights. In concluding that the judgment in *Al-Khawaja* was not determinative of the success of the appeals, it held that the European Court's decision (applying the sole or decisive factor test) was based on the previous case law of the European Court, which had not considered the impact of that rule on common law systems. Thus the judgment did not

---

[254] The Supreme Court remitted the case back to the judge to decide whether the child should be so called after making allegations of abuse against the stepfather.

[255] (1997) 25 EHRR 647.

[256] (2009) 49 EHRR 1.

[257] [2010] 2 WLR 47.

preclude exceptions to that rule or states from adopting their own provisions. This impasse is likely to be resolved shortly, as the case has been referred to the Grand Chamber of the European Court, whose decision will be available in 2011.

Article 7 – Prohibition of retrospective criminal law

Article 7 of the European Convention provides that no one shall be held guilty of any criminal offence on account of any act or omission which did not constitute a criminal offence under national or international law at the time when it was committed. Further, it provides that a heavier penalty may not be imposed than the one that was applicable at the time that a criminal offence was committed. Article 7 thus upholds the basic principle of the rule of law that laws should be prospective rather than retrospective, although the article itself only applies to criminal offences or penalties. The meaning of 'criminal offence' is the same as that of a 'criminal charge', employed in Article 6(1) of the Convention, and other penalties will not be caught by Article 7. Thus, in *R v B (RG)*[258] it was held that an order in 2003 extending a licence period to a sentence of imprisonment for an offence committed before 1 October 1991 did not amount to imposing a heavier penalty than was available at the time the offence was committed. This was because the licence was a preventive measure and not a punitive one.[259] Article 7 thus complements the right to a fair criminal trial under Article 6, above, in addition to insisting on the rules of legality and fairness inherent in other articles of the Convention which insist that procedures and penalties must be 'prescribed by law'.

Under this principle, the law should allow an individual to foresee the consequences of his actions and not impose liability on him or her after the event. This principle is particularly important where the law seeks to criminalise the behaviour of citizens and imposes criminal sanctions on such behaviour.[260] Therefore, Article 7 lays down two basic principles: that no one shall be guilty of an offence for an act which at the time of its commission was not an offence in domestic or international law; and that no one should be subjected to a heavier penalty than the one which existed at the time of the offence.

A clear breach of Article 7 was seen in the case of *Welch v United Kingdom*.[261] The applicant was convicted on five counts relating to drug offences and sentenced to 22 years' imprisonment. The trial judge imposed a confiscation order under the Drug Trafficking Act 1986, which came into force after the applicant's arrest but before his conviction. The Court held that the confiscation proceedings were clearly retrospective as they were made in respect of offences committed before the provision came into force. The Court also held that the proceedings clearly constituted a 'penalty' for the purpose of Article 7. In determining such the Court held that the following factors must be taken into account: whether the measure was imposed following conviction for a criminal offence; the nature and purpose of the measure; its characterisation under domestic law; the procedures involved in making and

---

[258] [2010] 1 Cr. App R 19.

[259] See also *AT and JK v Secretary of State for the Home Department* [2010] EWCA Civ 567, where it was held that an automatic deportation order under s.32 of the UK Borders Act 2007 was intended to apply retrospectively but not in breach of Article 7 as it was not taken in pursuance of the criminal law but was a preventive measure in the context of the law of aliens.

[260] See Beddard, The Rights of the Criminal under Article 7 ECHR (1996) ELRev 3.

[261] (1995) 20 EHRR 247.

implementing the provision; and its severity. Applying those criteria to the facts, the Court held that there was a strong indication of a regime of punishment and that taking into account a combination of punitive elements involved in the measure, it was a penalty within Article 7.[262]

However, the principles applied in that decision have been restricted by subsequent decisions. In *Taylor v United Kingdom*,[263] the European Commission held that the imposition of a confiscation order for offences committed before *as well as* those committed after the legislation came into force was not in violation of Article 7. The Commission held that the order was not a penalty for the offences committed before the Act's implementation, but rather one for the later offences. When committing those offences, the applicant was aware that he was liable to an order concerning the earlier proceedings because the Act was already in force. Further, in *R (Uttley) v Secretary of State for the Home Department*,[264] the House of Lords held that the 'maximum penalty' within Article 7 referred to the one that *could* have been imposed by the domestic court at the time of conviction, and not the one that would *probably* have been imposed. In this case the defendant had been sentenced to 12 year's imprisonment in 1995 for offences committed in 1983. He claimed that had he been sentenced to 12 year's imprisonment in 1983 he would have been eligible for release on expiry of two-thirds of his term, but that due to changes introduced by the Criminal Justice Act 1991 he was now subject to a licence. Their Lordships held that there had been no breach of Article 7 because in the present case, the maximum sentence that could have been lawfully imposed for rape was life imprisonment both before and after 1991. Similarly, in *R v Bowker*,[265] the Court of Appeal held that there is no violation of Article 7 where a defendant is subjected to a different penal policy than the one which applied at the time of the offence, provided the law under which he was sentenced was that which existed at the time of the offences. However, the European Court has insisted that the difference between the scope of the offence and its discretionary application must be clearly evident at the time of sentence. In *Kafkaris v Cyprus*[266] a prisoner had been given a life sentence for murder, which in practice invariably involved a 20-year fixed-term sentence. Later the law was changed and the sentence replaced by an indeterminate sentence and he was refused discretionary release. It was held that the imposition of an indeterminate life sentence constituted a breach of Article 7 as the scope and level of execution of the life sentence was not formulated with sufficient precision at the time of his sentence.[267]

Article 7 does not merely prohibit overt and deliberate attempts to impose criminal liability after the event. It also prevents a situation where the law's interpretation and application is changed or developed in a manner that offends against the principle of retrospectivity. In such a case the European Court will have to decide whether there has been a violation of Article 7, or whether the change was the result of the natural and foreseeable development of a particular legal rule. In *SW and CR v United Kingdom*,[268] the European Court held that there had been no violation of the applicants' rights under Article 7 when the applicants were

---

[262] Further, in *Tougher v Revenue and Customs Prosecution Officer*, decision of the Court of Appeal, 5 July 2007, it was held that confiscation orders which were in breach of Article 7 could, nevertheless, be enforced in the court's discretion so as to give effect to clear primary legislation.

[263] (1998) EHRLR 90.

[264] [2004] 1 WLR 2278.

[265] [2007] EWCA Crim 1608.

[266] (2009) 49 EHRR 35.

[267] However, as on the facts the prisoner had not received an increased sentence there had been no heavier penalty within Article 7.

[268] (1995) 21 EHRR 404.

found guilty of rape as a result of a decision of the domestic courts that a husband could no longer rely on the defence of 'marital rape'.[269] The Court held that provided the constituent elements of an offence were not essentially changed to the detriment of the accused, and that any progressive development is reasonably foreseeable, there will be no violation of Article 7. In this case, owing to the well-documented developments in case law, it was inconceivable that either applicant believed that the course of action he embarked upon was lawful. Again, in *Gay News* v *United Kingdom*,[270] the European Commission of Human Rights held that there was no violation of Article 7 when the applicants had been found guilty of blasphemy. The Commission held that the definition of blasphemy was sufficiently clear and that the House of Lords' decision on the question of intent merely clarified the common law position.

Further, Article 7 does not prohibit the prosecution of a conduct which is illegal within the established principles of international law. This would cover such things as war crimes and thus legalise the controversial War Crimes Act 1991. This matter was dealt with by the Grand Chamber of the European Court recently in the case of *Kononov* v *Latvia*.[271] In 2004 the applicant had been convicted of war crimes under the Latvian Criminal Code in respect of the killing of a number of suspected civilian collaborators in 1944 under his authority. Overturning the decision of the European Court,[272] which had decided that the applicant could not have foreseen that his conduct amounted to a breach of international law, the Grand Chamber held that there was a sufficiently clear basis in international law for his conviction. At 1944 international law was sufficiently clear that the summary killing of civilians, even if they were collaborators, was contrary to the principles of protecting the civil population and avoiding unnecessary suffering to combatants. However, it must be shown that the requisite components of the offence are satisfied. Thus, in *Korbelly* v *Hungary*,[273] the applicant's conviction for crimes against humanity (for murder) was found to be in breach of Article 7 as the domestic court had not satisfied itself that all the components of the offence had been satisfied in his case.

Further, in *SW*, above, the European Court held that the abandonment of the unacceptable idea of a husband being immune against prosecution for rape of his wife could not be said to be at variance with Article 7; on the contrary, it was in conformity with the fundamental objectives of the Convention, the very essence of which is respect for human dignity and human freedom.

Questions

What values does Article 7 of the Convention uphold?

Do you agree that the way in which the European and domestic courts have interpreted and applied that article have undermined those values?

Other Convention protocols

Protocol 7 of the convention also contains a number of additional guarantees with respect to due process. This includes the right of an alien lawfully resident in the territory of a state not

---

[269] *R* v *R* [1991] 4 All ER 481.
[270] (1982) 5 EHRR 123.
[271] (2010) 29 BHRC 137.
[272] (2008) 25 BHRC 317.
[273] (2010) 50 EHRR 48.

to be expelled except in pursuance of a decision reached in accordance with law (Article) 1. That article also provides the right of such a person to submit reasons against his expulsion, to have his case reviewed and to be represented for these purposes, although such rights may be lost when such expulsion is in the interests of public order or is grounded on reasons of national security. Article 2 provides for the right of those convicted of a criminal offence to have his conviction reviewed by a higher tribunal, the exercise of such right being governed by law. Article 3 provides for the right to compensation for those who have been wrongfully convicted, or pardoned on the ground that there had been a miscarriage of justice, and who have suffered punishment as a result of such conviction. Article 4 states that no one shall be liable to be tried or punished again in criminal proceedings for an offence for which he has already been acquitted or convicted in accordance with the law of the state.

Further reading

A number of texts on the European Convention contain excellent chapters on Article 6 of the Convention and its relevant case law. See, in particular, Harris, Warbrick, Bates and O'Boyle, *Law of the European Convention on Human Rights* (OUP 2009, 2nd edn), chapter 6; Ovey and White, *Jacobs and White: The European Convention on Human Rights* (OUP 2010, 4th edn), chapters 8 and 9; Janis, Kay and Bradley, *European Human Rights Law* (OUP 2007, 3rd edn), chapter 8; van Dijk and van Hoof, *Theory and Practice of the European Convention on Human Rights* (Intersentia 2006), chapters 10 and 11.

See also Mowbray, *Cases and Materials on the European Convention* (OUP 2007, 2nd edn), chapters 8 and 9, which details the essential case law of the European Court in this area.

Clayton and Tomlinson, *The Law of Human Rights* (OUP 2009, 2nd edn), chapter 11, provides comprehensive coverage of both European and domestic law in this area. See also Ashworth and Emmerson, *Human Rights and Criminal Justice* (Sweet & Maxwell 2007, 2nd edn) for an examination of various aspects of human rights and the trial process. Amos, *Human Rights Law* (Hart 2006), chapter 10, provides a useful account of domestic cases on Article 6 in the post-Human Rights Act era.

For discussion of the right to a fair trial and closed evidence, see Chamberlain, Special Advocates and Procedural Fairness in Closed Proceedings [2009] CJQ 314 (and update: [2009] CJQ 448); Craig, Perspectives on Process: Common Law, Statutory and Political [2010] PL 257; Hudson, Justice in Time of Terror [2009] Brit J Criminol 702.

Visit **www.mylawchamber.co.uk/fosterhumanrights** to access regular updates to major changes in the law, further case studies, weblinks, and suggested answers/approaches to questions in the book.

8

Freedom of expression: nature, purpose and restrictions

Introduction

In 2009 legislation was introduced to make it possible for a court to make an exploitation order with respect to convicted persons who have published their memoirs and derived a benefit from such publication.

In 2008 a new offence of being in possession of extreme pornographic images was introduced via s.63 of the Criminal Justice and Immigration Act 2008.

In 2008 the domestic law of blasphemy was abolished by s.79 of the Criminal Justice and Immigration Act 2008.

All these provisions, and many others, impact on the enjoyment of freedom of expression and other interests such as the prevention of crime, the protection of public morals and the enjoyment of religion. But how can we ensure that these provisions are necessary, proportionate and in conformity with human rights law?

This chapter introduces the reader to the basic arguments in favour of freedom of expression and the principles governing its restriction. The chapter begins by exploring the theories of free speech protection and its protection under Article 10 of the European Convention. It will then examine the protection of free speech in domestic law, in both the pre- and post-Human Rights Act eras. Finally, a number of domestic legal provisions affecting free speech are examined to judge their compatibility with free speech norms and the provisions and case law of the European Convention on Human Rights; including obscenity and indecency, official secrets and the control of prisoners' free speech. Chapter 9 will then explore the concept of press freedom and will provide a detailed study of the laws of defamation and confidentiality and of contempt of court.

Thus, this chapter will cover:

- An examination of the importance and nature of the right of freedom of expression.
- An examination and analysis of the scope of that right, including legitimate reasons for its restriction.
- An examination of the protection of freedom of expression under Article 10 of the European Convention on Human Rights.

- An examination and analysis of the protection of freedom of expression under domestic law, particularly in the post-Human Rights Act era.

- An examination of domestic law restrictions on freedom of expression with respect to obscenity and indecency, official secrets and prisoners' free speech and an analysis of their compatibility with human rights norms.

Nature and purpose of free speech

Freedom of expression has been described by the European Court of Human Rights as one of the essential foundations of a democratic society.[1] This reflects the fact that the promotion of freedom of expression is not only justified on grounds of individual liberty, but is also capable of achieving public benefits. Thus, Article 10 of the Convention is seen not only as essential to the person exercising that right, but also as supporting the democratic process through the promotion of a free press and the public's right to know, and the encouragement of open and responsible government.[2]

What is expression and speech?

Before examining the theories in favour of free speech, it is worth noting that freedom of expression, or freedom of speech, contains a number of characteristics which identify its constitutional status and values.[3] As we shall see, not all forms of expression engage this constitutional right and those actions will not therefore be worthy of the enhanced protection normally given to such rights.

The basic idea behind freedom of expression is that it involves the imparting and receiving of information and ideas. Freedom of expression thus consists of the manifestation, via communication, of that information and does not, therefore, cover every autonomous action of the individual. Consequently, many social activities and pursuits will not count as freedom of expression, even though they represent the individual's or group's decisions or choices. For example, taking part in a sport, or a pursuit such as fox-hunting, would not engage that person's Convention rights, including freedom of expression.[4] However, distributing leaflets or taking part in a protest either for or against such an activity would, as the purpose of that activity would be to communicate ideas to others.[5]

Although freedom of expression and freedom of speech are often used interchangeably, freedom of speech is merely one form of expression and (Article 10 of the European Convention) may be engaged by actions other than the spoken or written word.[6] Thus taking part in a protest will engage Article 10, as well as Article 11 (guaranteeing freedom of

---

[1] *Handyside* v *United Kingdom* (1976) 1 EHRR 737.

[2] See Part One of Beatson and Cripps (eds) *Freedom of Expression and Freedom of Information: Essays in Honour of Sir David Williams* (OUP 2002); Barendt, *Freedom of Speech* (OUP 2005, 2nd edn), chapter 1 – Why Protect Free Speech?

[3] See Barendt, *Freedom of Speech* (OUP 2005, 2nd edn), chapter 3 – The Scope of Freedom of Speech.

[4] *R (Countryside Alliance)* v *Attorney-General* [2007] 3 WLR 922 – fox-hunting did not engage the right to private life or freedom of assembly.

[5] See the cases on freedom of assembly, dealt with in chapter 10.

[6] See Barendt, n 3 above, pages 78–98.

peaceful assembly) and often a court will examine such cases solely under freedom of expression provisions.

Once it is satisfied that freedom of expression is engaged then the domestic and European courts have established that generally it covers every view, however objectionable or offensive.[7] For example, in *Livingstone v Adjudication Panel for England*[8] it was accepted that when Ken Livingstone (the then London Mayor) had been charged with bringing his office into disrepute by accusing a Jewish reporter of being a concentration camp guard, there had been an interference with his free speech which could not be justified unless he had acted unlawfully or there were otherwise satisfactory reasons to sanction him. In this case the comment had been made by Livingstone as an individual rather than as a public officer and it was unlikely that the public would think less of him because of that comment. This case can be contrasted with the more recent decision in *Gaunt v OFCOM*,[9] where the High Court was required to review a decision of the broadcasting authority that a radio presenter had broken its code when he had referred to a guest as a 'Nazi' and an 'ignorant pig'. The comments had been made during the course of a debate with a local councillor on whether people who smoked should be banned from becoming foster parents and the claimant argued that he was exercising his right of political expression. Rejecting that argument and upholding OFCOM's decision, the court accepted that the councillor was expected to receive a rough ride during the debate. That meant that the presenter would be protected when he used offensive expression, but such protection did not apply to gratuitous offensive insult or abuse or to repeated abusive shouting that served to express no real content. To call someone a 'Nazi' was capable of being highly insulting, and although the first use of the word, and its qualification as a 'health Nazi' was made in context and thus justified, subsequently the tone of the interview degenerated and amounted to no more than abusive shouting that served to convey to listeners no real content at all. The decision in *Gaunt* stresses that it is not the words themselves which lost protection, but the lack of context in which they were used. In other words, speech should make some contribution to a debate or idea, as opposed to mindless and unfocused words.[10]

Notwithstanding the engagement of Article 10, free speech cannot be enjoyed absolutely, for as we know it is a conditional right and subject to qualifications. However, it does mean that once Article 10 of the European Convention is engaged, then there must be legal and pressing reasons put forward to justify any interference. Thus, although obscene or indecent speech may be harmful, and ultimately restricted, it is generally recognised as speech and any interference must be justified under the terms of Article 10(2). This general principle must, however, be qualified in at least two respects. First, certain forms of hate (including racist) speech might fall foul of Article 17 of the European Convention (or a similar rule in domestic constitutional law), which prohibits activities which are intended to destroy the rights of others.[11] Secondly,

---

[7] *Handyside v United Kingdom* (1976) 1 EHRR 737.

[8] *The Times*, 9 November 2006; on the facts, it was held that the legislation, s.52 of the Local Government Act 2000, did not apply to conduct by public figures in their private lives.

[9] [2010] EWHC 1756 (Admin).

[10] Although it could be argued that Livingstone's remark made no contribution to any debate, it should be stressed that the question in that case was whether he had brought the office into disrepute when making that statement in his private capacity.

[11] See chapter 2 of this text, pages 77–8. Such expression needs to be extreme before it comes under Article 17. In *Gunduz v Turkey* (2005) 41 EHRR 5, it was held that there had been a violation of Article 10 when the applicant had been fined for stating that children born to couples who underwent a civil marriage were illegitimate. The views were part of a balanced public debate on television and were not excluded by Article 17.

although obscene or indecent speech counts as speech, it is clear that the domestic and European courts have given a wide margin of appreciation to member states in regulating and censoring such speech.[12] Similarly, the courts may attach *greater* weight to certain forms of freedom of expression, such as political speech,[13] and speech which seeks access to justice.[14] Thus, in *Sanders* v *Kingston*[15] it was held that a local councillor who made uninformed comments about deaths in Northern Ireland, calling on the people of Northern Ireland to apologise for killing soldiers and to hang their heads in shame for involving the English in their own quarrel, did not attract the special protection afforded to political speech because it was not an expression of his political opinion but merely his personal opinion.[16]

Theories of free speech

Freedom of expression is justified on four main bases.[17] With regard to individual liberty, free speech is said to promote both *moral autonomy* and *self-fulfilment*. However, freedom of speech can also promote public benefits in that it achieves the *discovery of the truth* as well as advancing *democracy*. These theories will be discussed below, but in general both the domestic courts and the European Court of Human Rights have given greater weight to speech that can be seen as promoting a public benefit over and above the enjoyment of individual liberty.[18] Thus, particularly in states which pride themselves on democratic principles, the law will tend to enhance the claims of public interest speech, giving precedence to speech which promotes freedom of the press and the public's right to be informed.

Moral autonomy and self-fulfilment

In chapter 1 of this text we explored the idea that individual liberty, and the enjoyment of specific human rights, were a good in itself, and that censorship and restriction on individual liberty were *prima facie* wrong. Accordingly, any interference with freedom of expression is seen as an attack on individual liberty and, in particular, on the right of moral autonomy – the right of the individual to make certain choices and to manifest those views by imparting them to others. The advantage of this argument is that speech is a good in itself and does not have to be justified on the basis that the information is in the public interest, or that its content is weak and unworthy of constitutional protection.[19] This argument is therefore particularly strong in defending speech from attack on the basis that it conflicts with public morality or the views and sensibilities of others. Domestic and international judges will, therefore, defend speech which shocks and offends and which attracts vehement disagreement and disapproval.[20]

Related to the argument on moral autonomy is the idea that freedom of speech promotes human self-fulfilment. Expression thus allows the individual to grow intellectually, morally

---

[12] See chapter 2 of this text, pages 67–9.
[13] *Lingens* v *Austria* (1986) 8 EHRR 407.
[14] *R* v *Secretary of State for the Home Department, ex parte O'Brien and Simms* [2000] 2 AC 115.
[15] *The Times*, 16 June 2005.
[16] He was, however, entitled to some protection under Article 10 and it was held that the fine imposed on him for bringing his office into disrepute was disproportionate.
[17] See in particular Barendt, *Freedom of Speech* (Clarendon 2005, 2nd edn), pages 6–23.
[18] See, in particular, *Sunday Times* v *United Kingdom* (1979) 2 EHRR 245; *Lingens* v *Austria* (1986) 8 EHRR 407.
[19] See LORD WOOLF MR in *A* v *B plc* [2002] 3 WLR 542.
[20] See *Handyside* v *United Kingdom* (1976) 1 EHRR 737.

and spiritually, and unless he or she is allowed to express their views and beliefs freely this growth will be thwarted. Again, this argument is based on individual freedom rather than any perceived public interest, and is grounded in the respect of the individual's human dignity and worth. However, as with the argument on moral autonomy, this argument is vulnerable to challenge where such speech is perceived to be causing a social or individual harm, and where the speech needs to be balanced against those competing claims. Thus, although the argument can defend speech from the laws such as obscenity, indecency, racial hatred or blasphemy, *in practice* such claims are more likely to trump freedom of expression, unless supported on other, utilitarian, grounds. For example, as we shall see, the European Court has given much greater protection to political speech, which could be said to promote democracy and open government, than pure artistic or commercial speech, which principally promotes ideas of individual autonomy and development.

Promotion of democracy and the discovery of the truth

Although individual liberty and the dangers of censorship are strong arguments for protecting freedom of expression, speech is likely to receive greater protection from the lawmakers and the judges if a public benefit is evident from the dissemination of that information. Most bills of rights and international treaties are founded on the rule of law and the promotion of democratic and open government, and if the enjoyment of individual rights can promote those principles, those rights will be protected to a greater extent. Thus, while insult and misinformation is unlikely to receive much protection when pitted against the privacy or reputation interest of another, speech that attempts to challenge or criticise government or public officials is more likely to trump such interests where it is seen as an attempt to offer opposition to public figures, and to provide the public with such views.[21] Consequently, the laws of defamation and confidentiality should be applied more liberally with regard to such views, and the law and judges should be tolerant of speech and other actions used in political or other protests.[22]

In particular, freedom of expression is seen as producing a public good because it may lead to the discovery of the truth.[23] The public, therefore, have a right to discover the truth and should not be restricted to receiving information which either the general majority or the government perceive as acceptable. The public must receive this information to make informed choices, and legal restriction, particularly in the form of prior restraint, is regarded as undesirable.[24] This recognises the importance of speech in advancing public awareness and knowledge in matters such as science and technology, but applies equally to opinions on political and moral matters. In combination with the presumption against censorship, this idea can be used to allow an individual, and in particular the press, to disseminate views about morality and politics. In turn it requires the law and the judiciary to safeguard such speech from unjustifiable interference, giving it an enhanced status over and above speech that merely promotes individual views and morality. Consequently, most states have developed principles of freedom of the

---

[21] See, in particular, Beatson and Cripps (eds), *Freedom of Expression and Freedom of Information: Essays in Honour of Sir David Williams* (OUP 2000), chapters 1, 2, 4, 5, 6 and 8.

[22] Contrast *Lingens v Austria*, n 18 above, with *Von Hannover v Germany* (2006) 43 EHRR 7. Both cases are dealt with in detail in the next chapter on press freedom.

[23] Mill, On Liberty, in Cowling (ed.), *Selected Writings of John Stuart Mill* (Cambridge University Press 1968).

[24] *Observer and Guardian v United Kingdom* (1991) 14 EHRRR 153.

press and the public right to know, and these principles are reflected in international treaties such as the European Convention and its case law. This advantage of free speech will, consequently, be very much in evidence when examining areas such as obscenity, indecency and blasphemy, where there is a danger of restricting the free flow of new or alternative ideas on sexual and religious matters purely on the grounds that such views disrupt the status quo. In addition, it can be used in combination with arguments on the promotion of democracy to assess the legality and necessity of defamation and confidentiality laws.

Restricting free speech

Freedom of speech and expression is a conditional right under the European Convention. Member states are allowed to interfere with the right provided the restriction is 'prescribed by law' and 'necessary in a democratic society' for the protection of one or more of a number of legitimate aims which are listed in Article 10(2) of the Convention.[25] By looking at paragraph 2, one can see that freedom of expression is capable of conflicting with a variety of rights and interests, some of which are rights protected under the Convention. In addition, a number of public interests, such as public morality, the due administration of justice and national security, are recognised as legitimate reasons for interfering with this basic right. Some of these reasons will be regarded as more legitimate than others, both by human rights theorists and the European Court itself, but it is clear that freedom of expression will be in constant competition with other interests.

For example, paragraph 2 provides that restrictions can be imposed for the 'protection of the rights of others'. This may be referring to the normal (non-fundamental) legal rights of other people, such as their rights under contract or their use of others' property. Although in such situations, freedom of expression may be regarded as a 'trump' right in relation to the competing claim, it may be necessary in some circumstances to interfere with freedom of expression in order to respect that claim.[26] In other cases freedom of expression will conflict with other Convention rights. For example, the 'rights of others' may be referring to the right to a fair trial, thus necessitating restrictions on free speech via the laws of contempt. The reference to the 'protection of reputation' in paragraph 2 obviously refers to the law of defamation, a legal right as discussed above, but as reputation is essential to one's privacy, that law also protects the fundamental right to private life contained in Article 8 of the Convention. There are numerous other examples (blasphemy, data protection, election restrictions), and in such cases the European Court will need to evaluate the importance of the competing fundamental rights and apply the doctrines of necessity and proportionality very carefully.

There will be a variety of legal provisions in domestic law, both statutory and under the common law, which seek to protect people, or the public at large, from the dangers of free speech, and which, therefore, interfere with the citizen's 'residual' right. Under a system which (still) retains parliamentary sovereignty, and which thus, in theory at least, allows *any* legal restriction on free speech, the courts, and indeed parliament, have to be careful to ensure that these legal provisions are imposed for legitimate reasons and that they possess the qualities

---

[25] See Jaconelli, Defences to Speech Crimes [2007] EHRLR 27; Turenne, The Compatibility of Criminal Liability with Freedom of Expression [2007] Crim L R 866.

[26] See, in particular, the restrictions on freedom of peaceful assembly, considered in chapter 10.

that will be recognised as lawful by bodies such as the European Court of Human Rights.[27] This will ensure that freedom of expression is not restricted simply because it comes into conflict with these individual or state interests. Such restrictions will need to be legitimate, applied for pressing reasons and be proportionate, and in considering such the legal system should recognise the fundamental nature of free speech and the dangers of its restriction. This may involve giving that right a 'trump' status, at least recognising such freedom of expression is the norm and that restrictions can only be justified in exceptional cases.[28]

Finally, it should be stressed that interferences with freedom of expression can take the form not only of prior restraint (or censorship) but also of penalties imposed after the speaker has been allowed to exercise their right. Thus, the domestic and European courts regard prior restraint as the most dangerous form of interference because it deprives that expression of its intended audience and the public are thus denied the opportunity to receive that information or idea.[29] However, it is clear that any sanction such as a fine, imprisonment or damages imposed on the speaker will constitute interference, and this will be the case even if the penalty was not actually imposed on the speaker.[30] This is because the imposition of that penalty, or its potential imposition, can have a 'chilling effect' on the speaker's decision to impart the information.[31]

Freedom of expression and the European Convention on Human Rights

Article 10 of the European Convention has been given effect to via the Human Rights Act 1998. Although it is not the sole provision on free speech, domestic law is now clearly informed by that article and the relevant case law of the European Court of Human Rights. Article 10 provides as follows:

> Everyone has the right to freedom of expression. This right shall include freedom to hold opinions and to receive and impart information and ideas without interference by public authority and regardless of frontiers.

The scope of Article 10

In *Handyside* v *United Kingdom*,[32] the European Court stated that freedom of expression constitutes one of the essential foundations of a democratic society, forming one of the basic conditions for its progress and for the development of every man. Further, the Court stressed that the protection afforded by Article 10 is applicable not only to information or ideas that are favourably received or regarded as inoffensive or as a matter of indifference, but also to those that offend, shock or disturb the state or any sector of the population. Such, in the

---

[27] Thus, these restrictions should be prescribed by law and necessary in a democratic society, as examined in chapters 2 and 3 of this text.

[28] See s.12 of the Human Rights Act 1998, considered below.

[29] See *Observer and Guardian* v *United Kingdom*, n 24, above. See also s.12(3) of the Human Rights Act 1998, below.

[30] See *Steel and Morris* v *United Kingdom* (2005) 41 EHRR 22, discussed in the next chapter.

[31] *Tolstoy* v *United Kingdom* (1995) 20 EHRR 442.

[32] (1976) 1 EHRR 737.

Court's view, are the demands of pluralism, tolerance and broadmindedness without which there is no democratic society.

Article 10 is concerned primarily with the right of the individual to be free from restrictions on their freedom of expression and does not provide the general right of freedom of information. Thus, in *Leander* v *Sweden*[33] it was held that the freedom to receive and impart information and ideas under Article 10 does not impose an obligation on the state to collect and disseminate information of its own motion.[34] For example, the Court has decided that a state did not have a positive duty to ensure public awareness in matters of public interest, such as environmental issues.[35] However, the state not only owes a negative duty not to interfere with freedom of expression, but must also take positive measures to protect a person's freedom of expression, including against threats from private persons.[36]

Freedom of expression, the public interest and press freedom

The European Court has placed special significance on the ability of free speech to impart information and ideas to the public and which is in the public interest. Thus, in *Sunday Times* v *United Kingdom*[37] the European Court stressed that the principles outlined in *Handyside* are of particular importance as far as the press is concerned, and that in assessing whether any interference was based on sufficient reason, account must be taken of any public interest aspect of the case. Accordingly, the Court is particularly vigilant in controlling any form of prior restraint. Thus, in *Observer and Guardian* v *United Kingdom*[38] the Court stated that although Article 10 did not prohibit prior restraints, the dangers inherent in such are that they call for the most careful scrutiny on the part of the Court, especially as far as the press is concerned. The fact that the information is in the public interest will, therefore, make it more difficult for the respondent state to justify any interference within Article 10(2). This has involved the Court in deciding what information is indeed in the public interest, and in this respect it has held that the dissemination of information relating to the private lives of celebrities does not serve a valid public interest so as to justify an interference with that person's private and family life.[39]

Correspondingly, the European Court has given special protection to freedom of speech in the context of press freedom. This might involve extending Article 10 to the media in circumstances where an individual would not be able to claim its protection. For example, in *Jersild* v *Denmark*[40] the conviction and fining of an employee of the Danish Broadcasting Company for aiding and abetting the expression of unlawful racist speech was found to be in violation of Article 10. Although the views of the group were not protected by Article 10, the punishment of a journalist for assisting in the dissemination of statements made by another

---

[33] (1987) 9 EHRR 433.

[34] There is, however, a right under the Convention (Article 8) to gain access to private information relating to one's private life: *Gaskin* v *United Kingdom* (1990) 12 EHRR 36.

[35] *Guerra* v *Italy* (1998) 26 EHRR 357.

[36] *X and Y* v *Netherlands* (1985) 8 EHRR 235. The principle in *X* was applied in *Gundem* v *Turkey* (2001) 31 EHRR 49, where it was found that the government had failed to take adequate steps to safeguard the applicant's newspaper against acts of intimidation and violence by both state authorities and others.

[37] (1979) 2 EHRR 245.

[38] (1991) 14 EHRR 153.

[39] *Von Hannover* v *United Kingdom*, n 22 above.

[40] (1994) 19 EHRR 1.

in an interview would seriously hamper the contribution of the press to discussion of matters of public interest. Similarly, the European Court has also given added protection to those who attempt to question and criticise government and public officials, insisting that those holding public office must be more tolerant of such criticism than a private individual.[41]

Article 10 and artistic and commercial speech

The European Court has given less protection to artistic and commercial speech, providing the respondent state with a wide margin of appreciation. For example, in *Müller v Switzerland*,[42] the European Court held that although Article 10 clearly included freedom of artistic expression, affording the right to take part in the public exchange of cultural and social information and ideas of all kinds, it stressed that those who promote their work are not immune from the possibility of limitations. In contrast, however, the Court has shown a good deal of tolerance to offensive artistic speech when such expression is used for satirical or political purposes.[43]

Similarly, with respect to commercial speech, the European Court has accepted that information of a commercial nature is not excluded from the scope of Article 10.[44] Thus, in *Autronic AG v Switzerland*[45] the European Court held that Article 10 applied to everyone, whether natural or legal persons, and that the article is applicable to profit-making bodies. The commercial applicant's claim will be stronger, of course, where such information serves a more public interest, such as the dissemination of commercial matters to the public. In *Markt Intern Verlag GmbH and Klaus Beermann v Germany*[46] it was noted that in a market economy an undertaking which seeks to set up a business inevitably exposes itself to close scrutiny and criticism of its practices by its competitors and that the specialised press should be able to disclose facts which would be of interest to readers and thereby contribute to the openness of business activities.[47] Nevertheless, the Court would be expected to give a reasonably wide margin of appreciation when the essential characteristic of the expression is a commercial one.[48] Thus, in *Hachette Filipacchi Presse Automobile v France*,[49] there had been no violation of Article 10 when the applicant companies had been prosecuted for advertising cigarettes contrary to French law. The Court noted that there was now a common consensus about the need to regulate such advertising and the incitement to smoke. Further, the prosecutions and fines (€10,000) were not disproportionate.

In addition, Article 10(2) provides that states shall not be prevented from requiring the licensing of broadcasting, television or cinema enterprises, although any restrictions must comply with the principles of freedom of expression. For example, in *Groppera Radio AG v*

---

[41] See *Lingens v Austria* (1986) 8 EHRR 407; *Barfod v Denmark* (1989) 13 EHRR 493; *Castells v Spain* (1992) 14 EHRR 445. These cases are dealt with in detail in the next chapter on press freedom.

[42] (1988) 13 EHRR 212. See also *Otto-Preminger Institute v Austria* (1994) 19 EHRR 34.

[43] See *Kunstler v Austria* (2008) 47 EHRR 5.

[44] Munro, The Value of Commercial Speech [2003] CLJ 134 485.

[45] (1990) 12 EHRR 485.

[46] (1989) 12 EHRR 161.

[47] See also *Barthold v Germany* (1985) 7 EHRR 383, where the European Court held that an injunction preventing a vet from distributing a statement to the general press criticising his fellow vets was contrary to Article 10.

[48] Thus, in *Jacobowski v Germany* (1994) 19 EHRR 64, the European Court held that there was no violation of Article 10 when a dismissed employee had been prohibited from distributing a newsletter that advertised his new business and which disseminated negative information about his former employers.

[49] (2009) 49 EHRR 23.

Switzerland[50] the Court stressed that any regulation must not be excessive and must be weighed against the interests of the applicants and others in the transmission of programmes.[51]

Questions

What constitutes speech and expression and why do you think it is given so much weight in both domestic and international law?

Why is freedom of speech a conditional right and for what reasons is it curtailed?

The protection of freedom of expression under the common law

Even before the Human Rights Act 1998, there was evidence that freedom of expression was regarded as a fundamental right. Although this is only rarely reflected in statutory form,[52] the courts had established freedom of expression as a constitutional right, protecting it from arbitrary and unnecessary interference.[53] Thus, the courts had long been prepared to interpret legislation and develop common law principles to provide the maximum possible enjoyment of free speech and could strike down administrative actions that interfered unnecessarily with freedom of expression. This presumption in favour of free speech could thus be used to challenge public actions, and the courts would attempt to safeguard such rights by insisting on substantial justification for any interference. In *R v Secretary of State for the Home Department, ex parte Brind*,[54] the House of Lords were adamant that any interference with freedom of speech had to be justified on very strong grounds, the courts starting with the presumption that any interference with freedom of expression was unlawful. Similarly in *R v Secretary of State for the Home Department, ex parte O'Brien and Simms*,[55] in declaring invalid a policy which restricted journalists visiting prisoners and using the content of such interviews for the purposes of publication, Lord Steyn stated that the starting point of the claim in this case was the right of freedom of expression, which in a democracy is a primary right and without which an effective rule of law is not possible.

This approach was also evident in the development of the common law, with the courts using freedom of speech and press freedom to interpret and develop the common law of defamation, confidentiality and contempt of court. For example, the law of defamation has been interpreted to prohibit democratically elected bodies from suing in defamation,[56] and the defence of qualified privilege has been developed so as to accommodate the right of the press to report on matters of public interest.[57] So too the law of confidentiality has been developed by the courts to allow a variety of public interest defences, thereby ensuring that the action impinges on freedom of expression only where such interferences are based on

---

[50] (1990) 12 EHRR 321.

[51] The compatibility of broadcasting censorship is considered below, pages 390–1.

[52] See, for example, s.43 of the Education (No 2) Act 1986 and the Public Interest Disclosure Act 1998.

[53] See Allan, Constitutional Rights and Common Law (1991) 11 OJLS 453.

[54] [1991] 1 AC 696.

[55] [2000] 2 AC 115.

[56] *Derbyshire County Council v Times Newspapers* [1993] 1 All ER 1011, discussed in chapter 9.

[57] *Reynolds v Times Newspapers* [1999] 4 All ER 609 and *Jameel v Wall Street Journal Europe* [2006] 3 WLR 642, also discussed in chapter 9.

pressing and necessary reasons. The House of Lords made a strong declaration of this constitutional right in the 'Spycatcher' litigation.[58] In that case it was stated that public authorities could not use the law of confidentiality to protect confidential information unless there was evidence of an overriding public interest outweighing the public interest in the free dissemination of information.[59] Further, in *Turkington v Times Newspapers*[60] the House of Lords accepted that the press often act as the agents of the public for the purpose of facilitating discussion on matters of public concern. However, the position of freedom of expression before the Human Rights Act was regarded as unsatisfactory for a number of reasons. First, the absence of a right to rely directly on Article 10 of the European Convention on Human Rights meant that restrictions on free speech were not subjected to the tests of necessity and proportionality so stringently applied by the European Court of Human Rights.[61] Secondly, the courts did not recognise the so-called constitutional right of free speech in a consistent manner. Thus, in *Harman v Home Office*,[62] a case where a reporter had been charged with contempt of court for disobeying a court order not to disclose details of litigation, Lords Scarman and Diplock disagreed with regard to the nature of the case. In Lord Scarman's opinion the case was concerned with the balance between freedom of expression and the impartiality and independence of the judiciary, whereas Lord Diplock was adamant that the case was not about these matters, but solely about the law of contempt of court.

Freedom of expression and the Human Rights Act 1998

The Human Rights Act should enhance the protection of free speech in a number of respects.[63] First, as with all other Convention rights, individuals will be able to rely directly on Article 10 of the Convention when bringing a claim under the Act alleging that a public authority has violated that right. This action may be brought directly under s.7 of the Act, or the individual may use Article 10 in other proceedings, such as judicial review, or in criminal or other proceedings brought by a public authority. Because of the Act's horizontal effect, a claimant may also raise Article 10 in private law proceedings, such as confidentiality and defamation. Secondly, the courts will be allowed to refer to the Convention case law and, in particular, the doctrine of proportionality, in deciding whether any interference with the right is legitimate and necessary.

More specifically, s.12 of the Human Rights Act requires the courts to have particular regard to freedom of expression in cases where freedom of expression is threatened in legal proceedings. Section 12 applies where a court is considering whether to grant relief which, if granted might affect the exercise of the Convention right to freedom of expression. In such a

[58] *Attorney-General v Guardian Newspapers* [1988] 3 All ER 852.

[59] Note, however, the judgment of Lord Keith, who concluded that he was discharging the injunctions not on the basis of press freedom or the public's right to know, but because the alleged confidential information had entered the public domain.

[60] [2001] 2 AC 277.

[61] *R v Secretary of State for the Home Department, ex parte Brind* [1991] 1 AC 696. This approach has led to a number of defeats for the government before the European Court of Human Rights. See, for example, *Sunday Times v United Kingdom* (1979) 2 EHRR 245 and *Goodwin v United Kingdom* (1996) 22 EHRR 123.

[62] [1983] 1 AC 280.

[63] See Fenwick and Phillipson, *Media Freedom under the Human Rights Act* (OUP 2006), chapter 3; Amos, Can We Speak Freely Now? [2002] EHRLR 750.

case, the Act first provides that if the respondent is neither present nor represented, then no relief should be granted by the court unless it is satisfied that the applicant has taken all practicable steps to notify the respondent, or that there are compelling reasons why the respondent should not be notified.[64] The purpose of this provision is to ensure as far as possible that free speech is not restricted without the respondent having the opportunity to argue that the restriction should not be allowed. It thus allows the court to be aware of all the relevant evidence before it takes the step of imposing a restriction on the fundamental right of free speech.[65]

In particular, s.12(3) deals with the scenario where a claimant seeks a temporary order to restrain publication pending a full trial, and states that no such order shall be made unless the court is satisfied that the applicant is likely to establish that publication should not be allowed. This provision deals with the problem of prior restraint, where an order is sought restraining publication before the material is published. Because this will preclude the dissemination of the information before the reader has the opportunity to receive and digest it, it is therefore seen as the most dangerous form of restriction.[66] The law on this matter was formerly regulated by the rules in *American Cyanamid v Ethicon Ltd*,[67] which requires the court to consider the strength of both parties' arguments, whether the claimant had a real prospect of success at full trial, and to decide where the balance of convenience lies before granting the order. The new provision appears to require the courts to give greater emphasis to freedom of speech in making such orders, although some of the case law under this provision suggests that the courts are unconvinced that s.12 will have a major impact on the application of the principles laid down in *American Cyanamid*.[68]

Thirdly, the Act states that a court, in considering the granting of relief which might affect freedom of expression, must have particular regard to the importance of the Convention right under Article 10.[69] This would appear to require the court to give freedom of expression an enhanced status in proceedings that involve a conflict between that right and other rights or interests. In addition, where the proceedings relate to material which the respondent claims, or which appears to the court, to be journalistic, literary or artistic material, the court must have particular regard to the extent to which the material has, or is about to, become available to the public; the extent to which it is, or would be, in the public interest for the material to be published; and any relevant privacy code. The requirement to consider whether the material has, or is about to, become available to the public would certainly cover the situation where the information has already reached the public domain. This was the real basis for the discontinuance of the injunctions in the 'Spycatcher' dispute,[70] and s.12(4) presumably strengthens this principle when the material in question is of a journalistic, literary or artistic nature.

---

[64] Section 12(2) Human Rights Act 1998.

[65] In *Re X (a Child)* [2009] EMLR 26, it was held that a judge should have considered s.12(2) of the Human Rights Act and informed the media of an impending injunction before an order was made excluding it from attending residence and contact proceedings concerning the child of well-known public figures.

[66] For an account of the law of prior restraint and its compatibility with the European Convention and the Human Rights Act 1998, see Munro, Prior Restraint of the Media and Human Rights Law (2002) Juridical Review 1. See also Robertson and Nicol, *Media Law* (Sweet & Maxwell 2002, 4th edn), pages 19–27.

[67] [1975] AC 396.

[68] See the cases of *Imutran v Uncaged Campaigns* [2001] 2 All ER 385; *Douglas v Hello! Magazine* [2001] QB 967; *Venables and Thompson v MGN* [2001] 2 WLR 1038, discussed below and in chapter 9.

[69] Section 12(4) Human Rights Act 1998.

[70] *Attorney-General v Guardian Newspapers* [1988] 3 All ER 852.

However, that rule is not absolute, and a court might still grant the order if they believe that further publication would cause greater harm to the claimant's interests. Thus, in *Barclays Bank PLC* v *Guardian News and Media Ltd*,[71] the court continued an injunction preventing the further dissemination of the claimant's financial documents pending full trial despite the fact that some of the information had already entered the public domain. The High Court held that although general availability of material on the internet would mean that such information would lose its confidential character, limited and partial dissemination, perhaps in some remote and specialist site that was not generally available to the public without a great deal of effort, would not result in a loss of confidentiality. The court stressed that s.12(4) and public domain was not a complete defence to the press and that the court had to apply proportionality in determining whether, in all the circumstances, the bank would probably have demonstrated at full trial that publication was disproportionate to their rights.

The provision also requires the court to consider whether the publication of the material is or would be in the public interest.[72] In such cases the courts must have particular regard to the advantages of upholding freedom of the press and the public's right to know, and they will inevitably have recourse to the case law of the Convention in giving those rights the necessary weight.

The case law under s.12 of the Human Rights Act

Since the coming into operation of the 1998 Act the courts have considered a number of cases that have required the balancing of freedom of speech with other human rights and other interests.[73] In these cases the courts had to consider whether the Act, particularly s.12, imposed on them a duty to give an enhanced status to freedom of expression, thus placing it above other claims. Early decisions displayed a good deal of caution, and in *Imutran* v *Uncaged Campaigns*[74] the court doubted whether s.12(3) was intended to have any additional impact on the question of whether the court should grant relief pending full trial. According to the court, although theoretically the test of likelihood used in s.12(3) was slightly higher in the scale of probability than the test of real prospect of success, the difference between the two was so small that the new test could be applied without any further consideration of how much more probable the claimant's success at trial would be. Also, in the court's view s.12(4) was not intended to direct the court to place even greater weight on the importance of free speech than it already did; the requirement to pay 'particular regard' merely contemplated specific and separate consideration being given to the factor.[75]

In other cases, however, the courts took a more robust attitude towards free speech and quite clearly placed great emphasis on it. For example, in *Attorney-General* v *Punch and Another*,[76] the Court of Appeal held that a newspaper would not be in contempt of court

---

[71] [2009] EWHC 591 (QB).

[72] In *A* v *B plc and Another* [2002] 3 WLR 542, the Court of Appeal stressed that any interference with freedom of expression must be justified irrespective of whether the public interest is served by the publication.

[73] See Amos, Are We Free to Speak Now? [2002] EHRLR 750; Fenwick and Phillipson, *Media Freedom and the Human Rights Act* (OUP 2006), chapter 3.

[74] [2001] 2 All ER 385.

[75] This latter point must now be read in the light of the Court of Appeal's decision in *A* v *B plc and Another* [2002] 3 WLR 542, although in that case Lord Woolf approved of the judgment in *Imutran* with regard to s.12(3) of the Act.

[76] [2001] 1 QB 1028.

simply because it published information in breach of a court order, unless that publication destroyed the essential purpose of the order.[77] Similarly, in *Attorney-General v Times Newspapers*[78] the Court of Appeal refused to require a newspaper to get clearance from the claimant and the court before publishing information which the newspaper thought to be already in the public domain. Again, in *R v Secretary of State for Health, ex parte Wagstaffe*,[79] it was held that the Secretary of State had acted unreasonably in deciding that an inquiry into the activities of Harold Shipman, a doctor who had been found guilty of murdering 15 of his patients, should be held in private. In the Divisional Court's view, because the inquiry related to a matter of great public interest, it would only be appropriate not to conduct that inquiry in public if there was a pressing social need to hold it in private.[80]

More recent case law has attempted to provide certainty in this area, but it is evident that there is a good deal of flexibility on what status is to be given to freedom of expression when it conflicts with other rights. With respect to the granting of interim injunctions, the House of Lords appears to have overruled the ambivalent approach adopted in *Imutran* (above), but nevertheless refused to lay down any hard and fast rules about the pre-dominance of free speech. In *Cream Holdings v Banjaree and Another*[81] the House of Lords confirmed that s.12 did not require the courts to give freedom of expression a higher order than other convention rights and that the test under s.12(3) on applications for interim injunctions was whether the applicant's prospects of success at trial were sufficiently favourable to justify the making of such an order in the particular circumstances of the case. Their Lordships stressed that the purpose of s.12(3) was to emphasise the importance of freedom of expression at the interim stage and that it set a higher threshold for granting interim orders against the press than the *American Cynamid* criteria (real prospect of success). However, their Lordships also held that the word 'likely' in the section does not mean 'more likely than not' and that there was no single inflexible test. As a general approach the courts should be very slow to make such orders where the applicant had not demonstrated that he would probably succeed at trial, although in some cases a lesser degree of likelihood would suffice.[82]

However, the ruling in *Cream Holdings* does not disturb the practice in defamation cases, which provides that interim injunctions should not be granted where the defendant intends to use the defence of justification and fair comment at the main trial, unless the defence is in the court's view *bound to fail*. Thus, in *Green v Associated Newspapers*[83] it was held that s.12(3) of the Human Rights Act 1998 was displaced by the rule in *Bonnard v Perryman*,[84] which was there to protect free speech from prior restraint and thus was not contrary to Article 8 of the

---

[77] This decision was, however, overruled on appeal: [2003] 1 AC 1046. The case is considered in chapter 9, under Contempt of Court, pages 491–3.

[78] [2001] 1 WLR 885.

[79] [2001] 1 WLR 292.

[80] However, in *Persey and Others v Secretary of State for the Environment, Food and Rural Affairs* [2002] 3 WLR 704, it was held that Article 10 of the Convention was not engaged in a case where a decision is made to hold an inquiry in private because Article 10 did not provide a right of access to information. In this case the Court of Appeal restricted *Wagstaffe* to its facts, stating that it had been decided on traditional grounds of judicial review. See also *Howard and Another v Secretary of State for Health* [2002] 3 WLR 738.

[81] [2005] 1 AC 253.

[82] On the facts, the House of Lords held that as the allegations of the claimant's corrupt business practices constituted information of strong public interest, the claimant was likely to fail at full trial. The case will be considered in more detail in the next chapter.

[83] [2005] QB 972.

[84] [1891] 2 Ch 269.

Convention.[85] Accordingly, in *LNS* v *Persons Unknown* (the John Terry case),[86] as the essential aim of the injunction was the protection of the claimant's personal and commercial reputation rather than his private and family life, the High Court refused to continue a super injunction which would have prohibited the disclosure by anyone of the fact that such an injunction was sought.

There has also been a good deal of confusion with respect to the status of freedom of expression under s.12 of the Human Rights Act 1998: some judges insisting that the section does not require an elevated status for Article 10, and others insisting that s.12 does require the court to give greater weight to free speech. All appear to be agreed that the starting point is always that any restriction on free speech is unlawful and needs to be justified on very strong grounds. With respect to the balancing of freedom of expression and the right to private life, the Court of Appeal in *Douglas* v *Hello! Magazine*[87] stated that s.12(4) requires the court to consider Article 10 of the Convention in its entirety, including the exceptions permitted within Article 10(2). Thus, it was not appropriate for the court to give freedom of speech additional weight over and above any competing right, such as the right to private life. Equally, under s.12(3), in deciding whether to give relief before trial, the court's task was to apply its mind to how one right was to be balanced on the merits against another right without building in additional weight on the one side, but articulating those rights by the principles of legality and proportionality and satisfying itself that at trial the balance was likely to be struck in favour of restraint of publication. However, in *Venables and Thompson* v *MGN*[88] the court held that because s.12 of the Act requires the court to pay special regard to freedom of speech it was no longer appropriate to conduct a pure balancing exercise, as may have been the case before the Act came into force. In the court's opinion s.12 required the court to give an enhanced status to freedom of speech and the right of the press to publish information. Accordingly, it was not appropriate to conduct a balancing exercise, but instead to apply the principle that any interference with the right in Article 10(1) had to be shown to fall within the exceptions permitted in Article 10(2), those restrictions being narrowly interpreted.[89] The Court of Appeal sounded a strong call for the protection of freedom of expression in *A* v *B plc and Another*,[90] where LORD WOOLF CJ held the effect of s.12 of the Human Rights Act was that courts would not be justified in interfering with freedom of expression simply because there was no identifiable public interest in particular material being published. In his Lordship's opinion, regardless of the quality of the material, *prima facie* the court should not interfere with its publication. Thus, any interference had to be justified. The effect of this judgment is that although there will be many cases where the court will need to balance freedom of expression with other interests, freedom of expression is a good in itself and must be preserved irrespective of its perceived quality. This aspect of the judgment seems to be called into doubt by subsequent cases where free speech has conflicted with privacy

---

[85] See also *Coys Ltd* v *Autocheris Ltd and Others* [2004] EMLR 25. In *Ingelheim Ltd* v *Vetplus, The Times,* 27 June 2007, the Court of Appeal held that the *Bonnard* test did not apply to trademark cases and that the *Cream Holdings* test would normally be applied.

[86] [2010] EMLR 16. The case will be examined in detail in chapter 9 of the text.

[87] [2001] 2 WLR 992.

[88] [2001] 2 WLR 1038.

[89] In this sense the court was following the approach adopted by the European Court of Human Rights in *Sunday Times* v *United Kingdom* (1979) 2 EHRR 245.

[90] [2002] 3 WLR 542.

interests, and it is now clear that the quality of the expression is relevant in determining the proportionality of any interference with free speech.[91]

In *Re S (Publicity)*[92] the House of Lords confirmed that freedom of expression under Article 10 does not have an automatic 'trump' status under the Act. In this case an order had been sought restraining the identification of a murderer (who was the child's mother) and her victim (the child's brother) in order to protect the welfare of a child who was in care. It was held that the court should conduct a balancing exercise between the child's right to private life and the right of freedom of expression. Their Lordships stressed that s.12(4) did not require the court to give pre-eminence to either article and the judge had to consider the magnitude of the interference proposed and then what steps were necessary to prevent or minimise that interference. Applying those principles to the present case, it was held that the murder incident was already in the public domain and anonymity would only have a mitigating effect. On the other hand, there was a clear and proper interest in knowing the name of the defendant in the murder trial.[93]

Despite the ruling in *Re S* it is proper for the courts to have *particular regard* to freedom of expression, and to require strong justification for its interference, even though they should not be led to give that right automatic pre-eminence. Thus, in *A Local Authority v A Health Authority and Another*[94] it was held that a local authority should be allowed to publish a report of an investigation into the management of a home for foster children and vulnerable adults unless a strong case could be made out against such publication. DAME BUTLER-SLOSS P held that in deciding whether to grant an injunction prohibiting the report's publication, the court by virtue of s.12(4) of the Human Rights Act had to have particular regard to the importance of freedom of expression. The correct approach was to publish unless that publication would be so disadvantageous to the children and others that the court was driven to restrain publication in whole or in part. In the present case the balance came down in favour of the children and those adults with a disability. However, in this case the owner of the home had failed to make out such a case and the court did not have jurisdiction to protect the interests of the NHS.

Questions

To what extent was freedom of expression accepted as a constitutional right before the Human Rights Act 1998?

How, if at all, has the Human Rights Act enhanced freedom of expression?

Freedom of information[95]

Although freedom of expression promotes the free flow of information and ideas, and access to such information is critical to that aim, the European Court of Human Rights has decided

---

[91] *McKennit v Ash* [2007] 3 WLR 194. This, and other cases are detailed in the next chapter and in chapter 10.

[92] [2005] 1 AC 593.

[93] See also *A Local Authority v PD and GD* [2005] EMLR 35, where it was held that an injunction prohibiting the naming of a child's father, who had killed his mother, was not, in the absence of exceptional circumstances, necessary to protect the privacy and best interests of the child.

[94] [2004] 2 WLR 926.

[95] For a comprehensive account of this area, see Carey, *Freedom of Information Handbook* (Law Society 2008, 2nd edn); Macdonald and Jones, *The Law of Freedom of Information* (OUP 2009, 2nd edn); and Wadham Blackstone's Guide to the Freedom of Information Act 2000 (OUP 2007, 3rd edn). See also Part Two of Beaston and Cripps (eds), *Freedom of Expression and Freedom of Information: Essays in Honour of Sir David Williams* (OUP 2000).

that Article 10 of the European Convention does not confer a right on individuals to receive information that others were not willing to impart.[96] Thus, although Article 10 prohibits interference with freedom of expression, it does not require its facilitation and does not impose an obligation on government to provide, in addition to existing means of communication, an open forum to achieve the yet wider dissemination of views. This distinction was accepted by the Court of Appeal in *Persey and Others v Secretary of State for Environment, Food and Rural Affairs*,[97] where it was held that the decision to hold an inquiry into the outbreak of foot-and-mouth disease in private was not in violation of Article 10. In that case the Secretary of State had set up three separate inquiries with the evidence, in particular the findings of the Lessons Learned Inquiry, for the most part to be received in private. The Court of Appeal held that Article 10 was not engaged by a government decision to hold a closed public inquiry, and upheld the distinction between freedom of expression and access to information.[98]

The Freedom of Information Act 2000

Liability for the disclosure of information relating to government is discussed below, but until recently there was little legislation on the government's duty to provide the citizen with information relating to its activities. A government White Paper on open government was published in 1993,[99] and a code of practice based on it committed the government to publishing 'facts and analysis of facts which the government considered relevant and important in framing major policy proposals and decisions'.[100] Under the code there was an obligation to provide certain information (rather than specific documents) concerning the running and funding of public services and an obligation to respond to requests for information relating to the policies, actions and decisions of departments and public authorities that came within the Code. The Code contained exemptions for certain areas, such as defence and law enforcement agencies, and information whose disclosure would harm the frankness and candour of internal discussion, which would cover cabinet and other governmental department discussions and advice. The Code was not legally enforceable, although such concerns could be investigated by the Ombudsman.

The Freedom of Information Act 2000 was part of the Labour government's constitutional reform package, and represented its commitment to open government and individual freedom. The Act was passed to make provision for the disclosure of information held by public authorities or by persons providing services for them and to amend the Data Protection Act 1998 and the Public Records Act 1958.[101] Section 1 of the Act provides a general right of access to information held by public authorities and entitles any person making a request

---

[96] *Leander* v *Sweden* (1987) 9 EHRR 433.

[97] [2002] 3 WLR 704.

[98] See also *Howard and Another* v *Secretary of State for Health* [2002] 3 WLR 738, where it was held that the Secretary of State was entitled to refuse public access to two inquiries that he had instigated into serious malpractice and criminal conduct by doctors. However, a decision to refuse a public inquiry may still be challenged on traditional judicial review grounds: see *R* v *Secretary of State for Health, ex parte Wagstaffe* [2001] 1 WLR 292.

[99] *Open Government* (Cm 2290).

[100] *Code of Practice on Access to Government Information*, para 3.

[101] Its central provisions came into force in 2005.

to a public authority for such information to be informed in writing whether it holds the information specified in the request and, if so, to have it communicated to him.[102] The public authority must comply with this request within 20 days,[103] and is entitled, under s.1(3), to request further information before complying with the request. If the authority refuses the request because the information in question is exempted under the Act, then it must, under s.17 of the Act, state that fact and specify the exemption in question, stating that the public interest in maintaining the exclusion outweighs the public interest in either disclosing whether the authority holds that information, or in disclosing that information.

Exemptions under the Act

The Act exempts the authority from the general duty under s.1, where the information in question is either reasonably accessible by other means,[104] or where the authority intends to publish such information at some future date.[105] In addition, there are a number of exemptions based on the information's subject matter. These include where the information is supplied by, or relates to, bodies dealing with security matters of specified bodies;[106] information not falling within s.23 but which is required for the purpose of safeguarding national security;[107] information where disclosure would, or would be likely to, prejudice the defence of the British Islands or any colony, or the capability, effectiveness or security of any relevant forces;[108] information which if disclosed would, or would be likely to, prejudice international relations,[109] relations between any administration in the United Kingdom and any other administration[110] or the economy.[111] The Act exempts information held for the purposes of criminal investigations and proceedings into crime, and information relating to law enforcement where that disclosure would, or would be likely to, prejudice, *inter alia*, the prevention or detection of crime or the apprehension or prosecution of offenders.[112] The exemptions relating to matters such as security intelligence, parliamentary privilege and court records are absolute,[113] but in

---

[102] The public authorities covered by this section are listed in Schedule 1 of the Act, and include central and local government, the police, the National Health Service, schools, universities and further education colleges and a variety of non-governmental organisations which carry out public functions, such as the Broadcasting Standards Commission. The Freedom of Information (Amendment) Bill 2006 proposed to exclude the House of Commons and the House of Lords (see below). See also *BBC v Sugar and the Information Commissioner* [2009] 1 WLR 430, dealt with below.

[103] Section 10 of the Freedom of Information Act 2000.

[104] Section 21.

[105] Section 22.

[106] Section 23. These bodies include, *inter alia*, the Security Service, the Secret Intelligence Service, GCHQ and the special forces.

[107] Section 24.

[108] Section 26.

[109] Section 27. Under s.27(2) information is also exempt if it is confidential information obtained from a state other than the United Kingdom or from an international organisation or international court.

[110] Section 28.

[111] Section 29.

[112] Sections 30 and 31. There are also exemptions in relation to the audit functions of public authorities (s.33), parliamentary privilege (s.34), the formulation of government policy (s.35), information whose disclosure would prejudice the effective conduct of public affairs (s.36), communications with Her Majesty or matters relating to conferring honours (s.37), and information in respect of legal professional privilege (s.42).

[113] In *Office of Government Commerce v Information Commissioner* [2009] 3 WLR 627, it was held that the law of parliamentary privilege deemed that parliamentary questions should not be answered by a ministerial statement as to the application of the Freedom of Information Act 2000 to a particular case.

other cases information can still be published if the authority in question considers that the public interest in disclosure outweighs the public interest in maintaining the exemption.[114]

Section 40 of the Act exempts information if it constitutes personal data information which is covered by s.1 of the Data Protection Act 1998. In *Common Services Agency* v *Scottish Information Commissioner*[115] the House of Lords held that the Scottish Commissioner had erred in not considering whether information relating to incidents of leukaemia in a particular area was personal data within the Act and whether its disclosure would breach the data protection principles. Further, in *Secretary of State for the Home Department* v *Information Commissioner*[116] it was held that the Information Tribunal was wrong to consider that information was only given in confidence where it would amount to a breach of confidence under the traditional law of confidentiality. That finding did not take into account the notion of the expectation of privacy as developed by the European Court and the domestic courts.[117]

In addition, under schedule 1, part IV of the Act a body will not be required to disclose information held by it for the purposes of journalism, art or literature. In *Sugar* v *BBC and the Information Commissioner*[118] the Court of Appeal gave guidance in this area. It was held that once information was held for a genuine journalistic purpose, it was exempt from the provisions of the Act even if it was also held for other purposes. A 'dominant purpose' test had not been included in the Act and such a test would lead to subjectivity and uncertainty. The court identified the three elements of functional journalism to include the process of collecting, writing and verification of material; the editing and presentation of material for publication; and the upholding of journalistic standards by supervision, training and review of journalists and their work. Whilst information being held for advertising revenue or property ownership would not be held for the purposes of journalism, in the present case a document which contained a review of past broadcasts was capable of coming within the exemption, even though that information had been elevated to a more strategic and managerial level.

On 6 October 2006 David Maclean MP introduced the Freedom of Information Bill before parliament. Clause 1 of the bill amended s.37 of the 2000 Act so as to exempt from that Act the House of Lords and the House of Commons and any information where it consists of correspondence between a member of parliament and any public authority. The aim of the bill was to promote the effective business of parliament and to secure the confidentiality of constituents whose information is passed from members of parliament to a variety of public authorities. In May 2007 the bill passed through the Commons and received its first reading in the House of Lords, but was subsequently lost. Subsequently, in *Corporate Officer of the House of Commons* v *Information Commissioner*,[119] it was held that the Information Commissioner and the Information Tribunal were entitled to disclose further details of the information provided by the House of Commons with respect to overnight accommodation and related allowances claimed by members of parliament. There was a legitimate public interest in the issues, particularly as it was conceded

---

[114] Section 2 of the Act. Refusals to disclose are subject to an appeal to the Information Commissioner under s.50 of the Act. In *Scottish Ministers* v *Scottish Information Commissioner, The Times*, 29 January 2007, it was held that the Commissioner had a duty to consider each document individually on its merits and not as a class of documents.

[115] [2008] 1 WLR 1550

[116] [2008] EWHC 892

[117] See also *British Union for the Abolition of Vivisection* v *Home Office and Information Commissioner* [2008] EWCA Civ 870.

[118] [2010] 1 WLR 2278.

[119] *The Times*, 22 May 2008.

that the scheme publicising such allowances was flawed. The privacy of the members of parliament had not been ignored and the tribunal's findings were based on any error. Members of parliament could not conduct their affairs on the basis that the legislation did not apply to them or that the Commons was entitled to dispense or suspend such legislation until it was amended or repealed. Given the flaws in the publication scheme, the provision of further information was inevitable.

Enforcement of the Act

The Act is enforced by an Information Commissioner, established under s.18 of the Act and who has, under s.47, a general duty to promote the following of good practice by public authorities and, in particular, to promote the observance by public authorities of the requirements under the Act and of any code of practice issued under s.45 and s.46 of the Act. The Commissioner has the power, under s.50, to receive complaints from persons who are not satisfied with the way in which their requests have been dealt with by public authorities, and to make a decision which he must then serve on the individual and the public authority in question. Under s.57 an appeal lies to the Information Tribunal, established under s.18 of the Act, and then, under s.59, to the High Court on a point of law.

The appeal procedure in the Act is intended to be exclusive, and in *Carruthers* v *South Norfolk District Council*[120] it was confirmed that an aggrieved individual could not bring judicial review proceedings with respect to a local authority's decision to refuse to disclose documents, and that the remedy lay exclusively with the right of appeal to the Commissioner. The Act then provides an appeal against 'decision notices' made by the Commissioner. In *BBC* v *Sugar and the Information Commissioner*[121] it was held that, although a decision of the Commissioner could only be the subject of an appeal where he had made a decision as to whether the provisions of the Act applied to a body and served notice of that decision, a decision that the Act did not apply – because an exemption applied – was still a decision which the Tribunal had power to reverse. In *Sugar*, the question was whether the applicant had made a *request to a public authority* for disclosure under s.1. The authority, the BBC, had commissioned a report as part of its coverage of the Middle East and S had requested to see it claiming that the BBC was a public authority and held the information for purposes other than journalism, art or literature. The Commissioner decided that the BBC was not a public authority and agreed with the BBC that the information was held for those purposes. The House of Lords held that it had been wrong to decide that the BBC, as a hybrid public authority, was not a public authority simply because of the nature of the information that was being requested.[122]

The Commissioner has the power, under s.50(4) of the Act, to issue enforcement notices on a public authority, notifying it of its breach of the Act and specifying any action that needs to be taken to comply. Any decision notice made by the Commissioner must be complied with unless an accountable person from the public authority certifies that it has not failed in its obligation;[123] otherwise, any failure to comply will amount to a contempt of court.[124] In addition, the authority may appeal against any decision made by the Commissioner to the Information Tribunal and from that body to the High Court.

---

[120] [2007] EWHC 478 (Admin).
[121] [2009] 1 WLR 430.
[122] Subsequently, in *BBC* v *Sugar and Information Commissioner*, n 118 above, it was held that the BBC had no obligation under the 2000 Act to disclose the information. See page 370 above.
[123] Section 51.
[124] Section 54.

Questions

What is the importance of freedom of information with respect to the enjoyment of free speech?

To what extent does the Freedom of Information Act 2000 facilitate freedom of information?

Domestic law restrictions on freedom of expression: defending the public interest

This chapter will now examine two areas where freedom of speech is compromised by the object of protecting the public interest: public morality (including laws on obscenity, indecency and blasphemy), and national security (including official secrets legislation and the law of confidentiality). The chapter will not provide an exhaustive account of these areas, but rather will examine the rationale behind these laws and whether they comply with the principles of freedom of expression, individual liberty and the public's right to know. In particular, the laws will be studied to see whether they comply with the principles and case law of the European Convention, and whether they have withstood any challenge in the post-Human Rights Act era.

Freedom of speech and protection of morals

Unlike other laws that reflect public or private morality, such as murder, theft or criminal damage, these laws are committed solely by a breach of such morals. In other words, the law will impose restrictions on speech or actions if they either threaten public morality, or cause offence either to the public at large or to particular individuals, without the necessity of proving the commission of a specific substantive offence. All legal systems will have *some* legal provisions controlling indecent, obscene or blasphemous speech, regulating expression which conflicts with the public's, or an individual's, sexual, religious or other morals. As such laws affect the exercise of freedom of speech and, to a limited extent, the right to private life, they need to be justified in accordance with principles of individual freedom studied throughout this text and, in particular, with the requirements of the European Convention and the Human Rights Act 1998. In addition, because of the vague and questionable nature of their aim – the protection of morality or the sensibilities of others – civil libertarians will be particularly sceptical of such laws and their necessity in a democratic liberal society.

▇ The law relating to obscenity and indecency

In the seventeenth century, the courts gave themselves power to punish moral subversion, taking such jurisdiction from the ecclesiastical courts.[125] Presently there exist a variety of laws

---

[125] *R v Sedley* (1663) 1 Sid 168. The poet, Sir Charles Sedley, and his fellow revellers climbed to the top of the Cock Inn and stripped themselves naked. They threw bottles of urine into the street below and preached blasphemy to the crowds. It was held that the courts had an inherent power to punish moral subversion, declaring that it was high time to punish such profane conduct.

that either criminalise indecent or obscene speech or behaviour, providing for legal sanctions on their breach, and/or allowing such expression to be restricted and regulated by certain agencies.[126] Thus, the law might either make it an offence to publish obscene material, or allow some regulating agency to refuse the broadcast of information if it regards it as unacceptable in some way. Both methods of control require justification, and the fact that the regulation of speech does not always carry with it legal liability is, at least initially, irrelevant to the principle of free speech, particularly as regulation allows some form of prior restraint.[127]

The distinction between obscenity and indecency

As we shall see, some of the laws in this area relate to the control of indecent speech and acts, while others relate to acts or speech that are classified as obscene. For example, the Indecent Displays (Control) Act 1981 makes it an offence to display any *indecent* matter in a public place, while the Obscene Publications Act 1959 makes it an offence to publish *obscene* articles, in other words those that are capable of depraving and corrupting its readership.[128] In one case, therefore, it is enough that the material is shocking or offensive, or lewd and disgusting,[129] whereas in other cases the material must go further and deprave and corrupt the morals of its likely readership, thereby attacking or threatening those morals in some way. The distinction between indecency and obscenity is important in relation to human rights protection, and in particular as to the necessity of certain legal provisions which interfere with freedom of speech. Obscene speech is generally regarded as capable of causing a greater social or individual harm as opposed to indecent speech, which merely causes offence or insult to the public or to an individual or group of individuals.[130]

Accordingly, the civil libertarian would expect interference with speech on grounds of indecency to be minimal; indeed some civil libertarians may regard *any* interference with speech on that ground as illegitimate because it restricts individual autonomy on the basis of either collective morality or individual distaste, both grounds in themselves being incapable of justifying restrictions on individual freedom. Despite this, many laws do impose restrictions on freedom of speech on the grounds that such speech would cause offence. In such cases, therefore, such laws need to be examined to see whether they are truly necessary, and to ensure that they interfere with free speech as little as possible.

---

[126] For a comprehensive coverage of these laws and how they impact on press freedom, see Robertson and Nicol, *Media Law* (Sweet & Maxwell 2002, 4th edn), pages 153–211, and Fenwick and Phillipson, *Media Freedom under the Human Rights Act* (OUP 2006), chapters 8–12.

[127] See *R (Pro Life Alliance) v BBC* [2004] 1 AC 185, considered below.

[128] Some provisions cover both definitions. For example, s.85 of the Postal Services Act 2000 (formerly s.11 of the Post Office Act 1953) makes it an offence to send an indecent *or* obscene article through the post (see also s.4 of the Unsolicited Goods and Services Act 1971). Further, the Customs and Excise Management Act 1979 prohibits the importation of indecent *and* obscene articles.

[129] In *R v Anderson* [1972] 1 QB 304, the Court of Appeal held that the meaning of obscenity in s.11 of the Post Office Act 1953 (now s.85 of the Postal Services Act 2000) was to be construed in accordance with its natural meaning so as to include something which was lewd and revolting. This equated with the general meaning of the word 'indecency', which generally covers something that can be described as lewd, crude or disgusting.

[130] In *O'Connor v United Kingdom* (2005) 45 EHRR SE1, the European Court held that the term 'indecency' was not so vague as to be in violation of Article 7 of the Convention (prohibiting retrospective criminal law). The fact that the term and its application to the facts were left to a jury did not violate Article 7. The judge's power to direct a jury on whether the material was capable in law of being indecent provided sufficient protection to the defendant.

The value of obscene and indecent speech and the reasons for interference and regulation

Although there are some arguments against the constitutional protection of indecent and obscene speech, both national and international bills of rights appear to recognise it as speech or expression, thus insisting that any interference is legitimate. For example, in *Miller* v *California*,[131] the United States Supreme Court held that pornography could qualify as speech and thus receive protection from unconstitutional interference. In that case the Court stated that such speech could be interfered with where the average person, applying contemporary community standards, would find that the work, taken as a whole, appeals to the prurient interest; where it describes, in a patently offensive way, sexual conduct specifically defined by the applicable state law; and where the work, taken as a whole, lacks serious literary, artistic, political or scientific value. The Court concluded that, in general, speech should not be penalised unless there is a demonstrable causal relationship between speech and antisocial conduct.[132] Equally, both English courts and the European Court of Human Rights have accepted that freedom of speech applies to views which shock and offend and which are heartily disapproved of by the recipient.[133]

If we accept that some, or all, obscene or indecent speech is 'speech', we must now examine whether it is legitimate to place restrictions on such speech. This involves deciding what reasons may legitimately be put forward to justify an interference with such speech and then determining whether the restrictions conform to standards of necessity and reasonableness. The strongest reason for such laws would appear to be the prevention of physical harm caused by the publication and dissemination of such speech. Thus, it might be argued that the control of such information could prevent the incitement of criminal acts. This would require strong evidence of a link between publication and crime, and pure conjecture would not suffice.[134] Accordingly, although it might be legitimate to prevent publication on the basis that such publication is likely to incite criminal activities, there should not be a notable difference between such evidence and evidence required to prove a specific incitement offence. This argument might also be extended to protect certain vulnerable individuals from physical harm. For example, one of the aims of the Obscene Publications Act might be to avoid corruption leading to physical attacks, and the offence of (taking) an indecent photograph of a child contrary to the Protection of Children Act 1978 might cause psychological harm to the participant as well as exposing children to future harm. This potential harm seems to be the basis of the offence of possessing extreme pornographic material. In a consultation paper produced by the Home Office it was recommended that a new criminal offence of being in possession of extreme pornographic material be created;[135] and s.63 of the Criminal Justice and Immigration Act 2008 creates a new offence of possession of violent and extreme pornography, carrying a maximum penalty of three years' imprisonment.[136]

---

[131] (1973) 413 US 15.

[132] In contrast, the Supreme Court has held that the distribution and possession of child pornography falls outside the First Amendment protection: *New York* v *Ferber* (1982) 485 US 747; *Osborne* v *Ohio* (1990) 495 US 103.

[133] See LORD DENNING MR in *Verall* v *Great Yarmouth BC* [1981] QB 202 and *Handyside* v *United Kingdom* (1976) 1 EHRR 737.

[134] The link between publication and crime was not established by the Williams Committee, *Report of the Committee on Obscenity and Film Censorship*, Cmnd 7722, 1979.

[135] *Consultation: On the Possession of Extreme Pornographic Material* (2005).

[136] See McGlynn and Rackley, Criminalising Extreme Pornography: A Lost Opportunity [2009] Crim LR 245; Attwood and Smith, Extreme Concern: Regulating 'Dangerous Pictures' in the United Kingdom [2010] J. Law & Soc. 171. The offence is considered at pages 382–4 below.

Another argument is that the dissemination of such information is capable of causing harm to society's morals. This paternalistic approach could be used to stop the destruction of or damage to public morality caused by such speech, and is evident in the common law offence of corrupting public morals, and, indirectly, in the offences under the Obscene Publications Act. To justify this, however, there should be evidence that there is a public morality worth protecting and that the publication is capable of harming that morality, as opposed to offending it. Even so, libertarians would argue that public morality could never justify interfering with self-autonomy and self-fulfilment. The central argument becomes stronger, however, if the purpose of the law is to protect the vulnerable from depravity or corruption, particularly if publication is likely to deprave and corrupt the thoughts and actions of the young, or the mentally or emotionally weak.[137]

The third argument, and the one which is the basis of most indecency offences, is that restriction and regulation protects society or individuals from shock or offence, or in certain cases, outrage. Thus, offences under the Indecent Displays (Control) Act 1981, the Post Office Act 1953 and the Postal Services Act 2000, and the variety of broadcasting controls, operate on the basis that publication or broadcast of such material will upset public morality or the sensibilities of individual citizens or viewers. Although this is a weak basis for restriction, particularly if it takes the form of prior restraint, the interferences are, it might be argued, minimal and limited – often delaying the information or imposing particular restrictions that, it is hoped, do not obstruct the central right of freedom of speech and expression. However, such controls do obstruct the principles of freedom of expression and individual choice and are particularly dangerous where the form of expression employed is the only, or only effective, method of expression.

There exists a fourth argument that the control of certain material, in particular pornography, is necessary in order to safeguard the dignity and integrity of certain sections of society. Thus, the traditional feminist argument against pornography is predicated on the assumption that such material constitutes violence against women and thus amounts to a form of discrimination.[138] This argument is not based *solely* on the link between the distribution of such material and the commission of sexual or other offences,[139] but on the idea that such information constitutes violence against women in itself. Therefore, as no one should be subjected to inhuman or degrading treatment, so too they should be protected from information that degrades them as human beings. Neither is this argument based on the right not to be shocked or offended; the feminist argument is not founded on arguments of taste and decency, but rather on the protection of women against discrimination and degradation. Although this argument has its basis in the protection of human rights and individual and group dignity, and would therefore appear to be a powerful basis for control, it is not reflected *directly* in any of the domestic laws on obscenity and indecency. Thus, although the argument might be relevant in deciding whether pornographic material prosecuted under the Obscene Publications Act is capable of depraving and corrupting its readership, or constitutes an extreme pornographic image under s.63 of the Criminal Justice and Immigration Act 2008, neither statute confronts the specific harm caused by possession and use of such material.[140]

---

[137] This argument was very influential in the European Court's decision in *Handyside* v *United Kingdom*, considered below.

[138] See Mackinnon, *Feminism Unmodified* (Harvard University Press 1997).

[139] In other words, it is based on arguments *in addition* to those based on actual physical harm caused to victims of pornography and other obscene material.

[140] See McGlynn and Rackley, Criminalising Extreme Pornography: A Lost Opportunity, n 136 above.

Whether any of the domestic provisions below are necessary and proportionate and in compliance with the European Convention depends on a number of related factors, including whether there is a legitimate aim for its suppression or sanction; whether the offences are sufficiently clear to be 'prescribed by law'; the *mens rea* required for the offence; the nature and severity of the penalty, and whether it imposes prior restraint; and whether there are any defences for 'legitimate' speech, particularly where such speech serves the public interest and the public's right to know.

The Obscene Publications Act 1959

This legislation is at the heart of discussions regarding the control of free speech on grounds of public morality. First, the Act has been the source of many *causes célèbres*, most notably the prosecution of Penguin Books for the publication of *Lady Chatterley's Lover*, thus highlighting the danger of obscenity and indecency law to works of artistic or literary merit.[141] Secondly, the Act imposes a severe restraint on the dissemination of material in that a successful prosecution under the Act will mean that the material will not be available to the public. Thus, unlike many other legal regulations concerning indecent material, publication of the offending material will not merely be restricted and so available at different locations or at a different time. If successful, an action under the Act will often stop publication, or future publication, completely, and the reader will be deprived of an opportunity to digest that information. Thirdly, the Act attempts to ensure that the desire to control harmful publications is balanced against the need to allow valuable free speech. Thus, s.4 of the Act provides a public good defence, allowing arguments to the effect that the publication of the material would enhance literary or other concerns.

Offences under the Act

Publication or possession for publication of obscene materials

Section 2 of the 1959 Act (as amended by the 1964 Act) makes it an offence for a person to publish[142] (whether for gain or not), or to have in their possession for publication for gain, an obscene article.[143] Consequently, it is not an offence to read such material, or to have it in one's possession, provided one does not intend to publish the material. The restriction on private life and freedom of expression is therefore indirect, and the Act concentrates on the publication of such information, attempting to prevent its dissemination. This offence does not require a specific *mens rea*, merely an intention to publish.[144] Therefore, it is not necessary to prove an intention to deprave and corrupt and the intention or motive of the publisher or original author are not relevant in determining liability.[145] Further, the question is whether the tendency of the article is to deprave and corrupt the likely readership, not whether it has been proved to

---

[141] *R v Penguin Books* [1961] Crim LR 176.

[142] Under s.1(3) of the Act a person publishes an article where they distribute, circulate, sell, let on hire, give or lend, or offer for sale or for letting on hire; or in the case of an article containing or embodying matter to be looked at or a record, a person shows, plays or projects it, or where the matter is data stored electronically, transmits that data.

[143] Under s.1(2), an article means any description of article containing or embodying matter to be read or looked at or both, any sound record, and any film or other record of a picture or pictures.

[144] Although liability is thus strict, there is a defence under s.1(5) where a person can prove that he had not examined the article in respect of which he is charged and had no reasonable cause to suspect that his publication of it would make him liable to be convicted of an offence under s.2.

[145] *R v Penguin Books* [1961] Crim LR 176.

have that effect. This equates with liability in the law of blasphemy, where it was the likely effect of the publication that was at issue, and where the lack of intention to cause outrage was irrelevant.[146] This would appear to be an arbitrary feature of the law, but the European Court and Commission have upheld these laws despite the absence of a specific intention.[147] These features of the offence are further compounded by the fact that expert evidence is generally not available to discover the intention of the author, or its likely effect on the readership.[148]

The definition of obscenity

The Act uses the concept of obscenity as opposed to indecency and the likely effect of the publication must be such that it would tend to *deprave and corrupt* its likely readership. In addition, s.2(4) states that a person publishing an article shall not be proceeded against for an offence at common law consisting of the publication of any matter contained or embodied in the article where the essence of the offence is that the matter is obscene. This would appear to give the Act exclusive jurisdiction over obscenity offences, and thus allow the defendant to rely on the public interest defence under s.4, below. However, it does not cover prosecutions for conspiracy or those where the nature of the charge is indecency.[149] Section 1 of the Act provides that an article is obscene if its effect or (where the article comprises two or more distinct items) the effect of any of those items is,[150] if taken as a whole, such as to tend to deprave and corrupt persons who are likely, having regard to all relevant circumstances, to read, see or hear the matter. The Act does not define these terms, but in *R v Penguin Books* it was held that 'deprave' meant to make morally bad, to pervert or corrupt morally, and 'corrupt' meant 'to render morally unsound or rotten, to destroy the moral purity of, to pervert or ruin a good quality.' Further, in *Knuller v DPP*[151] it was held that the Act applied to a publication that would produce a real social evil. The section thus concentrates on the likely effect on the reader, rather than its likely effect on public morals as a whole,[152] although when a person is likely to be *depraved and corrupted* is far from certain.

What is certain, at least in theory, is that the Act does not employ a test of indecency, and that it is not sufficient that the publication would merely shock and disturb its readership. In *R v Anderson* (n 150 and 152 above), the defendants were charged under the Post Office Act 1953 and under s.2 of the Obscene Publications Act 1959 for publishing and sending copies of the 'School kid's issue' of their magazine, *Oz*. The magazine contained items relating to lesbianism, homosexuality, oral sex and drug taking, and it was argued that it would deprave and corrupt its young readers. In summing up, the trial judge directed the jury that the test in the Act covered that which was repulsive, loathsome and lewd. On appeal, it was held that the sole test for

---

[146] *R v Lemon* [1979] AC 617.

[147] *Handyside v United Kingdom* (1976) 1 EHRR 737; *Gay News v United Kingdom* (1982) 5 EHRR 123.

[148] However, such evidence can be made available to explain particular concepts, such as drug taking, to an inexperienced jury, provided that does not attempt to explain the likely effect of the article on its intended readership. See *R v Skirving* [1985] QB 819; *DPP v A and BC Chewing Gum Ltd* [1968] 1 QB 159: in the latter case the court held that the Act applied to the obscene depiction of violence.

[149] See *DPP v Shaw* [1962] AC 220; *Knuller v DPP* [1973] AC 435, considered below.

[150] It is not generally permissible to extract the worst passages from the article; the article must therefore be assessed as a whole. However, when the article consists of separate pieces it is permissible to look at those passages in isolation and to found a conviction on that basis: *R v Anderson* [1972] 1 QB 304.

[151] [1973] AC 435.

[152] Although *public* morality is highly relevant, because the question is whether those morals are likely to be distorted by the reader as a result of reading the material.

obscenity under the Act was a tendency to deprave and corrupt, and that in the present case there was a grave danger that the jury might have understood 'obscene' as including filthy, loathsome or lewd.[153] This decision appears to provide some protection for offensive and challenging speech, although whether the jury can appreciate the difference between speech that is likely to deprave and corrupt, and that which they do not approve of, is another matter.

In addition, the section contains an implied 'defence' of aversion, and the defendant will escape liability if the likely effect of the publication is that it will cause revulsion in the reader. In *R v Calder and Boyars*[154] the defendants had been convicted in connection with the publication of the controversial novel *Last Exit to Brooklyn*, which depicted the decadent lifestyle of a young man living in Brooklyn. On appeal, it was held that as the book contained many words and incidents rightly described as obscene in the ordinary sense of the word, it was important to explain to the jury the specific defence that their true effect in context was the reverse of tending to deprave and corrupt. This will allow the court to consider whether the true effect of the publication is to revolt the reader and, possibly, to reinforce his existing morality. However, the 'defence' would not be available where the court is satisfied that the readership would be incapable of digesting the material in that way, and instead would, unlike the majority of society, be corrupted by the material.[155]

The scope of the Act

The Act is not concerned solely with the corruption of sexual morals, but covers other matters such as the depiction of violence, for example in *DPP v A and BC Chewing Gum Ltd*, mentioned above. The Act has also been applied to drugs, and a publication that corrupted moral views on this matter could face prosecution. For example, in *John Calder Publications v Powell*[156] it was held that obscenity and depravity were not confined to sex and could apply to publications that presented a distorted account of drug taking. In this case a book, *Cain's Book*, concerned the life of an imaginary junkie in New York and, in the court's view, highlighted the favourable effects of drug taking. The court noted that far from condemning such activities, it advocated them, and consequently there was a real risk that its readership might be tempted to experiment with drugs and to get the favourable sensations highlighted by the book. Again, in *R v Skirving*,[157] a pamphlet which claimed that cocaine was the greatest thing since sex, and which gave detailed instructions of use, was found to be rightly convicted under the Act.[158] It would also appear that the Act would apply to the corruption of religious morals and depraved or corrupted views on race.

Although the Act clearly prohibits publications likely to incite criminal or antisocial conduct, it has been held that the Act also covers corruption of the mind. In *DPP v Whyte*[159]

---

[153] The convictions under the 1959 Act were, therefore, quashed, although the court agreed that the meaning of obscene within s.11 of the Post Office Act was the ordinary meaning, which included shocking, lewd and indecent matter.
[154] [1969] 1 QB 151.
[155] Thus, in *Handyside v United Kingdom*, n 147 above, the fact that the readership was young and vulnerable was a weighty factor in deciding that the material was obscene, and that its prosecution was necessary in a democratic society.
[156] [1965] 1 QB 509.
[157] [1985] QB 819.
[158] An alternative course of action would be to prosecute for incitement to commit drugs offences. See *Marlow v United Kingdom*, considered below.
[159] [1972] AC 849. Husband and wife booksellers had been charged under the Act with having in their possession for gain a number of pornographic magazines, including the intriguingly entitled *Dingle Dangle No 3*.

it was held that the Act was principally concerned with the effect of the material on the mind of the reader, including the emotions of the persons who read it, and that it was not necessary to show that the reader would manifest those depraved thoughts in any physical way.[160] It was also established in this case that the Act was not concerned with once and for all corruption, and that it was no defence to prove that the likely readership was already corrupted. In this case it had been argued that their readers were inadequate, dirty old men, who were addicts of this type of material and whose morals were already in a state of depravity. Rejecting the plea that such people were incapable of corruption, it was held that the Act was concerned not only with the protection of the wholly innocent, but also with the protection of the less innocent from further corruption, and the addict from feeding or increasing his corruption. Consequently, if the likely effect of a book on unnatural sexual practices was to incite a substantial number of its readers to indulge in those practices, then the material could be said to deprave and corrupt. Similarly, if the likely effect of the publication would be to persuade that readership to think that such a practice was acceptable, then the material is still caught by the Act even though the reader is unlikely to indulge in such behaviour, either because of the deleterious effects of such actions, or because of the fear of being caught or prosecuted. The decision in *Whyte* highlights the paternalistic characteristics of the legislation, and questions the legitimacy of restricting the dissemination of material to adults when there is no evidence of any harmful effects from publication.[161]

A significant proportion of the likely readership

For an offence to be committed under the Act, it is usually essential to find that a significant number of the likely readership are likely to be depraved or corrupted. The court does not, therefore, use the test of the reasonable person, or of the person who is most likely to be corrupted by the material, but instead has to gauge the reaction of those who, having regard to all the relevant circumstances, are likely to see, hear or read the material. In deciding the likely readership, the courts will have regard to factors such as the nature and content of the material, its price and its intended market, including the possibility that it might, unintentionally, fall into the hands of persons other than the intended readership. In addition it has been held that the material must be likely to deprave and corrupt a certain proportion of that readership. This was defined in *R v Calder and Boyars*[162] as a significant proportion of the likely readership, which means neither just a few, nor on the other hand all, of its readers.[163]

The Court of Appeal considered this aspect of the offence in *R v Perrin*.[164] The defendant had been convicted under s.2 of the Act when he had published a web page, which contained pictures of people covered in faeces and which had been viewed by police officers. On appeal it was held that the judge had been correct in estimating the likely effect of the publication on those intended by the defendant to view the web page, including vulnerable young people. The prosecution was entitled to look beyond the officers' viewing of the material and ask

---

[160] This is also the case for prosecutions under the common law offence of corrupting public morals: *DPP v Shaw* [1962] AC 220.

[161] This argument is not used therefore in relation to the regulation of child pornography, where the nature of such material might be sufficient to justify regulation and the relevant penalties.

[162] [1969] 1 QB 151.

[163] In *DPP v Whyte* [1972] AC 849, the House of Lords held that significant proportion means more than a negligible number of readers, but may be much less than half. The number required might differ depending on the extent of the potential effect on the readership, and this would no doubt affect the thinking of the jury.

[164] [2002] EWCA Crim 747, 22 March 2002.

themselves whether any persons were likely to see the article, and if so whether the effect of the article was such as to tend to deprave and corrupt them.[165] In the Court's view, a jury need only be satisfied that there was a likelihood of vulnerable persons seeing the material, it did not have to demonstrate that such persons actually did or would see it. The Court also held that where there was no suggestion that the publication was for the public good, there was no reason why a jury should be directed that the effect of the article would tend to deprave and corrupt a significant proportion. It was sufficient that they were directed in accordance with the words of the Act and that the judge had made it clear that it was necessary for more than a negligible number of persons to be likely to see the material.

Powers of forfeiture and search and seizure

Section 3 of the Act provides the police with the power to search premises and to seize obscene articles, and also gives the courts the power to instigate forfeiture proceedings in relation to such articles. These powers can be used as an alternative to bringing proceedings under s.2 of the Act and can threaten both the right to a jury trial and the right to rely on the public interest defence in s.4 of the Act.[166] Under s.3(1) of the Act a magistrate may issue the police with a warrant to search specified premises, including stalls or vehicles, where he or she has been provided with information on oath that there is a reasonable suspicion that obscene publications are being kept for publication for gain. Under that provision, such material can then be seized and removed and, if the police do not decide to bring an action under s.2, the articles must then be brought before a magistrate, who will then issue a summons if satisfied that the articles are obscene.[167] In such a case the owner of the articles will be summonsed to appear to show reason why the goods should not be forfeited, and this will include the right to argue that the articles are not obscene, or that they are covered by the public interest defence.

The public interest defence

Section 4 of the Obscene Publications Act 1959 provides a defence to an action under the Act if it can be shown that the publication of the material can be justified in the public interest. The purpose of this provision was to afford some protection to material which, although having the potential to deprave and corrupt its likely readership, had a redeeming quality, thus giving it immunity from conviction. In particular, s.4(2) of the Act allows the defendant (and the prosecution) to introduce evidence to prove (or negate) the defence. Section 4 provides that a person shall not be convicted of an offence under s.2 of the Act, and a forfeiture order under s.3 of the Act shall not be made, if it proved that the article in question is justified as being for the public good on the grounds that it is in the interests of science, literature, art or learning, or of other objects of general concern.

It is important to note that the defence is not considered until there has been a finding of obscenity under the Act. Thus, by the time the defence is raised, a court or jury has already

---

[165] However, it was held in *R v Clayton and Halsey* (1962) Cr App R 227 that where the defendant is charged with the offence of selling or making available the publication to a single person, then it would have to be shown that that person was likely to be depraved or corrupted.

[166] Although the section allows the defendant to appear in court to defend forfeiture proceedings, in practice the forfeiture will be carried out without any such appearance. See Stone, Obscene Publications: The Problems Persist [1986] Crim LR 139.

[167] Section 3(3).

come to the conclusion that the likely effect of the article is that it will deprave and corrupt a substantial proportion of its readership. Accordingly, the court will not allow the defence to be used in a way that revisits the question of whether the article was likely to deprave or corrupt. For example, in *DPP v Jordan*,[168] the House of Lords held that the phrase 'other objects of general concern' did not cover the alleged therapeutic value of the material. It had been argued that certain hardcore pornographic articles had some psychotherapeutic value for various categories of persons, providing a relief for their sexual tensions by way of sexual fantasy and masturbation and acting as a safety valve to save them from psychological and antisocial and possibly criminal activities directed at others. However, Lord Wilberforce held that the words 'other objects of general concern' fell within the same dimension as science, art, literature, etc., and could not fall in the totally different area of the effect on sexual behaviour, which is covered by s.1 of the Act. Thus, it does not allow the argument that the article might have had an innocuous or beneficial effect to be raised again. At this stage, therefore, the court or jury will have to conduct a balancing exercise to see whether the already established detrimental effects of the publication are outweighed. In *R v Calder and Boyars*[169] it was held that in deciding whether a book properly found to be obscene should be published for the public good, the court had to consider whether the publication would be justified on the grounds listed in s.4, and that expert evidence on those matters was admissible, either to establish or negate those grounds. The jury had to decide on the balance of probabilities whether the publication was proved to be for the public good after they had considered the number of readers they believed would tend to be depraved and corrupted by the article, the strength of that tendency and the nature of the depravity and corruption.

It has been held that 'other objects of general concern' is wide enough to cover the sociological merits of a publication, thus inviting discussions on disturbing social events or phenomena such as drug taking or sexual promiscuity. For example, in *R v Calder and Boyars*[170] it was held that expert evidence could be put forward as to the sociological or ethical merit of a book, which it was claimed was obscene because of its depiction of sexual and other matters. However, controversially it has been held that the word 'education' does not allow evidence to be put forward solely on the basis that the article educated the readership. In *AG's Reference (No 3 of 1973)*,[171] therefore, it was held that the word 'learning' in s.4 could not be read so as to allow expert evidence to be available regarding the magazines in that they provided information to the readers about sexual matters. In the court's view, if learning was a noun, it must mean the product of scholarship, and cover something whose inherent excellence is gained by the product of the scholar. The defence could not be used, therefore, to argue that the article educated, or could have educated, the reader, and informed them of matters of which they were ignorant in the first place. This interpretation denies the argument for free speech with regard to the discovery of the truth, but provided it is not applied to material that has separate educational worth, it would appear that the inability to defend pornography on the basis that it widens the minds of its readers would not be in violation of Article 10 of the Convention.

---

[168] [1977] AC 699.
[169] [1969] 1 QB 151.
[170] [1969] 1 QB 151.
[171] [1978] 3 All ER 1166.

Possession of extreme pornographic images

Section 63 of the Criminal Justice and Immigration Act 2008 creates the offence of possessing extreme pornographic images.[172] The Act does not replace the existing offence contained in the Obscene Publications Acts (above), although one of its primary purposes is to identify the type of obscene image that might cause the greatest harm and which thus should be subject to prosecution policies. The offence was inspired by a consultation paper produced by the Home Office, which whilst not establishing a direct link between the possession of such material and sexual violence, concluded that extreme pornography might encourage an interest in violent or aberrant sexual activity, and thus recommended that a new criminal offence of being in possession of extreme pornographic material be created.[173] As we shall see the offence does not simply reflect those objectives and borrows from the 1959 Act and the principles of moral corruption inherent in the previous legislation.[174]

Section 63(1) of the Act provides that it is an offence for a person to be in possession of an extreme pornographic image,[175] in other words one that is both pornographic and constitutes an extreme image.[176] An image is then defined as pornographic if it is of such a nature that it must *reasonably be assumed* to have been produced solely or principally for the purpose of sexual arousal.[177] As with the Obscene Publications Acts, the provision employs an objective test to determine the purpose of the image, so that the actual intention of the producer of the image is not really relevant unless that intention points to the presumed intention. An extreme image is then defined as an image which is grossly offensive, disgusting or otherwise of an obscene character,[178] and portrays, in an *explicit and realistic way,*[179] any of the following acts: one which threatens a person's life; which results, or is likely to result, in serious injury to a person's anus, breasts or genitals; one which involves sexual interference with a human corpse; or one of a person performing an act of intercourse or oral sex with an animal (whether dead or alive). In addition, a reasonable person looking at the image would think that any such person or animal was real.[180]

Where a person is in possession of an image which forms part of a series of images, the question whether that image is of such a nature that it can be assumed to have been produced solely or principally for the purpose of sexual arousal is determined by the image itself, and (if the series of images is such as to be capable of providing a context for the image) the context in which it occurs in the series of images.[181] This means that where an image forms an integral part of a narrative constituted by a series of images, and having regard to those

---

[172] Under s.63(10) of the Act, proceedings for an offence may not be instituted in England and Wales, except by or with the consent of the Director of Public Prosecutions. The maximum penalty on conviction on indictment is three years' imprisonment for possession of images portraying life-threatening acts or acts threatening serious injury, and two years for depictions of necrophilia and bestiality; six months for all offences on summary conviction (s.67 Criminal Justice and Immigration Act 2008).

[173] *Consultation: On the Possession of Extreme Pornographic Material* (2005), at para 31.

[174] See McGlynn and Rackley, Criminalising Extreme Pornography: A Lost Opportunity [2009] Crim LR 245.

[175] An image is defined in s.63(8) of the Act as either a moving or still image (produced by any means), or data (stored by any means) which is capable of conversion into such an image.

[176] Section 63(2) Criminal Justice and Immigration Act 2008.

[177] Section 63(3).

[178] Section 63(6).

[179] This will exclude cartoons and drawings, which can quite often excite a strong response from the public or certain individuals.

[180] Section 63(7).

[181] Section 63(4).

images as a whole, they would not reasonably be assumed to have been produced solely or principally for the purpose of sexual arousal, the image may be found not to be pornographic, even though it might have been found to be pornographic if taken by itself.[182]

With respect to defences, where a person is charged under s.63, it is a defence to prove that that person had a legitimate reason for being in possession of the image concerned; had not seen the image concerned and did not know, nor had any cause to suspect, it to be an extreme pornographic image; or that the person was sent the image without any prior request, and did not keep it for an unreasonable time.[183] The section does not, therefore, provide any public interest defence as is available under the Obscene Publications Acts. Thus, once an image is regarded as extreme and pornographic there can be no argument that the detrimental effect of the publication is set off by its contribution to art, literature or other objects of general concern. The absence of such an express defence is mitigated by the fact that for an offence to be committed the image needs to be of such a nature that it must reasonably be assumed to have been produced *solely or principally* for the purpose of sexual arousal. Further, it could be argued that if someone was in possession of the images for artistic or other purposes that they would have a 'legitimate reason' for being in possession. Further, s.64 of the Act exempts films that have received a classification from the British Board of Film Classification, who will have already made a determination that the film is not obscene under the Obscene Publications legislation; although images taken from such films will be covered if they have been extracted from the film for pornographic purposes.[184] Finally, the requirement that the DPP consent to any prosecution under the Act also provides a safeguard against unnecessary charges.

In addition, where the offence relates to an image that portrays an act or act prohibited by s.63 (other than one of a person performing an act of intercourse or oral sex with an animal), then it is a defence to prove that the defendant directly participated in the act or any of the acts portrayed, and that the act or acts did not involve the infliction of any non-consensual harm on any person;[185] further, if it involved an act of sexual intercourse with a corpse that what was portrayed as a human corpse was not in fact a corpse.[186] This specific defence would appear to reflect the current law on consent to sexual harm and the need of such laws to be compatible with the right to private sexual life under Article 8 of the European Convention.[187]

The object of the Act is obviously to stop the possession of such images on the basis that they are by their very nature extreme and thus unacceptable for viewing, for example images of necrophilia for sexual gratification; although in other cases, such as depictions of violent rapes, the image must also meet the requirements of, for example, serious physical harm. In this sense the Act provides specific regulation of images that would otherwise be prosecuted under the Obscene Publications Acts. With respect to the compatibility of the legislation with Articles 8 and 10 of the Convention, it should be noted that the offence goes further than many existing provisions because it regulates possession rather than publication or possession with a view of publication. Thus, to justify the offence in terms of individual liberty, one would

---

[182] Section 63(4).

[183] Section 65(2).

[184] Section 64(3).

[185] Under s.66(3), harm inflicted on a person is non-consensual harm if the harm is of such a nature that the person cannot, in law, consent to it being inflicted on him- or herself; or where the person can, in law, consent to it being so inflicted, the person does not in fact consent to it being so inflicted.

[186] Section 66(2)(a)–(c).

[187] See *R v Brown* [1994] 1 AC 212; *Laskey, Jaggard and Brown v United Kingdom* (1997) 24 EHRR 39, considered in chapter 11 of this text at page 574.

have to argue that they pose a similar harm to, say indecent images of children, regulated by the Protection of Children Act 1978, see below. On the other hand, the Act only applies to images and not to literature, so therefore impacts on freedom of expression less than other measures. Further, European Convention case law provides little protection to extreme images and accordingly gives a wide margin of appreciation to the national authorities in regulating it.[188] The absence of a public interest or free speech defence therefore may be compatible with such jurisprudence. Thus, it may not be fatal provided the prosecution policy is aimed at extreme images with no possible worth.

Nevertheless, s.63 has attracted some criticism from commentators who believe either that the provision unreasonably interferes with private life on the basis of public distaste, or that its original intention to protect persons from sexual attacks has not been achieved. Thus, it has been argued that the provision should not have concerned itself with average depictions of consensual sado-masochistic activity, but with what might be seen as the really problematic images that glorify sexual violence through, for example, 'the deliberate misogynistic valorisation of rape'.[189] Thus it has been noted that most pro-rape websites will not be covered by the provision, despite there being some evidence of a link between such websites and a propensity to commit acts of sexual violence.[190]

Conspiracy to corrupt public morals

This common law offence, of conspiring to corrupt public morals, came to prominence in 1961 in the House of Lords' decision in *DPP* v *Shaw*.[191] In that case the defendants had published the *Ladies' Directory*, a booklet containing the contact numbers, predilections and prices charged by female prostitutes. They were charged with conspiracy (with the prostitutes) to corrupt public morals and the House of Lords confirmed that such an offence did exist at common law and that it had been committed in this particular case.[192] The House of Lords also held that such a charge would not breach s.2(4) of the Obscene Publications Act 1959, which insists that charges for publication of obscene material should not be the subject of proceedings outside the Act. That provision, in their Lordships' views, only applied to the offence of publication, and did not apply where, as in the present case, the basis of the charge was a conspiracy to corrupt public morals. The House of Lords held further that a specific intent was required to commit the offence, and that liability was based on the *corruption* of society's morals rather than causing mere shock and offence. However, there is no public interest defence available to the defendant and the offence could be used to circumvent that safeguard in cases where the material has arguable public interest content.[193]

---

[188] See, for example *Hoare* v *United Kingdom* [1997] EHRLR 678, considered at page 392 below, and *S and G* v *United Kingdom* (Application No 17634), considered under outraging public decency, below at page 385.

[189] See McGlynn and Rackley, Criminalising Extreme Pornography: A Lost Opportunity [2009] Crim LR 245, at page 249.

[190] Ibid., at page 250.

[191] [1962] AC 220.

[192] Similarly, in *Knuller* v *DPP* [1973] AC 435, the House of Lords upheld the convictions of the defendants when they had published a *Gentlemen's Directory*, consisting of a who's who of male homosexuals, and containing adverts such as 'alert young designer, 30, seeks warm, friendly, pretty boy under 23 who needs regular sex, reliability and beautiful surroundings. If the cap fits and you need a friend, write.' The House of Lords confirmed that there existed the offence of conspiracy to corrupt public morals, stating that to corrupt indicates that the conduct was destructive of the very fabric of society and meant more than being led morally astray.

[193] Such a defence was unlikely to have succeeded in *Shaw*, although it is extremely unlikely that the substance of the offence would be made out today.

Outraging public decency

In *Shaw* the House of Lords suggested that in addition to the offence of conspiracy to corrupt public morals, there existed at common law an offence of outraging public decency. This was confirmed by the House of Lords in *Knuller v DPP*,[194] where it was held that the offence existed at common law and could be brought both as a conspiracy charge and as a substantive offence. Section 2(4) of the Obscene Publications Act did not bar the action as the charge was one of conspiracy, and in any case the basis of liability for this offence was indecency rather than obscenity. No specific *mens rea* is required for this offence and, again, the s.4 defence is not available. On the other hand, the House of Lords stressed that for the offence of outraging public decency to be committed, the contents must be so lewd, disgusting and offensive that the sense of decency of members of the public would be outraged by seeing or reading them, and that outrage went beyond shocking the public. Further, the prospect of outrage must be related to the time and place of the exhibition – public decency is to be distinguished from public morals.

The decisions in *Shaw* and *Knuller* have been criticised on a number of grounds, most specifically that they allow the prosecution of material without allowing discussion on the publication's possible public interest merits. Although it is highly questionable whether the defendants in the above cases would have succeeded under any such defence, a later case fuelled the debate concerning the prosecution of material outside the Obscene Publications Act. The case, *R v Gibson and Sylverie*,[195] concerned the prosecution of an artist and a gallery owner in connection with the display of an exhibit at a gallery located in a shopping arcade. G had made a model's head and had attached to each of its ears an earring made out of a freeze-dried human foetus of 3–4 months' gestation. The model was displayed in a gallery, which was in a parade of shops, and following complaints, G and S, the gallery owners, were charged with conspiracy to corrupt public morals. The Court of Appeal confirmed that the charge of outraging public decency did not require an intention on behalf of the defendants to outrage, or an appreciation that there was a risk of such outrage coupled with a determination to run that risk, although the court felt that it made very little difference in this case. Following the conviction, a case was taken under the European Convention, claiming that the prosecution and conviction were contrary to the applicants' rights under Article 10 of the Convention. However, in *S and G v United Kingdom*,[196] the European Commission of Human Rights declared the case inadmissible. The European Commission restated the principles in *Handyside* and held that the relevant law was sufficiently clear, had a legitimate aim and was not disproportionate, even though there was no defence based on artistic merit. The defendants could have argued that the exhibition was not an outrage to public decency and thus have raised the issue of freedom of expression. In conclusion, the prosecution was within the state's margin of appreciation, taken for the legitimate aim of the protection of morals.

The Protection of Children Act 1978

Although the publication of child pornography is clearly covered by the Obscene Publications Act 1959, that legislation does not address fully the dangers involved in the possession and distribution of such material. For example, the 1959 Act only applies to the *publication of*

---

[194] [1973] AC 435.
[195] [1991] 1 All ER 441.
[196] Application No 17634.

obscene material and does not make it an offence to be in possession of such material.[197] Consequently, the Protection of Children Act 1978 was passed, which created a specific offence involving the taking and distribution of indecent photographs of children.[198] Section 1 of the Act provides that it is an offence for a person:

(a) to take, or to permit to be taken (or make) any indecent photograph (or pseudo photograph)[199] of a child; or

(b) to distribute or show such indecent photographs (or pseudo photographs); or

(c) to have in his possession such indecent photographs (or pseudo photographs) with a view to their being distributed or shown by himself or others; or

(d) to publish, or cause to be published, an advertisement likely to be understood as conveying that the advertiser distributes or shows such photographs (or pseudo photographs), or intends to do so.

This provision does not seek to protect members of the public from shock or offence; rather its purpose is to protect children from the harm that may result from both the taking and the distribution of such photographs. Unlike most other obscenity and indecency law, the offence can be committed by the mere possession of such a photograph,[200] provided it is possessed with a view to distribution to oneself or to others.[201] Although the section does not create an offence of strict liability, the provision may be breached quite easily. Thus, in *R v Smith and Jayson*[202] it was held that an offence of making or being in possession of an indecent photograph is not committed if a person opens an e-mail, unaware that it contains, or was likely to contain, an indecent image. However, where, as on the facts, a person voluntarily downloads an indecent image from the internet to his or her computer screen, the offence of making an indecent photograph has been committed because the computer's operator, in so downloading, causes the image to exist on the screen. In such a case the *mens rea* exists where a person carries out a deliberate and intentional act with the knowledge that the image was or was likely to be an indecent photograph (or pseudo photograph) of a child.[203]

---

[197] The 1978 Act makes it an offence to be in possession with a view to viewing them, or to their being distributed or shown *by himself* or others. See also s.160 Criminal Justice Act 1988.

[198] Section 69 of the Criminal Justice and Immigration Act 2008 extends the 1978 Act to photographs which consist of a tracing or other image, whether made by electronic or other means.

[199] Section 84 of the Criminal Justice and Public Order Act 1994 provided that the transmission of electronically stored data constitutes the publication of an article under s.1 of the OPA 1959; and made it an offence to make or take a pseudo photograph – 'an image whether made by computer graphics or otherwise howsoever, which appears to be a photograph'. The Act also provided that if the conveyed impression is that the person is a child then the pseudo photograph will be taken as showing a child and so shall be such a photograph where the predominant impression is of a child notwithstanding that some of the physical characteristics are those of an adult.

[200] In *R v Porter* [2006] EWCA Crim 560 the Court of Appeal held that a person could not be in possession of indecent photographs, contrary to s.160(1) of the Criminal Justice Act 1988 if he had deleted the images and could no longer retrieve or gain access to them.

[201] There is also a simple offence of possessing such a photograph under s.160 of the Criminal Justice Act 1988, although the Act provides a defence where the defendant is unaware of possession.

[202] *The Times*, 23 April 2002.

[203] In that case one defendant had opened an e-mail attachment, and the other had browsed the pseudo photograph on the internet. In both cases the browser software automatically saved the images to a temporary internet cache on their computers.

Again with regard to the necessary *mens rea*, the Court of Appeal in *R v Smethurst*[204] affirmed the previous decision in *R v Graham-Kerr*[205] that where a defendant was charged with making indecent photographs of children under s.1(1)(a) of the 1978 Act, his intention in making the photographs was not relevant in determining whether they were indecent. This decision reflects the position under other laws such as those under the Obscene Publications Act 1959 and the common law of blasphemy,[206] where the intention of the author is irrelevant. Furthermore, the Court of Appeal in *Smethurst* held that given the legitimate aim of protecting children from such offences this was within Article 10(2) of the Convention and thus compatible with the idea of free speech. This *obiter* appears to be well-founded, despite the absence of a public interest or artistic defence, provided the Act is not employed against photographs taken with genuine intentions, or ones that are ostensibly indecent but which highlight important issues such as child prostitution.[207]

Sending indecent, obscene and offensive messages

There are a number of statutory provisions which seek to prevent obscene, indecent or offensive material being sent through the post or via the telephone.[208] The purpose of these provisions is either to protect the recipient from unsolicited offensive material or to stop individuals from abusing the use of a public service. Although such legislation is not directly intended to prevent corruption or outrage of public or individual morals, they do use the basic morals and standards of society as a benchmark.[209] These provisions will in general be consistent with the right of individuals not to be exposed to such material against their will and will thus be compatible with Article 10 of the Convention. However, in limited cases the dissemination of the material may engage issues of genuine public interest and in such cases the legislation may impinge on true free speech and needs to be regulated within the parameters of Article 10, particularly as such provisions will not contain any public interest or public good defence.

For example, s.85 of the Postal Services Act 2000 makes it an offence to send an obscene or indecent package through the post, and if those terms are not construed accordingly when the speech in question strongly engages Article 10, there is a danger that the offence may be too easily committed. In *R v Kirk*[210] the Court of Appeal held that a judge had not misdirected a jury in stating that the words 'indecent' or 'obscene' in s.85 of the Postal Services Act 2000 might include that which was shocking and lewd. In the Court's view the words 'obscene' and 'indecent' were words that were readily understood by a jury and the judge had not misdirected them. Thus, the appellant's conviction for sending a package through the post to employees at an animal laboratory, describing it as equivalent to Auschwitz and including a Swastika was not flawed. Neither, in the Court's view was it or the prosecution in breach of the qualified right to free speech under Article 10.

---

[204] *The Times*, 13 April 2001.

[205] [1998] 1 WLR 1098.

[206] *R v Lemon* [1979] AC 617. But see *R (Green) v City of Westminster Magistrates Court* [2008] HRLR 12 (Admin), considered below under blasphemy.

[207] The Act does, therefore, have the potential for arbitrary use, particularly as the reason for the taking of the photograph, and the surrounding circumstances are irrelevant: *R v Owen* [1998] 1 WLR 134.

[208] Section 4 Unsolicited Goods and Services Act 1971; s.85 Postal Services Act 2000 (formerly s.11 Post Office Act 1953); s.127 Communications Act 2003. See also s.1 Malicious Communications Act 1998.

[209] See *DPP v Collins* [2006] 1 WLR 2223, below, in respect of the offence of making grossly offensive telephone calls under s.127 of the Communications Act 2003.

[210] [2006] Crim LR 850.

In addition s.127 of the Communications Act 2003 creates the offence of sending a grossly offensive message through a public electronic communications service. The meaning of that offence and that particular term was considered by the High Court in *DPP* v *Collins*.[211] The High Court held that the defendant had not committed the offence under s.127 because although the message (which included crude and derogatory references to ethnic and racial groups sent to his MP and the MP's secretary) would have been grossly offensive if the listener had been from such a group, there was no evidence that the caller cared who the listener was. The High Court also held that it was relevant that the messages were to be given to his MP. However on appeal,[212] the House of Lords held that the purpose of the offence was not to protect people from objectionable and unsolicited messages, but to prohibit the use of a public service for the transmission of communications that contravened the basic standards of society. Thus, the *actus reus* of the offence was complete when the message was sent, irrespective of the reaction of the recipient, or whether it was received at all. Whether a message was grossly offensive was a question of fact and had to be judged by considering the reaction of reasonable persons and the standards of an open and just multiracial society taking account of their context and all the circumstances. There could be no yardstick of gross offensiveness otherwise than by the application of reasonably enlightened contemporary standards to the particular message sent in the particular circumstances. The test was whether a message was couched in terms liable to cause gross offence to those to whom it related. With respect to the *mens rea*, their Lordships rejected the argument that liability was strict in the absence of an intention to be grossly offensive, but stated that a culpable state of mind would ordinarily be found when a message was couched in terms showing an intention to insult those to whom the message related. The same would be the case where the sender knows facts about the recipient that would render the message grossly offensive to that person, irrespective of whether it is ever received. In the present case at least some of the language used by the defendant could only have been chosen because of its highly abusive and offensive character and accordingly he should have been convicted.

Gross offensiveness is also the basis of the offence under s.1 of the Malicious Communications Act 1998, which makes it an offence to send a letter or article conveying, *inter alia*, a message which is grossly offensive where the purpose is to cause distress or anxiety to the recipient or other person to whom he intends the message to be communicated. The offence has been employed against protestors and activists and will be considered in chapter 10.[213]

The control of films, videos and the theatre

Obscene, indecent and offensive speech or acts in videos, films and theatrical performances are controlled by a combination of the general law on obscenity and indecency and by specific regulatory provisions.[214] Thus, the offences under the Obscene Publications Act 1959 apply to films, although the consent of the DPP is required before any action is brought under those provisions where the article in question is a moving picture film of a width of

---

[211] [2005] EWHC 1308 (Admin).

[212] [2006] 1 WLR 2223.

[213] *Connolly* v *DPP* [2008] 1 WLR 276.

[214] This area will be dealt with very briefly here. For a detailed account of the law and practice, see Bailey, Harris and Ormerod, *Civil Liberties: Cases and Materials* (OUP 2009, 6th edn), pages 630–52; Robertson and Nicol, *Media Law* (Sweet & Maxwell 2002, 4th edn).

not less than 19 millimetres.[215] In addition the Cinemas Act 1985 requires the licensing of premises for film exhibition and licensing authorities (each local authority) may grant a licence subject to such conditions as they think necessary in order to control the admission of children to cinemas and the suitability of films for children. The main task of the authority is to classify films in accordance to their suitable audience and in this respect they usually, although not always, follow the recommendations of the British Board of Film Censors, an independent body whose job it is to classify films.[216] With regard to the theatre, s.2 of the Theatres Act 1968 prohibits the presentation of an obscene performance of a play,[217] although under s.8 the consent of the Attorney-General is required before any prosecution is brought. Unlike written publications, it is not possible to bring obscenity or indecency charges other than under the 1968 Act, thus preserving the right of the defendants (the pre- senter or director of the performance) to the public interest defence under s.3 of the Act. In this sense, therefore, theatrical productions are given greater protection than the written word, where (as we have seen) it is possible to bring certain common law actions.[218]

Videos are subject to the Obscene Publications Act, but are regulated specifically by the Video Recordings Act 1984, which was passed to tackle the problem of the showing of 'video nasties' in the home environment. As with films, all videos are given a classification by the BBFC,[219] which must, when deciding to grant a licence, have special regard to any harm that may be caused to potential viewers, or, through their behaviour, to society by the manner in which the work deals with criminal behaviour, illegal drugs, violent behaviour or incidents, horrific behaviour or incidents or human sexual activity.[220] It is an offence under the Act to supply a video that has not been given a classification, or to supply a video to a person who is not old enough to view that film. The person denied a licence may appeal to the Video Appeals Committee and there is evidence that the Committee is taking a more liberal view than the BBFC.[221] In addition, the courts appear reluctant to interfere with the decisions of the Video Appeals Committee.[222]

Accordingly, given the opportunity to appeal to the Committee and the wide margin of appreciation afforded to such authorities by the European Court of Human Rights, it is unlikely that many acts of censorship would fall foul of Article 10 of the European

[215] Section 3A of the Obscene Publications Act 1959, as inserted by s.53 of the Criminal Law Act 1977. Under s.4A of the Obscene Publications Act it is not possible to bring obscenity or indecency charges outside the Act, thus preserving the defendant's right to use the s.4 public interest defence.

[216] The most recent classifications are U, PG, 12, 12A, 15, 18, 18R (suitable only for restricted distribution): see Munro, Sex, Laws and Videotape: The R18 category [2006] Crim LR 957. For the legal relationship between the local authority and the BBFC, see Ellis v Dubowski [1921] 3 KB 621; R v Greater London Council, ex parte Blackburn [1976] 1 WLR 550.

[217] A play is defined in s.18 of the Act as a dramatic piece, including a ballet, where what is done by one or more persons actually present and performing involves the playing of a role.

[218] For the application of the Theatres Act 1968 to actions in blasphemy, see R (Green) v Westminster Magistrates Court [2008] HRLR 12 (Admin), considered below under blasphemy and free speech.

[219] As with films shown in cinemas, but with the further classification of Uc (particularly suitable for children).

[220] Section 4A of the Video Recordings Act, as inserted by s.90 of the Criminal Justice and Public Order Act 1994.

[221] See Edwards, The Video Appeals Committee and the Standard of Legal Pornography [2001] Crim LR 305.

[222] R v Video Appeals Committee of the BBFC, ex parte BBFC [2000] EMLR 850. In that case the court held that the Committee had not erred in not refusing a licence (to a video initially refused an 18R classification) until the potential harm to children by the film's exhibition could be quantified. In the court's view the Committee had struck a correct balance between harm to children and freedom of expression and to refuse to classify a film until that harm was quantified would have unreasonably fettered its discretion.

Convention.[223] Indeed, in *Interfact v Liverpool City Council*[224] the High Court held that as the 1984 Act existed to make it more difficult to supply such videos to people under the age of 18, they were lawful, necessary and proportionate and thus compatible with Article 10(2) of the Convention.[225]

It should be noted that the 1984 Act and related prosecutions under it were challenged on the grounds that regulations implementing the Act were not in compliance with EC Directive 83/189.[226] However, although the Court of Appeal recognised that there had been a breach of the Directive, it nevertheless decided that existing convictions under the Act were valid and that there was no obligation on the courts to set them aside. However, it did refer the case to the Supreme Court to decide on this legal issue of public interest.

Broadcasting controls on obscene and indecent matter

Broadcasting authorities are given a wide range of powers to control taste and decency in carrying out their broadcasting duties.[227] Under the Communications Act 2003, OFCOM has a duty to draw up codes of practice to guide broadcasters on matters such as taste and decency,[228] and the way in which they portray sex or violence, together with a power to receive complaints regarding the breach of those standards.[229] Although these powers do not impose any criminal or civil liability on those who seek to disseminate their ideas, or those who simply wish to view or hear the material, these powers are nevertheless not to be under-estimated as ways in which freedom of speech may be interfered with. First, they do impose liability and sanctions on the broadcasting authorities themselves, thus having an effect on the freedom of the media to impart information and ideas. Secondly, they can be used by the broadcasting authorities as an effective way of imposing standards of decency and thus regulating the free flow of information and ideas through their medium.

These powers are subject to legal supervision, although it would be rare for the courts to interfere with the decision of the authorities, either because it was too restrictive of free speech, or because it had failed to apply rigorous enough standards in a particular case. For example, in *Attorney-General v McWhirter*,[230] the court rejected a complaint that the Independent Broadcasting Authority had failed in its duty to uphold decency by broadcasting a documentary about the life and work of the artist Andy Warhol. The court held that the IBA staff had directed their minds to their relevant duties and that its decision to allow the programme to be broadcast was not unreasonable.

As the broadcasting authorities are now public authorities for the purposes of s.6 of the Human Rights Act, they are under a duty not to breach Convention rights without lawful excuse. Thus, their decisions should be subject to intense review and any interference with

---

[223] In *Wingrove v United Kingdom* (1996) 24 EHRR 1, the European Court held that the Committee's decision not to grant a certificate to a potentially blasphemous video was within its wide margin of appreciation. Importantly, the Court noted that the Committee had considered the video's possible artistic merits, and the arguments under Article 10 of the Convention.

[224] [2005] 1 WLR 3118.

[225] The defendants had been prosecuted under s.12(1) of the Act of offering to supply a video classified as 18R at any other place other than a licensed sex shop, in this case by mail or telephone order.

[226] *R v Budimir* [2010] 3 CMLR 50.

[227] For a full account of the current law, see Fenwick and Phillipson, *Media Freedom under the Human Rights Act* (OUP 2006), chapter 11.

[228] Section 3 Communications Act 2003.

[229] Ibid.

[230] [1973] 1 QB 629.

freedom of expression should be shown to be necessary and proportionate. However, as shown in the *ProLife* case, below, the courts may be reluctant to interfere when the authority places public morality and decency ahead of free speech.

In *R (on the Application of ProLife Alliance) v BBC*[231] the claimants, who were opposed to abortion and who campaigned for absolute respect for the right to life, had submitted a video to the BBC which graphically illustrated the abortion process, and which the BBC refused to broadcast on grounds of taste and decency. An initial application for judicial review of the decision failed, but the Court of Appeal overturned that decision. The Court of Appeal held that the BBC had failed to give sufficient weight to the pressing imperative of free political expression and that it was only in the rarest of circumstances, if at all, that an election broadcast, which was otherwise truthful and unsensational, might properly be rejected on the grounds of taste, decency or the public interest, and this was not such a case. Although the broadcaster's views were entitled to be respected, their force and weight were modest at best. The court's constitutional responsibility to protect political speech was, on the other hand, overarching, and amounted to a duty to decide for itself whether the censorship was justified. In the Court's view it was difficult to think of a context in which the claims of freedom of expression were more pressing than where a registered political party was broadcasting their message at the time of a general election.[232]

However, on appeal the House of Lords overturned the decision of the Court of Appeal and held that the BBC were entitled to come to the conclusion that the broadcast should be banned on the grounds that it offended against good taste and indecency. In their Lordships' view the courts should be reluctant to interfere with the broadcasting authority's decision: the BBC's application of the statutory criteria could not be faulted and there was nothing to suggest that they had applied an inappropriate standard. Moreover, the Court of Appeal had erred and a challenge to the broadcaster's decision had become a challenge to the appropriateness of imposing a restriction on party broadcasts. The Court of Appeal had in effect carried out its own balancing exercise between the requirements of political speech and the protection of the public from being unduly distressed.

Although the decision of the House of Lords displays remarkable deference to the decisions of statutory bodies,[233] it *may* be defended on the grounds that the broadcasting authorities, whose main aim is to facilitate broadcasting, should be given a wide discretion with respect to whether they show material which might conflict with good taste and decency. Thus, had the BBC decided to show the video it is hoped that the courts would have shown similar deference in rejecting an application for judicial review of its decision not to restrict it.[234] Nevertheless, the decision has attracted severe criticism for its failure to subject restrictions on political speech to the most anxious scrutiny.[235]

Obscenity and indecency law and the European Convention on Human Rights

In relation to the case law of the European Convention on Human Rights the European Court has held that Article 10 of the Convention is wide enough to cover such speech. Thus, in *Handyside*

---

[231] [2004] 1 AC 185; [2002] 2 All ER 756.

[232] See, for example, the European Court decision in *Bowman v United Kingdom* (1998) 26 EHRR 1.

[233] See also *R v Radio Authority, ex parte Bull* [1997] 3 WLR 1094.

[234] In other words, a similar deference to that shown in *McWhirter*, above, n 230.

[235] See Scott, A Monstrous and Unjustifiable Infringement? Political Expression and the Ban on Advocacy Advertising (2003) 66 MLR 224; Barendt, Free Speech and Abortion [2003] PL 580; Geddis, 'If Thy Right Eye Offend Thee, Pluck it Out': *R v BBC, ex parte ProLife Alliance* (2003) 66 MLR 885.

v *United Kingdom*,[236] the European Court held that broadmindedness, tolerance and pluralism are hallmarks of a democratic society, and that accordingly Article 10 covers speech that shocks and offends. However, in that case the Court made it clear that such speech is more susceptible to interference than, for example, political expression, and that the domestic authorities would be given a wide margin of appreciation in regulating speech that causes harm to the morals of a particular state or the interests of particular individuals. The Court stressed that the domestic authorities were better placed than the international judge to assess the necessity for such laws and of particular restrictions. Accordingly it held that the conviction of the applicant for distributing a book to young people that dealt with a variety of sexual matters, and which the domestic courts felt encouraged sexual promiscuity, corresponded to a pressing social need even though the book freely circulated in other countries, and in some parts of the United Kingdom.

Thus, not only has the Court accepted that the protection of public morality and the sensibilities of others are legitimate aims for the purpose of Article 10(2), it has also made it clear that each member state has a wide discretion in deciding what laws to adopt and how to apply them.[237] This approach is also evident in *Müller* v *Switzerland*.[238] In this case several paintings, which portrayed various unnatural sexual acts, crudely depicted in large format, had been displayed in an art exhibition and were seized by the authorities. The applicants, the artists and promoters, were subsequently prosecuted and fined for displaying obscene materials and the paintings were held to be examined only by specialists. The paintings were returned to the owners eight years later. The applicants claimed that this amounted to an unjustified interference with their Article 10 rights. The European Court held that offensive and indecent material could be regulated by domestic law, provided it caused more than mere shock to the public. In the present case it was not unreasonable for the domestic courts to find that the paintings were likely to 'grossly offend the sense of sexual propriety of persons of ordinary sensibility'. The proceedings therefore fell within the state's margin of appreciation as being necessary in a democratic society and accordingly there had been no violation of Article 10.

The Court and Commission thus have also given little protection to hardcore pornography, particularly where it is likely to be viewed by unwitting or vulnerable individuals. In *Hoare* v *United Kingdom*[239] the applicants' convictions for obscenity for distributing hardcore pornographic videos was found not to be in violation of Article 10, primarily because there was an (unintended) risk that they may have fallen into the hands of young and vulnerable persons. However, in this case, the European Commission of Human Rights also noted the lack of any artistic merit in the articles, which might have counterbalanced their harmful effect. Thus, a greater tolerance has been shown in cases where the adult audience willingly encounters such material.[240]

A 'hands-off' approach was also evident in the admissibility decision in *Marlow* v *United Kingdom*,[241] albeit in a different context. In this case the applicant had published a book about the cultivation and production of cannabis. He was convicted for incitement to commit an offence under the Misuse of Drugs Act 1971, the prosecution case being that the book had been published as a grower's guide. The applicant claimed that the prosecution and conviction

---

[236] (1976) 1 EHRR 737. The case is dealt with in detail in the case study in chapter 2 of this text.
[237] See Fenwick and Phillipson, *Media Freedom under the Human Rights Act* (OUP 2006), pages 410–22.
[238] (1988) 13 EHRR 212.
[239] [1997] EHRLR 678.
[240] *Scherer* v *Switzerland* (1994) 18 EHRR 276.
[241] Application No 42015/98, decision of the European Court, 5 December 2000.

constituted an unjustified interference with his right to freedom of expression. In particular, he pleaded that the book was a genuine contribution to the debate about the legalisation of cannabis and that he had made it clear that the growing of cannabis was unlawful. In rejecting his application as manifestly ill-founded, the European Court held that the prosecution and conviction pursued a legitimate aim and that in the circumstances it was a necessary and proportionate act. The decision to maintain the offence of incitement to produce cannabis fell within the state's margin of appreciation and thus there had been no violation of Article 10. Although the case was not directly concerned with the law on public morality, the decision reflects the Court's willingness to offer each state a wide area of discretion with regard to the control of free speech that challenges domestic legal morals.[242]

However, the Court has displayed less tolerance to the interference of indecent speech when such expression serves a political purpose and constitutes political satire. Thus, in *Kunstler* v *Austria*[243] it was held that there had been a violation of Article 10 when the applicants' painting – depicting several outrageous sexual acts being performed by political and religious figures – was the subject of an injunction and an action for damages brought by a politician who claimed to have been debased by the painting. The European Court held that although states were given a wide margin of appreciation with respect to obscene and blasphemous material, in this case the painting had depicted political satire and that the law and the victims should be more tolerant of such depictions. It should be noted, however, that the reasons for interference were not based on public morals, but on the desire to protect individuals from attacks on their reputation and honour. The decision should not, therefore, be taken as questioning the stance adopted by the Court in cases such as *Muller* (above).

Questions

What purposes do the domestic laws of obscenity and indecency serve?

To what extent is the domestic law on obscenity and indecency compatible with Article 10 of the European Court of Human Rights?

Obscenity and indecency and EC law

In addition to complying with the standards laid down in the European Convention and its case law, the domestic law of obscenity and indecency must also comply with European Community law. Restrictions placed on the importation and distribution of such material might conflict with Article 28 of the EC Treaty, which prohibits quantitative restrictions on imports, although Article 30 of the same treaty allows such restrictions if they are justified on grounds of, *inter alia*, public morality. Thus, the domestic authorities are allowed to use their powers to seize such material,[244] provided such laws are regarded as proportionate to the legitimate aim of protecting public morals. In addition, it seems that the European Court of Justice will allow each member state a relatively wide margin of appreciation in determining the requirements of public morality in accordance with its own values.[245]

---

[242] Thus, the same decision would have been expected had the applicant been prosecuted under obscenity legislation, as in *R v Skirving*, above.

[243] (2008) 47 EHRR 5.

[244] See s.49 of the Customs and Excise Management Act 1979, which allows the authorities to seize obscene or indecent articles.

[245] *R v Henn and Darby* [1981] AC 850.

However, such restrictions must be necessary and proportionate and must not impose any additional restrictions on the articles simply because they are being imported. In *Conegate* v *Commissioner of Customs and Excise*[246] the European Court of Justice had to determine the legality of the seizure of life-size rubber dolls and other material and objects by customs authorities. The Court held that the seizure was unlawful because although they had been seized for the legitimate aim of public morality, the products in question were not liable to prosecution under the Obscene Publications Act 1959, being, at the most, indecent rather than obscene. The European Court of Justice held that a member state could not rely on grounds of public morality to prohibit the importation of goods where the same goods can be manufactured freely on its territory. This was the case even though those goods may have been subject to other restrictions prohibiting the sending or displaying of indecent material. In other words, EC law insists on the equal application of the law to all EC nationals, and since that decision the authorities only seize material that falls within the Obscene Publications Act: that is, material that tends to deprave and corrupt.[247]

Summary of obscenity and indecency law

The current laws on obscenity and indecency can be criticised on several grounds.[248] First, prosecution policies appear to be inconsistent, often depending on individual and subjective complaints and varying from district to district, and offering little guidance as to what should be prosecuted. Secondly, and related to the first criticism, the nature of obscenity and indecency offences is vague and it is often difficult for publishers to foresee conviction. Thirdly, there is still some uncertainty as to the aims of the various legal provisions and, most importantly, whether those aims are legitimate in terms of justifying the control of offensive speech. Fourthly, despite judicial guidance, the test of obscenity under the obscenity provisions is capable of being confused with indecency by jurors and magistrates, making interpretation and application of the law potentially subjective. Fifthly, most of the laws do not provide for a public interest or public good defence so as to balance the argument against censorship or other regulation. In particular, defences of public good, when available, can be circumvented by prosecution for other offences and the use of forfeiture proceedings.

The Williams Report into obscenity in 1977[249] concentrated on these aspects of the domestic law and made two principal recommendations: first, that conduct should not be suppressed by the law unless it can be convincingly demonstrated to carry a real prospect of harm to others; and secondly, that soft-core sex magazines should be taken from the counters of corner newsagents and placed on sale, together with pornography of much harder core, in soberly fronted 'adults only' sex shops.[250] These recommendations confront the nebulous nature of obscenity and indecency laws, and would support offensive and shocking speech unless it

---

[246] [1987] QB 254.

[247] In *R* v *Bow Street Magistrates, ex parte Noncyp* [1990] 1 QB 123, it was held that the authorities could seize imported material under the customs legislation even though the defendants could not rely on the public interest defence under s.4 of the Obscene Publications Act 1959.

[248] For a critical overview of obscene (and blasphemous) libel, see Kearns, The Ineluctable Decline of Obscene Libel: Exculpation and Abolition [2007] Crim LR 667.

[249] Williams Committee, *Obscenity and Film Censorship: Committee Report* 1979, Cmnd 7772.

[250] These are regulated by the Local Government (Miscellaneous Provisions) Act 1982, providing local councils with the power to grant licences for such premises. The courts are prepared to give the authorities a wide area of discretion in this respect: *Miss Behavin' Ltd* v *Belfast City Council*, [2007] WLR 1420.

could be shown to have an actual or real potential for causing harm,[251] thus excluding from the law's reach publications that cause shock or offence to individuals or which are an attack on some aspect of public morality. The proposal regarding the display of soft-core pornography has now been mainly taken over by a change in culture and morality, with most such publications being openly displayed in regular outlets. With regard to hardcore pornography, and other such depictions of violence, the recommendation respects the right of individuals to have access to such materials, but does not resolve the question of when the publication and reading of such materials causes harm to individuals or to society as a whole. As stated above, the new offence of possessing extreme pornographic images only partly reflect these proposals as the offence does not require a clear link between such possession and the committing of criminal acts.

Although there are many aspects of our obscenity and indecency laws which are open to question, the general conclusion is that they are compatible with the European Convention on Human Rights and the relevant case law of the Court and the Commission, which provides states with a wide margin of appreciation. Consequently, despite relatively regular calls for legal changes to be made in this area, it is likely that the law will continue in its present form, offering a great deal of flexibility and discretion to the enforcement agencies, and to courts and juries. Thus, the potentially wide and unruly scope of the law will be limited by modern attitudes to matters of taste and decency, leaving a wider range of material, which in the past would have been subject to legal action, untouched. This state of affairs is likely to continue so long as the Convention machinery remains reluctant to interfere with the state's decisions in this area.

With regard to the Human Rights Act 1998, there may be occasions in which the court or a jury may need to be mindful of the defendant's Convention rights and of the need to uphold freedom of expression. In theory, for example, judges and juries might restrict convictions to material that depraves and corrupts in the sense of causing likely physical harm, as opposed to corruption of an individual's thoughts. Similarly, the court could use their duty under s.6 of the Act to develop, or abandon, the common law offences of outraging public decency, and corrupting public morals. However, given the wide margin of appreciation allowed under the Convention, and the fact that the law is primarily used against material that has no clear literary or artistic merit,[252] it is unlikely that the Act will give rise to any substantial reinterpretation of the legislation or common law offences. For example, in R v Perrin[253] the Court of Appeal held that the purpose of the Obscene Publications Act 1959 was compatible with the European Convention on Human Rights. In the Court's view the offence of publishing an obscene article was prescribed by law and pursued a legitimate aim for the purpose of Article 10(2). Parliament had been entitled to conclude that prescription was necessary in a democratic society, and apart from the general right to freedom of expression, there was no public interest to be served by permitting a business for profit to supply material that most people would regard as pornographic or obscene. In particular, the fact that the legislation does not require evidence of an identifiable harm did not make the Act incompatible with the notion of freedom of expression.

---

[251] Covering, for example, offences such as those under the Protection of Children Act 1978.
[252] See Edwards, On the Contemporary Application of the Obscene Publications Act 1959 [1998] Crim LR 843.
[253] [2002] EWCA Crim 747.

Questions
Should existing laws on obscenity and indecency be retained?
What suggestions for reform would you propose in order to make those laws more compatible with human rights norms?

The law relating to blasphemy

Although the domestic law of blasphemy and blasphemous libel was abolished by s.79 of the Criminal Justice and Immigration Act 2008,[254] the study of the area is still important in two respects. *First*, as such laws may survive in other European states, the European Court of Human Rights will continue to consider claims alleging that such laws impose a disproportionate interference with freedom of expression. For that reason this chapter examines the relevant case law of the European Court and examines its impact on free speech jurisprudence. *Secondly*, the existence, or absence, of a law of blasphemy in a specific state impacts on the rights of religious followers to defend their faith from attack. Accordingly, in chapter 12 of the text we will examine how the absence of a specific law of blasphemy affects the right of religion under Article 9 of the European Convention; and will include a brief summary of the English law before it was repealed.[255]

Many legal systems will attempt to regulate speech or other actions in order to protect either the tenets of the country's religion, or the sensibilities of the followers of that religion. This may be done by applying the general criminal law, notably the law relating to breach of the peace, against such speech or actions, thus criminalising words or behaviour that threaten public order or safety. Alternatively, or in addition to the above, the state may devise particular blasphemy laws, which apply to speech or actions which attack those public or individual interests and which are regarded as worthy of criminal prosecution. The European Convention permits such laws provided they are necessary and proportionate in relation to a legitimate aim.[256] Equally, it permits the state to operate without such laws, such omission not necessarily being in violation of an individual's right to freedom of religion under the Convention.[257]

The law of blasphemy, or the lack of such law, thus gives rise to two, often related, human rights issues. First, any such law will be a *prima facie* interference with the right of free speech, and thus must be justified under the tests laid down in the Convention; it must be 'prescribed by law', pursue a legitimate aim, and its content and application must be judged as 'necessary in a democratic society'. Accordingly, there must be a sufficiently pressing social need for the law's existence and application, and the law should not impose a disproportionate interference on free speech in its desire to uphold that pressing need. Secondly, as any law of blasphemy should seek to protect, *inter alia*, the rights of freedom of thought, conscience and religion under Article 9 of the Convention, such laws should ensure that those rights are adequately protected. This has given rise to two major concerns: whether the state has a positive duty to pass and enforce blasphemy laws, and whether the domestic law has to provide protection in relation to all religions and all religious tenets enjoyed within their jurisdiction.

---

[254] See Parpworth, The Abolition of the Blasphemy Laws (2008) 172 JP 164.
[255] For an excellent account of this area see Ghandhi and James, The English Law of Blasphemy and the European Convention on Human Rights [1998] EHRLR 430. See also Kearns, The Uncultured God: Blasphemy Law's Reprieve and the Art Matrix [2000] EHRLR 512.
[256] *Otto-Preminger Institute* v *Austria* (1994) 19 EHRR 34; *Wingrove* v *United Kingdom* (1996) 24 EHRR 1.
[257] *Choudhury* v *United Kingdom* (1991) 12 HRLJ 172.

The justification for blasphemy laws

Among the reasons for justifying such laws, the desire to protect the rights of others to freedom of religion and religious enjoyment appears to be the strongest in that it seeks to protect the *fundamental* rights of others. Other reasons, however, are appreciatively weaker. For example, the desire to protect individuals from offence, or even outrage, to their religious sensibilities could be attacked on the basis that such reasons are contrary to free speech, which by its very nature is capable of shocking and offending its audience.[258]

Nevertheless, such reasons have been accepted as valid under the European Convention, particularly where such offence and outrage attacks the enjoyment of the individual's religious rights.[259] Blasphemy laws may also be justified on public interest grounds: to stop an attack on the religious views of society as a whole, blasphemous speech being seen as an attack on society and on public morality. Such reasons are open to attack on two principal grounds. First, it is often very difficult to assess the morality, or religious views, of a particular society and to find a common set of beliefs within that society. Secondly, even if such a consensus is to be found, arguments of self-autonomy and fulfilment militate against the criminalisation of such views merely because they conflict with the common consensus. Finally, such laws may exist to protect public safety and to prevent disorder or crime. Although the English courts have decided that a likely breach of the peace is not an essential requirement in a charge of blasphemy at common law, it is clear that one of the aims of blasphemy law might be to protect the peace and to guard society from the violent consequences of blasphemous speech.[260]

Blasphemy and the European Convention on Human Rights

The English law of blasphemy has been the subject of scrutiny by both the European Court and European Commission of Human Rights, and in each case the law and its application has survived allegations of its incompatibility with the Convention. The question whether domestic blasphemy laws were an unjustifiable interference with freedom of expression was considered in the case of *Gay News v United Kingdom*,[261] where the Commission upheld both the legitimacy and necessity of the law and its application. Indeed, the European Court has indicated that member states would be provided with a wide margin of appreciation in this area. For example, in *Otto-Preminger Institute v Austria*[262] the Court held that the state is better placed than the international judge to assess the need for blasphemy laws and their application in particular circumstances. The applicant, an arts association which ran a cinema, had advertised the showing of a film that depicted God as senile, Jesus as feeble-minded and Mary as a wanton woman. Criminal proceedings were brought against the applicant's manager, and later dropped, but court orders were issued for the seizure of the film, causing the showing of the film to be abandoned. The European Court held that speech causing gratuitous offence may be restricted, and that the concept of blasphemy could not be isolated from the society against which it is being judged, as well as the population where the showings were due to take place, which were strongly Catholic. Accordingly, the Austrian authorities had acted proportionately by

---

[258] *Handyside v United Kingdom* (1976) 1 EHRR 737.

[259] *Gay News v United Kingdom* (1982) 5 EHRR 123.

[260] *R v Lemon* [1979] AC 617. Public order was the basis of the unsuccessful attempt to prosecute the publication and distribution of Salman Rushdie's *Satanic Verses*: *R v Horseferry Road Stipendiary Metropolitan Magistrates, ex parte Siadatan* [1991] 1 QB 260; [1990] 3 WLR 1006.

[261] (1982) 5 EHRR 123.

[262] (1994) 19 EHRR 34.

acting to ensure religious peace in that region and to protect some people from an attack on their religious beliefs in an unwarranted and offensive manner.

This wide margin of appreciation was again evident in *Wingrove v United Kingdom*.[263] W had produced a video entitled *Visions of Ecstasy*, which described the ecstatic and erotic visions of Jesus Christ of a sixteenth-century nun. The British Board of Film Classification Censors had refused to give the video a licence on the basis, *inter alia*, that it would cause outrage at the unacceptable treatment of a sacred subject and would accordingly infringe the criminal law of blasphemy. An appeal to the Video Appeals Committee was dismissed. The applicant claimed that this constituted an unjustified interference with his right to freedom of expression under Article 10 of the Convention. The European Court noted that the British Board had acted under the Video Recordings Act 1984 and the national authorities had to be given a certain degree of flexibility in assessing whether the facts of a particular case came within the inevitably imprecise definition. Further, there was no general uncertainty as to the definition of blasphemy and the applicants could, with appropriate legal advice, have foreseen that certain scenes within the film could fall within the scope of the law. In those circumstances it could not be said that the law did not provide the applicant protection against arbitrary interference and accordingly the restriction was 'prescribed by law'. The Court also held that the interference corresponded to a legitimate aim, the protection of Christians against serious offence in their beliefs, which was a right protected by Article 9 of the Convention, and the fact that the law did not treat all religions alike did not detract from the legitimacy of that aim.

With respect to whether the restriction was necessary in a democratic society, although blasphemy laws were becoming increasingly rare in their application, there was as yet not sufficient common ground in the legal and social orders of the member states to conclude that blasphemy legislation was, in itself, unnecessary in a democratic society and thus incompatible with the Convention. Although there existed little scope for restrictions on political speech, or on questions of public interest, a wider margin of appreciation was generally available to states in relation to matters liable to offend intimate personal convictions in the sphere of morals and religion. However, in the Court's view, that did not preclude final European supervision, which was important given the open-endedness of blasphemy and the risks of arbitrary interferences. The fact that there had been prior restraint called for special scrutiny and made the more important any safeguards inherent in the law of blasphemy: in other words that there had to be a high degree of profanity and insult for there to be a violation of the law. As to the video itself, the Board and the Committee had noted that the video portrayed the crucified Christ in an act of overt sexuality in such imagery as to focus on the erotic feelings of the audience, rather than the character, a trait prevalent in pornography. Further, there had been no attempt to explore the meaning of that imagery beyond that voyeuristic experience. The reasons given to justify the interference could be considered relevant and sufficient and not arbitrary or excessive. Thus the interference was within the national authorities' margin and necessary in a democratic society.

The European Court has continued its hands-off approach in this area and it is clear that states are still allowed to operate moderate blasphemy laws. Thus, in *IA v Turkey*,[264] the European Court held that there had been no violation of Article 10 when the applicant had been fined for publishing a novel which, *inter alia*, alleged that the prophet Mohammad did not prohibit sexual intercourse with a dead person or a living animal. In the Court's view

---

[263] (1996) 24 EHRR 1.
[264] (2007) 45 EHRR 30.

the book was not merely provocative and shocking but constituted an abusive attack on the Prophet of Islam. Notwithstanding a degree of tolerance of criticism of religious doctrine within Turkish Society, believers could legitimately feel that certain passages of the book constituted an unwarranted and offensive attack on them. In addition the Court noted that the penalties were not disproportionate – the fine was small – and the book had not been seized. In contrast, in *Tatlav* v *Turkey*,[265] it was held that there had been a violation of Article 10 when the applicant had been prosecuted (his one year's sentence being substituted with a fine) when he published a book entitled the *Reality of Islam*, which claimed that religion had the effect of legitimising social injustices in the name of 'God's will'. The Court held that, although the book contained strong criticism of the religion, it did not employ an offensive tone aimed at believers or an abusive attack against sacred symbols. Further the book had been seized four years after its publication and on the basis of an individual complaint. In addition the applicant was faced with the threat of imprisonment, which would have a discouraging effect on authors.[266]

The European Court has also extended this deferential approach to cases where the state imposed bans or other controls on religious advertising. In *Murphy* v *Ireland*[267] it was held that there was no violation of Article 10 when the Irish broadcasting authority upheld domestic law and refused to allow the broadcast of the applicant's video dealing with the historical facts about Christ and evidence of resurrection. The European Court held that the restriction on the applicant's freedom of expression fell within the state's margin of appreciation, particularly as the applicant's advertisement was broadcast on satellite television. The interference was prescribed by law and pursued the legitimate aims of preserving public order and the protection of the rights of others. The authorities were entitled to have regard to the extreme sensitivity of the question of broadcasting of religious advertising in Ireland and to the fact that religion was a divisive issue in Northern Ireland. In coming to that decision the Court noted that there was much more scope for the restriction of religious views, where the margin of appreciation would be wider than in the case of restricting political opinion.

Freedom of speech and national security

The protection of national security is recognised as a legitimate aim by Article 10(2) of the European Convention, which allows freedom of speech to be compromised on grounds of national security, territorial integrity, public safety, the prevention of disorder and crime and the prevention of the disclosure of information received in confidence. All these aims can be related to laws which place restrictions on, and criminalise, speech and other activities which endanger sensitive aspects of government work, and are legitimate provided the restriction is both prescribed by law and necessary and proportionate. So too the case law of the European Convention recognises the need to protect the interests of the state, providing each member state with a relatively wide area of discretion in this area. Thus, the European Court has accepted that it is legitimate for a state to place legal restrictions on specified individuals, and others such

---

[265] Decision of the European Court, 2 May 2006 (Application No 50692/99).

[266] See also *Giniewski* v *France* (2007) 45 EHRR 23, decision of the European Court of Human Rights, 31 January 2006, where it was held that Article 10 had been violated when a journalist had been found guilty of group defamation when he had written an article suggesting that a Catholic doctrine had possible links with anti-Semitism and the origins of the Holocaust.

[267] (2004) 38 EHRR 13.

as the press, in order to safeguard the state from threats, and to promote confidence in sensitive areas of government.[268] For example, in *Leander* v *Sweden*[269] the Court held that the requirements of foreseeability in the special context of national security, in this case the secret controls of national security staff, were not the same as in other fields and that the state's margin of appreciation as to the best means of protecting national security is wide. However, such margin is not absolute, and in *Guja* v *Moldova*[270] it was held that the dismissal of a civil servant for disclosing two letters, not marked as confidential, to the press, alleging interference with criminal proceedings by a politician, was not necessary in a democratic society and thus in violation of Article 10. The public interest in that information was so important that it overrode the needs of confidentiality. Further, the servant had acted in good faith and for no personal interest; thus the punishment was not necessary and proportionate in all the circumstances.

The courts in the United States have, however, taken a more robust approach. In *New York Times* v *United States*[271] the government had sought injunctions against the New York Times to stop the publication of the 'Pentagon Papers', which detailed the government's involvement in Vietnam. The government had contended that such publication, being contrary to national security, was not constitutionally protected, but in rejecting that argument the Supreme Court held that the government had failed to show that publication would, as opposed to could, cause direct, immediate and irreparable harm to the nation. The Court held that in revealing the workings of government that led to the Vietnam War, the newspapers had nobly done precisely that which the founders of the Constitution hoped and trusted they would do. The Constitution tolerated absolutely no prior judicial restraints of the press predicated upon surmise or conjecture, and only allegation and proof that publication must inevitably, directly and immediately cause the occurrence of an event imperilling national security could support the issuing of a restraining order.

Domestic law and national security

Various laws, both civil and criminal, seek to protect national security, and in doing so impinge on the right of freedom of expression.[272] This is done either by imposing criminal liability on specified persons who disclose sensitive information, thus dissuading such persons from communicating information to the press or to the public, or by employing the civil law against such persons or those, including the press, who assist such persons in breaching their duties of confidentiality.[273] In the latter case, the government will seek temporary injunctions to stop the dissemination of this information and the law may, thus, allow prior restraint. Both domestic law and the law of the European Convention will need to consider the scope and legitimacy of these restrictions. In particular, human rights norms insist that the law is being used for a legitimate purpose – that there is evidence of a real and tangible

---

[268] *Observer and Guardian* v *United Kingdom* (1991) 14 EHRR 153.

[269] (1987) 9 EHRR 433.

[270] Application No 14277/04, decision of the Grand Chamber, 12 February 2008.

[271] (1971) 403 US 713.

[272] For a more detailed account of the law, see Bailey, Harris and Ormerod, *Civil Liberties: Cases and Materials* (OUP 2009, 6th edn), chapter 12. See also Whitty, Murphy and Livingstone, *Civil Liberties Law: The Human Rights Act Era* (Butterworths 2001), chapter 7.

[273] The government also rely on 'DA' notices, formerly 'D' notices, whereby the Defence Press and Broadcasting Advisory Committee issue notices agreeing that certain sensitive information will not be published.

harm – and that any restriction, criminal or civil, does not impose a disproportionate interference on individual free speech, and the public's right to know.

Official secrets legislation

The original legislation was passed to deal with various threats of spying and breaches of confidence and at present the majority of regulation is covered in the Official Secrets Act 1989. However, some provisions of the Official Secrets Acts 1911 and 1920 survive,[274] and will be considered here in so far as the provisions impact on freedom of expression or assembly. For example, s.1 of the 1911 Act, covering, *inter alia*, the unauthorised use of uniforms, falsification of reports, and personation, makes it an offence for any person for any purpose prejudicial to the safety or interests of the state to communicate[275] any official secret code word, password, sketch plan or other document or information which is calculated to be or might be or is intended to be directly or indirectly useful to an enemy.[276]

The section has a very wide potential, extending well beyond what might be regarded as clear acts of espionage.[277] In addition, the courts have adopted a strict approach in this area, and in *Chandler v DPP*[278] the House of Lords held that whether an activity was 'prejudicial to the interests of the state' was normally to be determined by reference to the views of the present government and not by the application of any objective standard. In this case the defendants had climbed over a perimeter fence of a US airbase in order to protest against nuclear weapons. They were charged with entering a prohibited place for a purpose prejudicial to the interests of the state, but claimed that their purpose, to safeguard the country against the threat of nuclear weapons, could not be regarded as prejudicial. Rejecting that claim, their Lordships held that the question was not a justiciable one and that with regard to the disposition of the armed forces the executive would be given an exclusive discretion. It was also held that the motive of the protestors was irrelevant for the purpose of establishing liability. The government's view was that it was in the interests of the state that the airfield be there and that those activities should not be disrupted. The protestors had entered the place with the intention of disruption and their motive in doing so was not relevant. Although the courts have continued to adopt this strict approach with respect to official secrets legislation in the post-Human Rights Act era,[279] it is very questionable whether the protestors' conviction could be regarded as necessary and proportionate in accordance with Article 10 of the European Convention.[280]

---

[274] Section 7 of the 1920 Act makes it an offence to attempt to commit an offence under the 1911 and 1920 Acts, to aid and abet and to do any act preparatory to the commission of such an offence. The 1920 Act will not be discussed in this section.

[275] Under s.12 of the Act, communication includes the transfer or transmission of information, and does not require the recipient to digest the information. This applies equally to the offences under the Official Secrets Act 1989, considered below.

[276] Information can be useful to the enemy even if it is not transmitted directly to an enemy of the state: *R v Parrott* (1913) 8 Cr App R 186.

[277] The potential impact is tempered by the requirement, under s.8, for proceedings to be initiated by the Attorney-General, and the fact that the provision is rarely used outside real cases of espionage.

[278] [1964] AC 763.

[279] *R v Shayler* [2002] 2 WLR 754, considered below.

[280] See *DPP v Percy, The Times*, 21 January 2002, considered in chapter 10, although that case was not concerned with official secrets legislation.

The Official Secrets Act 1989

The provisions of this Act relevant to freedom of expression were formerly contained in s.2 of the Official Secrets Act 1911, which made it an offence to disclose any official information without lawful authority. Official information covered any information acquired by a Crown servant in the course of their work, and liability was established automatically, irrespective of the nature or content of the information or of any potential damage caused by its disclosure.[281] This blanket liability caused concern among civil libertarians and in 1985 the law was discredited when a jury acquitted Clive Ponting, a senior civil servant, when he had been charged under s.2 for passing on unauthorised information relating to the sinking of the *General Belgrano* during the Falklands war. The trial judge directed the jury that he should be convicted and that his public duty to inform the public on matters of public interest could not excuse his specific duty under his contract. However, the jury acquitted, and soon afterwards the government published proposals for the reform of the law in this area.[282]

The 1989 Act improves the old law in two material respects. First, it creates particular categories of information that might attract liability for specified persons.[283] Secondly, a person will only be liable where the disclosure of the information would be damaging to those interests. The Act does not, however, create a public interest defence and, unlike the law of confidentiality (see below), does not provide a specific defence of prior publication where the information is already in the public domain. The Act now creates four categories of information where the disclosure will be an offence if shown to be damaging: security and intelligence (s.1);[284] defence (s.2);[285] international relations (s.3);[286] and crime and special investigation powers, including information relating to the interception of communications and activities authorised under warrant under specified legislation (s.4). The latter category covers any information or document the disclosure of which would, or if unauthorised would be likely to, result in either the commission of an offence; the facilitation of an escape from legal custody or the doing of an act prejudicial to the safekeeping of persons in custody; or the impeding of the prevention or detection of offences or the apprehension or prosecution of suspected offenders.

In the case of s.1 of the Act, a disclosure by a member or ex-member of the intelligence or security services (or a person who has been notified that he is subject to this provision) constitutes an offence irrespective of any damage, or likely damage, caused.[287] However, in the case of disclosure by a person who is or has been a Crown servant or government contractor,

---

[281] *R v Crisp and Homewood* (1919) 82 JP 121.

[282] *Reform of Section 2 of the Official Secrets Act 1911* (CM 408, 1988).

[283] The sections apply to a person who is or has been a member of the security and intelligence services, or who is otherwise notified that they are subject to the section (s.1); and to persons who are or have been a Crown servant or government contractor and who have had access to the relevant information or document (sections 1–4).

[284] Defined in s.1(9) of the Act as the work of, or in support of, the security and intelligence services and would cover the activities of bodies such as MI5 and MI6.

[285] Defined in s.2(4) as including the size, organisation, deployment, operations and training of the armed forces; its weapons and other equipment; defence policy and strategy and military planning and intelligence; and plans and measures for the maintenance of essential supplies and services needed in time of war.

[286] Defined in s.3(5) as the relations between states, between international organisations or between one or more states and such organisations, including any matter relating to a state other than the UK or to an international organisation which is capable of affecting the relations of the UK with another state or such organisation.

[287] As in the case of David Shayler, see below. Thus, defences of prior publication, or 'innocuous' publications, available in the laws of confidentiality and contempt, do not apply under the Act.

the disclosure is regarded as damaging if it either causes damage to the work of, or any part of, the security and intelligence service, or it is information that is such that its unauthorised disclosure would be likely to cause damage. The section also applies where the disclosure or document is of a description or class the unauthorised disclosure of which would be likely to have that effect, thus retaining an element of contents liability evident in the previous legislation. This aspect of the section is vulnerable to attack under the Human Rights Act 1998, particularly where there is no evidence of any harm or likely harm caused by the disclosure. In such a case the courts will have to decide whether the special status of government employees justifies such a wide provision.

With respect to the areas in sections 2–4 of the Act, a disclosure of information relating to defence is regarded as damaging if it has damaged, or is likely to damage, things such as the capability of the armed forces to carry out their tasks, leads to loss of life, or injury to members of the armed forces, or causes serious damage to the equipment or installation of those forces. Section 3 of the Act, covering information and documents relating to international relations, adopts the test of whether disclosure endangered the interest stated in the section, or where disclosure is likely to have that effect. Notably, s.3(3) provides that likely damage might be assumed from the fact that the information or document was confidential, or with respect to its nature or contents. As s.4 of the Act defines most categories of information in respect of the effect of such disclosure, the section does not further define damaging disclosures. However, s.4(3) of the Act states that the section also applies to information relating to interception of communications and activities authorised under warrant under various specified pieces of legislation, and in this respect, liability is imposed irrespective of any real or perceived harm.

Generally, the Act only applies to specified persons and its provisions might, therefore, be justified on the basis of the special relationship that members of security and intelligence services, or persons such as civil servants, have with their employers. However, the Act does apply to the public generally and can engage liability of such persons and, of course, of the press. Section 5 of the Act covers information resulting from unauthorised disclosures of information entrusted in confidence, and thus in certain cases further disclosure by an individual or the press will constitute an offence. This includes where the material was acquired as a result of a disclosure in contravention of s.1 of the 1911 Act, above; or acquired as a result of an unauthorised disclosure by a Crown servant or government contractor; or where it was entrusted to the recipient in confidence (or with a reasonable expectation of confidence) by such a person (or acquired as a result of an unauthorised disclosure at some stage by a person to whom it was so entrusted).[288]

Defences

Although the Act does not provide a general public interest defence, there are a number of defences and other safeguards in the legislation that might save its provisions from attack under the Human Rights Act or a challenge before the European Court of Human Rights.

---

[288] To be liable under s.5, the discloser must know, or have reasonable cause to believe, that it has been communicated in breach of s.1 of the 1911 Act, or that it is otherwise protected under, and damaging within, the 1989 Act. However, with respect to s.4 information, there is no need to prove such, or to show that the information was damaging, although the discloser must be aware or have reasonable grounds to believe that the material was protected under that section.

First, a person charged under the Act must be aware of the nature of the material and that its disclosure would be damaging, although the burden of proof in such a case is, ostensibly, on the person pleading the defence.[289] Secondly, s.7 of the Act lays down a procedure for authorised disclosures, and then s.7(4) of the 1989 Act provides that it is a defence for a person charged under the Act to prove that at the time of the alleged offence he believed that he had lawful authority to make the disclosure in question and had no reasonable cause to believe otherwise. Section 7(1) states that where the disclosure is by a Crown servant (or a person who is notified for the purposes of s.1 of the Act, above), a disclosure is made with lawful authority if, and only if, it is made in accordance with his official duty. It is important to note that this means his duty as a civil servant, and not as part of his general duty to the public interest, and accordingly s.7 does not include a general public interest defence.[290]

The compatibility of the Official Secrets Act 1989 was called into question in the case of *R v Shayler*.[291] The case raised a number of issues regarding the scope of sections 1 and 4 of the Act and, specifically, whether there was room for a 'public interest' defence to such charges. The case is detailed in the case study below, but for present purposes the House of Lords held that it was not possible to imply such a defence and, equally significantly, that the provisions were compatible with Article 10 of the European Convention on Human Rights.

CASE STUDY

R v Shayler [2002] 2 WLR 754

This case concerned a conflict between the right to freedom of expression and national security. It is an example of how freedom of expression can be compromised for the interests of the state and public good, and involved the courts in conducting a balancing exercise between those interests. The case also raises the question of the power of the courts to declare legislation incompatible with Convention rights, thus raising issues of parliamentary sovereignty and the proper constitutional role of the courts in the protection of human rights.

The defendant, a former member of the security service, was charged with unlawful disclosure of documents and information, contrary to sections 1 and 4 of the Official Secrets Act 1989. Section 1 of the Act makes it an offence for a person who is or who has been a member of the security and intelligence services to disclose any information or document relating to security and intelligence which is or has been in his possession by virtue of his membership of or work with such services, and s.4 of the Act makes it an offence for such a person to disclose any information document or other article, which, *inter alia*, relates to information obtained by reason of the interception of communications under the

---

[289] See *R v Keogh* [2007] 1 WLR 1500, examined in chapter 7 of this text, at pages 341–2.
[290] Section 7(2) states that with respect to a government contractor a disclosure is authorised only if it is made in accordance with an official authorisation for the purpose of his functions. With respect to any disclosure by any other person, s.7(3) provides that it must be made to a Crown servant for the purpose of his functions as such, or in accordance with an official authorisation.
[291] [2002] 2 WLR 754.

Interception of Communications Act 1985, or information obtained under the authority of the Security Services Act 1989 or the Intelligence Services Act 1994. The disclosures, which consisted of the disclosure of various secret documents to the press, which were later published as newspaper articles, did not comply with s.7(3) of the Act, which provides for a person to apply for permission to make an authorised disclosure.

The defendant had alleged that the security services had been involved in a plot to kill a head of state and also made allegations of gross incompetence relating to the service, and therefore asserted that the disclosures were in the public interest. At a preliminary hearing the judge ruled that no public interest defence was available to the defendant under either s.1 or s.4, and that those provisions were compatible with Article 10 of the European Convention on Human Rights, which guarantees freedom of expression. The judge then considered the defendant's defences of necessity and duress of circumstances, and held that although the conventional defence of duress was, in theory, available to a former member of the security service, the defence of necessity or duress of circumstances was not available. On appeal to the Court of Appeal ([2001] 1 WLR 2206), it was held that the judge had erred in deciding that the defences of necessity and duress of circumstances were not available to the defendant. Nevertheless, the Court of Appeal held that the judge had been entitled to make the rulings under the Act. In the Court of Appeal's view, there was no material before the court to suggest that such a defence was open to the defendants on the facts, and accordingly the judge's decision should be upheld.

The defendant appealed to the House of Lords on the following points:

1 Whether the offence under s.1 of the 1989 Act is committed, or is subject to a defence (either at common law or as a result of the coming into force of the Human Rights Act 1998) that (a) the disclosure was necessary in the public interest to avert damage to life or limb, or serious damage to property; or (b) to expose serious and pervasive illegality in the obtaining of warrants and surveillance of suspected persons.

2 Whether the offence of disclosing information obtained under warrants issued under the Interception of Communications Act 1985, contrary to s.4(1) of the 1989 Act is not committed, or is subject to a defence as claimed in point 1 above.

3 Whether an 'extended' defence based on the doctrine of necessity is available to a defendant charged under sections 1 and 4 of the 1989 Act and, if so, what is the scope of this extended defence.

The House of Lords held unanimously that the appeal should be dismissed and that the judge's decision was correct. Giving sections 1 and 4 of the 1989 Act their plain and ordinary meaning, and reading them in the context of the Act as a whole, it was plain that a defendant prosecuted under those provisions was not entitled to be acquitted if he showed that it was, or he believed that it was, in the public or national interest to make the disclosure in question. The provisions of the Act imposed no obligation on the prosecution to prove that the disclosure was not in the public interest and gave the defendant no opportunity to show that the disclosure was in the public interest or that he thought it was.

Further, those sections of the Act were compatible with Article 10 of the European Convention on Human Rights. The right to freedom of expression was not absolute and the broad language of Article 10(1) was qualified by Article 10(2), provided the restriction was necessary in a democratic society in the interests of national security. Although there could be no doubt that those provisions restricted the defendant's *prima facie* right to freedom of expression, the need to preserve the secrecy of the information relating to intelligence and military operations in order to counter terrorism, criminal activity, hostile activity and subversion had been recognised by the case law of the European Convention in relation to complaints made under Article 10 (*Leander* v *Sweden* (1987) 9 EHRR 433; *Murray* v *United Kingdom* (1995) 19 EHRR 193; *Klass* v *Federal Republic of Germany* (1978) 2 EHRR 214). There was much domestic authority pointing to the need for a security and intelligence service to be secure. The commodity in which such a service dealt was secret information and if the service is not secure those working against the interests of the state would be alerted and able to take evasive action. Further, the service's own agents might be unmasked, members of the service would feel unable to rely on each other, and those upon whom the service relied as sources of information would feel unable to rely on their identity remaining secret. However, the courts would insist on adequate safeguards to ensure that the restriction did not exceed what was necessary to achieve the end in question. The acid test was whether, in all the circumstances of the case, the interference with the Convention right prescribed by national law was greater than was required to meet the legitimate object that the state sought to achieve.

Assessing the Act in accordance with those principles, their Lordships noted that the ban on disclosure of such information imposed by the Act on a former member of the service was not absolute; rather it was a ban on disclosure without lawful authority, and a ban subject to two conditions. First, the former member might, under s.7(3)(a) make disclosure as appropriate to the staff counsellor, the Attorney-General, the Director of Public Prosecutions, the Commissioner of Metropolitan Police, the Prime Minister and other ministers, if he had anxieties relating to the work of the service which it had not been possible to allay through the ordinary processes of staff–management relations, or concerns of the lawfulness of what the service had done or was doing, or concerns about misbehaviour, irregularity, maladministration or incompetence. Secondly, if, following such disclosure, effective action was not taken or there remained facts which should in the public interest be revealed to a wider audience, the member might under s.7(3)(b) seek official authorisation to make disclosure to such an audience. Consideration of such a request should take into account the importance of freedom of expression and the need for any restriction to be necessary, responsive to a pressing social need and proportionate. Giving the leading speech, Lord Bingham held that although a sweeping, blanket ban admitting of no exceptions would be inconsistent with the general right of freedom of expression under Article 10(1) of the European Convention, and would not survive the rigorous and particular scrutiny required to give effect to Article 10(2), the procedures contained in s.7 of the Act provided sufficient and effective safeguards.

Further if the request were refused, the member is entitled to seek judicial review, and it would be expected that the courts would apply a rigorous review of the decision, in accordance with the approach set out by Lord Steyn in *R* v *Secretary of State for the Home Department, ex parte Daly* ([2002] 2 AC 532). Their Lordships also noted that by virtue of s.9(1) of the 1989 Act prosecutions could only be brought with the consent of the Attorney-General. Accordingly, those procedures, properly applied, provided sufficient and effective safeguards to ensure that unlawfulness and irregularity could be reported to those with the power and duty to take effective action, that the power to withhold authorisation to publish was not abused, and that proper discussions were not stifled. A member or former member of the security service should avail himself of those procedures and a former member, prosecuted for making an unauthorised disclosure, could not claim that if he had made a disclosure under s.7(3)(a) no notice or action would have been taken, or that if he had sought authorisation under s.7(3)(b) it would have been refused. The special position of those employed in the security and intelligence services, and the special nature of their work imposed duties and responsibilities on them within the meaning of Article 10(2) of the European Convention. If a person who had given a binding under-taking of confidentiality sought to be relieved, even in part, from that undertaking, he must seek authorisation and, if so advised, challenge any refusal. If that refusal was upheld by the courts, it must, however reluctantly, be upheld. Accordingly, sections 1 and 4 of the Act were compatible with Article 10 of the Convention.

Questions

1 How important was S's right to freedom of expression in these circumstances and what aspects of freedom of expression were raised by the case?
2 What is the rationale behind prosecutions under the Official Secrets legislation?
3 Was there a legitimate aim in preventing the speech in this particular case?
4 How does the decision accord with the role of the courts in protecting freedom of expression?
5 Should different considerations apply when freedom of speech threatens national security?
6 Do you think that the decision strikes a reasonable balance between freedom of expression and the protection of the national interest? In particular, do you think that the safeguards contained in s.7 of the Act are adequate to protect freedom of speech?*
7 Do you think that the decision is consistent with the Human Rights Act 1998?
8 Do you think the decision strikes a correct balance between the role of the domestic courts in protecting individual rights, and the power of parliament to pass restrictive legislation?
9 Is the decision consistent with the case law of the European Convention on Human Rights in this area?
10 In particular, if the case was taken before the European Court of Human Rights would the Court show deference to the domestic legislation and its application?

* Note: In *A* v *B*, *The Times*, 5 August 2008, the Court of Appeal held that the Investigatory Powers Tribunal had exclusive jurisdiction under s.65 of the Regulation of Investigatory Powers Act 2000 to hear a challenge to the refusal of the Director of the Security Service to consent to the publication of a book detailing an employee's work for the service.

Official secrets and the law of confidentiality

As an alternative to bringing prosecutions under the official secrets legislation, government bodies often resort to the civil law to protect their interests. Thus, it is often possible for the government to rely on the duty of confidentiality owed by its servants to prohibit the publication of information that is in breach of that duty, and such a duty can be imposed on a third party who intends to disclose it. In addition, a person may be guilty of contempt of court if they publish information that is already the subject of a pending confidentiality claim.[292] As temporary, interim injunctions are available in such cases, the advantage of such actions is that the government can restrict the publication of the information in advance by means of prior restraint.

The government may also employ the law of confidentiality, and breach of contract, to ensure that those who breach their duties as civil servants do not profit from any publication of unauthorised information. In *Attorney-General v Blake*[293] the House of Lords held that the government was entitled to account for the profits made by an officer in selling his memoirs. The applicant's claim before the European Court was subsequently declared inadmissible by the European Court of Human Rights. In *Blake v United Kingdom*[294] the European Court held that the decision of the House of Lords was sufficiently foreseeable to be prescribed by law and the order for profits was not disproportionate. Distinguishing its decision in *Observer and Guardian v United Kingdom*,[295] the Court held that even if the information that he published in 1990 was not confidential at that time, there were strong reasons to sanction him for divulging that information.[296]

The law of confidence is used in private law to protect various commercial and privacy interests, but it can also be used by public bodies, including the government, bringing into play fundamental issues of press freedom and the public's right to know versus national security.[297] The law of confidentiality was used in the 'Spycatcher' litigation – *Attorney-General v Guardian Newspapers (No 2)*.[298] This case confirmed that confidentiality could be used to restrain the publication of government information, but equally significantly the House of Lords held that a public body could only maintain an injunction so as to protect confidential information if they could prove that there was an overriding public interest justifying an interference with freedom of expression. Further, if information had entered the public domain it could no longer be the basis of an injunction to preserve confidentiality.[299]

When the case proceeded to the European Court of Human Rights – *Observer and Guardian v United Kingdom*[300] – the European Court held that the granting of the injunctions in the first period of the litigation (before the book was widely available) was necessary in a democratic society to preserve both national security and the Attorney-General's rights in relation to the full trial. The domestic courts had recognised that there was a conflict between two public interests and had weighed all relevant considerations carefully. Further, the newspapers had not

---

[292] *Attorney-General v Times Newspapers* [1991] 2 All ER 398, discussed in chapter 9 of this text.

[293] [2000] 4 All ER 385.

[294] (2007) 44 EHRR 29.

[295] (1991) 14 EHRR 153, considered below.

[296] However, the Court did find a violation of Article 6 with respect to the length of the civil proceedings. See chapter 7 of this text, page 336.

[297] See, for example, *Attorney-General v Jonathan Cape Ltd* [1976] QB 752, discussed in chapter 9 at page 462 of this text.

[298] [1990] 1 AC 109. The case concerned the publication by Peter Wright, a former intelligence employee, of his book *Spycatcher*, which gave details of certain undercover operations. The book had been published in the United States and various parts of the world, but was still made the subject of injunctions. The injunction proceedings were dealt with in two stages – pre-publication and post-publication.

[299] See also *Attorney-General v Times Newspapers Ltd* [2001] 1 WLR 885, where it was held that a newspaper did not have to prove that the information was already in the public domain. That, in the Court's judgment, would place too heavy a burden on the press and would thus constitute an unjustified interference with free speech and freedom of the press.

[300] (1991) 14 EHRR 153.

been subjected to a blanket ban on publication of material relating to the affair, provided they did not repeat this particular source. However, the injunctions granted after the information entered the public domain were unnecessary and disproportionate. In particular, the promotion of the efficiency and reputation of the security service was not in itself a sufficient reason to justify the interference with freedom of expression. The injunctions prevented the newspapers from carrying out their right and duty to inform the public about matters, already available elsewhere, which were clearly of great and legitimate public concern.[301]

The House of Lords' judgment was important in establishing that the government had to prove, at the very least, that the disclosure of such information was capable of damaging the public interest, and the principle was later applied in *Lord Advocate* v *Scotsman Publications Ltd and Others*,[302] where the House of Lords held that an injunction or interdict could not lie against a newspaper to prevent further publication when the Crown had conceded that a book of memoirs written by a former MI6 officer did not contain material harmful to national security and where publication had already taken place. However, in both cases the information was already in the public domain and, thus, the courts did not have to decide whether the public interest in the publication of confidential information was more important than the protection of national security. It is suggested that the decision of the European Court of Human Rights in *Observer* v *United Kingdom* indicates that if a threat to national security is a live issue, then the domestic courts would be given a wide margin of appreciation in balancing matters of national security with freedom of expression. Nevertheless, the 'defence' of prior publication is crucial in protecting newspapers against unnecessary injunctions, and it is noticeable that such latitude is not available when proceedings are brought under the official secrets legislation.

Despite deference in this area, there is evidence from the European Court that the prosecution of journalists for breaches of official secrets legislation needs to be strictly necessary and proportionate. For example, in *Stoll* v *Switzerland*,[303] the Court held that there had been a violation of Article 10 when the applicant had been fined for publishing an official document on holocaust compensation, which had been drawn up by an ambassador and received by the applicant in breach of confidence. In the Court's view, although there was a need to protect the work of the diplomatic corps, it had not been demonstrated that the disclosure of the government's strategy concerning the assets of holocaust victims and Switzerland's role in the Second World War was capable of prejudicing interests that were so precious that they outweighed freedom of expression in a democratic society. Similarly, in *Dammann* v *Switzerland*,[304] it was held that there had been a violation of Article 10 when a journalist had been prosecuted and fined for inciting a civil servant to disclose an official secret: the journalist had asked an administrative assistant to tell him whether a list of suspects of a recent robbery had any previous criminal convictions and she had supplied that information in breach of official secrecy law. The Court held that the robbery was a matter of great public interest and debate and, vitally, that the information in question could have been obtained by other means, such as consulting law reports or press records. These cases should not, however, be

---

[301] See also *Dupuis and Others* v *France*, decision of the European Court, 7 June 2007, where it was held that a prosecution for publishing a book which disclosed information received in confidence was disproportionate, as much of the information had already been made public and had attracted wide public debate.

[302] [1990] 1 AC 812.

[303] (2007) 44 EHRR 53. Upheld by the Grand Chamber (2008) 47 EHRR 59.

[304] Application No 77551/01, decision of the European Court, 25 April 2006.

taken as an indication of the European Court's reluctance to validate appropriate sanctions, including prior restraint, where there is potential for damage to national security.

Questions

How does domestic law seek to control speech which endangers national security?
Are those laws compatible with Article 10 of the European Convention?

Prisoners and freedom of expression

Article 10 of the European Convention on Human Rights provides that everyone has the right of freedom of expression, subject to the restrictions laid out in Article 10(2), which permits interference provided such interference is prescribed by law and necessary in a democratic society for achieving one of the legitimate aims listed therein. In this context the prison authorities will commonly rely on public safety or the protection of the rights of others, or more generally, on the prevention of disorder or crime, attempting to justify restrictions with the prisoner's correspondence and speech on the basis of good order and discipline within the prison.

With respect to Convention case law the majority of cases concerning prisoners' expression have been dealt with under Article 8 of the Convention.[305] However, there is some case law under Article 10 and there have been cases where the Court or Commission has specifically addressed the prisoner's freedom of expression under Article 10. For example, in *T v United Kingdom*,[306] it was held that there had been an unjustified interference with Article 10 when the prison authorities had placed a blanket ban on him sending his private writings out of prison. Again in *Bamber v United Kingdom*,[307] the European Commission held that there had been an interference with the prisoner's right of free speech when a prison regulation had been introduced prohibiting prisoners from talking directly to the media. On the facts, however, the Commission held that the interference was justified within Article 10(2) for the purpose of the prevention of crime and disorder, although it stated that the fact the exercise of that right would have caused distress to the prisoner's victim and their families was not justification in itself.

Although the Court and Commission has offered a wide area of discretion to the authorities, accepting that the prison regime warrants restrictions that would be regarded as impermissible outside the prison context,[308] it has accepted that the prisoner enjoys a qualified right to freedom of expression, and that such right can only be disturbed by legitimate and necessary restrictions. For example, in *Yankov v Bulgaria*,[309] the European Court held that a sanction of seven days' solitary confinement for writing defamatory comments about the state and the

---

[305] In *Silver v United Kingdom* (1983) 5 EHRR 347, the European Court held that it was unnecessary to pursue a further examination of the issue of freedom of expression, that right being guaranteed in Article 8.

[306] (1987) 49 DR 5.

[307] Decision of the European Commission of Human Rights, 11 September 1997.

[308] For example, in *McFeeley and Others v United Kingdom* (1981) 20 DR 44, the Commission held that it was permissible to restrict the prisoner's access to writing materials when there was evidence that the materials themselves were being used for an improper purpose. Further, in *Lowes v United Kingdom* (1992) 59 DR 244, it held that the withholding from the prisoner of a single issue of a magazine was justified on grounds of the prevention of disorder or crime.

[309] (2005) 40 EHRR 36.

judiciary was in violation of Article 10(2) of the Convention. The Court held that the prison authorities had failed to strike a fair balance between freedom of expression and the protection of the authority and reputation of state officials.

Despite the Convention's approach, there still remains some doubt, even in the post-Human Rights Act era, whether the prisoner retains the general right to freedom of expression under Article 10. In *R v Secretary of State for the Home Department, ex parte O'Brien and Simms*,[310] the House of Lords accepted that prisoners could use the right to freedom of expression in order to gain access to the courts and to justice. However, the decision did not uphold a prisoner's general right of freedom of expression. In that case, two prisoners serving life sentences for murder claimed that they had been victims of a miscarriage of justice and wished to conduct oral interviews with two journalists who had taken an interest in their cases. The prison authorities refused them permission, relying on a policy which prohibited face-to-face interviews. In the High Court,[311] LATHAM J accepted that the prisoners enjoyed a right of freedom of expression under Article 10 of the European Convention and that the blanket prohibition could not be justified as a minimum interference with that right. However, on appeal to the Court of Appeal it was held that the restrictions were both lawful and rational.[312] Significantly, the Court of Appeal rejected the idea that the prisoners' freedom of expression was engaged, noting that the case was not concerned with a prisoner's fundamental right of free speech, but rather with the relationship between the journalist and those responsible for the secure administration of prisons. On appeal, the House of Lords held that a blanket ban on interviews between prisoners and journalists was unlawful in that such a policy could deprive a prisoner of his fundamental and basic right to *seek justice*. The House of Lords stressed that the prisoners' claims were not based on the right to free speech in general. Also Lord Steyn was of the opinion that no prisoner could ever be permitted to have interviews with a journalist to publish pornographic material or to give vent to so-called hate speech.[313] Given the purpose of a sentence of imprisonment, a prisoner can also not claim to join in a debate on the economy or on political issues by way of interviews with journalists. In this respect the prisoner's right to free speech is outweighed by deprivation of liberty by the sentence of a court, and the need for discipline and control in prisons.

A more Convention-compliant approach was adopted by the domestic courts in *R (Hirst) v Secretary of State for the Home Department*.[314] Here it was claimed that a general policy insisting that prisoners seek the permission of the prison governor before speaking directly to the press was contrary to Article 10. It was held that the prisoner's right to freedom of expression was

---

[310] [1999] 3 All ER 400. See Foster, Do Prisoners Have the Right to Free Speech? [2000] EHRLR 393.

[311] *The Times*, 17 January 1997. See Foster, Free Speech and the Regulation of Prisoners' Correspondence (1997) NLJ 252.

[312] [1998] 2 All ER 491. The Court of Appeal accepted the reasons for the maintenance of the regulation: that staff ratios did not permit the supervision of the conversations so as to ensure the acceptability of their content and the potential impact of an article based on a live interview on the feelings of the victim.

[313] In *Morton v Governor of HMP Long Lartin* [2003] EWCA Civ 644, it was held that the refusal to allow the prisoner access to pornographic magazines was not in violation of his right to freedom of expression. In refusing permission to apply for judicial review, the Court of Appeal held that the governor had acted lawfully and reasonably and that the claimant had no reasonable prospect of success at trial. The Court stressed that each prison had the power to execute its own policy in accordance with the requirements of good order and discipline. A new Prison Service Order was introduced to allow general prisoners access to hardcore pornography. See Bamber, Prisoners Win the 'Human Right' to Hardcore Porn, *Daily Telegraph*, 10 November 2002.

[314] [2002] 1 WLR 2929. See Foster, Prisoners' Rights, Freedom of Expression and the Human Rights Act [2002] J Civ Libs 53.

not automatically curtailed by the fact of imprisonment itself and that any interference had to be justified by the principle of proportionality. Although the courts suggested that substantial safeguards would need to be put into place by the prison authorities, it held that the inflexible policy whereby the prisoner was denied the right to contact the media by telephone even where the purpose was to comment on matters of legitimate public interest was unlawful. The court confirmed that the right of prisoners to take part in political or economic debates might be curtailed as a necessary part of imprisonment.[315] However, in the present case it was held that talking to the media on matters relating to prisoners' rights did not fall into that restricted category.

After the promise of the decision in *Hirst*, the courts reverted to offering a wide margin of discretion in the case of *R (on the application of Nilsen) v Secretary of State for the Home Department and Others*,[316] a case which confirms the idea that a prisoner might indeed forgo his right to free speech on incarceration. Denis Nilsen had been sentenced to six life sentences for the murders of six young men and in 1992 he began to write an autobiography, detailing the murders, his life in prison and his views on the criminal justice system. The prisoner was informed that the material would be withheld from him on the basis that its publication would contravene paragraph 34(9)(c) of standing Order 5B,[317] the governor concluding that the material was intended for publication and that it did not represent a serious discussion about legitimate matters. The claimant argued that the Standing Order was *ultra vires* the Prison Act 1952 and contrary to Article 10 of the European Convention on Human Rights. The Court of Appeal held that the Home Secretary's powers extended beyond the prison walls and were not confined to good order and discipline within the prison. The Court noted that s.47 of the Prison Act 1952 spoke not only of regulation and management of prisons but control of prisoners. Further, one legitimate aspect of a sentence of imprisonment was to subject the prisoner's freedom to express himself outside the prison to appropriate control. Such a degree of restriction of the rights of prisoners was a justifiable element in imprisonment, not merely to accommodate the orderly running of the prison but as part of the penal objective of deprivation of liberty. Consequently, in considering what restrictions could properly be placed on prisoners, regard could be had to the expectations of right-thinking members of the democracy whose laws had deprived prisoners of their liberty. The Court did not believe that any penal system could readily contemplate a regime in which a rapist or a murderer would be permitted to publish an article glorifying in the pleasure that his crime had caused him. The wording of the regulation drew the line appropriately between what was and what was not acceptable conduct on behalf of a prisoner and fell within the Home Secretary's powers conferred by the Act.

The approach adopted by the Court in *Nilsen* accepts that some restrictions on prisoners' free speech can be lawfully imposed on the ground that the claimant is a prisoner. As a consequence the Court's review of the legality and acceptability of the restriction is weakened and the prison authorities are given a wider area of discretion to achieve the legitimate and

---

[315] Following the speech of Lord Steyn in *Simms*, above.
[316] [2005] 1 WLR 1028.
[317] This provides that 'General correspondence may not contain material which is intended for publication . . . (or if which sent would be likely to be published) if it . . . (c) is about the inmate's crime or past offences or those of others, except where it consists of serious representations about conviction or sentence or forms part of serious comment about crime, the process of justice or the penal system . . .'.

recognised aims of maintaining prison discipline and order.[318] It is submitted that the argument in favour of automatic forfeiture runs counter to the judgment of the European Court in *Golder* v *United Kingdom*, although some support for it can be found in the decision of the European Court in *Dickson* v *United Kingdom*,[319] considered in the case study in chapter 11.

Meanwhile parliament has reacted to the problem confronted in *Nilsen* by passing the Coroners and Justice Act 2009, which allows a court to make an 'exploitation proceeds order' in order to recover sums earned by convicted criminals from the publication of their memoirs.[320] Section 155(1) of that Act provides that a court can make such an order if it is satisfied, on the balance of probabilities, that a person is a qualifying offender and has obtained exploitation proceeds from a relevant offence. This involves the person having been convicted of an offence, or found not guilty by reason of insanity or disability,[321] and applies to serious offences, which are those tradable on indictment only.[322] The person must have received a benefit from such proceeds, which includes the exploitation of any material pertaining to the relevant offence or any steps taken or to be taken with a view to such exploitation.[323] Such exploitation may be by any means, including the publication of any material in written or electronic form, the use of any media from which visual images, words or sounds can be produced, and live entertainment, representations or interviews.[324] A person is regarded as having derived a benefit if they secure the benefit for another person, notwithstanding any legal right of either to provide or receive that benefit.[325] In making any order, and determining the recoverable amount, the court must take into account factors such as the nature and purpose of the exploitation, the degree to which the relevant material was integral and of central importance to the activity or product, the seriousness of the offence, and the extent to which the carrying out of the activity or supplying the product is in the public interest.[326] The latter factor will, at least in theory, allow the court to consider the public interest in the person's freedom of expression and the public's right to be informed, but whether such interests will be overridden by the desire to achieve the objects of the Act remains to be seen.

Questions
Should prisoners retain the right to freedom of expression during incarceration?
What are the advantages, and dangers, of allowing the prisoner the right to free speech?

---

[318] See also *R (Matthews)* v *Governor of Swaleside Prison* [2009] EWHC 2397 (Admin), where it was held that it was proportionate for the prison governor to refuse to allow a prisoner permission to submit an assignment on a postgraduate course he was enrolled on that would have involved research into domestic violence and would have involved the interviewing of existing prisoners. It was reasonable for the governor to conclude that such a research project was not appropriate until the prisoner had confronted his own guilt and behaviour.

[319] (2008) 46 EHRR 41. This was a case concerning the right to found a family, but the Grand Chamber did accept the idea that the authorities could consider public opinion on punishment and retribution in considering whether to allow the prisoner access to artificial insemination facilities.

[320] See Pannick, Why Putting a Pair of Handcuffs on Literature is Wrong, *The Times*, 5 November 2009, Law 85.

[321] Section 156(2) Coroners and Justice Act 2009.

[322] Ibid., s.159(2).

[323] Ibid., s.155(3).

[324] Ibid., s.160 (2).

[325] Ibid., s.160(3).

[326] Ibid., s.162(3).

Further reading

Textbooks

A number of texts on the European Convention contain excellent chapters on Article 10 of the Convention and its relevant case law: Harris, Warbrick, Bates and O'Boyle, *Law of the European Convention on Human Rights* (OUP 2009, 2nd edn), chapter 11; Ovey and White, *Jacobs and White: The European Convention on Human Rights* (OUP 2010, 5th edn), chapter 4; Mowbray's *Cases and Materials on the European Convention* (OUP 2007, 2nd edn), chapter 13. The latter is an excellent reference point on the case law of the European Court in this area.

For the protection of freedom of expression in domestic law, see Clayton and Tomlinson, *The Law of Human Rights* (OUP 2009, 2nd edn), chapter 7, for an expansive coverage of both domestic and European law in this area, and Amos, *Human Rights Law* (Hart 2006), chapter 12, for a very good account of the domestic case law.

In addition, there are a number of specialist texts examining freedom of expression: Beatson and Cripps (eds) *Freedom of Expression and Freedom of Information: Essays in Honour of Sir David Williams* (OUP 2002); Barendt, *Freedom of Speech* (2005 OUP, 2nd edn); Fenwick and Phillipson, *Media Freedom under the Human Rights Act* (OUP 2006); Macdonald and Jones, *The Law of Freedom of Information* (OUP 2003).

Articles

The following articles also provide interesting reading in specific aspects of freedom of expression: Amos, Can We Speak Freely Now? [2002] EHRLR 750; Hare, Methods and Objectivity in Free Speech Adjudication: Lessons from America [2005] ICLQ 49; McGlynn and Rackley, Criminalising Extreme Pornography: A Lost Opportunity [2009] Crim LR 245; Sedley, The Rocks or the Open Sea: Where is the Human Rights Act Heading? (2005) Law and Society 3; Jaconelli, Defences to Speech Crimes [2007] EHRLR 27.

Visit **www.mylawchamber.co.uk/fosterhumanrights** to access regular updates to major changes in the law, further case studies, weblinks, and suggested answers/approaches to questions in the book.

mylawchamber
unrivalled support for legal education

9

Press freedom and freedom of expression: defamation, confidentiality and contempt of court

Introduction

In February 2010, lawyers for a celebrity client attempted to get a 'super' injunction to stop the press from disclosing not only the personal affairs of the client, but also the simple fact that such an injunction was being sought. The injunction was refused and it became clear that it had been sought by John Terry, the then captain of the English football team, who wanted the injunction to stop the newspapers from reporting the details of an affair he had conducted with the former girlfriend of Wayne Bridge, a fellow England team mate.

The case raised the question of how the courts can effectively balance the conflicting rights of freedom of speech and respect for private life and reputation – both of which are guaranteed by respective articles of the European Convention on Human Rights. More specifically, it raised issues of whether celebrities enjoy the right to privacy, whether there is a public interest in the revelation of such facts and details, and the basis on which injunctions pending trial should be granted.

This chapter examines this and other privacy cases in detail. It also examines how the law achieves the delicate balance between free speech, press freedom and the public right to know on the one hand, and the right to privacy, reputation and the due administration of justice on the other.

This chapter examines how both the European Convention on Human Rights and relevant domestic law attempt to uphold the principles of freedom of expression as they relate to press freedom and the public's right to receive information. The chapter will first explore the basic nature and tenets of press freedom, explaining its importance and dangers. It will then examine how the laws of defamation, confidentiality and contempt of court impinge on press freedom and how domestic law attempts to achieve a balance between that right and the rights of others with respect to their reputation and confidentiality and the need to secure fair trials. Particular attention is paid to the question whether the law is consistent with the principles and case law of the European Convention on Human Rights.

Some of these areas are explored in other chapters, for example chapter 11 on privacy will examine the ways in which laws such as defamation and confidentiality can be used effectively to protect privacy; chapter 7 examined the right to a fair trial. However, this chapter will focus on how these areas of law impact on freedom of expression and freedom of the press.

Thus, this chapter will cover:

- An examination of the importance and nature of press freedom.

- An examination of how that right is protected under the European Convention on Human Rights.

- An examination of the extent to which those principles are upheld in domestic law, specifically under the Human Rights Act 1998.

- A specific examination of the laws of defamation, confidentiality and contempt of court as far as they impact on press freedom.

Press freedom and freedom of expression

Most legal systems, particularly those belonging to liberal democracies, will attempt to highlight the importance of press freedom, distinguishing individual speech from the dissemination of information and ideas by the media. For example, the US Constitution (Amendment 1) provides that Congress shall pass no law abridging the freedom of speech, *or of the press*, and the Supreme Court has given specific constitutional protection to the press.[1] The press is seen as the main vehicle for the dissemination of information and ideas. Further, it is seen as fulfilling the role of 'public watchdog', and the media are seen as the main vehicle for relaying individual and public criticism of the government and other public bodies.[2]

However, because the press provides mass coverage of information and ideas, and is, more than others, capable of influencing individual and public opinion, it is capable of causing greater harm if the speech that it transmits is indeed harmful. Libels and breaches of confidentiality will cause greater harm to an individual's reputation and private life because they have been published in the press and discussions of an impending court case will cause more harm to the parties to the action, and particularly to confidence in the judicial system, if published widely. These harms, to other people's human rights or to the public interest, are intensified by press coverage, resulting in caution on behalf of the legal system when deciding to grant special treatment to the press. Thus, every legal system will need to ensure that both press freedom and the responsibility to protect the rights of others from harm caused by the press are properly recognised and balanced.

Article 10 of the European Convention and press freedom

The European Court has placed special significance on the ability of free speech to impart information and ideas to the public on matters of public interest. Thus, in *Sunday Times* v *United Kingdom*[3] the European Court stressed that the principles outlined in *Handyside* v

---

[1] See *New York Times* v *United States* (1971) 403 US 713; *New York Times* v *Sullivan* (1964) 376 US 254.
[2] See Robertson and Nicol, *Media Law* (Penguin 2008, 5th edn), particularly chapter 1; Beatson and Cripps (eds) *Freedom of Expression and Freedom of Information: Essays in Honour of Sir David Williams* (OUP 2000), chapters 5–7; Fenwick and Phillipson, *Media Freedom under the Human Rights Act* (OUP 2006).
[3] (1979) 2 EHRR 245.

United Kingdom – that freedom of expression constitutes one of the essential foundations of a democratic society and forms one of the basic conditions for its progress and for the development of every man – are of particular importance as far as the press is concerned. Consequently, in assessing whether any interference was based on sufficient reason, account must be taken of any public interest aspect of the case, and the Court is particularly vigilant in controlling any form of prior restraint. Thus, in *Observer and Guardian* v *United Kingdom*[4] the Court stated that although Article 10 did not prohibit prior restraints, the dangers inherent in such are that they call for the most careful scrutiny on the part of the Court, especially as far as the press is concerned. The Court has also stressed that freedom of political expression is even wider when it is directed at the institutions of government, rather than at individual politicians or public figures. Thus, in *Castells* v *Spain*[5] it was held that in the democratic system, the actions or omissions of the government must be subject to the close scrutiny not only of the legislative and judicial authorities but also of the press and public opinion.

The European Court has, thus, given special protection to freedom of speech in the context of press freedom, extending Article 10 to the media in circumstances where, perhaps, an individual would not be able to claim its protection. For example, in *Jersild* v *Denmark*[6] the conviction and fining of an employee of the Danish Broadcasting Company for aiding and abetting the expression of unlawful racist speech was found to be in violation of Article 10. Although the views of the group were not protected by Article 10, the punishment of a journalist for assisting in the dissemination of statements made by another in an interview would seriously hamper the contribution of the press to discussion of matters of public interest. In other words, although the groups themselves may not have the right to air those views, there is a public interest in identifying that certain people hold such views and the media serve an essential function in that respect.[7] Similarly, penalties imposed on those exercising free speech are considered more seriously when the defendant is a member of the press. For example, in *Thorgeirson* v *Iceland*[8] the European Court held that the conviction and fining of a journalist for criminal defamation when he had published two, relatively moderate, articles about police brutality was disproportionate. In the Court's view, the articles were directed at a matter of serious public interest and were an attempt by the media to draw popular attention to matters of legitimate public concern.[9] Further, domestic laws should not be applied so as to unreasonably obstruct the press' duty to report, for example by denying access to a protest. Thus, in *Gsell* v *Switzerland*[10] it was held that there had been a violation of Article 10 when a journalist had been refused access to a protest on which he was to write an article.

---

[4] (1991) 14 EHRR 153.

[5] (1992) 14 EHRR 445. The applicant was a political opponent who had accused the government of a number of murders and who had been convicted of insulting the government. The European Court held that there had been an unjustified interference with the applicant's freedom of expression, particularly as he had been denied the opportunity to justify his allegations.

[6] (1994) 19 EHRR 1.

[7] See also *Demirel and Ates* v *Turkey*, judgment of the European Court, 9 December 2008, where it was held that there had been a violation of Article 10 when the owner and editor of a newspaper had been prosecuted for publishing declarations of an illegal organisation (the PKK). The article – stating the response of a member of the PKK to government accusations – did not contain material that was likely to incite violence, and merely contained a statement of the organisation's views.

[8] (1992) 14 EHRR 843.

[9] See further, *Dupuis and Others* v *France* (2008) 47 EHRR 52.

[10] Application No 12675/05.

He had been denied access under emergency provisions to deal with a clear and present danger, but the Court held that on the facts there was no basis for applying the emergency provisions as the risk posed by the protests was not unforeseeable and there was no evidence of the applicant causing a disturbance.

Specifically, the European Court has given added protection to those who attempt to question and criticise government and public officials, insisting that those holding public office must be more tolerant of such criticism than a private individual.[11] Thus, in *Lingens v Austria*[12] the Court noted that freedom of the press afforded the public one of the best means of discovering and forming an opinion of the ideas and attitudes of political leaders. As a consequence the limits of acceptable criticism are wider as regards a politician than as regards a private individual.

> **Questions**
> What do you understand by the term 'freedom of the press'?
> Why does the European Convention on Human Rights give an enhanced protection to press freedom within Article 10?

Press freedom under domestic law

Although press freedom might have been regarded by the judiciary as a common law constitutional right, the domestic courts traditionally regarded the press as a private entity, guilty of confusing the public interest with its own commercial interests. For example, in *Francome v Mirror Group Newspapers*,[13] LORD DONALDSON MR suggested that newspapers could report allegations of abuse to the proper authorities rather than in their own newspapers. However, more recently they have begun to recognise and safeguard press freedom. For example, in *Derbyshire County Council v Times Newspapers*[14] the House of Lords held that it would be contrary to democracy and the principles of press freedom if democratically elected councils were allowed to sue in defamation. Further, in *Reynolds v Times Newspapers*[15] the House of Lords developed the law of qualified privilege to allow the press a (restricted) defence against actions in defamation where the information was in the public interest.

A good illustration of the judicial acceptance of press freedom and the role of the press can be seen in the House of Lords' decision in *Turkington v Times Newspapers*.[16] In that case a newspaper had been sued in libel when they had published an allegedly libellous report of a press conference called by an action group. The question for the House of Lords was whether that report was of a 'public meeting' so as to attract a defence of qualified privilege.[17] The

---

[11] Although the European Court has accepted that it is permissible to criticise the judiciary, it has given a wide margin of appreciation to domestic authorities in its attempts to safeguard judges' reputations and the impartiality and independence of the judiciary. See *Barfod v Denmark* (1989) 13 EHRR 493, *Prager and Oberschlick v Austria* (1995) 21 EHRR 1; *De Haes and Gijsels v Belgium* (1997) 25 EHRR 1.

[12] (1986) 8 EHRR 407.

[13] [1984] 2 All ER 408.

[14] [1993] 1 All ER 1011.

[15] [1994] 4 All ER 609.

[16] [2001] 2 AC 277.

[17] Within s.7 of the Defamation (Northern Ireland) Act 1955.

House of Lords held that a meeting was public provided that those who arranged it had opened it to the public or, by issuing a general invitation to the press, had showed an intention that the proceedings of the meeting should be communicated to a wider public. Although the public at large had not attended this meeting, the invitation to the press to attend a meeting at which a matter of public concern was to be debated made the meeting public. Their Lordships stressed that the majority of persons could not participate in the public life of their society if they were not alerted to and informed about matters that called for consideration. It was largely through the media that they would be so alerted and informed and the proper functioning of a modern participatory democracy required that the media be free, active, professional and inquiring. A press conference attended by members of the press had become an important vehicle for promoting the discussion and furtherance of matters of public concern.

As we have seen in the previous chapter, s.12 of the Human Rights Act states that a court, in considering the granting of relief which might affect freedom of expression, must have particular regard to the importance of the Convention right under Article 10. In particular, where the proceedings relate to material which the respondent claims, or which appears to the court, to be journalistic, literary or artistic material, the court must have particular regard to the extent to which the material has, or is about to, become available to the public; the extent to which it is, or would be, in the public interest for the material to be published; and any relevant privacy code.[18] This allows the courts to have particular regard to the advantages of upholding freedom of the press and the public's right to know, and in giving the necessary weight to public interest speech.

Recently, the Supreme Court stressed the importance of the press' contribution to matters of public debate in the case of *Re Guardian News*.[19] In that case it held that there was sufficient public interest in publishing a report of a freezing order made against individuals suspected of terrorist offences, despite such publication interfering with their right to private and family life. In the Court's view, publication was necessary in the public interest in order to stimulate debate about the use of such orders. Although the suspects' right to private life was engaged, the Court did not accept that the public could not distinguish between a suspicion of terrorism and guilt of terrorism; and in any case publication of this information would assist the clarification of the public's perception and understanding of the issues. Further, failure to mention the suspects would lead to a disembodied story and the matter being given a lower priority in the media. The case is a good example of judicial acceptance and enforcement of press freedom and the public right to know and upheld many aspects of the European Court of Human Rights' jurisprudence in this area.[20]

The disclosure of confidential sources

An essential aspect of press freedom is that journalists and newspapers can insist that their sources remain confidential. Although there may be a number of good reasons why

---

[18] Section 12(4) Human Rights Act 1998.

[19] [2010] 2 WLR 325. See Bohlander, Open Justice or Open Session? [2010] J Crim Law 321.

[20] The case will also be examined in chapter 11 of this text. Contrast *Secretary of State for the Home Department* v *AP* [2010] 1 WLR 1652, where an anonymity order was imposed with respect to the identity of an individual subject to a control order because of potential threats of violence and interference with his private and family life.

individuals or the authorities want to find out who has divulged information to the press, it is vital that the press should not be required to disclose such information.[21] Such disclosures will destroy the confidence between the press and those who supply information to it, and as a consequence the press will be denied valuable information by the chilling effect of any such order for disclosure. However, as with most other rights, the right to refuse such disclosure so as to protect freedom of expression may be compromised where this essential aspect of free speech can be shown to be overridden by a more pressing social or individual interest. In this respect the law should ensure that the principle against press disclosure is only broken in the most exceptional cases and the European Court has stressed that each member state should be given a very narrow margin of appreciation with regard to its law and application.[22] Further, the European Court has insisted that the law provide adequate safeguards to ensure that there is an independent legal assessment as to whether the interests of criminal investigation override the public interest in the protection of journalistic sources.[23]

Section 10 Contempt of Court Act 1981

This stance is enshrined in domestic law in s.10 of the Contempt of Court Act, which puts into statutory form the power of the courts at common law to order the disclosure of sources. The section provides that no court may require a person to disclose, nor is any person guilty of contempt of court for refusing to disclose, the source of information contained in a publication for which he is responsible, unless it be established to the satisfaction of the court that disclosure is necessary in the interests of justice or national security or for the prevention of disorder or crime. As with Article 10 of the European Convention, this aspect of press freedom is stated as the primary right, which may only be interfered with if the court is satisfied that not only is there a legitimate aim, but also it is *necessary* to disclose that information in order to achieve that aim. Thus, in *Re an Inquiry under the Companies Security (Insider Dealing) Act 1985*,[24] it was held that the meaning of necessity in s.10 of the Act fell somewhere between indispensable on the one hand and useful and expedient on the other; in other words it must be shown that the disclosure was really needed. The section thus incorporates the principles of legitimacy, necessity and proportionality that are evident in both Article 10 of the Convention and the case law of the European Court of Human Rights. For example, in *Maxwell v Pressdram*,[25] the court refused to order the disclosure of a press source which the plaintiff had sought in order to expose the bad faith of the newspaper in pleading justification in a libel case. It was held that the plaintiff's claim in this respect could be dealt with at the full trial by the award of damages and thus the order for disclosure was not necessary within the terms of s.10.

---

[21] For a comprehensive account of this area, see Fenwick and Phillipson, *Media Freedom under the Human Rights Act* (OUP 2006), chapter 9; Tugendhat and Christie, *The Law of Privacy and the Media* (OUP 2002), chapter 14. See also Brabyn, Protection against Judicially Compelled Disclosure of the Identity of News Gatherers' Confidential Sources in Common Law Jurisdictions (2006) MLR 895.

[22] *Goodwin v United Kingdom* (1996) 22 EHRR 123.

[23] *Sanoma Utigevers BV v Netherlands* (Application No 38224/03), (2010) 51 EHRR 31.

[24] [1988] 1 All ER 203. In this case the House of Lords held that the term 'prevention of crime' did not apply solely to the prevention of a particular and identifiable crime, but applied equally to the prevention of leaks of information and criminal insider dealing generally.

[25] [1987] 1 All ER 656.

Although s.10 appears to be entirely consistent with Article 10 of the European Convention and with the general principles of press freedom, there have been a number of cases in which the courts have ordered the disclosure of press sources, suggesting that insufficient weight was being given to the principle of non-disclosure. For example, in *Secretary of State for Defence v Guardian Newspapers*,[26] the House of Lords ordered a newspaper to disclose the source of a leaked document containing information about the storing of nuclear weapons at an army base and allegations that parliament had been misled on the issue.[27] It was held that the mere fact that the identity of the person who leaked the document must be established was not by itself enough to satisfy the court that disclosure of the source was necessary in the interests of national security. Accordingly, the qualification under s.10 is not met merely by showing that the easiest way of identifying the person is calling upon the publisher to disclose it. Nevertheless, a majority of the House of Lords held that the disclosure of the source was necessary for the protection of national security. This was the case even though it was not shown that the leaking of the document caused any prejudice to national security, and even though the Ministry of Defence had not exhausted their efforts to reveal the identity of their source. The majority of their Lordships felt that the government's arguments were just enough to uphold the claim that the order was necessary, although the minority were not satisfied that sufficient evidence had been put forward to show the necessity of the disclosure.

Press freedom was also overruled in favour of the wider interest in justice in *X v Morgan Grampian (Publishers) Ltd*.[28] An individual had telephoned G, a journalist working for *The Engineer*, giving him information about a company, including the amount of a loan that it was attempting to raise and the company's projected results for the current accounting year. The company successfully obtained an injunction prohibiting the publication of this confidential information. It then sought an order forcing G to disclose the source of his information so as to assist it to take legal action against the informant, thus protecting the interests of the company from further disclosure. G had refused to disclose this information and was committed for contempt. The House of Lords held that the phrase 'the interests of justice' contained in s.10 meant the interests of the administration of justice generally so as to enable the courts to right serious wrongs or to give effective assistance. Further, it was held that it included contemplated legal proceedings, and that the company in this case was contemplating such proceedings.[29] Where disclosure appeared to be necessary in the interests of justice, the court in the exercise of its discretion would weigh the general public interest in maintaining the confidentiality of the source against the particular circumstances indicating the necessity of disclosure in the general interests of the administration of justice.

Applying those principles, it was held that the plaintiffs had established the need to identify G's informant so as to meet the interests of justice test in the section. There was a threat of severe damage to the plaintiff's business, and consequently to the livelihood of its employees, if disclosure was not ordered. In the absence of any other factor, for example

---

[26] [1985] AC 339.

[27] It transpired that the informant was Sarah Tisdall, a civil servant, who was subsequently charged under the Official Secrets Act.

[28] [1991] AC 1.

[29] In *British Steel Corporation v Granada Television Ltd* [1981] AC 1096, the House of Lords held that an application could be made even though the applicant was not contemplating legal proceedings against the informant, but rather was merely contemplating the informant's dismissal. This was confirmed by the House of Lords in *Ashworth Hospital Authority v MGN Ltd* [2002] 1 WLR 2033.

iniquity, the balance was clearly in favour of ordering disclosure. The public had no legiti-mate interest in the business of the plaintiffs and the information in question was in reality a piece of wholly unjustified intrusion into privacy. The House of Lords thus concluded that disclosure was necessary in order that the plaintiffs might take action against the source. The decision of the House of Lords indicated the courts' preference for maintaining commercial interests over and above the interests in freedom of expression and the freedom of the press. More importantly, the House of Lords combined the questions of the plaintiff's overriding right to confidentiality with the different, albeit related, question of whether the journalist should disclose his source. Whatever the merits of the plaintiff's commercial claims, they had been satisfied by the granting of the original injunction, and it is questionable whether such a factor should determine the necessity of disclosing the journalist's source, which needs to be shown to be necessary in the interests of justice. However, the courts do appear to accept that the greater the public interest in disclosing the leaked information, the greater protection they will grant to the anonymity of the source.[30]

The application of the law of contempt in that case was successfully challenged before the European Court of Human Rights in *Goodwin v United Kingdom*,[31] where G claimed that the order of disclosure and his subsequent conviction constituted an unjustifiable interference with his right to freedom of expression under Article 10. The European Court held that the interference with G's freedom of expression was 'prescribed by law', in that s.10 of the Act, as applied in the case by the House of Lords, was sufficiently precise and foreseeable to meet that test. The Court was also satisfied that the law and its application in this case pursued the legitimate aim of protecting 'the rights of others' – the company's rights to bring proceedings to vindicate its commercial interests. However, the measures taken against G were not neces-sary in a democratic society as required by Article 10(2). In the Court's view, without court protection of the right of the press to protect their sources, the ability of the press to provide reliable and accurate information would be adversely affected. Interference with that right would thus require an overriding requirement in the public interest, and accordingly the domestic law's margin of appreciation in such cases was circumscribed by the interest of preserving a free press. On the facts, the Court noted that a vital component of damage to the company had already been achieved by the original injunction. The additional benefit of unmasking the culprit and allowing legal action against him was not sufficient to outweigh the vital public interest in retaining confidentiality. In the present case there was no reasonable relationship of proportionality between the legitimate aim and the means employed to achieve it.

Since *Goodwin*, there have been a number of decisions that indicate that domestic courts find it difficult to fully embrace the principles enunciated in that case. For example, in *Camelot Group plc v Centaur Communications*,[32] the Court of Appeal ordered the disclosure of documents which led to the identification of a press source who had supplied information relating to the claimant's business to the defendant's newspaper. In that case a person employed by Camelot, the company running the national lottery, had sent some documents to a journalist that contained information on the company's accounts. The company sought the return of the document so that they could identify the employee and take necessary legal action. At first instance it was held that the court could not rely on the case law of the

---

[30] See *Interbrew SA v Financial Times* [2002] EMLR 24.
[31] (1996) 22 EHRR 123.
[32] [1999] QB 124.

European Court in deciding whether to grant the order,[33] but in the Court of Appeal it was accepted that such case law, including the decision of the European Court in *Goodwin*, was relevant. Nevertheless, it was held that the interests of the company in ensuring the loyalty of its employees and ex-employees outweighed the public interest attached to the protection of press sources. The Court of Appeal sought to distinguish the present case from the decision in *Goodwin* because in the present case there was a continuing threat of damage caused by the presence of a disloyal employee who might be causing unease and suspicion among fellow employees and who posed a risk that he might prove equally untrustworthy in other respects. In addition, in the Court's view there was no public interest in protecting the source.

The case law following the *Goodwin* judgment showed very little evidence that the courts had truly accepted the significance of s.10 of the 1981 Act and the principle of non-disclosure.[34] In addition, the courts were reluctant to accept that the disclosure of confidential information might further a wider public interest in allowing the public access to information concerning high-profile public companies, an argument which was particularly powerful in the *Camelot* case and which had been accepted by implication by the European Court of Human Rights in *Goodwin*. However, a more robust approach was taken in the case of *Saunders v Punch*.[35] The claimant had received an injunction against the defendants, prohibiting them from publishing an article relating to confidential legal correspondence. In addition, the claimant wanted an order requiring the defendants to reveal the sources of their information. It was held that although there was a great public interest in preserving the confidentiality of such correspondence, in this case the court's original injunction had gone a long way in protecting the claimant's interests and consequently an order for disclosure was not necessary in the interests of justice.

In the post-Human Rights Act era the courts finally began to recognise the importance of non-disclosure and to apply the principles established by the European Court in *Goodwin*. In *John v Express Newspapers*[36] the Court of Appeal seemed to adjust the balance in favour of press freedom and non-disclosure and to place a heavier onus on the claimant to show that the disclosure was necessary. In that case a draft opinion prepared by a barrister for a firm of solicitors had been left in the office and had come into the possession of a journalist, who destroyed it and notified the solicitors. The solicitors and their clients sought an order requiring the newspaper to disclose the identity of the source on the grounds that such disclosure was necessary in the interests of justice. Although the firm had not conducted an internal inquiry before seeking the order, the judge at first instance felt that such a source presented a real and continuing danger to the confidentiality of legal professional privilege and that in those circumstances the identification was compelling and overrode the need to protect journalistic sources. On appeal the Court of Appeal held that the judge had attached insufficient significance to the failure to conduct an internal inquiry and too much significance to

---

[33] *The Times*, 6 March 1998.

[34] The decision in *Camelot* was followed by the Court of Appeal in *O'Mara Books and Others v Express Newspapers and Others*, *The Times*, 6 March 1998. In that case a publisher and author of a biography of Sarah Ferguson had brought an action against the defendants for breach of copyright. The plaintiffs sought an order requiring the deputy editor to disclose the source of copyrighted information in his possession. It was held that since the commercial reputations of the plaintiffs were at issue, and that until the thief was identified they would remain vulnerable to repeat breaches, the interests of justice would require that the deputy editor should disclose his source.

[35] [1998] 1 All ER 234.

[36] [2000] 3 All ER 257.

the threat posed to legal confidentiality. In the present case it had not been established that disclosure was necessary in the interests of justice, and even if it had been, the judge should have exercised his discretion to refuse such disclosure. The Court of Appeal stressed that when orders were made requiring journalists to depart from their normal professional standards, the merit of their doing so in the public interest had to be clearly demonstrated. In the present case the decision at first instance would be in danger of being wrongly interpreted as an example of lawyers attaching disproportionate significance to professional privilege and undervaluing the interests of journalists and thus the public. The decision is more in line with *Goodwin* in that it stresses not only the obligation to provide strong evidence of the needs of the claimant, but also the higher status of the free speech interest in such cases.

The decisions in *Ashworth Security Hospital* v *MGN* and *Ackroyd*

The post-Human Rights Act approach is illustrated in a case involving the disclosure of the medical records of Ian Brady, Myra Hindley's accomplice. In *Ashworth Security Hospital* v *MGN Ltd*,[37] a hospital employee had supplied some medical information to a third party relating to Ian Brady which had been held on the hospital database. The defendants had subsequently published extracts from the database in the article and the third party was paid for that information. The hospital had unsuccessfully attempted to identify the employee and sought an order identifying the third party as the only means of discovering the source of the information. The High Court granted the order and the Court of Appeal upheld that order.[38] Dismissing the appeal, their Lordships held that the present case was an exceptional one and thus justified the disclosure of the source. The care of patients at the hospital was fraught with difficulty and danger, which was increased with the disclosure of their records. In order to deter the same or similar wrongdoing in the future, it was essential that the source be identified and punished. Further, the fact that the patient had attempted to put his confidential information into the public domain did not detract from the need to prevent staff from revealing medical records, and, in their Lordships' view, the disclosure was made worse because it had been purchased by a cash payment.

However, the House of Lords stressed that any disclosure order had to be both necessary and proportionate, the achievement of the legitimate aim being so important as to override the public interest in protecting journalistic sources. This approach was evident in subsequent proceedings related to the case. The source in the above case, who was an intermediary, was identified as a Mr Ackroyd, and proceedings were then instituted against him to force him to disclose his source. In *Mersey Care NHS Trust* v *Ackroyd*[39] the court followed the decision in *MGN* and ordered the disclosure of the journalist's source, an employee at the hospital. However, on appeal the Court of Appeal held that although there was a clear public interest in preserving the confidentiality of medical records, that fact alone could not automatically justify making a summary order for disclosure against a journalist without the case being considered at full trial.[40] At full trial, the High Court held that it was not necessary to disclose the journalist's source, stressing the vital public interest in protecting journalists' sources and concluding that the necessity of disclosure had not been convincingly established.[41] In

[37] [2002] 1 WLR 2033.
[38] [2001] 1 WLR 515.
[39] [2002] EWHC 2115 (QB).
[40] *Mersey Care NHS Trust* v *Ackroyd*, *The Times*, 21 May 2003.
[41] *Mersey Care NHS Trust* v *Ackroyd*, *The Times*, 9 February 2006.

particular, the High Court noted that the circumstances had changed since the original order – including the fact that since 1999 there had been no further disclosure and that thus the risk of further disclosures was lower. That decision was upheld by the Court of Appeal,[42] who stressed that for the court to order disclosure, it was necessary that there is an overriding interest in disclosure amounting to a pressing social need and that, given the problems experienced by the hospital in the 1990s and the importance of investigative journalism, the judge at first instance was entitled to regard Ackroyd's freedom of expression as being of a higher order when put in the scales against medical confidentiality. Although the Court of Appeal stressed that this decision should not lead to the conclusion that medial records were less private or confidential, or less deserving of protection, than was held by the Court of Appeal and the House of Lords in the original actions, it noted that the present circumstances were very different from those when the original action was first brought. In this case the purpose of the source was not to receive payment, Ian Brady had now given his consent to his notes being disclosed to the world, and Ackroyd, although guilty of wrongdoing, had not broken any duty of confidence owed towards Brady.[43]

Earlier case law had been less promising and appeared to give insufficient weight to press freedom, although such an approach needs to be re-evaluated in the light of the decision in *Ackroyd* and a recent decision of the European Court. In *Interbrew SA v Financial Times and Others*,[44] an order was granted ordering a newspaper to deliver up certain documents in its possession to identify a person who had provided the newspaper with deliberately misleading financial material relating to the claimants. At first instance,[45] the order was granted despite LIGHTMAN J stressing the need to protect journalistic sources and the chilling effect of court orders requiring such disclosure. This order was upheld on appeal to the Court of Appeal, where it was held that given the purpose of the source, and the legitimate aim of the claimant in ordering disclosure, the public interest in protecting the source of the leak was not sufficient to withstand the claimant's countervailing interest. The Court of Appeal also held that the source's motive in revealing the information was irrelevant to the application of s.10, although the purpose of a leak of information was highly material. Thus, if the purpose of the leak was to bring wrongdoing to the public interest, such a source would deserve a high degree of protection, whether the source was motivated by spite or not. However, the decision was overturned by the European Court of Human Rights. In *Financial Times and Others v United Kingdom*,[46] the European Court held that there had been a violation of Article 10 on the above facts. In the Court's view the interference was not necessary in a democratic society as the company had not sought an injunction to protect their interests and there was no evidence before the domestic courts that it had tried to identify the source. In those circumstances, and noting the chilling effect of identification of anonymous sources, the Court concluded that the threat of damage to the company and the interest in gaining damages for such was insufficient to outweigh the public interest in the protection of journalistic sources.

---

[42] *The Times*, 26 February 2007.

[43] The Court of Appeal saw no reason why an editor should not be asked to confirm that the source of an article was not a journalist whose own rights under Article 10 would fail to be considered if his or her identity was disclosed. Failure to do so might give rise to an action of summary disposal.

[44] [2002] EMLR 24.

[45] *The Times*, 4 January 2002.

[46] (2010) 50 EHRR 46.

In summary, even though the early case law often appeared inconsistent, the most recent case law does suggest that disclosure will only be granted in exceptional cases and that it will no longer be sufficient to assert that private commercial interests will be compromised by a failure to reveal such sources. This is in line with Article 10 of the Convention and within the true spirit of the *Goodwin* judgment, which clearly places the preservation of trust between the press and its sources above any other relationship of confidentiality.

Protection of sources versus the prevention of terrorism

Schedule 5 of the Terrorism Act 2000 provides for the production of material relating to terrorism where such production is in the public interest. This provision, formerly contained in Schedule 7 of the Prevention of Terrorism (Temporary Provisions) Act 1989, can in appropriate cases be used to order the media to disclose its sources, and thereby preclude the media from relying on the protection offered by s.10 of the Contempt of Court Act.[47] The use of this power was upheld in *DPP v Channel Four Television Company Ltd and Another*,[48] where the police had applied for an order disclosing the identity of an anonymous source that had alleged that the RUC and Loyalist paramilitaries had colluded in the assassination of a number of Republicans. The order had been granted but the television company refused to comply with it. It was held that it was not in the public interest for the identity of the source to be protected. In the court's view the television company should not have given the source an unqualified assurance of anonymity, and by doing so the company was in danger of encouraging breaches of the terrorism legislation, thus undermining the rule of law and helping to achieve the very result that the terrorists in Northern Ireland were seeking to bring about.

It is strongly arguable that the ruling is contrary to the case law of the European Court relating to press freedom and the public's right to know, and that the courts should apply the provision on a similar basis to s.10 of the 1981 Act, albeit allowing a wider margin of appreciation to the authorities because of the context of terrorism.[49] Indeed, more recently there is evidence that the courts are prepared to at least question the proportionality of such orders. Thus, in *Malik v Manchester Crown Court*,[50] the court quashed a production order made against a journalist under Schedule 5 of the Terrorism Act 2000 requiring him to disclose material relating to a book he was writing on the terrorist activities of certain individuals. The book had been written on the basis of information provided by someone (H) who had committed acts of terrorism. Quashing that specific order, the High Court held that its terms were too wide because it was drafted in such a way that would lead to the disclosure of M's sources other than H. The court provided more general guidance in this area and held that such orders could be made under Schedule 5 when it was likely that the material would be of substantial value; that is, when it was probable to be of a value that was more than minimal. In such cases the court must be satisfied that there were reasonable grounds for believing such material was of such value – a mere suspicion would not suffice. However, a court did not have to adopt a necessity test at this stage as such an investigation would be conducted at the

---

[47] In addition the press might be liable under s.19 of the Terrorism Act 2000 (as extended by s.38B of the Anti-Terrorism, Crime and Security Act 2001) for failing to report information that might be of assistance in preventing an act of terrorism or in arresting someone for carrying out such an act.

[48] [1993] 2 All ER 517.

[49] See Fenwick and Phillipson, *Media Freedom under the Human Rights Act* (OUP 2006), pages 374–5.

[50] [2008] EMLR 18.

second stage (whether it was in the public interest to disclose). On the facts the court held that there was evidence to make the order and that in general the journalist's right to keep his sources confidential was overridden by the public interest in detecting and punishing acts of terrorism. However, the terms of the order were too wide, and thus the order should be quashed.[51]

The right to order disclosure under this provision may also be refused if it would conflict with other human rights apart from press freedom. For example, *In the Matter of an Application by D*,[52] the Belfast High Court held that a journalist was not bound to disclose her sources to the police after she had interviewed members of the IRA regarding the killing of two soldiers. The Chief Constable had sought an order under the Terrorism Act 2000 requesting the disclosure of that information, but it was held that the journalist's right to life outweighed any need for such disclosure. On the facts there was a real and immediate risk to her life, which already existed and would have been increased by disclosure, and which the state and the court were bound to protect under Article 2 of the European Convention.

> **Questions**
> Why is the disclosure of press sources so damaging to freedom of expression and press freedom? How is the area covered in domestic law, and is that law compatible with Article 10 and the case law of the European Court of Human Rights?

The law of defamation and freedom of expression

The purpose of the law of defamation is to protect an individual's reputation from *untrue* statements which damage, or which are capable of damaging, that reputation.[53] This aim is recognised under Article 10(2) of the European Convention, which provides that freedom of expression can be restricted for the purpose of protecting the rights *or reputations* of others. In addition, as a person's right to reputation is part of his or her private life, under Article 8 of the European Convention, it is an aspect of one's fundamental Convention rights. Accordingly, the law of defamation must strike a proper balance between the protection of individual privacy and reputation on the one hand, and freedom of expression and press freedom on the other.[54] Before the Human Rights Act 1998, the law attempted to achieve this balance by ensuring that the law and its application did not unduly impinge on free speech, and in the post-Act era the courts can have specific reference to the case law of the European Court of Human Rights in this area, including the doctrine of proportionality.

The availability of defamation proceedings

Although the law of defamation seeks to protect a legitimate interest, the availability of defamation proceedings has an undoubted chilling effect on free speech and press freedom.

---

[51] See Cram, Terrorism Investigations and Coerced Disclosure of Journalists' Sources [2009] Comm Law 40.

[52] [2009] NI Cty 4.

[53] For a thorough account of defamation and freedom of expression, see Robertson and Nicol, *Media Law* (Penguin 2008, 4th edn), chapter 3. See also Barendt, *Freedom of Speech* (OUP 2005), pages 198–227.

[54] See Fenwick and Phillipson, *Media Freedom and the Human Rights Act* (OUP 2006), chapter 21.

In most jurisdictions the legal system will in some cases seek to bar or at least limit such proceedings on the basis that they interfere unduly with the public right to know. In English domestic law, although democratically elected bodies are barred from bringing defamation actions,[55] public officers, including politicians are not, and in such a case the press would need to rely on established defences.

However, both the domestic courts and the European Court of Human Rights have accepted that the law may need to be modified to accommodate the dangers to press freedom posed by large and powerful claimants. Thus, in *Jameel* v *Wall Street Journal*[56] the House of Lords held that Article 10 of the Convention did not justify barring a foreign claimant from seeking a remedy in defamation simply because they could not prove any financial loss resulting from the alleged defamatory article. In the court's view the right of journalists to free expression was not given such a high priority that such foreign corporations should be denied a remedy that would be available to domestic companies. However, the House of Lords also held that in such cases any damages awards should be small and kept within 'modest bounds'. Similarly, in *Steel and Morris* v *United Kingdom*,[57] the European Court of Human Rights held that although it was not incompatible with Article 10 to allow a multinational corporation to defend its reputation in defamation proceedings, in such a case the law had to ensure that sufficient protection was given to political protest speech that informed public opinion.[58]

In addition, in domestic law the courts have recognised that claimants are often able to hide behind a wall of secrecy, making it difficult for the press to prove a defence of justification. Accordingly, in *Derbyshire County Council* v *Times Newspapers*[59] the House of Lords held that democratically elected bodies were not able to sue in defamation, noting that if such bodies were allowed to sue they would be able to stifle public criticism of their activities. This decision was followed in *Goldsmith* v *Bhoyrul*,[60] where a political party had attempted to bring an action in defamation in relation to an article published by the defendants.

Where defamation proceedings can be instituted the courts must ensure that the rights of the claimant to his reputation and the right to a fair trial are adequately protected; even though this might involve some compromise of press freedom. Thus, in *Polanski* v *Conde Nast Publications*,[61] the House of Lords held that there had been a violation of Article 6 when a claimant in a defamation action had been refused permission by the court to give evidence by video link and instead was ordered to give evidence in court. The claimant, the well-known film director, had wished to avoid the risk of being arrested in the United Kingdom and deported to the United States to face charges of sexual abuse. The House of Lords held that despite his status as a fugitive the claimant was entitled to seek the assistance of the courts in seeking to enforce his civil rights. In the present case, his absence from the court would not prejudice the other party but a failure to give evidence by video link would gravely handicap the conduct of his case and of the proceedings. This reasoning was upheld by the

---

[55] *Derbyshire County Council* v *Times Newspapers* [1993] AC 534.

[56] [2006] 3 WLR 642.

[57] (2005) 41 EHRR 22. The case is dealt with in detail in the case study below, see page 433.

[58] See also *Panday* v *Gordon*, [2006] 1 AC 427, where the Privy Council held that the Constitution of Trinidad and Tobago did not prohibit the bringing of libel actions in respect of the expression of political views where the defendant's expression had been honest. An absolute right to express such views would be inconsistent with the right of private and family life.

[59] [1993] AC 534.

[60] [1997] 4 All ER 268.

[61] [2005] 1 WLR 637.

European Court in *Conde Nast Publications* v *United Kingdom*,[62] where it was held that such a procedure was not in violation of the magazine's Article 10 rights as that process assisted the principle of the equality of arms and helped the claimant in bringing his case before the court. The deprivation of such facilities would destroy the guarantee of equality of treatment and there had been no disadvantage to the applicants as a result of the admission of that evidence.

Defamation, the European Convention and the Human Rights Act 1998

As Article 10(2) of the European Convention provides for the restriction of free speech for the purpose of the protection of reputation and the rights of others, the law of defamation is not in general incompatible with the Convention or the reasonable restriction of free speech. However, the law needs to be sufficiently clear to meet the requirement of being 'prescribed by law', and any restriction on free speech in this area needs to be necessary and proportionate. Although the European Court has been prepared to offer a fairly wide margin of appreciation to member states in their attempts to balance free speech and reputation,[63] it has also insisted that defamation laws do not impose an unnecessary restriction on free speech. This is particularly so where the publication in question was in the public interest and issues of press freedom are raised.

In particular, the Court has insisted that domestic law makes allowance for the fact that the plaintiff was a public figure. In *Lingens* v *Austria*[64] the European Court recognised that politicians inevitably and knowingly open themselves to close scrutiny of their every word by journalists and the public at large, and must consequently display a greater degree of tolerance with regard to such criticism. Accordingly, the European Court found that the domestic law, which required defendants to prove the truth of both assertions of fact and opinion, and which provided that it was no defence to prove that the statement was made without malice, was an unnecessary interference with freedom of expression and press freedom. Similarly, in *Oberschlick* v *Austria*[65] it was held that the limits of acceptable criticism were wider with regard to a politician acting in his public capacity than in relation to a private individual. Although a politician was entitled to have his reputation protected, even when he was not acting in his private capacity, the requirements of that protection had to be weighed against the interests of open discussion of political issues.[66]

As a consequence of this approach, of course, the claimant's right to reputation and privacy (under Article 8 of the Convention) will be compromised, and in certain cases lost. For example, in *White* v *Sweden*,[67] the European Court held that there had been no violation of Article 8 when Swedish newspapers had published articles about the applicant (a well-known public figure whose alleged illegal activities, including the alleged murder of the Swedish

---

[62] Application No 29746/05, decision of the European Court, 8 January 2008.

[63] *Tolstoy Miloslavsky* v *United Kingdom* (1995) 20 EHRR 442.

[64] (1986) 8 EHRR 407.

[65] (1995) 19 EHRR 389. See also *Oberschlick Austria* v *(No 2)* (1998) 25 EHRR 357.

[66] See also *Raichinov* v *Bulgaria*, (2008) 46 EHRR 28, the prosecution of a civil servant for referring to the deputy prosecutor general as 'not a clean person' was a disproportionate interference with Article 10. The deputy was a high-ranking public official and the remark was made to a limited number of people.

[67] [2007] EMLR 1.

Prime Minister in 1986, had attracted public debate) accusing him of various criminal offences. In the Court's view the articles offered a balanced account, including denials of the allegations by the applicant and others. The domestic courts were entitled to find that the newspapers had a reasonable basis for publication and that the public interest in the articles' publication outweighed his right to private life under Article 8.

A particularly wide margin of discretion will be given to the press when making comments on matters of public interest, especially if there has already been public discussion of these matters. In such cases a speaker is allowed to use strong words in criticising public figures, especially if the comments are ones of opinion and not fact, and have some factual basis. Thus, in *Wirtschafts-Trend v Austria (No 3)*,[68] it was held that the press had not exceeded the standards of responsible journalism when describing a politician (who was fleeing the country following allegations of fraud) and his wife as 'Bonnie and Clyde'. The wife had commented on the allegations of fraud and hence should show more tolerance to the newspaper articles. Further, the articles had not suggested that she was actually involved in the fraud. Also, in certain cases the Court will consider what appears to be a statement of fact as one of opinion if made in the process of a public debate, thus providing the speaker with greater latitude. For example, in *Hrico v Slovakia*,[69] it was held that there had been a violation of Article 10 when the applicant had alleged that the judge had pre-decided a defamation case, and described the judgment and the proceedings as a legal farce. The criticisms were made because the judge was standing for election for a political party that had specific views on the matters that formed the basis of the defamation action and, given the public debate surrounding the judge's involvement and potential apparent bias, the fine was a disproportionate interference with the applicant's freedom of expression.[70] Similarly, in *Barasilier v France*,[71] when the applicant had distributed leaflets in an unauthorised meeting accusing a candidate of rigging the election, it was accepted that, given that the comments were made in the context of a general and heated debate and inquiry as to the legality of an election, they should be treated more as value judgments made in the context of a discussion on a matter of public interest. This principle can also apply where the target of the publication is not a public figure as such but nevertheless his (and others') activities have been subject to intense public scrutiny and debate.[72]

However, the Court has made it clear that the media's margin in this area is not unlimited. For example, in *Chauvy and Others v France*,[73] it held that there had been no violation of Article 10 when a journalist, a publishing company and a newspaper, were made criminally liable for a libel made in a magazine to the effect that the leader of the French Resistance may have been guilty of betrayal. The Court found that having regard to the magnitude of the libel

---

[68] Decision of the European Court, 13 December 2005.

[69] (2005) 41 EHRR 18.

[70] See also *Selisto v Finland* (2006) 42 EHRR 8, where the applicant had been fined for publishing an article which indirectly identified a surgeon and which suggested that he might have been drunk during an operation. In the Court's view the subject matter was one of overriding public interest, the surgeon had not been identified directly, and the surgeon had had a limited right to respond.

[71] Decision of the European Court, 11 April 2006.

[72] See the recent case of *Lecomte and Lyon Mag v France* (Application No 17265/05), where the European Court held that the press had not exceeded their discretion in naming and discussing the activities of a Muslim leader in the context of a prolonged and general report into Islamic terrorist networks in France.

[73] (2005) 41 EHRR 29.

and the size of the fine, the interference was not disproportionate to the aim of the protection of the rights and reputations of others.[74]

The European Court has also insisted that the law should not place unreasonable restrictions on the press when it seeks to rely on defences such as justification and fair comment. For example, in *Thoma v Luxembourg*,[75] the European Court held that it was disproportionate to attach liability to a broadcaster for quoting a defamatory article written by another journalist. The Court held that a requirement for broadcasters to distance themselves from a quotation that might damage the reputation of others was not reconcilable with the press's role of providing information on current events. Further, in *Bladet Tromso and Stensaas v Norway*,[76] the Court held that when the press are contributing to public debate on matters of legitimate concern, they should normally be entitled to rely on the contents of official reports without having to undertake independent research.[77] In that case the applicants had relied on a report on seal hunting that had been commissioned by the Ministry. The Ministry had then prohibited the report's public disclosure but the applicants nevertheless published extracts from the report, which contained defamatory statements against unnamed members of a shipping crew. The European Court held that the applicants did not have a duty to follow the Ministry's suggestion of censorship. The Court was particularly influenced by the fact that the issue had been a matter of intense public debate over a considerable period of time, thus allowing all sides of the argument to be aired. The European Court has also held that the remedies available to successful plaintiffs should not impose a disproportionate penalty on free speech, so as to unreasonably deter the publication of opinions.[78]

A number of issues relating to our domestic law of defamation law were raised in *McVicar v United Kingdom*.[79] The applicant had been sued in libel by the athlete Linford Christie after the publication of an article in which it was claimed that the athlete had regularly taken drugs to enhance his performance in races. The applicant alleged that the inability of a defendant in defamation proceedings to claim legal aid constituted a violation of Articles 6 and 10 of the Convention. He also claimed that the exclusion of witness evidence at the trial, the burden of proof that he faced in pleading justification, the order costs made against him and the injunction restricting future publication were in further violation of Article 10. With respect to Article 6, the European Court held that the applicant, a well-educated and experienced journalist who had received the benefit of a defence lawyer at least until the full trial, had not been prevented from presenting an effective defence. Further, the exclusion of the evidence was foreseeable and had not been applied arbitrarily. Given its finding under Article 6, the unavailability of legal aid did not constitute a violation of Article 10. Further, the exclusion of the witness evidence was made after a careful balance between the competing public interests at stake and was thus a necessary restriction on his freedom of expression. The Court also held that it was not disproportionate to require the applicant to pay the claimant's costs in

---

[74] See also *Standard Verlagsgesellshafy v Austria*, (Application No 37464/02), decision of the European Court, 22 February 2007 – no violation when the press had been liable under the Media Act when making allegations that the victim had deliberately misled parliament. The allegations were clearly statements of fact and were very serious in nature. See also *Lindon and Others v France* (2008) 46 EHRR 35.

[75] (2003) 36 EHRR 21.

[76] (2000) 29 EHRR 125.

[77] See *Gorelishlivi v Georgia*, decision of the European Court, 5 June 2005, where it was held that a journalist could rely on official parliamentary data when commenting on a member of parliament's property assets.

[78] *Tolstoy Miloslavsky v United Kingdom* (1995) 22 EHRR 442.

[79] (2002) 35 EHRR 22.

the case, and that the prohibition on further publication constituted a proportionate means of protecting the reputation and rights of the claimant, the allegations being very grave. Finally, the Court held that in all the circumstances of the case the requirement that the applicant had to prove on the balance of probabilities that the allegations were substantially true was a justified restriction on the applicant's freedom of expression.[80] However, the decision in *McVicar* needs to be read in the light of the European Court's ruling in *Steel and Morris v United Kingdom*,[81] where the Court stressed the need for equality of arms in defamation proceedings to counteract the rule on the burden of proof. The case is detailed in the case study below, see page 433.

The European Court has also ruled on the compatibility of the rules relating to defamatory comments on the internet, where owners can be liable for defamatory comments which are left on their sites. In *Times Newspapers (Nos 1 and 2) v United Kingdom*[82] it was held that there had been no violation of Article 10 when the newspaper was made liable for defamatory comments repeated on their internet site. The Court concluded that in the present case the internet publication rule did not operate as a disproportionate interference with freedom of expression as the paper had merely been requested to offer a suitable qualification to the initial publication. However, the Court accepted that the operation of the rule to proceedings brought a long time after initial publication might give rise to a disproportionate interference.[83]

The Human Rights Act 1998 allows the courts to consider the principles and case law of the Convention in the interpretation of statute and common law, and thus the courts can follow the guidance laid down by the European Court in the above cases.[84] More specifically, s.12 of the Act requires the court to have special regard to freedom of speech when granting any relief that might affect freedom of expression. Section 12(4) also requires the court to have special regard to material of a journalistic nature, and in such cases must consider the extent to which it would be in the public interest for the material to be published. Finally, s.12(3) provides that no relief should be granted to restrain publication before trial unless the court is satisfied that the applicant is likely to establish that publication should be allowed. This latter provision complements the rule against prior restraint laid down in *Bonnard v Perryman*[85] that injunctions will not be granted unless the defence is bound to fail at full trial and thus strengthens the position of free speech in this area.[86] Further, in *Green v*

---

[80] In some circumstances it might be a violation of Articles 6 and 10 to deny a defendant, or claimant, proper legal aid, or to order costs and grant further injunctions. In particular, the requirement that the defendant prove the truth of the allegations might constitute a violation of Article 10, especially where the public interest in freedom of expression and public debate is very high.

[81] (2005) 41 EHRR 22.

[82] [2009] EMLR 14.

[83] The new coalition government are considering introducing a single publication rule, which would mean that an action would need to be launched within a year of original publication: Verkaik, Overhaul of Libel Laws 'Will Have to Wait', *The Times*, 8 April 2010, page 2.

[84] See Wright, *Tort Law and Human Rights* (Hart 2001), chapter 6, where the author considers the compatibility of the law of defamation with Article 10 of the European Convention.

[85] [1891] 2 Ch 269.

[86] In *Dickson Minto WS and Others v Bonnier Media* (2002) SLT 776, the court refused a request by the petitioners for an interim interdict restraining the respondents from publishing allegedly defamatory remarks about a firm of solicitors. The Court held that it was by no means certain that the article would be found defamatory. It also had regard to the fact that the petitioners were solicitors whose conduct was a matter of public interest, in deciding that the balance of convenience lay in favour of publication.

Associated Newspapers,[87] the Court of Appeal confirmed that the rule in *Bonnard* v *Perryman* was not covered directly by s.12(3) and the decision in *Cream Holdings* v *Banjaree*,[88] to the effect that an injunction could be granted if the claimant was likely to succeed at full trial, was not applicable in defamation cases. In the Court of Appeal's view the retention of the rule in *Bonnard* was justified in order to protect free speech from prior restraint and thus was not contrary to Article 8 of the Convention.[89] Consequently, interim injunctions in defamation cases should only be granted where the defendant's chances of defending the claim at full trial appear hopeless.

Questions

How do actions in defamation threaten freedom of expression and press freedom?
How does both the European Convention and the Human Rights Act 1998 attempt to restrict that threat?

CASE STUDY

Steel and Morris v *United Kingdom* (2005) 41 EHRR 22

This case has been chosen because it raises the classic dilemma between free speech and the law of defamation: that is, whether the law should be used to suppress or penalise speech where the subject matter of the claim constitutes ideas expressed on matters of undoubted public interest. More specifically, the case addresses the question whether large corporations should be allowed to sue in the law of defamation and, if so, whether the law should take account of their wealth and influence in assuring that the litigation achieves a correct balance between free speech and the public right to know on the one hand, and the commercial and general reputation of large commercial entities on the other. The case involved the application of both Articles 10 and 6 of the Convention, the latter guaranteeing the right to a fair trial, and thus addresses a number of substantive and procedural aspects of defamation actions and freedom of expression. You should revisit this case study and the questions at the end when you have read the whole section on the law of defamation.

The applicants, well-known peace activists, had been involved in the distribution of a six-page leaflet entitled *What's wrong with McDonald's?* The leaflet made certain allegations about the fast-food company, claiming that it was guilty of abusive and immoral farming, deforestation, the exploitation of children and their parents through aggressive advertising, and the sale of unhealthy food. McDonald's issued a writ against the applicants claiming damages in libel and at the trial (known as the 'McLibel' case and the longest libel trial in English history: *McDonald's Corporation* v *Steel and Morris*, unreported, 19 June 1997), the applicants denied responsibility for publication, and also ➡

---

[87] [2005] 3 WLR 281.
[88] [2005] 1 AC 253, discussed in chapter 8, page 365.
[89] Confirmed in *Coys Ltd* v *Autocheris Ltd and Others* [2004] EMLR 25.

denied that the words in the leaflet (and later placed on a website) were defamatory. The applicants also raised defences of fair comment and justification. Both applicants were denied legal aid and represented themselves at the trial, although they did receive some legal assistance through volunteer lawyers. On the other hand McDonald's were represented by lawyers experienced in defamation law. The applicants' defences were rejected at first instance and the Court of Appeal upheld that decision (*The Independent*, 10 May 1999), although it did reduce the damages awarded by the trial judge so that £36,000 was awarded against Steel and £40,000 against Morris. McDonald's never sought to enforce those sums and the applicants were adamant that they would never pay.

The applicants petitioned the European Court of Human Rights claiming that the denial of legal aid at the trial deprived them of the right to a fair trial (guaranteed under Article 6) in that they were severely hampered with respect to the gathering of evidence and the general organisation of their case. Consequently, they claimed that there had been a violation of Article 6 of the European Convention. In addition they claimed that the trial and the damages award constituted an unnecessary and disproportionate interference with their right to freedom of expression as guaranteed by Article 10 of the Convention.

The decision of the European Court of Human Rights under Article 6

With respect to the claim under Article 6, the Court noted that it was central to the concept of a fair trial that the litigant was not denied the opportunity to present his or her case effectively before the court and was able to enjoy equality of arms with the opposing side. Whether a party was entitled to legal aid depended on the particular circumstances of the case, including the importance of what was at stake, the complexity of the relevant law and procedure and the person's capacity to represent him or herself effectively. In this case, in terms of what had been at stake, the Court noted that the financial consequences had been potentially severe. Further, with respect to the complexity of the case, it noted that the trial had lasted 313 days and that the factual case that had to be proved by the applicants was highly complex; extensive legal and procedural issues had to be resolved before the trial judge.

Against that background the Court noted that the applicants appeared to be articulate and resourceful and were successful in proving the truth of a number of allegations. They had also received some limited assistance from volunteer lawyers, including help in drafting their initial pleadings. However, for the bulk of the proceedings they had acted alone and in an action of such complexity neither the sporadic help nor the latitude granted to them by the court as litigants in person, was a substitute for competent and sustained representation by an experienced lawyer familiar with the case and the law of libel. The Court held that the denial of legal aid deprived the applicants of the opportunity to present their case effectively and contributed to an unacceptable inequality of arms with McDonald's, and that consequently there had been a violation of Article 6.

The decision of the European Court under Article 10

Turning to the claim under Article 10 of the Convention, the Court noted that the question in the present case was whether the interference with the applicants' right to free speech was necessary and proportionate, it being accepted that there was such interference and that it was prescribed by law and done in pursuance of a legitimate aim.

The Court first stated that where an allegedly defamatory statement amounted to a value judgement, the proportionality of any interference would depend on whether there existed a sufficiently factual basis for the impugned statement, since even a value judgement without any factual basis to support it could be excessive. The Court noted that the leaflet contained very serious allegations on topics of general concern, and that the Convention case law had long recognised that political expression on matters of public interest required a high level of protection under Article 10. Rejecting the government's contention that such principles should only apply to professional journalists and not to the applicants, the Court stated that in a democratic society even small and informal campaign groups, such as Greenpeace, had to be able to carry out their activities effectively. There existed a strong public interest in enabling such groups to contribute to the public debate by disseminating information on matters of general public interest such as health and the environment. However, the Court also stressed that this safeguard was subject to the proviso that journalists, and others engaging in public debate, acted in good faith in order to provide accurate and reliable information in accordance with the ethics of journalism. Although in a campaigning leaflet a certain degree of hyperbole and exaggeration was to be tolerated and expected, in this case the allegations had been of a very serious nature and had been presented as facts rather than value judgements.

The Court then addressed the applicants' specific claim that it was unfair for them to have to prove the truth of the allegations when they had denied publication and where they had simply distributed leaflets to the public. They had also argued that large multi-nationals such as McDonald's should not be allowed to bring actions in defamation without proving financial loss and when much of the information contained in the allegations was already in the public domain. Rejecting those arguments, the Court held that it was not in principle incompatible with Article 10 to require a defendant to prove the truth of those statements in accordance with the civil standard of proof. Nor should the fact that the claimants were a multinational company deprive it, in principle, of the right to bring proceedings or to require the defendants to prove the truth of the statements. Such companies inevitably laid themselves open to increased public scrutiny, but in addition to the public interest in free speech, there was a competing interest in protecting the commercial success and viability of companies, for the benefit of shareholders and for the wider economic good.

However, the Court added that notwithstanding the state's margin of appreciation in the operation of such laws and the relevant burden of proof, if a state does provide a remedy to such corporations, it was essential, so as to safeguard the countervailing interests in free speech and public debate, that a measure of procedural fairness and equality of arms was provided for. The more general interest in promoting the free circulation of information and ideas about the activities of powerful commercial entities and the possible chilling effect on others were also important factors to be considered in that context, bearing in mind the legitimate and important role campaign groups could play in stimulating public discussion. Consequently, the lack of procedural fairness and equality gave rise to a breach of Article 10. Further, the Court noted that under the Convention any award of damages for defamation had to bear a reasonable relationship of proportionality to the injury to reputation. In the present case, while no steps had been taken to enforce the damages award against the applicants, the fact remained that the substantial sums awarded against them had remained enforceable since the decision of the Court of Appeal in 1999, and in those circumstances the award of damages could be said to be disproportionate to the legitimate aim of protecting the corporation's reputation.

The Court thus found a violation of both Articles 6 and 10 of the Convention. It awarded the applicants compensation for the distress and anxiety caused by representing themselves in the long and complicated proceedings and also reimbursed their costs and expenses.

Questions

1 Why did the European Court of Human Rights (and the domestic courts) accept that multinational corporations such as McDonald's have the right to sue in the law of defamation?
2 In your view should such companies be allowed to sue, or should the principle in *Derbyshire County Council* v *Times Newspapers* be applied to bar such proceedings?
3 Should the law and the European Court make a distinction between the press and protest groups in deciding what latitude should be given to potentially defamatory speech?
4 Do you think that the applicants in this case were fulfilling a public duty in making these allegations?
5 How did the European Court of Human Rights accommodate the moral and practical problems of large and powerful claimants using the law of defamation to suppress allegedly untrue statements of fact?
6 Specifically, what role does, and did, Article 6 of the Convention play in resolving those problems?
7 How did the principles and values of Article 6 combine with those in Article 10 and how did they both shape the Court's judgment under Article 10?
8 Do you agree with the Court's judgment with respect to the lack of proportionality in the original damages, even though the award was never enforced?
9 With respect to its decision under Article 10, how does the outcome of this case affect the balance between free speech norms and the right to defend one's reputation.

The domestic law of defamation

This chapter will now examine the domestic rules relating to the enforcement of the law of defamation. This section will not provide an exhaustive account of the area, but rather will attempt to study the law with a view of identifying its central aims and assessing its compatibility with the values of free speech and the principles and case law of the European Convention, detailed above.

Definition of defamation

The law of defamation only protects an individual from statements that are untrue, and in this sense is much more limited than the right to privacy and the law of confidentiality, which can protect true, yet private, information. This characteristic will also be relevant in deciding the availability of defences, for the law will need to assess the extent to which it is in the public interest to publish untruths. A defamatory remark is one that causes a person to be shunned or avoided, or to be subjected to ridicule, hatred or contempt.[90] Alternatively, the statement must lower the person's reputation in the eyes of right-thinking members of society.[91] Thus, harm must be caused to the individual's reputation and it is not sufficient that he or she has been subjected to mere vulgar abuse. This requirement ensures that free speech is not interfered with merely because it causes upset to another person, thus upholding the right to free speech which merely shocks or offends the listener.[92] This distinction between mere vulgar abuse and a defamatory remark is essential in the area of political debate where opponents can often use derogatory and strong language. For example, to call a politician 'a bloody fool' might be considered either as mere vulgar abuse, or of implying incompetence in public office.[93] Certainly, vulgar abuse can amount to a defamatory statement if it does imply bad faith or other characteristics that would harm the claimant's reputation.[94]

Liability for defamation is, in general, strict and if a reasonable person would conclude that it was the claimant who was being referred to in the publication, the defendant is liable irrespective of the intent or negligence of the defendant.[95] However, in *O'Shea v Mirror Group Newspapers and Another*,[96] the High Court offered some protection against this rule. The defendants had published a photograph of a woman in a compromising pose who was the 'spit and image' of the claimant. The woman claimed that the picture implied that she had posed for the photograph and had agreed to advertise an explicit website. It was held that although it would have been assumed that the photograph was of the claimant, to apply the principle of strict liability to such a situation would be an unnecessary and disproportionate interference with freedom of expression and would be contrary to Article 10 of the Convention in that it would impose an impossible burden on a *bona fide* publisher if he were required to check that the true picture of someone resembled someone else.[97]

The defendant has the right to put forward an alternative meaning of the statement to the one claimed by the claimant, known as the *Lucas-Box* defence.[98] This allows the defendant to make a statement provided he can prove that the readership would not have attached a defamatory meaning to it. In *Lukowiak v Unidad Editorial SA*[99] an article was published stating that an Argentinian judge wished to summons British officers, including the claimant, for alleged war crimes, and that the claimant acknowledged having shot an Argentinian soldier who had surrendered. The defendants claimed that the article had not suggested that the claimant was guilty of a war crime, but merely suggested that there were reasonable grounds

---

[90] *Parmiter v Coupland* (1840) 6 M & W 105.

[91] *Sim v Stretch* (1936) 52 TLR 669.

[92] Ironically, this can protect remarks that have so little merit that they would probably not qualify as 'speech' for the purposes of Article 10 of the Convention, while leaving serious and articulate criticism subject to action.

[93] In *Oberschlick v Austria (No 2)*, n 65 above, it was accepted that calling a politician a *Trottel* (an idiot) was an attack on his reputation, yet one which in the context was within the speaker's right of freedom of expression.

[94] In *Liberace v Daily Mirror*, *The Times*, 17 June 1959, the plaintiff, an American entertainer, succeeded in an action for defamation when a newspaper referred to him as a 'winking, sniggering, chromium plated, ice-covered heap of mother love'. This, in the court's opinion, intimated that the plaintiff was homosexual, a fact which would have lowered his reputation among the public and his fans.

[95] *Hulton v Jones* [1910] AC 20. There is also strict liability regarding the objective meaning of the words used by the defendant: see *Bonnick v Morris and Others* [2002] 3 WLR 820.

[96] [2001] EMLR 943.

[97] MOORLAND J felt that the claimant would be adequately protected by the law of malicious falsehood if the publisher had acted in bad faith.

[98] *Lucas-Box v Associated Newspapers Group and Another* [1986] 1 WLR 147.

[99] *The Times*, 23 July 2001; [2001] EMLR 46.

to suspect that under Argentine law the claimant had, by his own account, committed a war crime against an Argentinian soldier. It was held that the words used by the defendants were incapable of bearing the lesser meaning suggested by the defendants because the article contained nothing which amounted to reasonable grounds to suspect a war crime, nor was there anything constituting a confession.[100]

Defences to an action in defamation

It is essential for the protection of press freedom and the public's right to know that defamation law also provides a series of defences, which not only ensure a fair balance between freedom of expression and the protection of reputation and privacy, but which also make a reasonable distinction between public and private figures, and information which it is in the public interest to disseminate. Before looking at these established defences, it should be noted that it is no defence for the defendant to claim that he or she was merely repeating a defamatory remark that had already been made by another.[101] This 'repetition rule' does not protect the press, who would either have to prove the truth of the repeated statement or rely on other defences. This rule was upheld in *Mark v Associated Newspapers*,[102] where the Court of Appeal decided that it did not conflict with either Article 10 of the European Convention or the case law of the European Court of Human Rights.[103] The Court made it clear, however, that the press would still be able to rely on the defence of qualified privilege (see below) in such a case, and that the courts should not easily attribute liability to the press for repeating defamatory statements as part of a public debate.

Justification

As defamation only applies to untrue statements, it is a defence that the statements made were true. This defence facilitates free speech in that it allows the public to receive information that is true, thus allowing the discovery of the truth.[104] The defence is available if the statement is true or substantially true, and thus the defendant does not have to prove that every aspect of the statement, or every allegation, is true. For example, if the defendant alleges that the claimant has been convicted of five acts of fraud, and in fact he has only been convicted three times, the defence would still be available. Similarly, under s.5 of the Defamation Act 1952 where more than one defamatory comment is made about a person and not all of them are justified, then the defence is still available if the words not proven do not materially injure the plaintiff's reputation having regard to the truth of the remaining charges. The defence was successfully pleaded in *Henry v BBC*,[105] where it had been alleged that the claimant (a senior hospital administrator) had been guilty of falsifying hospital waiting list figures.

---

[100] See also *Berezovsky and Another v Forbes Inc and Another* [2001] EMLR 45.

[101] *Stern v Piper* [1996] 3 All ER 385.

[102] [2002] EMLR 38, confirmed by the Court of Appeal in *Chase v Newsgroup Newspapers, The Times*, 31 December 2002.

[103] In *Jersild v Denmark* (1994) 19 EHRR 1 and, more recently, *Thoma v Luxembourg* (2003) 36 EHRR 21, the European Court has stressed that punishing journalists for disseminating statements made by another would seriously hamper the contribution of the press to discussion of matters of public interest and should not be envisaged unless there are particularly strong reasons for doing so.

[104] This is the case whether the information is in the public interest or not, although a person may still have a remedy for breach of his privacy rights under the law of confidentiality: see below.

[105] [2006] EWHC 386.

In the court's view, evidence suggested that the claimant was at the least aware of the manipulation of statistics regarding waiting lists and had actively participated in the concealment of such figures when investigations began.

One disadvantage from the perspective of free speech is that the onus of proving the truth of the allegations is placed on the defendant.[106] In many situations, particularly where the plaintiff is able to hide behind a wall of secrecy, defendants are unable to do this and are thus left without a defence. The courts have recognised this dilemma and have as a consequence developed other defences so as to facilitate press freedom and the public's right to know. Thus, in *Derbyshire County Council v Times Newspapers*[107] the House of Lords in deciding that democratically elected bodies were not able to sue in defamation had particular regard to the fact that the press often find it difficult to substantiate their stories. In that case it was accepted that quite often the facts that would justify a defamatory statement were known to be true, but that admissible evidence for proving those facts was not available. That might prevent the publication of matters that it was very desirable to make public. Accordingly, if such bodies were allowed to sue they would be able to stifle public criticism of their activities. This decision was followed in *Goldsmith v Bhoyrul*,[108] where a political party had attempted to bring an action in defamation in relation to an article published by the defendants. It was held that the principle that those who held office in government or who were responsible for public administration had always to be open to criticism should apply to political parties seeking power at an election and putting themselves forward for office or to govern. Defamation actions, or the threat of them, would constitute a fetter on free speech at a time when it was clearly in the public interest that there should be none.

To succeed in justification, the defendant must justify the essence or substance of any assault on the claimant. This rule was challenged in the case of *Berezovsky and Another v Forbes Inc and Another*,[109] where it was claimed that since the Human Rights Act 1998 the courts should recognise a defence of partial justification to a lesser charge than that which the libel made. Rejecting this plea, the Court of Appeal stated that s.12(4) of the Human Rights Act added little to the legal armoury of the press and that it remained for national legal systems to set their own thresholds of defamation and justification, subject to proportionality and the right to a legal remedy for breaches. In the Court's opinion, it was not a disproportionate invasion of the right of free speech to require a defendant, albeit a serious and reputable publisher, to be able to justify not a diminished version of a damaging assault on a claimant's reputation but the essence of that assault. Such a requirement met the legitimate purpose of protecting the claimant from damaging and unjustified falsehoods and it was not unacceptable to limit the defence of justification to the essential damage done by the publication, and to test exaggeration and error separately by allowing defences of qualified privilege and fair comment.[110]

---

[106] In *McVicar v United Kingdom* (2002) 35 EHRR 22, it was held that *on the facts* of the case there was no violation of Article 10 by requiring the applicant to prove that the allegations were substantially true. Thus, in appropriate cases, it might be in breach of Article 10 to require the defendant to prove that the statement was true. See now *Steel and Morris v United Kingdom*, detailed in the case study above, page 433.

[107] [1993] AC 534.

[108] [1997] 4 All ER 268.

[109] [2001] EMLR 45.

[110] See also *Armstrong v Times Newspapers* [2004] EWHC 2928 (QB) and *Jameel v Times Newspapers* [2003] EWHC 2609 (QB), with respect to failed attempts to raise the defence of justification, because the words were not capable of bearing a lesser meaning than that alleged by the claimant. The cases were eventually argued on qualified privilege.

In addition, the defendant cannot rely on matters that postdate publication, and the courts have confirmed that this is not a disproportionate restriction on press freedom.[111]

Fair comment

A person is allowed to publish a statement of opinion regarding another person and escape liability, provided that opinion amounts to fair comment. This is particularly important when the press make comments regarding the affairs and activities of politicians and other public officials. In a democratic society, such persons should be tolerant of comment and criticism, and the public should be allowed access to such views. This principle is reflected in the European Court of Human Rights judgment in *Lingens v Austria*.[112] In this case the applicant had, on the evidence of recent television interviews, accused the German Chancellor of being a Nazi sympathiser and an opportunist, calling him immoral and undignified. The European Court found that the prosecution of the applicant for criminal defamation was an unnecessary interference with freedom of expression. The words used by the applicants were value judgements made in the exercise of his freedom of expression and were based on undisputed facts and written in a balanced article in good faith. It was unreasonable that the applicant be placed under a duty to prove the truth of such statements.

Lord Diplock outlined the features and requirements of the defence in *Silkin v Beaverbrook Newspapers Ltd*.[113] First, the subject of the comment must be a matter of public interest and not merely of private interest. Further, people are entitled to hold and express freely strong views on matters of public interest, even though many might feel such views to be exaggerated, obstinate or prejudiced, provided they are views which are honestly held. His Lordship felt that it would be a sad day for freedom of speech if a jury were to apply the test of whether it agrees with the comment instead of asking whether this was an opinion, however exaggerated, obstinate or prejudiced, which was honestly held by the writer. His Lordship also opined that the defence was available to anyone, the reporter or newspaper editor having the same rights, no more or less, than every other citizen. This was to stress that a jury should not be prejudiced against the defendant simply because the information was to be published in a newspaper, or because of the reputation and standing of the newspaper.[114]

The defence is only available in relation to statements of opinion, rather than statements of fact. An example is provided in *Associated Newspapers v Burstein*,[115] where the Court of Appeal held that a critical review of the claimant's opera constituted a fair comment when the reviewer stated that he found the tone of the piece depressingly anti-American and that the idea that there is anything heroic about suicide bombers was, frankly, a grievous insult. The claimant had alleged that this intimated that he was a terrorist sympathiser, but the Court of Appeal held that the words clearly related to the artistic review of the piece in general and concluded that they were a fair comment on matter of public interest. Thus, to say that X is a bad politician is an opinion, but to say that X has misled Parliament is a fact and the defendant would have to rely on other defences such as privilege or justification. However, in *Keays*

---

[111] *Chase v Newsgroup Newspapers Ltd*, The Times, 31 December 2002.
[112] (1986) 8 EHRR 407.
[113] [1958] 1 WLR 743.
[114] This view, however, fails to take into account that in appropriate cases the press, as public watchdog, has a duty to publish such views.
[115] [2007] 4 All ER 319.

v *Guardian Newspapers and Others*[116] it was held that, in a libel action, the fact that a claimant had placed herself in the public arena invited public comment by the media and that articles commenting on her behaviour – that she had relied on her daughter's disability to seek publicity as retaliation against the father (a former MP) – should be construed as expressions of opinion rather than fact.[117]

Further, a statement of opinion which implies that there are facts to back it up, such as 'X is incapable of telling the truth', will require the defendant to verify those underlying facts. However, the defendant will not have to substantiate every allegation of fact, provided that the comment was fair in relation to those facts that were proved.[118] For example, if a newspaper accuses a politician of being unfit for public office, partly on the basis of attempting to falsify voting figures, and claiming that the politician has in the past been found guilty of doing such on two previous occasions, the defence of fair comment would still be available even if the politician had only been found guilty on one occasion.

In order to protect a person from arbitrary and unfair attacks on his or her reputation, the defence is qualified by a number of restrictions. First, the defence is not available when the defendant is activated by malice. Thus, as with the defence of qualified privilege, the defence is lost when the defendant has published in bad faith, although the defendant may still rely on the defence of justification in such circumstances. Secondly, the statement must concern a matter of public interest, in other words whether the public are *legitimately* interested in or concerned at what is going on, or what might happen to others.[119] Thirdly, although the statement must be one of opinion and not fact, as most opinions are based on facts, those facts on which the opinion is based must be proven to be true. For example, in *Kemsley* v *Foot*,[120] where a politician had published an article in a political magazine entitled 'Lower than Kemsley', in which he was strongly critical of newspapers owned by Beaverbrook Press, the House of Lords held that the plaintiff would have to substantiate certain facts to justify calling the plaintiff's newspaper 'low'. At this point the defendant will need to prove that his statement was a fair one given the facts that existed, and in *Telnikoff* v *Matusevitch*[121] the House of Lords held that, in deciding whether the statement was fact or opinion, the court should concern itself only with the article in question, and not any previous article. The claimant had written an article in a national newspaper, which was critical of the BBC Russian Service with regard to its recruitment policies. Five days later, the defendant published an article, suggesting that the tone of the article was racist and that it had in effect demanded a blood test for employment in the Russian Service and the dismissal of non-Russian staff. It was held that as

---

[116] [2003] EWHC 1565 (QB).

[117] See also *Unabhangige Initiative Informationsvielfalt* v *Austria* (2003) 37 EHRR 33 – an accusation levelled at a political party that they were guilty of 'racist agitation' was in the context of political debate a value judgement made in response to that group's strong views in relation to immigration control. See also *Albert-Englemann Gesselschaft mbH* v *Austria* (Application No 46389/99), decision of the European Court, 19 January 2006.

[118] Section 6 Defamation Act 1952.

[119] See LORD DENNING MR in *London Artists Ltd* v *Littler* [1969] 2 QB 375, who stated that the matter only has to be *of* public interest, rather than being *in* the public interest. However, see now *Jameel* v *Wall Street Journal Europe* [2007] 1 AC 359, which suggests the information should be in the public interest as opposed to information which the public are interested in.

[120] [1952] AC 345.

[121] [1991] 4 All ER 817.

many of the people reading the defendant's letter would not have read the plaintiff's previous article, the plaintiff would be likely to have been defamed having read the defendant's letter. The above decision may be at odds with Article 10 and may have to be modified in the post-Human Rights Act era. Thus, in *Lowe* v *Associated Newspapers*[122] it was held that a defendant relying on fair comment could rely on facts which were extrinsic to and not included in the relevant article where the subject matter had already been before the public. In this case the comments about the claimant's behaviour with respect to taking over a football club had been discussed in the public domain. Further, the Court of Appeal held that although the facts had to be known to the defendant at the time of publication, it was not essential that they were at the forefront of the defendant's mind.

Absolute privilege

In a number of situations immunity is given irrespective of the damage done to the defamed person, or the motive of the person publishing the defamatory material. In these situations the law has deemed that the free exchange of views or the publication of information is so important that it should always outweigh the rights of the individual to protect his or her reputation. For example, things said during court proceedings, whether by judges, counsel or witnesses, are entitled to absolute privilege, and in *Buckley* v *Dalziel*[123] that immunity was extended to witness statements made by a complainant.[124] The decision in *Buckley* was subsequently applied in the case of *Wescott* v *Wescott*[125] to initial oral complaints about an alleged crime and to subsequent witness statements. In holding that absolute privilege applied to a complaint made to the police, which instigated a criminal prosecution but which did not result in a prosecution, the Court of Appeal held that there was no logic in conferring immunity at the end of the process but not from its beginning. The question was whether the oral and written statements in the complaint could fairly be said to be part of the process of investigating a crime or potential crime with a view to a prosecution or possible prosecution in respect of the matter being investigated.

In addition, fair and accurate reports of court proceedings, provided they are published contemporaneously, are privileged[126] and communications between a solicitor and his client, provided such is in connection with litigation, are also privileged.[127] Situations that technically fall outside these provisions might attract a qualified privilege on the basis that the law wishes to protect the public interest in the free exchange of such information. Although it is open for the courts to extend the categories of absolute privilege, in *W* v *Westminster City Council*[128] the High Court refused to extend the scope of absolute privilege to statements made by a social worker in a child protection case conference. In the Court's view the availability of qualified privilege offered sufficient protection to the defendants.

---

[122] [2007] 2 WLR 595.

[123] [2007] 1 WLR 2933.

[124] See *Taylor* v *Director of the Serious Fraud Office* [1999] 2 AC 177, where it was held that immunity applied to statements made out of court if they were part of the process of crime investigation.

[125] [2009] 2 WLR 838.

[126] Section 14 Defamation Act 1996.

[127] See *Waple* v *Surrey County Council* [1997] 2 All ER 836.

[128] *The Times*, 7 January 2005. The case is considered below on the question of qualified privilege.

Proceedings in parliament

The importance of promoting free speech in parliamentary affairs is recognised in Article 9 of the Bill of Rights 1689, which provides that the freedom of speech and debates or proceedings in parliament ought not to be impeached or questioned in any court or place outside parliament.[129] This gives a person absolute immunity for things said during such proceedings, thus protecting parliamentary procedures from the interference of the court. The immunity is limited to those carrying out parliamentary functions and is not available to the press, who can, however, rely on the defence of qualified privilege, below. Equally, it will not be available to a member of parliament with respect to statements made outside parliament. Thus, in *Jennings v Buchanan*,[130] the Privy Council held that the affirmation in a newspaper of a statement made by an MP outside parliament did not attract absolute privilege even though the statement referred to a statement that was so privileged. The MP might be able to rely on qualified privilege, but freedom of expression in parliament did not require the absolute protection of such affirmations.

Neither can a claimant use such proceedings to prove the existence of malice, so as to negate a defence of fair comment.[131] This rule obviously impacts on press freedom because if a newspaper was sued in defamation and sought to rely on things said in parliament to justify the publication, Article 9 precludes such proceedings from being used. Because of this inequality, the courts had the power to stay a defamation action where it was of the opinion that the inability to rely on such proceedings to prove the truth of a statement would be unfair to the defendant.[132] However, under s.13 of the Defamation Act 1996 claimants in defamation actions may waive their privilege, allowing them to permit proceedings to be used as evidence in any libel action in which they are involved. Thus, a politician who wished to sue the defendant, but who was stopped from doing so because the defendant would not be able to have access to parliamentary proceedings, can waive that privilege and allow access to such proceedings. The inequality caused by s.13 throws doubt on the necessity of providing immunity in relation to such proceedings, and whether the situation is compatible with Article 10 of the European Convention is debatable.[133]

The compatibility of parliamentary privilege with an individual's right to bring defamation proceedings in relation to an attack on their reputation was raised in the case of *A v United Kingdom*.[134] The applicant had claimed that she had been defamed by a member of parliament during a parliamentary debate when she had been described as, *inter alia*, a 'neighbour from hell'. Her attempt to bring proceedings in defamation was barred by virtue of the absolute privilege offered to the member by Article 9 of the Bill of Rights and she claimed that this constituted an interference with her rights under Articles 6 and 8 of the

---

[129] In addition to the privilege granted by Article 9, the Parliamentary Papers Act 1840 grants absolute immunity to parliamentary papers published by either House of Parliament.

[130] [2005] 1 AC 115.

[131] See *Church of Scientology of California v Johnson-Smith* [1972] 1 QB 522. However, in *Jennings v Buchanan*, n 130 above, it was held that it was not in violation of Article 9 of the Bill of Rights 1689 for a claimant to rely on a statement made by the defendant in parliament as evidence that the defendant had actually made a subsequent allegation which was the subject of the action.

[132] See, for example, *Allason v Haines and Another* [1996] EMLR 143. See also *Prebble v Television NZ* [1994] 3 WLR 970.

[133] See Williams, 'Only Flattery is Safe': Political Speech and the Defamation Act 1996 (1997) 60 MLR 388.

[134] (2003) 36 EHRR 51.

European Convention, guaranteeing the right to a fair trial and private life respectively. The European Court held that the defence of absolute privilege attaching to parliamentary proceedings was necessary in a democratic society for the purpose of upholding freedom of speech in a democratic parliament. Thus, it found that there had been no violation of the applicant's Convention rights.[135] However, the European Court has held that such immunities will violate the right of access to the courts and the protection of private life if the rule is applied arbitrarily, for example, to remarks made outside the speaker's parliamentary duties. Thus, the Court has stressed that a state cannot use the principle of parliamentary immunity as a way of avoiding any scrutiny of parliamentary activity by the judiciary. Too broad an application of immunity could lead to too great a restriction on the right of access to a court.[136]

Qualified privilege

The defence of qualified privilege is available in a number of situations, which either do not fall into the category of absolute privilege, or fail to attract the defences of justification or fair comment. The defence is 'qualified' in that it is not available if it can be proved that the defendant has acted maliciously or in bad faith. As noted above, for a defendant to rely on the defences of justification or fair comment, he or she will need to prove the truth of certain facts. In many cases, however, the person *publishing* the information concedes that they cannot prove that such facts existed, but nevertheless the law may give a person the right to publish such information on the basis that the publication of such information may serve the public interest.

Fair and accurate reports of proceedings

Qualified privilege applies to the following: fair and accurate reports of (non-contemporaneous) judicial proceedings and of parliamentary proceedings (other than those contained in official reports, which are absolutely privileged); reports of various international courts and organisations; and meetings of local authorities (and their committees), statutory tribunals and inquiries, and of public companies. For the defence to be successful the reports must be fair and accurate and it is clear that the press will have to display a certain level of professional journalism in this respect. Thus, in *Charman* v *Orion Publishing*,[137] the defence of reportage failed when a book had been published making allegations of corruption against a police officer who had been found guilty of theft. In the Court's view the book was not a fair or disinterested account of the trial and the defendants had been irresponsible in relying on unsubstantiated reports from police officers involved in the trial.[138] However, the courts will give the press some leeway in this area. For example, in *Curistan* v *Times Newspapers*[139] it was held that although the defendant had defamed the claimant by linking him with money-laundering for the IRA, the article was a fair and accurate report of what had been alleged in parliament by an MP. Any information additional to the statement – that the claimant's company accounts had, contrary to the claimant's contention, been subject to some criticism

---

[135] See also *Zollman* v *United Kingdom*, admissibility decision of the European Court, 27 November 2003.
[136] *Cordova* v *Italy* (2005) 45 EHRR 43; *De Iorio* v *Italy* (2005) 45 EHRR 42.
[137] [2007] 1 All ER 750.
[138] The defendants nevertheless successfully pleaded qualified privilege in this case, see below, page 453.
[139] [2009] 2 WLR 149.

by the auditors – was closely associated with the parliamentary statement and the article contained no gratuitous or irrelevant commentary. Further, the article had merely indicated that there were grounds for suspecting that the allegations against the claimant were true, not that they were true.

The defence also applies to fair and accurate reports of a public meeting, provided the meeting is *bona fide* and held for a lawful purpose and for the furtherance of or discussion of a matter of public concern. In *Turkington v Times Newspapers Ltd* [140] the House of Lords had to consider whether a press conference was a public meeting so as to attract the defence. In this case a newspaper had been sued in libel when they had published a report of a press conference called by an action group supporting the release of a soldier convicted of murder. At the meeting critical references were made in relation to the plaintiffs, the soldier's previous solicitors. The plaintiffs sued in libel and the newspaper relied on the defence of qualified privilege, claiming that the article was a report of a 'public meeting'.[141] The House of Lords held that a meeting was public provided that those who arranged it had opened it to the public or, by issuing a general invitation to the press, had showed an intention that the proceedings of the meeting should be communicated to a wider public. Although the public at large had not attended this meeting, the invitation to the press to attend a meeting at which a matter of public concern was to be debated made the meeting public. Their Lordships paid particular regard to the role of the press in such cases, noting that the majority of persons could not participate in the public life of their society if they were not alerted to and informed about matters that called for consideration. It was largely through the media, including the press, that they would be so alerted and informed and the proper functioning of a modern participatory democracy required that the media be free, active, professional and inquiring. A press conference attended by members of the press had become an important vehicle for promoting the discussion and furtherance of matters of public concern, and there was nothing in the nature of such a conference that took it outside the ordinary meaning of 'public meeting'. In the present case the object of calling a press conference was to stimulate public pressure to rectify what the committee as promoters of the conference saw as a grave miscarriage of justice.[142]

The duty to impart information to others

Qualified privilege is also available where the defendant has a duty to impart information and does so to a person who has a duty to receive it. The best example of this is where information relating to a particular person is given by one public body to another, for example where a police officer relays information regarding a person's past criminal activity to the social services department of a local authority. In such a case, if the information is false, the defendant may claim that the public interest in giving and receiving such information outweighs any harm caused to the person so defamed. For example, in *Beech v Freeson*,[143] the defendant, a member of parliament, forwarded a complaint to the Law Society from one of

---

[140] [2000] 3 WLR 1670.

[141] Within s.7 of the Defamation (Northern Ireland) Act 1955.

[142] It was also held that the defendant could rely on the defence in respect of the publication of a press release that had not been read out at the meeting. The committee had treated the press release as having been read out, and such a procedure was normal at such events.

[143] [1972] 1 QB 14.

his constituents concerning the alleged improper behaviour of the claimant, a firm of solicitors. The letter of complaint contained a number of untrue and defamatory statements and the firm sued the defendant in defamation. It was held that the defendant could rely on qualified privilege; there was both a duty on the defendant's part to pass on the information, and a duty on behalf of the Law Society to receive it.[144]

The defence can also be employed with respect to statements made during elections. In *Culnane v Morris*[145] it was held that s.10 of the Defamation Act 1952, which provides that statements made by candidates in an election are not to be regarded as privileged on the ground that the statement was relevant to the election, was not to be interpreted to preclude an election candidate from relying on qualified privilege. Employing s.3 of the Human Rights Act 1998 it was held that the purpose of the section was to stop such publications receiving *special* immunity over and above the normal availability of qualified privilege; it was not to deprive such publications of the defence where that defence was otherwise satisfied.

This immunity can, however, be restricted by the courts in appropriate cases to ensure that the person providing the information acts responsibly. First, the defence will be lost if it can be shown that the defendant has acted with malice. In this respect the test is whether the defendants had acted *bona fide* in discharge of their moral duty to raise matters of concern, or whether they have acted for some other, unjustifiable motive.[146] Secondly, the courts will not allow the defence to be applied if it feels that it was inappropriate for such information to be disseminated to others. For example, in *Wood v Chief Constable of West Midland Police*[147] it was held that the defence could not succeed when a police officer had written letters to the Crime Fraud Prevention Bureau and a number of insurance companies informing it that the claimant's business partner had been charged with handling stolen goods and detailing the allegations against his partner and the claimant. As the partner had merely been arrested and charged, but had not been convicted particular care was needed, and in this case the statements of the officer were ill-considered and indiscriminate and did not contribute to the prevention of crime or the protection of victims of crime.[148] Similarly, despite the defendant having a duty to inform certain people, it might not be appropriate to inform others. Thus, in *Clift v Slough Borough Council*[149] it was held that although a local authority could place a person on a 'violent persons register' and publish that list to local authority departments whose staff faced customers, the defence of qualified privilege did not extend to publication to other departments.[150]

---

[144] See also *Horrocks v Lowe* [1975] AC 135, where a councillor defended proceedings brought by another councillor in relation to defamatory statements made at a council meeting, and *Watt v Longsdon* [1930] 1 KB 130, where it was held that a director of a board had the duty to pass on to the chair of the board information relating to the managing director, although there was no such duty to disclose such information to the plaintiff's wife.

[145] [2006] 2 All ER 149.

[146] *W v Westminster County Council* [2005] 4 All ER 96.

[147] [2005] EMLR 20.

[148] See also *W v Westminster City Council* [2005] 4 All ER 96, where it was held that allegations made in a child-care report against a father that he may be grooming a child for sex had been published unnecessarily.

[149] *The Times*, 25 January 2011

[150] See also *Levi v Bates* [2009] EWHC 1495, where it was held that the defence did not apply when a defamatory statement relating to the claimant's financial conduct was made in a football match programme. The purchasers of the programme did not have to have a genuine public interest in being informed about the club's financial affairs over recent years or the conduct of the claimant during that period.

However, in *Kearns and Others* v *General Council of the Bar*,[151] the Privy Council held that in a claim for qualified privilege in respect of persons who have existing relationships (such as communications between professional bodies), the rule that the allegation must be properly investigated and verified – applied in press cases, below – only goes to the question of malice, and is not relevant in deciding whether that communication is privileged or not. Thus, although such bodies must not act with malice and must act appropriately, it appears that the law will attach qualified privilege more readily to communications within an existing relationship than to those between strangers. In this case, therefore, communications between the Bar Council and a number of heads of chambers relating to the claimant's past activities were privileged regardless of the steps taken to verify the claims. On the other hand, it has been accepted that the 'Reynold's defence' (see below) is not simply available to the press and may be used by others who are seeking to defend defamation claims on grounds of public interest. Thus, in *Seaga* v *Harper*[152] the Privy Council held that the defence of qualified privilege applied to publications in the public interest made by any person and not just to those published by the media. In its view there was no reason why the *Reynolds* principle could not extend to others apart from the media, provided they met the conditions of responsible journalism identified in that case. Thus, a defendant can, in appropriate cases rely on both the 'traditional' principle of qualified privilege, above, or the public interest defence established in the context of press freedom, dealt with below. On the facts, the defendant, a politician who had defamed a police commissioner in a statement where the press were present, had not adhered to those principles as he had taken insufficient care to verify the information. Neither was the defendant able to rely on traditional qualified privilege because there was no duty-interest present in the case.

Qualified privilege and the press

The press will attempt to use the defence where they are unable to prove the truth of particular statements, but nevertheless maintain that the information should be published in the public interest. Initially, the courts appeared to reject the possibility that the press might have a public duty to impart information on matters of public interest, and that the public had a corresponding duty to receive such information. For example, in *Blackshaw* v *Lord*[153] it was held that there was no general duty on behalf of the press to disclose information to the public. Accordingly the defence was not available when a journalist had published an allegation of incompetence against a civil servant, claiming that he had committed a blunder that had cost his department £52 million. This approach was upheld in *Youngerwood* v *Guardian Newspapers*,[154] where it was held that the defendant did not have the right to disclose information against the claimant regarding his allegedly racist behaviour, irrespective of the truth or falsity of the allegations. In the Court's view there was no public interest in the promulgation of inaccurate allegations.

The decision in *Reynolds* v *Times Newspapers*

However, in *Reynolds* v *Times Newspapers*[155] the House of Lords held that in appropriate circumstances the defence might be used by the press to justify the publication of public interest

[151] [2003] 2 All ER 534.
[152] [2010] 1 WLR 312.
[153] [1984] QB 1.
[154] [1997] CLY 2036.
[155] [1999] 4 All ER 609.

information. In this case the claimant, the former Prime Minister of Ireland, had sued the defendant newspaper in libel over allegations that he had misled the Irish parliament and his cabinet colleagues. The House of Lords held that whether the defence of qualified privilege was available to a defendant who claimed that the publication was in the public interest depended on a number of factors which had to be assessed in relation to the particular facts of each case in order to determine whether the 'duty-interest test' had been satisfied. These factors included the seriousness of the allegation, the nature of the information, and the extent to which the subject matter was of public concern, thereby reflecting the importance of political information and the public's right to know. In addition, the court should take into account factors such as the source and status of the information, the steps taken to verify it, the urgency of the matter, the tone of the article, whether comment had been sought from the claimant and whether the article contained the gist of the claimant's side of the story, and the circumstances of the publication, including the timing. Applying those factors to the facts of the case, it was held that although the subject matter was undoubtedly of public concern, the article had made serious allegations without mentioning the claimants' explanation.[156] In those circumstances it was held that the allegations did not constitute information that the public had a right to know, and thus the publication was not permitted.

The House of Lords in *Reynolds* refused to accept that the press had a defence of public interest *per se*. Most notably, it was held that the common law should not develop political information as a generic category of information whose publication would, irrespective of the circumstances, attract immunity in the absence of malice. In their Lordships' view such a development would not attract adequate protection for reputation, which was an important part of the dignity of the individual. Moreover, it was unsound in principle to distinguish political discussion from discussion of other matters of public concern. In that sense the House of Lords was not prepared to offer the press the extent of constitutional protection that it is given in other jurisdictions, most notably the United States of America. For example, in *New York Times* v *Sullivan*,[157] the Supreme Court held that liability for defaming public figures was restricted to situations where the defamer had acted maliciously. Accordingly, a public official could not recover for defamatory falsehood unless he could prove that the statement was made without knowledge that it was false or with reckless disregard of whether it was false or not. Nevertheless, the House of Lords recognised that the defence does allow the court to give appropriate weight to freedom of speech by the media on matters of public concern, confining interference with freedom of speech to what was necessary in the circumstances of the case, and showing reluctance to find that a publication was not in the public interest, especially when the information was in the field of public discussion.

Despite the absence of a specific immunity given for political information, the political significance of the publication can be considered by the court. In *Roberts and Others* v *Searchlight Magazine and Others*,[158] an action had been brought by two members of the British National Party (BNP) with respect to an article which reported allegations made by other BNP members that the claimants were guilty of theft and making threats. In the court's view the principles laid down in *Reynolds* could apply to a reportage case, and that while *Reynolds* did not create a separate category of privilege for political information, the political significance of a publication

---

[156] Contrast the decision of the European Court of Human Rights in *Bladet Tromso*, n 76 above.
[157] (1964) 376 US 254.
[158] [2006] EMLR 23.

would often be an important factor in determining the merits of a privilege claim. Reporting both sides of a dispute in a political party was an important element in the doctrine of reportage, and the fact that the journalist or journal had a political stance contrary to the claimant did not deprive the former of the defence: what mattered was whether the matter was reported in an objective and disinterested way.

The defence was successfully relied on in the case of *Saad Al-Fagih v HH Saudi Research Marketing (UK) Ltd*.[159] In this case the claimant, a prominent member of a dissident political association, had sued the defendants concerning the publication of allegations made by one of his opponents that the claimant had spread malicious rumours about him and his family. The defendants had pleaded qualified privilege, but the trial judge had held that the defence was not available as the defendants had not sought to verify the rumours and had thus impliedly represented that the story was true. On appeal, the Court of Appeal held by a majority that the defendants could rely on the defence. The publication concerned a political dispute between the claimant and one of his opponents that had been conducted in the public arena and where the readership had a public interest in knowing exactly what allegations had been made. Provided the defendants did not suggest in any way that the allegations were true, the defence of qualified privilege ought to be available, notwithstanding the absence of verification. The decision appears more generous to press freedom than the decision in *Reynolds* and the cases above, and it appears that the Court of Appeal was influenced by the fact that the dispute between the claimant and his opponents had been conducted in public.[160]

However, post-*Reynolds* the courts established a number of restrictions to the use of the defence by the press. In *Loutchansky v Times Newspapers Ltd and Others (No 2)*,[161] the Court of Appeal laid down some guidance with respect to the defence and held that whether a particular publication attracted qualified privilege was to be decided by the court asking whether in the circumstances the 'duty-interest' test or the 'right to know' test was satisfied. Further, although in a modern democracy the public had an interest in the promotion of a free and vigorous press in order to keep them informed, the press had a corresponding duty to act responsibly. LORD PHILLIPS MR stated that to set the standard of journalistic responsibility too low would inevitably encourage too great a readiness to publish defamatory material. It was in the interests of the media as well as the defamed individual that, wherever possible, truths and not untruths should be told. However, setting the standards too high would be no less damaging to society because it would deter newspapers from discharging their proper function of keeping the public informed. His Lordship also stressed that as qualified privilege was a preliminary issue to be decided before the truth or falsity of the statement was established, the question to be posed was whether it was in the public interest to publish the article, true or false, rather than whether it was in the public interest to publish an untruth.[162] The Court

---

[159] [2002] EMLR 13.

[160] A liberal approach was also evident in the Privy Council decision in *Bonnick v Morris and Others* [2002] 3 WLR 820, where it was held that a journalist should not be penalised for making a mistake as to the meaning of particular words where there was another reasonable interpretation of the words used by him or her. In this case, as the words used by the journalist were capable of another, less controversial, meaning, then the journalist should not be precluded from relying on the defence of qualified privilege.

[161] [2002] 1 All ER 652.

[162] When the case was referred back to the High Court, GRAY J rejected the newspaper's defence of qualified privilege, finding that it had failed to live up to the standard of responsible journalism: *Loutchansky v Times Newspapers Ltd and Others* [2002] EWHC 2726 (QB).

of Appeal also held that the judge at first instance had erred by holding that the duty owed was such that a publisher would be open to legitimate criticism if he failed to publish the information in question. In the Court of Appeal's view, there may be occasions when one newspaper would quite properly decide to publish, yet a second newspaper, no less properly, would delay or abstain from publication.

More significantly, in *Loutchansky v Times Newspapers and Others (No 1)*[163] it was held that the defence could not be used by a defendant in relation to facts of which the defendant was unaware at the time of publication. In this case two newspaper articles had accused the claimant of serious international criminal activities. The defendants pleaded qualified privilege, relying on information that subsequently came to light, and the claimant asked for the plea to be struck out. It was held that in considering whether the publisher had a duty to publish the information in question the court had to consider all the circumstances surrounding the publication in the light of the matters known to the publishers at the time of the publication. The public had no right to know untrue defamatory statements about which the publisher had made no or insufficient enquiry before deciding on publication. The decision highlights the difficulty of the press relying on existing legal defences, particularly where sensitive information is not generally available at the time of publication.

Further, in *Baldwin v Rusbridger and Guardian Newspapers*[164] it was held that a newspaper already sued in libel could not claim privilege for the purpose of repeating a defamatory statement in the process of criticising the law of defamation. The newspaper had asserted that its previous statement was true but that the rules on defamation were unfair and prevented the truth from emerging. It was held that although the Press Complaints Commission Code of Practice obliged the media to report the outcome of any libel suit to which they were party fairly and accurately,[165] that duty could not be used as a shelter for undermining the decision itself. A defendant who wished to repeat a libel must in general be prepared to defend the statement afresh or risk paying further damages. In the court's view, there were powerful arguments against extending the law for journalists to allow privilege for attacks upon those who had criticised them before duly constituted courts of law. These limitations appear to be generally consistent with Article 10 of the Convention, and in *Times Newspapers v United Kingdom*[166] it was held that the striking out of the applicant's qualified privilege defence (in the domestic proceedings in *Loutchansky*) was both foreseeable by the applicants and proportionate to protecting the claimant from a serious factual defamatory statement.[167]

The courts were thus keen to establish that the press had followed these principles of professional journalism, and as a consequence a number of judgments displayed reluctance in extending the defence too far. For example, in *Grobbelaar v Newsgroup Newspapers*,[168] the Court of Appeal held that the defence was not available to protect the defendants when they had published an article in a national newspaper, asserting that the claimant was guilty of charges of fraudulent conduct relating to the throwing of football matches. The Court stated that newspapers would have to publish such material at their own financial risk and that there

---

[163] [2001] 3 WLR 404.

[164] *The Times*, 23 July 2001.

[165] The court noted, however, that the journalist and the newspaper would not have been the subject of legitimate criticism had they not published the article.

[166] Admissibility decision of the European Court, 11 October 2005.

[167] See Dunlop, Article 10, the Reynolds Test and the Rule in the *Duke of Brunswick* Case [2006] EHRLR 327.

[168] [2001] 2 All ER 437.

was no public benefit in allowing journalists to claim privilege in relation to such sensational and unfounded stories.[169] Again, in *Galloway v Telegraph Group Ltd*[170] the defence was unsuccessfully pleaded when the press had published an article accusing a member of parliament of benefiting financially from the regime of Saddam Hussein. The articles had been written on the basis of documents found in the presidential palace in Baghdad. It was held that the articles did not fairly and disinterestedly report the context of the relevant documents, and went beyond assuming them to be true, and drawing their own inferences as to the personal receipt of funds, something not imputed in the documents. In the Court's view, the newspaper was not under a moral or social duty to make the allegations about the claimant without any attempt at verification and without putting to him that they were proposing to publish allegations of personal enrichment. Such a decision, in the Court's view, struck a fair balance between Articles 10 and 8 and was thus consistent with the case law of the European Convention.[171]

These decisions not only protected individual claimants from damage to their reputation, but also stressed there was no genuine public interest in the dissemination of lies or fabricated stories. The court's cautious approach to the defence thus secured a fair balance between the Article 8 rights of claimants and the public right to know. For example, in *Armstrong v Times Newspapers*,[172] the Court of Appeal held that although the failure to put allegations to a claimant was not necessarily determinative of the defence of qualified privilege, generally there was no duty on behalf of a newspaper to publish allegations (in this case that the claimant had probably taken performance-enhancing drugs) without offering him an opportunity to respond. Further, in *Henry v BBC*[173] it was held that the BBC was not entitled to rely on qualified privilege when it broadcast allegations that the claimant had falsified information relating to NHS patient lists. Although the subject matter was of public interest it was not necessary to broadcast the material in that fashion, making specific allegations about the claimant.[174]

In *Lukowiak v Unidad Editorial SA*[175] the court considered the problem of qualified privilege and the international dissemination of potentially defamatory information. In this case the High Court held that when considering whether a multinational publication had a social or moral duty to publish information, the court should decide whether there was a duty to communicate the information to the world at large. Thus, it was not appropriate to draw fine distinctions between duties that might be owed in one jurisdiction and not another. In this

---

[169] More recently, in *Malik v Newspost Ltd and Others* [2008] EWHC 3063, it was held that qualified privilege was not available to a person who had sent in unsubstantiated allegations of fact to a newspaper which were seriously defamatory of an MP. There was no public interest in publishing that allegation irrespective of its truth or falsity. Further, the paper and editor had not corroborated the allegations or provided an opportunity for response.

[170] [2006] EMLR 11.

[171] The claimant was awarded £150,000 compensation, a sum which the Court of Appeal felt fairly reflected the seriousness of the allegations and the manner in which they had been placed into the public domain.

[172] [2006] 1 WLR 2462.

[173] [2005] EWHC 2787 (QB).

[174] See also *McKeith v MGN* [2005] EMLR 32. The newspaper had alleged that the presenter of *You are What You Eat* had deceived the public about her qualifications. In the court's view it was difficult to see that the newspaper had a duty to assert the worthlessness of her qualifications when it was well known that her doctorate took two years to complete and the allegations had not been put to her in advance of publication.

[175] *The Times*, 23 July 2001; [2001] EMLR 46.

case a Spanish newspaper had published an article that alleged that the claimant had been summoned by an Argentinian judge for war crimes during the Falklands dispute. The newspaper had a large circulation in Spain and a modest circulation in other jurisdictions, including the United Kingdom. In an action for defamation the defendants pleaded qualified privilege. In deciding that the defendants could rely on the defence, the court held that the article should be judged by the standards and obligations of modern journalism and that in the present case they had a moral duty to publish the information in the article in that they might well have been criticised for not following the story. However, the court held further that, applying the principles in *Reynolds*, the continuing publication of the information on the website, following receipt of the claimant's complaint, was not so protected.[176]

The decision in *Jameel*

Although the *Reynolds* defence is clearly circumscribed by the requirement to follow principles of responsible journalism, a subsequent decision of the House of Lords has stressed that the central issue in such cases is whether the public interest test is satisfied. Accordingly, breaches of professional journalism should not automatically defeat the defence where publication is clearly in the public interest.

In *Jameel* v *Wall Street Journal Europe*[177] the claimants were a Saudi Arabian trading company, one of a group of such companies owned by the other claimant. The defendants had published an article entitled 'Saudi officials monitor certain bank accounts – Focus is on those with potential terrorist ties', stating that the Saudi Arabian Monetary Authority was monitoring bank accounts associated with some of the country's leading businessmen in an attempt to prevent such accounts being used to fund terrorist organisations and their activities. The article named both claimants and stated that the companies could not be contacted for comment. The claimants pleaded that the article implicated them with terrorism and was thus defamatory and the defendants relied, *inter alia*, on qualified privilege.

The Court of Appeal,[178] rejecting the defence of qualified privilege, held that when considering whether the *Reynolds* privilege attached to the publication of a potentially defamatory article it was necessary to decide whether the publishers acted as responsible journalists in publishing that article; in the instant case, the defendants did not satisfy that test of responsible journalism because it had been requested to give the claimant the time to comment on the article, but did not do so. The House of Lords allowed the appeal with respect to the defence of qualified privilege. In their Lordships' view the Court of Appeal had denied the defence on the very narrow ground that it had failed to delay its publication until the claimant had been given the opportunity to comment on its contents. That decision subverted the liberalising effect of the House of Lords' decision in *Reynolds*, and the first question for the courts was whether the subject matter of the article was a matter of public interest. In the present case the subject matter was of high importance and of public interest and thus clearly satisfied that essential element of the test. Although it had to be established that the steps taken to gather and publish the information were responsible and fair, the standard of

---

[176] See also *Al Misnad* v *Azzaman Ltd* [2003] EWHC 1783 (QB), where it was held that in cases with an international dimension, account should be taken of the fact that journalists may for political reasons find it difficult to verify their sources. In such a case the defence of qualified privilege should not be struck out at the interlocutory stage.

[177] [2007] 1 AC 359. See Beattie, New Life for Reynolds 'Public Interest Defence'? [2007] EHRLR 81.

[178] [2005] 2 WLR 1614.

conduct required of a newspaper needed to be applied in a practical and flexible manner and, on the facts, the defendant clearly satisfied the requirements of responsible journalism.

The decision in *Jameel* will, it is hoped, have a positive effect on cases which involve a conflict between the protection of reputation and the undoubted public interest in free speech and public debate. The decision stresses the importance of the defendant seeking the claimant's views and comments before publication. Such an omission was fundamental in the *Reynolds* litigation and was clearly at the heart of the Court of Appeal's decision not to grant privilege in the present case. Their Lordships, on the other hand, were more concerned that the newspapers had acted in good faith and in accordance with the type of neutral investigative journalism that was anticipated in *Reynolds*. Thus, although the requirement to comply with professional journalism remains a clear prerequisite of the defence, the House of Lords reject the Court of Appeal's dogmatic approach towards certain omissions, particularly where, as in this case, the newspaper offered a subsequent opportunity to comment to the claimant.

Evidence of a more liberal approach is seen in the recent Court of Appeal decision in *Charman v Orion Publishing Ltd and Others*.[179] In that case a book entitled *Bent Coppers* had been written and published which had investigated police corruption and had made defamatory comments in respect to the claimant. The defence of qualified privilege had been rejected at first instance because the court felt that the book had failed to achieve the necessary neutral balance.[180] On appeal the Court of Appeal stated that once it was shown that the subject matter of the article was in the public interest then the inquiry shifted to whether the steps taken to gather and publish the information were responsible and fair, and that in assessing the responsibility of the article weight had to be given to the professional judgement of the journalist. The *Reynolds* principles were not intended to present an onerous obstacle to the media, but rather proper care was the essence of the responsible journalism and the test of whether the defendants had acted with proper professional responsibility. Further, the defendant's assertion that they did not intend to convey the imputation that the court did in the end impute to the words was a relevant fact to take into account. In the present case the judge had not considered the book as a whole and had not taken into account, to a sufficient degree, what the defendants had omitted and their editorial judgement.

However, this discretion will not be unlimited and in contrast in *Prince Radu of Hohenzollern v Houston and Another*[181] it was held that a publisher could not rely on qualified privilege (or reportage) when it failed to fairly and neutrally cover both sides of a debate concerning the possible fraudulent or illegitimate nature of the claimant's title and the claim that he was a member of the Romanian secret police. In this case serious allegations had been put into circulation without giving any opportunity for the claimant's side of the story to be stated on the alleged forgery of the deed conferring the title or the claimant's alleged service in the secret police.

Accordingly, despite the decision in *Jameel*, the press needs to ensure that it follows the standards of professional journalism. In particular, it needs to ensure that its records are updated, otherwise defamatory statements that would previously attract the defence will be withdrawn when it becomes apparent that the facts have changed. For example, in *Flood* v

---

[179] [2008] 1 All ER 750.
[180] [2007] 1 All ER 622.
[181] [2007] EWHC 2753 (QB).

Times Newspapers,[182] it was held that a newspaper could not rely on the defence of qualified privilege in naming a police officer suspected of corruption once it was clear that there was no evidence to justify that allegation. Accordingly, the defence was lost by failure to remove the allegation from the website. More generally, on appeal to the Court of Appeal in *Flood* it was held that the defence was not available even initially, and that whether a defence is available is a pure question of law to which there was only one correct answer.[183] In this case the Court of Appeal held that the newspaper could not rely on the defence where it had made serious and detailed allegations against the officer knowing that it was likely to be very damaging to his reputation and having done little to satisfy itself that the allegations were true. At the time of publication the allegations were no more than unsubstantiated, unchecked accusations from an unknown source, coupled with speculation. Although the newspaper had relied on a police dossier, that document had not named any officer and the mere fact that an allegation had been made in it was not enough to justify publication. The Court of Appeal's decision is a clear indication that the press will not be allowed *carte blanche* in its reporting practices simply because the subject matter of their investigation is a matter of public interest.

Unintentional or innocent dissemination and apologies

Although it is no defence that the plaintiff was unintentionally defamed, the law does provide limited defences in the case where either the defamatory effect of the publication was accidental, or where the actual publication of such material was innocent. For example, where a person making the statement neither knew nor had reason to believe that the statement referred to the aggrieved party, or was likely to be understood as referring to him, and was both false and defamatory of that party, the person making the statement is allowed to make an offer of amends to the other party.[184] This will be in the form of an offer of the publication of a correction and apology, in a manner that is reasonable and practicable, and the payment of agreed compensation.[185] Thus, it is quite common for newspapers and television companies to print or broadcast an apology in relation to such unintentional defamatory remarks, and for the potential claimant to accept some limited form of compensation.[186] In such cases the court will often reduce the amount of damages that would usually be paid in similar cases. Thus, in *Bowman* v *MGN Ltd*[187] the court reduced the claimant's damages by half when a newspaper had falsely accused him of conducting an affair with an actress; the court taking into account the newspaper's offer of apology and immediate retraction of the article once the truth was discovered.

In addition, a defence is available under s.1 of the Defamation Act 1996 in relation to the innocent dissemination of defamatory remarks. This defence applies where a person can show that he was not the author, editor or publisher of the statement and took reasonable care in relation to the publication, not knowing, or having reason to believe, that what he did caused or contributed to the publication of the defamatory statement.

---

[182] *The Times*, 23 October 2009.
[183] *Flood* v *Times Newspapers* [2010] EMLR 8.
[184] Section 4(3) Defamation Act 1996.
[185] Section 2(3) Defamation Act 1996.
[186] Such measures avoid unnecessary litigation and provide the public with an opportunity to be disabused of untruths. They can be contrasted with out-of-court settlements, which can often be used to put pressure on the press to retract statements which were made in the public interest, but which cannot be proved to be true.
[187] [2010] EWHC 895 (QB).

> **Questions**
>
> What defences are available to the press in defamation actions? Are those defences consistent with free speech and the case law of the European Court in this area?
>
> In particular, how compatible is the defence of qualified privilege with Article 10 of the Convention?

Remedies in defamation

The scope and extent of the claimant's remedies will determine the proportionality of that law and special care should be taken that such a law does not allow for unreasonable prior restraint or excessive damages. In relation to prior restraint, defendants in defamation proceedings are protected by the rule in *Bonnard* v *Perryman*[188] that no temporary order pending full trial can be given where the defendant intends to raise the defences of justification and/or fair comment at the full trial, unless the defence is bound to fail.[189] This is particularly important with regard to statements that have not yet reached the public domain, for it allows the public to receive the information. In *Holley* v *Smyth*,[190] it was held that the rule applies even if the defendant published the original material in bad faith. Further, in *Green* v *Associated Newspapers*,[191] the Court of Appeal confirmed that the rule in *Bonnard* was not covered directly by less generous rule in s.12(3) and the decision in *Cream Holdings* v *Banjaree*,[192] and that the retention of the rule in *Bonnard* was justified in order to protect free speech from prior restraint.[193]

It is important, therefore, for the courts to correctly identify the nature of a particular claim; for if it is in defamation the principles in *Bonnard* apply, whilst if the action is for breach of privacy/confidentiality, the principles in *Cream Holdings* will allow an interim injunction if the claimant is likely to succeed at full trial. Thus, in *LNS* v *Persons Unknown* (the 'John Terry' case),[194] the High Court refused to continue an injunction prohibiting the naming of the claimant and a person whom he was having an affair with where the judge felt that the essential aim of the injunction was the protection of his commercial reputation. Appling *Bonnard* v *Perryman* and *Greene* it was felt that such an interest was not capable of overriding freedom of expression.

A possible threat to this principle can be found in s.9 of the Defamation Act 1996, which allows the court to dispose of defamation cases via summary relief where satisfied that there is no defence which has a realistic prospect of success and there is no other reason why the claim should be tried. In such a case the court may make a number of orders including declaring that the statement was false and defamatory of the claimant, ordering that the defendant publish a suitable apology, awarding damages not exceeding £10,000, and granting an injunction to restrain further publication. Although this provision is intended to avoid unnecessary libel actions, and thus to protect defendants from crippling damages claims, it might also put pressure on such defendants to settle claims rather than imparting the information to the public at large.

[188] [1891] 2 Ch 269.
[189] This principle strengthens the requirement in s.12(3) and (4) of the Human Rights Act.
[190] [1998] 2 WLR 742.
[191] [2005] 3 WLR 281.
[192] [2005] 1 AC 253, discussed in chapter 8, page 365.
[193] Confirmed in *Coys Ltd* v *Autocheris Ltd and Others* [2004] EMLR 25.
[194] [2010] EMLR 16.

With regard to damages, the high sums awarded by juries for which English libel law is famous threaten freedom of speech and the freedom of the press as they can have a chilling effect on those who are considering publishing information that is critical of individuals and their activities.[195] This issue was raised before the European Court in *Tolstoy Miloslavsky* v *United Kingdom*,[196] where it was held that although member states should be given a wide margin of appreciation as to what would be an appropriate response to speech which did not enjoy the protection of Article 10, excessive awards should be avoided where they might have a chilling effect on freedom of expression. The applicant had been ordered to pay £1.5m in compensation to a person whom he had accused of handing over refugees to the Soviet authorities during the war. In the Court's view the award against the applicant was unforeseeably high and almost impossible to overturn on appeal. As domestic law failed to provide a requirement of proportionality in relation to such awards, the award was not proportionate under Article 10(2) and thus constituted an impermissible interference with the applicant's freedom of expression. Similar concerns were raised in *Rantzen* v *Mirror Group*,[197] where the Court of Appeal reduced the plaintiff's jury award of £250,000 to £110,000 on the basis that the sum of £250,000 was excessive whatever objective standards of reasonable compensation or necessity and proportionality were applied.[198] The Court of Appeal provided little guidance as to the appropriate measure of damages in a defamation action, or the grounds on which the court could overturn a jury award, and subsequent domestic law has attempted to establish some principles. Thus, in *John* v *MGN*[199] it was held that a jury should receive guidance on the appropriate level of damages from the party's counsel, and guidance from the court on the level of exemplary damages. In that case the Court of Appeal reduced the claimant's compensatory damages from £75,000 to £25,000, and the exemplary damages from £275,000 to £75,000 when the claimant, the pop star Elton John, had successfully sued in libel when the *Sunday Mirror* had alleged that he practised bizarre eating habits.[200]

In the post-Human Rights Act era, the courts will need to pay specific regard to the case law of the European Court, and under s.12 of the Act must pay particular regard to freedom of speech when granting relief that affects that right, especially where the statements are of a journalistic nature. This will involve avoiding excessive and unnecessary damages awards which would otherwise impact on freedom of expression. Thus, in *Grobbelaar* v *Newsgroup Newspapers Ltd*,[201] the House of Lords reduced an award of £85,000 granted to the plaintiff, a professional footballer who had been accused of taking bribes to fix matches. Noting that the claimant had been shown to act in a way in which no decent or honest footballer would act,

---

[195] In *Hays plc* v *Hartley* [2010] EWHC 1068 (QB), the court struck out a claim for damages against an intermediary journalist when the claimant had already received an apology from the newspaper. Such an award would have had a disproportionate effect on the defendant and would have constituted a disproportionate measure to vindicate the claimant's rights.

[196] (1995) 20 EHRR 442.

[197] [1994] QB 670.

[198] See also *Sutcliffe* v *Pressdram Ltd* [1991] QB 53, where it was held that in awarding the wife of Peter Sutcliffe (the 'Yorkshire Ripper') a sum of £600,000, the jury had failed to appreciate the real value and effect of so large a sum.

[199] [1997] QB 583.

[200] But note the decision in *Kiam* v *MGN Ltd* [2002] 2 All ER 219, where the Court of Appeal held that it should not interfere with a jury's award of aggravated compensatory damages for libel unless it regarded the amount awarded as substantially exceeding the most that any jury could reasonably have thought appropriate.

[201] [2002] 1 WLR 3024.

their Lordships felt that it would be an affront to justice to award substantial damages in this case and an award of £1 nominal damages was substituted. Again, in *Berezovsky v Russian Television and Broadcasting Co*[202] it was stressed that although evidence of bad reputation did not preclude a person from suing in defamation it could be used to mitigate any damages. In the present case, however, there were conflicting views on the claimant's status and reputation and he did not have a generally bad reputation. Thus, an unproven allegation that he was involved in a conspiracy to prevent his extradition could attract an appropriate award of £150,000.[203]

Nevertheless, provided the law contains some safeguards against excessive awards, both the domestic and European courts are prepared to sanction substantial sums in appropriate cases. For example, in *The Gleaner Company and Another v Abrahams*,[204] although the Privy Council held that the Jamaican Court of Appeal were entitled to reduce defamation damages by half because they had given an award that no reasonable jury would have thought reasonable to compensate the claimant, it held that the final award of £533,000 was not disproportionate to the enjoyment of freedom of expression given the evidence of loss of earnings and of actual psychological and physiological damage suffered by the claimant when he had been accused of corruption when in ministerial office. A similar approach was evident in the European Court's judgment in *Independent News and Media plc and another v Ireland*,[205] where damages of 300,000 Irish pounds had been awarded against the applicants in libel with respect to an article that linked an Irish politician to the illegal activities of a group of which the politician was the leader. The European Court held that the essential question was whether there were adequate safeguards existing in domestic law to ensure that a disproportionate sum was not awarded. In the Court's view, the Supreme Court had taken into account relevant factors such as the seriousness of the libel and the effect it had on the claimant's reputation and political ambitions. Having regard to the measure of appellate control over the awarded sum, and the margin of appreciation offered to each state in this context, the Court was not satisfied that there had been ineffective or inadequate safeguards against a disproportionate jury award.[206]

In addition, although costs awards might have a chilling effect on the press and other defendants, they have not been declared inconsistent with freedom of expression. The domestic courts have recognised that the granting of high costs in a libel action could have a stifling effect on freedom of expression and thus should be avoided.[207] However, in *Campbell v MGN*,[208] the House of Lords held that it was not in violation of Article 10 of the European Convention for a defendant in libel proceedings to be forced to pay the extra cost of solicitor's success fees which had been incurred by the claimant in bringing her libel action. This was the case even though those fees were twice as expensive as normal fees and the claimant did not need to avail herself of such a service because of her own personal wealth. In their

---

[202] [2010] EWHC 476 (QB).

[203] The court noted that had it been alleged that he had been involved in the murder of Alexander Litvinenko the award would have been substantially higher.

[204] [2004] 1 AC 638.

[205] (2006) 42 EHRR 46.

[206] See *Galloway v Telegraph Group Ltd* [2006] EMLR 11, where the Court of Appeal upheld an award of £150,000 for the publication of unsubstantiated allegations of personal enrichment made against an MP.

[207] *Pedder v News Group Newspapers* [2004] EMLR 19.

[208] [2005] 1 WLR 3394.

Lordship's view conditional fee arrangements (available to all) were not invalid simply because they were inconsistent with Article 10 and the scheme was within parliament's margin to choose to provide access to litigation in a way it deemed fit. (See the preface for developments.)

The rules relating to damages and costs are, however, subject to ensuring that the defendant is provided with the right to a fair trial when defending defamation actions. Thus, although personal wealth and power might be regarded as creating in some senses inevitable inequality, in *Steel and Morris* v *United Kingdom*[209] the European Court has insisted that the rules and procedures in defamation procedures must not deprive the defendant of the general right to equality of arms.

Reforming the present law of defamation?

At the time of writing, the Defamation Bill 2010, introduced by Lord Lester of Herne Hill, had been introduced into the House of Lords and was due to receive its second reading in July 2010. The Bill proposes a number of changes to the current law, intended to free the press and others from unnecessary libel actions and their financial and other consequences. Under the Bill the defences of justification and fair comment would be called truth and honest opinion respectively (clauses 2 and 4) and a new defence of responsible publication on a matter of public interest would be introduced (clause 1). In addition, the defences of absolute and qualified privilege with respect to the reporting of court and parliamentary proceedings would be expanded (clauses 6–8). The Bill also proposes that claimants would need to show evidence of substantial harm to their reputation to succeed in libel (clause 12), and that companies would need to show financial harm in such cases (clause 11). Finally, there would be presumption against jury trials in defamation proceedings, which can be rebutted if it is required in the interests of justice (clauses 14–15).

> **Question**
> Do you believe that the remedies for defamation and related actions strike a correct balance between the protection of reputation and the preservation of freedom of expression? Examine Lord Lester's Bill (above): do you feel those reforms are necessary and accommodate the interests of all parties to defamation cases?

Criminal libel and malicious falsehood

In certain cases defamatory statements give rise to criminal liability. Criminal libel is committed when the statement has been made in circumstances where the libel is likely to disturb the peace of the community or where it is likely seriously to affect the reputation of the claimant.[210] A claimant will require the permission of a judge to proceed with such an action,[211] and in *Goldsmith* v *Pressdram*[212] it was held that there must be a clear *prima facie* case to answer and that the public interest requires the institution of such proceedings. The offence could, in theory, be used against the press, and although in such a case the defendants can rely on

---

[209] (2005) 41 EHRR 22. See the case study on those proceedings, page 433.
[210] *R* v *Wicks* (1936) 25 Cr App Rep 168.
[211] Section 8 Law of Libel Amendment Act 1888.
[212] [1977] 2 All ER 557.

the above defences, apart from fair comment, justification is only available where the information is true *and* its publication is in the public interest.[213]

Such criminal proceedings will not be incompatible with freedom of expression and Article 10 of the Convention provided they are used in appropriate cases and the criminal sanction, including the monetary award, is proportionate. For example, in *Worme and Another v Commissioner of Police of Grenada*,[214] the Privy Council upheld the prosecution of two individuals for criminal libel after writing letters to a newspaper defaming the Prime Minister of Grenada. The protection of good reputation was in the public interest, as was the protection of the reputation of public figures from false accusations of misconduct in a public office. The criminal prosecution of the appellants, in respect of an allegation that the Prime Minister spent millions of dollars trying to bribe people to vote for him and his party, was justified, despite the sparse use of the law and the fact that it did not exist in every democratic society. However, there will be a violation of Article 10 where the law fails to give due strength to the public interest nature of the expression, and the fact that the proceedings are criminal will compound that violation. For example, in *Tonsberg Blad AS and Norway*,[215] the European Court held that there had been a violation of Article 10 when the press had faced a criminal prosecution for libel after it had published a number of articles suggesting that a pop singer had violated and manipulated planning laws. The Court held that a possible failure of a public figure to observe laws and regulations aimed at protecting serious public interests, even in the private sphere, might in certain circumstances constitute a matter of public interest. There had been no direct allegation that the pop star had committed a criminal offence, and given the strong public interest in the story, and given the fact that the property was on the council's list, the press were not obliged to fully verify the allegations.

A malicious falsehood is committed where a person maliciously publishes information about another that is false, and damage follows as a direct result of that publication. The law of malicious falsehood was relied on in *Kaye v Robertson*.[216] In that case the Court of Appeal confirmed that there was no general right to privacy in English law that would allow the claimant a remedy against the defendant who had conducted a sham interview with the claimant while he lay semiconscious in a hospital bed. Nevertheless, the claimant was allowed to sue in malicious falsehood on the basis that the defendants had told a deliberate untruth about the claimant and had thereby maliciously interfered with his right to sell his own story as an exclusive. The Court gave an order prohibiting the defendants from publishing the story in so far as it was suggested that the claimant had consented to it.

The law of confidentiality

While the law of defamation protects the individual from attacks on their reputations by untrue statements, the law of confidentiality protects a person or body from the dissemination of private or confidential information, whether such information is true or false. An action in confidentiality is therefore wider than one in defamation, and as it applies to

---

[213] Section 6 Libel Act 1843.
[214] [2004] 2 AC 430.
[215] (2008) 46 EHRR 40.
[216] [1991] FSR 62. The case will be dealt with in detail in chapter 11 on privacy.

protect information that is true, the arguments against its restriction on the grounds of press freedom and the public's right to know are stronger. In the absence of a constitutional right to privacy, the law of confidence has been used to provide individuals, and some public and private bodies, with protection against interference in respect of their confidential matters. This aspect of the law of confidence will be dealt with in chapter 11, and the rules relating to its scope and application will only be dealt with briefly in this section of the book. For the purposes of this chapter, the law of confidence imposes restrictions on freedom of speech and, in particular, on press freedom. The law of confidence will, therefore, provide sanctions for those who have exercised their right of free speech and who have caused damage to the claimant's financial or personal interests. Specifically, unlike the law of defamation, the law of confidentiality allows prior restraint on the basis that it is the most effective method of retaining the claimant's rights. Thus, the legal system must, if it is to protect free speech from unnecessary interference, ensure that the law is not too wide and that there are appropriate and adequate defences available to protect disclosures that are in some way in the public interest.[217]

Requirements of an action in confidentiality

The requirements for a successful action in confidentiality were laid down by MCGARRY J in *Coco v AN Clark (Engineers) Ltd*.[218] First, the claimant has to establish that the information was confidential, in other words that it has the necessary quality of confidentiality about it. Thus, the information must be sufficiently private in that it has not yet entered the public domain, and must not be too trivial. Secondly, the information must have been imparted in circumstances importing an obligation of confidence. Thirdly, there must be an unauthorised use of that information to the detriment of the plaintiff.

The above tests were formulated with respect to the protection of commercial secrets and in the modern era, where the law applies to the protection of personal information and privacy, the courts are now concerned with whether the claimant has a reasonable expectation of privacy or confidentiality with respect to the information, and whether the defendant should have realised that the information was private and confidential.[219] Thus, in *LNS v Persons Unknown*[220] (the John Terry case), the court distinguished between an action in confidentiality and an action for misuse of private information, the latter being more akin to an action in privacy. Nevertheless, in more traditional cases the claimant will need to show a duty of confidentiality. For example, in *Napier v Mitchell and Pressdram*,[221] the Court of Appeal refused to grant an injunction to a solicitor prohibiting a magazine from publishing details of a Law Society complaint made against him and the firm. The complainant owed no duty of confidentiality to the firm and was entitled to pass on the information to the magazine.

---

[217] Robertson and Nicol, *Media Law* (Penguin 2008, 5th edn), chapter 5; Fenwick and Phillipson, *Media Freedom under the Human Rights Act* (OUP 2006), Part IV.

[218] [1969] RPC 41.

[219] See now *Campbell v MGN Ltd* [2004] 2 AC 457, discussed in detail in chapter 11. For an examination of the growth of confidentiality into a privacy remedy, see Phillipson and Fenwick, Breach of Confidence as a Privacy Remedy in the Human Rights Act Era (2000) 63 MLR 600; Phillipson, Transforming Breach of Confidence? Towards a Common Law Right of Privacy under the Human Rights Act (2003) 66 MLR 726.

[220] [2010] EMLR 16.

[221] [2010] 1 WLR 934.

In the court's view the fact that the complaint was conducted in private did not make the findings confidential.

Consequently, in the modern era the right to freedom of expression might not only conflict with the claimant's commercial interests, but the court may also have to balance freedom of expression under Article 10 with the claimant's right to private life under Article 8. More specifically, the law seems to have dispensed with the requirement that the confidential information was imparted in breach of an enforceable relationship of confidentiality, although such a breach may well compound a breach of confidence.[222]

So too, the courts have been careful to ensure that the law of confidentiality does not stifle public interest debate, particularly where the speech relates to the workings of government. The House of Lords placed an important restriction on an action in confidentiality in *Attorney-General v Guardian Newspapers (No 2)*[223] – the 'Spycatcher' case. In this case the House of Lords held that the public interest in freedom of expression could only be overridden by the existence of a clear countervailing public interest. Thus, the disclosure of information can only be protected where there was no greater public interest to be gained in disclosing the information. This gives freedom of expression an enhanced status and places an important restriction on the use of the law of confidentiality to suppress free speech, particularly where the claimant is a public authority claiming that such suppression will promote the public interest. Further, the House of Lords held that in such cases it was incumbent on the Crown to show not only that the information was confidential, but also that it was in the public interest that it should not be published if it wished to restrain the disclosure of government secrets. Accordingly, as in the present case, if the information has already entered the public domain, it thereby loses its confidentiality and there is no public interest to override the interests in free speech. As the book had already been published, it would not be contrary to the public interest for the injunctions to be lifted, any public interest having already been damaged by the previous publications. This decision was followed in *Lord Advocate v Scotsman Publications*.[224] This case concerned the publication of *Inside Intelligence* – a book written by a former member of MI6. As in the 'Spycatcher' case, the book had already entered the public domain, but the Crown sought to restrain its publication by the newspaper on the basis that its publication would cause a loss of confidence in the security forces. It was held that as the book had already been published, and any damage was merely indirect, there was no basis for granting and maintaining the injunctions.

Defences to an action in confidentiality

If free speech and freedom of the press is to be maintained to a reasonable degree, it is essential that the law develop certain defences that are available to defendants in such proceedings. The common law, often influenced by free speech norms and the jurisprudence of the European Court of Human Rights, has developed a number of such defences and this area is now being developed in the light of the Human Rights Act 1998.

---

[222] See, for example, *HRH Prince of Wales v Associated Newspapers* [2007] 2 ALL ER 139; *McKennitt v Ash* [2007] EMLR 4.
[223] [1990] 1 AC 109. See also *Observer and Guardian v United Kingdom* (1991) 14 EHRR 153.
[224] [1990] 1 AC 812.

Where the information is in the public domain, or is stale

Information that enters the public domain loses its confidentiality and thus does not warrant protection.[225] When the information in question has already entered the public domain the claimant will be unable to prove that publication would be contrary to the public interest, or that it would cause any damage, and the defendant will be free to publish the information irrespective of whether the publication would be in the public interest.[226] The case of *Attorney-General v Times Newspapers*[227] provides further support for this principle and thus allows the courts to avoid any unnecessary restriction on free speech. In this case an order had prohibited the defendant newspaper from publishing information about the British Secret Intelligence Service, which had been disclosed to it by a former employee. The order had been varied to exclude information that had previously been published or which had been made generally accessible to the public at large. The Attorney-General claimed that that the latter phrase should be interpreted to allow publication only when the defendant could demonstrate to the court or to the Attorney-General that the information was already sufficiently in the public domain. The Court of Appeal held that having regard to Article 10 of the Convention it was not right to subject the defendants to a fetter on their freedom of expression by imposing on them the requirement to seek confirmation from the Attorney-General or the Court that facts which they intended to publish had been sufficiently brought into the public domain.[228]

It should be noted, however, that information does not lose its confidentiality simply because it is known to other people, and consequently the courts have the power to prohibit further disclosure, especially if the information has only reached a limited number of people and there are now plans to publish the information more widely.[229] Thus, in *Barclays Bank PLC v Guardian News and Media Ltd*,[230] the court continued an injunction preventing the further dissemination of the claimant's financial documents by the defendant newspaper pending full trial. The court held that although general availability of material on the internet would mean that such information would lose its confidential character, limited and partial dissemination, perhaps in some remote and specialist site that was not generally available to the public without a great deal of effort, would not result in a loss of such confidentiality. The defence of public domain, together with s.12(4) of the Human Rights Act 1998, was, therefore, not a complete defence and the court had to apply proportionality in deciding whether to continue the injunction. On the facts, although the documents related to how financial institutions operated in the economy and were thus a matter of most serious public debate, that did not give journalists complete freedom to publish in full confidential documents leaked in breach of a fiduciary duty.[231]

---

[225] It should be noted that the development of privacy via the law of confidentiality means that information might now retain its confidentiality despite its exposure to the public. See chapter 11.

[226] In *Dupuis and Others v France*, decision of the European Court, 7 June 2007, it was held that the prosecution of a book containing confidential information published some ten years after the prosecution of a politician was disproportionate as it was not likely to have had an impact on the administration of justice.

[227] [2001] 1 WLR 885.

[228] Note, however, the decision of the House of Lords in *Attorney-General v Punch* [2003] 1 All ER 301, dealt with under contempt of court and confidentiality, below.

[229] This is particularly so where the disclosure of the material affects the claimant's right to privacy: see, for example, *A v B plc and Another* [2002] 3 WLR 542, discussed in chapter 11.

[230] [2009] EWHC 591 (QB).

[231] The case will be examined below, at page 469.

In addition to allowing the publication of information that is already in the public domain, if the court is satisfied that the information in question is now 'stale news', the defendant will have a defence to publication or disclosure. Thus, in *Attorney-General* v *Jonathan Cape Ltd*,[232] the court refused to grant an injunction to restrain the publication of an ex-cabinet minister's memoirs, even though the doctrine of collective responsibility meant that such a publication was covered by the law of confidentiality. In the court's view, the publication of the diaries, ten years after the events, would do nothing to inhibit full discussion in the cabinet at the present time, or damage the doctrine of collective responsibility.

Defences of iniquity and public interest

The courts have established that there is no confidentiality in iniquitous behaviour. Thus, a defence to an action in confidentiality exists if the defendants can prove that the information in question revealed illegal or immoral behaviour on the part of the claimant.[233] For example, in *Initial Services* v *Putterill*[234] it was held that the defendants could successfully rely on that defence where publication would reveal that the plaintiffs had committed a criminal offence. In this case the defendant, a former employee of the plaintiffs, had disclosed to a newspaper allegations that the plaintiffs had repeatedly violated restrictive practices legislation by dealing with unregistered companies. It was held that the defendant could rely on the defence of iniquity.[235]

Quite apart from the defence of iniquity, the courts accepted that certain disclosures of confidential information should be permitted as being in the public interest. For example, in *Lion Laboratories* v *Evans*[236] it was held that the public interest defence was not limited to iniquity and that iniquity was merely an instance of a just cause and excuse for breaking a confidence. The plaintiffs had manufactured a breathalyser that had been successfully used by the police. Two employees of the plaintiffs disclosed documents to a national newspaper, revealing doubts as to the accuracy of the product, and the plaintiffs had successfully secured an injunction to stop publication. On appeal the Court of Appeal held that for the defendants to succeed in their defence they must prove a legitimate ground for supposing that it was in the public interest for the information to be disclosed and that the court had to perform a balancing exercise between the public interest and the plaintiff's right to confidentiality. The issue raised by the defendants was a serious question concerning the life and liberty of the subject, and thus the defendants should be allowed to put the information before the public. Accordingly, the courts need to consider first whether the nature of the subject matter is that such disclosure would be in the public interest, and secondly whether that public interest outweighs the protection of the claimant's claims to confidentiality.

Publication in the public interest?

Clearly, in *Evans* there was a strong public interest in such disclosure to the public, but the courts may have difficulty in deciding whether other information is of such interest, and

---

[232] [1976] QB 752.

[233] The courts have not gone so far as to preclude the claimant from relying on the law of confidentiality with respect to extramarital sexual encounters. See chapter 11, pages 623–7.

[234] [1968] 1 QB 396.

[235] Such employees are now protected from dismissal by the Public Interest Disclosure Act 1998.

[236] [1985] QB 526.

whether it should be disclosed to the public. In this context the courts traditionally drew a distinction between matters of public interest and matters which the public are interested in, thus attempting to place political and other public matters in the public interest category, while excluding information relating to a person's private life. The difficulty of such a distinction was shown in the controversial case of *Woodward v Hutchins*.[237] The plaintiff's agent had divulged information to the press regarding the sexual antics of the plaintiff and other pop stars. In an application for an interim injunction, LORD DENNING MR held that the defendants could raise the defence of public interest in relation to the disclosure. In his Lordship's view the defendant had been employed to produce a favourable image of not only the artists' public lives but also their private lives. Thus, if they seek publicity that is to their advantage, they cannot complain if a servant discloses the truth about them. If the image that they fostered was not a true one, then it is in the public interest that it should be corrected. Although the case involved proceedings at an interlocutory stage, the decision raised several issues regarding the balancing of press freedom and the right to private life.[238]

Although the decision in *Woodward* would be welcomed by both the press and the public, it might be argued that it gave too little weight to the privacy rights of public figures and in this respect would appear to be incompatible with the Human Rights Act 1998 and, perhaps, the case law of the European Court of Human Rights. Although the decision of the Court of Appeal in *A v B plc and Another*[239] (that any interference with press freedom had to be justified and that a court would not be justified in interfering with press freedom simply because there was no identifiable special public interest in any particular material being published) blurred the distinction between what is in the public interest and what the public are interested in, subsequent case law seems to make a clear distinction between the two. Thus, although it has been recognised that there may be a public interest in exposing public celebrities as liars,[240] it has been stressed that the public has no general right to be informed of the private details of a public figure's life merely because they are curious to know such detail.[241]

In addition to identifying the existence of a public interest, the courts will need to consider whether that interest is best served by disclosing that information to the public at large, rather than some more limited audience, such as the police or other authorities. In *Francome v Mirror Group Newspapers*[242] the defendant sought to rely on the defence so as to publish information relating to possible cheating in the horseracing world. It had acquired this information via illegal telephone tapping, but had claimed that the disclosure of such tapes was in the public interest. It was held that pending full trial it was impossible to see what public interest could be served by publishing the content of the tapes, which would not equally be served by giving them to the police or the Jockey Club. Any wider publication, in the court's

---

[237] [1977] 1 WLR 760.

[238] This approach was taken in the post-Human Rights Act case of *Theakston v MGN Ltd* [2002] EMLR 22. In that case a television presenter who had visited a prostitute in a brothel sought an injunction against the defendants to stop them publishing an article and photographs relating to the incidents. In refusing a temporary injunction, OUSELEY J held that there was a real public interest in the publication of the article given the claimant's portrayal as a respectable person to present programmes aimed at young viewers and the desire that he conduct himself appropriately in public.

[239] [2002] 3 WLR 542.

[240] *Campbell v MGN Ltd* [2004] 2 AC 457.

[241] *McKennitt v Ash* [2007] 3 WLR 194, following the decision of the European Court in *Von Hannover v Germany* (2005) 40 EHRR 1. Such cases are explored in detail in chapter 11.

[242] [1984] 1 WLR 892.

view, could only serve the interests of the newspaper. It is suggested that this approach is not consistent with Article 10 of the Convention and the role of a free press, and should be restricted to rare cases, perhaps those involving national security, where it is essential that the information be relayed to more appropriate authorities. It is suggested that this approach pays too little attention to the duty of the press to keep the public informed and is thus incompatible with both Article 10 and the Human Rights Act 1998. Thus, in *Jockey Club* v *Buffham*,[243] it was held that information revealing the apparent existence of wide-scale corruption within the racing world was of legitimate concern to the public, and the public interest in the disclosure outweighed the Jockey Club's right of confidence in respect of confidential documents that had come into the hands of the BBC.

The balancing of interests

Even where the defendant can establish that the disclosure of the information was in the public interest, it still needs to be established that that issue of public interest outweighs the claimant's legal right. This will involve the court in balancing the two conflicting claims and the success of the defence in such cases will often be dependent on the court's perceptions of the quality and strength of these competing claims. In the past the courts were liable to give undue weight to the commercial interests of the claimant, giving little or no protection to the claims of free speech and the public's right to know. An example is provided by the case of *Schering Chemicals* v *Falkman*.[244] In this case a person had been hired by the plaintiffs to give advice on how to deal with media questions relating to its controversial new drug, Primidos. That person decided to make a documentary about the drug and intended to sell it to Thames Television. In rejecting any public interest defence, the court held that the public interest in disclosing this information was outweighed by its duty to ensure that the employee's duty towards the company was not abused or exploited.[245]

The balancing exercise is particularly difficult where freedom of expression conflicts with another fundamental right. For example, in *X* v *Y*[246] the court was faced with a conflict between the public's right to know and the confidentiality of hospital patients' medical files. In that case an injunction had been sought by the area health authority to stop newspapers from disclosing the names of two doctors who had contracted AIDS. This information had been given to the press by an employee who had disclosed hospital records. The defendants relied on the public interest defence but it was held that the public interest in disclosure was substantially outweighed when measured against the public interest in maintaining loyalty and confidentiality. In the court's view, the record of hospital patients, particularly those suffering from this appalling condition, should be kept as confidential as the courts can properly keep them. The deprivation to the public of the information sought to be published

---

[243] [2003] 2 WLR 178.

[244] [1981] 2 WLR 848.

[245] The decision in the 'Spycatcher' case allowed the courts to give greater weight to freedom of expression. Theoretically, the courts should not grant an injunction unless the claimant can prove that there is an overriding public interest in displacing freedom of expression, but it should be noted that the decision was made in the context of information which was already in the public domain; it is more doubtful whether the courts would refuse injunctions with regard to truly confidential information on the grounds that the public interest in freedom of expression would be unduly threatened by the orders.

[246] [1998] 2 All ER 648.

will be minimal, given the wide-ranging public debate concerning AIDS and doctors which was being conducted in the press at that time.

Balancing freedom of expression and confidentiality under the Human Rights Act 1998

The above balancing exercise will continue under the Human Rights Act and in such cases the courts will need to strike an appropriate balance between the protection of privacy/confidentiality interests and press freedom. More specifically, s.12 of the Human Rights Act requires the courts to have particular regard to freedom of expression where freedom of expression is threatened in legal proceedings. Specifically, s.12(3) states that where a claimant seeks a temporary order to restrain publication pending a full trial, no such order shall be made unless the court is satisfied that the applicant is likely to establish that publication should not be allowed. Further, s.12(4) of the Act provides that where the proceedings relate to material which the respondent claims, or which appears to the court, to be journalistic, literary or artistic material, the court must have particular regard to the extent to which the material has, or is about to, become available to the public; the extent to which it is, or would be, in the public interest for the material to be published; and any relevant privacy code.[247]

With respect to s.12 and actions in confidentiality, two points are of central importance: the circumstances in which the courts will grant interim injunctions, and the weight that should be attached to the respective rights of free speech and confidentiality/privacy. With respect to the balancing of freedom of expression and the right to private life, the Court of Appeal in *Douglas* v *Hello! Magazine*[248] stated that s.12(4) requires the court to consider Article 10 of the Convention in its entirety, including the exceptions permitted within Article 10(2). Thus, it was not appropriate for the court to give freedom of speech additional weight over and above any competing right, such as the right to private life. However, in *Venables and Thompson* v *MGN*[249] the court held that because s.12 of the Act requires the court to pay special regard to freedom of speech it was no longer appropriate to conduct a balancing exercise, but instead to apply the principle that any interference with the right in Article 10(1) had to be shown to fall within the exceptions permitted in Article 10(2), those restrictions being narrowly interpreted.[250]

Both issues have since been clarified by the House of Lords. In *Cream Holdings* v *Banjaree and Another*[251] the House of Lords has accepted that s.12 does introduce a new, stricter test, but nevertheless confirmed that s.12 did not require the courts to give freedom of expression a higher order than other Convention rights and that the test under s.12(3) on applications for interim injunctions was whether the applicant's prospects of success at trial were sufficiently favourable to justify the making of such an order in the particular circumstances of the case. As a general approach the courts should be very slow to make such orders where the

---

[247] The scope and effect of s.12 is dealt with in detail in chapter 8 of this text, pages 362–7. See Rogers and Tomlinson, Privacy and Expression: Convention Rights and Interim Injunctions [2003] EHRLR (Special Issue) 37.

[248] [2001] 2 WLR 992.

[249] [2001] 2 WLR 1038.

[250] In this sense the court was following the approach adopted by the European Court of Human Rights in *Sunday Times* v *United Kingdom* (1979) 2 EHRR 245.

[251] [2005] 1 AC 253.

applicant had not demonstrated that he would probably succeed at trial, although in some cases a lesser degree of likelihood would suffice.[252] In that case the court recognised that the material in question – financial information relating to the company which alleged that it had taken part in corrupt business practices – was of serious public interest and accordingly the company was more likely to fail than to succeed at full trial. The House of Lords thus discharged an injunction prohibiting the disclosure of that information until trial.[253]

Further, in *Re S (Publicity)*[254] the House of Lords confirmed that freedom of expression under Article 10 does not have an automatic 'trump' status under the Act. In this case an order had been sought restraining the identification of a murderer (who was the child's mother) and her victim (the child's brother) in order to protect the welfare of a child who was in care. It was held that the court should conduct a balancing exercise between the child's right to private life and the right of freedom of expression. Their Lordships stressed that s.12(4) did not require the court to give pre-eminence to either article and the judge had to consider the magnitude of the interference proposed and then what steps were necessary to prevent or minimise that interference.

Whether the section has made a difference with respect to cases involving a conflict between freedom of expression and confidentiality can be answered, conditionally, by examining the relevant post-Act case law. With respect to cases pitting free speech against privacy claims, the courts have resolved such cases by applying the central principle of proportionality and resolving such cases on their merits. For example, in *Douglas and Others v Hello! and Others*[255] it was held that as English law now recognised the right to privacy under Article 8 of the European Convention the court was now required therefore to balance such a right with freedom of expression, according appropriate weight to each claim. Thus, as in this case the claimant's right to privacy was relatively weak – they had already sold their privacy rights as part of a commercial transaction – and the claimants could be adequately compensated by an award of damages if they succeeded at full trial, the balance of convenience was in favour of publication. In coming to that decision the Court noted that if the publication of the issue was killed by the injunction, the defendant would suffer loss that would be extremely difficult to quantify.[256]

Thus, although the courts may start from the position that any interference with freedom of expression needs to be justified on strong grounds, they are prepared to compromise it in favour of a stronger countervailing claim. Thus, in *Venables and Thompson v Newsgroup Newspapers*,[257] granting indefinite orders to restrain publicity of the claimants' identities, the High Court held that although it recognised the enormous importance of upholding freedom of expression, in the instant case it was necessary to grant such injunctions. The claimants

---

[252] The case will be considered again in chapter 11.

[253] See also *Northern Rock plc v Financial Times and Others* [2007] EWHC 2677 (QB) – injunction granted to restrain the publication on the newspaper group's website of sensitive and detailed financial information, but refused with respect to extracts from a document that had already been published by the mass media, thus making the interim injunction futile.

[254] [2005] 1 AC 593.

[255] [2001] 2 WLR 992.

[256] At full trial the court awarded the Douglases £14,600, incorporating £3750 each for distress. The Court of Appeal upheld this decision: *Douglas and Hello Ltd (No 3)* [2005] 3 WLR 881.

[257] [2001] 1 All ER 908. In December 2001 a newspaper was found guilty of contempt when it broke the terms of the court order: *Attorney-General v Greater Manchester Newspapers Ltd*, *The Times*, 7 December 2001.

were at serious risk of attack and the court had to have particular regard to Article 2 of the Convention, and thus the right of confidentiality should be placed above the right of the media to publish freely information about the claimants.

In cases involving the commercial or professional interests of the claimant, there are signs that the courts will give greater protection to freedom of expression than previously, especially where there is a strong public interest in publication. For example, in *Jockey Club* v *Buffham*[258] it was held that a broadcaster was entitled to make use of confidential documents obtained in breach of confidence by an ex-employee. The documents revealed apparent corruption in the racing world, a matter of legitimate concern to the public, and that interest clearly outweighed the Club's right of confidence in those documents. Further, in *Tiller Valley Foods* v *Channel Four Television*,[259] an interim injunction was refused preventing the defendants from broadcasting a programme made with the help of a journalist who had posed as an employee and who had reported on allegations of bad and unhygienic practices at the claimant's factory. In the judge's view the information was not confidential just because images of the factory had been taken without the claimant's consent. In any case its disclosure was justified in the public interest. However, the court must take into account any countervailing and genuine confidentiality and privacy claim. Thus, in *BKM* v *BBC*,[260] although a court refused an injunction to restrain the broadcast of a film exposing failings in the care provided at care homes, because the use of clandestine filming in this case was necessary in the public interest in investigating standards in care homes, it placed a condition to the effect that the broadcast should not interfere with the privacy of the residents more than was necessary (in this case by obscuring the identities of the residents).

Despite the court's willingness to uphold freedom of expression with respect to public interest information, they will not provide the press with an unlimited immunity in this respect. Thus, there will be cases where the commercial or private interests of the claimant outweigh the public interest in freedom of expression. In *Imutran* v *Uncaged Campaigns*,[261] the defendants, a body opposed to animal experimentation, had received confidential information relating to the claimant's business and intended to write an article on pig-to-primate organ transplantation on the basis of the information. The claimants had obtained an injunction prohibiting the defendants from infringing the claimant's copyright and from disclosing the confidential documents to anyone other than to and for the use of regulatory agencies. The claimant sought to have the injunctions continued until trial, and the defendants argued that having regard to s.12 of the 1998 Act the claimants were not likely to succeed and the injunctions should not be continued. SIR ANDREW MORRITT VC held that the word 'likelihood' in s.12(4) of the Human Rights Act was only slightly higher in the scale of probability than whether a case had a 'real prospect of success', the test established to decide whether an applicant should be granted an injunction pending a full trial. In his Lordship's opinion, s.12(4) was not intended to direct the court to place even greater weight on the importance of freedom of expression than it already did prior to the Act. It was held that in the instant case the claimant was likely to establish at the trial of the action that publication of its confidential documents should not be allowed. Moreover, the injunction did not go further than was necessary.

---

[258] [2003] 2 WLR 178.
[259] *The Times*, 23 May 2004.
[260] [2009] EWHC 3151 (Ch).
[261] [2001] 2 All ER 385.

A more recent example of the courts' reluctance to override commercial confidentiality can be seen in the interim proceedings in *Barclays Bank PLC v Guardian News and Media Ltd*,[262] where the High Court granted an injunction preventing the further dissemination of the claimant's financial documents by the defendant newspaper pending full trial. In coming to that decision the court stressed that the defence of public domain was not a complete defence and that the court had to apply the doctrine of proportionality in coming to its conclusion. In the present case, the documents related to how financial institutions operated in the economy and thus were a matter of most serious public debate, but that did not give journalists complete freedom to publish in full confidential documents that had been leaked in breach of a fiduciary duty. The court stated that it would be relevant for the court to ask if the debate could flourish without such full disclosure and that responsible journalists should also consider whether publication of personal details about the affairs of corporations that may not have even broken the law was appropriate. As the claimant's legal professional privilege was also at issue in this case and publication would have eroded that privilege, the court concluded that the bank would probably have demonstrated at full trial that publication was disproportionate.

Although the decisions in *Imutran* and *Barclays* might be thought to be confined to their own facts and context – where the defendant has made substantial use of the claimant's commercial or copyrighted work – it is feared that the courts may continue to place great weight on a person's commercial interests over and above freedom of expression on matters of public concern. As we shall see in chapter 11 the courts are beginning to provide greater protection to the individual's right to privacy where the defendant cannot display a true public interest (as opposed to a curiosity) in the dissemination of that information. However, in return the courts should offer an enhanced protection of such rights where the information is undoubtedly in the public interest. The case study below explores this dilemma, questioning whether the courts are capable of providing robust protection of public interest speech when it is in conflict with the claimant's right to confidentiality.

Questions

What interests does the law of confidentiality seek to protect? Is it necessary in a democratic society to protect those interests?

How does the law balance the right to confidentiality with the public interest in free speech? How would you define the public interest in this respect?

The law of copyright and freedom of expression

The law protecting a person's right to intellectual property is capable of inhibiting the free flow of information. Such restrictions will fall within the legitimate aim of protecting the rights of others, contained in the exceptions laid down in Article 10(2) of the European Convention, because a person's property rights will be in danger from the publication of such information. Although most breach of copyright cases do not give rise to serious issues relating to freedom of expression and the public's right to know, there may be cases where the publication of such protected information might be in the public interest, and in such a case the law should comply with the requirements of necessity and proportionality within Article 10(2).

---

[262] [2009] EWHC 591 (QB).

The courts refused to accept that there was a public interest defence to an action for breach of copyright in the pre-Human Rights Act case law,[263] and this stance was followed by the High Court in *Ashdown v Telegraph Group Ltd*.[264] In that case *The Sunday Telegraph* had published three separate items of a confidential record of a meeting held at Downing Street between various politicians, including several verbatim quotations from a nine-page minute. The claimant brought proceedings against the newspaper for breach of confidence and copyright infringement. The newspaper sought to rely on a defence of public interest in relation to the copyright action, but it was held that unless a copyright infringer could make out a specific defence under the Copyright Designs and Patents Act 1988, it was not open to him to defend the proceedings on the basis that the 1988 Act restricted freedom of expression further than was necessary and that the restriction was as a consequence contrary to Article 10(2) of the European Convention. The decision was upheld on appeal,[265] although the Court of Appeal held that the decision in *Yelland* and the decision of the High Court in the present case had taken too restrictive an approach by holding that there could be no public interest defence in an action for breach of copyright. The Court of Appeal held that now that the 1998 Act was in force there was the clearest public interest in giving effect to freedom of expression in those rare cases where this right trumped the rights conferred by the Copyright, Design and Patents Act 1988. In such circumstances the court felt that s.171(3) of the 1988 Act preserved the common law defence of public interest and thus permitted the defence of public interest to be raised, although in the court's opinion it would be rare for such a defence to justify the copying of a work to which copyright was attached. On the facts, the court held that although it was arguable that the newspaper was justified in making limited quotations from the meeting in order to demonstrate that it had indeed obtained the material so that it was in a position to give an authentic account of the meeting, extensive reproduction of the document was not necessary or justifiable. The claimant's work product had been deployed in furtherance of the newspaper's commercial interests and it was not arguable that a newspaper should be able to profit from such a use of copyright without paying compensation.

The Court of Appeal in *Ashdown* takes a more robust stance to that taken by the courts in the area of qualified privilege in the law of defamation. Thus, although the courts are prepared to accept that in rare cases the duty of the press to report matters of public interest should trump other rights, in practice they are reluctant to allow this to happen unless there is the strongest evidence to suggest that the tactics employed by the press were essential in order to receive the relevant information. As the question of whether the claimant had a copyright in the material is often a matter of chance, it is suggested that the fact that a breach of copyright was committed should not be given undue weight, particularly when the court is considering granting summary relief.[266]

The decision also shows the scepticism of the courts towards the press and their reluctance to accept that it is motivated by public concern rather than private commercial interests. The approach in *Ashdown* was certainly evident in the recent case of *HRH Prince of Wales v Associated Newspapers*,[267] detailed in the case study below, where both the High Court and the

---

[263] *Hyde Park Residence* v *Yelland* [2000] 3 WLR 215.
[264] [2001] Ch 685.
[265] [2001] 3 WLR 1368.
[266] Note that in *Imutran*, n 261 above, the claimant relied on copyright as well as the law of confidentiality.
[267] [2007] 2 All ER 139.

Court of Appeal rejected the argument that the disclosure of the Prince's diaries constituted fair dealing under s.30 of the Copyright, Design and Patents Act, or attracted the defence of public interest under s.171.

CASE STUDY

HRH Prince of Wales v *Associated Newspapers* [2007] 2 All ER 139

The case has been chosen because it is a high-profile example of freedom of expression, including press freedom and the public right to know, coming into conflict with an individual's right to confidentiality. This conflict was intensified because of the claimant's identity and social position and the courts needed to consider not only whether the right to privacy and confidentiality was lost in such cases, but also the extent to which the public interest debate could compromise any such right. The issue of press freedom and individual privacy is examined again in chapter 11 but this case study and the questions at the end concentrate on the issues of press freedom and the public right to know.

The claimant, Prince Charles, had written a number of private diaries detailing his private opinions and personal impressions of his official overseas tours. The diaries were photocopied by a member of his staff and sent to friends and family, but a copy of the Hong Kong diary, together with seven other journals relating to other tours, came into the hands of the defendant newspaper company. The *Mail on Sunday* then published an article, including an editorial comment, based on the Hong Kong diary, and including specific extracts from that journal. The Prince sought orders in the law of confidentiality restraining the newspaper from using or disclosing the contents of the seven other journals, claiming that the diaries set out his private and personal thoughts and were thus not matters in the public domain. Further, he claimed that the diaries were literary works and thus protected under the Copyright, Designs and Patents Act 1988; consequently he sought an order prohibiting further infringement of that copyright in all eight journals. At the original hearing the judge reserved his judgment and the diaries' contents were published in the national newspapers.

The defendant contended that the information was not private in that it did not constitute intimate personal information, but rather was information relating to the claimant's public life and thus related to a zone of his life that had previously been put in the public domain. The defendant further argued that as the information concerned the Prince's political opinions, the electorate had a right to know such information by virtue of the Freedom of Information Act 2000. Alternatively, as it related to his political behaviour, and involved him departing from constitutional convention, which demanded that the Heir to the Throne be politically neutral, there was a powerful public interest in the disclosure of such information to the public. This public interest thus outweighed any right of confidence the claimant might have in those diaries. With respect to the copyright claim the defendants argued that the publication constituted fair dealing for the purpose of reporting current events, or for the purpose of criticism and review, under s.30 of the 1988 Act.

Delivering his judgment ([2006] EWHC 552), BLACKBURNE J held that the claimant had established that he had a reasonable expectation of privacy in the contents of the Hong Kong journal and that there was no real prospect of the defendants proving otherwise. In his Lordship's view, it was clear that the claimant regarded his journals as private and confidential. Further, it was clear that the journals had not been obtained legitimately and that the newspaper's source of information was a former employee who would have been under an express duty of confidence with respect to the journals. The fact that the journal dealt with events most of which were a matter of public record was irrelevant; it was the claimant's impressions and musings prompted by those events which was significant about the journal. Thus, although the claimant's reflections could be said in the widest sense to be political, that did not mean that he had no reasonable expectation of privacy in respect of what he had written. In his Lordship's view it was equally immaterial that the claimant was a persistent and effective lobbyist (assuming that was established), was in a position to wield influence, was heir to the throne, and that he might be acting in breach of constitutional convention in the way he went about those matters. For that reason, the judge also rejected the claim under the Freedom of Information Act 2000, holding that the Act did not assist the defendants. In any case there was no evidence to suggest that the defendants had filed with a public authority any record of the tours to which the journals related.

His Lordship then stressed that the fact that the journal was not of a highly personal or private nature – in the sense that it did not deal with matters of an intimate or medical nature or about members of his family, and that its contents were a long way from the often salacious celebrity information often featured in privacy claims – did not rob the claimant of a reasonable expectation of privacy in respect of what he had written in his diary. By speaking out publicly both in speeches and in published articles on issues which in the widest sense were political, the claimant had not forfeited any reasonable expectation of privacy in respect of such matters that had been committed to a hand-written journal that had not been intended by him to be open to public scrutiny.

Turning to the newspaper's public interest defence, his Lordship held that it was impossible to say that the disclosures made by it from the journal's contents were necessary in a democratic society for the protection of the rights and freedoms of others and that as a consequence the claimant's entitlement to privacy in respect of the journal had been overridden by such a right. Not the least of the considerations that had to be weighed in the scales was the claimant's countervailing claim to his private space, which included the right to be able to commit his private thoughts to writing and keep them private, the more so as he was inescapably a public figure who was subject to constant and intense media interest.

His Lordship found that in the instant case the balancing exercise revealed that the interference with the claimant's right to privacy was not justified, while the interference with the defendant's right to freedom of expression was so justified. He also felt that the claimant had established an expectation of privacy with respect to the contents of the other diaries, but felt that they should not be covered by the order in the absence of the court knowing the content of those other journals. Thus, the claim for breach of confidence for the Hong Kong diary succeeded, but the claim in respect of the other diaries would go to trial (see below).

His Lordship also rejected the defences under the Copyright, Designs and Patents Act 1988. In the court's view the defence of fair dealing under the Act had no realistic prospect of success. As the journal had plainly not been made available to the public, and as the extracts quoted from the journal formed a substantial part of the whole work, the defendant's reliance on that defence was misplaced (see *Ashdown v Telegraph Group* [2001] 2 WLR 967). Further, taken as a whole the articles published by the defendants were not confined to dealing with current events. Having examined the articles, the court was of the impression that the selected passages from the journal had been chosen for the purpose of reporting on, the revelation of the contents of the journal as being an event of interest in itself. Thus, the claim under the 1988 Act succeeded with respect to the Hong Kong journal, but failed for the other journals for the same reasons.

The defendants appealed to the Court of Appeal, claiming, *inter alia*, that the journal was not confidential and private. Dismissing the appeal, the Court of Appeal held that the journal was obviously of a confidential and private nature and that the Prince had a reasonable expectation that its content would remain private (*Campbell v MGN Ltd* [2004] 2 AC 457). This was because the employees to whom the copies were circulated were all under a contractual duty of confidence and others who received copies had always treated them as confidential. In the Court's view it was significant that the contents of the journal had been disclosed in breach of confidence, and in such cases the test to be applied as to whether it was necessary to restrict freedom of expression in order to prevent disclosure of information received in confidence was not simply whether the information was a matter of public interest, but whether in all the circumstances it was in the public interest that the duty of confidence should be breached.

Further, in applying the test of proportionality, the nature of the relationship that gave rise to the duty of confidentiality might be important. There was an important public interest in employees respecting the obligations of confidence that they had assumed under their contracts, and in this case the public interest in disclosing the journal's contents did not outweigh the confidential nature of the information and the relationship of confidence under which it had been received. On the facts, therefore, the significance of the interference with the claimant's Article 8 rights outweighed the prospective interference with the defendant's Article 10 rights, and even in the absence of a breach of confidence the claimant would have had an unanswerable claim for breach of contract.

In subsequent proceedings the High Court granted summary judgment of the Prince's claim in breach of confidence and copyright with respect to the other seven journals: *HRH Prince of Wales v Associated Newspaper* [2007] EWHC 1685 (Ch).

Questions

1. In terms of freedom of the press and the public right to know, how highly would you regard the dissemination of the content of the journals?
2. Do you feel that members of the royal family, and major political figures, should be allowed to retain a right of confidentiality/privacy?
3. If so, should that right be lost with respect to matters that affect the performance of their public functions?
4. Why did the High Court believe that the journals were private and confidential? Do you agree with that finding?

5 Was it significant that these 'private' diaries concerned matters of political and/or constitutional importance?

6 How significant was it that the information had been taken and disseminated to the press in breach of a contractual duty of confidentiality and in breach of copyright?

7 Given the public interest nature of the information should it matter that the press in its articles concentrated on the revelation of the documents rather than discussing the actual constitutional and political issues raised in the journals?

8 Do you believe that both courts struck a fair balance between freedom of the press and the claimant's rights in confidentiality and copyright?

9 Is there an argument in cases such as this that any action brought by the claimant should be against the guilty employee, and that no action should be taken against the press?

10 If the case was referred to the European Court of Human Rights, what do you think the outcome would be?

Free speech and contempt of court

Introduction: the purpose of contempt of court

The law of contempt of court serves two essential purposes.[268] First, it seeks to safeguard the individual's fundamental right to a fair trial. If discussion takes place on the likely outcome of current legal proceedings, or information is published which would otherwise influence the outcome of such proceedings, then such expression is in danger of interfering with the rights of others. Such rights not only constitute a legitimate aim for the restriction of free speech as allowed under Article 10(2) of the European Convention, but also constitute a fundamental right, which is reflected in Article 6 of the Convention and is an established constitutional right in domestic law. Thus, a trial may be abandoned, or a retrial ordered, whenever there is a real risk of prejudice to the trial.[269] For example, in *R v Taylor*,[270] a murder trial was abandoned when a newspaper took part in an unremitting and misleading coverage of the defendant's trial. The *Sun* newspaper had published an incriminating photograph of a defendant in a murder trial kissing the husband of the victim at a wedding. The photograph had been distorted to portray a mouth-to-mouth kiss and the headline read 'Cheat's kiss'. It was held that the actions of the newspaper were part of unremitting and misleading press coverage and had led to a real risk of prejudice to the trial.[271]

---

[268] For a detailed account of the law and its impact on freedom of expression, see Robertson and Nicol, *Media Law* (Penguin 2008, 5th edn), chapter 7; Fenwick and Phillipson, *Media Freedom under the Human Rights Act* (OUP 2006), chapters 4–7. For a comparative approach, see Cram, *A Virtue Less Cloistered: Courts, Free Speech and Constitutions* (Hart 2002).

[269] In 2002 the jury was discharged in the trial of two professional footballers for assault when the *Sunday Mirror* published an article that suggested that the attacks might have been racially motivated. The newspaper was subsequently found in contempt of court and fined £75,000: *Attorney General v MGN Ltd* [2002] EWHC 907 (Admin).

[270] (1998) 93 Cr App R 361. The Attorney-General refused to bring contempt proceedings, and an action to challenge that decision was dismissed as such decisions were not subject to judicial review.

[271] The test was confirmed by the Court of Appeal in *R v Stone* [2000] Crim LR 465. The question of whether a retrial should be ordered where there has been extensive publicity had to be decided on the balance of probabilities as to whether the defendant would suffer serious prejudice to the extent that no fair trial could be held.

Secondly, the law seeks to uphold confidence in the judicial system, and in particular seeks to protect the impartiality and independence of the judiciary. Accordingly, unreasonable discussions of legal proceedings, or the bribing or pressurising of a juror, not only interferes with a party's right to a fair trial, but also undermines the public's confidence in the judicial system. This characteristic of the law of contempt is borne out by the fact that in many cases the relevant criminal proceedings are brought by the Attorney-General.

Although the law of contempt of court protects both such interests, the latter interest – the protection of the impartiality and independence of the judiciary – is the basis of liability. Thus a contempt is not committed simply because a court has decided, by, for example, abandoning a trial, that a person could not receive a fair trial because of some form of pre-trial publicity or discussion.[272] The decision to abandon the trial is based entirely on considerations of the individual's right to a fair trial, which should not to any reasonable degree be prejudiced by such publicity or discussion. Whether such publicity gives rise to liability in contempt, however, is decided by the application of slightly different rules and on wider grounds. This will involve considerations of public discussion versus the due administration of justice, thus raising questions of freedom of expression and the public's right to know. Thus, in *Attorney-General v MGN*,[273] although the publication of a number of stories about a person, giving information about his relationship with his girlfriend and details of his past criminal record, were sufficiently damaging for that person's trial to be abandoned, the court found the story's publication did not amount to contempt of court. In the court's view the articles did not pass the thresholds contained in the Contempt of Court Act 1981. Although the cumulative effect of the articles prejudiced the right to a fair trial, the court had to look at each publication separately, and in this case the effect of each individual article did not cause a substantial risk that the proceedings would be seriously impeded.[274]

Although the law of contempt pursues more than one legitimate aim, and its existence is essential to any society that practises the principles of due process and the rule of law, its scope and application must be restricted so as to accommodate principles of freedom of expression and the discussion of matters in the public interest. Thus, any study of this area needs to bear in mind the essential elements and principles of freedom of expression enshrined in the European Convention and its case law. In particular, the law should be careful to comply with the notions of necessity and proportionality that inform such case law and which supports the right and duty of the press to inform the public.[275]

---

[272] However, in *Attorney-General v Birmingham Post* [1998] 4 All ER 49, SIMON BROWN LJ commented that it was difficult to envisage a case which had caused a judge to discharge a jury not being regarded as sufficient to be regarded as contempt. In this case, during a murder trial a newspaper had published an article, suggesting that the murder had been committed by a notorious gang. The judge ordered a retrial and the newspaper was fined £20,000 for contempt.

[273] [1997] 1 All ER 456.

[274] Alternatively, a newspaper might be held in contempt even if its actions are not found to have actually prejudiced the proceedings, as a mere risk is sufficient. See *R v Thomson Newspapers Ltd, ex parte Attorney-General* [1968] 1 All ER 268.

[275] In *Bridges v California* 314 US 252 (1941), the United States Supreme Court held that utterances on pending judicial proceedings could only be punished as a contempt where there was a clear and present danger to the orderly and fair administration of justice. A reasonable tendency to interfere with those goals was not sufficient.

Contempt of court and the European Convention on Human Rights

As noted above, the law of contempt pursues at least two legitimate aims under Article 10(2) of the European Convention. The law of contempt is, therefore, at least in principle, entirely consistent with the principles of free speech in a democratic society. Of course, any such restriction will need to satisfy the tests laid down in Article 10(2); the law of contempt, and its application in individual cases, has to be 'prescribed by law' and 'necessary in a democratic society' for the purpose of achieving that legitimate aim(s).

In *Sunday Times* v *United Kingdom*[276] the European Court laid down a number of important principles relating to the legitimacy and proportionality of such restrictions. First, it held that contempt law could be sufficiently clear and certain so as to be 'prescribed by law', even though the law was not in statutory form. Secondly, the Court felt that, unlike laws based on public morality, the laws of contempt were based on more objective grounds, allowing for a more common European standard. Thirdly, as a consequence the Court could take a more robust approach in assessing the compatibility of those laws, affording the member states a relatively narrow margin of appreciation in deciding whether a restriction was necessary in a democratic society. Finally, the Court emphasised the importance of freedom of expression when the proceedings in question raised matters of great public interest. In that case, therefore, the Court felt that the press should not be prohibited from reporting on such matters unless it was absolutely certain that it would cause prejudice to the administration of justice.

Accordingly, the European Court will not allow domestic law to be used so as to unjustifiably restrict the publication of matter which is clearly in the public interest and which promotes public discussion. For example, in *News Verlags & Co GmbH* v *Austria*[277] the European Court held that an injunction placed on the applicant, restraining the publication of a photograph of a right-wing extremist, accompanied by an allegation that he was responsible for sending letter bombs as part of a political campaign, was a disproportionate interference with the applicant's freedom of expression under Article 10. The Court accepted that the rights of the defendant to a fair trial were at issue, but also noted that the defendant had courted publicity in the past and that the alleged offences were directed against democracy. In particular, the Court reaffirmed that the press had a duty to inform the public in relation to reporting and commenting on court proceedings. The injunctions restricted the choice of the newspaper as to its presentation of reports and created an absolute prohibition on publishing the picture, with or without such comments.

The European Court has to consider a number of issues in determining the question of necessity, including the importance of the subject matter of the speech and the potential threat to a fair trial and the administration of justice. In addition, the absence of an opportunity for the press to report on the matter objectively and fully will be a key issue. However, the European Court will not interfere if it is satisfied that the correct balance has been struck between freedom of speech and the protection of the administration of justice. In *Worm* v *Austria*[278] the applicant, a journalist, wrote an article about a former minister of finance who

---

[276] (1979) 2 EHRR 245.
[277] (2001) 31 EHRR 8.
[278] (1998) 25 EHRR 454.

at that time was involved in charges of tax evasion. The article was highly critical of the former minister and commented on the plausibility of his defence, opining that the court could do nothing less than convict him. The article was published shortly before the trial and the journalist was charged with exercising influence on criminal proceedings. His conviction was upheld and he was fined 48,000 Austrian schillings, which the publishers were jointly and severally liable for. The European Court held that the courts should be the appropriate forum for determining a person's guilt and that the public should have a respect for and confidence in the court's capacity to fulfil that function. Considering the question of necessity, although it was not the case that there should be no prior or contemporaneous discussion on the case in the general press or by the public, the press must not overstep the bounds imposed for the proper administration of justice and should not prejudice the chances of a fair trial. In the present case the domestic courts were entitled to conclude that the article was capable of influencing the outcome of the trial and the decision did not prohibit the journalist's ability to inform the public of his views in an objective manner. Given the limited amount of the fine, and the fact that his employers were liable for its payment, the sanction was not disproportionate and the conviction and sentence were thus necessary in a democratic society.[279]

> **Question**
> What purposes do contempt laws serve, and how are those purposes recognised in the European Convention on Human Rights?

Contempt of court in domestic law

The domestic law of contempt can be found both in statute and in the common law and consists of both civil contempt – disobedience of court orders – and criminal contempt, the interference with judicial proceedings and the administration of justice.

Civil contempt

Although the bulk of this chapter is devoted to criminal contempt, there exists also a principle of civil contempt. Civil contempt involves disobedience to a court order made during the course of civil proceedings and does not in the majority of cases impact on freedom of expression. However, such orders can raise real issues relating to freedom of expression. For example, in *Harman v Home Office*[280] a lawyer had breached a court order relating to the retention of confidential documents by showing the documents to a journalist. The House of Lords held that the lawyer was guilty of contempt of court even though the material had been read out in open court. The majority of their Lordships denied that the case raised issues of freedom of expression and press freedom, preferring to decide the case on the basis of the

---

[279] See also *Tourancheau and July v France*, decision of the European Court, 24 November 2005, where it was held that there was no violation of Article 10 when an editor and a journalist were convicted of contempt of court and fined €1500 each (suspended) when they had published an article explaining the details of a murder and revealing information from the case file while the matter was still under investigation.

[280] [1983] 1 AC 280.

simple question of whether there had been a contempt of court.[281] This approach, it is suggested, will not survive the Human Rights Act. Under s.12 of the Act the court must have particular regard to freedom of expression when making orders that interfere with that freedom, and case law in related areas suggests that it will not be sufficient that a party has deliberately broken a court order, if the essential purpose of that order has not been defeated by the disclosure.[282]

Criminal contempt

This offence can be committed in a variety of ways, including specifically criticising and scandalising the court. The purpose of this type of contempt is not simply to protect the feelings of the officers of the court, but also to maintain confidence in the administration of justice. This would include unruly and disrespectful words or behaviour in the courtroom, but might also involve unreasonable criticism of the judge in a subsequent publication.[283] Such prosecutions should not restrict reasonable free speech and the law should not be unduly sensitive of the feelings of judges. Thus, in *Kyprianou v Cyprus*,[284] the European Court held that there had been a breach of Articles 6 and 10 of the Convention when a lawyer had been sentenced to five days in prison for contempt of court when he had objected to the behaviour of the judge and other court officials when defending his client. The Court held that the domestic court had shown insufficient objectivity and detachment by saying that the judges had been deeply offended by the applicant's behaviour and that such language was inconsistent with Article 6. There had also been a breach of Article 10 because although the applicant had used certain objectionable words (he had accused court officials of passing secret notes and love letters during the proceedings), these had been used in the context of the applicant's attempt to secure a fair trial for his client.

Contempt can also be committed by disclosing jury secrets. Section 8 of the Contempt of Court Act 1981 makes it an offence to obtain, disclose or solicit any information relating to what has happened during a jury's deliberations.[285] Under this provision it is not necessary that the disclosure had, or might have, an adverse effect on the administration of justice, and thus the prohibition is absolute.[286] This leaves the provision vulnerable to challenge under the Human Rights Act as being a disproportionate interference with freedom of expression.[287]

---

[281] A subsequent application to the European Commission on Human Rights was the subject of a friendly settlement: *Harman v United Kingdom* (Application No 10038/82) (1984) DR 53.

[282] For example, if, as in the *Harman* case, the information has already entered the public domain. However, see the House of Lords' decision in *Attorney-General v Punch and Another* [2003] All ER 301 with regard to the law of contempt and confidentiality, below, at page 492.

[283] Thus, in *R v Gray* [1900] 2 QB 36, a person was guilty of contempt of court when he described a judge, who had just tried a charge of obscenity, as an impudent little man in horsehair, who would do well to master the duties of his own profession before undertaking the regulation of another. In the court's view this criticism amounted to scurrilous personal abuse of a judge as a judge. It was held, however, that reasonable criticism does not amount to contempt.

[284] (2007) 44 EHRR 27.

[285] It was held in *Attorney-General v Associated Newspapers* [1993] 2 All ER 535 that disclosure should be interpreted to cover any type of publication, whether obtained directly from a jury member, or indirectly via a third party.

[286] For a recent example, see *A-G v Seckerson* [2009] EMLR 20, where it was held that a newspaper and a juror were guilty of contempt under s.8 for disclosing the deliberations and opinions of the jury in a criminal trial, and that it was not necessary to show that any injustice had been caused.

[287] The Royal Commission on Criminal Justice recommended that the provision should be amended to allow research into jury verdicts: (1993) Cm 2263, chapter 11, para 8.

However, in *A-G v Scotcher* [288] the House of Lords held that s.8 was not incompatible with Article 10 of the European Convention. In that case the House of Lords held that although a juror would not commit an offence under s.8 of the Contempt of Court Act 1981 if he disclosed the jury's deliberations to the court with the genuine intention of avoiding a miscarriage of justice, there would be a contempt if he disclosed that information to a third party who had no authority to receive disclosures on behalf of the court and who might not pass on that information to the court; in this case the juror had written to the defendant's mother suggesting the jury had not treated the defendant fairly. This rule was not inconsistent with Article 10 as the juror can in relevant cases draw his concerns to the attention of the judge before the jury returned its verdict.[289]

This section of the book will, however, concentrate on situations where the publication of information is likely to prejudice ongoing judicial proceedings.[290] Liability in criminal law for contempt of court has its origins in the common law. However, since the Contempt of Court Act 1981, which was passed in response to the European Court of Human Rights' judgment in *Sunday Times v United Kingdom*,[291] the law can be found both in the common law and under the 1981 Act, depending on whether the contempt was intentional or based on strict liability. Section 6 of the 1981 Act preserves the common law of contempt by stating that nothing in sections 1–5 of the Act restricts liability for contempt of court in respect of conduct intended to impede or prejudice the administration of justice. As a consequence, proceedings may be governed under either the 1981 Act or the common law rules, the proceedings for each being subject to differing rules and defences. For example, for the common law offence to be committed an intention to prejudice is required, there must be a real risk of prejudice, proceedings need to be imminent, and there is no defence of 'public interest' as is provided under s.5 of the 1981 Act. On the other hand, liability under the Act is strict: there must be a substantial risk of serious prejudice, proceedings have to be active, and s.5 of the Act provides a 'public interest' defence.

This section of the chapter will start with an account of the common law of contempt before the 1981 Act was passed, including an account of the domestic and European Court rulings relating to the Thalidomide disaster. We will then look at the provisions of the Act in so far as they have changed the law of contempt in its strict liability form and, finally, explore the remaining common law principles as they apply to intentional prejudice of proceedings.

The common law of contempt and the Thalidomide case

Prior to the Contempt of Court Act 1981, common law contempt was committed whenever there was a real risk of prejudice to proceedings. The proceedings in question had to be within the *sub judice* period, starting from the period when the proceedings were imminent. Thus, discussion of relevant civil and criminal proceedings was forbidden when such proceedings were at risk of being prejudiced and the *actus reus* of the offence was the creation of

---

[288] [2005] 1 WLR 1867.

[289] Following the House of Lords' decision in *R v Mirza; R v O'Connor* [2004] 1 AC 118, jurors will be given clear advice by the trial judge as to when they can inform the judge about the wrongdoings of fellow jurors.

[290] For the purposes of contempt of court, a person must have interfered with the proceedings of a 'court'. This has been defined as a body that exercises a judicial rather than an administrative role, the label attached to the institution not being conclusive; *Attorney-General v BBC* [1980] 3 All ER 161.

[291] (1979) 2 EHRR 245. The case is detailed in the case study below, page 480.

the risk. Thus, in *R v Thomson Newspapers Ltd, ex parte Attorney-General*[292] a newspaper was found guilty of contempt for publishing derogatory statements regarding the defendant before his trial, even though it was later found that the information did not influence the jury. Liability for such contempt was strict, the *mens rea* for the offence being an intention to publish, although a contempt could be committed intentionally and that might determine the seriousness of the contempt and any relevant sanction.

The harshness of the common law principles was highlighted in the case of *Attorney-General v Times Newspapers Ltd*,[293] discussed below, and this case ultimately led to the passing of the Contempt of Court Act 1981, which to some extent reflected the approach of the European Court of Human Rights in the case of *Sunday Times v United Kingdom*.[294] This Act relaxed the law of contempt and is now the basis of strict liability contempt, although there had, even before the Strasbourg judgment, been proposals for the reform of the law.[295] The case, both in the domestic courts and in Strasbourg, raised fundamental issues relating to the balance of freedom of expression and the administration of justice. Accordingly, some time will be spent on the case and the decisions.

The case involved the publication of two articles commenting on the Thalidomide disaster at a time when some litigation between the parents and the Distillers company had still to be resolved. The High Court had granted injunctions against the *Sunday Times*, but on appeal the injunctions were discharged on the grounds that the proceedings were dormant. The House of Lords restored the injunctions, finding that the article had prejudged the case and had amounted to trial by media. The decision was criticised as giving too little weight to freedom of expression and the public's right to be informed on matters of genuine public concern.[296] In particular it was felt that the House of Lords had created a new test for establishing the *actus reus* of the offence, based on the principle of prejudgment, which negated the need to show a real risk of prejudice to the proceedings and attached liability to the mere act of prejudging legal issues in the newspaper.

CASE STUDY

Sunday Times v *United Kingdom* (1979) 2 EHRR 245

This case concerned the application of the domestic law of contempt of court to discussions by the press of issues that are the subject of ongoing legal proceedings. Accordingly the case involved a balance between the protection of the administration of justice and freedom of expression. The case is important in that it stresses the importance of freedom of expression and of the free press. It also provides guidance on how the European Convention should balance those rights with other interests, and what margin of appreciation should be allowed to the domestic law and the domestic courts in trying to achieve that balance.

---

[292] [1968] 1 All ER 268.
[293] [1974] AC 273.
[294] (1979) 2 EHRR 245.
[295] See *Report of the Committee on Contempt of Court* (1974) Cmnd 5794.
[296] See Miller, The Sunday Times Case (1974) 37 MLR 96.

The facts of the case were as follows. Distillers had manufactured the drug 'Thalidomide', which a number of women had taken during pregnancy, giving birth to babies with severe deformities. The drug was withdrawn from the market and by 1971 nearly 400 cases of negligence were pending against the company. The company was keen to settle out of court and had made offers of settlement to the relevant parties, which were being considered. In 1972 the *Sunday Times* published two articles. The first, headed 'Our Thalidomide Children: A Cause for National Shame', examined the settlement proposals, describing them as grotesquely out of proportion to the injuries suffered and criticising English law relating to the recovery and assessment of damages. The article suggested that Distillers, without surrendering on negligence, could and should think again. The newspaper proposed to publish a second article, which explored the history of the drugs' manufacture and questioned whether the company had exercised proper care in allowing the drug to come onto the market. The article concluded that there appeared to be no neat set of answers to the question whether they had adequately investigated the dangers of the drug. The Attorney-General contacted the newspapers regarding both articles and eventually decided to initiate proceedings with regard to the second article.

The High Court granted an injunction against the publication of the second article on the basis that it might prejudice the free choice and conduct of the parties to litigation. On appeal, the Court of Appeal discharged the injunctions on the basis that as the proceedings in question were dormant the public interest in discussion outweighed any potential prejudice to any party to litigation. However, the House of Lords restored the injunctions, holding that the Court of Appeal was wrong to consider the proceedings dormant (*Attorney-General* v *Times Newspapers* [1974] AC 273). In the House of Lords, Lord Reid held that although a balance must be struck between the public interest in freedom of speech and the public interest in protecting the administration of justice from interference, there was no difference in principle between a case which is thought to have news value and one which is not. Lord Diplock warned against the dangers of trial by newspaper and the House of Lords held that as the article had dealt with the question of negligence it had prejudged the case and had come close to trial by media. This would undermine the public confidence in the administration of justice and thus amounted to a contempt of court. The case was remitted to the Divisional Court to grant the injunctions, which were maintained until June 1976.

Meanwhile, the newspapers lodged an application under the European Convention claiming that the granting of the injunctions constituted a violation of their right to freedom of expression under Article 10 of the European Convention on Human Rights. The European Court of Human Rights acknowledged that there had been a restriction of the applicant's freedom of expression under Article 10 and that such restriction had to be justified within the terms of Article 10(2). The Court was satisfied that the domestic law of contempt was sufficiently clear to be 'prescribed by law' within Article 10(2). In the Court's opinion, it was not essential that the law had to be contained in statutory form, and it was satisfied that the common law of contempt was couched with sufficient certainty to allow persons to be guided in their future conduct. The Court was also satisfied that the law and its application in the present case pursued a legitimate aim within Article 10(2) in that the injunctions were granted for 'maintaining the authority and impartiality of the judiciary' and for the 'protection of the rights of others'. Thus the Court had to consider the essential question of whether the injunctions were 'necessary in a democratic society' for the purpose of achieving those aims.

The Court reiterated the principles laid down in the case of *Handyside v United Kingdom* (1976) 1 EHRR 737, that freedom of expression constitutes one of the essential foundations of a democratic society, and stated that those principles were of particular importance as far as the press is concerned. While accepting that the courts are the forum for the settlement of disputes, the Court held that this does not mean that there can be no prior discussion of disputes elsewhere. Furthermore, while the mass media must not overstep the bounds imposed in the interests of the proper administration of justice, it is incumbent on them to impart information and ideas concerning matters that come before the courts as in other areas of public interest. Not only do the media have the task of imparting such information and ideas: the public has a right to receive them. Thus, to assess whether the interference complained of was necessary in a democratic society account must be taken of any public interest aspect of the case.

The Court observed that in domestic law, following a balancing of the conflicting interests involved, an absolute rule was formulated to the effect that it was not possible to prejudge issues in pending cases. In this respect the Court noted that while it was not its function to pronounce itself on an interpretation of English law adopted in the House of Lords, it had to take a different approach. The European Court is not faced with a choice between two conflicting principles but with a principle of freedom of expression that is subject to a number of exceptions that must be narrowly interpreted. Thus it was not sufficient that the interference belonged to that class of exception listed in Article 10(2) which has been invoked; neither is it sufficient that the interference was imposed because its subject matter fell within a particular category or was caught by a legal rule formulated in general or absolute terms; the Court has to be satisfied that the interference was necessary having regard to the facts and circumstances prevailing in the specific case before it.

The Court went on to state that the Thalidomide disaster was a matter of undisputed public concern; fundamental issues concerning protection against and compensation for injuries resulting from scientific developments were raised and the public has the right to be properly informed. The families of numerous victims of the tragedy had a vital interest in knowing all the underlying facts and the various possible solutions. They could be deprived of this information only if it appeared absolutely certain that its diffusion would have presented a threat to the authority of the judiciary. Although, if the article had appeared at the relevant time Distillers might have felt obliged to develop their arguments, in public and in advance of the case, the facts of the case did not cease to be a matter of public interest merely because they formed the background to pending litigation. In conclusion, the Court felt that the interferences did not correspond to a social need sufficiently pressing to outweigh the public interest in freedom of expression. The article was couched in moderate terms and on a matter of great public interest and thus the restraint imposed was not proportionate to the legitimate aim pursued.

Questions

(NB Questions 8, 9 and 10 should be addressed after reading the whole chapter.)

1 To what extent did the domestic law allow considerations of freedom of expression and freedom of the press to be taken into account in deciding whether there had been contempt in this case?

2 In what respects did the approach adopted by the European Court in this case differ from that taken by the domestic courts?

3 Does the approach adopted by the European Court regard the protection of the impartiality and independence of the judiciary as an inferior claim to that of freedom of the press?

4 Why did the European Court feel that the domestic court's decision was in violation of Article 10?

5 Why did the Court regard the press reporting of this issue as so important?

6 Why did the Court grant a very narrow margin of appreciation in this case?

7 Do you think it was legitimate for the European Court to overrule the domestic courts in this case?

8 What changes were introduced in domestic law in response to this decision, and do you feel that those changes are sufficient to address the European Court's concerns in cases such as these?

9 Does the domestic case law after this decision suggest that the courts have followed the spirit of the Convention and the decision?

10 Is it inevitable that the courts would now decide the case in favour of the press, particularly after the passing of the Human Rights Act 1998?

Strict liability contempt and the 1981 Contempt of Court Act

In the light of the European Court's judgment in *Sunday Times v United Kingdom*, there was a clear need to address the question of how the law of contempt could accommodate freedom of expression, and, in particular, the public's right to be informed on proceedings raising issues of public interest, more reasonably and flexibly. The European Court had been particularly critical of the law's inability to accommodate the public interest argument in favour of free speech in the face of an absolute rule prohibiting prejudgment. In response to the judgment, parliament passed the Contempt of Court Act 1981, which adjusted the *actus reus* of strict liability contempt to make it more difficult to establish an offence, and provided a limited defence to allow discussion of proceedings in the public interest when the detrimental effect of such discussions was merely incidental to the discussion. The changes brought about by the Act apply only to contempts based on strict liability.[297] Thus, despite the changes introduced in the Act, the *mens rea* required for this type of contempt is merely the intention to publish.[298] This aspect of the law was, of course, a major factor in the *Sunday Times* judgment, and was a particularly harsh element of the common law offence.

[297] Despite liability being strict, s.1 of the 1981 Act provides a defence of ignorance if the publisher or distributor, having taken all reasonable care, does not know and has no reason to suspect that the proceedings are active or that the publication contains the type of material to give rise to liability under s.2 of the Act.

[298] Section 1 of the 1981 Act provides that the 'strict liability rule means the rule of law whereby conduct may be treated as a contempt of court as tending to interfere with the course of justice in particular legal proceedings regardless of intent to do so'.

The new test of liability

Section 2 of the Contempt of Court Act 1981 provides that the strict liability rule only applies in relation to publications,[299] and only to those publications which create a *substantial risk* that the course of proceedings in question will be *seriously impeded or prejudiced*.[300] Under this provision the rule only applies if the proceedings are active within the meaning of the section, as detailed in Schedule 1 of the Act. For criminal proceedings the starting point is the issue of a warrant for arrest, an arrest without warrant or the service of an indictment, and the ending point is acquittal, sentence, any other verdict or discontinuance of the trial. With regard to civil proceedings, the starting point is when the case is set down for a hearing or a date for the hearing is fixed, and not the date when the writ is issued. The ending point then comes when the proceedings are disposed of, discontinued or withdrawn. Appellate proceedings also come within the Act, running from when leave to appeal is applied for to when the proceedings are disposed of or abandoned.[301]

For liability to be established under the Act the court must be satisfied of two things: first, the publication must have created a *substantial risk* of prejudice or interference to the relevant proceedings; and secondly, as a result those proceedings will be *seriously impeded or prejudiced*. It is not sufficient, therefore, that an article presents a real risk – the common law test; the risk must be substantial. Further, even if there is a substantial risk that proceedings are going to be affected by that article, it must be shown that those proceedings will be *seriously impeded or prejudiced*. Thus, the contents of an article published before or during a criminal trial might well be remembered by a judge or juror, but for that article to be a contempt it would not only have to be shown to have a likely influence on the judge or juror, but also to have such an influence that the defendant's, or prosecution's, case would be materially and substantially prejudiced.

Both tests must be satisfied, and the meaning of those terms and the relationship between the two requirements was examined in the case of *Attorney-General v Newsgroup Newspapers*.[302] According to the Court of Appeal, a substantial risk was one that was 'not minimal' or 'not insubstantial', rather than having the meaning of 'weighty'. In addition, the effect of the publication on the particular proceedings had to be potentially serious. Thus there must be some risk that the proceedings in question will be affected, and a prospect that, if affected, the effect will be serious. Although the court stressed that the two elements of the section were separate and must be met in each case, it also noted that the two limbs of the test might overlap and that some factors, such as the proximity of the article to the trial, could be raised at either stage. In this case Ian Botham, then a well-known international cricketer, had brought libel proceedings against a newspaper over allegations of misconduct and drug taking while he was on tour in New Zealand. The trial of the case had been set for March 1987 and in

---

[299] Section 2(1) provides that 'publication' includes any speech, writing, programme included in a programme, service or other communication in whatever form, which is addressed to the public at large or any section of the public.

[300] Section 2(2) Contempt of Court Act 1981.

[301] As we shall see, because appeals do not involve juries, the courts are less likely to find that contempt has been committed by discussions between the end of the trial and the appeal. This is because it is unlikely that a judge would be influenced by such discussions. See, for example, *Re Lonrho* [1990] AC 154, discussed below. However, such a publication may still be in contempt if it was likely to influence one of the parties to abandon the case or one of the claims or defences in the action.

[302] [1987] 1 QB 1.

April 1986 the *News of the World* published an article about his behaviour on a tour in the West Indies. Botham issued a writ for libel, but the newspaper then declared its intention to run a story on the New Zealand tour, though this time based on independent investigations. Botham then asked the Attorney-General to stop the article on the basis that it was in contempt of court in that it raised substantially the same ground as the allegations made in 1984. Applying the above principles, the Court of Appeal held that as the libel trial would not take place for at least ten months it was not possible to say that there was a serious risk that the course of justice would be seriously prejudiced.

Although the case does much to clarify the meaning of both elements contained in s.2(2) of the Act, and the relationship between those elements, it is doubtful whether the ruling on the meaning of 'substantial' complies with the judgment of the European Court of Human Rights in the *Sunday Times* case. In that case the European Court concluded that the injunction should only have been granted if it could be shown that it was *absolutely certain* that the diffusion of that information would have a prejudicial effect on the proceedings. To allow liability in a case where the risk of prejudice is 'not insubstantial' might, therefore, lead to the courts giving too little weight to freedom of expression and the public's right to know. It should be noted, however, that the court has an opportunity to restrict the width of this ruling when considering whether there was evidence of serious prejudice, and it is hoped that at this stage the courts ensure that freedom of expression is not restricted apart from in the most pressing cases.

Was there a substantial risk of serious prejudice?

In the *Newsgroup Newspapers* case, the Court of Appeal reiterated that a court must address itself to both questions. First, was there a *substantial risk* that a juror would encounter the article, remember it and be affected by it so that he could not put it out of his mind during the trial? In answering this question, the Court stated that the following factors would be particularly relevant: the likely readership of the article; the proximity of publication of the article to the trial; whether the case had attracted the interests of the public; and the language used in the article, including whether any potentially influencing photographs were included with the article. Secondly, the court must ask if there is a substantial risk that a person would be *prejudiced* by the article, and that the effect of that prejudice would be *serious*. In answering this second question, the Court held that similar factors were relevant and thus had to be considered. Thus matters such as the proximity of the proceedings, the public profile of the case and the parties to the action and the language used in the publication are highly relevant factors to both the issues of substantial risk and serious prejudice.

A number of the above factors were at issue in the case of *Attorney-General v ITN and Others*.[303] ITN and several newspapers (national and local) had published the fact that Patrick Magee, who had been arrested for the murder of a special constable and the attempted murder of a police constable, had recently escaped from jail in Belfast where he was serving a life sentence for the murder of a member of the SAS. It was held that given the likely lapse of nine months between the publication of the material and the trial, the ephemeral nature of a single news item on TV news, and the limited circulation of one of the newspapers, no contempt of court had been committed. In particular, the court had regard to the very limited

---

[303] [1995] 2 All ER 370.

circulation of the only newspaper (the *Northern Echo*) that had been found to distribute a potentially offensive article; only 150 copies of the paper had been distributed in a specific area of London and thus the risk of prejudice was too low.[304]

The nature of the language used in the article will also be of relevance in deciding the likely effect of the article under both headings, and the court may have to draw the line between reasonable and unreasonable criticism of any person currently involved in legal proceedings. This is illustrated in the case of *Attorney-General* v *Hislop and Pressdram*.[305] Sonia Sutcliffe, the wife of the 'Yorkshire Ripper', had brought defamation proceedings against *Private Eye* magazine over an allegation that she had sold her story to the newspapers. With the trial approximately three months away, the magazine published two articles making allegations against Mrs Sutcliffe's character, alleging that she had covered for her husband and was currently defrauding the Department of Social Security. It was held that the articles constituted contempt under statute in that there was a substantial risk that the jurors might be prejudiced against her. The judge was satisfied that anyone reading the articles and finding themselves on a jury would be likely to remember them and in that case to mention the contents to the other jurors. The court noted that the articles went further than fair and temperate criticism and amounted to plain abuse.

Similarly, the court will have to consider whether the tone of the article is likely to influence the readership, or whether its content is likely to be dismissed. In *Attorney-General* v *Hat Trick Productions*[306] it was held that irreverent remarks made about the possible guilt of the Maxwell brothers, who at the time were facing charges of fraud over a pension scandal, constituted contempt of court. The remarks, made six months before the brothers' trial for fraud, were made by the presenter Angus Deayton on the programme *Have I Got News for You*. During the programme, Deayton stated that 'All have profited from the misfortune except the pensioners whose misfortune others have profited from. Mentioning no Maxwells, er, no names. The BBC is cracking down on references to Ian and Kevin Maxwell just in case programme makers appear biased against these two heartless, scheming bastards.' It was held that having regard to the strong implication of guilt, the relevance of the charges, the focus and repetition of the charges and that the words were strikingly prejudicial to the heart of the case, the defendants were guilty of contempt. The words could be taken by the public to be expressing the opinion of someone in the know and were, therefore, potentially influential and prejudicial.

The potential effect of the words on a jury are, therefore, particularly crucial to the question of whether there has been a contempt. Thus, in *Attorney-General* v *Times Newspapers*[307] the court found that the *Sun* newspaper was not in contempt of court when they referred to Michel Fagan, who had broken into the Queen's bedroom and who was facing charges of theft, as a glib liar with a long-standing drug problem. In the court's view the jury would have enough independence of mind so as to make the risk too remote to qualify as substantial. However, in the same case the court held that the *Daily Star* was in contempt when

---

[304] Although the court might regard a potentially prejudicial publication as normally having a short lifespan, getting lost in the public conscience after a relatively short period of time, this factor has to be looked at in the light of other factors such as the public profile of the case and the language used in the publication.

[305] [1991] 1 QB 514.

[306] *The Times*, 26 July 1996.

[307] *The Times*, 12 February 1983.

they had written an article asserting that Fagan had admitted to stealing the wine. However independent-minded a jury might be, and however cynical of the accuracy of newspaper reporting, there would inevitably be a real risk, whether the judge gave a warning or not, that the memory of what had been asserted in the newspaper would remain in the jurors' minds and would affect the outcome of their deliberations.

In many cases a court will need to determine the likely effect of a publication on members of a jury, and in particular whether such publicity is likely to influence members despite the instructions of the judge to ignore media comment on the case.[308] In this respect it has been held that the likelihood of a judge, as opposed to a juror, being influenced by such publications is not normally a substantial one. This distinction was evident in the decision in *Re Lonrho*.[309] In this case the Secretary of State had appointed inspectors to consider Mohammad Fayed's takeover of Harrods. He had sent the report to the Serious Fraud Office and had refused to publish it until the Office had completed their investigations. The Secretary then, without giving reasons, refused to refer the takeover to the Monopolies and Mergers Commission and Lonrho applied for judicial review of that decision. The Court of Appeal had rejected the action and before the appeal in the House of Lords a newspaper owned by Lonrho published the inspector's report. In the resulting contempt proceedings it was held that the likelihood of an appeal judge being influenced by a newspaper report on the Harrods takeover was not a substantial one. It was also held that there was no evidence to suggest that the Secretary of State's decision would be altered by the article and thus the publication of the report was not likely to prejudice the proceedings by putting pressure on the Secretary to alter his claim regarding the non-publication of the report or his failure to give reasons for his decision.

More recently, in *Chief Constable of Greater Manchester Police v Channel 5 Broadcast Ltd*[310] the Court of Appeal allowed an appeal against the granting of an injunction prohibiting Channel 5 from broadcasting a programme entitled *Gangsters*. The programme centred on the unlawful activities of two brothers, one of whom had been killed, and the police requested the order on the basis that their investigations were at a delicate stage and that the programme might deter potential witnesses from coming forward. The Court of Appeal held that there were insufficient grounds to conclude that the programme would create a substantial risk that the proceedings would be seriously impeded or prejudiced. The trial was some months off and a properly directed jury could cope with the fact that intimidation of witnesses in Manchester was rife. Further, since the killing there had been articles in both the local and national press and, given the brothers' notoriety, it could not be established that the showing of the programme would add substantially to the risk that already existed. The decision appears to accept that in modern times public discussion of serious criminal proceedings is inevitable and that the media should be allowed to report on such matters provided they do so responsibly and objectively.

---

[308] *Attorney-General v Guardian Newspapers* [1999] EMLR 904. See also the decision in *Attorney-General v Guardian Newspapers* [1992] 3 All ER 38, where it was held that the publication of the fact that one unidentified defendant out of six on trial in Manchester was awaiting trial on other charges in the Isle of Man was not likely to engender bias in a jury of ordinary good sense.

[309] [1990] AC 154.

[310] [2005] EWCA Civ 739.

The 'public interest' defence

Section 5 of the 1981 Act provides that a publication made as part of a discussion in good faith of public affairs or other matters of general public interest is not to be treated as a contempt of court under the strict liability rule if the risk of impediment or prejudice to the particular legal proceedings is merely incidental to the discussion. This provision, which only becomes relevant once the court is satisfied that the s.2 test for contempt has been satisfied, addresses the concerns of the European Court in the *Sunday Times* case and allows for more open discussion of cases that raise matters of serious public interest. This provision should allow the courts to balance freedom of expression with the interests of the administration of the justice and in particular give freedom of expression an added weight, to be displaced only in cases where the main thrust and effect of the publication is to prejudice the relevant proceedings. For example, if a public figure is currently facing criminal charges, it might be acceptable to publish an article commenting on the recent trend of public figures transgressing the law, provided the article does not centre on the person involved in the proceedings, or that particular case.

The defence has been raised in surprisingly few cases, but most famously in the case of *Attorney-General* v *English*.[311] While a Dr Arthur was on trial for the murder of a Down's Syndrome child, the *Daily Mail* published an article, written by the political commentator Malcom Muggeridge, in favour of a pro-life parliamentary candidate who had been born with no arms or legs. The author expressed the opinion that had the candidate been born today, the chances of her surviving would have been small; that surely someone would recommend letting her die of starvation. The article then concluded with the question: are babies not up to scratch to be destroyed before or after birth? The Attorney-General brought contempt proceedings against the editor of the newspaper and it was held that the test in s.2(2) of the Act had been satisfied in this case, in that the true course of justice had been put at risk by the article. On appeal it was held that the jury in the case would be likely to take the comments as referring to the trial and that, as at that stage the jury did not know what Dr Arthur's defence would be, the judge at first instance had not erred in deciding that the risk of prejudice in the present case was not too remote to qualify as contempt. However, the Court of Appeal held that the defence under s.5 should succeed. The main theme of the article was the candidate's election policy, and Dr Arthur was not mentioned by name. In the Court's opinion the risk, of the public and the jurors allowing themselves to be prejudiced in favour of finding him guilty on evidence that didn't justify it in court, could be described as incidental to any meaningful discussion in the publication.

Specifically, the Court of Appeal held that the trial judge's test, whether the article could have been written without the offending words, was not the correct test. The decision thus clarified that a discussion of public affairs could take place under s.5 beyond abstract debate and could include examples drawn from real life. In the Court's view, a discussion could include accusations without which the article would have been emasculated and would have lost its main point. In the present case, therefore, without the implied accusations the article would have been a contribution to a purely hypothetical issue. This principle was extended in the case of *Attorney-General* v *Times Newspapers*[312] to cover a situation where the case in

---

[311] [1983] 1 AC 116.
[312] *The Times*, 12 February 1983.

question is mentioned expressly. In that case comments about Michael Fagin, who had broken into the Queen's bedroom and was now facing criminal charges, to the effect that he was, *inter alia*, a penniless neurotic, were held to constitute a substantial risk of serious prejudice to his trial. However, they were held to fall within s.5 of the Act as they formed part of a discussion on the Queen's personal safety, a matter of public concern.[313]

In contrast, the s.5 defence will fail if the publication in question goes beyond a general discussion and becomes unduly focused on the particular proceedings or the parties thereto. In *Attorney-General v TVS Television Ltd and Southey and Sons*,[314] TVS had broadcast a programme entitled *The New Rachmans*, alleging that a minority of landlords in the Reading area were abusing the bed and breakfast provisions by deceiving the Department of Social Security and adopting bullying techniques against tenants. In addition, the second defendants published an article entitled 'Reading's new wave of harassment', which focused on the TV programme's exposé of 'bedsit barons'. As a result of the programme and the article a Crown Court trial of Reading landlords for fraud was abandoned at a cost of £215,000 and the defendants were charged with contempt. It was conceded that s.2 of the 1981 Act had been satisfied, and the question was whether the defendants could rely on the defence in s.5 of the Act. It was held that although there had been attempt to analyse the causes of this new wave of abuse by highlighting a shortage of accommodation in the south of England, the thrust of the discussion was more narrowly upon a small number of landlords in Reading. Thus, the s.5 defence could not succeed on the facts.[315] In giving guidance as to whether a risk was merely incidental, LLOYD LJ held that the court should look at the subject matter of the discussion and determine how closely it relates to the legal proceedings in dispute. The more closely it relates the easier it will be for the Attorney-General to show that the risk of prejudice is not merely incidental to the discussion.

It is arguable whether the combined effect of s.2 and s.5 of the 1981 Act satisfy the spirit of the decision in the *Sunday Times* case. On the face of it, the sections still require a mechanical application of the risk test irrespective of the (often) great public interest in publication of the offensive material. In that sense the provisions do not incorporate the overriding importance of public discussion, or the tests of necessity and proportionality that so dominated the European Court's findings. On the other hand, the courts have not been faced with a case of such public importance as the Thalidomide case, and until they are, it will remain uncertain how the provisions would be interpreted and applied so as to give proper weight to freedom of expression.

Intentional interference with the administration of justice

Section 6 of the Act states that nothing in the Act restricts liability for contempt of court in respect of conduct intended to impede or prejudice the administration of justice. Thus, the 1981 Act does not affect the position with regard to intentional prejudice of the administration of justice, including the intentional prejudicing of particular proceedings, and such an

---

[313] This appears to be a very liberal application of s.5. In the same case it was held that an allegation by a newspaper that Fagin had stabbed his stepson did not fall within the defence as it was not relevant to the subject of the Queen's safety.

[314] *The Times*, 7 July 1989.

[315] See also *Pickering v Liverpool Daily Post and Echo Newspapers plc* [1991] 2 AC 370.

offence will be based on the old common law rules. For example, the *actus reus* of the offence is that of creating a real risk of prejudice, and the *mens rea* is an intention to prejudice as opposed to a mere intention to publish. Significantly, the defence in s.5 of the 1981 Act is not available and the action applies to all proceedings that are imminent, as opposed to being active, as required under the 1981 Act. Under the common law, no formal steps need to be taken to initiate the proceedings, and with regard to criminal proceedings, the proceedings are imminent if it is surely obvious to everyone that a person was about to be arrested.[316]

The common law offence of contempt of court can be used as an alternative, or in addition, to liability under the 1981 Act, provided it can be shown that the action or publication in contempt of court was intentional. For example, in *Attorney-General* v *Hislop and Pressdram*,[317] the court found the defendants guilty of both common law and statutory contempt, with regard to two articles published three months before libel proceedings involving the defendants, which made a number of allegations regarding the claimant's character. It was held that the articles amounted to contempt at common law, as they constituted improper pressure on Mrs Sutcliffe to discontinue the first libel action. Significantly, this being found, the defendants were precluded from relying on the s.5 defence in relation to the statutory action because their intention to prejudice the proceedings negated the good faith inherent in that defence. Although in most cases this conclusion would be correct, it has been argued that there may be cases where a person intends to prejudice the proceedings, but their motive is to discuss public affairs. In such a case it would, therefore, be unfair to deprive that person of the s.5 defence.[318]

For an offence to be committed at common law the courts must be satisfied that the defendant intended to prejudice proceedings. The defendant must either wish to prejudice those proceedings or foresee that such prejudice was an inevitable consequence of publishing the material. Such an intention was satisfied in the case of *Attorney-General* v *Newsgroup Newspapers*.[319] In this case a doctor, who had been referred to as Doctor B, had been investigated over the alleged rape of an eight-year-old girl. The Crown Prosecution Service had found that there was insufficient evidence against the doctor and refused to bring proceedings against him. The *Sun* newspaper offered to assist the mother in a private prosecution and published various articles on the matter, with such headings as 'Beast must be named, says MP', 'Doc groped me, says girl', and 'Rape case Doc: the *Sun* acts'. The newspaper was charged with and found guilty of contempt of court at common law. The court found that the paper had in mind particular proceedings, which it was determined should take place. These proceedings were imminent as they were virtually certain to be commenced,[320] and the content of the articles posed a real risk of prejudice to a fair trial of the doctor, involving grave allegations against the doctor via prominent and widespread publicity. The court could see no possible other reason for publishing articles with such a heading if it was not to prejudice a fair trial by bringing to the notice of its readers extremely damaging material which would be inadmissible in a court of law. However, the court must be satisfied that the defendants clearly intended their publication to have a prejudicial effect. In this respect, the courts might

---

[316] *R* v *Savundranayagan and Walker* [1968] 1 WLR 1761.

[317] [1991] QB 514.

[318] See Fenwick, *Civil Liberties and Human Rights* (Cavendish 2007, 4th edn), pages 380–1.

[319] [1989] 2 All ER 906.

[320] Note, the proceedings were not active within the Contempt of Court Act 1981, but were nonetheless imminent under the common law test.

apply a distinction between cases (such as *Hislop* and *Newsgroup Newspapers* above) where the defendant has launched a personal or public campaign in relation to the case, and those where they have been merely negligent. For example, in *Attorney-General v Sports Newspapers*[321] the newspaper in question published the previous convictions for rape of David Evans, who at the time was facing charges relating to the abduction of a young girl. It was held that although there was a risk that the newspaper was aware of it, it could not be proven that they foresaw with virtual certainty that Evans's trial would be prejudiced as a result.

Contempt of court and the disclosure of sources

This aspect of press freedom has been dealt with earlier in this chapter, but is specifically connected with the law on contempt of court. Section 10 of the Contempt of Court Act 1981 provides that no court may require a person to disclose, *nor is any person guilty of contempt of court for refusing to disclose*, the source of information contained in a publication for which he is responsible, unless it be established to the satisfaction of the court that disclosure is necessary in the interests of justice or national security or for the prevention of disorder or crime. As with Article 10 of the European Convention, this aspect of press freedom is stated as the primary right, which may only be interfered with if the court is satisfied not only that there is a legitimate aim, but also that it is *necessary* to disclose that information in order to achieve that aim.

The law of confidentiality and contempt of court

It is possible to use the law of contempt in conjunction with principles of confidentiality and to charge a person with contempt for disclosing information in breach of an existing injunction that was imposed on that, or another, person for the purpose of safeguarding confidentiality. Thus, in *Attorney-General v Times Newspapers*[322] it was held that the publication of confidential material, which was the subject matter of a pending action and whose publication rendered the original action pointless, could constitute an interference with the administration of justice.[323] In that case it was held that the publication of extracts of the *Spycatcher* book after two newspapers had been injuncted for breach of confidence amounted to contempt of court.

The importance of this action is that it can be used to impose liability on a newspaper without the availability of either a general public interest defence under the law of confidentiality or a specific defence of public interest under s.5 of the Contempt of Court Act 1981. However, the principle has been given a limited interpretation, particularly in the post-Human Rights Act case law. Thus, in *Attorney-General v Newspaper Publishing Ltd*[324] it was held that a trivial breach of a court order that had been imposed on another party was insufficient to attract liability for contempt. In that case a court had allowed the party to a criminal trial

---

[321] [1991] 1 WLR 1194.

[322] [1992] 1 AC 191. See also *Attorney-General v Newspaper Publishing, The Times*, 28 February 1990.

[323] In *Attorney-General v Punch Ltd and Another* [2001] QB 1028 it was confirmed that this principle only applies to interlocutory (interim) injunctions, and not to final injunctions. See also *Jockey Club v Buffham* [2003] 2 WLR 178.

[324] [1997] 3 All ER 159.

to have disclosed to them a summary of documentation that was the basis of a public interest immunity claim. The judge had warned that breach of the court order would result in the matter being referred to the Attorney-General and *The Independent* published an account of the case which contained some information not referred to in the judgment and was committed for contempt. It was held that having regard to Article 10 of the European Convention and the importance of free speech, a trivial breach of a court order which had been imposed on other parties was insufficient to attract liability for contempt. The *actus reus* of the offence was not committed by any conduct that was inconsistent with a court order and it would need to be shown that the disclosure had caused a significant and adverse effect on the administration of justice.

More significantly, in the case of *Attorney-General* v *Punch and Another*[325] the Court of Appeal upheld freedom of expression by finding that contempt of court is not committed by mere disobedience of a court order, and by insisting that the breach must cause some identifiable and specific harm, for example the destruction of the confidentiality of the material which it had been the purpose of the injunction to preserve. In this case a court had granted an injunction against a third party (David Shayler) preventing him from disclosing information related to the security services and its activities, which had been obtained by him during the course of his employment. The order had been made to preserve confidentiality in relation to impending litigation against the third party for breach of the Official Secrets Act 1989 (dealt with in chapter 8). The defendants published an article containing much information covered by the injunction and the Attorney-General brought contempt proceedings against them. At first instance it was held that the defendants had contravened the order and that its breach could not be regarded as trivial. In the court's view the publication would have a significant and adverse effect on the administration of justice and the defendants had deliberately published the articles knowing that was in breach of the court order. However, on appeal to the Court of Appeal it was held that the purpose of the original orders was to preserve until trial the confidentiality of material whose disclosure arguably posed a risk of damaging national security. Re-publication of material that had already entered the public domain did not offend against that purpose, although the publication of new material could defeat it. The Court of Appeal also stressed that the offence can only be committed where the necessary *mens rea* has been established. In this case it had not been established that the defendants knew that the publication would interfere with the course of justice by defeating the purpose underlying the injunctions. It was not enough to establish that the editor had known that the publication was one that the defendants to the action were enjoined from making under the terms of the injunction. However, the ruling of the Court of Appeal was overturned by the House of Lords,[326] who confirmed that when a court issued an injunction to restrain publication of information relating to the security service pending an action in confidentiality, the purpose of that order was the prevention of publication during that period, and not the protection of national security. Thus, a deliberate breach of that order constituted contempt as it prejudged the issues that the trial court would be considering.[327]

---

[325] [2001] QB 1028. Overruled on appeal.

[326] [2003] 1 All ER 301. See Smith, Third Parties and the Reach of Injunctions [2003] CLJ 241.

[327] The House of Lords also held that a proviso imposed on the order that it did not apply to information that the Attorney-General consented to, was not censorship as the parties could always apply to the court for an alteration of that order if it became too restrictive.

The question of contempt and press freedom was raised in relation to the protective order made by the Family Division of the High Court, guaranteeing anonymity for Venables and Thompson, the boys found guilty of murdering a two-year-old boy.[328] In *A-G v Greater Manchester Newspapers Ltd*,[329] it was held that the newspaper had committed a contempt of court when it disclosed information relating to the location of the boys' Parole Board hearing and the region of the country where one of the boys was believed to be going on holiday. The court found that the information given in the article added information which, taken with other local knowledge, was likely to lead to the identification of the then whereabouts of one or both boys. It was argued on behalf of the newspaper that the released information was already available from Home Office records – available on the Home Office website and in public libraries – and thus was already in the public domain. The court agreed that in general information available in a public library was accessible to the public, but in this case such documentation provided detailed and complicated information and statistics not easy to digest by anyone not accustomed to its format or with insufficient background information to know where to look. For example, information posted on a public website would require some degree of background knowledge and persistence for it to become available to a member of the public.

Question

To what extent do you believe that the existing law on contempt of court is consistent with freedom of expression?

Contempt of court and restrictions on press reporting

Section 4 of the Contempt of Court Act 1981 provides that fair and accurate contemporaneous reports of legal proceedings, made in good faith, will not amount to contempt. This provision reflects the general principle of open justice and is in compliance with both Articles 6 and 10 of the European Convention.[330] However, as we have seen, Article 10 is a conditional right and may be compromised in certain situations. In addition, Article 6 provides that the press and public may be excluded from all or part of a trial in the interests of morals, public order or national security, or where the interests of juveniles or the protection of the private life of the parties so require. Both restrictions are subject to principles of legality and necessity and thus domestic law can only restrict the principle of open justice in particular circumstances.

Accordingly, there are a number of provisions that attempt to restrict the right of the press to report on legal proceedings. For example, s.4(2) of the Contempt of Court Act 1981 provides the courts with the power to order the postponement of the publication of such reports where it is felt that the report would create a substantial risk to the administration of justice in the proceedings which are the subject of the report, or to other present or imminent proceedings. This power to postpone the reporting of such proceedings can be used, for example,

---

[328] *Venables and Thompson v Newsgroup Newspapers Ltd* [2001] 1 All ER 908.
[329] *The Times*, 7 December 2001.
[330] See the decision of the Court of Appeal in *Clibbery v Allan* [2002] 2 WLR 1511, on the publication of information discussed in family proceedings held in public.

where the publication of that information would prejudice one of the parties to the action.[331] The courts have insisted that the power is used sparingly and in the light of freedom of expression and open justice, and both statute and case law have allowed the press to appeal against or make representations in relation to the order.[332] Thus, in *Re Central Independent Television plc and Another*,[333] the Court of Appeal overturned an order made by a court which postponed the reporting and broadcasting of proceedings so as to allow the jury to watch television or listen to the radio in their hotels. The Court of Appeal held that there was little evidence of a risk to the administration of justice as the previous reporting on the case had been fair and accurate. Further, alternative methods were available to the court to ensure that the jury was not exposed to prejudicial material. Similarly, in *ex parte Telegraph plc*,[334] it was stressed that orders should only be made when necessary, the court having to be satisfied not only that there was a substantial risk of prejudice to the administration of justice, but also that having regard to the need for open justice and fair reporting it was necessary to make such an order on particular terms.

Thus, the courts regard open justice and press freedom as of primary importance and are only prepared to compromise those interests in the most exceptional cases. For example, in *R v Beck, ex parte Daily Telegraph*,[335] the court confirmed that the public interest in the reporting of proceedings would normally outweigh any risk of prejudice to those proceedings. In this case an ex-social worker in charge of children's homes had been charged with a number of offences involving sexual abuse. Owing to the number of charges, the trial had been split into three and at the first trial the court made a s.4(2) order on the grounds that reporting would prejudice the two subsequent trials. On appeal to the Court of Appeal, although it was accepted that there was a substantial risk of prejudice, on the facts the Court held that the public interest in reporting outweighed such a risk. The Court of Appeal stressed that the public had the right to be informed in cases such as the present, which raised issues of great public concern, thus allowing them to ask questions of how such abuse had been allowed to take place.

This position will, of course, continue in the post-Human Rights Act era.[336] In *R v Sherwood, ex parte The Telegraph Group plc and Others*,[337] the Court of Appeal had to consider an appeal against a court order postponing the reporting of a murder trial. A police officer had been charged with the murder of a drug dealer and at the time of his appeal three other officers were being charged with misconduct relating to the same incident. It had already been decided that the trials be severed from the murder trial because the defendant was to rely on the negligence of the police force in planning and executing the operation. Accordingly

---

[331] In *R v Times Newspapers*, [2008] 1 WLR 234, the Court of Appeal quashed an order made under s.4 which had prohibited for an indefinite period the defendants from reporting a question and answer given in open court during a trial under the Official Secrets Act 1989. The Court of Appeal held that s.4 only permitted postponement of reporting during the proceedings in question. In addition, on the facts it found that it was difficult to see that the order made during the trial was necessary to prevent prejudice to the administration of justice as the trial would have continued even if the report had been published.

[332] Section 159 of the Criminal Justice Act 1988 provides a right of appeal in relation to trials on indictment, and a right to make representations against an order with respect to summary proceedings was recognised by the Court of Appeal in *R v Horsham Magistrates, ex parte Farquharson* [1982] 2 All ER 183.

[333] [1991] 1 All ER 347.

[334] [1993] 2 All ER 971.

[335] [1993] 2 All ER 177.

[336] See *R v Times Newspapers Ltd* [2008] 1 WLR 234.

[337] [2001] 1 WLR 1983.

the judge made a s.4(2) order, postponing the reporting of the murder trial until the completion of the other trials. On appeal against this order, the Court of Appeal held that when a judge was deciding whether to impose an order postponing the report of a trial until after the conclusion of a second related trial he should have regard to a three-stage test. In the Court's view the first question was whether reporting would give rise to a not insubstantial risk of prejudice to the administration of justice. Secondly, if such a risk was perceived to exist the court must be satisfied that an order under s.4(2) would eliminate it and that such a risk could not be overcome by less restrictive means. Finally, even if the judge were satisfied that there were not any other means of avoiding the risk, the order will not necessarily be made, for the judge will still have to ask whether the degree of risk should be regarded as tolerable in the sense of being the lesser of two evils. It was at this stage that value judgements might have to be made as to the priority between the two competing public interests. Having applied those principles the Court was satisfied that the judge was correct in applying the order in the present case. The evidence in the two trials was inextricably linked and justice required that the trials be severed. Thus, publicity would have inevitably defeated the object of that order and the judge had been correct in making the order. In contrast, in *R v B*,[338] the court adopted a more tolerant approach and held that it was not necessary to impose a reporting restriction under s.4 in respect of a forthcoming trial of a defendant for acts of murder and terrorism. The Court of Appeal held that even though the trial and conviction of his co-defendant had attracted wide publicity and debate on the reporting of the co-defendant's sentencing hearing, the press could and should be trusted not to publish anything prejudicial to the forthcoming trial and the jury could be trusted to act fairly.

In addition to the powers in s.4, s.11 of the Act provides that where a court has the power to allow a name or other material to be withheld from the public, it may give such directions prohibiting the publication of that name or material in connection with the proceedings as it considers necessary for the purpose for which it was upheld. This provision allows a court to extend the confidentiality relating to an individual's name or other matter, which has already been imposed on the parties to the proceedings, to another person, such as the press, thereby imposing on it the duty not to disclose such information. Section 11 does not give the courts any new powers in this respect and is referring to existing powers under statute or the common law.

As with the power under s.4(2), the power must only be used in exceptional cases and the court must be satisfied that there exist very strong grounds for imposing any restriction. Thus, it has been decided that an order should not be granted solely on the grounds of protecting a person's privacy,[339] although this might now have to be reviewed in the light of recent case law recognising the right to private life. However, the power has been used in cases involving blackmail trials,[340] where such an order is necessary to protect the subject matter of the blackmailer's actions and to encourage the victims of blackmail to give evidence in the future. It may also be appropriate to use such an order in cases involving national security. In *Attorney-General v*

---

[338] [2007] EMLR 5.

[339] *R v Westminster City Council, ex parte Castelli*, The Times, 14 August 1995. See also *R v Dover Justices, ex parte Dover DC and Wells* [1992] Crim LR 371: damage to the defendant's economic interests not sufficient; *R v Evesham Justices, ex parte McDonagh* [1988] 1 QB 553: protection of the defendant's comfort and feelings not sufficient.

[340] *R v Socialist Worker Printers and Publishers Ltd, ex parte Attorney-General* [1975] QB 637.

Leveller Magazine[341] a court had granted an anonymity order to a witness in proceedings under the Official Secrets Act. During the proceedings the witness disclosed details about his promotion, allowing a magazine to identify him and then publish details of his name and address. The magazine was charged with contempt but in the House of Lords it was held that there was no contempt because the witness had given away his own identity. Although the case was decided before the passing of the Contempt of Court Act 1981, it is felt that the release of such information into the public domain would mean that publication in breach of a s.11 order would not be in contempt.

Specific protection is given in relation to the reporting of proceedings involving children. Section 12 of the Administration of Justice Act 1960 forbids the press from reporting any aspect of wardship proceedings, and s.97 of the Children Act 1989 provides that no person shall publish any material which is intended, or likely, to identify a child as being involved in any proceedings. The latter provision was considered in *Re M (A Child)*,[342] where it was held that a court children and family reporter who encountered concerns about child abuse in private law proceedings had a discretion to report them to the relevant statutory authority without exposing himself to the risk of contempt. Where a child reporter made a discovery or received a direct report, an immediate report to the police or social services would be justified, and here the child reporter had to exercise an unfettered and independent discretion.[343] In addition in the post-Human Rights Act era, the provision should be applied proportionally with due regard to freedom of expression and open and fair justice. For example, in *Norfolk CC v Webster and Others*[344] it was held that a reporting restriction on care proceedings, prohibiting the press from attending and reporting on the case, was contrary to Article 6. The principles of open justice applied to such proceedings, albeit with exceptions, and there should be no automatic preference for privacy. In this case there was a public interest in exposing a possible miscarriage of justice and the case had already received public exposure.

Questions

Why does the law place restrictions on the press with respect to the reporting of court proceedings? Are those restrictions compatible with the Convention and the Human Rights Act?

---

[341] [1979] 1 All ER 745.

[342] [2002] 3 WLR 1669.

[343] However, the court stressed that the reporter must inform the judge of the steps he had taken at the earliest opportunity. These restrictions may in certain cases, continue after the ending of proceedings. In *Clayton v Clayton* [2006] 3 WLR 559, the Court of Appeal held that although the prohibition under s.97 on publication identifying children in family proceedings ceased to have effect when those proceedings ended, such a prohibition may extend beyond the ending of the proceedings, provided the court conducted a balancing exercise between the child's Article 8 rights and freedom of expression. In the present case a prohibition on a father making a video diary of his daughter, reliving his abduction of the child, was a proportionate interference with Article 10 given the impact on the child's privacy and welfare.

[344] [2007] EMLR 7.

Further reading

General

Students should read the relevant chapters of Fenwick and Phillipson, *Media Freedom under the Human Rights Act* (OUP 2006), chapters 2–3 on press freedom generally, chapters 4–7 on contempt of court, chapters 13–15 and 18 on confidentiality and privacy and copyright, and chapter 21 on defamation. They should also consult Barendt, Freedom of Speech (OUP 2005, 2nd edn), especially chapters 4, 6, 7 and 12; Robertson and Nicol, *Media Law* (Penguin 2008, 5th edn); Rozenburg, *Privacy and the Press* (OUP 2004). Mowbray's *Cases and Materials on the European Convention* (Oxford 2007, 2nd edn), chapter 11 provides an excellent reference point on the case law of the European Court in this area.

Defamation, confidentiality and contempt of court

The following texts and articles also provide interesting reading in specific aspects of defamation, confidentiality and contempt of court.

Brabyn, Protection against Judicially Compelled Disclosure of the Identity of News Gatherers' Confidential Sources in Common Law Jurisdictions (2006) MLR 895; Cram, *A Virtue Less Cloistered: Courts, Speech and Constitutions* (Hart 2002); Phillipson and Fenwick, Breach of Confidence as a Privacy Remedy in the Human Rights Act Era (2000) 63 MLR 600; McColgan, Privacy, Freedom of Expression and the Grant of Interim Injunctions [2008] CJQ 22; Millar, Whither the spirit of Lingens? [2009] EHRLR 277; Phillipson, Transforming Breach of Confidence? Towards a Common Law Right of Privacy under the Human Rights Act (2003) 66 MLR 726; Sanderson, Is Von Hannover a Step Backward for the Substantive Analysis of Speech and Privacy Interests? [2004] EHRLR 631; Thorgeirsdottir, Journalism Worthy of the Name: An Affirmative Reading of the ECHR [2004] Netherlands Human Rights Quarterly 601; Tugendhat and Christie (eds), *The Law of Privacy and the Media* (OUP 2002).

Visit **www.mylawchamber.co.uk/fosterhumanrights**
to access regular updates to major changes in the law,
further case studies, weblinks, and suggested
answers/approaches to questions in the book.

mylawchamber
unrivalled support for legal education

10 Freedom of association and assembly

Introduction

On 29 June 2010, the High Court granted an injunction to the Mayor of London ordering the removal of a number of protestors from Parliament Square, directly outside the Houses of Parliament: *Mayor of London* v *Hall and Others* (2010). They included Brian Haw, who had been protesting against war and for justice since 2001 and who had survived several legal attempts to remove him. The court order had been granted on the basis that the Mayor of London had a right of exclusive possession of Parliament Square Gardens and that he was entitled to demand that the camp being used by the protestors be dismantled because it interfered with his duty to maintain the area.

Should the Mayor's duties override Mr Haw's right to peaceful protest, and what factors should a court consider in making that decision? This chapter will examine this and many other cases where the courts have used domestic law, the Human Rights Act and the European Convention on Human Rights in their attempt to balance the fundamental right of protest with the public interest and the rights of others.

This chapter covers the fundamental democratic rights to form and take part in associations, including trade unions, and to organise and participate in peaceful assemblies. It also explores the legitimacy of restricting these conditional rights. The chapter begins by examining the reasons why these rights are important in liberal democracies and how they are protected and restricted under Article 11 of the European Convention on Human Rights. The chapter will then examine each right in turn, looking at its protection under the European Convention (together with an examination of the relevant case law of the European Court of Human Rights), and then its restriction in domestic law, paying particular attention to the legitimacy of such restrictions and their compatibility with the Convention and human rights norms.

Thus, this chapter will cover:

- An examination of the scope and importance of the democratic rights of freedom of association and freedom of peaceful assembly, including the necessity for lawful restrictions.

- An examination of the protection of those conditional rights under Article 11 of the European Convention on Human Rights.

- An examination of the protection of the right to freedom of association under Article 11, including an analysis of the case law of the European Court of Human Rights.

- An examination of the variety of domestic law restrictions on freedom of association, including an analysis of the compatibility of those provisions with the Convention and relevant human rights norms.

- An examination of the protection of the right to freedom of peaceful assembly under Article 11, including an analysis of the case law of the European Court of Human Rights.

- An examination of the variety of domestic law restrictions on freedom of peaceful assembly and an analysis of the compatibility of those provisions with the Convention and relevant human rights norms.

Nature and purpose of the rights of association and assembly

The rights of association and assembly are seen as fundamental in many respects. First, both the forming of associations and the right to take part in peaceful assembly unite people in their beliefs and opinions and is thus a democratically effective method of holding and imparting information and ideas. Thus, the rights of association and peaceful assembly are closely related to freedom of speech and expression under Article 10 of the Convention. By taking part in demonstrations, the participant is given the opportunity to impart information and ideas, and the public is provided with a direct and effective opportunity to receive those views.[1] Indeed, in many cases the European Court of Human Rights has held that it is unnecessary to deal with an allegation under Article 11, choosing instead to determine the matter under Article 10. For example, in *Steel* v *United Kingdom*,[2] once the Court had found that the applicant's freedom of expression had been interfered with by their arrest for taking part in an entirely peaceful demonstration, it did not find it necessary to entertain the applicant's claim that such action also interfered with their right of peaceful assembly under Article 11.[3]

Secondly, these rights are important to the promotion of democracy and pluralism. In a democratic society it is essential that those in authority face criticism and opposition and traditional views are challenged, and that individuals are given the opportunity to form certain ideas in common with others. Given the inability of most people to have access to the media in order to disseminate their views, the rights of association and assembly provide the perfect opportunity to take part in the democratic debate by imparting one's views and by challenging the actions and views of others. Thirdly, these rights are connected with self-development. Although freedom of assembly and association are defined as collective rights,

---

[1] For an analysis of protest as a means of expression see Barendt, Freedom of Assembly, in Beatson and Cripps (eds), *Freedom of Expression and Freedom of Information* (2000), Barendt, *Freedom of Speech* (OUP 2005), chapter 8; Fenwick, The Right To Protest, the Human Rights Act and the Margin of Appreciation (1999) 62 MLR 491; Fenwick and Phillipson, Public Protest, the Human Rights Act and Judicial Responses to Political Expression [2000] PL 627.

[2] (1998) 28 EHRR 603, considered below.

[3] See also *Vogt* v *Germany* (1995) 21 EHRR 205; *Chorherr* v *Austria* (1993) 17 EHRR 358.

they undoubtedly allow the individual to develop as an individual and to make individual choices based on his or her (shared) views.[4]

Association and assembly and Article 11 of the European Convention on Human Rights[5]

Article 11 of the Convention provides as follows:

> Everyone has the right to freedom of peaceful assembly and to freedom of association with others, including the right to form and to join trade unions for the protection of his interests.

Article 11 protects two basic rights: freedom of association with others, including the right to join a trade union, and the right to peaceful assembly. Article 11 of the Convention is, of course, a conditional right and restrictions may be placed on the exercise of those rights, provided they are prescribed by law and necessary in a democratic society in the interests of national security or public safety, for the prevention of disorder or crime, for the protection of health or morals or for the protection of the rights and freedoms of others.

Question

Why is freedom of association and peaceful assembly regarded as so fundamental in modern democracies and under the European Convention on Human Rights?

Freedom of association

Article 11 guarantees the right of association with others, and is a conditional right, subject to lawful and necessary restrictions on the grounds outlined above. In addition, Article 11(2) provides that the article does not prevent the imposition of lawful restrictions of these rights by members of the armed forces, of the police or of the administration of the state.[6] This particular provision was the subject of litigation under the European Convention in the famous 'GCHQ' case. The government had banned trade union membership at the government intelligence headquarters at Cheltenham on the grounds that such membership, and the threat of industrial action, would be injurious to national security.[7] In an action for judicial review the House of Lords held that the government had acted lawfully and fairly,[8] and proceedings were brought under the Convention claiming a violation of Article 11.[9] Declaring the application inadmissible, the European Commission of Human Rights held that the employees at the headquarters fell into the definition of 'members of the administration of

---

[4] The right of association includes the right of disassociation, and often the purpose of demonstrations is to disassociate the participants with a particular collective view of, for example, their government.

[5] For general reading in this area see Harris, O'Boyle and Warbrick, *Law of the European Convention on Human Rights* (OUP 2009, 2nd edn), chapter 12; Mowbray, *Cases and Materials on the European Convention on Human Rights* (OUP 2007), chapter 12; Clayton and Tomlinson, *Law of Human Rights* (OUP 2008, 2nd edn), chapter 16.

[6] See *Council of Civil Service Unions and Others v United Kingdom* (1987) 50 DR 228, upholding the government's banning of trade unions at GCHQ.

[7] Under Article 4 of the Civil Service Order in Council 1982.

[8] *Council of Civil Service Unions v Minister for Civil Service* [1985] AC 374.

[9] *Council of Civil Service Unions and Others v United Kingdom* (1987) 50 DR 228.

the state' and that the restrictions placed on their right of association were lawful under the terms of Article 11(2). In the Commission's opinion, an interference with the right under Article 11 could include the complete prohibition of that right. In this case, given the wide margin of appreciation offered to member states in cases involving national security, the Commission concluded that the measures taken, although drastic, were neither arbitrary nor in violation of the applicants' rights. However, this does not affect the right of association of those civil servants who are not working in national security.[10]

Article 11 includes the right to form trade unions, and member states have an obligation to ensure such a right is enjoyed by individuals employed by private employers, and by the state itself. Thus, in *Swedish Engine Drivers' Union v Sweden*[11] it was held that Article 11 imposed an obligation on the state when acting as an employer, rejecting the government's contention that the Convention only applied to the state in respect of its public powers. The right to form trade unions is not absolute although any restriction imposed by the state on the forming of trade unions would have to be convincingly established. For example, in *Tum Haber Sen and Cinar v Turkey*[12] it was held that there had been a violation of Article 11 when the applicant's trade union had been dissolved on the ground that civil servants could not form trade unions. No evidence had been provided to the Court as to why the union would threaten society so as to justify this measure. In addition, the absolute prohibition was contrary to the state's obligations under the International Labour Organisation (ILO) and the European Social Charter.

The European Court had consistently held that Article 11 does not secure any particular treatment of trade unions or their members, such as the right to negotiate or to conclude collective agreements.[13] For example, in *Wilson and Others v United Kingdom*,[14] the Court confirmed that the absence under United Kingdom law of an obligation on employers to enter into collective bargaining did not, on its own, give rise to a violation of Article 11.[15] However, in that case the Court held that under Article 11 a union should have the ability to strive for the protection of their members' interests, and that a scheme whereby an individual was only given an increase in contractual benefits if they agreed to the union being de-recognised was contrary to Article 11.[16] In this case the Court stressed that while the state did not have an obligation to compel employers to bargain with unions, it must ensure that trade union members are not prevented or restrained from using their union to represent them in their attempts to regulate their relations with their employers. More recently, however, the view expressed in the *Swedish Drivers'* case has been challenged, and in *Demir v Turkey*[17] the Grand Chamber referred to a number of international instruments on labour standards in holding

[10] *Demir v Turkey* [2009] IRLR 766.

[11] (1976) 1 EHRR 617.

[12] (2008) 46 EHRR 19.

[13] *Swedish Engine Drivers' Union v Sweden* (1976) 1 EHRR 617; *National Union of Belgian Police v Belgium* (1975) 1 EHRR 578; *Schmidt and Dahlstrom v Sweden* (1976) EHRR 632.

[14] (2002) 35 EHRR 20.

[15] See also the decision in *Unison v United Kingdom* (Application No 53574/99), admissibility decision, 10 January 2002, where it was held that the prohibition on the applicant's ability to take strike action and the lack of compulsion on employers to maintain collective bargaining was not in violation of Article 11.

[16] In *Associated Newspapers v Wilson; Associated Newspapers v Palmer* [1995] IRLR 258, the House of Lords held that such action did not constitute action taken against an individual for the purpose of deterring him from being a member of a trade union within (what is now) s.146 of the Trade Union and Labour Relations (Consolidation) Act 1992.

[17] [2009] IRLR 766.

that the right to bargain was indeed an inherent element of Article 11. In that case the Grand Chamber thus accepted that the right to bargain collectively with an employer has become one of the essential elements of the right to form and to join trade unions for the protection of interests under Article 11.

Article 11 also includes the right of that association to regulate its membership and affairs and the right to enforce its beliefs and principles, even where those principles conflict with individual beliefs. This aspect of the right to association was considered in the case of *ASLEF v United Kingdom*,[18] where the applicants claimed that their inability to legally expel a member for his right-wing views was contrary to their right of association under Article 11. The union had expelled one its members when they discovered he was standing for election for the BNP (formerly the National Front). His expulsion was ruled unlawful because domestic law prohibited discrimination on grounds of political association,[19] and the union petitioned the European Court claiming that such a position was inconsistent with Article 11. The European Court held that as an employee had the right to join or not join a particular trade union (see below) so too a trade union should be free to choose its own members; Article 11 did not impose an obligation on the union to admit whoever wished to join. Where associations were formed to espouse particular views or ideals (in this case social justice and equality), it would run counter to Article 11 if that association was not entitled to regulate its own membership. In this case, although the union's freedom of association was restricted by domestic law for a legitimate purpose – the right of others to espouse their political views – it failed to strike a fair balance between the rights of the association and the expelled member. There was no evidence that the member had suffered any financial or other hardship as a consequence of expulsion, and the union was fully entitled to believe that the member's values and position were inconsistent with its own.

The European Court has also decided that, while not containing an express right of non-association, Article 11 protects the right of an individual not to join an association when read in conjunction with Article 9 guaranteeing the right of thought, conscience and religion. In *Young, James and Webster v United Kingdom*[20] the European Court held that there had been a violation of Article 11 when domestic law allowed employers to dismiss employees who refused to join a trade union in accordance with a 'closed shop' agreement between unions and employers. The European Court held that such a right could be implied from both Articles 11 and 9 of the Convention (guaranteeing freedom of thought and conscience) and that on the facts the subjection of the applicants to dismissal for refusal to join that union was a disproportionate interference with that right.[21] However, in *Sibson v United Kingdom*[22] the European Court held that there had been no violation when the applicant was given a choice of trade unions, but wished to join one particular union. The applicant had resigned his employment after his employers had moved him when he had resigned his membership of the TGWU and had joined another union. His claim for unfair dismissal failed and he claimed that his rights under Articles 9 and 10 had been violated. Distinguishing *Young, James*

[18] (2007) 45 EHRR 34.
[19] By virtue of s.174 of the Trade Union and Labour Relations (Consolidation) Act 1992.
[20] (1982) 4 EHRR 38.
[21] As a consequence the law was changed making it unlawful to dismiss a person on the grounds of their trade union, or non-trade union membership. The current legal position thus complies with Articles 9 and 11 and also allows the union a greater leeway to control its membership: see *ASLEF v United Kingdom*, n 18 above.
[22] (1993) 17 EHRR 193.

and Webster, the European Court held that the applicant had no particular objection to trade union membership and had been faced with the choice of membership or dismissal. Whether there is a violation of Article 11 in such cases will depend on the extent of both the applicant's conscientious beliefs and the penalty for non-compliance. Thus, in *Sorensen and Rasmussen v Denmark*,[23] it was held that there had been a violation of Article 11 when the applicants had been, respectively, dismissed and forced to join a trade union other than one of their choice in compliance with a closed-shop agreement. The Court held that such a system struck at the foundation of freedom of choice and that current trends did not show that such agreements were essential to the effective enjoyment of trade union freedoms.

Outside the area of trade unions the Court has taken a broad approach in defining the term 'association' and has held that it covers political parties. Thus, in *United Communist Party of Turkey v Turkey*[24] the Court rejected the contention made on behalf of the government that the inclusion of trade unions in Article 11 necessarily excluded political parties. In the Court's view the mention of trade unions was intended as but one example among others of the form in which the right to freedom of association may be exercised. More importantly, in the Court's view, was that political parties were essential to the effective functioning of democracy. Consequently there was no doubt that political parties were included, despite not being specifically mentioned in Article 11. Article 11 would also apply to other associations where that group shares a common set of beliefs, political or otherwise. However, it was held in *Anderson v United Kingdom*[25] that Article 11 does not cover the right to associate for purely social purposes. So too, a prohibition on an association's right to participate in a particular activity would not engage Article 11 provided that association was still entitled to assemble generally.[26]

One of the features of a democratic society is pluralism, and therefore, the Convention would not sanction the proscription of an organisation merely because its views were contrary to those of the traditional majority parties in that society. In addition, because proscription is such a Draconian and severe step, based on potential harm, rather than specific criminal activities, it will be rare for the Court to sanction the criminalisation of political or other associations. Thus, in *United Communist Party of Turkey v Turkey*[27] it was held that the dissolution of a political party on the basis that it used the word 'communist' in its name, and that the party's constitution and programme contained statements likely to undermine territorial integrity and national unity, was in violation of Article 11. The Court held that the exceptions in Article 11 must, where political parties are concerned, be construed strictly and that only convincing and compelling reasons can justify restrictions on such parties' freedom of association. In particular, in deciding the question of necessity, the Court stated that it had to satisfy itself that the national authorities applied standards that were in conformity with the principles embodied in Article 11. The Court held that the mere use of the word 'communism' was insufficient to justify dissolution in the absence of other relevant and sufficient evidence. Neither, in the Court's opinion, did the party's views on the Kurdish problem

---

[23] (2006) 20 BHRC 258.

[24] (1998) 26 EHRR 121.

[25] (1998) 25 EHRR CD 172. No claim under Article 11 when the applicants had been barred from entering a shopping mall.

[26] In *R (Countryside Alliance) v Attorney-General* [2007] 3 WLR 922, the House of Lords held that the rights under Article 11 were not engaged when hunting with dogs was outlawed. In their Lordships' view the activity fell short of the kind of assembly whose protection was fundamental to the proper functioning of a democratic society. See now *Countryside Alliance v United Kingdom* (2010) 50 EHRR SE6.

[27] (1998) 26 EHRR 121.

provide sufficient evidence of separatism and division of the Turkish nation. It was quite clear that the party's views were based on democratic and peaceful ideals. So too, in *Linkov* v *Czech Republic*,[28] the European Court held that it was in violation of Article 11 to refuse to register the applicant's party as a political party on the grounds that it advocated an unconstitutional agenda. There was no evidence that the party was going to employ undemocratic or violent means and the party had been banned before it had begun its activities.[29]

In exceptional cases, however, the European Court has sanctioned the proscription of a particular organisation which was thought to pose a sufficient threat to the values of that society and, perhaps, of the European legal and social order. Thus in *Reefa Partisi Erbakan Kazan and Tekdal* v *Turkey*[30] the Court held that the dissolution of the applicant's party by the Turkish Constitutional Court on the ground that it had become a centre of activities against the principles of secularism was within the state's margin of appreciation and thus justified within the terms of Article 11(2). In the Court's view political parties which campaign for changes in legislation or to the legal or constitutional structure of the state are allowed the protection of Article 11, provided the means used to those ends are lawful and democratic. However, political parties whose leaders incite others to use violence and/or support political aims that were inconsistent with one or more of the rules of democracy cannot rely on the Convention to protect them from sanctions imposed as a result. The state could reasonably prevent the implementation of a political programme which was incompatible with Convention norms before it was given effect through specific acts that might jeopardise civil peace and the country's democratic regime.

The decision in *Reefah Partisi* is controversial because it allows for proscription of groups for reasons other than the direct prevention of violence.[31] In other words, the values or principles of that group may not simply be unpopular, but so abhorrent to democratic values that they fall outside the protection of Article 10. In making a distinction between such groups the European Court will have recourse to Article 17 of the Convention. That article provides that nothing in the Convention gives any person or group any right to engage in any activity or perform any act aimed at the destruction of any of the rights and freedoms in the Convention. Thus, the Court can use that article to distinguish groups whose purposes and activities are inimical to the notions of democracy embodied in the Convention from those whose ideas are merely inconsistent with other democratic, majority, views. Thus, the Court noted that a political party in employing its Convention rights might attempt to derive the right to conduct what amounts in practice to activities intended to destroy the rights and freedoms of others and thus bring about the destruction of democracy.[32]

The right of association under Article 11 protects the rights not only of the association itself, but also of individuals attached to it, and Article 11 can also be used to bolster the individual's freedom of thought and conscience and freedom of expression. Thus, in *Vogt* v

[28] Decision of the European Court, 7 December 2006.

[29] See also *Zhechev* v *Bulgaria* (Application No 57045/00), decision of the European Court, 21 June 2007 – refusal to register an association because it advocated restoring the monarchy and campaigning for changes to existing legal and constitutional frameworks was disproportionate in the absence of violent or undemocratic means and thus in violation of Article 11.

[30] (2002) 35 EHRR 2.

[31] See Sottiaux, Anti-Democratic Associations: Content and Consequences in Article 11 Adjudication [2004] (4) Netherlands Human Rights Quarterly 585.

[32] See Hare and Weinstein, *Extreme Speech and Democracy* (OUP 2009); Keane, Attacking Hate Speech under Article 17 of the European Convention on Human Rights [2007] Netherlands Human Rights Quarterly 241.

Germany[33] the Court held that the dismissal of a teacher because she was a member of the German Communist Party, and had taken part in its activities, was in violation of her right of freedom of expression under Article 10. The Court noted that her dismissal was disproportionate to that aim, given that her work as a teacher had been entirely satisfactory, that she had never acted in a way that was inconsistent with the compulsory declaration of allegiance to the German constitutional order, and that the Communist Party had never been banned. However, the Convention does not prohibit the interference with individual rights where there is evidence of a more pressing social harm caused by individual association. For example, in *Zdanoka v Latvia*,[34] it was held that the life-long prohibition of the applicant from standing for election because of her past membership and activities of the Communist Party of Latvia was proportionate and thus not in violation of Article 11 and Article 3 of the First Protocol to the Convention. In the Grand Chamber's view the relevant legislative ban had been introduced not to punish those who had been active in the party but to uphold the integrity of the democratic process by excluding from participation in the democratic legislature those who had taken an active and leading role in a party that was directly linked to the attempted violent overthrow of the democratic regime. The statutory exclusion was thus within the state's margin of appreciation, although the Grand Chamber noted that the state should keep the law under constant review.[35]

Questions

What types of association are protected under Article 11 of the European Convention and what rights does that article give to such bodies?

When is it permissible to restrict those rights?

Legal restrictions in domestic law on the right of association

The legal proscription of particular groups in domestic law has been reserved for the most extreme groups who pose major threats to public order or the security of the state. In such cases, the law does go further than criminalising certain words or behaviour that cause, or are likely to cause, particular harm, and renders illegal the very act of association with, or assistance of, that group. In most circumstances, however, the law will tolerate unpopular and antidemocratic bodies, provided they do not commit a breach of the law, or breach specific provisions intended to protect others from the worst excesses of those beliefs. Thus, although groups such as the BNP are not proscribed, their members are more vulnerable than others to prosecution for specific criminal law offences designed to protect the rights of others.[36] The law is not on the other hand prepared to take the more draconian step of proscribing the group irrespective of the peacefulness or otherwise of its activities, believing that such a step would be an affront to principles of democracy and pluralism.

---

[33] (1995) 21 EHRR 205.

[34] Decision of the European Court, 17 June 2004.

[35] Further, in *Ahmed v United Kingdom* [1999] IRLR 188, the Court upheld the prohibition of certain local authority officers from holding political office, finding that the need to secure public confidence in the carrying out of certain local authority posts justified the prohibition.

[36] These offences are detailed below, under freedom of assembly, and in chapter 12 on the right to religion.

As we have seen above, the European Convention on Human Rights allows such restrictions provided those restrictions are 'prescribed by law' and 'necessary in a democratic society' for the protection of one of the legitimate aims contained in Article 11. Such restrictions may also be supported by the member state's power to derogate from their normal obligations in times of war and other national emergency.[37] Alternatively, Article 17 of the Convention withdraws the protection of its substantive rights to those activities or actions aimed at the destruction of the rights and freedoms of others. Any domestic provision that permits proscription has to be viewed in the light of these permitted exceptions and of the Convention case law, which requires substantial justification for such interferences.

Public Order Act 1936

Section 1 of the Public Order Act 1936 makes it an offence to wear a uniform in any public place or at any public meeting that signifies association with any political organisation or with the promotion of any political object. This provision was passed in order to control the growth of fascist organisations in the 1930s and the consent of the Attorney-General is required before any prosecution is brought under the Act. The meaning of 'uniform' was considered in *O'Moran v DPP*.[38] A number of people had dressed in black berets, dark glasses and dark, but not identical, clothing. It was held that although the wearing of a uniform required some article of clothing, as opposed to, for example, a lapel badge, the wearing of a beret constituted the wearing of a uniform. It was also held that the wearing of a uniform could be associated with a political association either through evidence of previous association, or, as in the present case, from the circumstances surrounding the wearing of the uniform.

This provision overlaps heavily with terrorist provisions,[39] although it could still be used against associations that are otherwise lawful and which have not been proscribed. The provision is supported by s.2 of the 1936 Act, which prohibits the formation of military or quasi-military organisations. A 'quasi-military organisation' is one that is organised or trained, or organised and equipped, to be employed for the use or display of physical force in promoting any political object or act in such a manner as to arouse reasonable apprehension that they are organised and either trained or equipped for that purpose.[40] Section 2 provides that any person who takes part in the control or management of the association, or as a member of the association takes part in the organisation or training of members, is guilty of an offence.[41] Again, although many such groups will be proscribed under terrorism legislation, the provision does cover the activities of other groups. For example, in *R v Jordan and Tyndall*[42] the section was used successfully against two members of a fascist group who had engaged in the activities of the group. Members of the group in question, *Spearhead*, who were part of the British National Party and later the National Socialist movement, had been seen practising foot drill and carrying out attack and defence exercises during which they

---

[37] Under Article 15 of the European Convention.

[38] [1975] QB 864.

[39] A broader provision exists under s.13 of the Terrorism Act 2000 in relation to the wearing of items connected with proscribed organisations.

[40] Section 2 also covers organisations concerned with usurping the functions of the police or the armed forces, such as vigilante groups.

[41] Under s.2(2) of the Act any prosecution requires the consent of the Attorney-General.

[42] [1963] Crim LR 124.

exchanged Nazi salutes. The premises of the group had been searched and the police had found, *inter alia*, a tin of sodium chlorate, which could be used for making bombs, with the words 'jew killer' on it. It was held that there existed a reasonable apprehension that the group's members were organised for the use or display of physical force for promoting a political object. However, it was also stated that the apprehension of fear must be held by a person who is aware of all the facts and must not be based upon undue timidity or excessive suspicion or prejudice.

Proscribing terrorist groups: the Terrorism Act 2000, the Anti-Terrorism, Crime and Security Act 2001 and the Terrorism Act 2006

Most domestic legal systems will contain provisions allowing the authorities to compromise civil liberties in times of war or other emergency. In particular, laws will be passed giving those authorities increased powers regarding the control of terrorist activities, and these powers will permit greater interference with rights such as liberty of the person, fair trial, freedom of movement and, in certain cases, freedom of speech, association and assembly.[43] The law relating to the control of terrorism, including the proscription of particular organisations, is now contained in the Terrorism Act 2000,[44] as reinforced by the Anti-Terrorism, Crime and Security Act 2001, and the Terrorism Act 2006.[45] The Terrorism Act 2000 replaced the previous statutory provisions in this area contained in both the Prevention of Terrorism (Temporary Provisions) Act 1989 and the Northern Ireland (Emergency Powers) Act 1996, extending the definition of terrorism and giving the legislation a wide scope covering all manner of internal and international terrorism.[46] These provisions, together with the provisions regulating terrorist speech, will be examined in chapter 14 of the text.

Freedom of assembly

Although the right to association under Article 11 includes the right to take part in the activities of that group, including the right to demonstrate, the right of peaceful assembly will be treated separately. Demonstrations give rise to different and more direct problems with respect to public order and the rights of others and these difficulties will be reflected in a variety of domestic laws which will seek to regulate the right to demonstrate and balance it with other social or individual interests. This section will thus begin by looking at the right of peaceful assembly under the European Convention, and will then examine the variety of public order and other laws which affect that right.

---

[43] See Walker, *The Prevention of Terrorism in British Law* (Manchester University Press 1996, 2nd edn); Walker, *Blackstone's Guide to Anti-Terrorism Legislation* (OUP 2003).

[44] The Act followed a government consultation paper: *Legislation Against Terrorism: A Consultation Paper* Cm 1478 (Stationery Office 1998). For a critical account of the Act and of the law on terrorism, see Whitty, Murphy and Livingstone, *Civil Liberties Law: The Human Rights Act Era* (Butterworths 2001), chapter 3; Fenwick, *Civil Rights: New Labour, Freedom and the Human Rights Act* (Longman 2000), chapter 3.

[45] For a detailed and critical account of this Act, see Fenwick, The Anti-Terrorism, Crime and Security Act 2001: A Proportionate Response to 11 September? (2002) 65 MLR 724.

[46] For a general coverage of the terrorist legislation and its impact on freedom of association, see Fenwick, *Civil Liberties and Human Rights* (Cavendish 2007, 4th edn), pages 1363–1406.

Freedom of assembly under the European Convention

The right to peaceful assembly is protected conditionally by Article 11 and applies to most gatherings where people intend to impart information or ideas.[47] So too, a prohibition on an association's right to participate in a particular activity would not engage Article 11.[48] Article 11 protects the right to *peaceful* assembly, thus excluding any activity that is carried out with the intention of committing acts of violence. Consequently a person who intends to hold a violent assembly would not receive the protection of Article 11 in the first place. What is less certain, however, is whether a group which holds an assembly that is likely to incite violence from others receives the protection of Article 11. This is the classic dilemma with respect to the right to demonstrate and is explored in this chapter with respect to both the European Convention and domestic law. In the second place, such assemblies might bring into play Article 17 of the Convention and thus deprive the applicants of any protection under the Convention. That provision prohibits acts which are aimed at the destruction of the rights of others and may be used, in combination with Articles 10(2) and 11(2) to deny the Convention's protection to controversial demonstrations.

In the third place, Article 11 is a conditional right and Article 11(2) permits restrictions on even peaceful assemblies where those restrictions are necessary to preserve, for example, public order. Thus, even if demonstrators have no intention of committing or inciting acts of violence, the Convention might sanction an interference with the right of assembly where it was necessary to achieve the legitimate aim of preserving public order. For example, in *Rai, Allmond and Negotiate Now v United Kingdom*[49] the European Commission held that prior restraint was permissible provided the threat to public order was sufficiently pressing. In that case the Commission held that a refusal to allow the applicants to hold a rally in Trafalgar Square to discuss affairs concerning Northern Ireland was within the state's margin of appreciation. The ban was made for a legitimate aim of preventing public disorder and the policy of banning such meetings unless there were exceptional cases was both necessary and proportionate. In any case, the applicants could have held a meeting outside the vicinity of Trafalgar Square.[50]

Similarly, in *Chorherr v Austria*[51] the Court held that the arrest and subsequent detention of two peaceful protestors was not in violation of Articles 10 or 11. In this case the applicant and his friend were demonstrating against the purchase of fighter aircraft by the Austrian Armed Forces during a public military ceremony. The protestors distributed leaflets and wore huge rucksacks with slogans on them. A disturbance broke out when members of the public could not see the ceremony and the police asked the protestors to cease their demonstrations because they were causing public disorder. When they refused they were arrested for breach of the peace and detained for three hours. The European Court held that there had been no

---

[47] In *Anderson v United Kingdom* (1998) 25 EHRR CD 172, it was held that Article 11 does not cover the right to associate for purely social purposes.

[48] See *R (Countryside Alliance) v Attorney-General* [2007] 3 WLR 922, where the House of Lords held that Article 11 was not engaged as it did not cover social or sporting gatherings or pastimes. This was confirmed by the European Court of Human Rights: *Countryside Alliance v United Kingdom* (2010) 50 EHRR SE6.

[49] (1995) 19 EHRR CD 93.

[50] See also *Pendragon v United Kingdom* [1999] EHRLR 223, where the European Commission held that a banning order prohibiting persons from congregating at Stonehenge was necessary for the purpose of preserving public order, despite the lack of any evidence that the applicants were likely to contribute to any disorder.

[51] (1993) 17 EHRR 358.

violation of Article 10 and that member states had a margin of appreciation to determine what measures should be taken to ensure that lawful demonstrations and public events take place peacefully. The Court held that the measures taken against the applicant and his friend were not excessive, and the applicant must have realised, when he chose a public event for the venue of his protest, that he might cause a disturbance.[52] So too, in *Barraco* v *France*,[53] the Court found no violation of Article 11 when the applicant had been prosecuted for obstruction when taking part in a slow vehicle demonstration in the name of his union as part of a national day of protest. The applicant had had the opportunity to protest for a number of hours and the complete blockage of the highway went beyond normal disruption caused by demonstrations.[54]

A more liberal approach was taken in *Ollinger* v *Austria*,[55] where the European Court held that there had been a violation of Article 11 when the applicant's counter-demonstration against the holding of a meeting commemorating the deaths of SS officers in the Second World War had been prohibited under domestic law. The Court held that disruption to the commemorative meeting could not be sufficient reason in itself and that the possible disturbance to the public, who attended cemeteries on that day, was not serious enough given that the counter-demonstration would be attended by six people and that the organiser had promised that there would be no banner or chanting, and that there had been no evidence of violence in the past.[56]

Article 11 of the European Convention contains a positive right on behalf of every member state to ensure that everyone can enjoy the right of peaceful demonstration. Although this is not an absolute right, it has been held that demonstrators have the right to carry out their right of peaceful assembly free from unreasonable interference from others. In *Platform Ärzte für das Leben* v *Austria*,[57] a group of doctors were demonstrating against abortion and had two of their meetings disrupted by unlawful counter-demonstrations, in spite of a large police presence. The European Court held that on the facts there had been no violation of the applicants' rights under Article 11. The state had made it an offence to disrupt an unlawful meeting and in this case the police had refused to intervene because there were no serious assaults or lasting damage to property. The state's positive obligation is thus limited, and in *Appelby* v *United Kingdom*[58] it was held that there had been no violation of Article 11 when the applicants had been prohibited from holding a demonstration in a town centre shopping centre. Although the state had a duty to ensure there was sufficient opportunity for individuals to take part in freedom of assembly, the application of private law to stop the applicants campaigning against the building on a local playing field was not a disproportionate interference with their rights under Articles 10 and 11 of the Convention. The Court was persuaded by the

---

[52] Contrast *Steel* v *United Kingdom* (1999) 28 EHRR 603, discussed below.

[53] Decision of the European Court, 5 March 2009.

[54] Contrast *Patvi* v *Hungary*, decision of the European Court, 7 October 2008, where it held that there had been a violation when the authorities had prohibited a series of planned and peaceful demonstrations on the basis that they would cause disruption to traffic, but where that reason was not substantiated by the facts.

[55] (2008) 46 EHRR 38.

[56] For an analysis of that case and the jurisprudence of the European Court in this area, see Mead, Strasbourg Discovers the Right to Counter Demonstrate – A Note on *Ollinger* v *Austria* [2007] EHRLR 133; Mead, The Right to Peaceful Process under the European Convention on Human Rights – A Content Study of Strasbourg Case Law [2007] EHRLR 345.

[57] (1991) 13 EHRR 204.

[58] (2003) 37 EHRR 38.

fact that other avenues of protest were still open to them and that there was little evidence to suggest that the prohibition in this case had rendered their protest meaningless.

This positive obligation to facilitate peaceful assembly also includes the duty to provide demonstrators with fair and effective access to permission for such demonstrations and an effective remedy when such permission is refused. Thus, in *Baczkowski and Others v Poland*[59] it was held that there had been a violation of Article 11, and Article 13, of the Convention when the Mayor's refusal of the applicant's request to hold an assembly had only been quashed after the proposed date of the hearing. Although the meetings were actually held in contravention of the refusal it was held the initial refusal still constituted an interference with their rights as it could have discouraged the holding of the meeting. Domestic law should have imposed an obligation on the authorities to allow an effective challenge before the proposed meeting. In addition, as the Mayor had spoken out earlier against the rallies and the group's mandate (prohibition of discrimination against homosexuality), it could be inferred that the reasons given for the refusal (traffic problems) were not genuine and that the Mayor's initial reaction against the group had affected the decision-making process. Accordingly there was a violation of Article 14.

Further, any interference with peaceful assembly, whether in the form of prior restraint or via fines and other punishments, must meet the tests of legality and proportionality laid down by Article 11 and the case law of the Convention. First, any restriction has to be pre-scribed by law and related to one of the legitimate aims listed in Article 11(2). For example, in *Ivanov v Bulgaria*,[60] when two intended rallies had been banned on the grounds that the events would 'create conditions for breaches of public order', the Court concluded that the reasons given for the ban were inadequate and that the authorities had thus not provided relevant and sufficient reasoning for the ban.[61] However, the Court has not demanded that public order offences be defined with absolute certainty.[62] Thus, in *Lucas v United Kingdom*,[63] the European Court upheld the definition of breach of the peace in Scottish law – conduct which was alarming and disturbing, in its context, to any reasonable person – believing that it was sufficiently precise to provide reasonable foreseeability of actions which might fall into its remit.[64]

Penalties and prior restraints must also be proportionate. Thus, in those cases where a peaceful demonstration has been allowed to take place an individual also has the right not to be unjustifiably punished because of his involvement with the demonstration. In *Ezelin v France*[65] the applicant had been disciplined by the legal profession for taking part in a

---

[59] Application No 1543/06, decision of the European Court, 3 May 2007.

[60] (2005) 43 EHRR 119.

[61] In addition, with respect to the proportionality of the ban, the fact that there was reason to believe that the rallies were to be held by groups who harboured separatist views was not sufficient *per se* to ban the meetings. See also *Stefanec v Czech Republic*, decision of the European Court, 18 July 2006, where it was held that there had been a violation of Article 10 when the applicant had been convicted and fined for organising a banned demonstration. The offence of organising such a meeting had not been defined with sufficient certainty so as to allow the applicant to foresee that his involvement (announcing to the crowd that the meeting had been banned arbitrarily) would constitute an offence.

[62] See *Hashman and Harrap v United Kingdom* (1999) 30 EHRR 241, dealt with under breach of the peace, below.

[63] Admissibility decision of the European Court, 18 March 2003.

[64] In that case, therefore, the applicants' arrests for sitting in a road leading to a naval base were held to be in compliance with Articles 5, 10 and 11 of the Convention. See also *Steel v United Kingdom* (1998) 28 EHRR 603, dealt with under breach of the peace, below.

[65] (1991) 14 EHRR 362.

demonstration against the conviction of three militants. In the Court's opinion the measures taken against the applicant clearly interfered with his right of peaceful assembly, even though the penalty had been imposed after he had taken part in the demonstration. The applicant had joined a lawful assembly and there was no evidence that he had been party to any unlawful or antisocial activity that had taken place during the demonstration. A balance must be struck between the requirements laid down in Article 11(2) and those of free expression by words, gestures or even silence by persons assembled on the streets or other public places. The freedom to take part in a peaceful assembly cannot be restricted so long as the person concerned does not himself commit any reprehensible act on any such occasion. Accordingly, the sanction imposed on him was disproportionate to the legitimate aim of preserving public order.

So too, if a person is penalised for taking part in a demonstration there must be sufficient evidence that his actions posed a threat to, say, public order. For example, in *Christian Democratic People's Party* v *Moldova*,[66] the authorities had imposed a month's ban on the applicant's party's activities after it had taken part in an unauthorised demonstration outside the National Assembly Square. The Court held that, given the technicality of the breach and the fact that the meeting was held during the time of local elections, the measure might have a chilling effect on the group's future activities and was, therefore, out of proportion.[67]

Accordingly, in *Steel* v *United Kingdom*,[68] where two applicants were arrested for handing out leaflets outside a conference, the European Court held that as the police had no grounds for believing that their conduct would cause a breach of the peace such action was unlawful and disproportionate and in breach of the applicants' Convention rights. Where on the other hand the Court is satisfied that some breach of the peace was threatened, then it is likely to afford a good deal of discretion to the national authorities.[69]

Questions

How is freedom of assembly both protected and restricted under Article 11 of the European Convention?

What is the European Court's approach to restrictions on the right to peaceful assembly compared with other forms of expression?

Legal restrictions in domestic law on the right of assembly[70]

As with many other fundamental rights, the right of peaceful assembly has traditionally been regarded in domestic law as a residual right; everyone had the right to exercise the right

---

[66] (2007) 45 EHRR 13.

[67] See also *Christian Democratic People's Party* v *Moldova (No 2)*, decision of the European Court, 2 February 2010, where a refusal by the authorities for permission to hold a demonstration was held to be disproportionate as there was no evidence that the group would incite aggression; the previous peaceful protests by the group being evidence of its peaceful intentions.

[68] (1999) 28 EHRR 603.

[69] Thus, in *Steel* the Court held that the arrests of demonstrators who had disrupted a grouse shoot and had stood in front of a mechanical digger were justifiable under Articles 5 and 10 of the Convention.

[70] For general reading in this area see Mead, *The New Law of Peaceful Protest: Rights and Regulation in the Human Rights Act Era* (Hart 2010); Feldman, *Human Rights and Civil Liberties in England and Wales* (OUP 2002, 2nd edn), chapter 18; Bailey and Taylor, *Bailey, Harris and Jones, Cases and Materials on Civil Liberties* (Butterworths 2009, 6th edn), chapter 5.

provided there was no breach of the law. For example, in *Hubbard v Pitt*,[71] Lord Denning, speaking of the general right of assembly and the right of Englishmen to assemble together for the purpose of deliberating upon public grievances, stated that such was not prohibited as long as it was done peaceably and in good order and without threats or incitement to violence or obstruction to traffic.[72] In that case the defendants, a community action group, had taken part in a peaceful picket outside the offices of an estate agents owned by the plaintiff, protesting about the plaintiff's building policies and distributing leaflets and displaying placards during the protest. The plaintiff obtained a temporary injunction against the defendants on the basis that they had committed a public nuisance, and on appeal the Court of Appeal allowed a continuation of the injunction on the basis that it was arguable that the defendants had committed a private nuisance. Although the dictum of Lord Denning had little effect on the outcome of the case, and was principally ignored by the majority of the judiciary thereafter, it could be said to impact on some subsequent cases that reflected a more liberal approach.[73] Lord Denning's statement merely gives the right of assembly unless the law is broken, without imposing any restrictions on the legality or fairness of those legal restrictions. The statement does, however, make a declaration about the importance of peaceful assembly[74] and is of particular importance in the Human Rights Act era where the courts are under a duty to ensure that the law is not applied so as to impose unnecessary restrictions on this fundamental right.

Apart from the effect of the Human Rights Act 1998, in rare instances domestic law bestows a positive right to demonstrate. Thus, s.1 of the Public Meetings Act 1908 makes it unlawful to act in a disorderly manner at a public meeting for the purpose of preventing the transaction of the meeting's business, or to incite another person so to act.[75] This provision, however, is more likely be used against principally peaceful demonstrators who are carrying out a counter protest. Consequently, in the absence of a general statutory power to demonstrate, the right of peaceful assembly depended on the goodwill of the judiciary when enforcing the variety of legal provisions that impact on the right to demonstrate. An example of the acceptance of a constitutional right of assembly and association within the general common law can be seen in the case of *Verall v Great Yarmouth Borough Council*.[76] The plaintiffs, members of the National Front Party, had entered into a contract with the local authority to

---

[71] [1976] QB 142.

[72] Ibid., page 176.

[73] See, for example, *Hirst and Agu v Chief Constable of West Yorkshire* (1986) 85 Cr App R 143; *Jones and Lloyd v DPP* [1999] 2 All ER 257, considered below.

[74] Contrast, for example, the case of *Chandler v DPP* [1964] AC 763, where the House of Lords refused to take into account the fact that the defendants were taking part in the fundamental right to protest when entering upon military land in breach of the Official Secrets Act 1911.

[75] See s.43 Education Act 1986, which imposes duties on colleges and universities to ensure free speech for members, students, employees and visiting speakers and that the use of the premises is not denied on grounds of the beliefs and policies of particular persons. Again, although the section gives the right of free speech and assembly, the provision is more likely to be used to resist counter-demonstrations. See also s.95 and s.96 of the Representation of the People Act 2000, giving the right to hire a suitable room for the purpose of holding public meetings in furtherance of a person's candidature. This right must be afforded irrespective of the political nature of the part, see *Webster v Southwark LBC* [1983] QB 698, where the court upheld the right of a National Front candidate to make use of the provision.

[76] *The Times*, 22 November 1980.

use their premises to make an election address.[77] When the local authority changed power the newly elected council refused to allow the plaintiffs to use the hall, and the plaintiffs sued for breach of contract. The defendant council admitted liability but claimed that the remedy of specific performance should be denied to the plaintiffs because of the nature of the organisation. The Court of Appeal held that the plaintiffs should not be denied the remedy of specific performance. Stressing that freedom of expression applies to views of which many people would wholeheartedly disapprove the Court held that the conference should go ahead in the interests of speech and assembly.

Traditionally, English law has taken a very conservative approach to the control of demonstrations that threaten public order, and parliament has bestowed wide powers on the police and other authorities to ensure that demonstrations do not threaten such interests. Equally the courts have given the authorities a very wide margin of error in enforcing such legal powers, leaving the freedom to demonstrate largely unprotected. However, with the introduction of the Human Rights Act 1998, and a more enlightened approach of the judiciary, this traditional approach is being reconsidered and the right to demonstrate is beginning to attain some recognition.

The power to control processions and assemblies under the Public Order Act 1986

In addition to the powers granted to the police to enforce various public order offences committed during demonstrations, domestic law makes provision for controlling marches and other demonstrations both before they take place and during the demonstration itself.[78] This includes the right to impose conditions on such activities and, in exceptional cases, to prohibit them. These powers exist independently of other legal powers, but are useful to the authorities in ensuring that public disorder is averted and can be used either individually or in conjunction with their other statutory and common law powers in order to justify their actions. Because the powers exist primarily for the convenience of the authorities, and have a wide potential to interfere with or reduce the efficacy of demonstrations, it is essential that the courts strictly control their application.

Processions

Sections 11–13 of the Public Order Act 1986 curb the right to demonstrate in an attempt to preserve public order and the peace of the community against the threats posed by public processions.[79] These powers range from the requirement to give notice of such marches, to

---

[77] Under s.96 of the Representation of the Peoples Act 1983 there was a right to be provided with a suitable room for the purpose of holding meetings in furtherance of a person's candidature. This provision was applied in *Webster* v *Southwark London Borough Council* [1983] QB 698 to allow a National Front candidate to use a room for the purpose of an address in a parliamentary by-election.

[78] See Bonner and Stone, The Public Order Act 1986: Steps in the Wrong Direction? [1987] PL 202.

[79] A public procession is defined in s.16 of the Act as a procession in a public place, and a public place means any highway and any place to which at the material time the public or any section of the public has access, on payment or otherwise, as of right or by virtue of any express or implied permission. Procession is not defined in the Act but a procession was defined by Lord Goddard in *Flockhart* v *Robinson* [1950] 2 KB 498, page 502, as a body of persons moving along a route.

the power of the police to impose conditions on the organisation of the march. In exceptional circumstances a power is given to ban processions in advance.

The requirement to give notice

Section 11 of the Public Order Act 1986 imposes a duty on the organiser of a procession to give advance notice to the police in the relevant area six clear days before the date when it is intended to be held, unless it was not reasonably practicable to give any advanced notice.[80] If it is not reasonably practicable to give six days' notice then notice must be delivered as soon as is reasonably practicable. The requirement applies only to processions, and only to those processions held to demonstrate support or opposition to the views or actions of any person or body of persons, to publicise a cause or campaign, or to commemorate an event.[81]

Section 11(2) exempts processions commonly or customarily held in the police area in which the procession is proposed to be held, as well as funeral processions organised by funeral directors in the normal course of business. In *R (Kay) v Commissioner for Metropolitan Police Force*,[82] the House of Lords held that a cycle rally (Critical Mass) held to promote the interests of cyclists and to protest against motorists' abuse of cyclists was 'customarily held' within s.11 so as to exempt it from the notice provisions. The group started from the same point at the same time each month, and the fact that the route was irregular making it difficult for the police to anticipate the extent of any regulation required did not mean that it fell outside the exemption. In that case, it was also held (*obiter*) that for the section to be invoked the procession must involve some advanced planning and organisation. Section 11(1) applied to any proposal to hold a public procession and no offence (under s.11(7), below) could be committed if there were no organisers of that procession and if the procession was impromptu and lacked a specific route.

Assuming the section does apply, any notice must specify the date, time and proposed route and give the name and address of the person (or one of the persons) proposing to organise it.[83] The advantage of such a power as far as the police are concerned is that it allows the police to take advance action in readiness for the march, and the police will usually use this right in conjunction with its power to impose conditions under s.12 of the Act. Thus, under this provision the police can impose criminal liability for failure to comply with the notice requirement without having to prove an actual breach of the law during the procession, as the organiser will be guilty of an offence if the notice requirement has not been complied with or if the march deviates from the date, time and route specified.[84] The organiser does, however, have a defence if he or she did not know of, or had no reason to suspect, the failure to satisfy the requirements or of the change of date, time or route.[85] The organiser also has a defence where any deviation of time, place or route arose out of circumstances beyond his or her control or from something done with the agreement or direction of a police officer.[86] It must be noted, however, that compliance with these requirements does not

---

[80] Section 11(1) Public Order Act 1986.
[81] Section 11(1)(a) and (b).
[82] [2008] 1 WLR 2723.
[83] Section 11(3).
[84] Section 11(7).
[85] Section 11(8).
[86] Section 11(9).

provide any legal immunity for any subsequent disorder and does not preclude the police from using their general legal powers if disorder arises.

The power to impose conditions on processions

Section 12 provides the police with a convenient method of preventing disorder or disruption that they apprehend from the organisation of a particular procession by giving the police the statutory power to impose conditions on processions covered by the Act. Again, this power is in addition to any other power to preserve the peace or to ensure that obstructions do not take place, and a person would not be immune from an action in obstruction merely because they complied with the directions.

The section provides that where a senior police officer,[87] having regard to the time, place and circumstances in which the procession is to be held, or is intended to be held, reasonably believes that serious public disorder, serious damage to property or serious disruption to the life of the community may be caused by the procession, or where he reasonably believes that the purpose of the assembly is the intimidation of others,[88] he may give directions imposing on the persons organising or taking part in the procession such conditions which appear to him necessary in order to prevent such disorder, damage, disruption or intimidation.[89] This includes the power to impose conditions as to the route of the procession and to prohibit it from entering any public place specified in those directions. Unlike s.11 of the Act, s.12 imposes criminal liability on both the organiser and anyone taking part in a procession if they knowingly fail to comply with any condition, although there is a defence available to both if the failure arises from circumstances beyond the organiser's or other person's control.[90] It is also an offence for a person to incite a participant in the procession to commit an offence under the section,[91] and a police officer may arrest without warrant either an organiser or a participant if he reasonably suspects that person is committing an offence under the section.

The section allows conditions to be imposed on processions, including the possibility of the route being redirected, which might well have the effect of substantially reducing the impact of a procession. This is particularly controversial when the police are acting to avoid 'serious disruption to the life of the community', which might relate to interests as trivial as the convenience of shoppers, and unless the courts are prepared to control the discretion of the police in this area there is a danger that some conditions might impose a disproportionate interference with the right of peaceful assembly.

The power to ban processions

Section 13 of the Act gives a limited power to ban processions in advance. It states that if the Chief Constable of the district reasonably believes that because of the particular circumstances

---

[87] This means the chief officer of police where the conditions are being imposed before the event takes place, but in the case where the procession is already under way, or where the procession is assembling, it means the most senior officer at the scene: s.12(2). Directions from the chief of police must be given in writing: s.12(3).

[88] This intimidation must be with a view of compelling persons not to do an act they have the right to do, or to do an act they have the right not to do: s.12(1)(b). Thus, there must be a fear of coercion as well as intimidation. The fear of intimidation is more likely to be apprehended in the case of static assemblies such as industrial or commercial picketing.

[89] Section 12(1).

[90] Sections 12(4) and 12(5).

[91] Section 12(6).

existing in any district or part of a district that the powers under s.12 of the Act will not be sufficient to prevent the holding of public processions in that district from resulting in serious public disorder, he shall apply to the council of the district for an order prohibiting for such period not exceeding three months the holding of all public processions (or any class of public procession so specified) in the district.[92] Once such an order has been made it is then an offence to organise a procession, or to take part in a procession knowing that the march is prohibited under the section.

This power is exercised via the local authority, which, being aware of the local circumstances and the likely effect of such processions, are deemed to be the most appropriate body to decide on these matters. In any case, any order has to be approved by the Home Secretary, which suggests that such orders would only be made in exceptional cases. In addition, the powers under s.13 are subject to a number of conditions that should restrict the scope and regularity of the section's use. Most notably, the power is only available when the Chief Constable reasonably believes that the powers available to him under s.12 are inadequate to prevent the serious public disorder that is anticipated. Thus the Chief Constable has to consider the power to impose conditions on the procession under s.12, and, presumably, any other power to control public disorder, before having recourse to this exceptional power. Again, it is clear that the section can only be used when *serious public disorder* is anticipated, the other conditions being inadequate to trigger the power to apply for a ban. Nevertheless, the section permits a wide prior restraint on processions and the right to demonstrate and thus should be applied carefully and in accordance with the principles of freedom of assembly and free speech enshrined in the European Convention.

Although the provision has a potentially wide impact on the right to demonstrate, the courts, both domestic and European, have shown a marked reluctance to interfere with the exercise of these powers. For example, in *Kent v Metropolitan Police Commissioner*,[93] the Court of Appeal indicated that authorities would be given a wide discretion in this area provided there was some evidence to support their conclusions. The Commissioner had issued a ban on all processions for a period of 28 days, except those traditionally held on May Day and those of a religious character that were customarily held. The ban had been imposed in the wake of the Brixton disorders, at which there had been significant outbreaks of violence and covered an area of 786 square miles. The applicant, a leading member of the Campaign for Nuclear Disarmament, applied for a judicial review of the ban when it interfered with the group's plan to hold a procession during the period covered by the prohibition. The applicant claimed that the ban was unlawful in that it did not refer to a class of processions as required by the section. He also claimed that the extent of the prohibition, including its geographical boundary, was irrational and that the Commissioner had failed to direct himself properly as to the relevant matters. It was held that as the ban exempted May Day processions and certain religious processions, it did apply to a class of procession as required by the section. Also, the Commissioner was entitled to conclude that there was a risk that either the participants on

---

[92] Section 13(1). A safeguard against discrimination against a particular group or procession is provided via the requirement that the application for the prohibition must be in relation to the holding of all public processions, or of a particular class. Thus, the police cannot apply the power against a specific march, but must include all processions covered within the terms of the order. This is to stop the possible victimisation of particular political or other groups.

[93] *The Times*, 15 May 1981. The Commissioner had exercised his power under the Public Order Act 1936, the predecessor of s.13 of the 1986 Act.

the march or the police would be attacked by hooligans. The Court thus refused to interfere with his discretion, particularly as the Commissioner had received the approval of the Home Secretary, as required under the section. This approach suggests that the measures taken to deal with such problems will be left principally to the police and the Home Secretary. Although in the post-Human Rights Act era the courts will be under a duty to take into consideration the effect of such an order on the rights of free speech and peaceful assembly, a change of judicial attitude in this area is far from certain.

This reluctance is also evident in the case law under the European Convention. In *Christians Against Racism and Fascism v United Kingdom*[94] it was alleged that the imposition of a s.13 ban was in violation of Article 11. The domestic authorities had used their powers under the Public Order Act to ban processions in a particular area in order to stop one proposed National Front meeting, although its effect was to stop all public processions other than those of a religious character customarily held during that period. The applicants complained that as their procession was not likely to give rise to any disorder, the effect of the prohibition was disproportionate and thus in violation of Article 11. The European Commission of Human Rights declared the application inadmissible. It held that although a general ban on demonstrations could only be justified if there was a real danger of this resulting in disorder that could not be prevented by other less stringent means, nevertheless on the facts the police had adequate evidence to apply for this ban.

Public assemblies

Section 14 of the Public Order Act 1986 allows the police to impose conditions on static public assemblies. A public assembly was originally defined by s.16 of the 1986 Act as an assembly of 20 or more persons in a public place that is wholly or partly open to the air but that number was subsequently reduced to two or more persons.[95] The powers are similar to those that exist in relation to the imposition of conditions on processions, contained in s.12 of the Act, and apply in relation to the same circumstances. Thus, under s.14 a senior police officer, having regard to the time or place at which and the circumstances in which any public assembly is being held or is intended to be held, who reasonably believes that it may result in (a) serious public disorder, serious damage to property or serious disruption to the life of the community, or (b) where the purpose of the persons organising it is the intimidation of others, may give directions to the organisers or those taking part such conditions as appear to him necessary to prevent such disorder, damage, disruption or intimidation.[96] In *R (Brehony) v Chief Constable of Greater Manchester Police*,[97] it was held that where the conditions are imposed at the scene of the demonstration there was no duty to give reasons, but that when the conditions are imposed in advance the police should identify which head of s.14 ((a) or (b) above) they were acting under, and that if they apprehend serious public disorder, serious damage to property or serious disruption to community life, which and how many of those headings was being relied on. However, it also held that reasons do not have to be

---

[94] (1980) 21 DR 138.
[95] Section 16 Public Order Act 1986, as amended by s.57 of the Anti-Social Behaviour Act 2003. A public place is defined in s.16 as any highway and any place to which at the material time the public or any section of the public has access, on payment or otherwise, as of right or by virtue of express or implied permission.
[96] Section 14(1).
[97] *The Times*, 15 April 2005.

detailed provided they are sufficient to enable the demonstrators to understand why the decision was being made and whether it was reasonable or not. Further, in *Austin* v *Commissioner of the Police for the Metropolis*[98] it was held that it was not necessary that the police had s.14 in mind when giving such directions, provided they had a reasonable belief that the conditions in s.14 were evident on the facts. In *Brehony* the applicants had held a demonstration outside a supermarket in Manchester city centre over a period of time and had recently attracted a counter-demonstration. The Chief Constable wrote to them saying that in order to prevent public disorder or serious disruption to the life of the community over the Christmas period the demonstrations would be limited to an alternative location and must be of a limited duration. In the present case the High Court felt that sufficient reasons had been given and that the decision was reasonable, as there was a sufficient prospect of serious disruption to the life of the community of a large city on busy Saturdays leading up to the Christmas period.[99]

The conditions may relate to its maximum duration, or the maximum number of persons who may constitute it.[100] In addition, in *Austin* v *Commissioner of Police of the Metropolis*, above, it was held that the power to impose conditions could include a power to bring the procession to an end and that an instruction under s.14 of the same Act could include a direction that some or all of the assembly disperse by a specified route or that they stay in a particular place. As with s.12 of the Act, the police officer who gives the directions needs to be the chief of police where the assembly is intended to be held, and can be the most senior officer present where the assembly is being held.[101] A person who organises a public assembly and who knowingly fails to comply with a condition imposed under the section is guilty of an offence under the section, although it is a defence to such a charge that the failure arose from circumstances beyond his or her control.[102] Also, a person who takes part in a public assembly and knowingly fails to comply with such conditions is guilty of an offence.[103] A police officer can then arrest without warrant any person he reasonably suspects is committing any of the offences under the section.[104]

Again, the provision allows the police a convenient method of anticipating and avoiding public disorder, as can be seen in *Broadwith* v *DPP*.[105] The police had imposed conditions under s.14 by specifying that the assembly should be held in one location, with the demonstrators proceeding to another location at which another assembly could take place no earlier than 13.30. B arrived at the other location at 13.00 and was stopped from entering the road. When he refused to comply with the order he was arrested and charged with obstruction of a police officer in that he had refused to obey the instruction under s.14. B argued that the directions did not apply to him as he was on his own and that he had not been to the first assembly. The magistrates rejected this, and B appealed. It was held on appeal that the

---

[98] [2008] 2 WLR 415 (Court of Appeal). The appeal in the House of Lords was dismissed on other grounds. See below.

[99] See Hosseinbor, *The Right to Public Protest: Brehony* (2005) NLJ 833.

[100] The police also have the power to restrict numbers of demonstrators under their common law powers to preserve the peace. See, for example, *Piddington* v *Bates* [1961] 1 WLR 162, considered below.

[101] Section 14(2). If the directions come from the chief of police they must be in writing: s.14(3).

[102] Section 14(4).

[103] Section 14(5). An identical defence to that contained in s.12(4) is available to the defendant. Under s.14(6) it is an offence to incite a person to commit an offence under s.14(5).

[104] Section 14(7).

[105] [2000] Crim LR 924.

interpretation put on the directions by the magistrates was justified. The notice had made it clear that an assembly at the second location would not be permitted until 13.30 and B was clearly a demonstrator arriving on a bus with other demonstrators with his face covered. Although s.14 then applied to groups in excess of 20, those groups necessarily comprised individuals, against whom action might be taken to ensure that the assembly proceeded along permitted lines. B had arrived with the intention of demonstrating with the group and had deliberately tried to enter the second location. Accordingly, he had obstructed a police officer in the execution of his duty when the officer had attempted to carry out the provisions of the notice.

This decision shows that an officer can execute the conditions without any question as to their necessity at the time, and unless the imposition of the original conditions is subject to judicial control, the right to demonstrate can be interfered with on little or no substantive grounds.[106] The powers under s.14 of the 1986 Act are, of course, additional to the common law powers of the police to preserve the peace. Thus a police officer could use his or her powers to prevent a breach of the peace by issuing instructions to the demonstrators, either to supplement the content of the orders under s.14 or in a situation where such conditions have not been imposed under the section.[107]

Trespassory assemblies

Prior to 1994, although the police had a power under s.12 of the Public Order Act 1986 to impose conditions on static assemblies, and to use their general legal powers to preserve the peace to stop an assembly from taking place, there was no formal power to prohibit assemblies in advance. Sections 70 and 71 of the Criminal Justice and Public Order Act 1994 partially rectified this situation by expanding s.14 of the Public Order Act 1986, giving the police power to control trespassory assemblies.

Section 14A of the 1986 Act allows the relevant chief police officer[108] to apply to the local council for an order prohibiting for a specified period the holding of all trespassory public assemblies in the area.[109] Such an order may be applied for if the chief police officer reasonably believes that an assembly is intended to be held in any district at a place on land to which the public has no right of access or only a limited right of access, and that the assembly is either likely to be held without the permission of the landowner or to conduct itself in a way which would exceed that permission or the limit of the public's right of access. In addition to the requirement of trespass, the officer must also reasonably believe that the assembly might result in serious disruption to the life of the community, or, where the land, or a building or monument on it, is of historical, architectural, archaeological or scientific importance, in significant damage to the land, building or monument. Once an order is made it will operate to prohibit any assembly which is held on land to which the public has no, or a limited, right of access, and which takes place without the permission of the occupier or in excess of

---

[106] In *DPP* v *Jones* [2002] EWHC 110 (Admin), unreported, decision of the Divisional Court, 22 January 2002, it was held that *ultra vires* conditions imposed on a public assembly could be severed from valid conditions, thus allowing the remaining valid conditions to be used as the basis of a prosecution for failing to abide by such conditions.

[107] See, for example, the cases of *Piddington* v *Bates* [1961] 1 WLR 162, and *Moss* v *Mclachlan* [1985] IRLR 76, considered below.

[108] The power of the Commissioner for Police for the City of London and the Commissioner of Police of the Metropolis is executed directly through the Secretary of State: s.14A(4).

[109] Section 14A(1). An assembly is defined in s.14A(9) as an assembly of 20 or more persons. By s.14A(2) the granting of such an order by the council requires the consent of the Home Secretary.

any permission or the limits of the public's right of access.[110] The reference to limited right of access is clarified in the section, and limited in this sense is stated to mean that their use of it is restricted to use for a particular purpose (as in the case of a highway or road) or is subject to other restrictions.[111] Under the Act the order is restricted to a period of no more than four days and to a circle of no more than a radius of five miles from the specified centre.[112]

Further, s.14B creates specific offences in connection with such trespassory assemblies. Under this provision a person who organises an assembly knowing that it is prohibited by an order under s.14A is guilty of an offence.[113] So too, a person who takes part in such an assembly knowing that it is so prohibited commits an offence.[114] A constable in uniform may arrest without a warrant anyone whom he reasonably suspects to be committing an offence under the section.[115] Section 14C of the Act also gives the police the power to stop persons from proceeding to a trespassory assembly. Under this provision, if a constable in uniform reasonably believes that a person is on his way to an assembly within the area to which an order applies, which the constable reasonably believes is likely to be an assembly that is prohibited by that order, the constable may stop that person and direct any person not to proceed in the direction of the assembly. The power can only be exercised within the area to which the order applies, and a person who refuses to comply with such a direction which he knows has been given to him is guilty of an offence and a constable in uniform may arrest without warrant anyone he reasonably suspects to be committing an offence under the section.[116] The police already have a common law power to preserve the peace, and this has been used in the past to stop protestors from reaching particular destinations.[117] This provision gives the police a more formal power that can be used in the context of trespassory assemblies, and the courts should ensure that the power is not used to prohibit persons from going to a particular area so as to exercise their right of peaceful demonstration.[118]

The decision in *DPP* v *Jones and Lloyd*

The scope of these new powers and the extent to which it precluded the right of peaceful demonstration was considered in *DPP* v *Jones and Lloyd*.[119] The police had obtained an order under s.14A prohibiting the holding of trespassory assemblies within a four-mile radius of Stonehenge. A group of more than 20 people who had assembled on a grass verge on the roadside along the perimeter fence were asked to move by the police. When they refused they were arrested for committing a trespassory assembly. At their trial the defendants argued that as they had acted peaceably and there had been no obstruction, no offence had been

---

[110] Section 14A(5).

[111] Section 14A(9). This meaning of this was fundamental to the question of whether a demonstration is *prima facie* lawful, or whether a highway is restricted to the use of passage or repassage. See *DPP* v *Jones and Lloyd* [1999] 2 All ER 257, discussed below.

[112] Section 14A(6).

[113] Section 14B(1).

[114] Section 14B(2). Under s.14B(3) it is an offence to incite another person to commit an offence under subsection (2).

[115] Section 14B(4).

[116] Section 14C(4).

[117] See *Moss* v *McLachlan*, considered below.

[118] Thus, it is important that the decision in *DPP* v *Jones and Lloyd*, considered below, is not rendered redundant by police exercising their powers under s.14C to stop potentially lawful demonstrators from entering the relevant area and carrying out their right to take part in a peaceful and non-obstructive demonstration.

[119] [1999] 2 All ER 257.

committed. The defendants were charged and convicted but on appeal to the Crown Court it was found that there was no case to answer because in the court's opinion the holding of a peaceful, non-obstructive assembly was part of the public's limited right of access to the highway and thus not prohibited by the order. On appeal the Divisional Court had to decide whether an entirely peaceful assembly of more than 20 people was, *per se*, unlawful under s.14 simply because a banning order had been made, or whether the provision had retained the 'right' to assemble on the highway for the purpose of peaceful demonstration.

The Divisional Court[120] held that when an order under s.14A was in force, any meeting of 20 or more persons on the highway exceeded the public's right of access to the highway and constituted an offence even though the meeting was peaceful and did not obstruct the highway. The prosecution merely had to show that the assembly consisted of 20 or more persons and that the person charged had taken part knowing that the assembly was prohibited. It was not necessary that each of the 20 or more people present had exceeded the public's right of access. In any case, the 'right of access' in s.14A(9) referred to a right given by law. The holding of a meeting, demonstration or vigil, however peaceable, was nothing to do with the right of passage; such activities may be tolerated, but there is no legal right to pursue them.[121]

However, on appeal to the House of Lords it was held, by a majority of 3–2, that the public could have a right to use the highway for the purpose of conducting a peaceful assembly, provided that was a reasonable and usual activity and consistent with the primary right to use the highway for passage and repassage. Whether the use was so consistent with that primary right was a question of fact and degree for the court to determine on the particular facts. In the present case, the majority of their Lordships were satisfied that the Crown Court was entitled to find that the defendants' activities were peaceful and non-obstructive and therefore the appeals were allowed.[122] The central issue was whether the defendants had exceeded the limits of the public's right of access, and, thus, what those limits were. Disagreeing with the Divisional Court, Lord Irvine stated that s.14A did not in itself limit those rights and did not automatically prohibit the holding of any assembly that restricted the limited right of access to the highway by the public. The fundamental question was whether the public's right of access is limited to the right to pass or repass, including the right to carry out incidental activities related to that right, and thus eliminating the right to hold an assembly on the highway. After considering the relevant authorities,[123] his Lordship concluded that the public highway was a public place, which the public may enjoy for any reasonable purpose provided the activity in question does not amount to a public or private nuisance and does not obstruct the highway by unreasonably impeding the primary right of the public to pass and repass. To hold otherwise would, in his Lordship's opinion, mean that ordinary and useful activities such as making a sketch, handing out leaflets and collecting money for charity would not qualify as being incidental to the right of passage and would thus place an unrealistic and unwarranted restriction on commonplace day-to-day activities.

---

[120] [1997] 2 All ER 119.

[121] In the court's opinion, the fact that in previous cases the courts had found that a peaceful demonstration on the highway had not amounted to an obstruction, was not the same as holding that the demonstrator had a legal right to attend for those purposes. See, for example, *Hirst and Agu v Chief Constable of Yorkshire* (1986) 85 Cr App R 143. For a criticism of this decision see Fitzpatrick and Taylor, Trespassers Might be Prosecuted [1998] EHRLR 292; Fitzpatrick and Taylor, A Case of Highway Robbery? (1997) NLJ 338.

[122] For an account of the case and its effect on the right of peaceful assembly, see Clayton, Reclaiming Public Ground: The Right to Peaceful Assembly (2000) 63 MLR 252.

[123] *Harrison v Duke of Rutland* [1893] 1 QB 142; *Hickman v Maisey* [1900] 1 QB 752.

The majority decision appears to have been affected by human rights issues and, in particular, by reference to the European Convention on Human Rights. Thus, with regard to Article 11 of the Convention, Lord Irvine held that even if the common law of trespass was not as clear as he had stated, the Convention should be used to clarify its uncertain state. Article 11 guaranteed the right to peaceful assembly subject to necessary restrictions, and if the Divisional Court was correct in holding that an assembly on the highway was always trespassory, then there would not even be a *prima facie* right of assembly on the highway. In his Lordship's view, our law will not comply with the Convention unless its starting point is that assembly on the highway will not necessarily be unlawful. The decision establishes that a peaceful assembly for a reasonable period that did not unreasonably obstruct the highway was not necessarily unlawful. The decision of the House of Lords does not, however, establish that everyone has the right to demonstrate on the highway in all circumstances, nor that any right to demonstrate on the highway enjoys a higher status than any other activity simply because the person is exercising his or her right of assembly or free speech.[124] Nevertheless, the decision is arguably more generous to the right of assembly than the relevant case law of the European Convention.[125]

Questions

What restrictions do sections 12–14 of the Public Order Act 1986 (as amended) impose on the right to demonstrate? Are those restrictions compatible with Article 11 of the European Convention?

How important is the majority decision of the House of Lords in *DPP v Lloyd and Jones*?

Public order offences

In addition to the powers to control processions and assemblies in advance, there are a variety of common law and statutory offences that can be used to impose criminal liability on demonstrators. In most circumstances many of the offences are not of relevance to the rights under Articles 10 and 11 of the Convention, because the activities it regulated could not in any sense be associated with *peaceful* assembly or demonstration. However, some of the other, lesser, offences are of direct relevance to the right to demonstrate and go to the heart of the question whether the law gives sufficient weight to the right of free speech and the right to demonstrate, or whether it gives undue preference to the aim of preserving the peace and the right of others to be free from distress and shock.

Public order offences under the Public Order Act 1986

Riot, violent disorder and affray

Section 1 of the 1986 Act puts the offence of riot into statutory form. The offence is committed when 12 or more persons who are present together use or threaten unlawful violence[126] for a

---

[124] See Fenwick, *Civil Rights: New Labour, Freedom and the Human Rights Act* (Longman 2001), pages 151–2.

[125] See *Pendragon v United Kingdom* [1999] EHRLR 223.

[126] Violence is defined in s.8 of the Act as any violent conduct, including (apart from the offence of affray under s.3 of the Act) violent conduct towards property as well as towards persons. Violence is not restricted to conduct causing or intended to cause injury or damage, but includes any other violence (for example, throwing at or towards a person a missile of any kind capable of causing injury which does not hit or falls short).

common purpose, where the conduct of those persons (taken together) would cause a person of reasonable firmness present at the scene to fear for his personal safety.[127] In such a case any person using unlawful violence for the common purpose is guilty of the offence of riot. It is not necessary that the 12 or more use or threaten unlawful violence simultaneously[128] and that common purpose can be inferred from conduct.[129] For a person to be guilty of an offence under this section it is not necessary to prove that he or she intended that a person would fear for their personal safety, provided he or she intended to use violence or was aware that his or her conduct might be violent.[130] As with the offences of violent disorder and affray, no person of reasonable firmness need actually be, or be likely to be, present at the scene.[131] The offence can be committed in private as well as in public places[132] and a person guilty of riot is liable on conviction on indictment to a maximum of ten years' imprisonment and/or a fine.[133]

There is no doubt that the offence can be committed during political or other legitimate protest and many charges have been brought against those taking part in industrial picketing. Although the offence requires the use of violence, the fact that a common intention can be inferred from conduct, that no specific *mens rea* is required, and that no person of reasonable firmness need be present at the scene, means a person might face the severe penalties under this section in connection with relatively innocuous behaviour. However, the requirement that the DPP consents to proceedings offers some protection against the over-zealous use of police powers, and it is to be hoped that the provision is unlikely to be used unnecessarily against legitimate protestors.

Section 2 of the Act provides for the offence of violent disorder. This is committed when three or more persons who are present together use or threaten unlawful violence and their conduct (taken together) is such as would cause a person of reasonable firmness present at the scene to fear for his personal safety. In such a case each of the persons using or (unlike the offence of riot) threatening unlawful violence is guilty of the offence of violent disorder.[134] The offence does not require a common purpose and, as with the offence of riot, it is irrelevant that the three or more use or threaten violence simultaneously,[135] no person of reasonable firmness need be, or be likely to be, present at the scene[136] and the offence may be committed in a public or a private place.[137] Prosecutions do not require the consent of the DPP and the offence is triable either way, with a maximum penalty on indictment of five years' imprisonment.[138] As with the offence of riot, there is a danger that a person could be

---

[127] Section 1(1) Public Order Act 1986. Thus, although it is sufficient that the 12 or more people either use or threaten violence so as to constitute the prerequisite of the offence, for a person to be guilty of the offence, he or she must actually use violence.

[128] Section 1(2).

[129] Section 1(3).

[130] Section 6(1). The intention of the others need not be proven, only the person charged with the offence: s.6(7).

[131] Section 1(4).

[132] Section 1(5).

[133] Section 1(6). Under s.7(1) of the Act every prosecution for the offence must be brought with the consent of the Director of Public Prosecutions.

[134] Section 2(1). See *R v Hebron* [1989] Crim LR 839, where the defendant was convicted when he waved his fists and shouted 'Kill the bill', while others threw missiles at the police.

[135] Section 2(2).

[136] Section 2(3).

[137] Section 2(4).

[138] Section 2(5).

charged with an offence under s.2 for a relatively minor act of actual or threatened violence. This might be considered to be a threat to lawful protest if this act was to take place during a political or other protest, and the person charged did not associate himself with the acts or threats of violence of others.

Whereas the offences of riot and violent disorder contemplate the use or threat of collective, though not necessarily common, violence, s.3 of the 1986 Act covers the offence of affray, which can be committed by an individual.[139] Under s.3 of the Act a person is guilty of affray if he uses or threatens unlawful violence towards another person[140] and his conduct is such as would cause a person of reasonable firmness present at the scene to fear for his personal safety. Although no person of reasonable firmness need be present,[141] a person is only guilty of an affray if he uses or threatens violence towards another person. This requirement was confirmed by the House of Lords in *I v DPP*,[142] where the defendants' convictions for affray were quashed when it was established that although they had been carrying petrol bombs in public, they had not used them to threaten any person. The required *mens rea* is that the person intends or threatens to use violence or is aware that his conduct may be violent or threaten violence.[143] As with the offences of riot and violent disorder, the offence of affray can be committed in either a public or a private place.[144] A constable may arrest without warrant anyone he reasonably suspects is committing affray,[145] and a person accused of affray is triable either way, with a maximum penalty on indictment of three years' imprisonment, on conviction.[146]

Some protection of free speech and protest is given by the proviso that a threat of violence cannot be made by the use of words alone.[147] Thus, a person who merely uses threatening words against another is not guilty of an offence under s.3 of the Act, precluding an action under that section where, for example, during the course of a political or other protest, a person shouts threats at the police or at others such as a rival political group.[148] As with riot and disorder, the offence of affray may well be committed by a demonstrator in the context of an initially peaceful demonstration and might catch what might be regarded as reasonably incidental acts of protest. However, as the use or threat of unlawful violence is required for these offences, it is unlikely that the courts will be receptive to arguments that the provisions interfere unduly with the right of peaceful protest. Equally it is likely that the European Court of Human Rights would give a wide margin of appreciation to domestic authorities in penalising such acts.

---

[139] However, under s.3(2) of the Act where two or more persons use or threaten unlawful violence, it is the conduct of them taken together that must be considered for the purpose of establishing the offence.

[140] Unlike the offences of riot and violent disorder, threats of violence must be directed towards another person and not property: s.8.

[141] Section 2(4).

[142] [2001] 2 WLR 765.

[143] Section 6(2).

[144] Section 3(5). See *R v Davidson* [1992] Crim LR 31.

[145] Section 3(6). The offences of riot and disorder, above, because of the penalties, are arrestable offences and thus do not require a specific power of arrest.

[146] Section 3(7).

[147] Section 3(3). However, in *I v DPP* [2001] 2 WLR 765, it was held by the House of Lords that a person can threaten violence under this section by the mere act of carrying offensive or dangerous weapons. In that case it was held that a group seen carrying petrol bombs could be properly convicted of affray, even in the absence of any threat to use them. The convictions were quashed on other grounds, see above.

[148] In such circumstances, however, the person may be liable under s.4 or s.5 of the Act (see below).

Lesser public order offences

Sections 4 and 5 of the Public Order Act have a much greater relevance to the enjoyment of peaceful assembly. These provisions attach liability, for threatening behaviour and disorderly conduct, to conduct that might be considered as part and parcel of many heated, yet basically peaceful, demonstrations. In such cases the law has to distinguish between behaviour that is merely incidental to peaceful protest and which causes certain people an inevitable amount of distress and inconvenience, and behaviour that is unreasonable and which causes either a foreseeable fear of provocation of violence or unnecessary distress to others.

▉ Section 4 – Fear of provocation of violence

This offence involves the use towards another of threatening, abusive or insulting words or behaviour (or the distribution to another of any writing, sign or other visible representation which is threatening, abusive or insulting) with intent to cause that person to believe that immediate unlawful violence will be used against him or another by any person, or to provoke the immediate use of unlawful violence by that person or another, or whereby that person is likely to believe that such violence will be used or it is likely that such violence will be provoked.

For an offence to be committed under this provision the person must firstly employ threatening, abusive or insulting words or behaviour. As freedom of speech should include the right, within reasonable boundaries, to shock and offend, in defining the words used in the section, particularly 'insulting', the courts need to distinguish between words or actions which might be regarded as shocking and unpopular, and those which can truly be considered as insulting to a particular person or their beliefs. In *Brutus v Cozens*[149] it was held that the word 'insulting' should be given its normal, everyday meaning. This would appear to outlaw words or behaviour that are capable of producing very little harm to what might be considered a very low-level interest. However, the decision appears to accept that the law should be tolerant of words or actions that are capable of causing such a low level of harm. In that case a number of anti-apartheid demonstrators had disrupted proceedings at Wimbledon by sitting on the court, blowing whistles and distributing leaflets to the crowd. This had incited others to come onto the court holding banners and placards. The demonstrators were arrested under s.5 of the Public Order Act 1936. At first instance it was held that the defendants' conduct did not constitute insulting behaviour, but the Divisional Court held that the court of first instance was not entitled to come to that conclusion. In the Divisional Court's opinion insulting behaviour was such that affronted other people and evinced a disrespect or contempt for their rights and which reasonable persons would foresee as likely to cause resentment or disrespect. On appeal it was held by the House of Lords that the Divisional Court had erred in attempting to give the words a specific meaning and that the court of first instance was entitled to conclude that the defendant's actions were not insulting. Lord Reid stated that the meaning of the word 'insulting' was not a matter of pure law; the word 'insulting' means 'insulting', and nothing more, and an ordinary sensible person recognises an insult when he sees or hears it. Significantly it was held that words or actions were not insulting simply because they might cause resentment or affront. In his Lordship's view, it would be going too far to prohibit all speech and conduct likely to occasion a breach of the

[149] [1972] 2 All ER 1297.

peace because determined opponents might shrink from organising or at least threatening a breach of the peace in order to silence a speaker whose views they detest. Vigorous and distasteful or unmannerly speech or conduct is permitted provided it does not go beyond any of the three limits. Affront is too vague.[150]

Assuming that the words or behaviour employed by the defendants were threatening, abusive or insulting, it then has to be shown that the defendant either intended a particular consequence, or that such a consequence was likely. In *Jordan v Burgoyne*[151] it was held that the speaker should take his audience as he finds them and thus he or she will be responsible if those words to that group of people are likely to cause a breach of the peace, or other unlawful reaction. The defendant was addressing a crowd containing left-wing groups and Jewish organisations during which he expressed support for Hitler and condemned 'world Jewry'. The speech was met with a violent reaction from the crowd and the defendant was arrested and charged under s.5 of the Public Order Act 1936 of using threatening, abusive and insulting words likely to cause a breach of the peace. It was held that once he had used words that were threatening, abusive or insulting then the defendant had to take his audience as he found them.

Although this case was decided under a different provision, the principle would be likely to be applied in relation to s.4 and s.5 of the 1986 Act, although under s.6(3) of the 1986 Act a person is only guilty of an offence under s.4 if he intends the words or behaviour to be threatening, abusive or insulting, or is aware that it is so. Thus if, as in *Jordan*, the speaker is aware of the likely (insulting) nature of the words or behaviour to that group, and of their likely reaction, then liability will ensue. If, on the other hand, the speaker was not aware of the presence of those people, then it could be argued that he was not aware of the potentially insulting, etc. nature of his words or actions, or of the likely consequences of such. This might still leave the speaker liable in cases where he is aware of the presence of particularly sensitive persons in the audience and in such cases the courts should ensure that their oversensitive and unreasonable reactions do not result in liability being imposed on otherwise peaceful demonstrators. Although this provision insists that the defendant employs particular words or behaviour *and* causes a particular result, it is likely that if such words or actions are employed then a court will conclude that any ensuing fear or provocation of violence was the consequence of such words or actions.

The use of public order offences against the written word was given some protection in the case of *R v Horseferry Road Justices, ex parte Siadatan.*[152] In this case the courts insisted that for an offence to be committed under s.4 of the 1986 Act the words or behaviour must be intended or likely to provoke or to cause fear of *immediate* unlawful violence. The applicant had sought judicial review against the decision of the magistrates to dismiss an action under s.4 of the Act against the publishers of *The Satanic Verses*, which it was claimed contained abusive and insulting writing and was thus likely to provoke violence by Muslims because of its allegedly blasphemous content. It was held that 'violence' under the section meant immediate and unlawful violence, and that although the violence did not have to be instantaneous, there had to be sufficient proximity in time and place. Such a principle would not apply,

---

[150] These sentiments are echoed by SEDLEY LJ in *DPP* v *Redmond-Bate*, considered below, and are also relevant in determining whether a person has committed a breach of the peace at common law, or whether a police officer can reasonably apprehend a breach of the peace from a demonstrator's words or actions.

[151] [1963] 2 All ER 225.

[152] [1990] Crim LR 598.

however, to the situation where threatening, abusive or insulting words or images were distributed directly to an audience, and freedom of speech in such cases might well be compromised by the need to avoid a violent reaction to such representations.

Section 5 – Alarm and distress

Section 5 of the Public Order Act 1986 provides that an offence is committed where a person uses threatening, abusive or insulting words or disorderly behaviour (or displays any writing, sign, or visible representation which is threatening, abusive or insulting) within the hearing or sight of a person likely to be caused harassment, alarm or distress. Whereas s.4 is concerned with regulating conduct that threatens or incites violence, s.5 of the Act is concerned with the control of words or behaviour that causes the lesser harm of harassment, alarm or distress. As with s.4, the section covers the use of threatening, abusive or insulting words or behaviour, but also applies to what is referred to as 'disorderly behaviour'. The offence is only committed where the defendant was aware that others might be caused harassment, etc., although it is not necessary that such a consequence flows from such conduct, it being sufficient that a person present was *likely* to be caused such harassment, etc. Under the section, a person who engages in such conduct, or who displays any writing, sign or other visible threatening, abusive or insulting representation within the hearing or sight of a person likely to be caused harassment, alarm or distress, will engage the relevant police powers under the section. In such a case a police officer who reasonably suspects that a person has engaged in conduct in breach of s.5 may arrest that person without warrant if, after warning that person to stop such conduct, he or she engages in further such conduct immediately or shortly after the warning.

This provision provides the police with a very useful tool in controlling actions that are a fairly low-level threat either to public order and/or the rights and comfort of others. In the context of a demonstration, therefore, it could be used to order demonstrators to desist in certain conduct that is causing little more than annoyance to others. It is important, therefore, that the provision is construed strictly and is thus not used arbitrarily against the right of peaceful protest.[153] One safeguard in this respect is that as with s.4 of the Act the defendant must use words or behaviour that are either threatening, abusive or insulting, or which otherwise constitute disorderly behaviour. Thus, the result must be achieved by employing this unlawful conduct. A further safeguard is provided by s.6(4) of the 1986 Act, which states that a person is only guilty of an offence under s.5 if he intends, or is aware, that the words or behaviour (or his disorderly conduct) were, or were likely to be, threatening, abusive or insulting. For example, in *DPP v Clarke*[154] it was held that for an offence to be committed under s.5 it is not sufficient that the accused knew that the other person would be caused harassment, alarm or distress, it must also be shown that he intended his conduct to be threatening, abusive or insulting, or was aware that it might be. Anti-abortion protestors had displayed pictures of an aborted foetus outside an abortion clinic and had been charged with an offence under s.5. The magistrates found that although the displays were abusive and insulting, applying a subjective test the protestors did not intend them to be so and neither were they aware that they were so. An appeal against the court's finding in this respect was

---

[153] The Joint Committee on Human Rights, in its seventh report, Demonstrating Respect for Rights? A Human Rights Approach to Policing Protests, recommended the revision of s.5 of the Public Order Act 1986 so that the term 'insulting' be deleted.

[154] [1992] Crim LR 60.

dismissed, the Divisional Court finding that the court had acted properly on the evidence presented to it.

Therefore, although the actual offence under s.5 can be committed without a specific *mens rea* in the sense that the defendant does not have to intend the necessary consequences, the section does provide that the defendant must know, or appreciate, that the words or conduct are threatening, abusive or insulting. However, such an intention might be readily implied and the decision in *Clarke* can be contrasted with the case of *DPP v Fiddler*,[155] which arose from the same facts. In this case it was held that an offence had been committed under s.5 when an anti-abortion protester shouted and talked to people attending an abortion clinic and displayed plastic models and photographs of human foetuses. Here the court was prepared to find such an intention from the fact that the defendant was anti-abortion and a member of the group organising the protest. The decision in *Clarke*, therefore, might be regarded as exceptional, although after the Human Rights Act it is hoped that the courts adopt a similar approach in an attempt to protect demonstrators who employ provocative, yet reasonable, tactics.

In addition, s.4A of the 1986 Act adds the offence of threatening behaviour to the list of public order offences, making it unlawful to cause *intentional* harassment, alarm or distress. Under this provision it is an offence to use threatening, abusive or insulting words or behaviour, or disorderly behaviour, or to display any writing, sign or other visible representation which is threatening abusive or insulting, *with an intent* to cause a person harassment, alarm or distress, and thereby causing him or another person such. The defendant must *intend*, not just (as in s.5 of the Act) be aware of, such consequences, and, unlike the offence under s.5 of the Act, that consequence must occur. On the other hand, s.4A provides for greater sanctions and thus presents a potentially disproportionate interference with the right of protest.[156]

The offences under s.4A and s.5 of the Act provide a defence if the accused can prove that his conduct was reasonable.[157] The term is not defined in the Act, but is clear that conduct will not be regarded as reasonable simply because the defendants were seeking to exercise their right of free speech and assembly on matters of public concern. For example, in *DPP v Clarke*[158] the conduct of the demonstrators in displaying pictures of aborted foetuses was found not to be reasonable under the Act. Presumably the court in this case felt that it was unreasonable to impose such images on unwilling persons, and that such an act is not excusable simply because the defendants were attempting to impose their lawful views on others. It is likely, therefore, that the courts will continue to take a cautious approach and to reject the defence once it has found that the conduct was otherwise unlawful under the relevant sections. Any other approach would be a brave attempt by the courts to protect free speech from the sections' ambit and might be thought to undermine the intention of parliament in passing such provisions.

Nevertheless, a liberal approach was evident in *DPP v Percy*,[159] which involved the application of s.5 to a case of political protest. The defendants had taken part in a protest outside a US army base during which they had desecrated an American flag. They had been arrested and charged with a breach of s.5 of the Act and had appealed against their convictions on the

---

[155] [1992] 1 WLR 91.
[156] Both sections 4 and 4A attract a term of imprisonment not exceeding six months or a fine not exceeding level 5 on the standard scale, or both, while s.5 attracts a fine not exceeding level 3 on the standard scale.
[157] Section 5(3)(c) and s.4A(3)(b).
[158] [1992] Crim LR 60.
[159] *The Times*, 21 January 2002.

grounds that such proceedings were a disproportionate interference with their right of freedom of expression under Article 10 of the European Convention. Noting that s.5 required both proof of *mens rea*, and that s.6 of the Act provided a defence of reasonableness, it held that behaviour which was an affront to other people was not outlawed by the provision and that peaceful protest will only constitute an offence where the conduct goes beyond legitimate protest and moves into the realms of threatening, abusive or insulting behaviour which is calculated to insult (either intentionally or recklessly) and which is unreasonable. Although the court agreed with the judge at first instance when he had found that there was a pressing social need in a multicultural society to prevent the denigration of objects of veneration and symbolic importance for one cultural group, it felt that the use of the criminal law to control such behaviour constituted a disproportionate interference with freedom of expression. The district judge had placed too much emphasis on the appellant's insulting behaviour, in particular that her insulting behaviour could have been avoided, and insufficient weight on the presumption of freedom of expression. The decision confirms that free speech should not be restricted or penalised simply because it causes offence to others, but it might be regarded as generous given that the court accepted that the restriction had a legitimate aim.

A more conservative approach was adopted by the domestic courts in *Hammond v DPP*.[160] H, an Evangelical preacher, held up a large double-sided sign which, *inter alia*, bore the words 'Stop Homosexuality' and 'Stop Lesbianism' on each side while addressing a crowd in a town centre. A crowd gathered around him and began arguing and shouting and when the police officers arrived the crowd became outraged that H had not been arrested and eventually he was arrested for breach of the peace. Subsequently he was charged and convicted under s.5 of the 1986 Act.[161] On appeal against conviction the High Court accepted that the sign was not threatening or abusive, but considered whether it was insulting, considering its duty under s.3 of the Human Rights Act 1998 to interpret legislation compatibly with Articles 9 and 10 the European Convention on Human Rights. The court noted that the question was whether, first, the words on the sign went beyond legitimate expression and were something more than mere affront or disrespectful; and, secondly, whether the justices had erred in deciding that the defendant's conduct was not reasonable within s.5(3)(c). In the present case the restriction on the defendant's Convention rights were clearly prescribed by law and imposed for a legitimate aim – of preventing disorder. Further, the court found that although the right to freedom of expression included the right to shock and offend, and the defendant was preaching his sincerely and deeply held beliefs, it was open to the justices to find that the words on the sign were insulting and that the defendant's conduct was not reasonable. The words on the sign linked homosexuality to immorality and were directed specifically towards the homosexual and lesbian community.

The decision in *Hammond* may be justified by applying the principle that a speaker must take his audience as he or she finds them, applied in *Jordan v Burgoyne*, above. That principle is sound provided that the audience is not intolerant and unreasonable, for the danger in such cases is that the peaceful protestor may be held responsible for the consequences of their

---

[160] *The Times*, 28 January 2004. See Geddis, Free Speech Martyrs or Unreasonable Threats to Social Peace? – 'Insulting' Expression and Section 5 of the Public Order Act 1986 [2004] PL 853.

[161] Mr Hammond, in fact, died before the appeal, but the court felt that it was legitimate to proceed with the appeal. A subsequent application to the European Court was declared inadmissible on the grounds that his relatives were not victims: *Fairfield v United Kingdom* (Application No 24790/04), decision of the European Court, 8 March 2005.

peaceful protest when it excites a violent response, or undue distress, from those who are simply not tolerant of the protestor's views. Further, the decision may be defended on the basis that the protestor's views are indeed intolerant of other's rights and their lifestyles and as such are destructive of the rights of others. However, in any case the law should distinguish between views that are inconsistent with others' rights and which are aired peaceably, and those manifested in a blatantly offensive way: thus recognising the distinction between saying, for example, that homosexuality is immoral (however uninformed and idiotic), and saying that all homosexuals are perverts (an uninformed, idiotic and grossly insulting view).

The Crime and Disorder Act 1998

Section 1 of the Crime and Disorder Act 1998 provides for the granting of an antisocial behaviour order where a person has acted in a manner that caused or was likely to cause harassment, alarm or distress to one or more persons, and where such an order is necessary to protect persons in a specific local government area from further antisocial acts by that person. The provision is certainly not aimed at political protest, but could be used in cases where protestors have directed their actions against a particular person or group of persons and have caused, or are likely to cause, harassment, alarm or distress as a consequence. Such conduct is more likely to fall within other provisions, such as the Protection from Harassment Act 1997 and the Criminal Justice and Police Act 2001, which are considered below, and a defence of reasonableness is provided in s.1(5) of the Act, which provides that when a court is considering such an application it should disregard any act of the defendant which the defendant shows is reasonable.

That the provision can apply to political protest is amply illustrated in the Court of Appeal decision in *R (Singh) v Chief Constable of West Midlands*.[162] Singh and others had been taking part in a demonstration outside a theatre which had been showing a play entitled *Behtzi*, which the demonstrators felt was religiously offensive. When it was thought that the demonstrators had become unruly, the police issued a dispersal order under s.30 of Act, and when the protestors refused to comply with it they were arrested and cautioned. The area surrounding the theatre had been designated a relevant area under the Act because of the increasing acts of antisocial conduct taking place in the run-in towards Christmas and the demonstrators argued that the 2003 Act was never intended to apply to restrict the fundamental right to peaceful assembly; and specifically that the powers of the police under the orders should not apply to them as the orders had been issued to deal with a different category of conduct. It was held, first, that there was no reason why an authorisation in respect of one group of people (drunken revellers) could not be used in regard to unforeseen groups (the demonstrators). Further, it was abundantly clear that parliament had intended that provision to apply to protests; parliament had not expressly excluded protest groups and had parliament intended to limit the use of dispersal powers to antisocial behaviour of the kind specified in the original authorisation it would have done so expressly. The Court of Appeal also found that the provisions of the Act and their application in this case were compatible with the appellants' Convention rights to freedom of religion and free speech. The dispersal orders were prescribed by law and served the legitimate aims of preventing crime and disorder and protecting the rights of others (both of the theatre and theatre goers to go about their lawful

---

[162] [2006] 1 WLR 3374.

business). Further, the use of those powers had been necessary in a democratic society in that they achieved a balance between the rights of the protestors and the right to be protected from distressing conduct.

The decision in *Singh* illustrates the danger of applying law, passed for the purpose of regulating the carrying out of non-fundamental rights (such as getting drunk in a public place) to activities which fall squarely into the category of human rights (protesting on a matter of human rights and public interest). Although the Court of Appeal ultimately decides the legality of the measure by applying principles of legality and proportionality, it only does this once it accepts that the right to take part in political demonstrations is, in effect, no different from getting drunk in public. On that basis it is suggested that the decision is flawed and that the 2003 Act should not be applied to genuine political protests.

Questions

How do the above public order offences maintain a balance between preserving the right to demonstrate and protecting public order and safety?

Is the domestic courts' approach in this area consistent with free speech and the right to demonstrate?

Public order offences and racial and religious aggravation and incitement

In certain cases the law will make specific allowance for words or conduct that cause racial or religious hatred or offence, either by creating an identifiable offence or by increasing the sanctions for committing existing offences. The reason for such lawmaking may be to protect certain persons from discrimination, although such measures may also protect a person's right to freedom of thought, conscience and religion under Article 9 of the European Convention on Human Rights. For this reason the provisions will be examined in chapter 12 with respect to protection against racial or religious attacks. We will also examine them at this point because although there may be laudable reasons for criminalising, or further criminalising, certain behaviour, such laws raise a number of issues regarding freedom of speech and assembly.

Racial hatred and aggravation

Inciting racial hatred

The offence of inciting racial hatred is covered by Part III of the Public Order Act 1986.[163] In particular, sections 18–23 of the Act create a number of offences relating to the incitement of racial hatred. Section 17 defines racial hatred as hatred against a group of persons defined by reference to colour, race, nationality (including citizenship) or ethnic or national origins.[164] The offences exist for a number of reasons, including the protection of the (religious) rights

---

[163] This part of the Act not only creates a number of racial hatred offences, but also provides powers of entry, search and forfeiture.

[164] Under the 1986 Act 'persons' were those in Great Britain. Reference to Great Britain has now been omitted: s.38 Anti-Terrorism, Crime and Security Act 2001.

of others, the prohibition of discrimination, and the preservation of public order. They can be committed in a variety of media, and are by no means always related to the proper exercise of freedom of expression or freedom of assembly and association.[165] The offences do, however, have a particular effect on the right of association and on the manner in which certain groups manifest or disseminate their views.

Section 18 of the Act makes it an offence for a person to use threatening, abusive and insulting words or behaviour, or to display any such written material, where either that person intends thereby to stir up racial hatred, or, having regard to all the circumstances, such hatred is likely to be stirred up. The offence can be committed in a public or private place, unless the words or behaviour, etc. are used by a person in a dwelling and are not heard or seen by anyone other than persons inside the dwelling.[166] It is important to note that although the conduct causing the racial hatred can be merely insulting, the basis of the offence is not mere insult, requiring real or likely racial hatred to ensue. In this sense, therefore, the section requires evidence of, or at least potential for, real harm as opposed to mere shock and offence. On the other hand, the offence does not require a specific intent, and for that reason should be interpreted and applied carefully in relation to constitutional speech and protest. In addition, as with s.4 and s.5 of the Act, and where a person is not found to have intended to stir up racial hatred, it is a defence that he or she did not intend his words or behaviour, or the written material, to be, and was not aware that it might be, threatening, abusive or insulting.[167] Some protection is also granted by s.7 of the Act, which provides that no proceedings may be brought under this, and the other related provisions of the Act, except by or with the consent of the Attorney-General.[168]

In addition to s.18, which principally covers words or behaviour or the display of written material during demonstrations, the Act also makes it an offence, under s.19, to publish or distribute threatening, abusive or insulting written material which is intended or likely to stir up racial hatred. With regard to this offence, it is a defence for a person who has not been shown to have intended to stir up racial hatred to prove that he was not aware of the content of the material and did not suspect, or have reason to suspect, that it was threatening, abusive or insulting.[169] The Act also includes the offence of distributing, showing or playing a recording,[170] and under s.22 certain persons can be guilty of an offence if a programme involving threatening, abusive or insulting visual images or sounds is included in a programme service,[171] and that person either intends to stir up racial hatred, or it is likely that such hatred will be stirred up. Any action taken against broadcasters under this provision would need to be consistent with Article 10 of the Convention, and in particular the duty of the media to present information and ideas to the public.[172]

---

[165] In particular, the offence of racist chanting under s.3 of the Football (Offences) Act 1991 has little impact on freedom of expression as that right is defined under various bills of rights or international treaties.

[166] Under s.18(4), it is a defence if the accused was inside a dwelling and had no reason to believe that the words or behaviour, etc. would be heard or seen by a person outside that or any other dwelling.

[167] Section 18(5) Public Order Act 1986.

[168] Abu Hamza, the Imam of Finsbury Park Mosque, was convicted under s.18 with respect to addresses he made at the Mosque between 1997 and 2000.

[169] Section 19(2) Public Order Act 1986.

[170] Section 21 Public Order Act 1986.

[171] Those persons include any person providing, producing or directing the programme, and any person by whom offending words or behaviour are used.

[172] See, for example, *Jersild v Denmark* (1994) 19 EHRR 1.

Section 23 of the Act also makes it an offence to be in possession of racially inflammatory material. Under that section, a person who is in possession of written material which would form the basis of an offence in the above sections, with a view to such material being displayed, published, distributed, broadcast or included in a cable programme service whether by himself or another, will be guilty of an offence if either he intends to stir up racial hatred or such hatred is likely to be stirred up. Where it is not shown that the person intended to stir up racial hatred, it is a defence to prove that he was not aware of the content of the material or recording, and did not suspect, or had no reason to suspect, that it was threatening, abusive or insulting.

Provided these and other provisions are not allowed to interfere with words and actions which represent genuine and informed expression, then they seem to be pursuant to a legitimate aim and proportionate to the protection of the rights of others and of public order. In that respect they are potentially consistent with Articles 9, 10 and 11 of the European Convention. In addition, in the case of extreme groups and words or behaviour, Article 17 of the Convention, which precludes persons from relying on Convention rights when their actions are aimed at the destruction of the rights of others,[173] can be employed to justify any alleged violations of Convention rights.

Racially aggravated offences

In addition to the specific offences contained in Part III of the 1986 Act, the Crime and Disorder Act 1998 provides for increased penalties for certain offences, including s.4 and s.5 of the Public Order Act 1986, discussed above, where the offences are racially or religiously aggravated.[174] An offence is racially aggravated when at the time of committing the offence, or immediately before or after doing so, the offender demonstrates towards the victim of the offence hostility based on the victim's membership (or presumed membership) of a racial group, or where the offence is motivated (wholly or partly) by hostility towards members of a racial group based on their membership of that group.[175]

The meaning of racial group and racially aggravated insulting and abusive words was considered recently by the House of Lords in R v Rogers.[176] In that case the defendant had been found guilty of using racially aggravated abusive or insulting words when during an altercation with three Spanish women he referred to them as 'bloody foreigners' and told them to go back to their own country. The House of Lords held that membership of a racial group went beyond groups defined by their colour, race or ethnic origin and included nationality (including citizenship) and national origins. Further, the fact that the offender's hostility was based on other factors in addition to racism or xenophobia was irrelevant; the offences attacked the mischiefs of racism and xenophobia and the essence was the denial of equal respect and dignity to people who were seen as 'other', which was more deeply hurtful and damaging to the victims than the simple versions of the offence, and more damaging to the community as a whole.[177]

---

[173] This provision is considered in chapter 2, pages 77–8.

[174] Sections 28–32 Crime and Disorder Act 1998.

[175] Section 28 Crime and Disorder Act 1998. Racially (and now religiously) aggravated offences are triable either way, with a maximum penalty on indictment of two years' imprisonment.

[176] [2007] 2 WLR 280.

[177] See also DPP v Humphrey [2005] EWHC 822 (Admin), where it was held that the phrase 'you're fucking Islam', directed at an Asian policeman, were undeniably abusive, if not insulting. However, the words would need to be interpreted in the context in which they were used. See Shapiro, Free Speech, Hate Speech and Incitement (2006) NLJ 238.

Although this provision seeks to achieve a legitimate aim – the protection of the rights of others – and there may be an argument that racially motivated hate speech does not attract the protection of Article 10, there is a danger that the provision may be used to quash and penalise unpopular or politically incorrect speech. Thus, in the post-Act era the courts must be careful to not include speech or conduct which is merely politically unpopular or offensive speech. This dilemma was evident in the case of *Norwood* v *DPP*,[178] where both the domestic and European Courts upheld the conviction of the defendant for displaying a poster in the first-floor window of his flat which proclaimed 'Islam out of Britain' and 'Protect the British People'. The poster had been on display for some two months but was then seen by a passer-by who reported it to the police. The appellant was convicted under s.5 of the Public Order Act 1986, the District Judge finding that the poster was both abusive and insulting to Islam and its followers and was racially aggravated as it was motivated by hostility towards members of a religious group based on their membership of that group. In dismissing the appeal, the High Court stated that the act of displaying the poster clearly met the requirement of s.5: the appellant had displayed the poster intending it to be, or being at least aware that it might be insulting; and the words of the poster alone, and even more so when considered alongside the symbols of the twin towers and the crescent and star surrounded by the prohibition sign, were clearly racially directed and racially insulting. The poster was a public expression of attack on all Muslims in the UK, urging that all followers of the Islamic religion here should be removed from it and warning that their presence here was a threat to the British people. It could not, on any reasonable basis be dismissed as merely an intemperate criticism against the tenets of the Muslim religion, as distinct from an unpleasant and insulting attack on its followers. In addition, the display as a matter of plain common sense was capable of causing harassment, alarm or distress to those passing by who might see it. That would be the reaction of any right-thinking member of society concerned with the preservation of peace and the avoidance of religious and racial tension, as well as to any follower of the Muslim religion.

With respect to whether the conduct was in all the circumstances reasonable within Article 5(3), the court stated that where the prosecution has proved that an accused's conduct was insulting and that he intends it to be, or was aware that it might be so, it will in most cases follow that his conduct was objectively unreasonable, especially where, in the aggravated form, the prosecution has proved that the conduct was motivated by hostility towards a religious group. In this case the judge was entitled to reject the defence of reasonableness and there were also considerations under Article 9 (protection of freedom of religion) and Article 17 (the destruction of others' Convention rights) weighing against any defence in the present case.

The defendant then brought a case under the European Convention on Human Rights arguing that his conviction violated his right to freedom of expression under Article 10 and was discriminatory under Article 14. Relying principally on Article 17 of the Convention, the Court declared the case inadmissible. In the Court's view, the general purpose of that article is to prevent individuals or groups with totalitarian aims from exploiting in their own interests the principles enunciated in the Convention. Turning to the facts, the words and images on the poster amounted to a public expression of attack on all Muslims in the United Kingdom. In the Court's view, such a general and vehement attack against a religious group, linking the group as a whole with grave acts of terrorism, was incompatible with the values

[178] [2003] Crim LR 88; *Norwood* v *United Kingdom* (2005) 40 EHRR 11. The poster had been supplied by, and bore the initials of the British National Party, of which the appellant was a member and regional organiser.

of the Convention, notably tolerance, social peace and non-discrimination. Consequently, the poster fell outside the protection of Articles 10 and 11 of the Convention.

The decision in *Norwood* is in many respects inevitable given the specific desire of parliament to protect racial groups from verbal and other abuse. More generally, however, it is questionable that this type of speech and conduct should be denied the basic principles of free speech and proportionality simply because they are racially motivated. In particular, it is doubtful whether the defence of reasonableness under s.5(3) of the Act should in all but hardly imaginable cases be denied to the defendant. However outraged many of us may feel about right-wing, racially intolerant groups, a democratic society should be strong enough to tolerate such views in the absence of strong evidence of social or individual harm.

Religious hatred and aggravation

Inciting religious hatred, and religiously aggravated offences

The Anti-Terrorism, Crime and Security Act 2001 extended the principle of aggravated offences where the commission of the offence was activated on grounds of religious hatred. Consequently, s.28 of the Crime and Disorder Act 1998 was amended so as to extend to include the victim's membership of a religious group, and the definition of religious group is a group of persons defined by religious belief or lack of religious belief.[179] Although a person may have been liable under the laws of blasphemous libel for attacking religious views and principles, that law was restricted to the Christian faith and did not extend to other religions,[180] and did not protect the religious observer from all insult or attack.[181]

An offence of inciting religious hatred was included in clause 38 of the Anti-Terrorism, Crime and Security Bill 2001, but was dropped after objections, primarily in the House of Lords, that it would impose an undue restriction on freedom of expression.[182] Nevertheless, the Racial and Religious Hatred Act 2006 now contains an offence of incitement to religious hatred.[183]

Section 1 of the 2006 Act amends the Public Order Act 1986 to create an offence of stirring up hatred against persons on religious grounds by inserting a new Part 3A to the 1986 Act entitled 'Hatred Against Persons on Religious Grounds'. Religious hatred is defined as hatred against a group of persons defined by reference to religious (or lack of religious) belief[184] and s.29B now provides that it is an offence for any person who uses *threatening* words or behaviour, or displays any written material which is such, if *he intends* thereby to stir up religious hatred. The offence is therefore narrower than that of inciting racial hatred as the words or behaviour must be threatening (and not simply abusive or insulting) and the defendant has to intend the consequences (rather than them being simply likely). The offence can be committed in a public or private place unless the words or material were used or displayed inside a dwelling and are not heard or seen outside that or another dwelling.[185] The section does not

---

[179] Section 28(4) Anti-Terrorism, Crime and Security Act 2001.

[180] See *R v Chief Metropolitan Magistrates' Court, ex parte Choudhury* [1991] 1 QB 429.

[181] *R v Lemon* [1979] QB 10. The repealed law of blasphemy is discussed in chapter 8 of this book.

[182] See Fenwick, The Anti-Terrorism, Crime and Security Act 2001: A Proportionate Response to 11 September? (2002) 65 MLR 724, at page 730. See also Idriss, Religion and the Anti-Terrorism, Crime and Security Act 2001 [2002] Crim LR 890.

[183] See Addison, *Religious Discrimination and Hatred Law* (Routledge-Cavendish 2006).

[184] Section 29A Public Order Act 1986.

[185] Section 29B(2); it is also a defence if the accused can prove he was inside a dwelling and had no reason to believe he would be heard, or that the material would be seen, by a person outside that or another dwelling.

apply to words, behaviour or written material used or displayed solely for the purpose of being included in a programme service.[186]

Section 29 also covers a variety of other acts where the accused intends to stir up religious hatred and thus creates offences with respect to the publishing or distribution of written material,[187] the presentation or direction of a public performance of a play,[188] the distribution, showing or playing of a recording of visual images or sounds,[189] and the inclusion of visual images or sounds in a programme service (via providing, producing and directing such visual images or sounds, or by the use of such words and behaviour by any person during such a service).[190] The Act also now contains the offence of possessing inflammatory material.[191] Under this provision it is an offence for any person to have in his possession written material or a recording of visual images or sounds which is threatening and which (in the case of written material) he intends to be displayed, published, distributed or included in a programme service by himself or another, or (in the case of a recording) he intends to be distributed, shown, played or included in such a programme by himself or another.[192]

To meet concerns that the offence would impinge unduly on freedom of expression and freedom of the press the Act includes both a general free speech defence and immunity with respect to certain media reporting.[193] First, the Act states that nothing in these provisions should prohibit or restrict discussion, criticism or expressions of antipathy, dislike, ridicule, insult or abuse of particular religions or the beliefs or practices of their adherents, or proselytising or urging adherents of a different religion or belief system to cease practising their religion or belief system.[194] This will protect shocking or offensive views directed at religions and their followers, although such speech may be caught by other provisions of the Public Order Act 1986, or other public order offences studied in this chapter. The provision also recognises the right to try to persuade followers of a particular religion to abandon that religion in favour of another.[195] More specifically, the provision exempts fair and accurate reports of proceedings in parliament, or in the Scottish parliament, and of proceedings publicly heard before a court or tribunal exercising judicial authority, provided the report is published contemporaneously with the proceedings, or where that is not lawful or practicable as soon as publication is so practicable and lawful.[196]

Question

Is there a need to further restrict free speech and peaceful assembly with respect to the creation of racially and religiously aggravated crimes, above?

---

[186] Section 29B(5).

[187] Section 29C.

[188] Section 29D.

[189] Section 29E.

[190] Section 29F.

[191] Section 29G.

[192] Sections 29H and 29I provide powers of entry and search, and forfeiture of such materials.

[193] For a critical analysis of these provisions, see Hare, Crosses, Crescents and Sacred Cows: Criminalising Incitement to Religious Hatred [2006] PL 521; Fenwick and Phillipson, *Media Freedom under the Human Rights Act* (OUP 2006), pages 516–27.

[194] Section 29J.

[195] See *Kokkinakis v Greece* (1994) 17 EHRR 397, discussed in chapter 12, pages 672–3.

[196] Section 29K.

The law of trespass, nuisance and obstruction of the highway

As many demonstrations take place on either private land, or public land to which the demonstrators have limited access, laws which seek to protect either the propriety interests of landowners or the public's right to access and use such land can pose a threat to peaceful assembly. As with other laws the law and the courts should seek to balance those property and other rights with the right of peaceful protest in a manner which is compatible with Article 11 and the Human Rights Act 1998.

A public nuisance is committed when something occurs which inflicts damage, injury or inconvenience on all members of a class who come within the sphere or neighbourhood of its operation.[197] In *R v Rimmington and Goldstein*,[198] the House of Lords held that the common law offence of public nuisance was sufficiently clear to satisfy the tests of foreseeability and clarity required by Articles 7, 8 and 10 of the European Convention. In that case the defendant had been charged with and convicted of a public nuisance when he had sent over 500 postal packages containing racially offensive material to several members of the public over a period of nine years. A second defendant had, shortly after 11 September, sent a package through the post containing salt, which was mistaken for anthrax. It was held that the defendants had been convicted by simply adapting the original definition of the offence to new and novel facts of the case and that the offence and the conviction was a necessary and proportionate response to protect the public.[199]

In addition, the law of private nuisance can be used to control public demonstrations, where the actions of the demonstrators unreasonably interfere with a person's use of their land. For example, in *Hubbard v Pitt*[200] a temporary injunction was granted when a number of demonstrators carried out a protest outside the plaintiff's estate agent's business as a protest against property developers. A majority of the Court of Appeal held that there was a *prima facie* case that the conduct amounted to a private nuisance and on that basis granted a temporary injunction preventing the defendants from taking part in similar activities.

It is clear that many demonstrations and protests are capable of infringing these laws, including full-blown marches on the highway and other forms of protest such as stopping passers-by to discuss or to protest on certain matters. More recently, in *Church of Jesus Christ v Price*[201] it was held that the defendant had committed a private nuisance when he had over a period of some years demonstrated outside the claimant's Mormon church. Although the defendant had not used profane or foul language, and had not used or incited violence, local residents and visitors to the Church had been disturbed, intimidated, alarmed and offended by his behaviour and his actions had thus constituted harassment.[202] The court held further that activities on a highway that were neither obstructive nor violent could nevertheless

---

[197] *Halsbury's Laws of England*, 4th edn, vol. 34, para 305.

[198] [2006] 1 AC 459.

[199] On the facts, the House of Lords held that neither of the appellants had committed the offence of public nuisance because there was no common injury to a section of the public, but rather to a number of specific individuals.

[200] [1976] QB 142.

[201] [2004] EWHC 324 (Ch).

[202] An injunction was also granted under the Protection from Harassment Act 1997.

constitute a nuisance and that the relevant laws were a legitimate and proportionate interference with free speech. In the Court's view speech that promoted a person's religious beliefs should not necessarily be protected absolutely under Article 9. The laws of trespass and nuisance were again used successfully in *Heathrow Airport* v *Garman*,[203] where an injunction was granted to prevent protestors from gathering at Heathrow airport to protest about the environmental hazards of air transport. In the court's view, although there was no evidence to grant an injunction under the Protection from Harassment Act 1997, the increased risks of terrorist attacks caused by the protestor's actions warranted the granting of the injunctions in trespass and nuisance, tipping the balance of convenience in favour of the airport.

A more liberal approach was evident in the Court of Appeal's decision in *Tabernacle* v *Secretary of State for Defence*,[204] where the courts had to consider the legality of a bye-law which prohibited camping in a specified area outside a nuclear weapons site. Overruling the High Court's decision that the bye-law was both sufficiently certain and proportionate, the Court of Appeal held that those bye-laws violated the protestors' rights under Articles 10 and 11 of the Convention. The Court held that often it was difficult to distinguish between interfering with the essence of a protest and controlling the manner and form of its exercise; and that in the present case the manner and form of the protest – held over 23 years at a regular time and place – was the protest itself. So too no weight should have been attached to the fact that one was only entitled to attend on that land in accordance with the Secretary's order; there was no proper analogy between government held land and land of a private landowner. In the Court's view the bye-law's interference with protest was far from insignificant and the Secretary had to provide substantive objective justification amounting to a pressing social need. However, the regulations were not passed in response to high-profile public concerns or threats of violent public disorder and the Secretary viewed the camp's presence as no more and no less than a nuisance. The decision in *Tabernacle* should be contrasted with the more recent decision in *Mayor of London* v *Hall and Others*,[205] concerning the removal of protestors from Parliament Square.[206]

Section 137 of the Highways Act 1980 provides that it is unlawful to obstruct a highway without lawful authority. Not surprisingly, the domestic courts have not construed the words 'without lawful authority' in s.137 of the Highways Act to allow *any* peaceful protest on the grounds that the exercise of fundamental freedoms would automatically give rise to lawful authority under the section. However, they have shown some tolerance towards protestors in this area and a number of decisions have provided some protection. For example, in *Hirst and Agu* v *Chief Constable of Yorkshire*[207] it was held that the courts needed to consider the reasonableness of the protestors' actions in determining whether there had been an obstruction of the highway by the defendants. A number of people were protesting against the fur trade outside a store in a shopping arcade and were arrested and convicted for obstruction of the highway. On appeal it was held that the conviction should be quashed. The court of first instance in determining whether the defendants were guilty of an obstruction had failed to consider whether their actions constituted a reasonable use of the highway. If they had done so, the balance between the right to protest and the need for peace and good order would

[203] Unreported, decision of the High Court, 6 August 2007.
[204] *The Times*, 25 February 2009.
[205] [2010] HRLR 29.
[206] This case is detailed on page 542 below.
[207] (1986) 85 Cr App R 143.

have been properly struck and the freedom of protest on matters of public concern would be given the recognition it deserved.

It has also been established that in an action in public nuisance it is necessary to show that the defendants have acted unreasonably. In *R v Clarke (No 2)*,[208] the defendant had led a crowd through various streets in London to demonstrate against the visit of the King and Queen of Greece. He was convicted of inciting persons to commit a public nuisance by obstructing the highway, but on appeal the conviction was quashed on the ground that the jury had not been directed on the question of whether, given that there was an obstruction, there had been an unreasonable use of the highway.[209] The cases of *Hirst* and *Clarke* are significant in two respects. First, the courts have established that as far as actions for obstruction and nuisance are concerned a public highway is not to be restricted to passing and repassing, making any other activity automatically unlawful. This was confirmed by the House of Lords in *DPP v Jones and Lloyd*,[210] and thus allows the courts to consider peaceful protest as a *prima facie* lawful activity, along with other uses of the highway. Secondly, there is some evidence from those cases that the courts regard peaceful protest not only as a perfectly reasonable and normal activity, but also, because of its nature, a fundamental right. Thus, unless there is strong evidence of obstruction or unreasonable behaviour a person would appear to have at least the basis of a right to use the highway for such a purpose, particularly in the post-Human Rights Act era. This would allow the courts to give freedom of assembly on the highway an enhanced, although not absolute, status, protecting it from unnecessary restriction. This was evident in the decision in *Westminster CC v Haw*,[211] where the court refused to grant an injunction prohibiting the defendant from carrying out a constant protest outside near the Houses of Parliament. In the court's view there had been no unreasonable interference with the public's right to pass and repass on the highway, and the injunctions would interfere with the defendant's right of freedom of expression.

However, the law of obstruction is capable of being implemented in a harsh fashion and of interfering unduly with freedom of speech and association. For example, in *Arrowsmith v Jenkins*[212] it was held that the offence might be committed without any specific intention to obstruct on behalf of the defendant. The defendant had been given permission by the police to address a crowd in a street in Bootle. When the crowd caused an obstruction of the road the police asked the defendant to stop the address and when she refused she was arrested and subsequently convicted for obstruction of the highway. It was held that the defendant had been correctly convicted and that it was no defence that she had not intended an obstruction to occur. The obstruction had occurred because of her presence and thus she had unlawfully obstructed the highway. It is possible that this decision needs to be reviewed in the light of the Human Rights Act 1998 and the decision in *DPP v Redmond-Bate*,[213] although the courts might feel that given the specific nature of the offence it might be legitimate to impose strict liability in such circumstances. Nevertheless, in *Church of Jesus Christ v Price*[214] the court

---

[208] [1964] 2 QB 315.
[209] Similarly, in *Newsgroup Newspapers Ltd v SOGAT* [1986] ICR 716, it was held that a public nuisance is not committed by someone who causes a minor disruption of the highway for a legitimate purpose.
[210] [1999] 2 All ER 257.
[211] [2002] EWHC 1885 (QB).
[212] [1963] 2 QB 561.
[213] [1999] Crim LR 998, discussed below.
[214] [2004] EWHC 324 (Ch).

confirmed that activities on a highway that were neither obstructive nor violent could nevertheless constitute a nuisance. In that case the conduct of the defendant – harassing religious followers outside a Mormon church – was clearly unreasonable and intimidatory, but the statement is a reminder that one does not have an absolute right to conduct a peaceful assembly and that such a right may have to give way to other interests.

The Serious Organised Crime and Police Act 2005

Section 132 of the Serious Organised Crime and Police Act 2005 makes it an offence for any person to organise or take part in a demonstration in a public place that has been made a designated area without authorisation. The Act was passed to regulate demonstrations in areas such as Parliament Square, such as the one-man protest conducted outside parliament by the anti-Iraq war protestor Brian Haw.

Brian Haw had been taking part in a 24-hour-a-day protest on a pavement in Parliament Square against the government's policies towards Iraq since June 2001, placing a considerable number of placards on the pavement in support of his demonstration. As we have seen, Westminster Council sought an injunction to restrain him from obstructing the pavement, relying on s.130(1) of the Highways Act 1980 and s.222 of the Local Government Act 1972, which provides that a local authority may prosecute or appear in legal proceedings where it considers it expedient for the promotion or protection of the inhabitants in their area. Mr Haw claimed that his demonstration did not amount to a breach of s.137 of the Act, but rather that it was a reasonable use of the highway and consistent with his rights of freedom of expression and freedom of assembly under Articles 10 and 11 of the European Convention on Human Rights. The High Court held that there was an obstruction which was wilful but stressed that the use to which the defendant was putting the highway must be an unreasonable one. Noting that the location of the defendant's activities were particularly suitable, given his attempt to persuade parliament in relation to its policy towards Iraq, and that there was no evidence of any actual obstruction of any pedestrian seeking to walk along the pavement or of any violence or disorder or breach of the peace arising out of the defendant's presence, the court concluded that the obstruction for which the defendant was responsible was not unreasonable and thus the injunction would not be granted.

In response, s.132 of the 2005 Act made it an offence for any person to organise or take part in a demonstration in a public place that is in a designated area,[215] unless authorisation has been given. The section also makes it an offence for a person to 'carry on a demonstration by himself' in such a place, clearly covering one-man demonstrations such as the one organised by Brian Haw.[216] Section 133 of the Act then provides that a person seeking authorisation for a demonstration in such an area must give written notice of that effect to the Commissioner of Police of the Metropolis, such notice normally to be given not less than six days before the start of the demonstration, and in any event not less than 24 hours before such date. That

---

[215] This is an area designated by the Secretary of State, but no point in the specified area may be more than one kilometre in a straight line from the point nearest to it in Parliament Square.

[216] The provision does not, however, apply to processions as covered by the Public Order Act 1986, or to conduct that is lawful by virtue of s.220 of the Trade Union and Labour Relations Act 1992 (for example, lawful picketing in contemplation or furtherance of a trade dispute). In addition, if the protest is covered by s.132 of this Act, s.14 of the Public Order Act 1986 (allowing the imposition of conditions on public assemblies) does not apply to such a protest.

notice has to state the date and time of the start of the demonstration, how long it is to last and whether it is to be carried on by a person by himself or not. Having received such notice the Commissioner must then give authorisation for the demonstration, although in giving such may impose on the organisers or participants such conditions relating to the demonstration as in his reasonable opinion are necessary for the purpose of preventing any of the following: hindrance to persons wishing to enter or leave the Palace of Westminster, hindrance to the proper operation of parliament, serious public disorder or damage to property, disruption to the life of the community, security risks in the area or risk to the safety of members of the public (including those taking part in the demonstration).[217] The conditions can impose restrictions on the place where the demonstration may, or may not, be, the times at which it may be carried on and the period during which it may be carried on, the number of persons taking part, the number and size of the banners or placards used and the maximum permissible noise levels.[218] In addition, s.137 of the Act provides that a loudspeaker shall not be operated, at any time or for any purpose, in a street in a designated area, it now being an offence to do so unless the loudspeaker is exempted under the other provisions of the Act.

The exclusion zone, which extends up to 1000 yards from parliament, came into force on 1 August 2005 and Mr Haw claimed that the Act did not apply to continuing protests, such as his, that had started before the Act came into force. In *R (Haw) v Secretary of State for the Home Department and Another*,[219] the High Court held that Acts of parliament should be construed in favour of individual liberty, and that as parliament could not have intended to apply the Act to continuing demonstrations, secondary legislation purporting to do that was *ultra vires*. However, this decision was overturned on appeal, and the Court of Appeal held that on its proper construction the Act applied to all demonstrations, even those taking place before the Act was passed.[220] Further, in *Blum v DPP and Another*[221] it was held that the procedure under the 2005 Act for authorising demonstrations in a designated area was compliant with Article 11 of the European Convention. That being so, there was no duty on the authorities to justify the use of those powers on the individual facts of each case, even where a group's activities were entirely peaceful and harmless and where they had been prosecuted under the Act for taking part in an unauthorised demonstration.[222]

As with sections 11–14 of the Public Order Act 1986, above, the procedure under the 2005 Act provides the police authorities with a very flexible and useful tool in regulating conduct that would not normally constitute a breach of the criminal or civil law. Further, the Act, and its acceptance by the domestic courts, potentially circumvents the more liberal ruling in cases such as *Westminster CC v Haw*, above, where the law was willing to strike a proportionate balance between free speech and the proper use of the public highway. Nevertheless, the courts have insisted that restrictions imposed on such demonstrations comply with the principles

---

[217] Section 134(3) of the Act.

[218] Section 134(4).

[219] [2006] 2 WLR 50.

[220] [2006] 3 WLR 40. For an analysis of the case and the 2005 Act see Loveland, Public Protest and Parliament Square [2007] EHRLR 252.

[221] [2006] EWHC 3209 (Admin).

[222] In addition, The Serious Organised Crime and Police Act 2005 (Designated Sites under Section 128) (Amendment) Order 2007: SI 2007/930 came into force on 1 June 2006, making it an offence to trespass on designated sites. The order designated 16 sites, including Downing Street and Windsor Castle, and the offence is punishable by up to six months in prison.

of legality and necessity, and in *DPP* v *Haw*[223] it was held that conditions imposed on Brian Haw's protest outside parliament were too vague and unworkable to be prescribed by law and thus *ultra vires*.[224]

The Labour government had invited views from the public on the framework governing the right of protest in the vicinity of parliament and more generally sought views on wider existing legislative restrictions on the right of peaceful assembly. However, those proposals never became law and at the time of writing the above provision is still in force.[225] In the meantime, the protest camps, of Haw and other protestors, were ordered to be broken up by the use of the Mayor of London's powers under the Greater London Authority Act 1999. In *Mayor of London* v *Hall and Others*,[226] it was held that the Mayor of London had exclusive possession of Parliament Square gardens,[227] and was thus entitled to possession as against protestors who had set up a permanent protest camp in that area. Although the protestors' removal would interfere with their rights under Articles 10 and 11, there was a pressing social need to stop an indefinite camped protest in the gardens, to protect the rights of other visitors, to safeguard health and to prevent crime. The bye-laws did not impose a blanket ban on camping or taking part in a protest and the removal was necessary to allow the mayor to exercise his duties of management of the area under the 1999 Act, as there was strong evidence that the camp was attracting health hazards, homeless persons and illegal drinking. Subsequently, the Court of Appeal remitted for consideration whether one of the protestors, who had been conducting a separate protest, should be included in the original injunction.[228]

Questions

How do the laws of obstruction, trespass and nuisance strike a balance between the right to demonstrate and public safety, etc.?

How was that balance upset by the passing of the Serious Organised Crime and Police Act and by the ultimate prohibition of the protest outside parliament?

Aggravated trespass

Section 68 of the Criminal Justice and Public Order Act 1994 makes it an offence to trespass on land where other people are engaged in a lawful activity on that land, or adjoining land, and to do anything which is calculated to intimidate those persons so as to deter them from engaging in the activity, or to obstruct or disrupt that activity.[229] The section gives protection to lawful conduct on that land, and thus opens up the possibility of a defence if the protestors

---

[223] [2008] 1 WLR 379.

[224] The conditions included instructions that he must not use articles in connection with his demonstration that can conceal or contain other items and that he must maintain his site in a manner that allows any person present to tell at a glance that no suspicious items are present. In addition, if requested by a police officer in uniform, he had to confirm whether persons present were part of his demonstration or not. The judge accepted that counsel for Mr Haw had shown the conditions to be unworkable.

[225] See the end of the chapter for further information.

[226] [2010] HRLR 29.

[227] By virtue of the Greater London Authority Act 1999.

[228] *Hall and Others* v *Mayor of London, The Times*, 28 July 2010.

[229] The Anti-Social Behaviour Act 2003 deleted the words 'open air' from s.68 and s.69 of the Criminal Justice and Public Order Act 1994. Thus, the lawful activity that is disrupted does not have to be in the open air and the police can remove trespassers whether they trespass in the open air or not.

are attempting to prevent or disrupt unlawful action. In *DPP v Bayer and Others*,[230] it was held that the common law defence of protective force was not available to the defendant where the activity that was being disrupted was not unlawful. In this case protestors had tied themselves to tractors sowing genetically modified maize. In an action for aggravated trespass the court of first instance had allowed the defence of protective force because the defendants had genuinely believed that the sowing of such crops was damaging to adjoining property and animals. On appeal it was held that although the defence might apply in appropriate cases, the judge should have considered whether the defendants used reasonable force in order to defend property from actual or imminent damage constituting an *unlawful or criminal* act.[231] Further, in *R v Aycliff and Others*,[232] it was held that an act of aggression or crime against peace did not constitute an offence contrary to domestic law so as to constitute unlawful action and thus justify an act of trespass. However, although it was held that such a matter was not justiciable, allegations that the conduct of the soldiers at military bases constituted a war crime were so justiciable, both for the purposes of this Act and with respect to the question whether reasonable force had been used to prevent a crime under s.3 of the Criminal Damage Act 1971. On the facts, however, there was no evidence that the actions of the soldiers did constitute such an offence and the defendants had acted in order to protest rather than prevent crime.[233]

Section 69 of the 1994 Act then gives a senior police officer the power to give directions ordering certain people to leave the land if he reasonably believes that an aggravated trespass is taking, or is about to take, place. Such people include a person who is committing, has committed, or intends to commit the offence of aggravated trespass, or two or more persons who are present on the land with the common purpose of intimidating people so as to deter them from engaging in their lawful activity, or obstructing or disrupting that activity. The section is particularly appropriate to cover the activities of protestors who enter onto land in order to demonstrate against activities that are taking place on such land, such as fox-hunting or the building of motorways. It also provides the police and landowner with a convenient method of controlling and breaking up the activities of demonstrators, without having recourse to the civil law of trespass or of proving the ingredients of other public order offences.

For the offence to be committed a person must do something over and above entering the land; a mere act of trespass is not sufficient to attract liability. Thus, in *Barnard v DPP*[234] it was held that no offence had been committed when demonstrators had entered a mine in order to demonstrate against opencast mining. In order for an offence to be committed there had to be a distinct and overt act other than trespass which was intended to have the desired effect of disrupting the activity in question. In this case, therefore, the second element of the offence – that a person does something which was intended to have the effect of intimidating those persons engaged in a lawful activity so as to deter them from engaging in that activity

---

[230] [2004] 1 WLR 2856.

[231] The court did, however, state that the defence could apply to this offence, despite the absence of the words 'without lawful authority' in the section. The defence may be available, therefore, if landowners or others are carrying out unlawful activities, or carrying out lawful activities unlawfully, although the court stressed that the use of such protective force must be proportionate.

[232] [2005] 3 WLR 628.

[233] The court also clarified that the activity of preventing unlawful activities would not be a breach of s.68 even if the consequence of the activity was to prevent other, lawful actions taking place.

[234] *The Times*, 9 November 1999.

or of obstructing or disrupting the activity – was absent. It was held, however, that there might be circumstances where the act of coming onto land might constitute the second requirement, provided there was evidence of what the defendants were doing and that the occupation was a distinct and overt act from the original trespass. Thus, in *Winder* v *DPP*,[235] where hunt saboteurs ran onto land and ran after a chase it was held that they had committed the second element of the offence. Although the demonstrators had no intention that the running itself would disrupt the hunt, the act of running in this case was sufficiently closely connected to the intended disruption as to be more than merely preparatory. It was not necessary to prove an act which is itself intended to disrupt, obstruct or intimidate, provided the act is sufficiently separate from the original act of trespass and was sufficiently linked with the overall (presumably assumed) aim of disrupting a lawful activity. This is a particularly generous interpretation of the section and could impose liability for the mere act of trespass.[236]

The unfairness of the application of these provisions is highlighted in *Capon* v *DPP*.[237] The appellants had entered land in order to protest against fox-hunting and wanted to witness the pulling out of the fox from the hole to see if any offence was committed. The protestors entered into an argument with a police sergeant who, having had discussions with the hunt master, accused them of disrupting the hunt. As the protestors argued with the officer as to whether they were disrupting the hunt the officer told them that they were being arrested for aggravated trespass and at the police station they were charged with failing to leave land after a police direction to do so. It was held that although the appellants had not committed an act of aggravated trespass – the court accepting that they had positively tried to refrain from doing so and had accepted their side of the story – there was sufficient evidence for the police officer to have had a reasonable belief that they had been committing such an offence. The officer had given a clear direction under s.69 of the Act and all the protestors knew that the order had been given. Thus, even though a prosecution under s.68 would have failed, the appellants were obliged to comply with the officer's order and had, thus, committed the offence under s.69. This decision allows the police a very wide power to ask protestors to leave premises and, it is submitted, constitutes an arbitrary interference with free speech and freedom of peaceful assembly.

The power to remove masks – Criminal Justice and Public Order Act 1994

Under s.60(4A) of the Criminal Justice and Public Order Act 1994 a police officer has the power to require a person to remove any item which the officer reasonably believes the person is wearing in order to conceal his identity, and to seize anything which he reasonably believes the person intends to wear wholly or mainly for that purpose. In *DPP* v *Avery*[238] it

---

[235] *The Times*, 14 August 1996.

[236] The offence of aggravated trespass must also involve the disruption of another person's activity: *DPP* v *Tilly and Others*, *The Times*, 27 November 2001. In that case it was held that the disruption of farming by crop destruction was, in itself, insufficient to make out the offence of aggravated trespass. Farming or carrying out a business could not be an activity for such purposes and accordingly the defendants had not committed an act of aggravated trespass when they had entered upon land and damaged genetically modified crops.

[237] Unreported, decision of the Divisional Court, 4 March 1998. See Mead, Will Peaceful Protestors be Foxed by the Divisional Court Decision in *Capon* v *DPP*? [1998] Crim LR 870.

[238] *The Times*, 8 November 2001; (2002) Cr App R 31.

was held that in exercising that power the police officer did not have to comply with the normal requirements imposed by s.2(2)(b) and s.3 of the Police and Criminal Evidence Act 1984 to give his name, police station and the reasons for the request. In that case 200 demonstrators were gathered outside a dog-breeding site. The defendant was wearing a skeleton mask covering his face and was asked to remove it by a police officer. When he refused the officer attempted to remove the mask and the defendant assaulted the officer. The magistrates dismissed the case on the basis that the officer's powers under s.60 had to be exercised in accordance with the provisions of the Police and Criminal Evidence Act, but on appeal the Divisional Court held that as s.60(4A) did not confer the power to search upon the police officer, the provision was not governed by s.2 and s.3 of the 1984 Act.

The court accepted that the power under s.60(4A) created a significant power to interfere with the liberty of the subject, but nevertheless felt that such interference was legitimate. The court noted that the powers only arose in anticipation of violence and with the authorisation of a senior police officer, and accepted that the wearing of masks to conceal identity in the course of violent demonstrations could impede arrest, facilitate escape from the commission of an offence and impede proper measures by way of control in connection with future demonstrations. In fact, in this case there was no (immediate) threat of serious violence and it is strongly arguable that the powers are, in most cases, a convenient method of keeping control over demonstrators who might not otherwise be acting unlawfully. The decision that the powers of the police officer are not subject to the normal search powers adds weight to the allegation that such powers are arbitrary and possibly in violation of Article 5 of the European Convention.

The Protection from Harassment Act 1997

This Act was passed to protect individuals from persistent acts of harassment, primarily from 'stalkers'. However, the Act might in some circumstances be applied against demonstrators whose acts cause harassment to particular individuals.[239] Harassment is not specifically defined in the Act but s.1 of the Act states that a person should not pursue a course of conduct which amounts to harassment of another, that is to engage in a course of conduct which a reasonable person would consider amounted to harassment of another where the harasser knows or ought to know that this will be the effect of the conduct. Section 2 of the Act then makes it an offence to pursue a course of conduct that is in breach of s.1,[240] and under s.3 the harassed person can obtain an injunction ordering a person to desist from acts of harassment, and receive damages for acts of harassment. A defence that the conduct was reasonable is available under s.1(3).

---

[239] In *Daiichi and Others v Stop Huntington Animal Cruelty and Others* [2004] 1 WLR 1503, it was held that the Act could not be used by companies as such bodies were not victims within the Act. However, individuals, such as directors, who were non-corporate claimants, were entitled to protection. Also, in *Oxford University v Webb* [2006] EWHC 2490 (QB), it was held that the Animal Liberation Front was an organisation capable of being represented in a legal action despite its efforts to avoid legal or other status. The court stressed that care would need to be taken not to implicate all its members and all members should be notified of any injunction.

[240] The more serious offence of putting people in fear of violence is contained in s.4 of the Act, making it an offence to pursue a course of conduct which causes another to fear, on at least two occasions, that violence will be used against him.

The potential for the Act's provisions to be used against protestors is extremely wide, covering not only acts of violence, but also activities of protestors that cause mere inconvenience or annoyance. Accordingly, it is essential that the courts allow the employment of such powers very sparingly. Originally it was thought that the legislation was not appropriate in cases where the defendant was exercising his or her right to demonstrate. Thus, in *Huntington Life Sciences* v *Curtin*[241] it was held that the Act was clearly not intended by parliament to be used to clamp down on the discussion of matters of public interest or upon the rights of political protest and public demonstration which were so much part of our democratic society. In that case an antivivisection campaign had been launched against the plaintiffs and an injunction issued that stopped the groups, including the defendants who were a peaceful campaigning group, from continuing to commit acts of harassment or from entering the plaintiff's research sites. The Court of Appeal held that there was insufficient evidence to suggest that the defendants should have been covered by the injunctions and thus discharged the order as far as it applied to them.

However, if there is evidence that protestors have taken part in actions of harassment then the provision clearly applies and orders under the Act may be issued.[242] In addition, the order can be enforced to prohibit subsequent peaceful protest. For example, in *DPP* v *Moseley, Selvanayagam and Woodling*[243] it was held that the provision could be applied in the context of demonstrations and that it can affect acts of peaceful protest. One of the defendants had been served with a temporary injunction under s.3 of the Act. After she had been served with the injunction she and two other defendants continued to demonstrate against the fur trade at a fur farm. The defendants were charged with an offence under s.2 of the Act and sought to argue that their conduct was reasonable in all the circumstances. Although this plea was accepted at first instance, the High Court held that the defendant who was subject to the original order was precluded from relying on the defence as she had clearly broken the term of the original injunction. Although the other defendants, who were not subject to the original order, could rely on the defence under s.1(3), the court refused to look behind that order in the case of the other defendant.

The decision has been heavily criticised,[244] and shows that the 1997 Act can be used as a powerful tool to control the often entirely peaceful activities of protestors. Nevertheless, in *Silverton and Others* v *Gravett and Others*,[245] the High Court confirmed the legitimacy of the Act's application to demonstrations. The claimants, dealers in furs (and their families), had complained that the defendants had carried out various acts of harassment at retail outlets and at their homes, including damaging windows, obstructing customers, sending offensive letters and materials to shops, and publishing the home addresses of some of the claimants. The claimants had received temporary injunctions under the 1997 Act and in an action to make the injunctions permanent it was claimed that some of the actions complained of amounted to no more than an exercise of the rights of free speech and association under Articles 10 and 11 of the European Convention. The court accepted the evidence of the

---

[241] *The Times*, 11 December 1999. Noted in (1998) (3) 1 J Civ Libs 37.

[242] In *Heathrow Airport* v *Garman* [2007] EWHC 1957 (QB), it was held that there was no evidence to suggest that protestors were to condone or take part in acts of harassment so as to justify the granting of an injunction under the Act. However, an injunction was granted on other grounds.

[243] *The Times*, 23 June 1999.

[244] See Fenwick, *Civil Rights* (Longman 2000), page 237.

[245] Unreported, decision of the Queen's Bench Division, 19 October 2001.

claimants and held that the defendants' conduct constituted harassment under the 1997 Act, including the actions of an unincorporated body campaigning against cruelty to animals, and whose literature stated that it was currently concentrating on the claimant's fur shop. On the evidence, several unidentified members of the group were *probably* involved in the campaign of harassment against the claimants and their premises and one of the defendants had counselled and procured various acts of harassment.

Dealing with the arguments under Articles 10 and 11, the court noted that those rights were not absolute and could be restricted by the domestic law to prevent disorder or crime or to protect the reputation and rights of others. In the court's view, the prohibition of harassment imposed by the Act and by the common law constituted such a restriction. The court also held that it was possible for an injunction to bind people acting in concert with the defendants who were not party to this action but who had had notice of its terms,[246] and that the court had the power to impose an exclusion zone in an injunction to prevent harassment.[247] In the present case an exclusion zone for the street in which the shop was situated was reasonably required for the protection of the claimant's business. It was also necessary to include the claimant's homes in the zone. The decision highlights the often excessive ambit of such orders and their failure to distinguish between legitimate and unlawful actions. It is also of some concern that some of the defendants are covered by the order on the basis of the *probability* that they took part in, or orchestrated, previous acts of harassment.

The Act has been used regularly against animal rights protestors in recent years and is generally regarded by the courts to be a reasonable and Convention-compliant method of curtailing tactics which cause undue harassment to private individuals. In addition, the courts are prepared to apply quite stringent orders on such protestors. For example, in *Emerson Developments Ltd v Avery and Others*,[248] it was held that the claimants, employees of Huntington Life Sciences, were entitled to an order stopping the defendants from entering specified zones around the company's premises and the claimant's homes. More worryingly with respect to free speech, the court granted an order that the defendants cease publishing particular information relating to attacks on the company, which had been posted on their website.

Further, in *University of Oxford v Broughton*[249] an injunction was granted in the claimant's favour to prevent the defendants from demonstrating outside a research laboratory. On an application to continue the injunction, it was held that there was no requirement for the protected persons of an order to be named, and that their anonymity did not infringe the defendant's right to a fair trial under Article 6 as the defendants had no difficulty in identifying suitable targets for harassment and thus they could easily identify those protected by the injunction. The restrictions were a proportionate interference with the defendant's rights under the Convention and the order would be expanded to include the prohibition of photographing the protected persons. In subsequent proceedings,[250] it was held that where it

---

[246] Applying the decision of *Huntington Life Sciences Ltd v Curtin and Others*, The Times, 11 December 1999, and *DPP v Moseley and Others*, The Times, 23 June 1999, considered above.

[247] Following *Burris v Azadani* [1995] 4 All ER 802.

[248] Unreported, decision of the Queen's Bench Division, 26 January 2004.

[249] [2004] EWHC 2543 (QB).

[250] *University of Oxford v Broughton* [2008] EWHC 75 (QB).

was likely that activists would harass workers, students and staff at the university then the exclusion zone should be extended. However, the court refused the request to create a new zone to prevent activists from shouting at the site of graduation ceremonies, as the evidence did not suggest that this amounted to harassment within the Act.[251]

The Criminal Justice and Police Act 2001

Under s.42 of the Criminal Justice and Police Act 2001 a police constable is empowered to give directions to any person, *inter alia*, to leave the scene where they are outside or in the vicinity of a dwelling and the constable reasonably believes that those persons are present for the purpose (by his presence or otherwise) of representing to the resident or another individual or of persuading such a person that he should not do something that he is entitled or required to do or that he should do something that he is not under any obligation to do, and that the constable also believes on reasonable grounds that the presence of the person (either alone or together with any other person present) amounts to or is likely to result in the harassment of the resident, or is likely to cause alarm or distress to the resident.

The directions given under this section require the persons to whom they are directed to do all such things, including leaving the vicinity of the dwelling,[252] as the constable giving it may specify as the things he considers necessary to prevent any such harassment or alarm or distress.[253] They may be given orally and may be directed at persons individually or together.[254] Any person who knowingly contravenes such a direction will be guilty of an offence and liable on summary conviction to imprisonment for a term not exceeding three months.[255] The section then provides that a constable in uniform may arrest without warrant any person he reasonably suspects is committing an offence under the section.[256]

The provision was inserted into the Act following a number of incidents where workers and directors of such organisations were subjected to often intimidating activities from protestors. The provision, therefore, could be said to pursue a legitimate aim in the protection of the rights of such persons, who are fearful of their own safety or of intrusions into their privacy and their homes. However, the provisions do bestow a great deal of discretion on the police and the concern might be that in practice there is little or no distinction drawn between entirely peaceful protest that is causing no more than inconvenience, and activities of a violent or intimidatory nature which should deservedly be regulated and criminalised.

---

[251] Contrast *Novartis Pharmaceuticals* v *Stop Huntingdon Animal Cruelty and Others* [2010] HRLR 8, where an amendment to an injunction imposing restrictions on an animal right's protest was refused when the claimants had sought to stop the protestors from wearing masks and blood-splattered clothing. Such restrictions would haven been difficult to enforce in practice and would have constituted unreasonable interferences with the Article 10 rights of the protestors.

[252] Section 42(4). The order to leave may have immediate effect or may require the persons to leave within a specified time. Under s.42(5) the constable may make exceptions to the directions on such conditions as he thinks fit, including conditions relating to the distance from the premises that the persons are allowed to remain and the number of such persons allowed to remain in the vicinity.

[253] Section 42(2).

[254] Section 42(3).

[255] Section 42(7).

[256] Section 42(8).

The Communications Act 2003 and the Malicious Communications Act 1988

In addition to the above provisions, activists may be charged under provisions intended to protect recipients from offensive or distressing material. For example, under s.127 of the Communications Act 2003 it is an offence to send a grossly offensive message through a public electronic communications service.[257] In addition, s.1 of the Malicious Communications Act 1998 makes it an offence to send a letter or article conveying, *inter alia*, a message which is grossly offensive where the purpose is to cause distress or anxiety to the recipient or other person to whom he intends the message to be communicated.

The 1988 Act was employed against political activism in *Connolly* v *DPP*,[258] where it was held that the defendant had committed that offence when she had sent photographs of aborted foetuses to three pharmacists that sold the 'morning-after' pill. On appeal the defendant argued that the section did not apply to a lawful protest and that the provision and its application was contrary to the Human Rights Act 1998. The High Court held that although it was possible to interpret the meaning of the words 'indecent' and 'grossly offensive' so that the provision was not employed in violation of Article 10, the Act's interference with the defendant's free speech was justified under Article 10(2). The defendant's right to free speech was not of a higher order simply because it represented her religious views and did not justify the distress and anxiety that she intended to cause those who received the message. It was also significant that the recipients had not been targeted because they were in a position to influence a public debate on abortion. The most the defendant could hope for would be that the recipients ceased to sell the morning-after pill, and it was difficult to see what that would have contributed to the debate. The decision in *Collins* does display some respect for political protest, but it is difficult to imagine the courts siding with freedom of speech in cases where individuals are sent offensive and distressing material, however influential those people might be.

***

Questions

How does domestic law seek to protect the public and certain individuals from harassment and other harm caused by demonstrations and protest speech?

Do such laws strike a proper balance between public and individual safety and the right to demonstrate and is that balance compatible with the European Convention?

***

Demonstrations and breach of the peace

In addition to the specific criminal offences used to regulate protest activity, considered above, the police have a general duty to preserve the peace and this power, along with the power to commit people for breach of the peace, is a powerful weapon against protestors, even those who have acted in a perfectly peaceful manner. Breach of the peace can be used against a person both directly and indirectly. Directly, it can be used as the basis of a specific

***

[257] See *DPP* v *Collins* [2006] 1 WLR 2223. See also the Postal Services Act 2000. In *R* v *Kirk* [2006] EWCA Crim 525, the Court of Appeal upheld the appellant's conviction for sending a package through the post to employees at an animal laboratory, describing the premises as equivalent to Auschwitz and including a swastika emblem.

[258] [2008] 1 WLR 276.

criminal offence, as under s.4 of the Public Order Act 1986, or of arresting a person for committing or inciting a breach of the peace. Although breach of the peace is not a criminal offence as such, the police do have the legal power to arrest for breach of the peace and the courts can bind people over to keep the peace. Indirectly, the police may use a breach of the peace as the basis of taking action to control a potential breach of the peace and arrest a person who obstructs them in the execution of that duty. Thus, even if a demonstrator's action was not likely to cause a breach of the peace, if a police officer reasonably apprehends a breach of the peace by another person as a result of the presence of the demonstrator, and the demonstrator refuses to obey an officer's request to move on, the officer may wish to use his or her powers to arrest the demonstrator for obstruction in the course of his duty – his duty being to preserve the peace.[259]

A breach of the peace has been defined as an act done or threatened to be done which either actually harms a person, or in his presence his property, or is likely to cause such harm, or which puts someone in fear of such harm being done.[260] That definition clearly envisages the situation not only where a person is inciting a breach of the peace by his conduct or words, but also where the words or behaviour of a person are likely to result in another person committing a breach of the peace. Thus, the right to demonstrate may be under threat when the activities of the demonstrators are in themselves entirely peaceful, but nevertheless are likely to provoke an (unreasonable) violent reaction in others.

The law relating to breach of the peace can be used in a variety of ways by the police in order to control and keep the peace. First, an officer may arrest a person under their powers to deal with a breach of the peace when that person's conduct in itself would be likely to cause a breach of the peace. For example, in *Wise v Dunning*[261] the defendant was arrested for breach of the peace when, during his address to a group of Catholics, he waved a crucifix in his hand and referred to Catholics as 'rednecks'. Although the defendant claimed that he and his followers did not intend to use or threaten violence towards the crowd, the court was satisfied that the provocative nature of his conduct was likely to incite a breach of the peace.

In cases where there is no clear intention on behalf of the demonstrator to use or incite violence, the law must ensure that breach of the peace powers are not used, either directly or indirectly, to interfere unnecessarily with peaceful protest. However, the European Court has indicated that the domestic authorities will be provided with a wide margin of appreciation in the interpretation and application of breach of the peace powers. For example, in *Chorherr v Austria*[262] the European Court held that the police were entitled to arrest and detain a peaceful demonstrator whose actions were causing annoyance to the assembled crowd, the Court stating that the applicant must have known that his behaviour might cause a public disturbance. Of course, the domestic courts do not have to adopt such a cautious approach and, in any case, will have to distinguish between behaviour that is likely to cause a breach of the

---

[259] The authorities' power to control such activities is also subject to EC Law: *R v Chief Constable of Sussex, ex parte ITF Ltd* [1999] 2 AC 418; and to judicial review in general: *R v Coventry City Council, ex parte Phoenix Aviation* [1995] 3 All ER 37.

[260] *R v Howell* [1982] QB 416. Contrast LORD DENNING MR in *R v Chief Constable of Devon and Cornwall, ex parte Central Electricity Generating Board* [1982] QB 458, where he stated that there is a breach of the peace whenever a person who is lawfully carrying out his work is lawfully and physically prevented by another from doing it. This definition has not been accepted and would be inconsistent with Articles 10 and 11 of the European Convention.

[261] [1902] 1 KB 167.

[262] (1993) 17 EHRR 358. Dealt with above, at page 508.

peace and that which is not. An attempt to make this distinction was made in *Nicol and Selvanayagam v DPP*.[263] The defendants had been arrested when they had tried to disrupt an angling competition by blowing horns. It was held that for there to be a finding of breach of the peace, there had to be some interference with the rights of others and the conduct itself must be said to be unreasonable in respect to the other. Applying those principles and upholding the police action, it was held that although the actions of the demonstrators was not unlawful, it was nonetheless unreasonable and likely to cause a breach of the peace because on the facts the anglers were on the verge of using force against the protestors.

The decision in *Nicol* can be contrasted with the case of *Percy v DPP*.[264] The appellants had entered a military base in order to protest against the 'war machine'. They were arrested for conduct likely to cause a breach of the peace and the justices found that their presence at the airfield could have provoked the military police to react violently. On appeal it was held that although it was not necessary that violence be perpetrated by the *defendant*, violence or threatened violence was required before justices could exercise their powers to bind over to keep the peace. In the present case it was unlikely that the appellant's non-violent acts of trespass would provoke trained servicemen to violent reaction. A mere disturbance not involving violence could not amount to a breach of the peace. The difference between *Nicol* and *Percy* was that in *Percy* no violent reaction was likely from those present, while in *Nicol* the anglers were likely to react in such a way. The danger in applying this test is that the defendant has to take the other person as they find them and thus can often incur liability because of the unreasonable reaction of that other person. This is illustrated in *R v Morpeth Ward Justices, ex parte Ward*,[265] where the defendants had been arrested for attempting to disrupt a pheasant shoot. They had been met with a violent reaction by the shooters, and the police, fearing a breach of the peace, arrested them for conduct likely to cause a breach of the peace. Upholding the binding over orders, it was held that provocative, disorderly behaviour which is likely to have the natural consequence of causing violence, even if only to the persons of the provokers, is capable of being conduct likely to cause a breach of the peace.[266] The unfair repercussion of such cases is qualified by the requirement that the defendant's conduct must be unreasonable. However, without any formal mechanism for granting a higher status to the right of assembly as opposed to, for example, the right to fish or to build highways, the application of the law is capable of imposing undue restraints on peaceful demonstrators.[267]

Secondly, in the exercise of their power to preserve the peace, police officers may use reasonable force against a person in order to preserve the peace and use their common law powers as a defence to any possible action for assault. In *Humphries v O'Connor*[268] the plaintiff was walking through the streets of Swalinbar in Northern Ireland wearing an orange lily. As a result people were provoked and followed her, causing a great noise and threatening her with violence. The defendant, a police officer, removed the lily from the plaintiff's person and the plaintiff sued in trespass. It was held that a police officer was entitled to take direct action

---

[263] [1996] Crim LR 318.

[264] [1995] 1 WLR 1382.

[265] (1992) 95 Cr App R 215.

[266] See also *Kelly v Chief Constable of Hampshire, The Independent*, 23 March 1993; *Holmes v Bournemouth Crown Court*, unreported, decision of the Divisional Court, 6 October 1993.

[267] This dilemma will be revisited later in this section and it appears that the decision in *DPP v Redmond-Bate*, below, and the passing of the Human Rights Act 1998, has led to a more tolerant approach from the judiciary.

[268] (1864) 17 ICLR 1.

against a person not acting unlawfully where it was necessary to preserve the peace. The police's otherwise unlawful action was justified in order to prevent a breach of the peace, and the plaintiff's action failed.[269] Although the demonstrator is not charged with any criminal offence in such situations, it is dubious whether the police should receive immunity because they apprehend a breach of the peace from another quarter. It is thus arguable that such an action is an interference with the demonstrator's freedom of speech and assembly. The decision may also have to be reconsidered in the light of the decision in *DPP v Redmond-Bate*.[270]

Thirdly, and more controversially, a person may be arrested under s.89 of the Police Act 1997 for obstruction of a police officer in the execution of his or her duty when the police apprehend a breach of the peace and a person obstructs the officer in his or her attempt to deal with that anticipated breach. This power allows the police to restrain perfectly lawful and peaceful conduct on behalf of the protestor for the purpose of preserving the peace. Thus, although a person cannot be charged directly with a criminal offence because of the unlawful activities of others, a police officer might arrest a person acting entirely peaceably if that person refuses to cooperate with the officer in his or her attempt to quell the disorder caused by another person.

The anomaly of this power is evident by examining the cases of *Beatty* v *Gillbanks*[271] and *Duncan v Jones*.[272] In *Beatty* the defendants had been charged with unlawfully assembling to the disturbance of the peace when they had continued to hold a meeting of the Salvation Army. The meeting had attracted a crowd who began to threaten the demonstrators, and the defendants were asked to stop the meeting. On appeal their convictions were quashed, the court holding that there was no principle in English law that allowed a person to be punished for acting lawfully if he knows that in so doing he will induce another person to act unlawfully. This principle was, however, called into question by the decision in *Duncan*. The defendant, a well-known communist, was planning to address a crowd outside an employment exchange. Because the police feared a breach of the peace, she was asked to hold her meeting 175 yards away and when she refused she was arrested for obstruction of a police officer. It was not alleged that she had caused any obstruction: or that she or any other person at the meeting had caused or provoked a breach of the peace. Nevertheless her conviction was upheld. In the court's view there was evidence which would support her conviction: she must have known that a disturbance was a probable consequence of her holding the meeting (as there had been disturbances before) and she was not unwilling that such consequences would ensue. In such circumstances the officer was therefore entitled to apprehend a breach of the peace and to issue the request to her.[273]

This power is, however, subject to certain limitations. Under Article 11 of the European Convention on Human Rights, any restriction on the right of peaceful assembly must be prescribed by law and necessary in a democratic society for the achievement of a legitimate

---

[269] See also *O'Kelly* v *Harvey* (1883) 15 Cox CC 453, where it was held that a magistrate was justified in laying a hand on a man while dispersing a meeting of the Catholic Land League which was being threatened by the violent actions of Fermanagh Orangemen.

[270] [1999] Crim LR 998, considered below.

[271] (1882) 15 Cox CC 138.

[272] [1936] 1 KB 218.

[273] It was thought that the distinction between the cases was that in charges of obstruction the peaceful protestor is only incurring indirect criminal liability. However, the recent decision in *DPP v Redmond-Bate, The Times*, 23 July 1999, casts doubt on this distinction and appears to insist that the police must direct their actions at the source of the trouble and thus not interfere with entirely peaceful activities.

aim. Thus, the law relating to breach of the peace must be sufficiently clear to allow individuals to be aware of its powers and limitations, and for the domestic courts to check against its arbitrary use in practice. In addition, any interference caused by the use of the law must correspond to a pressing social need and be proportionate to the aim – usually the prevention of crime and disorder or the protection of the rights of others. After the Human Rights Act the courts must ensure that the powers are used in conformity with the European Convention and that they are not employed to restrict the right of peaceful assembly in an unnecessary manner.

Although traditionally the courts were very reluctant to interfere in decisions made by the police in respect of their duty to deal with a breach of the peace, recent case law suggests that the courts will be prepared to secure the protestors' right of peaceful assembly against the wide discretionary powers of police officers. Thus, early case law appeared to give an almost unfettered discretion to the police in deciding whether they had reasonable grounds for apprehending a breach of the peace, and in deciding what action to take in response. For example, in *Piddington v Bates*[274] it was held that the police were entitled to take action to restrict the number of pickets at a factory entrance and to arrest a person who attempted to push past a constable so as to join the picket line. Although there had to be facts from which a constable could reasonably anticipate a breach of the peace, in the present case the constable was in possession of such information. Based on the number of pickets (18) in ratio to the number of workers (eight), coupled with a telephone call received from the employer who anticipated trouble, the police officer was reasonably and fully entitled to think that there was a real danger of something more than peaceful picketing about to be carried out. More strikingly, in *Moss v McLachlan*[275] it was held that the police were entitled to arrest striking miners for obstruction, when they had refused to turn back when travelling to a colliery. The striking miners were two miles from one colliery and five miles from another, but the court held that, on the facts, the police were within the execution of their duty in apprehending a breach of the peace because of previous disorder that had occurred at the collieries.[276]

These, and other decisions, should be read in the light of the High Court decision of SEDLEY LJ in *DPP v Redmond-Bate*,[277] detailed in the case study below (pages 562–5). In this case SEDLEY LJ held that the arrest of two protestors for obstruction of a police officer in the execution of his duty was unlawful because the officer did not have reasonable grounds for believing that their conduct – the defendants were preaching on the steps of Wakefield Cathedral – would cause a breach of the peace. According to his Lordship, the officer should have concentrated on the *source* of the potential trouble, two or three people who were shouting insults at the defendants, and that as a consequence the arrest of the demonstrators had been unlawful. This decision casts doubts on the previous authorities, most notably *Moss v McLachlan*. The police will need to have strong evidence to apprehend a breach of the

---

[274] [1961] 1 WLR 162.

[275] [1985] IRLR 76.

[276] See also the decision in *Foy v Chief Constable of Kent*, unreported, 20 March 1984, where the court upheld the policy of the police to stop Kent miners at the Dartford Tunnel some 200 miles from their destination. However, in *Peterkin v Chief Constable of Cheshire*, *The Times*, 16 November 1999, damages were awarded to a hunt protestor who was arrested for conduct likely to cause a breach of the peace when he and others were on their way to a hunt. In the court's opinion there were no grounds for apprehending an immediate threat of any breach of the peace.

[277] *The Times*, 23 July 1999.

peace and the court will be more likely to question the police's assessment in any particular case. The decision also casts doubt on cases such as *Duncan* v *Jones*, although his Lordship attempted to distinguish that case on the grounds that the defendant's behaviour in that case was the source of the apprehended breach of the peace, whereas in the present case the only conduct that was reasonably capable of causing a breach of the peace was the reaction of the counter-demonstrators.

Breach of the peace, individual liberty and freedom of speech and the decision of the House of Lords in *Laporte*

Police powers with respect to breach of the peace impact not only on freedom of expression and protest, but also the right to individual liberty within Article 5 of the Convention. As we have seen, the police can use their powers to arrest and detain individuals who are thought to be a threat to the peace, and in *Albert* v *Lavin*[278] it was accepted that police officers can take reasonable steps to restrain an imminent breach of the peace, which might include using reasonable force against appropriate individuals. The scope of these powers and how they impact on peaceful protest was clarified in the House of Lords' judgment in *R (Laporte)* v *Chief Constable of Gloucestershire*.[279]

In this case the applicant, along with a number of other individuals, was travelling on a coach from London to RAF Fairford, Gloucestershire, to take part in a demonstration against the war in Iraq. Fearing a repetition of previous incidents of disruption at this site, the police decided to stop the coach from proceeding to the airbase but not to arrest anybody for breach of the peace at that stage. On the coach they seized a number of articles, including masks, spray paint, protective clothing, two pairs of scissors, a smoke bomb and five shields. Unable to identify the owners of these articles, the Chief Constable seized them and decided to re-route the coach back to London with all the protestors on it. The High Court held that the police action in preventing the coach from continuing to the base was not unlawful because the superintendent reasonably believed that, if the coaches were allowed to proceed, there would be breaches of the peace.[280] Further, although the instructions were applied in a blanket fashion, individual discrimination among a large number of uncooperative people was impracticable. The High Court also held that the initial decision to detain the protestors could be justified under the principle in *Albert* v *Lavin* (above) and that such restraint would not amount to detention under Article 5. However, any detention that went beyond that purpose would become unlawful, and as in this case there was no immediately apprehended breach of the peace by the applicant sufficient to justify even transitory detention, the detention on the coach for more than two hours went far beyond the type of transitory detention allowed under the principle in *Albert* v *Lavin*. The Court of Appeal upheld that decision,[281] and an appeal was made to the House of Lords. Allowing the protestors' appeal, the House of Lords held that there was nothing in domestic law which justified action short of arrest when a breach of the peace was not so imminent as to justify any arrest. In this case no breach of the peace was apprehended, and it is only when there is a reasonable apprehension of a

---

[278] [1982] AC 546.
[279] [2007] 2 WLR 46.
[280] [2004] 2 All ER 874.
[281] [2005] QB 678.

breach of the peace that the court can consider whether the preventive action was proportionate or reasonable. In the present case although it was reasonable to anticipate that there may be trouble from certain quarters at the place of the demonstration itself, it was not reasonable to anticipate that these people wanted a violent confrontation with the police, or that there would be an outburst of disorder on arrival of these passengers. Further, the action taken was disproportionate and unreasonable because the officer should have considered other options when he realised the coach passengers did not pose an imminent threat to the peace. It was not reasonable for the police to believe that there would be disorder once the coaches reached their destination because the police had put into place extensive precautions at the site. Further, *wherever possible*, the focus of preventive action should be on those about to act disruptively, not on peaceful protestors, although such action could be taken against an innocent person where it was reasonably apprehended that there was no other possible means of avoiding an imminent breach of the peace.

The House of Lords' decision enhances free speech and liberty in a number of respects. First, it confirms that the powers derived from *Albert* v *Lavin* only apply where the police reasonably apprehended a breach of the peace and that any other detention will constitute a violation of Article 5. Secondly, even if a breach of the peace has been reasonably anticipated, any action taken in furtherance of that belief should be reasonable and proportionate and should include other options that did not impact immediately on liberty and speech. Thirdly, although their Lordships appear to support the decision in *Moss* v *McLachlan* (above) on its facts, police discretion will now be heavily circumscribed by the courts' power to investigate the evidence surrounding the imminence of any threat to the peace.

The decisions in *Redmond-Bate* and *Laporte* are instructive in attempting to draw the line between conduct that may, and that which may not, lead to an apprehension of a breach of the peace on behalf of the police. Relying on previous decisions such as *Nicol and Selvanayagam* v *DPP*, SEDLEY LJ held that the conduct of the defendant must be unreasonable and intrusive of the rights of others. Significantly, his Lordship stressed that the demonstrators' right of free speech was protected even though it was regarded as offensive by others. In the light of this decision it is arguable whether cases such as *Nicol* and *ex parte Ward* are still good law. In *Redmond-Bate* there appeared to be no evidence of a breach of the peace in any case, and the rights of the counter-demonstrators were not compromised by the words or actions of the demonstrators. It is likely that the courts may take a different stance if the rights of others are attacked and therefore cases such as *Nicol* are probably still supportable in law, even though they give rather a weak recognition to the fundamental right of peaceful assembly. Equally, the decision of the House of Lords in *Laporte* not only clarifies and limits the powers of the police with respect to preserving the peace, but also suggests that the police should carefully consider their options, including utilising their extensive legal powers to deal with those who are actually threatening the peace or committing criminal offences, before allowing their residual power to deal with a breach of the peace to impact on the right to free speech and peaceful assembly.

A retreat from *Laporte*? – the decision in *Austin* v *Commissioner*

Despite this bold approach, it is expected that in certain circumstances the courts will allow the police to use their breach of the peace powers in relation to conduct which is entirely peaceful and harmless. For example, where the police apprehend a serious breach of the peace, which can be defused by taking an innocent person from the scene, then it is unlikely that the courts will refuse to sanction reasonable actions taken in consequence of that threat. Thus, if someone who is taking part in a peaceful protest or activity is met with great hostility by a large and unruly crowd, the police officer would appear to retain the power to remove that person from the scene, and to arrest that person if they failed to cooperate with the officer. In such a case the officer would have a defence to an action for assault, using the principle in *Humphries v O'Connor*, discussed above, and the courts are unlikely to disagree with the police officer that his or her actions were reasonable in the circumstances, even though the protestor's fundamental rights were compromised by the unlawful actions of others. Thus, although the decision in *Redmond-Bate* defends a fundamental principle and restricts the police's powers in such cases, it cannot be taken as authority for the proposition that peaceful protest is to be defended at all costs and in all circumstances. In such cases there would not necessarily be a violation of Article 11 of the European Convention, as that article presupposes that there may be justifiable restrictions on the right of peaceful protest. In addition, the European Court has indicated that the member states will be afforded a wide margin of appreciation in ensuring that public events and peaceful demonstrations take place.[282]

Further, where the police have reasonably apprehended a breach of the peace, they will in certain cases be given a broad discretion with respect to how they deal with that situation, particularly where there is potential for a high level of damage or violence. For example, in *Austin v Commissioner of the Police for the Metropolis*,[283] it was held that it was reasonable to detain the claimant, along with thousands of other demonstrators, for up to seven hours before allowing them to leave the area occupied by an unplanned mass demonstration. Although the High Court found that Article 5 had been engaged, it held that the measures were reasonable with respect to anticipated breaches of the peace and for the purpose of detaining them on reasonable suspicion of them having committed a variety of offences.[284] On appeal,[285] the Court of Appeal clarified the law after *Laporte*, and stressed that only where there was a reasonable belief that there were no other means whatsoever whereby a breach or imminent breach of the peace could be obviated could the lawful exercise by third parties be curtailed by the police. However, on the facts, the Court of Appeal concluded that the containment of persons inside the cordon was lawful because the situation was exceptional and the police had no alternative but to do what they did in order to avoid the imminent risk of serious violence by others. Further, the conditions of necessity remained throughout because no one had suggested an alternative release policy. There was no basis for believing that the police had acted unreasonably in deciding not to release the appellants on an individual basis.

The House of Lords upheld the Court of Appeal's decision,[286] and in addition decided that Article 5 of the Convention was not engaged in the present case because the police action did not constitute a detention within that article. In their Lordships' view, the intention of the police in the present case was to maintain the cordon only so long as was reasonably necessary to achieve a controlled dispersal and therefore the measures taken were proportionate, and thus

---

[282] See *Chorherr v Austria* (1993) 17 EHRR 358.

[283] *The Times*, 14 April 2005.

[284] In contrast, in *Epple v Germany* (Application No 77909/01), decision of the European Court, 24 March 2005, the European Court ruled that the detention of an individual for 19 hours for refusing to abide by an instruction not to visit a particular site was excessive and thus in breach of Article 5, even though the initial detention was lawful under Article 5(1)(b) for failure to carry out an obligation imposed by law.

[285] *The Times*, 29 October 2007.

[286] *Austin v Commissioner of the Police of the Metropolis* [2009] 1 AC 564.

there was no deprivation of liberty under Article 5. The case clarifies the decision in *Laporte*, and only applies when a breach of the peace is reasonably apprehended by the police.[287] However, the decision of the House of Lords with respect to Article 5 might need to be revisited in the light of the decision of the European Court of Human Rights in *Gillan and Quinton v United Kingdom*,[288] where it was held that stop and search powers conducted under the Terrorism Act 2000 were contrary to *Article 8* of the Convention. Although the decision was based on Article 8, rather than Article 5, the Court did not rule out the possibility that such powers entailed a deprivation of liberty under Article 5. If that is the case, and there was in fact a deprivation of liberty in *Austin*, then that detention and interference with the right to protest would need to be justified within the terms of Article 5 and constitute a necessary and proportionate measure in the circumstances; which the courts below the House of Lords in *Austin* felt was shown in the exceptional circumstances of the case.

Preserving the peace and private meetings

The police also appear to have a common law power to enter a private meeting to deal with a breach of the peace. Section 17(6) of the Police and Criminal Evidence Act 1984 preserves a constable's common law powers to enter premises without a warrant to deal with or prevent a breach of the peace. This power was considered in the context of the right of assembly in the case of *Thomas v Sawkins*.[289] A meeting had been planned to protest against the Incitement to Disaffection Bill and to demand the dismissal of the Chief Constable. The meeting was open to the public without payment and was attended by Sawkins, a police sergeant. When he was asked to leave and refused, Thomas attempted to eject him, and Sawkins and other officers resisted that attempt. Thomas then brought an action against Sawkins in assault for resisting his ejectment. It was held that the police were entitled to enter and remain on the premises during the meeting because they had reasonable grounds to believe that if they were not present there would be seditious speeches and other incitements to violence and a breach of the peace. It is questionable whether such a power is consistent with the Convention and the police would require strong evidence of any apprehended breach of the peace, as their actions involve not only a potential violation of Articles 10 and 11 of the Convention, but also the right to private life under Article 8.[290]

Conduct *contra bones mores*

Magistrates have an ancient power to bind a person over for conduct *contra bones mores* – conduct considered by the majority of society to be wrong.[291] This power might be used to

---

[287] For an analysis of the *Austin* decision, see Fenwick, Marginalising Human Rights: Breach of the Peace, 'Kettling', the HRA and Public Protest [2009] PL 737; Mead, Of Kettles, Cordons and Crowd Control – *Austin v Commissioner of the Police for the Metropolis* and the Meaning of 'Deprivation of Liberty' [2009] EHRLR 376.

[288] (2010) 50 EHRR 45. See Buxton, Terrorism and the European Convention [2010] Crim Law R 533.

[289] [1935] 2 KB 249.

[290] See, in particular, the decision in *McLeod v United Kingdom* (1999) 27 EHRR 493. In this case the European Court confirmed that the power to enter premises to deal with or stop a breach of the peace was compatible with Article 8 of the Convention, but that in the particular circumstances the entry onto the applicant's land was unnecessary.

[291] This is contained in the Justice of the Peace Act 1361 and its existence was confirmed by the Court of Appeal in *Hughes v Holley* [1988] 86 Cr App 130.

control conduct that is regarded as antisocial rather than illegal and is a convenient tool against demonstrators whose conduct has caused annoyance to others or to the public at large. The future of this ancient power was put in doubt by the decision of the European Court of Human Rights in *Hashman and Harrap v United Kingdom*.[292] The applicants had attended a hunt. The first applicant had blown a hunting horn and the second applicant had shouted at the hounds. Both were bound over to keep the peace and to be of good behaviour to the sum of £100. On appeal the Crown Court found that the applicants had deliberately attempted to interfere with the hunt and that their behaviour had been unlawful in exposing the hounds to danger. However, as the court found that there had been no violence or threat of violence, it found that there had been no breach of the peace. Nonetheless, the applicants' behaviour was *contra bones mores* and thus the applicants were bound over to be of good behaviour for one month. The applicants made an application under the European Convention, complaining that their rights under Articles 10 and 11 of the Convention had been violated. Dealing with the case under Article 10, the Court held that the violation of the applicants' freedom of expression could not be justified under paragraph 2 because the concept of *contra bones mores* was insufficiently precise to be 'prescribed by law' as required under that paragraph. In the Court's opinion, the concept failed to meet the requirement of foreseeability laid down by the case law of the European Court.[293] The criteria of behaviour which is wrong rather than right in the judgment of the majority of citizens failed to give the applicants sufficiently clear guidance as to how they should behave in the future.

However, the case was decided on its own facts, and does not rule out the possibility of the concept being used in the future, provided the nature and content of the order is sufficiently clear. Also, as the Court had decided the case on the question of whether the interference was sufficiently prescribed by law, it did not address the question of whether the interference was necessary and proportionate. It remains questionable, therefore, whether the desire to stop individuals from pursuing a course of conduct, which the majority of society regards as unacceptable, can ever be a sufficient justification for interfering with free speech and the right to peaceful assembly. It is hoped that the courts will refuse to allow this particular power to be used in cases where no breach of the peace or criminal conduct can be proven. If not, the right of free speech and assembly will be in danger of being suppressed on the inadequate grounds of convenience and intolerance.

Breach of the peace and the European Convention on Human Rights

Now that the Human Rights Act 1998 is in force, the courts will have to attempt to consider the case law of the European Court and Commission in this area. In this respect the European Court of Human Rights has held in the case of *Steel v United Kingdom*[294] that the law relating to breach of the peace and its use to restrict the right of peaceful demonstration is in general conformity with the European Convention. In that case one of the applicants had been arrested when, as part of a demonstration against a grouse shoot, she had walked in front of an armed member of the shoot, thereby preventing him from shooting. She was charged with

---

[292] (1999) 30 EHRR 241.
[293] See, in particular, *Sunday Times v United Kingdom* (1979) 2 EHRR 245.
[294] (1999) 28 EHRR 603.

causing a breach of the peace and was detained for 44 hours before appearing in court. At the trial the complaint of breach of the peace was proved and she was bound over to keep the peace for 12 months, with a penalty of £100 for any breach of that order. When she refused to be bound over she was imprisoned for 28 days. Another applicant had been arrested while taking part in a demonstration against the building of a motorway extension when she had stood in front of a digger and was charged with conduct likely to cause a breach of the peace, being detained for 18 hours before appearing in court. At her trial she was found to have committed a breach of the peace and was bound over for 12 months in the sum of £100. Again, she refused to obey the order and was committed to prison for seven days. The other applicants had been arrested for handing out leaflets and holding up banners against the sale of arms at a helicopter conference in London. The applicants had been detained for approximately seven hours, although the proceedings against them were subsequently dropped.

All applicants claimed that there had been a violation of their rights to liberty and security of the person, a fair trial and freedom of expression. The European Court held that although breach of the peace was not a criminal offence, it amounted to 'an offence' within Article 5(1)(c) of the Convention, which allows an arrest for the purpose of affecting an arrest or detention of someone who has committed an offence. With regard to whether that arrest was 'lawful' for the purpose of Article 5, the Court was satisfied that the concept of breach of the peace had been sufficiently clarified by the domestic courts so as to allow a person to foresee to a reasonable degree the legal consequences of his actions. In this respect the Court noted that domestic law only allowed a person to be arrested if he or she had caused a breach of the peace, or was reasonably feared to be likely to cause one. Applying those principles to the present cases, the Court held that in all but the case of the final applicants, the police had been justified in fearing that the applicant's behaviour would provoke a breach of the peace. The detention of those applicants for refusing to be bound over was compatible with Article 5(1)(b) – for non-compliance of a court order – and constituted a lawful and proportionate restriction of their freedom of expression under Article 10. However, in the case of those applicants who were merely handing out leaflets, their actions did not involve any behaviour that could have justified the police in apprehending a breach of the peace. Accordingly, their arrests and detentions were found to be unlawful under Article 5. Further, such restrictions were not 'prescribed by law' under Article 10(2), and having regard to the activities of the applicants, their treatment was not proportionate to the aim of preventing disorder and thus not necessary in a democratic society.

The judgment in *Steel* is, in some respects, a very cautious one. Not only does the Court uphold the general legality of the concept of breach of the peace, but it also regards the sanctions for its breach as generally proportionate to the aims of securing public order. Thus, once the Court was satisfied that an applicant's behaviour came within the concept of breach of the peace, it was prepared to uphold the sanctions imposed in the case as a necessary means of upholding the rule of law and the authority of the judiciary. Although the Court found the restrictions on the final applicants disproportionate, this was after it had found that the restrictions lacked a proper legal basis. The decision does not, therefore, suggest that the Court will insist that penalties imposed on demonstrators be strictly proportionate. Again, the decision that there had been a violation of Articles 5 and 10 in relation to the final applicants might be taken as indicating that the police authorities had clearly misapplied the domestic law, rather than that breach of the peace laws must accommodate reasonable activities, even though they might excite a violent response in others. As there was no evidence that the activities had caused, or were likely to cause, any breach of the peace, the Court's judgment may well have been different had there been such evidence, even though the applicant's activities might have been considered 'reasonable'.[295]

Freedom of assembly and European Union law

European Union law has an application to this area of law, both in justifying the restrictions on freedom of assembly when it interferes with community rights such as the free movement of goods, and of providing a test of proportionality when balancing such rights. These issues were raised in the case of *R* v *Chief Constable of Sussex, ex parte International Trader's Ferry Ltd*.[296] The Chief Constable of Sussex had decided to provide limited police presence at ports where protests were taking place against the export of live animals. The applicants claimed that this decision was both irrational and contrary to Article 34 (now Article 29) of the EC Treaty. The House of Lords held that any interference with the free movement of goods could be justified by reference to Article 36 (now Article 30) of the EC Treaty on public policy grounds – to secure adequate policing for the remainder of the district. Further, it was held that the Chief Constable's decision was a proportionate measure, which attempted to balance the right to carry out a lawful trade with the right of peaceful protest and the public cost of policing such a dispute.[297]

The decision in *International Trader's Ferry* suggests that both the European Court of Justice and the European Court of Human Rights would afford the domestic authorities a wide margin of appreciation in balancing the commercial interests of traders and the fundamental right to take part in peaceful protest. Thus, although in that case the courts upheld the interferences with the traders' interests, and as a consequence upheld the rights of the protestors, there is no reason to suggest that the domestic and European Courts would not have taken the same approach had the protestors brought an action against the police authorities for not adequately accommodating their right to peaceful protest.[298]

---

[295] The general decision in *Steel* was followed in the recent case of *Smith* v *Procurator Fiscal*, a decision of the Scottish courts, decision of the High Court of Justiciary, Appeal Court, 28 September 2001. The defendant had been charged with breach of the peace when she had lain down in a road outside a naval base used to hold nuclear weapons and had refused to move when requested. Upholding the convictions, the High Court held that it was clear that the definition of breach of the peace – which required that conduct had to cause alarm to ordinary people and threaten serious disturbance to the community, or, where there was no evidence of actual alarm, had to be flagrant in order to justify a conviction – was sufficiently clear and comprehensive to comply with the Convention and its case law. The decision appears to be consistent with the European Convention: *Lucas* v *United Kingdom* (2003) 37 EHRR CD 86.

[296] [1999] 2 AC 418. See Barnard and Hare, Police Discretion and the Rule of Law: Economic Community Rights versus Civil Rights (2000) 63 MLR 581.

[297] Contrast *R* v *Coventry City Council, ex parte Phoenix Aviation* [1995] 3 All ER 37, where the Divisional Court held that the Council could not interfere with the applicant's lawful trade activities solely because of the threat to public order. Such a decision would now have to be proportionate under both EC and European Convention Law.

[298] In *Eugen Schmidberger, Internationale Transport und Planzuge* v *Austria, The Times,* 27 June 2003, the European Court of Justice held that the Austrian Government had not acted unlawfully in refusing to ban a demonstration by environmentalists that blocked a motorway for 30 hours. Although there had been an interference with Articles 30 and 34 of the EC Treaty, that was justified on grounds of public policy and by the principles of freedom of expression.

Terrorism and freedom of assembly and association

The considerable powers to control and interfere with freedom of liberty, speech and assembly may be strengthened in the context of the fight against terrorism. In such circumstances the fear of terrorist activity might influence parliament in increasing police powers in this respect and this might be augmented by a deferential approach from the courts when such powers are challenged. The House of Lords' decision in *R (Gillan and Another) v Commissioner of the Police for the Metropolis*,[299] along with the appeal case before the European Court of Human Rights – *Gillan and Quinton v United Kingdom*[300] – provide contrasting judicial approaches to the interpretation and application of police powers of stop and search under the anti-terrorism provisions. The relevant provision and the cases will be examined in detail in chapter 14 of the text, although a brief review will be given here to assess the impact of them on the general right of freedom of expression and assembly.

Section 44 of the Terrorism Act 2000 provided the Home Secretary with a power to authorise a stop and search where he considers it expedient for the prevention of acts of terrorism and then bestows on police officers a power to stop a pedestrian in an authorised area and to search that person or anything carried by him. In this case the order had been confirmed by the Home Secretary (under s.46(4) of the Act) and was renewed on 9 September 2003 on the ground that it was near the anniversary of 11 September and that the Defence Systems and Equipment International Exhibition was being held at the Excel Centre in London. The claimants were each separately stopped and searched under this authorisation on their way to the exhibition – G was going to take part in a peaceful demonstration against the exhibition and the other claimant was a press reporter. Both were permitted to go on their way after the stop and search had been completed, but they argued that the authorisation was unlawful.

The House of Lords held that the word 'expedient' in s.44 had a meaning quite distinct from 'necessary' and that parliament had appreciated the significance of the power and thought it an appropriate measure to protect the public against the grave risks posed by terrorism, provided the power was subject to effective restraints, as it was under this legislation. In any case their Lordships doubted whether there had been any interference with Convention rights in this case: there was no deprivation of liberty as the applicants were merely being kept from proceeding or kept waiting, and the superficial search was not serious enough to amount to a violation of the applicant's right to private life under Article 8. Further, the House of Lords held it would be rare where such a power would give rise to an infringement of Articles 10 or 11, and if they did any interference would be justified under the exceptions provided under Articles 5, 8, 10 and 11.

However, those powers and the decision of the House of Lords were questioned before the European Court, and in *Gillan and Quinton v United Kingdom*[301] it was held that the powers were neither sufficiently prescribed by law nor proportionate. The Court concluded that the exercise of the police powers in the present case clearly interfered with the applicants' private life and then concluded that the powers under the 2000 Act were not sufficiently curbed by adequate legal safeguards so as to be in accordance with the law as required by Article 8(2).

---

[299] [2006] 2 AC 307. See O'Brien, Judicial Review under the Human Rights Act: Legislative or Applied Review [2007] EHRLR 550.
[300] (2010) 50 EHRR 45.
[301] (2010) 50 EHRR 45.

In particular, the Court was concerned with the breadth of the discretion conferred on the individual police officer; the officer's decision to stop and search an individual being based exclusively on a 'hunch' or 'professional intuition'. In general, the Court noted that although the powers of authorisation and confirmation were subject to judicial review, the breadth of the discretion involved meant that applicants faced formidable obstacles in showing that any authorisation and confirmation were unlawful; as shown in the applicants' case, judicial review or an action in damages to challenge the exercise of the stop and search powers by a police officer were unlikely to succeed. The absence of any obligation on the part of the officer to show a reasonable suspicion made it almost impossible to prove that that power had been improperly exercised. Consequently, the Court considered that the powers of authorisation and confirmation as well as those of stop and search under the Act were neither sufficiently circumscribed nor subject to adequate legal safeguards against abuse and were not 'in accordance with the law'.

The case was decided under Article 8 of the Convention (the right to private life), and, given its finding under Article 8, the Court held that it was not necessary to examine the applicants' complaints under Articles 10 and 11 (or Article 5). However, in its decision, the Court noted that there was a risk that such a widely framed power could be misused against demonstrators and protestors in breach of Articles 10 and 11. In that sense, therefore, the decision can be used by the domestic courts to subject a variety of domestic law powers that interfere with the right of peaceful demonstration to strict rules of legality and proportionality.[302]

Questions

How can the police's power to preserve the peace be reconciled with freedom of expression and the right to demonstrate?

Contrast the decisions of the House of Lords in *Laporte* and *Gillan*, above. What differences can you see in judicial approach in the two cases?

CASE STUDY

DPP v *Redmond-Bate* [1999] Crim LR 998

The case involves the classic dilemma in relation to demonstrations and the law. The apparently peaceful actions or words of the demonstrators provoke a violent, or potentially violent, reaction from others. The police, fearing a breach of the peace, decide to take action against the demonstrators and the courts must decide whether to uphold the demonstrators' fundamental right to protest peacefully, or to uphold the police's duty to preserve the peace. The case suggests that the domestic courts may develop a robust stance in this area, providing demonstrators with protection of such rights over and above that given by the European Court and Commission of Human Rights.

In this case three members of a Christian fundamentalist group, known as Faith Ministries, were on the steps of Wakefield Cathedral, addressing passers-by on their views on religion

---

[302] Following the decision, and the Grand Chamber's refusal to hear the case on appeal, the new coalition government announced plans for the immediate suspension of those powers pending their repeal. See Ford and Gibbs, No More Stop and Search in Curbs on Anti-terror Police, *The Times*, 9 July 2009.

and morality, having agreed with the police that they would be doing this. In response to a complaint made by an unidentified couple, a police officer had approached the speakers and warned them that they should not approach any person. The officer then left, but later returned to find that a large crowd had gathered and that some members of the crowd were showing hostility towards the speakers. A gang of youths who had been chanting and swearing were moved on by the officer and other members of the crowd were now shouting at the speakers, telling them to 'shut up' and shouting 'bloody lock them up'. Fearing a breach of the peace, the officer asked the speakers to stop addressing the crowd and when they refused they were all arrested for breach of the peace. Mrs Redmond-Bate was subsequently charged under s.89(2) of the Police Act 1997 for obstructing a police officer in the execution of his duty. She was convicted and her appeal to the Crown Court was dismissed. She now appealed to the Divisional Court, who had to consider two questions:

1 whether in the circumstances of the case it was reasonable for the police officer to arrest the appellant who had not conducted herself in a manner which would be said to be an offence under the Public Order Act 1986 when any apprehension by the police of violence or threat of violence which could be said to be likely to breach criminal law emanated from others present;

2 whether it was proper for the Court to conclude that such actual or threatened violence was or would be the natural consequence of the appellant's actions.

Delivering judgment, SEDLEY LJ held that the question whether a police officer reasonably apprehended a breach of the peace was an objective one for the court to decide, although one which had to be evaluated by the court without the benefit of hindsight. His Lordship also held that the question in this case had to be decided on the basis of where the threat was coming from, because, in his Lordship's opinion, it was there that the police officer's preventive action must be directed. His Lordship cited the case of *Beatty* v *Gilbanks* ((1882) 9 QBD 308), where it was held that Salvation Army marchers could not be guilty of an unlawful assembly merely because it was foreseeable that their march might cause others to react unlawfully and violently. In contrast, his Lordship then considered the case of *Wise* v *Dunning* ([1902] 1 KB 167), where a person was arrested for breach of the peace, when addressing a crowd of Roman Catholics, he had waved a crucifix over his head and referred to Catholics as 'Rednecks'.

His Lordship then referred to the case of *Duncan* v *Jones* ([1936] KB 218), where a woman had been arrested for obstruction of a police officer when she had refused to hold a meeting further down the road, the police officer anticipating that the meeting would occasion a breach of the peace. It was argued that that case was authority for the principle that a person who had acted in an entirely lawful manner could be arrested for obstruction if such an arrest was necessary to preserve the peace. It had been argued that the distinction between *Jones* and *Beatty* v *Gilbanks* was that a person arrested for obstruction was only indirectly responsible for their lawful behaviour. However, in his Lordship's opinion, the critical distinction between *Duncan* and *Beatty* v *Gilbanks* was that in the former case the threat to public order was coming from the speaker herself, while in the latter case the threat clearly came from another source. Thus, it was crucial in the present case to determine where the threat was coming from.

Referring to the case of *R v Nicol and Selvanayagam* (*The Times*, 22 November 1995), SEDLEY LJ confirmed that for a court to uphold a binding over order, the conduct in question must be a clear interference with the rights of others and that in all the circumstances the court must be satisfied that it was the defendant (rather than other persons) who was acting unreasonably. Turning to the present case, SEDLEY LJ held that the Crown Court had erred by stating that lawful conduct could, if persisted in, lead to a conviction for wilful obstruction of a police officer. In his Lordship's opinion that proposition had no basis in law and accordingly a police officer had no right to call upon a citizen to desist from lawful conduct unless such conduct would, by interfering with the rights and liberties of others, provoke violence in circumstances where it would not be entirely unreasonable for a constable to take steps to prevent it.

In coming to that conclusion, his Lordship considered the importance of Articles 9 and 10 of the European Convention, guaranteeing, respectively, freedom of thought, conscience and religion and freedom of speech. Although the Human Rights Act is not in force, it will require that the common law is compatible with the values of the European Convention. There is, therefore, good reason for policing the law to respect the Convention. Having regard to the decision of the European Court of Human Rights in *Steel v United Kingdom* ((1999) 28 EHRR 603), that the arrest of three protestors for taking part in entirely peaceful protest was disproportionate to the aim of preventing disorder, it must be the case that a police officer has no right to call upon a citizen to desist from lawful conduct. It is only if otherwise lawful conduct gives rise to a reason-able apprehension that it will, by interfering with the rights or liberties of others, provoke violence which, though unlawful, would not be entirely unreasonable, that a constable is empowered to take steps to prevent it. His Lordship also rejected the argument that the speaker would not be guilty of a breach of the peace provided that what he said was not offensive. In his Lordship's opinion, free speech included not only the inoffensive, but also the irritating, the contentious, the eccentric, the heretical, the unwelcome and the provocative provided it did not tend to provoke violence. Freedom only to speak inoffensively is not worth having. What Speakers' Corner illustrates is the tolerance which is both extended by the law to opinion of every kind and expected by the law in the conduct of those who disagree, even strongly, with what they hear. To proceed, as did the Crown Court, that from the fact that three women were preaching about morality, God and the Bible to a reasonable apprehension that violence is going to erupt is both illiberal and illogical.

On the facts, the situation perceived by the police officer did not justify him in per-ceiving a breach of the peace, much less a breach of the peace for which the three women would be responsible. The officer had done precisely the right thing with the three youths and sent them on their way. There was no suggestion of highway obstruction. Nobody had to stop and listen. If they did so, they were as free to express the view that the preach-ers should be locked up or silenced as the appellant and her companions were to preach. A police officer can only take action against either person when both are threatening violence or behaving in a manner that might provoke violence. Thus the police officer was not acting in the course of his duty when he required the women to stop addressing the crowd and the appellant was not therefore guilty of obstructing the officer.

Questions

1 Why did SEDLEY LJ overturn the decision of both the Magistrates' Court and the Crown Court? Were their decisions simply wrong on the facts or did they offend any human rights principles?

2 How, and in what respects, does SEDLEY LJ's judgment uphold the rights of freedom of expression and freedom of assembly?

3 How does SEDLEY LJ distinguish the cases of *Duncan* v *Jones* and *Beatty* v *Gilbanks*, and is that distinction satisfactory?

4 How practicable is it to apply a test that requires that conduct must interfere with the rights of others and be unreasonable before it attracts the power of the police to intervene?

5 Do you agree that the conduct of the demonstrators in this case was not unreasonable? If it wasn't, when would it have become so?

6 Is it practicable to require that the police deal only with those who are acting unreasonably and whose conduct is likely to cause a breach of the peace? What would be the situation if there had been a clearer violent, or potentially violent response from the crowd?

7 How does the decision in *Redmond-Bate* reflect the principles laid down in the European Court decision in *Steel* v *United Kingdom*?

8 Does the European Convention on Human Rights, and the relevant case law, require that lawful conduct should never be the subject of criminal liability or other restraint?

9 How is the decision in *Redmond-Bate* affected by the subsequent decisions of the domestic courts in *Laporte* and *Austin*?

Conclusions on freedom of assembly

With regard to freedom of assembly, although the traditional common law approach was sceptical of the right of peaceful assembly, and gave to the police and other authorities wide powers to control demonstrations and other assemblies for the purpose of controlling public order, there are signs that domestic law and its application is being relaxed in favour of free speech and peaceful assembly. Ironically, this development may have had less to do with the Human Rights Act 1998 and the case law of the European Convention, than the willingness of the domestic judiciary to interpret the law in the light of the right to demonstrate. Thus, the decisions in *Jones and Lloyd* v *DPP*, *DPP* v *Redmond-Bate*, *Percy* v *DPP* and *Laporte*, although taking into consideration the relevant articles of the Convention, seem to be the product of the constitutional right of liberty, free speech and assembly at common law. The cases certainly seem to go beyond the case law of the European Convention, which has, at least until very recently, displayed a reluctance to question the domestic authorities' power to balance freedom of expression with public order. On the other hand, there exist a variety of statutory and common law provisions that give the authorities a wide power to control demonstrations and which are often applied irrespective of the peaceful intentions of those taking part in the demonstration. These provisions must be interpreted carefully, although the case law of the Convention suggests that the Court will only interfere in exceptional circumstances, where the measures taken to control such freedoms are arbitrary and disproportionate. In addition, the decision of the House of Lords in *Austin* v *Commissioner of Police of the Metropolis*[303] serves

---

[303] [2008] 2 WLR 415.

as a reminder that the domestic courts are on occasion prepared to provide a wide margin of discretion to the police when the right to demonstrate is in conflict with public safety and the rights of others.

With respect to reform, before the May 2010 elections there had been proposals to repeal and amend a number of domestic provisions. The Labour government had issued a Green Paper seeking views on the framework governing the right to protest around parliament (under the Serious Organised Crime and Police Act 2005) and the general law on protests and demonstrations.[304] This was followed by a White Paper,[305] and the Governance of Britain Draft Constitutional Renewal Bill,[306] which recommended the repeal of the provisions under the 2005 Act. At the same time the Joint Committee on Human Rights published its seventh report of 2008–2009 on demonstrations,[307] recommending the repeal of the 2005 Act with respect to protests around parliament, the revision of s.5 of the Public Order Act 1986 and the clarification of arrest powers under terrorism legislation.

Clause 32 of the Constitutional Reform and Governance Bill 2009, which would have repealed sections 132–8 of the 2005 Act and replaced it with powers akin to those in s.12 of the Public Order Act 1986, was dropped from the Constitutional Reform and Governance 2009 Act, and at the time of writing there has been no change to the law regarding s.5 of the Public Order Act 1986. A private member's bill – the Constitutional Renewal Bill 2009 – recommended the repeal of sections 132–8, but that bill appeared to be lost following the general election in 2010. However, following the decision in *Gillan and Quinton* v *United Kingdom*,[308] the coalition government announced plans to repeal the police's power to stop and search under s.44 of the Terrorism Act 2000.

Question

How, if at all, has the Human Rights Act 1998 impacted on the right of peaceful assembly?

Further reading

Textbooks

A new text – Mead, *The New Law of Peaceful Protest: Rights and Regulation in the Human Rights Act Era* (Hart 2010) – provides an excellent coverage of the domestic law of demonstrations and its compatibility with the Human Rights Act and the European Convention.

A number of texts on the European Convention contain excellent chapters on Article 11 of the Convention and its relevant case law: Harris, Warbrick, Bates and O'Boyle, *Law of the European*

---

[304] *The Governance of Britain* (CM 7170), paras 164–6.
[305] *The Governance of Britain – Constitutional Renewal* (CM 73421, March 2008).
[306] *The Governance of Britain – Constitutional Reform Bill* (CM 7342-11, March 2008).
[307] 'Demonstrating respect for rights? A human rights approach to policing protests' (2008–2009), available at www.publications.parliament.uk/pa/jt200809/jtselect/jtrights/47/47i.pdf. See also the government's response: Cm 7633, May 2009.
[308] (2010) 50 EHRR 45. The case is detailed in this chapter and chapters 6 and 11.

Convention on Human Rights (OUP 2009, 2nd edn), chapter 12; Ovey and White, *Jacobs and White: The European Convention on Human Rights* (OUP 2010, 5th edn), chapter 14; Mowbray's *Cases and Materials on the European Convention* (OUP 2007, 2nd edn), chapter 12.

For the protection of freedom of association and assembly in both domestic law and international law, see Clayton and Tomlinson, *The Law of Human Rights* (OUP 2009, 2nd edn), chapter 16, which provides an expansive coverage of the topic. See also Barendt, *Freedom of Speech* (OUP 2005), chapter 8.

Articles

The following articles also provide interesting reading in specific aspects of freedom of association and assembly: Sottiaux, Anti-Democratic Associations: Content and Consequences in Article 11 Adjudication [2004] (4) Netherlands Human Rights Quarterly 585; Fenwick, The Right To Protest, the Human Rights Act and the Margin of Appreciation (1999) 62 MLR 491; Fenwick, Marginalising Human Rights: Breach of the Peace, 'Kettling', the HRA and Public Protest [2009] PL 737; Fenwick and Phillipson, Public Protest, the Human Rights Act and Judicial Responses to Political Expression [2000] PL 627; Geddis, Free Speech Martyrs or Unreasonable Threats to Social Peace? – 'Insulting' Expression and Section 5 of the Public Order Act 1986 [2004] PL 853; Hare, Crosses, Crescents and Sacred Cows: Criminalising Incitement to Religious Hatred [2006] PL 521; Keane, Attacking Hate Speech under Article 17 of the European Convention on Human Rights [2007] Netherlands Human Rights Quarterly 241; Mead, Strasbourg Discovers the Right to Counter Demonstrate – A Note on *Ollinger* v *Austria* [2007] EHRLR 133; Mead, The Right to Peaceful Process under the European Convention on Human Rights – A Content Study of Strasbourg Case Law [2007] EHRLR 345; Mead, Of Kettles, Cordons and Crowd Control – *Austin* v *Commissioner of the Police for the Metropolis* and the Meaning of 'Deprivation of Liberty' [2009] EHRLR 376.

Visit **www.mylawchamber.co.uk/fosterhumanrights**
to access regular updates to major changes in the law,
further case studies, weblinks, and suggested
answers/approaches to questions in the book.

11 The right to private and family life

Introduction

In *S and Marper* v *United Kingdom*, the European Court of Human Rights held that the retention of the DNA and other records of those acquitted of criminal charges was a disproportionate interference with their right to private life.

In *Countryside Alliance* v *United Kingdom*, the same Court held that the statutory banning of hunting with hounds did not interfere with the private life of the participants.

In *Mosley* v *News Group Newspapers*, the domestic courts held that a newspaper had unjustifiably interfered with M's right to private life when it reported details of his sado-masochistic encounter with a number of women.

In *Dickson* v *United Kingdom*, the European Court held that the secretary of state had acted disproportionately in refusing a request by a life sentence prisoner to make use of artificial insemination facilities so to allow him and his wife to start a family whilst he was in prison.

All these cases involved a court deciding whether someone had a right to private and/ or family life, and if so whether it had been interfered with and whether there was justification for that interference. This chapter examines the concept of private and family life and how that right is protected and restricted in both domestic law and under the European Convention on Human Rights. It also examines how the often difficult balance between those rights and other interests is maintained.

This chapter examines the protection of private life (or privacy) under both Article 8 of the European Convention on Human Rights and in domestic law. In addition, it will examine some aspects of the right to family life, as guaranteed by Article 8, and the right to marry and found a family, as guaranteed by Article 12. However, the chapter will not provide detailed analysis of all aspects of family and private life and will thus exclude many aspects of family and child law which warrant independent and specialist study. Although the terms 'privacy' and 'private life' are mostly used interchangeably, the term privacy will be used specifically when dealing with areas such as press freedom versus individual privacy and access to personal information.

The chapter will look at the notion of privacy and private life and its scope for protection under Articles 8 and 12 of the European Convention. The chapter will then examine the growth of the domestic law of privacy, both before the passing of the Human Rights Act 1998 and in the post-Act era, measuring its compatibility with the Convention and any relevant case law. It will then provide an analysis of specific areas of privacy, such as privacy and press freedom, access to personal information, privacy and personal autonomy and integrity, privacy and surveillance, the right to private sexual life and the right to private and family life of prisoners.

Thus, this chapter will cover:

- An examination of the importance, nature and scope of the right to privacy and private and family life.

- An examination and analysis of the scope and extent of the state's obligation under the European Convention to protect private and family life.

- An examination of the domestic law's efforts to protect private and family life, both before and after the Human Rights Act 1998.

- An examination of the application of privacy interests with respect to issues such as privacy and press freedom, access to personal information, personal autonomy, surveillance, sexual privacy and prisoners' right to private and family life.

Nature and scope of the right to privacy and private life

The protection of the right to privacy and private life gives rise to a number of legal and constitutional difficulties. First, it is necessary to define 'privacy' and its boundaries for the purposes of recognising its legal existence. As the notion of privacy and private life is often nebulous, domestic law might be reluctant to pass or develop a specific law of privacy, preferring to rely on established legal principles, such as the laws of trespass and confidentiality, which recognise and protect more tangible rights and interests.[1] Secondly, the law will need to determine the extent of the right to privacy and, more specifically, when it is legitimate to violate that right. As Article 8(2) of the European Convention admits, privacy and other related rights can be compromised for a variety of legitimate reasons: the detection of crime can justify surveillance techniques; public morality may justify the control of even private acts of sexuality, or sexual preference; and freedom of speech and press freedom may justify intrusions into an individual's private life and justify the disclosure of confidential information. Although any law will require the setting of boundaries and the provision of defences, the already vague character of privacy may dissuade the legislators and judges from making or developing the law in this area. Thirdly, even if domestic law decides to enact and develop a law of privacy, it will then need to achieve a balance between the enjoyment of that right and the protection of other individual rights and public interests. Again, although this is true of any legal right, the absence of developed principles of legality and proportionality before the coming into operation of the Human Rights Act, and the uncertain character of privacy and private life, contributed to a general reluctance to accommodate this right in domestic law and still poses acute dilemmas for the legal system.

---

[1] As evidenced in cases such as *Malone v Metropolitan Police Commissioner (No 2)* [1979] Ch 344 and *Kaye v Robertson* [1991] FSR 62, considered later in the chapter.

What is privacy?

What do we actually mean when we talk of the right to privacy or the right to private life? In one sense, when we talk of the right to privacy we are referring to the general right to be left alone, a desire to be allowed to enjoy a particular space, either alone or with others, which the state or others should not be allowed to penetrate. This can refer to one's property as well as to one's physical person, and can also allow the enjoyment of privacy with others, such as family and friends.[2] Thus, laws of trespass and nuisance are capable of protecting these privacy interests, although more specific laws that identify personal space may be needed to provide fuller protection of individual privacy.[3] The right to privacy, or more specifically, the right to private life, may also refer to the right to make choices about one's life, such as whom you may marry or associate with, what literature you are allowed to read, whether you should undertake an operation, and decisions relating to your sexual orientation or activity. The right to personal autonomy and physical and human dignity demands that you should be allowed to make these choices without undue interference by the state or other individuals.

The right to privacy may refer more specifically to the protection of information that is personal to you or an associate: the revelation of personal or family secrets or any other information that one would prefer to keep either to oneself or within a particular group of associates. In domestic law, the laws of confidentiality, data protection and defamation seek to protect unwanted disclosures of information that are either personal to that particular individual or otherwise damaging to his or her reputation or honour. However, such laws are surrounded by technical limitations and do not always protect the true spirit of privacy. These limitations, and the distinction between privacy and confidentiality, were illustrated in *R v Broadcasting Complaints Commission, ex parte Granada Television*.[4] Two parents of murdered children complained to the BCC that Granada TV had, without their prior permission and without notification, broadcast programmes that identified and dealt with their children's cases. Under s.143 of the Broadcasting Act 1990 the BCC had a duty to consider and adjudicate upon complaints of unwarranted infringements of privacy in, or in connection with, the obtaining of material included in television or sound programmes. The applicants claimed that as the deaths had been reported publicly in the past, the matter was in the public domain and could not form the basis of an infringement of privacy under s.143. The BCC upheld the complaints, finding that the programmes had been guilty of an unwarranted infringement of privacy by not forewarning the parents. The fact that a matter had once been in the public domain could not prevent its resurrection, possibly several years later, from being an infringement of privacy, and whether there was an unwarranted infringement was a matter of fact and degree for the decision of the BCC.[5] As we shall see, the principles evident in this case have informed the development of the law of confidentiality under the Human Rights Act 1998.[6]

The right to privacy or private life thus reflects a number of values and principles: personal autonomy and dignity; reputation and honour; bodily integrity; and the formation and

---

[2] But see *R (Countryside Alliance) v Attorney General* [2007] 3 WLR 922, where it was held that the hunting ban imposed by the Hunting Act 2004 did not engage the landowners' or the hunters' right to private and home life under Article 8. See also *Friend v United Kingdom; Countryside Alliance v United Kingdom* (2010) EHRR SE6.

[3] Such as laws to stop harassment or intrusions into private life by the press, discussed below.

[4] [1995] EMLR 163.

[5] In addition, the word 'privacy' was not confined to matters concerning the individual complainant but extended to the family of such persons.

[6] Discussed under both the law of confidentiality, and privacy and press freedom, below. See also chapter 9, pages 466–9.

continuance of personal and other relationships. At the heart of these values lies the right of individual liberty: the right of the individual to exist as such in the context of an organised state. The right to privacy is thus eternally in conflict with the power of the state to regulate individual and group conduct, and with the obligation of the state and its law to ensure that individual privacy is not enjoyed at the unreasonable expense of other rights. The chapter will now examine how the right to private (and family) life is defined and protected under the European Convention on Human Rights. This will provide the basis of an examination of domestic law in this area, and its compatibility with the Convention.

Questions

What do you understand by the right to privacy or the right to private life?

What values does that right uphold?

Privacy and the European Convention on Human Rights

Article 8 provides that everyone has the right to *respect* for their private and family life, their home and correspondence. Article 8 clearly goes further than protecting a person's right to privacy in the sense discussed above. In addition to protecting an individual's right to private life, it also covers his right to family life, his home and his correspondence. Nevertheless, the protection of private life is clearly wide enough to cover privacy issues relating to the protection of, and access to, personal information, and interference with privacy and the home by surveillance techniques, as well as such matters as sexual privacy and physical integrity. In particular, because the right to private life is enjoyed alongside the right to family life, Article 8 envisages the right to form private relationships with other people, and does not merely contain a negative duty to leave individuals alone.

The scope of Article 8

Article 8 includes the right to be free from unlawful and unreasonable interferences with those interests – either from the actions of the state or the actions of other individuals or groups of individuals. Also, in certain cases the state may be responsible for providing the physical and other resources necessary for the enjoyment of these rights. Thus, in *Marckx* v *Belgium*,[7] it was accepted that a state might have an obligation to ensure that an individual leads a normal family life by recognising the status of illegitimate children.[8] Where the claim is that the state has interfered with an individual's Article 8 rights, the applicant has the burden of proving that there was such interference,[9] although it is not always necessary to show that the state has committed a specific act of interference.[10]

---

[7] (1979) 2 EHRR 330.

[8] See also *Airey* v *Ireland* (1979) 2 EHRR 305.

[9] For example, proving that state officials intercepted the applicant's correspondence. See *Halford* v *United Kingdom* (1997) 24 EHRR 523.

[10] For example, in *Dudgeon* v *United Kingdom* (1982) 4 EHRR 149, the European Court accepted that the mere existence of laws prohibiting certain sexual activity constituted an interference with private life, and in *Klass* v *Federal Republic of Germany* (1978) 2 EHRR 214, the European Court held that the mere existence of legislation permitting secret surveillance constituted a menace that struck at the right of communication.

571

The Article covers a variety of private and family interests, including the right to respect for one's physical integrity, the right to one's own space, and the right to communicate private information with others. In addition it has been used to allow individuals to have access to personal information, going further than Article 10 in that respect.[11] The right to private and family life also includes the right to a private sexual life, including the right to choose and practise one's sexual identity, and to forge relationships with others and to enjoy the benefits of family and home life.[12] Article 8 can also be used in conjunction with other articles so as to further protect other Convention rights, such as the right to be free from ill-treatment, freedom of expression, and freedom of thought, conscience and religion. In addition, the right to privacy is related to individual liberty and, for example, a wrongful or arbitrary arrest can involve a breach of Article 5 as well as Article 8.[13] Article 8 refers to the right to private life rather than the right to privacy, but otherwise the scope of the article is very similar to other international rights to privacy, covering a variety of individual and collective interests.[14]

Article 8 is a conditional right and interferences with the exercise of the right by a public authority are permitted under Article 8(2) provided they are in accordance with law and necessary in a democratic society in the interests of national security, public safety or the economic well-being of the country, for the prevention of disorder or crime, for the protection of health or morals, or for the protection of the rights and freedoms of others. Although paragraph 2 states that there shall be no interference by a *public authority* with the exercise of the right in Article 8, the European Court has accepted that the state is responsible for ensuring that an individual's Article 8 rights are not interfered with, either by state officials or by private individuals.[15]

The right to respect of private life

The European Court has given a broad interpretation to the term 'private life', extending the protection of Article 8 beyond the concept of interference with a person's private space. Thus, in *Niemietz* v *Germany*,[16] the European Court held that it would be too restrictive to limit the notion of private life to an 'inner circle' in which the individual may live his own personal life as he chooses, and thus respect for private life must also comprise, to a certain degree, the right to develop and establish relationships with other human beings. Further, the Court held that Article 8 applied to individual activities of a professional or business nature since it is in their working lives that the majority of people have a significant opportunity of developing relationships with the outside world. Accordingly, in the area of secret surveillance the Court has found a violation of the right to private life in cases not only where the act was committed

---

[11] See *Gaskin* v *United Kingdom* (1989) 12 EHRR 36; *MG* v *United Kingdom* (2003) 36 EHRR 3. Contrast *Leander* v *Sweden* (1987) 9 EHRR 433, where it was held that Article 10 does not provide the general right to freedom of information.

[12] See Feldman, The Developing Scope of Article 8 of the European Convention on Human Rights [1997] EHRLR 265.

[13] Note in particular the case of *Gillan and Quinton* v *United Kingdom* (2010) 50 EHRR 45 with respect to stop and search powers, considered in chapters 6, 10 and 14 of this text.

[14] Article 17 of the International Covenant on Civil and Political Rights 1966 provides protection against arbitrary or unlawful interferences with privacy, family, home and correspondence (and to unlawful attacks on one's honour and reputation), and the right to the protection of the law against such interference.

[15] See *X and Y v Netherlands* (1985) 8 EHRR 235.

[16] (1992) 16 EHRR 97.

in or on the applicant's home,[17] but also where the interception was carried out on business premises.[18]

On the other hand, both the domestic and European courts have refused to accept that every activity, including pastimes, is a manifestation of the right to private life. Thus in *Friend v United Kingdom; Countryside Alliance v United Kingdom*,[19] the European Court declared as inadmissible applications alleging that the ban on hunting with hounds was in breach of Article 8 of the European Convention. The Court held that not every activity a person might engage in with others was protected by the article, and that hunting, by its very nature, was essentially a public activity and the hunting community could not be regarded as an ethnic or national minority or represent a particular lifestyle which was indispensable to a person's identity. Thus, the activity must not only be sufficiently private, but also sufficiently central to that person's private lifestyle.[20]

Article 8 protects a person's right to physical and moral integrity, and in *X and Y v Netherlands*[21] it was held that a state owes a positive duty to protect those interests from attack. The protection of this aspect of private life is supplemented by Article 3, which prohibits the subjection of individuals to torture and other forms of ill-treatment,[22] and again the Court has held that this article can have a horizontal effect by imposing a duty on the state to safeguard the rights of the applicant.[23] The European Court has also held that the term 'private life' covers an individual's health, so that where a government engages in activities that have hidden adverse consequences on the health of others, respect for private and family life requires that an effective procedure be established to allow such persons to seek relevant information.[24]

The right to private sexual life

The right to a private sexual life raises a number of Convention rights, including the right to private life under Article 8, and the right to marry under Article 12. In addition domestic law can often discriminate against certain individuals on the grounds of their sexual preferences or orientation, thus bringing into play Article 14 of the Convention.[25] The case law of the European Convention clearly establishes the right to a private sexual life. In *Dudgeon v United Kingdom*[26] it was held that the right to 'private life' under Article 8 includes the right to private sexual life and that an individual's sexual life is one of the most intimate aspects of private life as guaranteed by the Convention. Accordingly, any interference with an individual's private

---

[17] *Klass v FRG* (1978) 2 EHRR 214; *Malone v United Kingdom* (1984) 7 EHRR 14; *Khan v United Kingdom* (2000) 31 EHRR 45.

[18] *Halford v United Kingdom* (1997) 24 EHRR 523, where the European Court held that an individual was entitled to a private telephone conversation on work premises.

[19] (2010) 50 EHRR SE.

[20] See also *Pretty v United Kingdom* (2002) 35 EHRR 1.

[21] (1985) 8 EHRR 235.

[22] For example, in *Raninen v Finland* (1997) 26 EHRR 563, the Court accepted that Article 8 might afford protection in relation to the conditions of detention that do not attain the level of severity required by Article 3. On the facts, the Court held that the handcuffing of the applicant did not violate Articles 3 or 8.

[23] See *A v United Kingdom* (1999) 27 EHRR 611, where having found a violation of Article 3 because the state had not protected the applicant from ill-treatment by his stepfather, the Court did not find it necessary to consider a separate complaint under Article 8.

[24] *McGinley and Egan v United Kingdom* (1998) 27 EHRR 1.

[25] The rights of homosexuals and transsexuals to a private and family life will be studied in detail in chapter 13 of this text, on discrimination and human rights.

[26] (1982) 4 EHRR 149.

sexual life would need to be justified on very strong grounds. This reflects the need to promote individual autonomy and choice and to protect the enjoyment of private life from interference on the sole ground that it conflicts with majority public opinion and approval.

Nevertheless, Article 8 is a qualified right and the European Court has sanctioned interference with private sexuality on grounds such as health and morals. For example, in *Laskey, Jaggard and Brown* v *United Kingdom*[27] it was held that in certain circumstances a state was entitled to regulate and criminalise such behaviour, even where it took place between consenting adults. The case arose from the prosecution of several men who had performed a number of sado-masochistic acts on each other. The men had been found guilty of offences of malicious wounding and assault causing actual bodily harm, and the House of Lords confirmed that it was no defence to such charges that the victim had consented to the assault.[28] It was argued before the European Court of Human Rights that they had been subjected to an unjustified interference with their right to private life under Article 8, but the Court held that the prosecutions and subsequent convictions were necessary in a democratic society for the protection of health and morals. The Court held that the applicants' activities were not entirely a matter of private morality and that the state was entitled to regulate the infliction of such harm via the criminal law. Further, the degree of harm that the victim could consent to was principally a question for the state to determine at its discretion. The Court concluded that on the facts before it, given the intensity of the organisation of the acts, the limited number of charges that were eventually brought, and the reduced sentences, the interference corresponded to reasons that were relevant and sufficient, and were not disproportionate to the aims of that law.[29] The approach taken in *Laskey* was followed subsequently in *KA and AD* v *Belgium*,[30] where it was held that there had been no violation of Article 8 when two individuals had been convicted, fined, suspended from public service and imprisoned for assault occasioning actual bodily harm for taking part in filmed sado-masochistic acts. In the Court's view, given the intensity and dangerousness of some of the acts the measures taken against the applicants were necessary and proportionate, particularly as they had not honoured a promise to stop the actions if the participants so requested.

However, the European Court is more likely to intervene where there is evidence of discrimination. Thus, the decision in *Laskey* was distinguished in the later case of *ADT* v *United Kingdom*,[31] where the Court reaffirmed the right of private sexual life and the principle of individual choice. The applicant had been charged under s.13 of the Sexual Offences Act 1956 with committing an act of gross indecency with four other men. As more than two people were present, the defence that the participants were over 18 and that they consented was not available and accordingly the applicant was convicted. The applicants brought a claim under Article 8 of the European Convention claiming that his right to private life had been interfered with and, further, that there had been a violation of Article 8 in conjunction with Article 14, because the law only applied to acts between men. The European Court held that there had been an interference with the applicant's right under Article 8, and that such interference was clearly prescribed by law. With respect to the question of necessity, the Court held that

---

[27] (1997) 24 EHRR 39.

[28] *R* v *Brown* [1994] 1 AC 212.

[29] The Court also held that there was no evidence of bias against the applicants on the grounds of their homosexuality so as to constitute a violation of Article 14 of the Convention.

[30] Decision of the European Court of Human Rights, 17 February 2005.

[31] (2001) 31 EHRR 33.

although state interference might be justified where groups of men gather to perform sexual activity, and the possibility of such activities being publicised becomes inevitable, the facts of the case did not indicate the existence of such circumstances. The applicant had been involved in sexual activities with a restricted number of friends and it was unlikely that others would become aware of what was going on. Although the activities were on videotape, the applicant had been prosecuted for the activities themselves. Consequently, because the activities were private, the margin of appreciation would be narrow, and the reasons submitted for the maintenance in force of laws criminalising homosexual acts between men in private, and the prosecution and conviction in the present case, were not sufficient to justify the legislation and the interference.[32]

The European Court was, therefore, able to distinguish its judgment in *Laskey, Jaggard and Brown* and to restate the general principle that the state and its law has no place in the regulation of private sexual life among consenting adults. Nevertheless, the Court refused to look at the relevant law *in abstracto*, and thus did not declare the legislation itself in violation of Article 8. This leaves open the possibility that the Court will tolerate a certain level of discrimination in this field. Similar public morality is used to justify a number of obscenity and indecency laws, where the European Court has offered the state a very wide margin of error.[33] In addition, although there is evidence of some change of attitude on behalf of the European Court, it has sanctioned a good deal of interference with the private lives of homosexuals and, until recently, transsexuals.

The domestic courts must also ensure that legislation intended to restrict and criminalise sexual activity does not unduly interfere with an individual's right to private sexual life. However, it can grant a good deal of judicial deference to parliament in this area. For example, in *R v G*[34] the House of Lords held that it was not incompatible with a child's Article 8 rights to charge a 15-year-old boy with rape of a girl under 13.[35] Even though he could have been charged with a lesser offence under the Act the state was entitled to charge him with the offence of rape where that accurately described what he had done. Their Lordships noted that parliament had decided to use that description because a girl under the age of 13 was incapable of consenting to intercourse and it would have been open to criticism had it not provided the complainant with that protection. Neither did it constitute unlawful discrimination under Article 14, as the possibility of unwanted pregnancies justified the distinction between males and females with respect to committing the offence.

Homosexuality and the European Convention on Human Rights

The European Court has, on a number of occasions, ruled on the compatibility of criminal legislation and other domestic practices which discriminate against an individual on grounds of their sexual orientation.[36] In *Dudgeon v United Kingdom*[37] the European Court held that some regulation and inequality of treatment might be justified with respect to homosexuality.

---

[32] As the Court had found a violation of Article 8, it did not deem it necessary to consider the applicant's claim under Article 14. However, as the fact that the legislation only applied to men was taken into account by the Court in assessing necessity, it is likely that there was a violation of Article 14.

[33] *Handyside v United Kingdom* (1976) 1 EHRR 737.

[34] [2009] 1 AC 92.

[35] Under s.5 of the Sexual Offences Act 2003.

[36] This area, and the area of transsexuals and the Convention, will be dealt with in detail in chapter 13 of this text.

[37] (1982) 4 EHRR 149.

In that case the Court held that domestic law which placed an absolute prohibition on, *inter alia*, acts of buggery, irrespective of the age of the participants, constituted an interference with the applicant's right to respect for his private life. The Court was also satisfied that the restriction pursued legitimate aims under Article 8(2) – 'the protection of the rights and freedoms of others' and 'the protection of morals'. In the Court's view, some degree of regulation of male homosexual conduct, by means of the criminal law, could be justified and accepted that in so far as the applicant was prevented from having sexual relations with males under 21 years of age any restriction was justified as being necessary for the protection of the rights of others.[38]

The decision in *Dudgeon* still left states the right to distinguish between heterosexual and homosexual conduct.[39] However, although this margin of appreciation is still available, more recent case law suggests a very narrow margin would be offered to individual states. Thus, in *Sutherland* v *United Kingdom*[40] the European Commission found that the disparate age of consent in the United Kingdom regarding homosexual sex was in violation of Article 8, the Commission noting that medical evidence showed that a person's sexual orientation was decided and settled at the age of 16 and that men aged 16–21 were not in need of special protection from homosexual recruitment.[41]

The decision in *Sutherland* suggests that the Court is no longer prepared to afford the state any substantial discretion in this area, particularly where there is no evidence that such restrictions reflect the morality of the general public.[42] This is reflected in the European Court's judgments in *Smith and Grady* v *United Kingdom* and *Lustig-Prean and Beckett* v *United Kingdom*.[43] In these cases the European Court held that the investigations into the applicants' sexual orientation, and their subsequent dismissals from the armed forces on the grounds of their homosexuality, constituted especially grave interferences with the applicants' private lives, which were not justified on the grounds of national security and public order. In the Court's view, there was no substantive evidence that the applicants' homosexuality affected the performance of their functions, and the negative attitudes of heterosexual personnel toward homosexuals could not justify the interferences in question.[44] The Court has also

---

[38] The Court concluded that although there was evidence that the majority of the population may have disapproved of homosexuality, there was no evidence to suggest that the practice of homosexuality had been injurious to moral standards or that there had been any public demand for stricter enforcement of the law. See also *Norris v Ireland* (1988) 13 EHRR 186; *Modinos v Cyprus* (1993) 16 EHRR 485.

[39] In *Frette v France* (2002) 38 EHRR 438, it was held that it was permissible under Article 14 to distinguish between heterosexuals and homosexuals with respect to adoption rights. This decision seems to have been modified in *EB v France* (2008) 47 EHRR 21, which was then accepted as sound in *Re P and Others* [2009] 1 AC 173. These cases are detailed in chapter 13, at pages 724–5.

[40] *The Times*, 13 April 2001.

[41] The case was referred to the European Court of Human Rights, but was struck out following a friendly settlement whereby the government secured the passing of the Sexual Offences (Amendment) Act 2000, which equalised the age of consent for both homosexual and heterosexual sex. In *BB v United Kingdom* (2004) 39 EHRR 635, it was held that there had been a violation of Articles 8 and 14 when the applicant had been convicted with the buggery of a 16-year-old man. Although the law had since been changed so as to equalise the age of consent for homosexual and heterosexual sex, the applicant had been convicted before the change in the law and had thus been subjected to that discriminatory law.

[42] See also *SL v Austria* (2003) 37 EHRR 39, where the European Court held that differential age limits for heterosexual and homosexual sex were not justified and were thus contrary to Article 14 of the Convention.

[43] (2000) 29 EHRR 493; (2000) 29 EHRR 548.

[44] See *Brown v United Kingdom* (Application No 52770/99), where the government agreed a settlement of £52,500 covering all claims and expenses when the applicant had been discharged from the armed forces on the grounds of his homosexuality.

challenged domestic laws which discriminate against homosexuals with respect to property and other rights connected to personal and stable relationships.[45]

Transsexuals and the European Convention

As with the regulation of homosexuality, the Convention rights of transsexuals have been raised before the European Court on a number of occasions. In *Rees* v *United Kingdom*,[46] the Court held that there had been no violation of the Convention when the applicant's request to register his new sex was refused by the domestic authorities; the right to respect for private life did not include a positive obligation on a state to give individuals the unconditional right to label the sexual identity of their choice. The Court also held that the right to marry under Article 12 referred to a right between persons of the opposite biological sex; that such a restriction did not have the effect of destroying the very essence of the right. That decision was followed in *Cossey* v *United Kingdom*,[47] where the Court held that it was necessary to balance the right of such individuals with the interests of the community, and confirmed that the right to marry as restricted by English law did not undermine the existence of that right under Article 12. Although that approach was modified in *B* v *France*,[48] where the European Court held that French law which denied the applicant the right to change the sex or even name on the birth certificate was not compatible with Article 8, the Court's general stance was applied in subsequent cases such as *Sheffield and Horsham* v *United Kingdom*[49] and *X, Y and Z* v *United Kingdom*.[50] In those case it held that given transsexuality raised complex scientific, legal, moral and social issues in respect of which there was no generally shared approach, Article 8 could not be taken to imply an obligation for a member state to formally recognise the rights of such individuals to assume full legal and civil status, including the right to marry.

However, in *Goodwin* v *United Kingdom*,[51] the European Court reconsidered its stance, effectively overruling the above cases. In that case the Grand Chamber held that domestic law had subjected transsexuals to a serious interference with both their legal rights and their right to private life, which had led to feelings of vulnerability, anxiety and humiliation. Rejecting the government's arguments with respect to their margin of discretion, the Court noted that no concrete or substantial hardship or detriment to the public interest had been demonstrated as likely to flow from any change to the status of transsexuals, and that society should tolerate a certain inconvenience to enable individuals to live in dignity and worth in accordance with their chosen sexual identity. The Court also held that although Article 12 referred to the right of a man and a woman to marry, it was not persuaded that at this date such terms restricted the determination of gender to purely biological criteria. While it was for the contracting state to determine the conditions under which a person could claim legal recognition as a transsexual, there was no justification for barring transsexuals from enjoying the right to marry under any circumstances.

---

[45] See *Karner* v *Austria* (2004) 38 EHRR 24, where the denial of a homosexual partner of his right to succeed a tenancy shared by him and his partner before his partner's death was held in violation of Articles 8 and 14 of the Convention. The Civil Partnership Act 2004 provides legal recognition to same-sex relationships and allows lesbian and homosexual couples to register their partnership. The relevant law is discussed in chapter 13 of this text.

[46] (1986) 9 EHRR 56.

[47] (1990) 13 EHRR 622.

[48] (1992) 16 EHRR 1.

[49] (1998) 27 EHRR 163.

[50] (1997) 24 EHRR 143.

[51] (2002) 35 EHRR 18.

The judgment clearly left the British government with some discretion in deciding how to give effect to the judgment, including the extent to which transsexuals will be recognised and any conditions attached to that recognition.[52] Nevertheless, the judgment is an important one in respect of the rights of transsexuals. Further, it is illustrative of the European Court's ability and willingness to interpret the Convention in the context of changing circumstances, and to protect the rights of previously oppressed groups. Further, in *Van Kuck v Germany*,[53] it was prepared to impose a positive obligation on the state when it held that a domestic court's refusal to order reimbursement of top-up costs of a transsexual's gender reassignment surgery was a violation of his right to private life under Article 8. In the Court's view, as gender identity was one of the most intimate aspects of a person's private life, it was disproportionate to require the applicant to prove the medical necessity of the treatment.[54]

Private life and personal integrity

The right to private life as guaranteed by Article 8 of the Convention can protect a person's right to physical integrity and autonomy and thus protect them from attacks on their person or personal dignity.[55] This aspect of privacy or private life is supplemented by Article 3 of the Convention, which provides that no one shall be subject to torture or to inhuman or degrading treatment and punishment, and often a claim is made under both articles. For example, in *Costello-Roberts v United Kingdom*,[56] a claim was made under Articles 3 and 8 of the Convention where a seven-year-old boy had been subjected to corporal punishment at school. The European Court held that Article 8 of the Convention could afford protection going beyond that provided by Article 3 where it was satisfied that the treatment had adverse effects on the applicant's physical or moral integrity. On the facts, however, the Court held that there had been no violation of Articles 3 or 8.[57]

This aspect of Article 8 would protect individuals from subjection to medical treatment without their own or parent's consent, and in *Glass v United Kingdom*[58] the European Court found a violation of Article 8 when medical staff ignored the wishes of the parents and administered drugs to their seriously ill child. The Court held that although the treatment fulfilled a legitimate aim, the onus was on the authority to apply for the domestic court's permission to administer the treatment once it was clear that the parents were opposed to the treatment. The question of physical integrity and medical treatment has been raised on a number of occasions in the domestic courts and those cases are dealt with later in this chapter.

---

[52] See now the Gender Recognition Act 2004, discussed in chapter 13, pages 733–4. In *Grant v United Kingdom* (2007) 44 EHRR 1, the European Court held that there had been a violation of Articles 8 and 14 when a male to female transsexual had been denied a pension on her sixtieth birthday because biologically she was a male. The Court held that although the United Kingdom had acted swiftly to pass the Gender Recognition Act 2004 the applicant still remained a victim and there was no reason why she should not be regarded as a victim from the date of the judgment and until that Act came into force. In *R v United Kingdom* (Application No 35749/05), the Court declared inadmissible a claim that the inability of a transsexual to change a birth certificate until that person had divorced was contrary to her, and her partner's, Convention rights.

[53] (2003) 37 EHRR 51.

[54] See also *L v Lithuania* (Application No 27527/03), decision of the European Court of Human Rights, 11 September 2007, where it was held that the failure to bring promptly into effect legislation facilitating gender reassignment was in breach of Article 8.

[55] See Feldman, Human Dignity as a Legal Value [1999] PL 682, and [2000] PL 61.

[56] (1993) 19 EHRR 112.

[57] The case is discussed in chapter 5, dealing with the case law of the European Convention under Article 3.

[58] (2004) 39 EHRR 15.

The European Court has also dealt with cases under Article 8 which have raised issues about the right to life and the right to self-determination. In *Pretty* v *United Kingdom*[59] the applicant argued that there had been a violation of her right to respect for private and family life when her husband had been refused permission to end her life. The Court held that the notion of personal autonomy was an important principle underlying the interpretation of Articles 8 and that the ability to conduct one's life in a manner of one's choosing might also include the opportunity to pursue activities perceived to be of a physically or morally harmful or dangerous nature for the individual concerned. The very essence of the Convention is respect for human dignity and human freedom, and without negating the principle of sanctity of life protected under the Convention, it was not prepared to exclude that the prevention of the applicant from exercising her choice to avoid what she considered to be an undignified and distressing end to her life constituted an interference with her right to respect for private life under Article 8. On the facts, however, the Court found that the interference was justified within Article 8(2). The Court did not consider that the blanket nature of the ban on assisted suicide was disproportionate; neither was it arbitrary for the law to reflect the importance of the right to life by prohibiting assisted suicide while providing for a system of enforcement that gave due regard in each particular case to the public interest in bringing a prosecution, as well as to the fair and proper requirements of retribution and deterrence.[60]

However, a further challenge to the law and its practice was made more recently, in *R (Purdy)* v *DPP*,[61] where it was held that the DPP had acted unlawfully by refusing to publish guidance as to the circumstances in which individuals would or would not be prosecuted for assisting suicides under the Suicide Act 1961. Preferring the decision of the European Court to that of the decision of the House of Lords in the *Pretty* litigation, the House of Lords held that the claimant's Article 8 rights were engaged and that as such any interference with that right had to be sufficiently clear so as to be in accordance with law, as required by Article 8(2). The lack of such guidelines offended the principles of foreseeability and accessibility inherent in that provision and thus was in breach of Article 8.

Following the decision in *Purdy*, changes to the previous law were made and the DPP has issued such guidelines, indicating in what circumstances a person might be prosecuted under the Act.[62] First, s.59 of the Coroners and Justice Act 2009 has replaced the existing offences under the Suicide Act 1961 and the Criminal Attempts Act 1981 with one offence of encouraging or assisting suicide. This offence requires an intention to encourage or assist and s.2A provides clearer guidance on acts that are capable of doing so. The new policy, whilst not changing the law on suicide or legalising euthanasia, provides guidelines as to when a prosecution would be brought, thus providing clarity for prosecutors and the 'victim' and their families, etc. In particular, prosecutors should consider (assuming there is sufficient evidence of an offence) whether any prosecution would be in the public interest, taking into account factors such as the victim's age (whether they were under 18), their mental capacity and whether they had reached a voluntary, clear, settled and informed decision to commit suicide. Equally, the prosecutor should take into account the motives of the 'suspect' and whether the encouragement was offered purely out of compassion.

---

[59] (2002) 35 EHRR 1.
[60] The case is dealt with in detail as a case study in chapter 4.
[61] [2010] 1 AC 345.
[62] The guidelines are set out in *Policy for Prosecutors in Respect of Cases of Encouraging Assisting Suicide* (2010).

Of course, any change in the law and policy will need to comply with the obligation of the state under Article 2 to preserve an individual's life, as well as its duty to protect the right to private and family life. In this respect in *Burke v United Kingdom*,[63] the European Court dismissed the applicant's claims under Articles 2 and 8 after being satisfied that there was nothing incompatible with the Convention about the GMC's policy guidance on the provision and withdrawal of artificial nutrition and hydration. The Court was satisfied that where a competent patient had indicated a desire to be kept alive by artificial nutrition then a doctor who ignored that advice would be in breach of Article 2 and guilty of murder. The applicant thus faced no risk of dying in breach of Article 2 of the Convention; the domestic law and its operation did not pose a significant risk that his Convention rights would be jeopardised.[64]

The right to private life and abortions

Although it has been held that the unborn child is not entitled to specific protection under the European Convention,[65] the issue of abortions gives rise to a number of issues under Article 8: most notably whether a woman has the right to an abortion and whether the father has a right to prevent it. Convention case law recognises that the decision to terminate a pregnancy engages the woman's right to private life under Article 8, although the Commission has stressed that pregnancy does not pertain uniquely to the woman's right to private life and that regulation of that process will not constitute a violation of Article 8 in every case.[66] On the other hand, the domestic law should not impose an unreasonable restriction on the woman's choice. For example, in *Tysia v Poland*,[67] it was held that there had been a violation of Article 8 when the applicant had been denied an abortion on the grounds that the threat to her eyesight by the pregnancy did not constitute grounds for an abortion on therapeutic grounds. The Court found that the uncertainty of what amounted to an abortion on such grounds and the lack of a procedure to resolve such issues in cases of disagreement (including the lack of a legal remedy to enforce her right to an abortion) created a situation of prolonged uncertainty for the applicant and thus amounted to a breach of her right to private life.[68] The woman also has a right to access information with respect to her decision whether to terminate.[69]

Abortions may also give rise to claims from others who are affected by the decision to terminate. In *X v United Kingdom*[70] the European Commission held although the unborn child was not to be regarded as an 'other' for the purpose of Article 8(2),[71] the father of the

---

[63] Application No 19807/06.

[64] Upholding the domestic court's decision in *R (Burke) v General Medical Council and Others* [2005] 3 WLR 1132.

[65] *Vo v France* (2005) 40 EHRR 12, considered in chapter 4 of this text. The hospital had carried out an abortion on the applicant's child by mistake. Although the foetus had no rights under Article 2, a mother would be able to bring an action under the Convention for breach of her private and family rights.

[66] *Bruggermann and Scheuten v Germany* (1977) DR 100.

[67] Decision of the European Court, 20 March 2003.

[68] In *D v Ireland* (Application No 26499/02), the European Court declared inadmissible a claim about the lack of abortion services in the applicant's country on the grounds that she had not exhausted domestic remedies in discovering whether she was entitled to an abortion.

[69] *Open Door Counselling v Ireland* (1993) 15 EHRR 244. See preface for recent developments.

[70] (1980) DR 244.

[71] Under Article 8(2) the rights under Article 8 can be compromised for the protection of 'the rights and reputation of others'.

woman who had aborted her child was a victim for the purpose of a claim under Article 8 of the Convention. Nevertheless, the Convention recognises the woman's rights to private life under Article 8, and to life under Article 2, and the Convention machinery gives a wide margin of appreciation to each state to balance the relevant interests in an area which it recognises is a delicate one.[72]

Private life and personal identity

The right to private life includes the right to obtain and retain one's right to personal identity.[73] The European Court has accepted that a person's name concerns a person's private life and is, therefore, protected under Article 8. In *Burghatz v Switzerland*[74] it was held that there had been a violation of Article 8 when the authorities had refused the applicant's request to register his surname as a combination of his family name and his wife's name. Further, in the Court's view there was no objective justification why men could not combine the names when under domestic law women could. As we have seen, above, in a series of cases the Court held that Article 8 did not impose a positive obligation on the state to allow transsexuals to amend their birth certificates.[75] In those cases the Court accepted that the refusal came within the state's margin of appreciation, but they were overturned in *Goodwin v United Kingdom*,[76] where the European Court held that the failure of the government to recognise the post-operative identity of transsexuals for the purposes of matters such as pensions, birth certificates and the right to marry was in violation of both Articles 8 and 12 of the Convention.

The right to respect of family life

The right to family life is specifically protected by both Article 8 and Article 12 of the Convention: the latter article providing that men and women of marriageable age have the right to marry and found a family, according to the national laws governing the exercise of that right. The right to family life also interrelates with the right to liberty of the person and in a number of cases the domestic courts have had to decide on the legality and proportionality of control orders issued under the Prevention of Terrorism Act 2005, which impose restrictions on an individual's movement, liberty and enjoyment of private and family life.[77]

Articles 8 and 12 do not just apply to the traditional idea of families based on marriage, but also extend to other relationships.[78] Thus, in *X, Y and Z v United Kingdom*[79] it was held

---

[72] See *H v Norway* (1992) 73 DR 155; *Boso v Italy* (Application No 50490/99).

[73] In *Jaggi v Switzerland* (Application No 58757/00), decision of the European Court, 13 July 2006, it was held that there had been a violation of Article 8 when the applicant had been refused permission to have a DNA test carried out on a dead person with a view of discovering whether that person was his biological father.

[74] (1994) 18 EHRR 101.

[75] *Rees v United Kingdom* (1986) 9 EHRR 56; *Cossey v United Kingdom* (1990) 13 EHRR 622; *Sheffield and Horsham v United Kingdom* (1999) 27 EHRR 163.

[76] (2002) 35 EHRR 18.

[77] See *Secretary of State for the Home Department v AP, The Times*, 17 June 2010; *BX v Secretary of State for the Home Department* [2010] EWHC 990 (Admin). These cases are considered in chapter 14, at pages 771–2.

[78] *Marckx v Belgium* (1979) 2 EHRR 330.

[79] (1997) 24 EHRR 143.

that family life applied to a number of *de facto* relationships other than marriage, and that it covered a transsexual (X) who had lived with his partner ostensibly as her male partner, had been granted treatment by artificial insemination to allow his partner to have a child, and had acted as the child's father since the birth.[80]

The state is under an obligation not to interfere with, or to place obstacles in the way of, the enjoyment of that relationship, and any such interference must be justified on very strong grounds. For example, in *P, C and S v United Kingdom*,[81] the European Court held that there had been a violation of Article 8 when the domestic authorities removed the applicant's baby from her immediately after the birth for fear that the applicant might harm the child. Although the mother's previous behaviour gave rise to grave concern over the child's welfare and safety, the immediate removal of the child, as opposed to allowing the mother to have supervised contact with her while in hospital, constituted a draconian step that was not supported by relevant and sufficient reasons.

There have been a number of cases where the decision to take a child into care has been challenged on the basis that it unduly interferes with the parents' and children's right to private and family life. Such decisions have not been capable of challenge at domestic common law,[82] although they are reviewable by the European Court of Human Rights and its case law can inform the domestic courts in actions brought under the Human Rights Act 1998. The European Court will insist that any decision to take a child into care be made on cogent evidence and for legitimate reasons and that it does not involve a disproportionate interference with anyone's Article 8 rights. For example, in *MAK and RK v United Kingdom*[83] it was held that there had been a violation of Article 8 when a parent had been wrongfully suspected of abuse after their child's injuries had been misdiagnosed. The Court found that the child should have been seen by a dermatologist at an early stage so as to explain the bruising on her body, and that there had been a further breach of Article 8 when she had been medically treated and photographed without her parents' consent.[84] In contrast, in *RK and AK v United Kingdom*,[85] it was held that there had been no violation when the applicants' child had been placed into care when the authorities had wrongly concluded that she had been assaulted when taken into hospital with a fractured leg; it being subsequently confirmed that she suffered from brittle bone disease. The Court held that the authorities had acted on substantive evidence and that the action was thus proportionate to the protection of the child.[86]

---

[80] On the facts, the Court decided that there had been no violations of Articles 8 and 12, but see now the decision in *Goodwin v United Kingdom* (2002) 35 EHRR 18. In *R (Rose) v Secretary of State for Health and Others, The Times*, 22 August 2002, it was held that the right to family life was engaged in respect of the claimant's relationship with an unknown sperm donor.

[81] (2002) 35 EHRR 31.

[82] In *JD v East Berkshire Community Health NHS Trust* [2005] 2 AC 373, the House of Lords held that in the absence of bad faith there was no duty of care owed by investigative authorities of child abuse towards parents – as opposed to children – and that this was not affected by Article 8 of the Convention; affirmed in *Lawrence v Pembrokeshire County Council* [2007] 1 WLR 2991.

[83] (2010) 51 EHRR 14.

[84] The Court also found a violation of Article 13 as their civil action had failed and there was thus no effective remedy at the time (pre-Human Rights Act) to compensate for those violations of Convention rights.

[85] (2009) 48 EHRR 39.

[86] However, again the Court found a violation of Article 13 as the parents did not have available to them a procedure to challenge the authority's actions and to claim compensation.

This obligation also includes a duty to allow families to take part in proceedings or decisions that affect the position of the family.[87] Thus, in *TP and KM v United Kingdom*[88] it was held that the local authority's failure to allow a mother an opportunity to refute allegations of abuse against her daughter by her partner, resulting in the child being taken into care, constituted a violation of Article 8. Equally there may be a violation of Article 8 if there is some other form of procedural irregularity. Thus, in *AD and OD v United Kingdom*,[89] the European Court found a violation of Article 8 (in conjunction with Article 13) when the local authority had placed a child in foster care after they had mistakenly diagnosed the child at risk from its mother and partner. Although there had been sufficient reason to conduct the risk assessment, the delays in returning the child and flaws in the procedure for conducting the risk assessment had led to a disproportionate interference with the applicants' private and family life rights.[90]

In certain cases the state may also be in violation of Article 8 if it deports an individual and such an act would disproportionately interfere with that person's private and family life. For example, in *Omojudi v United Kingdom*[91] the European Court found a violation of Article 8 when the applicant had been deported after living in the United Kingdom for 26 years having been given indefinite leave to remain. Despite his conviction for a sexual offence (considered to be at the lower end of the scale by the Court) and other offences, his ties to the country and his family were too strong and thus his deportation was regarded as disproportionate in all the circumstances. Similarly, in *EM (Lebanon) v Home Secretary*,[92] the House of Lords held that there had been a flagrant violation of the applicants' Article 8 rights when the applicant was deported to Lebanon after she had looked after her son for seven years in the United Kingdom. As she would by national law automatically lose custody to the father, such an act would have severely interfered with her and her son's family life. In contrast, in *Onur v United Kingdom*,[93] the European Court held that there had been no violation of Article 8 when the applicant had been deported back to his native Turkey after being convicted of serious property offences committed in the United Kingdom. Despite the applicant having lived in the UK for 19 years and forming a relationship and fathering a daughter, the offences were serious and he must have expected that he was liable for deportation. In addition the Court noted that the problems for relocation in Turkey were not exceptionally difficult. The same considerations can apply to cases of extradition, although it has been held that a court should only allow the right to private and family life to outweigh the interest in extradition when the consequences of such interference were exceptionally serious.[94] Control orders, including curfews may also engage Articles 8 and 5 of the Convention,[95] although the courts have allowed proportionate restrictions on movement and family life and contact.[96]

---

[87] Thus, in *P, C and S v United Kingdom*, n 81, above, it was held that there had been a violation of Article 8 when the applicants had been denied the right to legal representation in both care order and adoption proceedings relating to their daughter.

[88] (2002) 34 EHRR 2.

[89] (2010) 51 EHRR 8.

[90] Further, there was a violation of Article 13 with respect to the mother, as she was not entitled to bring an action in negligence against the authorities (see *RK and AK*, above). As the child was able to bring such a claim (*JD*, above) there was no violation of Article 13 in his respect.

[91] (2010) 51 EHRR 10.

[92] [2009] 1 AC 1198.

[93] (2009) 49 EHRR 38.

[94] *Norris v United States* [2010] 2 AC 487.

[95] See *AP v Secretary of State for the Home Department*, *The Times*, 17 June 2010, discussed in chapters 6 and 14 of this text.

[96] *BX v Secretary of State for the Home Department* [2010] EWHC 990 (Admin).

Thus, not all interference with the family relationship will amount to a breach of Article 8, unless discriminatory and disproportionate. For example, in *Abdulaziz, Cabales and Balkandali* v *United Kingdom*[97] there was no violation of Article 8 when the immigration authorities refused to allow the applicants' foreign husbands to enter the country. Article 8 did not impose an obligation on the state to respect the choice by married couples of the country of their matrimonial residence and to accept the non-national spouses for settlement in that country. Nevertheless, the Court found a violation of Article 8 in conjunction with Article 14 of the Convention because the applicants had been discriminated against on grounds of their gender. On the other hand, the deportation of an individual, which interferes with his or her enjoyment of private and family life, needs to be justified within Article 8 and must, therefore, represent a legitimate and proportionate act on behalf of the state.[98] Further, Article 8 does not guarantee the right to divorce, although in certain circumstances an individual might have the right to separate from his or her partner.[99] In *Johnston* v *Ireland*,[100] the applicant wished to divorce his wife in order to allow him to marry his new partner, but Irish constitutional law prohibited divorce. It was held that Article 8 could not extend so as to impose an obligation on the part of the state to introduce measures permitting the divorce and remarriage of an individual.

Restrictions on the right to marry and to found a family

Article 12 complements Article 8 of the Convention, guaranteeing the right to family and private life, by providing a right to marry and to found a family. The rights under Article 12 are primarily negative, requiring the state to refrain from imposing undue impediments on the rights – they do not generally impose an obligation on the state to provide the necessary facilities to allow individuals to enjoy those rights. Using that logic, although compulsory sterilisation of an individual would raise an issue under Article 12, the refusal to afford artificial insemination facilities would appear not to engage the article. This, however, does not fully reflect the European Court's jurisprudence and in some cases there will be an obligation on the state to provide positive assistance; although the Court will be reluctant to impose too onerous a duty in such cases.

For example, in *Dickson* v *United Kingdom*,[101] the Court drew a distinction between negative and positive obligations in deciding that it was within the state's margin of appreciation to refuse artificial insemination facilities to a prisoner and his wife. In the European's Court's view the present restriction did not limit a general entitlement already in place in a prison environment, but rather concerned the state's refusal to take steps exceptionally to allow something (to beget children) that was not an already existing general right. As a consequence, the extent of such obligations will vary considerably from case to case, having regard to the diversity of situations obtaining in the contracting states and its resources, and given the margin of appreciation afforded to the national authorities in this respect, it had not been shown that the decision was arbitrary or unreasonable or that it failed to strike a fair balance between the competing interests. However, on appeal to the Grand Chamber of the European Court of Human Rights,[102] it was held that whether the breach was of a positive

---

[97] (1985) 7 EHRR 471.
[98] See *Moustaquim* v *Belgium* (1991) 13 EHRR 802; *El Boujaidi* v *France* (1997) 30 EHRR 223.
[99] *Airey* v *Ireland* (1979) 2 EHRR 305.
[100] (1986) 9 EHRR 203.
[101] (2007) 44 EHRR 21.
[102] (2008) 46 EHRR 41.

or negative right, in either case it had to be shown that there was a proper balance between the enjoyment of that right and any other conflicting public interest. In the present case that balance had not been achieved by the policy or its judicial review because both started from the basis that the right should not be afforded unless exceptional circumstances were present.[103]

On the face of it, Article 12 leaves the right to marry and found a family entirely at the discretion of the member states and their national law, with respect to both the threshold of 'marriageable age' and any conditions or restrictions on such a right. However, although the European Court and Commission has offered member states a very wide margin of appreciation with regards to the eligibility to marry, both have interpreted Article 12 to mean that any restriction on the right to marry must not destroy the very essence of the right contained in the article. In addition, although the right to marry is subject to a number of implied restrictions, the case law also makes it clear that any exception must follow the basic principles of legality and reasonableness that inform other conditional rights. Thus, in *F v Switzerland*[104] it was held that a prohibition under domestic law on the applicant's right to marry after his divorce was contrary to Article 12. Under Article 150 of the Swiss Civil Code, a court could fix a period of up to three years in which a person was not allowed to marry after a divorce. The applicant was found to have been solely responsible for the breakdown of his third marriage and the court applied a three-year prohibition, delaying his subsequent marriage. Although the domestic law had a legitimate aim – the stability of marriage in society – the Court doubted whether the particular means used were appropriate for achieving that aim. The measure affected the very essence of the right to marry and was disproportionate to the aim pursued.

A further example can be seen in the recent case of *B and L v United Kingdom*,[105] where it was held that there had been a violation of Article 12 when the applicants had been denied the right to marry because of their relationship as former father- and daughter-in-law. The European Court held that the legal prohibition of such marriages,[106] unless both parties' former spouses were dead, constituted a disproportionate interference with their right to marry under the Convention. Further, the Court held that the procedure for exceptionally granting the right to marry in such cases – whereby the individuals had to apply to parliament for a private Act of parliament to be passed – was arbitrary and uncertain. The Court noted that there was a legitimate aim in outlawing such marriages, viz, the protection of the integrity of family life and of children's interests. However, the interference was not necessary or proportionate; the fact that such relationships did not establish criminal liability detracted from the argument that such prohibition was necessary, and in this case there was no evidence of emotional or other pressure as the applicants were already living together with the woman's child.[107]

Whether a restriction does destroy the fundamental character of the right to marry will depend not only on the particular facts, but also on the interpretation of the article by the Convention machinery. The European Court and Commission had consistently held that the right to marry applies only to persons of the opposite sex on the basis that Article 12 is concerned with the protection of marriage as the basis of the family and therefore marriages

---

[103] The case is dealt with as a case study at the end of this chapter.
[104] (1987) 10 EHRR 411.
[105] (2006) 42 EHRR 11.
[106] Under s.1(5) of the Marriage Act 1949.
[107] Subsequently the Marriage Act 1949 (Remedial Order) 2007 was passed, complying with the Court's ruling.

that are incapable of such fall outside its ambit.[108] However, the Court's interpretation of Article 12, and Article 8, was questioned in *Goodwin v United Kingdom*,[109] where the European Court accepted that transsexuals were in effect deprived of their right to marry because they remained able only to marry a person of their former opposite sex. This infringed the very essence of the applicant's right to marry, and the state's margin of appreciation in this area could not be used to bar such a person from enjoying the right to marry under any circumstances.

Thus, a state's margin of discretion must not be used in order to apply a restriction or qualification that destroys the essence of this fundamental right. Accordingly, in *Hamer v United Kingdom*,[110] the European Commission of Human Rights held that a prohibition of the right to marry placed on convicted prisoners was inconsistent with Article 12. In the Commission's view the imposition by the state of any substantial period of delay on the exercise of the right of a prisoner to form a legal relationship was an injury to the substance of that right. Further, its exercise by a prisoner involved no threat to prison security and the restriction could not be justified by the fact of imprisonment itself.[111] On the other hand, it has been held that the authorities are allowed to place some restrictions on a prisoner's rights to found a family. Accordingly, prisoners do not have the right to conjugal visits,[112] or the immediate right to start a family.[113]

The Court will also be reluctant to interfere with domestic law where it places a reasonable restriction on a person's right to found a family. In *Evans v United Kingdom*,[114] the European Court held that there had been no violation of Article 8 when the applicant had been refused permission to be treated with embryos created between her and her former partner, when that partner had withdrawn his consent. In the domestic courts it was held that any interference with the woman's right was necessary for achieving the purpose of the domestic legislation, viz, the regulation of IVF treatment, and that such interference was proportionate and objectively justifiable.[115] The European Court held that given the lack of European consensus in this area and the moral sensitivities concerned, the state should be afforded a wide margin of appreciation with respect to the decision to legislate and the content of that law. In the Court's view there were strong policy considerations for adopting a 'bright line' rule which provided legal certainty and helped to maintain public confidence in the law in a highly sensitive field. Further, the Article 8 rights of the male donor were not necessarily less worthy than those of the female.[116]

---

[108] *Rees v United Kingdom* (1986) 9 EHRR 56; *Cossey v United Kingdom* (1990) 13 EHRR 622; *Sheffield and Horsham v United Kingdom* (1998) 27 EHRR 163.

[109] (2002) 35 EHRR 18.

[110] (1982) 4 EHRR 139.

[111] See also *Draper v United Kingdom* (1980) 24 DR 73, where the European Commission held that there was a violation of Article 13 even though the prisoner's incarceration made it impossible for the parties to cohabit at the time of the marriage.

[112] See *X v United Kingdom* (1975) DR 2; *ELH* and *PBH v United Kingdom* [1998] EHRLR 231; *X and Y v Switzerland* (1978) DR 241.

[113] *X v United Kingdom*, above, approved by the domestic courts in *R (Mellor) v Secretary of State for the Home Department* [2001] 3 WLR 533. But see *Dickson v United Kingdom* (2008) 46 EHRR 41.

[114] (2006) 33 EHRR 21.

[115] *Evans v Amicus Healthcare Ltd* [2004] 3 WLR 681.

[116] The decision was upheld by the Grand Chamber of the European Court: *Evans v United Kingdom* (2008) 46 EHRR 34.

The European Court has also held that Article 12 does not guarantee the right to divorce. In *Johnston v Ireland*[117] the applicant had separated from his wife and wished to marry another woman, who had a child, but they were prohibited from doing so as divorce was unlawful under the Irish Constitution. The Court held that neither Article 12 nor Article 8 guaranteed the right to divorce. The words 'right to marry' contained in Article 12 covered the formation of marital relationships and not their dissolution; the Convention text had deliberately omitted any reference to such rights on the dissolution of a marriage.[118] Alternatively, the Court felt that the restriction in question, imposed in a democratic society that adhered to the principle of monogamy, did not injure the substance of the right. However, in *F v Switzerland*,[119] the European Court held that if national law *did* allow divorce, it must not place unreasonable restrictions on a person's right to remarry.

The right to marry under Article 12 was considered recently by the House of Lords in *R (Baiai and Others) v Secretary of State for the Home Department and Others*[120] with respect to restrictions placed by the Home Secretary on those subject to immigration control. Under that scheme the Secretary would need to provide permission to marry via a Certificate of Approval. Further, the Secretary's policy was to refuse approval to anyone who did not have a valid right to enter and remain in the United Kingdom for more than six months, and with more than three months of that period outstanding. It was held that although the scheme had a legitimate aim – to avoid sham marriages – it was applied in a blanket fashion and was thus disproportionate to that aim. In order to be proportionate, a scheme had to investigate individual cases and had to show that the marriages that were targeted did indeed make substantial inroads into immigration control. In the present case the regulations and the policy did not merely prevent sham marriages – which would have been legitimate – but restricted the right to marry to a greater extent.[121]

The right to respect for the home

Article 8 specifically protects the right to a home and this right is often linked with the right to family and private life. However, not every activity carried out on one's property will engage Article 8. In *R (Countryside Alliance) v Attorney General*,[122] it was held that the hunting ban imposed by the Hunting Act 2004 did not engage the landowners' right to private and home life under Article 8. The House of Lords held that even if the ban did prevent their land from being used for specific purposes and threatened their livelihoods that did not arise from a breach of Article 8. Article 8 protected the right to home life and the term 'home' did not cover land over which the owner permitted a sport to be conducted. The House of Lords also held that fox-hunting did not amount to an activity of private life for the purposes of Article 8 of the European Convention. The Court noted that the activity was carried on in the open air, involved a large number of participants and was available to all comers, thus making it

---

[117] (1986) 9 EHRR 203.

[118] In contrast, Article 16 of the Universal Declaration of the Human Rights included rights after marriage.

[119] (1987) 10 EHRR 411.

[120] [2009] 1 AC 287.

[121] In July 2010 the government laid a remedial order under the Human Rights Act 1998 to abolish the scheme: Asylum and Immigration (Treatment of Claimants, etc.) Act 2004 (Remedial) Order 2010.

[122] [2007] 2 WLR 922.

inclusive rather than exclusive. This decision was upheld by the European Court of Human Rights, which held that the concept of home did not include land over which the owners practised or allowed sport to be practised and there was no evidence that the applicants would indeed lose their homes as a result of the ban or that it had created serious difficulties for earning one's living.[123]

In particular, Article 8 protects persons from destruction of and eviction from their home.[124] For example, in *Akdivar* v *Turkey*[125] it was held that there had been a violation of Article 8 when the government's security forces deliberately burned down the applicants' homes and contents in retaliation for a terrorist attack at a nearby gendarme station. Although the right to a home can be compromised for legitimate public interest grounds, the Court requires stronger justification for a violation of this article than, for example, the right to property under Article 1 of the First Protocol. Thus, in *Gillow* v *United Kingdom*[126] the Court held that there was an unjustified violation of Article 8 when local housing laws prohibited the applicants from returning to their family home, having left the area and let the property. The applicants still had sufficient links with the area to establish that the house was still their 'home' within Article 8 and the refusal to allow them a licence to occupy the house was disproportionate to the legitimate aim of the economic well-being of the community. In addition, the law should provide sufficient procedural and substantive safeguards to protect the right to the home. For example, in *McCann* v *United Kingdom*,[127] there was a violation of Article 8 when the applicant had been ejected from his home when the council had persuaded his ex-wife (who had formerly occupied the house) to sign a notice to quit. The Court found that the summary procedure which deprived the applicant of his right of residency without arguing the proportionality of that ejection before an independent tribunal constituted a disproportionate interference with the applicant's rights.

The European Court has considered the compatibility of planning laws with the right to respect for the home, and of family life, and it is clear that it is prepared to offer a reasonably wide margin of appreciation in this area. In *Buckley* v *United Kingdom*,[128] the applicant was refused planning permission to place three caravans for her and her family to live in on her land. The Court held that the right to a home under Article 8 was not restricted to a lawful home and that as she had intended to make the land and her caravans her home, her right under Article 8 was engaged. Nevertheless, those measures were prescribed by law and pursued the legitimate aims of highway safety and environmental and public health (public safety, economic well-being and the protection of health and morals and the rights of others). Although the decision-making process needs to be fair and take due account of any Convention rights, in this case the decision of the planning authorities had not exceeded the margin of appreciation and the means employed to enforce the law were not disproportionate.[129]

---

[123] *Friend* v *United Kingdom; Countryside Alliance* v *United Kingdom* (2010) 50 EHRR SE6.
[124] The Convention does not guarantee the right to a home. In *R (Bishop)* v *Bromley LBC* [2006] EWHC 2148 (Admin) it was held that a decision to transfer a local authority's day-care services to another centre was not sufficiently serious to engage Article 8, and even if that were the case the decision was justified on grounds of the economic well-being of the country.
[125] (1996) 1 BHRC 137.
[126] (1986) 11 EHRR 335.
[127] (2008) 47 EHRR 40.
[128] (1996) 23 EHRR 101.
[129] See also *Coster, Beard and Chapman* v *United Kingdom* (2001) 33 EHRR 20.

However, the Court will insist that the domestic laws and procedures are fair and non-discriminatory. For example, in *Connors v United Kingdom*,[130] it found a violation of Article 8 when the applicant and his family, who were gypsies, were evicted from council-owned property which had been their base for the previous 15 years. In the Court's opinion the eviction was not attended by sufficient procedural safeguards, namely the requirement to establish proper justification for the serious interference with their Convention rights and to provide necessary and detailed reasons. The Court noted that the law and the state had placed considerable obstacles in the way of gypsies pursuing an actively nomadic lifestyle while at the same time excluding from procedural protection those who decided to take up a more settled lifestyle.[131]

This wide margin of appreciation is also evident in cases where the individual complains of interference with the enjoyment of his property. In *Hatton v United Kingdom*,[132] a number of residents living on the flight path of Heathrow Airport complained that the introduction of a scheme to regulate flights had increased night-time noise, especially in the early morning, which interfered with their right to respect for their private and family lives and their homes. The Court held that the government owed a positive duty to take reasonable and appropriate measures to secure those rights and that the authorities were required to minimise, as far as possible, the interference with such rights by trying to find alternative solutions and by generally seeking to achieve their aims in the least onerous way as regards human rights. In order to do that, a proper and complete investigation and study with the aim of finding the best possible solution that would, in reality, strike the right balance, should precede the relevant project. On the facts, the European Court held that the government's modest steps at improving the night noise climate did not constitute the measures necessary to protect the applicants' position.[133] However, on appeal to the Grand Chamber,[134] it was held that the authorities *had* achieved a proper balance. It held that given the fact that only a limited number of people were affected by the noise, and that their house prices had not devalued (thus giving them the opportunity to move), there had not been a disproportionate interference with their rights for the purpose of achieving economic benefit.[135]

This margin of appreciation will be narrower where the applicant can prove that there has been exceptional hardship. In *Fadeyeva v Russia*,[136] there had been a violation of Article 8 when the applicant had been subjected to pollution from a nearby steel works. The domestic courts had refused her claim for resettlement to another area, placing her on a general waiting list rather than giving her priority. The European Court was satisfied that her health and quality

---

[130] (2005) 40 EHRR 9.

[131] The decision in *Connors* was not followed domestically. In *Price v Leeds City County* [2006] 2 AC 465, it was held that a possession order from a local authority ordering a family of gypsies to leave its land was not, in the absence of exceptional circumstances, contrary to Article 8 and the decision in *Connors*.

[132] (2002) 34 EHRR 1.

[133] See also *Lopez Ostra v Spain* (1994) 20 EHRR 277, where the European Court held that there had been a violation of Article 8 when the applicant's home had been subject to serious pollution from a private tannery reprocessing plant.

[134] *Hatton v United Kingdom* (2003) 37 EHRR 28.

[135] See *Powell and Rayner v United Kingdom* (1990) 12 EHRR 355, where it was held by the European Commission that the noise from aircraft flying over the applicants' homes was justified as being necessary for the economic well-being of the country. The Grand Chamber in *Hatton* did, however, find that there had been a violation of Article 13 of the Convention, because the domestic judicial review proceedings could only question the bare legality and rationality of the executive decisions.

[136] (2007) 45 EHRR 10.

of home life had been affected by living by the plant. Although the consideration of others on the waiting list, and the economic benefits of the plant, constituted legitimate aims for not providing her with priority housing, in the applicant's case the state had failed to offer any effective solution to help her move from the dangerous area. The Court held that although it would be going too far to suggest that the state or the polluting enterprise were under an obligation to provide the applicant with free housing, in this case despite the knowledge that the plant was operating in breach of environmental standards, the state had offered no measures to reduce the pollution to acceptable levels. Despite the wide margin, the state had failed to strike a fair balance between the interests of the community and the applicant's enjoyment of her Article 8 rights.

The right to private and family life and the home are compromised by police powers allowing entry into an individual's property, and such acts must be carried out legitimately and proportionately. In *McLeod* v *United Kingdom*[137] the police, fearing a breach of the peace, had entered the applicant's house to allow her ex-husband to remove property from the matrimonial home. This had caused distress to the applicant's mother, who had informed the police that the applicant was not at home. The Court held that the means employed by the police in the present case were disproportionate to the aim of preventing disorder or crime. Although the Court was satisfied that the common law power of the police to enter premises was in accordance with law, it felt that the police officers had not struck the right balance and should have realised on discovering that the applicant was not present that the risk of disorder was small. Similarly, in *Keegan* v *United Kingdom*,[138] it was held that there had been a breach of Article 8 when the police broke into the applicant's home in the early hours of the morning in the mistaken belief that an armed robber lived on the premises. In the Court's view the police could have avoided their mistake by conducting appropriate investigations, and although they had not acted with malice, on the facts, their actions were disproportionate to the aim of detecting crime.[139] The Court will also insist that powers to enter and search private premises are curtailed by procedural safeguards so as to avoid arbitrary state action.[140]

The right to respect for correspondence

Article 8 protects the right to communicate with others and overlaps with the right to freedom of expression contained in Article 10 of the Convention. Article 8 provides specific protection for correspondence between one person and another and it is clear that this covers not purely personal correspondence with friends or relatives, but also business communications. Thus, in *Halford* v *United Kingdom*[141] it was held that Article 8 applied to telephone conversations

---

[137] (1999) 27 EHRR 493.

[138] (2007) 44 EHRR 33.

[139] The Court also found a breach of Article 13 because of the law's insistence that malice had to be proven to found a case for damages, despite the distress caused to the applicants. The domestic courts had dismissed their claim in the absence of malice, despite there being evidence that the police had not taken basic steps to verify the details before entering the building: *Keegan* v *Chief Constable of Merseyside* [2003] 1 WLR 2187.

[140] In *Ernst and Others* v *Belgium* (2004) 39 EHRR 35, it was held that there had been a violation of Article 8 when commercial and private premises were searched to find documents in respect of a prosecution for breach of confidence. The Court held that the search warrants were drafted in wide terms – to seize any document or object that might assist the investigation – and gave no information about the investigation concerned, the premises to be searched or the objects to be seized. Furthermore, the applicants were not informed of the reasons for the searches.

[141] (1997) 24 EHRR 523.

held on business premises provided the individual had a legitimate expectation that their private conversations would be respected.[142]

A number of cases have been brought under Article 8 in connection with interferences with legal and other privileged correspondence. For example, in *Golder v United Kingdom*[143] the refusal to allow a prisoner to contact a solicitor for the purpose of bringing a civil action against a prison officer constituted a violation of Articles 6 and 8 of the Convention. The Court also found a violation of Articles 6 and 8 in the cases of *Silver v United Kingdom*,[144] where a number of prison regulations interfering with the prisoner's right of correspondence were declared in violation of Articles 6 and 8, either on the basis that they were not sufficiently accessible to be in accordance with law, or that they were so excessive and thus not necessary for the prevention of disorder and crime.[145] Similarly, in *Foxley v United Kingdom*[146] the applicant was the subject of an order under the Insolvency Act 1986, allowing his mail to be redirected to a trustee in bankruptcy. In all, 71 letters were redirected, including some of a legal nature, and the applicant claimed that this constituted a violation of Articles 6 and 8 of the Convention. In its view, there was no justification for a procedure whereby legally privileged letters were opened, copied and committed to file before being forwarded to the applicant. There was no evidence to suggest that the privileged channel of communication was being abused and thus there was no pressing social need justifying the interference with that correspondence.

Questions

What aspects of privacy and private life are protected by Article 8 of the European Convention?
What values do Articles 8 and 12 of the Convention uphold?
To what extent does the European Court allow states a margin of appreciation in these areas?

The protection of privacy in domestic law

The absence of a distinct law of privacy

One of the key features of the traditional method of protecting civil liberties was the absence of a legal right to privacy.[147] Although the rule of law demanded that any interference with a person's liberty has a legal basis,[148] this principle only applied when the claim itself was recognised in law. Thus, in *Malone v Metropolitan Police Commissioner (No 2)*[149] it was held that

---

[142] This case, and other surveillance cases, are discussed later in this chapter.

[143] (1975) 1 EHRR 524.

[144] (1983) 5 EHRR 347.

[145] See also *Campbell v United Kingdom* (1992) 15 EHRR 137, where the Court held that restrictions placed on a prisoner's right to communicate with his legal adviser, including the right of authorities to open legal correspondence, constituted an unjustified interference with the applicant's right to correspondence.

[146] (2001) 31 EHRR 25.

[147] However, there were, and still are, certain systems of self-regulation of the media, such as the Press Complaints Commission and the Broadcasting Complaints Commission, which recognised and gave limited redress for breach of privacy.

[148] *Entick v Carrington* (1765) 19 St Tr 1029.

[149] [1979] Ch 344.

the plaintiff had no remedy when the police had tapped his telephone for the purpose of detecting possible criminal activities. The plaintiff could not rely on Article 8 of the European Convention because it had not been incorporated into English law, and the domestic laws of trespass and confidentiality did not provide him with a remedy. The police were allowed to tap his telephone simply because they had committed no civil wrong in doing so. The decision in *Malone* established that no general right of privacy existed in domestic law. Thus, although various aspects of privacy and private life were recognised in a number of legal areas, unless the individual's claim clearly fell within those legal claims, a violation of his or her privacy was left without remedy.[150]

Although the courts often referred to the individual's fundamental right to privacy, they refused to apply Article 8 directly, or to recognise an individual's legal right to privacy.[151] For example, in *R v Ministry of Defence, ex parte Smith*,[152] although the Court of Appeal seemed to recognise that the applicants' fundamental rights had been interfered with by their dismissal from the armed forces on the grounds of their sexual orientation, the Court was adamant that there could be no reliance on the right to private life under Article 8 of the Convention. As a consequence, the principal violation of the right to private life – the intrusive techniques employed by the armed forces to identify the applicants' sexual orientation – did not feature in the court's assessment of the rationality of the policy.[153]

In the area of press intrusion, although a person was able to rely on a number of legal principles in order to indirectly protect his or her right to privacy, in some cases those legal rules failed to give appropriate and effective redress. For example, in *Kaye v Robertson*[154] it was held that English law did not recognise the right of privacy and thus an individual could not rely on that concept to obtain legal redress. The plaintiff was lying critically ill in hospital and was interviewed by a reporter who had sneaked into the hospital room. At first instance he had received an injunction restraining the paper from publishing the interview and the photographs. On appeal, however, it was held that the injunction could not be sustained under the law of libel, as it was not inevitable that at full trial the court would find that the plaintiff had been defamed. The court did find that the plaintiff could succeed in an action in malicious falsehood, as the words were false, published maliciously, and special damage had followed from their publication. The damage in this case was that the plaintiff would lose his right to sell his story as an exclusive. An injunction would, therefore, be granted allowing the story to be published provided it was not claimed that the plaintiff had given his consent.[155] In this case the court accepted that there had been a monstrous invasion of the plaintiff's privacy, but held that that alone did not entitle him to relief in English law.

A similar ruling was given in *R v Central Independent Television*.[156] In this case, Central Independent Television broadcast a trailer for a programme on the police detection and arrest

---

[150] See also *R v Health Secretary, ex parte C, The Times*, 1 March 2000.

[151] See, for example, *R v IRC, ex parte Rossminster* [1980] AC 852; *Haig v Aitken* [2000] 3 All ER 80.

[152] [1996] 1 All ER 257.

[153] The applicants successfully sought a remedy under the European Convention on Human Rights: *Smith and Grady v United Kingdom* (2000) 29 EHRR 493; *Lustig-Prean and Beckett v United Kingdom* (2000) 29 EHRR 548.

[154] [1991] FSR 62.

[155] With regard to the law of trespass, the court found that there was no evidence that the taking of his photograph caused him any injury by setting back his recovery.

[156] [1994] 3 All ER 641.

of a purveyor of child pornography. During the trailer Mrs R recognised the front door to her house and realised that the programme was about her ex-husband, who had been found guilty of indecent assault and who had been sentenced to six years' imprisonment. The film was to show the outside and interior of her house and would include her voice as the husband was being arrested. She was concerned that her house would be identified, and that her child would now be associated with her ex-husband's conviction, and thus sought to stop the programme. She received an injunction to stop them showing the interior of the house and the recording of her voice, and the exterior of the house and the street, but she wished to stop them using the husband's face and name because of the possible link between him and her family. The Court of Appeal held that the court's jurisdiction to protect the child did not extend to protecting the child from publicity which was not directed at the child or those who cared for them and that accordingly the judge had been wrong in making a provision that the husband's name and identity be taken out. Giving judgment, HOFFMANN LJ held that although there was room for constitutional argument as to whether in a matter so fundamentally trenching upon the freedom of the press a right of privacy should be created, it would be more appropriate for the remedy to be provided by the legislature rather than the judiciary.[157]

Inevitably, the limitations of the domestic law in this area exposed the United Kingdom to challenge before the European Court of Human Rights. In *Peck v United Kingdom*[158] the European Court held that the disclosure of local authority CCTV footage to the media showing the applicant in a state of distress constituted a serious interference with the applicant's right to respect for private life. In the Court's view, the disclosure of private, intimate, information could only be justified by an overriding requirement in the public interest and in the present case the disclosure was not accompanied by sufficient safeguards and thus constituted a disproportionate and unjustified interference with the applicant's private life under Article 8. The Court also found a violation of Article 13 because domestic law failed to provide an effective remedy, particularly as review excluded any consideration by the courts of the question whether the interference answered a pressing social need or was proportionate.

Despite the incorporation of the Convention (including Article 8) into domestic law, the House of Lords has confirmed the absence of a specific common law action in privacy. In *Wainwright v Secretary of State for the Home Department*,[159] a woman and her disabled child who were visiting friends and relatives in prison in January 1997 were subjected to a strip search by prison officers and had brought an action in trespass. The Court of Appeal held that the Human Rights Act 1998 could not be relied on so as to introduce a retrospective right to privacy that did not exist at common law. The Court also held that the decision to search the claimants had not been disproportionate to the need to clear drugs from the prison, but that in any case the judge should not have been concerned with proportionality as the events in question took place before the 1998 Act came into force.[160] Dismissing the appeal, the House of Lords held that there was no general cause of action in English law for invasion of individual privacy, and that although the courts had in the post-Act era developed the law of confidentiality in a manner which resembled the right to private life under Article 8 of the Convention, those cases only applied to that cause of action and were not authority

---

[157] In the post-Human Rights Act era the case would be dealt with by balancing the respective interests in private life and freedom of expression. See below, and chapter 6, pages 603–4.
[158] (2003) 36 EHRR 719: the case is examined in detail in the case study at the end of this chapter.
[159] [2004] 2 AC 406.
[160] [2002] 3 WLR 405.

for the proposition that there now existed a separate action in privacy. Moreover, their Lordships held that the absence of a specific law of privacy in domestic law did not conflict with the United Kingdom's obligations under the European Convention; the Convention did not require that an individual be able to make a separate claim for breach of privacy,[161] merely requiring that domestic law provide an adequate remedy when Article 8 had been violated. In their Lordships' opinion the Human Rights Act 1998 now provided a statutory remedy with respect to violations committed by public authorities, and thus there was no need for the common law to be developed so as to provide a specific claim in the tort of privacy.[162]

In their Lordships' view, therefore, it was not essential to develop a common law action in privacy. In the post-Act era, victims of privacy breaches could bring claims against public authorities under the 1998 Act (or in related proceedings) and in other cases (including as in the present when the act precedes the Act) the claimant could rely on (adequate) common law remedies. However, the subsequent proceedings before the European Court of Human Rights further exposed the limitations of the traditional common law remedies. In *Wainwright v United Kingdom*,[163] although the European Court did not find a violation of Article 3,[164] it concluded that the interference with private life in this case could not be considered necessary in a democratic society. In the Court's view, where procedures were laid down for the proper conduct of searches to be carried out on outsiders to the prison the authorities were required to comply strictly with any such safeguards and by rigorous precautions protect the dignity of those being searched as far as possible. In this case it was clear that the authorities had not carried out those searches in accordance with those safeguards and thus there was a violation of Article 8. Further, the Court found a violation of Article 13 of the Convention, guaranteeing the right to an effective remedy. Although the applicants had been allowed to bring a civil action for damages in connection with the events, that claim had failed save the claim for battery brought by Mrs Wainwright's son. Individuals should have available to them a means of obtaining redress for any alleged interference with their Convention rights, and in the present case the substance of the applicants' claims had failed primarily because the domestic courts failed to recognise a general tort of invasion of privacy.[165]

The European Court's finding under Article 8 was thus in conflict with the domestic courts' assessment of the facts, and the House of Lords' belief that the courts did not have to develop a common law of privacy in order to comply with the European Convention. Thus, once the European Court applied the principles of legality and proportionality to the facts, it found a clear violation of Article 8, a violation that the domestic courts were unable to find by applying

---

[161] See *Winer* v *United Kingdom* (1986) 48 DR 154.

[162] Their Lordships stated *obiter* that even had the Act been in force at the time, it was doubtful whether the claimants would have succeeded in their claim with respect to Article 8 because it did not follow that a negligent act (as in the present case) would give rise to liability for damages simply because it affected the privacy of the individual.

[163] (2007) 44 EHRR 40.

[164] In the Court's opinion the search served a legitimate preventive measure in respect of the endemic drug problems within the prison and that although the officers had failed to comply with their own procedures and had demonstrated 'sloppiness' and a lack of courtesy, and the procedure had caused obvious distress to the applicants, it did not reach the minimum level of severity prohibited by Article 3.

[165] With respect to just satisfaction under Article 41, although the Court noted that it did not, as a matter of practice, make aggravated or exemplary damages awards, having regard to the undoubted and more than transient distress suffered by the applicants it awarded each applicant €3000 each for non-pecuniary loss.

the common law rules relating to trespass and assault. More importantly, its decision under Article 13 casts doubt on the House of Lords' dicta that the passing of the Human Rights Act 1998 and the existence of common law remedies was sufficient to comply with the Convention. In *Wainwright*, although the claimants had recourse to a legal remedy with respect to the searches, the restrictions on those remedies, including the absence of proportionality, was clearly exposed. The case also raised concerns that the Act's provisions do not apply retrospectively to actions occurring before it came into force. Consequently, the House of Lords' refusal to allow the Act to have a retrospective effect on the development of the common law meant that the claimants needed to have recourse to the Convention procedure.

Questions

How was privacy protected in domestic law before the passing of the Human Rights Act 1998? How satisfactory was that protection with respect to the United Kingdom's obligations under the European Convention?

Privacy and the Human Rights Act 1998

The passing of the Human Rights Act 1998 provided an opportunity for the law to develop a legal remedy for the protection of privacy and private life.[166] First, the victim of a violation of Article 8 of the Convention can bring an action under the Act itself, claiming that a public authority has violated the right to private life.[167] In cases such as *Malone*, therefore, the claimant will be able to bring a direct action against the police authorities under s.7 of the 1998 Act. Secondly, as courts are public authorities within the Act, they have a duty to develop and interpret the law, both public and private, to ensure that (Article 8) rights are not violated, and to provide a remedy if none existed prior to the Act. For example, in a case such as *Kaye v Robertson*, above, the court will have the opportunity to expand the common law of confidentiality to protect the claimant from interference with his privacy interests (see below). Thirdly, under s.12(4) of the 1998 Act the courts have a duty to take into account the contents of any privacy code in deciding whether to grant relief which affects freedom of expression. Such provisions must, therefore, be balanced against freedom of expression in cases involving press freedom and the right to privacy.[168]

Thus, after the Human Rights Act, the private law of confidentiality, defamation and copyright, etc., will need to be refined so as to accommodate the horizontal application of the Human Rights Act and the right to privacy needs to be protected by both the passing, modification and reinterpretation of privacy legislation, and the development of private common law rules and principles. Almost immediately after the Act came into operation the courts began to use these new powers to develop a law of privacy. Thus, in *Douglas v Hello! Magazine*[169] the

---

[166] See Singh and Strachan, The Right to Privacy in English Law [2002] EHRLR 129.

[167] See *R (Bernard and Another) v Enfield LBC, The Times*, 8 November 2002, where damages were awarded against the local authority for its failure to respect the claimants' right to private and family life.

[168] See Markensinis, Privacy, Freedom of Expression, and the Horizontal Effect of the Human Rights Bill: Lessons from Germany (1999) 115 LQR 47; Singh, Privacy and the Media after the Human Rights Act [1998] EHRLR 712.

[169] [2001] 2 WLR 992.

Court of Appeal accepted that the common law had reached the point where the right to privacy could now be recognised, and in *Venables and Thompson* v *MGN*[170] the same law of confidentiality was expanded so as to protect the claimants from a threat to their lives, which in the court's view were under threat because of the proposed disclosure of information relating to their identity and whereabouts.

As we shall see, this development was achieved not by creating a new law of privacy as such, but by expanding the existing law of confidentiality and data protection in the light of Article 8 of the European Convention.[171] For example, in *R* v *Wakefield MBC, ex parte Robertson*[172] the law of confidentiality and data protection was used to prohibit the electoral authorities from passing on the claimant's personal details for various marketing purposes. In the court's view, the refusal of the authorities to allow the claimant to have his name removed from an electoral register before that register was sold to a commercial concern was a breach of his right to private life and his right to vote under Article 3 of the First Protocol to the Convention. In this case, therefore, the court used Article 8, and the principles of proportionality, to inform the application of existing data protection law.[173]

A legitimate expectation of privacy?

In such cases the courts first need to establish which aspects of a person's private life fall within Article 8 of the European Convention. This may involve the court in distinguishing between information relating to a person's private life and information that relates to his or her public rights or duties. As we shall see with respect to modern confidentiality claims, the courts will pose the question whether the claimant had a legitimate expectation of privacy? For example, in *R* v *Law Society, ex parte Pamplin*,[174] it was held that information relating to an allegation about the claimant's conduct as a solicitor, which had been passed on from the Chief Constable of Lancashire to the Law Society, related to the claimant's employment and thus was part of his public life. Although such a distinction is dubious, and often impossible to separate, the courts will need to make some form of distinction, either to decide whether the claim falls into Article 8, or on the reasonableness and proportionality of the interference. Again, in *H* v *Tomlinson*,[175] the Court of Appeal held that there was no arguable case that the disclosure by a head teacher of allegedly defamatory comments to a statutory disciplinary panel investigating the exclusion of a child from school for violent conduct was in breach of his right to private life. The report made to the panel did not simply discuss the boy's conduct in the home, but his public arrest outside his home for violence. The boy could not reasonably expect that such information would not have been made public to a statutory body set up to consider whether his conduct justified his exclusion, particularly as he had a history of using violence.

---

[170] [2001] 2 WLR 1038.

[171] See the Court of Appeal decision in *A* v *B plc and Another* [2002] 3 WLR 542, and the House of Lords' decision in *Campbell* v *MGN Ltd* [2004] 2 AC 457, considered below.

[172] [2002] 2 WLR 889.

[173] Section 11 of the Data Protection Act 1998 and Article 14 of European Directive 95/46/EC. Shortly after the decision, the Minister for Local Government published draft regulations to allow for two registers, one only being available for limited purposes such as crime prevention. The new scheme has been declared compatible with the Human Rights Act: *R (Robertson)* v *The Secretary of State and Others, The Times,* 11 August 2003.

[174] *The Independent,* 9 August 2001.

[175] [2008] EWCA Civ 1258.

The court will be especially influenced by the public nature of the information and activity concerned. Thus, in *Author of a Blog* v *Times Newspaper*[176] it was held that the contributor to a 'blog' on a website – a serving police officer commenting on police practices – was not entitled to an injunction restraining the defendants from identifying him. Those who used 'blog' sites had no reasonable expectation of privacy as the site was public, as opposed to cases where claimants had sought to suppress intimate and private information; in this case there was a significant public element in the information sought to be restricted.[177] In contrast, in *Re Attorney General's Reference No 3 of 1999*,[178] the House of Lords held that a defendant acquitted of rape had an expectation of privacy because although the fact of acquittal was not private information, the fact that there had been a link between his DNA and the commission of the offence was personal information. Such information suggested he was guilty and his right to a fair trial and privacy thus engaged Article 8.[179]

That the question of the legitimacy of any privacy claim is complex and open to argument is clear from the case of *Wood* v *Commissioner of Police of the Metropolis*.[180] In this case the police had taken photographs of the claimant whilst attending the AGM of a company who had been targeted by an anti-arms group of which the claimant was associated. The High Court held that Article 8 had not been engaged as he had no reasonable expectation of privacy at the time.[181] This was because he had attended as a media coordinator of a high profile national pressure group and that as a member of the anti-arms group was actively and publicly canvassing those attending the meeting. In those circumstances it would not have been surprising if press interest had led to photographs, in a public street, being taken. That decision was overturned by the Court of Appeal, who, relying on Convention case law,[182] disagreed with the High Court that the images were being retained for very limited purposes and that their retention was not part of the compilation of a general dossier of information concerning the claimant so as to constitute an interference with Article 8 rights. The Court found that as it was clear that these photographs would be retained and used, their taking thus amounted to a sufficient intrusion into private life. Further, once it was evident that the claimant had committed no offence, the police had failed to show that the retention was necessary and proportionate. It is clear therefore that the question of whether there is an expectation of privacy is inextricably linked with the legality and necessity of official intervention; the Court of Appeal in this case being insistent on regulating what would otherwise be arbitrary powers.[183]

---

[176] [2009] EMLR 22.

[177] Alternatively the court found that there was a public interest in free speech outweighing any privacy interest.

[178] [2010] 1 AC 145.

[179] On the facts the House of Lords held that freedom of expression outweighed that expectation of privacy. The present government has abandoned plans to offer pre-trial anonymity to rape defendants and instead will negotiate with the Press Complaints Commission to ensue anonymity on the press: Minister in U-turn on Rape Charge Anonymity, *Guardian*, 26 July 2010, page 6.

[180] [2009] 1 WLR 123.

[181] [2008] HRLR 34.

[182] *S and Marper* v *United Kingdom* (Retention of DNA Samples) (2009) 49 EHRR 50. The case is detailed later in this chapter, at page 639.

[183] Contrast *Re East Sussex Council and Others* [2009] EWHC 935 (Fam), where it was held that reporting restrictions banning the press publishing photographs of three teenagers and a two-month-old girl, were no longer viable as the images were now extensively in the public domain. The restrictions would have constituted a disproportionate interference with the media's attempts to clarify earlier misinformation relating to the paternity.

The publicity given to court proceedings has also raised issues in this area. In *Clibbery* v *Allan*[184] it was held that no confidentiality was attached to personal information conveyed in the course of family proceedings.[185] In that case a party to proceedings in the Family Division had sought an injunction prohibiting the defendant from disclosing details of their case to a national newspaper. Upholding a refusal to grant the injunction, the Court of Appeal conceded that there may be cases where genuinely confidential or sensitive personal information may need to be restricted, but that the ban on disclosure in this case was not necessary and did not correspond to a pressing social need. Although different considerations applied in cases concerning children,[186] whether proceedings were protected by secrecy depended on whether the administration of justice would be impeded or prejudiced by the publication. The general rule was that it was not a contempt of court to report what happened in chambers and that the principle of open justice was to be derogated from only to the extent that it was strictly necessary to do so, and applied equally to publication of information. Although having a liberalising effect on freedom of expression, the decision can be questioned on the basis that it gives too little effect to privacy and confidentiality.[187]

Justified interference?

The courts will also have to decide whether the right to private life can take precedence over other interests, particularly where privacy conflicts with other Convention rights such as freedom of speech. In this respect the courts can, of course, be guided by the case law of the European Convention, which often places freedom of expression over and above the privacy interests of public figures.[188] However, the courts will need to be careful to accommodate the right to private life, and the courts have stressed that when privacy conflicts with freedom of expression, they should not give the latter a trump or superior status.[189] Such a balancing exercise is often difficult and a certain area of discretion will be given to the authorities. For example, in *R (X)* v *Chief Constable of the West Midlands Police*[190] it was held that although the chief constable of the police had to have regard both to the principles of natural justice and Article 8 of the

---

[184] [2002] 2 WLR 1511.

[185] See also *Revenue and Customs Commissioners* v *Banerjee* [2009] 3 All ER 330, where it was held that a taxpayer was not entitled to an order of anonymity with respect to her tax proceedings. The case is detailed in chapter 7, at page 325.

[186] See, for example, *Re X (a Child)* [2009] EMLR 26, where an order was made excluding the media from attending residence and contact proceedings concerning the child of well-known public figures. The court noted that although cases concerning children of celebrities were not to be treated differently, there would inevitably be more intense media coverage of such that would impact on the child's interests.

[187] See also *R (Axon)* v *Secretary of State for Health* [2006] 2 WLR 1130, where it was held that parental rights under Article 8 had not been violated when an under-16 patient's confidentiality was preserved when seeking advice on contraception. Since the relevant guidance provided that advice would only be given when the young person understood the implications of such advice, there was no interference with family life under Article 8. Alternatively, any interference constituted a proportionate measure in ensuring that young people were not discouraged from seeking advice.

[188] See, for example, *Lingens* v *Austria* (1986) 8 EHRR 407 in relation to the law of defamation and Article 10 of the European Convention. Contrast the decision in *Von Hannover* v *Germany* (2005) 40 EHRR 1. The balancing of press freedom and privacy is considered in detail below.

[189] See the House of Lords' decision in *Re S (Publicity)*, discussed in chapter 9, page 467. See *O'Riordan* v *DPP*, *The Times*, 31 May 2005, where it was held that the offence under s.1 and s.5 of the Sexual Offences (Amendment) Act 1992 of publishing information likely to divulge the identity of a young victim of a sexual offence was not incompatible with Article 10 of the European Convention.

[190] [2005] 1 WLR 65.

European Convention in deciding whether there was a pressing social need to disclose details of allegations of sexual abuse to potential employers under s.115(7) of the Police Act 1997, such rules were flexible. The police had provided information about two incidents of alleged sexual abuse by the applicant to a social work agency to whom the applicant had applied for employment. At first instance it was held that the applicant should have been given the right to stress that one allegation had proved to be incorrect and was attributable to another person, and that the police had broken the rules of natural justice by not contacting the applicant and allowing him to make representations before disclosing such information.[191] However, on appeal, the Court of Appeal held that there was no presumption against disclosure and that the constable was under a duty to disclose that information if it might be relevant unless there was a good reason for not making a disclosure. In the Court's view, it imposed too heavy an obligation on the Chief Constable to require him to give an opportunity to make representations to him prior to performing his statutory duty: X had had ample opportunity to set out his account during his police interview and was able to explain his position to his potential employers or to correct the certificate under the Act.[192]

The courts will be particularly concerned that such disclosures are subject to necessary safeguards which will adequately protect the individual's right to privacy. Thus in *R (L) v Commissioner of the Police of the Metropolis*,[193] it was held that s.115(7) of the Police Act 1997, which allowed the police to include certain personal information on an individual in an enhanced criminal record certificate, was not incompatible with Article 8, provided the words 'ought to be included' were interpreted so that the chief constable gave proper consideration to the applicant's right to private life. The police would, therefore, have to consider whether such information would interfere with the person's private life and whether such interference was justified and proportionate on the facts. For example, in *R (F and Thompson) v Secretary of State for Justice*,[194] the Supreme Court held that s.82 of the Sexual Offences Act 2003 – which subjected sex offenders to indefinite notification requirements that affected their travel arrangements – was disproportionate and thus incompatible with Article 8 of the European Convention. This was because the requirements were not subject to review or dependent on the ability of the offender to prove that they were no longer a risk. Further, in *R (Wright and Others) v Secretary of State for Health*[195] the House of Lords held that Article 8 was violated when nurses had been placed on a provisional list that would prevent them from working as carers with vulnerable adults. Their Lordships held that the powers under the Care Standards Act 2000 to prevent the employee from working in that field were potentially disproportionate given the social stigma created by that listing. Their Lordships noted that the scope of the ban was very wide and that although the lists were not made public, the fact was likely to get about and the stigma would be considerable. The scheme under the Act should

---

[191] [2004] 1 WLR 1518.

[192] See also *Stone v Kent CC and Others* [2006] EWHC 1668 (Admin), where it was held the public interest required publication in full of a report following an independent inquiry into a person who had been convicted of two murders and one attempted murder, and who had cooperated with the report. Although there was a great interest in protecting the privacy of medical records, the strong public interest in the claimant's behaviour and his treatment, together with his concession that some publication was necessary, outweighed his claim of privacy.

[193] [2010] 1 AC 410.

[194] [2010] 2 WLR 992.

[195] [2009] 1 AC 739.

be devised in such a way as to ensure that the procedures were fair in the light of the importance of the interests at stake. In particular, the low threshold for provisional listing added to the risk of arbitrary and unjustified interferences and thus contributed to the overall unfairness of the scheme.

> **Questions**
> To what extent has the right to privacy and private life been incorporated into domestic law by the passing of the Human Rights Act 1998?
> Do you believe that domestic law now recognises a right to privacy?

Privacy-related domestic law

As the courts appear reluctant to develop a specific law of privacy, the development of privacy rights will, it appears, rely on the expansion of existing law. This section of the chapter considers those areas of domestic law that seek to protect the various aspects of private life identified above, highlighting the impact of the European Convention on the interpretation and application of those laws.

The protection of reputation and confidential information

The laws of defamation and confidentiality have already been discussed in chapter 9 of this book dealing with free speech and the protection of reputation and confidentiality. In that chapter we examined how the respective laws imposed restrictions on the right of free speech, and in particular on press freedom, and how those laws sought a balance between free speech and press freedom on the one hand and the individual's right to private life and reputation on the other. Although those two aims are inextricably linked, this section of the book will concentrate on the latter issue: whether the laws of defamation and confidentiality provide adequate protection of a person's privacy.

Defamation and the protection of privacy

Both domestic law and European Convention case law recognise that a central purpose of the law of defamation is to protect an individual's right to private life.[196] Thus the protection of a person's reputation is a legitimate aim under the heading 'the rights of others' and also raises specific issues under Article 8 of the Convention.[197] The inability of a person to seek redress for a violation of their reputation is thus a *prima facie* violation of Article 8,[198] and the courts must also ensure that the relevant law provides a proportionate remedy for such

---

[196] *Tolstoy Miloslavsky* v *United Kingdom* (1995) 20 EHRR 442. This includes the reputations of multinational corporations: *Steel and Morris* v *United Kingdom* (2005) 41 EHRR 22.

[197] Article 17 of the International Covenant on Civil and Political Rights 1966 and Article 12 of the Universal Declaration of Human Rights 1948 specifically mention this right by stating that no one shall be subjected to arbitrary or unlawful interference with their privacy, family, home or correspondence, or to unlawful attacks on their honour and reputation.

[198] See *A* v *United Kingdom* (2003) 36 EHRR 51, where it was claimed that the inability to sue a member of parliament for allegedly defamatory comments was a violation of Article 8. The application failed on its merits.

violation.[199] This will include a duty on behalf of the courts to ensure that damages in defamation cases adequately compensate the claimant for any privacy interests violated by the untruth.

Although the law of defamation provides a remedy in a case where the claimant's private or public reputation is attacked, it does not provide a remedy for general intrusions into a person's privacy or private life.[200] First, the remedy only applies to information that is untrue; private information that is true is thus left unprotected under this area of law. Secondly, the claimant must show that his reputation has been damaged. Thus, in *Kaye v Robertson*[201] the Court of Appeal refused the plaintiff a remedy in libel on the basis that the public would not have thought less of him had he sold his story to the newspapers while in a critical medical state.[202] Finally, the claimant is not normally entitled to an injunction before the full trial,[203] and must, therefore, wait for the untruth to be published, or published further, and then rely on damages as his remedy.

Confidentiality and the protection of privacy

Although the original purpose of the law of confidentiality was to protect the commercial interests of the claimant, the law can be, and has been, used to safeguard privacy interests.[204] Thus a claimant may use the law to stop the publication of personal information, or to compensate him or her after such publication. Although in such cases a person's commercial interests may have been affected by disclosure, in many cases the main damage has been caused to the person's privacy rights. A person who has had details of his or her sex life published in the newspapers may well have suffered financially because of such disclosures because they threaten his or her professional reputation and standing; nevertheless, in such cases a person's privacy interests have been infringed: private and confidential information has been made public and the person's privacy has been invaded. Such individuals will as a consequence seek a remedy in the law, either in the form of injunctive relief or by the payment of compensation, and as the law of confidentiality allows remedies based on prior restraint, it can be an effective tool in protecting the rights of the individual.[205]

The development of the law of confidentiality as a privacy remedy

The law of confidentiality and copyright was used to protect private confidential information in *Prince Albert v Strange*[206] in order to prevent an employee from exploiting private drawings owned by the plaintiffs, members of the Royal Family, which had been given to his employers by the plaintiffs. The court found that the employee had obtained the drawings in breach of

---

[199] The balance between the protection of reputation and of freedom of expression has already been discussed in chapter 9 of this text.

[200] *Corelli* v *Wall* (1906) 22 TLR 532.

[201] [1991] FSR 62.

[202] The plaintiff did, however, obtain a limited remedy in the tort of malicious falsehood.

[203] *Bonnard* v *Perryman* [1891] 2 Ch 269, upheld in the post-Human Rights Act era in *Green* v *Associated Newspapers* [2005] 3 WLR 281.

[204] The requirements of an action in confidentiality have already been outlined in chapter 9 on freedom of expression and the protection of reputation and confidentiality.

[205] Confidentiality can also be protected indirectly by the courts restraining publication of information, which if disclosed would pre-empt issues of confidentiality that are to be raised in other proceedings. See *H v N (A Health Authority); H v Associated Newspapers* [2002] EMLR 23, where the court restrained the defendants from identifying a person who had contracted AIDS.

[206] (1842) 2 De G & Sm 652.

confidence, and awarded an injunction to prevent any commercial exploitation. The law was then applied to protect information pertaining to private confidential relationships, such as marriage. For example, in *Argyll* v *Argyll*,[207] the court granted an injunction to the plaintiff to stop the newspapers from disclosing intimate details of his marriage relationship, which had been provided by his wife.[208]

Although the law protected private information, the case law had appeared to require some form of contractual agreement to attach liability for breaches of confidence. However, in *Stephens* v *Avery*[209] it was held that it was not necessary that the relationship in question was legally binding. In that case the plaintiff had confided in her friend about a sexual relationship that she had had with a woman who had subsequently been killed by her husband. In breach of a promise to keep the information confidential, the defendant had sold the story to the newspapers and the plaintiff sought an injunction to prevent publication. It was held that the fact that the matter was concerned with sexual relations outside marriage did not take away the law's protection.[210] Further, the sexual conduct of the plaintiff was not so morally shocking in this case as to stop the newspaper from spreading the story all over its pages; the wholesale revelation of the sexual conduct of an individual could not properly be called trivial 'tittle tattle'. The court also held that the relationship of the parties was not the determining factor in an action of confidentiality; rather it was the acceptance of the information on the basis that it would be kept secret that affected the conscience of the recipient. In the present case the plaintiff's clear statement imposed the clearest duty on the defendant. The court also held that the fact that information was now known by two people did not mean that the information had lost its confidentiality; information only ceased to be incapable of protection when it was in fact known to a substantial number of people.[211]

There was also authority to the effect that the law of confidentiality could be used in cases where confidential information was acquired by illegal means. Thus, in *Francome* v *Mirror Group Newspapers*,[212] the *Daily Mirror* was offered tape recordings of the plaintiff's bugged telephone conversations. The plaintiff, pending an action for trespass and breach of confidence, sought an interim injunction. It was held that although the users of a telephone take the risk of crossed lines and of official telephone tapping, they are entitled to regard their conversations as confidential and anyone overhearing the conversations knows this. Accordingly, there was an arguable case that the plaintiff had a right of confidentiality in his telephone call and a temporary injunction was granted.[213]

---

[207] [1967] Ch 302.

[208] In this case it was accepted that the right to confidentiality was not lost merely because the plaintiff had published certain information himself, as his revelations were reasonable and sober. Contrast *Lennon* v *Mirror Group Newspapers* [1978] FSR 573, where an injunction was refused because both parties had brought their private affairs into the public domain to such an extent that an injunction to protect confidential information would have been inappropriate.

[209] [1988] 2 WLR 1280.

[210] See subsequent decisions in *A* v *B plc* and *CC* v *AB*, considered below.

[211] See also *Barrymore* v *Newsgroup Newspapers Ltd* [1997] FSR 600, where an injunction was granted to stop the further publication of extracts of letters written by the claimant, a television personality, to his homosexual lover. In this case the court held that the information about the relationship is for the relationship and not for a wider purpose.

[212] [1984] 2 All ER 408.

[213] See also *Jockey Club* v *Buffham, The Times*, 4 October 2002. It has subsequently been held that the mere fact that information has been acquired illegally does not automatically mean that there has been a breach of confidence: *Campbell* v *MGN Ltd* [2004] 2 AC 457, discussed below.

Despite the development of the law of confidence to protect certain aspects of privacy, it was clear that the law did not protect the right of privacy as such. The law did not protect the individual merely because private information was disclosed or an individual's privacy was invaded. For example, in *Kaye v Robertson*[214] the Court of Appeal held that the right was unknown to English law, even though it was satisfied that the action of the newspapers in conducting and publishing an interview with him when he lay critically ill in hospital was a monstrous invasion of privacy.

However, subsequent cases seemed to suggest that there was no requirement of any duty to keep such information private, along with a breach of that duty. Thus, in *Shelley Films Ltd v Rex Features Ltd*[215] the defendant was restrained by an injunction from publishing photographs which had been taken without permission on the set of a film. Similarly, in *Hellewell v Chief Constable of Derbyshire*[216] the court seemed to accept that a breach of confidence had taken place when the police took a photograph of the plaintiff, a suspect at a police station, for their 'Stop watch' scheme, although a remedy was refused on the basis that it was in the public interest to publish. In that case LAWS J opined that if a person with a telephoto lens were to take a photograph of another engaged in some private act, his subsequent disclosure of the photo would amount to a breach of confidence. Most famously, an injunction was granted in *HRH Princess of Wales v MGN Newspapers*,[217] where photographs of the Princess of Wales had been taken while she was exercising in a private gymnasium. She sought injunctions to stop their publication on the grounds of breach of contract and confidentiality and an interim injunction was granted to stop the publication of the photographs, the court appearing to accept that the information – a photographic image – was capable of being classified as confidential. These cases established that the duty of confidentiality could be imposed unilaterally and did not have to be founded on the breach of any express or implied agreement of the parties[218] and provided the basis of the development of the law of confidentiality under the Human Rights Act 1998 (see below).

Confidentiality and the Human Rights Act 1998

Since the coming into operation of the Human Rights Act 1998, the law of confidentiality has been used to develop a law of privacy that is consistent with Article 8 of the European Convention.[219] In *Douglas v Hello! Magazine*[220] it was held that although previous authority had established that there was no law of privacy as such in English law, under the Human Rights Act 1998 the courts had the duty to remedy the deficiencies of the common law so as to comply with the United Kingdom's obligations under the European Convention.[221] In that case the Court of Appeal recognised that the claimants had an expectation of privacy and

---

[214] [1991] FSR 62.

[215] [1994] EMLR 134.

[216] [1995] 1 WLR 804.

[217] Unreported, 8 November 1993.

[218] See also *Creation Records Ltd v Newsgroup Newspapers Ltd* [1997] EMLR 444, where the court granted an injunction to stop the further publication of a photograph of the pop group Oasis, taken surreptitiously at a photo session to promote the group's new album.

[219] See Strachan and Singh, The Right of Privacy in English Law [2002] EHRLR 129; Phillipson, Transforming Breach of Confidence? Towards a Common Law Right of Privacy under the Human Rights Act [2003] MLR 726; Wright, *Tort Law and Human Rights* (Hart 2002), chapter 7.

[220] [2001] 2 WLR 992. See Morgan, Privacy, Confidence and Horizontal Effect: 'Hello' Trouble [2003] CLJ 442.

[221] Relying on decisions of the European Court in cases such as *A v United Kingdom* (1999) 27 EHRR 611.

confidentiality with respect to photographs taken at their wedding, a decision which was later upheld by the House of Lords.[222] In particular the Court noted that the decision of the European Commission of Human Rights in *Earl Spencer* v *United Kingdom*[223] appeared to suggest that the domestic law of confidentiality did, or at least should, provide a remedy for invasion of an individual's privacy. LORD JUSTICE SEDLEY LJ stated that English law has reached the point at which it can be said with confidence that the law recognises and will appropriately protect a right of personal privacy. In his Lordship's view, this was the case because the domestic law was now in a position to respond to an increasingly invasive social environment by affirming that everybody has the right to some private space. Specifically, his Lordship held that the courts were now under a duty to give appropriate effect to Article 8 of the European Convention, which guarantees the right to private life, and that the courts had to give horizontal effect to the Convention via the interpretation and application of domestic law.[224] His Lordship also held that there was nothing in s.12 of the Human Rights Act that required the courts to give freedom of expression an enhanced status over and above the right to private life contained in Article 8. Both rights were to be articulated by the principles of legality and proportionality contained in the Convention itself.

In *Venables and Thompson* v *MGN Ltd*,[225] it was accepted that although it might not be possible to rely on a free-standing application under the Convention, because the defendants were not public authorities within the Act, nevertheless the duty of the courts was to act compatibly with Convention rights in adjudicating upon existing common law causes of action. In this case the claimants, the young killers of James Bulger, were seeking an injunction against the defendant newspapers to prohibit them from disclosing details of their new identities and their whereabouts, on the basis that such disclosure would violate, *inter alia*, their right to life and private life under Articles 2 and 8 of the European Convention. After stressing the importance of freedom of expression, both under Article 10 of the Convention and s.12 of the Human Rights Act 1998, DAME ELIZABETH BUTLER-SLOSS P was satisfied that the law of confidence could extend to cover the injunctions sought in this case. In her Ladyship's view, there was a well-established cause of action in the tort of breach of confidence in respect of which the injunctions could be granted.[226] Accepting that the common law continued to evolve, and noting the decision of the Court of Appeal in *Douglas* v *Hello!*, her Ladyship stated that the duty of confidence now arose in equity independently of any transaction or relationship between the parties.

With respect to the facts, her Ladyship held that it was the duty of the court, where necessary, to take appropriate steps to safeguard the physical safety of the claimants, including the adoption of measures even in the sphere of relations of individuals and/or private organisations between themselves. The court concluded that on release the claimants would be in a most exceptional situation and the risks to them of identification were real and substantial. There were compelling reasons to grant the injunctions to protect the relevant information, and in these exceptional circumstances it was necessary to place the right to confidence above the right of the media

---

[222] *OBG Ltd and Others* v *Allan and Others* [2008] 1 AC.

[223] (1998) 25 EHRR 105.

[224] His Lordship relied on *X* v *Netherlands* (1985) 8 EHRR 235.

[225] [2001] 2 WLR 1038.

[226] It was important for the court to establish this, because then the consequent restriction on freedom of expression would have a legal basis and thus be prescribed by law for the purpose of Article 10(2) of the European Convention.

to publish freely.[227] A similar approach was adopted some years later when one of the boys had been convicted of downloading indecent images of children and the court awarded an injunction to prevent his, and the other boy's, identity being disclosed, noting that there was still a real and high risk of them being attacked.[228] In giving judgment, BEAN J stated that it is a fundamental duty of the State to ensure that suspects, defendants and prisoners are protected from violence and not subjected to retribution or punishment except in accordance with the sentence of a court.

Although the facts in the above case were exceptional, the courts have provided protection in cases where there was no real threat to the claimant's life. Thus, in *X (Mary Bell) and Another v News Group Newspapers and Another*,[229] the court granted a lifetime injunction prohibiting the identification of the whereabouts of Mary Bell, who had been found guilty of the murder of two young children at the age of 11. Unlike the decision in *Venables*, above, the court did not recognise any threat to the claimant's, or her daughter's life, but felt that the exceptional circumstances justified the protection of their right to private and family life. The court considered the fragility of Mary Bell's mental health and the danger that her rehabilitation and new life would be frustrated by intense media and public attention.

In the above cases privacy protection has been achieved, not by the creation of a new tort or action in privacy, but by the development of the law of confidentiality, and in *A v B plc and Another*,[230] the Court of Appeal held that it was not necessary for the courts to develop a separate tort of privacy. Giving judgment, LORD WOOLF CJ stated that it was most unlikely that any purpose would be served by a judge seeking to decide whether there existed a new cause of action in tort protecting privacy. In his Lordship's view, in the great majority, if not all situations, where the protection of privacy was justified, an action for breach of confidence would, where appropriate, provide the necessary protection. This was confirmed by the House of Lords in *Campbell v MGN Ltd*,[231] and in *Wainwright* (above, pages 593–5) the House of Lords confirmed that the dicta of SEDLEY LJ in *Douglas* related specifically to the law of confidentiality.

In cases such as *Campbell*, discussed below under privacy and press freedom, the courts began to develop the law of confidentiality so as to better reflect the new privacy interests that it was needed to recognise if domestic law was to become Convention compliant. Thus, in *Campbell* the majority of their Lordships concluded that the information in question – details of her drug treatment – was such that the claimant had a *reasonable expectation of privacy*. Correspondingly, the defendant newspapers ought to have known that there was a reasonable expectation that the information would be kept confidential. This replaced the former tests of confidentiality, which were more suited to cases of commercial and industrial secrets,[232] and which insisted on a breach of some form of confidential relationship.

However, despite the development of this more flexible test of confidentiality, the courts will treat the claimant's case more seriously when there has been a formal breach of confidence.

---

[227] See also *Carr v News Group Newspapers Ltd* [2005] EWHC 971, where a lifelong injunction was granted protecting the claimant, Maxine Carr, from revelations as to her identity and whereabouts. The court was persuaded by actual threats against the claimant's life.

[228] *Venables and Thompson v News Group Papers Ltd* [2010] EWHC (QB).

[229] [2003] EMLR 37.

[230] [2002] 3 WLR 542.

[231] [2004] 2 AC 457.

[232] *Coco v Clark* [1968] FSR 415, considered in chapter 9, page 460.

Thus, in *HRH Prince of Wales* v *Associated Newspapers*,[233] the Prince of Wales was granted an injunction to stop the publication of his stolen political diaries on grounds of breach of confidence and copyright, the court paying particular attention to the fact that the diaries were misappropriated by someone in a position of trust. Similarly, in *Attorney-General* v *MGN Ltd*,[234] an injunction was granted on behalf of the Royal Family to stop the further publication of material acquired by a former employee of the Royal household and in breach of an express covenant in his contract of employment.[235]

Balancing confidentiality/privacy and freedom of expression

It is often necessary for the courts to conduct a balancing exercise in order to determine which Convention or other claim should succeed on the facts. This matter has been examined in chapter 9 of this text (pages 466–9), but this dilemma is particularly acute when the right to private or family life comes into conflict with another Convention right, for example freedom of expression or another aspect of private life.[236] Thus, although the cases below mainly concern privacy versus freedom of expression there may be a more general public interest in compromising privacy, and in doing so disclosure may uphold the rights of others. For example, in *Brent LBC* v *K*[237] it was held that there was a clear public interest in permitting a local authority to disclose to another authority the fact that a person working in a care home had been found guilty of assaulting her child. Thus, despite the potential disadvantages to the mother's enjoyment of her private and family life, the need for public safety and the interests of the woman's patient outweighed any Article 8 rights and justified disclosure.

With respect to the balance between privacy and free speech, in *Re S (Publicity)*[238] the House of Lords confirmed that freedom of expression under Article 10 did not have an automatic 'trump' status and that when freedom of expression came into conflict with another Convention right s.12(4) of the Human Rights Act did not require the court to give pre-eminence to either article. Instead, the judge had to consider the magnitude of the interference proposed and then what steps were necessary to prevent or minimise that interference. In *Re S* an order had been sought restraining the identification of a murderer (who was the child's mother) and her victim (the child's brother) in order to protect the welfare of a child who was in care. It was held that the court should conduct a pure balancing exercise between the child's right to private life and the right of freedom of expression and the interests of open justice. On the facts it was held that the trial judge was entitled to give precedence to freedom of expression, and to follow the general principle in relation to the reporting of criminal proceedings unless the child's interests clearly outweighed the public interest in free speech. Similarly,

---

[233] [2007] 2 All ER 139.

[234] Unreported, decision of the Chancery Division, 20 November 2003.

[235] The employee was in fact a journalist employed by the *Daily Mirror* and the latter had written extensive articles based on information provided by him. See also *Archer* v *Williams* [2003] EMLR 38, where Mary Archer was granted an injunction restraining her former employee from disclosing confidential details of Lord and Lady Archer in breach of an express clause in her contract of service. She was also granted £2500 damages when the employee disclosed that Lady Archer had had a facelift, details of which later appeared in a newspaper.

[236] See Delany and Murphy, Towards Common Principles Relating to the Protection of Privacy Rights? [2007] EHRLR 568.

[237] [2007] EWHC 1250 (Fam).

[238] [2005] 1 AC 593. See Fenwick, Clashing Rights, the Welfare of the Child and the Human Rights Act (2004) 67 MLR 900.

in *Re LM*,[239] it was held that a restriction on the reporting of an inquest into a child's suspicious death should not be granted as there was insufficient evidence of any lasting harm to the child's siblings so as to override freedom of expression.[240]

The key factor, therefore, is proportionality and whether publication would be a disproportionate and unnecessary interference with the individual's confidentiality and privacy. For example, in *Barclays Bank PLC v Guardian News and Media Ltd*,[241] the court granted an injunction pending full trial preventing the further dissemination of the claimant's financial documents by the defendant newspaper, stressing that s.12(4) of the 1998 Act and prior publication was not a complete defence and the court had to apply proportionality. Although the documents in question related to how financial institutions operated in the economy and thus were a matter of most serious public debate, that did not give journalists complete freedom to publish, in full, confidential documents leaked in breach of a fiduciary duty. It would be relevant to ask if the debate could flourish without such full disclosure, and responsible journalists should consider whether publication of personal details about the affairs of corporations that may not have even broken the law was appropriate. Accordingly, at full trial the bank would probably have demonstrated that publication was disproportionate.

Again, in *T v British Broadcasting Corporation*,[242] the High Court granted an injunction to prevent the identification of a vulnerable mother in a broadcast about adoption. The programme reported on the practice of 'current planning', where a child who was taken from his natural parents would be fostered pending a decision whether to adopt or not. The programme showed details of the process as it has been applied to T, who was suffering from a mental disorder, and her daughter, showing footage of the last contact between the two and indicating that T had problems with anger management. In granting the injunction, EADY J held that it was necessary to conduct a balancing exercise as to whether T's rights should take priority, and that it was not necessary to ask whether the programme was not in the best interests of T before conducting that exercise. In this case, there was medical opinion to the effect that the programme would cause greater distress than any benefit to T and such evidence was relevant. T was vulnerable and unable to truly consent to or appreciate the programme. There was a real risk that she would be greeted with a hostile and abusive reaction from viewers (although that need not be proved for the injunction to be granted), and the broadcast constituted a massive intrusion into her privacy and autonomy, undermining her dignity as a human being. In the present case the broadcaster's Article 10 rights would not be proportionate to the exposure of T's raw feelings and her relationship with her daughter, and the public interest could be served without identification.

The claim in favour of publication might be particularly strong where the information in question promotes not only freedom of expression but also some other Convention rights. For example, in *Torbay BC v News Group Newspapers*,[243] the High Court discontinued an injunction and allowed the publication of a girl's story concerning her pregnancy at the age of 12. The court recognised that the right to communicate one's story was protected not only by Article 10 of the ECHR, but also by Article 8, which protected an individual's physical and social

---

[239] *The Times*, 20 November 2007.

[240] On the other hand, the court held that it was necessary to place a restriction on the press identifying the siblings as such a measure constituted a proportionate response to their privacy interests under Article 8.

[241] [2009] EWHC 591 (QB).

[242] [2007] EWHC 1683 (QB).

[243] [2004] EMLR 8.

identity. Although the father's rights justified maintaining the injunction as far as he was concerned, it did not prevent the girl or the press from telling his story anonymously, and an injunction wide enough to do that would infringe the girl's and the newspaper's rights. Again, in *BKM v BBC*,[244] it was held that although clandestine recording in a care home for the elderly engaged and interfered with the residents' right to private life, there was not a sufficiently serious infringement to outweigh the right to freedom of expression as the public interest in such a film justified the recording. The use of clandestine filming in this case was necessary in the public interest in investigating standards in care homes and the care home was unlikely to succeed at full trial in proving that the broadcast should not be shown. However, in refusing the injunction the court placed a condition to the effect that the identity of the residents be obscured so that the broadcast should not interfere with the privacy of the residents more than was necessary.

The outcomes of such conflicts are, thus, often difficult to predict, depending as they do on the particular facts. All that can be said is that the courts will attempt to reach a proportionate outcome, recognising both claims appropriately. For example, in *H v Associated Newspapers; H v N*,[245] the Court of Appeal made an order that a newspaper should not identify either a former health worker who had retired from the health service because he had been diagnosed HIV positive or the health authority for which he had worked. Nevertheless, the court held that the risk that those who knew the details of the claimant's retirement would suspect that he was the healthcare worker in this particular action did not justify the restraint imposed on the newspaper not to disclose his speciality. That restraint, in the court's opinion, would inhibit debate on a matter of public interest and was not justified. Similarly, an order restraining the newspaper from soliciting information that might directly or indirectly lead to the disclosure of the identity or whereabouts of the claimant and his patients was, in the court's opinion, a particularly draconian fetter on freedom of expression and, therefore, too wide to be justified.[246]

The right of the press to report on pending litigation raises a number of balancing issues, and recently the Supreme Court has attempted to stress the importance of press freedom and the public right to know in these cases. Thus, in *Re Guardian News and Media*,[247] the Supreme Court held that there was sufficient public interest in publishing a report of freezing orders made against individuals suspected of terrorist offences, despite such publication interfering with their right to private and family life. The publication was necessary in the public interest in order to stimulate debate about the use of such orders and it did not accept that the public could not distinguish between those *suspected* and those *guilty* of terrorism. In any case, the Supreme Court held that publication of this information would assist the clarification of the public's perception and understanding of the issues, and failure to mention the suspects

---

[244] [2009] EWHC 3151 (Ch).

[245] [2002] EMLR 425. See also *A Health Authority v X* [2002] 2 All ER 780, where the Court of Appeal stressed it was for a court of law and not the area health authority to resolve the conflict between the private/public interests in the confidentiality of medical records and any other public interest.

[246] See also *Green Corns Ltd v Claverley Group Ltd* [2005] EMLR 31. Here, it was held that where a newspaper had published the addresses of homes for troubled children, which had resulted in a campaign by local residents to have the homes abandoned, it was necessary to place a restraint on the publication of addresses in subsequent newspaper articles. The public interest did not justify the publication and re-publication of such sensitive information as the addresses of the children and their past mental and social problems.

[247] [2010] 2 WLR 325.

would lead to a disembodied story and the matter being given a lower priority in the media.[248]

Further, in *Re Attorney General's Reference No 3 of 1999*[249] the House of Lords discharged an anonymity order relating to a defendant acquitted of rape, finding that the defendant's right to privacy was outweighed by the broadcaster's right to freedom of expression. The House of Lords held that although the defendant had an expectation of privacy – because such information suggested he may have been guilty – there was a legitimate reason for interference. This was because it was in the public interest to make a programme about his acquittal and the fact that it was related to the removal of the double jeopardy rule; it was equally in the public interest to name him in order to give credibility to the programme. Their Lordships also noted that the defendant's acquittal had already been in the public domain and that he could not complain that as a result of the programme an application was made to retry him for that offence. Although there was a danger of trial by media, his right to privacy did not outweigh the public interest in freedom of expression.[250] This case should not be read as giving press freedom a trump status and it is clear that factors such as prior publication were relevant in the case.[251]

Questions

How has the domestic law of confidentiality been adapted to accommodate the right to privacy? How have the domestic courts managed to balance confidentiality with freedom of expression and what difficulties have they experienced in carrying out that exercise?

Trespass and nuisance and the protection of privacy

The law of trespass is capable of protecting various aspects of private and family life guaranteed under Article 8 of the Convention. For example, the law of trespass to the person, alongside the law of assault and false imprisonment, can protect an individual from interferences with his or her physical person.[252] In addition, the law of trespass to land can impact on the right to private and home life, and must now be applied consistently with relevant Convention rights.[253] Although the law of trespass to land is primarily concerned with the protection of property rather than privacy as such, it is capable of protecting specific aspects of a person's right to private life. This can be seen in cases such as *Hickman v Maisey*.[254]

---

[248] Contrast *Secretary of State for the Home Department v AP (No 2)* [2010] 1 WLR 1652, where the Supreme Court extended an anonymity order imposed to protect the identity of those involved in control order proceedings.

[249] [2010] 1 AC 145.

[250] Further, their Lordships took into account the fact that the rape victim had waived anonymity and that his name had been published since his acquittal.

[251] In contrast, in *A v Norway*, decision of the European Court, 9 April 2009, there was a violation of Article 8 when a recently released prisoner had been identified by newspapers as a suspect in a rape and murder investigation and who had brought an unsuccessful defamation action against the media. The domestic courts had dismissed his action by finding that the press had acted in the public interest in publishing photographs and the allegations of guilt. The European Court held that the applicant had been persecuted at a time of his potential rehabilitation and that such stories had caused psychological and moral harm to his integrity.

[252] See, for example, *St George's Healthcare NHS Trust v S* [1998] 3 All ER 673, considered below.

[253] See, for example, *McLeod v United Kingdom* (1999) 27 EHRR 493, concerning the right of the police to enter private property to ensure that the peace is preserved.

[254] [1900] 1 QB 752.

The plaintiff owned land on which he allowed racehorse owners to train their horses. The defendant had watched the horses from the highway that crossed the plaintiff's land, which was owned by the plaintiff, with a view to gaining information about the horses, and the plaintiff sought an injunction to stop the defendant from using his land in this way. In granting an injunction the court noted that the intention and object of the defendant were all-important in deciding whether the defendant's use of the highway was a reasonable and lawful one.[255]

Similarly, as the law of nuisance prevents interference with the enjoyment of a person's property rights, it might also engage Article 8 of the European Convention and be used to protect certain privacy interests. For example, in *Khorasandjian v Bush*[256] an interim injunction was granted restraining the defendant, an ex-boyfriend who persistently hounded the plaintiff with telephone calls, from using violence to, harassing, pestering or communicating with the plaintiff. It was held that there was no reason why someone other than the owner of land, or their partner, could not obtain an injunction to stop a person from making persistent telephone calls, and as a partner of such a person also had such a right, there was no reason why the child of the owner should not have the same rights as the partner. Although this decision was overturned by the House of Lords' judgment in *Hunter v Canary Wharf*,[257] where it was held that an action in nuisance must be based on a proprietary interest, it would appear that the courts have the power under the Human Rights Act to extend the private law so as to provide a remedy in such cases. More specifically, the claimant in such a case would be able to rely on the Protection from Harassment Act 1997, which protects individuals from 'stalkers' and other similar acts of harassment.

The law of nuisance can now be developed and interpreted in the light of the Human Rights Act, although the domestic courts have insisted that the Convention should not override the domestic laws in this respect. In *Marcic v Thames Water Utilities*,[258] it was claimed that a water company had failed to take any steps to remedy the discharge of sewage on to the claimant's land. The Court of Appeal held that the claimant did have a claim under the law of nuisance, and that his right to damages at common law displaced any claim he would have under the Human Rights Act. Nevertheless, the court held that the scope of the law of nuisance, and the type and extent of damages available in such a case, can and should be informed by Article 8 and its relevant case law. However, on further appeal the House of Lords held that the claimant's common law action had been displaced by the statutory scheme provided by the Water Industry Act 1991, and that such a scheme was compliant with the European Convention, as it struck a fair balance between the claimant's Article 8 rights and the interests of the public and of other customers. On the other hand, in *Dennis v Ministry of Defence*,[259] it was held that there had been an actionable nuisance when the claimants were subjected to highly intrusive noise caused by low-flying combat aircraft, and relying on Article 8 of the Convention, the court held that in this case the noise was not justified on grounds of public

---

[255] Contrast *Bernstein v Skyviews* [1978] 1 QB 479, where it was held that the flying over the plaintiff's land and the taking of one photograph was not a trespass, primarily because the plaintiff had no right in the sky above, and in any case the Civil Aviation Act allowed reasonable flights over land, the taking of one photo not being unreasonable.

[256] [1993] QB 727.

[257] [1997] 2 All ER 426.

[258] [2004] 2 AC 42.

[259] *The Times*, 6 May 2003.

interest and that it should award an appropriate amount in damages to represent just satisfaction for breach of the claimant's Convention rights.[260]

The Protection from Harassment Act 1997

The Act was passed to protect individuals from activities such as 'stalking'. It protects an individual against harassment by making it an offence to pursue a course of conduct that amounts to harassment of another.[261] The Act also provides, in s.3, a civil remedy for an actual or apprehended breach of the Act, allowing for the award of damages for any anxiety and other loss caused by the harassment, and for the award of an injunction to restrain the defendant from pursuing such conduct.[262] The Act is capable of protecting the individual from a number of intrusions into their privacy and private life, and the courts have allowed its use beyond mere physical or mental threats.[263] Thus in *DPP* v *Moseley*,[264] it was held that the Act could be used to protect individuals from the unreasonable actions of protestors who were protesting against the fur trade outside a fur farm. As we have already seen, this decision has implications for freedom of speech and assembly,[265] but in some cases it might provide a legitimate protection from unreasonable intrusions into one's private life.[266]

More significantly, it was held in *Thomas* v *Newsgroup Newspapers*[267] that a person could maintain an action against a newspaper which had published an article that had led to the person receiving distressing communications from the public. In that case the *Sun* newspaper had published an article explaining how police officers had been disciplined after making racist comments about an asylum seeker. The article, headed ' "Beyond a joke": police sarges busted after refugee jest', explained how the officers had been disciplined after 'a black clerk' (the claimant) had reported them for making the comments. The article published the claimant's name and workplace, and subsequently several *Sun* readers wrote in to the newspaper and had their letters published under the heading 'Don't punish cops over a joke made in private'. The claimant also received a good deal of hate mail, which, she claimed, had caused her considerable distress. An action was brought under the 1997 Act, claiming that the articles amounted to racism and harassment. The defendants sought to have the action struck out as disclosing no reasonable grounds of action, and in particular that the action was contrary to Article 10 of the European Convention. Refusing to strike the action out, the Court of Appeal

---

[260] See now *Dobson* v *Thames Water Utilities* [2007] EWHC 2021 (TCC), where it was accepted that damages for a nuisance which also amounts to a breach of Article 8 might not give just satisfaction in every case and the court might grant compensation under s.8 of the HRA for any inconvenience, mental distress and physical suffering.

[261] Section 2 of the Protection from Harassment Act 1997.

[262] Under s.3 the claimant may also apply for the issue of a warrant for the arrest of the defendant where he or she considers that the defendant has done anything that he is prohibited from doing under the injunction.

[263] In *Wainwright* v *Secretary of State for the Home Department* [2002] 3 WLR 405, the Court of Appeal stated that an action might have been available to a number of persons who had been unlawfully searched by prison officers when visiting relatives and friends, provided the searches amounted to a course of conduct within s.3 of the Act. In this case, however, the events had taken place before the Act's implementation.

[264] *The Times*, 23 July 1999.

[265] See chapter 10, pages 545–8.

[266] See also s.42 of the Criminal Justice and Police Act 2001, giving the police the power to give directions stopping the harassment of a person at his or her home.

[267] [2002] EMLR 4.

held that the publication of press articles calculated to incite racial hatred of an individual was a course of conduct capable of amounting to harassment under the 1997 Act.

In the Court's view, it was not the conduct that made up an offence of harassment, but rather the effect of that conduct. A pleading that did no more than allege that a series of articles caused distress was liable to be struck out; what was required were clear facts that suggested harassment. With regard to the motives of the action, it was for the defendants to show that the motive for their actions were reasonable, reasonableness being dependent in each case upon the particular circumstances. In this case it was arguable that the reference in the articles to the claimant's colour was not reasonable and that it was foreseeable that *Sun* readers would send hate mail after the article was published. Further, the newspaper had made no attempt to disassociate itself from those letters. The particular facts of the case, including the racial content, should distinguish it from the more general case where public or other figures complain of unreasonable tactics employed by the press that result in intrusions into their privacy and private life.[268]

Although the courts often have to balance a person's privacy against another's right to free speech, the domestic courts have vigorously protected individuals from unreasonable harassment. For example, in *Howlett* v *Holding*,[269] it was held that an order under the 1997 Act could be made even where the defendant was exercising his right of freedom of expression. The defendant had pursued a campaign against the claimant (a local councillor) after she had spoken out against the defendant in a planning application. The campaign involved flying abusive and derogatory banners and dropping leaflets from his aircraft, and placing her under surveillance in order to see whether she was committing benefit fraud. The court held that the anguish suffered by the claimant was out of all proportion to the value attached to his right of free speech and was thus a necessary restriction under Article 10(2).[270]

The 1997 Act can also be used to protect individuals from arbitrary and abusive conduct of state officials. For example, in *KD* v *Chief Constable of Hampshire*,[271] it was held that a police officer had subjected the claimant to harassment under the 1997 Act when during the conducting of an investigation into the claimant's daughter's allegations of sexual abuse he had asked her intimate questions about her sexual life and touched her inappropriately. The court held that in the post-Human Rights Act era the 1997 Act had to be read in line with Article 8 and the claimant's right to private life. In this case the claimant should be awarded £20,000 for the distress caused by the questioning, the physical assaults (which formed part of the harassment) as well as the persistent denial of the charges by the defendant.

Privacy and press freedom

The most topical and controversial aspect of privacy concerns the protection of private life from press and media intrusion. The inability of the law to protect individuals from invasion

---

[268] Under s.32 of the Crime and Disorder Act 1998, the penalties for a breach of the 1997 Act are increased if the offence is racially aggravated as defined in s.28 of the Crime and Disorder Act.

[269] *The Times*, 8 February 2006.

[270] See also *R* v *Debnath* [2005] EWCA Crim 3472, where it was held that a restraining order prohibiting the defendant from publishing any information about the complainant or his fiancée, irrespective of whether it was true or false, was not in breach of Article 10.

[271] [2005] EWHC 2550 (QB).

of their private life, as evidenced by cases such as *Kaye* v *Robertson*, above, resulted in a number of recommendations for increased regulation of the media and for the creation of specific privacy laws.[272] Notwithstanding these proposals, the law and the system of self-regulation remained principally intact and cases of press intrusions into private life were dealt with within the existing criminal and civil law. However, with the passing of the Human Rights Act, the individual has a number of remedies available to him or her where they feel that their right to privacy has been violated. First, they may apply to the Press Complaints Commission itself and ask it to investigate an allegation of privacy violation. As we shall see, the Commission's code specifically mentions breach of privacy, and thus provides some quasi-legal protection of such rights. Secondly, if they are not satisfied with that finding, they may take judicial review proceedings to challenge it. Thirdly, they may take direct action against the Commission under the Human Rights Act for its failure to protect individual privacy. Finally, and more controversially, they may take legal action against the newspapers themselves, requiring the courts, as public bodies under the Act, to employ Article 8 in the interpretation and application of existing private law rights, or alternatively to develop a law of privacy.

Self-regulation

The Press Complaints Commission replaced the Press Council (which insisted on the claimant dropping all legal action before investigation) and has the task of investigating complaints into various acts of misbehaviour by the press. The Commission operates under its own code of practice, and although it can make findings, and request the publication of apologies, corrections, etc., it has no power to fine or punish. Similarly, the Commission may request newspapers to publish their findings, but has no legal power to order this.

The Code of Practice

The Code of Practice, initially based on the recommendations of the Calcutt Report, contains rules relating to privacy violation by the press and thus provides some recognition of privacy, which can be supplemented by various legal remedies.[273] However, in most cases the prohibition of intrusion into private life is subject to a defence of public interest, which includes situations where intrusion or publication is in the interests of the detection or exposure of crime or serious misdemeanours, the protection of public health or safety, or for preventing the public from being misled by some statement or action of an individual or organisation. The Code states that in any case where the public interest is invoked, the Commission will require a full explanation by the editor demonstrating how the public interest was served. In

---

[272] See, for example, *Report of the Committee on Privacy and Related Matters*, Cm 1102, 1990 (Calcutt Report) advocating the creation of the Press Complaints Commission to replace the Press Council, but rejecting the introduction of a tort of privacy; *Review of Press Self Regulation*, Cm 2135, proposing the introduction of a statutory tribunal to operate its own code and to have the power to impose fines and compensation and the creation of criminal liability for certain acts of press intrusion; The National Heritage Select Committee, Fourth Report of the Committee 294–91, *Privacy and Media Intrusion*, HC 291–1 (1993), proposing the introduction of a tort of privacy; the government White Paper, *Privacy and Media Intrusion*, Cm 2918, 1995, proposing the setting up of an insurance fund scheme to compensate victims of newspaper intrusion to be administered by the Press Complaints Commission.

[273] The industry framed a revised code of practice, which was ratified by the PCC on 7 August 2006.

cases involving children, editors must demonstrate an exceptional public interest to override the normally paramount interests of the child.

The most relevant provision relating to privacy and press intrusion is contained in clause 3 of the Code, which states that everyone has the right to private and family life, home, health and correspondence, and that publications intruding into private life without consent must be justified by editors. The clause further provides that it is unacceptable to photograph individuals in private places without their consent. A breach of clause 3 is stated to be excusable if justified in the public interest. In this respect, a 'private place' is defined by the code as property, whether public or private, where there is a reasonable expectation of privacy, thus excluding obviously public places or places where one would not expect to have complete privacy. This gives rise to problems of classifying certain locations, such as beaches, as well as inviting arguments on the question of whether any intrusion might be in the public interest.[274]

In addition, clause 4 of the Code provides protection against press harassment. Under this clause journalists and photographers must not obtain or seek to obtain information or pictures via harassment or persistent pursuit. In addition, they must not photograph individuals in private places without their consent; must not persist in telephoning, questioning or pursuing or photographing individuals after having been asked to desist; must not remain on their property after having been asked to leave; and must not follow them. Further, editors must ensure that those working for them do not breach these principles. Again, these prohibitions are subject to the public interest defence. The code contains specific rules relating to the privacy of children,[275] victims of sexual assault[276] and listening devices.[277] It also contains rules on common concerns regarding press intrusion such as intrusions into private grief,[278] and the identification of relatives or friends of persons accused or convicted of crime, which is prohibited unless it is necessary for the public's right to know.[279] Many of these clauses represent the current legal position, but the development of the law of privacy in the courts should mean that certain guidelines, such as dealing with cases with sympathy and discretion, are not merely platitudes. Clause 9 of the Code covers the issue of press intrusions in places such as hospitals, a problem raised in the famous case of *Kaye v Robertson*.[280] Journalists and photographers making enquiries at such institutions should identify themselves to a responsible person and obtain permission before entering non-public areas. The clause stresses that the other restrictions on privacy intrusions are particularly relevant to enquiries about individuals in such institutions, although the public interest defence is still available in this situation. Again, with the development of privacy protection by the courts, the clause is not merely of rhetorical value and probably represents the true, albeit uncertain, legal state.

If the Press Complaints Commission fail to uphold the privacy rights of the applicant, then an application may be brought under the Human Rights Act 1998, claiming a violation of Article 8 of the European Convention on Human Rights. The Commission are without doubt a public authority for the purpose of s.6 of the Act and are, thus, under a duty to uphold the

---

[274] See *R v Press Complaints Commission ex parte Ford* [2002] EMLR 5, considered below.
[275] Clauses 6 and 7 of the Code.
[276] Clause 12.
[277] Clause 8.
[278] Clause 5 of the Code, which states that enquiries and approaches should be carried out with discretion and sympathy. The public interest defence is not available in respect of this clause.
[279] Clause 10.
[280] [1991] FSR 62.

Convention rights of any person who is subject to their decisions. Of course, in deciding whether there has been a violation of a person's right to privacy under Article 8 of the Convention, the Commission will need to balance such a right with the right of free speech and freedom of the press enshrined in its own code and Article 10 of the Convention, and inevitably the Commission will give a generous interpretation of the public interest defence to the press.

The Commission's adjudications are subject to judicial review by the traditional courts, which in turn is under a duty to safeguard the Convention rights of both individuals and the press and to ensure that the balance between privacy and free speech has been properly maintained. The decision of the High Court in *R v Press Complaints Commission, ex parte Ford*[281] indicates that the courts may give a wide margin of appreciation to the Commission in deciding where the balance properly lies. Anna Ford, the famous newsreader, had applied for permission to quash the decision of the Commission, which had refused to uphold her complaint that photographs of herself and a friend on a beach in Majorca, which had been published by the *Daily Mail* and *Hello!* magazine, were in breach of the Commission's code of practice. The Commission had dismissed the claim on the basis that the beach was a publicly accessible place, and accordingly the complainant had no reasonable expectation of privacy. On an application for judicial review of that decision it was held that the type of balancing operation carried out by a specialist body such as the Commission was, even after the Human Rights Act, a field of activity to which the courts should and would defer. The Commission was a body whose membership and expertise made it better equipped than the courts to resolve the difficult exercise of balancing the conflicting rights of the claimant to privacy and of the newspapers to publish. The courts should only interfere with the decisions of the Commission when it was clearly desirable to do so, and in this case none of the criticisms of the determination had any merit or reached the threshold for obtaining permission.

The decision suggests that the courts may be sympathetic to the Commission's stance that public figures ought to be tolerant of intrusions into their privacy in public places and that such individuals would need to show a gross intrusion into their private lives before their claims are upheld. However, the decision should not be taken as authority that the photographing of individuals in public places is not in violation of Article 8 of the Convention, and will always be justified on the grounds of press freedom.[282] Thus, if a person were to maintain a direct action in such circumstances, the court would need to decide whether there had been a violation of Article 8 and whether such interference was necessary for the protection of freedom of speech.[283]

---

[281] [2002] EMLR 5.

[282] The decision in *Ford* can be contrasted with the case of *R v Press Complaints Commission, ex parte Attard*, unreported, decision of the High Court, 7 October 2002, where an injunction was granted to the parents of conjoined twins who had complained to the Commission that the *Manchester Evening News* had taken and published photographs of the twins without their permission. The Commission had rejected the majority of the complaints on the basis that the parents had already sold their story to another newspaper and had agreed to the publication of some pictures.

[283] See, for example, *Theakston v MGN Ltd* [2002] EMLR 22, discussed below. Express Newspapers made an out-of-court settlement of £40,000 to the comedian Les Dennis and his actress wife, who had claimed breach of privacy when the *Star* newspaper had published sneak photographs of the couple while they were on holiday; see Showbiz Couple win Human Rights Case Against *Star*, *Guardian*, 21 December 2001.

> **Question**
> Do you believe that self-regulation can ever be an effective mechanism in balancing privacy with press freedom?

Privacy, press freedom and the courts

The passing of the Human Rights Act 1998 has provided a direct opportunity for those whose privacy has been invaded by the press to seek a legal remedy for such intrusion. This section will first consider the relevant case law of the European Court in this field and then examine the domestic law and how it has struck a balance between press freedom and individual privacy.

Privacy, press freedom and the European Convention on Human Rights

Although the question of press intrusion into private life has dominated arguments surrounding the domestic law of privacy, there is limited case law under the European Convention on Human Rights in this area. Article 8 of the Convention, guaranteeing the right to private and family life, is wide enough to accommodate the individual's right to privacy. In addition, that right is qualified and thus subject to the restrictions permitted within Article 8(2), most notably the rights of others to freedom of expression. Until recently, however, there was little guidance to be gained from the case law as to how that conflict may be resolved.

The European Commission has accepted that an individual should have some available remedy when their private life has been violated, although it has provided the state with a wide discretion as to the type and extent of that remedy. For example, in *Winer v United Kingdom*[284] the European Commission held that provided an individual was allowed to sue in defamation with respect to untrue statements, the state did not have an obligation to provide him with a remedy in respect of statements that were true. The law of defamation provided him with some protection of his Article 8 rights, and that was sufficient to satisfy Article 8. That decision, however, should not be taken as establishing a general principle and in some cases the state would have to provide a suitable remedy for breach of the individual's privacy. Thus, in *Barclay v United Kingdom*,[285] the Commission accepted that the applicants had a right to a remedy in respect of the filming of their family home by television reporters.[286]

An individual is obliged to pursue any relevant domestic remedies, and in *Earl Spencer v United Kingdom*[287] the European Commission rejected a claim because the applicant had failed to exhaust all effective domestic remedies by bringing a claim in the law of confidentiality. In this case the applicant had complained about a series of articles written about his sister (Lady Diana Spencer) concerning her medical and mental health problems. The Commission declared the case inadmissible for refusal to exhaust all effective domestic remedies, and as a consequence the merits of the case were not considered. The case might, however, suggest that the domestic law of confidence *did* provide a remedy for breach of privacy, and was thus

---

[284] (1986) 48 DR 154.

[285] (1999) Application No 35712/97.

[286] The application failed on its merits. In the domestic courts it was held that the Broadcasting Complaints Commission had rightfully rejected the applicants' complaint because at that stage the relevant programme had not been broadcast: *R v BCC, ex parte Barclay and Another, The Times*, 11 October 1996.

[287] (1998) 25 EHRR CD 105.

in conformity with Article 8.[288] It seems clear now that even though the case law of the Convention does not require such a specific remedy in every case, the development of privacy remedies in respect of press intrusion is required in appropriate cases. Further, although the early case law of the European Court of Human Rights indicates that the private rights of public individuals would only trump freedom of expression in exceptional cases,[289] that principle now needs to be viewed in the light of the European Court's decision in *Von Hannover* v *Germany*,[290] below.

The decision of the European Court in *Von Hannover* v *Germany*

The applicant, Princess Caroline von Hannover (better known as Princess Caroline of Monaco) had attempted to prohibit the publication of photographs taken of her, and herself with family and friends, by the German paparazzi. The photographs included pictures taken of her while shopping, relaxing with her children and in the company of male friends, including her husband. The German Constitutional Court dismissed most of her claims, regarding her as a public figure and concluding that she had to tolerate the publication of photographs of herself in a public place, even though they showed her in scenes from her daily life rather than engaged in her official duties. The applicant brought an application before the European Court of Human Rights, complaining that the decisions of the German courts infringed her right to respect for her private and family life under Article 8 of the Convention.

The European Court held that the publication of the various photographs of her in her daily life fell within the scope of her private life as covered by Article 8 and that as a result it was necessary to balance the applicant's right against freedom of expression. In the Court's view, although freedom of expression extended to the publication of photographs, in this case the photographs did not involve the dissemination of 'ideas', but rather of images containing very personal or very intimate 'information' about an individual. Further, the Court noted that photographs appearing in the tabloid press were often taken in a climate of continual harassment, inducing in the person concerned a very strong sense of intrusion into their private life or even of persecution. Thus, the decisive factor in cases such as these lay in the contribution that the published photographs and articles made to a debate of general interest. In the present case the photographs showed the applicant in scenes from her daily life, and thus engaged in activities of a purely private nature. The photographs had been taken secretly and without her consent and made no contribution to a debate of public interest, since the applicant exercised no official function and the photographs and articles related exclusively to details of her private life. The Court stressed that while the general public might have a right to information, including, in special circumstances, on the private lives of public figures, they did not have such a right in this instance: the general public did not have a legitimate interest in knowing the applicant's whereabouts or how she behaved generally in her private life even if she appeared in places that could not always be described as secluded and was well known to the public. In any case, even if such a public interest existed, that interest, and the commercial interest of the press in publishing such material, had to yield to the applicant's

---

[288] Although a remedy in the law of confidence may be available in the post-Human Rights Act era, it is questionable whether the case law before the Act supported a claim in those circumstances.

[289] See, for example, *Lingens* v *Austria* (1986) 8 EHRR 407; *Oberschlick* v *Austria* (1991) 19 EHRR 389. See Tierney, Press Freedom and the Public Interest: The Developing Jurisprudence of the European Court of Human Rights [1998] EHRLR 419.

[290] (2005) 40 EHRR 1.

right to the effective protection of her private life. The Court noted that the protection of private life was essential to the development of every human being's personality and that everyone, including people known to the public, had a legitimate expectation that his or her private life would be protected. In conclusion, therefore, the German courts had not struck a fair balance between the competing interests of free speech and respect for private life and accordingly there had been a violation of Article 8.[291]

The principle established in *Von Hannover* can be contrasted with those cases where the Court has held that public figures must be more tolerant than private individuals of intrusions into their private lives and of attacks on their reputation.[292] Those cases concerned politicians and discussions of traditional political and public interest, rather than the private affairs of such individuals, thus heightening the importance of free speech and lessening the privacy claim. In contrast, in *Tammer v Estonia*[293] the Court sided with the private reputation of a well-known figure over freedom of expression and the public right to know. In that case the Court held that the fining of a journalist and newspaper for attacking the reputation and honour of the applicant – the wife of a politician who was no longer performing public duties and who had written her private memoirs – was a justifiable interference with freedom of expression as the impugned remarks related to aspects of the applicant's private life (her suitability as a mother). In the Court's view, since the applicant had now resigned from her governmental position the use of the impugned terms were no longer justified by considerations of public concern and neither did they deal with matters of general public importance. The decision in *Von Hannover*, therefore accepts the distinction between politicians and other well-known figures, stressing that a former public figure generally has the right to lose the trappings of that status once they retire from public life.

Equally importantly, the Court in *Von Hannover* makes a clear distinction between information whose dissemination is in the public interest and information which the public are interested in. This distinction has been gradually accepted in domestic law and thus both the European and domestic courts are more likely to give precedence to freedom of expression over individual privacy when that speech has a genuine public interest value, such as engendering a debate on political, constitutional or social issues.[294]

Since *Von Hannover* the European Court has attempted to establish whether there exists a genuine public interest in publication. Thus, in *Standard Verlags GMBH v Austria (No 2)*,[295] it held that there had been no violation of freedom of expression when the applicants had been fined for publishing an article reporting on rumours about the then Austrian President's

---

[291] See also *Plon (Societe) v France* (2006) 42 EHRR 36, where the European Court held that there had been no violation of Article 10 when the family of the late President Mitterand had obtained an interim injunction shortly after his death stopping the publication of a book about the President's illness. However, Article 10 was violated when that prohibition was continued in force after the informant had been sanctioned by the courts, and once the information became public property.

[292] See the decisions in *Lingens v Austria* and *Oberschlick v Austria*, n 289 above, and considered in chapter 9, pages 429.

[293] (2003) 37 EHRR 43.

[294] See Sanderson, Is Von Hannover a Step Backward for the Substantive Analysis of Speech and Privacy Interests? [2004] EHRLR 631. Subsequently, an unsuccessful legal action was brought by Caroline and her husband before the German courts where a story about them renting their holiday home in Kenya was accompanied by a photograph of the couple in a public street in Kenya. It was held that the claimants had no expectation of privacy as the intrusion was tied to a story of public concern and the intrusion was not significant. Noted by Clark [2009] Entertainment Law Review 107.

[295] Decision of the European Court, 4 June 2009.

marriage. The Court applied the principles in *Von Hannover* and found that the articles contained 'idle gossip' and thus did not contribute to any debate of general interest. However, *Von Hannover* was distinguished in *Hachette Fipacchi Associes v France*,[296] where it held that there had been a violation of Article 10 when a newspaper had been fined for publishing a story about the famous French singer Johnny Halliday's extravagant tastes, together with publicity and stage photographs of the singer. The Court noted that the photographs were already public, that the story was based on the singer's previous revelations about his lifestyle and that the story was not offensive. The domestic measure was thus a disproportionate interference with freedom of expression and press freedom. We shall see that prior publication, and prior self-publicity, are relevant factors in determining privacy claims in domestic law.

Question

What is the European Court's stance with respect to balancing freedom of expression with individual privacy?

Privacy, press freedom and the domestic courts

As we have seen, there are a variety of legal remedies available to individuals who believe that their private life has been infringed by the press. These remedies will continue to be available in the post-Human Rights Act era, although the Act impacts on this area in two material respects. First, the courts have a duty to develop the law in line with Convention rights, including the right to privacy. Thus, as seen above, the courts have begun to develop the existing law to accommodate the right to privacy as protected under Article 8. Secondly, s.12 of the Act specifically requires the courts to have regard both to various aspects of freedom of expression and relevant privacy codes in determining cases that interfere with freedom of expression.

The principal dilemma facing the courts is how to balance the individual's right to private life with the right of the press to disseminate information to the public. There was some authority before the Human Rights Act to the effect that the disclosure of details of the private lives of public celebrities was in the public interest. Thus, in *Woodward v Hutchins*,[297] it was held that there was a public interest in the disclosure of the private sexual activities of a number of pop celebrities. LORD DENNING MR noted that the defendant, the claimant's agent, had been employed to represent the plaintiffs in a favourable light, and consequently the public had an interest in receiving information that refuted that image. That decision, which, it should be noted, was delivered at an interlocutory stage, was viewed with a good deal of scepticism, assuming as it does that public celebrities are seen as role models and that the public has a genuine interest in the majority of their activities. As we shall see those principles are controversial and have been the subject of a good deal of case law in the post-Act era.[298]

Balancing press freedom and privacy under the Human Rights Act: the early case law

Early case law seemed to suggest that although public figures enjoyed a right to private life, such enjoyment would have to be compromised by their public status and the public's right

---

[296] (2009) 49 EHRR 23.

[297] [1977] 1 WLR 760.

[298] For a thorough analysis of the basis of personal privacy claims and the domestic and European case law on the balance between privacy and freedom of expression, see Gomerry, Whose Autonomy Matters? Reconciling the Competing Claims of Privacy and Expression (2007) 27 LS 404.

to receive information about their private lives. The Court of Appeal attempted to provide some guidelines in this area in *A v B plc and Another*.[299] In this case it was confirmed that the law of confidence could apply to information regarding a sexual relationship outside marriage.[300] More controversially, at first instance the court granted an injunction prohibiting the press from disclosing details about the extramarital relationship of a professional footballer, even though the relationship was known to a number of other persons, and despite the defendant's plea that such disclosure was in the public interest. The judge was strongly influenced by the fact that the information in question could not be regarded as being in the public interest so as to justify its disclosure.[301] However, the ambit of that decision was severely limited on appeal to the Court of Appeal. In the opinion of LORD WOOLF CJ, in most if not all cases, the law of confidentiality would provide the necessary protection against any alleged violation of the claimant's privacy. Whether a duty of confidence did exist would depend on all the circumstances of the relationship between the parties at the time of the threatened or actual breach of confidence. The bugging of someone's home or the use of other surveillance techniques were obvious examples, but in any case where a person could reasonably expect his privacy to be respected, this gave rise to liability unless the intrusion could be justified. The Court also held that the fact that the information was obtained illegally did not mean that its publication could be restrained, but that might be a compelling factor when it came to the court exercising its discretion to grant an injunction.

With regard to the protection of intimate sexual detail, LORD WOOLF CJ established that there was a significant difference between the confidentiality that attached to sexual relations in transient relationships, and that attached to sexual relations within marriage or other stable relationships. Thus, where the alleged breach of privacy was the result of the reporting of the information to a third party by the party to the relationship, it was a material factor that the two people had shared a sexual relationship outside marriage, particularly where one of them wished to exercise their right to freedom of expression under Article 10 of the Convention. In such circumstances the right to have such confidence respected, although not extinguished, will be undermined. The Court of Appeal also considered whether it was relevant that the claimant was a public figure. In the Court's view, although such a person was entitled to a private life, he must expect and accept that his actions would be more closely scrutinised by the media and that even trivial facts could be of great interest to readers and other observers of the media. Further, a public figure might hold a position where higher standards of conduct might rightly be expected from the public, and the higher the profile the more likely that might be the position. In such circumstances the public had an understandable and so a legitimate interest in being told the information and the courts should not act as censors or arbiters of taste merely because the publication had given a more lurid account of the details than the court found acceptable.

Applying those principles, the Court of Appeal held that the original order was clearly flawed. The degree of confidentiality to which the claimant was entitled, notwithstanding that the two women involved did not wish their relationship to remain confidential, was very modest. Such relationships did not belong to the categories that the court should be astute to protect when the other parties to the relationship did not wish them to remain confidential.

---

[299] [2002] 3 WLR 542.
[300] This general position had been accepted in *Stephens v Avery* [1988] 2 All ER 477.
[301] [2001] 1 WLR 2341.

Although the Court would not go so far as to say that such relationships could never be entitled to any confidentiality, the present situation was at the outer limits of relationships that required protection. The judgment suggests that the circumstances in which public-profile individuals can use the Human Rights Act 1998 to protect their right to private life will be rare, and will be limited to those circumstances where the privacy claim is very strong and thus sufficient enough to override the presumption in favour of free speech. In particular, in deciding that there is a sufficient interest in such matters because the public are under-standably interested in such matters, and by holding that the quality and tone of the article is for the newspaper reader and the Press Commission to determine, seems to suggest that freedom of expression will trump the right to privacy in most cases.[302]

This restrictive approach had been taken in the earlier case of *Theakston* v *MGN Ltd*.[303] The claimant, a well-known television presenter had, by his own admission, visited a brothel and had a sex act performed on him by a prostitute, although he claimed that he did not know that it was a brothel. Other persons entered a room and took photographs and the defendants intended to publish those photographs, along with an article describing the incident. The claimant sought a temporary injunction to stop the publication of the articles and the photo-graphs. The court granted the injunction with regard to the photographs but not in respect to the article. The court held that the principle of confidentiality could not be extended to all acts of intimacy and that on the scale of circumstances that should be protected from disclosure, a transitory engagement with a prostitute in a brothel was far removed from sexual activities in a private home. Neither the prostitute's personal knowledge of the events nor the nature of events in a brothel had the inherent quality of confidentiality. In the present case there had been no express stipulation as to confidentiality between the claimant and the prostitute, and the relationship was not in itself confidential.[304]

The decision in *Campbell* v *MGN*

The stance taken in *A* and *Theakston* was modified somewhat by the House of Lords' decision in *Campbell* v *MGN Ltd*,[305] a case in which the courts recognised that public figures have a reasonable expectation of privacy despite their status, one which cannot be overridden simply because the public are interested in reading the details of such private affairs. The claimant, an internationally well-known model, had sued the defendants when the *Daily Mirror* had published articles revealing that the claimant, contrary to her previous assertions, was a drug addict and was attending Narcotics Anonymous. Details of those meetings were published in the article along with photographs of her leaving a clinic. She sued both in confidentiality and under the Data Protection Act 1998, claiming that although the newspaper was entitled to publish the fact that she was a drug addict, the details relating to where she was receiving the treatment and the details of her attendance were private and confidential and that there was no public interest justifying its publication.

---

[302] See Mead, It's A Funny Old Game – Privacy, Football and the Public Interest [2006] EHRLR 541.

[303] [2002] EMLR 22.

[304] In granting the injunction in relation to the publication of the photographs, although the court found that a brothel was not a private place for the purpose of clause 3 of the Press Commission's Code of Practice, which states that no photographs should be taken of people in a private place without their consent, it found that the claimant had a reasonable expectation that photographs taken in a brothel without consent would remain private and that on that basis the claimant was likely to establish his case at trial.

[305] [2004] 2 AC 457.

At first instance it was held that the details did have the necessary quality of confidence and that the claimant was entitled to damages, including aggravated damages.[306] However, on appeal the Court of Appeal overturned the decision at first instance and restated the principles laid down in *A v B plc*.[306a] The Court held that although the public would not have an interest in private facts which a fair-minded person would consider it offensive to display, the public did have a legitimate interest in being told information, including trivial facts, about a public figure. Although the fact that an individual had achieved public prominence did not mean that their private lives could be laid bare by the media, where a public figure chose to make untrue pronouncements about his or her private life, the press would normally be entitled to put the record straight. In this case, the disclosure of the claimant's attendance at Narcotics Anonymous was not of sufficient significance to shock the conscience so as to justify the interference of the court. Such information was justified in order to provide a factual account of her drug addiction, and had the detail necessary to carry credibility. Provided the disclosure was justifiable in the public interest, a journalist had to be given reasonable latitude as to the manner in which the information was conveyed to the public; otherwise freedom of expression would be unnecessarily inhibited.[307]

However, on further appeal the House of Lords held that on the facts there had been an unjustifiable interference with her right to respect for her private life.[308] In the present case, the judge at first instance had been right to regard details of her attendance at Narcotics Anonymous as imposing a duty of confidence; the details of such attendance were obviously private and the therapy was at risk if the duty of confidence which the participants owed to each other was breached by making those details public. Further, although the choice of language and any decision to accompany those words with photographs were editorial matters, decisions about the publication of private matters raised issues that were not simply about presentation and editing and those decisions were thus open to review by the courts. On the facts it was not enough to deprive her of her right to privacy that she was a celebrity and that her private life was newsworthy and it was hard to see that there was any compelling need for the public to know the name of the organisation she was attending for the therapy or for the details of it to be set out. However, in the majority's view had it not been for the publication of the photographs they would have been inclined to regard the balance between the rights as about even, the proper conclusion being that the restriction on freedom of expression was disproportionate.

Although *Campbell* did not disturb the basic principle that a public figure should endure greater invasions into their private lives or that there is a general public interest in discovering private information about such individuals, it cast doubts on the right of the press to choose the manner in which they are to report matters of public interest. The decision in *Von Hannover*, however, may suggest that their Lordships were too generous towards press freedom and that the courts should give even greater protection to the privacy claim. On the other hand, the

---

[306] [2002] HRLR 28. The Court awarded damages of £3500. For an account of damages in privacy breaches, see Witzleb, Monetary Remedies for Breach of Confidence in Privacy Cases (2007) 27 LS 430.

[306a] [2003] 2 WLR 80.

[307] See also *Mills v Newsgroup Newspapers* [2001] EMLR 41.

[308] [2004] 2 AC 457. A subsequent appeal to the European Court upheld the House of Lords' decision: *MGN v United Kingdom, The Times*, 18 January 2011.

fact that the claimant in *Campbell* had lied to the public, distinguishes that case from cases such as *Von Hannover*, where the only public interest is mere curiosity. The decisions in *Von Hannover* and *Campbell* would also suggest that the court's reluctance to interfere with the decisions of the Press Complaints Commission, unless its determination is perverse, or the press intrusion gross,[309] may have to be modified.[310]

Post-*Campbell*: enhancing privacy and compromising press freedom?

The decisions in *Von Hannover* and *Campbell* had an instant impact on the domestic courts and, in *McKennitt v Ash*,[311] EADY J noted the law's recent desire to protect individual privacy from press and other intrusion by stating that there was a significant shift taking place between, on the one hand, freedom of expression for the media and the corresponding interest of the public to receive information, and, on the other hand, the legitimate expectation of citizens to have their private lives protected. In his Lordship's view, it was clear that even where there was a genuine public interest in the media publishing articles or photographs, sometimes such interests would have to yield to the individual citizen's right to the effective protection of private life.[312]

In that case, Loreena McKennitt, a well-known folk singer, sought an injunction to prevent the further publication of a book written by the defendant, a former friend and confidant. The book detailed many aspects of the claimant's private and family life, including information with respect to her relationships and the emotional impact of those relationships. At first instance the High Court granted the injunction and also awarded her £5000 in damages representing the distress caused by the publication. The judge found that the author and publisher of the book must have appreciated the claimant's legitimate expectation of privacy and that its publication would cause her distress. Upholding the decision at first instance the Court of Appeal held that the judge had been correct in finding that the claimant had a reasonable expectation of privacy with respect to that information.[313] The Court of Appeal also held that the judge at first instance had been correct in balancing the claimant's private life with the defendant's Article 10 rights. In the court's view the defendant had no story to tell of her own as opposed to the claimant's, and accordingly the right to freedom of expression under Article 10 clearly had to yield to Article 8.[314]

---

[309] *R v Press Complaints Commission, ex parte Ford* [2002] EMLR 5. The case is considered in more detail in the section on the Press Complaints Commission, above.

[310] See, for example the case of *R v Press Complaints Commission, ex parte Attard*, decision of the High Court, 7 October 2001, where the court overruled the decision of the Commission, which had held that the applicants' privacy had not been violated when newspapers published pictures, because the applicants had already agreed to the publication of the pictures by another newspaper.

[311] [2006] EMLR 10.

[312] Ibid., at paragraph 57.

[313] [2007] 3 WLR 194. The Court of Appeal rejected the defendant's argument that the confidential relationship which existed between her and the claimant devalued the private nature of the information and thus defeated the claimant's privacy claim. The Court of Appeal also rejected the claim that the singer's limited disclosure of her private life – about the death of her fiancé – placed the information in the public domain and thus opened up the whole area of her private life to intrusive scrutiny.

[314] It is now likely that the decision in *Beckham v Morris* (unreported) should not be followed. In that case the High Court refused to grant the Beckhams an injunction pending trial to prohibit the claimant's nanny from breaching her contract of confidentiality and selling a story to the tabloids relating information about the Beckhams' marriage and lifestyle. The judge accepted that there was a public interest in the story.

Most significantly, with respect to the defence of public interest, applying the principles laid down in *Von Hannover*, it was held that the claimant was not a public figure in whom there was a legitimate interest to justify or require exposure of her private life. In the Court's view, even if the claimant was a public figure in the relevant sense, there were no special circumstances to justify or require the exposure of her private life.[315] The Court of Appeal in this case also felt that its decision in *A v B plc* was in some ways inconsistent with the decision in *Von Hannover*, and that the dicta of LORD WOOLF LJ in *A* needed to be qualified in the light of the House of Lords' decision in *Campbell*. Accordingly, in the present case the claimant's popularity as a singer and the fact that she was well known did not place her private life in the public domain and justify any public interest in the disclosure of details of her private life.

This approach was also followed by the High Court in *CC v AB*,[316] a case which casts further doubt on the Court of Appeal's decision in *A v B plc* and which reiterates the importance of upholding individual privacy save in cases where there is a clear countervailing claim in freedom of expression. The applicant, who had been having an affair with the respondent's wife, sought an injunction against the respondent to prevent him from publicising that affair, believing that disclosing the applicant's and the wife's identity would be harmful to him and his family, and to the emotional and mental state of the woman with whom he had the relationship.[317] The respondent had written several abusive messages to the applicant, threatening to make the affair public, but claimed that a party to an adulterous relationship could not as a matter of law obtain injunctive relief against a wronged party and so prevent the disclosure of that relationship. It was held that there was no such general rule and that it was clear from the case law that intimate personal relationships could fall within the law of confidentiality,[318] the principle applying also to an adulterous relationship, which could attract a reasonable expectation of privacy. On the facts, it was held that although the applicant was unlikely to obtain a blanket restraint on any communication about the fact of the adulterous relationship, it was necessary to protect his right to private and family life from the respondent's actions. Consequently, an order was made restraining the latter from communicating, directly or indirectly with the media, or on the internet, on the subject of the claimant's former relationship with the respondent's wife.[319] In addition, the court refused to accept the respondent's claim that publication was in the public interest. Applying the well-established principle that there was a real difference between what was in the public interest and what the public were interested in, in this case there was no public interest in allowing the respondent to go to the media for no better reasons than spite, money-making or to spread 'tittle tattle'.[320]

---

[315] The Court of Appeal rejected the claim that the claimant's treatment of the defendant and other acquaintances justified the publication of the book and the revelation of otherwise confidential information.

[316] [2007] EMLR 11.

[317] Unlike the case of *A v B plc*, above, the woman in the relationship did not want to sell her story or for the information to become public.

[318] *Stephens* v *Avery* [1988] Ch 499.

[319] Contrast *D v L* [2004] EMLR 1, where the Court of Appeal refused to restrain the former lover of the claimant from disclosing the contents of a tape-recorded message containing information relating to the claimant's sexual proclivities. Although the claimant could rely on the long-term relationship and the illegal method of obtaining the information to found a claim in confidentiality, the matter was already in the public domain and there was no evidence to suggest that L was to abuse the information.

[320] In addition, the court was satisfied that the respondent's threats and conduct amounted to harassment, and an order would be made under the Protection from Harassment Act 1997.

The decisions in the above cases make it clear that celebrities or other public figures do not forgo their privacy simply because they are well known and have put themselves into the public domain. Thus, in *X and Y* v *Person Unknown*[321] a court upheld a 'John Doe' injunction, forbidding 'persons unknown' from revealing details about the breakdown in the marriage between a famous model and her husband. In the court's view it did not follow that an individual who was photographed and described in print, and about whom speculation was published regarding his or her private life, had behaved so as to forfeit the entitlement to privacy with regard to intimate personal relationships or the conduct of their private life generally. This principle would not, however, prevent the courts from taking into account truly iniquitous behaviour, and self-publicity might warrant certain unobjectionable intrusions into the private lives of public figures. For example, in *A* v *B and C and D*[322] the High Court refused to grant an injunction to stop the publication of details regarding the claimant's drug use and other personal details because firstly he did not have a legitimate expectation of privacy in such matters and secondly some of that information had already reached the public domain.

Thus, there may be cases where the courts will not protect a public figure's privacy, because of the conduct of that individual, and/or the public interest in discovering the truth. In *Lord Browne* v *Associated Newspapers Ltd*[323] the Court of Appeal refused to continue a wide interim injunction prohibiting a newspaper from giving details of the claimant's homosexual affair with a young man. The claimant, Lord Browne, the then chief executive of BP, had obtained a previous injunction prohibiting any information given by the man to the newspapers about the relationship, but had lied to the court about how he had been introduced to the young man. The newspaper now wished to publish details about that affair, provided to it by the young man, including how the claimant had lied to the court. On an application for renewal of the injunction the judge allowed the publication of allegations to the effect that the claimant may have misused his position in granting favours and facilities to the man, together with the bare fact of the relationship with that man. The claimant now appealed. Clarifying the decision in *McKennitt*, the Court of Appeal held that the mere fact that the information in question was imparted in the course of a relationship of confidence did not create an expectation of privacy. The judge at first instance had been entitled to conclude that the newspaper could publish the bare fact that the claimant was having an affair with the young man, because without publication of that fact the other information about possible abuse of power would not have made sense. The Court of Appeal also accepted that there was a public interest in the revelation of those details which the judge had allowed, and that the fact and content of the lie were relevant to the balance to be struck between Article 8 and 10. As a result it was not likely that the claimant would have succeeded at full trial.

That decision does show that the expectation of the privacy of public figures may be diminished in appropriate cases and for appropriate reasons. In this case the court appeared to recognise that the claimant was entitled to confidentiality in that relationship. However, as there were allegations that he had misused his position and possibly broken duties of confidentiality that he owed towards the company, the court accepted that there was a clear public interest in the dissemination of that information. So too, the fact that he had lied in

---

[321] [2007] EMLR 10.
[322] [2005] EWHC Q651 (QB).
[323] [2007] 3 WLR 289.

judicial proceedings was relevant in determining the extent to which his privacy should be respected.

The decision in *Mosley* v *News Group Newspapers*

Much controversy has surrounded the high-profile decision in *Mosley* v *News Group Newspapers Ltd,*[324] a case involving the publication by the press of photographs and graphic details of the sexual antics of Max Mosley, the president of the FIA (the governing body of Formula 1) and grandson of Oswald Mosley. The case is important in that it assesses both the legal expectation of sexual privacy of public figures and whether the press are entitled to claim a public interest defence in such cases.

The claimant sought damages from the defendants after they had published an article entitled 'F1 Boss Has Sick Nazi Orgy With 5 Hookers' together with video footage of him taking part in a sado-masochistic event attended by him and five women. The articles alleged that the sex sessions had a Nazi theme and had mocked the way in which Holocaust victims had been treated in concentration camps. A follow-up story was published by the defendants, based on the confessions of one of the women who had taken clandestine photographs of the event. The claimant alleged that publication constituted a breach of his right of privacy.

In giving judgment for the claimant, it was held that the claimant had a reasonable expectation of privacy in relation to sexual activities, albeit unconventional, carried on between consenting adults on private property, and that, consequently, the clandestine recording of that event on private property engaged the claimant's rights under Article 8. As a consequence, serious reasons had to exist to justify any interference with that right and the court had to determine whether the degree of intrusion in the present case was proportionate to the publication of such information.[325] In the court's view it was highly questionable that in modern society the principle of iniquity could be applied so as to deprive the claimant of his right of privacy in cases involving sexual activity, fetishist or otherwise, that had been conducted in private. Consequently the woman had committed both a breach of confidentiality and a violation of the claimant's Article 8 rights.

Turning to the public interest defence, the court found that despite the defendants' assertions, there was no evidence to suggest that the events had a Nazi theme or that the participants had mocked victims of the Holocaust. In the absence of that evidence, although there had been bondage, beatings and domination typical of sado-masochistic behaviour, there was no public interest or other justification for the recording and publication of these private events. Although such behaviour would be viewed by some people with distaste and moral disapproval, in the light of modern rights-based jurisprudence that did not justify intrusion on the personal privacy of the claimant. The court thus found an unjustified breach of his rights in confidentiality and privacy. In granting damages, the court stressed that it was necessary to provide the claimant with an adequate financial remedy so as to acknowledge the infringement of his right to privacy and to compensate him for the injury to feelings, the embarrassment and the distress caused by the publication. On the facts, although no amount of damages could fully compensate him for the damage done to him and what could be achieved by a monetary award in such cases was limited, a proper award in all the circumstances would be a sum of £60,000.

[324] *The Times*, 30 July 2008.
[325] The court also recognised that the woman in question owed a duty of confidentiality towards the claimant and the other participants as those taking part in such activities might be expected not to reveal private conversations and activities.

The decision followed the line of domestic cases which favoured individual privacy over and above the public's 'right' to access details of private sexual affairs, albeit outside the context of marriage or other stable relationships. It is suggested that the decision might have been better justified on the basis that the specific publication of those details constituted an objectionable intrusion into the claimant's private life, *despite* the presence of a clear potential public interest in publication. Thus the domestic courts have consistently defended individuals from the publication of intrusive photographs, recognising that they involve a more intimate and distressing violation of privacy,[326] and the principle that repeated publication of the images would only serve to humiliate the claimant could have been used in *Mosley* without undermining the public interest in disclosure of that information. Instead, in the court's view, only if the press were able to show that the claimant was taking part in sexual activities that had a Nazi theme could they rely on the public interest defence. As a consequence, the fact that the claimant, the President of the FIA, and grandson of the wartime fascist Oswald Mosley, was taking part in sado-masochistic sex scenes with prostitutes, was of insufficient public interest to disturb his legitimate expectation of privacy.

As an important postscript to the decision, despite being awarded damages the claimant intends to bring an action before the European Court of Human Rights. This is because the domestic courts refused to award interim relief because the information was already in the public domain by the time the claimant sought to prevent publication,[327] and Mosley is seeking to establish that the press have a duty to inform the potential victim of its intention to publish prior to publication. Thus, Mosley's claim is that only by offering such notification will the domestic law of confidentiality and privacy represent an effective remedy for a violation of Article 8. The press, on the other hand, will argue that such a duty will represent a disproportionate interference with freedom of expression, as it will deprive them in effect of the prior publication defence and allow prior restraint as a matter of course. A possible compromise, and one which the court utilised in the substantive hearing in *Mosley*, is to insist that the rules of responsible journalism – generally applied to defamation cases where the defendant seeks to rely on the defence of qualified privilege[328] – apply to privacy cases. This factor is then taken into account in deciding whether the press could rely on the defence of public interest.[329]

The decision in *LNS* (The John Terry case)

Pending the outcome of Mosley's application to the European Court, the domestic courts were provided with another opportunity to balance press freedom with sexual privacy in *LNS v Persons Unknown*,[330] commonly known as the John Terry case as it involved revelations that the then England football captain had conducted an affair with the ex-girlfriend of one of his team mates. In this case the High Court was asked to continue an injunction prohibiting the naming of the claimant and the person with whom he was having an affair. The claimant

---

[326] *Jagger* v *Darling* [2005] EWHC 683.

[327] *Mosley* v *News Group Newspapers Ltd* [2008] EWHC 687 (QB) – injunction refused because the information was already in the public domain.

[328] See *Reynolds* v *Times Newspapers* [1999] 4 All ER 609.

[329] Equally, the courts could award the claimant in this type of case a truly nominal sum in damages. Thus in *Reynolds* v *Times Newspapers*, although the press failed in their defence of qualified privilege, the jury awarded damages of one pound to the Prime Minister of Ireland, accepting that his reputation had suffered little because of publication.

[330] [2010] EMLR 16.

had applied for a 'super injunction', which would prohibit the disclosure by anyone of not only the claimant and any relevant information but also of the fact that such an injunction was being sought.[331]

Refusing the injunction the court felt that the essential aim of the injunction was the protection of the claimant's (mainly) commercial reputation. Accordingly, in deciding whether to grant the injunction the court followed the principle established in *Bonnard v Perryman*,[332] to the effect that the order should not be granted unless any defence to be raised at full trial by the newspaper was *bound to fail*. As the court treated the application as one which concerned the defamation of the claimant, as opposed to the protection of his privacy, the case does not formally add to the jurisprudence on privacy versus press freedom. Nevertheless, several observations made by the court are worthy of note in the context of the reasonable expectation of privacy and public interest defences which can be used as guidance for future cases.

First, the court distinguished between traditional actions in confidentiality and modern actions for misuse of private information. In the former action, the information must have the necessary quality of confidence, and have been imparted in circumstances importing an obligation of confidence to the claimant; whereas, in a claim for misuse of private information, a claimant must establish that he had a reasonable expectation of privacy in relation to the information of which disclosure was threatened. Assuming both requirements were met then the court would have to consider, in a confidentiality claim, whether it would be in the public interest to publish, and in the misuse of private information case, whether there was a justification for disclosure, such as public interest or public domain, as required by Article 8(2), and whether a permanent injunction would be a necessary and proportionate remedy, having regard to the right to freedom of expression under Article 10. Applying those tests to the facts, the court felt that the claimant was not likely to establish that there had been a breach of a duty of confidence owed to him, or that he was likely to succeed in defeating a public interest defence.[333]

Secondly, the court's judgment on the claimant's privacy claim gave some guidance as to how individual and family privacy might be balanced with free speech. For example, it found that whilst the claimant had shown that there was a real threat that the defendant would publish information about the *fact* of the relationship, he was not likely to succeed in establishing that publication of the fact of the relationship should not be allowed. This was because there was no evidence that the newspaper intended to publish information or photographs that would be regarded as highly offensive or objectionable according to the test laid down in cases such as *Campbell* and *Mosley*. In this sense the analogy would be cases such as *Browne*, where the mere disclosure of a relationship would not be in breach of a person's privacy.

Thirdly, the court clarified to some extent the position of the public interest defence in such cases. It held that whilst it was one of the essential features of the protection of private life that people were entitled to live freely according to their own choices, it was not the case that the conduct of a person in private had to be unlawful before another person could be permitted to criticise it in public. The freedom to live as one chose was one of the most valuable freedoms, but so was the freedom to criticise (within the limits of the law) the conduct of other

---

[331] Such injunctions were sought to stop publication of parliamentary debates: see Geddis, What We Cannot Talk About We Must Pass Over in Silence [2010] PL 443.

[332] [1891] 2 Ch 269.

[333] For the reasons detailed below in respect of the privacy claim.

members of society as being socially harmful or wrong. Again it must be stressed that the court in this case recognised that the nub of the application was a desire to protect what was in substance his reputation, in particular having regard to his business with various sponsors. Accordingly, his true privacy interests are lessened by this concession. Nevertheless, the court concluded that an injunction was not necessary or proportionate having regard to the level of the gravity of the interference with his private life that would occur in the event of publication of the fact of the relationship, or that he could rely on the interference with the private life of anyone else, such as his family. That conclusion was based *primarily* on the fact that the court was unable – because of the procedure of the application for a super injunction – to hear the defendant's public interest arguments; thus the court could not be satisfied that the claimant was likely to succeed at full trial. However, it may have been partly based on the court's acceptance that these revelations *might* have been in the public interest; although the judge refused to pass comment on the social utility or otherwise of the revelations in this case. If that is the case, then the fact that John Terry was arguably a public figure and role model, the captain of the national football team, and that these activities may have affected his standing and performance as a captain and footballer may have created a lesser expectation of privacy and a potential public right to know.

Questions

What principles can we take from the Mosley and John Terry cases?

Do you think that either or both claimants are public figures or that there was a true public interest in any of those disclosures?

Photographs and privacy

The decisions in cases such as *Campbell* and *Mosley* reflect the domestic courts' robust approach in defending individuals from the publication of photographs, the courts recognising that they involve a more intimate and distressing violation of privacy. Thus, in *Jagger v Darling*,[334] an injunction was granted to Elizabeth Jagger (the daughter of Sir Mick Jagger) to stop further publication of CCTV footage taken in the defendant's nightclub, showing the claimant engaged in sexual activities with another celebrity. Granting the injunction the judge held that there was no genuine public interest in the publication of the images and that repeated publication of the images would only serve to humiliate the claimant. The claimant had a reasonable expectation of privacy and the balance clearly was in favour of restricting publication.[335]

On the other hand, it is clear that the taking of an individual's photograph without their consent will not provide an automatic right in confidentiality in the absence of other circumstances. Thus, in *Sir Elton John v Associated Newspapers*[336] the court refused to grant an injunction to restrain the publication of photographs taken by the press of the claimant in the absence of any harassment. Although the photographs and story would have been unflattering and offensive – because they caught the celebrity rock star in a casual and scruffy state – that, in the court's view, was insufficient to ground an action in confidentiality. Further, the fact that the photographs were taken without his consent did not *per se* give rise to an action,

---

[334] [2005] EWHC 683.

[335] See also the decision in *Theakston*, above.

[336] Unreported, decision of the High Court, 23 June 2006.

the court stressing that there had to be some form of harassment to engage the protection offered by the *Von Hannover* case.

Subsequently, a flexible approach to protection against publication of photographs, taking into account all the circumstances of the claim, was adopted by the Court of Appeal in *Murray* v *Big Pictures*.[337] In this case the author JK Rowling, and her husband and son, sought an injunction and damages against Express Newspapers to stop the further publication of a photograph taken of the boy by use of a long-range lens when he was walking in the street with his parents. The parents had not given their consent to the photograph and subsequently it appeared in a newspaper, along with a quotation, attributed to JK Rowling, setting out her thoughts on motherhood and family life. An action was brought both in the law of confidentiality and under the Data Protection Act 1998.

At first instance the claim was struck out as disclosing no possible course of action,[338] PATTEN J rejecting the idea that the taking of the photograph without consent was unlawful *per se*, and noting that there was no evidence that the boy's parents were either aware of the photograph being taken or were in any way distressed by it being taken. Neither was there any evidence that the boy had been exposed to physical danger or any other harm. His Lordship drew a distinction between someone engaged in family and sporting activities and something as simple as a walk down a street or a visit to the grocers to buy milk. The former activity was part of a person's private recreation time intended to be enjoyed in the company of family and friends and applying *Von Hannover* any publicity was intrusive and could adversely affect the exercise of such activities. However, if a simple walk down the street qualified for protection, it was difficult to see what would not. Thus, there was an area of routine activity which, when conducted in a public place, carried no guarantee of privacy and although anodyne and trivial events might be of considerable importance and sensitivity to a particular person, the facts in the present case were not sufficient to engage Article 8.

On appeal it was held that the High Court had been wrong to strike out the claimant's case, and whether there was a reasonable expectation of privacy depended on all the circumstances of the specific case, including the attributes of the claimant and the activity in which they were engaged, the place at which it happened, the nature and purpose of the intrusion, the absence of consent, the effect on the claimant and the circumstances in which, and the purposes for which, the information reached the hands of the publisher. Once the reasonable expectation test was satisfied, the court would then have to consider how the balance should be struck between the claim in privacy and the right to publish; the question whether the publication of those facts would be highly objectionable to a reasonable person being relevant. Applying those tests, the Court of Appeal stated that it was at least arguable that the appellants had a reasonable expectation of privacy; and in particular the fact that the photographed appellant was a child was relevant and of greater significance than the judge at first instance recognised.[339]

This flexible approach allows the court to afford protection against offensive and intrusive photographs in appropriate cases and appears to follow the jurisprudence of the European

[337] [2008] 3 WLR 1360

[338] *Murray* v *Express Newspapers* [2007] EMLR 22.

[339] See also *Recklos* v *Greece*, decision of the European Court, 15 January 2009, where it was held that the taking of a baby's photograph in a hospital without the parent's consent constituted a violation of Article 8. There was no public interest in taking the photograph and the retention of the photographs contrary to the parents' wishes was an aggravating factor contributing to the finding of a breach.

Court in this field. For example, in *Egeland and Hanseid* v *Norway*,[340] it was held that there had been no violation of Article 10 when two journalists had been prosecuted and fined for taking photographs of accused persons outside a court hearing without their consent, contrary to national law. The European Court noted that the photographs had been taken without her consent and directly after she had been informed of her conviction for a triple murder; she was in tears and in great distress and thus at her most vulnerable psychologically. The public interest in the photographs and the trial did not outweigh the woman's right to privacy and the interest in the fair administration of justice, and the relatively modest fine was not disproportionate.[341]

Privacy versus press freedom: conclusions

Decisions in cases such as *McKennitt* and *Mosley* are examples of the change in judicial direction with respect to the balance between freedom of expression and the protection of privacy. This change has been prompted by the decision of the European Court in *Von Hannover*, above, and has been achieved by modifying at least two principles that are always present in such cases. The first relates to the strength of the privacy claim of the claimant, particularly with respect to sexual information. In *A* v *B plc* LORD WOOLF CJ was almost dismissive of the claimant's right to hide his adulterous relationship, feeling that such information and relationships lay at the lower end of privacy rights. In *Mosley*, however, such information is readily accepted as private, almost irrespective of the nature and propriety of the relationship in question. The second modification relates to the circumstances in which the public interest should demand the disclosure of information relating to the private lives of public figures. In cases before *Von Hannover*, the public right to be informed of the misdemeanours and activities of celebrities was justified on the basis that such people were role models and that the public had a genuine, thus legitimate interest in receiving such information.[342] The decision in *Von Hannover*, however, called those decisions into question, restricting the public interest defence to matters of genuine, and more formal, political and public concern, and in most cases excluding information relating to the private lives of celebrities. The distinction between public officials and public celebrities, and information of genuine public concern and mere 'tittle tattle' may create elitism with respect to the sorts of matters the public *should* be interested in, but probably reflects the jurisprudence of the European Convention. However, the move to protect privacy from the mere inquisitiveness of the media and the public will be undermined if the courts do not, at the same time, protect freedom of expression and press freedom in cases where the information in question is clearly in the public interest: as in the case of *HRH Prince of Wales* v *Associated Newspapers*,[343] where the Court of Appeal upheld injunctions to prohibit the publication of private diaries which included information of undoubted public, and in that case constitutional, interest. In this respect, the decision of the Court of Appeal in *Browne*, and the *obiter* comments in *LNS*, above, are welcomed.

---

[340] (2010) 50 EHRR 2.

[341] See also *Callaghan* v *Independent News and Media Ltd* [2009] NIQB 1, where the Northern Ireland High Court awarded an injunction to prevent a newspaper from publishing an unpixelated photograph of a sex offender due for release. Such publication would have been a disproportionate interference with the offender's expectation of privacy and would have constituted a threat to his life and private life. The court noted that there existed ways in which he could be monitored by the police and the prison service without such identification.

[342] See *Woodward* v *Hutchins*, *A* v *B plc* and *Theakston*, considered earlier.

[343] [2007] 2 All ER 139.

> **Questions**
> How have the domestic courts attempted to balance the right to individual privacy with free-
> dom of press and the public right to know?
> Do you believe that they have got that balance right?

Personal information and the right to private life

The right to privacy and private life does not merely protect people from direct intrusions into
their private life or information, in other words with interferences with their right to be let
alone, but also protects their right to have access to information that is personal to them.
Accordingly, to enjoy privacy and private life it will be necessary to have laws which not only
prohibit, or regulate, other people's right of access to the individual's private information, but
also allow that individual to gain access to such information. Also, there may be cases where
there are two competing privacy claims, as illustrated in the European Court's judgment in
Gaskin v *United Kingdom*.[344] The applicant wished to have access to files in order to bring
an action against people who were responsible for alleged abuse when he was in care as a
child. The law at that time only allowed such access when the contributor of the confidential
information waived their right to confidentiality. It was held that a system that applied that
presumption of confidentiality without balancing the interests of the persons seeking the
information represented an unnecessary restriction on the right to private life.[345] Similarly, in
MG v *United Kingdom*[346] it was held that there had been a violation of Article 8 when the
applicant had been denied access to full details on his social service records, which he sought
in order to confirm that he had been physically abused as a child. Noting that at the relevant
time the applicant had no legal right of access, and no appeal against any refusal, it found
that there had been a violation of Article 8.[347]

The principle in *Gaskin* was applied in the domestic courts in *R (Rose)* v *Secretary of State
for Health and Others*.[348] The claimant sought to review the Secretary's decision not to introduce legislation to give individuals conceived via IVF the right to obtain information about
anonymous donors. The High Court held that although the state did not have to take every
possible step to promote the emotional well-being of its citizens, respect for private and
family life required that everyone should be able to establish details of their identity as individuals, including the right to obtain information about a biological father. The fact that
in this case there was no relationship beyond an unidentified biological connection did not
prevent Article 8 from being engaged, and the claimants were thus entitled to claim that
the Secretary of State had acted unlawfully by failing to make the necessary regulations under
the Human Fertilisation and Embryology Act 1990.

This aspect of private life is, however, subject to interference where the public interest, or the
protection of the rights of others, is at issue. In particular, both domestic and international

---

[344] (1989) 12 EHRR 36.
[345] As a consequence parliament passed the Access to Personal Files Act 1989.
[346] (2003) 36 EHRR 3.
[347] The Court noted that the applicant would now enjoy a right of appeal under the Data Protection Act 1998,
which came into force after the applicant's requests.
[348] *The Times*, 22 August 2002.

law recognise the need for access, and to deny access, to personal information, and the European Court has indicated that a wide margin of appreciation will be available to individual states, particularly where issues of national security are raised. For example, in *Leander* v *Sweden*[349] the Court held that, provided there existed adequate and effective guarantees against abuse, the Convention would give a state a wide margin of appreciation in maintaining a system of secret surveillance for the protection of national security. In particular, with regard to whether the system of surveillance was in accordance with law, the Court held that the requirement of foreseeability in the special context of secret controls of staff in sectors affecting national security cannot be the same as in other fields. In this case the applicant had worked in a museum adjacent to a naval base in a restricted military zone but his contract was terminated pending security clearance. The applicant was denied such clearance, and refused access to information held about him on security files and which could only be accessed in exceptional circumstances. On the facts, the Court held that the effect of the regulations were mitigated by sufficient safeguards, particularly as any decision to release such information was supervised by members of parliament.

The law relating to data protection

Domestic law includes a number of legal provisions preventing unauthorised access to and use of personal information. For example, the Computer Misuse Act 1990 makes it an offence to secure unauthorised access to computerised data, including the accessing of information not covered by any authority.[350] In particular, the Data Protection Act 1998 provides for the statutory protection and regulation of personal data. Personal data is defined as data which relates to a living individual who can be identified from those data or from those data and other information which is in the possession of, or is likely to come into the possession of, the data controller. It includes any expression of opinion about the individual and any indication of the intentions of the data controller or any other person in respect of the individual.[351] However, in *Durant* v *Financial Services Authority*,[352] the Court of Appeal held that not all information relating to an individual held in a data register constituted 'personal data' so as to require the registered data controller to disclose it to the individual. In that case an individual had sought disclosure of various bank records which mentioned his name and which the bank held. It was held that not all information retrieved from a computer against an individual's name or unique identifier was personal data. In the Court's view the information must have affected the subject's privacy in personal, family, business or professional life. The Act was aimed at protecting data, and not simply documents and the mere fact that a document was retrievable by the individual's name did not make it personal data.[353]

The Act replaces previous legislation in this area,[354] and represents parliament's response to the EU Data Protection Directive 1995. The Act establishes a number of data protection

---

[349] (1987) 9 EHRR 433.

[350] See also the Access to Health Records Act 1990, allowing individuals access to health records.

[351] Section 1 Data Protection Act 1998.

[352] *The Times*, 2 January 2004.

[353] On the facts, the Court of Appeal held that the Act could not be used by individuals as a means of third-party discovery with a view to litigation – in this case the individual wanted to pursue an action against the bank.

[354] The Data Protection Act 1984, which was based on the recommendations of the Data Protection Committee: *Computers and Privacy*, Cmnd 6353.

principles, which are contained in Schedule 1 of the Act. These principles provide the basis of the Act's provisions and seek to provide control over the use of stored personal information, whether on manual or computerised files.

The data protection principles

The Act and its enforcement are guided by a number of data protection principles, which are contained in Schedule 1 of the Act. Principle 1 provides that personal data should be processed fairly and lawfully.[355] In particular it shall not be processed unless at least one of the requirements in Schedule 2 of the Act are met. Thus, the data subject must have given consent to the processing, unless the processing is necessary for a number of legitimate reasons, including the administration of justice, the exercise of statutory functions, the functions of a minister or government department or for the exercise of other functions of a public nature exercised in the public interest, or for the purposes of legitimate interests pursued by the data controller or a third party. Further, in the case of sensitive personal data,[356] principle 1 states that at least one of the conditions in Schedule 3 should be met. These conditions include the requirement that the subject has given his or her explicit consent to the processing, or where the subject has deliberately made the information public. Schedule 3 then gives a number of exceptions to such consent, including where the processing is necessary for medical purposes, or for the administration of justice, or for the exercise of statutory functions or functions of a minister or government department, or for the purposes of legitimate interests pursued by non-profit-making bodies.

Principle 2 elaborates on the above by providing that such data shall be obtained only for one or more specified, and lawful, purposes, and that any further processing shall not be incompatible with that purpose(s). Principle 3 then provides that such data shall be adequate and relevant, and not excessive in relation to the above purpose(s). The data shall be accurate, and where necessary kept up to date, shall not be kept for longer than is necessary to achieve the above purpose(s), shall be processed in accordance with the rights of data subjects under the Act, and appropriate technical and organisational measures must be taken against unauthorised or unlawful processing and against accidental loss or destruction of such data. Personal data should not be transferred to a country or territory outside the European Economic Area unless that jurisdiction can ensure an adequate level of protection for the rights and freedoms of data subjects in relation to the processing of personal data.

Right of access to personal data

Section 7 of the Act provides that an individual has the right to be informed by the data controller as to whether any personal data is being processed on behalf of that data

---

[355] In *Johnson v Medical Defence Union Ltd, The Times*, 10 April 2007, it was held that a continuous and single operation of processing data, part of which consisted of retrieval of information from a computer and part of which involved a mental process of selection and analysis, did not amount to processing of data under s.1. In this case the defendant's use of computer file information to investigate the claimant's professional activities did not fall within s.1 so as to amount to unfair processing.

[356] Sensitive personal data is defined in s.2 of the Act as personal data consisting of information as to the racial or ethnic origin of the data subject; his political opinions, religious or other similar beliefs; whether he is a member of a trade union; his physical or mental health or condition; his sexual life; the commission or alleged commission of any offence, or any proceedings for any such offence.

controller.[357] Such an individual is entitled to be given a description of the personal data, the purpose for which it is being processed and the recipients or classes of recipients to whom it is or may be disclosed. The individual also has the right to have communicated to him in an intelligible form the relevant personal information data as well as any information available to the data controller as to the source of that data. Under s.7(4) of the Act, the data controller need not comply with the request where to do so would involve disclosing information relating to another individual, unless that other has consented to such disclosure or it is reasonable in all the circumstances to comply with the request without gaining such consent. In *Durant v Financial Services Authority*[358] the Court of Appeal held that the legitimate interests of identifiable third parties were highly relevant but not determinative of the reasonableness of the decision to disclose personal data where consent had not been sought. There may also be compelling reasons not to give full disclosure to the applicant. For example, in *Roberts v Nottingham Healthcare NHS Trust*,[359] it was held that a patient at a mental institution who wished to challenge a restriction order was not entitled to disclosure of a psychology report as there were compelling medical and ethical reasons to refuse disclosure. Further, the refusal did not impinge on his right to a fair trial as other reports were available as evidence and the trust did not rely on it in any proceedings.

Enforcement of the Act

The Act can be enforced in a number of ways, through both the criminal and civil law. Thus, the Act not only creates specific criminal offences for breach of the Act's principles, but also provides a remedy of compensation to the aggrieved individual: see below. In addition, a breach of its provisions would in many cases engage Article 8 of the European Convention and thus an individual could bring an action against a public authority under the Human Rights Act 1998. The Data Protection Act's obligations apply to private persons, and Article 8 and its case law can be used to determine those duties and any relevant remedies as part of the horizontal effect of the Human Rights Act. As we shall see, the remedies provided under the Act can be used in conjunction with other remedies such as the law of confidentiality.

The principles and rights under the Act are enforced through the Data Protection Commissioner. The Commissioner has the power to make rulings on whether the Act has been breached, and it is an offence under s.47 of the Act to fail to comply with such a ruling. Before a ruling is made, the Commissioner must serve an enforcement notice on a data controller, and can do so only when he is satisfied that such a person has contravened any of the data protection principles.[360] The enforcement notice will require the data controller to take the necessary steps to comply with the principle or principles in question. In addition it may require the controller to take or refrain from taking such steps as are specified in the notice, and/or to refrain from processing any personal data, or personal data of a specified description, or to refrain from processing such after any specified time. An appeal against the Commissioner's decision lies, under s.48, to the Tribunal, and s.49 provides an appeal against the Tribunal's rulings to the High Court on a point of law.

---

[357] The data controller is defined as the person who (alone, jointly or in common with other persons) determines the purposes for which and the manner in which any personal data is, or is to be, processed.

[358] Note 352, above.

[359] [2008] EWHC 1934.

[360] An individual who thinks that they are the subject of a contravention of those principles may apply to the Commissioner, under s.42, asking for him to make a relevant assessment.

Right to prevent processing likely to cause damage or distress

Section 10 states that an individual is entitled at any time by notice in writing to a data controller to require that such a person, at the end of a period as is reasonable in the circumstances, to cease, or not to begin, processing (or processing for a specified purpose or in a specified manner) any personal data in respect of which he is the data subject. This request must be made on the grounds that such processing is causing or is likely to cause substantial damage or distress to him or to another, and that such damage or distress is or would be unwarranted. Upon such a request the data controller must reply within 21 days, informing the individual that he has complied or intends to comply with the request, or informing that person why he feels the request is unjustified.[361]

The right to compensation and other remedies

Section 13 of the 1998 Act provides that an individual who suffers damage by reason of any contravention of the requirements of the Act by a data controller is entitled to compensation from the data controller for that damage. Further, an individual is entitled to compensation from the data controller for any distress suffered by reason of such contravention, provided the individual suffers damage by reason of that contravention, or the contravention relates to the processing of personal data for the special purposes of journalism, art or literature.[362] The section provides a defence where the defendant can prove that he had taken such care as in all the circumstances was reasonably required to comply with the relevant requirement.[363] An action under the Data Protection Act 1998 can also be combined with a claim in confidentiality so as to protect the individual's right to private life under Article 8.[364]

Journalism, literature and art

Although the 1998 Act does not contain a specific public interest defence, s.32 attempts to give some protection to freedom of the press by exempting from the requirements of the Act data which have been processed for special purposes as defined in s.2 of the Act, that is, for the purposes of journalism, or for artistic or literary purposes.[365] Such data is only exempt if the processing is undertaken with a view to the publication by a person of any such material, and the data controller reasonably believes that publication would be in the public interest having regard to the importance of freedom of expression and that in all the circumstances compliance with that provision is incompatible with the special purposes.[366]

---

[361] Section 10(3).
[362] Section 13(2).
[363] Section 13(3).
[364] See, for example, the decisions in *R v Wakefield MBC and Another, ex parte Robertson* [2002] 2 WLR 889, and *Campbell v Mirror Group Newspapers* [2004] 2 AC 457.
[365] The s.13 exemption applies to the data protection principles (apart from principle 7 relating to the taking of relevant technical and organisational measures); and sections 7, 10, 12, 12A and 14(1) to (3) of the Act.
[366] In *Campbell v Mirror Group Newspapers* [2003] 2 WLR 80, the Court of Appeal held that where the data controller was responsible for the publication of hard copies that reproduced data that had previously been processed by means of equipment operating automatically, the publication formed part of processing and thus fell within the scope of s.32, overruled [2004] 2 AC 457.

> **Question**
>
> How does data protection law enhance the right to individual privacy and the protection of personal information?

Privacy and physical integrity

The right to private life as guaranteed by Article 8 of the Convention can protect a person's right to physical integrity and autonomy and thus protect him or her from attacks on their person or personal dignity.[367] This aspect of privacy or private life is supplemented by Article 3 of the Convention, which provides that no one shall be subject to torture or to inhuman or degrading treatment and punishment, and often a claim is made under both articles.[368]

The question of physical integrity and medical treatment has also been raised on a number of occasions domestically and the courts have established a presumption that a person is entitled to consent to or refuse medical treatment provided they possess the mental capacity to make relevant decisions.[369] Thus, in *St George's Healthcare NHS Trust v S*[370] the Court of Appeal held that a trespass had been committed on a pregnant woman who was forced to have a Caesarean section. The woman, who had been diagnosed with depression at the time and had been admitted to hospital for an assessment under the Mental Health Act 1983, was found to have full mental capacity and to be aware of the consequences of her refusal of any intervention at her birth. The Court of Appeal held that every person of full age and capacity had the right to autonomy and bodily integrity. The applicant was not suffering from a clinically recognised mental disorder and her irrational thought processes could not justify the removal, under compulsion, of the foetus from her body. Accordingly her detention for the purpose of carrying out that operation was unlawful and a trespass had been committed.[371] The position may be different, however, where there is evidence that the patient is suffering from a short-term incapacity, which negates their ability to make the necessary decision.[372]

The Convention does not rule out compulsory medical treatment of those who are detained on grounds of their mental health when such treatment is intended to address their

---

[367] See Feldman, Human Dignity as a Legal Value [1999] PL 682; [2000] PL 61.

[368] See, for example, *Costello-Roberts* v *United Kingdom* (1993) 19 EHRR 112; *Pretty* v *United Kingdom* (2002) 35 EHRR 1, discussed earlier in this chapter.

[369] See Feldman, *Civil Liberties and Human Rights in England and Wales* (OUP 2002, 2nd edn), pages 275–301. Medical treatment may also raise aspects of the right to family life. In *Re Vaccination: A v B; D v E, The Times*, 15 August 2003, it was held that immunisation against childhood diseases was in the best interests of the child despite the mother's objections; her objections were outweighed by the potential benefit of the whole course of immunisation and Article 8(2) allowed the court to interfere with those wishes where to do so would protect the child.

[370] [1998] 3 All ER 673.

[371] However, in *Simms v Simms and Another* [2003] 1 All ER 669, it was held that it was lawful to carry out experimental treatment on a helpless and mentally incapacitated individual with parental consent. In the court's view a patient not able to consent to pioneering treatment should not be deprived of that choice where he would have been likely to consent had he been competent.

[372] Thus, in *Re MB (An Adult: Medical Treatment)* [1997] 2 FCR 541, it was held that it was lawful to carry out a Caesarean section on a woman who wanted the operation, but who because of her panicked state, was incapable of giving consent for the anaesthetic.

illness.[373] Further, in *R (B) v Home Secretary and Others*,[374] it was held that the test of strict medical necessity to justify compulsory medical treatment did not apply unless that treatment reached the appropriate degree of severity to engage Article 3 – in other words that it would result in intense physical or mental suffering. In the present case there was no evidence that the patient would suffer such a detriment, and the above test did not apply to breaches of Article 8, where the court would simply have to establish that the interference was prescribed by law and necessary to achieve a legitimate aim. On the facts, the court held that the compulsory treatment with anti-psychotic medication of a convicted rapist did not infringe his human rights where the treatment was convincingly shown to be a medical necessity, and that it was not necessary also to show that the treatment was required to prevent the patient causing harm to himself or to others.[375]

The right of prisoners to refuse food, and the right of authorities to force-feed such individuals, was considered in the case of *Secretary of State for the Home Department v Robb*.[376] The Secretary had sought a declaration regarding the legal liability of the Home Office in a case where the prisoner was refusing food. It was held that a prisoner retained his right to self-autonomy during incarceration and that the authorities would have no duty to intervene unless there was a risk of suicide or of danger to others. A prisoner was capable of making the decision to refuse food provided he or she retained their mental faculties. This effectively overrules older authority to the effect that prison authorities could force-feed prisoners on grounds of necessity,[377] although in the case of mental patients the authorities are allowed to intervene if the act of hunger strike was a symptom of their mental illness.[378] The principle in *Robb* was applied in the recent case of *Re W (Adult: Refusal of Treatment)*,[379] where it was held that a prisoner with mental capacity had the right to refuse treatment to a self-inflicted wound that was potentially life-threatening. A secure prisoner had cut open his leg and forced objects into it, and then refused medical treatment. Giving judgment, DAME BUTLER-SLOSS P held that a mentally competent patient had an absolute right to refuse consent to medical treatment for any reason, rational or irrational, or for no reason at all, even where the decision would lead to his or her own death.

The principle that a prisoner has the general right to refuse treatment which thereby threatens their life was applied in *Re B (Consent to Treatment: Capacity)*,[380] where it was held that a seriously physically disabled patient who was mentally competent had the same right to personal autonomy as any other person with mental capacity. Mrs B, a severely disabled person who

---

[373] *Herczegfalvy v Austria* (1993) 15 EHRR 47.

[374] *The Times*, 2 February 2006.

[375] See also *Munjaz v Mersey Care NHS Trust; S v Airedale NHS Trust* [2006] 2 AC 148, where the House of Lords held that there was no violation of Articles 3 or 8 where a mental health patient had been secluded in breach of the authorities' code of practice. The authorities could depart from the Code if they had cogent reasons for doing so and that, on the facts, such reasons did exist.

[376] [1995] 1 All ER 677.

[377] *Leigh v Gladstone* (1909) 26 TLR 139.

[378] *R v Collins, ex parte Brady* [2000] Lloyd's Rep Med 355. However, see *R (Wilkinson) v Broadmoor Hospital* [2002] 1 WLR 419, on the question of how the necessity of the treatment is to be assessed. See also *R (N) v Dr M and Other, The Times*, 12 December 2002, where the Court of Appeal held that a mental health patient who had refused medical treatment should only be treated if medical necessity was convincingly shown. The Court of Appeal held that the standard of proof was not criminal, but that the court must be satisfied convincingly that the treatment was in the patient's best interests.

[379] *The Independent*, 17 June 2002.

[380] [2002] 2 All ER 449.

required artificial ventilation to stay alive, sought an order from the court to the effect that she could refuse medical treatment that was keeping her alive. In granting the order, DAME ELIZABETH BUTLER-SLOSS was satisfied that the claimant had the capacity to make decisions regarding her future medical treatment. In that case, therefore, there was a presumption that a patient had the mental capacity to consent to or refuse medical or surgical treatment. In the present case the mental capacity of the patient was not an issue and the patient, having been given the relevant information and offered the alternative options, chose to refuse treatment and that decision had to be respected, considerations of the best interests of the patient being irrelevant.

Although the case law protects individual bodily autonomy from non-consensual treatment, it has been held that Articles 2, 3 and 8 of the Convention do not give a right to die as such. This dilemma was raised in the case of *R (Pretty) ex parte v DPP and Another*,[381] the details of which have been dealt with in chapter 4 and earlier in this chapter. It was held that the law drew a distinction between the withdrawal of life-saving treatment, and the taking of action lacking any medical justification and intended solely to terminate the life of another. Article 2 was concerned with the right to life and not the right to die. It was also held that if the claim under Article 8 of the Convention should fail; any infringement was justified within Article 8(2) of the Convention.

Privacy and the retention of DNA samples

Both the domestic and European courts have considered Article 8 with respect to the retention and use of DNA samples and fingerprint evidence, collected under the Police and Criminal Evidence Act 1984, once a suspect had been cleared of an offence. In *R v Chief Constable of South Yorkshire, ex parte LS and Marper*,[382] the House of Lords held that the retention and use of such evidence was not contrary to Article 8; given the limited use made of such samples the majority felt that Article 8 had not been engaged because there had been no significant violation of the right to private life. Although Baroness Hale dissented on that point, she agreed that any violation was justified within the terms of Article 8(2).[383]

An application was then made under the European Convention, and in *S and Marper v United Kingdom*[384] the Grand Chamber of the European Court held that there had been a violation of Article 8 of the Convention. The applicants claimed that the retention of their fingerprints, cellular samples and DNA profiles interfered with their right to respect for private life because the samples were crucially linked to their individual identity and concerned a type of personal information that they were entitled to keep within their control, and that their retention provoked social stigma and psychological implications in the case of children, making the interference with the right to private life all the more pressing in respect of one of the applicants.

The Grand Chamber first considered the question whether Article 8 was engaged, noting that the concept of 'private life' covered the physical and psychological integrity of the person and that the mere storage of data relating to the private life of an individual was capable of

---

[381] [2001] 1 All ER 1. See also *Pretty v United Kingdom* (2002) 35 EHRR 1.

[382] [2004] 1 WLR 2196.

[383] Contrast *Jones v Chief Constable of West Midlands*, unreported, 23 March 2006, where it was held that a teacher who had been charged but not prosecuted for striking a child was entitled to demand that her fingerprints, DNA and photograph taken by the police should be destroyed. She was awarded £250 for false imprisonment and assault.

[384] (2009) 48 EHRR 50.

amounting to an interference within the meaning of Article 8.[385] Further, it accepted that cellular samples contained sensitive information about an individual, including information about their health and containing a unique genetic code of great relevance to both the individual and his relatives. With regard to DNA profiles, these contained substantial amounts of unique personal data and the possibility created by DNA profiles for drawing inferences about ethnic origin made their retention all the more sensitive and thus capable of affecting the right to private life. Furthermore, fingerprints contained unique information about the particular individual, and their retention without their consent could not be regarded as insignificant. Accordingly, it found that the retention of cellular samples, DNA profiles and finger prints amounted to an interference with the applicants' right to respect for their private lives within Article 8(1).

Having found a *prima facie* violation of Article 8(1), the Court accepted that the retention of the applicants' fingerprints and DNA records had a clear legal basis and pursued a legitimate aim of the detection and prevention of crime. With respect to the question of necessity and proportionality, it stressed that the protection of personal data was of fundamental importance to a person's enjoyment of private and family life, and that the retention of an unconvicted person's data may be especially harmful in the case of minors, given their special situation and the importance of their development and integration in society. Accordingly, the domestic law had to afford appropriate safeguards so as to prevent the use of such personal data being inconsistent with the guarantees of Article 8. In its view, although the interests of data subjects and the community as a whole in protecting personal data might be outweighed by the legitimate interest of the prevention of crime, the intrinsically private character of that information required careful scrutiny of any measure authorising its retention and use by the authorities without the individual's consent. Applying those principles, the Grand Chamber held that the blanket and indiscriminate nature of the powers of retention of the fingerprints, cellular samples and DNA profiles of persons suspected but not convicted of offences failed to strike a fair balance between the competing public and private interests. The state had overstepped any acceptable margin of appreciation in that regard, and the retention of such information constituted a disproportionate interference with the applicants' right to respect for private life.

Following the decision, legislative changes were made by the Labour government with respect to the retention and storage of such samples. Section 64 of the Crime and Security Act 2010 provided that adults convicted of an offence would have their DNA samples retained indefinitely, but those arrested but not convicted would have their profiles retained for six years irrespective of the offence. With respect to those under the age of 18, for those convicted of a serious offence or more than one minor offence there would be indefinite retention, whereas those convicted of a single minor offence would have the sample retained for five years. Those between 16 and 17 who were arrested but not convicted of a serious offence would have their profiles retained for six years, and all other under-18s who were arrested but not convicted, for three years. However, those provisions did not come into force and at the time of writing the 2010 coalition government announced that its intention was to scrap the retention of DNA samples of all those who have been arrested but not convicted of a criminal offence. It is likely that any provisions would mirror those adopted in Scotland, whereby

---

[385] The Court noted that it was accepted that fingerprints, DNA profiles and samples were personal data within the meaning of the Data Protection Act 1998.

those arrested but not convicted of sexual or violent crimes would have samples retained for three years. It is suggested that such a system is likely to be compliant with Article 8 and the Grand Chamber's decision in *Marper*.

Powers of surveillance, interception of communications and the right to privacy

The police and other state authorities will employ a variety of techniques for the purpose of ascertaining information in the prevention or detection of crime, or criminal activities. Most of these techniques will involve some form of intrusion into the individual's private or family life or home and will thus engage Article 8 of the European Convention and/or domestic legal remedies. The general powers of the police to enter and search premises are beyond the scope of this chapter, although it is clear that such powers must be exercised in accordance with the principles and case law of Articles 5 and 8 of the Convention.[386] This section of the chapter will examine specific practices such as telephone tapping, 'bugging', interception of communications and other covert surveillance techniques. First, it will examine the relevant European Convention principles and case law, in particular those cases that have involved the United Kingdom. The section will then examine the present domestic legal provisions to see whether such provisions are compatible with the Convention and the Human Rights Act 1998.[387]

Surveillance and the European Convention on Human Rights

Where these techniques involve a *prima facie* violation of a Convention right, they must pass the tests of legitimacy and reasonableness laid down by the European Court of Human Rights. In particular, such techniques must be in accordance with law, pursue a legitimate aim recognised in Article 8, and be necessary and proportionate in relation to that aim.[388]

The European Court has accepted that surveillance and other techniques engage the protection of Article 8. Thus, in *Klass v Federal Republic of Germany*[389] it was held that the mere existence of legislation allowing telephone tapping by state authorities involved, for those affected, a menace of surveillance that strikes at freedom of communication and therefore constitutes an interference of the right to private life and correspondence within Article 8. Accordingly, any interference with Article 8 has to be justified and at the very least the power to carry out the relevant activity must be in accordance with law. In the Court's view, the rule of law implies that interference by the executive authorities should be subject to an effective control, which should normally be assured by the judiciary. In a field where abuse is potentially so easy and could have harmful consequences for democratic society,

---

[386] See Bailey, Harris and Ormerod, *Civil Liberties: Cases and Materials* (OUP 2009, 6th edn), pages 576–600. See also Cheney, Dickson, Skilbeck, Uglow and Fitzpatrick, *Criminal Justice and the Human Rights Act 1998* (Jordan 2001), chapter 3.

[387] For a detailed examination of this area, see Fenwick, *Civil Rights, New Labour, Freedom and the Human Rights Act* (Longman 2000), chapters 8–10; Fenwick, *Civil Liberties and Human Rights* (Cavendish 2007), chapter 10.

[388] See Benjamin, Interception of Internet Communications and the Right to Privacy [2007] EHRLR 637.

[389] (1978) 2 EHRR 214.

it was in principle desirable to entrust supervisory control to a judge. However, as the legislation in question had inbuilt safeguards against abuse, the lack of judicial supervision was not fatal to the government's case and the Court held that the interference was both lawful and proportionate under Article 8(2).[390] The decision in *Klass* appears to allow the state a reasonably wide margin of appreciation provided the practices have a proper legal basis, the Court stressing that democratic societies were under threat from highly sophisticated forms of espionage and terrorism, which could justify the need to resort to covert methods of surveillance.

The principles in *Klass* were applied in *Malone* v *United Kingdom*,[391] where the Court found that the present state of domestic law on telephone tapping was obscure and open to differing interpretations and that accordingly it did not satisfy Article 8(2). At that time the rules on telephone tapping were contained in government circulars that were not publicly accessible. In the Court's view, domestic law in this area had to be laid down with reasonable precision in accessible legal rules that sufficiently indicate the scope and manner of exercise of discretion conferred on the relevant authorities. The inherent secrecy surrounding telephone tapping carried with it a danger of abuse, and it could not be said with any reasonable certainty what elements of the powers to intercept were incorporated in legal rules and what elements remained within the discretion of the executive. To that extent, therefore, the minimum degree of legal protection to which citizens are entitled under the rule of law was lacking.[392]

As a consequence of the ruling in *Malone*, parliament passed the Interception of Communications Act 1985, which put the practice of telephone tapping on a statutory footing. This allowed the legitimacy and necessity of the tapping to be tested, and in *PG and JH v United Kingdom*,[393] the European Court suggested that a member state would be afforded a good deal of discretion in this area. In this case the police had obtained permission to place a covert listening device in the applicants' flat and had requested itemised billing for calls from his telephone. Such information had been used against the applicants in subsequent criminal proceedings. The Government conceded that the authorities lacked the power to place the listening device, and the Court found a violation of Article 8 in that respect. However, with regard to the use of the applicant's telephone, the Court held that as the information had been obtained and used in the context of an investigation and trial concerning a suspected conspiracy to commit robbery, the measures were justified under Article 8(2), as necessary in a democratic society for the prevention of crime. In contrast, in *Liberty* v *United Kingdom*,[394] it was held that there had been a violation of Article 8 when Liberty and other human rights' groups had had their telephone calls and other communications, including privileged legal

---

[390] Contrast the decision in *Amann* v *Switzerland* (2000) 30 EHRR 843, where it was held that the tapping of the applicant's telephone conversation with a business client, who had telephoned from the former Soviet Embassy, amounted to a violation of Article 8. It was held that the national law was not sufficiently clear to alert those who may be affected of the risk that it would occur.

[391] (1984) 7 EHRR 14. The application had been brought after the applicant had brought an unsuccessful action against the police for tapping his telephone in the process of a criminal investigation: *Malone v Metropolitan Police Commissioner (No 2)* [1979] Ch 344.

[392] See also *Harman and Hewitt* v *United Kingdom* (1992) 14 EHRR 657, where the activities of MI5 in placing the applicants under surveillance were declared not to be in accordance with law. As a consequence, parliament made provision for such powers in the Security Services Act 1989.

[393] *The Times*, 19 October 2001.

[394] (2009) 48 EHRR 1.

correspondence, intercepted by an Electronic Test Facility operated by the Ministry of Defence. The European Court found that the power to intercept and read communications, *at that time* under s.3(2) of the Interception of Communications Act 1985, was not in accordance with law because it gave an unlimited discretion to the authorities. Further, any safeguards against abuse were not made public or accessible. In the Court's view, such inaccessibility was not justified for national security reasons because subsequently relevant codes of practice had been made publicly available.[395]

Although the 1985 Act complied with the basic thrust of the European Court's ruling, the Act did not apply to all methods of interception. For example, in *Halford* v *United Kingdom*[396] the European Court held that there had been a violation of Article 8 when the police authorities had tapped the applicant's telephone conversation held on her employer's premises. The European Court held that telephone calls made from business premises were covered by the notion of private life under Article 8, and that employees who made calls on internal telecommunications systems had a reasonable expectation of privacy.[397] Since domestic law did not regulate the interception of such calls, it could not be said that the interception was in accordance with law, and accordingly there had been a violation of Article 8.[398]

The practice of placing covert listening devices on individuals or their property, on the other hand, had not been placed in legal form, and in *Khan* v *United Kingdom*[399] the European Court held that the absence of domestic law warranting and regulating the use of such devices meant that there had been an unjustified interference with the applicant's private life and correspondence under Article 8. The police had placed a bugging device on the home of the applicant's associate and had gathered information that was later used in his criminal trial.[400] The Court held that as this interference had been authorised via unpublished Home Office guidelines, such restriction was not in accordance with law.[401] Subsequently, the United Kingdom has been defeated in a number of other cases where it has been unable to provide legal authority for the employment of such techniques, resulting in a finding of a violation not only of Article 8, but also of Article 13 for failure to provide an effective remedy for breach of the individual's Convention rights.[402] For example, in *Govell* v *United Kingdom*[403] the European Commission held that the police complaints and disciplinary system into the misuse of police powers was not sufficiently independent to provide an effective remedy within Article 13. Similarly, in *PG and JH* v *United*

---

[395] For a commentary on the case, see Goold, *Liberty and Others* v *United Kingdom* [2009] PL 5.

[396] (1997) 24 EHRR 523.

[397] In *PG and JH* v *United Kingdom, The Times*, 19 October 2001, the European Court held that the principles in *Klass* and *Malone* applied to recording devices operated without the knowledge and consent of the individual on police premises.

[398] Such practices are now covered by the Regulation of Investigatory Powers Act 2000: see below.

[399] (2000) 31 EHRR 45.

[400] Nevertheless, the Court found that there had been no violation of Article 6. The fact that the evidence had been used to determine his guilt was not, necessarily, in violation of his right to a fair trial. Contrast *Allan* v *United Kingdom* (2003) 36 EHRR 12.

[401] The practice was, by the time of the decision, covered by s.93 of the Police Act 1997.

[402] See *Chalkley* v *United Kingdom* (2003) 37 EHRR 30, where a violation of Article 8 was found when the applicant's telephone conversation had been taped by a covert listening device when at the relevant time there had been no statutory scheme regulating such practices. See also *Hewitson* v *United Kingdom* (2003) 37 EHRR 31; *Lewis* v *United Kingdom* (2004) 39 EHRR 9.

[403] (1997) EHRLR 438.

Kingdom[404] it was held that the domestic courts were not in a position to provide an effective remedy within Article 13 and that the complaints procedure did not meet the requisite levels of independence demanded by that Article.[405]

Similar breaches have been found with respect to the covert filming of prisoners in their cells. In *Perry v United Kingdom*,[406] a film of the applicant had been taken secretly when he was in a prison cell and was then used for identity purposes. The Court held that the applicant's right to respect for his private life had been interfered with by this process and that police had gone beyond the normal use of that type of camera. Further, as the police had failed to follow the procedures set out in the relevant code of practice under the Police and Criminal Evidence Act 1984, and had not obtained his consent or informed him of his rights the filming was not in accordance with law and accordingly in violation of Article 8.[407] Also, in *Wood v United Kingdom*,[408] the European Court found a violation of Article 8 when the applicant's conversation with other detainees in a prison cell had been recorded and used in evidence in his criminal trial. The government conceded that the taping had been done without legal authority and that the applicant had no available remedy for that breach. Accordingly there was a violation of Articles 8 and 13.

A further gap in domestic law was raised in the case of *Copland v United Kingdom*[409] with respect to the monitoring of employees' correspondence. The applicant was employed as the personal assistant to a college principal and for a period of 18 months her telephone, e-mail and internet usage had been monitored at the instigation of the college in order to ascertain whether she was making excessive use of those facilities. The applicant argued that this constituted a violation of her right to private life, but the government contended that as her calls had not been intercepted, or the content of her communications examined, the monitoring of her use of the facilities did not constitute a violation of Article 8. The European Court held that the collection and storage of personal information relating to the applicant's use of those forms of communication interfered with her right to respect for her private life and correspondence. Further, the Court held that although there may be circumstances where it was legitimate for an employer to monitor and control the employee's use of the telephone and internet, etc., in the present case it was not necessary to consider whether the aims of the employer were legitimate, or whether the interference was necessary and proportionate. As there was no law regulating this aspect of monitoring of correspondence, the interference was not in accordance with law and thus in violation of Article 8.

Surveillance and domestic law

Before the series of cases against the United Kingdom government referred to above, the power to intercept communication and to carry out other surveillance techniques was governed by

---

[404] *The Times*, 19 October 2001. See also *Armstrong v United Kingdom* (2003) 36 EHRR 30, where it was held that the obtaining of evidence from a covert surveillance operation and the recording of conversations in the home of the applicant's co-defendant were in violation of Article 8 because there was at the time no statutory system to regulate the use of such devices, and *Taylor-Sabori v United Kingdom* (2003) 36 EHRR 17, where the interception of pager messages was held to be in violation of Article 8.

[405] The position is now governed by the Regulation of Investigatory Powers Act 2000, considered below.

[406] (2004) 39 EHRR 3.

[407] The Court awarded the applicant €1500 for non-pecuniary loss under Article 41.

[408] *The Times*, 23 November 2004.

[409] (2007) 45 EHRR 37.

largely secret administrative guidance. The domestic courts upheld these activities on the basis that their exercise did not infringe any legal claim and thus did not require any legal justification.[410] Accordingly, these powers were left unchallenged, although in *R v Secretary of State for Home Affairs ex parte Ruddock*[411] it was held that at the very least an individual had a legitimate expectation that the police would follow the current policies on telephone tapping. Following the European Court's rulings, legislation was put into place to regulate the variety of surveillance techniques and these provisions are now either contained in or regulated by the Regulation of Investigatory Powers Act 2000. These powers are not covered in any detail in this section of the chapter, but should be studied in the light of the European Convention and Court's insistence that such laws should be open and clear, subject to sufficient independent scrutiny, and only applied in necessary cases and in a proportionate manner.

Interception of communications

The power to intercept communications, including the power to tap telephones, was contained in the Interception of Communications Act 1985, which was passed in response to the European Court's ruling in *Malone*, above. The position is now governed by Part I of the Regulation of Investigatory Powers Act 2000. Under s.1 of the Act it is an offence intentionally and without lawful excuse to intercept communications by either a postal service or a telecommunications system.[412] An interception will be lawful where it is carried out with the individual's consent,[413] or under the authority of a warrant that has been issued under s.5 of the Act.

The power to issue a warrant is vested in the Home Secretary and any application must come from a person specified in s.6 of the Act, which includes Chief Constables, the Director-General of the Security Service, the Chief of the Secret Intelligence Service, the Director-General of the National Criminal Intelligence Service and the Commissioners of Customs and Excise. The warrant must not be issued unless the Home Secretary believes that it is necessary for the following purposes: the interests of national security; the prevention or detection of serious crime;[414] for safeguarding the economic well-being of the United Kingdom; or giving effect to an international mutual assistance agreement for the prevention or detection of serious crime.[415] In addition, the Home Secretary must believe that the conduct authorised by the warrant is proportionate to what is sought to be achieved by that conduct. This incorporates the principles of legitimacy and proportionality into the powers, although the Home Secretary's assessment in these respects should not be conclusive. Under s.8 of the Act the warrant must specify the subjects of the interception warrant, and any details relating to the addresses and

---

[410] *Malone v Metropolitan Police Commissioner (No 2)* [1979] Ch 344.

[411] [1987] 2 All ER 518.

[412] This includes a private telecommunications system so as to comply with the European Court's decision in *Halford v United Kingdom* (1997) 24 EHRR 523. For a critical overview, see Ormerod and McKay, Telephone Intercepts and their Admissibility [2004] PL 15.

[413] Section 3. This includes the situation where the person has reasonable grounds for believing that the correspondents have consented.

[414] Serious crime is defined in s.81(3) of the Act and includes an offence either for which a person over the age of 21 would reasonably expect to be sentenced to imprisonment for a term of three years or more, or where the conduct involves the use of violence, results in substantial financial gain or is conducted by a large number of persons in pursuit of a common purpose.

[415] Section 5(3).

telephone numbers of the individuals or premises concerned, and the means by which the interception is to take place.

An important element of decisions such as *Malone* is that any system is surrounded by sufficient safeguards to avoid abuse, and in particular that there are opportunities for judicial or equivalent review. In this respect, an independent Interception of Communications Officer, who must, under s.57, have held high judicial office and who must report to parliament via the Prime Minister, supervises the system of interceptions. In addition, a Tribunal is established by s.65 of the Act to consider and determine any complaints made to them relating to, *inter alia*, the conduct of the intelligence services and conduct for or in connection with the interception of communications. The Tribunal must consist of members who have held high judicial office and its jurisdiction is to consider and determine complaints in relation to the scope of the 2000 Act.[416] The Tribunal must apply the principles applicable by a court on an application for judicial review, and in the post-Human Rights era this would allow it to scrutinise decisions that are in violation of the individual's Convention rights and, in particular, the principles of proportionality. The Tribunal has the power under s.67 of the Act to award compensation, and may make an order quashing or cancelling any warrant or authorisation. Section 67 also states that the determinations of the tribunal shall not be subject to appeal or be liable to be questioned in any court.

These safeguards were held by the European Court to be Convention compliant in the recent case of *Kennedy* v *United Kingdom*.[417] In this case Kennedy had been sentenced to life imprisonment for murder and alleged that on his release his business mail, telephone and e-mail communications were being intercepted because of his high-profile case and his subsequent involvement in campaigning against miscarriages of justice. He complained to the Investigatory Powers Tribunal (IPT) that his communications were being intercepted in violation of his private life and sought the prohibition of any communication interception by the intelligence agencies and the destruction of any product of such interception. He also requested specific directions to ensure the fairness of the proceedings before the IPT, including an oral hearing in public, and a mutual inspection of witness statements and evidence between the parties. The Tribunal examined the applicant's specific complaints in private, and ruled that no determination had been made in his favour in respect of his complaints; which meant either that there had been no interception or that any interception which took place was lawful.

Dismissing his claims under Articles 6, 8 and 13 of the Convention, the Court found that the interference in question pursued the legitimate aims of preventing crime and had been carried out on the basis of the 2000 Act as supplemented by the Interception of Communications Code of Practice. In the Court's view, the Act defined with sufficient precision the cases in which communications could be intercepted; the state not being compelled to exhaustively list national security offences as those were by nature difficult to define in advance. Finally, as only communications within the United Kingdom were concerned in the present case, the domestic law described more fully the categories of persons who could be subject to an interception of their communications.

---

[416] Section 65(2). It is also stated that for the purposes of such claims it is the only appropriate tribunal to consider claims under s.7(1) of the Human Rights Act 1998. In *A v B* [2010] 2 WLR 1, the Supreme Court held that the Investigatory Powers Tribunal had exclusive jurisdiction to hear a challenge to the refusal of the Director of the Security Service to consent to the publication of a book detailing an employee's work for the service.

[417] *The Times*, 3 June 2010.

With respect to the processing, communication and destruction of data, the Court noted that the overall duration of interception measures could be left to the discretion of the domestic authorities, provided adequate safeguards were put in place. In this case the renewal or cancellation of interception warrants were under the systematic supervision of the Secretary of State and warrants for internal communications related to one person or one set of premises only, thus limiting the scope of the authorities' discretion to intercept and listen to private communications. The law also strictly limited the number of persons who had access to the intercept material, of which only a summary would be disclosed whenever sufficient, and required the data to be destroyed as soon as they were no longer needed. The Court also noted the roles of both the independent Commissioner, who ensured that the legal provisions were applied correctly, and the extensive jurisdiction of the Tribunal, which examined any complaint of unlawful interception of communications. Any person could apply to the Tribunal, which had access to closed material and could require the Commissioner to order disclosure of all relevant documents, and which could, on finding a breach, quash any interception order, require destruction of intercepted material and order compensation. Further, the publication of its rulings enhanced the level of scrutiny over secret surveillance activities in the United Kingdom. Accordingly, the relevant domestic provisions indicated with sufficient clarity the procedures concerning interception warrants as well as the processing, communicating and destruction of data collected. Thus, as there was no evidence of any significant shortcomings in the application and operation of the surveillance regime in the present case there had been no violation of Article 8.

With respect to the claim under Article 6, the Convention allowed restrictions on the right to fully adversarial proceedings where strictly necessary in the public interest. Further, restrictions on the Tribunal's proceedings were justified by considerations of confidentiality, whilst the nature of the issues justified the absence of an oral hearing. The Court further noted that under Article 6 national security might justify the exclusion of the public from the proceedings, and that it was sufficient that an applicant be informed in terms that the authorities neither confirmed nor denied the surveillance. Thus, bearing in mind the importance of secret surveillance to the fight against terrorism and serious crime, the Court considered that the restrictions on the applicant's rights in the context of the proceedings before the Tribunal were both necessary and proportionate and were not contrary to Article 6.[418]

In conclusion, therefore, although the legislation provides certain safeguards and complies with basic aspects of the rule of law, it does provide wide powers to intercept private and privileged communications. For example, in Re Mc E and Others,[419] the House of Lords accepted that the Act permitted the covert surveillance of legally privileged communications between lawyers and their clients notwithstanding the statutory right of people in custody to consult with their lawyers. Their Lordships held that the Act was clearly intended to apply to all communications and to override the common law and statutory protection of such rights. The House of Lords held that there was no absolute prohibition on such surveillance but that in the circumstances the surveillance had been disproportionate. In particular, the House of Lords noted that it was regrettable that, following the Divisional Court's finding that the

---

[418] Having regard to its conclusions in respect of Article 8 and Article 6, the Court considered that the Tribunal offered to the applicant an effective remedy insofar as his complaint was directed towards the alleged interception of his communications, and thus dismissed his claim under Article 13.

[419] [2009] 1 AC 908.

monitoring of legal consultations in police stations or prisons could not lawfully be authorised under the Code, the Secretary of State had taken no steps to characterise such surveillance as intrusive surveillance, so as to ensure the safeguards that went with that level of surveillance.

The bugging of private premises

The Police Act 1997 was also passed to satisfy the European Convention and its case law, which required that such interferences be in accordance with law.[420] The Act gave the police the power to enter property and to carry out surveillance techniques without the need to obtain a warrant, provided they obtained authorisation under the Act.[421] In other words, the Act made lawful activities that would otherwise engage criminal or civil liability, enabling the police to obtain authorisation for those activities. The Act is supplemented by provisions of the Regulation of Investigatory Powers Act 2000, which provides for a Chief Surveillance Commissioner and Surveillance Commissioners,[422] and Assistant Surveillance Commissioners,[423] who have the responsibility of supervising and controlling the authorisation procedures.

Authorisation is provided by the authorising officer[424] who may permit the taking of action in respect of property or wireless telegraphy where he or she reasonably believes that it is necessary for such action to be taken on the ground that it is likely to be of substantial value in the prevention or detection of serious crime,[425] and that the action it seeks to achieve cannot reasonably be achieved by other means.[426] The authorisation must normally be in writing, but under s.95 may be given orally in cases of emergency. When authorisation has been granted, a Surveillance Commissioner must be notified, and such person has the power to quash or cancel it if he or she is satisfied that there were no reasonable grounds for believing that the conditions for its issue were satisfied, or that such conditions have ceased to apply.[427] This power does not normally affect any action taken in relation to the authorisation, but s.97 of the Act states that in certain cases the authorisation does not take effect until the Commissioner approves it. Under that section approval is needed first where the property specified is used wholly or mainly as a dwelling or as a bedroom in a hotel, or constitutes office premises; and secondly where the authorising officer believes that the authorised action is likely to result in any person acquiring knowledge of matters relating to legal privilege, confidential personal information or confidential journalistic material.[428]

---

[420] See *Khan v United Kingdom* (2000) 31 EHRR 45. By the time the European Court made its judgment, the Police Act was already in force.

[421] Section 92 states that no entry or interference with property or with wireless telegraphy shall be unlawful if it is authorised by an authorisation having effect under the Act.

[422] Section 81. The Chief Surveillance Commissioner must by virtue of s.107 of the Police Act make an annual report to parliament.

[423] Section 61.

[424] This is defined in s.92(5) as a Chief Constable, the Commissioner, or Assistant Commissioner of Police of the Metropolis, the Commissioner of Police for the City of London, the Chief or Deputy Chief Constable of the RUC, the Directors-General of the National Criminal Intelligence Service and the National Crime Squad, and a designated customs officer. Section 93 allows the authorisation to be given to designated persons when it is not practicable for the above to give it.

[425] Defined in s.93(4) of the Act in virtually the same way as with the interception of communications: see s.81(3) RIPA, above.

[426] Section 93(2) Police Act 1997.

[427] Section 101 Police Act 1997.

[428] Under s.97(3), this safeguard does not apply where the authorising officer believes that the case is one of emergency.

Complaints regarding the operation of these powers are now made to the Tribunal, established under s.65 of RIPA, whereas appeals by authorising officers against decisions of the Commissioner in relation to the refusal or quashing of any order are made to the Chief Surveillance Commissioner, under s.104 of the Police Act. It has been questioned whether these provisions, including those relating to the challenge of such powers, comply with the requirements of Article 8 of the Convention, or the rights under Articles 5 and 6,[429] but in *R v Lawrence*[430] the Court of Appeal held that the scheme provided by the Act, now under RIPA, constituted sufficient statutory oversight for the purposes of Article 8 and its case law.

Covert surveillance

The Regulation of Investigatory Powers Act 2000 governs particular covert surveillance techniques adopted by the various authorities.[431] Under s.48 of the Act, surveillance includes monitoring, observing, listening to persons, their movements, their conversations or their other activities; recording anything monitored, observed or listened to in the course of surveillance; and surveillance by or with the assistance of a surveillance device. Section 26 governs 'directed surveillance', 'intrusive surveillance' and the conduct of 'covert human intelligence sources'. 'Directed surveillance' is covert surveillance that is not intrusive, but which is undertaken for the purposes of a specific investigation or operation and which is likely to result in the obtaining of private information about a person. 'Intrusive surveillance' on the other hand is surveillance that relates to activity in residential premises or in a private vehicle, and which either involves the presence of an individual in residential premises or a private vehicle, or is carried out by means of a surveillance device. A 'covert human intelligence source' is one that establishes or maintains a relationship with a person for the covert purpose of using the relationship to obtain access to information or of disclosing information obtained from the relationship.

Authorisation for such surveillance is governed by sections 28–32 of the Act and can be given by relevant persons prescribed by order made under s.30.[432] Any authorisation must be on relevant grounds, including national security, the economic well-being of the United Kingdom, the prevention or detection of crime, public safety, public health or tax collection, and must be necessary and proportionate in relation to those aims. In the case of intrusive surveillance, s.32 states that authorisation must come from the Home Secretary or senior authorising officers, such as Chief Constables, and the grounds are limited to national security, the economic well-being of the United Kingdom and the prevention or detection of serious crime. With regard to covert intelligence sources, the person authorising the use of the source must be satisfied that there are proper arrangements in place for the supervision of the operation of the source.[433]

---

[429] See Fenwick, *Civil Rights: New Labour, Freedom and the Human Rights Act 1998* (Longman 2000), pages 372–7.

[430] [2002] Crim LR 584.

[431] In *R v Rosenburg* [2006] EWCA Crim 6, it was held that surveillance via a neighbour's camera of the defendant's activities, although done with the knowledge of the police, and used in a criminal prosecution as evidence, was not police surveillance for the purpose of RIPA 2000.

[432] Under s.30 this must be a person holding such an office, rank or position with relevant public authorities as are prescribed for the purpose of this subsection by an order under this section. With regard to the police, the relevant rank is superintendent, or an inspector in cases of emergency.

[433] The monitoring and appeal processes are similar to those which apply under the Police Act 1997, above.

◼ Closed circuit television cameras and other monitoring

Public authorities, including the police and local councils, have a number of powers to take and collect images of individuals, and issues of privacy arise from such practices, especially where that information is passed on to others and perhaps to the public.[434] In *Peck v United Kingdom*, considered below in the case study, the European Court held that there had been a violation of Article 8 of the Convention when CCTV footage of the applicant in a distressed condition had been released for use in various newspapers and television programmes without sufficient safeguards to ensure his anonymity. Further, in *Martin v United Kingdom*,[435] it was alleged that the use by the local authority of hidden cameras to monitor the applicant and her home following allegations of disorderly behaviour was in violation of Article 8 of the Convention. The European Court struck the case out following a friendly settlement whereby the applicant received €4000 and expenses in compensation. Such powers are now regulated under the Regulation of Investigatory Powers Act 2000 but are still subject to review by the Investigatory Appeal Tribunal.[436]

Assuming that the authorities have legal power to carry out such practices, whether there is a violation of Article 8 in such cases will depend on all the facts, including the level of intrusion. In *R (Ellis) v Constable of Essex Police*,[437] the Divisional Court held that a proposed offender naming scheme, whereby the identities of burglars and other offenders be identified in order to reduce crime, should be postponed in order for the authorities to consider whether it would impose a disproportionate interference on the offender's and his family's private and family life. Whether the operation of the scheme was lawful or not would depend upon the circumstances of the offenders solicited for the scheme and how it operated in practice. However, in *R (Stanley and Other) v Metropolitan Police Commissioner and Another*,[438] it was held that there had been no illegality or violation of Article 8 of the Convention when the police and the local authority had distributed leaflets containing photographs, names and addresses and ages of a number of young people who had been issued with Anti-social Behavioural Orders. In the court's view, where the purpose of publicity was to inform, reassure and assist in enforcing orders it would not be disproportionate to provide such detail.[439]

The taking of images by private individuals, and the subsequent use of that information, also gives rise to legal uncertainty. Such actions may constitute a breach of confidentiality and other laws, such as trespass, but a *prima facie* breach of privacy might not preclude the admissibility of such information. For example, in *Jones v Warwick University*[440] a court rejected a claim that evidence obtained by an insurance company when they had trespassed on an individual's property in order to prove that her personal injury claims were exaggerated

---

[434] The Information Commissioner operates a UK CCTV code of practice regulating the use of such devices. See Reid, Nearly all Cameras Illegal says Watchdog, *The Times*, 31 May 2007.

[435] (2007) 44 EHRR 31.

[436] For example, the Tribunal decided that Poole District Council had acted unlawfully in monitoring local parents whom the council suspected of lying about their address in order to win a place at a school outside their catchment area: *Paton and Others v Poole District Council* (IPT/09/01/C).

[437] *The Times*, 17 June 2003.

[438] *The Times*, 22 October 2004.

[439] On the facts it was held that the colourful language used in the leaflets in this case was necessary in order to attract the attention of the readership. It was also proportionate to give this information (via the internet) to people not in the relevant locality, as many people may have been affected by such behaviour.

[440] [2003] 3 All ER 760.

should not be admitted in court. Although the actions violated the claimant's privacy, it was held that such evidence was admissible. Further, in *Martin v McGuiness*,[441] the Court of Session held that evidence gathered by a private investigator, which infringed an individual's right to private life under Article 8, was admissible in personal injury litigation provided the inquiries and surveillance was reasonable and proportionate in the circumstances.[442]

Questions

What has been the European Court of Human Right's approach to the use of surveillance techniques by public authorities?

Do you believe that existing domestic law is compatible with the right to privacy and the case law of the European Court in this area?

CASE STUDY

Peck v *United Kingdom* (2003) 36 EHRR 41

This case has been chosen as an example of individual privacy being compromised by the actions of both public bodies and the media. It concerned the disclosure of CCTV footage of the applicant when he was in a public place and in a distressed medical state. Both the domestic and the European Court proceedings are examined to see how the dispute was resolved both under domestic law and under the European Convention on Human Rights. In particular it provides an example of how a privacy dispute was resolved in the pre-Human Rights Act era, and how that case should have been dealt with by employing Convention principles and case law.

The facts

The applicant, Geoffrey Peck, was suffering from depression. In August 1995 he was walking down Brentwood High Street with a kitchen knife in his hand and attempted to commit suicide by slitting his wrists. Unbeknown to the applicant, he was being filmed by closed-circuit television, although the footage did not show him cutting his wrists. Police and medics were called to the scene and the applicant was later detained for a short period under the Mental Health Act 1983, but released and taken home. In October 1995 Brentwood Council issued a press feature in their CCTV News, containing two photographs from the footage along with an account of the incident. The applicant's face was not specifically masked and the article explained that the applicant had been spotted with a knife in his hand and that he was clearly unhappy but not looking for trouble. Three days later the local newspaper – the *Brentwood Weekly News* – used a photograph of the ➡

---

[441] *The Times*, 23 April 2003.

[442] See also *Amwell View School Governors v Dogherty*, unreported, 15 September 2006 (EAT), where it was held that there was no violation of Article 8 when a claimant in an unfair dismissal action had secretly taped the disciplinary hearing held by the employers and sought to use such evidence in the tribunal. The governors' private and family lives were not compromised as they had been acting in a public and quasi-judicial capacity. However, the tribunal should not have admitted recordings of the deliberations of the governors for that would compromise open discussion and encourage satellite litigation.

incident on a front-page article about the closed-circuit television system and again the applicant's face was not specifically masked. The next day an article entitled 'Gotcha' appeared in another local newspaper – the *Yellow Advertiser* with a circulation of approximately 24,000 – containing a photograph from the footage and describing how the police had defused a potentially dangerous affair. A follow-up article was published three days later, using the same photograph and there was evidence to suggest that a number of people recognised the applicant.

One day after the publication of the last article, Anglia Television broadcast a programme to approximately 350,000 people containing extracts of the footage although the applicant's face had been masked at the Council's request. The applicant became aware of these articles and programmes in late October but chose not to take any legal action because of his depression. The footage was then supplied to the producers of the BBC programme *Crime Beat*, which had on average nine million viewers. The Council imposed a number of conditions relating to its showing, including that no one should be identifiable and that all faces should be masked. However, in trailers for the programme the applicant's face was not masked and although the producers assured the Council that his face was masked in the main programme, several of his friends and family recognised him from the programme.

The applicant then made a number of television appearances to complain about the situation. He also complained to the Broadcasting Standards Commission regarding the programme on the BBC, alleging an unwarranted infringement of his privacy and claiming that he had been treated unjustly and unfairly. The Commission upheld his complaints. The applicant also complained to the Independent Television Commission concerning the Anglia television programme and the Commission found that there had been a breach of the Commission's Code as his face had not been properly obscured. As a result of the finding, an apology was given by Anglia TV. The applicant's complaint to the Press Complaints Commission regarding the article in the *Yellow Advertiser* was dismissed on the basis that the incidents had taken place in a public place and no criminal stigma had been attached to the applicant.

An application for judicial review of the Council's decision to release the footage was also unsuccessful, the High Court finding that the Council had an implied legal power to release such information to other bodies when that was necessary to fulfil its statutory power to operate the scheme. Further it was held that the Council had not acted irrationally in conveying this particular information to the relevant bodies in the manner that it did (*R v Brentwood Council, ex parte Peck* [1998] EMLR 697). In the court's view the council could not be said to have acted irrationally; they did not know the identity of the individual so could not have consulted with him before releasing the information; further they acted in good faith without any aim to gain financially and had given instructions to the recipients of the footage to mask the individual's face. It was not the fault of the Council that the media had not followed these instructions. Finally, with respect to the claim based in privacy, although such practices might occasion a breach of privacy, in the absence of a clear domestic law of privacy the authorities were simply bound to have and carry out effective codes of practice so as to avoid abuse.

The applicant applied under the European Convention, invoking Article 8 before the European Court of Human Rights, and claiming that the use of the footage was an unjustified interference with his right to private life. He further claimed that there had been a violation of Article 13 in that he had not been applied with an effective remedy in domestic law to redress that interference.

The decision of the European Court of Human Rights

With regard to the claim under Article, 8, the Court observed that the disclosure of the footage had resulted in the applicant's actions being observed to an extent far exceeding any exposure to a passer-by or to security observation and to an extent surpassing that which the applicant could have foreseen. Accordingly, the disclosure by the Council of that footage had resulted in a serious interference with the applicant's right to respect for private life. The Court was satisfied that this interference was prescribed by law in that s.163 of the Criminal Justice and Public Order Act 1994, which enabled local authorities to operate such schemes, together with s.111 of the Local Government Act 1972, which allows local authorities to do anything to facilitate the discharge of their functions, was sufficiently clear and certain to be acceptable within the terms of Article 8(2). The Court also considered that the powers bestowed on the Council under that provision served a legitimate aim in that such powers were necessary for the detection and deterrence of criminal activities and that the publication of such footage served the legitimate aims of public safety, the prevention of disorder and crime and the protection of the rights of others.

However, the Court held that the reasons for the interference with the applicant's rights were neither relevant nor sufficient so as to be considered as necessary in a democratic society for the purposes of achieving the legitimate aim. The Court stressed that the disclosure of private, intimate information could only be justified by an overriding requirement in the public interest and that the disclosure of such information without the consent of the individual called for the most careful scrutiny by the European Court (Z v Finland (1997) 25 EHRR 371). In the Court's view, the aims of the coverage and its release could not justify the direct disclosure by the Council to the public of stills of the applicant in CCTV News without it obtaining the applicant's consent or masking his identity. Neither could it justify its disclosure to the media without it taking steps to ensure so far as possible that his identity would be masked. Particular scrutiny and care was needed given the crime prevention objective and the context of the disclosures. The disclosure of the material in CCTV News and to the Yellow Advertiser, Anglia Television and the BBC were not accompanied by sufficient safeguards and thus constituted a disproportionate and unjustified interference with the applicant's private life under Article 8. In coming to that conclusion the Court held that the applicant's voluntary media appearances after the initial coverage did not diminish the serious nature of the interference, neither did they reduce the need for care concerning disclosures. The applicant had been the victim of a serious interference with his right to privacy and it could not be held against him that he had tried afterwards to expose and complain about that wrongdoing through the media.

With respect to the applicant's claim under Article 13 of the Convention the Court held that the action in judicial review did not provide him with an effective remedy in relation to the violation of his Article 8 rights. In the Court's view, the threshold at which the High Court could impugn the decision of the Council was placed so high that it effectively excluded any consideration by it of the question whether the interference answered a pressing social need or was proportionate. In addition, the lack of legal power of both the Broadcasting Standards Commission and the Independent Television Commission to award damages meant that those bodies could not provide an effective remedy to the applicant. Moreover, although the applicant was aware of the Council's disclosure prior to the *Yellow Advertiser* article and the BBC broadcasts, neither the BSC nor the ITC had the power to prevent such publications or broadcasts. (See, for example, *R v Broadcasting Complaints Commission, ex parte Barclay* (1997) 9 Admin LR 265, where it was held that an allegation of breach of privacy could only relate to the actual broadcast of a programme.) The Court also noted that at the relevant time the applicant did not have an actionable remedy in breach of confidence, the information in question not having the necessary quality of confidentiality required by the law at that time, and re-publication of confidential information would have been classed as information in the public domain. Accordingly, the applicant had been left with no effective remedy for breach of his Convention right of private life and there had been a violation of Article 13.

The Court awarded the applicant just satisfaction under Article 41 of the Convention of €11,800 for non-pecuniary damage and €18,075 for costs and expenses.

Questions
1 What aspects of the applicant's privacy rights were engaged in this case?
2 Do you feel that any privacy claim in such cases should be lost, either for the protection of the individual or for the wider public interest?
3 Why was the domestic challenge to the local authority's actions unsuccessful?
4 To what extent did the domestic courts consider the human rights of the applicant in coming to that decision?
5 Why did the European Court find a violation of Article 8 of the Convention, and how did its decision-making process differ from the domestic courts?
6 Why did the European Court find a violation of Article 13 of the Convention?
7 What deficiencies in the domestic law of privacy are highlighted by the European Court's decision?
8 How do you think the case would be decided by the domestic courts in the post-Human Rights Act era?

Prisoners and the right to private and family life

Although the prisoner's private and family life will be compromised by the fact of incarceration, the prisoner, and his family and friends,[443] continue to enjoy the basic rights under Articles 8 and 12 of the Convention, subject, of course, to legitimate and proportionate restrictions.[444]

---

[443] See Borroks-Gordon and Bainham, Prisoners' Families and the Regulation of Contact [2004] J Soc Wel & Fam L 263; Tabib and Mole, Imprisoned Parents and the Right to Family Life (2006) International Family Law Journal 97.

[444] Note, in *R (Foster) v Governor of High Down Prison*, decision of the High Court, 22 July 2010, it was held that a prisoner had no right to smoke under Article 8 and thus a withdrawal of smoking privileges did not engage Article 8. This followed the decision of the Court of Appeal in *R (G) v Nottingham Healthcare NHS Trust* [2009] EWCA Civ 795.

Prisoners and the right to private life, correspondence and contacts

Article 8 has been used on a number of occasions by prisoners seeking to challenge regulations and practices which place restrictions on the prisoner's correspondence and contacts. In *Golder v United Kingdom*[445] the European Court held that there had been an interference with the prisoner's right to correspondence under Article 8 when he had been refused permission to correspond with his solicitor with a view of bringing a civil action against a prison officer. Significantly, the European Court held that Article 8 contained no implied restrictions excluding prisoners from its protection. Prisoners, like other individuals, enjoyed the right to private and family life and any restriction had to be justified on the grounds and under the conditions prescribed in Article 8(2). Similarly, in *Silver v United Kingdom*[446] the European Court held that there had been a violation of Article 8 when the prisoners' correspondence with their families, friends and legal advisers had been interfered with. In that case the Court had held that many of the interferences were not in accordance with the law because they were not published and thus not accessible to the prisoners. In other instances the Court found the interferences to be disproportionate and based on the presumption that prisoners did not have the right of correspondence, rather than any pressing social need to preserve prison discipline or public order.

The Court has taken a particularly robust approach when the correspondence relates to the prisoner's right to access the courts and legal advice and will demand clear and strong justification for any interference. For example, in *AB v Netherlands*,[447] the European Court held that there had been a violation of Article 8 when the prisoner's correspondence with his legal adviser and the European Commission had been interfered with. In the Court's view there was no justification for interference with his correspondence with the Commission and the fact that his adviser was an ex prisoner and not a formal lawyer did not justify a lack of protection of his legal correspondence. As there was no requirement in Dutch law that the adviser had to be a lawyer the interference was not in accordance with law. However, provided the prisoner has an opportunity to seek judicial review where his correspondence has been unlawfully interfered with, it is not necessary that the prisoner be compensated for such when there is no evidence that they have suffered any loss or damage.[448]

An equally hands-on approach has been taken by the European Court with respect to medical correspondence, despite the domestic courts being prepared to show considerable deference in this area. In *R (Szuluk) v Home Secretary and Another*,[449] a prisoner suffering from a life-threatening condition brought an action when the prison medical officer examined correspondence between him and his medical advisers in accordance with prison regulations.[450] The Court of Appeal found that the practice was necessary in a democratic society for the prevention of crime and the protection of the rights of others, noting that short of withdrawing all scrutiny, there was no less invasive measure available to the prison service. However, in *Szuluk v United Kingdom*,[451] the European Court held that such correspondence should be

---

[445] (1975) 1 EHRR 524.
[446] (1983) 5 EHRR 347.
[447] (2003) 37 EHRR 48.
[448] *Watkins v United Kingdom* (Application No 35757/06).
[449] *The Independent*, 4 November 2004.
[450] Prison Service Order 1000, chapter 36.
[451] (2010) 50 EHRR 10.

given protection equal to that of legal correspondence and there was no pressing need to depart from that principle in this case. Accordingly, it found that the interference was disproportionate and in violation of Article 8.

Although any interference with a prisoner's general correspondence has to be in accordance with the law,[452] and must relate to a legitimate aim and be necessary in a democratic society,[453] the European Court indicated that they would give to member states a wide margin of appreciation. For example, in *Boyle and Rice v United Kingdom*[454] the European Court rejected a number of claims made by prisoners in relation to restrictions placed on their correspondence and visiting rights. The European Court held that when assessing the obligations of contracting states under Article 8, regard must be had to the ordinary and reasonable requirements of imprisonment and to the resultant degree of discretion that the national authorities must be allowed in regulating a prisoner's contact with his family.[455] In general, therefore, the Convention machinery has taken a 'hands-off' approach with regard to prison regulations which interfere with the prisoner's private and family life, stating that the prison authorities are better placed to determine the type and level of restrictions in this area. For example in *Messina v Italy (No 2)*,[456] it was held that a strict regime of prison visits, imposed on the applicant because of his Mafia-related activities, did not constitute a disproportionate interference with his right to family life under Article 8.[457] However, the Court will insist on basic principles of legality and necessity. Thus, in *Wisse v France*,[458] it was held that there had been a violation of Article 8 when prisoners' conversations with visitors were recorded. Such provisions were not properly prescribed by law and failed to maintain even some degree of privacy. Further, they had been adopted for reasons other than prison security.

Many domestic prison regulations impose restrictions on the prisoner's right of private and family life and their right to correspondence.[459] All such restrictions on rights of private and family life need to be justified as legitimate and proportionate.[460] Indeed, recent changes

---

[452] See also the decisions of the European Court in *Domenichini v Italy* (2001) 32 EHRR 4, and *Petra v Romania* (2001) 33 EHRR 5. See also *Labita v Italy*, decision of the European Court of Human Rights, 6 April 2000.

[453] See *McCallum v United Kingdom* (1991) 13 EHRR 596. Here the European Court held that restrictions placed on the prisoner's correspondence as part of formal disciplinary proceedings and to address his uncooperative behaviour in prison were in violation of Article 8.

[454] (1988) 10 EHRR 425.

[455] Thus in that case the prisoners could not, *inter alia*, complain when their visiting and contact rights had been reduced by reason of their transfer to another prison with a less generous regime.

[456] Judgment of the European Court, 28 September 2000.

[457] See also *Erdem v Germany* (2002) 35 EHRR 15, where the European Court held that the regulation of a terrorist prisoner's correspondence was not in violation of Article 8. Given the threat presented by terrorism and the necessity of the state to monitor correspondence in evaluating that threat, the interference was not disproportionate to the legitimate aims pursued. See also *Stitic v Croatia* (Application 29660/03) – regulation of correspondence (right to receive parcels) as part of a punishment for attempted drug smuggling was proportionate.

[458] Decision of the European Court, 20 December 2005.

[459] Many of these restrictions will, of course, restrict the rights of the prisoner's family and friends. These individuals are able to bring actions against the prison authorities if the latter have acted unlawfully and/or in violation of those persons' Convention rights. See, for example, *Wainwright v Secretary of State for the Home Department* [2004] 2 AC 406, and *Wainwright v United Kingdom* (2007) 44 EHRR 40 on the legality of strip searches on those visiting prisoners.

[460] See Livingstone and Owen, *Prison Law* (OUP 2008), chapter 7.

to the Prison Rules in these areas have attempted to ensure that the provisions are compliant with the European Convention. For example, the Prison (Amendment) (No 2) Rules 2000,[461] which give the Secretary the power to impose restrictions and conditions on communications permitted between a prisoner and other persons, are now subject to the qualifications that such restrictions and conditions must, in her opinion, not interfere with the Convention rights of any person and must be proportionate to the aims laid down in Article 8(2) of the European Convention for prison security or good order and discipline.[462] Despite these safeguards, the courts will give a wide area of discretion to the prison authorities where there appears to be a strong justification for imposing restrictions on the prisoner's right to family and other contacts. Thus, in *R (on the application of B) v Governor of Wakefield Prison*,[463] it was held that Rule 4(1) of the Prison Rules did not prevent the Secretary of State from introducing a rational policy on the restriction of prison visits and that the weight attached to the relevant factors of visiting rights and prison security and the protection of others was essentially a matter for the decision maker.[464]

A similar approach was adopted in *R (Taylor) v Governor of Riley Prison*.[465] The prisoner had sought judicial review of a blanket policy of 'call enabling', which restricted the amount of numbers that the prisoner could use to 20 and which provided that such numbers had to be given to the prison authorities in advance. The prisoner claimed that the system unjustifiably interfered with his rights under Article 8 and that the blanket ban was disproportionate. The High Court held that having regard to the growing problem of drugs in the prison, the system of 'call-enabling' was a justified interference of the prisoner's right under Article 8. The system had been introduced to deal with that problem and thus related to the legitimate aim of preventing crime within the prison. Further, in this particular prison and on this particular occasion the means adopted to achieve that objective were necessary, proportionate and thus justified.

In fact, in *R (RD) v Secretary of State for the Home Department*,[466] it was held that prisoners had no general right under Article 8 to make telephone calls and that the prisoner's claim that the extortionate rate for such calls infringed his rights under the Convention did not engage Articles 8 or 14. Further the claim under Article 14 failed because prisoners could not compare themselves with those in the community.[467] Further, in *Potter v Scottish Ministers*,[468] the Court of Session held that the practice of including a pre-recorded message on all outgoing telephone calls, informing the recipient that the call was being made from a prison, was not an

---

[461] Statutory Instrument 2000 No 2641.

[462] Rule 4, substituting Rule 34 of the Prison Rules 1999.

[463] [2001] EWHC 917 (Admin).

[464] The courts have given a wide margin of appreciation to the hospital authorities with respect to restrictions placed on the visiting rights of patients detained in high-security hospitals. See *R v Secretary of State for the Home Department, ex parte LM* [2001] FLR 406. See also the decision in *R v Ashworth Security Hospital Authority and Another, ex parte N, The Times*, 26 June 2001 where it was held that the policy of random monitoring of telephone calls for high-risk patients was not a disproportionate interference with the applicant's rights of private life and correspondence under Article 8 of the Convention.

[465] [2004] EWHC 2564.

[466] [2008] EWCA Civ 676.

[467] The National Consumer Council later investigated the issue and has made a complaint to OFCOM re the charges, which were eight times greater than those made to ordinary pay-phone customer ('Prison charges under scrutiny', *Financial Times*, 24 June 2008). OFCOM subsequently upheld the complaint.

[468] [2010] CSOH 85.

unlawful and disproportionate interference with the prisoner's right to private and family life. In the Court's view the procedure was necessary to protect vulnerable people from unwanted calls and to protect their reasonable expectation of privacy. If the procedure impacted on the prisoner's Article 8 rights at all, which the court doubted, it did so only tangentially and in any case was not disproportionate. The court also considered the fact that telephones were provided by prison authorities not as a matter of legal obligation and thus alongside conditions for their use. However, the court did opine that a blanket monitoring and recording of calls would be disproportionate, and the European Court has held that the provision of telephone facilities should not be based on discrimination.[469]

Prisoners and the right to private sexual life

Although the European Court has confirmed that the right to private life includes the right to a private sexual life, there is little authority for the prisoner's claim to a private sexual life. Thus, the European Commission has held that it is not in violation of Article 12, or 8, of the Convention to impose a prohibition on conjugal visits. For example, in *X v United Kingdom*[470] the European Commission held that there was no violation of the prisoner's convention rights when prisoners were not allowed conjugal visits, and this stance has been maintained in subsequent cases.[471] Thus, in *ELH and PBH v United Kingdom*[472] the European Commission declared inadmissible a claim by a prisoner and his wife that the refusal of conjugal visits constituted a violation of Articles 8, 9 and 12 of the Convention. Any restriction on the applicant's private and family life were justified by reference to prison security and the Commission noted that the prisoner might be able to make use of the facility of artificial insemination offered by the Prison Service (see below).

Despite the above approach, prisoners enjoy a limited right to sexual life.[473] In *R v Secretary of State for the Home Department, ex parte Fielding*,[474] the High Court made a declaration that a policy whereby male prisoners were only provided with condoms if they could prove that they were at specific risk of contracting AIDS or HIV was unlawful.[475] The case was not decided on Convention principles, although LATHAM J held that Article 8 could inform the court on the question of the rationality of the policy, and the court held that prisoners did not have a general right to be supplied with condoms on demand.[476]

---

[469] In *Petrov v Bulgaria* (Application No 15197/02), it was held that there had been a violation of Articles 8 and 14 when a person in pre-trial detention was prevented from having telephone contact with his unmarried partner. In the Court's view it was not apparent why married and unmarried partners should be given disparate treatment with regard to maintaining contact by telephone whilst in custody.

[470] (1979) 2 DR 105.

[471] See also *ELH and PBH v United Kingdom* [1998] EHRLR 231.

[472] See note 471, above.

[473] The Prison Service has recently amended the Rules to allow homosexual partners to be classified as close relatives, thus making it easier for partners of homosexual prisoners to visit. In addition, homosexual prisoners in relationships with prisoners in other prisons are now entitled to 'inter-prison visits'.

[474] Unreported, decision of the High Court, 5 July 1999. Noted by Foster (1999) 149 NLJ 1082.

[475] For an analysis of the impact of the Human Rights Act on AIDS/HIV-related issues, see Valette, AIDS Behind Bars: Prisoners' Rights Guaranteed (2002) Howard Journal of Criminal Justice 107.

[476] See also *R v A Hospital, ex parte RH*, decision of the Administrative Court, 30 November 2001, where the applicant, who was detained under the Mental Health Act 1983, unsuccessfully challenged the hospital's policy of not providing condoms to patients, claiming that it was irrational and contrary to his Convention right to private life.

The domestic courts have also recognised the prisoner's right of sexual identity, and in *R (AB)* v *Secretary of State for Justice*[477] it was held that the Secretary of State had violated Article 8 by refusing to transfer a pre-operative transgender woman to a female prison. The court found that the Secretary had failed to consider the claimant's Article 8 claims, which were clearly engaged by an interference with her personal autonomy and the fact that the refusal would bar her eligibility for surgery and her progress to full gender reassignment, and had thus made a disproportionate decision. Further, the risk arguments for refusing to transfer the prisoner were not clear or weighty enough to override her Article 8 rights.

Prisoners and the right to family life under Articles 8 and 12

The mere fact of imprisonment impacts on the prisoner's family and private life,[478] and in certain cases the imposition of a custodial sentence may be seen as an infringement of the prisoner's fundamental rights. Thus, in *R* v *Gwent Magistrates' Court, ex parte Stokes*[479] it was held that the committal to prison of a single mother of four children for non-payment of fines and compensation orders should only be made as a last resort and that any term of imprisonment should be proportionate to any interference with the prisoner's right to family life under Article 8 of the Convention.[480] On the other hand, as we have seen, once imprisoned there will be an inevitable, although not unlimited, interference with the prisoner's right to family life.[481]

Article 12 of the Convention guarantees the right to marry in accordance with the law, and in *Hamer* v *United Kingdom*,[482] the European Commission of Human Rights held that the prohibition on prisoners marrying while in prison struck at the very essence of the right guaranteed by Article 12 of the Convention and thus constituted a clear violation of that provision.[483] The issues of family and private life have been raised in two important cases where the prisoner has been denied a request to begin a family via artificial insemination. In *R* v *Secretary of State for the Home Department, ex parte Mellor*,[484] a prisoner serving a life sentence for murder claimed that he had the right to artificially inseminate his wife. He had met and married his wife while in prison and wished to start a family. The Secretary of State had a policy allowing artificial insemination in exceptional cases, but refused the applicant permission on the grounds that he and his wife could start a family on his release. The Secretary of State also took into account the fact that as the relationship had not been tested outside prison it would not be in the best interests of any child for permission to be granted.

---

[477] [2010] All ER 151.
[478] See Borroks-Gordon and Bainham, Prisoners' Families and the Regulation of Contact [2004] J Soc Wel & Fam L 263; Tabib and Mole, Imprisoned Parents and the Right to Family Life (2006) International Family Law Journal 97.
[479] [2001] EWHC 569 (Admin), decision of the Administrative Court, 30 August 2001.
[480] See also *R* v *Mills* [2002] Cr App R 52, where the Court of Appeal held that where an alternative was available, a mother responsible for the care of young children who had committed a non-violent act of dishonesty should not be sentenced to imprisonment.
[481] *Boyle and Rice* v *United Kingdom* (1988) 10 EHRR 425.
[482] (1982) 4 EHRR 139.
[483] In *R (Crown Prosecution Service)* v *Registrar-General of Births, Deaths and Marriages* [2003] 2 WLR 504, it was held that it was not lawful to prevent a prisoner from marrying even where the marriage would make the wife a non-compellable witness for the prosecution in his forthcoming trial.
[484] [2001] 1 WLR 533.

The High Court held that those articles did not guarantee to a prisoner the right to found a family while in prison. The decision was upheld by the Court of Appeal, which found that the restriction was for a legitimate aim and was proportionate in the circumstances. Although the Court of Appeal held that the prisoner might, in exceptional circumstances, be able to claim the right to artificially inseminate his wife, it was satisfied that no such circumstances existed in the present case.

This approach was also adopted by the Scottish courts in *Dickson v Premier Prison Service*,[485] where it was held that it was not irrational or unlawful to refuse a prisoner's request to allow him to artificially inseminate his wife, even though on his release his wife would be 51 years of age and unlikely to be able to conceive. The court held that the likelihood of procreation on his release was only the starting point for the Secretary of State to consider. He was entitled to take into account the fact that his wife was claiming benefits, the welfare of the child, the implications of creating single-parent families and public concern about deterrence and punishment. An appeal under the European Convention was initially unsuccessful, and in *Dickson v United Kingdom*[486] the European Court held that the policy rightly took into account matters which reflected public concern and the Secretary's application of those factors to the particular case was both legitimate and proportionate.[487] However, on reference to the Grand Chamber it was held that there had been a violation of Article 8 on the facts.[488] Although the Grand Chamber accepted that the Secretary of State could legitimately take into account the welfare of the child in making his decision, it held that the policy, and its review by the courts, did not strike a proper balance between the competing interests on the one hand of the applicants and on the other of the public interest in regulating and refusing such facilities.[489] The decision and the approach of the Grand Chamber should ensure that such policies and restrictions are subjected to more intense scrutiny, although it is more doubtful whether either court will intervene lightly with policies related to matters such as conjugal and other visits where there has been evidence that the competing issues have been balanced.

A more robust approach has been taken with respect to challenges to prison mother and baby policies. The right of mothers to keep their babies with them during their sentence was raised in *R v Secretary of State for the Home Department, ex parte P and Q*,[490] where the Court of Appeal held that a blanket policy subjecting every mother to its provisions irrespective of individual family circumstances was unlawful. The Prison Service was required to consider whether a proposed interference with the child's family life was justified by the legitimate aims recognised by Article 8(2) of the Convention and to strike a fair balance between those aims. Adopting those principles the Court of Appeal held that although the Prison Service was entitled to adopt a policy which attempted to balance the rights of family life

---

[485] [2004] EWCA Civ 1477. See Codd, Regulating Reproduction: Prisoners' Families, Artificial Insemination and Human Rights [2006] EHRLR 39. See also Jackson, Prisoners, Their Partners and the Right to Family Life [2007] 19 (2) CFLQ 239.

[486] (2007) 44 EHRR 21.

[487] See Codd, The Slippery Slope to Sperm Smuggling: Prisoners, Artificial Insemination and Human Rights (2007) 15 Med Law Rev 220.

[488] (2008) 46 EHRR 41.

[489] The decision of the European Court and the Grand Chamber are examined in detail in the case study below.

[490] [2001] 3 WLR 2002.

with the best interests of the child, and that the policy had been properly applied in the case of one of the prisoners, in the case of the other prisoner there was evidence that the policy would have a disproportionately detrimental effect on the child and the mother which was in contravention of the right to private and family life within Article 8. The case is important in recognising the principle that a prisoner does not forgo their fundamental rights on incarceration, and is a good example of the courts insisting that fundamental rights should not be compromised by inflexible policies that bind the administration and which fail to take account of the particular circumstances of any particular case.[491]

Notwithstanding the fact that restrictions on private and family life need to be justified as being for a legitimate purpose and proportionate, it is expected that the courts will continue to provide the authorities with a relatively wide margin of appreciation in this area, and uphold restrictions which are reasonably related to factors such as good order and discipline.[492] The principle laid down in *P and Q* was considered in *R v Secretary of State for the Home Department, ex parte Craven*,[493] where the court upheld a restriction placed on the applicant that he should only enter his home town of Newcastle, where the murder had taken place and where the victim's family still lived, in order to pass through the area so as to visit his family or to travel to work. The court was satisfied that the exclusion zone reasonably accommodated the competing interests of both families and that the interference was justified under Article 8(2) for the purpose of protecting the rights of others.[494] Similarly, in *R (C) v Ministry of Justice*,[495] it was held that the imposition of polygraph testing as a condition of the prisoner's release was not in breach of Article 8 as it was justified on grounds of public safety given the seriousness of his crime (rape).[496]

Questions

To what extent should prisoners retain their right to private and family life while in prison?
To what extent have the European and domestic courts recognised such rights?

---

[491] Contrast *B v S* [2009] EWCA Civ 548, where it was held that there was no violation of Article 8 when a woman had been committed to prison without being allowed initially to have her baby with her (because a written application had to be made). Although the Article 8 rights of the baby had been engaged and the judge had not given sufficient weight to this when sentencing, this did not demand that her sentence be postponed for six months.

[492] In *R v Ashworth Hospital Authority, ex parte E, The Times,* 17 January 2002, it was held that the decision of a special hospital to refuse a male patient's request to dress as a woman was justified under the terms of Article 8(2) of the Convention on security and therapeutic grounds.

[493] [2001] EWHC 850 (Admin).

[494] See also *R (Gunn) v Secretary of State for Justice* [2009] WHC 1812 (Admin), it was held that there had been no violation of Article 8 when a prisoner had been banned from entering the city of Nottingham, where he had family and friends and where his criminal activities had taken place. The condition did not stop him having contact with his family and were based on a real concern that he would carry on his illegal activities and intimidate others including witnesses.

[495] [2010] HRLR 10.

[496] It was also held not to be in breach of Article 14 simply because the pilot use of the scheme only applied to certain geographical areas.

CASE STUDY

Dickson v United Kingdom (2007) 44 EHRR 21; (2008) 46 EHRR 41

This case has been chosen because it raises the controversial question of whether a prisoner's human rights (and the rights of the prisoner's family members) should be compromised or limited as a result of incarceration. The case concerned a prisoner's request to be allowed to artificially inseminate his wife while he was in prison. Judicial review proceedings challenging the Home Secretary's refusal of that request were dismissed and the prisoner and his wife took their complaint before the European Court of Human Rights and, subsequently to the Grand Chamber of the Court. Essentially the case raises the question whether it is permissible for the executive, and the courts, to consider the status of the applicant as a prisoner, and public perception of prisoners and due punishment, in deciding whether a restriction of human rights is permissible and necessary.

The applicants were a prisoner serving a life sentence for murder and his wife, a former prisoner whom he married in 2001. As the first applicant's minimum term would not expire until 2009, by which time the second applicant would be 51 and thus not capable of child-bearing, they sought permission to make use of artificial insemination facilities. This procedure, introduced to avoid the facility being used as an alternative to conjugal visits, provided that permission would be granted in exceptional cases, and that in considering permission in particular cases the Secretary would have regard to the following factors:

- the likely release of the prisoner;
- whether the couple were in a stable relationship;
- whether both parties want the procedure;
- whether the medical authorities are satisfied that the couple are medically fit to participate in the procedure;
- whether there is evidence of satisfactory arrangements for the welfare of the child;
- whether there is any evidence to suggest that it would not be in the public interest to provide facilities in the particular case.

In May 2003 the Secretary of State wrote to the applicants refusing permission citing the following reasons: that the couple had met in prison and that the relationship had not been tested in the outside world; that there was insufficient provision in place to provide independent welfare for any child that might be conceived, or immediate support network for the mother and child; any child would be without a father for an important part of its childhood; and in the light of the violence of the first applicant's crime – he had been convicted of murder – there would be a legitimate public concern that the punitive and deterrent elements of his sentence would be circumvented if he were allowed to father a child by artificial insemination.

The applicants made an application for judicial review of the Secretary's policy and decision, and in Dickson v Premier Prison Service ([2004] EWCA Civ 1477), it was held that the policy and the decision was not irrational. Relying on the Court of Appeal decision in *R (Mellor)* v *Home Secretary* ([2001] 3 WLR 533) the Court of Appeal held that the likelihood of procreation on his release was only the starting point for the Secretary of State to consider, and that he was entitled to take into account the fact that the prisoner's wife was claiming benefits, the welfare of the child, the implications of creating single-parent families and public concern about deterrence and punishment. After the failure of the judicial review proceedings the applicants brought an action under Articles 8 and 10 of the Convention, claiming that the refusal of permission constituted a violation of their right to private and family life and their right to found a family.

The decision of the European Court in *Dickson* (2007) 44 EHRR 21

The Court stressed that prisoners did not forgo their Convention rights following conviction and sentence, and continue to enjoy all fundamental rights save for the right to liberty. However, the Court noted that it remained the case that any measure depriving a prisoner of liberty by definition has some effect on the normal incidents of liberty and inevitably entails limitations and controls on the exercise of Convention rights, including a measure of control on prisoner's contacts with the outside world and, for present purposes, on the possibility of begetting a child. Such control would not be in violation of the prisoner's Convention rights, provided the nature and extent of such control is compatible with the Convention.

The Court then considered whether there was any interference with the applicants' rights in this case or alternatively whether the state had failed in its positive obligation to provide such rights. In the Court's view, although restrictions on the conjugal rights of prisoners was to be classified as an interference with a Convention right, in the present case the restriction did not limit a general entitlement already in place in a prison environment, for example, controlling the mechanics of contact with family and visits. Rather, it concerned the state's refusal to take steps exceptionally to allow something (to beget children) that was not an already existing general right or entitlement. Therefore, in effect the applicants' complaint was that in refusing the appropriate facilities, the state had failed to fulfil a *positive* obligation to secure respect for their private and family life.

As a consequence, the extent of such obligations will vary considerably from case to case having regard to the diversity of situations obtaining in the contracting states and its resources. The issues raised in the present case display little common ground and there was no European consensus in favour of granting such facilities to prisoners. Further, although more than half the states allow for conjugal visits, the fact that the Court does not require contracting states to make provision for such visits, suggests that the state enjoys a wide margin of appreciation in this area in determining the steps to be taken to comply with the Convention with due regard to the needs and resources of the community and of individuals. Regard must be had to the fair balance that has to be struck between the general interest of the community and the interests of the individual and the aims mentioned in Article 8(2) have only certain relevance, with any state obligation not imposing an impossible or disproportionate burden on the authorities (*Osman* v *United Kingdom* (2000) 29 EHRR 245).

Considering the policy, the Court accepted that it had two principal aims – the maintenance of public confidence in the penal system and the welfare of any child conceived as a result of the process, which related, therefore, to the general interests of society as a whole. As to the first aim the Court stated that although there was no room in the Convention system for automatic forfeiture of rights by prisoners based purely on what might offend public opinion, the maintenance of public confidence in the penal system has a legitimate role to play in the development of penal policy within prisons. Further, in developing and applying the policy it was valid for the authorities to retain certain criteria that concerned the interests of any child to be conceived. The very object of a request for artificial insemination is the conception of a child and the state has positive obligations to ensure the effective protection and the moral and material welfare of children.

As to the policy itself the Court noted that in contrast to the law concerning the disenfranchisement of prisoners (successfully challenged in *Hirst v United Kingdom (No 2)* (2006) 42 EHRR 41), it did not operate in a blanket manner irrespective of individual circumstances. Requests for artificial insemination were carefully considered on individual merit and in accordance with the published criteria, which the Court does not find arbitrary or not related reasonably to the underlying aims of the policy. In addition there was evidence to suggest that the Secretary of State had allowed access to the facilities in previous cases, including two cases which had been subsequently struck out by the European Commission on other grounds (*PG v United Kingdom*, Application No 10822/84, and *G and RS v United Kingdom*, Application No 17142/90).

With respect to the present case, although the applicants had promised to bear the cost of the process, and gaining permission was the only realistic chance of the applicants having a child together, the Secretary of State had given careful consideration to all these factors before concluding that they were outweighed by the nature and gravity of the first applicant's offence, the welfare of the child and the lack of material and other support in place for the mother and child. Further, this decision had been reviewed by the Court of Appeal and considered lawful, rational and proportionate. Having regard to the margin of appreciation afforded to the national authorities in this respect, it had not been shown that the decision in the particular case was arbitrary or unreasonable or that it failed to strike a fair balance between the competing interests. Accordingly, there had been no violation of Article 8.

The case was appealed to the Grand Chamber of the European Court in accordance with Article 43 of the Convention.

The decision of the Grand Chamber of the European Court

The Grand Chamber first established that the applicants' Article 8 rights were engaged; the refusal of artificial insemination concerning their private and family lives which incorporates the right to respect for their decision to become genetic parents. The Grand Chamber then referred to its decision in *Hirst v United Kingdom (No 2)* to confirm that prisoners did not forfeit their Convention rights on imprisonment and that any restriction must be justified on each individual case. In this respect the Grand Chamber accepted that such restrictions might flow from the necessary and inevitable consequences of imprisonment or from an adequate link between the restriction and the circumstances of the prisoner in question; although it could not be based solely on what would offend public opinion.

The Grand Chamber then considered whether the state's refusal in this case consisted of a positive or negative obligation to comply with Article 8 of the Convention. Although it recognised that the article imposed both negative and positive obligations, it felt that it was not necessary in this case to decide whether it would be more appropriate to analyse the case as one concerning a positive or a negative obligation. This was because in either case the central issue was whether a fair balance was struck between the competing public and private interests involved.

The Grand Chamber then considered the three reasons put forward by the government to justify any interference with the applicants' rights. First it rejected the contention that losing the opportunity to beget a child was an inevitable and necessary consequence of imprisonment. Although the inability to beget a child might be a consequence of imprisonment it was not an inevitable one as the granting of such facilities would not inevitably involve any security issues, or impose any significant administrative or financial demands on the state. Secondly, the argument with respect to the undermining of public confidence in the prison system and the circumvention of the punitive and deterrent element of the sentence were partially accepted by the Grand Chamber. Thus, although there was no place for restrictions on the basis that the enjoyment of rights might offend public opinion, it was accepted that the maintaining of public confidence in the penal system has a role to play in the development of penal policy. However, with respect to the government's argument that the restriction, of itself, contributed to the overall punitive element of imprisonment, it referred to the evolution in European penal policy of the importance of rehabilitation. Thirdly, it accepted that the national authorities should, as a matter of principle, concern themselves with the welfare of any child. The state has a positive obligation to protect children (*Z v United Kingdom* (2002) 34 EHRR 3), although that duty should not go so far as to prevent parents who so wish from attempting to conceive a child in circumstances such as the present, especially as the second applicant was at liberty and could have taken care of any child until her husband's release.

The Grand Chamber then considered the balance between those accepted and competing interests and the role of the margin of appreciation in that exercise; noting that where (as in this case) a particularly important aspect of family life is at stake the margin of appreciation in general will be restricted. Where on the other hand there is no common European consensus on the relevant issue the margin will be wider; although that margin will not be all-embracing and the national authorities must be shown to have balanced those interests (*Hirst (No 2)*). Although the Grand Chamber noted that almost half the states had provided for conjugal visits (thus obviating the need for artificial insemination facilities), it also stressed that there was still no positive obligation to do so which arose from the Convention. However, although this particular policy had been subject to review, the Grand Chamber was of the view that the policy effectively excluded any real weighting of the competing interests thus preventing the required assessment of the proportionality of a restriction in any particular case. The policy placed an inordinately high exceptionality burden on the applicants when seeking those facilities: being required to show that the refusal of such facilities would prevent conception altogether and that their circumstances were exceptional. Thus the policy set the threshold so high against the applicants from the outset and did not allow a balancing exercise and a proportionality test as required by the Convention. In addition there was no evidence that the Secretary of State had formed the policy after consideration of the impact on Convention rights, the policy not having been considered by parliament or within the context of its compatibility with Convention rights (the policy being formed before the Human Rights Act 1998).

Although the policy did not constitute a blanket ban (as in *Hirst (No 2)*), the policy did not permit the required proportionality assessment in the individual case. The absence of such an assessment as regards a matter of significant importance to the applicants meant that the acceptable margin of appreciation had been exceeded and thus there had been a violation of Article 8, it not being necessary to consider the separate claim under Article 12.

Questions

1 Do you think that a prisoner should enjoy the (qualified) right to private and family life while in prison?

2 Should there be any restriction on the prisoner's 'right' to found a family while in prison?

3 Do you consider the Secretary of State's policy and its application in this case to be rational and consistent with the notion of prisoners' rights?

4 In particular, do you think the decisions of the Court of Appeal in *Dickson* and *Mellor* are consistent with the principles laid down in *Golder* v *United Kingdom*?

5 Do you agree with the European Court's initial ruling that the applicants' claim in this case arose from the state's positive obligation to provide the facility, rather than from a negative obligation not to interfere with their existing right? What is the Grand Chamber's view on this aspect and should a state's positive obligations to provide resources for the enjoyment of such rights be less extensive than its negative obligation not to violate that right?

6 To what extent do you feel that the European Court's first decision undermined the notions of prisoners' rights?

7 Why did the Grand Chamber disagree with the first Court decision and decide that there had been a violation of Article 8 in this case?

8 To what extent does the Grand Chamber accept that incarceration and public confidence in the penal system provide a legitimate reason for restricting prisoners' rights?

9 Do you agree that it is permissible to take the interests of any child into account when determining whether prisoners and their partners can start a family?

10 To what extent does the Grand Chamber's decision resolve the question of what restrictions it is permissible to place on prisoners' Convention rights, and the level of the margin of appreciation given to the national authorities in this respect?

Further reading

General texts

A number of texts on the European Convention contain excellent chapters on Articles 8 and 12 of the Convention and its relevant case law: Harris, Warbrick, Bates and O'Boyle, *Law of the European Convention on Human Rights* (OUP 2009, 2nd edn), chapter 9; Ovey and White, *Jacobs and White: The European Convention on Human Rights* (OUP 2010, 4th edn), chapter 11; Janis, Kay and Bradley, *European Human Rights Law* (OUP 2007, 3rd edn), chapter 11. In addition, Mowbray's *Cases and Materials on the European Convention* (OUP 2007, 2nd edn), chapters 10 and 14, is an excellent reference point on the case law of the European Court in this area. Clayton and Tomlinson, *The Law of Human Rights* (OUP 2009, 2nd edn), chapters 12 and 13 provide comprehensive coverage of both European and various domestic law provision; Amos, *Human Rights Law* (Hart 2006), chapter 11 provides a useful account of domestic cases on Article 8 in the post-Human Rights Act era. See also Colvin (ed.), *Developing Key Privacy Rights* (Hart 2002) for a discussion of a wide number of privacy issues.

Texts on press freedom and privacy

With respect to specialist texts on press freedom and privacy students should consult: Moore, *Privacy, the Press and the Law* (Palladian 2003); Rozenberg, *Privacy and the Press* (OUP 2004); Tugendhat and Christie, *The Law of Privacy and the Media* (OUP 2002, with supplement); and Fenwick and Phillipson, *Media Freedom under the Human Rights Act* (OUP 2006), chapters 13–17.

Articles

The following articles also provide expert commentary and analysis of the scope and case law of Article 8: Barber, A Right to Privacy? [2003] PL 602; Brazell, Confidence, Privacy and Human Rights: English Law in the Twenty-First Century [2005] EIPR 405; Chadwick, The Value of Privacy [2006] EHRLR 495; Gomery, Whose Autonomy Matters? Reconciling the Competing Claims of Privacy and Freedom of Expression (2007) 27 LS 404; Moreham, Privacy in the Common Law [2005] 121 LQR 628; Morse, Rights Relating to Personality, Freedom of the Press and Private International Law [2005] CLP 133; Mulheron, A Potential Framework for Privacy? A Reply to *Hello!* (2006) MLR 679; Phillipson, Transforming Breach of Confidence? Towards a Common Law Right of Privacy under the Human Rights Act (2003) MLR 726. See also the *European Human Rights Law Review* (Special Issue) on Privacy and the Law (Sweet & Maxwell 1996).

For articles on the rights of homosexuals and transsexuals, see Campbell and Lardy, Transsexuals – the ECHR in Transition [2003] NILQ 209; Catley, A Long Road Nearing the End [2003] JSWFL 277; Morris and Nott, Marriage Rites and Wrongs (2005) (1) JSWFL 43.

Visit **www.mylawchamber.co.uk/fosterhumanrights** to access regular updates to major changes in the law, further case studies, weblinks, and suggested answers/approaches to questions in the book.

Introduction

In *Ghai* v *Secretary of State for Justice*, it was claimed that the prohibition of open air funeral pyres interfered with the right to manifest religious beliefs under Article 9 of the European Convention on Human Rights, which guarantees freedom of thought, conscience and religion.

In *R (Watkins Singh)* v *Aberdare Girls' High School Governors*, it was argued that the refusal of a school to allow a girl to wear a 'Kara' – a slim bracelet expected to be worn by Sikhs at all times – was contrary to the Race Relations Act 1976 and the Equality Act 2006.

In *London Borough of Ealing* v *Ladele*, it was argued that it was a breach of the Equality (Religion and Belief) Regulations to discipline a registrar who refused to participate in civil partnerships.

All the above cases raised issues of potential racial or religious discrimination or possible breaches of the individual's right to freedom of religion under Article 9 of the European Convention. This chapter examines the right to freedom of religion, both under the Convention and in domestic law, and cases such as these will be studied in order to assess how the law balances this right with others' rights or the general public interest.

This chapter covers the fundamental democratic right to thought, conscience and religion contained in Article 9 of the European Convention on Human Rights and various other international human rights treaties. The main purpose of the chapter is to examine how that right is protected under both the European Convention and the Human Rights Act 1998 and the extent to which it can and is compromised when in conflict with other individual rights or state interests. The chapter begins by examining the reasons why this right is so fundamental in liberal democracies and how it relates to other human rights such as freedom of expression and freedom from discrimination. The chapter will then analyse the scope of Article 9 of the Convention, along with the relevant case law under that and related articles, so as to examine the extent to which the right is protected and restricted by the European, and domestic courts. There will then be a brief overview of relevant domestic laws that specifically seek to protect the right to religion, such as anti-discrimination laws.

In addition, the chapter will examine a number of specific areas where freedom of religion, thought and conscience conflicts with or interrelates with the enjoyment of other Convention rights, such as freedom of expression and the right to education. Thus, this section of the chapter will examine topical and controversial areas such as the control of religious hate speech, blasphemy and religion and the right to wear religious dress.

Thus, this chapter will contain:

- An examination of the scope and importance of the democratic right of freedom of thought, conscience and religion.

- An examination of the protection of that right under Article 9 of the European Convention on Human Rights and related articles.

- An examination and analysis of the case law of the European Court of Human Rights and the domestic courts in this area.

- A brief overview of domestic laws on the protection of religion including religious discrimination laws.

- An examination of how freedom of religion, thought and conscience impacts on the protection, and restriction, of free speech.

- An examination of how the freedom impacts on the right to education.

Freedom of thought, conscience and religion and human rights

Given that religious and racial persecution was perhaps the main reason behind the modern international human rights movement, including the ratification of the European Convention on Human Rights, it is inevitable that such instruments provide specific protection to freedom of religion.[1] Thus, although freedom of religion, thought and conscience often overlaps with other human rights – such as freedom of expression, association and assembly and the right to private life – human rights treaties will dedicate a specific article to the right to hold and manifest religious or other conscientious beliefs. For example, Article 18 of the International Covenant on Civil and Political Rights 1966 provides that everyone shall have the right to freedom of thought, conscience and religion, including the right to adopt a religion and to manifest that religion and belief in worship, observance, practice or teaching. Further, the second paragraph of that article provides that no one shall be subject to coercion which would impair his freedom to have or to adopt a religion or belief of his choice.

This represents the fundamental nature of those beliefs or opinions to the individual or to the group as a whole, allowing the law to provide *enhanced* protection to such individuals or associations and the manifestation of their views. Thus, an attempt by one person or group to persuade others as to the qualities of their religion (or the disadvantages of another religion) certainly constitutes speech for the purpose of Article 10 of the European Convention; and would also engage Article 11 when done as part of a demonstration. Equally, taking part in religious ceremonies or practices would engage the right to private and/or family life under Article 8; and restrictions on that right would in many cases involve a violation of Article 14,

---

[1] For a comprehensive analysis of the right and its protection in international law, see Taylor, *Freedom of Religion* (Cambridge University Press 2005). See also Evans, *Religious Liberty and International Law in Europe* (Cambridge University Press 1997).

prohibiting discrimination in the enjoyment of one's Convention rights. However, the inclusion of a specific right of religion, thought and conscience reflects the fundamental character of that association and the beliefs and tenets of the individual. In other words, belonging to a religious group is not simply exercising the right to association; and religious worship is not simply the manifestation of ideas and information. Both represent the basic and root beliefs of that individual or group of how they wish to live their lives; and this can be the case even in largely secular societies or where the beliefs are not based on formal religion as such.

In theory, therefore, human rights documents and their enforcement machinery will offer greater protection to those who belong to or manifest the views of such groups. This may involve giving more substantive protection against restrictions on religious speech or assembly, or imposing greater positive obligations on the state to ensure individuals and groups can enjoy their religious or other beliefs. In practice, however, the right under Article 9 to *manifest* those views will be restricted by other rights and interests and as we shall see both the European and domestic courts have allowed it to be compromised in largely the same manner as other conditional rights, such as freedom of expression.

Questions

Why is freedom of thought, conscience and religion so fundamental in human rights law?
Why is separate provision made for this right in both domestic bills of rights and international treaties?

Freedom of religion under the European Convention on Human Rights

Article 9 of the European Convention on Human Rights provides as follows: everyone has the right to freedom of thought, conscience and religion; this right includes freedom to change his religion or belief and freedom, either alone or in community with others and in public or private, to manifest his religion or belief, in worship, teaching, practice and observance.[2] Article 9(2) then provides that freedom to *manifest* one's religion or beliefs shall be subject only to such limitations as are prescribed by law and are necessary in a democratic society in the interests of public safety, for the protection of public order, health or morals, or the protection of the rights and freedoms of others.

A number of initial points should be made with respect to Article 9.[3] First, the general right to freedom of thought, conscience and belief is an absolute right in the sense that is not subject to the qualifications laid down in paragraph 2 of the article, which only applies to the *manifestation* of such views. This ensures that individuals or groups are free from persecution on grounds of their thoughts, beliefs or religion or their association with any relevant group. It is important, therefore, to make the distinction between discrimination on the grounds of conduct which manifests that belief and discrimination based solely on that belief. In *McFarlane v Avon Ltd*,[4] a counsellor had been dismissed for refusing to provide advice for

---

[2] The words in Article 9 are identical to Article 18 of the Universal Declaration of Human Rights 1948.

[3] For a more comprehensive coverage of Article 9, see Clayton and Tomlinson, *Law of Human Rights* (OUP 2008, 2nd edn), chapter 13; Mowbray, *Cases and Materials on the European Convention on Human Rights* (OUP 2007), chapter 11.

[4] (2010) IRLR 196.

same-sex couples on the grounds that it conflicted with his Christian views about relation-ships. The applicant argued that it was not permissible to distinguish between his belief and his conduct as both were protected, but the Employment Appeal Tribunal held that in cases such as the present there was a clear and evidently genuine basis for drawing that distinction. In this case, therefore, the fact that the individual's motive for the conduct was a wish to manifest his Christian beliefs did not mean that the belief itself was the ground of the employer's action in dismissing him. However, the Tribunal did concede that in some cases an objection to the manifestation of that belief and one to the belief itself might be indistin-guishable and thus automatically discriminatory.

Secondly, although Article 9 is absolute in that sense, even that fundamental aspect of the right is not exempt from Article 15 of the Convention, which allows states to derogate from the Convention in times of war or other public emergency. Thirdly, as noted above, the right to manifest one's religion etc. is a conditional right and subject to restrictions which accord with the principles of legality and necessity already noted in this text: although the state's margin of appreciation in this respect might be circumscribed by the fundamental nature of Article 9. Fourthly, as with many of the other Convention rights, Article 9 imposes on the state a positive obligation (albeit limited) to ensure that individuals and groups are not hindered in their enjoyment of their Article 9 rights. This obligation might involve in certain cases a positive duty to provide resources for such enjoyment, but more usually it will involve an obligation to ensure that those freedoms are not threatened or destroyed by other indi-viduals and counter-religious groups.

The scope of Article 9

It should be stressed that Article 9 is not limited to *religious* beliefs or convictions, but applies equally to other thoughts and convictions.[5] In *Kokkinakis v Greece*,[6] the European Court recog-nised that in its religious dimension Article 9 enshrined one of the most vital elements that go to make up the identity of believers and their conception of life. However, it also noted that equally freedom of thought and conscience was a precious asset for atheists, agnostics, sceptics and the unconcerned. The article thus protects a wide range of beliefs provided they are deeply held. For example, in *Arrowsmith v United Kingdom*,[7] the European Commission of Human Rights accepted that pacifism was a philosophy protected by Article 9. In that case the Commission accepted that the applicant's commitment to the philosophy of securing one's political or other objectives without resorting to the threat or use of force against another human being under any circumstances was a philosophy that fell within the ambit of Article 9.[8] Further, in *H v United Kingdom*,[9] the Commission accepted that veganism fell within Article 9's protection and a prisoner's vegan convictions engaged his Article 9 rights.[10]

[5] Similarly, Article 2 of the First Protocol to the Convention, considered below, protects a parent's right to have their children educated in conformity with their religious *and deeply held personal convictions*.

[6] (1993) 17 EHRR 397.

[7] (1978) 3 EHRR 218.

[8] See also *Grainger PLC v Nicholson* [2010] 2 All ER 253, where it was held that a belief in man-made climate change and the alleged moral obligation to act was capable, if genuinely held, of being a philosophical belief for the purpose of the Equality (Religion or Belief) Regulations 2003.

[9] (1993) 16 EHRR CD 44.

[10] In that case, however, the punishment of the prisoner for refusing to work with meat in the prison kitchen was held to be necessary and proportionate.

On the other hand, the Court has stressed that Article 9 does not apply to every opinion and conviction held by the individual. In *Pretty* v *United Kingdom*,[11] the applicant claimed that by denying her the right to die the state had interfered with her beliefs as protected by Article 9. The Court held that the applicant's claims did not involve a form of manifestation of a 'religion or belief, through worship, teaching, practice or observance' as described in the second sentence of the first paragraph in Article 9. The term 'practice' did not cover each act that was motivated or influenced by a religion or belief and although the applicant's views reflected her commitment to the principle of personal autonomy, that claim was merely a restatement of her complaint that there had been a violation of her right to private and family life under Article 8 of the Convention. So too, in *Friend* v *Lord Advocate*,[12] the House of Lords held that the restriction on hunting with hounds did not engage the right to thought, conscience and religion under Article 9. In their Lordships' view the right to engage in a recreational activity, however fervent or passionate, could not be equated with beliefs of the kind protected by Article 9. In any case, the legislation did not compel any individual to act against their conscience or to refrain from holding and giving visible expression to beliefs about the practice of hunting in the way they dressed. This decision was confirmed by the European Court of Human Rights, when it declared the applicants' case under the Convention manifestly ill-founded and thus inadmissible.[13]

Further, not every manifestation of views held by someone who has a conviction will engage Article 9.[14] Thus, in *Arrowsmith* v *United Kingdom* (above) the applicant was not allowed to argue that her conviction for disaffection for distributing leaflets outside an army base was a manifestation of her convictions as a pacifist. In the Commission's view her actions did not reflect her pacifist views, but rather her opposition to British military involvement in Northern Ireland.[15] The decisions in *Pretty* and *Arrowsmith* deny the applicant an enhanced claim that Article 9's engagement might have provided. Nevertheless, in such cases the applicant's deeply held beliefs can be reflected in the alternative claim: Pretty's claim being based on the fundamental right of self autonomy, and Arrowsmith's freedom of expression constituting political speech. That is the case even though the alternative claim might fail on the fact, as it did in both these cases.

Once it is accepted the individual's beliefs come within Article 9, the European Court has held that the article implies the freedom to manifest one's beliefs. Thus, in *Kokkinakis* v *Greece*[16] it was held that while freedom of religion is primarily a matter of individual conscience, it also implies the right to manifest one's religion because bearing witness in words and deeds is bound up with the existence of religious convictions. Accordingly, Article 9 gives the right to manifest those views either in public with others, or alone. It also includes the right to try to convince other people of those views so as to put into effect the right of an

[11] (2002) 35 EHRR 1.

[12] [2008] HRLR 11.

[13] *Friend* v *United Kingdom; Countryside Alliance* v *United Kingdom*, (Application Nos 16072/06 and 27809/08); (2010) 50 EHHR 6 SE.

[14] See the decision in *R (Playfoot)* v *Millais School Governing Body, The Times*, 23 July 2007, where the High Court insisted that there must be some form of religious obligation to engage in the practice.

[15] See also *C* v *United Kingdom* (1983) 37 D & R 142.

[16] (1993) 17 EHRR 397. Contrast *C* v *United Kingdom* (1983) 37 DR 142, where it was held that Article 9 did not give the right of a pacifist to take action in the public sphere (non-payment of taxes) for the purpose of promoting his beliefs.

individual to change one's religion, a right which is recognised in the wording of Article 9. The Court has thus recognised the practice of proselytism, although as we shall see that right is subject to the restrictions laid down in Article 9(2).

Article 9 also imposes a positive obligation on the state to allow individuals the right to manifest and enjoy their beliefs peacefully and without undue interference.[17] This certainly includes the obligation to protect the group and its followers from physical and other attacks when such behaviour interferes with the manifestation of their religion or other belief. This would include the duty to apply the law's protection to that group and the negative duty not to treat any such group in a discriminatory fashion with respect to the application of such laws. In *97 Members of the Gladni Congregation of Jehovah's Witnesses v Georgia*,[18] the Grand Chamber of the Court found a violation of, *inter alia*, Article 9 when the applicants complained that the authorities had failed to take appropriate action against a group of Orthodox extremists who had led a number of attacks on various religious groups. The extremists had burst into the applicant's meeting and violently assaulted a number of the congregation. At the meeting one member had his head shaved by one of the extremist group and after the meeting the extremists searched members of the congregation and threw away their religious possessions. Criminal proceedings were brought against the group and its leader but suspended for lack of evidence despite the attack being shown on television and the leader of the group conducting a television interview displaying satisfaction at the attack. The Grand Chamber held that the failure by the authorities to take appropriate action against the extremists and to ensure that that groups tolerated the existence of the applicants' religious community and to enjoy the free exercise of their right to freedom of religion amounted to a violation of Article 9.[19] In addition the Grand Chamber held that the attitude of the authorities in respect of the applicants' complaints and the applicants' treatment by the legal system was not compatible with the principles of equality before the law and thus gave rise to a violation of Article 14 of the Convention.[20]

To a lesser extent the state will also need to protect the group and its followers from verbal abuse and speech which offends or attacks its beliefs. However, although the European Court has accepted that the right to enjoy one's beliefs can be used to justify an interference with freedom of expression on the basis that any restriction protects 'the rights of others' in Article 10(2),[21] it has not insisted that domestic law pass and maintain a law of blasphemy for that purpose. Thus, in *Choudhury v United Kingdom*[22] it was held that Article 9 did not guarantee a right to bring proceedings against those who have offended the religious or other sensitivities of an individual or group of individuals. This decision will be considered in more detail below.

The state's duty to facilitate freedom of religion and conscience might allow the individual to claim his or her Article 9 rights against a private body, including an employer, although the Court and Commission have given a wide margin of discretion in this area. For example, in

---

[17] *Dubowska and Skup v Poland* (1997) 24 EHRR CD 75.

[18] Application No 71156/01, decision of the Grand Chamber of the European Court, 3 May 2007.

[19] The Court also concluded that the treatment accorded to some of the applicants by the group and the inactivity of the authorities to take any action amounted to a breach of Article 3.

[20] See also *Religiongemeinschaft Zeugen Jehovas v Austria*, decision of the European Court, 31 July 2008, where it found a violation of Articles 9 and 14 when the Austrian authorities had refused to recognise the applicant's sect and then granted them inferior legal status in comparison with other religious groups.

[21] *Otto-Preminger Institute v Austria* (1995) 19 EHRR 34; *Lemon v United Kingdom* (1982) 28 DR 77; *Wingrove v United Kingdom* (1996) 24 EHRR 1.

[22] (1991) 12 HRLJ 172.

Stedman v *United Kingdom*[23] the European Commission held that employees accepted reasonable restrictions on their right to manifest their religion by applying for and taking their respective employment. Accordingly, the applicant's dismissal for refusing, on religious grounds to work on a Sunday did not breach her Article 9 rights; she had been dismissed for refusing to abide by her contract and not because of her religious beliefs. Similarly, in *Ahmad* v *United Kingdom*[24] the European Commission dismissed the applicant's claim that his Article 9 rights had been violated when he resigned after being refused permission to take Friday afternoons off work to attend prayers at a mosque. In *Ahmad* the Commission noted that the applicant had willingly entered into employment on clear contractual terms and had failed to raise the matter for six years. Presumably, therefore, Article 9 rights may be engaged in appropriate cases, and the domestic law can, of course, provide for such benefits and facilities.[25]

The rights under Article 9 are complemented by Article 14 of the Convention, which states that the enjoyment of Convention rights and freedoms shall be secured without discrimination on any ground such as race, colour, language, religion, political or other opinion, national or social origin or other status. Article 14 is not an absolute right and does not secure to everyone complete equality of treatment. Thus, in the *'Belgian Linguistic' case*[26] the European Court held that Article 14 is only violated if the difference in treatment has no objective or reasonable justification. Further, Article 14 does not provide a 'free-standing' right not to be discriminated against, and any claim under that article must be related to a violation of another Convention right. Thus, in *Choudhury* v *United Kingdom*,[27] the European Commission held that as freedom to manifest one's religion under Article 9 did not include the right of a person to insist that the state pass and maintain sufficient blasphemy laws, the applicant's claim under Article 14 failed even though the domestic law of blasphemy excluded the applicant's religion from its protection.

Questions

What sorts of beliefs and thoughts does Article 9 protect?

Why does the European Court take pains to exclude every action or thought from the scope of Article 9?

Restrictions on the manifestation of thought, conscience and religion

Article 9 includes the right to manifest one's religion or beliefs, but this right is subject to limitations that are prescribed by law and necessary in a democratic society in the interests of public safety, for the protection of public order, health or morals, or for the protection of the rights and freedoms of others. In addition, all aspects of Article 9 are subject to Article 15 of the Convention, which allows derogations in times of war or other public emergency, and Article 17, which allows restrictions on individual rights where the individual's aim is the destruction of other person's Convention rights.

---

[23] (1997) 23 EHRR CD 168.
[24] (1981) 4 EHRR 126.
[25] The relevant laws on religious discrimination will be considered below.
[26] (1968) 1 EHRR 252.
[27] (1991) 12 HRLJ 172.

In *Kokkinakis v Greece*[28] the European Court stressed that any interference with that right is contrary to Article 9 unless that interference is prescribed by law and necessary in a democratic society for the achievement of one of the legitimate aims laid down in Article 9(2). An interference with an individual's rights under Article 9 will not, therefore, be allowed simply on the grounds that his or her beliefs are contrary to the established religion. In that case the applicant, a converted Jehovah's Witness, had been imprisoned for three months after being found guilty of proselytism after he and his wife had called on the wife of a figure of the local Orthodox Church and engaged her in a religious discussion. The European Court accepted that the domestic law which prohibited proselytism pursued the legitimate aim of protecting people who held religious views from attempts to influence them by immoral and deceitful means. However, it found that the measures taken against the applicant in the present case were not necessary in a democratic society. In the Court's view a distinction had to be made between bearing Christian witness and improper proselytism: the former representing true and legitimate evangelism and the latter a corruption or deformation of it, amounting to improper pressure and possible brainwashing. On the facts, the domestic courts had not identified how the applicant had attempted to use improper means to convince her of his views and thus the state had failed to show that the conviction met a pressing social need and was thus necessary in a democratic society.

The decision in *Kokkinakis* is important in allowing religious and other believers to manifest their views, even to those who may be hostile to their beliefs. The decision thus upholds the principle of pluralism so inherent in Article 9 and the European Convention. This protects Article 9 rights from arbitrary interference simply because the applicant's views are inconsistent with the established religion of that state. For example, in *Manossakis v Greece*,[29] it was held that the conviction of a number of Jehovah's Witnesses simply for establishing a place of worship of a denomination other than the Orthodox religion, and holding an unauthorised meeting, was in violation of Article 9, particularly as the authorities had failed to take appropriate action to provide such authorisation.

However, although Article 9 permits the establishment of contrary views and even proselytism, it does not allow the exertion of improper pressure in carrying out those rights. For example, in *Larrisis v Greece*[30] it was held that there had been no violation of Article 9 when officers in the Greek army had been prosecuted for proselytism when they had attempted to persuade soldiers under their command to join the Pentecostal Church. Although the European Court stated that not every discussion about religion between personnel of unequal rank would amount to improper pressure, the restriction on such discussions would be justified where there was evidence of harassment or an abuse of power. In the present case the applicants had engaged the soldiers in theological discussions for long periods of time and had tried to persuade the soldiers to join the church. In those circumstances the domestic law was entitled to take special measures to protect the rights and freedoms of subordinate members of the armed forces.[31] The Court will therefore take into account the position and

---

[28] (1993) 17 EHRR 397. Contrast *C v United Kingdom* (1983) 37 DR 142, where it was held that Article 9 did not give the right of a pacifist to take action in the public sphere (non-payment of taxes) for the purpose of promoting his beliefs.

[29] (1996) 23 EHRR 387.

[30] (1999) 37 EHRR 329.

[31] On the other hand, the applicants' convictions for proselytism with respect to visits made to civilians' houses was held to be in violation of Article 9 as there was no evidence of improper behaviour and the civilians were not under the same pressure as the junior personnel.

professional duties of the applicant. For example, in *Kalac* v *Turkey*[32] the European Court found that there had been no violation of Article 9 when a military judge had been compulsorily retired for being a member of and taking part in the activities of a fundamentalist sect and thus 'adopting unlawful fundamentalist opinions'. The European Court held that there had been no interference with the applicants' Article 9 rights and accepted the government's claim that his retirement merely removed from the military a person who had manifested his lack of loyalty to the foundation of the Turkish nation, which it was the task of the armed forces to guarantee. The Court concluded, therefore, that his treatment was not based on his religious beliefs but rather his conduct which was incompatible with his position and the fundamental tenets of Turkish society.

Although the Court has upheld the fundamental right to manifest one's religion, including persuading others, it has also accepted that the manifestation of those views may have to be compromised in order to comply with society's needs or the rules of particular institutions, provided such rules do not impinge on the very essence of that person's Article 9 rights.[33] In *Leyla Sahin* v *Turkey*,[34] the Grand Chamber of the European Court held that there had been no violation of Article 9, or Article 2 of the first protocol, when the applicant had been denied access to a university's facilities and to an exam for wearing an Islamic headscarf. The Grand Chamber accepted that the restrictions on religious dress imposed by the university constituted an interference with her right to manifest her religion, but held that they were both legitimate and necessary in a democratic society. In its judgment the Grand Chamber noted that the ban was imposed to uphold principles of secularism and equality, and that in the context of the universities, where the values of pluralism, respect for the rights of others and, in particular, equality before the law of men and women were being taught, it was understandable that the authorities would consider it contrary to such values to allow religious attire to be worn on its premises. The Court also noted that all students, including Muslim students, were free, within the limits imposed by the educational organisational constraints, to manifest their religion in accordance with habitual forms of observance. Despite the Turkish government's plans to lift the ban, the Court is still willing to offer each state a wide margin of appreciation in this area, and in *Atkas and Others* v *France*[35] it held that there had been no violation of Article 9 when pupils had been excluded from school for wearing religious symbols. Upholding *Sahin*, the Court stressed that the ban was necessary to uphold secularism in the country as well as the state's role as the neutral and impartial organiser of the exercise of various religions and faiths.

Questions

Why is the right to manifest religious or other deeply held beliefs subject to the limitations laid down in Article 9(2)?

What sorts of reasons justify such restriction and what level of margin of appreciation should be afforded to each sate in this respect?

---

[32] (1997) 27 EHRR 552.

[33] See Leader, Freedoms and Futures: Personal Priorities, Institutional Demands and Freedom of Religion (2007) 70 MLR 713.

[34] (2007) 44 EHRR 5.

[35] Decision of the European Court, 17 July 2009.

The protection of religion in domestic law

This brief section of the chapter will outline some of the measures taken in domestic law to protect religious freedom; either to prohibit discrimination on racial and religious grounds, or to provide positive assistance to the enjoyment of that right. It is not intended to provide a detailed account of such laws but rather to place such laws in the context of the right to religion contained in the European Convention and the Human Rights Act 1998. The topics of race and religious hate speech and blasphemous speech are covered later in the chapter.

Section 13 of the Human Rights Act 1998

Section 13 of the Human Rights Act 1998 provides that if a court's determination of any question arising under the Act might affect the exercise by a religious organisation (itself or its members collectively) of the Convention right to freedom of thought, conscience and religion, it must have *particular regard* to the importance of that right.[36] The section was included because of concerns expressed by church organisations during the passage of the Human Rights Bill, particularly about the right to employ suitable teachers in religious schools and that to impose requirements for religious marriages would be threatened by actions under the 1998 Act.

The section does not give any specific guidance as to what aspects of that right and its enjoyment are to be given special weight, and in that sense it adds little to the general position that interference with any Convention right must be necessary and proportionate.[37] Nevertheless, the courts will be obliged to take this right into account in developing the law in favour of the enjoyment of the rights contained in Article 9, including allowing interferences with other Convention rights, such as freedom of expression, for the purpose of protecting an individual's, or group's, Article 9 rights.

Despite the inclusion of s.13, the courts have refused to give freedom of religion anything like an enhanced status when balancing it against other rights or interests. This cautious approach has been achieved either by refusing to accept that Article 9 rights have been interfered with, or by giving the authorities a wide margin of discretion in balancing that right with other claims. For example, in *R (Begum)* v *Denbigh High School Governors*[38] it was held that an individual's right to manifest their religion had to be enjoyed in the context of reasonable rules intended to benefit society and the rights of others. Consequently, a schoolchild's right to manifest her religion by wearing full Muslim dress at school had not been interfered with by the relevant school-uniform policy. That approach has been followed in subsequent cases, dealt with below,[39] mirroring the jurisprudence of the case law of the European Court and reiterating that the right to manifest religion has to be enjoyed in the context of society's laws and practices. Thus, in *R* v *Taylor*[40] the Court of Appeal summarily dismissed any claim

---

[36] For a detailed discussion of this area, see Cumper, The Protection of Religious Rights under Section 13 of the HRA [2000] PL 254.

[37] See Wadham and Mountfield, *The Human Rights Act 1998* (Blackstone Press 2000, 4th edn), page 67.

[38] [2007] 1 AC 100. The case is examined in detail in the case study, below.

[39] *R (Playfoot)* v *Millais School Governing* Board, *The Times*, 23 July 2007; *R (X)* v *Headteachers and Governors of Y School* [2007] HRLR 20.

[40] [2002] 1 Cr App R 37.

that Article 9 gave the right to an individual to transgress the Misuse of Drugs Act 1971 by relying on the defence that he was using the drug for religious purposes.

The domestic courts have also refused to place too onerous a duty on the relevant authorities when they seek to balance such interests, insisting only that the final decision is reasonable and proportionate. Thus in *Begum*, above, the House of Lords held that the school did not have to carry out a specific balancing exercise to see whether any interference with religious rights was necessary; the question was whether the policy as applied was proportionate. That principle was upheld in *R (Swami Suryanada) v Welsh Ministers*,[41] where the Court of Appeal upheld a policy of destroying diseased cattle even when it conflicted with a Hindu community's religious beliefs. The High Court had granted a judicial review of the decision to slaughter the community's bullock on the grounds that the ministry had failed to conduct a proper balancing exercise so as to properly assess the animal's risk.[42] However, on appeal the Court of Appeal held that the authorities had been entitled to apply the slaughter policy to the applicants and not to make an exception because of the *prima facie* interference with their Article 9 rights. The policy was a result of government and EU policy and pursued the legitimate aims of the elimination of disease and public safety, and it was important that the procedure be applied uniformly to eradicate those risks. A similar approach was taken by the High Court in *Ghai v Secretary of State for Justice*,[43] where it was held that although the criminalising of open air funeral pyres interfered with the right to manifest religious beliefs under Article 9, such interference was justified under Article 9(2) because a significant number of people would find both the principle and reality of such cremations offensive.[44]

Protection against religious discrimination

Freedom from discrimination on grounds of religion is enshrined in Article 14 of the Convention (given effect to via the Human Rights Act 1998), which forbids discrimination in the enjoyment of such rights on grounds of a person's status, including their religion. That article does not give a general right to freedom from discrimination in the enjoyment of rights that are not protected within the Convention, for example freedom from discrimination in employment. Nevertheless, national law may intervene to protect certain groups from discrimination, thus bolstering the individuals' Convention rights and providing a greater right to equality in the law.

With specific reference to religion and Article 9, until recently domestic law did not grant specific protection against religious discrimination,[45] although some religious groups were protected indirectly by the Race Relations Act 1976, which covered discrimination on racial grounds.[46] Thus, in *Mandla v Dowell Lee*,[47] the House of Lords held that a person's religion

---

[41] [2007] EWCA Civ 893.

[42] [2007] EWHC 1736 (Admin).

[43] *The Times*, 18 May 2009.

[44] On appeal the Court of Appeal held that such a ceremony was in fact in compliance with s.2 of the Cremation Act 1902 because the structure that an orthodox Hindu found acceptable was a 'building' within that provision. The traditional definition of an 'inclosure of brick or stonework covered in by a roof' was not an exclusive definition: [2010] 3 All ER 380.

[45] In Northern Ireland religious and political discrimination in employment is covered by the Fair Employment (Northern Ireland) Act 1976.

[46] For a sound coverage of discrimination law (including religious discrimination), see McColgan, *Discrimination Law: Text, Cases and Materials* (Hart 2005); Connolly, *Discrimination Law* (Sweet & Maxwell 2006).

[47] [1983] AC 548.

could equate with their 'ethnic origins' and thus bring them within the scope of the Act. Under this criterion, groups such as Sikhs (as in *Mandla*) and Jews would be covered,[48] although groups whose only common factor is religion or religious culture, such as Rastafarians, would not.[49]

Specific protection against religious discrimination was provided by the implementation of the Employment Equality (Religion or Belief) Regulations 2003, which made discrimination on the grounds of religion and belief unlawful in the employment field, thus providing similar protection to that already available to those discriminated on grounds of sex, race and disability. Regulation 2(1) defines religion or belief as 'any religion, religious belief, or similar philosophical belief' thus including any denomination of a particular religion (such as Catholicism). The reference to 'similar philosophical belief' would also allow the protection of non-religious beliefs and conviction. This would be in line with Article 9 of the European Convention on Human Rights, which recognises freedom of thought and conscience, provided the conviction is deeply held.[50] In addition, although the 2003 regulations may not have protected non-believers, the inclusion of the words 'lack of religion or belief' in the amended definition contained in the Equality Act 2006[51] (below) would give protection to those individuals, again complying with the Convention and its case law,[52] and s.10 of the Equality Act 2010 lists religion and belief as protected characteristics, thus protecting individuals from discrimination, harassment and victimisation.

As with cases under Article 9 of the Convention, not every refusal to accommodate requests to manifest one's religion will be unlawful and freedom from discrimination under the regulations is circumscribed by reasonable restrictions. Thus, in *Azmi v Kirklees MBC*[53] it was held that the employers had not been guilty of discrimination when they had suspended a Muslim woman from employment for refusing to remove her veil when working with children as a teaching assistant. The Employment Appeal Tribunal held that she had been suspended for refusing to obey a contractual instruction and that the dress code policy was enforced in order to ensure effective teaching – the wearing of a full face veil being obstructive of such as children would be deprived of non-verbal signals from the teacher. The policy was not based on religion and had been applied proportionately and free from discrimination. The Appeal Tribunal stressed that not every manifestation of a religious belief would give rise to an issue of discrimination under the regulations and that every case had to be dealt with on its merits. So too in *McClintock v Department of Constitutional Affairs*[54] the Employment Appeal Tribunal had held that a Christian magistrate had not been unfairly and constructively dismissed when he resigned in objection to having to carry out his duty to place children with same-sex couples. It was held that his objections had not been based on his philosophical views (because his main concern was to the lack of research as to the benefits of such placing), but that in any

---

[48] Subsequently, in *R (E) v JFS Governing Body* [2010] 2 WLR 153, the Supreme Court held that the criterion of being Jewish by virtue of Jewish matrilineal descent was a test of ethnic origin within the Race Relations Act 1976. Accordingly, the decision of a Jewish school not to admit a child who did not conform within Jewish orthodox laws to the requirements of Jewish descent constituted direct racial discrimination.

[49] *Crown Suppliers v Dawkins* [1993] ICR 517. Discrimination against Muslims would be unlawful if it related to national origins, for example if it constituted discrimination against Pakistanis.

[50] See, for example, *Arrowsmith v United Kingdom* (1978) 3 EHRR 218.

[51] See s.77 Equality Act 2006.

[52] *Kokkinakis v Greece* (1994) 17 EHRR 397.

[53] *The Times*, 17 April 2007.

[54] *The Times*, 5 December 2007.

case the department was fully justified in insisting that all magistrates apply the law of the land without exception based on moral or principled objection.

In such cases, even if the individual's refusal is based on a belief protected by Article 9 (or any relevant domestic discrimination laws), that belief may be overridden by other rights or considerations. Thus, in *London Borough of Ealing* v *Ladele*,[55] the Court of Appeal held that it was not a breach of the Employment Equality (Religion or Belief) Regulations 2003 to discipline a registrar who refused to participate in civil partnerships. The Court of Appeal held that the Equality Act (Sexual Orientation) Regulations 2007, which protected individuals from sexual orientation discrimination, took precedence over any right which a person would otherwise have by virtue of religious belief or faith to practise discrimination on the grounds of sexual orientation. In the Court's views, even had the refusal been based on her religious views, the regulations offered no choice to both her and her employer to insist that such duties be carried out. Again, in *McFarlane* v *Relate Avon Ltd*[56] the Employment Appeal Tribunal held that an employer was justified in dismissing a counsellor who refused to give advice to same-sex couples on the grounds that it conflicted with his Christian beliefs. In the Employment Appeal Tribunal's view, there was a legitimate distinction between the holding of that belief and conduct which was motivated by that belief; in the latter case the reason for dismissal was the conduct and thus reasonable restrictions may be placed on that conduct in accordance with Article 9(2). In this case dismissal was a proportionate response as it was reasonable for the employer to insist on compliance of the policy of equality for all couples without compromising the policy for an employee's religious views; hence it was not appropriate to ask whether it was practical for the employer to accommodate the employee's individual wishes.[57]

A more general right to freedom from discrimination on grounds of religion or belief (or lack of religion or belief) is now contained in the Equality Act 2006, now fully in force, and supplemented by the Equality Act 2010.[58] Section 45 of the 2006 Act makes it unlawful for a person to discriminate against another on grounds (or supposed grounds) of religion or belief (whether or not that is that person's religion or belief). The section covers direct and indirect discrimination as well as victimisation, and although there is no positive obligation on the part of the employer to offer the employee facilities to allow religious observance, discrimination against a particular religious group with respect to, for example, allowing time off work, would be unlawful. This position would appear to be compatible with Convention case law, which does not provide an absolute positive right to manifest one's religion and requires such practices to be constrained by commitment to reasonable employment terms.[59]

Article 9 and the right to education

The right to religion and conscience under Article 9 is complemented by Article 2 of the First Protocol to the Convention, which provides that no person shall be denied the right to

---

[55] [2010] 1 WLR 995.

[56] (2010) IRLR 196.

[57] In *Catholic Care* v *Charity Commission for England and Wales, The Times*, 13 April 2010, it was held that the Commission could reject Charity Care's request to amend its objectives so that it only provided an adoption service to heterosexuals. Such a change would have amounted to unlawful discrimination against persons on grounds of their sexual orientation.

[58] The effect on discrimination law generally of the Equality Act 2010 will be dealt with in chapter 13.

[59] See *Stedman* v *United Kingdom* (1997) 27 EHRR CD 28, discussed above.

education. More specifically the article states that in the exercise of any functions which it assumes in relation to education and teaching the state shall respect the right of parents to ensure such education and teaching in conformity with their own religious and philosophical convictions.[60] This (conditional) right to insist that one's children are taught in conformity with one's religious and philosophical convictions is further restricted by the government's reservation to the article, which states that its obligations are restricted to the provision of efficient instruction and training and the avoidance of unreasonable public expenditure.[61] Further, it has been held that it does not include a right to be taught at a particular school if other institutions offer tuition which is consistent with such beliefs. Thus, in *Kjeldsen, Busk Madsen and Pedersen v Denmark*,[62] it was held that parents had no right to insist that their children did not receive compulsory sex education in state schools when they had the option of sending them to private schools or teaching them at home. This principle of alternative facilities is not inflexible and in that case the Court also found that the lessons were in the public interest and did not subject the children to any form of indoctrination.

Despite these restrictions the articles combine with Article 9 of the Convention to ensure some recognition of a right to education in conformity with the religious or conscientious beliefs of the child and the parents. Thus, in *Folgero and Others v Norway*,[63] the Grand Chamber of the European Court found a violation of Article 2 when parents had been refused full exemption from compulsory religious teaching in Norwegian schools. In 1997 the school system changed so that two separate subjects – Christianity and philosophy of life – were taught together under one subject of Christianity, religion and philosophy which involved teaching the established Christian faith in Norway and providing an awareness of other religions and philosophies. The law provided for partial exemption from the teaching of the subject and the parents' request for full exemption was refused. The Grand Chamber held that although the system served the purpose of avoiding sectarianism and of creating greater understanding of other faiths, the content of the curriculum showed a marked disparity between the teaching of Christianity and other faiths and thus infringed the applicants' rights under Article 2. Although Article 2 allowed the state a margin of appreciation with respect to the weight to be given to the accepted and majority religion, given the purpose of the new system to create greater awareness and the difficulty of gaining partial exemption, there had been a violation of Article 2.[64]

Article 2 has been employed by parents to challenge the use (and non-use) of corporal punishment in schools. For example, in *Campbell and Cosans v United Kingdom*[65] it was held that the imposition of corporal punishment in a school attended by the applicants' children constituted a violation of Article 2 because it interfered with the parents' convictions on discipline, which the Court accepted as falling within the phrase philosophical

---

[60] This provision has been dealt with in outline in chapter 2, see pages 89–91.

[61] In *X v United Kingdom* (1980) 23 DR 228, it was held that the state had the right to regulate scarce resources by restricting access to certain courses to the most able students.

[62] (1976) 1 EHRR 711.

[63] Application No 15472/02, decision of the Grand Chamber of the European Court, 29 June 2007.

[64] See also *Luatsi v Italy*, decision of the European Court, 3 November 2009, where it was held that there had been a breach of Article 9 (and Article 2 of the First Protocol) when the applicants' children had to attend school where crucifixes were displayed in the classroom. This was contrary to the children's right to religion and the parents' right to have their children educated in line with their religious convictions.

[65] (1982) 4 EHRR 243.

convictions.[66] In the Court's view, the duty to respect parental convictions could not be overridden by the alleged necessity of striking a balance between the conflicting views involved and although the right to education guaranteed by Article 2 by its very nature calls for regulation by the state, such regulation should never injure the substance of the right or conflict with other rights in the Convention and its protocols.

However, Article 2 does not guarantee parents the right to insist that their children *are* subject to reasonable physical punishment at school. In *R (Williamson) v Secretary of State for Education*,[67] it was held that the banning of corporal punishment in schools via the Education Act 1996 was not incompatible with Article 2. In this case parents and teachers at a number of independent schools claimed that the statutory ban was in conflict with the views of a fundamental Christian belief that part of education in the Christian context was that teachers should be able to stand in the place of parents and administer physical punishment to children guilty of indiscipline. In rejecting their claim, the House of Lords stressed that there was a difference between freedom to hold a belief and freedom to express or manifest it; the latter being subject to necessary and proportionate restrictions. Although the lower courts had been wrong in deciding that the case did not engage the parents' Article 2 rights,[68] the restriction in this case was necessary in a democratic society. Article 2 was engaged in this case because it could not be argued that a belief in even mild forms of punishment violated the child's integrity to such an extent that it fell outside the ambit of Articles 2 and 9. Further, the parents' views in this case were a clear manifestation of their beliefs which the law materially interfered with. However, the ban pursued a legitimate aim in protecting the rights and freedoms of vulnerable children and securing their well-being. Corporal punishment involved the infliction of deliberate physical violence and the legislation was intended to protect children from the distress, pain and other harmful effects of that form of punishment. Thus, although parliament was bound to consider the religious and philosophical beliefs of parents, it was entitled to decide that the manifestation of those beliefs in this manner was not in the best interests of children.

On the other hand, the right to education, including parental choice, might have to bow to wider issues of public interest and the rights of others. Thus, in *Leyla Sahin v Turkey*[69] the Grand Chamber held that although the exclusion of the applicant from University for wearing religious dress did engage the right to education, it ruled that the ban did not constitute an infringement of that right. In the Court's view, the rules were foreseeable and proportionate and did not destroy the very essence of the applicant's rights under that article; balancing as they did the rights of religious observance with the protection of secularism.[70] Similarly, in *R (Begum) v Denbigh High School Governors*[71] it was held that a schoolchild who had been

---

[66] As a consequence of the Court's ruling the Education (No 2) Act 1986 was passed, prohibiting corporal punishment in state schools.

[67] [2003] 1 All ER 385.

[68] *R (Williamson) v Secretary of State for Education* [2003] 3 WLR 482. The Court of Appeal held that the case did not fall within Article 2 or Article 9 because the parents could administer reasonable chastisement at home.

[69] (2007) 44 EHRR 5.

[70] See Lewis, What Not to Wear: Religious Rights, the European Convention and the Margin of Appreciation [2007] ICLQ 395.

[71] [2007] 1 AC 100. The case is detailed in a case note below. For a detailed examination of the case, see Hill and Sandberg, Is Nothing Sacred? Clashing Symbols in a Secular World [2007] PL 488; Idriss, Lacite and the Banning of the 'Hijab' in France [2005] LS 260. See also McGoldrick, *Human Rights and Religion: The Islamic Headscarf Debate in Europe* (Cambridge University Press 2007). At the time of writing the Turkish government is considering lifting the ban.

refused entry to school because of her unwillingness to comply with a dress code had not been denied the right to education under Article 2 of the First Protocol. The disruption to her schooling had been caused by her unwillingness to comply with a rule that the school was entitled to adhere to, and of her failure to secure prompt admission to another school where her religious convictions could be accommodated.

The decision in *Begum* was followed in *R (X) v Headteachers and Governors of Y School*,[72] where it was claimed that the school's refusal to allow a Muslim schoolgirl to wear a niqab veil at school did not interfere with her Article 9 rights. The girl had claimed that the rule interfered with her Article 9 rights and was disproportionate because in the past her sisters had been allowed to wear the veil. The court stated that a rule that required certain behaviour at an institution did not constitute an infringement of a person's right to manifest their religion simply because that rule did not conform to the individual's religious beliefs, particularly where that individual could choose whether to avail themselves of the institution's service or other services which did not include the rule. Article 9 did not provide a right to manifest one's religion at any time and place of one's choosing. In this case the school had offered her an alternative school and a school was entitled to have its own policies. Thus, even if her Article 9 rights had been interfered with, the interference was justified within Article 9(2) as being in the interests of public safety or for the protection of the rights and freedoms of others.

Claimants in such cases thus have to clear several hurdles. First, their claim must engage Article 9 in that it relates to an identifiable belief and a recognised practise of it. Secondly, there must be an actual interference with that right and not simply a case where the manifestation of that belief is made more inconvenient.[73] Finally, the court needs to be satisfied that the manifestation of that belief outweighs other interests, such as the maintenance of school rules: interests which the courts are reluctant to upset simply to allow a person to practise their religious beliefs. The difficulty facing the engagement and success of Article 9 claims in this context is shown in the recent case of *R (Playfoot) v Millais School Governing Body*.[74] In this case a schoolgirl claimed that the school's refusal to allow her to wear a purity ring as an expression of her Christian faith breached her Article 9 rights. The High Court held firstly that as there was no religious compulsion for her to wear the ring, the wearing of it was not sufficiently and intimately linked to her belief in chastity before marriage. Further, applying *Begum*, any right to manifest her religion had not been interfered with as she had voluntarily accepted the school policy, which did not allow the wearing of rings at school unless that rule would have a disproportionately harsh result on a pupil, and there were other means open to her to practise her belief without undue hardship and inconvenience.

The above cases were distinguished in *R (Watkins Singh) v Aberdare Girls' High School Governors*,[75] a case brought under the Race Relations Act 1976 and the Equality Act 2006. In this case it was held that the refusal of a school to allow a girl to wear a 'Kara' – a slim bracelet expected (but not required) to be worn by Sikhs at all times – was contrary to both s.1 of the 1976 Act and s.45 of the Equality Act 2006, which make it unlawful to discriminate on grounds of, respectively, race and religion. In coming to its decision as to whether the claimant had suffered a disadvantage or detriment, the High Court recognised the critically

---

[72] [2007] HRLR 20.

[73] The decisions in *Sahin* and *Begum* are somewhat inconsistent in this respect, although even where there has been an interference the Court will still examine its proportionality, ensuring the same conclusion in most cases.

[74] *The Times*, 23 July 2007.

[75] [2008] EWHC 1865.

important religious significance of the item to the girl as she genuinely attached exceptional importance to wearing the Kara and therefore satisfied the subjective requirement identified by the House of Lords in *Williamson*, above, with respect to the legitimacy of her religious belief. In the court's view, the no jewellery policy constituted indirect discrimination on the grounds of religion and it was not necessary to show that the item was a *requirement* of her religion. In this respect, therefore, the decision in *Playfoot*, above, is, it appears, no longer, sound authority. With respect to justification, the school had failed to justify the prohibition and exclusion on objective grounds because, as opposed to cases involving religious dress in cases such as *Begum*, the Kara was less visible and ostentatious and did not interfere with the general uniform policy. The court also distinguished *Playfoot* on this point as, unlike the policy in that case, in the present case there was no evidence that the prohibition of this jewellery impacted on the issue of equality of dress and appearance; it being accepted in *Playfoot* that the banning of jewellery would diminish the feeling of inequality among students with respect to wealth and appearance.

The case law in this area is, therefore, complex: some cases denying the engagement of Article 9 in school policy and exclusion cases, and others accepting that Article 9 applies yet is overridden on the facts of the case by the countervailing interests of the school and other pupils. It is suggested that a more consistent approach would be to accept that all these cases (provided the belief is genuine) engage Article 9 and that the policy needs to be justified in terms of Article 9(2). If that is the case, cases such as *Begum* and *X* can be easily reconciled, whilst the *Playfoot* case would appear inconsistent with *Watkins Singh* and basic principles of proportionality.

Questions

How is Article 9 of the Convention complemented by Article 2 of the First Protocol to the Convention?

Do you agree that the domestic and European Courts have provided sufficient protection in this area?

Return to these questions once you have examined the case study below.

CASE STUDY

R (On the Application of Begum) v *Headteacher and Governors of Denbigh High School* [2007] 1 AC 100

As we have seen, the right to manifest one's religious or other deeply held personal convictions may come into conflict with either the rights of others or the needs of society as a whole. The right to wear clothes or other symbols that associate a person with their religion or beliefs is certainly capable of engaging one's Article 9 rights, but the law often insists that that right needs to be balanced with the above interests. The right to wear such symbols in educational institutions has given rise to much social and legal debate and the case below has been chosen to highlight the moral and legal difficulties in accommodating Article 9 rights in this context: in particular in examining the weight given to such rights by the law and the judiciary.

The facts

Shabina Begum attended Denbigh High School in Luton, where approximately 79 per cent of its pupils are Muslim. The school's uniform policy – designed in consultation with the governing body of the school, parents and local Mosques – allowed the wearing of the shalwar kameez if pupils did not wish to wear the traditional school uniform. This rule was prompted by the fact that as Sikh and Hindu schoolgirls also wore the shalwar kameez, religious differentiation among pupils would be minimised. Shabina happily wore the garment for two years but then insisted on wearing a jilbab (a long cloak covering the whole body except the hands and face). The school informed Shabina that she had to wear the correct uniform, which included the shalwar kameez and the traditional hijab, but Shabina refused as she felt that the garment did not comply with the strict requirements of Islam. The school refused to allow her to attend the school in breach of its uniform policy and because Shabina could not get entry into a local school which allowed the wearing of the jilbab, and claimed that two other schools were too far from her home, as a result she lost two years' education before she found another suitable school.

Legal challenge

Shabina brought judicial review proceedings seeking a declaration that the school had unlawfully excluded her contrary to sections 64–8 of the School Standards and Framework Act 1998, and had denied her access to appropriate education in breach of Article 2 of the First Protocol to the European Convention. She claimed further that she had been denied the right to manifest her religion in breach of Article 9(1) of the Convention. The High Court dismissed her claim (*The Times*, 18 June 2004), ruling that, on the facts, she had not been excluded from school and that accordingly her Convention rights had not been breached.

In the High Court's view the school sincerely wanted Shabina to attend school and did not impede her access; rather it insisted that when she came to school she was dressed in accordance with the school-uniform policy. The girl, entirely of her own volition, chose not to attend the school unless it agreed to her wearing the jilbab, and that did not amount to exclusion. Further, the High Court held that any violation of Article 9(1) that had taken place fell clearly within Article 9(2) as being necessary in a democratic society for the 'protection of the rights and freedoms of others' in that the school-uniform policy aimed to protect a not insignificant number of Muslim female pupils at Denbigh High School who do not wish to wear the jilbab and who do or might feel pressure on them either from inside or outside the school if the policy was not enforced.

On appeal the Court of Appeal overruled the decision of the High Court and found a breach of her Convention rights ([2005] 1 WLR 3372). In the Court's view the school had undoubtedly excluded the girl as it had sent her away because she was not willing to comply with the discipline of wearing the prescribed school uniform, and she was unable to return to school for the same reason. The fact that the girl's view that Islamic law required her to wear a jilbab was held only by a minority of Muslims was irrelevant to the question of whether her Convention rights were engaged. Although the right to manifest one's religion was limited, it was for the school, as an emanation of the state, to justify the limitation on her freedom created by its uniform policy and the way in which it was enforced. Distinguishing this case from the European Court's decision in *Leyla Sahin* v *Turkey* ((2005) 41 EHRR 8), the Court of Appeal noted that the United Kingdom was not a secular state and provided for religious education and worship in schools, placing a duty on schools to ensure that religious education was given to pupils and that each pupil should take part in acts of collective worship every day, unless withdrawn by their parents. In the present case the school had approached the issues from an entirely wrong direction and did not attribute to the girl's beliefs the weight they deserved. The school had started from the premise that its uniform policy was there to be obeyed rather than from the premises that she had a right recognised by English law and that the onus lay on it to justify its interference with that right. Accordingly, the school had unlawfully denied her the right to manifest her religion in accordance with Article 9 and had denied her access to suitable and appropriate education in violation of Article 2. The school appealed to the House of Lords.

Had Shabina been excluded?
Restoring the decision of the original judge, their Lordships held that Shabina had not been excluded from her school. Relying on the decision in *Spiers* v *Warrington Corporation* ([1954] 1 QB 51), LORD BINGHAM held that the school did not intend to exclude Shabina and was always perfectly willing to take her in provided that she was properly dressed in accordance with the uniform policy adopted by the school. Furthermore, although the decision to prevent her from entering school was taken on disciplinary grounds, that did not amount to 'exclusion' under the 1998 Act. Shabina was not directed to stay away from the school; rather she was directed and encouraged to return to school wearing the *correct* school uniform. The decision not to return to school was that of Shabina's who could have returned to the school at any time.

Had there been an interference with her religious beliefs?
Their Lordships held unanimously that Shabina's right to religious freedom had not been violated under Article 9. Although it was conceded that Shabina sincerely held her religious beliefs at all times and that Article 9(1) had been engaged, the main questions were whether her freedom to manifest her belief was subject to interference and, if so, whether such interference was justified under Article 9(2). What amounted to interference depends on all the circumstances, including the extent to which in the circumstances an individual can reasonably expect to be at liberty to manifest his beliefs in practice (*R (Williamson)* v *Secretary of State for Education* [2003] 1 All ER 385). Article 9 does not protect every act motivated or inspired by a religion or belief, and in exercising his freedom to manifest his religion, an individual may need to take his specific situation into account (*Kalaç* v *Turkey* (1999) 27 EHRR 552). Further, in *Leyla Sahin* v *Turkey* (above) it was established that the European Court will not readily find an interference with the right to manifest a religious belief where a person has voluntarily accepted a situation which does not accommodate that practice and where there were other means open to them to practise or observe their religion without undue inconvenience.

In particular, their Lordships took into consideration the lengths made by Denbigh High School and its governors to create an acceptable and cohesive uniform policy;

appointing a representative working party to re-examine its dress code in response to requests by several Muslim girls, consulting parents, students and staff and sending letters to parents reminding them of the school's rules on dress. This great effort on the school's part showed a very sincere effort to significantly contribute to the social cohesion in a catchment area that was racially, culturally and religiously diverse. The rules were very clearly communicated to those affected by them, including Shabina's family, who had chosen for her a school outside their own catchment area. Shabina's right was not infringed because there was nothing to stop her from going to a single-sex school where her religion did not require a jilbab or to a local school whose rules permitted it. Arrangements could have been made to transfer Shabina to one of these schools but she did not take up the chance of doing so.

Their Lordships stressed that Article 9 does not require that one should be allowed to manifest one's religion at any time and place of one's own choosing. While Shabina had the right to freedom of religion, she could not manifest that freedom in such a way as to prejudice the school's ability to ensure discipline and order and to run things in the way it wanted. Shabina could have sought the help of the school in order that she could change schools, but instead she and her brother sought a confrontation, claiming that she had a right to attend the school of her own choosing in the clothes she chose to wear. Thus, on the facts, there had been no interference with her Article 9 rights.

Procedure, proportionality and the margin of appreciation

LORD BINGHAM believed that BROOKE LJ's approach in the Court of Appeal – to the effect that the school should have started from the premise that the exclusion was wrong and then sought to justify its necessity – was mistaken. The focus of the Convention was not whether a challenged decision is the product of a defective decision-making process, but whether an applicant's Convention rights have been violated. Article 9 of the Convention is concerned with substance and not procedure and does not confer a right to have a decision made in a particular way by a public body. What matters in any case is the practical and proportionate outcome of the decision and whether on the facts it constitutes a violation of Article 9, not the quality of the decision-making process that led to it.

Considering whether any interference with Shabina's Convention rights was necessary in a democratic society, LORD BINGHAM stressed that the proportionality of the measure had to be judged objectively with respect to its aims and the effect that it had on such rights. Thus, it was illogical to find (as did the Court of Appeal) that the school's actions were disproportionate, while at the same time acknowledging that on reconsideration the same action could very well be maintained and properly so. In *Sahin* (above) the European Court of Human Rights recognised not only the high importance of the rights protected by Article 9, but also the need in some situations to restrict the freedom to manifest religious belief and to uphold the value of religious harmony and tolerance between competing groups. Further, there was a need to recognise the principles of pluralism and broadmindedness together with the need for compromise and balance and the role of the state in deciding what is necessary to protect the rights and freedoms of others given the variation of practice and tradition among member states in this area.

Applying those principles to the present case the school was fully justified in acting as they did. The school had taken immense pains to devise a uniform policy that respected Muslim beliefs but in an inclusive, unthreatening and uncompetitive manner. The rules were as far from being mindless as uniform rules could be, being acceptable to mainstream Muslim opinion and allowing the school to enjoy a period of harmony and success. Some schoolgirls expressed their concern that if the jilbab were to be allowed, they would face pressure to adopt it even if they did not wish to do so. Assuming the honesty of the school on this matter, this was evidence that the decision not to permit the wearing of the jilbab was objectively proportionate in the prevailing circumstances. The uniform policy was thoughtful and proportionate in response to reconciling the complexities of the situation.

Moreover, the Court of Appeal's comments with respect to the difference between the present case and that prevailing in *Sahin* – that the UK was not a secular state and that schools are under a statutory duty to provide religious instruction – missed the point. LORD HOFFMANN observed that Turkey has a national rule about headscarves, by virtue of its constitution, and justification for the interference with the manifestation of a religious belief is considered at a national level. In the UK, there is no such national rule on these matters and parliament has considered it desirable to delegate to individual schools the power to decide whether to impose requirements about uniforms that may interfere with the manifestation of religious beliefs. In conclusion it would be irresponsible of any court, lacking the experience, background and detailed knowledge of the headteacher, staff and governors of the school, to overrule their judgement on such a sensitive matter.

The right to education

Their Lordships unanimously held that Article 2 of the First Protocol to the Convention had not been breached. Shabina had not been denied access to education by the school because of its position over the school-uniform policy. While a two-year interruption in the education of any child was a subject of profound regret, the interruption was the result of Shabina's unwillingness to comply with a rule to which the school was entitled to adhere to. Article 2 confers no right to go to a particular school and is only infringed where a claimant has been unable to obtain an education from the system as a whole. In the present dispute there was nothing to suggest that Shabina could not have found a suitable school if she had notified her requirements in good time to the local education authority. The school had referred the matter of Shabina's non-attendance at school to the Education Welfare Service, who made a number of attempts to persuade Shabina to return to school. However, Shabina remained unwilling to return. If the school was entitled to have a school-uniform policy that did not allow Shabina to wear a jilbab, it followed that the school (by requiring her to wear the correct school uniform) did not commit any breach of her Convention right to education.

Questions

1 Why did the High Court and the House of Lords believe that Shabina had not been excluded from school?
2 On what basis did the House of Lords conclude that Shabina's Convention rights had not been interfered with in this case?

3 How did the Court of Appeal's decision differ in the above respects? Which decision do you agree with in those respects?

4 How did the Court of Appeal draw a distinction between the present case and the decision of the European Court in *Sahin* v *Turkey*? Why did the House of Lords refuse to accept that distinction?

5 What flaws did the House of Lords identify in the Court of Appeal's decision? Do you agree that the Court of Appeal's approach and decision was flawed?

6 Should a body such as the school be required to approach this type of question logically and sequentially, asking itself the same questions that a court will ultimately address?

7 Should the question be whether the school acted fairly in all the circumstances or whether an interference with her Convention rights could and should have been avoided?

8 Overall, were Shabina's Convention rights given due weight and respect, or was the decision of the House of Lords based on pragmatism?

9 How does the decision reflect the jurisprudence of the European Court in this area and under Article 9 and if the case had been taken to the European Court of Human Rights what do you think the outcome would have been?

10 Are the cases subsequent to *Begum* reconcilable with *Begum* and Article 9?

Freedom of expression and Article 9

Certain speech or expression will engage the speaker's Article 9 rights in addition to Article 10 because such views or actions do not merely reflect their political or social views, but represent the speaker's religious or other conscientious beliefs. In such cases international human rights law may provide an enhanced protection to such speech, and any restrictions on such speech imposed by domestic law needs to be examined in the light of those principles. Equally, certain speech will threaten an individual's or a group's Article 9 rights and again the domestic system will need to offer some protection against such threats while balancing that with the speaker's Convention rights. More specifically, the domestic courts will need to take into account s.13 of the Human Rights Act 1998, which provides that they should have particular regard to the importance of the right under Article 9 when making a determination that might affect the exercise by a religious organisation (itself or its members collectively) of the Convention right to freedom of thought, conscience and religion.

This section of the chapter examines the situations where free speech complements, or conflicts with, the right under Article 9. It will examine cases where the speakers are using Article 9 to enhance their Article 10 rights, examining the extent to which the courts will engage Article 9 in that respect. It will also consider cases where the speech is potentially destructive of others' Article 9 rights and thus may require restriction to protect those rights or more general democratic values.

Upholding pro-religious speech

Although the European Convention guarantees both the right of free speech and the right to manifest one's religion, the European Court has permitted the state to impose restrictions on religious expression. Thus, in *Murphy v Ireland*,[76] it was held that there was no violation of Article 10 when the Irish broadcasting authority refused to allow the broadcast of the applicant's video dealing with the historical facts about Christ and evidence of the resurrection. The European Court held that the restriction on the applicant's freedom of expression fell within the state's margin of appreciation, particularly as the applicant's advertisement was broadcast on satellite television. The interference was prescribed by law and pursued the legitimate aims of preserving public order and the protection of the rights of others, and the authorities were entitled to have regard to the extreme sensitivity of the question of broadcasting of religious advertising in Ireland and to the fact that religion was a divisive issue in Northern Ireland.

Nevertheless, Article 10 rights may be enhanced by the engagement of Article 9 and there is some evidence that the domestic courts will recognise the speaker's Article 9 rights when deciding whether a restriction on freedom of expression is lawful and proportionate. In *Redmond-Bate v DPP*,[77] three members of a Christian fundamentalist group were addressing passers-by on their views on religion and morality on the steps of Wakefield Cathedral, and were subsequently arrested for obstruction of a police officer when they refused to move on. In declaring the arrest unlawful SEDLEY LJ had regard not only to Article 10 but also to the speakers' rights under Article 9 and rejected the argument that the speaker would not be guilty of a breach of the peace provided what he said was not offensive. In his Lordship's opinion, free speech included not only the inoffensive, but also the irritating, the contentious, the eccentric, the heretical, the unwelcome and the provocative, provided it does not tend to provoke violence. Thus, to argue that the fact that three women were preaching about morality, God and the bible would lead to a reasonable apprehension that violence is going to erupt was both illiberal and illogical.

Redmond-Bate was decided before the implementation of the Human Rights Act and in any case SEDLEY LJ did not formally recognise the enhanced nature of religious speech. Domestic law has tended to deal with this issue on a case-by-case basis, being tolerant of such speech in general, but finding a breach of the law if there is evidence of sufficient harm, irrespective of the religious content of the speech. For example, in *Dehal v Crown Prosecution Service*,[78] it was stressed that a prosecution should not be brought under public order offences unless there was clear evidence that there had been a threat to public order. In that case therefore the court quashed a conviction under s.4 of the Public Order Act 1986 when the defendant had placed a poster in a temple which was critical of the temple's president. Employing the *dicta* in *Redmond-Bate* the court held that it was not sufficient that the words used were irritating and that the Crown had failed to establish that there had been a threat to public order so as to justify the use of the criminal law. On the other hand, in *Connolly v DPP*,[79] the High Court upheld a conviction under s.1 of the Malicious Communications Act 1998 of sending a letter conveying a grossly offensive message when the defendant sent photographs of aborted foetuses to three pharmacists who sold the morning-after pill. The High Court held that although it was possible to interpret the meaning of the words 'indecent' and 'grossly offensive' so that the provision was not employed in violation of Article 10, the defendant's

---

[76] (2004) 38 EHRR 13.
[77] [1999] Crim LR 998.
[78] [2005] EWHC 2154 (Admin).
[79] [2008] WLR 276.

right to free speech was not of a higher order simply because it represented her religious views. Further, on the facts, it did not justify the distress and anxiety that she intended to cause to those who received the message.

That pragmatic approach has also been adopted with respect to various public order offences.[80] For example, in *DPP* v *Clarke*[81] it was held that there had been no breach of s.5 of the Public Order Act 1986 (causing harassment, alarm and distress by the use of threatening, abusive or insulting words or behaviour) when anti-abortion protestors had displayed pictures of an aborted foetus outside an abortion clinic. The magistrates found that although the displays abusive and insulting, the protestors did not intend them to be so and neither were they aware that they were so. There was no specific mention of Article 9 in *Clarke* and in any case in *DPP* v *Fiddler*,[82] which arose from the same facts, it was held that an offence had been committed when an anti-abortion protest shouted and talked to people attending an abortion clinic and displayed plastic models and photographs of human foetuses. In this case the court was prepared to find the relevant intention to commit the offence from the fact that the defendant was anti-abortion and a member of the group organising the protest.

In general, therefore, the courts have adopted a conservative approach to religious speech as evidenced in the following two cases. In the first case – *Hammond* v *DPP*[83] – an Evangelical preacher was convicted under s.5 when he had addressed a crowd in a town centre and held up a large double-sided sign which bore the words 'Stop Homosexuality' and 'Stop Lesbianism'. On appeal, although the High Court accepted that it was its duty under s.3 of the Human Rights Act 1998 to interpret legislation compatibly with Articles 9 and 10 of the European Convention on Human Rights, it held that the court at first instance was entitled to conclude that his words and actions were insulting and, in the circumstances, unreasonable. Although the defendant was preaching his sincerely and deeply held beliefs, it was open to the justices to find that the words on the sign were insulting and that the defendant's conduct was not reasonable, particularly as the words on the sign linked homosexuality to immorality and were directed specifically towards the homosexual and lesbian community.

The second case concerned s.1 of the Crime and Disorder Act 1998, which provides for the granting of an antisocial behaviour order where a person has acted in a manner that caused or was likely to cause harassment, alarm or distress to one or more persons, and where such an order is necessary to protect persons in a specific local government area from further such acts. In *R (Singh)* v *Chief Constable of West Midlands*,[84] Singh and others had been taking part in a demonstration outside a theatre which had been showing a play entitled *Behtzi*, which the demonstrators felt was religiously offensive. The area surrounding the theatre had been designated under the Act because of the increasing acts of anti-social conduct taking place in the run-in towards Christmas, and when the police issued a dispersal order under the Act which the protestors refused to comply with they were arrested and cautioned. The Court of Appeal held that the Act could apply to acts of protest and that, further, the provisions of the Act and their application in this case were compatible with the appellants' Convention

---

[80] These offences, including the Protection from Harassment Act 1997, are detailed in chapter 10.

[81] [1992] Crim LR 60.

[82] [1992] 1 WLR 91.

[83] *The Times*, 28 January 2004. See Geddis, Free Speech Martyrs or Unreasonable Threats to Social Peace? – 'Insulting' Expression and Section 5 of the Public Order Act 1986 [2004] PL 853.

[84] [2006] 1 WLR 3374.

rights to freedom of religion and free speech. The use of the dispersal orders in this case achieved a balance between the rights of the protestors and the right to be protected from distressing conduct. That decision appears to pay scant regard to the protestors' right to freedom of religion and free speech, instead adopting a pragmatic approach to the protection of public order.

Less surprisingly, the speaker's right to religious free speech is likely to be given little weight when it conflicts with national security. In *R v Secretary of State for the Home Department, ex parte Farrakhan*,[85] the claimant (a US citizen and leader of a group called Nation of Islam) challenged a refusal by the Home Secretary to relax an order excluding him from entering the country, a decision based on the assertion that his presence would not be conducive to the public good and that he was likely to commit racial hatred offences. In overruling a decision of the High Court,[86] the Court of Appeal held that the Secretary of State had struck a proportionate balance between the legitimate aim of the prevention of disorder and freedom of expression. The Court of Appeal stressed that despite the application of the principle of proportionality to the decision, the Secretary of State was far better placed to reach an informed decision as to the likely consequences of admitting that person into the country than the court.

Questions

Should the right to freedom of expression be enhanced when Article 9 of the Convention is engaged?

Is there any evidence to suggest that the domestic courts believe that to be the case?

Restricting anti-religious speech

Some speech may be harmful to religious groups and its followers and thus the enjoyment of their right to freedom of thought, conscience and religion guaranteed by Article 9. In such cases the domestic law and the Convention may wish to restrict that speech in one of two ways. First, it may attempt to define it as 'hate speech' and thus place it outside the protection of Article 10 of the European Convention or the equivalent constitutional guarantee of free speech.[87] Secondly, while accepting that such speech is worthy of some protection, it may seek to justify the restriction or penalty as lawful and necessary within the terms of Article 10(2) of the Convention. In any case the domestic law will have to balance its obligation not to unduly interfere with freedom of expression with its obligation to ensure that the individual and group's Article 9 rights are enjoyed in practice.

Hate speech and Article 17 of the European Convention

Article 17 provides that nothing in the Convention shall be interpreted as implying for any state, group or person any right to engage in any activity or perform any act aimed at the destruction of any of the rights and freedoms set forth herein or at their limitation to a greater extent than is provided for in the Convention. Thus, although in most cases a breach of the applicant's free speech can be justified within Article 10(2), Article 17 operates to disqualify

---

[85] [2002] 3 WLR 481.
[86] *The Daily Telegraph*, 9 October 2001.
[87] See Barendt, *Freedom of Speech* (OUP 2005), pages 170–92.

the applicant from even relying on the Convention right, allowing the Court to dispense with the case on the grounds that the claim is inconsistent with the terms of the Convention.[88]

The provision is aimed at extremist groups whose primary aim is the destruction or denial of the human rights and fundamental freedoms of others, and can be employed where such activities are clearly racially or religiously biased. Thus, in *Glimerveen and Hagenbeek* v *Netherlands*,[89] Article 17 was applied where the applicants had been prosecuted for the possession of leaflets likely to cause racial hatred, the leaflets suggesting that certain religious and other groups were not welcome in the country. The European Commission declared the applicants' case inadmissible, stating that Article 10 did not extend to such views. Although Article 17 protects individuals and groups from, *inter alia*, religious attacks and persecution, it is subject to limitations and the Court must make a distinction between activities that are destructive of the rights of others and those which are simply offensive and unpopular. In *Lehideux and Irsoni* v *France*[90] the Court held that the expression of ideas did not constitute an 'activity' within the meaning of Article 17 and that any measures taken under it must be proportionate to the threat to the rights of others.

Such restrictions, therefore, cannot simply protect religious groups from mere offence, but must meet the tests laid down in the Convention's conditional rights, the article being reserved for those rare cases where the person or group has resorted to acts of violence or clear racial hatred. Thus, in *Gunduz* v *Turkey*[91] the European Court held that the applicant's conviction for making hate speech on a television broadcast – the leader of an Islamic sect had opposed democracy and opined that children born to couples who had undergone a civil marriage were illegitimate – was not necessary in a democratic society. The Court held that while expressions that sought to spread or justify hatred based on intolerance did not enjoy the protection of Article 10, the mere fact of defending sharia law without calling for violence could not be regarded as hate speech. The Court also took into account the fact that the statement was made as part of a television programme which was intended to present the sect's views on democracy and Islam and which offered counterbalancing views.[92]

Nevertheless, Article 17 has been employed, often in combination with Article 10(2) to deny protection to racist speech. In *Norwood* v *United Kingdom*,[93] the European Court confirmed that the applicant's conviction for displaying a poster in the first-floor window of his flat which proclaimed 'Islam out of Britain' and 'Protect the British People' was compatible with the Convention. In upholding the conviction the domestic courts had found that the judge at first instance was entitled to consider Article 9 and Article 17 in rejecting any defence of reasonableness. The applicant's claim that his conviction violated his right to freedom of expression under Article 10 and was discriminatory under Article 14 was declared inadmissible by the Court. In the Court's view, the general purpose of that article was to prevent individuals or groups with totalitarian aims from exploiting in their own interests the principles enunciated in the Convention. On the facts, the words and images on the poster

---

[88] See Keane, Attacking Hate Speech under Article 17 of the European Convention on Human Rights [2007] Netherlands Human Rights Quarterly 241; Hare and Weinstein, *Extreme Speech and Democracy* (OUP 2009).

[89] (1979) 18 DR 187.

[90] (2000) 30 EHRR 665.

[91] (2005) 41 EHRR 5.

[92] See also *Jersild* v *Denmark* (1994) 19 EHRR 1, where the European Court defended the media's right to broadcast hate speech that would not have attracted the speaker's Article 10 rights.

[93] (2005) 40 EHRR SE11.

amounted to a public expression of attack on all Muslims in the United Kingdom, and such a general and vehement attack against a religious group, linking the group as a whole with grave acts of terrorism, was incompatible with the values of the Convention, notably tolerance, social peace and non-discrimination. Consequently, the poster fell outside the protection of Articles 10 and 11 of the Convention.[94]

> **Question**
> What is hate speech and is there a case for excluding it from the protection of Article 10?

Domestic laws on religious hate speech

English domestic law makes provision for conduct that incites racial or religious hatred as well as words and conduct causing harassment, alarm or distress. This provides some protection to an individual's, or a group's, right to freedom of thought, conscience and religion within Article 9. These offences have been covered in chapter 11 of this text with respect to freedom of association and assembly, but for present purposes this section of the text will concentrate on how such provisions assist the enjoyment of Article 9 rights. Nevertheless, such provisions not only restrict free speech, but also in many cases religious speech and those issues will be discussed where relevant.

Inciting racial and religious hatred

The offence of inciting racial hatred is covered by sections 18–23 of the Public Order Act 1986, which creates a number of incitement offences and defines racial hatred as hatred against a group of persons defined by reference to colour, race, nationality (including citizenship) or ethnic or national origins.[95] For example, s.18 makes it an offence for a person to use threatening, abusive and insulting words or behaviour, or to display any such written material, where that person either intends thereby to stir up racial hatred, or, having regard to all the circumstances, such hatred is likely to be stirred up. Although the offences can be committed by the use of insulting words or behaviour, they do not protect individuals from mere offence and insult, it being necessary to show that racial hatred is likely to be stirred up. Further, under s.7 no proceedings may be brought except by or with the consent of the Attorney-General.[96]

The Act also makes it an offence to publish or distribute threatening, abusive or insulting written material which is intended or likely to stir up racial hatred (s.19), and under s.23 it is an offence to be in possession of racially inflammatory material with a view to such material being displayed, published, distributed, or broadcast and the person either intends to stir up racial hatred or such hatred is likely to be stirred up.

The Racial and Religious Hatred Act 2006 now contains an offence of incitement to *religious* hatred, thus providing potentially broader protection to religious groups and its

---

[94] Contrast the decision in *Dehal v Crown Prosecution Service* [2005] EWHC 2154 (Admin), considered above, at page 690.

[95] This does not specifically cover religion, but certain racial groups may also constitute religious groups. Further, religious incitement is now specifically covered under the Act, see below.

[96] In 2006 Abu Hamza, the Imam of Finsbury Park Mosque, was convicted, *inter alia*, of using threatening words with intent to stir up racial hatred with respect to addresses he made at the Mosque between 1997 and 2000. An appeal against other convictions was unsuccessful: *R v Abu Hamza* [2007] 2 WLR 226.

followers, while, of course, further restricting some religious speech. Section 1 of the 2006 Act inserts a new Part 3A to the 1986 Act, above, and defines religious hatred as hatred against a group of persons defined by reference to religious (or lack of religious) belief.[97] It is now an offence for any person to use *threatening* words or behaviour, or to display any written material which is such, if *he intends* thereby to stir up religious hatred.[98] The scope of the offence is narrower (and even less protective of religious sensibilities) than that of inciting racial hatred, reflecting concerns that it would impose an undue interference on free speech.[99] Thus, the words or behaviour must be threatening (and not simply abusive or insulting) and the defendant has to intend the consequences (rather than them being simply likely). Further, the section does not apply to words, behaviour or written material used or displayed solely for the purpose of being included in a programme service.[100]

More specifically, the Act states that nothing should prohibit or restrict discussion, criticism or expressions of antipathy, dislike, ridicule, insult or abuse of particular religions or the beliefs or practices of their adherents, or proselytising or urging adherents of a different religion or belief system to cease practising their religion or belief system.[101] Thus, shocking or offensive views directed at religions and their followers will not necessarily come within the Act, although the right to protect one's religion from such attacks might be provided by the Public Order Act 1986, below. With respect to the protection of religious speech, the section also recognises the right to try to persuade followers of a particular religion to abandon that religion in favour of another, a right which the European Court has regarded as fundamental to the manifestation of religion and conscience.[102]

Racially and religiously aggravated offences

The offences of incitement to racial or religious hatred apply to the most exceptional hate speech and conduct and thus provide limited protection to religious groups and their followers who wish to manifest their views without harassment and offence. However, the law does provide some protection (and further restriction on religious speech) via the creation of racially and religiously aggravated offences. Thus, sections 28–32 of the Crime and Disorder Act 1998 provide for increased penalties for certain public order offences where the offences are racially or religiously aggravated.

An offence is racially aggravated when at the time of committing the offence, or immediately before or after doing so, the offender demonstrates towards the victim of the offence hostility based on the victim's membership (or presumed membership) of a racial group, or where the offence is motivated (wholly or partly) by hostility towards members of a racial group based on their membership of that group.[103] Further, the Crime and Disorder Act 1998 was

---

[97] Section 29A Public Order Act 1986.

[98] Section 29B Public Order Act 1986. The new section creates a number of related offences which are detailed in chapter 10, pages 535–6.

[99] For a critical analysis of these provisions, see Hare, Crosses, Crescents and Sacred Cows: Criminalising Incitement to Religious Hatred [2006] PL 521; Fenwick and Phillipson, *Media Freedom under the Human Rights Act* (OUP 2006), pages 516–27.

[100] Section 29B(5).

[101] Section 29J.

[102] See *Kokkinakis* v *Greece* (1994) 17 EHRR 397, discussed above at page 672.

[103] By s.28 Crime and Disorder Act 1998.

amended so as to include the victim's membership of a religious group, and the definition of 'religious group' is a group of persons defined by religious belief or lack of religious belief.[104]

The scope of these offences was considered in *R* v *Rogers*,[105] where the House of Lords upheld the defendant's conviction for using racially aggravated abusive or insulting words when he had referred to three Spanish women as 'bloody foreigners' and told them to go back to their own country. The House of Lords held that membership of a racial group went beyond groups defined by their colour, race or ethnic origin and included nationality (including citizenship) and national origins. Their Lordships noted that the offences attacked the mischiefs of racism and xenophobia and the essence was the denial of equal respect and dignity to people who were seen as 'other'. Consequently, such remarks were more deeply hurtful and damaging to the victims than the simple versions of the offence, and more damaging to the community as a whole. In that case the fact that the offender's hostility was based on other factors in addition to racism or xenophobia was irrelevant, but the context in which the words are used might be relevant in determining liability.[106]

Such provisions provide some protection to the rights of others to belong to and take part in their religion, although such protection should always be balanced with arguments on free speech. The line needs to be drawn carefully between views hostile to religion and unreasonable attacks on such and in this respect the decisions in *Norwood* v *DPP* and *Norwood* v *United Kingdom*, are illustrative. The details of those cases are given above with respect to Article 17 of the Convention, but the domestic court regarded the display of the poster as a public expression of attack on all Muslims in this country, and not, on any reasonable interpretation, merely an intemperate criticism against the tenets of the Muslim religion. Further, the High Court stated that once the prosecution has proved that an accused's conduct was insulting and that he intends it to be, or was aware that it might be so, it will in most cases follow that his conduct was objectively unreasonable, especially where that conduct was motivated by hostility towards a religious group. Equally, the European Court found that the poster constituted a general and vehement attack against a religious group, linking the group as a whole with grave acts of terrorism. Such views were, therefore, incompatible with the values of the Convention and outside the protection of Articles 10 and 11 of the Convention.[107]

Question

Do you believe that domestic laws on causing racial and religious hatred and offence offer adequate protection against hate speech and the protection of religion?

Protecting religion from blasphemous speech

A state's law of blasphemy seeks to regulate speech or other expression so as to protect either the tenets of the country's religion or the sensibilities of its followers. The European Convention on

---

[104] Section 28(4) Anti-Terrorism, Crime and Security Act 2001.

[105] [2007] 2 WLR 280.

[106] In *DPP* v *Humphrey* [2005] EWHC 822 (Admin), it was held that the phrase 'you're fucking Islam', directed at an Asian policeman, was undeniably abusive, if not insulting. However, the courts should hear evidence with respect to the context in which they were used.

[107] Note also s.127 of the Communications Act 2003, which makes it an offence to send a grossly offensive message through a public electronic communications service. This might be used to regulate offensive racial or religious views, although the purpose of the Act is not solely to protect a person's sensibilities: *DPP* v *Collins* [2006] 1 WLR 2223.

Human Rights recognises these aims in two respects. First, Article 10(2) permits restrictions on free speech for the protection of the rights of others (including, of course, the right of thought, conscience and religion under Article 9). Secondly, Article 9 of the Convention provides the individual with the right to manifest their religion, and it could be argued, the right to be protected from blasphemous speech. This section of the text considers whether Article 9 of the Convention and the, now abolished, domestic law of blasphemy provided adequate protection to freedom of religion.[108] In particular, it considers the extent to which a state has a positive duty to pass and enforce blasphemy laws, and whether any such laws need to protect all religions and religious tenets.[109]

It should be noted at this stage that the UK domestic law of blasphemy and blasphemous libel was abolished by s.79 of the Criminal Justice and Immigration Act 2008.[110] Nevertheless, the area remains important with respect to the protection of religion from religious attacks as the absence of such a law might impact on that protection and call into question the efficacy of alternative claims (such as incitement to racial and religious hatred, above) in protecting religion and religious sensibilities. For that reason the text will provide a brief outline of the law of blasphemy under the European Convention; references will also be made to the UK domestic law on blasphemy wherever relevant so as to allow the reader to appreciate the controversies created by the law and its reform.

Blasphemy and the European Convention on Human Rights

Although blasphemy laws conflict with freedom of expression, the Convention machinery has afforded each state with a generous margin of appreciation in passing and applying such laws. This in turn has provided religious groups and followers with a good deal of protection of their Article 9 rights when they are under threat from blasphemous expression.

For example, in *Otto-Preminger Institute v Austria*[111] the European Court noted that the state is better placed than the international judge to assess the need for blasphemy laws and their application in particular circumstances and that accordingly it should be given a wide margin of appreciation in this context. The European Court also recognised the right under Articles 9 and 10(2) of others to follow their religion free from gratuitous offence. In that case an arts association had advertised the showing of a film that depicted God as senile, Jesus as feeble-minded and Mary as a wanton woman. Criminal proceedings were brought against the applicant's manager, and later dropped, but court orders were issued for the seizure of the film, causing the showing of the film to be abandoned. The European Court held that the concept of blasphemy could not be isolated from the society against which it is being judged, as well as the population where the showings were due to take place, which in this case, were strongly Catholic. Accordingly, the Austrian authorities had acted proportionately by acting to ensure religious peace in that region and to protect some people from an attack on their religious beliefs in an unwarranted and offensive manner.

---

[108] The law of blasphemy as it affects freedom of expression has been considered in chapter 8 of this text.

[109] For an excellent account of this area, and of the European Court's judgment in *Wingrove v United Kingdom*, see below, Ghandhi and James, The English Law of Blasphemy and the European Convention on Human Rights [1998] EHRLR 430. See also Kearns, The Uncultured God: Blasphemy Law's Reprieve and the Art Matrix [2000] EHRLR 512.

[110] See Parpworth, The Abolition of the Blasphemy Laws (2008) 172 (11) JP 164; Bennion, Farewell to the Blasphemy Laws (2008) 172 (28) JP 448.

[111] (1994) 19 EHRR 34.

The European Court has continued its hands-off approach in this area and it is clear that states are still allowed to protect individuals and groups from unreasonable attack via moderate blasphemy laws. For example, in *IA* v *Turkey*,[112] the European Court held that there had been no violation of Article 10 when the applicant had been fined for publishing a novel which, *inter alia*, alleged that the prophet Mohammad did not prohibit sexual intercourse with a dead person or a living animal. In the Court's view the book was not merely provocative and shocking but constituted an abusive attack on the Prophet of Islam. Notwithstanding a degree of tolerance of criticism of religious doctrine within Turkish society, believers could legitimately feel that certain passages of the book constituted an unwarranted and offensive attack on them.

However, blasphemy laws should not attempt to safeguard followers from any attack on their religion. In *Tatlav* v *Turkey*,[113] it was held that there had been a violation of Article 10 when the applicant had been fined when he published a book entitled the *Reality of Islam*, which claimed that religion had the effect of legitimising social injustices in the name of 'God's will'. The Court held that although the book contained strong criticism of the religion, it did not employ an offensive tone aimed at believers or an abusive attack against sacred symbols. Further, the book had been seized four years after its publication and on the basis of an individual complaint. In addition the applicant was faced with the threat of imprisonment, which would have a discouraging effect on authors.

UK blasphemy laws and the European Convention

The European Court and Commission have also ruled on the compatibility of UK blasphemy law. For example, in *Gay News* v *United Kingdom*,[114] the European Commission had to decide whether a prosecution of a poem which described, *inter alia*, acts of sodomy and fellatio with the body of Christ immediately after his crucifixion was necessary in a democratic society. This action was brought following the House of Lords' decision in *R* v *Lemon*,[115] which involved the private prosecution, brought by Mary Whitehouse, the famous 'good taste' campaigner, of a poem which had been published in an issue of *Gay News*. The poem, entitled 'The Love that dares to speak its name', also, allegedly, ascribed to him during his lifetime promiscuous homosexual practices with the Apostles and other men. The defendant claimed that it was not his intention to blaspheme or to cause outrage, but rather to explore matters such as the crucifixion from a homosexual viewpoint.

The defendant was convicted and the case was referred to the House of Lords on the question of the relevant *mens rea* of the offence; was it essential that the publisher and author intended to insult the feelings of a religious group, or could the offence be committed by the mere intention to publish the article? The House of Lords confirmed that the offence of blasphemy still existed at common law, and that it was not necessary to prove that the words would lead to a breach of the peace.[116]

---

[112] (2007) 45 EHRR 30.

[113] Decision of the European Court, 2 May 2006.

[114] (1983) 5 EHRR 123. The details of the case are given in chapter 8 on freedom of expression, page 397.

[115] [1979] AC 617.

[116] Subsequently the High Court have stated that any publication must be such as tends to endanger society as a whole, by endangering the peace, depraving public morality, shaking the fabric of society or tending to cause civil strife: *R (Green)* v *Westminster Magistrates Court* [2008] HRLR 12 (Admin), dealt with below.

In *Lemon*, Lord Scarman held that although it was no longer an offence to deny the existence of God or Jesus Christ, or to speak or publish opinions hostile to the Christian religion, it was an offence if the publication contained any contemptuous, reviling, scurrilous or ludicrous matter relating to God, Jesus Christ or the Bible. On the facts, therefore, the jury was entitled to conclude that the article would outrage the feelings of any member or sympathiser with the Christian religion. On the question of the relevant *mens rea*, it was held that the offence is satisfied by proof only of an intention to publish material, which in the opinion of the jury is likely to shock and arouse resentment among believing Christians.[117]

On appeal under the European Convention it was noted by the Commission that it might be necessary in a democratic society to attach criminal sanctions to material that offends against religious feelings, provided the attack is serious enough and that the application of the law is proportionate to the appropriate aim. The Commission held that the prosecution of a poem which described, *inter alia*, acts of sodomy and fellatio with the body of Christ immediately after his crucifixion was necessary in a democratic society. In the Commission's view the domestic law was sufficiently clear and had several legitimate aims, including the protection of the rights of others. Further, the fact that the offence was one of strict liability and is, thus, committed irrespective of the publisher's intention and the intended audience did not make it disproportionate *per se*.

This wide margin of appreciation was also applied in *Wingrove* v *United Kingdom*,[118] where the European Court upheld the banning of a potentially blasphemous video, finding that any interference corresponded to a legitimate aim of protecting Christians against serious offence to their beliefs. Further, the Court noted that although blasphemy laws were becoming increasingly rare in their application, there was as yet not sufficient common ground in the legal and social orders of the member states to conclude that blasphemy legislation was unnecessary in a democratic society and thus incompatible with the Convention. Although there existed little scope for restrictions on questions of public interest, a wider margin of appreciation was generally available to states in relation to matters liable to offend intimate personal convictions in the sphere of morals and religion; although that did not preclude final European supervision, which was important given the open-endedness of blasphemy and the risks of arbitrary interferences.

Thus Article 9 (and Article 10(2)) does not provide an absolute right to be free from religious attacks, simply because the individual or group might find that attack offensive and is genuinely sensitive to such attacks. Of more concern, however, is the fact that a specific religious group cannot demand that the state pass and operate such laws, and indeed are allowed to operate such laws in a manner which discriminates against, or in favour of, specific religions. This had been recognised, indirectly, in *Wingrove* v *United Kingdom* (above) when it held that the fact that domestic law did not treat all religions alike did not detract from the legitimacy of the aim of protecting the religious rights of others and the necessity of any subsequent restriction.

In addition, the European Commission has ruled on whether UK domestic law should provide specific protection to religion and religious sensibilities via clear and equal blasphemy

---

[117] However, there must be shown to be an attack on that religion and not on another object or person. See *R (Green)* v *Westminster Magistrates' Court*, n 116, considered below.

[118] (1996) 24 EHRR 1, detailed in chapter 8, page 398.

laws. In *R v Chief Magistrates Court, ex parte Choudhury*,[119] the Court of Appeal confirmed that the English law of blasphemy did not apply to any religion other than Anglicanism, believing that to extend the law to cover other religions would create difficulties in recognising different views of various sects within a particular religion and would encourage intolerance, divisiveness and unreasonable interference with freedom of expression. The case followed the publication of Salman Rushdie's *Satanic Verses*, which a number of people claimed that it vilified Islam. Following that decision an application was made under the European Convention claiming that that state of affairs was in contravention of Articles 9 and 14 of the Convention, which guaranteed the right to religion and freedom from discrimination. However, in *Choudhury v United Kingdom*[120] the European Commission held that Article 9 did not include a positive obligation upon the state to protect religious sensibilities and that there was no right to demand that the state operated a law of blasphemy so as to protect the religious beliefs and activities of certain individuals. Thus, the right to freedom of religion did not compel freedom for adherents of all religions to bring legal proceedings in respect of scurrilous abuse. Further, with respect to the claim under Article 14 that the unequal application of blasphemy laws discriminated against the applicant's religion, the Commission held that as there was no positive obligation of a state to protect the right to be free from offence under Article 9, it could not be a breach of Article 14 to deny a group or individual protection against such attacks.

This leads to the incongruous situation that although the existence and application of blasphemy laws is considered a legitimate aim for the purposes of Article 10(2) of the Convention – that is the protection of the rights of others (the right to religion under Article 9) – Article 9 does not itself guarantee that protection. It is, therefore, in the discretion of the state to decide whether to operate blasphemy laws; equally, within its discretion to choose which religions to protect, it may discriminate against specific religions.[121]

Although now only of historical importance with respect to domestic law, given the abolition of the specific offence of blasphemy, the High Court decision in *R (Green) v Westminster Magistrates' Court*[122] provides an interesting example of how a liberal judicial attitude towards free speech can reduce the effect of religious protection laws. In this case the High Court dismissed an application for judicial review which had been brought in relation to a Magistrates' Court refusal to issue a summons for the private prosecution for blasphemous libel of the theatre performance and television broadcast of a work entitled *Jerry Springer: The Opera*. The case had been brought by a member of an organisation known as Christian Voice, who claimed that several scenes in the performance were blasphemous. In particular, he claimed that the second part of the piece, which imagines Mr Springer's descent into Hell and in which his guests appeared as Satan, Christ, God, Mary and Adam and Eve, amounted to a scurrilous and ludicrous portrayal of venerable Christian figures and thus a contemptuous and reviling attack on the Christian religion.

The application for review was rejected by their Lordships on two essential grounds. First, it was held that the Theatres Act 1968 and the Broadcasting Act 1990 precluded any action in

[119] [1991] 1 QB 429.
[120] (1991) 12 HRLJ 172.
[121] The matter could be resolved by the introduction of a free-standing right to equality, as is contained in Article 26 of the International Covenant on Civil and Political Rights, and the, as yet, unratified, Protocol 12 of the European Convention.
[122] [2008] HRLR 12.

the common law of blasphemy with respect to theatre productions and broadcasts. The 1968 Act provides (in s.2(4)) that no person shall be proceeded against in respect of a performance of a play for an offence at common law where it is the essence of the offence that the performance or what was said in the performance was obscene, indecent, offensive, disgusting or injurious to morality.[123]

Secondly, and more controversially, their Lordships felt that the claimant had failed to make out a *prima facie* case that the play and the broadcast were blasphemous. Thus, although the judges were prepared to accept that the content of the play might cause deep offence to some (though not most) practising Christians and that it was couched in not merely tasteless but arguably contemptuous and reviling terms, it was clear that the play had as the object of its attack not religion, but the exploitative television chat show hosted by Springer. The word 'attack' focused attention on the need for what has been said to be properly regarded as immoderate or offensive treatment of Christianity or sacred objects. The District Judge was thus entitled to consider that the matters relied on as constituting blasphemy could not in the context be regarded as such because the play as a whole was not and could not reasonably be regarded as aimed at, or an attack on, Christianity or what Christians held sacred.

These *obiter* comments regarding the nature of the attack are highly contentious, both legally and morally. It is uncertain how the court in the instant case distinguished the facts from those in *R v Lemon*, where it was made clear that the intention of the author was not relevant in determining whether material was blasphemous. In the present case, although the object of the ridicule was intended to be Mr Springer and the modern phenomenon of tasteless reality television, the producers and broadcasters were prepared to use venerable religious objects to make their point, a tactic which is likely to cause grave offence to some Christians, who would fail to see the distinction between attacking the religion directly and using its objects in a possibly scurrilous manner in order to attack Mr Springer and his show. Indeed, in that case their Lordships opined that insulting a person's religious sensibilities would not normally amount to an infringement of the right of religion under Article 9 of the Convention, as the right to hold and practise one's religion is generally unaffected by such insults. Although the decision may be thought to have a liberating effect on free speech, the fact that the *actus reus* of the offence requires civil strife or the like to be induced makes it likely to be committed when the religion and society in question are prone to a more radical reaction to scurrilous religious attacks. In addition, the fact that the common law offence only applied to the Christian faith deepens the arguments about its unequal application.

It appears, therefore, that both the European Court and the domestic courts offer, or offered, little direct protection against blasphemous speech within the context of Article 9. Under the European Convention such sensibilities can be indirectly protected when free speech has been restricted on such grounds, the European Court in particular offering a relatively wide margin of appreciation in that area. However the absence, or abolition, of such laws does not appear to give rise to a violation of Article 9 *per se*. In such a case it must be asked whether groups have an alternative effective remedy to protect their rights under Article 8. In the context of UK domestic law that requires an appraisal of the effectiveness, and appropriateness, of existing public order laws in safeguarding such interests.

---

[123] A similar provision is contained in Schedule 15 of the Broadcasting Act 1990, which covered the action in respect to the television broadcast of the show.

Questions

How does the European Court draw a distinction between acceptable criticism and comment of religions and religious views and words or actions which can justifiably be restricted within Article 10(2)? Is this distinction a viable one?

Why is domestic law allowed to decide whether or not to have blasphemy laws and to distinguish between different religions with respect to that law's extent?

Do you feel that the abolition of the UK blasphemy laws leaves religious groups and followers with adequate protection against anti-religious speech?

Further reading

General

For a comprehensive coverage of religion and human rights, see Taylor, *Freedom of Religion; UN and European Human Rights Law and Practice* (Cambridge University Press 2005).

A number of texts contain excellent chapters on Article 9 of the Convention and its relevant case law: Harris, Warbrick, Bates and O'Boyle, *Law of the European Convention on Human Rights* (OUP 2009, 2nd edn), chapter 10; Ovey and White, *Jacobs and White: The European Convention on Human Rights* (OUP 2010, 5th edn), chapter 12; Clayton and Tomlinson, *Law of Human Rights* (OUP 2009), chapter 14. In addition, Mowbray's *Cases and Materials on the European Convention* (OUP 2007, 2nd edn), chapter 11 provides an excellent reference point on the case law of the European Court in this area.

Freedom of religion and education

There has been a good deal of literature written with respect to freedom of religion and the right to wear religious dress, and, in particular, the Shabina Begum and Leyla Sahin cases. See Hill and Sandberg, Is Nothing Sacred? Clashing Symbols in a Secular World [2007] PL 488; Lewis, What Not to Wear: Religious Rights, the European Convention and the Margin of Appreciation [2007] ICLQ 395. See also McGoldrick, *Human Rights and Religion: The Islamic Headscarf Debate in Europe* (Cambridge University Press 2007); Idriss, Lacite and the Banning of the 'Hijab' in France (2005) LS 260 for a wider discussion of the issue. See also Leader, Freedoms and Futures: Personal Priorities, Institutional Demands and Freedom of Religion (2007) 70 MLR 713, for a more general debate on the accommodation of religious freedom in society.

Hate speech, blasphemy, free speech and religion

See Barendt, *Freedom of Speech* (OUP 2005), pages 170–92 and Fenwick and Phillipson, *Media Freedom under the Human Rights Act* (OUP 2006), chapter 9 for an overview. See also Hare and Weinstein, *Extreme Speech and Democracy* (OUP 2009).

There are also some excellent articles in these areas: Geddis, Free Speech Martyrs or Unreasonable Threats to Social Peace? – 'Insulting' Expression and Section 5 of the Public Order Act 1986 [2004] PL 853; Hare, Crosses, Crescents and Sacred Cows: Criminalising Incitement to Religious Hatred [2006] PL 521; Ghandhi and James, The English Law of Blasphemy and the European Convention on Human Rights [1998] EHRLR 430; Keane, Attacking Hate Speech under

Article 17 of the European Convention on Human Rights [2007] Netherlands Human Rights Quarterly 241; Kearns, The Uncultured God: Blasphemy Law's Reprieve and the Art Matrix [2000] EHRLR 512; Parmar, The Challenge of Defamation of Religions to Freedom of Expression and International Human Rights [2009] EHRLR 353.

Visit **www.mylawchamber.co.uk/fosterhumanrights**
to access regular updates to major changes in the law,
further case studies, weblinks, and suggested
answers/approaches to questions in the book.

13 Human rights and freedom from discrimination

Introduction

In *Pretty* v *United Kingdom* Diane Pretty, a woman suffering from motor neurone disease argued that the failure of the law to allow her husband to assist her suicide was contrary to her human rights. Specifically, she argued that the refusal of the law to make a distinction between able-bodied persons (who could terminate their own lives within the law) and disabled persons (such as herself who could not), was discriminatory. The European Court had to decide whether the like treatment of all persons within the law was capable of being discriminatory, and if so whether that discriminatory treatment was justified on legitimate grounds.

This chapter will examine the right not to be discriminated against in the context of the enjoyment of human rights, and will study a host of cases that pose the above questions and examine how the European and domestic courts resolve those issues.

A basic tenet of human rights protection is that people are treated equally and not discriminated against on impermissible grounds, such as their sex, race or religion. With respect to the enjoyment of Convention rights this is enshrined in Article 14 of the Convention (given effect to via the Human Rights Act 1998), which forbids discrimination in the enjoyment of Convention rights on grounds of a person's status. Although that article does not give a general right to equality under the law or freedom from discrimination in the enjoyment of rights that are not protected within the Convention, nevertheless discrimination in areas such as housing, education and employment might give rise to a claim under a substantive Convention right, for example the right to private life, in combination with Article 14.[1] In addition, national law may intervene to protect certain groups from discrimination, thus bolstering the individuals' Convention rights and providing a greater right to equality in the law.

This chapter examines how the right to equality and freedom from discrimination can impact and enhance the enjoyment of the human rights and civil liberties that we have

---

[1] See, for example, *Smith and Grady* v *United Kingdom* (2000) 29 EHRR 493, with respect to breach of private life and discrimination in the employment field.

identified in the earlier chapters of this text. It is not intended to give an exhaustive account of discrimination law, but rather to examine how the European Convention and national law protects individuals and groups from discrimination in the enjoyment of their Convention rights.[2] It will begin with a brief summary of the arguments in favour of equality and the importance of anti-discrimination provisions in respect of the protection of human rights. Particular attention will then be paid to Article 14 of the European Convention and how that provision has been interpreted by the European Court of Human Rights, and by the domestic courts under the Human Rights Act 1998; the limitations of Article 14 as an effective safe-guard against discrimination will also be examined.

The chapter will then provide a brief overview of the domestic law on equality and freedom from discrimination as it impacts on the enjoyment of human rights, including the variety of statutory provisions covering discrimination and the establishment and func-tions of the Commission for Equality and Human Rights Commission under the Equality Acts 2006 and 2010.

The chapter will then conclude by examining how both European and domestic law has responded to discrimination on grounds of sexuality, in particular against homosexuals and transsexuals: including the case law of the European Court of Human Rights, the protection afforded under European Union law and the domestic protection of those groups under the Human Rights Act 1998 and other legislation such as the Civil Partnership Act 2004 and the Gender Recognition Act 2004.

Thus, this chapter will cover:

- An examination of the importance of equality and non-discrimination in the protection of human rights and civil liberties.

- An examination of Article 14 of the European Convention on Human Rights and its effectiveness in securing equality and freedom from discrimination in the enjoyment of Convention rights.

- An analysis of the relevant case law of the European Court of Human Rights and the domestic courts under Article 14 of the Convention, including an analysis of the effective-ness of that case law in protecting against inequality and discrimination.

- An overview of the various anti-discrimination and equality laws in England and Wales as they affect the enjoyment of human rights and civil liberties, including the provisions of the Equality Acts 2006 and 2010 and the role of the Commission on Equality and Human Rights.

- An examination of how the case law of the European Court of Human Rights, EU law and domestic law affects discrimination on grounds of sexuality, including the rights of homo-sexuals and transsexuals.

---

[2] For a detailed coverage of domestic discrimination law, see Monohagan, *Equality Law* (OUP 2007); McColgan, *Discrimination Law: Text, Cases and Materials* (Hart 2005, 2nd edn); Connolly, *Townshend-Smith on Dis-crimination Law: Text, Cases and Materials* (Cavendish 2004, 2nd edn); Connolly, *Discrimination Law* (Sweet & Maxwell 2006); Fredman, *Discrimination Law* (Clarendon 2002). See also Fenwick, *Civil Liberties and Human Rights* (Routledge-Cavendish 2007, 4th edn), chapter 15.

Equality and freedom from discrimination as a human right

In chapter 1 of this text we examined the idea that protection of fundamental human rights is essential to maintaining the dignity and integrity of the human being and that many domestic bills of rights and international human rights treaties are based on the idea of equality and freedom from discrimination. These documents insist that the rights identified therein are enjoyed free from discrimination on grounds such as sex, race, national origin and religion, and advocate that the rights are available to all, irrespective of personal or group characteristics. For example, the preamble to the United Nations Charter 1945 and the Universal Declaration of Human Rights 1948 both reaffirm 'faith in the dignity and worth of the human person and in the equal rights of men', and Article 2 of the Universal Declaration provides that everyone is entitled to the rights and freedoms set forth in this Declaration, without distinction of any kind, such as race, colour, sex, language, religion, political or other opinion, national or social origin, property, birth or other status. These statements not only respond to the discrimination and victimisation of certain peoples leading up to the drafting and ratification of such treaties, but also reflect the principle expounded by theorists such as Ronald Dworkin, who believes that every state has a duty to treat all of its citizens with equal concern and respect.[3]

Within the practice of human rights adjudication this should ensure that every human being, particularly those belonging to oppressed and minority groups, are allowed to enjoy the basic rights identified in these treaties. Thus, as we have seen, the rights contained in the European Convention on Human Rights have been used consistently by groups such as prisoners,[4] sexual minorities,[5] and those suspected of terrorist crimes,[6] the judiciary rejecting state arguments that such individuals or groups have either forgone their basic human rights or that they must be compromised in the context of the maintenance of societal interests such as public safety or national security.[7] Consequently, the European Court has insisted that such groups or individuals are not automatically excluded from the enjoyment of Convention rights,[8] and that it would be contrary to principles of equality and dignity to allow the majority the right to insist that all individuals abide by its standards.[9] This principle has been followed by the domestic courts in the post-Human Rights Act era, and in one case Baroness Hale stressed that one essential purpose of human rights instruments was to secure the protection of essential rights of members of minority groups, even where they are unpopular with the majority.[10]

---

[3] Dworkin, *Taking Rights Seriously* (Duckworth 1977). See also McColgan, Principle of Equality and Protection from Discrimination in International Human Rights Law [2003] EHRLR 157; Singh, Equality: The Neglected Virtue [2004] EHRLR 141.

[4] *Golder v United Kingdom* (1979) 1 EHRR 524.

[5] *Dudgeon v United Kingdom* (1982) 4 EHRR 149; *Goodwin v United Kingdom* (2002) 35 EHRR 18.

[6] *A v Secretary of State for the Home Department* [2005] 2 AC 68.

[7] See Livingstone and Harvey, Protecting the Marginalised: The Role of the European Convention on Human Rights [2000] 51 NILQ 445.

[8] *Golder v United Kingdom*, n 4 above.

[9] *Dudgeon v United Kingdom* and *Goodwin v United Kingdom*, n 5 above.

[10] *Ghaidan v Mendoza* [2004] 2 AC 557, at para 132.

This principle complements the idea that to discriminate against an individual on impermissible grounds is an affront to their basic dignity. To discriminate against an individual thus not only deprives them of protection under the law but also is capable of degrading them as human beings. Thus, in *Ghaidan* v *Mendoza*, above, a case involving the discriminatory treatment of homosexual partners, Lord Nicholls described discrimination as invidious and the antithesis of fairness, demeaning both those who have unfairly benefited from and those who are unfairly prejudiced by it.[11] Similarly, Baroness Hale identified that treating people with less value causes pain and distress and violates their dignity as an individual, as well as being damaging to society as a whole.[12] Indeed, as we shall see, discrimination against an individual may, in extreme cases, amount to inhuman and degrading treatment in violation of Article 3 of the Convention.[13]

Question

Why is discrimination and inequality seen as an affront to human dignity?

Prohibition of discrimination and the European Convention on Human Rights

Equality and freedom from discrimination are basic principles of the European Convention and the jurisprudence of the European Court of Human Rights. Thus, Article 1 of the Convention provides that member states must secure the rights laid down in the Convention to *everyone* within their jurisdiction, and this obligation is augmented by Article 14 of the Convention, below, which seeks to ensure that those rights are enjoyed equally and free from discrimination, and which the European Court utilises to interpret substantive Convention rights.

Before considering Article 14 of the Convention, it is worth noting that some provisions of the Convention do allow certain individuals or groups to be treated differently with respect to the enjoyment of their Convention rights. For example, Article 16 of the Convention provides that nothing in Articles 10, 11 and 14 shall be regarded as preventing the High Contracting Parties from imposing restrictions on the political activity of aliens, thus restricting the rights of political aliens to enjoy their rights of freedom of expression, freedom of association and peaceful assembly. In addition, Article 17 provides that nothing in the Convention shall be interpreted as implying for any state, group or person any right to engage in any activity or perform any act aimed at the destruction of any of the rights and freedoms set forth herein or at their limitation to a greater extent than is provided for in the Convention. The provision is aimed particularly at extremist groups, whose primary agenda is the destruction or denial of the human rights and fundamental freedoms of others, and is subject to limitations, most notably that any measures taken under Article 17 must be proportionate to the threat to the rights of others.[14] Further, Article 18 of the Convention provides that the

---

[11] Ibid., at para 10.

[12] Note 10 above.

[13] *East African Asians Case* (1973) 3 EHRR 76.

[14] *Lehideux and Irsoni* v *France* (2000) 30 EHRR 665. In this case the court held that the expression of ideas did not constitute an 'activity' within the meaning of Article 17.

restrictions permitted under this Convention to the said rights and freedoms shall not be applied for any purpose other than those for which they have been prescribed. This provision stops the imposition of restrictions on the enjoyment of Convention rights when such restrictions cannot be justified under the Convention's other provisions, thus eliminating arbitrary discrimination.

Article 14 of the European Convention and freedom from discrimination

Article 14 of the European Convention states that the enjoyment of the rights and freedoms set forth in the Convention shall be secured without discrimination on any ground such as sex, race, colour, language, religion, political or other opinion, national or social origin, association with a national minority, property, birth or other status.

The article seeks to ensure that everyone enjoys the rights and freedoms laid down in the Convention and its protocols, irrespective of their sex, race or colour, etc., and that individuals are not denied that enjoyment, or any appropriate redress for breach on such grounds. Thus, unless otherwise permitted under the specific terms of the Convention,[15] everyone should enjoy equally the right to private life, liberty and freedom of speech and association, etc., and should not, on any of the grounds listed in Article 14, be denied such rights to any greater extent than is normally permitted.

As we shall see, the article is conditional in the sense that once Article 14 and the substantive rights are engaged, and discriminatory treatment is found to have taken place,[16] the Court will examine the facts to see whether there was a legitimate reason for that discriminatory treatment and whether the means employed by that treatment are proportionate to that legitimate aim. Also, as the Court will often show a good deal of deference to the state when reviewing these measures it will enquire as to whether the state has exceeded its margin of appreciation in this respect.[17] In this sense, therefore, the Court will follow a similar methodology than the one employed for other conditional rights such as freedom of expression, although the domestic courts have warned against taking too formal an approach, noting that the questions of whether the article is engaged and whether there was justification for the treatment, often overlap.[18]

Grounds of discrimination covered by Article 14

With respect to the groups covered by Article 14, the article goes beyond discrimination based on sex, race, religion and colour, covering, for example, discrimination based on a person's political association. On the other hand, discrimination on certain grounds, including sex and race, will be viewed more seriously, and consequently it will be more difficult to justify such discrimination when the Court considers whether there are objectively good grounds for any such discrimination (see below). Thus, in *Ghaidan v Mendoza*,[19] the House of Lords made a distinction between grounds which could be called values, such as race, sex and political

---

[15] See, for example, Article 16 of the Convention, considered above which restricts the political activities of aliens.
[16] Including whether the comparable situation was truly analogous.
[17] *Chassagnou and Others v France* (2000) 29 EHRR 615.
[18] *Ghaidan v Mendoza* [2004] 2 AC 557.
[19] Ibid.

association, and others which could be termed 'questions of rationality', such as a person's education, wealth, occupation or ability. In the former case, their Lordships could foresee very few cases where discrimination on such basis would be acceptable and the courts would, thus, subject any such differences to intense scrutiny. In the latter category of cases, however, there may be good public interest reasons for distinguishing between people in those groups and the courts would offer a good deal of discretion to the elected branches of government.

To succeed in a claim under Article 14, the victim must be discriminated against on one of the grounds enumerated above, or on grounds of their 'other status'. The term would include such grounds as the person's sexual orientation,[20] or their disability,[21] and would thus normally relate to the type of grounds specifically listed in the article. The domestic courts have adopted a relatively narrow approach and have held that the phrase 'other status' used in Article 14 refers to a personal characteristic of the applicant, and that such a characteristic had to be sufficiently analogous to the specific grounds that were enumerated in the article itself.[22] Further, in *R (Clift)* v *Secretary of State for the Home Department*,[23] the House of Lords held that although the list of grounds on which discrimination could occur was neither exhaustive nor unlimited, a personal characteristic could not be defined by the differential treatment of which a person had complained. Thus, in that case a prisoner had been treated differently with respect to his release process because of the length of his sentence and thus what he had done, rather than because of any personal characteristic.[24] Similarly, in *R (RJM)* v *Secretary of State for Work and Pensions*[25] the Court of Appeal held that being homeless or a 'rough sleeper' was not a personal characteristic and that accordingly such a person did not have a status for the purposes of Article 14 of the Convention. The Court of Appeal noted that it was relevant that the European Court had not as yet recognised that category and that his 'status' was not analogous to any of the specified grounds in Article 14. Further, although a status was not disqualified under Article 14 simply because it had resulted from personal choice, a status was less likely to be within Article 14 if it derived from personal choice.[26]

This approach may lead to undue inflexibility in specific cases, and in *Clift* v *United Kingdom*[27] the European Court disagreed with the decision of the House of Lords, above, and held that a prisoner who had been discriminated against with respect to his release because of the length of his sentence had in fact been subject to unjustifiable discrimination on grounds of his status within Article 14. The Court held that the applicant's status, a prisoner who had been sentenced to more than 15 years in prison, was one covered by Article 14 as that status did not have to be personal in the sense of being innate and inherent, and that,

---

[20] *Smith and Grady* v *United Kingdom* (2000) 29 EHRR 493; *ADT* v *United Kingdom* (2001) 31 EHRR 33.

[21] *Pretty* v *United Kingdom* (2002) 35 EHRR 1.

[22] *R (S)* v *Chief Constable of South Yorkshire* [2004] 1 WLR 2196.

[23] [2007] 1 AC 484.

[24] See now *Clift* v *United Kingdom, The Times*, 13 July 2010, discussed below. The offending legislation has subsequently been repealed: see now s.145 of the Coroners and Justice Act 2009.

[25] [2006] EWCA Civ 1698.

[26] Consequently, it was held that the withdrawal of disability benefits when he was homeless did not violate that article. Moreover, the Court of Appeal found that if he did come within Article 14 the difference in treatment was justified and it was permissible to distinguish between the homeless and those who did have accommodation.

[27] *The Times*, 13 July 2010.

unlike the situation where the difference in treatment is based purely on the gravity of the offence,[28] his treatment was different because of the length of the sentence. Although the Court recognised that the two were related, it noted that there were other factors that were relevant to the sentence, including the judge's perceived risk to the public of the prisoner. Accordingly, where early release schemes applied to prisoners depended on the length of sentence there was a risk that unless they were objectively justified they may lead to arbitrary detention. With respect to whether the prisoner was in an analogous position with the other prisoners, the Court held that the purpose of excluding the applicant from the early release scheme was not to punish him but to reflect the unacceptability of the risk of his release, and in that case no distinction could be drawn between long-term prisoners serving less than 15 years, long-term prisoners serving 15 years or more, and life prisoners. As the methods of assessing risk were in principle the same for all prisoners, the applicant was in an analogous position with the other categories. Finally, although the Court accepted that the difference in treatment between those serving less than 15 years and those serving more might be capable of justification, in this case the government had failed to demonstrate how the approval of the Secretary of State for the release of the latter group addressed concerns for public security. In addition it was not justifiable to treat these prisoners less favourably than life-sentence prisoners, when lifers often posed greater risks to the public on release.

Relationship of Article 14 with other substantive rights

Article 14 does not provide a 'free-standing' right not to be discriminated against, and any complaint of discriminatory treatment under this article must be related to the alleged violation of another Convention right. Thus, it would not be possible for a person to make a claim under Article 14 in relation to discrimination in employment, or the provision of welfare benefits, unless such treatment constituted an alleged violation of another Convention right such as the right to private or family life or freedom from inhuman or degrading treatment. Consequently the Court has noted that, although the application of Article 14 does not presuppose a *breach* of the substantive provision, there is no room for its application unless the facts at issue fall *within the ambit* of one or more of those provisions.[29]

What is less certain, however, is how the line between ambit and breach is applied in practice. Thus, in some cases, a claim under Article 14 has been rejected where it is decided that the Convention right in question does not cover the substantive claim made by the applicant. For example, in *Choudhury* v *United Kingdom*,[30] the European Commission of Human Rights concluded that freedom to manifest one's religion under Article 9 of the Convention did not include the right of a person to insist that the state pass and maintain sufficient blasphemy laws to protect that person from religious offence. The applicant then complained that domestic law, which only covered the Anglican faith, was discriminatory under Article 14 because it failed to cover faiths other than the established church and thus discriminated against those others with respect to the enjoyment of their right to religion under Article 9. However, the applicant's claim under Article 14 was dismissed on the basis that as the applicant's substantive claim was not covered by Article 9 then it could not be discriminatory to deprive them of that claim by discriminatory law. It is suggested that the

---

[28] *Gerger* v *Turkey* (Application No 24919/94).
[29] *Abdulaziz, Cabales and Balkandali* v *United Kingdom* (1985) 7 EHRR 471.
[30] (1991) 12 HRLJ 172.

Commission's decision in *Choudhury* is flawed because, as we shall see, the Court can find a violation of Article 14 in conjunction with another article even when it is satisfied that the claim under the substantive article would have failed, either on its merits, or because the article would not normally (in the absence of discrimination) impose an obligation on the state to uphold that claim. Indeed, in cases where the Court is satisfied that there has been a violation of the substantive article, it will often refuse to consider in addition the claim under Article 14.[31] Thus, it is clear that the European Court may find a violation of a Convention right when that alleged violation is considered together with a violation of Article 14.

For example, in the *'Belgian Linguistics' case*[32] the European Court stated that although Article 14 had no separate existence, a measure which was in itself in conformity with another Convention article might infringe that article when read in conjunction with Article 14 because of its discriminatory effect. In this case the government had ordained that children taught in schools in specific regions of the country would only be taught in the official language of that region and that public funding would not be available to private schools which did not teach in the official language. A number of parents alleged that this was in violation of the right of education under Article 2 of the First Protocol in conjunction with Article 14. Specifically, they alleged that as French speakers living in particular communes their children were unable to be taught in French, whereas if they had lived in other communes, lessons in French at nursery and primary level would have been available had there been sufficient parental demand. In addition, Dutch classes were available to all children, wherever they resided. The European Court cited the example that, although there was no right under Article 2 of the First Protocol to obtain from the public authorities the creation of a particular kind of educational establishment, nevertheless a state which had set up such an establishment could not, in laying down entrance requirements, take discriminatory measures within the meaning of Article 14. Further, the Court stated that in the present case the articles in conjunction do not guarantee to a child or his parents the right to obtain instruction in a language of his choice, but rather ensures that the right to education is secured by each state to everyone within its jurisdiction without discrimination on the grounds, for instance, of language. The Court thus moved on to examine the possible justifications for the present distinctions and concluded that there was no possible justification for this anomaly.

This case shows that Article 14 can be used to complement the substantive articles and that it should be used as an aid to each article's interpretation.[33] A further example is provided in *Abdulaziz Cabales and Balkandali* v *United Kingdom*,[34] where it was held firstly that there had been no violation of the applicants' right to family life under Articles 8 and 12 of the

---

[31] See, for example, *Smith and Grady* v *United Kingdom* (2000) 29 EHRR 493, where the Court, having found a disproportionate interference with the applicants' private lives by their dismissals from the armed forces on grounds of their homosexuality, did not consider their separate claim under Article 14. In that case, therefore, it was clear that the discriminatory nature of the treatment contributed to the Court's finding on necessity and proportionality under Article 8.

[32] (1968) 1 EHRR 252.

[33] It is suggested, therefore, that unless the applicant's claim clearly does not engage the substantive article, the claim under Article 14 should not be rejected out of hand, but that the Court move on to the question of the necessity of the measure, taking into account, *inter alia*, its discriminatory effect. The decision in *Choudhury* is made even more absurd by the fact that the Convention accepts that the protection of religious sensibilities is a legitimate aim in restricting freedom of speech. See chapter 8 of this text, pages 397–9.

[34] (1985) 7 EHRR 471.

Convention when the government had refused permission for their spouses to enter and remain in the United Kingdom. Nevertheless, the European Court found a violation of Article 14 of the Convention because the rules relating to the entry of such persons into the country were applied more harshly to women who wished to bring their husbands into the country. Thus, although the Court recognised that it was legitimate for a state to construct immigration rules in a manner so as to protect the domestic labour market, that reason was not sufficiently important to justify a difference of treatment based on the grounds of sex.

Further, an act of discrimination within Article 14 can constitute a violation of another article. In the *East African Asians Case*[35] the European Commission of Human Rights held that the discriminatory treatment of the applicants in relation to the government's refusal to allow them to enter and remain permanently in the country constituted inhuman and degrading treatment within Article 3. The Commission held that to single out a group of persons publicly for differential treatment on the basis of race might, in certain circumstances, constitute a special form of affront to human dignity. On the facts, it concluded that the racial discrimination to which the applicants had been subjected constituted an interference with their human dignity, which in the special circumstances – they had been expelled from East Africa as part of an 'Africanisation' policy – amounted to degrading treatment within Article 3. It is worth noting that the Commission placed a special importance on discrimination based on grounds of race, and that the Court has been less willing to find a violation of Article 3 in other cases of discrimination, such as on grounds of sexual orientation.[36] Further, such discrimination is less likely to be justified on objective grounds (see below).

It is also clear that Article 14 covers not only direct discrimination, where the individual or group are treated less favourably on impermissible grounds, but also indirect discrimination, where that person or group suffers discrimination because of the state's refusal to accommodate their differences. For example, in *Pretty* v *United Kingdom*[37] it was argued that English law with respect to suicides discriminated against the applicant on the grounds of her disability because she had been treated in the same manner as others whose situations were fundamentally different, namely those who had the physical capability to attempt suicide and thus avoid criminal liability. Her claim was, therefore, that the law's refusal to allow others to assist her suicide without threat of legal action effectively prevented her from exercising her right of self-determination within Article 8 of the Convention. The European Court accepted that discrimination under Article 14 might occur where states, without an objective and reasonable justification, failed to treat differently persons whose situations are significantly different. However, as we shall see below, the Court found that on the facts the refusal to treat her differently was objectively justified in the interests of the prevention of crime and the rights of others.

Consequently, the European Court has accepted that Article 14 imposes a positive obligation on states to prevent discrimination taking place, including, as above, the obligation to consider the material differences of the individual's status and to reflect such differences in its domestic law. For example, in *Thlimmenos* v *Greece*[38] the European Court found a violation

---

[35] (1973) 3 EHRR 76.

[36] For example, in *Smith and Grady* v *United Kingdom*, n 31, above, the Court was not satisfied that the serious intrusion into the applicants' private sexual lives on grounds of their sexual orientation crossed the threshold necessary to find a breach of Article 3.

[37] (2002) 35 EHRR 1.

[38] (2001) 31 EHRR 15.

of Article 14, in conjunction with Article 9, when the applicant, a Jehovah's Witness, had been refused entrance into the professional body of chartered accountants because he had been previously convicted of refusing to serve in the armed forces. The European Court held that Article 14 applied to the applicant's case because the state had failed to treat him differently according to his religious beliefs. Thus, although Article 9 may not guarantee the right to be a conscientious objector,[39] by failing to distinguish between his objection, which was based on religious conviction and engaged Article 9, and other individuals' objections, which might not engage the person's Convention claims, the law had discriminated against him on grounds of his religion. The Court thus went on to examine whether that failure to treat the applicant differently was justified and proportionate, and found that although it may have been necessary to punish the applicant for his refusal, it was not proportionate that he be barred from a profession for that reason.

The case also provides further evidence that the applicant does not have to show a clear violation, or even full engagement, of another substantive article of the Convention to succeed under Article 14. Thus, notwithstanding the Court's refusal to consider whether Article 9 in fact covered the right to conscientious objection, the Court still found that the applicant had been treated in a discriminatory fashion with respect to his religious beliefs. This decision casts further doubts on the European Commission's decision in *Choudhury*, above, because even if there may be no positive obligation within Article 9 to pass and enforce blasphemy laws in order to protect religious sensibilities, there was no doubt that the applicant's claim in that case was based on his religious views, and that the domestic law deprived him of the right to vindicate those beliefs within the law as he would be able to do so had he been a follower of the established religion.

Protocol No 12 – prohibition on discrimination

This protocol, as yet not ratified by the United Kingdom government, seeks to impose a general prohibition on discrimination, thus establishing a general right of freedom from discrimination. Unlike Article 14, Protocol No 12 thus establishes a principle of equality before the law, similar to the right in Article 26 of the International Covenant on Civil and Political Rights 1966, which provides that all persons are equal before the law and are entitled without any discrimination to the equal protection of the law.[40]

Article 1 of Protocol No 12 provides that the enjoyment of any right set forth by law shall be secured without discrimination on any ground such as sex, race, colour, language, religion, political or other opinion, national or social origin, association with a national minority, property, birth or other status, guaranteeing freedom from discrimination in relation to the enjoyment of any legal right available under domestic law. Article 1 of the protocol also provides that no one shall be discriminated against by a public authority on any such ground.

Under Protocol 12 no one should be discriminated against in the enjoyment of those rights on any of the above grounds, although the state may be able to justify such unequal treatment by reference to justified reasons that have been accepted and applied in relation to Article 14. The protocol would also provide protection in cases such as *Choudhury v United*

---

[39] The European Court refused to consider the issue of whether Article 9 guarantees such a right.

[40] See Moon, The Draft Discrimination Proposal to the European Convention on Human Rights: A Progress Report [2000] EHRLR 49. See also Wintemute, 'Within the Ambit': How Big is the 'Gap' in Article 14 European Convention on Human Rights? (Part 1) [2004] EHRLR 366; Filling the Article 14 'Gap': Government Ratification and Judicial Control of Protocol No 12 ECHR: (Part 2) [2004] EHRLR 484.

Kingdom,[41] where, presumably, the protocol would operate to allow all persons the 'right' to protect their religious sensibilities against blasphemous speech. In such a case the law of blasphemy should be applied generally, unless there was a justifiable reason for not extending it to all, or particular, religious groups.

Questions

What is the purpose and scope of Article 14 of the Convention? How does it interact with other substantive rights and the underlying principles of the European Convention?

How would the ratification of Protocol No 12 enhance protection against discrimination?

Justifiable discrimination

Article 14 is not an absolute right and the European Court has held that Article 14 does not secure to everyone complete equality of treatment in the enjoyment of the rights and freedoms contained in the Convention. For example, in the *'Belgian Linguistic'* case[42] the Court held that despite its general wording, Article 14 did not forbid every difference in treatment in the exercise of the rights and freedoms contained in the Convention. In that case, therefore, the Court noted that the principle of equality in Article 14 is only violated if the difference in treatment has no objective or reasonable justification. Such justification had to be assessed in relation to the aims and effects of the measures under consideration, regard being had to the principles that normally prevail in democratic societies. The Court also held that any such difference must pursue a legitimate aim and that there must be a reasonable relationship of proportionality between the means employed and the aim sought to be realised.

In addition each state would be given a margin of appreciation in deciding the nature and scope of the differences, at the same time allowing the Court to review the conformity of such measures with the Convention. Thus, in the *'Belgian Linguistic' case* the Court stressed that the competent national authorities are frequently confronted with situations and problems which on account of inherent differences call for different legal situations. Accordingly, in deciding whether there has been an arbitrary distinction, the Court should not disregard those legal and factual features which characterise the life of the society in the state which has to answer to the measure in dispute. The national authorities thus remain free to choose the measures which they consider appropriate in those matters which are governed by the Convention, and the Court's review should only concern the conformity of those measures with the requirements of the Convention.

At the very least the European Court will insist that any discriminatory treatment must be based on factors other than the person's sex or other status. For example, in *Willis v United Kingdom,*[43] the applicant applied for the equivalent of a widow's payment and Widowed Mother's Allowance when he was forced to leave his employment to look after his children after his wife died, but no such payments were available to him under domestic law. The Court held that there had been a violation of Article 14 taken in conjunction with Article 1 of the First Protocol to the Convention. The only reason for his being refused the benefits was that he was a man; a female in the same position would have had a right to such payments,

---

[41] (1991) 12 HRLJ 172.
[42] (1968) 1 EHRR 252.
[43] (2002) 35 EHRR 21.

enforceable under domestic law. Further, it considered that the difference in treatment between men and women was not based on any objective and reasonable justification.[44] Similarly, in *PM v United Kingdom*,[45] the European Court held that there had been a violation of Article 14, in conjunction with Article 1 of the First Protocol, when the applicant had been denied tax relief in respect of maintenance payments made to his daughter because he had not been married to the girl's mother. The Court held that there appeared to be no reason to treat him differently from a married father, who would have been eligible for relief. Although the purpose of the deductions served a legitimate aim – to make it easier for married fathers to support a new family – it was difficult to see why unmarried fathers would not have similar difficulties.

However, where the Court is satisfied that there is a legitimate reason for the provision and the initial distinction it will be prepared to give the state a reasonably wide area of discretion with respect to the implementation of that measure. For example, in *Burden and Burden v United Kingdom*,[46] the European Court held that there was no violation of Article 14, in conjunction with Article 1 of the First Protocol when two sisters who had lived together all their lives were unable to apply for exemption from inheritance tax on either's death, as could married couples or (after 2004) civil partners. The Court stressed that states enjoyed a wide margin of appreciation in respect of levying taxes where a balance needed to be struck between the requirement to raise revenue and issues of social policy; the states themselves being in the better position to judge how that balance should be struck and the Court refusing to interfere unless a taxation scheme was manifestly without reasonable foundation or was discriminatory under Article 14. The Court held that the exclusion of sibling relationships from family relationships able to obtain the benefit of the scheme was within the state's margin of appreciation, encouraging as it did stable sexual relationships. The fact that the state could have drawn the dividing line at a different place did not in itself amount to discrimination. The decision was upheld by the Grand Chamber of the European Court,[47] which stressed that the relationship between adult siblings on the one hand and between spouses or civil partners on the other was qualitatively different: the very essence of the sibling relationship being consanguinity, whereas the precise opposite was true of marriage or civil partnership. Marriage conferred a special status on those who entered into it, which was protected by Article 12 of the Convention. The relationships of marriage and civil partnership involved a public undertaking carrying with it rights and obligations of a contractual nature, which set those relationships apart from other types of cohabitation. Accordingly, there had been no discrimination and no violation of Article 14.[48]

---

[44] See also *Booth v United Kingdom*, 3 February 2009, where the Court applied *Willis* and found a breach of Article 1 of the First Protocol in conjunction with Article 14 with respect to the non-payment of widowers' benefits. However, the Court rejected the complaints with respect to the rules on widow's pensions (now abolished) as the rules were objectively justified in order to protect older widows.

[45] (2006) 42 EHRR 45.

[46] (2007) 44 EHRR 51.

[47] (2008) 47 EHRR 38.

[48] Dissenting, Judge Borrego Borrego stated that where a state decided to extend a tax exemption to one extra-marital group, it was obliged to employ at least a minimum of reasonableness in deciding not to apply that benefit to other groups of people in a relationship of similar proximity; in this case, therefore, making consanguinity an impediment in that regard was simply arbitrary. In the Judge's view the Court had disregarded the inherent injustice in the lack of provision of the inheritance tax exemption in the case of close relatives and had failed to consider the issue of the state's margin of appreciation and its limits.

Further, in *Stec and Others* v *United Kingdom*[49] the Grand Chamber of the European Court held that there had been no violation of Article 14 (in conjunction with Article 1 of the First Protocol) when eligibility for earnings-related benefits depended on the differential retirement ages for men and women (65/60). The Grand Chamber held that the ages were introduced to correct the disadvantaged economic position of women and that the retention of those ages was within the state's margin of appreciation. In its view, although that distinction had become outdated and unjustified it was not unreasonable for the state to implement a gradual process to bring about equality with respect to pension ages by the year 2020.[50] The Court has also accepted differential treatment with respect to nationality and residence, again providing a wide margin of appreciation. For example, in *Carson* v *United Kingdom*,[51] the European Court held that the exclusion of pensioners, who were now resident in other countries that did not have arrangements with the United Kingdom, from the cost of living increases in pension benefits was within the very wide margin of appreciation of the state and its economic policies and thus objectively justified under Article 14. The decision was upheld by the Grand Chamber,[52] which also held that people who live outside the United Kingdom were not in a relevantly similar position to residents in the United Kingdom or countries which were party to specific agreements whereby their pensions would be 'uprated'.

These decisions are evidence of the European Court's deference when the discrimination is the result of implementation of economic or social policy which impacts on the individual's welfare or property rights.[53] However, it will be prepared to offer a good deal less discretion in respect to interferences with the individual's other rights, such as privacy and self-determination.[54] Notwithstanding this, in *Pretty* v *United Kingdom*,[55] the Grand Chamber held that there was objective and reasonable justification for not distinguishing in law between those who are and those who are not physically capable of committing suicide. When considering the applicant's claims under Article 8 the Court had already found that there were sound reasons for not introducing into the law exceptions to cater for those who are deemed not to be vulnerable, and similar cogent reasons existed under Article 14 for not seeking to distinguish between those persons. The state was entitled to believe that the building into the law of an exemption for those judged incapable of committing suicide would seriously undermine the protection of life which the 1961 Act was intended to safeguard.[56]

---

[49] (2006) 43 EHRR 47.

[50] See also *Barrow and Others* v *United Kingdom*, *The Times*, 11 September 2006, where the European Court held that there was no violation of Article 14 of the Convention when the applicant claimed that her invalidity benefit stopped at 60, whereas for a man it would have continued until 65. In the Court's view the state was entitled to operate a different retirement age for men and women, and was entitled to change that policy slowly and gradually.

[51] (2009) 48 EHRR 41.

[52] (2010) 51 EHRR 13.

[53] See also *R (RJM)* v *Secretary of State for Work and Pensions* [2009] 1 AC 311, where the House of Lords held that the exclusion from disability premiums of those who were without accommodation was justified and not in breach of Article 14 as the condition of accommodation would encourage those seeking support to get shelter.

[54] The position of Article 14 with respect to the control of private sexual life, including the position of homosexuals and transsexuals, is covered in the final section of this chapter.

[55] (2002) 35 EHRR 1.

[56] See also *AL (Serbia)* v *Home Secretary* [2007] HRLR 7, where it was held that it was justifiable discrimination under Article 14 to distinguish between an asylum seeker who was part of a family and one (as the applicant) who was not for the purpose of adopting an amnesty policy.

Despite the latitude given to states under Article 14, the courts (both European and domestic) will insist that there is a legitimate reason for any discrimination and that there is cogent evidence that such a distinction is capable of achieving its objective. This will be particularly so where the restriction impinges on fundamental human rights and is based on grounds, such as race or nationality. Thus, in *A v Secretary of State for the Home Department*[57] the House held that the measures allowing detention without trial of foreign terrorist suspects were unlawful under Article 14. The provisions allowed foreign nationals to be deprived of their liberty but not UK nationals, and the individuals were therefore treated differently because of their nationality or immigration status. Although their Lordships accepted that some distinction might be made between those groups in an immigration context, such a distinction could not form the legitimate basis of depriving one group of their Convention right to liberty of the person as protected by Article 5. In contrast, in *AL (Serbia) v Secretary of State for the Home Department*,[58] the House of Lords held that it was not in breach of Article 14 to offer an indefinite leave to stay concession to children who entered the country with their families, but not to those who entered the country without them. Although the latter group had been discriminated against on grounds of their 'other status' within Article 14, the difference in treatment was objectively justified as it was implemented in order to reduce the backlog of asylum claims and to benefit family groups; the favourable treatment given to family groups being an aspect of the respect afforded by the state to family life under the Convention. The Court was not therefore looking at differential treatment in relation to exactly the same Convention rights of the applicants and the comparators, as the latter group's private *and family* rights were at issue.

Questions

What guidelines has the European Court of Human Rights established for the purpose of determining when it is permissible to discriminate against an individual or group in the enjoyment of their Convention rights?

What role does and should the margin of appreciation play in this respect?

Freedom from discrimination in domestic law

In addition to the protection provided by Article 14 of the European Convention (above) – given effect to via the Human Rights Act 1998 and applying to the enjoyment of the rights laid down in the Convention – domestic law (and various EU laws) provide specific protection against discrimination on particular grounds, making it unlawful to discriminate on such grounds, empowering certain agencies to enforce those laws, and providing the victim with some form of legal remedy.

Domestic anti-discrimination laws

At present the domestic law contains provisions prohibiting discrimination (by both state agencies and private individuals or bodies) on grounds of sex,[59] race, colour, nationality and

---

[57] [2005] 2 AC 68.
[58] [2008] 1 WLR 1434.
[59] The Sex Discrimination Act 1975 and the Equal Pay Act 1970.

national origins,[60] religion,[61] disability,[62] age,[63] gender reassignment[64] and sexual orientation.[65] Many of these provisions have been introduced to comply with both the European Convention on Human Rights and EU law, and in addition to enforcing specific domestic laws both Article 14 and relevant EU law can be relied on directly by victims in the domestic courts.

In addition to the above provisions which provide the victim with a remedy for discriminatory treatment, certain legislation makes it unlawful to incite hatred against or, cause harassment alarm or distress to, certain groups.[66] This criminal legislation provides further protection to such groups, ensuring their safety and the enjoyment of their Convention rights free from unreasonable harassment and outrage. This protection now extends to hatred based on a person's sexual orientation. Section 126 of the Criminal Justice and Immigration Act 2008 makes it unlawful to incite hatred on grounds of a person's sexual orientation, covering threatening words or materials which incite hatred against homosexual, lesbian, bisexual, transgendered and heterosexual people.[67]

The Equality Acts 2006 and 2010

The purposes of the Equality Act 2006 were 'to make provision for the establishment of the Commission for Equality and Human Rights (below); to make provision about discrimination on grounds of religion and belief;[68] to enable provision to be made about discrimination on the grounds of sexual orientation;[69] to impose duties relating to sex discrimination on persons performing public functions; and to amend the Disability Discrimination Act 1995.' Although the Act provides for a more effective and comprehensive system of enforcement of anti-discrimination law it did not provide a comprehensive consolidation of various anti-discrimination provisions. However, the Equality Act 2010 does consolidate the provisions of the 2006 Act and provides a full list of 'protected characteristics' that are protected against discrimination, harassment or victimisation. These characteristics are age, ability, gender reassignment, marriage and civil partnership, pregnancy and maternity, race, religion or belief, sex, and sexual orientation,[70] and subsequent sections define those characteristics.[71] Further, the 2010 Act places a new duty on public bodies to consider socio-economic disadvantages when making strategic decisions about how to exercise their functions,[72] and a duty on public

---

[60] The Race Relations Act 1976.

[61] The Employment Equality (Religion or Belief) Regulations 2003.

[62] Disability Discrimination Acts 1995 and 2005.

[63] Employment (Equality) Age Regulations 2006.

[64] The Sex Discrimination (Gender Reassignment) Regulations 1999 (adding s.2A to the Sex Discrimination Act 1975) and the Gender Recognition Act 2004.

[65] Employment Equality (Sexual Orientation) Regulations 2003, and the Equality Act (Sexual Orientation) Regulations 2007 (SI 2007/1263).

[66] These offences are considered in chapters 10 and 12 with respect to the right of assembly and association and the right to religion.

[67] The offence caries a maximum sentence of seven years' imprisonment and any action must be brought with the consent of the Attorney-General.

[68] This aspect of the Act is discussed in chapter 12, pages 679–80.

[69] See the Equality Act (Sexual Orientation) Regulations 2007 (SI 2007/1263), which came into force in April 2007.

[70] Section 3 Equality Act 2010.

[71] Sections 5–12 Equality Act 2010.

[72] Section 1 Equality Act 2010.

bodies and those carrying out public functions to ensure that their functions are carried out in a manner which avoids, *inter alia*, any conduct which is prohibited by the Act.[73]

The Equality and Human Rights Commission[74]

As we have seen, the central provisions of the Human Rights Act 1998 attempt to enhance the powers of the judiciary to enforce Convention rights and thus to provide for more coherent and stable human rights enforcement in the United Kingdom. However, those provisions are primarily concerned with enhancing judicial powers and the rights of victims to more effective legal redress. In addition there have been moves to improve the human rights culture on a more general level, and to provide a system whereby the state's duties to respect human rights under both the 1998 Act and in international law is monitored. In this respect the work of the Joint Parliamentary Committee on Human Rights has provided invaluable information and advice to the government on the operation of the Act and the potential compatibility of government policy and parliamentary legislation with human rights.[75]

More specific to this section of the book, s.1 of the Equality Act 2006 creates a body corporate known as the Equality and Human Rights Commission, and s.3 of the Act states that it shall exercise its functions with a view to encouraging and supporting the development of a society in which there is respect for and protection of each individual's human rights and the dignity and worth, where each individual has an equal opportunity to participate in society, and where there is mutual respect between groups based on the understanding and valuing of diversity and on shared respect for equality and human rights. Those very laudable yet general objectives are then supplemented by more specific functions with respect to promoting understanding of the importance of equality and diversity,[76] human rights,[77] and good relations among members of different groups and members of groups and others.[78]

The Commission will replace the existing bodies responsible for monitoring and enforcing anti-discrimination laws (the Equal Opportunities Commission, the Commissioner for Racial Equality and the Disability Rights Commissioner). It is then given specific powers to monitor the effectiveness of equality and human rights legislation,[79] including the power to issue codes of practice with respect to existing legislation on discrimination.[80] The Commission will take over the previous bodies' powers to offer legal assistance to persons bringing legal actions in these areas. However, although the Commission is given a remit with respect to the recognition and protection of human rights (s.9), it will lack the enforcement powers that it possesses with respect to the enforcement of anti-discrimination law (above). In that sense, therefore, there will be no formal mechanism by which Convention or other human rights are upheld under the 1998 Act or the law generally.

---

[73] Part 2, sections 149–57 Equality Act 2010.

[74] It was decided to replace the title of the Commission for Equality and Human Rights so as to place emphasis on its role with respect to equality and human rights, rather than the fact that it was a commission.

[75] For an explanation of the Joint Committee's remit and a critical analysis of its work, see Klug and Widbore, Breaking New Ground: The Joint Committee on Human Rights and the Role of Parliament in Human Rights Compliance [2007] EHRLR 231. The Committee's website (www.parliament.uk/parliamentary_committtees/joint_committee_on_human_rights.cfm) provides full details of its work and documentation.

[76] Section 8 Equality Act 2006.

[77] Section 9 Equality Act 2006.

[78] Section 10 Equality Act 2006.

[79] Sections 11 and 12 Equality Act 2006.

[80] Section 14 Equality Act 2006.

Questions

To what extent is it necessary to augment the Convention right not to be discriminated against by specific domestic laws on anti-discrimination?

How effective will the new Commission on Human Rights and Equality be in this respect?

Sexual privacy and freedom from discrimination

This section of the chapter focuses on discrimination on the grounds of a person's private sexual life or choices. In particular, it examines how Article 14 of the European Convention, and other EU and domestic law, has been used to combat and address discrimination on grounds of sexual orientation and gender reassignment, exploring the potential of anti-discrimination principles on the protection of the rights of homosexuals and transsexuals. As this chapter focuses on Article 14 of the Convention, this section will begin by examining the relevant case law of the European Court in these areas before examining how domestic law has responded to that case law and the principles of equality contained in both Article 14 and relevant EU law.

The criminalisation of certain sexual activity, including the censoring of sexual material, engages the right to private sexual life as guaranteed under Article 8 of the European Convention. Further, as the individual should not be discriminated against by reason of their sexuality or sexual activity, either by the enforcement against them of the criminal law, or by a reduction of legal and civil status because of their preference or orientation, Article 14 of the Convention is clearly engaged. The case law of the European Court of Human Rights has been instrumental in challenging such legal restrictions and the limited legal and civil status of homosexuals and transsexuals, and in turn many of its judgments have effected legal change in domestic law.[81]

The right to private sexual life and the European Convention

As we have seen in chapter 11 of this text on privacy, the case law of the European Convention clearly establishes the right to a private sexual life,[82] recognising that sexual life is one of the most intimate aspects of an individual's private life and subjecting any interference with that to rigorous scrutiny. Nevertheless, the European Court has sanctioned interference with private sexuality on grounds such as health and morals, and in *Laskey, Jaggard and Brown* v *United Kingdom*[83] it held that in certain circumstances a state was entitled to regulate and criminalise such behaviour, even where it took place between consenting adults.[84] In that case

---

[81] For general discussion in this area, see Waaldijk and Clapham, *Homosexuality: A European Community Issue* (Martinus Nijhoff 1993); Wintemute, *Sexual Orientation and Human Rights: The US Constitution, the ECHR and the Canadian Charter* (Clarendon 1995); Moran, *Sexuality, Morality and Justice* (Cassell 1999); Wintemute and Andenas, *Legal Recognition of Same-Sex Partnerships* (Hart 2001).

[82] *Dudgeon* v *United Kingdom* (1982) 4 EHRR 149.

[83] (1997) 24 EHRR 39.

[84] The details of the case are given in chapter 11 of this text, pages 574–5. See also *KA and AD* v *Belgium*, decision of the European Court of Human Rights, 17 February 2005, where it was held that there had been no violation of Article 8 when two individuals who had taken part in filmed sado-masochistic acts had been convicted, fined, suspended from public service and imprisoned for assault occasioning actual bodily harm.

the Court held that not all sexual activities were entirely a matter of private morality and that the state was entitled to regulate the infliction of serious physical harm via the criminal law.[85] Notwithstanding this discretion on the part of the state, the Court will ensure that such laws are not enforced in a discriminatory manner, for example differentiating between sexual orientation.[86]

Homosexuality and the European Convention on Human Rights

Legal systems and constitutions may seek to differentiate between heterosexual and homo-sexual activity,[87] and the European Convention has been used on numerous occasions to challenge those distinctions and subject them to the principles of legality and necessity. A number of domestic laws and practices have impinged on the enjoyment of Convention rights by homosexuals, many of which have been tested under the European Convention.[88] As we shall see, although some of these provisions have been amended following European Court rulings – in particular the Sexual Offences Act 2003 rid domestic law of many of these discriminatory provisions – the European Court has been less proactive in addressing other forms of sexual orientation discrimination in other aspects of family and social life.

Although the European Court has recognised an individual's right to private sexual life and sexual choice, it has not prohibited all legal regulation with respect to one's sexual orientation. In *Dudgeon v United Kingdom*[89] the European Court held that some regulation and inequality of treatment might be justified. The applicant was a practising homosexual living in Northern Ireland where the law placed an absolute prohibition on, *inter alia*, acts of buggery, irrespective of the age of the individuals. The European Court was satisfied that there had been an interference with the applicant's private life. According to the Court, the main-tenance in force of the impugned legislation constituted a continuing interference with the applicant's right to respect for his private life, which includes his right to his sexual life. The Court was also satisfied that the restriction was in accordance with law and that it pursued a legitimate aim under Article 8(2). In the Court's view it was artificial to draw a distinction between 'the protection of the rights and freedoms of others' and 'the protection of morals'. The latter may imply the safeguarding of the moral ethos or moral standards of the society as a whole, but may also cover protection of the moral interests and welfare of a particular

---

[85] In *Pay v Lancashire Probation Service, The Times*, 7 November 2003, the Employment Appeal Tribunal held that an employer was entitled to dismiss an employee in connection with his sado-masochistic activities outside work; although Article 10 of the Convention was engaged, the dismissal was a proportionate response to those activities. It was also held that Article 8 of the Convention was not engaged because his activities had been published on a website and did not therefore impact on his private and family life.

[86] *ADT v United Kingdom* (2001) 31 EHRR 33, examined below.

[87] In the United States it was held in *Bowers v Hardwick* (1986) 478 US 186, that the rights under the 5th and 14th Amendments – that no person may be deprived of their liberty (which includes their right to privacy and private life) – bore no resemblance to the claimed constitutional right of homosexuals to engage in acts of sodomy. However, in *Romer v Evans* (1996) 517 US 620, the Supreme Court invalidated an amendment to the Colorado constitution, which made it an offence for any state body to recognise homosexuality, lesbianism or bisexuality as categories that could be granted protection against discrimination. It was held that if the concept of equal protection means anything it must mean that a bare desire to harm a politically unpopular group cannot constitute a legitimate governmental interest.

[88] See *Dudgeon v United Kingdom* and *ADT v United Kingdom*, considered below.

[89] (1982) 4 EHRR 149.

section of society. According to the Court, some degree of regulation of male homosexual conduct, by means of the criminal law, can be justified as necessary. The overall function of the law in this field is to preserve public order and decency and to protect the citizen from what is offensive or injurious; this necessity may even extend to consensual acts committed in private, notably where there is a call to provide sufficient safeguards against exploitation and corruption of others, particularly those who are specially vulnerable because they are young, weak in body or mind, inexperienced or in a state of special physical, official or economic dependence. The Court thus accepted the European Commission's opinion, that in so far as the applicant was prevented from having sexual relations with males less than 21 years of age any restriction was justified as being necessary for the protection of the rights of others.

With respect to whether the restrictions were necessary in a democratic society, the Court noted that the nature of the aim of the restriction and the nature of the activities involved affected the scope of the margin of appreciation. The present case concerned a most intimate aspect of private life and accordingly there must exist particularly serious reasons before interferences on the part of public authorities can be legitimate for the purpose of Article 8(2). In comparison with the time when the laws were enacted there had been an increased tolerance and understanding shown towards homosexuals. Thus, although there was evidence that the majority of the population may have disapproved of homosexuality there was no evidence to suggest that the practice of homosexuality had been injurious to moral standards or that there had been any public demand for stricter enforcement of the law. In those circumstances, there was no pressing social need to make such acts criminal offences.[90]

Although the decision in *Dudgeon* contained a strong warning to states regarding the imposition of majority norms on private sexual behaviour, the judgment still left states the right to distinguish between heterosexual and homosexual conduct.[91] Although this margin of appreciation is still available, the decision of the European Commission in *Sutherland* v *United Kingdom*[92] suggests that the state must provide strong evidence of a pressing social need before making such a distinction. In that case the Commission found that the disparate age of consent in the United Kingdom regarding homosexual sex was in violation of Article 8. In coming to its decision, the Commission found that medical evidence showed that a person's sexual orientation was decided and settled at the age of 16, and that men between 16 and 21 were not in need of special protection from homosexual recruitment. Thus, it could not accept that society was entitled to indicate disapproval of homosexual conduct or that its preference for a heterosexual lifestyle constituted an objective, reasonable justification for an inequality of treatment under the criminal law.[93] The decision in *Sutherland* suggests that the Court is no longer prepared to afford the state any substantial discretion in

---

[90] Similar judgments were made in *Norris* v *Ireland* (1988) 13 EHRR 186 and *Modinos* v *Cyprus* (1993) 16 EHRR 485, where the Court held that the mere existence of the laws constituted a violation of the applicants' right to private life.

[91] See *Frette* v *France* (2004) 38 EHRR 1, discussed below with respect to adoption rights of homosexuals.

[92] *The Times*, 13 April 2001 (Application No 25186/94). The applicant had not been charged under the Sexual Offences Act in 1956, but claimed that the existence of the law and its discriminatory effects was an interference with his right to private life and that he and his partner worried about the possible enforcement of the law.

[93] The case was referred to the European Court of Human Rights, but was struck out following a friendly settlement whereby the government secured the passing of the Sexual Offences (Amendment) Act 2000, which equalised the age of consent for both homosexual and heterosexual sex.

this area, particularly where there is no evidence that such restrictions reflect the morality of the general public.[94] Thus, in *BB v United Kingdom*,[95] it was held that there had been a violation of Article 14 in conjunction with Article 8 when the applicant had been charged with buggery of a 16-year-old man, contrary to s.12 of the Sexual Offence Act 1956. Although the law has subsequently been changed so as to equalise the age of consent for homosexual and heterosexual sex, the applicant had been charged and convicted before the change in the law and had thus been subjected to that discriminatory law which violated his Convention rights.

Consequently, domestic law should not make such arbitrary distinctions with respect to sexual activity in either the criminal law or prosecution policies. In *ADT v United Kingdom*,[96] the applicant had been charged under s.13 of the Sexual Offences Act 1956 with committing an act of gross indecency with four other men, and as more than two people were present, the defence that the participants were over 18 and that they consented was not available. The applicants argued that there had been a violation of Article 8 in conjunction with Article 14 because the law only applied to acts between men. The Court held that although state interference might be justified where groups of men gather to perform sexual activity,[97] in this case the applicant had been involved in sexual activities with a restricted number of friends and it was unlikely that others would become aware of what was going on. In this case although the activities were on videotape, the applicant had been prosecuted for the activities themselves and as the activities were private the margin of appreciation would be narrow. The reasons submitted for the maintenance in force of laws criminalising homosexual acts between men in private, and the prosecution and conviction in the present case, were not sufficient to justify the legislation and the interference. Because the Court found a violation of Article 8, it did not deem it necessary to consider the applicant's claim under Article 14. However, as the fact that the legislation only applied to men was taken into account by the Court in assessing necessity under Article 8, it is clear that there was a violation of Article 14.[98]

The European Court has also protected homosexuals from discriminatory treatment outside the criminal law. Thus, in *Smith and Grady v United Kingdom* and *Lustig-Prean and Beckett v United Kingdom*,[99] it held that the investigations into the applicants' sexual orientation, and their subsequent dismissals from the armed forces on the grounds of their homosexuality, constituted especially grave interferences with the applicants' private lives, which were not justified on the grounds of national security and public order. In the Court's view, there was no substantive evidence that the applicants' homosexuality affected the performance of their functions, and the negative attitudes of heterosexual personnel towards homosexuals could not justify the interferences in question.[100] The Convention, and other international instruments,

---

[94] See, for example, the Court's decision in *SL v Austria* (2003) 37 EHRR 799, where it was held that differential age limits for heterosexual and homosexual sex were no longer justified and thus were contrary to Article 14 of the Convention. The Court noted that although the domestic law had been upheld previously as proportionate, subsequent views of the law had made the laws incompatible. The relevant law had, in fact, been repealed subsequent to the applicant's convictions.

[95] *The Times*, 18 February 2004.

[96] (2001) 31 EHRR 33.

[97] See *Laskey, Jaggard and Brown v United Kingdom*, n 83 above.

[98] The offence was repealed in the Sexual Offences Act 2003 (Schedule 7).

[99] (2000) 29 EHRR 493; (2000) 29 EHRR 548.

[100] See also *Perkins and R v United Kingdom* (Application Nos 43208/98 and 44875/98), decision of the European Court of Human Rights, 22 October 2002.

can also impose a positive obligation on the state to prevent discrimination and persecution on grounds of sexual orientation. For example, the deportation of a homosexual who would face persecution in the receiving state could constitute a breach of Articles 3 and 8 of the European Convention as well as being in breach of international law relating to refugees.[101]

Despite these decisions, the European Court has not embraced the notion of full equality for homosexuals in the enjoyment of their Convention rights and has accepted that certain differential treatment may be justified within the state's margin of appreciation. For example, in *Frette* v *France*,[102] it was held that it was permissible under Article 14 to distinguish between heterosexuals and homosexuals with respect to adoption rights. The applicant, a homosexual, had applied for prior authorisation to adopt a child but had been refused because of his 'choice of lifestyle'. This decision had been upheld by the domestic courts on the grounds that despite his clear personal qualities and high natural aptitude for bringing up children, his lifestyle did not provide the requisite family, educational and psychological safeguards for adopting a child. The European Court held that the right to adopt a child was not guaranteed under Article 12 (the right to marry), but engaged Article 8. Nevertheless, the Court held that because there was little consensus among the member states as to adoption rights of homosexuals it should provide a wide margin of appreciation to the respondents in determining the interests of such children. Accordingly, by a bare majority, it found that the state had not violated Articles 8 and 14.[103]

This approach, and the decision in *Frette*, has now been questioned both by the European Court itself and the domestic courts. Thus, in *EB* v *France*,[104] the European Court held that there had been a violation of Article 14 (in conjunction with Article 8) when the applicant – a homosexual living with another woman – had had her request for adoption refused on the grounds of the lack of paternal referent. In the Court's view the grounds for the refusal were found to be based implicitly and unreasonably on her homosexuality and as such *prima facie* in breach of Article 14. The Court held that the lack of a paternal referent in the household was not *necessarily* a problem in itself and could lead to an arbitrary refusal, serving as a pretext for rejecting the application on the ground of sexual orientation. Although the applicant's partner's ambivalent attitude to adoption was relevant, and the child's best interests required detailed examination of the role she would play in the child's daily life, in that respect sexual orientation was irrelevant. On the facts, the applicant's sexual orientation had consistently been at the centre of the domestic authorities' deliberations on her application and was a decisive factor in the refusal of her application. Further, the Court noted that such grounds alone could not be objectively justified as state law allowed applications from homosexuals, thus making this decision clearly arbitrary. This more liberal approach was adopted by the domestic courts, and in *Re P and Others*[105] the House of Lords held that it was held that the Northern Ireland courts had acted unlawfully and in breach of Articles 8 and 14

---

[101] In *HJ (Iran)* v *Secretary of State for the Home Department* [2010] 3 WLR 386, the Supreme Court held that a homosexual fearing persecution would still be a refugee under Article 1 of the Status of Refugees 1951 (United Nations) even if he could in reality live discreetly as a homosexual in that county and thus be free from harm.

[102] (2004) 38 EHRR 1.

[103] The Court did, however, find a violation of Article 6 as the applicant had been precluded from taking part in the deliberations of the proceedings.

[104] (2008) 47 EHRR 21.

[105] [2009] 1 AC 173.

when they had refused to grant adoptive rights to a couple because they were not married. Their Lordships held that Article 14 of the Adoption (Northern Ireland) Order 1987 unjustifiably discriminated against unmarried couples and that to apply a 'bright line' rule in such a case was irrational, defied everyday experience and was contrary to the main principle of the Order, which was to consider whether adoption by particular persons would be in the best interests of the child. Although the adoption of children was a matter of social policy, often best left to parliament, parliament was not allowed to discriminate on an irrational basis. In coming to that decision the House of Lords relied on *EB v France*, which in their Lordships' view overrode *Frette v France* and pointed strongly in favour of the view that discrimination against persons on the grounds of marital status in this area was not acceptable.

A similarly liberal approach was evident in the case of *Karner v Austria*,[106] where it was held that the denial of a homosexual partner of his right to succeed a tenancy shared by him and his partner before his partner's death was in violation of Articles 8 and 14 of the Convention. The Court noted that the case raised the question of the respect for human rights and the elucidation and safeguarding of the standards of human rights protection under the Convention. Noting that, but for his sexual orientation, he could have been accepted as a life companion entitled to succeed to the lease under domestic law it concluded that the respondent state had not offered convincing and weighty reasons justifying the applicant's exclusion from the protection of the domestic law and that accordingly there had been a breach of Article 14 in conjunction with Article 8.

Domestic law has also gone some way to redress discrimination against homosexuals with respect to their right to marry and to private and family life. Such liberalism was evident to a certain extent in the pre-Human Rights Act era. For example, in *Fitzpatrick v Sterling Housing Association Ltd*[107] the House of Lords held that although a same-sex couple could not be said to be living as husband and wife for the purposes of the Rent Act 1977, the couple could be regarded as living as members of a family, that phrase being applied in the light of modern and unprejudiced opinion.[108] Similarly, there was evidence of a more liberal judicial approach with regard to adoption and custody rights. Thus, even though the Adoption Act 1976 restricted joint adoption to a married heterosexual couple, it was held that although issues such as sexual orientation could be taken into consideration, they would not be allowed to prevail over what was in the best interests of the child.[109]

In the post-Human Rights era, the courts have a duty to interpret and apply domestic law in this area in a Convention-friendly manner, taking into account the case law of the European Court. As a result the decision in *Fitzpatrick* (above) was rationalised by the House of Lords in *Ghaidan v Mendoza*,[110] where it was held that the Rent Act 1977 was incompatible with Article 14 of the European Convention, but could be interpreted to give a homosexual

---

[106] (2003) 38 EHRR 44.

[107] [1993] 3 WLR 1113.

[108] See the approach of the European Court of Human Rights in *X, Y and Z v United Kingdom* (1997) 24 EHRR 143. See now *Ghaidan v Mendoza*, considered below.

[109] See *Re W (A Minor) (Adoption: Homosexual Adopter)* [1997] 3 All ER 620. In *Re G (Children)* [2006] 2 FLR 614, the Court of Appeal held that the non-biological mother of children conceived during a same-sex relationship should be granted primary care of those children. On appeal to the House of Lords it was held that the Court of Appeal had allowed the unusual facts of the case to distract itself from universally accepted principles relating to the paramount interests of the child: [2006] 1 WLR 2305.

[110] [2004] 2 AC 557.

the right to inherit his partner's tenancy. According to the majority of their Lordships it was possible to interpret the words 'living together as man and wife' in paragraph 2(2) of the Housing Act 1977, thus avoiding the conflict with the individual's Convention rights.

The Civil Partnership Act 2004 and the right to private and family life

The decision in *Mendoza*, and the desire to arrest discrimination against homosexuals with respect to the enjoyment of their rights to private and family life led to the passing of the Civil Partnership Act 2004,[111] which gave legal recognition and protection to same-sex relationships in areas such as housing, pensions and inheritance, and allowed lesbian and homosexual couples to register their partnership in a civil ceremony.[112] The Act allows two people to register a civil partnership by signing a formal civil partnership document;[113] a civil partnership being defined as a relationship between two people of the same sex formed when they register as civil partners of each other.[114] Under the Act non-religious premises must be used, although under the Equality Act 2010 the prohibition of such premises being used is lifted, although there is no obligation on any religious organisation to host such ceremonies.[115]

Before the 2004 Act was passed the domestic courts had upheld differential treatment between homosexuals and heterosexuals as compatible with the European Convention. For example, in *M v Secretary of State for Work and Pensions*[116] a majority of the House of Lords held that the statutory framework for assessing child support contributions for non-resident parents, which distinguished between parents in heterosexual and homosexual relationships, was not in violation of Article 8. The majority held that the link with family life in the present case was tenuous and that the Convention did not demand entire equality with respect to the treatment of homosexuals. In the majority's view the provisions struck a fair balance and it was within the state's margin of appreciation and given the passing of the Civil Partnership Act, above, the court's decision in this case would have had little if any retrospective effect.[117] However, recently the European Court found that such differences were incompatible with Article 1 of the First Protocol of the Convention and that such discrimination was not justified. In *JM v United Kingdom*[118] the Court held that Article 1 was certainly engaged as the sums paid were taken from the applicant's own financial sources; it declined to rule on the engagement of Article 8. With respect to Article 14 the Court noted that the only reason for the difference in treatment was the sexual orientation of the applicant, and that as the purpose of the domestic law was to avoid placing an excessive burden on absent parents living in new circumstances, it could see no reason for such difference in treatment. In particular, the Court could see no reason why the applicant's housing costs should be taken into account differently than would have been the case had she formed a relationship with a man. This discrimination has now been removed by the 2004 Act, but the Court saw that as immaterial in finding a breach in this case.

[111] For a detailed coverage of the Act and its passage and interpretation, see Bamforth, Malik and O'Cinnedide, Discrimination Law: Theory and Context (Sweet and Maxwell 2007), at pages 726–45.
[112] See also s.2 of the Human Fertilisation and Embryology Act 2008, which provides both women in a lesbian relationship with the legal status of a parent when one of them has a child following fertility treatment.
[113] Section 2 Civil Partnership Act 2004.
[114] Section 1(1) Civil Partnership Act 2004.
[115] Section 202 Equality Act 2010.
[116] [2006] 2 AC 91.
[117] The case is noted by Wintemute in [2006] EHRLR 722.
[118] *The Times*, 11 October 2010.

Despite Convention case law and the passing of the Act it is clear that not all inequality in this area will fall foul of the Convention. Thus, in *Wilkinson v Kitzinger and Another*,[119] it was held that the domestic courts did not have a duty to recognise a same-sex marriage entered into validly under Canadian law as equally valid in English law. It was noted that the Civil Partnership Act 2004 has been passed by parliament to provide the same benefits to civil marriages as traditional ones, save the name, and that this was within the state's margin of appreciation and thus not in violation of Articles 8 or 14.[120] Parliament had passed this law not because it felt obliged to comply with rulings of the European Court but as a policy choice. It had declined to alter the deep-rooted and almost universal recognition of marriage as a relationship between a man and a woman while at the same time recognising the right of same-sex couples to respect for their private and family life. The Act accorded such couples all the rights, responsibilities, benefits and advantages of civil marriage save the name and to remove all the legal, social and economic disadvantages suffered by them. To the extent that by reason of that distinction it discriminated against such partners, that discrimination was legitimate, reasonable and proportionate and fell within the state's margin of appreciation.

This approach appears to be consistent with the jurisprudence of the European Court of Human Rights, and in *Schalk and Kopf v Austria*[121] it was held that a refusal to allow a same-sex couple to enter into a contract of marriage was not in violation of their Convention rights. With respect to their claim under Article 12, the Court accepted their argument that in today's society the procreation of children was no longer a decisive element in a civil marriage, and that the inability to conceive a child could not be regarded in itself as removing the right to marry.[122] However, that finding did not oblige member states to provide for access to marriage for same-sex couples. The Court observed that among Council of Europe member states there was no consensus regarding same-sex marriage. Further, although Article 9 of the Charter of Fundamental Rights of the European Union did not include a reference to men and women, thus possibly allowing for the conclusion that the right to marry must not in all circumstances be limited to marriage between two persons of the opposite sex, the Charter left the decision whether or not to allow same-sex marriage to regulation by member states' national law.[123] The Court thus stressed that national authorities were best placed to assess and respond to the needs of society in this field, given that marriage had deep-rooted social and cultural connotations differing largely from one society to another, and concluded that Article 12 did not impose an obligation to grant a same-sex couple like the applicants access to marriage.

With respect to the claim under Article 14 the Court firstly concluded that the relationship of the applicants, a cohabiting same-sex couple living in a stable partnership, fell within the notion of 'family life', just as the relationship of a different-sex couple in the same situation would. Accordingly, different treatment based on sexual orientation required particularly serious reasons by way of justification. Although it had to be assumed that same-sex couples were just as capable as different-sex couples of entering into stable committed relationships, having regard to the conclusion reached that Article 12 did not impose an obligation on states to grant same-sex couples access to marriage, the Court was unable to find that such an

[119] *The Times*, 21 August 2006.
[120] The case is noted by Booth and Burke in [2007] Fam Law 253.
[121] Application No 30141/04.
[122] Applying *X, Y and Z United Kingdom* (1997) 24 EHRR 143.
[123] Article 9 of the Charter provides that 'The right to marry and the right to found a family shall be guaranteed in accordance with the national laws governing the exercise of these rights'.

obligation could be derived from Article 14 taken in conjunction with Article 8. It did not follow that if a state chose to provide same-sex couples with an alternative means of recognition, it was obliged to confer a status on them which corresponded to marriage in every respect. The fact that Austrian law (the Registered Partnership Act) retained some substantial differences compared to marriage in respect of parental rights corresponded largely to the trend in other member states, and in the present case the Court did not have to examine every one of these differences in detail. The decision is obviously pertinent to UK law in this area and it would appear that the domestic legislation is within the margin of appreciation allowed by each member state.[124]

> **Questions**
> How instrumental has the European Convention and the European Court of Human Rights been in recognising the human rights of homosexuals?
> To what extent should such individuals and groups be treated with complete equality under the Convention and within the law?

Homosexuals and European Community law

Article 141 (formerly Article 119) of the EC Treaty provides that each member state shall ensure that the principle of equal pay for male and female workers for equal work or work of equal value is applied. In addition, Equal Treatment Directive 76/207 provided that there shall be no discrimination whatsoever on the grounds of sex either directly or indirectly by reference in particular to marital or family status.[125] These provisions gave rise to claims that it would be unlawful to discriminate on grounds of sexual orientation, but in *R v Ministry of Defence, ex parte Smith*,[126] the Court of Appeal held that the Directive only applied to gender discrimination,[127] and this was confirmed by the European Court of Justice in *Grant v South West Trains*,[128] which held that the equal treatment directive applies to discrimination based on sex gender, and not sexual identity or orientation.[129]

This position was also accepted by the domestic courts in the post-Human Rights Act era, and in *Advocate-General for Scotland v MacDonald*[130] the House of Lords held that the word 'sex' could not be interpreted to cover discrimination on the grounds of a person's sexual

---

[124] In addition, a heterosexual couple are to take their case to the European Court, challenging a registry office's refusal to conduct a civil partnership ceremony: Couple Fight for Civil Partnership, *The Daily Telegraph*, 22 January 2010.

[125] It also provides that this is without prejudice to the rights of states to exclude from its field of application those occupational activities, for which by reason of their nature or the context in which they are carried out, the sex of the worker constitutes a determining factor.

[126] [1996] 1 All ER 257.

[127] Although the applicants brought a successful action under Articles 8 and 14 of the European Convention, that decision was made on the basis of the rights in the Convention, and did not affect the interpretation of either domestic sex discrimination law or the provisions of the EC Treaty or Directive.

[128] [1998] IRLR 206. See Bamforth, Sexual Orientation Discrimination after *Grant v South West Trains*, (2000) 63 MLR 694.

[129] Under the then domestic law discriminatory treatment against homosexuals was unlawful if the individual could prove that a homosexual of a different sex would have been treated more favourably; see *Smith v Gardner Merchant* [1998] IRLR 510.

[130] [2004] 1 All ER 339.

orientation, and that this interpretation was not affected by the Human Rights Act 1998. Similarly, in *Pearce* v *Governing Body of Mayfield School*,[131] where it was argued that homophobic taunts made by children against a lesbian teacher constituted sex discrimination under the 1975 Act, the claim was dismissed on the basis that as the acts complained of took place before the Human Rights Act came into force, it could not be used to interpret the Sex Discrimination Act so as to comply with Articles 8 and 14 of the Convention, and the European Court of Human Right's ruling in *Smith and Grady* v *United Kingdom*.[132] Thus, although the treatment amounted to a violation of Articles 8 and 14 of the Convention and an individual could now bring a claim under the 1998 Act against a public authority for breach of those rights, no remedy could be given retrospectively. This discrepancy was covered by the passing of the Employment Equality (Sexual Orientation) Regulations 2003,[133] passed in response to the EU Employment Equality Work Directive for Equal Treatment in Employment and Occupation,[134] the regulations making it unlawful to discriminate on grounds of sexual orientation in employment and vocational training.[135] Part 3 of the Equality Act 2006 extended the law's protection against discrimination on such grounds beyond the employment field, and such measures came into existence in April 2007.[136] Further, the Equality Act 2010 provides that sexual orientation is a protected characteristic, and thus protects against discrimination, harassment or victimisation.[137]

Transsexuals and the law

The recognition and treatment of transsexuals gives rise to a number of Convention issues. First, the refusal to allow such individuals to change their sexual identity raises issues under Article 8 of the European Convention, guaranteeing the right to private life. Such treatment may also, in exceptional circumstances, raise a claim under Article 3, which prohibits degrading treatment. Secondly, the refusal to recognise that change may engage Article 12, which guarantees the right to marry and found a family, such a claim usually being made in conjunction with Article 8, and/or Article 3. Thirdly, the treatment of transsexuals can give rise to claims under Article 14 of the Convention, which guarantees that individuals enjoy their Convention rights free from discrimination. The success of the latter claim will usually depend on whether the applicant succeeds in the other claims, and often the Court will refuse to consider a separate complaint under Article 14 if it has already established a violation of another substantive Convention right. Finally, a claim may be made under Article 13 where national law has failed to provide an effective remedy for any possible Convention violation.[138]

---

[131] Heard jointly with *MacDonald*, above.

[132] (2000) 29 EHRR 493.

[133] SI 2003/1661.

[134] 2000/78/EC.

[135] The regulations were challenged as being incompatible with EC law, but the claim failed: *R (Amicus)* v *Secretary of State for Trade and Industry* (2004) IRLR 430.

[136] Equality Act (Sexual Orientation) Regulations 2007 (SI 2007/1263). For a detailed coverage of EU law in this area, see Waaldijk and Bonini-Baraldi, *Sexual Orientation Discrimination in the European Union: National Laws and the Employment Equality Directive* (Asser Press 2006).

[137] Sections 4 and 12 Equality Act 2010.

[138] For general literature in this area, see Whittle, *Respect and Equality* (Routledge-Cavendish 2002); Campbell and Lardy, Transsexuals – the ECHR in Transition [2003] NILQ 209; Catley, A Long Road Nearing the End [2003] JSWFL 277.

Transsexuals and the European Convention on Human Rights

The Convention rights of transsexuals have been raised before the European Court on a number of occasions. In the first case, *Rees* v *United Kingdom*,[139] Rees was a female to male transsexual whose request to register his new sex was refused by the domestic authorities. The European Court held that the right to respect for private life did not include a positive obligation on a state to give them the unconditional right to label the sexual identity of their choice. A balance had to be drawn between the interest of the applicant and the public in deciding whether a violation of his private life had occurred, and the Convention could not force the United Kingdom government to adopt a system of civil status as in other member states that would make a change of sex more easily incorporated. Such a scheme would lead to falsification and such information being denied to people who had a legitimate interest in receiving it, such as the armed forces. The Court also held that the right to marry under Article 12 referred to a right between persons of the opposite biological sex; that such a restriction did not have the effect of destroying the very essence of the right.

The decision in *Rees* was followed in *Cossey* v *United Kingdom*.[140] Cossey, a male to female transsexual, claimed that domestic law, which did not allow her to change her sex on his birth certificate, or to marry a person of the same biological sex was in violation of Articles 8 and 12 of the Convention. The European Commission distinguished *Rees* on the question of Article 12 as the applicant had a partner and was ready to marry, but the Court held that there had not been any material change in the practice of member states since the *Rees* case to allow the Court to change that decision. In the Court's view, it was necessary to balance the right of the applicant with the interests of the community. Further, it held that the right to marry as restricted by English law did not undermine the existence of that right under Article 12. The biological approach was a valid one and the practice of some states in allowing a marriage between two people born male was not a uniform practice and did not indicate the need to deviate from the traditional approach to the concept of marriage.

This conservative approach was abandoned somewhat in *B* v *France*.[141] B had been born male and in 1972 had sex-change surgery. Since that time she had lived with a man and wished to marry. In 1978 she wished to change her birth certificate but this was refused because her change in sex had been brought about intentionally and by artificial processes. The European Court held that the case was distinguishable from *Rees* and *Cossey*, since French law denied the right to change the sex of even one's name on the birth certificate. Even having regard to the margin of appreciation, the fair balance that has to be struck in such cases had not been attained. The Court noted that the applicant found herself in a daily situation which taken as a whole was not compatible with the respect due to her private life.

However, the Court adopted its general stance in *Sheffield and Horsham* v *United Kingdom*.[142] The applicant had been born a man and had married and undergone a sex change. She had obtained a divorce as a condition of the surgery being carried out. Her former spouse then received a court order barring the applicant from having access to the child on the basis that contact with a transsexual would be against the best interests of the child. Although the applicant could change her name on her driving licence and passport, she had to disclose the

---

[139] (1986) 9 EHRR 56.
[140] (1990) 13 EHRR 622.
[141] (1992) 16 EHRR 1.
[142] (1998) 27 EHRR 163.

change of sexual identity for certain other purposes and her original sex was also relevant for the purposes of National Insurance, social security and pensions. Horsham was born a man and had undergone reassignment surgery in 1992. The authorities issued a passport in her new sex but refused to allow her to change her birth certificate, although she had been issued with a new birth certificate in the Netherlands. The European Court held that there had been no violation of Articles 8 or 12. Since the cases of *Rees* and *Cossey* there was insufficient evidence to establish the existence of any common European approach to the problems created by the legal recognition of post-operative gender status. Also the Court was not satisfied that the applicants had suffered a sufficient detriment so as to outweigh the state's margin of appreciation in this area: the disclosures that the applicants would have to make did not occur with such a degree of frequency so as to impinge to a disproportionate extent on their right to respect for their private lives. The Court also held that the applicants' ability to contract a marriage under domestic law did not give rise to a breach of Article 12.[143]

Different issues were raised in the case of *X, Y and Z v United Kingdom*.[144] X, a female to male transsexual, had been in a stable relationship with Y since 1979 and in 1992 the couple had a child (Z) via artificial insemination. X's application to be registered as Z's father was refused, although Z was allowed to take X's name. The couple applied to have the birth registered in their joint names as mother and father but were told that the father's name must remain blank. The European Commission held that there had been a violation of Article 8 and the case was distinguishable from earlier cases on the ground that the interference con-cerned the applicants' private *and* family life. However, the European Court found that there had been no violation, although it accepted that family life was not restricted to marriage relationships and that in this case the concept of family life was relevant to the applicants' *de facto* relationship. The claims made by the applicants raised new issues than those raised in previous cases – parental rights and the status of children born by artificial insemination.

With respect to the necessity of the domestic position, the Court held that as there was little common ground the state should be given a wide margin of appreciation. The community as a whole had an interest in maintaining a coherent system of family law that placed the best interests of the child at the forefront. It was not clear that a change in the law would be beneficial to the child and in those circumstances the state could be cautious in chang-ing the law, since it was possible that an amendment might have undesirable and unforeseen ramifications for children in Z's position. Furthermore, it might lead to inconsistencies if a female to male transsexual could become a father in law while still being treated for other purposes as a female and capable of marrying a man. Given that transsexuality raised complex scientific, legal, moral and social issues in respect of which there was no generally shared approach, Article 8 in that context could not be taken to imply an obligation for a member state government to formally recognise as the father of a child a person who was not the biological father.

However, the issue of transsexual rights was raised again before the European Court of Human Rights in *Goodwin v United Kingdom* and *I v United Kingdom*,[145] and on this occasion the European Court took the opportunity to review its previous stance in this area. The applicants

---

[143] In a strong dissenting judgment, JUDGE VAN DIJK noted that society and individual third parties should be required to accept a certain inconvenience to enable their fellow citizens to live in dignity and worth in the same society in accordance with the sexual identity chosen by them at great personal cost.

[144] (1997) 24 EHRR 143.

[145] (2002) 35 EHRR 18 and *The Times*, 12 July 2002, respectively.

were both post-operative male to female transsexuals. G claimed that following her gender reassignment she had faced sexual harassment at work and had also faced discrimination with regard to the payment of her National Insurance contributions; she had to pay contributions up to the age of 65 and had to enter into a special arrangement to avoid her employer asking questions. She also claimed that her inability to change her National Insurance number allowed her employer to discover her previous name and gender. The other applicant, I, claimed that she was unable to be admitted onto a nursing course because she refused to present her birth certificate. Both applicants complained that the lack of legal recognition of their post-operative gender amounted to a violation of Articles 8, 12 and 14 of the European Convention.

The Grand Chamber of the European Court held that there had been a violation of Articles 8 and 12 of the Convention, and that no separate issue arose under Article 14. The Court found that the applicants had been subjected to a serious interference with both their legal rights and their right to private life, which had led to feelings of vulnerability, anxiety and humiliation. Although the Court accepted that important repercussions would follow from a change in the system of birth registration and other fields, it did not accept that these problems were insuperable. No concrete or substantial hardship or detriment to the public interest had been demonstrated as likely to flow from any change to the status of transsexuals. Further, society might reasonably be expected to tolerate a certain inconvenience to enable individuals to live in dignity and worth in accordance with their chosen sexual identity. In particular, the Court noted that the government had done nothing to respond to the Court's continual request to keep the need for legal reform under review. The government could, therefore, no longer claim that the matter fell within its margin of appreciation.

The Court also found a violation of Article 12. It held that although Article 12 referred to the right of a man and a woman to marry, it was not persuaded that at this date such terms restricted the determination of gender to purely biological criteria. There were now other important factors, such as the acceptance of the condition of gender identity disorder by the medical professions and the provision of relevant treatment. In the Court's view, it would be artificial to claim that post-operative transsexuals had not been deprived of their right to marry. The applicants in this case lived as women and would only wish to marry a man, and their inability to do so infringed the very essence of the right to marry. Although fewer countries permitted the marriage of transsexuals in their assigned gender than recognised the change of gender itself, this did not leave the matter entirely within the state's margin of appreciation. While it was for the contracting state to determine the conditions under which a person could claim legal recognition as a transsexual, including the formalities applicable to future marriages, there was no justification for barring transsexuals from enjoying the right to marry under any circumstances.[146]

The judgment clearly left the government with some discretion in deciding how to give effect to the judgment, including the extent to which transsexuals will be recognised and any conditions attached to that recognition. Nevertheless, the judgment is an important one in respect of the rights of transsexuals. Further, it is illustrative of the European Court's ability

---

[146] See also *Van Kuck* v *Germany* (2003) 37 EHRR 973, where it was held that a domestic court's refusal to order reimbursement of top-up costs of a transsexual's gender reassignment surgery was a violation of his right to private life under Article 8 of the Convention. In the Court's view, as gender identity was one of the most intimate aspects of a person's private life, it was disproportionate to require the applicant to prove the medical necessity of the treatment.

and willingness to interpret the Convention in the context of changing circumstances, and provides an example of the interaction between the margin of appreciation and the European Court's supervision of domestic law and practices.

In the meantime the domestic courts had refused to recognise the validity of marriages entered into between persons who had undergone reassignment. Thus, in *Bellinger* v *Bellinger*,[147] the House of Lords held that although after the decision in *Goodwin* domestic law was incompatible with Articles 8, 12 and 14 of the Convention, it was not the role of the courts to reinterpret clear legislation. Any fundamental change in the law must, therefore, be made by parliament. The possible incompatibility of that approach with the Convention was exposed in *Grant* v *United Kingdom*,[148] where the European Court held that there had been a violation of Articles 8 and 14 when the applicant, a male to female transsexual, had been denied a pension on her 60th birthday because biologically she was a male. The European Court held that although the United Kingdom government had acted swiftly to pass the Gender Recognition Act 2004, below, to address the decision in *Goodwin*, the applicant still remained a victim and there was no reason why she should not be regarded as such from the date of the judgment and until that Act came into force.

The Gender Recognition Act 2004

As indicated above, following the decision in *Goodwin* the Lord Chancellor's Department announced its intention to introduce new legislation to give formal recognition in the acquired gender, including the right to marry and to change their birth certificates, and the Gender Recognition Act 2004 was given the Royal Assent on 1 July 2004, providing transsexuals with, *inter alia*, the right to marry and to be treated as the sex they have adopted as their acquired gender.[149]

Section 1 of the Act provides that any person over the age of 18 can make an application to the Gender Recognition Panel for a gender recognition certificate on the basis of either living in the other gender or having changed gender under the law of another country. The act's protection extends beyond those who have undergone full gender reassignment and under s.2 of the Act protection applies where the person has or has had gender dysphoria (in other words gender identity disorder) and has lived in the acquired gender for two years prior to the application and intends to live in it permanently. Under s.3 of the Act, the panel may reject an application if not provided with the relevant medical and psychological evidence from registered practitioners.

Because the Panel requires evidence of the person living as the acquired gender, and subsequent decisions regarding reassignment surgery will require such evidence, any decision or policy which unreasonably frustrates the aim of the Act will be incompatible with the individual's Convention rights. For example, in *R (AB)* v *Secretary of State for Justice*,[150] it was held that it was proper for the Secretary of State to consider the fact that a prisoner had been granted a gender recognition certificate under the Gender Recognition Act 2004 in deciding whether to transfer her to a female prison. The claimant was a post-tariff life sentence prisoner who had begun the process of gender reassignment treatment and who wished to be transferred to a female prison. The Secretary of State had refused that request on the grounds

---

[147] [2003] 2 AC 467.
[148] (2007) 44 EHRR 1.
[149] The Act came into force in April 2005.
[150] [2010] 2 All ER 151.

of both cost and the risk to female prisoners and argued that Article 8 did not require him to fulfil a positive duty to facilitate the claimant's request. The court held that the decision was both *Wednesbury* unreasonable and contrary to Article 8. It held that the decision effectively barred her from qualifying for surgery and thus impacted on her personal autonomy in a manner which went beyond the nature of imprisonment. Further, preventing the transfer and frustrating her ability to realise her intended gender was likely to disrupt the current stable regime leading to an increase in her risk profile and segregation in even her current prison regime. Thus, the decision had failed to consider the effect on the claimant's progress towards full gender reassignment and the alternative costs of keeping her within a male prison; further, the secretary had failed to recognise that she would pose a risk in both male and female prisons.

That decision does not mean that the individual can progress to their new gender irrespective of cost, and in that case the court accepted that the deployment of resources can justify infringement of Article 8 rights provided the reasons are weighty, clear and proportionate. For example, in *AC v Berkshire West Primary Care Trust*,[151] it was held that a policy adopted by the trust which classified breast augmentation for those seeking treatment for gender identity disorder as 'non-core' was neither irrational nor discriminatory against transsexual patients. The trust were allowed to have policies which prioritised the funding of specific operations provided the policy was not inflexible and did not preclude exceptional cases, such as where the individual is suffering from an exceptionally severe disorder because of the lack of treatment. In the present case the claimant had been treated equally with other, non transsexual patients with the same symptoms; although there would not be a comparator if the claimant had sought genital reconstruction surgery. Previously, in *R v North West Lancashire HA, ex parte A*,[152] it had been accepted that it was lawful and rational to have a policy on the prioritisation of funding operations, including gender reassignment. However, on the facts it was held that the authority had acted irrationally because its policy on funding surgery did not reflect its medical judgement that gender dysphoria was an illness worthy of medical treatment.

The 2004 Act and related case law follow the general spirit of the decision in *Goodwin*, and it has been accepted by the European Court as being compatible with the Convention even though it does not provide for full equality of treatment. Thus, in *R and F v United Kingdom*,[153] the European Court declared inadmissible a claim that the requirement for a transsexual to divorce before registering for a gender recognition certificate under the 2004 Act was in violation of her Convention rights. The Court held that the regulations were within the state's margin of appreciation and left the applicants with a genuine and real choice, either to divorce and register, or to enter into a civil partnership under the Civil Partnership Act 2004.

Transsexuals and European Community law

Transsexuals have won the right to equal treatment in the area of employment and are now covered by domestic discrimination laws, which prohibit discrimination in this field. This situation was the result of the European Court of Justice's decision in *P v S and Cornwall CC*[154] that the principles of equal treatment applied to discrimination arising from an individual's

---

[151] [2010] EWHC 1162 (Admin).
[152] [2000] 1 WLR 977.
[153] Application No 35748/05, admissibility decision of the European Court, 28 November 2006.
[154] [1996] ECR I-2143.

gender reassignment. P had been dismissed when he notified his employers of his intention to undergo a sex change. The dismissal took effect after the final operation was completed, although he was given notice after some minor operations and after he had gone through a period of dressing and behaving like a woman. The employment tribunal rejected his claim under the Sex Discrimination Act 1975 on the basis that the word 'sex' in the Act did not apply to discrimination on grounds of gender reassignment. The case was referred to the European Court of Justice, which noted that the principle of equal treatment indicated that there should be no discrimination whatsoever on the grounds of sex: it was simply the expression of the principle of equality, a fundamental principle of Community law and a fundamental human right. The scope of the directive could not be confined simply to discrimination based on the fact that a person was one or another sex and it also applied to discrimination arising from the gender reassignment of the person concerned. The Court held that he was treated unfavourably by comparison with persons of the sex to which he or she was deemed to belong before undergoing gender reassignment. To tolerate such discrimination would be tantamount, in regard to such a person, to a failure to respect the dignity and freedom to which he or she was entitled.

The directive was used directly in domestic law in *A v Chief Constable of West Yorkshire Police*,[155] where it was held that a male to female transsexual police officer had been discriminated against when her application for employment had been refused because she could not carry out searches on female suspects. Such a refusal contravened the EC Directive and was not justified under s.7 of the Sex Discrimination Act 1975. That decision was upheld by the House of Lords; in their Lordship's view, no one searched by a transsexual could reasonably object to the search.[156] Specifically, the Sex Discrimination (Gender Reassignment) Regulations 1999 were passed, adding s.2A to the Sex Discrimination Act 1975 and making it unlawful to (directly) discriminate against a person on grounds of gender reassignment in employment (including matters of pay) and training,[157] and gender reassignment is a protected characteristic under the Equality Act 2010.[158] In addition, transsexuals can continue to rely directly on EU law, and in *KB v National Health Service Pensions Agency and Another*[159] the European Court of Justice held that national law which made it impossible for a transsexual to marry their partner, and thus to become a spouse for the purpose of entitlement to a survivor's pension under an occupational pension scheme, was discriminatory and thus constituted a breach of the EC principles of equal pay.[160]

---

[155] [2003] 1 All ER 255.

[156] Contrast *Croft v Royal Mail Group plc*, The Times, 24 July 2003, where the Court of Appeal held that there had been no direct sex discrimination on the grounds of gender reassignment when an employee who was in the pre-operative stage of reassignment had been refused permission to use the female toilets at work. In the Court's view, the measures taken by the employer – to allow the person to use the disabled toilet rather than the female toilets – were appropriate and did not amount to sex discrimination.

[157] See Griffiths, The Sex Discrimination (Gender Reassignment) Regulations 1999 (1999) J Civ Libs 230. Section 4A(3) of the 1975 Act also contains a right to be free from harassment on such grounds.

[158] Section 7 Equality Act 2010.

[159] [2004] ICR-541.

[160] Having established that the relevant legislation was contrary to those principles, the European Court of Justice then decided that the question of whether such a situation constituted a violation of Article 141 EC in this particular case should be decided by the national courts. See also *Richards v Secretary of State for Work and Pensions*, The Times, 5 May 2006, where the European Court of Justice held that the applicant, a male to female transsexual, was discriminated against by not receiving her pension at 60 because the law refused to recognise her reassignment. She will receive a backdated lump sum payment for loss of her pension.

European Community law is, of course, superior to domestic law and can augment the rights under the Human Rights Act 1998 and domestic legislation, even before such provisions have come into force. Thus, in *Timbrell v Secretary of State for Work and Pensions*,[161] the Court of Appeal held that a male to female transsexual could rely on an EEC directive to claim a female pension despite the fact that the Gender Recognition Act 2004 had not been passed at the time of the discrimination. The directive was precise and unequivocal and obliged the Secretary of State to provide protection in domestic law.

Questions

Why in *Goodwin* v *United Kingdom* did the European Court of Human Rights change its previous stance with respect to the human rights and civil status of transsexuals?

Do you feel that the current position under both the Convention and domestic law is consistent with the dignity and liberty of transsexuals?

Further reading

Textbooks

There are useful chapters on Article 14 of the European Convention in the following texts: Mowbray, *Cases and Materials on the European Convention on Human Rights* (OUP 2007), chapter 16; Van Dijk and Van Hoof, *Theory and Practice of the European Convention on Human Rights* (Intersentia 2006), chapters 30 and 33; Harris, O'Boyle and Warbrick, *The Law of the European Convention on Human Rights* (OUP 2009), chapter 15; Ovey and White, *The European Convention on Human Rights* (OUP 2010, 5th edn); Janis, Kay and Bradley, *European Human Rights Law: Text, Cases and Materials* (OUP 2008), chapter 11. In addition, Amos, *Human Rights Law* (Hart 2006), chapter 15, contains excellent coverage of domestic case law under Article 14.

For a detailed coverage of domestic discrimination law, see Bamforth, Malik and O'Cinneide, *Discrimination Law: Theory and Context, Text and Materials* (Sweet and Maxwell 2008); Monohagan, *Equality Law* (OUP 2007); McColgan, *Discrimination Law: Text, Cases and Materials* (Hart 2005, 2nd edn); and Connolly, *Townshend-Smith on Discrimination Law: Text, Cases and Materials* (Cavendish 2004, 2nd edn).

Articles

The following articles explore the ambit and efficacy of Article 14: Baker, Comparison Tainted by Justification against a 'Compendious Question' in Article 14 Discrimination [2006] PL 476; Baker, The Enjoyment of Rights and Freedoms: A New Conception of the 'Ambit' under Article 14 ECHR (2006) MLR 714; Baker, Article 14: A Protector, Not a Prosecutor, in Fenwick, Phillipson and Masterman, *Judicial Reasoning under the UK Human Rights Act* (Cambridge University Press 2007); Livingstone, Article 14 and the Prevention of Discrimination in the European Convention on Human Rights [1997] EHRLR 25; Monaghan, Constitutionalising equality: new horizons [2008] EHRLR 20; Wintemute, 'Within the Ambit': How Big is the 'Gap' in Article 14 European Convention

---

[161] [2010] EWCA Civ 701.

on Human Rights? (Part 1) [2004] EHRLR 366; Filling the Article 14 'Gap': Government Ratification and Judicial Control of Protocol No 12 ECHR: (Part 2) [2004] EHRLR 484.

Discrimination on grounds of sexual orientation and gender reassignment

There is a good deal of literature in this area, much of which is referred to in the footnotes of this chapter; specifically, students should consult the following: Bamforth, Same-sex Partnerships: Some Comparative Constitutional Lessons [2007] EHRLR 47; Campbell and Lardy, Transsexuals – the ECHR in Transition [2003] NILQ 209; Catley, A Long Road Nearing the End [2003] JSWFL 277; Johnson, An Essentially Private Manifestation of Human Personality: Constructions of Homosexuality in the European Court of Human Rights [2010] HRLR 67; Whittle, *Respect and Equality* (Routledge-Cavendish 2002); in addition to other sources referenced in this chapter.

Visit **www.mylawchamber.co.uk/fosterhumanrights**
to access regular updates to major changes in the law,
further case studies, weblinks, and suggested
answers/approaches to questions in the book.

14 Human rights and terrorism

Introduction

Since the terrorist attacks in New York and London, additional measures have been taken by various governments to counter the threat of terrorism. These measures inevitably impact on the civil liberties and human rights of suspected and convicted terrorists as well as the population as a whole, and question whether the relevant state is in breach of its own and international human rights law.

In the United Kingdom the government introduced a measure, via parliament, to allow the detention without trial of foreign nationals suspected of committing terrorist offences, and in *A v Secretary of State for the Home Department* (2005) the House of Lords declared such measures incompatible with the rights to liberty and freedom from discrimination. When those measures were replaced with control orders, which placed geographical and other restrictions on suspected terrorists, the House of Lords and the Supreme Court ruled such measures incompatible with the right to liberty (*JJ v Secretary of State for the Home Department* (2008)) and private and family life (*AP v Secretary of State for the Home Department* (2010)).

These measures, and their challenge, raise fundamental issues of basic rights and the rule of law, parliamentary sovereignty and the separation of powers, the constitutional role of the courts, and the role of international human rights law in maintaining a balance between state security and human rights.

This chapter will examine the role of domestic and international law in protecting human rights and civil liberties in the context of the fight against terrorism. Rather than providing an extensive picture of relevant domestic regulations concerning terrorism,[1] this chapter will bring together a number of instances where fundamental rights have been interfered with for reasons of national security and the fight against terrorism and where those interferences have been challenged in both the domestic and European courts. This will include an examination of the relevant legal provisions and case law in areas such as the proscription of terrorist groups and freedom of association (including the suppression of terrorist speech), the protection of the right to life and freedom from torture in the terrorist context, the

---

[1] For an excellent account of the general law relating to human rights and terrorism, see Fenwick, *Civil Liberties and Human Rights* (Routledge 2007, 4th edn), chapter 14.

extended powers of detention of terrorist suspects (including the impact of such detention on private and family life), and the due process of terrorist suspects during detention and subsequent trials and other proceedings. The chapter will use a number of case examples to illustrate the way in which human rights are protected and compromised in this context and these areas will be studied in the light of the principles of human rights law governing the lawful derogation of rights in times of emergency.

Thus, this chapter will cover:

- An examination of the reasons why human rights and civil liberties will need to be compromised in the context of terrorist threats and the extent to which such rights should and can be compromised.

- A re-examination of the relevant rules and principles contained in both the European Convention on Human Rights and the Human Rights Act 1998, which govern the situations in which states are allowed to derogate from their human rights obligations in times of emergency.

- An examination of the relevant domestic law concerning the proscription of terrorist groups and their impact on the right to freedom of association and related fundamental rights.

- An examination of the manner in which domestic and international law protects the right to life and freedom from torture in the terrorist context.

- An examination of the most controversial provisions governing the arrest, questioning and detention of terrorist suspects, together with key cases involving the challenge of such powers.

- An examination of the provisions governing the trial of terrorist suspects and other legal proceedings intended to control the movement of such suspects, for example control orders.

Restricting human rights and civil liberties in emergency and terrorist situations

As we have seen earlier in the text (in chapters 2 and 3), the dilemmas posed by seeking to protect individual human rights and fundamental principles of fairness are particularly acute in times of war or other public emergency, such as the threat of terrorism. In such situations the need to secure public safety and national security can justify the compromising of individual liberty and other rights, and it might be argued that fundamental human rights have to come second to the protection of the state and its citizens. As the former Prime Minister, Tony Blair, famously stated in the aftermath of the London bombings in 2005, 'the rules of the game have changed'. Indeed, following an increase in terrorist attacks around the world the British government introduced new measures to provide greater powers to the police and other authorities with respect to the arrest and detention of those suspected of terrorism.[2]

---

[2] These measures, beginning with the Anti-Terrorism, Crime and Security Act 2001, are discussed later in this chapter and are referred to in chapters 6 and 7 of this text.

Thus, if we were to take the substantive articles of the European Convention on Human Rights (and the Human Rights Act 1998) as an example, we can imagine virtually all of those rights being compromised to some extent in order to counter a terrorist threat, as outlined below.

Article 2 – The right to life

In order to protect public safety against terrorist threats it might, in exceptional circumstances, be necessary to take the life of one or a number of individuals in circumstances which would not normally justify the taking of life. For example, the shooting by the London Metropolitan Police of the Brazilian Jean Charles De Menezes in 2005 raised issues as to what measures could and should be taken by the authorities to protect the lives of others, and the extent to which Article 2, which allows the taking of life in such cases where it is 'absolutely necessary', permits those authorities a greater level of discretion and judgement in the context of terrorism.[3]

Article 3 – Prohibition of torture

Although the prohibition of torture and other ill-treatment is absolute, there are arguments that the prohibition should be compromised in the terrorist context. For example, some argue that there should be a right to torture terrorists in order to gain valuable information which would secure the lives of others.[4] Less controversially, perhaps, many member states of the Council of Europe have argued that the prohibition on deporting or extraditing individuals to countries where they face the risk of torture and ill-treatment should be modified in the context of terrorist offences.[5] Although these arguments have been defeated,[6] there may still be some compromise of human rights on matters such as prison conditions and the enjoyment of private and family lives of terrorist suspects or convicted criminals.[7]

Article 5 – Liberty and security of the person

In response to threats of terrorism it is common for states to introduce measures which will allow the police, and other authorities, greater powers of arrest, questioning and detention. These powers, the state will argue, are necessary to protect the public and to effectively combat serious crime, and in particular terrorist crime which can pose greater problems of detection and regulation. In such cases the state may wish to reduce the objective standard to justify arrest, to extend the periods of questioning and detention and, in exceptional cases, allow detention without trial; thus compromising or abandoning some of the basic principles of liberty and fairness.

International and domestic law will allow such 'derogations' provided they are necessary and proportionate,[8] and the courts will be called upon to rule on the compatibility of those provisions with human rights law. This will raise issues of the rule of law and the separation

---

[3] See *McCann v United Kingdom* (1995) 21 EHRR 97, discussed below, at pages 759–60.

[4] See Ginbar, *Why Not Torture Terrorists?* (OUP 2008), where the author reviews the arguments for and against before rejecting the arguments in favour.

[5] See *A v Netherlands* (Application No 4900/06); *Ramzy v Netherlands* (Application No 25424/06); *N v Sweden* (Application No 23505/09), considered below at page 762.

[6] See cases in n 5, and *Saadi v Italy* (2009) 49 EHRR 30.

[7] See *Sanchez v France* (2006) 43 EHRR 54, with respect to prison conditions, and *R (A) v Secretary of State for the Home Department* [2004] HRLR 12, with respect to suspected prisoners' right to access to journalists.

[8] Article 15 of the European Convention on Human Rights and s.14 of the Human Rights Act 1998, discussed below.

of powers and in this chapter we will examine a number of battles between the judiciary and government on issues such as detention without trial and the imposition of control orders.[9]

Article 6 – The right to a fair trial

The state may wish to compromise the rights to due process and a fair trial in this context in order to protect the rights of others or to more effectively allow the successful prosecution of terrorist crime. For example, a state might introduce special procedures to allow for the prosecution of terrorist offences so as to protect otherwise vulnerable witnesses. Further, it may restrict media access to such trials, reverse the criminal burden of proof, or restrict the participants' access to relevant evidence for reasons of national security. Such measures compromise the right to open justice and the right to a fair trial as guaranteed by Article 6 of the Convention, and although some derogation is allowed, the courts will be called upon to rule on the compatibility of specific measures so as to ensure that the basis principles of fairness are adhered to.

Specifically, both the domestic and European courts have been asked to rule on proceedings related to the granting of control orders under the Anti-Terrorism, Crime and Security Act 2001, whereby evidence can be withheld from the 'controlee' and their lawyers. The government has argued that such measures are necessary to protect national security and the safety and identity of informants, although the courts have insisted that such procedures secure basic standards of justice and allow access to sufficient detail to ensure a fair trial.[10]

Articles 8–11 and 14 – The right to private and family life, freedom of religion, expression and assembly and association, and freedom from discrimination

A number of anti-terrorism provisions are capable of impacting on the enjoyment of the 'democratic' rights contained in Articles 8–11 of the European Convention on Human Rights. These rights are conditional in the sense that they can be interfered with for a legitimate aim and are necessary and proportionate to achieve such an aim. During threats of terrorism the state will argue that measures need to be taken to further restrict these rights in order to protect the rights of others, public safety and national security. Such measures might include the 'proscription' of certain groups, the creation of offences of supporting such groups, and the imposition of curfews or other measures restricting the movement and liberty of the individual.

The proscription of terrorist groups, whereby mere membership of such a group is made illegal, inevitably impact on the right to freedom of association, guaranteed by Article 11 of the European Convention. Governments will argue that such proscription is necessary to secure the successful fight against terrorism, but human rights law will be pleaded in order to test the necessity of such a measure. Such measures will be accompanied by a variety of offences making it unlawful to recruit members to, or to support, such groups, and these offences (for example glorifying terrorism under s.1 of the Terrorism Act 2006) will impact on freedom of expression, and the right to peaceful assembly and association.

In addition, as membership of such groups is often based on religious tenets, these provisions will often restrict the individual or group's right to hold and practise their religious or

---

[9] *A v Secretary of State for the Home Department* [2005] 2 AC 68, detailed as a case study in this chapter, and *JJ and Others v Secretary of State for the Home Department* [2008] 2 WLR 642, dealt with below at page 771.
[10] See *A v United Kingdom* (2009) 49 EHRR 29; *AF v Secretary of State for the Home Department* [2010] 2 AC 269, discussed below at pages 767 and 776, respectively.

philosophical beliefs, thus engaging Article 9 of the European Convention in combination with Articles 10 and 11. Further, measures taken to restrict liberty and movement, in addition to engaging Article 5, above, can impact on the enjoyment of private and family life, both of suspected or convicted terrorists, and of the general public.[11] Such measures may, for example, restrict the access of a prisoner to his family and friends, and control orders (above) may impose restrictions on the controlee's family and private life.[12] Finally, as many of the measures are taken against specific nationals or groups with a religious or other philosophy (above), it is likely in all the above circumstances that Article 14 of the Convention will be engaged. Article 14 guarantees that Convention rights are enjoyed free from discrimination and the courts will have to address whether provisions which inevitably impact on such groups to a greater extent are objectively justified.[13]

In all these cases, both international and domestic law have to decide where the balance lies between the protection of human rights and the protection of the state, and how that balance is achieved will, inevitably, fuel debate between politicians, judges and the public. International law allows states to 'derogate' from their normal treaty obligations in times of war or other emergencies which threaten the life of the nation,[14] and similar provisions exist in the domestic Human Rights Act.[15] Although this right to derogate will be subject to certain procedural limitations, the real dilemma is faced when the domestic lawmakers decide the extent to which the law must erode civil liberties, and the domestic judges decide the extent to which they are going to subject that decision to judicial control.

To allow the government and parliament an unqualified margin of discretion in such cases might appear to accord with democracy: fundamental issues of public safety and national security will be decided by elected and accountable politicians free from supervision by unelected judges. However, as the House of Lords have recently reminded us, the protection of individual liberty and other rights to due process are part and parcel of a civilised, democratic society, and an attack on such individual freedoms might be regarded as an affront to those collective democratic goals.[16] This does not resolve the substantive issue of whether the courts should ultimately decide the legality and reasonableness of government measures intended to combat terrorism, but at least it reminds us of the advantages of upholding human rights, from both the individual and the collective perspective. It should also defeat the argument that in times of terrorism we simply cannot afford to protect individual human rights, for such an argument ignores the fact that democratic societies cannot afford *not* to uphold them.[17]

---

[11] See, for example, the stop and search powers under s.44 of the Terrorism Act 2000, discussed below, at pages 756–9.

[12] See, for example, the recent decision of the Supreme Court in *AP* v *Secretary of State for the Home Department* [2010] 1 WLR 1652.

[13] Article 14 was instrumental in the House of Lords' decision in *A* v *Secretary of State for Home Department* [2005] 2 AC 68, discussed throughout this chapter.

[14] See, for example, Article 15 of the European Convention on Human Rights, discussed in chapters 2 and 3, and Article 4 of the International Covenant on Civil and Political Rights 1966.

[15] Section 14, Human Rights Act 1998.

[16] See, in particular, Lord Hoffmann in *A* v *Secretary of State for the Home Department*, n 13.

[17] See Sottiaux, *Terrorism and the Limitation of Rights* (Hart 2008); Feldman, Human Rights, Terrorism and Risk: The Role of Politicians and Judges [2006] PL 364; Dickson, Law versus Terrorism: Can Law Win? [2005] EHRLR 11; Walker, Prisoners of 'War all the Time' [2005] EHRLR 50; McKeever, The Human Rights Act and Terrorism in the UK [2010] PL 110.

> **Question**
>
> Why are human rights and civil liberties under threat in times of emergency? Why is it important that they survive in such times?

Compromising human rights in times of terrorism and Article 15 of the European Convention on Human Rights

As we have seen in chapters 2 and 3 of the text, international human rights law makes specific provision for the 'derogation' by member states of their human rights obligations during times of war and other emergencies, including threats of terrorism. This allows states to utilise specific procedures under human rights treaties, notifying the agencies of a state of war or emergency and of specific measures that they are going to take to deal with that situation. Before re-examining those provisions and the limit of the right to derogate, it should also be noted that even outside the context of official derogation, the European Court, and the domestic courts, will inevitably offer the state a wider margin of appreciation in balancing human rights with other rights and interests. Thus, in this chapter we will examine cases where the courts, employing basic principles of review and deference, have granted greater discretion and judgement to the authorities in matters such as arrest, detention, conditions of imprisonment, freedom of assembly and freedom of expression.

This part of the text, however, deals with the specific right of derogation, contained in Article 15 of the European Convention,[18] which makes specific provision for war and emergency situations and provides as follows:

> In times of war or other public emergency threatening the life of the nation any High Contracting Party may take measures derogating from its obligations under this Convention to the extent strictly required by the exigencies of the situation, provided that such measures are not inconsistent with its other obligations under international law.

Article 15 of the Convention thus recognises that different considerations may apply to the safeguarding of human rights in times of war or other situations of emergency; allowing member states to make provisions or taking action in order to deal with that emergency situation without breaching its obligations under the Convention. As outlined above, with an increased threat to national security, territorial integrity and public safety, it is common for a state to grant greater powers to arrest and detain individuals, and to restrict freedom of association, assembly and free speech. These measures will have an impact, or an increased impact, on the enjoyment of individual rights and liberties, and the obligations of the state under such treaties as the European Convention.[19] As a consequence they must be monitored closely so that they comply with basic human rights norms.

Article 15 qualifies the right of derogation and any measures will need to be passed or carried out for a legitimate, and objectively justified, purpose and will also need to be

---

[18] A similar provision is contained in Article 4 of the International Covenant on Civil and Political Rights 1966.

[19] For a detailed analysis on Article 15 and terrorism law, see Warbrick, The Principles of the European Convention on Human Rights and the Response of States to Terrorism [2002] EHRLR 287. See also Allain, Derogation from the European Convention of Human Rights in the Light of 'Other Obligations in International Law' [2005] EHRLR 490; Walker, Prisoners of 'War all the Time' [2005] EHRLR 50.

reasonable and proportionate. First, a High Contracting Party can only take such measures as are strictly required by the exigencies of the situation and by using the phrase *strictly* required it indicates that the measures must correspond to a very pressing social need and meet a strict test of proportionality. Although the member state will be afforded a wide margin of error in such situations, Article 15 gives the Convention organs the right to provide an objective review of the emergency and the measures necessary to deal with it. Secondly, the measures taken by the member state must not be inconsistent with its other obligations under international law and any derogation must comply with other internationally accepted standards applying to war or other emergency situations. Thirdly, Article 15 provides that no derogation is allowed in respect of Article 2 (the right to life), (excluding deaths resulting from lawful acts of war), Article 3 (prohibition of torture, etc.), Article 4(1) (prohibition of slavery or servitude) or to Article 7 (prohibition of retrospective criminal law). Thus, certain rights should never be transgressed, whatever the circumstances or possible justification, and certain things should never be carried out in defence of the state and of social justice. Finally, any High Contracting Party using the right of derogation must keep the Secretary-General of the Council of Europe informed of the measures which it has taken, along with the reasons for the derogation; the state must also inform the Secretary-General when such measures have ceased to operate and that the provisions of the Convention are being fully executed.

The European Court and Commission of Human Rights have provided guidance on the operation of Article 15 and in *Lawless v Ireland (No 3)*,[20] although the Court stressed that the measures governments can take when derogating are strictly limited to what is required by the exigencies of the situation, it held that the government should be afforded a certain margin of error or appreciation in deciding what measures were required by the situation. Thus, it was not the Court's function to substitute for the government's assessment any other assessment of what might be the most prudent or most expedient policy to combat terrorism, and it must arrive at its decision in the light of the conditions that existed at the time that the original decision was taken, rather than reviewing the matter retrospectively. Further, the domestic courts have appeared to draw a distinction between the question of whether there was a public emergency (primarily a political question for politicians to decide) and whether the measures were proportionate (primarily a legal question for the courts to determine).[21]

The Court offered a very wide margin to the state in *Brannigan and McBride v United Kingdom*.[22] The case concerned the United Kingdom's derogation of Article 5 following the European Court's decision in *Brogan v United Kingdom*,[23] where it held that the detention provisions contained in the Prevention of Terrorism Act 1978 were in contravention of Article 5(3) of the Convention, which guarantees the right of detained persons to be brought promptly before a judge or other officer. The government had then lodged a derogation in respect of Article 5(3), claiming that the emergency position in Northern Ireland justified such derogation. This derogation was challenged in *Brannigan and McBride*, but the European Court held that it was justified, even though the derogation had not been lodged before the Court's decision in *Brogan*. The Court accepted the government's contention that there was

---

[20] (1961) 1 EHRR 15.
[21] In *A v Secretary of State for the Home Department* [2005] 2 AC 68.
[22] (1993) 17 EHRR 539.
[23] (1989) 11 EHRR 117.

an emergency situation, and held that the derogation was not invalid merely because the government had decided to keep open the possibility of finding a means in the future of ensuring greater conformity with Convention obligations. As we shall see, below, this margin of appreciation is not limitless and the Court will review the measures to ensure that they are not arbitrary, disproportionate and discriminatory.

Derogations and the Human Rights Act 1998

Section 1(2) of the Human Rights Act allows the government to avoid giving effect to the Convention to the extent that it has lodged a derogation order within the provisions of s.14 of the Act and United Kingdom derogations existing at the time of the Act's implementation were contained in Schedule 3 of the Act. The Act contained the government's derogation notices of 1988 and 1989, which were made after the European Court's decision in *Brogan* v *United Kingdom*, above. This derogation was withdrawn by an order made under the Human Rights Act[24] when the relevant statutory provisions were replaced by the Terrorism Act 2000.

As we have seen in chapter 3 of the text, the Home Secretary used his powers under s.14 to make the Human Rights Act 1998 (Amendment No 2) Order 2001, which derogated from Article 5(1) of the European Convention. This followed the passing of the Anti-Terrorism, Crime and Security Act 2001,[25] which provided for an extended power to arrest and detain foreign nationals whom it is intended to remove or deport from the United Kingdom, but where such removal or deportation is not for the time being possible, primarily because such a person would face treatment in violation of the Convention if returned to that particular country. The derogation was necessary in order to comply with the European Court's judgment in *Chahal* v *United Kingdom*,[26] where the European Court held that to comply with Article 5 deportation proceedings had to be prosecuted with due diligence, and that it was in breach of the Convention to deport an individual to a country where they would face ill-treatment. These powers were challenged as being incompatible with Articles 5 and 15 of the Convention, and in *A and Others* v *Secretary of State for the Home Department*[27] the House of Lords held that the measures were incompatible as they were disproportionate because they failed to deal with the threat of terrorism from persons other than foreign nationals; permitted suspected foreign terrorists to carry on their activities in another country provided there was a safe country for them to go; and permitted the detention of non-al-Qaeda supporters even though the threat relied on to justify the measures was from that specific source. It was also held that the measures contravened Article 14 because the appellants were treated differently because of their nationality or immigration status.

Following the decision in *A*, the 2001 derogation was withdrawn and parliament passed the Prevention of Terrorism Act 2005, which introduced a system of control and supervision orders to deal with such suspects, and these measures will be examined later in this chapter. These powers were passed as non-derogating orders as the government believed them to be

---

[24] Human Rights Act (Amendment) Order (2001) SI 2001/1216.
[25] See Warbrick, The Principles of the European Convention on Human Rights and the Responses of States to Terrorism [2002] EHRLR 287.
[26] (1997) 23 EHRR 413.
[27] [2005] AC 68.

compatible with Articles 5 and 6 of the Convention, but have been successfully challenged in the domestic court. Thus, in *Secretary of State for the Home Department v JJ and Others*,[28] the House of Lords held that control orders imposed on the applicants under s.2 of the Prevention of Terrorism Act 2005 were capable of impacting on liberty of the person as opposed to the right of movement and were therefore derogating orders that the Secretary had no jurisdiction to make. The provisions have also been challenged under Article 6 as being contrary to the right to a fair trial as the proceedings are conducted via the use of closed evidence.[29]

These provisions and cases have already been dealt with in earlier chapters and will be examined again later in this chapter. However, at this stage it is interesting to note how the domestic courts have reacted to challenges of domestic laws that impact on fundamental rights and which have been passed to secure national security and public safety, especially in the context of the fight against terrorism.

The domestic courts and the protection of human rights in the terrorist context

The domestic courts have often been called upon to adjudicate on the legality of interferences with fundamental human rights in the context of terrorism. Such challenges are now normally made under the Human Rights Act 1998, and can involve the interpretation and application of derogation powers under the European Convention and the Human Rights Act 1998, above. The Act has been used extensively in areas such as detention and the regulation of control orders, but as we shall see other cases can be resolved by reference to basic common law principles of fairness and due process, which survive the passing of the Act and which can be used co-extensively with Convention principles and case law.

Common law rights and principles are thus still applicable in the Human Rights Act era, and in certain cases the domestic courts prefer to rely on them to control excessive interference with basic liberty. For example, in *A v Secretary of State for the Home Department (No 2)*[30] the House of Lords ruled out evidence that may have been obtained via torture by relying on both international and common law prohibition. In coming to that decision, their Lordships referred to the common law rejection of such practices and both European and United Nations treaties and instruments on torture, and stated that although it was within the power of parliament to allow such evidence to be admitted, there was no evidence to suggest that the Anti-Terrorism, Crime and Security Act 2001 intended to override the common law and international position. Another example is provided by the Supreme Court's recent ruling in *HM Treasury v Mohammed Jabar Ahmed and Others*,[31] where the Supreme Court considered the legality of the Terrorism Order 2006, which allowed for freezing orders to be placed on the funds of those who were reasonably suspected of committing acts of or facilitating terrorism. Using traditional principles of interpretation and legality it held that the Order was *ultra vires* of s.1 of the United Nations Act 1946, which had been passed to give effect to a UN resolution intended to suppress terrorism. The Supreme Court held that if the rule of

---

[28] [2007] 3 WLR 642.
[29] *Re MB* [2007] 3 WLR 681. See also *AF v Secretary of State for the Home Department* [2010] 2 AC 269.
[30] [2006] 2 AC 221. The case is detailed as a case study in chapter 5.
[31] [2010] 2 AC 534.

law meant anything, what amounted to decisions that were necessary and expedient within s.1 could not be left to the uncontrolled judgement of the executive. By introducing a test based on reasonable suspicion the Treasury had exceeded its powers of implementing the 1946 Act, and was a clear example of an attempt to adversely affect the basic rights of the citizen without the clear authority of parliament. The absence of any indication that parliament intended to impose restrictions on the freedom of individuals when debating the Act meant that it was impossible to say that it confronted the matter and was prepared to accept the political cost when the measure was enacted.[32] However, the limitations of this method of protection were exposed by the passing of the Terrorist Asset-Freezing (Temporary Provisions) Act 2010, which specified that the order of 2006 was validly made under the 1946 Act. Any judicial challenge to the new Act would have to be made under the Human Rights Act, alleging a breach of rights under the European Convention.

In such cases it is inevitable that the courts will offer a good deal of deference to the authorities, most notably parliament, in striking the necessary balance between fundamental human rights and national security. Such deference was evident in *R v Secretary of State for the Home Department, ex parte Farrakhan*,[33] a case which had some characteristics of the terrorism cases, and where a challenge had been made to the refusal by the Home Secretary to relax an order excluding the claimant from entering the country. The Home Secretary had asserted that the claimant's presence would not be conducive to the public good and that he was likely to threaten public order and commit offences of racial hatred, but the High Court held that there was a complete absence of evidence so as to establish objective justification for the exclusion order.[34] However, the decision was overruled by the Court of Appeal, which held that the Secretary of State had on the facts struck a proportionate balance between the legitimate aim of the prevention of disorder and freedom of expression. The Court of Appeal stressed that, despite the application of the principle of proportionality, there were a number of factors present in the case that made it appropriate to accord a particularly wide margin of discretion to the Secretary: that it was an immigration decision; that the decision was personal to the Secretary of State, taken after detailed consideration involving widespread consultation; that the Secretary was far better placed to reach an informed decision as to the likely consequences of admitting that person into the country than the court; and that the Secretary was democratically accountable for his decision.[35]

This deference will naturally be greater when challenges are made to primary legislation, where the power to declare such legislation incompatible with the Convention will involve the courts assessing that legislation's legality, necessity and proportionality, and where the courts will be expected to display deference to legislation passed by a democratically elected parliament, particularly where that body has contemplated the possible human rights arguments in passing such provisions. For example, in *R v Shayler*,[36] the House of Lords held that

---

[32] The Court noted further that the Al-Qaeda order, which allowed designation of a person by a Sanctions Committee without judicial review, denied any effective remedy and thus was also *ultra vires*.

[33] [2002] 3 WLR 481.

[34] *The Daily Telegraph*, 9 October 2001.

[35] See also *R (Abbasi) v Secretary of State for Foreign and Commonwealth Affairs*, *The Times*, 8 November 2002, where it was held that the courts could interfere with a decision relating to foreign policy which impinged on an individual's fundamental human rights, although the decision maker would not be required to give more than due consideration to the individual's position.

[36] [2002] 2 WLR 754.

sections 1 and 4 of the Official Secrets Act 1989 were not incompatible with Article 10 of the European Convention simply because the Act did not provide the defendant, a former security officer, with a defence of public interest. Lord Bingham held that the special position of those employed in the security and intelligence services, and the special nature of their work, imposed duties and responsibilities that made it appropriate for them to seek the necessary authorisation from their superiors and accordingly sections 1 and 4 of the 1989 Act were compatible with Article 10.

However, despite this judicial deference, the courts have made it clear that when fundamental human rights are at issue they will not show the executive, or parliament, undue deference simply because the decision or act involved high levels of sensitive policy.[37] As we shall see later in this chapter, in *A v Secretary of State for the Home Department*[38] the House of Lords ruled that the detention of foreign nationals suspected of terrorism under s.21 of the Anti-Terrorism, Crime and Security Act 2001 was a disproportionate response to the threat of terrorism. In that case Lord Bingham held that where the conduct of government was threatened by serious terrorism, difficult choices had to be made and that while any decision of a representative democratic body commanded respect, the degree of respect would be conditioned by the nature of the decision made. In his view the traditional *Wednesbury* approach was no longer appropriate and the domestic courts themselves had to form a judgment whether a Convention right was breached, the intensity of the review being greater under proportionality. In Lord Bingham's view, even in terrorist situations, judicial control of the executive's interference with individual liberty was essential and the courts were not precluded by any doctrine of deference from scrutinising such issues.[39] Lord Bingham justified this approach by reference to the Human Rights Act 1998, which he noted had expressly conferred new powers of review and interpretation on the domestic courts. In his Lordship's view, given that these powers were specifically granted by parliament itself, the courts were operating under a wholly democratic mandate.

Equally, the normal deference shown towards legislation passed by Parliament has not stopped the domestic courts from attempting to achieve a Convention-friendly interpretation, where that is possible and appropriate. This was evident in the House of Lords' decision in *Attorney-General's Reference (No 4 of 2002)*,[40] where the question was whether s.11(2) of the Terrorism Act 2000, which made it an offence to belong or profess to belong to a proscribed organisation, imposed an evidential rather than a legal burden on the defendant so as to make that provision compatible with Article 6 of the Convention. Section 11(2) of the Act appeared to place the burden on the defendant to prove that he had not taken part in the activities of the organisation. The majority of their Lordships held that this contravened the presumption of innocence under Article 6(2), but that it was possible to read that provision down in such a way as to avoid a legal burden. Such an interpretation was possible even

---

[37] In *Machado v Home Secretary* [2005] 2 CMLR 43, the Court of Appeal held that an administrative decision that involved issues of public policy as well as human rights issues required a more intensive review than the test of whether the decision maker's response was within the range of reasonable responses open to it.

[38] [2005] 2 AC 68.

[39] Nevertheless, the majority of the House of Lords (Lord Hoffmann dissenting) did respect the Home Secretary's decision that there existed an emergency threatening the life of the nation, recognising that that decision at least was essentially political. For a commentary on this case and the role of the courts, see Feldman, Human Rights, Terrorism and Risk: The Roles of Politicians and Judges [2006] PL 364.

[40] [2005] 1 AC 264.

though parliament had when passing the legislation intended to impose a legal burden in such cases. Although parliament had had that intention when passing the 2000 Act, having regard to its intention in passing s.3 of the Human Rights Act 1998, that provisions such as s.11 should not be incompatible with Convention rights, it was permissible to eradicate that incompatibility by employing s.3.

Question

How would you assess the domestic courts' efforts to uphold fundamental rights in times of emergency and threats of terrorism?

The control of terrorism and the freedom of association

Anti-terrorism provisions will inevitably include the power to proscribe certain groups in addition to creating specific terrorist offences prohibiting certain acts which support or further the aims of that group. These provisions will impact on the rights to freedom of association and assembly and free speech and will need to be justified on grounds of legality and proportionality, possibly by using Article 15 of the Convention with respect to derogation.

Although freedom of association is regarded as fundamental under the European Convention, in exceptional cases the European Court has sanctioned the proscription of a particular organisation which was thought to pose a sufficient threat to the values of that society and the underlying values of democracy. Thus, in *Reefa Partisi Erbakan Kazan and Tekdal* v *Turkey*[41] the Court held that the dissolution of the applicant's party on the ground that it had become a centre of activities against the principles of secularism was within the state's margin of appreciation and thus justified within the terms of Article 11(2). Although it accepted that political parties which campaign for changes in legislation or to the legal or constitutional structure of the state are allowed the protection of Article 11, provided the means used to those ends are lawful and democratic, groups whose leaders incite others to use violence or support political aims that were inconsistent with one or more of the rules of democracy could not rely on the Convention. The decision in *Reefa Partisi* was made in the context of political groups but its reasoning may also be used in measuring the legality of anti-terrorist provisions which proscribe or restrict the right of association.

The Terrorism Act 2000 and the Anti-Terrorism, Crime and Security Act 2001

Most domestic legal systems will contain provisions allowing the authorities to compromise civil liberties in times of war or other emergency. In particular, laws will be passed giving those authorities increased powers regarding the control of terrorist activities, and these powers will permit greater interference with rights such as liberty of the person, fair trial, freedom of movement and, in certain cases, freedom of speech, association and assembly.[42] The law relating to the control of terrorism, including the proscription of particular organisations, is now

---

[41] (2002) 35 EHRR 2.
[42] See Walker, *The Prevention of Terrorism in British Law* (Manchester University Press 1996, 2nd edn); Walker, *Blackstone's Guide to Anti-Terrorism Legislation* (OUP 2003).

contained in the Terrorism Act 2000,[43] as reinforced by the Anti-Terrorism, Crime and Security Act 2001.[44] The Terrorism Act replaces the previous statutory provisions in this area contained in both the Prevention of Terrorism (Temporary Provisions) Act 1989 and the Northern Ireland (Emergency Powers) Act 1996, extending the definition of terrorism and giving the legislation a wide scope covering all manner of internal and international terrorism.[45]

As with the previous legislation, the Act contains powers to proscribe groups and to make it an offence both to belong to them and take part in the activities, and assist such groups. For the purposes of the Act an organisation is proscribed if it is listed in Schedule 2 of the Act or if it operates under the same name as such an organisation,[46] and the Secretary of State can, by order, add to or delete groups from the Schedule.[47] In R v Z,[48] the House of Lords held that the Real Irish Republican Army could be regarded as a proscribed organisation under s.3 of the Terrorism Act 2000 even though it was not specifically listed under the legislation. The historical context of the legislation was paramount in concluding that the 'IRA' included all manifestations, representations and emanations of the IRA.

Such an order requires the Secretary of State to lay a draft for the approval of both Houses of Parliament.[49] Section 3 of the Terrorism Act 2000 allows the Secretary of State to add to the list of proscribed organisations if he believes that the organisation is concerned in terrorism.[50] An organisation will be concerned in terrorism if it commits or participates in acts of terrorism, prepares for terrorism, promotes or encourages terrorism or is otherwise concerned in acts of terrorism.[51] Section 1 of the Terrorism Act 2000 defines terrorism as the use or threat, for the purpose of advancing a political, religious or ideological cause, of action designed to influence the government or to intimidate the public or a section of the public, which involves serious violence against any person or serious damage to property, endangers the life of any person, or creates a serious risk to the health or safety of the public or a section of the public, or is designed seriously to interfere with or seriously to disrupt an electronic system. This definition is wider than in previous legislation, which only applied to terrorism connected with the affairs of Northern Ireland and, in particular circumstances, to international terrorism.[52] Thus, although the previous legislation was used to proscribe groups connected with terrorist activities in connection with Northern Ireland,[53] the new definition will

[43] The Act followed a government consultation paper: *Legislation Against Terrorism: A Consultation Paper*, Cm 4178 (Stationery Office 1998). For a critical account of the Act and of the law on terrorism, see Whitty, Murphy and Livingstone, *Civil Liberties Law: The Human Rights Act Era* (Butterworths 2001), chapter 3; Fenwick, *Civil Rights: New Labour, Freedom and the Human Rights Act* (Longman 2000), chapter 3.
[44] For a detailed and critical account of this Act, see Fenwick, The Anti-Terrorism, Crime and Security Act 2001: A Proportionate Response to 11 September? (2002) 65 MLR 724.
[45] For a general coverage of the terrorist legislation and its impact on freedom of association, see Fenwick, *Civil Liberties and Human Rights* (Cavendish 2007, 4th edn), pages 1363–406.
[46] Section 3(1) Terrorism Act 2000.
[47] Section 3(4). Those groups who were proscribed under the previous legislation continue to be proscribed.
[48] [2005] 2 WLR 1286.
[49] Section 123(4). Under s.123(5) an order may be made without approval in cases of emergency.
[50] Section 3(4). See The Terrorism Act 2000 (Proscribed Organisations) (Amendment) Order 2002 SI 2002 No 2724, which adds a number of Islamic groups to those proscribed under the Act.
[51] Section 3(5).
[52] Section 20 of the Prevention of Terrorism (Temporary Provisions) Act 1989. Under s.1(4) the Terrorism Act applies wherever terrorist action takes place.
[53] Under the Prevention of Terrorism (Temporary Provisions) Act 1989 a total of 14 groups were proscribed, including the Irish Republican Army, and all its splinter groups, and a variety of Loyalist and Republican paramilitary groups.

cover not only those groups, and other international terrorist groups, but also groups who use the above action to 'influence the government or to intimidate the public or a section of the public'. Groups such as animal rights activists, therefore, some of whom have employed such techniques in the past, risk proscription, with the result that association with such groups, which espouse quite legitimate causes, will be illegal by itself.[54] The curtailment of the right of association of such groups, who represent a genuine and strongly supported cause, and who provide the public with valuable information relating to such matters, questions whether such measures are disproportionate and thus in contravention of Articles 10 and 11 of the Convention.

Section 5 of the Act establishes the Proscribed Organisations Appeal Commission, which hears appeals against the Secretary of State's refusal to remove an organisation from the list of proscribed groups. In *R v Secretary of State for the Home Department, ex parte Kurdistan Workers Party and Others*[55] it was held that this procedure should be used to challenge the procedural and substantive legality of any decision. The applicants' organisations had been proscribed under the Act by statutory instrument and the groups challenged the Secretary of State's decision in judicial review proceedings, claiming a violation of Articles 8, 10, 11 and 14 of the Convention. It was held that the applicants needed to bring proceedings before the Proscribed Organisations Appeal Commission, set up under s.5 of the Act, rather than bring proceedings for judicial review in the Administrative Court. However, the court was of the opinion that the challenges were arguable, or at least contained a sufficient number of arguable points, to get over the threshold in respect of the main issues.

Once a group is proscribed, s.11 of the Act makes it an offence to belong, or profess to belong, to a proscribed organisation.[56] Although the offence does not require a specific *mens rea*, and it is not necessary that the person did not know that the group were proscribed, there is a defence under s.11(2) of the Act if the person charged with the offence can prove that the organisation was not proscribed on the last or only occasion on which he became a member, and that he has not taken part in its activities at any time while it was proscribed. Section 12 of the Act also makes it an offence to solicit support, other than money or other property, for a proscribed organisation,[57] or to arrange, manage or assist in managing a meeting which he knows is to support or further the activities of a proscribed organisation, or to be addressed by a person who belongs or professes to belong to such an organisation.[58] The organiser of a meeting will be liable only if they know that the meeting was to be held for the above purposes, but given the penalties involved,[59] and the fact that the provision can cover small meetings which might not involve any inflammatory words or actions, the provision imposes

---

[54] See *Legislation Against Terrorism: A Consultation Paper*, Cm 4178 (Stationery Office 1998), para 3, explaining the reason for inclusion of such groups.

[55] [2002] EWHC 644 (Admin). The case was joined with two other applications: *R v Secretary of State for the Home Department, ex parte People's Mojahedin Organisation of Iran and Others; R v The Same, ex parte Nisar Ahmed.*

[56] In *R v Hundal and Dhaliwal, The Times*, 13 February 2004, the Court of Appeal held that a person in the United Kingdom could commit the offence of belonging to a proscribed organisation under s.11 of the Terrorism Act 2000 even where he or she had joined that organisation in another country that did not proscribe the group. Such a finding was not in violation of Article 7 of the European Convention because the person was only in violation of the law once he or she entered the United Kingdom, thus rendering him or her liable to the relevant legislation.

[57] Section 12(1).

[58] Section 12(2).

[59] The maximum punishment is ten years' imprisonment.

what might, in certain circumstances, be regarded as a disproportionate restriction on free speech and freedom of association and assembly. The section also makes it an offence to address any such meeting in order to encourage support for a proscribed organisation or further its activities.[60] Again, given the sanctions, and the possible innocuous content of the address, considerable evidence of harm is required to justify the resultant infringements on civil liberties.

With regard to a person's association with a proscribed group, s.13 of the Act makes it an offence to wear an item of clothing, or wear, carry or display an article in such a way or in such circumstances as to arouse reasonable suspicion that the person in question is a member or supporter of a proscribed organisation. The offence does not require any specific *mens rea* and could be committed by any person who expresses their support of a proscribed group, or, presumably, any of its views, via the wearing of such items. Although it does not prohibit a person from expressing agreement with the views of such groups, unless they did so in such a way as to arouse suspicion that they were professing to belong to such a group,[61] the provision might apply to a person who, say, wears a badge, or holds up a placard, expressing views in agreement with that group. Accordingly, this provision, along with all the other provisions in the Act, has to be applied very carefully so as not to catch legitimate speech and dissent.[62]

These provisions may, of course, be used extensively following the terrorist attacks on the World Trade Center in New York with the Secretary of State using his power to add various groups to the list of proscribed organisations. In doing so, he must ensure that a proper balance is created between outlawing groups whose ideals and actions are totally inconsistent with both public safety and democratic principles, and interfering with the human rights of those whose views and ideals may be inconsistent with those of the majority, but who do not pose any such threats.[63]

Proscription and the Terrorism Act 2006

The Terrorism Act 2006 adds to the above provisions on proscription and the regulation of terrorist support by introducing new offences designed to curb and penalise the support of such groups. Sections 21–22 of the Act amend s.3 of the Terrorism Act 2000, above, so as to extend the Home Secretary's power of proscription to organisations which promote or encourage terrorism where the activities of the organisation include the unlawful glorification of the commission or preparation of acts of terrorism, or where those activities are carried out in a manner that ensures that the organisation is associated with statements containing any such glorification.[64] This provision complements s.1 of the 2006 Act, which introduces the offence of encouragement of terrorism, dealt with below. As with s.1 of the Act, although the

---

[60] Section 12(3). A meeting is defined as one at which three or more persons are present, either in a public or private place.

[61] Under s.11 of the Act. In addition, such an action might, in certain circumstances, be regarded as likely to incite a breach of the peace, see below.

[62] In *O'Driscoll* v *Secretary of State for the Home Department and Another* [2002] EWHC 2477 (Admin), the High Court held that s.16 of the Act, which makes it an offence to be in possession of property for the use of terrorism, was sufficiently certain to be prescribed by law and was not inconsistent with Article 10 of the Convention.

[63] See Warbrick, The Principles of the European Convention on Human Rights and the Response of States to Terrorism [2002] EHRLR 287.

[64] See now s.3(5A) Terrorism Act 2000.

offence did not directly retain the offence of glorifying terrorism, both s.1 and s.21 use that vague term in describing the type of conduct that amounts to encouragement for the purpose of either committing an offence or supplying the Secretary of State with evidence of the need for proscription. The Act states that the glorification of any conduct is unlawful if there are persons who may become aware of it who could reasonably be expected to infer that what is being glorified is being glorified as conduct that should be emulated in existing circumstances or conduct that is illustrative of a type of conduct that should be so emulated.[65] Section 22 of the 2006 Act deals specifically with name changes made to proscribed organisations and amends s.3(6) of the 2000 Act by providing that where the Home Secretary believes that a listed organisation is operating wholly or partly under a name that is not specified in Schedule 2 of the Act, or where that organisation is otherwise for all practical purposes the same as a listed organisation, he or she may provide that the name that is not so specified be treated as another name for a listed organisation.

In addition to the new provisions on proscription the Act creates a series of new offences with respect to the preparation of acts of terrorism. For example, s.5(1) of the 2006 Act provides that a person commits an offence if, with the intention of committing an act of terrorism or assisting another to commit such an act, he engages in *any* conduct in prepara-tion for giving effect to that intention. This offence will cover actions that are not directly or imminently related to the commission of a terrorist offence, and s.5(2) states that it is irrelevant whether the intention and preparations relate to one or more acts of terrorism, acts of terrorism of a particular description or acts of terrorism generally.[66] In addition, s.6 of the Act creates an offence of providing training or instruction to persons knowing that the person intends to use those skills for terrorist purposes, and an offence of receiving such instruction for such purposes.[67] The skills are detailed in s.6(3) of the Act and include the making, handling and use of a noxious substance (or of substances or a description of such sub-stances, and the use of techniques for doing anything else that is capable of being done for the purposes of terrorism). It also includes the design or adaptation for the purposes of terrorism, or in connection with the commission or preparation of an act of terrorism, or in connection with assisting the commission or preparation by another of such an act, of any method or technique for doing anything.[68]

Questions

What human rights issues are raised with respect to the proscription of associations?
Do you feel that UK terrorism laws are consistent with the European Convention in this respect?

---

[65] Section 3(5B) Terrorism Act 2000. Under s.3(5C) 'glorification' includes any form of praise or celebration. Two groups have been proscribed under the new provisions: see Militant Islamist Groups Banned under Terror Law, *The Times*, 18 July 2006.

[66] Under s.5(3) the maximum penalty is life imprisonment.

[67] Section 8 of the Act also makes it an offence to attend at any place (whether in the United Kingdom or not) where terrorist training is being provided or is available. For the offence to be committed the person must know that such training was being provided or if he could not reasonably have failed to understand that such training was being provided: s.8(2). Under s.8(3) it is immaterial that the person received the instruction or training himself and under s.8(4) the maximum penalty is ten years' imprisonment and a fine.

[68] Under s.6(5) the maximum penalty is ten years' imprisonment and an unlimited fine.

Restricting free speech on grounds of terrorism

The proscription and regulation of associations and their activities inevitably impacts on freedom of expression and the exchange of ideas and information. This section examines specific offences intended to regulate speech that might incite, encourage or lend support to such organisations and their causes; such measures will be examined to identify whether they are compatible with the principles of free speech examined in chapters 8 and 9 of the text.

In addition to the offence of encouraging terrorism, below, the freedom of expression of certain groups or individuals might be compromised by the government policy. For example, the Home Secretary's power to deport or refuse entry to individuals on the grounds that their presence is not conducive to the public good or they are likely to commit public order or terrorist offences might affect freedom of expression. Thus, as we have seen, in *R v Secretary of State for the Home Department, ex parte Farrakhan*[69] the Court of Appeal upheld that the Home Secretary's refusal to allow the claimant – a black Muslim and founder of the Nation of Islam Group – entrance to the country, on the assertion that his presence would not be conducive to the public good and that his addresses were likely to threaten public order and amount to racial hatred. In addition, the courts have given a wide margin of discretion to prison authorities in restricting the free speech and correspondence rights of those detained on grounds of terrorism. In *R (A) v Secretary of State for the Home Department*[70] it was held that the refusal to allow the prisoners to be interviewed by journalists unless the interviews were conducted within earshot of an official at all times and tape-recorded by the Prison Service was not irrational or disproportionate. The claimants were all asylum seekers who had been detained by virtue of s.21 of the Anti-Terrorism, Crime and Security Act 2001 on the basis that they were suspected of terrorist activities and whose presence in the United Kingdom was believed to be a risk to national security. They claimed that the restrictions imposed on those visits were inconsistent with their rights under Article 10 of the Convention.[71] The High Court held that the requirement of good order and discipline generally required a degree of monitoring when inmates were interviewed, and that in this case the additional dimension of national security provided ample justification for the extra measures imposed on these claimants. The restrictions imposed fell within Article 10(2) of the Convention and the balance struck by the Home Secretary in determining the conditions of the interviews was not one with which the court should interfere.

Inciting and glorifying terrorism under the Terrorism Act 2006

To deal with the problem of speech which was intended to, or might be seen as encouraging or defending acts of terrorism, s.1 of the Terrorism Act 2006 creates a new offence of encouraging terrorism. In addition s.2 of the Act creates an offence of disseminating terrorist publications. The offences apply to speech which falls short of direct incitement to commit an offence and apply to speech which merely encourages such conduct.[72] The offences are capable of being committed by even the mainstream media, and there is no public interest

[69] [2002] 3 WLR 481.
[70] [2004] HRLR 12.
[71] See *R v Home Secretary, ex parte O'Brien and Simms* [2000] 2 AC 115, dealt with in detail in chapter 8.
[72] For a more detailed explanation and analysis of these provisions, see Fenwick and Phillipson, *Media Freedom under the Human Rights Act* (OUP 2006), pages 527–33; Hunt, Criminal Prohibitions on Direct and Indirect Encouragement of Terrorism [2007] Crim LR 441.

or press freedom defence as such contained in the section. In addition, under s.336(5) of the Communications Act 2003 the Secretary of State has the power to direct a person who holds a broadcasting licence from including in their licensed services any matter specified in his notice to them. This power, then contained in the Broadcasting Act 1981, was used by the government in the 1980s to control terrorist propaganda and the ban was unsuccessfully challenged by journalists and broadcasters, the House of Lords confirming that the measure was lawful and rational.[73]

Section 1(1) of the Act provides that a person commits an offence if he publishes a statement that is likely to be understood by some or all of the members of the public to whom it is published as a direct or indirect encouragement or other inducement to them to the commission, preparation or instigation of acts of terrorism.[74] For the offence to be committed the person must either intend members of the public to be directly or indirectly encouraged or induced by the statement to commit, prepare or instigate acts of terrorism, or be reckless in that respect.[75] The section then provides that statements that are likely to be so understood by members of the public include every statement which glorifies the commission or preparation of acts of terrorism and statements from which those members of the public could reasonably be expected to infer that what is being glorified is being glorified as conduct that should be emulated by them in existing circumstances.[76] In deciding how the statement is likely to be understood a court must take into account the content of the statement as a whole and the circumstances and manner of its publication,[77] although it is irrelevant whether any person was in fact encouraged.[78] There is a partial defence in s.1(6) of the Act where the accused can show that the statement neither expressed his views nor had his endorsement, and that it was clear, in all the circumstances of the statement's publication, that it did not express his views or have his endorsement.

In addition, s.2 of the 2006 Act provides that a person is guilty of an offence if they, *inter alia*, distributes or circulates a terrorist publication where they intend an effect of their conduct to be a direct encouragement or other inducement to the commission, preparation and encouragement of acts of terrorism or to be the provision of assistance of such acts, or where they are reckless as to such consequences.[79] The provisions in s.1 above, relating to the likely effect of the publications and the tests for determining such are employed in this section,[80] and there is a similar defence where it can be shown that the material does not express the person's views or endorsement.[81]

Whether the provisions are compatible with Article 10 of the European Convention is difficult to predict and will depend on how they are used by the authorities and interpreted by the courts. Although the government has not lodged a derogation under the Human

---

[73] *R v Secretary of State for the Home Department, ex parte Brind* [1991] 1 AC 696.

[74] Section 1(7) of the Act provides a maximum penalty of seven years' imprisonment and a fine.

[75] Section 1(2) Terrorism Act 2006.

[76] Section 1(3) Terrorism Act 2006.

[77] Section 1(4) Terrorism Act 2006.

[78] Section 1(5) Terrorism Act 2006.

[79] The section also applies to giving, selling or lending such publications, the offer of such publications for sale or loan, the provision of a service to others that enables them to access such material, the transmission of such electronically, and the possession of such with a view of it being disseminated as above. The maximum sentence is seven years' imprisonment and a fine: s.2(10) Terrorism Act 2006.

[80] See s.2(3)–(5) Terrorism Act 2006.

[81] Section 2(10) Terrorism Act 2006.

Rights Act with respect to these provisions, it is clear that it feels they were introduced and are justified in the present circumstances, where Britain faces terrorist threats. In that sense it could be argued that the courts, and the European Court of Human Rights, would provide the government with a generous margin of appreciation if the provisions and any prosecution were challenged under the Human Rights Act or via the Convention machinery. In particular, the government would rely on the argument that any speech in support or defence of terrorist acts would not attract the protection of Article 10 and that in combination with Article 17 of the Convention such views would fall outside the protection of the Convention and the Human Rights Act. On the other hand if the provisions are used to prosecute speech or material which constitutes unpopular, but non-inflammatory, support for proscribed groups or their activities, then there is the danger that they could be used to suppress democratic views from those who do not support the mainstream argument against proscribed groups or the relevant underlying political arguments.[82] In addition, given that the section's talk of the likely effect of the speech on members of the public, there is a danger that such reaction may be different depending on who manifests that view. Certain racial or political groups and its individual members may thus be subjected to discrimination, exposing the provisions to challenge under Article 14 of the Convention.

Terrorism and freedom of assembly

The considerable powers to control and interfere with freedom of liberty, speech and assembly may be strengthened in the context of the fight against terrorism. In such circumstances the fear of terrorist activity might influence parliament in increasing police powers in this respect and this might be augmented by a deferential approach from the courts when such powers are challenged. The House of Lords' decision in *R (Gillan and Another) v Commissioner of the Police for the Metropolis*,[83] along with the appeal case before the European Court of Human Rights – *Gillan and Quinton v United Kingdom*[84] – provide contrasting judicial approaches to the interpretation and application of police powers of stop and search under the anti-terrorism provisions, and these cases will be examined next.

In this case the Commissioner had made an order under s.44 of the Terrorism Act 2000 authorising police officers to stop and search persons in the whole of the Metropolitan Police District. Section 44 provides the Home Secretary to authorise a stop and search where he considers it expedient for the prevention of acts of terrorism and then bestows on police officers a power to stop a pedestrian in an authorised area and to search that person or anything carried by him. The order had been confirmed by the Home Secretary (under s.46(4) of the Act) and accordingly officers could stop and search any person without the need to prove any relevant suspicion. The order was renewed on 9 September 2003 on the grounds that it was near the anniversary of 11 September and that the Defence Systems and Equipment International Exhibition was being held at the Excel Centre in London. The claimants were

---

[82] For example, if after a terrorist bombing, a person were to state that given the absence of political representation of that proscribed group it is hardly surprising that the groups resort to such tactics, and indeed such tactics appear to be the only reasonable measure available to the group, would, or should that constitute an offence under the Act?

[83] [2006] 2 AC 307. See O'Brien, Judicial Review under the Human Rights Act: Legislative or Applied Review [2007] EHRLR 550.

[84] (2010) 50 EHRR 45.

each separately stopped and searched under this authorisation on their way to the exhibition – G was going to take part in a peaceful demonstration against the exhibition and the other claimant was a press reporter. Both were permitted to go on their way after the stop and search had been completed, but they argued that the authorisation was unlawful on the grounds, *inter alia*, that they should only be given in respect of an imminent terrorist threat to a specific location and that no appropriate guidance had been given to the Metropolitan police officers as to how they should use their powers. Dismissing the applications, the Divisional Court held that the authorisations were both lawful and proportionate.[85] The Court noted that the relevant senior police officer had a broad discretion as to the width of the authorisation: the Act envisaging that an authorisation could cover the whole of a police area in response to a general threat of terrorist activity on a substantial scale. On the facts, there were no grounds for setting the authorisation aside and the conduct of the police officers did not show that the authorisations and the use of the powers were exercised for an irrelevant purpose or irrationally. The threat posed by terrorist activity and the risk that the threat could become a reality in London provided justification for any possible violation of the claimant's rights under the European Convention. Although the police had to take particular care to ensure that such powers were not used arbitrarily or against any particular group of people, on the facts, there was just enough evidence that the arms exhibition was an occasion that concerned the police sufficiently to persuade them that s.44 powers were necessary. The Court of Appeal upheld the decision of the High Court,[86] and the claimant appealed to the House of Lords.

Dismissing the appeal, the House of Lords held that the word 'expedient' in s.44 had a meaning quite distinct from 'necessary'. In their Lordships' view there was every indication that parliament had appreciated the significance of the power that it was conferring and thought it an appropriate measure to protect the public against the grave risks posed by terrorism, provided the power was subject to effective restraints, as it was under this legislation. The Act informed the public that the powers were, if duly authorised and confirmed, available; further it defined and limited those powers with considerable precision and anyone stopped had to be told by the constable all he needed to know. The constable was not free to act arbitrarily and would be open to civil suit if he did. In any case their Lordships doubted whether there had been any interference with Convention rights in this case: there was no deprivation of liberty as the applicants were merely being kept from proceeding or kept waiting,[87] and the superficial search was not serious enough to amount to a violation of the applicants' right to private life under Article 8 of the Convention. Further, the House of Lords held it would be rare where such a power would give rise to an infringement of Articles 10 or 11, and if they did any interference would be justified under the exceptions provided under Articles 5, 8, 10 and 11.[88] The decision displays a 'hands-off' approach from the domestic courts, which were clearly reluctant to interfere with specific powers bestowed by parliament on the police in an effort to combat terrorism.

---

[85] *The Times*, 12 August 2004.

[86] [2004] 3 WLR 1144.

[87] Contrast this finding with that of their Lordships in *R (Laporte)* v *Chief Constable of Gloucestershire* [2007] 2 WLR 46. These cases are also discussed in chapter 6 of this text, with respect to liberty of the person.

[88] The majority of their Lordships felt that the police would not have the right to use the power simply because a person was of Asian origin or appearance. However, Lord Scott thought that any such discrimination was valid by virtue of the authority of the 2000 Act.

However, those powers and the decision of the House of Lords were questioned before the European Court, and in *Gillan and Quinton* v *United Kingdom*[89] it was held that the powers were neither sufficiently prescribed by law nor proportionate.

The Court first concluded that the exercise of the police powers in the present case clearly interfered with the applicants' private life. Distinguishing such searches from those imposed on travellers at airports, the Court noted the coercive nature of the powers and the public nature of the search. The Court then considered whether the powers under the 2000 Act were sufficiently curbed by adequate legal safeguards so as to be in accordance with the law as required by Article 8(2). In the Court's view they were not. First, the relevant provisions only required that the search power be 'expedient' rather than necessary. The authorisation of such powers was subject to confirmation by the Secretary of State within 48 hours and was renewable after 28 days. However, the Secretary could not alter the geographical coverage of an authorisation and although he or she could refuse confirmation or substitute an earlier time of expiry, in practice this had never been done. Indeed, an authorisation for the Metropolitan Police District had been continuously renewed in a 'rolling programme' since the powers had first been granted. Although an additional safeguard was provided by the Independent Reviewer appointed under the 2000 Act, his powers were confined to reporting on the general operation of the statutory provisions and he had no right to cancel or alter authorisations.[90]

The Court was also concerned with the breadth of the discretion conferred on the individual police officer; the officer's decision to stop and search an individual being based exclusively on a 'hunch' or 'professional intuition'. Not only was it unnecessary for him to demonstrate the existence of any reasonable suspicion; he was not required even subjectively to suspect anything about the person stopped and searched. The sole proviso was that the search had to be for the purpose of looking for articles which could be used in connection with terrorism, a very wide category covering many articles commonly carried by people in the streets. Provided the person concerned was stopped for the purpose of searching for such articles, the police officer did not even have to have grounds for suspecting the presence of such articles. The Court was also struck by the statistical and other evidence showing the extent to which police officers resorted to the powers of stop and search under section 44 of the Act and found that there was a clear risk of arbitrariness in granting such broad discretion to the police officer; in particular the risks of the discriminatory use of the powers against such persons was a very real consideration and the statistics showed that black and Asian persons were disproportionately affected by the powers.

In general, the Court noted that although the powers of authorisation and confirmation were subject to judicial review, the breadth of the discretion involved meant that applicants faced formidable obstacles in showing that any authorisation and confirmation were unlawful; as shown in the applicants' case, judicial review or an action in damages to challenge the exercise of the stop and search powers by a police officer were unlikely to succeed. The absence of any obligation on the part of the officer to show a reasonable suspicion made it almost impossible to prove that that power had been improperly exercised. Consequently, the Court considered that the powers of authorisation and confirmation as well as those of

---

[89] (2010) 50 EHRR 45.

[90] This was despite the fact that in every report from May 2006 onwards he had expressed the clear view that the powers could be used less and that he expected them to be used less.

stop and search under sections 44 and 45 were neither sufficiently circumscribed nor subject to adequate legal safeguards against abuse and were not 'in accordance with the law'.

It must be stressed that the case was decided under Article 8 of the Convention (the right to private life), rather than under Articles 10 and 11. Nevertheless the principles established by the Court in this case would appear to be equally applicable to those rights. Given its finding under Article 8, the Court held that it was not necessary to examine the applicants' complaints under Articles 10 and 11 (or Article 5). However, in its decision, the Court noted that there was a risk that such a widely framed power could be misused against demonstrators and protestors in breach of Article 10 and 11. In that sense, therefore, the decision can be used by the domestic courts to subject a variety of domestic law powers that interfere with the right of peaceful demonstration to strict rules of legality and proportionality.[91]

> **Question**
>
> Do you consider the above provisions of the Terrorism Act 2006 to be compatible with Articles 10 and 11 of the European Convention?

The right to life, freedom from torture and the threat of terrorism

Articles 2 and 3 of the Convention are regarded as 'absolute' rights and are not subject to the principles of proportionality – in that they are not subject to the normal balancing act between their enjoyment and the achievement of other legitimate aims – or to the right of derogation under Article 15 of the Convention. Nevertheless, the European and domestic courts have, indirectly, considered the threat of terrorism when deciding whether the right has been violated on the facts of the case. In addition, there have been (largely unsuccessful) attempts by member states to dilute the absolute character of Article 3 in the context of anti-terrorism measures. This section of the chapter will thus examine the interpretation and application of these articles in cases where measures have been taken to combat terrorism.

The right to life in the terrorist context

As we have seen in chapter 4 of the text, although the right to life is absolute, Article 2(2) allows the use of fatal force in order to protect another or other individuals from unlawful violence. In such cases the state is allowed to use fatal force where it is *absolutely necessary* and for this exception to apply the most exceptional circumstances should exist. It might of course be argued that the state's 'right' to take life might be greater in the terrorist context and this possibility was considered by the European Court in *McCann v United Kingdom*.[92] In this case security intelligence had been gathered to the effect that three IRA terrorists were to enter Gibraltar and commit an act of terrorism, probably via a car bomb. Three people were seen

---

[91] Following the decision, and the Grand Chamber's refusal to hear the case on appeal, the new coalition government announced plans for the immediate suspension of those powers pending their repeal: see also Ford and Gibbs, No More Stop and Search in Curbs on Anti-terror Police, *The Times*, 9 July 2010.

[92] (1995) 21 EHRR 97.

near a car, and believing that the car contained a bomb and that it was to be detonated, members of the SAS shot dead the three people. The European Court held that the SAS members had used no more force than was necessary in the circumstances, suggesting that in the context of the perceived threat of terrorist actions the personnel should be provided by courts with a greater level of deference with respect to their judgement in deciding to use fatal force. Thus, the Court would be reluctant to interfere where it is alleged that unreasonable force has been used by officers at the scene. In those cases the Court might be reluctant to question the judgement of the individual officers, who having little time to reflect have to make an instant decision.[93]

Despite this the Court held that there had been a violation of the right to life through the careless planning of the operation by the security authorities because the authorities had fed misinformation to the soldiers and crucial assumptions had been made which turned out to be untrue. Further, the Court stated that the wording of Article 2 (absolutely necessary) indicated that a stricter and more compelling test of necessity must be employed than, for example, when deciding whether an interference with freedom of speech is necessary in a democratic society under Article 10(2). Thus there is no reason to believe that the European Court or the domestic courts would dilute the fundamental character of Article 2 simply because the death occurred in the fight against terrorism. On the other hand, it is clear that the special threat to public safety caused by terrorist acts, or other serious crime, will inform the courts' views on whether the requirements of Article 2(2) have been met.

The fight against terrorism has also raised issues surrounding the rendition of terrorist suspects to states where they may face the death penalty. Member states of the Council of Europe can agree to the additional protocols under the Convention, agreeing not to carry out the death penalty. Protocol No 6 provides that the death penalty shall be abolished and that no one shall be condemned to such penalty or executed and once a member state signs the Protocol then the death penalty exemption contained in Article 2 of the Convention ceases to operate. In addition Protocol No 13 to the European Convention provides for the abolition of the death penalty in all circumstances and was signed by the United Kingdom government in May 2002.

Consequently, any death penalty carried out in the jurisdiction of the United Kingdom would be contrary to that Protocol and thus contrary to the United Kingdom's Convention responsibilities. In addition, the death penalty might also give rise to liability under Article 3 of the Convention in that the circumstances surrounding the death penalty may well constitute inhuman and degrading treatment.[94] Ratification of Protocol Nos 6 and 13 thus gives rise to a specific problem for states such as the United Kingdom which might deport or extradite a person to face the death penalty in another country, which is either not a party to the Convention, or has not ratified Protocol No 6. In such a case, the United Kingdom government's decision to deport or render that person would appear to be in breach of that protocol.

These issues have been raised recently where occupying British troops had surrendered individuals suspected of committing terrorist offences who then may face the death penalty.[95]

---

[93] See the Court's decision in *McCann*, above, with respect to the liability of the soldiers. See also the European Commission's decisions in *Stewart v United Kingdom* (1984) 39 DR 162, where it was held that the shooting of a 13-year-old boy by armed troops in Northern Ireland during a riot was not a violation of Article 2, and the admissibility decision of the European Court in *Caraher v United Kingdom* (Application No 24520/94). See also *Brady v United Kingdom* (Application No 85752/97).

[94] *Soering v United Kingdom* (1989) 11 EHRR 439.

[95] This issue has been examined in chapters 4 and 5 of this text.

In *R (Al-Saadoon and Mufdhi) v Secretary of State for Defence*,[96] it was held that it was not unlawful for British troops to hand over two Iraqi nationals who were suspected of committing terrorist killings to the Iraqi authorities to face a criminal trial and the death penalty as the victims were not within the authority's jurisdiction as the British troops did not have exclusive control over the relevant territory. In any case it was held that the government troops were obliged under international law to hand over the individuals, unless there was a real risk that the detainees' Article 3 rights were to be violated. Although the death penalty was outlawed in the United Kingdom, it was not in breach of the Convention or international law as there was insufficient evidence that international law prohibited executions by hanging because it was in violation of the prohibition of inhuman treatment. However, in *Al-Saadoon and Mufdhi v United Kingdom*,[97] the European Court of Human Rights held that the handing over of the detainees to the Iraqi authorities constituted a violation of Articles 2 and 3. In the European Court's view, the United Kingdom authorities had exclusive control over the detention facilities which held the applicants. As the applicants were likely to face the death penalty, the Court had to consider whether the United Kingdom was in breach of its Convention obligations. As the death penalty was now considered as constituting inhuman and degrading treatment, from the date of the United Kingdom's ratification the respondent's obligation under Article 2 of the Convention dictated that it should not enter into any arrangement which involved it in detaining individuals with a view to transferring them to stand trial on capital charges or in any way subjecting individuals within its jurisdiction to a real risk of being sentenced to the death penalty and executed. Further, the applicants' well-founded fear of being executed gave rise to a significant degree of mental suffering and thus constituted inhuman treatment within the meaning of Article 3.[98]

The decision prohibits the rendition of terrorist suspects where they face the death penalty in another jurisdiction, and as we shall see the European Court has taken an equally robust approach in cases where individuals face the risk of other forms of torture and ill-treatment.

The prohibition of torture and inhuman and degrading treatment and punishment in the terrorist context

Article 3 prohibits torture and inhuman and degrading treatment and punishment in unqualified terms. Further, Article 15 does not allow derogation from Article 3 in times of war or emergency. Accordingly Article 3 would appear to apply in full force in the context of combating terrorism. In *Ireland v United Kingdom*,[99] it was alleged that the application of the so-called 'five techniques', which involved detained suspects being subjected to intense noise, wall-standing, and deprivation of food and sleep, constituted a breach of Article 3. The Court found that the application of the techniques to the applicants constituted both inhuman treatment, as they were applied in combination, with premeditation and, for hours at a stretch, causing if not bodily injury, at least intense physical and mental suffering and acute

---

[96] [2009] 3 WLR 957.

[97] (2010) 51 EHRR 9.

[98] The Court also rejected the government's contention that they had no choice but to respect Iraqi sovereignty and transfer the applicants. It had not been shown that the respect of their human rights would inevitably damage sovereignty because the domestic authorities had neither negotiated with the Iraqi authorities nor explored the possibility of trying the applicants in the domestic courts.

[99] (1978) 2 EHRR 25.

psychiatric disturbances. Further, the Court held that the techniques were degrading since they were such as to arouse in their victims feelings of fear, anguish and inferiority capable of humiliating them and possibly taking away their physical or moral resistance. However, the techniques did not amount to torture, which the Court felt was treatment constituting *deliberate* inhuman treatment causing *very serious and cruel suffering*. Although the European Court stressed that the distinction between 'torture' and the other terms would be a question of degree, it did not contemplate the possibility that the terrorist context would in any way compromise the absolute nature of Article 3 and its prohibition of ill-treatment.

Further, in *Chahal v United Kingdom*,[100] in respect to deportation, the European Court has stressed that as the prohibition under Article 3 against ill-treatment is absolute, once substantial grounds have been shown for believing that an individual would face a real risk of being subjected to a violation of Article 3 on return, the activities of the person, however undesirable, cannot be a material consideration.

Recently, the European Court has been asked to relax the judgment in *Chahal* where the individual is suspected of terrorism. In *A v Netherlands; Ramzy v The Netherlands*,[101] the defendant states, together with four intervening states including the United Kingdom, argued that such removals do not violate Article 3 when it is strictly necessary to secure national security and is in the interests of the state's execution of their international relations. However, the Court reiterated the absolute prohibition of torture under Article 3 and stated that it was not possible to weigh the risk of ill-treatment against the reasons put forward for the expulsion in order to determine whether the state's responsibility was engaged under the article. Specifically, the Court stressed that the existence of domestic laws and accession to international human rights treaties by states who were not a party to the European Convention could not by itself ensure adequate protection from ill-treatment; particularly as reliable sources had reported practices which were contrary to the Convention and which were actively tolerated and pursued by the authorities.[102]

This decision in *A v Netherlands*, above, follows the approach taken in *Saadi v Italy*,[103] where it was held that there would be no compromise of Article 3 and the test of assessing risk in such cases. In that case the Court found that there was a real risk of the applicant being subjected to ill-treatment in breach of Article 3, and that the considerable difficulties facing states with respect to terrorist violence did not call into question the absolute nature of Article 3. Thus, it was not possible to weigh the risk that a person might be subjected to ill-treatment against his dangerousness to the community if he was not sent back. Further, the argument that the risk had to be established by solid evidence where the individual was a threat to national security was not consistent with Article 3 and its absolute nature. The test was whether there were substantial grounds for believing that there was a real risk and in this case there was strong evidence that those found guilty of terrorist offences had been subjected to torture and that the authorities had failed to investigate relevant allegations of such.[104]

---

[100] (1997) 23 EHRR 413.

[101] Application No 25424/05.

[102] The application in *Ramzy* was struck out as the Court and his lawyers could not locate him.

[103] (2009) 49 EHRR 30.

[104] In *AS (Libya) v Secretary of State for the Home Department, The Times*, 16 April 2008; [2008] HRLR 28, the Court of Appeal upheld the Appeals Commission's findings that the deportation of two suspected terrorists to Libya would have been in breach of Article 3. The correct test was whether there were substantial grounds for believing that they would face a risk of suffering contrary to Article 3; and that meant no more than there must be a proper evidential basis for concluding that there was such a risk.

Nevertheless, where there is no reason to doubt those assurances the Court will consider the importance of upholding extradition agreements and diplomatic relations between the states when determining the extent of the risk to the individual. Thus, in *Cahuas v Spain*,[105] the European Court found that there had been no violation of Article 3 when the applicant had been deported to Peru to face terrorist charges. Spain had received assurances that he would not face the death penalty or a life sentence and Peru was party to international human rights treaties.

On the other hand, the domestic courts have been prepared to take into consideration the policies of extradition and punishment in deciding whether on the facts the necessary threshold required for a finding of inhuman or degrading treatment has been breached by prison conditions in the receiving country. For example, in *R (Bary and Others) v Secretary for the Home Department*,[106] it was held that there was no violation of Article 3 when the claimants had been extradited to the United States to face charges of terrorism, because the administrative measures applicable in the United States, together with the tough prison conditions in super-maximum security prisons, did not cross the necessary threshold. It was also noted that there were sufficient protective measures available to the claimants under US law to safeguard them against abuse. These cases, although decided outside the context of terrorism, would be relevant in determining the acceptability of prison and other conditions awaiting terrorist suspects in the receiving country, but do not apply where there is a real risk of torture or other forms of ill-treatment outside lawful detention.

This decision in *Bary* needs to be examined in the light of the admissibility decision in the case of *Babar Ahmad and Others v United Kingdom*,[107] which concerned the United Kingdom's intended extradition to the United States of four suspected international terrorists, including the Muslim cleric Abu Hamza. In that decision the Court declared admissible his and the other applicants' claims that if extradited they would face inhuman and degrading prison sentences and conditions. Specifically, they claimed that they would be subjected to special administrative measures – including solitary confinement and restrictions on communication with their legal representatives – and life imprisonment without parole and/or extremely long sentences in a 'supermax' prison in the United States such as ADX Florence where special administrative measures would be applied to them. The European Court held that the applications raised serious questions of fact and law which needed to examine them on the merits. It also declared admissible their complaint that their conditions of detention might be made even stricter by the imposition of special administrative measures in ADX Florence.[108]

Admissibility of torture evidence and Article 3

Various legal and moral issues are raised when there is evidence that individuals have been subjected to torture or ill-treatment in breach of Article 3 or other international rules prohibiting such treatment. This aspect of the prohibition of torture has been dealt with in chapter 5 of the text, but it will be discussed briefly in the context of Article 3 and anti-terrorism

---

[105] (2009) 48 EHRR 24.
[106] *The Times*, 14 October 2009.
[107] European Court of Human Rights (Application Nos 24027/07, 11949/08 and 36742/08).
[108] The case is examined in detail in chapter 5, at pages 259–61.

provisions where the courts will need to assess the admissibility of such evidence in the light of principles of the prohibition of torture, or open justice.

In *A v Secretary of State for the Home Department (No 2)*,[109] the House of Lords held that the government could not rely on evidence that may have been extracted by torture to prove the grounds on which to justify the imposition of a control order.[110] The appellants had been detained under s.21 of the Anti-Terrorism, Crime and Security Act 2001 and claimed that certificates issued by the Home Secretary to justify their detention should be cancelled because he may have based his suspicion on evidence that was obtained by torture inflicted on persons in other countries.

The House of Lords held that although the European Court of Human Rights had been reluctant to lay down any common rules on the use of evidence, it nevertheless had insisted that each state must ensure that proceedings were fair; recognising that the way in which evidence was gathered might make those proceedings unfair.[111] Accordingly, the House of Lords would take a similar view where complaints of coercion and torture appear to be substantiated. Further, it was common ground that the international prohibition on the use of torture enjoyed the enhanced status of a *jus cogens* or peremptory norms of general international law recognised as one from which no derogation was allowed. States were now obliged not only to refrain from authorising or conniving at torture, but also to suppress and discourage it and not condone it. Specifically, Article 15 of the UN Convention required the exclusion of statements made as a result of torture as evidence in any proceedings, and it would be remarkable if national courts, exercising universal jurisdiction, could try a foreign torturer for acts of torture committed abroad but receive evidence obtained by such torture. Lord Bingham stated that the rationale of the exclusionary rule was found not only in the unreliability of torture evidence but also its offensiveness to civilised values and its degrading effect on the administration of justice, thus damaging the integrity of the proceedings. Nor should the above principles be undermined by measures directed to counter international terrorism. All states were strongly urged by the international community to cooperate and share information to counter terrorism, but human rights and humanitarian law could not be compromised or infringed. Consequently, a body should refuse to admit the evidence if it concluded, on a balance of probabilities, that it was obtained by torture.

The domestic courts have also rejected attempts by the government to claim public interest immunity with respect to official documents that were needed to verify claims that individuals have been tortured. Thus, in *R (Binyam Mohamed) v Secretary of State for Foreign and Commonwealth Affairs*,[112] the Court of Appeal ordered the publication of documents passed between the UK and US authorities relating to a suspected terrorist's detention and treatment so that they could be used in legal proceedings. The Court rejected the Secretary's claim of public interest immunity in respect of the information and noted that confidentiality as to working arrangements between allied intelligence services was not absolute. On the facts, in balancing national security with the public interest in open justice those reports should be included as they did not contain any information which would pose a risk to national

---

[109] [2006] 2 AC 221.
[110] See also *Yasser Al-Sirri v Home Secretary* [2009] EWCA Civ 222, where it was held that the Immigration Tribunal had erred by giving any, albeit limited, weight to evidence that it conceded might have been obtained from torture.
[111] *Saunders v United Kingdom* (1996) 23 EHRR 313.
[112] [2010] 3 WLR 554.

security but did contain information that it was in the public interest to disclose. The Court of Appeal rejected the claim that such correspondence was automatically confidential to the receiving country, and that disclosure would lead to less productive intelligence sharing. It also noted that some of the allegations had entered the public domain because of a court action pursued by the suspect in the United States.[113] Further, in *Aamer v Secretary of State for Foreign and Commonwealth Affairs*[114] the court ordered the disclosure of documents that a detainee at Guantanamo Bay required to prove before a US task force that his original confessions during detention were induced by torture.[115]

The right to liberty of the person in the context of terrorism

The right to personal liberty (under Article 5) is especially susceptible to interference in times of emergency and the state is likely to introduce a variety of powers to increase powers of arrest and detention to deal with terrorist threats. These measures and the accompanying case law have been referred to throughout the text, particularly in chapter 6, and this section will summarise those rules, including the power of derogation under Article 15, and highlight the difficulties of balancing civil liberty with national security and public safety.

Powers of arrest

The European Court laid down the requirements of a 'lawful arrest' within paragraph 5(1)(c) in *Fox, Campbell and Hartley v United Kingdom*,[116] stating that a 'reasonable suspicion' presupposed the existence of facts that would satisfy an objective observer that the person might have committed the offence. However, the Court stressed that in respect of terrorism the test differs from that applied in conventional crime, provided the essence of reasonableness is not impaired. Thus, in the present case, as the only evidence was that the applicants had committed offences seven years previously the Court was not satisfied that those minimum standards were met.[117] Thus, the Court will give a wide, though not unlimited, discretion with regard to the investigation of terrorism, insisting on some objectivity, albeit watered down by the exigencies of the situation. Further, in *Murray v United Kingdom*,[118] it held that the fact that the domestic provision was couched in subjective terms, merely requiring a suspicion that was honestly and genuinely held, was not decisive but nevertheless instructive.

More recently, in *O'Hara v United Kingdom*,[119] although the European Court confirmed that the exigencies of dealing with terrorist crime could not stretch the notion of reasonableness

---

[113] Subsequently, the new coalition government announced plans to compensate detainees who were allegedly mistreated by British troops held in foreign custody: Payouts for Detainees over Torture Claims, *The Times*, 7 July 2010.

[114] [2009] EWHC 3316 (Admin).

[115] See also *Al Rawi and Others v Security Service* [2010] EWHC 1496 (QB), where guidance on the interrogation and treatment of detainees was disclosed in proceedings which alleged ill-treatment at Guantanamo Bay.

[116] (1990) 13 EHRR 157.

[117] In *Brogan v United Kingdom* (1989) 11 EHRR 117, the European Court held that it was sufficient to arrest a person on suspicion of being involved in terrorism as that phrase was defined in the relevant legislation and that in that case the applicants were questioned about specific acts and allegations.

[118] (1995) 19 EHRR 193.

[119] (2002) 34 EHRR 32.

so as to impair the safeguards of Article 5(1)(c), it was prepared to modify the normal requirements of objectivity. The Court stressed that the reasonableness of the suspicion on which an arrest must be based formed an essential safeguard against arbitrary arrest and detention and that there must exist some facts which would satisfy an objective observer that a person may have committed an offence. Nevertheless, that had to be considered in all the circumstances, particularly that terrorist crime posed particular problems as the police may have to rely on evidence which is reliable but which cannot be disclosed for fear of jeopardising others. The decision in *O'Hara* suggests that current domestic arrest powers with respect to terrorism are probably consistent with Article 5 of the Convention, provided they are executed in good faith. Under s.31 of the Terrorism Act 2000 the police have the power to arrest, without a warrant, a person whom the officer *reasonably* suspects of being a terrorist, and thus the provision requires objectivity.[120]

A similar deference has been shown by the Court with respect to Article 5(2), which guarantees that everyone who is arrested shall be informed properly, in a language which he understands, of the reasons for his arrest and of any charge against him. For example, in *Fox, Campbell and Hartley* v *United Kingdom*[121] it was held that an interval of a few hours between the arrest and the provisions of reasons did not violate Article 5(2). Although the fact that the applicants were simply told that they were being arrested under s.11 of the Northern Ireland (Emergency Provisions) Act 1978 on suspicion of being terrorists, and that was not sufficient to comply with the requirement that a person should know why he was being detained, the fact that they were questioned in relation to specific acts and allegations satisfied Article 5(2). Similarly, in *Murray (Margaret)* v *United Kingdom*,[122] it was held that although the reasons for the applicant's arrest had not been brought to her attention at the time of her arrest, she had been notified adequately during her subsequent interrogation and thus an interval of a few hours did not fall outside the definition of promptness.

Article 5(3) and pre-trial detention

The right under Article 5(3) to be brought promptly before a judicial body lies at the heart of basic liberty and is especially controversial in the context of terrorist crime. In *Brogan* v *United Kingdom*,[123] where the applicants had been detained for periods between four and a half and six days and eventually released without charge, the European Court held that the requirement that they be brought before a court 'promptly' was violated, despite the circumstances of terrorism. The Court concluded that even the shortest of the periods was inconsistent with the notion of promptness and to justify so lengthy a period of detention would involve a serious weakening of this procedural guarantee to the detriment of the individual.[124] Such rulings call into question the compatibility of current domestic detention powers with respect to the prevention of terrorism. Initially, a person arrested under s.41 of the Terrorism Act 2000 can be detained for up to 48 hours, but that period may be extended to up to 28 days

---

[120] However, as terrorism covers not only the commission of terrorist offences, but also 'being concerned' with such, there is the danger that individuals could be detained on the basis of association with others rather than any clear connection with criminal activities.

[121] (1990) 13 EHRR 157.

[122] (1995) 19 EHRR 193.

[123] (1989) 11 EHRR 117.

[124] See also *O'Hara* v *United Kingdom* (2002) 34 EHRR 32.

by a judge.[125] The current law requires judicial approval and review and in *R (I) v City of Westminster Magistrates' Court*[126] it was held that s.41 was not incompatible with Article 5 because although there was no power to release on bail, there was judicial control over whether there was to be further detention.[127]

Liberty and Article 15 of the European Convention

In chapters 2 and 3 of the text we examined how Article 15 of the European Convention on Human Rights allowed states to derogate from their obligations under the Convention, and in chapter 6 we examined how Article 15 impacts on the right to liberty and security of the person. Those basic principles have also been mentioned earlier in this chapter with respect to the protection of human rights during times of terrorism, and to see how the courts have attempted to interpret that power so as to balance human rights and national security. In this section we will examine the case law surrounding the detention of foreign suspects under anti-terrorism legislation, using the case of *A v United Kingdom* as a case study. As we have already examined the domestic proceedings in *A v Secretary of State for the Home Department* as a case study in chapter 6 we will not provide detail of those proceedings at this stage; although we will remind ourselves of the decision and the events leading up to it so as to better understand the Strasbourg proceedings.

In *A v Secretary of State for the Home Department*[128] we will recall that the House of Lords declared as incompatible the government's derogation from Article 5(1) with respect to s.23 of the Anti-Terrorism, Crime and Security Act 2001, which provided for an extended power to arrest and detain foreign nationals, whom it is intended to remove or deport from the United Kingdom, but where such removal or deportation is not for the time being possible. They held that there did exist a public emergency threatening the life of the nation so as to allow derogation, but that the actual measures to deal with that emergency were disproportionate and discriminatory because the appellants were treated differently because of their nationality or immigration status.

The case study below will now examine the subsequent challenge before the European Court of Human Rights.

CASE STUDY

A v United Kingdom (2009) 49 EHRR 29

The legal and political arguments concerning the detention without trial of foreign suspects under the now repealed provisions of the Anti-Terrorism, Crime and Security Act 2001 have resurfaced due to the recent decision of the European Court of Human Rights in *A v United Kingdom*.[129] In that case the Court found the government in violation

---

[125] A district judge can approve an extension up to 14 days and a High Court judge up to 28 days. Any extension must not exceed 7 days at a time.

[126] [2008] EWHC 2146.

[127] Any detention had to be justified before a Magistrate and then, if an extension was granted, by a High Court judge – and thus sufficient protection for the individual for the purpose of Article 5.

[128] [2005] 2 AC 68.

[129] Application No 3455/05, decision of the European Court, 19 February 2009.

of Article 5 of the Convention, which guarantees the right to liberty of the person and compensation for those who have their liberty taken away in breach of the Convention. In 2004 the House of Lords held that such detention was incompatible with Articles 5 and 14 of the European Convention on Human Rights; guaranteeing liberty of the person and the enjoyment of Convention rights without discrimination.[130] However, as the domestic courts have no power under the Human Rights Act 1998 to strike down clear primary legislation, such detention could not give rise to a claim for compensation as the public authorities are immune from such actions because of their right, and duty, to carry out the clear intention of parliament. Thus, the House of Lords were limited to declaring the relevant provisions incompatible with the Convention; a measure which prompted the introduction by the government of control orders to replace detention without trial, but without retrospectively granting a remedy to those subjected to the illegal detention. Hence, the applicants sought a remedy before the European Court of Human Rights, claiming that such detention was in breach of Article 5 and thus attracted liability in damages under Article 5(5). They also claimed that there had been a violation of Article 3 as they had been subjected to, potentially, indefinite detention, which constituted inhuman and degrading treatment. (The provisions in the 2001 Act were replaced by a system of control orders under the Prevention of Terrorism Act 2005, which have in turn been subject to judicial challenge (see below).)

The applicants then filed an application under the European Convention and the European Court of Human Rights had to decide the following issues:

- Whether the detentions were so arbitrary and indefinite that they subjected the applicants to inhuman and degrading treatment in breach of Article 3 of the Convention.
- Whether the provisions were indeed in breach of the applicants' right to liberty of the person under Article 5(1); including whether the derogation, ruled in breach of the Convention and the Human Rights Act by the House of Lords, complied with Article 15 of the Convention.
- Whether the applicants had been provided with an effective remedy to challenge the lawfulness of the detention, as provided by Article 5(4).
- Whether the applicants had been denied an enforceable right to compensation as required by Article 5(5).

The applicants claimed that their indefinite detention in high-security conditions amounted to inhuman and degrading treatment because of the anxiety and uncertainty caused by such detention. The Court accepted that such uncertainty would cause the applicants anxiety and stress that may have been sufficiently serious to affect their mental health. However, it found that on the facts the applicants had not been without any prospect of release so as to equate their detention with an irreducible life sentence, which would have made their detention contrary to Article 3. The applicants had been able to challenge the legality of their detention and their initial certification under the Act, which needed to be reviewed on a six-monthly basis. These remedies were no less effective under Article 13 of the Convention simply because the domestic courts were unable to challenge the relevant primary legislation. Further, the applicants had available to them

---

[130] *A v Secretary of State for the Home Department* [2005] 2 AC 68.

legal remedies to challenge their conditions of detention, which they had failed to use; consequently the failure to use these remedies made their claim with respect to conditions of detention inadmissible under Article 35 of the Convention. Accordingly, their claim under Article 3 was dismissed.

With respect to the claim under Article 5(1) the Court confirmed that the right to liberty should be protected regardless of nationality. In the present case, apart from Moroccan and French nationals who had been detained for short periods before leaving the country, there was no evidence that the other applicants were being detained pending 'action being taken with a view of deportation', as required by Article 5(1)(f). Consequently their continued detention was unlawful unless a valid derogation under Article 15 existed. In this respect, as the House of Lords had already ruled on Article 15, the European Court stressed that it would only come to a contrary conclusion if the Lords' decision was manifestly unreasonable. The Court first found that although the United Kingdom was the only state to lodge a derogation in response to the threat from al-Qaeda, it was for the national authorities to make its own assessment on the basis of facts known to it. Weight needed to be given to the judgement of the government and parliament of the United Kingdom as well as the assessment of the domestic courts and accordingly the Court found that there was an emergency threatening the life of the nation. Equally, the Court saw no reason or evidence for it to disagree with the reasoning and decision of the House of Lords with respect to whether the measures were proportionate and thus strictly required by the exigencies of the situation. The House of Lords had carefully approached the relevant issues and could not be said to have afforded insufficient weight to views of government and parliament. The European Court thus concluded that the measures were indeed disproportionate, even in the context of an accepted public emergency.

The European Court then considered the claim that there had been a violation of Article 5(4) in that the applicants had not been able to challenge the legality of their detention in the domestic courts. In particular it was alleged that the procedure before the Special Immigration Appeals Commission (SIAC) was unfair because it had regard to closed evidence that was not made available to the applicants and their lawyers. The European Court confirmed that Article 5(4) required a detained person to be given an opportunity to challenge any allegation that formed the basis of their detention and that generally that would require the disclosure of any evidence against the detainee. Although there may be a strong public interest in not disclosing such material, for non-disclosure to be lawful the detainee must still have the possibility of effectively challenging those allegations. The European Court accepted that the SIAC and the use of special advocates provided sufficient guarantees of independence and protection against unfairness.

However, whether Article 5(4) was satisfied depended on whether the allegations made against the applicants were sufficiently specific to allow them to provide the lawyers and the special advocate with information in order to refute such allegations; if the open material merely consisted of general assertions and the SIAC upheld the certificates solely on closed materials, then Article 5(4) would not be satisfied. On the facts, although allegations against some of the applicants had been specific and related to possession of specific documents, others had been general, such as being a member of a named extremist group linked to al-Qaeda, and in another case alleging fund-raising, no evidence suggesting a link between the money and acts of terrorism had been provided. Consequently, in respect of the latter applicants there had been a violation of Article 5(4) and it was not necessary to consider a separate claim under Article 6 of the Convention. Further, as no enforceable claim was available to the applicants in the domestic courts for breach of Article 5 (because of the clear legality of the domestic provisions) there had been a clear violation of Article 5(5), which guarantees such a remedy.

In considering the applicants' claims for just satisfaction the European Court noted that it had not found a breach of Article 3 and thus could not consider compensation for mental suffering allegedly arising from the nature of the sentence and the conditions of detention. Nevertheless, as there had been breaches of Article 5(1), (4) and (5) with respect to various applicants it could consider awarding monetary compensation if necessary; although it had the discretion to decide that judgment alone was sufficient satisfaction. Although the Court had made no award in *McCann v United Kingdom*,[131] because the immediate victims had intended to carry out a terrorist act, the present case was distinguishable because it had never been established that the applicants had engaged, or attempted to engage, in such acts.

In this case the applicants had been detained for long periods of time which would normally require large sums in satisfaction. However, in this case the government had acted in good faith and the measures in question had been passed and applied for the genuine purpose of dealing with an emergency, which the domestic courts accepted existed. Although both courts found the measures disproportionate, a core part of those findings was based on the discriminatory effect of the provisions. Further, as the provisions had been subsequently replaced by control orders it could not be assumed that the applicants would not have been subjected to some loss of liberty even if these violations had not taken place. Accordingly, the Court awarded sums (between €2300 and €3900) which were substantially lower than those granted in other cases of unlawful detention.

Questions

1 Why was it necessary for the applicants to petition Strasbourg even though the provisions were declared incompatible with the Convention and the Human Rights Act?

2 Why did the European Court find that there has been no violation of Article 3 of the Convention? Do you agree with that finding? (Revisit chapter 5 on this point.)

3 Why did the European Court find that there had been a violation of Article 5(1) of the Convention?

4 What decision did the Court make with respect to Article 15 and the right to derogate? Is this evidence of a more liberal approach to Article 15? (See chapters 2 and 3 of the text on this issue.)

5 Why did the European Court find a violation of Article 5(4) of the Convention? Revisit this question when you have read the decision in *AF v Home Secretary*, below, with respect to closed proceedings.

6 On what basis did the Court award the applicants damages for breach of Article 5?

7 Why did the domestic courts not award the applicants compensation in the domestic courts?

8 Do you agree with the limited damages granted to the applicants? Do you feel that such applicants should get no compensation?

---

[131] (1995) 21 EHRR 97.

Control orders and liberty of the person

Following the decision of the House of Lords in *A*, the 2001 derogation was withdrawn and parliament passed the Prevention of Terrorism Act 2005, which introduced a system of control and supervision orders to deal with such suspects.[132] These powers were passed as non-derogating orders – the government believing them to be compatible with Articles 5 and 6 of the Convention.[133] However, in *JJ and Others* v *Secretary of State for the Home Department*,[134] the House of Lords held that control orders imposed on the applicants under s.2 of the Prevention of Terrorism Act 2005 were in breach of Article 5 of the Convention. Consequently, the orders, which purported to be non-derogating orders because the Home Secretary regarded them as restrictions on liberty rather than deprivations of liberty, were, in fact, derogating orders that the Secretary had no jurisdiction to make.[135]

In *JJ and Others*, the orders were imposed on a number of asylum seekers from Iraq and Iran and obliged them to remain within their residences (a one-bedroom flat) at all times apart from a period of six hours a day. All visitors had to be screened and the residences were subject to spot searches by the police, and when the individuals were allowed to leave they were restricted to confined urban areas. Applying the principles in *Guzzardi*, it was noted that the orders impacted severely on liberty and were expected to last indefinitely. In their Lordships' view the effect of the orders was that they were practically in solitary confinement for an indefinite duration, being located in an unfamiliar area, devoid in reality of social contacts, with their lives wholly regulated by the Home Office. Further, the House of Lords held that the lower courts were correct in quashing such orders as beyond the power of the Home Secretary and thus treating them as a nullity. In the majority's view, defects in those orders could not be cured by amending specific obligations, and it would be contrary to principle to decline to quash orders made without lawful power and which deprived individuals of their liberty. The judge at first instance had, thus, been entitled to conclude that the restrictions imposed physical restraints on those concerned and that that prevented the individuals from pursuing the life of their choice.[136]

However, the courts have not declared such orders as contrary to Article 5 *per se*, insisting that whether Article 5 is engaged depends on the cumulative effect of the restrictions. Thus, in *Secretary of State for the Home Department* v *E*[137] the House of Lords distinguished the case of *JJ*, above, and held that Article 5 was not engaged when the individual lived in his own home with his family and was able to leave that home for 12 hours a day with no geographical restriction. Further, he had ample opportunity to engage in everyday activities and make

---

[132] These measures were examined in chapters 6 and 7 of this text and will be examined below.

[133] The orders have also been challenged as being contrary to Article 6 of the Convention, and those proceedings will be examined in more detail below.

[134] [2008] 3 WLR 642.

[135] Applying the decision of the European Court of Human Rights in *Guzzardi* v *Italy* (1981) 3 EHRR 333, their Lordships held that the orders impacted severely on liberty, were expected to last indefinitely, and prevented the individuals from pursuing the life of their choice. Contrast the decision of the House of Lords in *Secretary of State for the Home Department* v *E* [2007] 3 WLR 720. These cases are examined in chapter 6 of this text.

[136] Lord Hoffmann dissented, stressing that the courts should not give an over-expansive interpretation to Article 5 and believing that the measures were simply a restriction on movement.

[137] [2007] 3 WLR 720.

a wide range of social contacts.[138] Further, in *Secretary of State for the Home Department v AF*[139] the House of Lords held that an order which prohibited the individual from leaving his flat for more than ten hours a day and which imposed electronic tagging and restricted him to a certain geographical area outside the flat, did not constitute a deprivation of liberty. The domestic courts have thus stressed that whether the imposition of a curfew within the control order amounts to a deprivation of liberty under Article 5 will depend on all other considerations and conditions of the order, the essential issues being whether there is a sufficient element of confinement.[140] However, the courts have also held that a control order contains no implied power to conduct a personal search, and that such an act would constitute a violation of Articles 5 and 8.[141]

More recently, the Supreme Court has held that whether such orders do engage and breach the right to liberty under Article 5 might depend on whether such restrictions impinge on the right to private life contained in Article 8. Thus, in *AP v Secretary of State for the Home Department*,[142] it was held that a condition in a control order which restricted the controlee's rights under Article 8 could tip the balance when determining whether there had been a deprivation of liberty under Article 5, even where that restriction might be regarded as a proportionate interference with private and family life.[143] In the Supreme Court's view, in cases where a control order imposed a curfew of between 14 and 18 hours a day other restrictions apart from confinement could be relevant; although in cases where the curfew was less than 16 hours a day the other conditions would have to be particularly destructive of the life of the controlee for the court to strike it down. In the present case it was relevant that the controlee lived some distance from his family – he lived in Manchester and the family in London – and that the curfew thus caused in practice the substantial isolation of the controlee.

The right to a fair trial in the context of terrorism

As with the right to liberty under Article 5, the right to a fair trial may have to be compromised in the context of the prosecution of terrorism, provided the very essence of that right is not jeopardised. This section will examine various provisions which ostensibly violate the basic tenets of the right to a fair trial, but which it is argued constitute necessary adjustments to that right so as to secure the rights of others or the effective administration of justice.

---

[138] See also *Rideh v Secretary of State for the Home Department* [2007] EWHC 2237 (Admin), where it was held that a modification to the individual's control orders did not involve a restriction on his liberty, and that any interference with his right to private and family life was necessary and proportionate. The court did, however, recognise that, in general, the mental state of an individual could have an impact on the severity of the restrictions.

[139] [2007] 3 WLR 681.

[140] *Secretary of State for Home Department v AP* [2009] EWCA Civ 731. See also *Home Secretary v GG and NN* [2009] EWHC 142 (Admin), where it was held that a control order imposing a 16-hour curfew on an individual and which required him to move to another town did not amount to a derivation of liberty under Article 5.

[141] *Home Secretary v GG and NN* [2010] 2 WLR 731; *BH v Secretary of State for the Home Department* [2009] EWHC 2938.

[142] [2010] 3 WLR 51.

[143] See *BX v Secretary of State for the Home Department* [2010] EWHC 990 (Admin), where it was held to be proportionate to relocate the individual away from London to the West of England to stop him associating with extremists.

In particular, the section will examine the compatibility of closed proceedings under the Prevention of Terrorism Act 2005, but will begin with some examples where the context of terrorism has informed Article 6.

Since the coming into force of the Human Rights Act 1998, there have been claims that anti-terrorist provisions purporting to reverse the burden of proof are contrary to the presumption of innocence contained in Article 6(2) of the Convention. For example, the compatibility of s.16 and s.16A of the Prevention of Terrorism Act 1989, which appeared to reverse the normal burden of proof when a person is charged with being in possession of articles for terrorist purposes, was considered in the pre-Human Rights Act case of *R v DPP, ex parte Kebilene*.[144] In this case, the courts considered whether the DPP should give consent to a prosecution under s.16 and s.16A of the Prevention of Terrorism Act 1989, which placed a legal burden of proof on the accused to prove that the items found in his possession were neither not in his possession nor not in his possession for a terrorist purpose. The House of Lords held that the DPP's decision to proceed with a prosecution was not subject to judicial review, but that in any case Convention case law did not necessarily preclude the reversal of the burden of proof, provided such does not interfere fundamentally with the defendant's right to a fair trial and the principle of the presumption of innocence.[145]

Further, in *Attorney-General's Reference (No 4 of 2002)*,[146] the House of Lords considered the compatibility of s.11 of the Terrorism Act 2000, which makes it an offence to belong to or take part in the activities of a proscribed organisation and which provides a defence if the charged can prove that he had not taken part in such activities at any time at which it was proscribed. The question for the House of Lords was whether the provision imposed a *legal* burden on the defendant, in which case the presumption of innocence would be violated, or simply an *evidential* burden, in which case the defendant would have to adduce some evidence but the burden of proving beyond reasonable doubt that the offence had been committed would still remain with the prosecution. The House of Lords held that parliament had intended that s.11(2) impose a legal burden on the defendant and that in such a case a conviction would be a disproportionate breach of Article 6 because a person could be convicted on the basis of conduct which was not criminal at the date of commission. However, in their Lordships' view that section could be read down so as to impose an evidential burden only, in which case the provision could remain compatible with Article 6 and the Human Rights Act.[147]

Closed evidence and control orders

The legality of relying on undisclosed material has been considered by both the domestic and European courts with respect to the making of control orders under s.3 of the Prevention of Terrorism Act 2005. Before examining the relevant case law the procedure for making such orders and the rules on the gathering of the necessary evidence are outlined below.

---

[144] [1999] 4 All ER 801.

[145] When the *Kebilene* case was returned to trial the incompatibility issue was in fact resolved by the court interpreting the provisions so as to require the prosecution to discharge the ultimate, legal, standard of proof: decision of the Crown Court, 14 February 2000.

[146] [2005] 1 AC 264.

[147] The implications of that case on the court's powers of interpretation under s.3 of the Human Rights Act 1998 are discussed in chapter 3, pages 140–1.

Under s.2 of the Act, non-derogation orders can be made by the Secretary where he has reasonable grounds for suspecting that the individual is or has been involved in terrorism-related activity and considers it necessary for the purpose of protecting members of the public from a risk of terrorism to impose obligations on that person. Under s.3 of the Act the Secretary, having decided that there are grounds for making such an order, must normally (except in cases of urgency or where the individual was detained under Part 4 of the 2001 Act) apply to a court for permission to make an order, and must be granted such permission. When such an application is made the Secretary must set out the order for which he seeks permission and then the court must consider whether the Secretary's decision that there are grounds for making the order is 'obviously flawed'. If it feels that it is obviously flawed it will quash the order,[148] but otherwise it will give directions for a hearing in relation to the order.[149] At the initial stage the proceedings can occur in the absence of the individual, without his being notified of the application or reference, and without his being given an opportunity of making any representations to the court.[150] If the order is confirmed, then at the hearing the court will consider whether the Secretary's decision to make the order and his decisions on any obligation imposed by the order are 'flawed'.[151] Further, s.11(2) of the 2005 Act states that the reviewing court under s.3 is the appropriate tribunal for the purpose of s.7 of the Human Rights Act 1998 in relation to proceedings which call a control order decision into question.

When considering control orders the court will follow a special procedure involving the use of 'closed evidence' submitted to the court. Under the Act's schedule special rules of court can be made in respect of control order proceedings which must secure that all relevant material is disclosed and that the Secretary has the opportunity to make an application to the relevant court for permission not to disclose relevant material otherwise than to the court and appointed persons where the court considers that disclosure would be contrary to the public interest. These rules are contained in the Civil Procedure Rules, which require the court to give effect to the above objective in such a way as to ensure that information is not disclosed contrary to the public interest, and that if it requires that a summary of the information is given to the party or the legal representative that such disclosure would not be contrary to the public interest. In cases where disclosure, or a summary of disclosure, is not given the rules must also make provision so that information relevant to the case is either withdrawn from the court's consideration or that the Secretary cannot rely on such information. These allow the court to conduct the proceedings in private and to exclude the controlee and his representative from all or part of the hearing and allow the court to receive evidence that would not, but for the rule, be admissible in a court of law.

Specifically, with respect to dealing with closed material, Rules 76.22 and 76.29 provide that the Secretary must apply to the court for permission to withhold the closed material from the person controlled or his legal representatives, filing his statement explaining the reasons for withholding such information. The material will then be considered by the Special Advocate, who is a security-cleared specialist lawyer appointed to deal with the material for the interests of the controlee, whilst not representing that individual. The Special Advocate will thus have access to that closed information and will be able to cross-examine witnesses

---

[148] Section 3(6) Prevention of Terrorism Act 2005.
[149] Section 3(2).
[150] Section 3(5).
[151] Section 3(10).

on behalf of the controlled person, but cannot disclose any such information to the individual or the legal representative. In addition, if the Special Advocate challenges the need to withhold all or any of the closed material the court must arrange a hearing to determine the issue, unless the Secretary and the Special Advocate agree that the court may decide it without a hearing.

In *Re MB*,[152] the House of Lords held that the use of closed materials by a judge in reviewing the legality of a control order was not necessarily in violation of the Convention, provided there were appropriate safeguards in place. Acting under the 2005 Act the Secretary had obtained the court's permission on a 'without notice' application to make a non-derogating order against an Iraqi national (MB) who was suspected of involvement with terrorism-related activity and whom the Secretary wished to prevent from travelling to Iraq to fight against the coalition forces. At the full hearing the court took into consideration the Secretary's evidence, which included an open statement that explained the object of the obligations that were to be imposed on the individual and an explanation of how he had been stopped from boarding flights to Syria and to Yemen and that his explanation for taking those flights was unconvincing. The open statement asserted that he was an Islamic extremist and that the Secretary considered him to be involved in terrorism-related activities. It was accepted, therefore, that the evidence in the open statement added little to the case against the individual and that the Secretary's justification lay in the closed material, which the Special Advocate did not challenge and which was agreed not to be given even in summary form to the individual or his legal representative. The order was thus approved on the basis of the closed material and the individual then sought judicial review claiming that the procedure for approving and reviewing control orders was incompatible with Article 6 of the Convention.

Assessing whether the proceedings under the Act, including the use of closed evidence, was compatible with the right to a fair trial, their Lordships noted that evidence could only be withheld if strictly necessary and that any difficulties caused to the defence by such non-disclosure had to be counterbalanced by any measures taken by the court: what was sufficient depending on the circumstances of each case and noting that there was a difference between background information not essential to the outcome of the defence, and evidence which was crucial to its determination. Although their Lordships were not confident that the Strasbourg Court would hold that every control order hearing in which that advocate was used would comply with Article 6, with strenuous effort it should usually be possible to accord to the individual a substantial measure of procedural justice. If, despite all efforts to afford justice, it was not possible to do so, Convention rights demanded that the judge be in a position to quash the order. However, that would not be necessary in every case and in the present case it was not appropriate to make a declaration of incompatibility with respect to the 2005 Act. Instead, Schedule 1 of the Act could (using s.3 of the Human Rights Act 1998) be interpreted to read 'except where to do so would be incompatible with Article 6 and the right of a controlled person to a fair trial'. In the present case the appellant's cases should be remitted to the court to consider whether they did receive a fair trial.[153]

---

[152] [2007] 3 WLR 681.

[153] Further, in *MT and Others v Secretary of State for the Home Department* [2008] 2 WLR 159, the Court of Appeal held that the Special Immigration Appeals Commission were entitled to use such material in assessing whether the claimant's deportation was lawful and consistent with his Convention rights. The Court of Appeal held that the commission had been entitled to rely on such material and that although there had to be rigorous scrutiny of the question of whether there was a real risk of a breach of Article 3, the presence of the individual and the giving of individual evidence was not a necessary component of that requirement.

The House of Lords held that the Special Immigration Appeals Commission were entitled to use such material in assessing whether the claimant's deportation was lawful and consistent with his Convention rights. It was argued that in determining whether such deportation would be in violation of Article 3 of the Convention, the Commission had to ensure that such proceedings were fair and that by relying on closed material and not allowing the individuals concerned to be present during the proceedings, there had been manifest unfairness. The Court of Appeal held that the Commission had been entitled to rely on such material and that although there had to be rigorous scrutiny of the question of whether there was a real risk of a breach of Article 3, the presence of the individual and the giving of individual evidence was not a necessary component of that requirement.

However, in *A v United Kingdom*[154] the Grand Chamber of the European Court held that there had been a violation of Article 5(4) of the Convention when the lack of access to closed evidence to the detainees and their lawyers meant that they were deprived of their right to effectively challenge the continued legality of that detention. Subsequently, in *Secretary of State for the Home Department v AF*,[155] the House of Lords, relying on the decision of the Grand Chamber in *A*, held that where closed evidence was relied on by the Secretary the controlled person had to be given sufficient information about the case against him to enable him to give effective instructions to the special advocate. The House of Lords held that the decision in *A* made it clear that non-disclosure could not go so far as to deny a person knowledge of the essence of the case against him; although in the interests of national security it might be acceptable not to disclose the source of evidence that founded the suspicion of involvement in terrorism.

Their Lordships also stated that provided that this requirement was satisfied, there could be a fair trial notwithstanding that the controlee was not provided with the detail or the sources of the evidence forming the basis of the allegation; but that where the open material consisted purely of general assertions and the case against the controlee was based solely or to a decisive degree on closed materials, the requirements of a fair trial would not be satisfied, however cogent the case based on the closed materials might be. In their Lordships' view there were strong policy considerations that supported a rule that a trial procedure could never be considered fair if a party to it was kept in ignorance of the case against him. First, there are many cases where it was impossible for the court to be confident that disclosure would make no difference. Reasonable suspicion might be established on grounds that established an overwhelming case of involvement in terrorism-related activity but, because the threshold was so low, reasonable suspicion might also be founded on misinterpretation of facts in respect of which the controlee was in a position to put forward an innocent explanation. A system that relied on the judge to distinguish between the two was not satisfactory, however able and experienced the judge. Secondly, there would be feelings of resentment if a party to legal proceedings was subject to sanctions on grounds that led to his being suspected of involvement in terrorism without any proper explanation of what those grounds were. Further, if the wider public were to have confidence in the justice system, they needed to be able to see that justice was done rather than being asked to take it on trust. As in none of the cases had the disclosure required by the decision of the European Court been given to the individuals, the House of Lords referred their cases back to the judge for further consideration in the light of this finding. Subsequently, in *Secretary of State for the Home*

---

[154] (2009) 49 EHRR 29.
[155] [2009] 3 WLR 74.

Department v *AF and AE*,[156] the control orders in question were quashed with retrospective effect from the day they were made.

The decision of the House of Lords in *AF* thus retreats from the flexible approach taken by their Lordships in *MB*, replacing it with a stricter method of review based on the jurisprudence of the European Court of Human Rights. As with the decision of the House of Lords in *A* on the question of detention without trial, it thus provides evidence of the domestic court's ability and willingness to apply both Convention and common law principles to question measures that threaten not only the individual's right to a fair trial, but also the public interest in observing justice and due process. In January 2011 the government announced plans to replace control orders with increased surveillance.

Conclusions

This book started by examining the various dilemmas created by the adjudication of human rights disputes; and the balance between civil liberty and public safety and national security in the successful prosecution of the war against terror is perhaps the most difficult. The passing of various anti-terrorism provisions, and their challenge before the domestic and European Courts, has excited a great deal of legal, constitutional and political debate and as we have seen in this chapter the battle between parliament and government on the one hand and the courts on the other has raised fundamental issues relating to parliamentary and national sovereignty, the separation of powers and the rule of law.

The majority decision of the House of Lords in *A* represented a robust judicial approach towards the protection of fundamental constitutional rights. Although the courts have been given additional powers via the Human Rights Act 1998 to protect Convention rights from unnecessary encroachment, the success of such cases depend primarily on the courts' desire to carry out their constitutional role to the full and to uphold principles and values which they regard as central to democracy and the rule of law. Nevertheless, the decision gave rise to concern with respect to parliamentary sovereignty and the separation of powers. The provisions of the 2001 Act had been passed by a democratically elected legislature, which, it is argued, should be the final arbiters of where the balance lies between on the one hand the safeguarding of individual liberty, and on the other the protection of national security and public safety. For many, therefore, the decision threatens the doctrine of sovereignty, allowing unelected and unaccountable judges to gainsay the wishes of parliament. Such judicial power has, of course, been sanctioned by parliament itself, as the Human Rights Act 1998 increases the power of judges to ensure that executive actions, and, to a lesser extent, primary legislation, is compatible with the rights laid down in the European Convention and incorporated into domestic law by the 1998 Act. The decision of the House of Lords in *A* is thus of fundamental importance to the recognition of basic democratic rights and values and should be welcomed as such despite its controversial constitutional ramifications. It is essential in a state with no entrenched and superior bill of rights that the courts act as the guardians of individual rights and uphold values central to that society. The fact that the decision was achieved by respecting parliament's will, as expressed in the Human Rights Act 1998, to uphold rights in a manner consistent with the government's international law obligations, should also give the decision democratic

---

[156] [2010] EWHC 42 (Admin).

credence, as too does their Lordships' reliance on a joint parliamentary report, which had suggested that the measures were unnecessary and unlawful.[157]

On the other hand, the judges will still be blamed for not showing due deference to the will of parliament and of not offering parliament a sufficient level of discretion in dealing with the sensitive issue of counterterrorism. In such cases it might be expected that the courts offer the executive, and especially parliament, a wide margin of appreciation. It must also be noted that although the House of Lords struck down the derogation order made under the Human Rights Act, it did not have the power to strike down or disapply the provisions of the 2001 Act. Consequently, parliamentary sovereignty is maintained and the decision whether to repeal or maintain the offending primary legislation is left with government and, ultimately, parliament. This situation, of course, necessitated an 'appeal' to Strasbourg, thus highlighting the limits of the Human Rights Act and its method of incorporation. Of course, as the Human Rights Act was passed to enable domestic law to be compatible with the standards and case law of the European Convention, whether the decision of the House of Lords was democratically sound depends on whether the derogation would ultimately be accepted if tested before the European Court of Human Rights. In *A* v *United Kingdom* the European Court countenanced the decision of the House of Lords on this issue without deciding the matter afresh. Nevertheless, the decision does suggest that the English courts acted within their duty to apply the Convention in domestic law, even if the decision provided less clarity as to the margin of error allowed to the state and the domestic courts by the European Court when the derogation is directly challenged as in cases such as *Brannigan and McBride* v *United Kingdom*.[158]

The decision of the European Court in *A* on the other hand highlights the fact that the method of 'incorporation' favoured by the Human Rights Act might not be capable of providing effective redress where there has been a clear, but lawfully sanctioned, violation of a Convention right. The European Court's judgment exposes the inadequacy of the domestic remedies in respect of Convention breaches which are clearly authorised by primary legislation passed by a still sovereign parliament. Further, the observations of the European Court on the legality of using closed evidence in legal proceedings have been constructive in informing the jurisprudence of the domestic courts with respect to Article 6 and control orders in cases such as *AF* v *Secretary of State*, examined above.

All these cases suggest that the domestic courts will subject anti-terrorist measures, including derogating measures, to the strictest scrutiny. Thus, whilst showing some deference to parliament and the executive, especially when deciding whether a state of emergency exists, they have showed little reluctance to pass judgment on the compatibility of specific provisions that impact on fundamental rights of liberty and due process. Equally, the European Court has resisted arguments by member states that the absolute character of Article 3 should be compromised in the context of the fight against terrorism, and the domestic courts have taken a similar approach with respect to the admissibility of torture evidence. The balance between human rights and public safety and national security continues to be complex, although the courts and human rights law appear to be holding out against arbitrary interference with human rights and fundamental notions of liberty and fairness.

[157] Parliamentary Joint Committee on Human Rights, the Report of the Newton Committee of Privy Counsellors on *Anti-Terrorism, Crime and Security Act 2001*: Review December 2003 (HC 100). Their Lordships also referred to *Opinion 1/2002 of the Council of Europe Commissioner for Human Rights* (CommDH 2002/7) and a variety of statements of European and UN human rights bodies.

[158] (1993) 17 EHRR 539

Further reading

Textbooks

For a thorough account of police powers and anti-terrorist legislation, see Fenwick, *Civil Liberties and Human Rights* (Routledge 2007, 4th edn), chapters on liberty of the person (chapter 11) and anti-terrorism and human rights (chapter 14). See also Stone, *Civil Liberties and Human Rights* (OUP 2010, 8th edn), chapters 3 and 6, and Bailey, Harris and Jones, Civil Liberties: Cases, Materials and Commentary (OUP 2009, 6th edn), chapter 6. For more specialist treatment of the area see Ranstrop and Wilkinson *Terrorism and Human Rights* (Routledge 2007) and Walker, *The Anti-Terrorism Legislation* (OUP 2009, 2nd edn).

Articles

See Bates, Anti-terrorism Control Orders; Liberty and Security Still in the Balance (2009) LS 99; Ewing, The Continuing Futility of the Human Rights Act [2008] PL 668; Feldman, Human Rights, Terrorism and Risk: The Roles of Politicians and Judges [2006] PL 364. See also Finnis, Nationality, Alienage and Constitutional Principle [2007] LQR 123; Shah, From Westminster to Strasbourg: *A and Others* v *UK* (2009) (3) HRLR 473; Walker, Prisoners of 'War all the Time' [2005] EHRLR 50.

For discussion on closed evidence and control orders, see Chamberlain, Special Advocates and Procedural Fairness in Closed Proceedings [2009] CJQ 314 (and update: [2009] CJQ 448); Craig, Perspectives on Process: Common Law, Statutory and Political [2010] PL 257; and Hudson, Justice in Time of Terror [2009] Brit J Criminol 702.

Visit **www.mylawchamber.co.uk/fosterhumanrights**
to access regular updates to major changes in the law,
further case studies, weblinks, and suggested
answers/approaches to questions in the book.

mylawchamber
unrivalled support for legal education

Index